KODANSHA'S ROMANIZED
JAPANESE-ENGLISH DICTIONARY

KODANSHA'S
ROMANIZED
JAPANESE-ENGLISH
DICTIONARY

Timothy J. Vance
University of Hawaii

Based on THE NEW WORLD
JAPANESE–ENGLISH DICTIONARY FOR JUNIORS
By Masatoshi Yoshida & Yoshikatsu Nakamura

KODANSHA INTERNATIONAL
Tokyo • New York • London

Note: This dictionary has been adapted for native English language speakers from *The New World Japanese-English Dictionary for Juniors* by Masatoshi Yoshida & Yoshikatsu Nakamura published by Kodansha Ltd.

Distributed in the United States by Kodansha America, Inc. 114 Fifth Avenue, New York, 10011, and in the United Kingdom and continental Europe by Kodansha Europe Ltd., 95 Aldwych, London WC2B 4JF. Published by Kodansha International Ltd., 17-14, Otowa 1-chome, Bunkyo-ku, Tokyo 112 and Kodansha America, Inc.

95 96 97 98 99 10 9 8 7 6 5 4 3 2

ISBN 4-7700-1603-4

Library of Congress Cataloging-in-Publication Data
Vance, Timothy J.
  Kodansha's romanized Japanese-English dictionary/
Timothy J. Vance. —1st ed.
      p. cm.
  Based on: Chūgaku nyū wārudo Wa-Eijiten, 1990
  1. Japanese language—Dictionaries—English. I. Yoshida, Masatoshi, 1913 - Chūgaku nyū wārudo Wa-Eijiten. II. Nakamura, Yoshikatsu, 1921 - III. Title.
PL679.V36 1993
495.6'321—dc20   92-45652 CIP

CONTENTS

INTRODUCTION

Kodansha's Romanized Japanese–English Dictionary is an up–to–date work of practical reference in a portable and handy format. It aims to be as comprehensive as possible within self–imposed limits, but at the same time, and more importantly, to be easily accessible and useful to beginners. Moreover, maximum priority has been given to ease of reference: first by listing all entries in alphabetical order; second, by giving headwords, compounds, derivatives, and set phrases in both romanized Japanese and standard written Japanese.

This dictionary is based on a Japanese–English dictionary compiled for junior–high–school students and published by Kodansha in 1990 (『中学ニューワールド和英辞典』 *The New World Japanese–English Dictionary for Juniors*). This original dictionary has been completely rewritten to meet the very different needs of English–speaking students of Japanese at the beginning and intermediate levels. We are extremely grateful to the editors of the original dictionary, Masatoshi Yoshida and Yoshikatsu Nakamura, for graciously consenting to let their work serve as the basis for this revision.

The following people provided invaluable help in the revision process: Haruko Cook, Kazue Kanno, Kathy Kitsutani, Masako Lackey, Naoko Maeshiba, Sachiko Matsunaga, Pamela Morley, Machiko Netsu, Miki Ogasawara, Katsue Reynolds, Yumiko Sato, Yutaka Sato, Rieko Sawyer, Nobue Suzuki, Kishiko Vance, Shinichiro Yokomizo. We would also like to thank Michael Brase, Taro Hirowatari, Paul Hulbert, and Koji Tokumasu at Kodansha International for their hard work in getting this dictionary into production.

Timothy J. Vance
Supervising Editor
Noriko Kawaura
Janice Omura
Barbara Riley
Assistant Editors

ORGANIZATION OF ENTRIES

1. Entry Words

a. Romanization

Each entry word is given first in romanization and then in standard Japanese script—hiragana, katakana, and kanji. The romanization used throughout this dictionary is a version of the popular Hepburn system with some modifications.

Long vowels are marked with macrons (as in **kūkō** 空港); two identical vowels in a row thus indicate a separation of some kind. For example, adjectives such as **kanashii** 悲しい are romanized with **ii** because the second **i** can be replaced in related forms such as **kanashiku, kanashikatta**, etc. The word **mizuumi** 湖 is romanized with **uu** because there is a syllable break between the two vowels: **mi-zu-u-mi**.

Word-final short vowels that are typically followed by a conspicuous glottal stop (indicated by a small **tsu** っ in hiragana) are marked with a breve in romanization. An example is the entry word **ă** あっ.

The so-called mora nasal (written ん in hiragana) is always romanized as **n**. The **n** is followed by an apostrophe to distinguish it from the ordinary **n** sound only before a following vowel or **y**. For example, the **n'** in **kin'en** 禁煙 represents the mora nasal, whereas the **n** in **kinen** 記念 represents the ordinary **n** sound. At the end of a word or before a following consonant, the letter **n** alone is unambiguous. For example, in **gohan** ご飯 or **hantai** 反対, the **n** can only be the mora nasal.

b. Hyphens

Some entry words are actually fixed phrases in which the individual words cannot ordinarily be used separately. In such cases, the individual words are separated by hyphens in the romanization, as in the example below.

 ói-ni 大いに *very, greatly* [→ **hijō ni** 非常に]

The definitions provided for such entries are for the entire combination.

Hyphens are also used in the romanization of entry words containing an honorific prefix (**o–** or **go–**) when the base word can also occur without the prefix. For example, there is a hyphen in the romanization of the entry word **o–jama** お邪魔 because **jama** also occurs, but there is no hyphen in the romanization of the entry word **gohan** ご飯 because **han** does not normally occur.

c. Accent

Except for entry words that are prefixes or suffixes rather than independent words, the romanization of each entry word includes an indication of accent. Interested users who are unfamiliar with the accent system of standard Tokyo Japanese should consult a textbook or other source for a full description. An acute accent mark over a vowel indicates the point in the word after which there is a drop in pitch. (If the acute accent mark appears over a long vowel, there is a drop in pitch during the vowel.) If no acute accent mark appears on the romanization of an independent word, the word is unaccented (that is, it contains no drop in pitch). Accent is marked only on entry words and nowhere else in this dictionary.

There is considerable variation in word accent even among Tokyo speakers. The accents given in this dictionary are taken primarily from the NHK pronunciation and accent dictionary (『日本語発音アクセント辞典』改訂新版, 日本放送出版協会, 1985年). When the NHK dictionary lists two or more alternative accents for a given word, only the first alternative appears in this dictionary.

Some entry words in this dictionary are not listed in the NHK dictionary. In each such case, the accent pattern in this dictionary follows the one given in *Daijirin* (『大辞林』三省堂, 1988年).

d. Japanese Orthography

The romanization of each entry word is followed by a representation in the ordinary Japanese writing system. Whenever such representations include kanji, the kanji are used unless they are so obscure that, in the judgment of the editors, even educated Japanese would be unlikely to know them. Consequently, many representations of entry words include kanji that do not appear on the Ministry of Education's list of 1,945 kanji for general use (**Jōyō–kanji–hyō** 常用漢字表).

For some entry words there are alternative Japanese representations involving different kanji but no consistent usage distinction. In such cases, the alternative representations are separated by a comma, as in the following example.

atatákai 暖かい，温かい…

When there is a consistently observed distinction in kanji usage, different senses of what is presumably the same word are treated as separate entries.

For example, **atsui** 暑い and **atsui** 熱い are listed as separate entry words even though the relationship between the two is obvious. As lexicography, this practice is questionable, but it simplifies cross referencing (see Section 2.j below).

e. Verb Conjugation

As in all Japanese dictionaries, verbs and adjectives are listed in the informal nonpast affirmative form. If a verb or adjective listed in this dictionary is irregular, it is marked with the notation {Irreg.} immediately after the ordinary Japanese writing of the entry word. Unless there is an explicit notation to the contrary, any verb listed in this dictionary with final **-iru** or **-eru** is **ichidan.** If a verb ending in **-iru** or **-eru** is **godan,** its entry in this dictionary contains the notation {5} immediately after the ordinary Japanese representation of the entry word. The following entries illustrate how these notations are used.

    kúru 来る {Irreg.}···

    hashíru 走る {5}···

For details, consult Appendix 1.

2. Definitions

a. Entry Structure

For some entry words only a single definition is provided, but most entries include more than one definition. The following schematic entry shows how definitions are positioned in this dictionary.

    entry word エントリー・ワード① *definition 1ai, definition 1aii;*
      definition 1bi, definition 1bii
      ② *definition 2ai, definition 2aii; definition 2bi, definition 2bii*

If the definitions can be divided into clearly distinct ranges of meaning, those ranges are numbered. In the schematic entry above, two clearly distinct meaning ranges of the entry word are distinguished. Within each clearly distinct range, closely related meanings are separated by semicolons. In the schematic entry above, there are two closely related meanings within each clearly distinct meaning range. Commas separate synonymous definitions. In the schematic entry above each meaning is represented by two synonymous definitions.

There is no clear dividing line between synonymous definitions and closely related definitions, but the distinction between commas and semicolons is useful in the placement of cross references and notes (see Sections 2.j and 2.k below).

A few definitions include diagonal slashes to separate alternative words and avoid repetition. The following entry illustrates.

masáru 勝る *to be / become better, to be / become superior*

b. Parts of Speech

The entries in this dictionary do not include part-of-speech labels, but the part of speech of any entry word will be clear to users who know basic Japanese grammar.

The definitions for verbs are consistently given in the English infinitive form (that is, containing the word *to*), and this convention serves to distinguish verbs from other parts of speech. For example, the verb **kakeru** 賭ける is defined as *to bet, to wager,* whereas the noun **kake** 賭け is defined as *bet.*

The definitions for nouns do not contain articles (*the* or *a/an*) except when the presence of an article can serve to avoid potential confusion with a different part of speech or a different noun meaning. For example, **ido** 井戸 is defined as *a well* to make clear that it is not an adverb meaning *well,* and **doresu** ドレス is defined as *a dress* to make it clear that it does not mean *dress* in the sense of *attire.*

Part-of-speech labels are used in some explanatory notes (see Section 2.k below).

c. Comparing Alternative Definitions

Needless to say, none of the entries in this dictionary has a perfect set of definitions, but a great deal of effort has gone into making the definition sets as precise as possible within realistic limits. Many potential misunderstandings can easily be avoided simply by making sure to look at all the alternative definitions provided. For example, *to escape* is given as a definition both for **moreru** 漏れる and for **nigeru** 逃げる, but the basic difference between the meanings of these two Japanese words is clear from the alternative definitions provided in each entry, as shown below.

moréru 漏れる *to leak out, to escape…*
nigéru 逃げる *to run away, to flee, to escape…*

d. Tildes

In many entries definitions are given not for the entry word alone but for a short phrase containing the entry word. A tilde (〜) is used to show the position of the entry word in the phrase, and both romanization and ordinary Japanese writing are given for the word(s) with which the entry word combines. For example, in the entry below, the definition given is not for **attō** alone but for **attō suru.**

attō 圧倒 ～**suru** ～する *to overwhelm*…

Three types of phrases are especially common in this dictionary. The first is noun followed by **suru** する, the type illustrated in the entry above. An entry of this form indicates that although the entry word is a kind of noun, it does not ordinarily occur as a subject or object in sentences. Instead it combines with **suru** to to serve as a predicate.

The second common type is noun followed by **no** の, as in the entry below.

chūko 中古 ～**no** ～の *used, secondhand*…

An entry of this form indicates that although the entry word is a kind of noun, it does not ordinarily occur as a subject or object in sentences. Instead, it combines with **no** to modify a following noun. In most cases, an entry word of this type can also combine with a form of the copula (**da**, **desu**, etc.) to serve as a predicate or with **ni** to serve as an adverb.

The third common type is adjectival noun followed by **na** な, as in the entry below.

junshin 純真 ～**na** ～な *pure-hearted, innocent*…

An entry of this form indicates that although the entry word is a kind of noun, it does not ordinarily occur as a subject or object in sentences. Instead, it combines with **na** to modify a following noun. In most cases, an entry word of this type can also combine with a form of the copula (**da**, **desu**, etc.) to serve as a predicate or with **ni** to serve as an adverb.

In some cases, a short phrase containing the entry word has the same meaning as the entry word alone. Parentheses are used to show that the phrase combination is optional. For example, the following entry indicates that the definition applies to **harubaru** alone as well as to **harubaru to**.

harubáru はるばる（～**to** ～と） *all the way, covering a great distance*…

There are also cases in which two alternative short phrases have the same meaning. Diagonal slashes are used to show the alternatives, as in the following entry.

junsui 純粋 ～**na**／**no** ～な／の *pure*…

In entries which contain numbers indicating clearly distinct ranges of meaning (see Section 2.a above), the placement of phrases with tildes indicates which definitions apply to the phrase. Placement before the first number indicates that all the definitions apply to the phrase. For example, in the entry below, all the definitions apply to **dame na**.

damé 駄目 ～**na** ～な①…

Placement after a number, on the other hand, indicates that only the definitions in that particular meaning range apply to the phrase. For example, in the entry below, only the definitions in meaning range ① apply to **tsurutsuru no.**

　tsúrutsuru つるつる　① ～**no** ～の…

e. Speech–Level Labels

Some entry words are labeled as belonging to a particular speech level. The following labels are used.

【COL.】 Words marked as colloquial are characteristic of casual conversation and are not likely to be used in formal situations.

【CRUDE】 Words marked as crude are felt to be inappropriate in polite conversation.

【FORMAL】 Words marked as formal are characteristic of formal situations and are not likely to be used in casual conversation. This category includes predicate words that are more polite than semi-formal (see below).

【HON.】 This label is used for two types of words. One type is predicate words which express respect for someone by honoring the subject of a sentence. The other type is nouns that express respect for their referents. Especially important among words of the second type are kinship terms which are used to refer to the relatives of someone outside one's own family. Some of these honorific kinship terms can also be used to address one's own relatives who are higher in status. (For example, it is normal to address one's older brother as **onīsan**, but it is not normal to address one's younger brother as **otōto-san.**)

【HUM.】 This label is used for two types of words. One type is predicate words which express respect for someone else by humbling the subject of a sentence. The other type is nouns that express respect for someone else by humbling their referents.

【SEMI-FORMAL】 This label refers to predicate words in what the Japanese refer to as **desu-masu-tai** ですます体. The semi-formal style, in contrast to the informal style, expresses politeness toward the person(s) the speaker is addressing.

In an entry which contains numbers indicating clearly distinct ranges of meaning (see Section 2.a above), the placement of a speech–level label indicates the definitions to which it applies. Placement before the first number indicates that a speech–level label applies to all the definitions of the entry word. For example, in the entry below, the label means that **chinpira** is colloquial in all its definitions.

　chinpira ちんぴら 【COL.】 ① *young hoodlum, young tough*
　　② *low-ranking gangster, punk*…

Placement after a number, on the other hand, indicates that a label applies only to the definitions in that particular meaning range. For example, the label in the entry below means that **tairageru** is colloquial only in meaning range ②.

    tairagéru 平らげる① *to put down, to suppress; to subjugate*
      ② 【COL.】 *to eat up completely*

Many speech-level labels include a cross reference, as in the entry below.

    myónichi 明日 【FORMAL for **ashita** 明日】 *tomorrow*

To avoid lengthy repetitions, no definitions are provided for some of the entry words which are followed by speech-level labels containing cross references. The entry below refers the user to **mama** for definitions.

    manmá まんま 【COL. for **mama** まま】

f. Parenthesized Material

Many individual definitions in this dictionary contain parenthesized material to specify a meaning precisely. The parenthesized portion of such a definition would not ordinarily be used in a natural English translation of a Japanese sentence containing the entry word, but a definition without the parenthesized portion would be misleadingly broad. The following entry illustrates.

    sakubun 作文① *(school) composition, (school) essay*···

g. Collocations

Many individual definitions in this dictionary include material in angle brackets. Such material is not part of the meaning of the entry word; it simply provides a context that makes the intended meaning of the definition clear. For example, in the entry below, the definition under ② means *record* in the sense that *record* has in the collocation *world record*. (The entry word **rekōdo** alone does NOT mean *world record*.)

    rekōdo レコード···
      ② ⟨*world*⟩ *record*···

h. Superordinate Terms

In may cases, the intended meaning of a potentially ambiguous definition is specified by providing a superordinate term in double parentheses following the definition. A superordinate term denotes a broad category within which the definition falls. The two entries below illustrate.

    tánku タンク *tank* ⟪container⟫···

    sénsha 戦車 *tank* ⟪vehicle⟫···

i. American and British Usage

In cases where a difference in usage between American English and British English is common knowledge, the labels ⟨US⟩ and ⟨UK⟩ precede the appropriate definitions. The following entry illustrates.

sákkā サッカー ⟨*US*⟩ *soccer,* ⟨*UK*⟩ *football*

There are certainly many additional differences of which the editors are unaware, and no attempt whatever has been made to deal with differences in other English-speaking countries. American spellings are used exclusively throughout, and the English translations of the example sentences (see Section 5 below) are all based on the norms of American English usage.

j. Cross References

Three types of cross references appear in this dictionary (in addition to the cross references contained in speech-level labels; see Section 2.e above). A cross reference to a synonym is marked with a single-pointed arrow (→), and a cross reference to an antonym is marked with a double-pointed arrow (⇔).

When a cross reference is to a word or phrase that is not itself an entry word, the entry word under which the item referred to appears is given in parentheses and marked with the notation **s.v.** For example, in the entry below, the cross reference means that **miryoku-teki na** is a synonym for **chāmingu na** and that **miryoku-teki na** is listed under the entry word **miryoku**.

chāmingu チャーミング ～**na** ～な *charming, attractive*
[→**miryoku-teki na** 魅力的な (s.v. **miryoku** 魅力)]

A pointing hand (☞) marks a cross reference to another location in the dictionary and is used to avoid repeating the same definition in more than one place. The reference may be to an alternative form of the same word (an abbreviation or a longer form), as in the first entry below, or simply to another entry word under which the item in question is defined, as in the second entry below.

tóiretto トイレット [☞**toire** トイレ]
to iu という [☞**iu** 言う]

When a cross reference refers to another item within the same entry, the notation (above) or (below) appears at the end of the cross reference, as in the following entry.

dékki デッキ…
③ [☞**tēpu-dekki** テープデッキ (below)]
・tēpu-dekki テープデッキ *tape deck*

In entries which contain numbers separating clearly distinct ranges of meaning or semicolons separating closely related meanings (see Section 2.a above), the placement of a cross reference indicates the definitions to which it applies. Placement before the first number indicates that a cross reference applies to all the definitions of the entry word. For example, in the entry below,

the cross reference means that **nibui** is an antonym for all the definitions of
surudoi.

    surudói 鋭い [[⇔**nibui** 鈍い]] ① *sharp, good for cutting…*
      ② *keen, acute, sensitive…*

Placement at the beginning of a set of closely related meanings separated by
semicolons (and directly after a number if there is one) indicates that a cross
reference applies to all the closely related meanings in that particular meaning range. For example, in the entry below, the cross reference means that **katahō** is a synonym for all the definitions in meaning range ① but not for
those in other meaning ranges.

    ippṓ 一方① [[→**katahō** 片方]]
      one side (of two); one (of two), one (of a pair)…

Placement at the end of a list of definitions indicates that a cross reference
applies only to the single set of synonymous definitions that immediately precede it. For example, in the entry below, the cross reference means that **oginau** is a synonym for **tasu** in the sense of *to supply, to supplement* with but not
in the sense of *to add* in general in meaning range ① or in the sense of *to add*
in arithmetic in meaning range ②.

    tasu 足す① *to add; to supply, to supplement with* [→**oginau** 補う②]
      ② *to add* 《in arithmetic》 …

Many cross references include a number to indicate reference to a single
meaning range of a specified entry word. The cross reference to **oginau** in
the entry just above is an example.

All cross references are enclosed in square brackets, but the brackets are double ([[ ]]) when the cross reference applies to more than a single set of synonymous definitions. The cross references to **nibui** and **katahō** in the entries
above illustrate.

k. Explanatory Notes
Many definitions are accompanied by explanatory notes enclosed in bold angles (《 》). Some of these notes are as short as a single word, while others
are quite lengthy.

In entries which contain numbers separating clearly distinct ranges of meaning or semicolons separating closely related meanings (see Section 2.a above),
the placement of a note indicates the definitions to which it applies. The rules
for placement are the same as those for cross references (see Section 2.j
above). Placement before the first number indicates that a note applies to all
the definitions of the entry word. For example, the note in the following
entry means that for all the given definitions of **nakunaru**, the subject must
be inanimate.

nakunaru 無くなる «The subject must be inanimate.»

① *to become lost*⋯

② *to run out, to be used up*⋯

③ *to disappear, to go away*⋯

Placement at the beginning of a set of closely related meanings separated by semicolons (and directly after a number if there is one) indicates that a note applies to all the closely related meanings in that particular meaning range. For example, the note in the entry below means that all the definitions of **sakeru** are to be understood as intransitive verbs.

sakéru 裂ける «intransitive» *to tear, to rip; to split, to crack*⋯

Placement at the end of a list of definitions indicates that a note applies only to the single set of synonymous definitions that immediately precede it. For example, the note in the following example means that **tō** can refer to a building at a Buddhist temple that is usually called a *pagoda* in English.

tố 塔 *tower; pagoda* «at a Buddhist temple»

Part-of-speech labels are used in some explanatory notes. The terms *noun, verb, adverb, adjective, adjectival noun,* and *particle* refer to the Japanese parts of speech traditionally called **meishi** 名詞, **dōshi** 動詞, **fukushi** 副詞, **keiyōshi** 形容詞, **keiyōdōshi** 形容動詞, and **joshi** 助詞, respectively. (The terminology used in textbooks written for English-speaking learners varies, but every good textbook has labels for these six categories.)

In a few cases an explanatory note is given instead of a definition rather than as a supplement to a definition. This practice is resorted to when no appropriate English equivalent is available. The following entries illustrate.

–nin 一人 «counter for people; see Appendix 2»

háikei 拝啓 【FORMAL】 «opening phrase used in formal letters» [⇔**keigu** 敬具]

l. Works Consulted

The works listed below were important sources of useful information during the process of revising the definitions in this dictionary for English-speaking users.

文化庁『外国人のための基本語用語辞典』第 2 版 [Agency for Cultural Affairs, *Dictionary of Basic Japanese Usage for Foreigners.* 1975.]

Eleanor Harz Jorden & Mari Noda, *Japanese: The Spoken Language*, 3 vols. Yale University Press, 1987–1990.

Samuel E. Martin, *A Reference Grammar of Japanese*, revised ed. Tuttle, 1987.

Akira Miura, *English Loanwords in Japanese.* Tuttle, 1979.

Momoo Yamaguchi & Setsuko Kojima, *A Cultural Dictionary of Japan.* Japan Times, 1979.

3. Phrases

Many entries in this dictionary include as examples short phrases containing the entry word. These phrases are given in romanization followed by a representation in the ordinary Japanese writing system. For the most part, kanji usage in these representations is limited in accordance with Ministry of Education conventions. Consequently, many words are represented in kanji as entry words (see Section 1.d above) but in hiragana as elements of phrases.

In some cases, repetition is avoided by combining two or more phrases into a single example by enclosing alternative words in special brackets (〔　〕). In the entry below, the combined phrase represents the two phrases **tsuyoi hifu** (defined as *strong skin*) and **yowai hifu** (defined as *delicate skin*).

hífu 皮膚 *skin* 《of a person or animal》 ⋯

　• tsuyoi〔yowai〕hifu 強い〔弱い〕皮膚 *strong*〔*delicate*〕*skin*

In many phrases, the capital letters A and B are used to stand for arbitrary nouns in order to illustrate patterns of usage. The phrase given in the following entry illustrates.

machigaéru 間違える ⋯

　② *to mistake*

　• A o B to machigaeru AをBとまちがえる *to mistake A for B*

There are also cases in which two alternative phrases have the same meaning. Diagonal slashes are used to show the alternatives (as in phrases marked by tildes; see Section 2.d above). The following entry illustrates.

futsū 普通 *usually, commonly, ordinarily* ⋯

　• futsu no/na 普通の／な *usual, common; ordinary, unremarkable* ⋯

When a phrase has two or more distinct meanings, the sets of definitions are separated by semicolons, as in the entry below.

honé 骨 *bone* ⋯

　• hone o oru 骨を折る *to break a bone; to take pains, to make efforts*

Even if the definitions involve clearly distinct ranges of meaning (as in the entry above), semicolons are used; numbers are used only for distinct meaning ranges of entry words (see Section 2.a above). Otherwise, the format conventions for phrase definitions are the same as those for entry-word definitions (see Section 2 above).

4. Compounds and Derivatives

Many entries in this dictionary include compounds and/or derivatives containing the entry word. A compound or derivative is given in romanization with a hyphen separating the entry word from what it is combined with. For example, in the following entry the hyphen in the romanization of the compound **mukashi-banashi** separates the entry word **mukashi** from **banashi**.

> **mukashi** 昔 *long ago*···
> · mukashi-banashi 昔話 *tale of long ago, legend*···

As noted in Section 1.a above, the so-called mora nasal (written ん in hiragana) is always romanized as **n**, and the **n** is followed by an apostrophe to distinguish it from the ordinary **n** sound only before a following vowel or **y**. Before a hyphen, however, the letter **n** alone is unambiguous; it must represent the mora nasal. Consequently, no apostrophe is used before a hyphen in a compound or derivative. For example, in the entry below, the **n** in **pan-ya** can only be the mora nasal.

> **pan** パン *bread*···
> · pan-ya パン屋 *bakery; baker*

The romanization of a compound or derivative is followed by a representation in the ordinary Japanese writing system. Whenever such representations include kanji, the kanji are used unless they are so obscure that, in the judgment of the editors, even educated Japanese would be unlikely to know them. (This same practice is followed for entry words; see Section 1.d above.)

The ordinary Japanese representation of a compound or derivative is followed by one or more definitions. When a compound has two or more distinct meanings, the sets of definitions are separated by semicolons. The definitions for **pan-ya** in the entry above illustrate. As with phrases (see Section 3 above), even if the definitions involve clearly distinct ranges of meaning, semicolons are used; numbers are used only for distinct meaning ranges of entry words (see Section 2.a above). Otherwise, the format conventions for compound and derivative definitions are the same as those for entry-word definitions (see Section 2 above).

Some of the compounds included in this dictionary contain an alternative form of the entry word with a different initial consonant. For example, in the entry below, the compound **bentō-bako** contains **bako** rather than **hako**.

> **hako** 箱 *box, case*···
> · bentō-bako 弁当箱 *lunch box*···

This kind of consonant alternation is widespread in Japanese. Users who are unfamiliar with it should consult a textbook.

5. Example Sentences

Many entries in this dictionary include one or more sample sentences to illustrate typical usages of an entry word, a phrase, a compound, or a derivative. Each example sentence is preceded by the symbol ¶ and given first in romanization, followed by a representation in the ordinary Japanese writing system and an English translation. For the most part, the kanji usage in the ordinary Japanese representations is limited in accordance with Ministry of Education conventions. Consequently, many words are represented in kanji as entry words (see Section 1.d above) or as compounds or derivatives (see Section 4 above) but in hiragana as parts of sample sentences.

The English translations of sample sentences tend to be literal at the expense of naturalness. For example, the translation of the example sentence in the following entry would be more natural as English with *smells bad* or *stinks* rather than *is bad-smelling*, but these more natural translations would obscure the fact that **kusai** is an adjective.

> **kusái** 臭い *bad-smelling, smelly*
> ¶Kono heya wa kusai desu.
> この部屋は臭いです。
> *This room is bad-smelling.*

When a fairly literal translation of a sample sentence seems likely to be misleading or difficult to comprehend, two translations are provided. The first is natural enough to be easily understood as English, and the second, appended as an note is labeled as literal. There is no such thing, of course, as an absolutely literal translation; the label simply means relatively literal. The sample sentence in the following entry illustrates.

> **toshí** 年 ① *year*
> ¶Yoi o-toshi o o-mukae kudasai.
> よいお年をお迎えください。
> *Have a happy New Year!* «Literally: *Please greet a good year.*»···

A few of the sample sentences in this dictionary are proverbs and are identified as such with a note. Many proverbs include archaisms like the obsolete copula form **nari** in the proverb given in the entry below.

> **tokí** 時 ① *(amount of) time, time span*···
> ¶Toki wa kane nari.
> 時は金なり。 «proverb»
> *Time is money.*

List of Symbols

SYMBOL	USE	SEE
{}	to enclose a notation about verb or adjective conjugation	1.e
/	to separate alternative words	2.a, 2.d, 3
~	to indicate the location of an entry word in a phrase	2.d
( )	to enclose optional material	2.d, 2.f
	to enclose notes within cross references	2.j
【 】	to enclose a speech-level label	2.e
⟨ ⟩	to enclose material with which a word being defined collocates	2.g
⟨⟨ ⟩⟩	to enclose a superordinate term	2.h
⟨US⟩	to mark a definition as American usage	2.i
⟨UK⟩	to mark a definition as British usage	2.i
[ ]	to enclose a cross reference that applies to a single set of definitions	2.j
[[ ]]	to enclose a cross reference that applies to more than a single set of definitions	2.j
→	to indicate that a cross reference is to a synonym	2.j
⇔	to indicate that a cross reference is to an antonym	2.j
☞	to indicate that a cross reference is to a definition listed elsewhere	2.j
⟪ ⟫	to enclose explanatory notes	2.k, 5
⌈ ⌉	to enclose alternative words in a combined phrase	3
¶	to mark the beginning of an example sentence	5

A

ǎ あっ *Oh!, Ah!* 《an interjection expressing surprise, alarm, or dismay》
¶Ǎ, abunai
あっ、危ない！
Oh! Look out! 《Literally: *Oh! Dangerous!*》
¶Ǎ, wakatta.
あっ、わかった。
Oh! I understand.
¶Ǎ, nōto o wasuremashita.
あっ、ノートを忘れました。
Ah! I forgot my notebook.

ā ああ *Oh!, Ah!* 《an interjection exprssing surprise or dismay》
¶Ā, dō shiyō.
ああ、どうしよう。
Oh! What shall I do?
¶Ā, bikkuri shita!
ああ、びっくりした！
Oh! What a surprise! 《Literally: *Oh! I was surprised!*》

ā ああ 【COL. for **hai** はい】 *yeah* 《Generally restricted to male speakers.》
¶Ā, wakatta yo.
ああ、わかったよ。
Yeah, I understand!
¶"Kore o moratte ii no?" "Ā, ii yo."
「これをもらっていいの？」「ああ、いいよ」
"May I have this?" "Yeah, fine!"

ā ああ *like that, in that way* 《Like other Japanese demonstratives beginning with **a-**, **ā** has two uses. One is to refer to something which is in sight and relatively far both from the speaker and from the listener(s). The other is to refer to something not in sight but which is familiar both to the speaker and to the listener(s).》 [⇔**kō** こう; **sō** そう]
•ā iu ああいう *that kind of* [→**anna**
あんな]

abareru 暴れる *to become violent, to get rowdy, to run amok*
¶Kodomo-tachi wa ie no naka de abarete imasu.
子供たちは家の中で暴れています。
The children are being rowdy in the house.

abékku アベック 【COL.】 *couple* 《man and woman》

abiru 浴びる *to pour all over oneself; to take* 《a bath or shower》
¶Kodomo-tachi wa kawa de mizu o abimashita.
子供たちは川で水を浴びました。
The children poured water all over themselves in the river.
¶Watashi wa itsu-mo neru mae ni shawā o abimasu.
私はいつも寝る前にシャワーを浴びます。
I always take a shower before going to bed.

abiseru 浴びせる *to pour all over, to shower with*

ábu 虻 *horsefly*

abunai 危ない ① *dangerous* [→**kiken na** 危険な] [⇔**anzen na** 安全な]
¶Abunai!
危ない！
Watch out! 《Literally: *Dangerous!*》
¶Koko de sukī o suru no wa abunai yo.
ここでスキーをするのは危ないよ。
It's dangerous to ski here!
② *in danger*
¶Sono ko wa inochi ga abunai desu.
その子は命が危ないです。
That child's life is in danger.

abura 油 ① *oil*
•abura o sasu 油を差す *to apply oil* 《to a machine for lubrication》
¶Kono jitensha ni abura o sashite kudasai.
この自転車に油を差してください。
Please oil this bicycle.
② *grease*

abura 脂 (*animal*)*fat* [→**shibō** 脂肪]
¶Kono niku wa abura ga oo-sugiru ne.

この肉は脂が多すぎるね。
This meat has too much fat, doesn't it.
• abura-kkoi 脂っこい *fatty, greasy*

ácherī アーチェリー *archery*

áchi アーチ ① *arch* ((shape))
② *archway*

achíkochi あちこち *here and there*
¶Yukue-fumei no kodomo o achikochi
sagashite imasu.
行方不明の子供をあちこち探しています。
*We are looking for the lost child here
and there.*
¶Sengetsu Kyōto-jū o achikochi tazunete
mawarimashita.
先月京都中をあちこち訪ねて回りました。
*I went around visiting here and there all
over Kyoto last month.*

achira あちら 【FORMAL for **atchi**
あっち】《Like other Japanese demonstratives beginning with a–, **achira** has two
uses. One is to refer to something which
is in sight and relatively far both from
the speaker and from the listener(s). The
other is to refer to something which is
not in sight but which is familiar both to
the speaker and to the listener(s).》
　① [[⇔**kochira** こちら①; **sochira**
そちら①]] *that way; over there*
¶Higashi wa achira desu.
東はあちらです。
East is that way.
¶Achira ni tsuitara denwa o kudasai.
あちらに着いたら電話をください。
*Please give me a phone call when you
get there.*
¶Aoki-sensei wa achira desu.
青木先生はあちらです。
Mr. Aoki is over there.
　② *that person* [⇔**kochira** こちら②]
¶Achira wa donata desu ka.
あちらはどなたですか。
Who is that person?
• achira-gawa あちら側 *the other side,
that side over there*
¶Kawa no achira-gawa wa Chiba-ken
desu.
川のあちら側は千葉県です。

*The other side of the river is Chiba
Prefecture.*

áchisuto アーチスト *artist*

adana あだ名 *nickname, sobriquet*
¶Otōto no adana wa "Usagi" desu.
弟のあだ名は「うさぎ」です。
*My younger brother's nickname is
"Rabbit."*
¶Seito-tachi wa sensei ni "Koara" to iu
adana o tsukemashita.
生徒たちは先生に「コアラ」というあだ名
をつけました。
*The pupils gave the teacher the nickname
"Koala."*

adáputā アダプター (*electrical*)*adapter*

ádobaisu アドバイス *advice* [→**jogen**
助言]
¶Seito-tachi wa sensei no adobaisu ni
shitagatta.
生徒たちは先生のアドバイスに従った。
*The pupils followed their teacher's
advice.*
• adobaisu suru アドバイスする *to advise*
¶Sensei wa besuto o tsukusu yō ni to
watashi-tachi ni adobaisu shimashita.
先生はベストを尽くすようにと私たちにアドバ
イスしました。
Our teacher advised us to do our best.

adobárūn アドバルーン *balloon from
which an advertising banner is suspended*

ádoresu アドレス *address* [→**jūsho**
住所]

adoribu アドリブ *ad-lib*
• adoribu de shaberu アドリブでしゃべる *to
talk ad-lib*
• adoribu de ensō suru アドリブで演奏する
to perform ad-lib 《on a musical instru-
ment》

afuréru 溢れる *to overflow*
¶O-furo no o-yu ga afurete iru yo.
おふろのお湯があふれているよ。
The hot water in the bath is overflowing!
¶Keiko-san no me ni wa namida ga
afurete imashita.
桂子さんの目には涙があふれていました。
Tears were overflowing in Keiko's eyes.

Afurika アフリカ *Africa*
- Afurika-jin アフリカ人 *an African*
- Afurika-tairiku アフリカ大陸 *the African Continent*

afutāsábisu アフターサービス *after-sales service*

agaru 上がる ① *to go up, to rise* [⇔ **sagaru** 下がる②]

¶Tako wa dondon takaku agatte ikimashita.

たこはどんどん高く上がっていきました。

The kite went up higher and higher.

¶Okujō ni agatte oshaberi o shimashita.

屋上に上がっておしゃべりをしました。

We went up on the roof and had a chat.

¶Kion wa sanjūroku-do made agarimashita.

気温は36度まで上がりました。

The temperature rose to 36 degrees.

¶Kon-gakki wa seiseki ga sukoshi agaru deshō.

今学期は成績が少し上がるでしょう。

My grades will probably go up a little this term.

② *to end, to be finished*

¶Ame ga agarimashita.

雨が上がりました。

The rain stopped.

③ *to get nervous*

¶Shiken no toki agatte shimaimasu.

試験の時上がってしまいます。

I get nervous at exam time.

④ 【HON. for **taberu** 食べる; **nomu** 飲む①】 [[→**meshiagaru** 召し上がる]] *to eat; to drink*

¶Kudamono o agatte kudasai.

果物を上がってください。

Please have some fruit.

ageru 上げる *to raise, to put higher*

¶Kotae no wakaru hito wa te o agenasai.

答えのわかる人は手を上げなさい。

People who know the answer, raise your hands.

¶Haha ga raigetsu kozukai o agete kureru yo.

母が来月小遣いを上げてくれるよ。

My mother will raise my allowance next month!

ageru 揚げる *to fly* 《a kite》; *to raise* 《a flag》
- tako o ageru たこを揚げる *to fly a kite*
- hata o ageru 旗を揚げる *to raise a flag*

ageru 挙げる ① *to hold* 《a ceremony》

¶Ano futari wa kyōkai de kekkon-shiki o agemasu.

あの二人は教会で結婚式をあげます。

Those two are going to have their wedding at church.

② *to give, to cite* 《an example》

¶Rei o mō hitotsu agete kudasai.

例をもう1つあげてください。

Please give another example.

ageru 上げる《In either use of this word the recipient must not be the speaker, the speaker's group, or a person or group with whom the speaker is identifying.》

① *to give* 《to someone》

¶Haha no tanjōbi ni sētā o agemasu.

母の誕生日にセーターを上げます。

We are going to give our mother a sweater for her birthday.

¶Kore o tomodachi ni agemashō.

これを友達に上げましょう。

I'll give this to my friend.

② *to do the favor of* 《following the gerund (-te form) of another verb》

¶Tomodachi no shukudai o tetsudatte agemasu.

友達の宿題を手伝ってあげます。

I help my friend with her homework.

¶Sono hito ni eki e no michijun o oshiete agemashita.

その人に駅への道順を教えてあげました。

I showed that person the way to the station.

¶Nan-demo ki ni itta mono o katte ageru yo.

何でも気に入った物を買ってあげるよ。

I will buy you anything you like!

ageru 揚げる *to deep-fry*

agó 顎 *jaw; chin*
- ago-hige 顎髭 *beard*

agura あぐら *sitting cross-legged*
- agura o kaku あぐらをかく *to*

sit cross-legged

ái 愛 *love, affection* [→**aijō** 愛情]

¶Kodomo ni taisuru haha no ai wa totemo fukai desu.

子供に対する母の愛はとても深いです。

A mother's love for her child is very deep.

ái 藍 ① *Japanese indigo plant*
② *indigo dye*

•ai-iro 藍色 *indigo color*

aida 間 ① *time during, time while* [→**uchi** 内②]

¶Natsu-yasumi no aida ni hon o takusan yomimasu.

夏休みの間に本をたくさん読みます。

I will read a lot of books during the summer vacation.

¶Benkyō shite iru aida wa shizuka ni shite kudasai.

勉強している間は静かにしてください。

While I am studying, please be quiet.

• nagai aida 長い間 *for a long time*

② *area between; time period between*

¶Sono shima to Honshū no aida ni wa hashi ga kakatte iru.

その島と本州の間には橋が架かっている。

A bridge has been built between that island and Honshu.

¶Shichi-ji to hachi-ji no aida ni denwa shite kudasai.

7時と8時の間に電話してください。

Please telephone between 7:00 and 8:00.

③ *connection between, relationship among*

¶Sono gēmu wa kodomo-tachi no aida de ninki ga aru.

そのゲームは子供たちの間で人気がある。

That game is popular among children.

¶Sore wa Hamada-san to watashi no aida no himitsu deshita.

それは浜田さんと私の間の秘密でした。

That was a secret between Mr. Hamada and me.

aidagara 間柄 *relationship* 《between people》

áidia アイディア *idea* [→**kangae** 考え②]

¶Sono toki ii aidia ga ukabimashita.

その時いいアイディアが浮かびました。

A good idea occured to me at that time.

áidoru アイドル ① *idol, worshipped object*

② *idol, idolized person, popular famous person*

aijin 愛人 *(illicit)lover*

aijō 愛情 *love, affection*

¶Junko-san wa kazoku ni tsuyoi aijō o motte iru.

淳子さんは家族に強い愛情を持っている。

Junko has a strong love for her family.

•aijō o komete 愛情を込めて *with love, with affection*

aikagi 合鍵 *duplicate key*

aikawarazu 相変わらず *as ever, as before, as usual, still*

¶Michiko-san wa aikawarazu shinsetsu desu.

道子さんは相変わらず親切です。

Michiko is as kind as ever.

¶Yumi-san wa aikawarazu tenisu ni muchū desu.

由美さんは相変わらずテニスに夢中です。

Yumi is still crazy about tennis.

¶Kimura-san wa aikawarazu benkyō-ka desu.

木村さんは相変わらず勉強家です。

As before, Ms. Kimura is a studious person.

aikídō 合気道 *aikido* 《a Japanese martial art》

aikoku 愛国 *love of one's country*

•aikoku-sha 愛国者 *patriot*

•aikoku-shin 愛国心 *patriotic feeling*

aikyō 愛嬌 *charm, amiability*

aikyū アイキュー *IQ* [→**chinō-shisū** 知能指数 (s.v. **chinō** 知能)]

aimai 曖昧 〜**na** 〜な *vague, ambiguous, obscure*

¶Yōko-san wa yoku aimai na henji o shimasu.

洋子さんはよくあいまいな返事をします。

Yoko often gives a vague answer.

ainiku 生憎 *unfortunately*

¶Ainiku obāsan wa rusu deshita.

あいにくおばあさんは留守でした。

Unfortunately, your grandmother was out.

• ainiku no／na あいにくの／な *unfortunate, inopportune*

¶Ainiku no tenki desu ne.
あいにくの天気ですね。
It's bad weather, isn't it.

Áinu アイヌ *Ainu* 《the aboriginal people of northern Japan》

• Ainu-go アイヌ語 *the Ainu language*

airon アイロン *iron* ((appliance))

• A ni airon o kakeru Aにアイロンをかける *to iron A*

áisatsu 挨拶 *greeting, courteous expression*

¶Watashi-tachi wa maiasa aisatsu o kawashimasu.
私たちは毎朝あいさつを交わします。
We exchange greetings every morning.

• aisatsu suru あいさつする *to greet*

¶Seito-tachi wa kōchō-sensei ni "Ohayō gozaimasu" to aisatsu shimasu.
生徒たちは校長先生に「おはようございます」とあいさつします。
The students greet the principal, "Good morning."

aishō 愛称 *nickname, pet name*

aishō 相性 *compatibility in temperament*

• aishō ga ii 相性がいい *to be congenial, to be compatible*

¶Ano futari wa aishō no ii pea desu.
あの二人は相性のいいペアです。
Those two are a congenial pair.

aisó 愛想 *amiability, affability; courtesy, civility*

• aiso ga ii 愛想がいい *amiable, affable*

aisō 愛想 [☞**aiso** 愛想]

aisuhókkē アイスホッケー *ice hockey*

aisukurímu アイスクリーム *ice cream*

aisúru 愛する {Irreg.} *to love*

¶Michiko-san o aishite iru yo.
美知子さんを愛しているよ。
I love Michiko!

¶Ōji wa Shinderera o aisuru yō ni natta.
王子はシンデレラを愛するようになった。
The prince fell in love with Cinderella.

aisusukéto アイススケート ① *ice skates* ② *ice skating*

aité 相手 ① *partner, companion*

¶Yōko-san o aite ni Eigo no renshū o shimashita.
洋子さんを相手に英語の練習をしました。
I practiced English with Yoko as my partner.

• sake no aite 酒の相手 *drinking partner* ② *opponent, rival*

• tenisu no aite テニスの相手 *tennis opponent*

• aite ni totte fusoku wa nai 相手にとって不足はない *to be a worthy opponent*

• asobi-aite 遊び相手 *playmate*

• hanashi-aite 話し相手 *person to talk with*

• sōdan-aite 相談相手 *adviser*

aitsu あいつ 【CRUDE】 *that person* 《Like other Japanese demonstratives beginning with **a**–, **aitsu** has two uses. One is to refer to a person who is in sight and relatively far both from the speaker and from the listener(s). The other is to refer to a person who is not in sight but who is familiar both to the speaker and to the listener(s).》 [⇔**koitsu** こいつ; **soitsu** あいつ]

áitsuide 相次いで *one after another, in succession*

áizu 合図 *sign, signal*

• aizu suru 合図する *to make a sign, to signal*

¶Junbi ga dekitara, aizu shimasu.
準備ができたら、合図します。
When the preparations are done, I'll signal.

aizuchi 相槌 《This term refers to words or short phrases that are used to assure a person speaking that one is listening. Words for yes (**hai** はい, **ē** ええ, **un** うん) are the most common, but other typical **aizuchi** include **naruhodo** なるほど, **Soo desu ne** そうですね, etc.》

• aizuchi o utsu 相づちを打つ *to use aizuchi*

aji 味 *flavor, taste*

¶Kono jūsu wa suppai aji ga shimasu.
このジュースは酸っぱい味がします。
This juice has a sour taste.

¶Aji wa dō desu ka.
味はどうですか。
How does it taste?

¶Kono kēki wa aji ga hen desu.
このケーキは味が変です。
This cake has a strange flavor.

áji 鯵 *horse mackerel*

Ajia アジア *Asia*
- Ajia-jin アジア人 *an Asian*
- Ajia-tairiku アジア大陸 *the Asian Continent*

ajisai あじさい *hydrangea* ((flower))

ajiwáu 味わう ① *to taste, to sample the flavor of*

¶Sono sūpu o ajiwatte mite kudasai.
そのスープを味わってみてください。
Please taste that soup.

② *to experience* [→**keiken suru** 経験する]

áka 赤 *red* 《as a noun》

¶Shingō ga aka ni narimashita.
信号が赤になりました。
The traffic light turned red.
- koi 〔usui〕 aka 濃い〔薄い〕赤 *dark 〔light〕 red*
- aka-denwa 赤電話 *red pay telephone* 《One of several types of public telephone in Japan, red pay telephones accept only 10-yen coins and are found near store and restaurant entrances.》
- aka-enpitsu 赤鉛筆 *red pencil*
- aka-shingō 赤信号 *red (traffic)light*

ákachan 赤ちゃん *baby*
- otoko 〔onna〕 no akachan 男〔女〕の赤ちゃん *baby boy 〔girl〕*

akai 赤い *red* 《as an adjective》
- akaku naru 赤くなる *to turn red; to blush*

¶Watashi wa hazukashikute kao ga akaku narimashita.
私は恥ずかしくて顔が赤くなりました。
I was ashamed, and my face turned red.

akaji 赤字 *deficit, red ink* [⇔**kuroji** 黒字]

akanbō 赤ん坊 *baby* [→**akachan** 赤ちゃん]

akari 明かり ① (*artificial*)*light, lamplight*

¶Akari ga tsuite imasu.
明かりがついています。
The light is on.

¶Akari o keshite kudasai.
明かりを消してください。
Turn off the light, please.

② *light, illumination* [→**hikari** 光り]
- tsuki no akari 月の明かり *the light of the moon*

akarui 明るい [[⇔**kurai** 暗い]]
① *light, illuminated, bright*

¶Sora ga akaruku natte kimashita.
空が明るくなってきました。
The sky has gotten light.

¶Kon'ya wa tsuki ga totemo akarui ne.
今夜は月がとても明るいね。
Tonight the moon is very bright, isn't it.

¶Akarui uchi ni kaette kinasai.
明るいうちに帰ってきなさい。
Come back home while it's still light.
- akarui iro 明るい色 *bright color*

② *cheerful*

¶Keiko-san wa itsu-mo akarui ne.
恵子さんはいつも明るいね。
Keiko is always cheerful, isn't she.

¶Shōjo wa akaruku hohoemimashita.
少女は明るくほほえみました。
The girl smiled cheerfully.

akashia アカシア *acacia*

ákēdo アーケード ① *arcade, passageway with an arched roof*

② *shopping arcade* 《i.e., a roofed-over passageway or street with shops on both sides》

akegata 明け方 *daybreak, dawn*

¶Akegata ni kaji ga okorimashita.
明け方に火事が起こりました。
A fire broke out at dawn.

akeru 空ける ① *to vacate, to make empty, to make room on／in*

¶Wakai josei wa rōjin ni seki o akemashita.
若い女性は老人に席を空けました。

The young woman made room on the seat for an elderly person.

¶Minna kyūkyū-sha no tame ni michi o akemashita.

みんな救急車のために道を空けました。

Everyone made way for the ambulance.

② *to empty out* «the contents»

¶Kabin kara mizu o akete kudasai.

花瓶から水を空けてください。

Please empty the water out of the vase.

③ **ana o～** 穴を～ *to make a hole*

¶Kabe ni ana o akemasu.

壁に穴を空けます。

I will make a hole in the wall.

akeru 明ける ① **yo ga～** 夜が～ *day breaks, night ends*

¶Yo ga akeru mae ni shuppatsu shimasu.

夜が明ける前に出発します。

We will leave before day breaks.

② *to begin* «The subject is a year.»

¶Toshi ga akemashita.

年が明けました。

The new year began.

③ **tsuyu ga～** 梅雨が～ *the rainy season ends*

¶Mō sugu tsuyu ga akemasu.

もうすぐ梅雨が明けます。

The rainy season will end soon.

akeru 開ける *to open, to unclose* «transitive» [⇔**shimeru** 閉める]

¶Kyōka-sho no gojup-pēji o akenasai.

教科書の50ページを開けなさい。

Open your textbooks to page 50.

¶Doa o akete oite wa ikenai yo.

ドアを開けておいてはいけないよ。

You mustn't leave the door open!

¶Futsū jū-ji ni mise o akemasu.

普通10時に店を開けます。

We usually open the store at 10:00.

áki 秋 *autumn, fall* [⇔**haru** 春]

¶Jimu-san wa kono aki ni Amerika ni kaerimasu.

ジムさんはこの秋にアメリカに帰ります。

Jim is going back to the United States this fall.

• aki-bare 秋晴れ *clear sky typical of autumn*

aki 空き *vacancy, opening, space*

• aki-bin 空き瓶 *empty bottle*

• aki-ya 空き家 *vacant house*

akíraka 明らか ～**na** ～な *clear, plain, obvious*

¶Akiraka na shōko wa arimasen.

明らかな証拠はありません。

There is no clear evidence.

¶Akiraka ni okāsan wa tsukarete iru yo.

明らかにお母さんは疲れているよ。

Clearly mother is tired!

akiraméru 諦める *to give up on, to abandon as hopeless*

¶Tomodachi o sagasu no o akiramemasu.

友達を探すのをあきらめます。

I will give up searching for my friend.

akireru 呆れる *to become appalled*

¶Seiji-ka no kotoba ni wa akiremashita.

政治家の言葉にはあきれました。

I was appalled at the politician's words.

¶Jibun no fu-chūi ni akirete shimaimasu.

自分の不注意にあきれてしまいます。

I am appalled at my carelessness.

akiresúken アキレス腱 *Achilles tendon*

akíru 飽きる *to get tired of, to get sick of*

¶Watashi wa tsumaranai eiga ni akite shimatta.

私はつまらない映画に飽きてしまった。

I got tired of the boring movie.

¶Appuru-pai wa mō akimashita.

アップルパイはもう飽きました。

I'm sick of apple pie already.

akka 悪化 *worsening*

• akka suru 悪化する *to worsen* «transitive or intransitive»

akódion アコーディオン *accordion*

• akódion-kāten アコーディオンカーテン *accordion door*

akogareru あこがれる *to long, to yearn*

¶Yamanaka-san wa meisei ni akogarete imasu.

山中さんは名声にあこがれています。

Ms. Yamanaka is longing for fame.

¶Otōto wa kashu ni naru koto ni akogarete imasu.

弟は歌手になることにあこがれています。

My younger brother is yearning to be a singer.

áku 悪 *badness, wickedness, evil* [⇔ **zen** 善]

¶Ano hito demo zen to aku no kubetsu wa wakaru yo.

あの人でも善と悪の区別はわかるよ。

Even that person knows the difference between good and evil!

•aku-eikyō 悪影響 *bad influence*

•aku-i 悪意 *ill will*

•aku-ji 悪事 *evil deed*

aku 空く *to become vacant, to become empty; to become available for use*

¶Seki ga yatto hitotsu akimashita.

席がやっと1つ空きました。

At last one seat became vacant.

¶Kondo no Nichiyōbi wa aite imasu ka.

今度の日曜日は空いていますか。

Are you free this coming Sunday?

aku 開く *to open, to become open* [⇔**shimaru** 閉まる]

¶Yūbin-kyoku wa ku-ji ni akimasu.

郵便局は9時に開きます。

The post office opens at 9:00.

¶Kono bin wa nakanaka akanai ne.

この瓶はなかなか開かないね。

This bottle just won't open, will it.

¶Sono mise wa nijūyo-jikan aite imasu.

その店は24時間開いています。

The store is open 24 hours a day.

akuarángu アクアラング *aqualung*

akubi 欠伸 *yawn*

•akubi o suru あくびをする *to yawn, to give a yawn*

¶Yamada-san wa ōki na akubi o shimashita.

山田さんは大きなあくびをしました。

Mr. Yamada gave a big yawn.

ákuma 悪魔 *devil, demon* [⇔**tenshi** 天使]

•akuma no yō na 悪魔のような *devilish, fiendish*

akurobátto アクロバット ① *acrobatics* [→**kyokugei** 曲芸]

② *acrobat* [→**kyokugei-shi** 曲芸師 (s.v. **kyokugei** 曲芸)]

ákusento アクセント *accent, stress* «on a syllable»

ákuseru アクセル *accelerator* (*pedal*)

ákusesarī アクセサリー ① *fashion accessory* «Usually refers to a jewerly item.»

② *accessory, appurtence* [→**fuzoku-hin** 付属品 (s.v. **fuzoku** 付属)]

ákushon アクション ① *action, act, behavior* [→**kōdō** 行動]

② (*violent*)*action* «in movies, etc.»

•akushon-eiga アクション映画 *action movie*

•akushon-sutā アクションスター *action movie star*

ákushu 握手 *handshake, shaking hands*

•akushu suru 握手する *to shake hands*

¶Watashi wa aite to akushu shimashita.

私は相手と握手しました。

I shook hands with my opponent.

áma 尼 ① *Buddhist nun*

② *Christian nun*

áma アマ [☞**amachua** アマチュア]

áma 海女 *woman diver* «A traditional occupation in Japan, **ama** use no breathing equipment and dive for seaweed, shellfish, etc.»

amachua アマチュア *an amateur* [⇔**puro** プロ]

•amachua-supōtsu アマチュアスポーツ *amateur sports*

amádo 雨戸 *rain door* «a sliding door or shutter on a Japanese house that is closed to keep out the rain»

amaeru 甘える *to presume on the love or kindness* «of someone»; *to act like a baby* «toward someone in order to get that person to satisfy one's selfish desires»

¶Imōto wa tokidoki haha ni amaemasu.

妹は時々母に甘えます。

My younger sister sometimes acts like a baby toward my mother.

amai 甘い ① *sweet* (*-tasting*)

¶Amai mono ga suki desu.

甘い物が好きです。

I like sweet things.

② *lenient, indulgent*

¶Minami-sensei wa saiten ga amai desu.
南先生は採点が甘いです。
Mr. Minami's grading is lenient.
　③ *overly optimistic, naive*
¶Chotto kangae ga amai yo.
ちょっと考えが甘いよ。
Your thinking is a bit overly optimistic!

Ama-nó-gawa 天の川 *the Milky Way*

amarí 余り *the rest, remainder, surplus*
[→**nokori** 残り]
¶Bentō no amari o inu ni yatta yo.
弁当の余りを犬にやったよ。
I gave the rest of my lunch to the dog!

-amari －余り *over, more than* 《Added
to bases denoting quantities.》
¶Ikeda-san-tachi wa is-shūkan-amari
Hawai ni ita.
池田さんたちは1週間あまりハワイにいた。
*The Ikeda's were in Hawaii for over a
week.*

amari あまり ① （〜**ni** 〜に） *too, too
much*
¶Amari ni samui desu.
あまりに寒いです。
It's too cold.
¶Amari tabesuginai de ne.
あまり食べすぎないでね。
Don't eat too much, OK?
¶Amari atsui node tsumetai shawā o
abita.
あまり暑いので冷たいシャワーを浴びた。
It was too hot, so I took a cold shower.
¶Karēraisu ga amari karakatta node,
zenbu wa taberaremasen deshita.
カレーライスがあまり辛かったので、全部は
食べられませんでした。
*Since the curry and rice was too
(spicy)hot, I couldn't eat it all.*
　② 〈*not*〉 *very,* 〈*not*〉 *much,*
〈*not*〉 *many* 《in combination with a
negative predicate》
¶Jazu wa amari suki ja nai desu.
ジャズはあまり好きじゃないです。
I don't like jazz very much.
¶Watashi wa amari eiga o mi ni ikimasen.
私はあまり映画を見に行きません。

I don't go to see movies very much.
¶Sakana wa amari imasen deshita.
魚はあまりいませんでした。
There weren't very many fish.
¶Masao-san wa amari shaberimasen ne.
正男さんはあまりしゃべりませんね。
Masao doesn't talk very much, does he.

amarírisu アマリリス *amaryllis*
((plant))

amáru 余る *to remain as surplus, to be
left over*
¶O-kane wa ikura amarimashita ka.
お金はいくら余りましたか。
How much money was left over?
¶Sanjū kara jūsan o hiku to jūnana
amaru deshō?
30から13を引くと17余るでしょう？
*If you subtract 13 from 30, 17 is left
over, right?*

amayádori 雨宿り *taking shelter from
the rain*
¶Koko de amayadori o shimashō.
ここで雨宿りをしましょう。
Let's take shelter here from the rain.

amayakásu 甘やかす *to indulge, to
spoil, to pamper*
¶Okāsan wa Jirō o amayakashite
shimatta ne.
お母さんは次郎を甘やかしてしまったね。
Mother spoiled Jiro, didn't she.

áme 雨 *rain*
¶Ame wa hiru-goro ni yamimashita.
雨は昼ごろにやみました。
The rain stopped around noon.
¶Ame no hi wa kirai desu.
雨の日は嫌いです。
I dislike rainy days.
• ame ga furu 雨が降る *rain falls*
¶Ashita wa ame ga furu deshō.
あしたは雨が降るでしょう。
Tomorrow it will probably rain.
¶Nihon de wa Roku-gatsu ni ame ga ōku
furimasu.
日本では6月に雨が多く降ります。
In Japan it rains a lot in June.
• ame ni au 雨にあう *to get caught in the
rain*

ame 飴 *sweetened-starch candy*
amēba アメーバ *amoeba*
Amerika アメリカ ① *America, the Americas*

② *the United States* [→**Beikoku** 米国]
• Amerika-gasshūkoku アメリカ合衆国 *the United States of America*
• Amerika-Indian アメリカインディアン *American Indian*
• Amerika-jin アメリカ人 *an American*
¶ Amerika-jin no tomodachi ga imasu ka.
アメリカ人の友達がいますか。
Do you have any American friends?
• Chūō-Amerika 中央アメリカ *Central America*
• Kita-Amerika 北アメリカ *North America* [→**Hokubei** 北米]
• Minami-Amerika 南アメリカ *South America* [→**Nanbei** 南米]
• Raten-Amerika ラテンアメリカ *Latin America*

amí 網 *net*
• ami de toru 網で捕る *to catch with a net*
¶ Ogawa de sakana o ami de torimashita.
小川で魚を網で捕りました。
I caught a fish with a net in the stream.
• ami ni kakaru 網にかかる *to become caught in a net*
• ami-dana 網棚 *shelf with a net bottom* 《typical overhead luggage rack on a Japanese train》
• ami-do 網戸 *window screen; screen door*

amímono 編み物 *knitting*
• amimono o suru 編み物をする *to do knitting*

aminosan アミノ酸 *amino acid*
āmóndo アーモンド *almond*
ámu 編む *to knit, to weave; to braid*
¶ Chichi ni tebukuro o ande agemashita.
父に手袋を編んであげました。
I knitted mittens for my father.

án 案 ① *proposal, suggestion* [→**teian** 提案]
¶ Sono an wa kyohi saremashita.
その案は拒否されました。

That proposal was rejected.

② *idea* [→**kangae** 考え]; *plan* [→**keikaku** 計画]
¶ Nani-ka ii an wa arimasen ka.
何かいい案はありませんか。
Don't you have any good ideas?

án あん *sweet bean paste*
• an-pan あんパン *sweet bean-paste bun*
aná 穴 *hole*
¶ Chichi wa niwa ni ana o horimashita.
父は庭に穴を掘りました。
My father dug a hole in the garden.
• ana ga aku 穴が開く *a hole appears* 《in something》
• ana o akeru 穴を開ける *to make a hole* 《in something》

anáta あなた ① *you* 《There are several Japanese words for *you*, and **anata** is the most commonly used in translation from English. In general, however, Japanese speakers prefer to use names or titles rather than words for *you*. It is not appropriate to use **anata** to refer to a social superior. Other words for *you* include **kimi** 君, **omae** お前, and **kisama** 貴様.》
¶ Anata wa heikin yori se ga takai ne.
あなたは平均より背が高いね。
You are taller than average, aren't you.
¶ Watashi no kami wa kuro de, anata no wa kinpatsu desu.
私の髪は黒で、あなたのは金髪です。
My hair is black, and yours is blonde.
¶ Anata-jishin ga sore o yatta no desu.
あなた自身がそれをやったのです。
You did that yourself.

② *dear, darling* 《when used by a wife to her husband》

anaúnsā アナウンサー *announcer*
anaúnsu アナウンス *announcement* 《made over a microphone》
• anaunsu suru アナウンスする *to announce*
anda 安打 *hit* 《in baseball》
• anda o utsu 安打を打つ *to get a hit*
• anda suru 安打する *to hit safely*
andánte アンダンテ *andante*
andāráin アンダーライン *underline*

•A ni andārain o hiku アンダーラインを引
く to underline A

¶Sono tango ni andārain o hikimashita.

その単語にアンダーラインを引きました。

I underlined that word.

andāshátsu アンダーシャツ *undershirt*

andāsurō アンダースロー *underhand throw* 《in baseball》

ane 姉 *older sister* [⇔**ani** 兄; **onēsan** お姉さん; **imōto** 妹]

¶Ane wa suchuwādesu desu.

姉はスチュワーデスです。

My older sister is a stewardess.

anemone アネモネ *anemone*

angai 案外 (〜**ni** 〜に) *unexpectedly*

¶Kono mondai wa angai muzukashii ne.

この問題は案外難しいね。

This problem is unexpectedly difficult, isn't it?

•angai na 案外な *unexpected, surprising*

angō 暗号 *code*

¶Supai wa angō de tsūshin o okurimashita.

スパイは暗号で通信を送りました。

The spy sent a communication in code.

ánguru アングル *angle, viewpoint* [→**kakudo** 角度②]

¶Iroiro na anguru de butsuzō no shashin o totta.

いろいろなアングルで仏像の写真を撮った。

I took photos of the Buddhist image from various angles.

áni 兄 *older brother* [⇔**ane** 姉; **onīsan** お兄さん; **otōto** 弟]

¶Watashi ni wa ani ga san-nin imasu.

私には兄が３人います。

I have three older brothers.

animḗshon アニメーション (*movie*) *animation*

•animēshon-eiga アニメーション映画 *animated cartoon*

anji 暗示 *suggestion, hint*

¶Hayakawa-san wa anji ni kakari-yasui desu.

早川さんは暗示にかかりやすいです。

Mr. Hayakawa is easily influenced by suggestion.

•anji suru 暗示する *to suggest, to hint at*

•jiko-anji 自己暗示 *autosuggestion*

ánkā アンカー ① *anchor* 《of a ship or boat》[→**ikari** 錨]

¶Sono fune wa minato ni ankā o oroshimashita.

その船は港にアンカーを下ろしました。

The boat dropped anchor in the harbor.

② *anchor* 《in a relay》

¶Yoshida-kun wa rirē de ankā o tsutomemashita.

吉田君はリレーでアンカーを務めました。

Yoshida served as anchor in the relay.

ánkēto アンケート *questionnaire*

¶Ankēto ni kinyū shite kudasai.

アンケートに記入してください。

Please fill out the questionnaire.

anki 暗記 *memorization, learning by heart*

¶Nogi-san wa anki ni tsuyoi desu.

野木さんは暗記に強いです。

Mr. Nogi is good at memorization.

•anki suru 暗記する *to memorize, to learn by heart*

¶Kono kashi o anki shinasai.

この歌詞を暗記しなさい。

Learn these lyrics by heart.

ánko あんこ 【COL. for **an** あん】

ankóru アンコール *encore*

¶Domingo wa ankōru o ni-kyoku utaimashita.

ドミンゴはアンコールを２曲歌いました。

Domingo sang two encores.

•ankōru suru アンコールする *to ask for an encore*

¶Chōshū wa sono kashu ni ankōru o motometa.

聴衆はその歌手にアンコールを求めた。

The audience asked that singer for an encore.

anmari あんまり 【COL. for **amari** あまり】

anmonia アンモニア *ammonia*

anna あんな *that kind of* 《Like other Japanese demonstratives beginning with a-, **anna** has two uses. One is to refer to something which is in sight and relatively far both from the speaker and from the listener(s). The other is to refer to something which is not in sight but which is familiar both to the speaker and to the listener(s).》 [⇔**konna** こんな; **sonna** そんな]

¶Anna hito wa kirai desu yo.
あんな人は嫌いですよ。
I dislike that kind of person!

¶Anna shiai o mita koto ga nai desu.
あんな試合を見たことがないです。
I have never seen that kind of game.

•anna ni あんなに *to that extent, that much*

¶Anna ni kangaenakute mo ii desu yo.
あんなに考えなくてもいいですよ。
You don't have to think so hard!

annái 案内 ① *guiding, going along to show the way*

•annai suru 案内する *to guide, to show the way*

¶Oba wa Kyōto o annai shite kuremashita.
伯母は京都を案内してくれました。
My aunt showed me around Kyoto.

¶Kono hito o heya ni annai shite kudasai.
この人を部屋に案内してください。
Please show this person into the room.

② *information, notification*

¶Tenrankai no annai ga kimashita.
展覧会の案内が来ました。
Notification of the exhibition came.

•annai suru 案内する *to inform, to notify*

•annai-jo 案内所 *information desk; information booth*

•annai-nin 案内人 *guide* ((person))

•annai-sho 案内書 *guidebook*

•annai-zu 案内図 *guide map*

ano あの *that, those* 《as a noun modifier》《Like other Japanese demonstratives beginning with **a**–, **ano** has two uses. One is to refer to something which is in sight and relatively far both from the speaker and from the listener(s). The other is to refer to something which is not in

sight but which is familiar both to the speaker and to the listener(s).》 [⇔**kono** この; **sono** その]

¶Ano hito wa dare desu ka.
あの人はだれですか。
Who is that person?

¶Ano toki nani o shite ita no desu ka.
あの時何をしていたのですか。
What were you doing at that time?

anō あのう *uh, um, er* 《a pause filler》 [→**ēto** ええと]

anpáia アンパイア *umpire*

¶Senshu-tachi wa anpaia ni shitagaimashita.
選手たちはアンパイアに従いました。
The players obeyed the umpires.

•anpaia o suru アンパイアをする *to umpire*

anpéa アンペア *ampere*

•–anpea －アンペア《counter for amperes; see Appendix 2》

ánpu アンプ *amplifier*

ánraku 安楽 *comfort, ease*

•anraku na 安楽な *comfortable, easy*

¶Sobo wa anraku ni kurashite imasu.
祖母は安楽に暮らしています。
My grandmother is living comfortably.

•anraku-isu 安楽椅子 *easy chair*

•anraku-shi 安楽死 *euthanasia*

ansei 安静 *rest, peace and quiet*

•ansei ni shite iru 安静にしている *to be resting in bed*

¶Ni-, san-nichi ansei ni shite inasai.
2、3 日安静にしていなさい。
Rest in bed for two or three days.

•zettai-ansei 絶対安静 *complete rest*

¶Otōsan wa sūjitsu zettai-ansei ga hitsuyō desu.
お父さんは数日絶対安静が必要です。
Your father must have a complete rest for several days.

anshin 安心 [[⇔**shinpai** 心配]] *relief; peace of mind, ease of mind*

•anshin suru 安心する *to be relieved; to put one's mind at ease*

¶Sono shirase o kiite anshin shimashita.
その知らせを聞いて安心しました。

I was relieved to hear the news.
¶Sono koto ni tsuite wa anshin shite kudasai.
その事については安心してください。
Please put your mind at ease about that.

anshitsu 暗室 *darkroom*

anshō 暗唱 *recitation from memory*
•anshō suru 暗唱する *to recite from memory*

antei 安定 *stability*
•antei suru 安定する *to become stable, to stabilize*
¶Watashi-tachi wa antei shita seikatsu o nozonde imasu.
私たちは安定した生活を望んでいます。
We are hoping for a stable life.
¶Kono tēburu wa antei shite imasu.
このテーブルは安定しています。
This table is stable.

antena アンテナ *antenna* 《for electronic signals》

anzan 暗算 *mental calculation, doing arithmetic in one's head*
¶Ōmura-san wa anzan ga tokui desu.
大村さんは暗算が得意です。
Mr. Omura is good at mental calculation.

anzen 安全 *safety* [⇔**kiken** 危険]
•anzen na 安全な *safe* [⇔**abunai** 危ない]
¶Kono heya ni ireba anzen desu.
この部屋にいれば安全です。
If you stay in this room you are safe.
¶Anzen daiichi
「安全第一」《on a sign》
Safety First
•anzen-ben 安全弁 *safety valve*
•anzen-beruto 安全ベルト *safety belt*
•anzen-chitai 安全地帯 *safety zone; refuge*
•anzen-hoshō 安全保障 *security*
•anzen-pin 安全ピン *safety pin*
•anzen-sōchi 安全装置 *safety device*
•anzen-unten 安全運転 *safe driving*

áo 青 ① *blue* 《as a noun》
•koi 〔usui〕 ao 濃い 〔薄い〕 青 *dark* 〔*light*〕 *blue*

② *green* 《as a noun》《The range of **ao** includes both *blue* and *green*, but **midori** is typically used for *green*.》[→**midori** 緑]
¶Shingō ga ao ni kawarimashita.
信号が青に変わりました。
The traffic light changed to green.
•ao-ba 青葉 *green leaves*
•ao-shingō 青信号 *green (traffic)light*
•ao-zora 青空 *blue sky*

aógu 仰ぐ [[→**miageru** 見上げる]]
① *to look up at*
¶Watashi-tachi wa aozora o aogimashita.
私たちは青空を仰ぎました。
We looked up at the blue sky.
② *to look up to, to respect*
¶Watashi wa Ishii-san o shidō-sha to shite aoide iru.
私は石井さんを指導者として仰いでいる。
I look up to Mr. Ishii as my leader.

aógu 扇ぐ *to fan*
¶Haha wa sensu de kao o aoide imasu.
母は扇子で顔をあおいでいます。
My mother is fanning her face with a folding fan.

aói 青い ① *blue* 《as an adjective》
¶Sono ningyō wa aoi me o shite imasu.
その人形は青い目をしています。
The doll has blue eyes.
② *green* 《as an adjective》《The range of **aoi** includes both *blue* and *green*, but **midori no** 緑の is typically used as a noun modifier for *green*.》
•aoi ringo 青いりんご *green apple*
③ *pale* 《because of illness or fear》
¶Kaoiro ga aoi desu yo. Dō-ka shita no desu ka.
顔色が青いですよ。どうかしたのですか。
Your face is pale! Is something the matter?
¶Kawamoto-san wa sore o mite aoku narimashita.
川本さんはそれを見て青くなりました。
Ms. Kawamoto saw that and turned white.

aojirói 青白い *pale, pallid*
•aojiroi kao 青白い顔 *pale face*

aomuke 仰向け 〜**ni** 〜に *facing upward, on one's back* [⇔**utsubuse ni** うつぶせに]
¶Shōnen wa aomuke ni taoremashita.
少年はあお向けに倒れました。
The boy fell over on his back.

apáto アパート ① <*US*>*apartment,* <*UK*>*flat*
¶Watashi-tachi wa apāto ni sunde imasu.
私たちはアパートに住んでいます。
We live in an apartment.
　② <*US*>*apartment building,* <*UK*>*block of flats*
¶Kono apāto ni wa yonjū-setai ga sunde iru.
このアパートには40世帯が住んでいる。
Forty families live in this apartment building.

apíru アピール ① *appeal, attraction*
• apīru suru アピールする *to appeal*
　② *appeal, entreaty*
• apīru suru アピールする *to appeal* [→**yobikakeru** 呼びかける②]

appíru アッピール [☞**apīru** アピール]

appuríke アップリケ ① *appliqué, sewing on decorative patches*
　② *appliqué, decorative patches*

apurōchi アプローチ *approach, method*
• apurōchi suru アプローチする *to approach*

ára あら *Oh!; Why!* «*an interjection expressing surprise or dismay; generally restricted to female speakers*»
¶Ara mā.
あらまあ。
Oh, dear!
¶Ara, Kyōko-san mo iru wa.
あら、京子さんもいるわ。
Why, Kyoko's here too!

arai 荒い ① *rough, violent*
¶Kyō wa nami ga arai desu.
きょうは波が荒いです。
Today the sea is rough.
　② *coarse, vulgar*
¶Kazuko-san wa kotoba-zukai ga arai desu.
和子さんは言葉づかいが荒いです。
Kazuko's way of speaking is coarse.

arai 粗い ① *coarse, not fine*
¶Kono nuno wa me ga arai desu ne.
この布は目が粗いですね。
This cloth's weave is coarse, isn't it.
　② *rough, not smooth*
• arai hada 粗い肌 *rough skin*

arakajime 予め *in advance* [→**maemotte** 前もって]
¶Watashi-tachi wa arakajime junbi o totonoemashita.
私たちはあらかじめ準備を整えました。
We made preparations in advance.

arakáruto アラカルト *a la carte item*

arare 霰 *snowy hail*
• arare ga furu あられが降る *snowy hail falls*

árashi 嵐 *storm*
¶Arashi ga ki-sō desu.
嵐が来そうです。
It looks as if a storm is going to come.
¶Arashi ga osamarimashita.
嵐が治まりました。
The storm abated.
¶Otoko-tachi wa arashi no yoru ni dete ikimashita.
男たちは嵐の夜に出ていきました。
The men went out on a stormy night.

arasói 争い ① *dispute, quarrel, fight* [→**kenka** 喧嘩]; *trouble, conflict, strife*
• arasoi ga okoru 争いが起こる *a dispute arises*
　② *competition, rivalry* [→**kyōsō** 競争]

arasóu 争う ① *to argue, to quarrel, to fight* [→**kenka suru** 喧嘩する]
¶Tokidoki sasai na koto de ane to arasoimasu.
時々ささいな事で姉と争います。
I sometimes quarrel with my older sister over trivial things.
　② *to compete for*
¶Watashi-tachi wa o-tagai ni ittō-shō o arasoimashita.
私たちはお互いに１等賞を争いました。
We competed with each other for the first prize.

arasu 荒らす *to damage, to ruin*
¶Usagi ga hatake o arashimashita.
うさぎが畑を荒らしました。
Rabbits damaged the field.

arasuji 粗筋 *summary, outline, synopsis*

aratamáru 改まる ① *to change, to be replaced by something new*
• toshi ga aratamaru 年が改まる *the new year comes*
② *to change for the better, to improve* 《intransitive》
¶Haruko-chan no seikaku mo daibu aratamatta yo.
春子ちゃんの性格もだいぶ改まったよ。
Haruko's disposition has also improved a great deal!
③ *to become formal, to become ceremonious*
¶Sonna ni aratamaru hitsuyō wa nai desu yo.
そんなに改まる必要はないですよ。
There's no need to become so formal!

arataméru 改める ① *to change, to replace with something new*
¶Kono keikaku o aratamemashō ka.
この計画を改めましょうか。
Shall we change this plan?
② *to change for the better, to improve, to correct* 《transitive》
[→**kaizen suru** 改善する]
¶Kanemaru-san wa warui shūkan o aratamemashita.
金丸さんは悪い習慣を改めました。
Mr. Kanemaru improved his bad habits.
¶Ayamari ga areba aratamete kudasai.
誤りがあれば改めてください。
If there are errors, please correct them.
③ *to examine, to check*
¶O-kyaku-san no kippu o aratamemashita.
お客さんの切符を改めました。
I checked the customers' tickets.

aratámete 改めて *again, anew* [→**futatabi** 再び]
¶Aratamete ukagaimasu.
改めて伺います。

I will call on you again.
¶Ato de aratamete o-denwa shimasu.
あとで改めてお電話します。
I will phone again later.

arau 洗う *to wash*
¶Kao o arainasai.
顔を洗いなさい。
Wash your face.
¶Ringo o mizu de araimashita.
りんごを水で洗いました。
I washed the apples with water.
¶Te o sekken de kirei ni araimashita ka.
手を石けんできれいに洗いましたか。
Did you wash your hands clean with soap?

arawaréru 表れる, 現れる *to appear, to come in sight; to be manifested, to show*
¶Eiga-sutā ga totsuzen butai ni arawaremashita.
映画スターが突然舞台に現れました。
A movie star suddenly appeared on the stage.
¶Taiyō ga kumo no aida kara arawaremashita.
太陽が雲の間から現れました。
The sun came out from behind the clouds.
¶Kanjō ga sensei no kao ni arawarete imasu.
感情が先生の顔に表れています。
Emotion is showing on the teacher's face.

arawásu 表す, 現す ① *to show, to make manifest; to express* [→**hyōgen suru** 表現する]
¶Yamada-san wa jibun no kanjō o kao ni arawasanai.
山田さんは自分の感情を顔に表さない。
Mr. Yamada does not show his feelings on his face.
¶Egao de kansha no kimochi o arawashimashita.
笑顔で感謝の気持ちを表しました。
I expressed my feeling of gratitude with a smiling face.
• sugata o arawasu 姿を現す *to appear, to show oneself, to come in sight*

② *to stand for, to mean, to represent* [→**imi suru** 意味する]

¶ "Yū enu" wa nani o arawasu no desu ka.

「UN」は何を表すのですか。

What does "UN" stand for?

arawásu 著す *to write and publish, to author*

arayúru あらゆる *all, every* [→**subete no** すべての]

¶ Kore wa arayuru shurui no hana ni kan-suru hon desu.

これはあらゆる種類の花に関する本です。

This is a book about all kinds of flowers.

¶ Arayuru doryoku o shimashita.

あらゆる努力をしました。

I made every effort.

are あれ *that (one)* 《Like other Japanese demonstratives beginning with **a-**, **are** has two uses. One is to refer to something which is in sight and relatively far both from the speaker and from the listener(s). The other is to refer to something which is not in sight but which is familiar both to the speaker and to the listener(s).》[⇔ **kore** これ; **sore** それ]

¶ Are wa nan desu ka.

あれは何ですか。

What is that?

¶ Are wa Yamada-kun da yo.

あれは山田君だよ。

That's Yamada! 《This use of **are** instead of **ano hito** あの人 to refer to a person is not very polite.》

• are kara あれから *after that; since then*

¶ Are kara nani o shimashita ka.

あれから何をしましたか。

What did you do after that?

¶ Are kara chichi ni tegami o kaite imasen.

あれから父に手紙を書いていません。

I have not written a letter to my father since then.

• are-kore (to) あれこれ(と) *in a manner involving this and that*

¶ Watashi-tachi wa are-kore to

oshaberi shimashita.

私たちはあれこれとおしゃべりしました。

We chatted about this and that.

are あれ *Dear!; Heavens!* 《an interjection expressing surprise or dismay》

¶ Are, dare mo inai yo.

あれ、だれもいないよ。

Heavens, there's no one here!

aréguro アレグロ *allegro*

areru 荒れる ① *to become rough* 《when the subject is the sea, etc.》

¶ Umi wa kinō arete imashita.

海はきのう荒れていました。

The sea was rough yesterday.

② *to become stormy* 《when the subject is the weather》

¶ Kyō wa tenki ga areru sō desu.

きょうは天気が荒れるそうです。

They say the weather will become stormy today.

③ *to become ruined, to become dilapidated*

¶ Tonari no ie wa sukkari arete shimaimashita.

隣の家はすっかり荒れてしまいました。

The house next door became completely dilapidated.

④ *to become chapped, to become rough*

¶ Haha no te wa daidokoro-shigoto de arete imasu.

母の手は台所仕事で荒れています。

My mother's hands are rough from kitchen work.

arérugī アレルギー *allergy*

• arerugī-taishitsu アレルギー体質 *allergic constitution*

ari 蟻 *ant*

• ari no gyōretsu ありの行列 *line of ants*

• ari no su ありの巣 *ant nest*

aribai アリバイ *alibi*

arifureta ありふれた *commonplace, very common, not at all unusual* 《Used only as a noun modifier, not as a predicate.》

¶ Tarō wa arifureta namae desu.

太郎はありふれた名前です。

Taro is a very common name.

¶Sumiko wa arifureta doresu o kite iru yo.

澄子はありふれたドレスを着ているよ。

Sumiko is wearing a commonplace dress!

arigatái 有り難い *welcome, meriting gratitude*

¶Mizu o ip-pai moraetara arigatai n da kedo.

水を1杯もらえたらありがたいんだけど。

If I could get a glass of water, it would be welcome.

¶Sō itte kudasatte totemo arigatai desu.

そう言ってくださってとてもありがたいです。

I am very grateful to you for saying so.

•arigatai koto ni ありがたいことに *fortunately*

¶Arigatai koto ni ame ga yamimashita.

ありがたいことに雨がやみました。

Fortunately, the rain stopped.

arígatō 有難う *Thank you*

ありがとうございます 【FORMAL for **arigatō**】 *Thank you very much* «for what you are doing or going to do»

ありがとうございました 【FORMAL for **arigatō** 】 *Thank you very much* «for what you have done»

¶"Go-chūkoku dōmo arigatō gozaimashita." "Dō itashimashite."

「ご忠告どうもありがとうございました」「どういたしまして」

"Thank you very much for your advice." "You're welcome."

áru アール *are* «unit of area»

•-āru －アール«counter for ares; see Appendix 2»

áru 或る *certain, unspecified* «Used only as a noun modifier, not as a predicate.»

¶Takagi-san wa aru daigaku ni hairimashita.

高木さんはある大学に入りました。

Mr. Takagi entered a certain university.

áru ある {Irreg.} ①«The subject ordinarily must be inanimate.»

there is∕are; to be (located); to exist [→**sonzai suru** 存在する]

¶Tēburu no ue ni tokei ga arimasu.

テーブルの上に時計があります。

There is a watch on the table.

¶Watashi no kaban ga isu no shita ni arimasu.

私のかばんがいすの下にあります。

My bag is under the chair.

¶Migi ni magaru to ginkō ga arimasu yo.

右に曲がると銀行がありますよ。

When you turn right, there is a bank!

¶Kono hoteru ni wa heya ga rokujū-shitsu arimasu.

このホテルには部屋が60室あります。

There are sixty rooms in this hotel.

② *to have, to possess* «What is possessed is treated as a grammatical subject and marked with **ga** が rather than with **o** を.»

¶Ani wa kuruma ga ni-dai arimasu.

兄は車が2台あります。

My older brother has two cars.

③ *there is∕are, to take place, to happen*

¶Nani-ka atta n desu ka.

何かあったんですか。

Did something happen?

¶Yūbe kaji ga arimashita.

ゆうべ火事がありました。

Last night there was a fire.

¶Kinō pātī ga atta yo.

きのうパーティーがあったよ。

Yesterday there was a party!

¶Kyō sūgaku no shiken mo arimashita.

きょう数学の試験もありました。

Today there was also a math exam.

arubáito アルバイト *part-time job; side job*

¶Ane wa eigo gakkō de arubaito o shite imasu.

姉は英語学校でアルバイトをしています。

My older sister is working part-time at an English school.

•arubaito-gakusei アルバイト学生 *student with a part-time job*

arubamu アルバム ① *album* «for photographs, stamps, etc.»

② *(record)album*

arufabétto アルファベット *alphabet*

• arufabetto-jun アルファベット順 *alphabetical order*

¶ Hon wa chosha-mei no arufabetto-jun ni naraberarete imasu.

本は著者名のアルファベット順に並べられています。

The books are arranged according to author.

arúiwa 或いは ① *or* [→**mata-wa** または]

¶ Satoko ka aruiwa Hideko ga machigatte iru.

里子かあるいは秀子がまちがっている。

Either Satoko or Hideko is wrong.

② *perhaps* 《This word typically occurs in sentences ending with an expression of possibility (such as **ka mo shirenai** かもしれない). Since such a sentence has virtually the same meaning whether or not **aruiwa** is present, **aruiwa** is redundant in a sense, but it serves as a signal of how a sentence will end.》

¶ Aruiwa haha no iu tōri ka mo shiremasen.

あるいは母の言うとおりかもしれません。

Perhaps it is as my mother says.

arukari アルカリ *alkali* [⇔**san** 酸]

• arukari no アルカリの *alkaline*

• arukari-sei アルカリ性 *alkalinity*

arukōru アルコール *alcohol*

• arukōru-chūdoku アルコール中毒 *alcoholism*

arúku 歩く *to walk*

¶ Kyō mo zuibun arukimashita.

きょうもずいぶん歩きました。

I walked a great deal today too.

• aruite 歩いて *on foot, by walking*

¶ Kōen made aruite jup-pun desu.

公園まで歩いて10分です。

It's 10 minutes to the park on foot.

¶ Aruite sugu desu.

歩いてすぐです。

It's a short walk. 《Literally: *Walking, it's nearby.*》

¶ Aruite zuibun arimasu.

歩いてずいぶんあります。

It's a long walk. 《Literally: *Walking,*

there's quite a lot.》

arumi アルミ *aluminum*

• arumi-hoiru アルミホイル *aluminum foil*

• arumi-sasshi アルミサッシ *aluminum* (*window*)*sash*

aruminyūmu アルミニウム 《Note the mismatch between the katakana spelling and the pronunciation.》 [☞**arumi** アルミ]

áruto アルト ① *alto* (*voice*)

② *alto* (*singer*)

③ *alto* (*part*)

asá 麻 *hemp*

ása 朝 *morning*

¶ Watashi wa asa roku-ji ni okimasu.

私は朝6時に起きます。

I get up at 6:00 in the morning.

¶ Nichiyōbi no asa ni yūfō o mita yo.

日曜日の朝にＵＦＯを見たよ。

I saw a UFO on Sunday morning!

¶ Kawamura-kun wa asa kara ban made benkyō shimasu.

川村君は朝から晩まで勉強します。

Kawamura studies from morning till night.

• asa-gohan 朝ご飯 *breakfast* [→**chōshoku** 朝食]

ásaban 朝晩 *morning and night*

aságao 朝顔 *morning-glory* ((flower))

ásahi 朝日 *morning sun, rising sun*

asai 浅い *shallow* [⇔**fukai** 深い]

¶ Kono kawa wa koko ga asai desu.

この川はここが浅いです。

This river is shallow here.

¶ Haha wa nemuri ga asai desu.

母は眠りが浅いです。

My mother's sleep is shallow.

¶ Sono kizu wa asai desu ne.

その傷は浅いですね。

That wound is shallow, isn't it.

• keiken ga asai 経験が浅い *to have little experience*

asari あさり *short-necked clam*

asátte 明後日 *the day after tomorrow*

• shi-asatte 明明後日 *the day after the day after tomorrow*

áse 汗 *sweat*

• ase o kaku 汗をかく *to sweat*

- ase o fuku 汗をふく *to wipe off sweat*
- ase–bisshori no 汗びっしょりの *sweaty all over, dripping with sweat*
- hiya–ase 冷や汗 *cold sweat*

aséru 焦る {5} *to become hurried; to get impatient* [→**iraira suru** いらいらする]; *to get excited, to get flustered*

¶Shiken ga jiki ni hajimaru node, asette imasu.
試験がじきに始まるので、焦っています。
The examination starts soon, so I'm flustered.

¶Asette wa ikemasen.
焦ってはいけません。
You mustn't get flustered.

ashí 足 ① *foot*

¶Ashi ga shibirete imasu.
足がしびれています。
My foot is asleep.

- ashi ga hayai 足が速い *fast at running, fleet-footed*
- ashi no ura 足の裏 *sole of the foot*
  ② *leg* 《*including the foot*》

¶Chichi wa ashi ga nagai desu.
父は足が長いです。
My father's legs are long.

¶Ashi o kunde suwaru no wa kitsui desu.
足を組んで座るのはきついです。
Sitting with your legs crossed is hard.

- ashi–ato 足跡 *footprint*
- ashi–dori 足取り *gait, steps*
- ashi–moto 足元 *the area at one's feet*

¶Ashimoto ni go–chūi kudasai.
足元にご注意ください。
Please watch your step.

- ashi–oto 足音 (*the sound of*)*footsteps*

ashíkubi 足首 *ankle*

ashísutanto アシスタント *assistant*

ashitá 明日 *tomorrow*

¶Ashita wa watashi no tanjōbi desu.
あしたは私の誕生日です。
Tomorrow is my birthday.

¶Ashita no gogo ni pātī o hirakimasu.
あしたの午後にパーティーを開きます。
We'll have a party tomorrow afternoon.

¶Ashita no ima–goro mata kimasu.

あしたの今ごろまた来ます。
I'll come again at about this time tomorrow.

¶Mata ashita.
またあした。
See you tomorrow.

asobi 遊び *play, game, recreation, amusement*

¶Daigaku-sei wa taitei asobi ga dai-suki desu.
大学生はたいてい遊びが大好きです。
College students are almost all very fond of play.

- asobi ni iku 遊びに行く *to go and visit, to go for a visit*
- asobi ni kuru 遊びに来る *to come and visit, to come for a visit*

¶Chikai uchi ni uchi e asobi ni kite kudasai.
近いうちにうちへ遊びに来てください。
Please come to my house for a visit soon.

- asobi–aite 遊び相手 *playmate*
- asobi–ba 遊び場 *playground*

asobu 遊ぶ ① *to play, to enjoy oneself, to have fun*

¶Kodomo-tachi wa kōen de asonde imasu.
子供たちは公園で遊んでいます。
The children are playing in the park.

¶Toranpu o shite asobimashita.
トランプをして遊びました。
We played cards.

¶Watashi-tachi wa kaigan de tanoshiku asobimashita.
私たちは海岸で楽しく遊びました。
We enjoyed ourselves at the seashore.
  ② *to be idle*

¶Kinō wa ichi–nichi asonde shimaimashita.
きのうは1日遊んでしまいました。
I was idle all day yesterday.

asoko あそこ *that place* (*over there*), *there* 《*Like other Japanese demonstratives beginning with* **a**–, *asoko has two uses. One is to refer to a place which is in sight and is relatively far both from the* speaker and from the listener(s). The other is to refer to a place which is not in sight but which is familiar both to the speaker and to the listener(s).» [⇔**koko** ここ; **soko** そこ]

¶Asoko ni entotsu ga miemasu.

あそこに煙突が見えます。

A chimney is visible over there.

assári あっさり *simply, easily*

¶Taguchi-kun wa muzukashii mondai o assari toku yo.

田口君は難しい問題をあっさり解くよ。

Taguchi solves the difficult problems easily!

• assari sita あっさりした *plain, simple*

¶Watashi wa assari shita tabemono ga suki desu.

私はあっさりした食べ物が好きです。

I like plain food.

ásu アース <*US*>(*electrical*)*ground,* <*UK*>(*electrical*)*earth*

asú 明日 *tomorrow* [→**ashita** 明日]

asufáruto アスファルト *asphalt*

asuparágasu アスパラガス *asparagus*

ataeru 与える *to give*

¶Sono shirase wa sensei ni shokku o ataeta.

その知らせは先生にショックを与えた。

That news gave the teacher a shock.

¶Sakamoto-san ni ittō-shō o ataemashō.

坂本さんに1等賞を与えましょう。

Let's give the first prize to Ms. Sakamoto.

atai 値 *value, worth* [→**kachi** 価値]

• A ni atai suru Aに値する *to be worth A*

¶Kono hon wa ichi-doku ni atai suru to omoimasu.

この本は一読に値すると思います。

I think this book is worth reading.

átakamo あたかも *just like, just as if* [→**marude** まるで]

atákku アタック ① *attack* [→**kōgeki** 攻撃]

• atakku suru アタックする *to make an attack*

② *strenuous effort* «toward a difficult goal»

• atakku suru アタックする *to make a strenuous effort*

atamá 頭 ① *head*

¶Chichi wa atama o kaku kuse ga arimasu.

父は頭をかくくせがあります。

My father has a habit of scratching his head.

• atama ga itai 頭が痛い *one has a headache*

• atama o karu 頭を刈る *to cut a person's hair*

¶Rihatsu-ten de atama o katte moraimashita.

理髪店で頭を刈ってもらいました。

I had my hair cut at the barbershop.

② *head, mind, brains* [→**zunō** 頭脳]

• atama ga ii 頭がいい *to be smart, to be bright*

• atama o tsukau 頭を使う *to use one's head*

• atama ga furui 頭が古い *to have old-fashioned ideas*

• atama ni kuru 頭に来る *to get angry*

¶Aitsu ni wa hontō ni atama ni kita yo.

あいつには本当に頭にきたよ。

I really got angry at that guy!

atamakin 頭金 *down-payment*

atarashii 新しい ① *new* [⇔**furui** 古い]

¶Atarashii kuruma ga hoshii desu.

新しい車が欲しいです。

I want a new car.

¶Atarashiku kaiten shita depāto ni ikimashō.

新しく開店したデパートに行きましょう。

Let's go to the newly-opened department store.

• atarashii nyūsu 新しいニュース *hot news*

② *fresh* [→**shinsen na** 新鮮な]

¶Kono tamago wa atarashii desu ka.

この卵は新しいですか。

Are these eggs fresh?

átari 辺り *area around, vicinity* [→**hen** 辺①]

¶Boku wa atari o mimawashimashita.

僕はあたりを見回しました。

I looked around me.

¶Watashi ga modotte kuru made kono atari ni inasai.

私が戻ってくるまでこのあたりにいなさい。

Stay around here until I return.

atari 当たり ① *hitting, striking, contact*

② *hit* 《*on a mark, target, etc.*》

③ *hit, success*

¶Sono shibai wa atari desu.

その芝居は当たりです。

That play is a hit.

④ *correct guess*

• magure-atari まぐれ当たり (*lucky*)*fluke*

• ō-atari 大当たり *big hit*

atarimae 当たり前 ～**no** ～の *natural, obvious, unsurprising* [→**tōzen no** 当然の]

¶Kodomo ga dekinai no wa atarimae da yo.

子供ができないのは当たり前だよ。

It's obvious that a child can't do it!

ataru 当たる ① *to hit, to strike, to make contact*

¶Bōru ga musuko no atama ni atarimashita.

ボールが息子の頭に当たりました。

A ball hit my son's head.

• hi ga ataru 日が当たる *the sun shines 〈on〉, sunlight strikes*

② *to hit* 《*a mark, target, etc.*》[⇔**hazureru** 外れる②]

• kuji ni ataru くじに当たる *to draw a winning lot, to win a lottery prize*

③ *to be exposed, to expose oneself* 《*to a natural phenomenon*》

¶Watashi-tachi wa hi ni atatte atatamarimashita.

私たちは火に当たって暖まりました。

We warmed ourselves at the fire.

④ *to prove correct* [⇔**hazureru** 外れる③]

¶Tenki-yohō wa atarimashita.

天気予報は当たりました。

The weather forecast proved correct.

¶Sono yosō mo atatta ne.

その予想も当たったね。

That prediction also proved

correct, didn't it.

⑤ *to be called on, to be assigned*

¶Kyō wa jugyō de go-kai mo atatta yo.

きょうは授業で５回も当たったよ。

I was called on five times in class today!

⑥ *to correspond, to be equivalent*

¶Eigo no "red" wa Nihon-go no "aka" ni atarimasu ne.

英語の「red」は日本語の「赤」に当たりますね。

English "red" corresponds to Japanese "aka", doesn't it.

¶Kotoshi wa Kodomo no hi ga Nichiyōbi ni atarimasu.

今年は子供の日が日曜日に当たります。

This year Children's Day falls on Sunday.

⑦ *to get poisoned, to get ill* 《*from eating or exposure to something*》

• sakana ni ataru 魚に当る *to get ill from eating fish*

atashi あたし 【COL.】 *I, me* 《*There are several Japanese words for I／me. The word **atashi** is ordinarily restricted to female speakers and is less formal than **watashi**. Other words for I／me include **watashi** 私, **watakushi** 私, **boku** 僕, and ore 俺.*》

atasshukēsu アタッシュケース *attaché case*

atatakái 暖かい, 温かい ① *warm* 《*in temperature*》[⇔**suzushii** 涼しい]

¶Kyō wa atatakai desu ne.

きょうは暖かいですね。

It's warm today, isn't it?

¶Kyonen no fuyu wa atatakakatta desu.

去年の冬は暖かかったです。

Last year's winter was warm.

¶Nani-ka atatakai nomimono ga hoshii desu.

何か温かい飲み物が欲しいです。

I want something warm to drink.

• atatakai hi 暖かい日 *warm day*

② *warm, providing warmth*

¶Kyō wa atatakai sētā o kite imasu.

きょうは暖かいセーターを着ています。

Today I'm wearing a warm sweater.

③ *warm (-hearted), kind, kindhearted* [→**shinsetsu na** 親切な] [⇔**tsumetai** 冷たい②]

¶Takeyama-san wa atatakai hito desu.

竹山さんは暖かい人です。

Mr. Takeyama is a warm person.

atatamáru 暖まる，温まる *to warm up* 《intransitive》[⇔**hieru** 冷える]

¶Sūpu ga yoku atatamarimashita yo.

スープがよく温まりましたよ。

The soup has warmed up well!

¶Takibi ni atatte atatamarimashō.

たき火に当たって暖まりましょう。

Let's warm ourselves at the bonfire.

¶Sore wa kokoro ga atatamaru hanashi desu.

それは心が温まる話です。

That's a heartwarming story.

atataméru 暖める，温める *to warm up* 《transitive》

¶Yōko-san wa gyūnyū o atatamemashita.

洋子さんは牛乳を温めました。

Yoko warmed up the milk.

¶Heya o sugu ni atatamete kuremasen ka.

部屋をすぐに暖めてくれませんか。

Will you warm up the room right away?

atchí あっち【COL. for **achira** あちら】

ate 当て ① *aim, objective* [→**mokuteki** 目的]

• ate mo naku 当てもなく *aimlessly, with no particular objective*

② *hope, expectation* [→**kitai** 期待]

• A o ate ni suru Aを当てにする *to count on A, to put one's hopes on A*

¶Tomodachi no tasuke o ate ni shite wa ikenai yo.

友達の助けを当てにしてはいけないよ。

You shouldn't count on your friends' help!

-ate －宛 *addressed to, for* 《Added to names.》

¶Kono tegami wa Takako-san-ate desu.

この手紙は孝子さんあてです。

This letter is addressed to Takako.

atehamáru 当てはまる *to be applicable, to hold true*

¶Sono kisoku wa kono baai ni mo atehamarimasu.

その規則はこの場合にも当てはまります。

That rule applies in this case too.

atena 宛名 *addressee's name* 《on a letter, etc.》

¶Tegami ni atena o kakinasai.

手紙にあて名を書きなさい。

Write the addressee's name on the letter.

ateru 当てる ① *to make ⟨something⟩ hit ⟨something else⟩* [→**butsukeru** ぶつける]

• A ni B o ateru AにBを当てる *to make A hit B*

¶Naifu o mato ni ateru no wa muzukashii desu.

ナイフを的に当てるのは難しいです。

It is difficult to make a knife hit the target.

② *to place, to put, to hold* 《one thing to the appropriate place on another》

¶Yūko-san wa me ni hankachi o atemashita.

祐子さんは目にハンカチを当てました。

Yuko held a handkerchief to her eyes.

③ *to guess* [→**suisoku suru** 推測する]

¶Dare-mo kodomo no toshi o ateraremasen deshita.

だれも子供の年を当てられませんでした。

Nobody was able to guess the child's age.

• atete miru 当ててみる *to take a guess at*

④ *to call* 《on a person by name》

¶Sensei wa Kumi-chan ni ateta yo.

先生は久美ちゃんに当てたよ。

The teacher called on Kumi!

⑤ *to expose, to subject*

¶Akachan o tsuyoi hi ni atete wa ikemasen.

赤ちゃんを強い日に当ててはいけません。

You mustn't expose a baby to strong sun.

⑥ *to succeed* [→**seikō suru** 成功する]

• kuji de ateru くじで当てる *to win a prize in a lottery*

¶Oda-san wa kuji de issen-man-en

atemashita yo.
小田さんはくじで1000万円当てましたよ。
Ms. Oda won 10,000,000 yen in a lottery!

áto 後 ① *the area behind* [→**ushiro** 後ろ]
•A no ato o oikakeru Aの後を追いかける *to run after A, to chase after A*
¶Inu ga kodomo no ato o oikakete imasu.
犬が子供のあとを追いかけています。
The dog is running after the child.
•A no ato ni tsuku Aの後に付く *to follow along behind A*
¶Watashi-tachi wa sensei no ato ni tsuite ikimashita.
私たちは先生のあとについていきました。
We followed along behind our teacher.
•ato o furikaeru 後を振り返る *to look back, to look behind one*
•ato ni sagaru 後に下がる *to step back*
•ato ni nokoru 後に残る *to remain behind*
② *time after, time later* [⇔**mae** 前①]
¶Chōshoku no ato de tenisu o shimasu.
朝食のあとでテニスをします。
After breakfast I play tennis.
¶Shukudai o shita ato de terebi o mimasu.
宿題をしたあとでテレビを見ます。
I watch TV after I do my homework. 《A verb preceding **ato** is always in the past tense.》
¶Ato de denwa o shite kudasai.
あとで電話をしてください。
Please phone me later.
③ *the rest, remainder* [→**nokori** 残り]
¶Ato wa ashita yarimasu.
あとはあしたやります。
I will do the rest tomorrow.
④ *another, more* 《preceding a word that specifies a quantity》
¶Gakkō-seikatsu wa ato ik-kagetsu de owari desu.
学校生活はあと1か月で終わりです。
My school life will be over in a month.
¶Ato go-fun matte kudasai.

あと5分待ってください。
Please wait five more minutes.
•ato-aji 後味 *aftertaste*

áto 跡 *mark, trace; track, trail*
¶Usagi no tōtta ato ga mitsukarimashita.
うさぎの通った跡が見つかりました。
Tracks from a passing rabbit were found.
¶Masao-san no Eigo wa shinpo no ato ga miemasen.
正雄さんの英語は進歩の跡が見えません。
Masao's English shows no trace of progress.
•ashi-ato 足跡 *footprint*
•kizu-ato 傷跡 *scar*

atokátazuke 後片付け *clearing away afterwards; straightening up afterwards*
¶Watashi-tachi wa pātī no atokatazuke o shita.
私たちはパーティーの後片づけをした。
We straightened up after the party.
•tēburu no atokatazuke テーブルの後片づけ *clearing the table*

atorákushon アトラクション *side entertainment* 《offered to attract customers to the main entertainment》

atorie アトリエ *atelier, 〈artist's〉 studio*

atsui 厚い ① *thick, large from front to back* [⇔**usui** 薄い①]
¶Zuibun atsui hon desu ne.
ずいぶん厚い本ですね。
It's a really thick book, isn't it.
¶Pan o atsuku kitte kudasai.
パンを厚く切ってください。
Please cut the bread thick.
② *warm, friendly, cordial*
¶Watashi-tachi wa atsui motenashi o ukemashita.
私たちは厚いもてなしを受けました。
We received a warm welcome.

atsúi 熱い *hot* 《describing something tangible at a high temperature》[⇔**tsumetai** 冷たい]
¶Kono miso-shiru wa atsui yo.
このみそ汁は熱いよ。
This miso soup is hot!

atsúi 暑い *hot* «describing a high air temperature or how a person feels when the air temperature is high» [⟺**samui** 寒い]
¶Kyō wa totemo atsui desu ne.
きょうはとても暑いですね。
Today it's very hot, isn't it.

atsukai 扱い *treatment, handling*
• kodomo-atsukai suru 子供扱いする *to treat like a child*

atsukau 扱う *to treat, to deal with, to handle*
¶Kyaku o teinei ni atsukaimashō.
客をていねいに扱いましょう。
Let's treat the customers politely.
¶Sono kabin wa teinei ni atsukatte kudasai.
その花瓶はていねいに扱ってください。
Please handle the vase carefully.
¶Ano mise wa manga wa atsukatte imasen.
あの店は漫画は扱っていません。
That store doesn't handle comic books.

atsukurushíi 暑苦しい *stuffy, sultry*
¶Atsukurushii heya kara demashita.
暑苦しい部屋から出ました。
I went out of the stuffy room.
• atsukurushii yoru 暑苦しい夜 *sultry night*

atsumáru 集まる ① *to gather, to meet, to get together* «intransitive»
¶Seito-tachi wa sensei no mawari ni atsumarimashita.
生徒たちは先生の周りに集まりました。
The pupils gathered around the teacher.
¶Tosho-iin wa maishū Getsuyōbi ni atsumarimasu.
図書委員は毎週月曜日に集まります。
The library committee members meet every Monday.
¶O-shōgatsu ni wa shinseki ga ōzei atsumaru yo.
お正月には親せきが大勢集まるよ。
A lot of relatives get together at New Year's!
② *to be collected, to be gathered*
¶Kanari no o-kane ga atsumarimashita.
かなりのお金が集まりました。

Quite a lot of money was collected.
¶Sono jiken no shiryō wa sugu ni atsumarimashita.
その事件の資料はすぐに集まりました。
Data on that incident were gathered easily.
③ *to center, to converge*
¶Zen'in no shisen ga sensei ni atsumarimashita.
全員の視線が先生に集まりました。
Everyone's eyes converged on the teacher.

atsuméru 集める *to gather, to collect* «transitive»
¶Kōchi wa mawari ni senshu o atsumemashita.
コーチは周りに選手を集めました。
The coach gathered the players around him.
¶Watashi no shumi wa kitte o atsumeru koto desu.
私の趣味は切手を集めることです。
My hobby is collecting stamps.

atsúryoku 圧力 *pressure*
• atsuryoku o kakeru 圧力をかける *to apply pressure*

atsusa 厚さ *thickness*
¶Koko no kōri no atsusa ga sanjus-senchi desu.
ここの氷は厚さが30センチです。
The thickness of the ice here is 30 centimeters.

átsusa 熱さ *heat* «of something tangible»

átsusa 暑さ *heat* «of the air» [⟺**samusa** 寒さ]
¶Kyō no atsusa wa hidoi ne.
きょうの暑さはひどいね。
Today's heat is terrible, isn't it.

attakái 暖かい, 温かい 【COL. for **atatakai** 暖かい, 温かい】

attō 圧倒 ～**suru** ～する *to overwhelm*
¶Teki wa wareware o attō shimashita.
敵はわれわれを圧倒しました。
The enemy overwhelmed us.
• attō-teki na 圧倒的な *overwhelming*

áu 合う ① *to fit, to be the right size and shape*
¶Kono sētā wa watashi ni pittari au yo.

このセーターは私にぴったり合うよ。
This sweater fits me perfectly!

② *to suit; to match*

¶Midori ga haha ni totemo yoku aimasu.
緑が母にとてもよく合います。
Green suits my mother very well.

¶Sono burezā to shatsu wa yoku atte imasu.
そのブレザーとシャツはよく合っています。
That blazer and shirt match well.

③ *to coincide, to agree* [→**itchi suru** 一致する]

¶Watashi wa chichi to iken ga awanai yo.
私は父と意見が合わないよ。
My opinion and my father's don't agree!

• ki ga au 気が合う *to get along, to be like-minded*

④ *to become correct, to become accurate*

¶Kono tokei wa atte imasu ka.
この時計は合っていますか。
Is this clock correct?

áu 会う *to see, to meet*

• A ni／to au Aに／と会う *to see A, to meet A*

¶Tanaka-san ni aimashita ka.
田中さんに会いましたか。
Did you see Mr. Tanaka?

¶Ato de aimashō.
後で会いましょう。
Let's meet later.

¶Doko de Nakano-san to au yotei desu ka.
どこで中野さんと会う予定ですか。
Where are you planning to meet Mr. Nakano?

¶Kaeri-michi de sensei ni battari aimashita.
帰り道で先生にばったり会いました。
I ran into the teacher on my way home.

áu 遭う *to meet* 《with an unpleasant experience》

• hidoi me ni au ひどい目にあう *to have a bad experience*

-au －合う *to do to each other, to do mutually* 《Added to verb bases.》

¶Futari wa mukai-atte tatte imashita.

二人は向かい合って立っていました。
The two of them were standing facing each other.

áuto アウト ～no ～の *out* 《in baseball》
[⇔**sēfu no** セーフの]

¶Battā wa auto desu.
バッターはアウトです。
The batter is out.

autopútto アウトプット (*computer*)*output* [→**shutsuryoku** 出力] [⇔**inputto** インプット]

autoráin アウトライン *outline, summary* [→**gairyaku** 概略]

awá 泡 *bubble; foam*

• awa-datsu 泡立つ *to bubble, to foam*

áwabi あわび *abalone* ((fish))

áware 哀れ *pity; grief*

• aware na 哀れな *pitiful* [→**kawaisō na** かわいそうな]

awarému 哀れむ *to pity*

awaséru 合わせる ① *to put together, to unite, to join, to combine*

¶Kono ni-mai no ita o awasete kureru?
この2枚の板を合わせてくれる？
Will you put these two boards together?

¶Ittō-shō o toru tame ni chikara o awasemashō.
1等賞を取るために力を合わせましょう。
Let's combine our efforts in order to win first prize.

② *to add up, to total* [→**gōkei suru** 合計する]

• awasete 合わせて *altogether, in all*

¶Awasete ichi-man-en ni narimasu.
合わせて1万円になります。
It comes to 10,000 yen in all.

③ *to adjust, to set, to fit, to make match*

• tokei o awaseru 時計を合わせる *to set a clock*

¶Michiko-san wa ongaku ni awasete suberimashita.
美知子さんは音楽に合わせて滑りました。
Michiko skated to the music.

awatadashíi 慌ただしい *busy, rushed, hurried*

¶Ōsaka de awatadashii ichi-nichi

o sugoshimashita.
大阪で慌ただしい1日を過ごしました。
I spent a busy day in Osaka.

¶Otōto wa awatadashiku shita ni orite ikimashita.
弟は慌ただしく下に降りていきました。
My younger brother went downstairs in a hurry.

awateru 慌てる ① *to get confused, to get flustered*

¶Unten-shu wa jiko de awatemashita.
運転手は事故で慌てました。
The driver got flustered in the accident.

② *to get in a great hurry*

¶Imōto wa awatete hashitte itta yo.
妹は慌てて走っていったよ。
My younger sister ran away in a great hurry!

• awate-mono 慌て者 *hasty person; scatterbrain*

ayamachí 過ち *mistake, error* [→**machigai** 間違い]

¶Onaji ayamachi o ni-do to shite wa ikemasen.
同じ過ちを二度としてはいけません。
You must not make the same mistake twice.

¶Dare ni mo ayamachi wa aru mono.
だれにも過ちはあるもの。《proverb》
To err is human.《Literally: *In everyone there are mistakes.*》

ayamarí 誤り *mistake, error* [→**machigai** 間違い]

ayamáru 誤る *to make a mistake in, to do wrongly* [→**machigaeru** 間違える]

• hōshin o ayamaru 方針を誤る *to take the wrong course*

• sentaku o ayamaru 選択を誤る *to make a wrong choice*

ayamáru 謝る *to apologize for* [→**wabiru** 佗びる]

¶Kikuko-san wa jibun no machigai o ayamarimashita.
菊子さんは自分のまちがいを謝りました。
Kikuko apologized for her own mistakes.

¶Jon-san wa "Chikoku shite sumimasen" to ayamarimashita.

ジョンさんは「遅刻してすみません」と謝りました。
"I'm sorry for being late," apologized John.

ayame あやめ *iris*((flower))

ayashii 怪しい ① *suspicion-arousing, suspicious* [→**utagawashii** 疑わしい②]

¶Sono hito ga ayashii to omoimashita.
その人が怪しいと思いました。
I thought that person was suspicious.

• ayashii jinbutsu 怪しい人物 *suspicious character*

¶Yūbe ayashii oto ga kikoemashita.
ゆうべ怪しい音が聞こえました。
We heard a suspicious sound last night.

② *doubtful, questionable* [→**utagawashii** 疑わしい①]

¶Tanaka-kun no yakusoku wa ayashii desu.
田中君の約束は怪しいです。
Tanaka's promises are questionable.

ayashímu 怪しむ ① *to suspect, to become suspicious of* [→**utagau** 疑う②]

② *to doubt* [→**utagau** 疑う①]

ayatóri あやとり *cat's cradle*

• ayatori o suru あやとりをする *to play cat's cradle*

ayauku 危うく《in combination with a predicate indicating something undesirable about to happen or likely to happen》

¶Ayauku densha ni noriokureru tokoro deshita.
危うく電車に乗り遅れるところでした。
I nearly missed the train.

áyu 鮎 *ayu*《a fresh-water fish commonly eaten in Japan》

azárashi あざらし *seal*((animal))

azáyaka 鮮やか 〜**na** 〜な *bright, vivid*

¶Kono bara wa azayaka na aka desu.
このばらは鮮やかな赤です。
These roses are a bright red.

azukáru 預かる *to keep, to hold, to look after*《for someone》

¶Kono o-kane o azukatte kudasai.
このお金を預かってください。
Please look after this money.

¶Tonari no inu o shibaraku

azukarimashita.

隣の犬をしばらく預かりました。

We looked after the neighbor's dog for a while.

azukéru 預ける *to entrust, to leave* «in someone's care»

¶Kamera o sensei ni azukemashō.

カメラを先生に預けましょう。

I'll leave my camera with the teacher.

¶Ginkō ni gosen-en o azukemashita.

銀行に5000円を預けました。

I put 5,000 yen in the bank.

azukí 小豆 *red bean*

B

ba 場 ① *place* [→**basho** 場所]
② *occasion, time* [→**baai** 場合]
③ *scene* «in a play, etc.» [→**bamen** 場面①]
• -ba 一場 «counter for scenes; see Appendix 2»

bá バー *bar, barroom,* <*UK*>*pub*

baai 場合 ① *case, instance, occasion, time*

¶Kono baai wa kore ga tadashii kotae desu.

この場合はこれが正しい答えです。

In this case, this is the correct answer.

¶Fuzakete iru baai ja nai yo.

ふざけている場合じゃないよ。

This is no time to be joking!

② (〜**ni** 〜に) «following a clause» *when; if*

¶Ame no baai ni wa taiiku-kan de shiki o okonaimasu.

雨の場合には体育館で式を行ないます。

If it rains, we will hold the ceremony in the sports center.

¶Kaigai e iku baai ni wa pasupōto ga hitsuyō da.

海外へ行く場合にはパスポートが必要だ。

A passport is necessary when

going overseas.

bābékyū バーベキュー *barbecue*

bachí 罰 *punishment, penalty* [→**batsu** 罰]
• bachi ga ataru 罰が当たる *to suffer punishment*

badomínton バドミントン *badminton*

bágen バーゲン *bargain sale*

¶Kore o bāgen de katta yo.

これをバーゲンで買ったよ。

I bought this at a bargain sale!

• bāgen-sēru バーゲンセール [☞**bāgen** バーゲン (above)]

bággu バッグ *bag* [→**fukuro** 袋]; *satchel* [→**kaban** 鞄]

bai 倍 *double, twice as much, twice as many*

¶Otōto wa watashi no bai no o-kane o motte iru yo.

弟は私の倍のお金を持っているよ。

My younger brother has twice as much money as I do!

-**bai** 一倍 «counter for multiples; see Appendix 2»

¶Fuji-san wa kono yama no yaku go-bai no takasa ga aru.

富士山はこの山の約5倍の高さがある。

Mt. Fuji is about five times as high as this mountain. «Literally: *Mt. Fuji has a height of about five times this mountain.*»

báibai 売買 *buying and selling*
• baibai suru 売買する *to buy and sell, to deal in*

Báiburu バイブル *Bible* [→**Seisho** 聖書]

baikin 黴菌 *germ*

báikingu バイキング ① *smorgasbord* ② *viking*

báiku バイク *motorbike, motorcycle*

baindā バインダー *binder* «for documents, etc.»

baiorin バイオリン *violin*
• baiorin o hiku バイオリンを弾く *to play a violin*
• baiorin-sōsha バイオリン奏者 *violinist*

baiotekunóroji バイオテクノロジー *biotechnology*

baipasu バイパス *by-pass* (*road*)

baiten 売店 (*sales*)*stand*, (*merchandise*)*stall*
- eki no baiten 駅の売店 *station sales stand*

bájji バッジ *badge*

báka 馬鹿 ① *fool*
- baka na ばかな *foolish, silly* [⇔**kashikoi** 賢い]
¶Baka na koto wa yoshinasai.
ばかな事はよしなさい。
Stop doing foolish things.
- A o baka ni suru Aをばかにする *to make a fool of A, to make fun of A*
② ～**ni naru** ～になる *to become nonfunctional*
¶Kono neji wa mō baka ni natta yo.
このねじはもうばかになったよ。
This screw doesn't hold anymore! 《Literally: This screw has become nonfunctional.》
- baka-shōjiki 馬鹿正直 *foolish honesty, naive honesty*

bakabakashíi ばかばかしい *absurd, ridiculous*

bákansu バカンス *vacation, holiday*

bákari ばかり ① *only, nothing but* [→ **dake** だけ①]
¶Tarō wa neko no koto bakari kangaete iru yo.
太郎は猫のことばかり考えているよ。
Taro only thinks of the cat!
- bakari de naku ばかりでなく *not only*
¶Oba wa Eigo bakari de naku Doitsu-go mo dekiru.
伯母は英語ばかりでなくドイツ語もできる。
My aunt can speak not only English, but also German.
② ～**da** ～だ *to have just* 《following a past-tense verb》
¶Watashi wa gakkō ni tsuita bakari desu.
私は学校に着いたばかりです。
I've just arrived at school.
③ ～**ni** ～に *just because, simply as a result of* 《following a past-tense verb》
¶Eigo o shiranakatta bakari ni warawareta.
英語を知らなかったばかりに笑われた。
Just because I didn't understand

English, I was laughed at.

–**bakari** －ばかり *about, or so* 《Added to number bases.》 [→ –**gurai** －ぐらい①]
¶Hawai ni wa is-shūkan-bakari imasu.
ハワイには1週間ばかりいます。
I will be in Hawaii for about a week.

bakemonó 化け物 *ghost, goblin, monster*

báketsu バケツ *bucket*
¶Baketsu de mizu o kyōshitsu made hakobimasu.
バケツで水を教室まで運びます。
They carry water to the classroom in a bucket.

bakkin 罰金 *a fine*
¶Supīdo-ihan de ichiman-en no bakkin o haratta.
スピード違反で1万円の罰金を払った。
I paid a fine of 10,000 yen for a speeding violation.
- bakkin o hatasu 罰金を課す *to levy a fine*

bákku バック ① *background, backdrop* [→**haikei** 背景①]
② *backing, support* [→**haikei** 背景②]; *backer, supporter*
③ ～**suru** ～する *to back up, to move backwards* 《intransitive》
¶Sukoshi bakku shite kudasai.
少しバックしてください。
Back up a little, please.

bakkuáppu バックアップ *backing, support*
- bakkuappu suru バックアップする *to back up, to support*

bakkubōn バックボーン *backbone, strength of character*

bakkumírā バックミラー *rearview mirror*

bákkuru バックル *buckle*

bakudai 莫大 ～**na** ～な *huge, enormous*
¶Roketto kaihatsu ni wa bakudai na hiyō ga kakaru.
ロケット開発にはばく大な費用がかかる。
Rocket development takes enormous expenditure.

bakudan 爆弾 *bomb*

¶Bakudan o toshi ni otoshimashita.

爆弾を都会に落しました。

They dropped bombs on cities.

• genshi–bakudan 原子爆弾 *atomic bomb*
• jigen–bakudan 時限爆弾 *time bomb*
• kaku–bakudan 核爆弾 *nuclear bomb*
• suiso–bakudan 水素爆弾 *hydrogen bomb*

bakugeki 爆撃 *bombing attack*

• bakugeki suru 爆撃する *to bomb*
• bakugeki–ki 爆撃機 *bomber* ((airplane))

bakuhatsu 爆発 *explosion*

¶Kōjō no chika de bakuhatsu ga arimashita.

工場の地下で爆発がありました。

There was an explosion in the basement of the factory.

• bakuhatsu suru 爆発する *to explode*

bakuteria バクテリア *bacteria* [→**saikin** 細菌]

bakuzen 漠然 ～**to** ～と *vaguely, obscurely*

• bakuzen to shite iru 漠然としている *to be vague, to be obscure*
• bakuzen to shita 漠然とした *vague, obscure* [→**aimai na** 曖昧な]

¶Bakuzen to shita kaitō de wa ukeireraremasen.

漠然とした回答では受け入れられません。

Vague answers will not be accepted.

bamen 場面 ① *scene* 《in a play, etc.》; *setting*

¶Bamen ga kawarimashita.

場面が変わりました。

The scene changed.

② *situation, circumstances*

• abunai bamen 危ない場面 *dangerous situation*

ban 晩 *night, evening* [→**yoru** 夜]

¶Watashi–tachi wa itsu–mo ban no shichi–ji ni yūshoku o taberu.

私たちはいつも晩の７時に夕食を食べる。

We usually have dinner at 7:00 in the evening.

¶Doyōbi no ban ni Michiko–san ni aimasu.

土曜日の晩に美知子さんに会います。

I'll see Michiko on Saturday night.

¶Oji wa Go–gatsu tsuitachi no ban ni tsukimashita.

叔父は５月１日の晩に着きました。

My uncle arrived on the night of May 1.

¶Ken–san wa asa kara ban made hataraita yo.

健さんは朝から晩まで働いたよ。

Ken worked from morning until night!

• –ban －晩《counter for nights; see Appendix 2》
• ban–gohan 晩ご飯 *evening meal, dinner* [→**yūshoku** 夕食]
• hito–ban–jū 一晩中 *all night long*
• kon–ban 今晩 *tonight* [→**kon'ya** 今夜]
• mai–ban 毎晩 *every night*
• myō–ban 明晩 *tomorrow night*
• saku–ban 昨晩 *last night* [→**sakuya** 昨夜]

bán 番 ① *one's turn*

¶Sā, dare no ban desu ka.

さあ、だれの番ですか。

All right, whose turn is it?

② *keeping watch, guarding* [→**mihari** 見張り①]

• ban ni tatsu 番に立つ *to go on guard, to stand guard*
• A no ban o suru Aの番をする *to keep an eye on A, to watch over A*

¶Watashi wa sūtsukēsu no ban o shimasu.

私はスーツケースの番をします。

I will keep an eye on the suitcase.

• ban–nin 番人 *guard, watchman; caretaker*

–ban －番 ① 《counter for numbers; see Appendix 2》

¶Zaseki wa nan–ban desu ka.

座席は何番ですか。

What number is your seat?

② 《counter for positions in a sequence or ranking; see Appendix 2》

¶Katō–kun wa kurasu de san–ban desu.

加藤君はクラスで３番です。

Kato is third in the class.

• –ban–sen －番線《counter for railroad−station track numbers; see Appendix 2》

¶Nagoya−yuki no densha wa ni−ban−sen kara demasu.

名古屋行きの電車は 2 番線から出ます。

The train for Nagoya leaves from Track No. 2.

bā́nā バーナー *Bunsen burner*

bánana バナナ *banana*

banchi 番地 *lot number* 《as part of an address》

¶Kono tegami wa banchi ga machigatte iru yo.

この手紙は番地がまちがっているよ。

This lot number on this letter is wrong!

• −banchi −番地《counter for lot numbers; see Appendix 2》

¶Kono ie wa nan−banchi desu ka.

この家は何番地ですか。

What lot number is this house?

bándo バンド ① *belt* 《(clothing)》〔→**beruto** ベルト①〕

② *band* 《on a watch, etc.》

bándo バンド (*musical*)*band*

• burasu−bando ブラスバンド *brass band*

• rokku−bando ロックバンド *rock band*

báne ばね (*metal*)*spring*〔→**zenmai** 発条〕

bangárō バンガロー *bungalow*

bangó 番号 *number* 《used as an identifier》

¶Kippu no bangō wa nan−ban desu ka.

切符の番号は何番ですか。

What number is your ticket?

¶Bangō ga chigaimasu.

番号が違います。《on the telephone》

You have the wrong number. 《*Literally: The number is wrong.*》

• bangō−jun 番号順 *numerical order*

• denwa−bangō 電話番号 *telephone number*

bangumi 番組 (*entertainment*)*program*

¶Tokidoki kodomo no bangumi o mimasu.

時々子供の番組を見ます。

I sometimes watch children's programs.

banken 番犬 *watchdog*

bankoku 万国 *all the countries of the world*

• bankoku−hakurankai 万国博覧会 *international exposition, world's fair*

bánku バンク *bank* 《(financial institution)》〔→**ginkō** 銀行〕

• dēta−banku データバンク *data bank*

bannen 晩年 *one's later years*

¶Sofu wa bannen o hitori de kurashimashita.

祖父は晩年を一人で暮らしました。

My grandfather lived his later years alone.

bannō 万能 ~**no** ~の *all−around, able to do anything well; effective in all circumstances*

• bannō−senshu 万能選手 *all−around player*

banpaku 万博〔☞**bankoku−hakurankai** 万国博覧会 (s.v. **bankoku** 万国)〕

bansō 伴奏 (*musical*)*accompaniment*

¶Piano no bansō de utaimashō.

ピアノの伴奏で歌いましょう。

Let's sing to accompaniment of the piano.

¶Sensei wa piano de baiorin no bansō o shita.

先生はピアノでバイオリンの伴奏をした。

The teacher accompanied the violin on the piano.

• bansō suru 伴奏する *to play accompaniment*

bansōkō 絆創膏 *sticking plaster* 《for an injury》

bánto バント *bunt* 《in baseball》

• banto suru バントする *to bunt*

• gisei−banto 犠牲バント *sacrifice bunt*

banzái 万歳 *hurrah , hurray*

¶Banzai, katta zo!

万歳、勝ったぞ!

Hurray, we won!

bara 薔薇 *rose*

¶Bara wa totemo ii nioi ga shimasu ne.

ばらはとてもいいにおいがしますね。

Roses smell very nice, don't they.

• bara no ki ばらの木 *rose bush*

• bara-iro ばら色 *rose color, pale red*

barabara ばらばら ① 〜**no** 〜の *separate, scattered; in pieces*

¶ Watashi-tachi wa barabara ni ie o demashita.

私たちはばらばらに家を出ました。

We left home separately.

• barabara ni naru ばらばらになる *to scatter, to disperse; to come apart*

• barabara ni suru ばらばらにする *to scatter, to disperse; to take apart*

¶ Otōto wa sono omocha o barabara ni shimashita.

弟はそのおもちゃをばらばらにしました。

My younger brother took that toy apart.

② (〜**to** 〜と) *in big drops, peltingly*

• ame ga barabara furu 雨がばらばら降る *rain falls in big drops*

baransu バランス *balance, equilibirium* [→**tsuriai** 釣り合い]

• baransu o ushinau バランスを失う *to lose one's balance*

• baransu ga toreru バランスが取れる *to become balanced*

barásu ばらす 【COL.】 ① *to reveal, to divulge, to disclose*

• himitsu o barasu 秘密をばらす *to reveal a secret*

② *to take apart, to take to pieces*

bárē バレエ *ballet*

¶ Musume wa barē o naratte imasu.

娘はバレエを習っています。

My daughter is studying ballet.

bárē バレー [☞**barēbóru** バレーボール]

barēbóru バレーボール ① (*the game of*)*volleyball*

• barēbōru o suru バレーボールをする *to play volleyball*

② *a volleyball*

Barentaíndē バレンタインデー *Valentine's Day*

barerína バレリーナ *ballerina*

baréru ばれる 【COL.】 *to be revealed, to be divulged, to be disclosed*

barikan バリカン *barber's clippers*

barikēdo バリケード *barricade*

• barikēdo o kizuku バリケードを築く *to set up a barricade*

bariki 馬力 *horsepower*

• -bariki −馬力《*counter for horsepower; see Appendix 2*》

¶ Kono kuruma ni wa nihyaku-bariki no enjin ga tsuite imasu.

この車には200馬力のエンジンがついています。

There is a 200-horsepower engine in this car.

bariton バリトン ① *baritone* (*voice*)

② *baritone* (*singer*)

③ *baritone* (*part*)

barométā バロメーター *barometer* [→**kiatsu-kei** 気圧計 (s.v. **kiatsu** 気圧)]

barukónī バルコニー *balcony*

básha 馬車 *horse-drawn carriage; horse cart*

basho 場所 *place* [→**tokoro** 所①]

¶ O-hiru o taberu basho o mitsukemashita.

お昼を食べる場所を見つけました。

I found a place to eat lunch.

• basho o tori-sugiru 場所を取りすぎる *to take up too much space*

bassuru 罰する{Irreg.} *to punish*

• kado ni bassuru 過度に罰する *to punish excessively*

básu バス *bus*

¶ Hakubutsukan made basu de ikimashō ka.

博物館までバスで行きましょうか。

Shall we go to the museum by bus?

• basu ni noru バスに乗る *to get on a bus; to ride on a bus*

• basu o oriru バスを降り *to get off a bus*

• basu-gaido バスガイド *guide accompanying passengers on a tourist bus*

• basu-tei バス停 *bus stop*

• kankō-basu 観光バス *sightseeing bus*

básu バス *bath* [→**furo** 風呂]

• basu-taoru バスタオル *bath towel*

básu バス ① *bass* (*voice*)

② *bass* (*singer*)

③ *bass* (*part*)

basukétto バスケット ① *basket* [→**kago** 籠]

② [☞**basukettobōru** バスケットボール①]
basukettobōru バスケットボール ① (*the game of*)*basketball*
② *a basketball*
básuto バスト ① *bust* (*measurement*)
② *bust* ((sculpture))
bátā バター *butter*
• batā o nuru バターを塗る *to spread butter*
bátafurai バタフライ *butterfly* ((swimming stroke))
batán ばたん 〜**to** 〜と *with a bang, with a thud*
• batan to to o shimeru ばたんと戸を閉める *to shut the door with a bang*
• batan to taoreru ばたんと倒れる *to fall over with a thud*
bāten バーテン [☞**bātendā** バーテンダー]
bāténdā バーテンダー *bartender*
baton バトン *baton*
• baton-gāru バトンガール (*girl*) *baton twirler*
bátsu 罰 *punishment, penalty*
bátsu ばつ *an "X" mark* 《indicating that something is incorrect or unacceptable》
batsugun 抜群 〜**no** 〜の *outstanding, excellent*
¶Masako-chan no Eigo wa batsugun da yo.
政子ちゃんの英語は抜群だよ。
Masako's English is outstanding!
batta ばった *grasshopper*
báttā バッター *batter, hitter* [→**dasha** 打者]《in baseball》
• battā-bokkusu バッターボックス *batter's box*
battári ばったり (〜**to** 〜と) ① *unexpectedly* 《modifying a verb that denotes meeting》
• battari A ni au ばったりAに会う *to meet A unexpectedly, to run into A*
¶Ongaku-kai de battari Furuno-san ni aimashita.
音楽会でばったり古野さんに会いました。
I ran into Ms. Furuno at the concert.

② *suddenly, with a flop* 《modifying a verb that denotes falling over》
¶Sono rōjin wa battari to mae ni taore mashita.
その老人はばったりと前に倒れました。
The elderly person suddenly fell flat on his face.
bátterī バッテリー *battery* 《in baseball》
• batterī o kumu バッテリーを組む *to team up as the battery*
batterī バッテリー (*electric*)*battery* [→**denchi** 電池]
• batterī ga agaru バッテリーが上がる *a battery goes dead*
battingu バッティング *batting, hitting* 《in baseball》
bátto バット (*baseball*)*bat*
• batto o furu バットを振る *to swing a bat*
baundo バウンド *bound, bounce*
• baundo suru バウンドする *to bound, to bounce*
bawai 場合 [☞**baai** 場合]
bázā バザー *bazaar*
béddo ベッド (*Western-style*)*bed*
¶Watashi wa itsu-mo beddo de nemasu.
私はいつもベッドで寝ます。
I always sleep on a bed.
¶Dekakeru mae ni beddo o totonoenasai.
出かける前にベッドを整えなさい。
Make the bed before you go out.
• beddo-kabā ベッドカバー *bedspread*
• beddo-rūmu ベッドルーム *bedroom*
• beddo-taun ベッドタウン *bedroom town*
• daburu-beddo ダブルベッド *double bed*
• nidan-beddo 二段ベッド *bunk bed*
béiju 米寿 *88th birthday* 《a special birthday in Japan》
béika 米価 *rice price*
Beikoku 米国 *the United States* [→**Amerika** アメリカ②]
-**beki** ーべき 〜**da** 〜だ *should, ought to; must* 《Added to the informal affirmative nonpast-tense form of a verb (i.e., the form listed in dictionaries). Instead of **suru** する, the classical form **su** す may appear before -**beki**.》
¶Sugu ni isha ni mite morau-beki desu.

すぐに医者にみてもらうべきです。
You should see a doctor immediately.
¶Hontō no koto o iu-beki desu.
ほんとうのことを言うべきです。
You must tell the truth.

bēkingupáudā ベーキングパウダー *baking powder*

bekkyo 別居 *residing separately*
• bekkyo suru 別居する *to reside separately*

bēkon ベーコン *bacon*
• bēkon-eggu ベーコンエッグ *bacon and eggs*

bén 便 *convenience*
• A wa B no ben ga ii AはBの便がいい
A is convenient to／for B
¶Uchi wa chikatetsu no ben ga ii desu.
うちは地下鉄の便がいいです。
My house is convenient to the subway.

bén 弁 *valve*

bénchi ベンチ *bench*

béngi 便宜 *convenience* 《*for a person*》
• bengi o hakaru 便宜を図る *to be accomodating*

béngo 弁護 （*verbal*）*defense, arguing on behalf of*
• bengo suru 弁護する *to defend, to argue on behalf of*
¶Watashi wa jibun de bengo dekimasu.
私は自分で弁護できます。
I can defend myself.
• bengo-shi 弁護士 *lawyer*

beniyaíta ベニヤ板 *plywood*

bénjin ベンジン *benzene*

benjó 便所 【CRUDE for **toire** トイレ】
bathroom, lavatory 《Toilets and bathtubs are traditionally in separate rooms in Japan. This word refers to a place containing a toilet.》
• kōshū-benjo 公衆便所 *public lavatory*

benkai 弁解 *excuse, exculpatory explanation* [→**iiwake** 言い訳]
¶Mō benkai no yochi wa nai desu.
もう弁解の余地はないです。
There's no longer any room for excuses.
• benkai suru 弁解する *to make an excuse, to exculpate oneself*

bénki 便器 *toilet fixture*

benkyō 勉強 *study, studying*
• benkyō suru 勉強する *to study*
¶Mariko wa nesshin ni Nihon-shi o benkyō shite imasu.
真理子は熱心に日本史を勉強しています。
Mariko is studying Japanese history enthusiastically.
¶Nani o benkyō shita no desu ka.
何を勉強したのですか。
What did you study?
• benkyō-beya 勉強部屋 *room for studying*
• benkyō-jikan 勉強時間 *study hours*
• benkyō-ka 勉強家 *person who studies hard*

benpi 便秘 *constipation*
• benpi suru 便秘する *to become constipated*

bénri 便利 ～**na** ～な *convenient, handy* [⇔**fuben na** 不便な]
¶Denshi-renji wa totemo benri desu.
電子レンジはとても便利です。
A microwave oven is very convenient.
¶Basu de iku no ga benri desu.
バスで行くのが便利です。
Going by bus is convenient.
¶Kore wa benri na dōgu desu ne.
これは便利な道具ですね。
This is a handy tool, isn't it.

benron 弁論 *discussion, debate, oratory*
• benron-bu 弁論部 *debate club, debate team*
• benron-taikai 弁論大会 *oratory contest*

benshō 弁償 *compensation payment*
• benshō suru 弁償する *to pay for*
¶Watta kabin o benshō shimasu.
割った花瓶を弁償します。
I will pay for the vase I broke.

bentō 弁当 *lunch* 《*to be carried along and eaten later*》
¶Shibafu no ue de bentō o tabemashō yo.
芝生の上で弁当を食べましょうよ。
Let's eat our lunch on the grass!
• bentō-bako 弁当箱 *lunch box*

berabō べらぼう 【COL.】 ～**na** ～な

unreasonable, absurd, extreme
• berabō na nedan べらぼうな値段
unreasonable price

beranda ベランダ *veranda*

bĕru ベール *veil*

béru ベル ① *electric bell*
¶Beru ga natte iru yo.
ベルが鳴っているよ。
The bell's ringing!
② *signaling bell* 《on a bicycle, etc.》
• hijō-beru 非常ベル *alarm bell*

béruto ベルト ① *belt* ((clothing)) [→
bando バンド①]
¶Beruto o yurumeta hō ga ii desu.
ベルトを緩めたほうがいいです。
It would be better to loosen your belt.
¶Zaseki no beruto o o-shime kudasai.
座席のベルトをお締めください。
Please fasten your seat belts.
② *belt* ((machine part))
• anzen-beruto 安全ベルト *safety belt*

berutokonbéyā ベルトコンベヤー *belt conveyer*

bessō 別荘 *summer house, country house, villa*

bĕsu ベース ① *base* 《in baseball》 [→**rui** 塁]
② *base, basis, standard*
③ *base* (*of operations*) [→**konkyo-chi** 根拠地 (s.v. **konkyo** 根拠)]
• bĕsu-appu ベースアップ *increase in base wages*
• bĕsu-kyanpu ベースキャンプ *base camp* 《for an expedition, etc.》

bĕsu ベース [☞**basu** バス (*bass*)]
• bĕsu-gitā ベースギター *bass guitar*

bésuto ベスト *vest*

bésuto ベスト *one's best* (*effort*) [→**saizen** 最善]
¶Sono shiai ni katsu tame besuto o tsukushimasu.
その試合に勝つためベストを尽くします。
I will do my best to win the game.

besuto– ベスト– *best, top* 《Added to noun bases.》
• besuto-serā ベストセラー *best seller*
• besuto-ten ベストテン *the top ten*

beteran ベテラン *veteran, old hand, person of long experience*

betsu 別 ① ～**no**／**na** ～の／な *another, other, different, separate* [→**hoka no** 外の, 他の]
¶Betsu no baggu o misete kudasai.
別のバッグを見せてください。
Please show me another bag.
¶Sore wa mattaku betsu no hanashi desu.
それはまったく別の話です。
That's a completely different story.
¶Kinō betsu no isha ni mite moraimashita.
きのう別の医者にみてもらいました。
I had a different doctor look at it yesterday.
② ～**ni** ～に *particularly, in particular* 《in combination with a negative predicate》
¶Hōkago betsu ni suru koto ga nai.
放課後別にすることがない。
I don't have anything in particular to do after school.

–betsu –別 ～**no** ～の *classified by, according to* 《Added to noun bases.》
¶Nenrei-betsu no jinkō o hyō ni shimashita.
年齢別の人口を表にしました。
I made a chart of the population classified by age.
¶Sanka-sha wa chiiki-betsu ni narande imasu.
参加者は地域別に並んでいます。
The participants are lined up according to region.

betsubetsu 別々 ～**no** ～の *separate* (*from each other*)
¶Ane to watashi wa betsubetsu no heya o motte imasu.
姉と私は別々の部屋を持っています。
My older sister and I have separate rooms.
¶Issho ni shokuji shita ga, betsubetsu ni haratta.
いっしょに食事したが、別々に払った。
We ate together, but paid separately.

betsumei 別名 *different name,*

pseudonym, alias
bí 美 *beauty*
- bi-gaku 美学 *(the study of)esthetics*

biahōru ビアホール *beer hall*

bídeo ビデオ ① [☞**bideotēpu** ビデオ
テープ]
② [☞**bideotēpu-rekōdā** ビデオ
テープレコーダー (s.v. **bideotēpu** ビデオ
テープ)]

bideotēpu ビデオテープ *videotape*
- bideotēpu ni toru ビデオテープに撮る *to
record on videotape*
- bideotēpu-rekōdā ビデオテープレコーダー
videotape recorder, VCR

bifuteki ビフテキ *(beef-)steak* [→**sutēki** ステーキ]

bíjin 美人 *beautiful woman, a beauty*
¶Ojōsan wa bijin desu ne.
お嬢さんは美人ですね。
Your daughter is a beauty, isn't she.

bíjinesu ビジネス *business ((activity))*
- bijinesu-hoteru ビジネスホテル *inexpensive hotel catering to business people*
- bijinesu-man ビジネスマン *businessper-
son* [→**jitsugyō-ka** 実業家 (s.v. **jitsugyō**
実業)]; *office worker, company employee* [→**kaisha-in** 会社員 (s.v. **kaisha**
会社)]

bíjon ビジョン *vision, conception of the
future*
- bijon no aru hito ビジョンのある人 *a person of vision*

bíjutsu 美術 *art, the fine arts*
- bijutsu-gakkō 美術学校 *art school*
- bijutsu-hin 美術品 *work of art*
- bijutsu-kan 美術館 *art museum*
- bijutsu-tenrankai 美術展覧会 *art exhibition*

bíkā ビーカー *beaker*

bikkúri びっくり ～**suru** ～する *to be
surprised* [→**odoroku** 驚く]
¶Takai nedan ni bikkuri shimashita.
高い値段にびっくりしました。
I was surprised at the high price.
- bikkuri-bako びっくり箱
jack-in-the-box

bimyō 微妙 ～**na** ～な *subtle,*

difficult to discern
bín 瓶 *bottle*
- bin-zume no 瓶詰めの *bottled*
- aki-bin 空き瓶 *empty bottle*
- honyū-bin 哺乳瓶 *baby bottle*

bín 便 *(airline)flight; (scheduled)ship;
(scheduled)train*
¶Tsugi no bin de iku koto ni shimashita.
次の便で行くことにしました。
I decided to go on the next flight.
- -bin ー便《counter for number of
flights or flight numbers; see Appendix
2》

bínbō 貧乏 *poverty*
- binbō na 貧乏な *poor, indigent, destitute* [⇔**kanemochi no** 金持ちの]
¶Kono chihō no hitobito wa totemo
binbō desu.
この地方の人々はとても貧乏です。
The people of this region are very poor.

biníru ビニール *vinyl*
- binīru-hausu ビニールハウス *vinyl greenhouse*

binkan 敏感 ～**na** ～な *sensitive,
acutely-sensing* [⇔**donkan na** 鈍感な]
¶Inu wa nioi ni binkan desu.
犬はにおいに敏感です。
Dogs are sensitive to smell.

binsen 便箋 *letter-writing paper*

bira ビラ *handbill, leaflet, poster*

bíri びり 【COL.】 *last place, bottom
rank*
¶Tarō wa biri de gōru ni haitta yo.
太郎はびりでゴールに入ったよ。
Taro reached the goal last!
¶Kinō no tesuto de kurasu no biri datta
yo.
きのうのテストでクラスのびりだったよ。
*I was bottom of the class on yesterday's
test!*

birōdo ビロード *velvet*

bíru ビール *beer*
- ippai no bīru 1杯のビール *one glass of
beer*
- ippon no bīru 1本のビール *one bot-
tle/can of beer*
- kan-bīru 缶ビール *canned beer*

• nama-bīru 生ビール *draft beer*
bíru ビル *a building*
　• chō-kōsō-biru 超高層ビル *skyscraper*
bírusu ビールス *virus* [→**uirusu** ウイルス]
bisshóri びっしょり *to the point of being drenched*
　• bisshori nureru びっしょりぬれる *to get soaking wet*
　• bisshori no びっしょりの *drenched, soaked*
bisukétto ビスケット *sweet cracker, <UK>biscuit*
bitámin ビタミン *vitamin*
bíto ビート *(musical)beat*
bíwa びわ *loquat*
biyō 美容 *enhancing a person's beauty*
　• biyō-in 美容院 *beauty parlor, beauty shop*
　• biyō-shi 美容師 *hairdresser, beautician*
　• biyō-taisō 美容体操 *slim-down calisthenics*
bíza ビザ *visa*
　• biza o toru ビザを取る *to get a visa*
　• kankō-biza 観光ビザ *tourist visa*
bízu ビーズ *bead*
bō 棒 *stick, rod, pole*
　• bō-takatobi 棒高跳び *the pole vault*
bóchi 墓地 *graveyard, cemetery*
　• kyōkai-bochi 教会墓地 *churchyard*
bōchō 膨張 *swelling, expansion*
　• bōchō suru 膨張する *to swell, to expand*
¶Tetsu wa netsu de bōcho shimasu.
鉄は熱で膨張します。
Iron expands with heat.
bodíbiru ボディービル *body building*
bodíchékku ボディーチェック *body search, frisk*
bodígádo ボディーガード *bodyguard*
bōdō 暴動 *riot; rioting*
bōei 防衛 *defense, protection* [→**bōgyo** 防御] [⇔**kōgeki** 攻撃]
　• bōei suru 防衛する *to defend*
　• Bōei-chō 防衛庁 *the Defense Agency* 《in the Japanese government》
　• bōei-hi 防衛費 *defense expenditures*

bōeki 貿易 *trade, commerce*
　• bōeki suru 貿易する *to trade*
¶Nihon wa kazu-ōku no kuni to bōeki shite imasu.
日本は数多くの国と貿易しています。
Japan trades with numerous countries.
　• bōeki-fū 貿易風 *trade wind*
　• bōeki-gaisha 貿易会社 *trading company*
　• gaikoku-bōeki 外国貿易 *foreign trade*
　• hogo-bōeki 保護貿易 *protective trade*
　• jiyū-bōeki 自由貿易 *free trade*
bōenkyō 望遠鏡 *telescope*
¶Ani wa bōenkyō de hoshi o kansatsu suru koto ga suki desu.
兄は望遠鏡で星を観察することが好きです。
My older brother likes to observe the stars with a telescope.
　• tentai-bōenkyō 天体望遠鏡 *astronomical telescope*
bōfū 暴風 *intense wind, gale*
　• bōfū-u 暴風雨 *rainstorm*
bōgai 妨害 *obstruction, interference, disturbance* [→**jama** 邪魔]
　• bōgai suru 妨害する *to obstruct, to interfere with, to disturb*
¶Kōtsū o bōgai shinai de ne.
交通を妨害しないでね。
Don't obstruct traffic, OK?
bógyo 防御 *defense, protection* [→**bōei** 防衛]
　• bōgyo suru 防御する *to defend, to protect*
bōhan 防犯 *crime prevention*
bōhatei 防波堤 *breakwater*
bōifuréndo ボーイフレンド *casual boyfriend* 《as opposed to a steady boyfriend or lover》 [⇔**gárufurendo** ガールフレンド]
boikótto ボイコット *boycott*
　• boikotto suru ボイコットする *to boycott*
boin 母音 *vowel* [⇔**shiin** 子音]
bóirā ボイラー *boiler*
bóisukáuto ボーイスカウト ① *the Boy Scouts*
② *boy scout*
bōken 冒険 *adventure, risky*

undertaking

¶Mukashi wa Chūgoku e no kōkai wa inochi gake no bōken deshita.

昔は中国への航海は命がけの冒険でした。

Long ago a voyage to China was a desperate and risky undertaking.

- bōken suru 冒険する *to venture to do, to risk doing*
- bōken-ka 冒険家 *adventurer*
- bōken-shin 冒険心 *spirit of adventure*
- dai-bōken 大冒険 *great adventure*

bokéru 惚る *to become senile*

bókkusu ボックス *box* [→**hako** 箱]
- battā-bokkusu バッターボックス *batter's box*
- denwa-bokkusu 電話ボックス *telephone booth*

bōkō 暴行 *act of violence, assault*

bókō 母校 *alma mater*

bókoku 母国 *native country*
- bokoku-go 母国語 *native language*

bóku 僕 *I, me* 《There are several Japanese words for *I / me*. The word **boku** is ordinarily restricted to male speakers and is less formal than **watashi**. Other words for *I / me* include **watashi** 私, **watakushi** 私, **atashi** あたし, and **ore** 俺.》

bokuchiku 牧畜 *stock farming, stock raising*

bokujō 牧場 *stock farm, <US>ranch; pasture* 《where farm animals graze》

¶Kotani-san wa Hokkaidō de bokujō o keiei shite iru.

小谷さんは北海道で牧場を経営している。

Mr. Kotani is running a ranch in Hokkaido.

- bokujō-nushi 牧場主 *rancher*

bókushi 牧師 *Protestant minister, pastor*

bókushingu ボクシング *boxing*
- bokushingu o suru ボクシングをする *to box*

bokusō 牧草 *grass (for grazing), pasturage*
- bokusō-chi 牧草地 *meadow, pasture*

bōmei 亡命 *defection, fleeing to another country*

- bōmei suru 亡命する *to defect, to take political asylum*
- bōmei-sha 亡命者 *defector*

bon 盆 *(serving)tray*

Bón 盆 *the Buddhist festival of the dead* 《Celebrated on July 15 in some areas of Japan and on August 15 in other areas.》《This word is almost always used with the prefix **o-** : **o-Bon** お盆.》
- Bon-odori 盆踊り *Bon dance*

bónasu ボーナス *salary bonus* 《Japanese employees usually receive such a salary bonus twice a year in June and December》

bónbe ボンベ *gas cylinder*
- sanso-bonbe 酸素ボンベ *oxygen cylinder*

bonchi 盆地 *(geographical)basin*
- Nara-bonchi 奈良盆地 *the Nara Basin*

bóndo ボンド *bonding agent, glue* [→**setchakuzai** 接着剤]

bōnénkai 忘年会 *year-end party*

bonsai 盆栽 *bonsai, dwarf tree in a pot*
- bonsai o tsukuru 盆栽を作る *to grow a bonsai*

bon'yári ぼんやり （～to ～と）

① *vacantly, absent-mindedly, blankly*

¶Otoko no hito ga mon no soba ni bon'yari to tatte iru.

男の人が門のそばにぼんやりと立っている。

A man is standing by the gate vacantly.

- bon'yari suru ぼんやりする *to become blank, to become vacant; to behave absent-mindedly, to daydream*

¶Masashi wa gozen-chū zutto bon'yari shite imasu.

雅史は午前中ずっとぼんやりしています。

Masashi has been absent-minded all morning.

② *dimly, vaguely*

¶Sofu no koto wa bon'yari oboete iru dake da.

祖父のことはぼんやり覚えているだけだ。

I only remember my grandfather vaguely.

bōon 防音 ～**no** ～の *soundproof; sound-insulated*
- bōon suru 防音する *to soundproof;*

to sound-insulate

• bōon-sōchi 防音装置 *soundproofing device; anti-noise device*

borántia ボランティア (*community-service*)*volunteer*

bōrei 亡霊 *dead person's spirit, ghost* [→**yūrei** 幽霊]

bōringu ボーリング *bowling*

• bōringu-jō ボーリング場 *bowling alley*

bóro ぼろ *rag; ragged clothes*

• boro-gutsu ぼろ靴 *worn-out shoes*

bōru ボール ① *ball* 《used in a game》[→**tama** 球]

¶Yakyū-senshu wa bōru o batto de uchimashita.

野球選手はボールをバットで打ちました。

The baseball player hit the ball with the bat.

¶Sentā wa kantan ni bōru o torimashita.

センターは簡単にボールを捕りました。

The center fielder caught the ball easily.

• tenisu no bōru テニスのボール *tennis ball*

② *pitch out of the strike zone, ball*

bōrupen ボールペン *ballpoint pen*

boruto ボルト *volt*

• -boruto －ボルト《*counter for volts; see Appendix 2*》

¶Hyaku-boruto no denryū ga nagarete imasu.

100ボルトの電流が流れています。

A 100-volt current is flowing.

boruto ボルト *bolt* ((*fastener*))

bóryoku 暴力 *violence, force*

• bōryoku o furuu 暴力をふるう *to use violence*

boryúmu ボリューム ① (*sound*)*volume*

¶Hiroshi wa terebi no boryūmu o sukoshi ageta yo.

浩はテレビのボリュームを少し上げたよ。

Hiroshi turned the TV volume up a little!

② *volume, amount*

bōshi 帽子 *hat*

• bōshi o kaburu [nugu] 帽子をかぶる [脱ぐ] *to put on* [*take off*] *a hat*

¶Bōshi o kabutta mama de

heya ni hairanaide.

帽子をかぶったままで部屋に入らないで。

Don't enter the room with your hat on.

• bōshi-ya 帽子屋 *hat store; hatter*

boshū 募集 ① *recruitment*

• boshū suru 募集する *to recruit*

¶Rika-bu wa buin o boshū shite imasu.

理科部は部員を募集しています。

The science club is recruiting members.

¶Sutaffu boshū

「スタッフ募集」《on a sign》

Staff Wanted

② *raising, collection, solicitation* 《of contributions》

• boshū suru 募集する *to raise, to collect*

¶Ichi-oku-en no kifu-kin o boshū shimashita yo.

1億円の寄付金を募集しましたよ。

They raised donations of 100 million yen!

• boshū-kōkoku 募集広告 *want ad*

bōsózoku 暴走族 *motorcycle gang*

bósu ボス *boss* 《of henchmen》[→**oyabun** 親分]

bōsui 防水 ～**no** ～の *waterproof; water-resistant*

• bōsui suru 防水する *to waterproof; to make water resistant*

bosutonbággu ボストンバッグ *Boston bag*

botan ボタン *button*

¶Shatsu no botan ga toremashita.

シャツのボタンが取れました。

A shirt button came off.

• botan o kakeru ボタンをかける *to button a button*

• botan o hazusu ボタンを外す *to unbutton a button*

• botan-ana ボタン穴 *buttonhole*

bótan 牡丹 *peony*

bótchan 坊ちゃん ① 【HON.】(*young*)*son; little boy*

② *spoiled and naive young man*

bōto ボート *rowboat*

¶Ken-chan wa mizuumi de bōto o koide imasu.

健ちゃんは湖でボートをこいでいます。

Ken is rowing a boat on the lake.

¶Tanken-ka wa bōto de kawa o watatte imashita.

探検家はボートで川を渡っていました。

The explorers were crossing the river by rowboat.

• bōto ni noru ボートに乗る *to get in a rowboat; to ride in a rowboat*

• kashi-bōto 貸しボート *rowboats for hire*

bōya 坊や *little boy*

bōzu 坊主【CRUDE】*Buddhist priest, Buddhist monk*

bú 部 ① *part, portion* [→**bubun** 部分]

• -bu －部《counter for parts; see Appendix 2》

¶Dewa, dai-ichi-bu kara hajimemashō.

では、第1部から始めましょう。

Well then, let's begin with Part One.

② *department, division*

• bu-chō 部長 *department head, division head*

• bungaku-bu 文学部 *literature department*

• senden-bu 宣伝部 *publicity department*

• yakyū-bu 野球部 *baseball club, baseball team*

-**bu** －部《counter for copies; see Appendix 2》

¶Sono repōto o ichi-bu okutte kudasai.

そのレポートを1部送ってください。

Please send me one copy of that report.

buáisō 無愛想 ～**na** ～な *curt, unfriendly, surly*

¶Ano ten'in wa buaisō desu ne.

あの店員は無愛想ですね。

That sales clerk is surly, isn't he.

búbun 部分 *part, portion* [⇔**zentai** 全体]

¶San-ka no saisho no bubun o yonde kudasai.

3課の最初の部分を読んでください。

Please read the first part of Lesson 3.

• bubun-teki na 部分的な *partial*

¶Otōto no hanashi wa bubun-teki ni wa hontō desu.

弟の話は部分的にはほんとうです。

My younger brother's story

is partly true.

budō 葡萄 ① *grape*

② *grapevine*

• budō-batake 葡萄畑 *vineyard*

• budō-shu 葡萄酒 *(grape)wine* [→**wain** ワイン]

• hoshi-budō 干し葡萄 *raisin*

buhin 部品 *part* 《of a machine, etc.》

• yobi-buhin 予備部品 *spare part*

búi ブイ *buoy*

buiaipī VIP《Generally not written out in katakana.》 *V. I. P.*

buji 無事 ～**na** ～な *free from mishap, safe*

¶Ani wa buji ni Sendai ni tōchaku shimashita.

兄は無事に仙台に到着しました。

My older brother arrived in Sendai safely.

bujoku 侮辱 *insult*

• bujoku suru 侮辱する *to insult*

¶Hito o bujoku suru no wa yoku nai desu yo.

人を侮辱するのはよくないですよ。

It's not good to insult people!

búki 武器 *weapon, arms* [→**heiki** 兵器]

• buki o toru 武器を取る *to take up arms*

búkimi 不気味 ～**na** ～な *eerie, weird*

bukka 物価 *prices, the cost of things*

¶Hawai wa bukka ga takai desu ne.

ハワイは物価が高いですね。

In Hawaii prices are high, aren't they.

• bukka ga agaru〔sagaru〕物価が上がる〔下がる〕*prices rise〔fall〕*

búkku ブック *book* [→**hon** 本]

• bukku-endo ブックエンド *bookend*

• bukku-kabā ブックカバー *book jacket; (protective)book cover*

Búkkyō 仏教 *Buddhism*

būmu ブーム *boom, sudden increase in activity*

• būmu ni naru ブームになる *to boom*

¶Ima wa kōsō-kenchiku ga būmu ni natte imasu.

今は高層建築がブームになっています。

Now high-rise building is booming.

bún 文 [[→**bunshō** 文章]]
① *sentence*
¶Kono bun no imi o setsumei shite kudasai.
この文の意味を説明してください。
Please explain the meaning of this sentence.
② *text, piece of writing*
¶Eigo de mijikai bun o kakimashita.
英語で短い文を書きました。
I wrote a short text in English.

bún 分 *part, portion*
• -bun －分《counter for parts; see Appendix 2》
• -bun －分 *portion for, supply for* 《Added to number bases.》
¶Kyūjo-tai ga mikka-bun no shokuryō o motte imashita.
救助隊は3日分の食料を持っていました。
The rescue party had a three-day food supply.
¶Ani wa karē o san-nin-bun tabeta yo.
兄はカレーを3人分食べたよ。
My older brother ate enough curry for three people!

bunbṓgu 文房具 *stationery item*
• bunbōgu-ya 文房具屋 *stationery store; stationer*

bundṓki 分度器 *protractor*

búngaku 文学 *literature*
• bungaku-sakuhin 文学作品 *a literary work*
• bungaku-sha 文学者 *literary person*
• bungaku-shi 文学史 *history of literature*
• Ei-bungaku 英文学 *English literature*
• Nihon-bungaku 日本文学 *Japanese literature*

bungo 文語 *literary language, written language* 《This word denotes a variety of a language used in written texts that differs from a colloquial variety used in conversation. In the case of Japanese, it refers specifically to classical Japanese.》
[⇔**kōgo** 口語]
• bungo-tai 文語体 *literary writing style*

búnka 文化 *culture*
¶Pateru-san wa Nihon bunka ni kyōmi ga arimasu.
パテルさんは日本文化に興味があります。
Ms. Patel is interested in Japanese culture.
• Bunka no hi 文化の日 *Culture Day* 《a Japanese national holiday on November 3rd》
• bunka-sai 文化祭 *cultural festival; school festival*
• bunka-teki na 文化的な *cultural*

bunkai 分解 *taking apart, dismantling, breaking down into components*
• bunkai suru 分解する *to take apart, to break down into components*
¶Musume wa sono omocha no jidōsha o bunkai shita.
娘はそのおもちゃの自動車を分解した。
My daughter took that toy car apart.

bunkatsu 分割 *division, partition*
• bunkatsu suru 分割する *to divide, to partition*

bunko 文庫 ① *book storehouse*
② *series of books published in uniform pocket-size editions*
• bunko-bon 文庫本 *pocket-size edition of book*

bunmei 文明 *civilization*
• bunmei-shakai 文明社会 *civilized society*
• gendai-bunmei 現代文明 *modern civilization*
• kodai-bunmei 古代文明 *ancient civilization*

bunpō 文法 *grammar*
¶Bunpō no ayamari ga ōi desu yo.
文法の誤りが多いですよ。
There are a lot of grammatical mistakes!
• bunpō-teki na 文法的な *grammatical*
• Ei-bunpō 英文法 *English grammar*
• Nihon-bunpō 日本文法 *Japanese grammar*

bunpu 分布 *distribution, arrangement*
• bunpu suru 分布する *to become distributed*
• bunpu-zu 分布図 *distribution chart; distribution map*

búnraku 文楽 *traditional Japanese puppet play*

bunretsu 分裂 *division, split, fission*
• bunretsu suru 分裂する *to divide, to split* «intransitive»
¶ Sono seitō wa futatsu ni bunretsu shimashita.
その政党は二つに分裂しました。
That political party split into two.
• kaku-bunretsu 核分裂 *nuclear fission*

bunrui 分類 *classification, division into types*
• bunrui suru 分類する *to classify, to divide into types*
¶ Koko no hon o shomei de bunrui shimashita.
ここの本を書名で分類しました。
I classified the books here by titles.

bunseki 分析 *analysis*
• bunseki suru 分析する *to analyze*

búnshō 文章 [[→**bun** 文]] ① *text, piece of writing*
② *sentence*

bunsū 分数 *fraction* «in arithmetic»

buntan 分担 *apportionment, sharing* «of a burden»
• buntan suru 分担する *to divide and share, to apportion*
¶ Hiyō o minna de buntan shimashō ka.
費用をみんなで分担しましょうか。
Shall we all share the expenses between us?
¶ Sono shigoto o chichi to buntan shimasu.
その仕事を父と分担します。
I will divide that work with my father.

buntsū 文通 *exchanging letters, correspondence*
• buntsū suru 文通する *to exchange letters, to correspond*
¶ Jū-nen-mae kara Kyōko-san to buntsū shite imasu.
10年前から京子さんと文通しています。
I've been corresponding with Kyoko for the past 10 years.

bún'ya 分野 *field* (*of endeavor*)
¶ Ano gakusha wa sūgaku ni atarashii bun'ya o hiraita.
あの学者は数学に新しい分野を開いた。
That scholar opened a new field in mathematics.

búrabura ぶらぶら（～**to** ～と）
① *danglingly, swingingly*
• burabura suru ぶらぶらする *to dangle, to swing back and forth* «intransitive»
• ashi o burabura saseru 足をぶらぶらさせる *to swing one's legs*
② *strollingly*
• burabura suru ぶらぶらする *to take a stroll*
¶ Kōen o burabura shimashō ka.
公園をぶらぶらしましょうか。
Shall we take a stroll through the park?
③ *idly, loungingly*
• burabura suru ぶらぶらする *to be idle, to loaf, to loiter*
¶ Kyō chichi wa uchi de burabura shite imasu.
きょう父はうちでぶらぶらしています。
Today my father is loafing around at home.

buraindo ブラインド（*window*)*shade;* (*window*)*blinds*
• buraindo o ageru〔orosu〕ブラインドを上げる〔下ろす〕*to raise*〔*lower*〕*a shade／blinds*

búranko ぶらんこ *swing* ((toy))
• Buranko ni norō yo.
ぶらんこに乗ろうよ。
Let's go on the swings!

burasagaru ぶら下がる【COL.】*to hang down* «intransitive»
¶ Ranpu ga tenjō kara burasagatte imasu.
ランプが天井からぶら下がっています。
A lamp is hanging from the ceiling.

burasageru ぶら下げる【COL. for **tsurusu** 吊るす】*to hang, to suspend*

búrashi ブラシ *brush* ((implement))
[→**hake** 刷毛]
• A ni burashi o kakeru Aにブラシをかける *to brush A*
• ha-burashi 歯ブラシ *toothbrush*
• hea-burashi ヘアブラシ *hairbrush*

burasubándo ブラスバンド *brass band*

buraunkan ブラウン管 *cathode-ray tube*

buráusu ブラウス *blouse*

búrei 無礼 *rudeness, impoliteness* [→ **shitsurei** 失礼]
- burei na 無礼な *rude, impolite*

burēkā ブレーカー *(circuit)breaker*

burēki ブレーキ *brake*
- ¶Kono burēki wa kikanai yo.
- このブレーキは利かないよ。
- *This brake doesn't work!*
- burēki o kakeru ブレーキをかける *to apply the brake, to put on the brakes*

burézā ブレザー *blazer*
- burezā-kōto ブレザーコート [☞**burezā** ブレザー (above)]

-buri －振り ① *way, manner* 《Added to verb bases and to noun bases denoting actions.》
- ¶Ano hito no hanashi-buri ga suki desu.
- あの人の話し振りが好きです。
- *I like that person's manner of speaking.*
- ¶Tamura-kun no benkyō-buri wa sugoi desu yo.
- 田村さんの勉強振りはすごいですよ。
- *Tamura's way of studying is amazing!*
② ～**no** ～の *the first in* 《Added to bases denoting periods of time.》
- ¶Rok-kagetsu-buri no enzetsu deshita.
- 6か月振りの演説でした。
- *It was the first speech in 6 months.*
- ¶Furukawa-san wa go-nen-buri ni Hawai e ikimasu.
- 古川さんは5年ぶりにハワイへ行きます。
- *Ms. Furukawa will go to Hawaii for the first time in five years.*

búri 鰤 *yellowtail* 《(fish)》

burífu ブリーフ *briefs* 《(underwear)》

buríjji ブリッジ ① *bridge* 《spanning a river, etc.》 [→**hashi** 橋]
② *bridge* 《on a ship》
③ *(dental)bridge*
④ *bridge* 《in wrestling》

buríjji ブリッジ *bridge* 《(card game)》

buriki ブリキ *tin plate* 《i.e., iron or steel coated with tin》
- buriki-kan ブリキ缶 <*US*>*tin can*, <*UK*>*tin*

burōchi ブローチ *brooch*

buromáido ブロマイド *still (photograph)of a celebrity*

burū ブルー *blue* 《as a noun》

burudóggu ブルドッグ *bulldog*

burudōzā ブルドーザー *bulldozer*

burujoa ブルジョア *wealthy person who lives extravagantly*

burūsu ブルース *blues* 《(music)》
- burūsu o utau ブルースを歌う *to sing the blues*

búshi 武士 *samurai warrior*
- bushi-dō 武士道 *the way of the samurai, the samurai code of honor*

bushō 無精, 不精 ～**na** ～な *lazy, indolent, eager to spare oneself effort*
- ¶Otōto wa sukoshi bushō desu.
- 弟は少し無精です。
- *My younger brother is a little lazy.*

búshu 部首 *radical* 《of a Chinese character》

busō 武装 *arming, being armed*
- busō suru 武装する *to arm oneself, to become armed*

busshitsu 物質 *matter, material, substance*
- busshitsu-bunmei 物質文明 *material civilization*
- busshitsu-teki na 物質的な *material, tangible* [⇔**seishin**-**teki na** 精神的な]

buta 豚 *pig*
- buta-goya 豚小屋 *pigpen, pigsty*
- buta-niku 豚肉 *pork*
- yaki-buta 焼き豚 *roast pork*

bútai 舞台 *stage* 《for performances》
- butai ni tatsu 舞台に立つ *to appear on the stage*
- butai-haiyū 舞台俳優 *stage actor*
- butai-shōmei 舞台照明 *stage lighting*
- butai-sōchi 舞台装置 *stage set*

bútikku ブティック *boutique*

būtsu ブーツ *boot* 《(footwear)》

bútsu ぶつ 【COL.】 *to strike, to hit* 《The subject and the direct object must both be animate; the hitting may be intentional or accidental.》
- ¶Aite no atama o butsu no wa

fauru da yo.

相手の頭をぶつのはファウルだよ。

Hitting the opponent on the head is a foul!

bútsubutsu ぶつぶつ *murmuringly, mutteringly; complainingly*
- butsubutsu iu ぶつぶつ言う *to murmur, to mutter* [→**tsubuyaku** 呟やく]*; to complain*

butsudan 仏壇 *household Buddhist altar* 《Ordinarily a wooden cabinet containing a Buddha figure and memorial tablets bearing the names of deceased family members.》

butsukaru ぶつかる *to hit, to run into, to collide*
¶Sono fune wa ōki na iwa ni butsukarimashita.

その船は大きな岩にぶつかりました。

That ship hit a big rock.
- konnan ni butsukaru 困難にぶつかる *to run into difficulties*

butsukeru ぶつける ① *to throw at and hit with*
¶Inu ni ishi o butsukete wa ikenai yo.

犬に石をぶつけてはいけないよ。

You mustn't throw stones at dogs!

② *to hit, to bump* 《one thing on another》
¶Hashira ni atama o butsukemashita.

柱に頭をぶつけました。

I hit my head on the post.

bútsuri 物理 ① *principles of physics*
② [☞**butsuri-gaku** 物理学 (below)]
- butsuri-gaku 物理学 (*the study of*) *physics*
- butsuri-gaku-sha 物理学者 *physicist*

butsuzō 仏像 *image of Buddha*

buttai 物体 *physical object*

búzā ブザー *buzzer*
- buza o narasu ブザーを鳴らす *sound a buzzer*

byó 秒 *second* 《of time》
- -byō －秒《counter for seconds; see Appendix 2》
¶Ip-pun wa rokujū-byō desu.

1分は60秒です。

One minute is 60 seconds.
- byō-shin 秒針 *second hand*
- byō-yomi 秒読み *countdown*

byōbu 屏風 《*free-standing*》*folding screen*

byōdō 平等 *equality, impartiality*
- byōdō na／no 平等な／の *equal, even, impartial*
¶Futari wa rieki o byōdō ni wakemashita.

二人は利益を平等に分けました。

The two divided the profits equally.
- danjo-byōdō 男女平等 *equal rights for men and women*

byōin 病院 *hospital, infirmary*
¶Kega-nin wa byōin ni shūyō saremashita.

けが人は病院に収容されました。

The injured person was admitted to the hospital.
- daigaku-byōin 大学病院 *university hospital*
- kyūkyū-byōin 救急病院 *emergency hospital*
- sōgō-byōin 総合病院 *general hospital*

byōki 病気 *sickness, illness* [⇔**kenkō** 健康]
¶Sofu wa me no byōki ni kakatte imasu.

祖父は目の病気にかかっています。

My grandfather is suffering from an eye disease.
¶Imōto wa is-shūkan byōki de nete imasu.

妹は1週間病気で寝ています。

My younger sister has been sick in bed for a week.
- omoi〔karui〕byōki 重い〔軽い〕病気 *serious* 〔*slight*〕*illness*
- byōki no 病気の <*US*>*sick, ill*
- byōki ni naru 病気になる *to become ill*
- byōki ga naoru 病気が治る *an illness gets better*

byōnin 病人 *ill person*

byōsha 描写 *depiction, portrayal; description*
- byōsha suru 描写する *to depict, to portray; to describe*

byōshitsu 病室 *sickroom*
byúffe ビュッフェ *buffet restaurant*

C

cha 茶 *tea* [→**o-cha** お茶①]
• cha-saji 茶匙 *teaspoon*
• cha-no-yu 茶の湯 *the tea ceremony* [→**sadō** 茶道]
cháhan チャーハン *fried rice*
cháimu チャイム *chime*
¶Hora, chaimu ga natte iru yo.
ほら、チャイムが鳴っているよ。
Listen, the chimes are ringing!
chairo 茶色 *brown* «as a noun»
• usui chairo 薄い茶色 *light brown*
• koge-chairo 焦げ茶色 *dark brown*
-chaku 一着 ① «counter for suits, dresses, etc.; see Appendix 2»
② «counter for places in the order of finish in a race; see Appendix 2»
chakujitsu 着実 ～**na** ～な ① *steady (-going), constant*
¶Ane no ryōri no ude wa chakujitsu ni agatte imasu.
姉の料理の腕は着実に上がっています。
My older sister's cooking skill is steadily improving.
¶Keikaku wa chakujitsu ni susunde imasu.
計画は着実に進んでいます。
The plan is progressing steadily.
② *sound, trustworthy*
• chakujitsu na eigyō 着実な営業 *sound management*
chakuriku 着陸 *landing* «of an airplane, etc.» [⇔**ririku** 離陸]
• chakuriku suru 着陸する *to land*
¶Hikōki wa buji ni Narita-kūkō ni chakuriku shimashita.
飛行機は無事に成田空港に着陸しました。
The plane landed safely at Narita Airport.

chakuseki 着席 *taking a seat*
• chakuseki suru 着席する *to take a seat*
¶Daihyō-zen'in ga chakuseki shimashita.
代表全員が着席しました。
The representatives all took their seats.
chámingu チャーミング ～**na** ～な *charming, attractive* [→**miryoku-teki na** 魅力的な (s.v. **miryoku** 魅力)]
chanbara ちゃんばら 【COL.】 *sword battle*
• chanbara-eiga ちゃんばら映画 *sword battle movie* «typically involving **samurai**»
chánneru チャンネル *(television)channel*
• channeru o kirikaeru チャンネルを切り替える *to change the channel*
• -channeru 一チャンネル «counter for channels; see Appendix 2»
¶Yon-channeru de yakyū o miyō.
4チャンネルで野球を見よう。
Let's watch baseball on Channel 4.
• channeru-arasoi チャンネル争い *dispute over which channel to watch*
cha-no-ma 茶の間 «a room in a traditional Japanese house where the family has meals and relaxes»
chánpion チャンピオン *champion*
chánsu チャンス *chance, opportunity* [→**kikai** 機会]
• zekkō no chansu 絶好のチャンス *best chance*
• chansu o nogasu チャンスを逃す *to miss a chance*
chanto ちゃんと *neatly, precisely; properly, in accordance with accepted standards*
¶Shōjo wa chanto fuku o kimashita.
少女はちゃんと服を着ました。
The little girl put on her clothes properly.
• chanto shita ちゃんとした *neat, precise; proper, up-to-standard*
charénjā チャレンジャー *challenger* «in sports»
cháerenji チャレンジ [[→**chōsen** 挑戦]]
① *challenge, invitation to combat*
• charenji suru チャレンジする *to challenge (to combat)*
② *taking on a challenge*

• charenji suru チャレンジする *to make a challenge*

• A ni charenji suru Aにチャレンジする *to make a challenge at A*

chárití チャリティー *charity* [→**jizen** 慈善]

• charití-shō チャリティーショー *charity show*

chátā チャーター 〈*vehicle*〉*charter*

• chātā suru チャーターする *to charter*

• chātā-ki チャーター機 *chartered plane*

chawan 茶碗 ① *rice bowl*
② *teacup*

• chawan-mushi 茶碗蒸し *thick steamed custard soup served in a teacup with a lid*

chékku チェック ① *check, verification*

• chekku suru チェックする *to check*
② *check* (*mark*)

• chekku-auto チェックアウト 〈*hotel*〉 *check-out*

• chekku-in チェックイン 〈*hotel*〉 *check-in*

chékku チェック *check* (*pattern*)

¶Tomomi wa chekku no sukāto o haite iru.

友美はチェックのスカートをはいている。

Tomomi is wearing a checked skirt.

chékku チェック 〈*bank*〉 *check* [→ **kogitte** 小切手]

chén チェーン *chain* [→**kusari** 鎖]

• chēn-sutoa チェーンストア *chain store*

• taiya-chēn タイヤチェーン *tire chain*

chéro チェロ *cello*

• chero-sōsha チェロ奏者 *cellist*

chésu チェス *chess*

chi 血 *blood* [→**ketsueki** 血液]

• chi ga deru 血が出る *blood comes out*

• chi no shimi 血の染み *blood stain*

• chi-darake no 血だらけの *blood-covered*

¶Kega-nin no kao wa chi-darake da yo.

けが人の顔は血だらけだよ。

The injured person's face is covered with blood!

chiagáru チアガール 〈*girl*〉*cheerleader*

chían 治安 *public peace, public order*

chíbi ちび 【COL.】 *short person,*

shrimp [⇔**noppo** のっぽ]

chíbusa 乳房 〈*woman's*〉*breast*

chichí 父 *father* [⇔**haha** 母; **otōsan** お父さん]

¶Chichi wa tsuri ga dai-suki desu.

父は釣りが大好きです。

My father loves fishing.

• Chichi no hi 父の日 *Father's Day*

• chichi-oya 父親 *father, male parent* [⇔**haha-oya** 母親 (s.v. **haha** 母)]

chichí 乳 ① *mother's milk*
② *breast; teat*

• ushi no chichi o shiboru 牛の乳を搾る *to milk a cow*

chídori 千鳥 *plover*

chié 知恵 *wisdom*

chífu チーフ *a chief, a head*

chífusu チフス *typhus*

chigai 違い *difference, distinction*

¶Jūdō to karate no chigai wa nan desu ka.

柔道と空手の違いは何ですか。

What is the difference between judo and karate?

chigai-nái 違いない [☞**ni chigai-nai** に違いない]

chigau 違う ① *to be different, to differ* [→**kotonaru** 異なる]

¶Ojōsan no seikaku wa okāsan to wa chigaimasu.

お嬢さんの性格はお母さんとは違います。

The daughter's character is different from her mother's.

② *to be wrong, to be incorrect*

¶Sono kotae wa chigau to omou yo.

その答えは違うと思うよ。

I think that answer is wrong!

¶"Kore desu ka." "Īe, chigaimasu."

「これですか」「いいえ、違います」

"Is this it?" "No, it isn't." 《Using **chigau** as in this example is a relatively gentle way of contradicting someone. It is not nearly as abrupt as saying *You're wrong* in English.》

chigíru 千切る{5} ① *to tear into pieces*

¶Makiko-chan wa sono kami o

futatsu ni chigitta.
真紀子ちゃんはその紙を二つにちぎった。
Makiko tore that paper in two.

② *to pluck off, to tear off*
• hana o chigiru 花をちぎる *to pick a flower*

chiheisen 地平線 *horizon (between sky and land)* [⇔**suihei-sen** 水平線 (s.v. **suihei** 水平)]
¶Taiyō ga chiheisen ni chikazukimashita.
太陽が地平線に近づきました。
The sun approached the horizon.
• chiheisen-jō ni 地平線上に *above the horizon*
• chiheisen-ka ni 地平線下に *below the horizon*

chihō 地方 ① *area, region* [→**chiiki** 地域]
② *the parts of a country away from the capital, the provinces*
¶Itoko wa chihō ni sunde imasu.
いとこは地方に住んでいます。
My cousin lives in the provinces.
• chihō-kōmuin 地方公務員 *provincial civil servant*
• chihō-shinbun 地方新聞 *local newspaper, provincial newspaper*
• chihō-shoku 地方色 *local color*
• Kantō-chihō 関東地方 *the Kanto region*

chii 地位 *position, post, rank*
• chii no takai hito 地位の高い人 *person of high position*
• shakai-teki-chii 社会的地位 *social position*

chiiki 地域 *area, district*
• kōgyō-chiiki 工業地域 *industrial area*

chiji 知事 *governor《of a prefecture, state, etc.》*
• Chiba-ken-chiji 千葉県知事 *the Governor of Chiba Prefecture*

chijimaru 縮まる *to shrink, to contract, to shorten 《intransitive》*

chijimeru 縮める *to shorten, to reduce 《transitive》*[→**tanshuku suru** 短縮する]
¶Sukāto o sukoshi chijimeta hō ga ii darō.

スカートを少し縮めたほうがいいだろう。
It would probably be better to shorten the skirt a little.
• kubi o chijimeru 首を縮める *to duck one's head*

chijimu 縮む *to shrink 《intransitive》*
¶Kono sētā wa sentaku de chijinde shimatta ne.
このセーターは洗濯で縮んでしまったね。
This sweater shrank in the laundry, didn't it.

chijin 知人 *an acquaintance* [→**shiriai** 知り合い]

chijireru 縮れる *to become curly*
• chijireta kami 縮れた髪 *curly hair*

chijō 地上 *(the area)aboveground* [⇔**chika** 地下]
¶Sono biru wa chijō gojuk-kai, chika san-gai desu.
そのビルは地上50階、地下3階です。
That building is 50 stories aboveground and three stories underground.

chika 地下 *(the area)underground* [⇔**chijō** 地上]
¶Atarashī eki ga chika gojū-mētoru ni kensetsu sareta.
新しい駅が地下50メートルに建設された。
The new station was built 50 meters underground.
• chika-dō 地下道 <US>*underpass*, <UK>*subway*
• chika-gai 地下街 *underground shopping center*
• chika-ni-kai 地下2階 *second floor underground*
• chika-shitsu 地下室 *basement room*
• chika-sui 地下水 *underground water*
• chika-tetsu 地下鉄 <US>*subway*, <UK>*underground*

chikagoro 近ごろ *recently, lately* [→**kono-goro** このごろ]

chikai 地階 *basement*

chikai 近い *near, close* [⇔**tōi** 遠い]
¶Ichiban chikai yūbin-kyoku wa doko desu ka.
いちばん近い郵便局はどこですか。
Where is the nearest post office?

¶Kurisumasu ga chikai desu ne.

クリスマスが近いですね。

Christmas is near, isn't it.

¶Sofu wa nanajū ni chikai desu.

祖父は70に近いです。

My grandfather is nearly 70.

• chikai uchi ni 近いうちに *soon, in the near future*

¶Chikai uchi ni mata sono hito ni aimasu.

近いうちにまたその人に会います。

I will see that person again soon.

chikáku 近く *the area nearby* 《This word is the adverbial form of **chikai** 近い and has the predictable meanings as well.》

¶Sobo wa mainichi chikaku no kōen ni sanpo ni ikimasu.

祖母は毎日近くの公園に散歩に行きます。

My grandmother goes for a walk in a nearby park every day.

¶Watashi wa gakkō no chikaku ni sunde imasu.

私は学校の近くに住んでいます。

I live near the school.

-**chikaku** -近く *nearly* 《Added to bases denoting specific quantities.》

¶Hikōki wa sanjup-pun-chikaku oku-remashita.

飛行機は30分近く遅れました。

The plane was nearly 30 minutes late.

chikámichi 近道 *shortcut*

¶Sore wa tosho-kan e no chikamichi desu.

それは図書館への近道です。

That's a shortcut to the library.

• chikamichi o suru 近道をする *to take a shortcut*

¶Takabatake-san wa chikamichi o shite kōen e ikimashita.

高畑さんは近道をして公園へ行きました。

Mr. Takabatake took a shortcut to the park.

chikará 力 ① *power, strength*

• chikara ga tsuyoi〔yowai〕力が強い〔弱い〕*to be strong〔weak〕*

¶Sono senshu wa totemo chikara

no tsuyoi hito desu.

その選手はとても力の強い人です。

That athlete is a very strong person.

• hōritsu no chikara 法律の力 *the power of the law*

② *ability* [→**nōryoku** 能力]

¶Murakami-san ni wa sono shigoto o hitori de yaritogeru chikara ga aru to omoimasu.

村上さんにはその仕事を一人でやり遂げる力があると思います。

I think Ms. Murakami has the ability to do that work by herself.

③ *effort, exertion* [→**doryoku** 努力]

• chikara o awaseru 力を合わせる *to combine efforts*

• chikara-ippai (ni) 力一杯 (に) *with all one's strength*

¶Hiroshi wa chikara-ippai jitensha no pedaru o koida.

浩は力いっぱい自転車のペダルをこいだ。

Hiroshi is pumping the bicycle pedals with all his strength!

chikatetsu 地下鉄 <US>*subway*, <UK>*underground*

¶Tōkyō kara Kōrakuen made chikatetsu de ikimashita.

東京から後楽園まで地下鉄で行きました。

I went from Tokyo to Korakuen by subway.

chikáu 誓う *to swear, to pledge*

¶Shinnyū-shain wa saizen o tsukusu koto o chikatta.

新入社員は最善を尽くすことを誓った。

The new employee promised to do his best.

chikayóru 近寄る *to get near, to approach* [→**chikazuku** 近づく]

¶Sono saru ni chikayoranai de.

その猿に近寄らないで。

Don't go near that monkey.

chikazukéru 近づける [[⇔**tōzakeru** 遠ざける]] ① [[→**yoseru** 寄せる]] *to bring near, to put close; to let approach*

② *to begin to associate with, to become friendly with*

chikazúku 近づく *to get near, to approach*
　¶Basu wa shūten ni chikazukimashita.
バスは終点に近づきました。
The bus approached the last stop.
　¶Gaikoku-jin ga watashi no hō e chikazuite kimashita.
外国人が私のほうへ近づいてきました。
A foreigner approached me.

chikétto チケット *ticket* [→**kippu** 切符]

chíkin チキン *chicken* (*meat*)

chikoku 遅刻 *arriving after the starting time, being late*
　•chikoku suru 遅刻する *to be late*
　¶Ikegami-kun wa kesa gakkō ni jup-pun chikoku shita yo.
池上君はけさ学校に10分遅刻したよ。
Ikegami was ten minutes late for school this morning!

chikú 地区 *district, region, area* [→**chiiki** 地域]; *zone* [→**chitai** 地帯]
　¶Kono gakkō wa chiku no daihyō deshita.
この学校は地区の代表でした。
This school was the district representative.
　•jūtaku-chiku 住宅地区 *residential area*
　•shōgyō-chiku 商業地区 *business district*

chikúbi 乳首 *nipple*

chikushō 畜生 【CRUDE】 *Damn it!*

chikyū 地球 *the* (*planet*)*earth*
　¶Chikyū wa taiyō no mawari o mawatte imasu.
地球は太陽の周りを回っています。
The earth revolves around the sun.
　•chikyū-gi 地球儀 *globe* ((*map*))

chimei 地名 *place name*

chiméishō 致命傷 *fatal wound*

chimeiteki 致命的 ～**na** ～な *fatal*

chímu チーム *team*
　¶Sono chīmu ni hairitai desu.
そのチームに入りたいです。
I want to join that team.
　•chīmu-wāku チームワーク *teamwork*

chinbotsu 沈没 *sinking* (*in water*)
　•chinbotsu suru 沈没する *to sink*
　¶Fune wa shibaraku shite chinbotsu shimashita.
船はしばらくして沈没しました。
The ship sank after a while.

chíngin 賃金 *wages*

chinmoku 沈黙 *silence, not talking*
　•chinmoku suru 沈黙する *to become silent, to stop talking* [→**damaru** 黙る]
　¶Keikan wa sono aida zutto chinmoku o mamotte ita.
警官はその間ずっと沈黙を守っていた。
The police officer maintained his silence the whole time.
　¶Tsui ni daitōryō wa chinmoku o yaburimashita.
ついに大統領は沈黙を破りました。
At last the president broke his silence.

chínō 知能 *intelligence, mental powers*
　¶Inu wa usagi yori chinō ga takai.
犬はうさぎより知能が高い。
A dog is more intelligent than a rabbit.
　《*Literally: A dog's intelligence is higher than a rabbits*》
　•chinō-shisū 知能指数 *intelligence quotient* [→**aikyū** アイキュー]
　•chinō-tesuto 知能テスト *intelligence test*

chinpánjī チンパンジー *chimpanzee*

chinpira ちんぴら 【COL.】 ① *young hoodlum, young tough*
　② *low-ranking gangster, punk*

chinretsu 陳列 *exhibiting, display*
　•chinretsu suru 陳列する *to exhibit, to put on display*
　¶Takusan no e ga koko ni chinretsu sarete imasu.
たくさんの絵がここに陳列されています。
Many pictures are being exhibited here.
　•chinretsu-hin 陳列品 *item on exhibit*
　•chinretsu-mado 陳列窓 *display window*
　•chinretsu-shitsu 陳列室 *showroom*

chíppu チップ *tip, gratuity*
　¶Chichi wa hoteru no bōi ni chippu o watashita.
父はホテルのボーイにチップを渡した。
My father handed a tip to the hotel bellboy.

chirashi 散らし *handbill*

chirí 塵 *dust* [→**hokori** 埃]*; bits of trash*
- chiri-tori 塵取り *dustpan*

chíri 地理 *geography*

chirigami 塵紙 *kleenex, tissue* [→**tisshupēpā** ティッシュペーパー]*; toilet paper* [→**toiretto-pēpā** トイレットペーパー (s.v. **toiretto** トイレット)]

chiru 散る{5} ① *to fall and be scattered on the ground* 《when the subject is blossoms, leaves,etc.》
¶Ko-no-ha ga chitte imasu.
木の葉が散っています。
Leaves are falling.
¶Sakura ga sukkari chitte shimaimashita.
さくらがすっかり散ってしまいました。
The cherry blossoms have all fallen.
② *to scatter, to disperse* 《intransitive》 [⇔**atsumaru** 集まる]
- gunshū ga chiru 群衆が散る *a crowd disperses*
- ki ga chiru 気が散る *to become distracted*

chiryō 治療 *(medical)treatment*
¶Sono hito wa mada chiryō o ukete imasu.
その人はまだ治療を受けています。
That person is still undergoing treatment.
- chiryō suru 治療する *to treat*

chísa 小さ ～**na** ～な《Used only as a modifier, never as a predicate.》[[→**chīsai** 小さい]] [[⇔**ōki na** 大きな]] *small, little; soft* 《sound》
¶Chīsa na koe de iu to, kikoenai yo.
小さな声で言うと、聞こえないよ。
I can't hear you when you speak softly!

chīsái 小さい [[⇔**ōkii** 大きい]] *small, little; soft* 《sound》
¶Kono shatsu wa boku ni wa chīsai to omoimasu.
このシャツは僕には小さいと思います。
I think this shirt is small for me.
¶Chīsai toki, pairotto ni naritakatta.
小さいとき、パイロットになりたかった。
When I was a little, I wanted to become a pilot.

¶Kono ningyō wa totemo chīsai ne.
この人形はとても小さいね。
This doll is very small, isn't it.
- chiisai koe 小さい声 *soft voice, low voice*

chisei 知性 *intellect*
- chisei-teki na 知性的な *intellectual*

chíshiki 知識 *knowledge*
¶Mori-sensei wa kanari kabuki no chishiki ga arimasu.
森先生はかなり歌舞伎の知識があります。
Mr. Mori has quite a knowledge of kabuki.
- chishiki-jin 知識人 *an intellectual*
- kiso-chishiki 基礎知識 *basic knowledge*

Chishima-réttō 千島列島 *the Kurile Islands*

chishitsúgaku 地質学 *(the study of) geology*

chísso 窒素 *nitrogen*

chissoku 窒息 *suffocation, asphyxiation*
- chissoku suru 窒息する *to suffocate, to be asphyxiated*

chitai 地帯 *zone; region* [→**chiiki** 地域]
- anzen-chitai 安全地帯 *safety zone; safety island, refuge*
- shinrin-chitai 森林地帯 *forest region*

chitchái ちっちゃい 【COL. for **chiisai** 小さい】

chiteki 知的 ～**na** ～な *intellectual, mental*

chitsújo 秩序 *order, discipline*
- hō to chitsujo o tamotsu 法と秩序を保つ *to preserve law and order*
- shakai-chitsujo 社会秩序 *public order*

chittómo ちっとも 【COL.】 〈*not*〉 *at all* 《Always occurs in combination with a negative predicate.》
¶Boku wa chittomo tsukarete inai yo.
僕はちっとも疲れていないよ。
I'm not tired at all!

chízu チーズ *cheese*
- chīzu-kēki チーズケーキ *cheesecake*
- kona-chīzu 粉チーズ *powdered cheese*

chízu 地図 *map*

¶Sekai no chizu o mite miyō.

世界の地図を見てみよう。

Let's have a look at a map of the world.

¶Rondon o chizu de sagashinasai.

ロンドンを地図で捜しなさい。

Look for London on the map.

• chizu-chō 地図帳 *atlas*

• dōro-chizu 道路地図 *road map*

• Nihon-chizu 日本地図 *map of Japan*

chō 腸 *intestines*

• dai-chō 大腸 *large intestine*

• shō-chō 小腸 *small intestine*

chō 蝶 *butterfly*

-chō -兆 *trillion* 《see Appendix 2》

• it-chō-en 1兆円 *one trillion yen*

chochiku 貯蓄 [[→**chokin** 貯金]]
saving money; savings

• chochiku suru 貯蓄する *to save money*

chōchin 提灯 *paper lantern*

chōchō 町長 *town mayor*

¶Tomodachi no otōsan wa chōchō ni erabareta yo.

友達のお父さんは町長に選ばれたよ。

My friend's father was elected town mayor!

chōchō 蝶々 [☞**chō** 蝶]

chōdai 頂戴 ① ～**suru** ～する 【HUM. for **morau** 貰う①】 [→**itadaku** 頂く①]

 ② ～**suru** ～する 【HUM. for **taberu** 食べる; **nomu** 飲む】 [→**itadaku** 頂く③]

 ③ *please give me*

¶Sono chokorēto o chōdai.

そのチョコレートをちょうだい。

Please give me that chocolate.

 ④ *please (be good enough to)* 《following the gerund (-te form) of a verb》

¶Kore o tsukatte chōdai.

これを使ってちょうだい。

Please use this.

chōdo 丁度 *just, exactly*

¶Basu wa chōdo ni-ji ni shuppatsu shimasu.

バスはちょうど2時に出発します。

The bus will leave at exactly 2:00.

¶Nishizawa-san wa chōdo densha ni maniatta.

西沢さんはちょうど電車に間に合った。

Mr. Nishizawa was just in time for the train.

¶Ane wa chōdo shukudai o owatta tokoro desu.

姉はちょうど宿題を終ったところです。

My older sister has just finished her homework.

¶Chōdo sono toki, kaichō ga heya ni haitte kita.

ちょうどその時、会長が部屋に入ってきた。

Just then, the chairperson came into the room.

chōeki 懲役 *penal servitude*

chōhei 徴兵 *conscription, (military) draft*

chōhōkei 長方形 *rectangle*

chōjo 長女 *oldest daughter* [⇔**chōnan** 長男]

¶Yōko-san wa chōjo desu.

洋子さんは長女です。

Yoko is the oldest daughter.

chōjō 頂上 *summit, top* 《of a mountain》 [⇔**fumoto** ふもと]

¶Watashi-tachi wa yama no chōjō made noborimashita.

私たちは山の頂上まで登りました。

We climbed to the top of the mountain.

chōkaku 聴覚 *hearing, auditory sense*

chōkan 朝刊 *morning edition of a newspaper* [⇔**yūkan** 夕刊]

chōkan 長官 *chief, director* 《of a government agency》; *cabinet secretary* 《in the United States government》

• Kokumu-chōkan 国務長官 *the Secretary of State*

chōki 長期 *long period of time* [⇔**tanki** 短期]

• chōki-keikaku 長期計画 *long-range plan*

chokin 貯金 ① *saving money; depositing money* 《in a bank, etc.》

• chokin suru 貯金する *to save money; to save* 《money》; *to deposit money; to deposit* 《money》

¶Oji wa yūbin-kyoku ni chokin shite imasu.

伯父は郵便局に貯金しています。
My uncle saves money at the post office.
② *savings, money on deposit*
¶Okusan wa ginkō kara chokin o orosh-imashita.
奥さんは銀行から貯金を下ろしました。
His wife withdrew her savings from the bank.
• chokin-bako 貯金箱 *savings box, piggy bank*
• chokin-tsūchō 貯金通帳 *passbook, bankbook*
• yūbin-chokin 郵便貯金 *postal savings*
chokkaku 直角 *right angle*
• chokkaku-sankaku-kei 直角三角形 *right triangle*
chokkan 直感 *intuition*
• chokkan de 直感で *by intuition*
chokkei 直径 *diameter*
¶Kono en no chokkei wa ni-mētoru desu.
この円の直径は2メートルです。
The diameter of this circle is two meters.
chokki チョッキ <*US*>*vest*, <*UK*>*waistcoat*
chōkō 聴講 *auditing* 《of classes》
• chōkō suru 聴講する *to audit*
• chōkō-sei 聴講生 *auditor* ((student))
chōkoku 彫刻 *sculpture, engraving*
• chōkoku suru 彫刻する *to sculpt, to en-grave*
¶Sensei wa dairiseki de zō o chōkoku shimashita.
先生は大理石で像を彫刻しました。
The teacher sculpted an image in marble.
• chōkoku-ka 彫刻家 *sculptor*
chokorēto チョコレート *chocolate*
chōku チョーク *chalk*
¶Kokuban ni chōku de namae o kaki-nasai.
黒板にチョークで名前を書きなさい。
Write your name with chalk on the black-board.
chokusen 直線 *straight line*
• chokusen o hiku 直線を引く *to draw a straight line*
chokusetsu 直接（〜**ni** 〜に）*directly*

[⇔**kansetsu ni** 間接に]
¶Shachō to chokusetsu renraku o to-rimasu.
社長と直接連絡を取ります。
I will get in touch directly with the com-pany president.
¶Sono shitsumon wa chokusetsu sensei ni shite kudasai.
その質問は直接先生にしてください。
Please ask the teacher that question directly.
• chokusetsu no 直接の *direct*
• chokusetsu-mokuteki-go 直接目的語 *direct object*
• chokusetsu-zei 直接税 *direct tax*
chokutsū 直通 〜**no** 〜の *di-rect* 〈*flight*〉, *through* 〈*train*〉; *nonstop*
• chokutsū suru 直通する *to go straight through, to go directly*
• chokutsū-ressha 直通列車 *through train; nonstop train*
chōkyori 長距離 *long distance* [⇔**tan-kyori** 短距離; **chūkyori** 中距離]
• chōkyori-kyōsō 長距離競走 *long-distance* (*running*) *race*
• chōkyori-denwa 長距離電話 *long-distance telephone call*
chōmán'in 超満員 *crowded beyond capacity* (*with people*)
chōmíryō 調味料 (*food*)*seasoning*
chōnán 長男 *oldest son* [⇔**chōjo** 長女]
¶Ano ko ga uchi no chōnan desu.
あの子がうちの長男です。
That child is our oldest son.
chonmage ちょんまげ *samurai topknot*
chōnóryoku 超能力 *supernatural power*
chōónpa 超音波 *ultrasonic waves*
chōónsoku 超音速 *supersonic speed*
chōrei 朝礼 *morning assembly* 《at a school, factory, etc.》
chōsa 調査 *investigation, survey*
¶Sono jiko no chōsa wa susunde imasu.
その事故の調査は進んでいます。
The investigation of that accident is prog-ressing.

- chōsa suru 調査する *to investigate, to do a survey on*

chōsei 調整 *regulation, adjustment*
- chōsei suru 調整する *to regulate, to adjust*

chōsen 挑戦 ① *challenge, invitation to combat*
- chōsen suru 挑戦する *to challenge (to combat)*
¶Aite wa sono chōsen ni ōjiru deshō.
相手はその挑戦に応じるでしょう。
The opponent will probably accept that challenge.
② *taking on a challenge*
- chōsen suru 挑戦する *to make a challenge*
- A ni chōsen suru Aに挑戦する *to challenge A, to take on A*
¶Chanpion ni chōsen shitara dō desu ka.
チャンピオンに挑戦したらどうですか。
How about taking on the champion?
- chōsen-sha 挑戦者 *challenger*

Chōsén 朝鮮 *Korea* «sometimes used pejoratively»
- Chōsen-minshushugi-jinmin-kyōwa-koku (Kita-chōsen) 朝鮮民主主義人民共和国（北朝鮮） *The Democratic People's Republic of Korea (North Korea)*
- Chōsen-ninjin 朝鮮人参 *ginseng*

chōsetsu 調節 *adjustment, regulation*
- chōsetsu suru 調節する *to adjust, to regulate*

chósha 著者 *writer, author*

chōshi 調子 ① *condition, state* [→**guai** 具合①]
- chōshi ga ii 調子がいい *to be in good condition; to be operating well; to be feeling well*
¶Ano pitchā wa kyō wa chōshi ga ii ne.
あのピッチャーはきょうは調子がいいね。
That pitcher is in good condition today, isn't he.
- chōshi ga warui 調子が悪い *to be in bad condition; to be operating badly; to be feeling unwell*
¶Fumiko-san wa karada no chōshi ga warukatta yo.

文子さんは体の調子が悪かったよ。
Fumiko wasn't feeling well!
¶Chōshi wa dō desu ka.
調子はどうですか。
How are you feeling?
② *way (of doing)* [→**hōhō** 方法, **guai** 具合②]
¶Sono chōshi de tsuzukete kudasai.
その調子で続けてください。
Please continue it in that way.
③ *tune, tone; pitch, key*
¶Kashu wa hikui chōshi de uta o utaimashita.
歌手は低い調子で歌を歌いました。
The singer sang low key.
- chōshi ga atte iru 調子が合っている *to be in tune*
¶Kono piano wa chōshi ga atte imasu.
このピアノは調子が合っています。
This piano is in tune.
- chōshi ga kurutte iru 調子が狂っている *to be out of tune*
④ *rhythm, tempo* [→**hyōshi** 拍子]
⑤ [[→**kuchō** 口調]] *tone (of voice); tone, style (of expression)*
⑥ *spirit, impetus*
- chōshi ni noru 調子に乗る *to get carried away, to become elated*
- chōshi-hazure no 調子外れの *out of tune; off-key*

chósho 長所 *strong point* [⇔**tansho** 短所]
¶Yumi-san no chōsho wa nintai desu.
由美さんの長所は忍耐です。
Yumi's strong point is patience.
¶Dare demo chōsho o motte iru yo.
だれでも長所を持っているよ。
Everyone has strong points!

chōshoku 朝食 *breakfast* [→**asa-gohan** 朝ご飯 (s.v. **asa** 朝)]
¶Maiasa shichi-ji ni chōshoku o tabemasu.
毎朝７時に朝食を食べます。
I eat breakfast at 7:00 every morning.
¶Chichi no chōshoku wa gyūnyū ip-pai to tōsuto ni-mai desu.
父の朝食は牛乳１杯とトースト２枚です。

My father's breakfast is a glass of milk and two slices of toast.

chōshū 聴衆 *audience*

¶Hōru wa ōzei no chōshū de man'in deshita.

ホールは大勢の聴衆で満員でした。

The hall was filled with a large audience.

chosúichi 貯水池 *reservoir* «i.e., an artificial water-storage pond»

chóten 頂点 *top, zenith, peak*

chōtsúgai ちょうつがい *metal hinge*

chotto ちょっと ① *a little while, a moment*

¶Chotto matte kudasai.

ちょっと待ってください。

Wait a moment, please.

¶Chotto denwa o tsukatte ii desu ka.

ちょっと電話を使っていいですか。

May I use the phone for a while?

② *a little, a few* [→**sukoshi** 少し]

¶Kono mondai wa san-nen-sei ni wa chotto muzukashii.

この問題は3年生にはちょっと難しい。

This problem is a little difficult for third-years students.

¶Tomato mo chotto moraō ka na.

トマトもちょっともらおうかな。

May I take a few tomatos too.

③ «Frequently, **chotto** is used simply to make a request sound less demanding. In such cases, a literal translation such as *a little while* or *a little* will be inappropriate.»

¶Chotto kono shashin o mite.

ちょっとこの写真を見て。

Look at this picture.

¶Chotto tōshite kudasai.

ちょっと通してください。

Please let me through.

④ *Say, I say* «Used to get a person's attention.»

¶Chotto Kyōko-chan, kore wa dō?

ちょっと京子ちゃん、これはどう？

Say, Kyoko, how about this?

chōwa 調和 *harmony, accord*

• chōwa suru 調和する *to harmonize,*

to become in harmony

¶Kono kagu wa jūtan no iro to chōwa shite iru.

この家具はじゅうたんの色と調和している。

This furniture goes well with the color of the carpet.

chōyaku 跳躍 (*upward*)*jump*

• chōyaku suru 跳躍する *to jump* (*upward*) [→**tobiagaru** 跳び上がる]

chozō 貯蔵 *storing*

• chozō suru 貯蔵する *to store*

chū 注 *annotation, note*

• kyaku-chū 脚注 *footnote*

chú 中 *mediocrity, the average*

• chū-ijō 中以上 *above average*

¶Kono gakusei no kaiwa-ryoku wa chū-ijō desu.

この学生の会話力は中以上です。

This student's speaking ability is above average.

-chū – 中 «Added to noun bases.»

①(~**ni** ~に) *during*

¶Jugyō-chū oshaberi o shite wa ikenai yo.

授業中おしゃべりをしてはいけないよ。

You mustn't talk during class!

¶Rōma-taizai-chū ni e o benkyō shimashita.

ローマ滞在中に絵を勉強しました。

During my stay in Rome, I studied painting.

② ~**no** ~の *in the midst of, under*

¶Chichi no kuruma wa shūri-chū desu.

父の車は修理中です。

My father's car is being repaired.

¶Sensei-gata wa ima, kaigi-chū desu.

先生方は今、会議中です。

The teachers are in a meeting now.

• kōji-chū no 工事中 *under-construction*

chūbu チューブ ① *tube, pipe* [→**kuda** 管]

② *inner tube*

③ *squeeze-tube container*

Chūbu-chíhō 中部地方 *the Chubu area of Japan* «Niigata, Toyama, Ishikawa, Fukui, Nagano, Yamanashi, Shizuoka, Aichi, and Gifu Prefectures»

chūdan 中断 *interruption, stoppage*
• chūdan suru 中断する *to interrupt, to stop in progress*
¶Gakusei wa benkyō o chūdan shite, kōen ni dekaketa.
学生は勉強を中断して、公園に出かけた。
The student stopped studying and went out to the park.

chūdoku 中毒 ① *poisoning, toxic effects*
• chūdoku suru 中毒する *to get poisoned, to suffer toxic effects*
• chūdoku o okosu 中毒を起こす *to get poisoned, to suffer toxic effects*
¶Chichi wa nama-gaki o tabete chūdoku o okoshimashita.
父は生がきを食べて中毒を起こしました。
My father ate raw oysters and got poisoned.
② *addiction*
• arukōru-chūdoku アルコール中毒 *alcoholism*
• gasu-chūdoku ガス中毒 *gas poisoning*
• shoku-chūdoku 食中毒 *food poisoning*

chūgákkō 中学校 [☞**chūgaku** 中学]

chūgaku 中学 *junior high school*
¶Watashi wa chūgaku no ichi-nen-sei desu.
私は中学の1年生です。
I am a first-year student in junior high school .
• chūgaku-sei 中学生 *junior-high-school student*

chūgen 中元 *midsummer gift*

Chūgoku 中国 *China*

Chūgoku-chíhō 中国地方 *The Chugoku region of Japan* 《Okayama, Hiroshima, Yamaguchi, Shimane, and Tottori Prefectures》

chúi 注意 ① *attention, notice* [→**chūmoku** 注目]
¶Shidō-sha no setsumei ni chūi o harainasai.
指導者の説明に注意を払いなさい。
Pay attention to the leader's explanation.
• chūi suru 注意する *to pay attention, to give heed*

② *care, caution* [→**yōjin** 用心]
• chūi suru 注意する *to take care, to be careful*
¶O-karada ni jūbun chūi shite kudasai.
お体に十分注意してください。
Please take good care of yourself.
¶Toriatsukai chūi
「取り扱い注意」《on a sign》
Handle With Care
¶Ashimoto chūi
「足元注意」《on a sign》
Watch Your Step
¶Zujō chūi
「頭上注意」《on a sign》
Watch Your Head
③ *warning, admonition*
• chūi suru 注意する *to warn, to admonish, to caution*
¶O-isha-san no chūi ni shitagatta hō ga ii yo.
お医者さんの注意に従ったほうがいいよ。
You had better follow the doctor's warning!
• chūi-bukai 注意深い *careful, cautious*

chūíngamu チューインガム *chewing gum* [→**gamu** ガム]

chūjí 中耳 *middle ear*
• chūji-en 中耳炎 *middle ear infection*

chūjitsu 忠実 ～**na** ～な *faithful, loyal*
¶Kono inu wa shujin ni chūjitsu desu.
この犬は主人に忠実です。
This dog is faithful to its master.

chūjun 中旬 *the middle third of a month* [⇔**jōjun** 上旬, **shojun** 初旬; **gejun** 下旬]
¶Jū-gatsu no chūjun ni kensa ga arimasu.
10月の中旬に検査があります。
There's an inspection in the middle of October.

chūkan 中間 *the area about halfway between; the area between*
¶Hamamatsu wa Ōsaka to Tōkyō no chūkan ni arimasu.
浜松は大阪と東京の中間にあります。
Hamamatsu is about halfway between Osaka and Tokyo.

• chūkan-hōkoku 中間報告 *interim report*

• chūkan-shiken 中間試験 *midterm examination*

Chūkaryōri 中華料理 *Chinese cuisine, Chinese food*

chūkei 中継 *relay broadcast*
• chūkei suru 中継する *to broadcast by relay*
• chūkei-hōsō 中継放送 *relay broadcast*
• butai-chūkei 舞台中継 *relay broadcast of a play from the stage*
• eisei-chūkei 衛星中継 *satellite relay broadcast*
• yakyū-chūkei 野球中継 *relay broadcast of a baseball game*

chūko 中古 ～**no** ～の *used, second-hand*
• chūko-sha 中古車 *used car*

chūkoku 忠告 *advice*
¶Watashi wa chichi no chūkoku ni shitagaimasu.
私は父の忠告に従います。
I will follow my father's advice.
• chūkoku suru 忠告する *to advise*
¶Chichi oya wa musuko ni motto benkyō shiro to chūkoku shita.
父親は息子にもっと勉強しろと忠告した。
The father advised his son to study more.

chūkyóri 中距離 *middle distance, intermediate distance* [⇔**chōkyori** 長距離; **tankyori** 短距離]
• chūkyori-kyōsō 中距離競走 *middle-distance (running)race*

chūmoku 注目 *attention, notice*
• chūmoku suru 注目する *to pay attention, to take notice*
¶Seiji-ka wa minna kono mondai ni chūmoku shimashita.
政治家はみんなこの問題に注目しました。
The politicians all paid attention to this problem.
• chūmoku o hiku 注目を引く *to attract attention*
• chūmoku ni atai suru 注目に値する *to be noteworthy*

• chūmoku no mato 注目の的 *the center of attention*

chūmon 注文 *order, requisition*
• chūmon suru 注文する *to order*
¶Hon-ya ni hon o ni-satsu chūmon shimashita.
本屋に本を2冊注文しました。
I ordered two books from the bookstore.

chūnen 中年 *middle age, one's middle years*
• chūnen no 中年の *middle-aged*

chūō 中央 *the center, the middle* [→ **mannaka** 真ん中]
¶Shi-yakusho wa shi no chūō ni arimasu.
市役所は市の中央にあります。
The city hall is in the center of the city.
• Chūō-Ajia 中央アジア *Central Asia*
• chūō-bu 中央部 *central part*

chúrippu チューリップ *tulip*

chūritsu 中立 *neutrality*
• chūritsu o mamoru 中立を守る *to maintain neutrality*
• chūritsu no tachiba 中立の立場 *neutral standpoint*
• chūritsu-chitai 中立地帯 *neutral zone*
• chūritsu-koku 中立国 *neutral country*
• chūritsu-teki na 中立的な *neutral*
• chūritsu-teki na taido 中立的な態度 *neutral attitude*

chūryūkáikyū 中流階級 *the middle class*

Chúsei 中世 *the Middle Ages* 《the Kamakura and Muromachi Periods in Japanese history》
• Chūsei no 中世の *medieval*

chūséishi 中性子 *neutron* [⇔**yōshi** 陽子; **denshi** 電子]

chūsen 抽選 *lottery, drawing* [→**kuji** くじ②]; *drawing lots* [→**kuji-biki** くじ引き (s.v. **kuji** くじ)]
¶Chūsen de atatta yo.
抽選で当たったよ。
I won the lottery!
¶Chūsen de junban o kimeyō.
抽選で順番を決めよう。
Let's decide the order by drawing lots.
• chūsen suru 抽選する *to draw lots*

- chūsen-ken 抽選券 *lottery ticket*

chūsha 注射 *injection, shot*
- chūsha suru 注射する *to inject*
- chūsha o ukeru 注射を受ける *to get a shot*
¶ Isha wa akachan ni penishirin o chūsha shita.
医者は赤ちゃんにペニシリンを注射した。
The doctor injected penicillin into the baby.
- chūsha-ki 注射器 *syringe*
- yobō-chūsha 予防注射 *preventive injection, innoculation*

chūsha 駐車 *parking*
- chūsha suru 駐車する *to park*
¶ Hana-ya-san wa kuruma o mise no mae ni chūsha shimashita.
花屋さんは車を店の前に駐車しました。
The florist parked his car in front of his shop.
¶ Chūsha kinshi
「駐車禁止」《on a sign》
No Parking
- chūsha-ihan 駐車違反 *parking violation*
- chūsha-jō 駐車場 <*US*>*parking lot,* <*UK*>*car park*

chūshi 中止 *suspension, calling off*
- chūshi ni naru 中止になる *to be suspended, to be called off*
¶ Sono shiai wa ō-ame no tame chūshi ni narimashita.
その試合は大雨のため中止になりました。
That game was called off because of heavy rain.
- chūshi suru 中止する *to suspend, to call off*
¶ Bōisukauto wa kyanpu o chūshi shita.
ボーイスカウトはキャンプを中止した。
The boy scouts called off their camp.

chūshin 中心 *the center, the middle* [→ **mannaka** 真ん中]*; core, heart*
¶ Tōkyō wa Nihon no shōgyō no chūshin desu.
東京は日本の商業の中心です。
Tokyo is the business center of Japan.
- chūshin-bu 中心部 *central part*

¶ Eki wa machi no chūshin-bu ni arimasu.
駅は町の中心部にあります。
The station is in the central part of the town.
- chūshin-ten 中心点 *central point*

chūshoku 昼食 *lunch* [→**hiru-gohan** 昼ご飯 (s.v. **hiru** 昼)]
¶ Chūshoku wa sumasemashita ka.
昼食は済せましたか。
Did you have lunch?
¶ Boku-tachi wa chūshoku o tabete, tenisu o shita.
僕たちは昼食を食べて、テニスをした。
We ate lunch and then played tennis.
¶ Chūshoku ni supagetti o tabemashita.
昼食にスパゲッティを食べました。
I had spaghetti for lunch.
- chūshoku-jikan 昼食時間 *lunchtime*

chūshōteki 抽象的 ~**na** ~な *abstract, not concrete* [⇔**gutaiteki na** 具体的な]

chūto 中途 ~**de** ~で *halfway, in the middle* [→**tochū de** 途中で]
- chūto de hikikaesu 中途で引き返す *to turn back on the way*
- chūto-hanpa na 中途半端な *half-done, incomplete*
¶ Shukudai o chūto-hanpa ni shite wa ikenai yo.
宿題を中途半端にしてはいけないよ。
You mustn't leave your homework half-done!

Chūtō 中東 *the Middle East*

D

da だ *to be* 《This word is the informal nonpast form of the copula, which follows nouns and nominal adjectives and expresses meanings roughly equivalent to *be identical to* or *be characterized by*. For details, see Appendix 1.》
¶ Boku mo gakusei da yo.

僕も学生だよ。
I'm a student too!

¶Seito-tachi wa totemo shizuka da ne.
生徒たちはとても静かだね。
The students are very quiet, aren't they.

¶Musume wa ashita jūyon-sai da yo.
娘はあしたで14歳だよ。
My daughter will be fourteen years old tomorrow!

dáburusu ダブルス *doubles* 《in sports》
[⇔**shingurusu** シングルス]
• danshi-daburusu 男子ダブルス *men's doubles*
• joshi-daburusu 女子ダブルス *women's doubles*
• kongō-daburusu 混合ダブルス *mixed doubles*

dachō 駝鳥 *ostrich*

daenkei 楕円形 *ellipse, oval*

dagákki 打楽器 *percussion instrument*

dageki 打撃 ① (*physical*)*blow, hit*
¶Arashi wa kome no shūkaku ni dageki o ataemashita.
あらしは米の収穫に打撃を与えました。
The storm dealt a blow to the rice crop.
② (*psychological*)*blow, shock* [→ **shokku** ショック]
③ *batting, hitting*
¶Kaneyama-senshu no dageki wa subarashii yo.
金山選手の打撃はすばらしいよ。
Kaneyama's batting is wonderful!

dái 代 *a person's time* 《as head of a family, company, country, etc.》
¶Kono ie wa sofu no dai ni tateraremashita.
この家は祖父の代に建てられました。
This house was built in my grandfather's time.
• –dai －代《counter for number of people in succession to a headship; see Appendix 2》
¶Kono hito wa nijū-dai-me no daitōryō deshita.
この人は20代目の大統領でした。
This person was the 20th president.

–dai －代 *decade of a person's life*

《Added to numerals that are multiples of 10.》
• nijū-dai 20代 *one's twenties*
• yonjū-dai 40代 *one's forties*

dái 代 *charges, fare, fee*
• basu-dai バス代 *bus fare*
• denwa-dai 電話代 *telephone charges*

dái 台 *stand, rest, platform, pedestal*
• fumi-dai 踏み台 *footstool*
• senmen-dai 洗面台 *washstand*

dái 題 *title* 《of a book, etc.》

dai– 大－ *big, great* 《Added to noun and adjectival noun bases.》
• dai-kōzui 大洪水 *great flood*
• dai-seikō 大成功 *great success*
• dai-suki na 大好きな *greatly liked; greatly fond*

dai– 第－ *–th* 《Added to number bases to make ordinal numbers.》
¶Kore wa seikō e no dai-ip-po desu.
これは成功への第一歩です。
This is the first step to success.

–dai －台《counter for vehicles, machines; see Appendix 2》

daibén 大便 *feces*

dáibingu ダイビング ① (*competitive*)*diving* 《into a pool, etc.》
② (*underwater*)*diving*
• sukai-daibingu スカイダイビング *skydiving*
• sukin-daibingu スキンダイビング *skin diving*

daibu 大分 *very, much* [→**zuibun** 随分]; *rather, pretty* [→**kanari** かなり]
¶Daibu kuraku natte kita ne.
だいぶ暗くなってきたね。
It's gotten very dark, hasn't it.
¶Kibun wa daibu yoku narimashita.
気分はだいぶよくなりました。
I feel much better.
¶Kyō wa daibu atsui desu ne.
きょうはだいぶ暑いですね。
Today is rather hot, isn't it.

daibúbun 大部分 [[→**hotondo** 殆ど]]
① *mostly, almost completely*
¶Sakura no hana wa daibubun chitte

shimaimashita.

桜の花は大部分散ってしまいました。

The cherry blossoms have almost completely fallen.

¶Kyō no shigoto wa daibubun owatte imasu.

きょうの仕事は大部分終わっています。

Today's work is almost over.

② *majority, greater part* [→**ōku** 多く②]

¶Daibubun no gakusei ga sono teian ni sansei desu.

大部分の学生がその提案に賛成です。

Most of the students are in agreement with that proposal.

¶Kono ie wa daibubun ga ki de dekite imasu.

この家は大部分が木でできています。

Most of this house is made of wood.

daibutsu 大仏 *great statue of Buddha*

• Nara no daibutsu 奈良の大仏 *the Great Buddha at Nara*

dáichō 大腸 *large intestine, colon*

daidái 橙 *bitter orange* ((fruit))

• daidai-iro 橙色 *(the color)orange* [→ **orenji** オレンジ②]

daidokoro 台所 *kitchen*

• daidokoro-shigoto 台所仕事 *kitchen work*

daigaku 大学 *university; college*

¶Ani wa kotoshi daigaku ni hairimashita.

兄は今年大学に入りました。

My older brother entered college this year.

¶Ane wa rainen daigaku ni ikimasu.

姉は来年大学に行きます。

My older sister will go to college next year.

• daigaku-in 大学院 *graduate school*

• daigaku-nyūshi 大学入試 *college entrance examination*

• daigaku-sei 大学生 *college student*

• daigaku-sotsu 大学卒 *college graduate*

• tanki-daigaku 短期大学 *junior college*

daihon 台本 *script, scenario* [→**kyaku-hon** 脚本]

daihyō 代表 ① *representing,*

representation

• daihyō suru 代表する *to represent*

② *a representative*

¶Akiko-chan wa watashi-tachi no kurasu no daihyō desu.

明子ちゃんは私たちのクラスの代表です。

Akiko is our class representative.

• daihyō-dan 代表団 *delegation*

dáiichi 第一 〜no 〜の *first, foremost*

• daiichi ni 第一に *first, first of all*

¶Mazu daiichi ni shukudai o shinakereba naranai.

まず第一に宿題をしなければならない。

First of all I have to do my homework.

¶Anzen daiichi

「安全第一」《on a sign》

Safety First

• daiichi-inshō 第一印象 *first impression*

daiji 大事 ① 〜na 〜な [[→**taisetsu na** 大切な]] *important* [→**jūyō na** 重要な]; *precious* [→**kichō na** 貴重な]

• daiji ni suru 大事にする *to take good care of; to value*

¶Dōzo kono hon o daiji ni shite kudasai.

どうぞこの本を大事にしてください。

Please take good care of this book.

② *very important matter, serious matter*

dáijiesuto ダイジェスト *digest, summary*

dáijin 大臣 (*government*)*minister*

• Gaimu-daijin 外務大臣 *Foreign Minister*

• Monbu-daijin 文部大臣 *Education Minister*

daijóbu 大丈夫 〜na 〜な *all right, OK, safe*

¶Kusuri o nonda kara, daijōbu desu.

薬を飲んだから、大丈夫です。

I took the medicine, so I'm all right.

¶Kono ike de sukēto shite mo daijōbu desu ka.

この池でスケートしても大丈夫ですか。

Is it safe to skate on this pond? 《Literally: *Even if one skates on this pond is it safe?*》

daikin 代金 *price, cost, charge*

¶Kono raketto no daikin wa ikura desu ka.

このラケットの代金はいくらですか。

What is the cost of this racket?

daikon 大根 *daikon, Japanese radish*

dáiku 大工 *carpenter*

• daiku-dōgu 大工道具 *carpenter's tools*

daiméishi 代名詞 *pronoun*

daimyō 大名 *daimyo, Japanese feudal lord*

dainamáito ダイナマイト *dynamite*

dainamíkku ダイナミック ~**na** ~な *dynamic*

dainashi 台無し *ruination*

• dainashi ni suru 台なしにする *to ruin, to spoil*

• dainashi ni naru 台なしになる *to be ruined, to be spoiled*

¶Pikunikku wa ame de dainashi ni natta yo.

ピクニックは雨で台無しになったよ。

The picnic was spoiled by the rain!

dainingukítchin ダイニングキッチン *a room used as both a dining room and a kitchen* [→**díkē** DK]

dairekutoméru ダイレクトメール *direct mail*

dairi 代理 ① *acting on another's behalf, acting in another's place, acting by proxy*

¶Ono-sensei ga Sugi-sensei no dairi o shimashita.

小野先生が杉先生の代理をしました。

Mr. Ono acted on Mr. Sugi's behalf.

¶Watashi no dairi de Sonoda-san ga sono kai ni shusseki shita.

私の代理で園田さんがその会に出席した。

Mr. Sonoda attended the meeting in my place.

② *person acting on another's behalf, proxy*

• dairi-nin 代理人 [☞**dairi** 代理② (above)]

• dairi-ten 代理店 *agency* 《for business transactions》

• buchō-dairi 部長代理 *acting department head*

dairíseki 大理石 *marble* ((stone))

dáisánsha 第三者 *third party, disinterested person*

daisū 代数 *algebra*

daitai 大体 ① *approximately, about* [→**oyoso** およそ]

¶Watashi wa daitai jūichi-ji-goro nemasu.

私は大体11時ごろ寝ます。

I go to bed at about 11:00.

• daitai no 大体の *rough, approximate*

② *in general, for the most part, almost completely*

¶Kono sakubun wa daitai yoku dekite imasu.

この作文は大体よくできています。

This composition is good for the most part.

¶Dai-go-ka wa daitai sumasemashita.

第5課は大体済せました。

I've almost finished Lesson 5.

③ *gist, substance, main points*

• daitai no 大体の *general, rough*

④ *originally, to begin with* [→**motomoto** 元々]

daitán 大胆 ~**na** ~な *bold, daring*

daitásū 大多数 *the great majority*

¶Seito no daitasū wa oyogemasu.

生徒の大多数は泳げます。

The great majority of the students can swim.

daitōryō 大統領 *president* (*of a country*)

• -daitōryō -大統領 《Added to a surname as a title.》

¶Rinkān-daitōryō wa ansatsu saremashita.

リンカーン大統領は暗殺されました。

President Lincoln was assassinated.

• daitōryō-senkyo 大統領選挙 *presidential election*

• Amerika-gasshūkoku-daitōryō アメリカ合衆国大統領 *the President of the United States of America*

• fuku-daitōryō 副大統領 *vice-president*

dáiya ダイヤ (*written*)*train schedule*

¶Jiko de daiya ga midarete imasu.

事故でダイヤが乱れています。
The schedule has been disrupted by an accident.

dáiya ダイヤ ① [☞**daiyamondo** ダイヤモンド]

② *diamonds* ((playing-card suit))

daiyamóndo ダイヤモンド *diamond*

daiyaru ダイヤル *dial*

• daiyaru o mawasu ダイヤルを回す *to turn a dial*

¶Chichi wa unten shi-nagara rajio no daiyaru o mawashite imashita.
父は運転しながらラジオのダイヤルを回していました。
My father was turning the radio dial while he was driving.

¶Watashi wa bangō o machigaete daiyaru o mawashita.
私は番号をまちがえてダイヤルを回した。
I dialed the wrong number. «Literally: I made a mistake on the number and turned the dial.»

daizu 大豆 *soybean*

dakai 打開 *breakthrough to a solution, overcoming* «of a difficult situation»

• dakai suru 打開する *to make a break-through in, to overcome*

dákara だから *that's why, for that reason* «This word is simply a combination of the copula **da** だand the clause-conjoining particle **kara** から, but the combination can be used initially in a sentence. The combination **desukara** ですから, with the semi-formal copula form, can also be used sentence-initially in the same way.»

¶Ame ga furidashita. Dakara gaishutsu o yameta yo.
雨が降りだした。だから外出をやめたよ。
It started to rain. That's why we gave up on going out!

dake だけ ① *only, just*

¶Nobuko-san dake ga wakarimasu.
信子さんだけがわかります。
Only Nobuko understands.

¶Sore o haha dake ni hanashimashita.
それを母だけに話しました。
I told that only to my mother.

¶Shippai shita no wa watashi dake de wa arimasen.
失敗したのは私だけではありません。
I am not the only one who failed.

¶Sukoshi dake tabete chōdai.
少しだけ食べてちょうだい。
Eat just a little.

¶Terebi de mita dake desu.
テレビで見ただけです。
I only saw it on television.

② *extent* [→**teido** 程度]

¶Dekiru dake nonde kudasai.
できるだけ飲んでください。
Please drink as much as you can.

dakishiméru 抱き締める *to hug tightly*

dákko だっこ 【COL.】 *picking up and holding in one's arms* «The direct object is a child, pet, etc.»

• dakko suru だっこする *to pick up and hold in one's arms*

daku 抱く *to hold in one's arms, to embrace*

¶Haha wa akachan o yasashiku dakima-shita.
母は赤ちゃんを優しく抱きました。
The mother held her baby gently.

dakyō 妥協 *compromise*

• dakyō suru 妥協する *to compromise*

damáru 黙る *to stop talking, to become silent*

¶Sensei ga kita node, watashi-tachi wa damarimashita.
先生が来たので、私たちは黙りました。
We stopped taking, when the teacher came in.

¶Hamano-san wa gozen-chū zutto damatte imashita.
浜野さんは午前中ずっと黙っていました。
Mr. Hamano kept quiet all morning.

damásu 騙す *to cheat, to deceive*

¶Kantoku wa haiyū o damashimashita.
監督は俳優をだましました。
The director deceived the actor.

damé 駄目 ～**na** ～な ① *no good, use-less; futile* [→**muda na** 無駄な]

¶Kono denchi wa dame desu yo.
この電池はだめですよ。

This battery is no good!

¶Hamanaka-san wa doryoku shimashita ga, dame deshita.

浜中さんは努力しましたが、だめでした。

Ms. Hamanaka made efforts, but they were futile.

② *impermissable, unacceptable* 《This meaning is particularly common in combination with a conditional clause of some kind. Translations of such combinations into English ordinarily use *must not* or *may not* rather than *unacceptable if* and *must* or *have to* rather than *unacceptable if not.*》 [→**ikenai** いけない①]

¶Kono kawa de oyoide wa dame desu.

この川で泳いではだめです。

You must not swim in this river.

¶"Gaishutsu shite mo ii?" "Dame da yo."

「外出してもいい？」「だめだよ」

"May I go out?" "You may not!"

¶Motto benkyō shinai to dame da yo.

もっと勉強しないとだめだよ。

You must study more!

dámu ダム *dam*

dan 段 (*stair-*)*step; rung*
- ishi-dan 石段 *stone steps*

danbō 暖房 (*indoor*)*heating* [⇔**reibō** 冷房]

¶Kono heya wa danbō ga kiki-sugite imasu.

この部屋は暖房が利きすぎています。

The heating in this room is turned up too high.
- danbō-sōchi 暖房装置 *heating equipment*

danbóru 段ボール *corrugated cardboard*
- danbōru-bako 段ボール箱 *corrugated cardboard box*

danchi 団地 (*apartment*)*housing development*

¶Itoko wa danchi ni sunde imasu.

いとこは団地に住んでいます。

My cousin lives in a housing development.

dandan 段々 *gradually, little by little* [→**shidai-ni** 次第に]

¶Shiai wa dandan omoshiroku narimashita.

試合はだんだんおもしろくなりました。

The game gradually became interesting.

¶Dandan kuraku natte kimashita.

だんだん暗くなってきました。

It has gradually gotten darker.

dangén 断言 *unequivocal assertion*
- dangen suru 断言する *to assert unequivocally*

dango 団子 *round flour dumpling*

daní ダニ *tick* ((*insect*))

dánjo 男女 *man and woman, men and women; boy and girl*
- danjo-byōdō 男女平等 *sexual equality*
- danjo-dōken 男女同権 *equal rights for men and women*
- danjo-kyōgaku 男女共学 *coeducation*

dankai 段階 ① *grade, rank*
② *step, stage, phase*

danketsu 団結 *unity, solidarity*
- danketsu suru 団結する *to unite, to band together*

¶Jimoto no hito-tachi to danketsu shite hatarakimashō.

地元の人たちと団結して働きましょう。

Let's work united with the local people.

danna 旦那 ① *husband* [→**otto** 夫]
② *patron* 《*of a woman*》
- danna-san 旦那さん 【HON. for **danna** (above)】

dánpingu ダンピング *dumping* (*on the market*)
- danpingu suru ダンピングする *to dump*

danpuká ダンプカー *dump truck*

danraku 段落 *paragraph*

dánro 暖炉 *fireplace; heating stove*

danryoku 弾力 *elasticity; flexibility*

danryū 暖流 *warm* (*ocean*)*current* [⇔**kanryū** 寒流]

dánsā ダンサー (*professional*)*dancer*

dansei 男性 *a man* [⇔**josei** 女性]
- dansei-teki na 男性的な *manly*

dánshi 男子 [[⇔**joshi** 女子]] *boy; man* [→**dansei** 男性]
- danshi-chūgakkō 男子中学校 *boys' junior high school*

- danshi-kōkō 男子高校 *boys' high school*
- danshi-seito 男子生徒 *schoolboy*
- danshi-chīmu 男子チーム *men's team*

dánsu ダンス *dance; dancing*
- dansu o suru ダンスをする *to dance*
- dansu-pātī ダンスパーティー *party with dancing*
- fōku-dansu フォークダンス *folk dance*
- shakō-dansu 社交ダンス *social dance*

dantai 団体 *group (of people)*

¶Dantai de kōdō suru no wa suki ja nai yo.

団体で行動するのは好きじゃないよ。

I don't like to act in a group!
- dantai-kyōgi 団体競技 *team sport*
- dantai-ryokō 団体旅行 *group tour*
- dantai-seikatsu 団体生活 *living in a group*
- dantai-waribiki 団体割引 *group discount*

danwa 談話 *talk, casual conversation, chat*
- danwa suru 談話する *to have a talk, to have a casual conversation*

danzen 断然 ① *resolutely, decisively*

¶Shachō wa jūgyōin no yōkyū o danzen kyozetsu shimashita.

社長は従業員の提案には断然反対です。

The company president was resolutely against his employees' proposal.

② *absolutely, decidedly*

¶Kono eiga no hō ga danzen omoshiroi yo.

この映画のほうが断然おもしろいよ。

This movie is decidedly more interesting!

-darake -だらけ 【COL.】 ~**no** ~の *full of; covered with* 《Added to noun bases denoting something viewed with disfavor.》

¶Kono Nihon-go no tegami wa machigai-darake da yo.

この日本語の手紙はまちがいだらけだよ。

This Japanese letter is full of mistakes!

¶Kono ningyō wa hokori-darake desu.

この人形はほこりだらけです。

This doll is covered with dust.

darashinái だらしない ① *slipshod, careless, sloppy*

¶Ano hito wa fukusō ga darashinai ne.

あの人は服装がだらしないね。

That person's attire is sloppy, isn't it.

② *(morally)loose*

¶Darashinai seikatsu o shite wa ikenai yo.

だらしない生活をしてはいけないよ。

You mustn't lead a loose life!

dáre 誰 *who* 《as a question word》

¶Ano onna no hito wa dare desu ka.

あの女の人はだれですか。

Who is that woman?

¶Dare ga uta o utatte iru no?

だれが歌を歌っているの？

Who is singing?

¶Kore wa dare no pen desu ka.

これはだれのペンですか。

Whose pen is this?

¶Dare ni ai-tai no desu ka.

だれに会いたいのですか。

Who do you want to see?

¶Dare o sagashite iru no desu ka.

だれを捜しているのですか。

Who are you looking for?
- dare demo だれでも *everyone, anyone, no matter who it is*

¶Dare demo sono tango o shitte iru yo.

だれでもその単語を知っているよ。

Everyone knows that word!

¶Dare demo watashi-tachi no kurabu ni hairemasu.

だれでも私たちのクラブに入れます。

Anyone can join our club.
- dare-ka だれか *someone, somebody*

¶Dare-ka ga yatte kureru yo.

だれかがやってくれるよ。

Someone will do it for us!

¶Dare-ka tetsudatte kuremasen ka.

だれか手伝ってくれませんか。

Won't somebody help me?
- dare-mo だれも *nobody, no one, ⟨not⟩ anyone* 《Always occurs in combination with a negative predicate.》

¶Dare-mo chikoku shimasen deshita.

だれも遅刻しませんでした。

Nobody was late.

¶Dare-mo kega o shita hito wa imasen deshita.

だれもけがをした人はいませんでした。

Nobody was injured.

daritsu 打率 *batting average* 《in baseball》

dáriya ダリヤ *dahlia*

darō だろう ① *probably is ╱ are* 《When it follows a noun or anominal adjective, this word is the informal tentative form of the copula da だ. For details, see Appendix 1. With falling intonation, it simply makes an assertion tentative.》

¶Koko wa shizuka darō.

ここは静かだろう。

This place is probably quiet.

② *probably* 《With falling intonation following a predicate, **darō** marks a sentence as tentative.》

¶Sono ressha wa jikan-dōri ni tsuku darō.

その列車は時間どおりに着くだろう。

That train will probably arrive on time.

¶Kamiyama-san ga kono e o kaita darō.

上山さんがこの絵をかいただろう。

Mr. Kamiyama probably drew this picture.

③ *right?, don't you think?* 《With rising intonation, **darō** urges the listener to agree with the speaker. Rising intonation can be used on either **darō** ① or **darō** ② (above).》

¶Konsāto wa tanoshikatta darō?

コンサートは楽しかっただろう？

The concert was fun, right?

darúi だるい *languid, heavy-feeling, listless*

¶Zenshin ga darui desu.

全身がだるいです。

My whole body is listless.

Daruma 達磨 ① *Bodhidharma* 《the monk who introduced Zen from India into China》

② *a doll portraying Bodhidharma sitting in Zen meditation* 《The most common type of Daruma doll is made of

plaster and sold with no pupils painted in the eyes. Such a doll is used as a good-luck charm by painting in one pupil when a wish is made and painting in the other pupil when the wish comes true.》

dasanteki 打算的 〜**na** 〜な *calculating, mercenary*

dásha 打者 *batter, hitter* 《in baseball》

• ichiban-dasha 1番打者 *leadoff hitter*

• kyō-dasha 強打者 *slugger*

dashí 出し *broth,* (*soup*)*stock*

dassen 脱線 *derailment*

• dassen suru 脱線する *to jump the rails, to become derailed*

¶Ressha ga tonneru no naka de dassen shita.

列車がトンネルの中で脱線した。

The train was derailed inside the tunnel.

dásshu ダッシュ (*running*)*dash*

• dasshu suru ダッシュする *to dash*

dásshu ダッシュ *dash* ((punctuation mark))

dásu ダース *dozen*

• -dāsu −ダース《counter for dozens; see Appendix 2》

¶Enpitsu o ichi-dāsu kaimashita.

鉛筆を1ダース買いました。

I bought a dozen pencils.

dásu 出す ① [[⇔**ireru** 入れる①]] *to take out; to put out*

¶Jōkyaku wa poketto kara kippu o dashimashita.

乗客はポケットから切符を出しました。

The passenger took the ticket out of her pocket.

¶Mado kara kao o dasu no wa abunai desu.

窓から顔を出すのは危ないです。

Putting your head out of the window is dangerous.

② *to let out* [⇔**ireru** 入れる②]

¶Kodomo ga saru o ori kara dashite shimaimashita.

子供が猿をおりから出してしまいました。

A child let the monkey out of the cage.

③ *to hold out, to present* [→**sashidasu** 差し出す①]

¶Ano hito ga hannin da to iu shōko o dashinasai.

あの人が犯人だという証拠を出しなさい。

Present evidence that this person is a crook.

④ *to show, to expose, to exhibit*
• genki o dasu 元気を出す *to cheer up*
• kuchi ni dasu 口に出す *to voice, to put into spoken words*
• supīdo o dasu スピードを出す *to speed up*

⑤ *to hand in, to turn in, to submit* [→ **teishutsu suru** 提出する]

¶Sā, tōan o dashinasai.

さあ、答案を出しなさい。

OK, hand in your test papers.

⑥ *to send, to mail* [→**okuru** 送る①]
• henji o dasu 返事を出す *to send a reply*

⑦ *to publish, to put out*
• hon o dasu 本を出す *to publish a book*

⑧ *to serve, to offer*

¶Haha wa o-kyaku-san ni kōcha to kēki o dashita.

母はお客さんに紅茶とケーキを出した。

My mother served the guest tea and cake.

-dasu －出す *to begin to* 《Added to verb bases.》

¶Yuki ga furi-dashimashita.

雪が降りだしました。

It began to snow.

¶Seito-tachi wa kyōshitsu o sōji shi-dashimashita.

生徒たちは教室を掃除しだしました。

The students began to clean the classroom.

-date －建て 〜の 〜 no *-story, -floor* 《Added to bases consisting of a number containing the counter **-kai** －階.》

¶Nijuk-kai-date no manshon ga tachimashita.

20階建てのマンションが建ちました。

A twenty-story condominium was built.

¶Kawamura-san no ie wa ni-kai-date desu.

川村さんの家は2階建てです。

Ms. Kawamura's house is two stories.

• ni-kai-date-basu 2階建てバス *double-decker bus*

datsuzei 脱税 *tax evasion*
• datsuzei suru 脱税する *to evade paying taxes*

dátte だって ① 【COL. for **demo** でも①】 *even, even if it is*

② 【COL. for **demo** でも②】 *no matter* 《following a phrase beginning with a question word》

③ 【COL. for **demo** でも④】 *however, but* 《at the beginning of a sentence》

④ 【COL.】 *the reason is* 《at the beginning of a sentence》

¶Mō taberarenai. Datte mazui n da yo.

もう食べられない。だってまずいんだよ。

I can't eat any more. The reason is, it's foul!

de で《noun-following particle》 ① *in, at, on* 《indicating a place which is the site of some activity》

¶Haha wa Ōsaka de umaremashita.

母は大阪で生まれました。

My mother was born in Osaka.

¶Kūkō de tomodachi o demukaemashita.

空港で友達を出迎えました。

I met a friend at the airport.

¶Nogi-san wa nōjō de hataraite iru ne.

野木さんは農場で働いているね。

Mr. Nogi is working on a farm, isn't he.

② *by means of, with, using*

¶Denwa de hanasu no wa kirai desu.

電話で話すのは嫌いです。

I don't like talking on the telephone.

¶Enpitsu de kaite kudasai.

鉛筆で書いてください。

Please write with a pencil.

¶Koko made wa basu de kimashita.

ここまではバスで来ました。

I came this far by bus.

¶Eigo de supīchi o shimashita.

英語でスピーチをしました。

I made a speech in English.

③ *of, from* 《indicating materials or ingredients》

¶Kono hashi wa ishi de dekite imasu.

この橋は石でできています。

This bridge is made of stone.

¶Chīzu wa gyūnyū de tsukurimasu.

チーズは牛乳で作ります。

Cheese is made from milk.

④ *because of, on account of, from*

¶Ame de shiai wa chūshi ni narimashita.

雨で試合は中止になりました。

The game was called off because of rain.

¶Uchi no inu wa atama no kega de shinimashita.

うちの犬は頭のけがで死にました。

Our dog died from a head injury.

⑤ *in* 《indicating a period of time》

¶Uehara-san wa sanjup-pun de modo-rimasu.

上原さんは30分で戻ります。

Ms. Uehara will be back in 30 minutes.

⑥ *at, for* 《indicating a point on a scale》

¶Kono kamera o hassen-en de kaimashita.

このカメラを8000円で買いました。

I bought this camera for 8,000 yen.

¶Ano densha wa sugoi sokuryoku de hashitte iru yo.

あの電車はすごい速力で走っているよ。

That train is running at incredible speed!

¶Ane wa jūhas-sai de ryūgaku shimashita.

姉は18歳で留学しました。

My older sister studied abroad at eighteen.

⑦ *by, according to* 《indicating an information source or criterion》

¶Watashi no tokei de chōdo ni-ji desu.

私の時計でちょうど2時です。

It's exactly 2:00 by my watch.

¶Enpitsu wa dāsu de uru deshō?

鉛筆はダースで売るでしょう？

Pencils are sold by the dozen, right?

deáu 出会う *to happen to meet, to come across, to run into*

¶Ichiba de gūzen Yōko-san ni deatta yo.

市場で偶然洋子さんに出会ったよ。

I happened to run into Yoko at the market!

débyū デビュー *debut*

• debyū suru デビューする *to debut,*

to make one's debut

¶Tadashi wa jūyon-sai de kashu to shite debyū shita.

正は14歳で歌手としてデビューした。

Tadashi made his debut as a singer at the age of fourteen.

deddobṓru デッドボール *pitch that hits a batter* 《in baseball》

• deddobōru o kuu デッドボールを食う *to be hit by a pitch*

deddohīto デッドヒート *dead heat*

• deddohīto o enjiru デッドヒートを演じる *to run a dead heat*

defure デフレ *(monetary)deflation* [⇔ **infure** インフレ]

defureshon デフレーション [☞**defure** デフレ]

de-gozaimásu でございます 【FORMAL for **da** だ】《The word gozaimsu is a verb with the semi-formal -**masu** ending. The informal nonpast (the form of a verb that ordinarily appears in a dictionary) is **gozaru** ござる, but such informal forms are not used in modern Japanese.》

déguchi 出口 *exit, exit doorway* [⇔ **iriguchi** 入り口]

dehairi 出入り [☞**deiri** 出入り]

de-irassháru でいらっしゃる 【HON. for **da** だ】

deiri 出入り *going in and out*

• deiri suru 出入りする *to go in and out*

¶Sono inu wa mado kara deiri shimasu.

その犬は窓から出入りします。

The dog goes in and out through the window.

• deiri-guchi 出入り口 *combined entryway and exit*

déjitaru デジタル 〜**no** 〜の *digital*

• dejitaru-dokei デジタル時計 *digital watch; digital clock*

dekái でかい 【COL. for **ōkii** 大きい】 *big*

dekakeru 出掛ける *to go out* 《to do something》; *to set out, to leave* [→ **shuppatsu suru** 出発する]

¶Sanpo ni dekakemashō ka.

散歩に出かけましょうか。

Shall we go out for a walk?

¶Haha wa ima dekakete imasu.

母は今出かけています。

My mother is out now.

¶Chichi wa ashita Kōbe e dekakemasu.

父はあした神戸へ出かけます。

My father will leave for Kobe tomorrow.

dekiagaru 出来上がる *to be completed*

dekígoto 出来事 *occurrence, event*

¶Kore wa nichijō no dekigoto desu.

これは日常のできごとです。

This is an everyday occurrence.

¶Rajio wa kinō no mezurashii dekigoto o hōdo shita.

ラジオはきのうの珍しいできごとを報道した。

The radio reported yesterday's unusual events.

¶Kotoshi no ōki na dekigoto ni tsuite hanashimasu.

今年の大きなできごとについて話します。

We will talk about the major events of this year.

dekíru できる ① *to be able to do, can do* «This is the potential form of **suru** する. What a person is able to do is treated as a grammatical subject and marked with **ga** が rather than with **o** を.»

¶Sukēto ga dekimasu ka.

スケートができますか。

Can you skate?

¶Mita-san wa Eigo ga yoku dekiru sō desu.

三田さんは英語がよくできるそうです。

They say that Ms. Mita can speak English well.

¶Dekireba, denwa o kudasai.

できれば、電話をください。

If you can, please give me a telephone call.

• dekiru dake できるだけ *to the extent one can, to the extent possible*

¶Ashita wa dekiru dake hayaku shuppatsu shimashō.

あしたはできるだけ早く出発しましょう。

Tomorrow let's start out as early as possible.

¶Dekiru dake hon o yominasai.

できるだけ本を読みなさい。

Read as many books as you can.

② *koto ga~* ことが~ *to be able to* «following a nonpast-tense verb»

¶Watashi-tachi wa shiai ni katsu koto ga dekimashita.

私たちは試合に勝つことができました。

We were able to win the game.

¶Itsu-ka Kasei ni iku koto ga dekiru deshō.

いつか火星へ行くことができるでしょう。

Someday one will probably be able to go to Mars.

③ *to be completed, to get finished*

¶Chōshoku no yōi ga dekimashita yo.

朝食の用意ができましたよ。

Breakfast is ready! «Literally: The breakfast preparations are finished!»

dekitate 出来立て *~no ~*の *freshly made, just finished*

¶Kono kukkī wa dekitate desu.

このクッキーはできたてです。

These cookies are freshly baked.

dekkái でっかい 【COL.】 [☞**dekai** でかい]

dékki デッキ ① *deck* «of a boat» [→**kanpan** 甲板]

② *railroad car vestibule*

③ [☞**tēpu-dekki** テープデッキ (below)]

• tēpu-dekki テープデッキ *tape deck*

dékoboko 凸凹 *unevenness, bumpiness*

• dekoboko na 凸凹な *uneven, bumpy*

déma デマ *false rumor*

demado 出窓 *bay window*

demae 出前 *delivery of ordered meals*

démo デモ *demonstration* «i.e., a public exhibition of protest, etc.»

• demo o suru デモをする *to demonstrate*

• demo-shinkō デモ行進 *demonstration march*

• demo-tai デモ隊 *demonstrator group*

démo でも 《The examples of **demo** given here can all be analyzed as a combination of the gerund (-te form) of the copula **da** だ with the particle **mo**. Other examples (romanized as two words **de mo** in this

dictionary)are combinations of the particle **de** with the particle **mo**.》 ① *even,*
even if it is

¶Chīsa na kodomo demo sonna koto wa dekiru yo.

小さな子供でもそんなことはできるよ。

Even little children can do such a thing!

¶Koko wa fuyu demo yuki ga hotondo furimasen.

ここは冬でも雪がほとんど降りません。

Even in winter it hardly snows here.

• A demo B demo　AでもBでも *either A or B, whether it's A or B*

¶Kyō demo ashita demo ii desu.

きょうでもあしたでもいいです。

Either today or tomorrow is all right.

② *no matter* 《following a question word or a phrase beginning with a question word》

¶Kono toranpu no naka kara dore demo ichi-mai hiite kudasai.

このトランプの中からどれでも1枚引いてください。

Please pull out any one from these cards.

③ *or something*

¶Shinbun demo yonde machimashō.

新聞でも読んで待ちましょう。

Let's read a newspaper or something and wait.

④ *however, but* 《at the beginning of a sentence》 [→**shikashi** しかし]

demokuráshī デモクラシー *democracy*
[→**minshushugi** 民主主義]

demukaeru 出迎える *to go out and meet* 《an arriving person》

¶Eki made itoko o demukaemashita.

駅までいとこを出迎えました。

I went to meet my cousin at the station.

den'atsu 電圧 *voltage*

dénchi 電池 *battery*

• denchi ga kireru 電池が切れる *a battery goes dead*

• kan-denchi 乾電池 *dry battery*

• taiyō-denchi 太陽電池 *solar battery*

denchū 電柱 *utility pole, telephone pole*

den'en 田園 *the country, rural area;*

suburban area with greenery

• den'en no 田園の *rural, pastoral*

• den'en-toshi 田園都市 *garden city*

dengen 電源 *electric power supply*

• dengen o kiru 電源を切る *to shut off the power*

dengon 伝言 [[→**kotozuke** 言付け]]
message 《that someone asks one person to give to another person》;
giving a message

¶Kore wa Ōtake-san e no dengon desu.

これは大竹さんへの伝言です。

This is a message for Ms. Otake.

• dengon suru 伝言する *to give a message, to send word*

¶Onīsan ni dengon shite kudasai.

お兄さんに伝言してください。

Please give your older brother the message.

• dengon-ban 伝言板 *message board*

denki 伝記 *biography*

¶Meiji-tennō no denki o yonda koto ga arimasu.

明治天皇の伝記を読んだことがあります。

I have read a biography of the Meiji Emperor.

dénki 電気 ① *electricity*

¶Kono kikai wa denki de ugokimasu.

この機械は電気で動きます。

This machine works by electricity.

② *electric light* [→**dentō** 電灯]

• denki o tsukeru 〔kesu〕電気をつける〔消す〕 *to turn on* 〔*off*〕 *a light*

• denki-gama 電気釜 *electric rice cooker*

• denki-kigu 電気器具 *electrical appliance*

• denki-mōfu 電気毛布 *electric blanket*

• denki-sutando 電気スタンド *electric lamp*

denkyū 電球 *light bulb*

¶Rokujū-watto no denkyū wa mō nai desu.

60ワットの電球はもうないです。

There are no more 60-watt light bulbs.

• denkyū ga kireru 電球が切れる *a light bulb burns out*

dénpa 電波 *electric wave, radio wave*

denpō 電報 *telegram, cablegram*
¶Denpō de kekka o shirasete kudasai.
電報で結果を知らせてください。
Please let me know the result by telegram.
¶Kesa ojīsan kara denpō ga todoita yo.
けさおじいさんから電報が届いたよ。
This morning a telegram arrived from grandfather!
• denpō o utsu 電報を打つ *to send a telegram*
• denpō-ryōkin 電報料金 *telegram fee*
• shikyū-denpō 至急電報 *urgent telegram*

denpun 澱粉 *starch* 《in or extracted from food》

dénryoku 電力 *electric power*
• denryoku-gaisha 電力会社 *electric power company*

denryū 電流 *electric current*

densen 伝染 *contagion*
• densen suru 伝染する *to spread (by contagion); to be contagious*
¶Infuruenza wa densen suru ne.
インフルエンザは伝染するね。
Influenza is contagious, isn't it.
• densen-byō 伝染病 *contagious disease*

densen 電線 *electric wire, electrical cable*

densetsu 伝説 *legend*
• densetsu-jō no 伝説上の *legendary*

densha 電車 *(electric)train; streetcar*
¶Kono densha wa Nara ni ikimasu ka.
この電車は奈良に行きますか。
Does this train go to Nara?
¶Musume wa densha de tsūgaku shite imasu.
娘は電車で通学しています。
My daughter commutes to school by train.
• densha-chin 電車賃 *train fare*
• tsūkin-densha 通勤電車 *commuter train*

dénshi 電子 *electron* [⇔**yōshi** 陽子; **chūsei-shi** 中性子 (s.v. **chūsei** 中性)]
• denshi-keisan-ki 電子計算機 *(electronic)computer* [→**konpyūtā** コンピューター]

• denshi-kenbikyō 電子顕微鏡 *electronic microscope*
• denshi-ongaku 電子音楽 *electronic music*
• denshi-orugan 電子オルガン *electronic organ*
• denshi-renji 電子レンジ *microwave oven*

dentaku 電卓 *small electronic calculator*

dentō 伝統 *tradition*
¶Sono gakkō wa nanajū-nen no dentō ga arimasu.
その学校は70年の伝統があります。
That school has a 70-year tradition.
• dentō-teki na 伝統的な *traditional*
¶Sumō wa Nihon no dentō-teki na supōtsu desu.
相撲は日本の伝統的なスポーツです。
Sumo is a traditional sport of Japan.

dentō 電灯 *electric light*
• keichū-dentō 懐中電灯 <*US*>*flashlight*, <*UK*>*torch*

denwa 電話 ① *telephone*
¶Denwa ga natte iru yo.
電話が鳴っているよ。
The telephone is ringing!
¶Yūbe Yōko-san to denwa de hanashimashita.
ゆうべ洋子さんと電話で話しました。
Last night I talked with Yoko on the telephone.
¶Denwa o karite mo ii desu ka.
電話を借りてもいいですか。
May I use your telephone?
• denwa ni deru 電話に出る *to answer the phone; to come to the phone*
② *telephone call*
¶Kondō-san, denwa desu yo.
近藤さん、電話ですよ。
Mr. Kondo, there's a telephone call for you! 《Literally: Mr. Kondo, it's a telephone call!》
¶O-denwa o arigatō gozaimashita.
お電話をありがとうございました。
Thank you for your telephone call.
• denwa suru 電話する *to telephone, to call*

• denwa o kiru 電話を切る *to cut off a phone call* 《*ordinarily by hanging up*》

• A ni denwa no kakeru Aに電話をかける *to make a telephone call to A*

• A kara denwa ga kakaru Aから電話がかかる *a telephone call comes from A*

• denwa-bangō 電話番号 *telephone number*

• denwa-chō 電話帳 *telephone directory*

• denwa-chū no 電話中の (*in the midst of talking*) *on the phone*

• denwa-guchi 電話口 *the area at the telephone*

• denwa-kōkan-shu 電話交換手 *telephone operator*

depáto デパート *department store*

¶ Okāsan wa depāto e kaimono ni itta yo.
お母さんはデパートへ買物に行ったよ。
Mother went shopping at the department store.

déppa 出っ歯 【COL.】 *buck teeth*

derákkusu デラックス 〜**na** 〜な *deluxe*

derikéto デリケート 〜**na** 〜な *delicate*

déru 出る ① *to go out, to come out, to exit, to leave*

• A kara／o deru Aから／を出る *to exit (from) A, to leave A*

¶ Gakusei-tachi wa yatto kyōshitsu kara demashita.
学生たちはやっと教室から出ました。
The students finally came out of the classroom.

② *to leave, to start off, to depart* [→**shuppatsu suru** 出発する]

¶ Basu ga deru tokoro da yo.
バスが出るところだよ。
The bus is about to leave!

③ *to appear, to emerge, to come out* [→**arawareru** 現われる]

¶ Me ga sorosoro deru deshō.
芽がそろそろ出るでしょう。
The buds will probably appear soon.

¶ Sono hon wa raigetsu demasu.
その本は来月出ます。
That book will come out next month.

④ *to attend, to take part*

¶ Ōmori-san mo kono kai ni demasu.
大森さんもこの会に出ます。
Mr. Omori will also attend this meeting.

¶ Santosu-san wa benron-taikai ni deru tsumori da.
サントスさんは弁論大会に出るつもりだ。
Ms. Santos is planning to take part in the speech contest.

⑤ *to graduate from* [→**sotsugyō suru** 卒業する]

¶ Musuko wa Rikkyō-daigaku o demashita.
息子は立教大学を出ました。
My son graduated from Rikkyō University.

deshabáru 出しゃばる *to meddle, to act obtrusively*

¶ Kawai-san wa kesshite deshabaranai hito desu.
川合さんは決して出しゃばらない人です。
Mr. Kawai is the type that never meddles.

deshí 弟子 *pupil, disciple; apprentice*

deshó でしょう 【SEMI-FORMAL for **darō**】

déssan デッサン *rough sketch* [→**suketchi** スケッチ②]

désu です ① 【SEMI-FORMAL for **da**】

② 【SEMI-FORMAL】 《This word is used to mark the semi-formal style of adjectives in both the nonpast and past tenses.》

¶ Kono hon wa takai desu.
この本は高いです。
This book is expensive.

¶ Shiken wa hijō ni muzukashikatta desu.
試験は非常に難しかったです。
The exam was extremely difficult.

déta データ *data*

detarame でたらめ 【COL.】 *nonsense, bunk; random talk, haphazard talk; nonsensical behavior, haphazard behavior*

• detarame na でたらめな *nonsensical, absurd; random, haphazard*

¶ Ano hito wa itsu-mo detarame o itte iru ne.

あの人はいつもでたらめを言っているね。
That person is always talking nonsense, isn't he.

dēto デート *date* 《with a person》
• dēto suru デートする *to go on a date*
¶Hiroshi wa kyō Natsuko to dēto suru n da yo.
弘はきょう夏子とデートするんだよ。
Hiroshi is going to go on a date with Natsuko today!

dé-wa では *well then, in that case* [→ **sore-de-wa** それでは]

dezáin デザイン ① *design, plan* ② *designing*
• dezain suru デザインする *to design*
• gurafikku-dezain グラフィックデザイン *graphic design*

dezáinā デザイナー *designer*

dezáto デザート *dessert*
¶Dezāto ni wa aisukurīmu o tabeta.
デザートにはアイスクリームを食べた。
I had ice cream for dessert.

dīkē DK《Generally not written out in katakana.》 [☞**dainingukitchin** ダイニングキッチン]

dīpīī DPE《Generally not written out in katakana.》 *developing, printing, and enlarging* 《Typically appears on camera store signs.》

dirékutā ディレクター *director* 《of movies, television shows, etc.》

disukásshon ディスカッション *discussion* [→**tōron** 討論]
• disukasshon suru ディスカッションする *to have a discussion*

disukáunto ディスカウント *discount* [→ **waribiki** 割引]
• disukaunto-sutoa ディスカウントストア *discount store*

dísuko ディスコ *disco*

disukujókkī ディスクジョッキー *disk jockey*

dīzeruénjin ディーゼルエンジン *diesel engine*

-do 度 ① 《counter for number of times; see Appendix 2》 [→**-kai** 回②]
¶Tsuki ni ichi-do Yōko-san ni

tegami o kakimasu.
月に一度洋子さんに手紙を書きます。
I write a letter to Yoko once a month.
② 《counter for degrees (of arc or of temperature); see Appendix 2》
¶Kion wa ima jū-do desu.
気温は今10度です。
The temperature is now ten degrees.
¶Chokkaku wa kyūjū-do desu.
直角は90度です。
A right angle is 90 degrees.

dó 胴 *torso, trunk*
• fune no dō 船の胴 *ship's hull*

dó 銅 *copper; bronze*
• dō-ka 銅貨 *copper coin*
• dō-medaru 銅メダル *bronze medal*
• dōzō 銅像 *bronze statue*

dó どう *how* 《as a question word》《In many uses, natural English translations have *what* rather than *how*.》
¶Konsāto wa dō deshita ka.
コンサートはどうでしたか。
How was the concert?
¶"Bunka" wa Eigo de dō iimasu ka.
「文化」は英語でどう言いますか。
How do you say "bunka" in English?
¶Kōhī o mō ip-pai dō desu ka.
コーヒーをもう1杯どうですか。
How about another cup of coffee?
¶Dō shita n desu ka.
どうしたんですか。
What's the matter?
¶Kono hon o dō omoimasu ka.
この本をどう思いますか。
What do you think of this book?
• dō iu どういう *what kind of, what* [→ **donna** どんな]
¶Kono tango wa koko de wa dō iu imi desu ka.
この単語はここではどういう意味ですか。
What meaning does this word have here?
• ka dō ka かどうか *whether or not* 《This expression generally follows an informal-style predicate, but the word preceding **ka dō ka** cannot be the copula form **da** だ. When **ka dō ka** is added to a clause that would end with **da**, the

da does not appear.》

¶Sore wa honmono ka dō ka wakarimasen.

それは本物かどうかわかりません。

*I don't know whether or not that's the
real thing.*

¶Ashita kuru ka dō ka Yamashita-san ni
tazuneta.

あした来るかどうか山下さんに尋ねた。

*I asked Mr. Yamashita whether or not
he will come tomorrow.*

• dō-ka どうか *somehow* 《Often used in
requests.》

¶Dō-ka ku-ji made ni sumasete kudasai.

どうか9時までに済ませてください。

Please finish it somehow by 9:00.

• dō-ka suru どうかする *to have something go wrong*

¶Kono kikai wa dō-ka shite iru yo.

この機械はどうかしているよ。

*There's something wrong with this
machine!*

dóa ドア *door* [→**to** 戸]

dōbutsu 動物 *animal*

¶Tori mo sakana mo ningen mo dōbutsu
desu.

鳥も魚も人間も動物です。

*Birds, fish, and human beings are all
animals.*

• dōbutsu-en 動物園 *zoo*
• dōbutsu-gaku 動物学 *zoology*
• dōbutsu-gaku-sha 動物学者 *zoologist*
• dōbutsu-kai 動物界 *the animal kingdom, the animal world*

dóchira どちら 【FORMAL】 ① *which
one* 《Used when there are only two alternatives.》 [⇔**dore** どれ]

¶Akiko-san no raketto wa dochira desu
ka.

明子さんのラケットはどちらですか。

Which one is Akiko's racket?

¶Taiyō to chikyū to dochira ga ōkii desu
ka.

太陽と地球とどちらが大きいですか。

Which is larger, the sun or the earth?

¶Gyūniku to buta-niku to dochira ga
suki desu ka.

牛肉と豚肉のどちらが好きですか。

Which do you like better, beef or pork?

② *which way; where*

¶Dochira e o-dekake desu ka.

どちらへお出かけですか？

Where are you going?

• dochira-ka どちらか *one or the other*

¶Ano futari no dochira-ka ga kono
shigoto o ashita made ni oenakereba
narimasen.

あの二人のどちらかがこの仕事あしたまでに
終えなければなりません。

*One or the other of those two has to
finish this work by tomorrow.*

¶Dochira-ka ga machigatte imasu.

どちらかがまちがっています。

One or the other is wrong.

• dochira-mo どちらも *both* 《in combination with an affirmative predicate》; *neither one* 《in combination with a negative
predicate》

¶Watashi-tachi wa dochira-mo ongaku
ni kyōmi ga arimasu.

私たちはどちらも音楽に興味があります。

Both of us have an interest in music.

¶Chichi wa Eigo mo Furansu-go mo
dochira-mo dekiru.

父は英語もフランス語もどちらもできる。

*Father can speak both English and
French.*

¶Sono gakusei-tachi wa dochira-mo
shiranakatta yo.

その学生たちはどちらも知らなかったよ。

*I didn't know either one of those
students!*

• dochira-sama どちら様 【HON. for
dare 誰】 *who* 《as a question word》
[→**donata** どなた]

dodai 土台 *foundation, base* [→**kiso**
基礎]

dōfū 同封 〜**no** 〜の *enclosed in the
same envelope*

• dōfū suru 同封する *to enclose in the
same envelope*

¶Saikin no shashin o dōfū shimasu.

最近の写真を同封します。

I enclose a recent photograph.

dōgú 道具 *tool, utensil*
- dōgu–bako 道具箱 *toolbox*
- daidokoro–dōgu 台所道具 *kitchen utensils*
- daiku–dōgu 大工道具 *carpenter's tools*

dōhō 同胞 *fellow countryman, compatriot*

dōi 同意 *agreement, approval* [→**sansei** 賛成]
- dōi suru 同意する *to agree, to give one's approval*
¶Watashi wa Nakatsu–san ni dōi shimasu.
私は中津さんに同意します。
I agree with Ms. Nakatsu.
¶Kachō wa sono keikaku ni dōi shimashita.
課長はその計画に同意しました。
The section chief agreed to that plan.

dō itashimashite どういたしまして *not at all* 《Used as a response to a thank-you (= *you're welcome*), an apology, or a compliment.》
¶"Dōmo arigatō gozaimashita." "Dō itashimashite."
「どうもありがとうございました」「どういたしまして」
"Thank you very much." "Not at all."

dóitsu どいつ 【CRUDE】 *which person*

dōji 同時 ~**no** ~の *simultaneous, concurrent*
¶Sono futari wa dōji ni shuppatsu shimashita.
その二人は同時に出発しました。
Those two started out simultaneously.
- dōji–tsūyaku 同時通訳 *simultaneous interpretation*

dóji どじ 【COL.】 *goof, blunder* [→**hema** へま]
- doji o fumu どじを踏む *to blunder, to make a goof*
- doji na どじな *goof-prone, blundering*

dōjō 同情 *sympathy, compassion*
- A no dōjō o eru 〔ushinau〕 Aの同情を得る〔失う〕 *to gain 〔lose〕 A's sympathy*

- dōjō suru 同情する *to feel sympathy, to feel compassion*
¶Higai-sha ni dōjō shimasu.
被害者に同情します。
I feel sympathy for the victim.

dojō どじょう *loach; mudfish*

dōkan 同感 *agreement, shared opinion, shared feeling*

dokeru どける *to remove, to get out of the way*
¶Sono hako o tēburu kara dokete kudasai.
その箱をテーブルからどけてください。
Please remove that box from the table.

dōki 動機 *motive, motivation*
¶Jogingu o hajimeta dōki wa nan desu ka.
ジョギングを始めた動機は何ですか。
What was your motivation to start jogging?

dókidoki どきどき ~**suru** ~する *to throb with a fast heartbeat*

dokkingu ドッキング *docking* 《of spacecraft》
- dokkingu suru ドッキングする *to dock*

dóko どこ *what place, where*
¶Watashi no baggu wa doko desu ka.
私のバッグはどこですか。
Where is my bag?
¶Sasaki-san wa doko ni sunde imasu ka.
佐々木さんはどこに住んでいますか。
Where does Ms. Sasaki live?
¶Doko e ikimashō ka.
どこへ行きましょうか。
Where shall we go?
- doko-ka どこか *somewhere*
¶Shūmatsu ni doko-ka ni ikimasu ka.
週末にどこかに行きますか。
Will you go somewhere on the weekend?

dókoro-ka どころか *far from, quite the opposite of, to say nothing of* 《This expression generally follows an informal-style predicate in the nonpast tense, but the word preceding **dokoro-ka** cannot be the copula form **da** だ. When **dokoro-ka** is added to a clause that would end with **da**, the **da** does not appear.》

¶Harue-san wa warau dokoro-ka okotte shimatta.

春江さんは笑うどころか怒ってしまった。

Far from laughing, Harue got angry.

¶Pasokon dokoro-ka wā-puro mo kaenai yo.

パソコンどころかワープロも買えないよ。

I cannot even buy a word processor, to say nothing of a computer!

¶Sore wa yūeki dokoro-ka gai ni naru yo.

それは有益どころか害になるよ。

Far from beneficial, that'll be harmful!

dokú 毒 *a poison*

¶Tabako no sui-sugi wa karada ni doku da yo.

たばこの吸いすぎは体に毒だよ。

Smoking too much is bad for your health!

• doku-gasu 毒ガス *poison gas*
• doku-hebi 毒蛇 *poisonous snake*
• doku-kinoko 毒茸 *poisonous mushroom*

doku どく *to get out of the way* 《intransitive》

dókuji 独自 ～**no** ～の *original, one's own*

• dokuji no hatsumei 独自の発明 *original invention*

dokuritsu 独立 *independence*

¶Amerika wa sen-nanahyaku-nanajū-roku-nen ni dokuritsu o sengen shima-shita.

アメリカは1776年に独立を宣言しました。

The United States declared its independence in 1776.

• dokuritsu no 独立の *independent*
• dokuritsu suru 独立する *to become independent*
• Dokuritsu-kinen-bi 独立記念日 *Independence Day*
• dokuritsu-koku 独立国 *independent country*
• dokuritsu-shin 独立心 *independent spirit*

dokusai 独裁 *dictatorship, despotism, autocracy*

• dokusai suru 独裁する *to rule dictatorially*
• dokusai-seiji 独裁政治 *dictatorial government*

dokusen 独占 *exclusive possession; monopoly*

• dokusen suru 独占する *to get for oneself alone; to monopolize*

¶Ane wa ni-kai o dokusen shite iru yo.

姉は2階を独占しているよ。

My older sister has the second floor all to herself!

dókusha 読者 *reader*

• dokusha-ran 読者欄 *readers' column*

dokushin 独身 ～**no** ～の *unmarried, single*

¶Ani wa mada dokushin desu.

兄はまだ独身です。

My older brother is still single.

dókusho 読書 *reading a book, reading books*

• dokusho suru 読書する *to read a book, to read books*

¶Musume wa dokusho ga suki desu.

娘は読書が好きです。

My daughter likes reading books.

• dokusho-shitsu 読書室 *reading room*

dokushō 独唱 *vocal solo*

• dokushō suru 独唱する *to sing a solo*
• dokushō-kai 独唱会 *solo recital*

dokusō 独奏 *instrumental solo*

• dokusō suru 独奏する *to play a solo*
• dokusō-kai 独奏会 *solo recital*

dokusō 独創 *originality, inventiveness*

• dokusō-teki na 独創的な *original, creative, inventive*

dokutoku 独特 ～**no** ～の *unique, special*

¶Ano tetsugaku-sha ni wa dokutoku no kangae-kata ga arimasu.

あの哲学者には独特の考え方があります。

That philosopher has a unique way of thinking.

• –dokutoku no －独特の *unique to, peculiar to* 《Added to noun bases.》
• Nihon-dokutoku no 日本独特の *unique to Japan*

dōkutsu 洞窟 *cave* [→**horaana** 洞穴]

dókyō 度胸 *courage, nerve* [→**yūki** 勇気]

dōkyo 同居 *living together* 《in the same household》
- dōkyo suru 同居する *to live together*

dōkyū 同級 *the same grade in school*
¶Hiromi-chan to Yōko-chan wa dōkyu desu.
弘美ちゃんと洋子ちゃんは同級です。
Hiromi and Yoko are in the same grade.
- dōkyū-sei 同級生 *student in the same grade*

dokyuméntarī ドキュメンタリー *a documentary*

dōmei 同盟 *alliance, union, league*
- dōmei suru 同盟する *to ally, to form an alliance*
- dōmei-koku 同盟国 *allied country*

dṓmo どうも ① *very, quite* [→**totemo** とても]
¶Dōmo arigatō.
どうもありがとう。
Thank you very much.
¶Dōmo sumimasen.
どうもすみません。
I'm very sorry.
② *somehow, for some reason* [→**nan-da-ka** 何だか]
¶Dōmo neko ga kirai desu.
どうも猫が嫌いです。
I don't like cats for some reason.

domóru 吃る *to stutter, to stammer*

dṓmu ドーム *dome*

dōmyaku 動脈 *artery* 《blood vessel》 [⇔**jōmyaku** 静脈]

dón どん ～**to** ～と *with a banging noise, with a bang*
¶Jū ga don to narimashita.
銃がどんと鳴りました。
A gun sounded with a bang.
¶Yōi, don.
用意、どん。
Ready, go! 《when starting a race》

donáru 怒鳴る *to shout at, to yell at*
¶Sensei wa okotte, seito-tachi o donarimashita.

先生は怒って、生徒たちをどなりました。
The teacher got angry and shouted at the students.

dónata どなた 【HON. for **dare** 誰】 *who* 《as a question word》
¶Donata desu ka.
どなたですか。
Who is it?

dṓnatsu ドーナツ *doughnut*

donburi 丼 ① *large ceramic bowl* 《used to serve food》
② [☞**donburi-mono** 丼物 (below)]
- donburi-mono 丼物 *meal served in a large ceramic bowl*

dóndon どんどん ① (～**to** ～と) *with a bam-bam, poundingly*
¶Keikan wa to o dondon tatakimashita.
警官は戸をどんどんたたきました。
The police officer banged on the door.
② *rapidly; more and more; on and on*
¶Watashi-tachi wa dondon arukimashita.
私たちはどんどん歩きました。
We walked on and on.

donguri 団栗 *acorn*

donkan 鈍感 ～**na** ～な *insensitive, unfeeling* [⇔**binkan na** 敏感な]

dónna どんな *what kind of*
¶Kyōto de wa donna tokoro o tazunemashō ka.
京都ではどんな所を訪ねましょうか。
What kind of places shall we visit in Kyoto?
¶Donna ongaku ni kyōmi ga arimasu ka.
どんな音楽に興味がありますか。
What kind of music are you interested in?
¶Donna fukusō demo kekkō desu.
どんな服装でも結構です。
It doesn't matter what you wear.
¶Kazoku no tame nara, donna koto demo shimasu.
家族のためなら、どんなことでもします。
I will do anything for my family.
- donna ni どんなに *to what extent, how much*
¶Donna ni takai desu ka.
どんなに高いですか。

How expensive is it?

dóno どの *which* 《as a noun-modifying question word》

¶Dono hon ga sensei no desu ka.
どの本が先生のですか。
Which book is the teacher's?

¶Dono supōtsu ga ichiban suki desu ka.
どのスポーツがいちばん好きですか。
Which sport do you like best?

¶Dono seki ni suwatte mo ii desu yo.
どの席に座ってもいいですよ。
Sit in whichever seat you like!

• dono A …mo どのA…も *every A* 《in combination with an affirmative predicate》; 〈*not*〉 *any A* 《in combination with a negative predicate》

¶Dono kōho-sha mo sonna koto o shimashita.
どの候補者もそんなことをしました。
Every candidate did that kind of thing.

¶Dono seito mo sono mondai o tokenakatta.
どの生徒もその問題を解けなかった。
No student could solve that problem.

¶Dono shitsumon ni mo sugu ni wa kotaeraremasen.
どの質問にもすぐには答えられません。
I can not answer any of the questions right away.

• dono kurai どのくらい [☞**dono gurai** どのぐらい (below)]

• dono gurai どのぐらい *about how many, about how much, about to what extent*

¶Kago no naka ni kuri wa dono gurai arimasu ka.
かごの中に栗はどのぐらいありますか。
About how many chestnuts are there in the basket?

¶Eki made basu de dono gurai kakarimasu ka.
駅までバスでどのぐらいかかりますか。
About how long does it take to go to the station by bus?

• dono yō ni どのように *how, in what way* [→**dō** どう]

don'yóri どんより ～**suru** ～する *to become cloudy, to become gray*

¶Kyō wa sora ga don'yori shite imasu ne.
きょうは空がどんよりしていますね。
Today the sky is gray, isn't it.

dōnyū 導入 *introduction* 《of one thing into another》

• dōnyū suru 導入する *to introduce*

dōongo 同音語 *homonym*

dorái ドライ ～**na** ～な *unsentimental, pragmatic-minded* [⇔**uetto na** ウェットな]

doraiáisu ドライアイス *dry ice*

doraibā ドライバー *screwdriver* [→**neji-mawashi** ねじ回し (s.v. **neji** ねじ)]

doráibā ドライバー *driver* 《of a car, etc.》 [→**unten-sha** 運転者 (s.v. **unten** 運転)]

doráibu ドライブ *drive, automobile trip*

• doraibu-in ドライブイン *drive-in*

doraiyā ドライヤー *drier* 《machine》

dórama ドラマ *a drama, a play* [→**geki** 劇]

doramachíkku ドラマチック ～**na** ～な *dramatic*

dóramu ドラム *drum* 《musical instrument》 [→**taiko** 太鼓]

• doramu o ensō suru ドラムを演奏する *to play the drums*

doramukan ドラム缶 *drum* 《can》

dóre どれ *which one* 《Used when there are more than two alternatives.》 [⇔**dochira** どちら①]

¶Kono san dai no supōtsukā no uchi de dore ga ichiban suki desu ka.
この3台のスポーツカーのうちでどれがいちばん好きですか。
Out of these three sportscars which do you like best?

• dore demo どれでも *any one*

¶Dore demo erande kudasai.
どれでも選んでください。
Please choose any one.

• dore-ka どれか *one of them*

¶Dore-ka o Yasuko-chan ni agenasai.
どれかを安子ちゃんにあげなさい。
Give one of them to Yasuko.

• dore-mo どれも *every one, all of them* 《in combination with an affirmative predi-

cate»; *none of them* «in combination
with a negative predicate»
¶Kono rekōdo wa dore-mo suki desu.
このレコードはどれも好きです。
I like every one of these records.
¶Dore-mo kaimasen deshita.
どれも買いませんでした。
I didn't buy any of them.
•dore-kurai どれくらい [☞**dore-gurai**
どれぐらい (below)]
•dore-gurai どれぐらい *about how many,
about how much, about to what extent*
[→**dono gurai** どのぐらい (s.v. **dono**
どの)]
dorei 奴隷 *slave*
dorésshingu ドレッシング (*salad*)*dressing*
dóresu ドレス *a dress*
dōrí 道理 *reason, logic, rationality* «of
something»
•dōri ni kanau 道理にかなう *to become
reasonable, to become rational*
¶Sono yōkyū wa dōri ni kanatte imasu.
その要求は道理にかなっています。
That request is reasonable.
-dōri -通り ～**no** ～の *according to, in
keeping with* «Added to noun bases.»
¶Basu wa jikan-dōri ni tsukimashita.
バスは時間どおりに着きました。
The bus arrived on time.
•keikaku-dōri no 計画どおりの *accord-
ing-to-plan*
•moji-dōri no 文字どおりの *literal*
doríburu ドリブル *dribbling* «in sports»
•doriburu suru ドリブルする *to dribble*
dóriru ドリル ① *drill* ((tool))
② *drill, study by repetitive practice*
dōro 道路 *road, street* [→**tōri** 通り]
•dōro-chizu 道路地図 *road map*
•dōro-hyōshiki 道路標識 *road sign*
•dōro-kōji 道路工事 *road repair; road
construction*
•kōsoku-dōro 高速道路 *superhighway,
<US>expressway, <UK>motorway*
•yūryō-dōro 有料道路 *toll road*
doró 泥 *mud*
¶Basu ga watashi no doresu ni doro

o hanemashita.
バスが私のドレスに泥を跳ねました。
A bus splashed mud on my dress.
•doro-darake no 泥だらけの *mud-
covered*
•doro-michi 泥道 *muddy road, muddy
path*
•doro-mizu 泥水 *muddy water*
dorobō 泥棒 *thief; burglar; robber* [→
gōtō 強盗②]
¶Yūbe sono mise ni dorobō ga hairimashita.
ゆうべその店に泥棒が入りました。
A thief broke into that store last night.
doróppu ドロップ *candy drop*
dóru ドル *dollar*
•-doru -ドル«counter for dollars; see
Appendix 2»
dōryō 同僚 *colleague, fellow worker*
dóryoku 努力 *effort, exertion*
¶Kore kara mo doryoku ga hitsuyō desu.
これからも努力が必要です。
*From now on, too, effort will be neces-
sary.*
•doryoku suru 努力する *to make efforts,
to strive, to exert oneself*
¶Eigo no chikara o nobasō to doryoku
shite imasu.
英語の力を伸ばそうと努力しています。
*I am making efforts to improve my
English.*
•doryoku-ka 努力家 *hard worker*
dōsa 動作 (*bodily*)*movement,
*(*bodily*)*action*
¶Sono shōnen wa dōsa ga hayai desu.
その少年は動作が早いです。
That boy's movements are fast.
dōse どうせ *in any case, anyway* «Used
to express the feeling that something unpleasant is unavoidable.»
¶Dōse ano hito wa shippai suru deshō.
どうせあの人は失敗するでしょう。
*In any case, that person will probably
fail.*
¶Dōse yaru nara, saizen o tsukushi-
mashō.
どうせやるなら、最善を尽くしましょう。

If we're going to do it anyway, let's do our best.

Dosei 土星 *(the planet)* Saturn

dōsei 同棲 *living together, cohabitation* 《*especially by an unmarried couple*》
• dōsei suru 同せいする *to live together*

dōsei 同性 *the same sex*
• dōsei-ai 同性愛 *homosexuality*

doshaburi 土砂降り *heavy rain, downpour*

dōshi 動詞 *verb*

-dōshi －通し ～**no** ～の *continually* 《Added to verb bases.》
¶Yo-dōshi unten shite sukījō ni tsukimashita.
夜通し運転してスキー場に着きました。
I drove all through the night and arrived at the ski resort.

-dōshi －同士《Added to noun bases.》 *fellow; of each other*
• gakusei-dōshi 学生同士 *fellow students*
• koibito-dōshi 恋人同士 *lovers (of each other)*

dōshite どうして ① *why* [→**naze** なぜ]
¶Dōshite sonna ni tsukarete iru no?
どうしてそんなに疲れているの？
Why are you so tired?
¶Dōshite Eigo o benkyō shite iru n desu ka.
どうして英語を勉強しているんですか。
Why are you studying English?
② *how, in what way* [→**dō** どう]
¶Kono kikai wa dōshite ugokasu n desu ka.
この機械はどうして動かすんですか。
How does one operate this machine?

dōshite-mo どうしても *no matter what (one does)*
¶Dōshite-mo Amerika ni ikimasu.
どうしてもアメリカに行きます。
I will go to the United States no matter what.
¶Kono doa wa dōshite-mo akanai yo.
このドアはどうしても開かないよ。
This door won't open no matter what!
¶Dōshite-mo ano hito no namae ga omoidasenai.
どうしてもあの人の名前が思い出せない。
No matter what I do, I can't remember that person's name.

dosō 土葬 *burial, interment* 《*of a dead body*》[⇔**kasō** 火葬]
• dosō suru 土葬する *to bury, to inter*

dōsṓkai 同窓会 ① *alumni association* ② *alumni meeting*

dosoku 土足 *having one's shoes on*
• dosoku de 土足で *with one's shoes on*
¶Kōsha ni dosoku de haitte wa ikenai yo.
校舎に土足で入ってはいけないよ。
You mustn't enter the school building with your shoes on!
¶Dosoku genkin
「土足厳禁」《on a sign》
Remove your shoes 《*Literally: Shoes are prohibited.*》

dōtai 胴体 *torso, trunk* [→**dō** 胴]
• hikōki no dōtai 飛行機の胴体 *airplane fuselage*

dótchi どっち【COL. for **dochira** どちら】

dotchimichi どっちみち【COL.】 *either way, in any case, anyway*
¶Dotchimichi Horita-san ni au tsumori datta.
どっちみち堀田さんに会うつもりだった。
I was planning to see Mr. Horita anyway.

dote 土手 *earth embankment, earth levee*

dōteki 動的 ～**na** ～な *dynamic* [⇔**seiteki na** 静的な]

dōten 同点 *tie score*
• dōten ni naru 同点になる *to become tied*

dōtoku 道徳 *morals, morality*
• dōtoku-teki na 道徳的な *moral*
• kōshū-dōtoku 公衆道徳 *public morality*
• kōtsū-dōtoku 交通道徳 *standards of behavior for drivers*

dōwa 童話 *fairy tale* [→**otogibanashi** おとぎ話]

dowasure 度忘れ ～**suru** ～する *to have slipped one's mind*

¶Ano hito no namae o dowasure shimashita.

あの人の名前を度忘れしました。

That person's name has slipped my mind.

dō̄-yara どうやら ① *perhaps* 《in combination with a word indicating likelihood, such as **rashii** らしい ① or a word ending in -**sō** −そう.》

¶Dō-yara yuki ga furi-sō desu ne.

どうやら雪が降りそうですね。

It looks as if perhaps it's going to snow, doesn't it.

② *somehow or other, barely, with difficulty*

¶Dō-yara gakkō ni maniaimashita.

どうやら学校に間に合いました。

I was barely in time for school.

dōyō 動揺 ① *trembling, swaying, jolting*

• dōyō suru 動揺する *to tremble, to sway, to jolt*

② *agitation, unrest, disturbance*

• dōyō suru 動揺する *to become agitated, to become disturbed*

¶Sono shirase ni minna ga dōyō shimashita.

その知らせにみんなが動揺しました。

Everyone became agitated at that news.

dōyō 同様 ～**no** ～の *same, similar* [→ **onaji** 同じ]

• shinpin-dōyō no 新品同様の *as good as new, just like new*

Doyóbi 土曜日 *Saturday*

dō̄zo どうぞ *please, if you please* 《Used both in requests and in offers. In offers, phrases such as *here you are* or *go ahead* are often used as natural English translations.》

¶Dōzo o-hairi kudasai.

どうぞお入りください。

Please come in.

¶Dōzo kochira e.

どうぞこちらへ。

This way, please.

¶"Shio o totte kudasai." "Hai, dōzo."

「塩を取ってください」「はい、どうぞ」

"Please pass me the salt." "Here you are."

dōzō 銅像 *bronze statue*

dyúetto デュエット *duet*

E

e へ《noun-following particle》 ① *to, for, toward* [→**ni** に③]

¶Chichi wa Kyūshū e ikimashita.

父は九州へ行きました。

My father went to Kyushu.

¶Shachō wa raishū Nyūyōku e tachimasu.

社長は来週ニューヨークへたちます。

The company president will leave for New York next week.

¶Hikōki wa nishi e tonde imashita.

飛行機は西へ飛んでいました。

The airplane was flying toward the west.

¶Kore wa sensei e no okurimono desu.

これは先生への贈り物です。

This is a present for the teacher.

② *into, onto* [→**ni** に④]

¶Seito wa heya e kakekomimashita.

生徒は部屋へ駆け込みました。

The student ran into the room.

¶Ningyō o hako no naka e iremashita.

人形を箱の中へ入れました。

I put the doll inside the box.

¶Neko ga tēburu e tobiagarimashita.

猫がテーブルへ跳び上がりました。

The cat jumped up onto the table.

e 柄 *handle*

¶Kono kanazuchi no e wa ki de dekite imasu.

この金づちの柄は木でできています。

The handle of this hammer is made of wood.

• hōki no e ほうきの柄 *broomstick*

é 絵 *picture, painting, drawing* 《not a photograph》 [⇔**shashin** 写真]

¶Akiko-san wa e ga jōzu desu.

明子さんは絵が上手です。
Akiko is good at drawing pictures.
¶Kore wa Pikaso no e desu.
これはピカソの絵です。
This is a painting by Picasso.
•e o kaku 絵をかく *to paint／draw a picture*

ě えっ *What?, What!* 《This exclamatory interjection expresses surprise or doubt. It frequently precedes a question asking for repetition or confirmation of surprising information.》
¶Ě, Satō-san mo yasumu n desu ka.
えっ、佐藤さんも休むんですか。
What? Satō isn't going to come, either?

ē ええ *yes* [→**hai** はい①] [⇔**īe** いいえ]
¶"Demasu ka." "Ē, demasu."
「出ますか」「ええ、出ます」
"Are you going to leave?" "Yes, I am."
¶"Kēki wa mō arimasen ne." "Ē, arimasen."
「ケーキはもうありませんね」「ええ、ありません」
"There's no more cake, is there." "No, there isn't." 《In response to a question that presumes a negative answer, ē is used to mean *Yes, your presumption is correct.* A natural English translation will often have *no* rather than *yes*.》

eakon エアコン *air conditioner*
earobíkusu エアロビクス *aerobics*
ebi 海老 *shrimp, prawn; lobster*
échiketto エチケット *etiquette* [→**sahō** 作法]
¶Sō suru koto wa echiketto ni hanshite imasu.
そうすることはエチケットに反しています。
To do so is against etiquette.

eda 枝 *branch, bough, limb, twig*
•eda o oru 枝を折る *to break a branch*
•eda o kiru 枝を切る *to cut a branch*
•eda o dasu 枝を出す *to put out branches, to grow branches*
edamame 枝豆 *green soybean*
egáku 描く ① *to draw, to paint* [→**kaku** 描く]
② *to describe, to depict*

égao 笑顔 *smiling face*
¶Kachō wa egao de haitte kimashita.
課長は笑顔で入ってきました。
The section chief came in with a smiling face.

egoísuto エゴイスト *egoist*
ehágaki 絵はがき *picture postcard*
ehón 絵本 *picture book*
Eibun 英文 ① *English text*
② *English sentence*
eien 永遠 ～**no** ～の *eternal, permanent* [→**eikyū no** 永久の]
•eien ni 永遠に *eternally, permanently, forever*

éiga 映画 *movie, film*
¶Eiga o mi ni ikimashō.
映画を見に行きましょう。
Let's go and see a movie.
¶Kono eiga wa mō mimashita yo.
この映画はもう見ましたよ。
I've already seen this movie!
•eiga-fan 映画ファン *movie fan*
•eiga-haiyū 映画俳優 *movie actor, movie actress*
•eiga-kan 映画館 *movie theater*
•eiga-kantoku 映画監督 *movie director*
•eiga-ongaku 映画音楽 *movie music*
•eiga-sai 映画祭 *film festival*
•eiga-sutā 映画スター *movie star*

Eigo 英語 *the English language*
¶Ashita Eigo no shiken ga aru yo.
あした英語の試験があるよ。
There's an English test tomorrow!
¶Okamoto-san no imōto-san wa Eigo no sensei desu.
岡本さんの妹さんは英語の先生です。
Mr. Okamoto's younger sister is an English teacher.

eigyō 営業 *business (operations)*
•eigyō suru 営業する *to operate a business, to carry on business*
•eigyō-chū no 営業中の *open-for-business*
¶Kono mise wa eigyō-chū desu.
この店は営業中です。
This store is open for business.
•eigyō-jikan 営業時間 *business hours*

Eikáiwa 英会話 *English conversation*

eikyō 影響 *influence*
- eikyō suru 影響する *to influence*
- eikyō o ataeru 影響を与える *to have an influence*

¶Terebi wa watashi-tachi ni fukai eikyō o ataemasu.

テレビは私たちに深い影響を与えます。

Television has a big influence on us.

- eikyō o ukeru 影響を受ける *to receive an influence*

eikyū 永久 〜no 〜の *permanent, eternal* [→**eien no** 永遠の]
- eikyū ni 永久に *permanently, eternally, forever*
- eikyū-shi 永久歯 *permanent tooth*

eisákubun 英作文 ① *English composition*
② *English composition* (*course*)

eisei 衛生 *health maintenance, hygiene*
- eisei-teki na 衛生的 *sanitary*

¶Kono nagashi wa eisei-teki de wa arimasen.

この流しは衛生的ではありません。

This sink is not sanitary.

- kōshū-eisei 公衆衛生 *public health*
- seishin-eisei 精神衛生 *mental health maintenance*

eisei 衛星 *satellite*
- eisei-chūkei 衛星中継 *satellite transmission*

¶Sono bangumi wa eisei-chūkei de hōsō saremasu.

その番組は衛星中継で放送されます。

That program will be broadcast by a satellite transmission.

- eisei-hōsō 衛星放送 *satellite broadcasting*
- eisei-tsūshin 衛星通信 *satellite communication*
- jinkō-eisei 人工衛星 *artificial satellite*
- kishō-eisei 気象衛星 *weather satellite*
- tsūshin-eisei 通信衛星 *communication satellite*

eisha 映写 *projection* (*on a screen*)
- eisha suru 映写する *to project*
- eisha-ki 映写機 *projector*

Eiwajíten 英和辞典 *English–Japanese dictionary*

Eiyaku 英訳 *English translation*

¶Kaneda-san wa Sōseki no shōsetsu o Eiyaku de yonda.

金田さんは漱石の小説を英訳で読んだ。

Mr. Kaneda read Soseki's novel in English translation.

- Eiyaku suru 英訳する *to translate into English*

¶Yamamura-kyōju wa sono shōsetsu o Eiyaku shimashita.

山村教授はその小説を英訳しました。

Prof. Yamamura translated that novel into English.

eiyō 栄養 *nourishment, nutritiousness*

¶Kono sarada wa eiyō ni tonde imasu.

このサラダは栄養に富んでいます。

This salad is rich in nourishment.

- eiyō no aru tabemono 栄養のある食べ物 *nutritious food*
- eiyō-shi 栄養士 *dietician*

eiyū 英雄 *hero, heroine*
- eiyū-teki na 英雄的な *heroic*
- eiyū-teki na kōi 英雄的な行為 *heroic deed*
- kokumin-teki-eiyū 国民的英雄 *national hero*

eizō 映像 *picture, image projected on a screen*
- terebi no eizō テレビの映像 *television picture*

éizu エイズ *AIDS*

éjiki 餌食 *prey*

¶Ano kotori wa neko no ejiki ni natta yo.

あの小鳥は猫のえじきになったよ

That bird became cat's prey!

éki 駅 〈*railway*〉 *station*

¶Mainichi eki made musume o mukae ni ikimasu.

毎日駅まで娘を迎えにいきます。

Every day I go to the station to meet my daughter.

- eki-ben 駅弁 *box lunch sold at a station*
- eki-biru 駅ビル *station building*

- eki-chō 駅長 *stationmaster*
- eki-den 駅伝 *long-distance running relay race*
- eki-in 駅員 *station employee*
- norikae-eki 乗り換え駅 *transfer station*
- shihatsu-eki 始発駅 *first station* 《from which a train or bus starts》
- shūchaku-eki 終着駅 *last station* 《at which a train or bus stops》

ekisáito エキサイト ~**suru** ~する *to get excited* [→**kōfun suru** 興奮する]
¶Kanshū wa shiai ni hijō ni ekisaito shimashita.
観衆は試合に非常にエキサイトしました。
The spectators get very excited by the game.

ekishibishongému エキシビションゲーム *exhibition game*

ékisu エキス *extract (solution)*
- gyūniku no ekisu 牛肉のエキス *beef extract*

ekitai 液体 *liquid* [⇔**kitai** 気体; **kotai** 固体]

ekizochíkku エキゾチック ~**na** ~な *exotic*

ekkususen エックス線 *x-ray (radiation)* [→**rentogen** レントゲン①]
- ekkususen-kensa エックス線検査 *x-ray examination*

ékubo 笑窪 *dimple* 《which appears in the cheek during a smile》
¶Keiko-chan wa warau to ekubo ga dekiru ne.
恵子ちゃんは笑うとえくぼができるね。
Keiko gets dimples when she smiles, doesn't she.

emerárudo エメラルド *an emerald*

én 円 ① *circle* [→**maru** 丸]
- en o kaku 円をかく *to draw a circle*
② *yen* 《the Japanese monetary unit》
- -en －円《counter for yen; see Appendix 2》
¶Teika wa sen-en desu.
定価は1000円です。
The list price is 1,000 yen.
- en-daka 円高 *rise in the value of the yen*

- en-yasu 円安 *fall in the value of the yen*

enban 円盤 *disk; discus*
- sora o tobu enban 空を飛ぶ円盤 *flying saucer*
- enban-nage 円盤投げ *the discus throw*

énbun 塩分 *salt content*

enchō 延長 ① *lengthening, extension* 《in space》
- enchō suru 延長する *to lengthen, to extend*
¶Kono dōro wa rainen enchō sareru ka mo shiremasen.
この道路は来年延長されるかもしれません。
This road may be extended next year.
② *prolongation, extension* 《in time》
- enchō suru 延長する *to prolong, to extend*
¶Abe-san wa taizai o mō ichi-nichi enchō shimashita.
阿部さんは滞在をもう1日延長しました。
Ms. Abe extended her stay for another day.
- enchō-sen 延長戦 *overtime game; extra-inning game*

éndō えんどう *pea*

enérugī エネルギー *energy*

engan 沿岸 *coast, shore*
¶Boku no kyōri wa Nihon-kai no engan ni arimasu.
僕の郷里は日本海の沿岸にあります。
My hometown is on the coast of the Japan Sea.
- engan-gyogyō 沿岸漁業 *coastal fishery*
- engan-sen 沿岸線 *coastline, shoreline*

engawa 縁側 *wooden veranda* 《projecting outside a ground-floor room under the eaves in traditional Japanese architecture》

engei 園芸 *gardening, horticulture*
- engei-yōgu 園芸用具 *gardening tool*

engējiríngu エンゲージリング *engagement ring* [→**kon'yaku-yubiwa** 婚約指輪 (s.v. **kon'yaku** 婚約)]

engeki 演劇 *theatrical performance, drama, play* [→**geki** 劇]

• engeki-bu 演劇部 *drama club*

éngi 演技 *acting, performance*

¶Sano-san no engi wa subarashikatta desu.

佐野さんの演技はすばらしかったです。

Ms. Sano's performance was wonderful.

• engi suru 演技する *to act, to perform* 《*intransitive*》

engi 縁起 *omen, portent*

• engi ga ii 縁起がいい *to be auspicious*

• engi ga warui 縁起が悪い *to be inauspicious, to be ominous*

énjin エンジン *engine*

• enjin o kakeru 〔tomeru〕 エンジンをかける 〔止める〕 *to start* 〔*stop*〕 *an engine*

• dīzeru-enjin ディーゼルエンジン *diesel engine*

• tābo-enjin ターボエンジン *turbocharged engine*

enjínia エンジニア *engineer, engineering specialist* 〔→**gishi** 技師〕

enjiru 演じる *to play* 《*a role*》

¶Ōkawa-san wa Hamuretto-yaku o enjimashita.

大川さんはハムレット役を演じました.

Mr. Okawa played the part of Hamlet.

¶Nihon wa kono mondai de jūyō na yakuwari o enjimasu.

日本はこの問題で重要な役割を演じます。

Japan plays an important role in this problem.

énjo 援助 *help, assistance, aid*

• enjo suru 援助する *to help, to assist, to aid*

enkai 宴会 *banquet*

enki 延期 *postponement*

• enki suru 延期する *to put off, to postpone*

¶Kondo no Doyōbi made kai o enki shimasu.

今度の土曜日まで会を延期します。

We will put off the meeting until this coming Saturday.

énnichi 縁日 *day of a fair at a Buddhist temple or Shinto shirine*

e-no-gu 絵の具 *paints* (*for pictures*)

• e-no-gu no chūbu 絵の具のチューブ *tube of paint*

• e-no-gu-bako 絵の具箱 *paintbox*

• e-no-gu-fude 絵の具筆 *paintbrush*

• abura-e-no-gu 油絵の具 *oils, oil paint*

• suisai-e-no-gu 水彩絵の具 *watercolors*

enpitsu 鉛筆 *pencil*

¶Shin ga oreta node, enpitsu o kezurimashita.

しんが折れたので、鉛筆を削りました。

The lead broke, so I sharpened the pencil.

• enpitsu-ire 鉛筆入れ *pencil case*

• enpitsu-kezuri 鉛筆削り *pencil sharpener*

• aka-enpitsu 赤鉛筆 *red pencil*

• iro-enpitsu 色鉛筆 *colored pencil*

énryo 遠慮 *reserve, modesty,* (*polite*)*hesitation, diffidence*

• enryo suru 遠慮する *to be reserved, to hesitate* (*out of politeness*)

¶Enryo shinai de nan-demo kiite kudasai.

遠慮しないで何でも聞いてください。

Please don't hesitate; ask me anything.

• enryo-gachi na 遠慮がちな *reserved, diffident*

• enryo-naku 遠慮なく *without reserve, without hesitating* (*out of politeness*)

¶Enryo-naku hanashite kudasai.

遠慮なく話してください。

Please speak without reserve.

¶Enryo-naku sandoitchi o tabete-kudasai.

遠慮なくサンドイッチを食べてください。

Please eat the sandwiches without hesitating out of politeness.

ensei 遠征 ① (*military*)*expedition, foray*

• ensei suru 遠征する *to make an expedition, to go on a foray*

② (*exploratory*)*expedition*

• ensei suru 遠征する *to make an expedition*

¶Ikkō wa raigetsu Eberesuto e ensei shimasu.

一行は来月エベレストへ遠征します。

The party will make an expedition to

Mt. Everest next month.

③ *tour* 《by a sports team》
- ensei suru 遠征する *to make a tour, to go on the road*
- ensei-chīmu 遠征チーム *visiting team*
- ensei-gun 遠征軍 *expeditionary force; visiting team*

ensen 沿線 *the area along* 《a transportation route》
¶Watashi-tachi no gakkō wa tetsudō no ensen ni arimasu.
私たちの学校は鉄道の沿線にあります。
Our school is in the area along the railroad.

enshi 遠視 *far-sightedness,* <*UK*>*long-sightedness* 《i.e., a vision defect》[⇔**kinshi** 近視]
- enshi no hito 遠視の *far-sighted person,* <*UK*>*long-sighted person*

enshū 円周 *circumference*
- enshū-ritsu 円周率 *pi* 《π》

enshutsu 演出 *production, staging* 《of a play, movie, etc.》
- enshutsu suru 演出する *to produce, to stage, to put on*
¶Tsugi no geki wa Asano-san ga enshutsu shimasu.
次の劇は浅野さんが演出します。
Mr. Asano will stage the next play.
- enshutsu-ka 演出家 *production director*

énso 塩素 *chlorine*

ensō 演奏 《*musical instrument*》*performance*
- ensō suru 演奏する *to perform, to play*
¶Ano pianisuto no ensō wa subarashii desu.
あのピアニストの演奏はすばらしいです。
That pianist's performances are wonderful.
¶Noguchi-san wa piano de sonata o ensō shimashita.
野口さんはピアノでソナタを演奏しました。
Ms. Noguchi played a sonata on the piano.
- ensō-kai 演奏会 *concert, recital*
- ensō-sha 演奏者 *performer*

ensoku 遠足 *one-day outing,*
(school)field trip
¶Boku-tachi wa Kamakura e ensoku ni ikimashita.
僕たちは鎌倉へ遠足に行きました。
We went to Kamakura on a field trip.

éntorī エントリー *entry* (*in a race*)
- entorī suru エントリーする *to enter*
¶Sono marason ni wa nanajū-nin ga entorī shita.
そのマラソンには70人がエントリーした。
Seventy people entered that marathon.

entotsu 煙突 *chimney, smokestack*

énzeru エンゼル *angel* [→**tenshi** 天使]

enzetsu 演説 *speech, address*
¶Seiji-ka wa jōzu na enzetsu o shimashita.
政治家は上手な演説をしました。
The politician made a good speech.
- enzetsu suru 演説する *to make a speech, to deliver an address*

épisōdo エピソード ① *episode, digression in a longer story*
② *anecdote*

Ēpurirufūru エープリルフール ① *April Fools' Day*
② *an April fool* [→**Shi**–**gatsu**–**baka** 四月馬鹿 (s.v. **shi** 四)]

épuron エプロン *apron* [→**maekake** 前掛け]

érā エラー *error*
- erā o suru エラーをする *to make an error*
¶Ano shōto wa yoku erā o suru ne.
あのショートはよくエラーをするね。
That shortstop often makes errors, doesn't he.

erábu 選ぶ *to choose, to select; to elect*
¶Mari-san wa kono jisho o erabimashita.
真理さんはこの辞書を選びました。
Mari chose this dictionary.
¶Hoshii hon o erabinasai.
欲しい本を選びなさい。
Select the book you want.
¶Boku-tachi wa Tanaka-kun o iin-chō ni eranda yo.
僕たちは田中君を委員長に選んだよ。
We elected Tanaka committee

chairperson.

erái 偉い ① *great, eminent* 《describing a person or a person's actions》

¶Kyūrī-fujin wa erai gakusha deshita.

キュリー夫人は偉い学者でした。

Madam Curie was a great scholar.

② *important, high-ranking*

¶Tsuda-san wa erai yakunin desu.

津田さんは偉い役人です。

Mr. Tsuda is a high-ranking official.

③ *terrible, awful* [→**hidoi** ひどい]

¶Erai ame deshita ne.

偉い雨でしたね。

It was terrible rain, wasn't it.

erebḗtā エレベーター 《*US*》*elevator*, 《*UK*》*lift*

¶Erebētā de jūni-kai made agarimashita.

エレベーターで12階まで上がりました。

I went up to the 12th floor on the elevator.

éreganto エレガント 〜**na** 〜な *elegant* [→**yūga na** 優雅な]

¶Konya wa ereganto na doresu o kimasu.

今夜はエレガントなドレスを着ます。

Tonight I will wear an elegant dress.

erekutoroníkusu エレクトロニクス *electronics*

erí 襟 *collar* 《on an article of clothing》

eríto エリート *the elite; member of the elite*

¶Kon'yaku-sha wa ginkō ni tsutomeru erīto desu.

婚約者は銀行に勤めるエリートです。

Her fiance is a member of the elite who work in banking.

• erīto-ishiki エリート意識 *elitist attitude*

ḗru エール *a cheer* 《by spectators at a sporting event》

• ēru o kawasu エールを交す *to exchange cheers*

éru 得る *to get, to obtain*

¶Hayashi-san wa benron-taikai de ittō-shō o emashita.

林さんは弁論大会で1等賞を得ました。

Mr. Hayashi got first prize in the oratory contest.

esá 餌 ① (*animal*)*food, feed*

¶Kono tori no esa wa nan desu ka.

この鳥のえさは何ですか。

What does this bird eat?

• A ni esa o yaru Aにえさをやる *to feed A*

¶Dobutsu ni esa o yaranai de kudasai.

動物にえさをやらないでください。

Please don't feed the animals.

② *bait*

éshaku 会釈 *greeting nod*

• eshaku suru 会釈する *to nod in greeting*

éssē エッセー *essay*

ḗsu エース ① *ace* (*player*)

¶Nakahara-kun wa chīmu no ēsu desu.

中原君はチームのエースです。

Nakahara is the ace of the team.

② *ace* ((playing card))

esuefu SF 《Generally not written out in katakana.》 *science fiction*

esukarḗtā エスカレーター *escalator*

esukarḗto エスカレート 〜**suru** 〜する *to escalate* 《intransitive》

Esukímō エスキモー *Eskimo*

Esuperánto エスペラント *Esperanto*

étchi エッチ 〜**na** 〜な *obscene, lewd*

ḗto ええと *uh, um, er* 《a pause filler》 [→**anō** あのう]

¶"Pātī ni wa nan-nin kimasu ka." "Ēto, hachi-nin desu."

「パーティーには何人来ますか」「ええと，8人です」

"How many people will come to the party?" "Um, eight."

etsuran 閲覧 *perusal, reading*

• etsuran suru 閲覧する *to read, to peruse*

• etsuran-shitsu 閲覧室 *reading room*

F

fainpurḗ ファインプレー *fine play* 《in sports》

fáiru ファイル (*document*)*file*

- fairu suru ファイルする *to file, to put on file*

fáito ファイト *fight, fighting spirit* [→ **tōshi** 闘志]

fákkusu ファックス [☞**fakushimiri** ファクシミリ]

fakushímiri ファクシミリ *facsimile, fax*

fán ファン *fan, enthusiast*
- fan-kurabu ファンクラブ *fan club*
- fan-retā ファンレター *fan letter*
- eiga-fan 映画ファン *movie fan*
- yakyū-fan 野球ファン *baseball fan*

fandḗshon ファンデーション ① *foundation* ((make-up))
　② *foundation garment*

fanfāre ファンファーレ *(musical)fanfare*

fántajī ファンタジー *fantasy*

fásshon ファッション ① *fashion, style, vogue* [→**ryūkō** 流行①]
　② *clothing fashion*
- fasshon-moderu ファッションモデル *fashion model*
- fasshon-shō ファッションショー *fashion show*

fásunā ファスナー *zipper* [→**jippā** ジッパー]

fāsuto ファースト ① *first base* [→**ichirui** 一塁]
　② *first baseman* [→**ichirui-shu** 一塁手 (s.v. **ichirui** 一塁)]

fáuru ファウル ① *foul (ball)* [⇔**fea** フェア②]
- fauru o utsu ファウルを打つ *to hit a foul*
　② *foul, rule violation* [→**hansoku** 反則]
- fauru-bōru ファウルボール [☞**fauru** ファウル① (above)]
- fauru-guraundo ファウルグラウンド *foul ground, foul territory*

féa フェア ① ～**na** ～な *fair, equitable* [→**kōsei na** 公正な]
　② *fair ball* [⇔**fauru** ファウル①]
- fea-bōru フェアボール [☞**fea** フェア② (above)]
- fea-purē フェアプレー *fair play*

fénshingu フェンシング *fencing* ((sport))

fénsu フェンス *fence*

férī フェリー *ferry (-boat)*

ferībōto フェリーボート [☞**ferī** フェリー]

feruto フェルト *felt*

fésutibaru フェスティバル *festival*

fībā フィーバー *fever, wild enthusiasm* [→**nekkyō** 熱狂]
- fībā suru フィーバーする *to become fevered*

fígyua フィギュア [☞**figyuasukēto** フィギュアスケート]

figyuasukḗto フィギュアスケート *figure skating*

fíkushon フィクション *fiction* [⇔**nonfikushon** ノンフィクション]

fināre フィナーレ *finale*

fīrudo フィールド *the field* ≪where field events are held in track and field≫
- fīrudo-kyōgi フィールド競技 *field events*

fírumu フィルム *(photographic)film*
　¶Firumu ga san-bon hitsuyō desu.
　フィルムが3本必要です。
　Three rolls of film are necessary.
- karā-firumu カラーフィルム *color film*

fírutā フィルター *filter*
- firutā-tsuki-tabako フィルターつきたばこ *filter-tipped cigarette*

fíto フィート *foot* ≪unit of measure≫
- -fīto -フィート≪counter for feet; see Appendix 2≫

foabōru フォアボール *base on balls, walk* [→**shikyū** 四球]

fóku フォーク *fork* ((eating utensil))
- fōku-bōru フォークボール *fork ball*

fōkudánsu フォークダンス *folk dance*

fōkusóngu フォークソング ① *(traditional)folk song* [→**min'yō** 民謡]
　② *American-style popular folk song*

fōmu フォーム *(athletic)form*
　¶Kurokawa-san no fōmu wa ii.
　黒川さんのフォームはいい。
　Ms. Kurokawa's form is good.

fú 府 *prefecture* ≪Used to refer only to Osaka and Kyoto Prefectures.≫

- Kyōto—fu 京都府 *Kyoto Prefecture*
- Ōsaka-fu 大阪府 *Osaka Prefecture*

fū 風 ① *way, manner*
¶Konna fū ni kaite kudasai.
こんなふうに書いてください。
Please write it in this way.

② *appearance, air, manner*
- darashinai fū o suru だらしない風をする
to take on a sloppy appearance

-fū -風 〜**no**/**na** 〜の/な《Added to noun bases.》① *-style*
¶Hosokawa-san wa Chūgoku-fū no ie ni sunde imasu.
細川さんは中国風の家に住んでいます。
Mr. Hosokawa lives in a Chinese-style house.

② *-like, having the air of, having the look of*
¶Otōsan wa geijutsu-ka-fū deshita.
お父さんは芸術家風でした。
Her father looked like an artist.

fu- 不 *un-, non-; bad*《Added to noun and adjectival noun bases.》
- fu-meiryō na 不明瞭な *unclear* [⇔ **meiryō na** 明瞭な]
- fun-ninki 不人気 *unpopularity* [⇔ **ninki** 人気]
- fu-seiseki 不成績 *bad results, poor showing*

fuan 不安 *unease, anxiety*
¶Gakusei wa shiken no kekka ni fuan o kanjite ita.
学生は試験の結果に不安を感じていた。
The student was feeling anxious about his examination results.
- fuan na 不安な *uneasy, anxious*

fúben 不便 *inconvenience*
- fuben o shinobu 不便を忍ぶ *to put up with an inconvenience*
- fuben na 不便な *inconvenient* [⇔**benri na** 便利な]
¶Jitensha no nai seikatsu wa totemo fuben desu.
自転車のない生活はとても不便です。
Life without a bicycle is very inconvenient.
¶Uchi wa kaimono ni fuben na

tokoro ni arimasu.
うちは買い物に不便な所にあります。
My house is in an inconvenient place for shopping.

fúbo 父母 *father and mother, parents*
[→**ryōshin** 両親]

fúbuki 吹雪 *snowstorm*

fuchí 縁 *edge, rim*
¶Shōnen wa gake no fuchi ni suwatte imasu.
少年はがけの縁に座っています。
The boy is sitting on the edge of the cliff.

fuchūi 不注意 *carelessness, inattention*
[⇔**chūi** 注意②]
¶Sono jiko wa unten-shu no fuchūi kara okotta.
その事故は運転手の不注意から起こった。
That accident occurred because of the driver's carelessness.
- fuchūi na 不注意な *careless, heedless*
[⇔**chūi-bukai** 注意深い (s.v. **chūi** 注意)]
¶Fuchūi na hatsugen o shinai yō ni shinasai
不注意な発言をしないようにしなさい。
Take care not to make careless statements.

fuda 札 *card, tag, label*
- azukari-fuda 預かり札 *claim check*
- na-fuda 名札 *name tag; nameplate*
- ne-fuda 値札 *price tag*
- ni-fuda 荷札 *baggage label*
- shō-fuda 正札 *price tag*

fúdan 普段 (〜**ni** 〜に) *usually, ordinarily* [→**futsū** 普通]
¶Kyō wa fudan yori osoku uchi o demashita.
きょうはふだんより遅くうちを出ました。
Today I left home later than usual.
- fudan no ふだんの *usual, common, everyday*

fude 筆 *writing brush; painting brush* 《for pictures》
- fude-bako 筆箱 *pencil box*
- fude-ire 筆入れ *pencil case*

fúdo フード *hood* 《on an article of clothing》

fudṓsan 不動産 *real estate*

fue 笛 *flute, pipes, woodwind instrument; whistle*

fuéru 増える *to increase* «intransitive» [⇔**heru** 減る]
¶Kōtsū-jiko no kazu mo daibu fuemashita.
交通事故の数もだいぶ増えました。
The number of traffic accidents also increased considerably.
¶Machi no jinkō wa kore kara kyū ni fueru deshō.
町の人口はこれから急に増えるでしょう。
The population of the town will probably increase rapidly from now on.
¶Shimano-san wa taijū ga nijuk-kiro fueta yo.
島野さんは体重が20キロ増えたよ。
Mr. Shimano's gained 20 kilograms!
«Literally: As for Mr. Shimano, weight increased 20 kilograms.»

fúfu 夫婦 *married couple, husband and wife* [→**fusai** 夫妻]
¶Ano fūfu wa shiawase-sō desu ne.
あの夫婦は幸せそうですね。
That husband and wife look happy, don't they.
• fūfu-genka 夫婦喧嘩 *quarrel between husband and wife*
• shinkon-fūfu 新婚夫婦 *newly-married couple*

fugṓkaku 不合格 *failure* «to meet a standard or pass a test» [⇔**gōkaku** 合格]
¶Musuko no fugōkaku wa machigai-nai desu.
息子の不合格はまちがいないです。
My son's failure is certain.
• fugōkaku no 不合格の *unqualified, failed, rejected*
• fugōkaku ni naru 不合格になる *to fail, to be rejected*

fúgu 河豚 *globefish, blowfish* «This fish is considered a great delicacy in Japan, but proper preparation requires special training because its internal organs contain a deadly poison.»

fuhei 不平 *dissatisfaction, discontent*

[→**fuman** 不満]
• fuhei o iu 不平を言う *to express dissatisfaction, to complain*
¶Chichi wa yoku tabemono no fuhei o iimasu.
父はよく食べ物の不平を言います。
My father often complains about the food.

fui 不意 ～**no** ～の *unexpected* [→**omoigakenai** 思い掛けない]; *sudden* [→**totsuzen no** 突然の]

fuji 藤 *wisteria*

fujin 夫人 *wife*
• -fujin 夫人 *Mrs.* «Added to a family name or a given name a title.»

fujin 婦人 *woman, lady*
• fujin-fuku 婦人服 *ladies' wear*
• fujin-keikan 婦人警官 *policewoman*

fújiyū 不自由 *inconvenience* [→**fuben** 不便]; *difficulty caused by the lack of something necessary*
• fujiyū na 不自由な *inconvenient; difficult*
• fujiyū suru 不自由する *to be inconvenienced, to have difficulty, to be in need*
¶Masami-chan wa kozukai ni fujiyū shite imasu.
正美ちゃんは小遣いに不自由しています。
Masami is in need of more pocket money.

fuka 鱶 *shark* [→**same** 鮫]

fukái 不快 ～**na** ～な [[→**fuyukai na** 不愉快な]] ① *unpleasant, distasteful* ② *displeased*

fukái 深い *deep* [⇔**asai** 浅い]
¶Kono ike wa dono gurai fukai desu ka.
この池はどのぐらい深いですか。
About how deep is this pond?
¶Ueki-ya wa ana o fukaku hotte imasu.
植木屋は穴を深く掘っています。
The gardener is digging the hole deep.
¶Shichō wa sono mondai o fukaku kangaete imasu.
市長はその問題を深く考えています。
The mayor is thinking deeply about that problem.
• fukai umi 深い海 *deep sea*

- fukai kangae 深い考え *deep thought*
- fukai kiri 深い霧 *dense fog*
- fukai nemuri 深い眠り *deep sleep*

fukánō 不可能 〜**na** 〜な *impossible* [⇔**kanō na** 可能な]

¶Hitori de soko ni iku no wa fukanō desu.

一人でそこに行くのは不可能です。

It is impossible to go there alone.

fukása 深さ *depth*

¶Kono ido no fukasa wa nan-mētoru desu ka.

この井戸の深さは何メートルですか。

How many meters deep is this well?

《*Literally: The depth of this well is how many meters?*》

fuke ふけ *dandruff*

fūkei 風景 *scenery, landscape* [→**keshiki** 景色]; *view, vista* [→**nagame** 眺め]

- fūkei-ga 風景画 *landscape picture*

fukéiki 不景気 (*economic*)*depression, bad times, hard times* [→**fukyō** 不況]

¶Kotoshi wa fukeiki desu.

今年は不景気です。

This year times are bad.

fukéru 更ける *to grow late, to become late* 《The subject is a night or a season.》

- yo ga fukeru 夜が更ける *to become late at night*
- aki ga fukeru 秋が更ける *to become late in autumn*

fukéru 老ける *to grow old*

¶Haha wa mō fukete shimaimashita.

母はもう老けてしまいました。

My mother has already grown old.

fuketsu 不潔 〜**na** 〜な *unclean, dirty* [→**kitanai** 汚い①] [⇔**seiketsu na** 清潔な]

fukidásu 吹き出す／噴き出す ① *to begin to blow* 《The subject is a wind.》

¶Kita no kaze ga fukidashimashita.

北の風が吹き出しました。

A north wind began to blow.

② *to burst into laughter*

¶Watashi-tachi wa sono hanashi o kiite, fukidashita yo.

私たちはその話を聞いて、吹き出したよ。

We heard that story and suddenly burst out laughing!

③ *to spurt out, to spew out, to spout out*

¶Kizuguchi kara chi ga fukidashite imasu.

傷口から血が噴き出しています。

Blood is spurting out from the wound.

fukígen 不機嫌 〜**na** 〜な *in a bad mood, grouchy, displeased*

¶Kesa sensei wa fukigen desu ne.

けさ先生は不機嫌ですね。

The teacher is in a bad mood this morning, isn't he.

fukikésu 吹き消す *to blow out, to extinguish by blowing*

- rōsoku o fukikesu ろうそくを吹き消す *to blow out a candle*

fukín 付近 *neighborhood, vicinity* [→**kinjo** 近所]

¶Kono fukin ni wa shōten ga ōi desu.

この付近には商店が多いです。

There are many stores in this neighborhood.

fukín 布巾 *kitchen towel, dish towel*

fukísoku 不規則 〜**na** 〜な *irregular* [⇔**kisoku-teki na** 規則的な (s.v. **kisoku** 規則)]

fukitobásu 吹き飛ばす *to blow off* 《transitive》《The subject is typically a wind.》

¶Yane o fukitobasu hodo tsuyoi kaze desu.

屋根を吹き飛ばすほど強い風です。

It's a wind strong enough to blow off roofs.

fukitsu 不吉 〜**na** 〜な *inauspicious, ominous*

fukkatsu 復活 *revival, restoration, resurrection*

- fukkatsu suru 復活する *to be revived, to be restored, to be resurrected*
- Fukkatsu-sai 復活祭 *Easter*

fukṓ 不幸 [[⇔**kōfuku** 幸福]] *unhappiness; misfortune*

- fukō na 不幸な *unhappy; unfortunate*

¶Ano hito wa fukō na jinsei o okurimashita.

あの人は不幸な人生を送りました。

That person lived an unhappy life.

• fukō ni mo 不幸にも *unfortunately*

fukṓhei 不公平 *unfairness, partiality* [⇔**kōhei** 公平]

• fukōhei na 不公平な *unfair, partial, inequitable*

¶Ryūgaku-sei wa fukōhei na atsukai o ukemashita.

留学生は不公平な扱いを受けました。

The foreign student received unfair treatment.

¶Kono wake-kata wa watashi ni totte fukōhei desu.

この分け方は私にとって不公平です。

This way of dividing it is unfair for me.

fukú 服 *clothes, clothing*

fukú 吹く ① *to blow* 《intransitive》《The subject is a wind.》

¶Kaze ga hageshiku fuite imasu.

風がはげしく吹いています。

The wind is blowing hard.

② *to blow on*

¶Atsui ocha o fuite samashita.

熱いお茶を吹いてさました。

I blew on the hot tea and cooled it down.

③ *to play* 《a wind instrument》; *to play* 《music on a wind instrument》

¶Nozaki-san wa toranpetto o fukimasu.

野崎さんはトランペットを吹きます。

Mr. Nozaki plays the trumpet.

④ *to spout out, to spew out* 《intransitive》[→**fukidasu** 吹き出す③]

⑤ *to spout out, to spew out* 《transitive》

• kujira ga shio o fuku 鯨が潮を吹く *a whale spouts*

fuku 拭く *to wipe* [→**nuguu** 拭う]

¶Mado o kirei ni fukinasai.

窓をきれいにふきなさい。

Wipe the windows clean.

¶Watashi wa sara o fuite imasu.

私は皿をふいています。

I am wiping the dishes.

fuku- 副- *vice-, assistant-* 《Added to noun bases.》

• fuku-daitōryō 副大統領 *vice-president* 《of a country》

• fuku-kaichō 副会長 *vice-chairperson*

• fuku-kōchō 副校長 *vice-principal*

• fuku-shachō 副社長 *vice-president* 《of a company》

• fuku-shihai-nin 副支配人 *assistant manager*

fukugōgo 複合語 *compound word*

fukujū 服従 *obedience, submission* [⇔**hankō** 反抗]

• fukujū suru 服従する *to submit, to give obedience*

fukuméru 含める *to add, to put in, to include* [⇔**nozoku** 除く]

• A o fukumete Aを含めて *including A*

¶Watashi o fukumete go-nin ga kaigi ni demasu.

私を含めて5人が会議に出ます。

Including me, five people will attend the meeting.

fukúmu 含む *to contain, to include*

¶Orenji wa bitamin-shī o ōku fukunde iru.

オレンジはビタミンCを多く含んでいる。

Oranges contain a lot of vitamin C.

¶Kono nedan wa shōhi-zei o fukunde imasu.

この値段は消費税を含んでいます。

This price includes consumption tax.

fukurahagi 腫ら脛 *calf* 《of the leg》

fukuramasu 膨らます *to make swell, to inflate*

¶Bīchi-bōru o fukuramashimashita.

ビーチボールを膨らましました。

I inflated the beach ball.

fukuramu 膨らむ *to swell, to bulge, to become inflated*

¶Ho ga kaze de fukurande imasu.

帆が風で膨らんでいます。

The sails are swelling in the wind.

fukureru 膨れる ① *to swell, to expand*

• pan ga fukureru パンが膨れる *bread rises*

② 【COL.】 *to get sulky*

fukuró 袋 *bag*

- kaimono-bukuro 買い物袋 *shopping bag*
- kami-bukuro 紙袋 *paper bag*

fukurō 梟 *owl*

fukusánbutsu 副産物 *by-product*

fukusáyō 副作用 *side-effect, harmful after-effect*

fukusei 複製 ① *replica, reproduction* ② *making a replica, reproducing*
- fukusei suru 複製する *to make a replica of, to reproduce*

fukusha 複写 ① *copy, duplicate, reproduction* [→**kopī** コピー]
② *copying, duplicating, reproducing*
- fukusha suru 複写する *to copy, to duplicate, to reproduce*

fukusha-ki 複写機 *copying machine, duplicator*

fukushi 副詞 *adverb*

fukúshi 福祉 *welfare, well-being*
- shakai-fukushi 社会福祉 *social welfare*

fukushū 復習 *review of what one has learned* [⇔**yoshū** 予習]
- fukushū suru 復習する *to review*
¶Mō kyō no jugyō o fukushū shimashita.
もうきょうの授業を復習しました。
I have already reviewed today's classes.
¶Sā, rok-ka o fukushū shimashō.
さあ、6課を復習しましょう。
Now, let's review Lesson 6.

fukushū 復讐 *revenge*
- fukushū suru 復しゅうする *to take revenge*
¶Taishō wa teki ni fukushū shimashita.
大将は敵に復しゅうしました。
The general took revenge on the enemy.

fukusō 服装 *dress, attire* [→**minari** 身なり]
¶Wakatsuki-san wa fukusō ni kamawanai hito desu.
若月さんは服装に構わない人です。
Ms. Wakatsuki is a person who doesn't care about the way she dresses.
¶Shachō wa itsu-mo kichin to shita fukusō desu.
社長はいつもきちんとした服装です。
The company president always wears

neat clothes. 《Literally: *As for the company president, it's always neat attire.*》

fukusū 複数 *the plural* [⇔**tansū** 単数]

fukutsū 腹痛 *stomachache*
¶Hidoi fukutsū ga shimasu.
ひどい腹痛がします。
I have a terrible stomachache.

fukuzatsu 複雑 ～**na** ～な *complicated, complex* [⇔**tanjun na** 単純な①]
¶Kono fukuzatsu na kikai no atsukai-kata ga wakarimasu ka.
この複雑な機械の扱い方がわかりますか。
Do you know how to handle this complicated machine?

fukyō 不況 (*economic*)*depression,* (*economic*)*slump* [→**fukeiki** 不景気]
- fukyō no 不況の *depressed, slumping*

fukyū 普及 *spread, diffusion*
- chishiki no fukyū 知識の普及 *the spread of knowledge*
- fukyū suru 普及する *to spread, to become more widespread*
¶Konpyūtā wa saikin hiroku fukyū shimashita.
コンピューターは最近広く普及しました。
Computers have recently spread widely.

fuman 不満 *dissatisfaction, discontent* [→**fuhei** 不平]
- fuman no 不満の *dissatisfied, displeased*
¶Seito-tachi no kōi ni fuman desu.
生徒たちの行為に不満です。
I am dissatisfied with the students' conduct.

fumikiri 踏切 *crossing* 《where a road crosses a railroad track》

fuminshō 不眠症 *insomnia*

fumotó 麓 *foot* 《of a mountain》 [⇔**chōjō** 頂上]
¶Yama no fumoto ni gorufu-jō ga arimasu.
山のふもとにゴルフ場があります。
There is a golf course at the foot of the mountain.

fumu 踏む *to step on*
¶Neko no ashi o funda yo.
猫の足を踏んだよ。

You stepped on the cat's paw!

-fun 一分 ① «counter for minutes past the hour when telling time; see Appendix 2»

¶Yumi-san wa jūni-ji yonjup-pun ni ie o demasu.

由美さんは12時40分に家を出ます。

Yumi leaves home at 12:40.

② «counter for minutes; see Appendix 2»

¶Gakkō wa eki kara aruite jūgo-fun desu.

学校は駅から歩いて15分です。

The school is fifteen minutes from the station on foot.

fún 糞 *animal feces, manure*

funabin 船便 *sea mail*

funayoi 船酔い *seasickness*

fúnbetsu 分別 *discretion, good judgment, good sense*

¶Katayama-san no kōdō wa funbetsu ga kakete imasu.

片山さんの行動は分別が欠けています。

Mr. Katayama's actions are lacking in discretion.

• funbetsu no aru hito 分別のある人 *person of good judgment, sensible person*

fúne 船 *boat, ship*

¶Takeyama-san wa fune de Shikoku ni ikimashita.

竹山さんは船で四国に行きました。

Mr. Takeyama went to Shikoku by ship.

¶Watashi-tachi wa Yokohama-yuki no fune ni norimashita.

私たちは横浜行きの船に乗りました。

We boarded a ship for Yokohama.

fun'íki 雰囲気 *atmosphere, ambience*

¶Kono kaigō ni wa yūkō-teki na fun'iki ga arimasu.

この会合には友好的な雰囲気があります。

There is a friendly atmosphere at this meeting.

funka 噴火 *(volcanic)eruption*

• funka suru 噴火する *to erupt*

• funka-kō 噴火口 *(volcanic)crater*

funmatsu 粉末 *powder, dust* [→**kona** 粉①]

funsō 紛争 *dispute, conflict* [→**arasoi** 争い]

funsui 噴水 ① *spouting water, fountain*

② *fountain* «device for producing spouting water»

fúrafura ふらふら（〜**to** 〜**と**）① *dizzily; totteringly, unsteadily*

• furafura suru ふらふらする *to feel dizzy, feel faint; to be unsteady, to totter*

¶Kyō wa netsu de furafura shite imasu.

きょうは熱でふらふらしています。

Today I feel dizzy with a fever.

② *aimlessly, for no particular purpose, without conscious thought*

• furafura suru ふらふらする *to waver, to be unable to decide what to do*

¶Musuko wa daigaku o demashita ga, mada furafura shite hataraite imasen.

息子は大学を出ましたが、まだふらふらして働いていません。

My son graduated from college, but still unable to decide what to do, he's not working.

furai フライ *fly (ball)* «in baseball»

• furai o utsu フライを打つ *to hit a fly*

furai フライ *deep-frying*

• furai ni suru フライにする *to deep-fry*

• ebi-furai 海老フライ *deep-fried shrimp*

furaipan フライパン *frying pan*

furásshu フラッシュ *(photographic)flash*

• furasshu o taku フラッシュをたく *to use a flash*

furasuko フラスコ *flask* «used in chemistry, etc.»

furátto フラット *(musical)flat* [⇔**shāpu** シャープ]

-furatto ーフラット *flat* «Added to numbers denoting short time periods.»

¶Yoshida-kun wa hyaku-mētoru o jūichi-byō-furatto de hashiru koto ga dekimasu.

吉田君は100メートルを11秒フラットで走ることができます。

Yoshida can run the 100 meters in 11 seconds flat!

furēmu フレーム ① *frame, enclosing edge* [→**waku** 枠]

- megane no furēmu 眼鏡のフレーム *eye-glasses frames*
  ② *frame, framework, supporting part of a structure*
- jitensha no furēmu 自転車のフレーム *bicycle frame*

furéndo フレンド *friend* [→**tomodachi** 友達]

fureru 触れる ① *to bring (gently) into contact*
- A ni te o fureru Aに手を触れる *to touch A with one's hand*
  ¶Kore ni te o furenai de kudasai.
  これに手を触れないでください。
  Please do not touch this.
  ② *to come (gently) into contact*
  ¶Kore wa kūki ni fureru to sugu kataku narimasu.
  これは空気に触れるとすぐ固くなります。
  This gets hard as soon as it comes into contact with the air.
- me ni fureru 目に触れる *to catch one's eye*
- te de A ni fureru 手でAに触れる *to touch A with one's hand*
  ③ *to come into conflict, to infringe*
- hōritsu ni fureru 法律に触れる *to come into conflict with the law*
  ④ *to touch, to refer*
  ¶Sensei wa sono mondai ni fureru deshō.
  先生はその問題に触れるでしょう。
  The teacher will probably touch on that problem.

furésshu フレッシュ 〜na 〜な *fresh* [→**shinsen na** 新鮮な]

fúri 不利 *disadvantage*
- furi na 不利な *disadvantageous, unfavorable, adverse* [⇔**yūri na** 有利な]
  ¶Jōkyō wa yotō ni furi desu.
  状況は与党に不利です。
  The circumstances are unfavorable to the ruling party.

furí 振り *pretense, false show*
- furi o suru 振りをする *to pretend, to make a pretense*
  ¶Ikeda-san wa tokidoki byōki no furi o shimasu.

池田さんは時々病気のふりをします。
Ms. Ikeda sometimes pretends to be sick.
¶Musuko wa benkyō shite iru furi o shite imasu.
息子は勉強している振りをしています。
My son is pretending to be studying.

furī フリー 〜na／no 〜な／の ① *free, unconstrained* [→**jiyū na** 自由な]
② *free-lance*
- furī no jānarisuto フリーのジャーナリスト *free-lance journalist*
  ③ *free (of charge)* [→**muryō no** 無料の]
- furī-pasu フリーパス *free pass ((ticket))*
- furī-surō フリースロー *free throw*

furigána 振り仮名 *small kana printed alongside or above a Chinese character to show its pronunciation*

furikáeru 振り返る{5} *to look back*
¶Shinobu wa furikaette, sayonara o iimashita.
忍は振り返って、さよならを言いました。
Shinobu looked back and said good-by.

furiko 振り子 *pendulum*

furimúku 振り向く *to look back at*
¶Haha wa watashi no hō o furimuite hohoemimashita.
母は私の方を振り向いてほほえみました。
My mother looked back at me and smiled.

fūrin 風鈴 *wind chime*

fúriru フリル *frill*

furīsutáiru フリースタイル *freestyle*

furízā フリーザー *freezer*

furó 風呂 *bath*
¶Furo ga wakimashita.
ふろが沸きました。
The bath has heated up.
¶Mainichi o-furo ni hairimasu.
毎日おふろに入ります。
I take a bath every day.
- furo-ba 風呂場 *bathroom* 《Toilets and the bathtubs are traditionally in separate rooms in Japan. This word refers to a room for taking a bath.》 [→**yokushitsu** 浴室]

• furo-oke 風呂槽 *bathtub* [→**yokusō** 浴槽]

• furo-ya 風呂屋 *public bathhouse* [→ **sentō** 銭湯]

furóa フロア *floor* 《i.e., bottom surface of a room》[→**yuka** 床]

furoku 付録 ① *supplement* 《in a magazine, newspaper, etc.》

② *appendix* 《in a book》

furonto フロント ① *front desk, reception desk*

② *front office* 《of a professional sports team》

furontogárasu フロントガラス <*US*>*windshield*, <*UK*>*windscreen*

furoshiki 風呂敷 *wrapping cloth* 《a square piece of cloth used to wrap items for easy carrying》

• furoshiki ni tsutsumu ふろしきに包む *to wrap in a wrapping cloth*

• furoshiki-zutsumi 風呂敷包み *bundle in a wrapping cloth*

fúru 降る *to fall* 《The subject must be a form of precipitation.》

¶Ashita wa ame ga furu deshō.
あしたは雨が降るでしょう。
It will probably rain tomorrow.

¶Yuki ga hageshiku futte imasu.
雪がはげしく降っています。
It is snowing hard.

furu 振る *to shake, to wave, to swing, to wag*

¶Keiko-chan wa watashi ni te o futte imasu.
恵子ちゃんは私に手を振っています。
Keiko is waving her hand to me.

¶Inu wa shippo o furimashita.
犬はしっぽを振りました。
The dog wagged its tail.

• batto o furu バットを振る *to swing a bat*

• kubi o yoko ni furu 首を横に振る *to shake one's head*

furueru 震える *to tremble, to quiver*

¶Shōjo wa samusa de furuemashita.
少女は寒さで震えました。
The girl trembled from the cold.

¶Jushō-sha no koe wa sukoshi furuete imashita.
受賞者の声は少し震えていました。
The prize winner's voice was trembling a little.

furuhon 古本 *used book, secondhand book*

• furuhon-ya 古本屋 *used-book store; used-book dealer*

furúi 古い *old, not new* [⇔**atarashii** 新しい]

¶Kono tera wa hijō ni furui desu.
この寺は非常に古いです。
This temple is very old.

¶Yōko-san wa furui tomodachi desu.
洋子さんは古い友達です。
Yoko is an old friend.

¶Ojīsan wa furui kitte o atsumete imasu.
おじいさんは古い切手を集めています。
Grandfather collects old stamps.

furukusái 古臭い *old-fashioned, outmoded*

furumai 振る舞い *behavior, conduct*

furumáu 振る舞う *to behave, to conduct oneself*

¶Sono shōnen wa gyōgi-yoku furumaimashita.
その少年は行儀よくふるまいました。
That boy behaved politely.

furúsato 古里 *place where one was born and raised, hometown* [→**kokyō** 故郷]

¶Hayashi-san no furusato wa Akita desu.
林さんのふるさとは秋田です。
Ms. Hayashi's hometown is Akita.

furusupído フルスピード *full speed*

• furusupído de フルスピードで *at full speed*

furúto フルート *flute*

• furūto-sōsha フルート奏者 *flutist*

furútsu フルーツ *fruit* [→**kudamono** 果物]

• furūtsu-kēki フルーツケーキ *fruit cake*

• furūtsu-pārā フルーツパーラー *cafe specializing in cake, drinks, etc., garnished with fruit*

furuu 振るう ① *to wield, to put to use, to exercise, to exhibit* [→**hakki suru**

発揮する]

• ude o furuu 腕をふるう *to exhibit one's ability*

• bōryoku o furuu 暴力をふるう *to use violence*

② *to prosper, to thrive, to do well*

¶ Konban wa ano tōshu wa zenzen furuwanakatta ne.

今晩はあの投手は全然ふるわなかったね。

Tonight that pitcher didn't do well at all, did he.

furyō 不良 ① *delinquency, immorality*

• furyō no 不良の *delinquent, immoral, bad*

② *a delinquent, an undesirable*

③ *poor quality, inferiority, poor condition*

• furyō no 不良の *poor, low-quality, inferior*

• furyō-hin 不良品 *inferior article, defective item*

• furyō-shōjo 不良少女 *delinquent girl*

• furyō-shōnen 不良少年 *delinquent boy*

fusá 房 ① *tassel, tuft*

② *cluster, bunch* 《*of fruit or flowers hanging from a branch*》

• budō no fusa ぶどうの房 *a bunch of grapes*

• hito-fusa 一房 *one tuft; one bunch*

fusagaru 塞がる ① *to become blocked, to become clogged*

¶ Dōro wa yuki de fusagatte imashita.

道路は雪でふさがっていました。

The road was blocked with snow.

② *to become occupied, to become taken, to become in use*

¶ Kono seki wa fusagatte imasu ka.

この席はふさがっていますか。

Is this seat occupied?

fusagu 塞ぐ *to stop up, to block*

¶ Kono ana o fusaide kudasai.

この穴をふさいでください。

Please stop up this hole.

¶ Torakku ga semai michi o fusaide imashita.

トラックが狭い道をふさいでいました。

A truck was blocking the narrow road.

fusái 夫妻 *husband and wife* [→**fūfu** 夫婦]

• -fusai －夫妻 *Mr. and Mrs.* 《*Added to a surname as a title.*》

¶ Pātī wa Suzuki-fusai no otaku de arimasu.

パーティーは鈴木夫妻のお宅であります。

The party will be at Mr. and Mrs. Suzuki's house.

• go-fusai ご夫妻 【HON. for **fusai** (above)】

• yūjin-fusai 友人夫妻 *a friend and his/her spouse*

fusaku 不作 *bad crop* [⇔**hōsaku** 豊作]

fusawashíi 相応しい *suitable, fitting, appropriate* [→**tekisetsu** na 適切な]

¶ Kono doresu wa pātī ni fusawashii.

このドレスはパーティーにふさわしい。

This dress is suitable for a party.

fuségu 防ぐ ① *to defend, to protect* [→**mamoru** 守る②]

¶ Jūmin wa machi o gōtō kara fusegimashita.

住民は町を強盗から防ぎました。

The residents defended the town against the robbers.

② *to prevent, to protect against*

¶ Jiko o fusegu tame ni kisoku o mamorinasai.

事故を防ぐために規則を守りなさい。

Obey the rules to prevent accidents.

③ *to keep away, to ward off*

¶ Kono kemuri wa ka o fusegu no ni yakudatsu deshō.

この煙は蚊を防ぐのに役立つでしょう。

This smoke will probably be useful to ward off mosquitoes.

fusei 不正 *injustice, unfairness* [⇔**kōsei** 公正]*; dishonesty; illegality*

• fusei o hataraku 不正を働く *to do wrong*

• fusei na 不正な *unjust, unfair; dishonest; illegal*

fūsen 風船 *balloon* ((*toy*))

• fūsen-gamu 風船ガム *bubble gum*

fuséru 伏せる ① *to lay upside down, to lay face down; to turn upside down*

¶Chawan o shokutaku no ue ni fusemashita.
茶わんを食卓の上に伏せました。
I laid the bowls upside down on the table.

• me o fuseru 目を伏せる *to look downward*

• karada o fuseru 体を伏せる *to lie down face down*

② *to lie down face down*
¶Shōjo wa shibafu no ue ni fusete imasu.
少女は芝生の上に伏せています。
The girl is lying down on the grass.

③ *to keep secret*
¶Watashi no namae o fusete kudasai.
私の名前を伏せてください。
Please keep my name secret.

fúsha 風車 *windmill*

fūshi 風刺 *satire*
• fūshi suru 風刺する *to satirize*

fushí 節 ① *joint, node*
• take no fushi 竹の節 *bamboo joint*
② *joint* «where two bones come together» [→**kansetsu** 関節]
• yubi no fushi 指の節 *knuckle*
③ *knot* «in wood»
④ *tune, melody* [→**merodī** メロディー]

fushigi 不思議 *marvel, wonder, strangeness*
• fushigi na 不思議な *strange, wonderful*
¶Sensei ga sonna koto o shita to wa fushigi desu.
先生がそんなことをしたとは不思議です。
It's a wonder that the teacher did such a thing.
¶Yoku fushigi na yume o mimasu.
よく不思議な夢を見ます。
I often have strange dreams.
¶Uematsu-san wa fushigi na jiken ni makikomareta.
上松さんは不思議な事件に巻き込まれた。
Mr. Uematsu got involved in a mysterious incident.
• fushigi na koto ni 不思議なことに *strangely*
• Sekai no Nana-fushigi 世界の七不思議 *the Seven Wonders of the World*

fushínsetsu 不親切 *unkindness* [⇔**shinsetsu** 親切]
• fushinsetsu na 不親切な *unkind*

fushízen 不自然 ～**na** ～な *unnatural* [⇔**shizen no／na** 自然の／な]

fushō 負傷 *getting injured, getting wounded*
• fushō suru 負傷する *to get injured, to get wounded*
• fushō-sha 負傷者 *injured person, wounded person*

fūsoku 風速 *wind speed*
¶Fūsoku wa jū-mētoru desu.
風速は10メートルです。
The wind speed is ten meters (per second).
• fūsoku-kei 風速計 *wind gauge*

fusoku 不足 *insufficiency, shortage, lack*
• fusoku suru 不足する *to become insufficient, to run short, to become lacking*
¶Ano shima de wa shokuryō ga fusoku shite imasu.
あの島では食糧が不足しています。
Food is short on that island.
¶Mikami-san wa nintai ga fusoku shite imasu.
三上さんは忍耐が不足しています。
Mr. Mikami is lacking in patience.
• mizu-busoku 水不足 *water shortage*
• suimin-busoku 睡眠不足 *lack of sleep, insufficient sleep*
• undō-busoku 運動不足 *lack of exercise, insufficient exercise*

fusuma 襖 *sliding door* «of the type used between rooms in Japanese houses.»

futa 蓋 *lid, cover, cap*
¶Sono hako no futa o totte kudasai.
その箱のふたを取ってください。
Please take the lid off that box.
• futa o suru ふたをする *to put a lid* «on something»
¶Ano bin ni futa o shimashita ka.
あの瓶にふたをしましたか。
Did you put the cap on that bottle?

futago 双子 *twins*
¶Ano futari wa futago desu.

あの二人は双子です。
Those two are twins.

futan 負担 *burden, onus*
• futan suru 負担する *to bear, to accept* 《a burden, responsibility, etc.》

futarí 二人 *two* 《when counting people; see Appendix 2》
¶Ane ni wa musuko ga futari imasu.
姉には息子が二人います。
My older sister has two sons.

futatabi 再び *again, once again, once more*
¶Hanagata-sensei wa kokyō o futatabi otozuremashita.
花形先生は故郷を再び訪れました。
Dr. Hanagata visited her hometown again.

futatsu 二つ *two* 《see Appendix 2》
¶Sono ringo o futatsu ni kitte kudasai.
そのりんごを二つに切ってください。
Please cut that apple in two.

fūtō 封筒 *envelope*
¶Tegami o fūtō ni irete, dashimashita.
手紙を封筒に入れて、出しました。
I put the letter in an envelope and mailed it.

futo ふと *by chance; unexpectedly; suddenly*
¶Keiko-san wa futo sora o miagemashita.
恵子さんはふと空を見上げました。
Keiko happened to look up at the sky.
¶Ii kangae ga futo atama ni ukabimashita.
いい考えがふと頭に浮かびました。
A good idea suddenly occurred to me.

futói 太い *thick, large in diameter* [⇔ **hosoi** 細い]
¶Imōto wa futoi ki no miki ni yorikakatte imasu.
妹は太い木の幹によりかかっています。
My younger sister is leaning against a thick tree trunk.
¶Koko ni futoi sen o hiite kudasai.
ここに太い線を引いてください。
Please draw a thick line here.
¶Chichi no ude wa futoi yo.

父の腕は太いよ。
My father's arms are big!
• futoi koe 太い声 *big and deep voice*
¶Endō-san wa futoi koe o shite imasu.
遠藤さんは太い声をしています。
Mr. Endo has a big, deep voice.

futokoro 懐 *the inside of the part of a kimono covering the chest*
¶Haha-oya wa akanbō o futokoro ni daite imasu.
母親は赤ん坊を懐に抱いています。
The mother is holding her baby inside her kimono.

futomomo 太股 *thigh* [→**momo** 股]

futon 布団 *Japanese-style bedding, futon* 《Traditional Japanese bedding is folded up and put in closets during the day and laid out on the floor at night. There are three kinds of futon: (1)the lower, mattress type; (2)the thin sheet type placed directly on the sleeping person; (3)the upper, quilt type.》
• futon o shiku 布団を敷く *to lay out bedding*
• futon o tatamu 布団を畳む *to fold up bedding*
• hada-buton 肌布団 *sheet futon*
• kake-buton 掛け布団 *upper futon, quilt futon*
• shiki-buton 敷布団 *lower futon, mattress futon*

futóru 太る *to become fatter, to gain weight* [⇔**yaseru** 痩せる]
¶Akagi-san wa futotte kimashita.
赤木さんは太ってきました。
Mr. Akagi has gotten fat.
¶Musuko wa ichi-nen-kan de nijuk-kiro futorimashita.
息子は1年間で20キロ太りました。
My son gained 20 kilograms in one year.
• futotte iru 太っている *to be fat*
• futotta hito 太った人 *fat person*

futósa 太さ *thickness, diameter*
¶Kono kuda no futosa wa go-senchi desu.
この管の太さは5センチです。
The diameter of this pipe is

five centimeters.

futsū 不通 *suspension, interruption* 《of transportation or communication》
- futsū ni naru 不通になる *to be suspended, to stop running*

¶Shinkansen wa ōyuki no tame futsū ni natte imasu.

新幹線は大雪のため不通になっています。

The Shinkansen is not running because of heavy snow.

futsū 普通 *usually, commonly, ordinarily* [→**fudan** (**ni**) 普段 (に)]

¶Watashi wa futsū shichi-ji ni uchi o demasu.

私は普通 7 時にうちを出ます。

I usually leave home at 7:00.

- futsū no／na 普通の／な *usual, common; ordinary, unremarkable*

¶Kōtsū-jūtai wa Tōkyō de wa futsū desu.

交通渋滞は東京では普通です。

Traffic jams are common in Tokyo.

¶Kyōko-chan wa futsū no onna no ko desu.

京子ちゃんは普通の女の子です。

Kyoko is an ordinary girl.

- futsū-ka 普通科 *general course of study*
- futsū-yūbin 普通郵便 *ordinary mail*

futsuka 二日 《see Appendix 2》 ① *two days*
② *the second* 《day of a month》

futtō 沸騰 *boiling*
- futtō suru 沸騰する *to come to a boil*

¶Yakan no o-yu ga futtō shite imasu.

やかんのお湯が沸騰しています。

The kettle is boiling. 《Literally: The water in the kettle is boiling.》

- futtō-ten 沸騰点 *boiling point*

futtobōru フットボール（*American*)*football*

futtowāku フットワーク *footwork*

fūun 不運 *bad luck, misfortune* [⇔ **kōun** 幸運]
- fuun na 不運な *unfortunate, unlucky*
- fuun ni mo 不運にも *unfortunately, unluckily*

fuyásu 増やす *to increase* 《transitive》

¶Haha wa raigetsu kara kozukai o fuyashite kuremasu.

母は来月から小遣いを増やしてくれます。

From next month, mother will increase my allowance.

fuyō 不要 〜**no** 〜の *unnecessary* [⇔ **hitsuyō na** 必要な]

¶Sono chūkoku wa fuyō desu.

その忠告は不要です。

That advice is unnecessary.

fuyō 不用 〜**no** 〜の *useless*

¶Kono kamera wa watashi ni wa fuyō desu.

このカメラは私には不用です。

This camera is useless to me.

fuyú 冬 *winter* [⇔**natsu** 夏]

¶Kyonen no fuyu wa samukatta desu.

去年の冬は寒かったです。

Last winter was cold.

¶Fuyu wa yuki ga ōi desu.

冬は雪が多いです。

In winter there's a lot of snow.

- fuyu-fuku 冬服 *winter clothes*
- fuyu-yasumi 冬休み＜*US*＞*winter vacation*, ＜*UK*＞*the winter holidays*

fuyúkai 不愉快 〜**na** 〜な [[⇔**yukai na** 愉快な]] ① *unpleasant, distasteful*

¶Kinō fuyukai na keiken o shimashita.

きのう不愉快な経験をしました。

Yesterday I had an unpleasant experience.

② *displeased*

¶Ano toki watashi wa fuyukai deshita.

あのとき私は不愉快でした。

I was displeased then.

fuzakéru ふざける ① *to joke, to kid around*
- fuzakete iu ふざけて言う *to say in jest, to say jokingly*
② *to romp, to frolic, to play around*

¶Uchi no naka de fuzakeru no wa yoshinasai.

うちの中でふざけるのはよしなさい。

Stop playing around in the house.

fūzoku 風俗 *customs, folkways, manners*
- fūzoku-shūkan 風俗習慣 *manners*

and customs

fuzoku 付属 〜**no** 〜の *attached, affiliated, accessory*

• fuzoku suru 付属する *to be attached, to belong, to be affiliated*

¶ Kono chūgakkō wa daigaku ni fuzoku shite imasu.

この中学校は大学に付属しています。

This junior high school is affiliated with the university.

• fuzoku-hin 付属品 *accessory item*

G

ga 蛾 *moth*

ga が《noun-following particle marking the subject of a clause》

¶ Neko ga sakana o tabemashita.

猫が魚を食べました。

The cat ate the fish.

¶ Boku wa sūgaku ga suki desu.

僕は数学が好きです。

I like math. 《Note that the English translation of a noun marked with **ga** will not necessarily be the subject of the English clause in which it appears.》

ga が《clause-conjoining particle》 *but; and* 《following a clause providing background information for the following clause》

¶ Ane ni wa ketten ga arimasu ga, watashi wa suki desu.

姉には欠点がありますが、私は好きです。

My older sister has some faults, but I like her.

¶ Chichi ni wa ani ga imasu ga, totemo kenkō desu.

父には兄がいますが、とても健康です。

Father has an older brother, and he is in good health.

gabyō 画鋲 *thumbtack*

-gachi ーがち 〜**no** 〜の *having a tendency to, apt to* 《Added to verb bases.》

¶ Ano seito wa chikoku shi-gachi desu.

あの生徒は遅刻しがちです。

That student has a tendency to be late.

gachō 鵞鳥 *goose*

gádo ガード *railroad bridge, railroad overpass*

gádoman ガードマン *guard, watchman* [→**keibi-in** 警備員 (s.v. **keibi** 警備)]

gādoréru ガードレール *guardrail*

gái 害 *harm, damage* [→**songai** 損害]

¶ Arashi wa sakumotsu ni ōki na gai o ataemashita.

あらしは作物に大きな害を与えました。

The storm did great damage to the crops.

¶ Tabako wa karada ni gai ga arimasu.

たばこは体に害があります。

Smoking is harmful to one's health.

《Literally: *Tobacco has harm to the body.*》

• gai-suru 害する {Irreg.} *to harm, to damage, to hurt*

¶ Watashi wa Akira-san no kanjō o gai-shimashita.

私は明さんの感情を害しました。

I hurt Akira's feelings.

gáibu 外部 *the outside, outer part* [⇔**naibu** 内部]

gaichū 害虫 *harmful insect*

gáidansu ガイダンス *guidance counseling* 《at a school》

gáido ガイド ① *guide* 《person》 ② [☞**gaido-bukku** ガイドブック (below)]

• gaido-bukku ガイドブック *guidebook*

gaijin 外人 *foreigner*

gaiken 外見 *outward appearance*

¶ Gaiken de hito o handan shite wa ikemasen.

外見で人を判断してはいけません。

You mustn't judge a person by appearance.

gaikō 外交 *diplomacy*

• gaikō-kan 外交官 *diplomat*

gaikoku 外国 *foreign country*

¶ Gaikoku e itta koto ga arimasu ka.

外国へ行ったことがありますか。

Have you ever been to a foreign country?

• gaikoku-go 外国語 *foreign language*

• gaikoku-jin 外国人 *foreigner* [→**gaijin** 外人]

• gaikoku-seihin 外国製品 *foreign manufactured product*

• gaikoku-yūbin 外国郵便 *foreign mail*

gáimu 外務 *foreign affairs*

• Gaimu-shō 外務省 *Ministry of Foreign Affairs*

gáinen 概念 *general idea; concept*

gairaigo 外来語 *borrowed word, loanword* 《With respect to Japanese, this term ordinarily refers only to relatively recent loanwords, mostly from European languages, and not to the many loanwords from Chinese.》 [⇔**kango** 漢語; **wago** 和語]

gairyaku 概略 *outline, summary* [→**gaiyō** 概要]

gaishoku 外食 *eating out* 《at a restaurant, etc.》

• gaishoku suru 外食する *to eat out*

gaishutsu 外出 *going out* 《i.e., temporarily leaving one's home or workplace》

• gaishutsu suru 外出する *to go out*

¶Gogo wa gaishutsu shimasu.

午後は外出します。

In the afternoon I'll go out.

¶Ani wa ima gaishutsu shite imasu.

兄は今外出しています。

My older brother is out now.

gaitō 街灯 *streetlight*

gaiya 外野 *outfield* [⇔**naiya** 内野] 《in baseball》

• gaiya-seki 外野席 *outfield bleachers*

• gaiya-shu 外野手 *outfielder*

gaiyō 概要 *outline, summary* [→**gairyaku** 概略]

gaka 画家 *artist who paints or draws*

gake 崖 *cliff*

• gake-kuzure 崖崩れ *cliff landslide*

gakí 餓鬼 ① *urchin; brat*
② 【CRUDE for **kodomo** 子供】 *child, kid*

• gaki-daishō 餓鬼大将 *bully, boss of the kids*

gakka 学科 (*school*)*subject*

¶Watashi no suki na gakka wa ongaku desu.

私の好きな学科は音楽です。

The subject I like is music.

gakkai 学会 ① *academic society, academic organization*
② *academic conference*

gakkai 学界 *the academic world, academic circles*

gakkári がっかり ～**suru** ～する *to become disappointed, to become discouraged*

¶Tanaka-san no henji o kiite gakkari shimashita.

田中さんの返事を聞いてがっかりしました。

I was disappointed when I heard Mr. Tanaka's reply.

gakki 学期 (*academic*) *term,* (*academic*) *in-session period*

¶Tsugi no gakki wa Ku-gatsu ni hajimarimasu.

次の学期は9月に始まります。

The next term begins in September.

• gakki-matsu-shiken 学期末試験 *end-of-term examination, final examination*

gakki 楽器 *musical instrument*

• da-gakki 打楽器 *percussion instrument*

• gen-gakki 弦楽器 *string instrument*

• kan-gakki 管楽器 *wind instrument*

• kenban-gakki 鍵盤楽器 *keyboard instrument*

gakkō 学校 *school*

¶Gakkō e iku tokoro desu.

学校へ行くところです。

I'm about to go to school.

¶Uchi no Jirō wa kotoshi kono gakkō ni hairimashita.

うちの次郎は今年この学校に入りました。

Our Jiro entered this school this year.

¶Kyōko-chan wa kinō gakkō o yasunda yo.

京子ちゃんはきのう学校を休んだよ。

Kyoko was absent from school yesterday!

¶Gakkō wa san-ji ni owarimasu.

学校は3時に終わります。

School ends at 3:00.

¶Ashita wa gakkō wa yasumi desu.

あしたは学校は休みです。

Tomorrow the school has a day off.

• gakkō-kyūshoku 学校給食 *school lunch*
• gakkō-seikatsu 学校生活 *school life*
• gakkō-tomodachi 学校友達 *schoolmate, school friend*

gakkyū 学級 (*school*)*class,* (*school*)*grade* 《i.e., students grouped according to year of study》
• gakkyū-iin 学級委員 *class officer*

gaku 額 *sum* (*of money*) [→**kingaku** 金額]

¶Kono kikai ni ōki na gaku o haraimashita.

この機械に大きな額を払いました。

I paid a large sum of money for this machine.

gaku 額 *picture frame*

gákubu 学部 *college, faculty* 《division of a university》

gakuchō 学長 (*college*)*president*

gakudan 楽団 *band; orchestra*

gakufu 楽譜 *musical score*

gakuhi 学費 *school expenses*

gákui 学位 (*academic*)*degree*

gakúmon 学問 *learning, knowledge, scholarship*
• gakumon no aru hito 学問のある人 *a person of learning*

gakunen 学年 ① *school year, academic year*

¶Ōbei de wa atarashii gakunen ga Ku-gatsu ni hajimarimasu.

欧米では新しい学年が9月に始まります。

In Europe and America the new school year begins in September.

② *year in school,* (*school*)*grade* [→**gakkyū** 学級]
• gakunen-matsu-shiken 学年末試験 *annual examination,* (*academic year*)*final examination*

gakureki 学歴 *school career, academic background*

gakuryoku 学力 *scholarly attainments; scholastic ability*

¶Kono seito wa gakuryoku ga arimasu.

この生徒は学力があります。

This student does have scholastic ability.

• gakuryoku-tesuto 学力テスト *scholastic achievement test*

gakusei 学生 *student* 《Typically refers to a college student.》

[⇔**sensei** 先生]

¶Kono daigaku no gakusei wa hotondo Tōkyō-shusshin desu.

この大学の学生はほとんど東京出身です。

The students at this university are almost all from Tokyo.

• gakusei-fuku 学生服 *student uniform*
• gakusei-jidai 学生時代 *one's student days*
• gakusei-seikatsu 学生生活 *student life*

gakusha 学者 *scholar*

gákushi 学士 *bachelor's degree holder*
• gakushi-gō 学士号 *bachelor's degree*

gakushū 学習 *learning, study* [→**ben-kyō** 勉強]
• gakushū suru 学習する *to study* [→**manabu** 学ぶ]

gama 蒲 *cattail* ((plant))

gamagáeru 蒲蛙 *toad*

gáman 我慢 *patience, endurance, forbearance* [→**shinbō** 辛抱]
• gaman suru 我慢する *to stand, put up with, to tolerate*

¶Sore o gaman shinakute mo ii desu yo.

それを我慢しなくてもいいですよ。

You don't have to put up with that!

¶Atama ga itakute gaman dekinai yo.

頭が痛くて我慢できないよ。

I have a headache and I can't stand it!

• gaman-zuyoi 我慢強い *patient, forbearing*

gámen 画面 ① *screen* 《for movies, etc.》 ② *screen* 《of a television, computer, etc.》

gámu ガム (*chewing*)*gum*
• fūsen-gamu 風船ガム *bubble gum*

gán 雁 *wild goose*

gán 癌 *cancer*

ganbáru 頑張る *to strive, to persevere*

¶Ano hito mo isshōkenmei

ganbarimashita.
あの人も一生懸命頑張りました。
That person also strove as hard as she could.

ganjitsu 元日 *New Year's Day* [→**gantan** 元旦]

ganjō 頑丈 ~**na** ~な *strong, tough, solid*

gánko 頑固 ~**na** ~な *stubborn, obstinate*

gánnen 元年 *first year of an imperial reign*
- Heisei-gannen 平成元年 *the first year of the Heisei Era* 《1989》
- Meiji-gannen 明治元年 *the first year of the Meiji Era* 《1868》

gánrai 元来 *originally, from the beginning; by nature, essentially*

gánsho 願書 (*written*)*application*
- nyūgaku-gansho 入学願書 *application for admission to a school*

Gantan 元旦 *New Year's Day* [→**Ganjitsu** 元日]

gappei 合併 ① *amalgamation, merger, combining*
- gappei suru 合併する *to amalgamate, to merge, to combine* 《transitive or intransitive》
  ② *annexation, incorporation*
- gappei suru 合併する *to annex, to incorporate*

garakuta がらくた 【COL.】 *rubbish, junk*

garasu ガラス *glass* ((substance))
- garasu o waru ガラスを割る *to break glass*
- garasu no hahen ガラスの破片 *broken piece of glass, glass fragment*
- garasu-seihin ガラス製品 *glass manufactured item*
- mado-garasu 窓ガラス *window pane*

gárēji ガレージ *garage*

garō 画廊 *art gallery*

gáron ガロン *gallon*
- -garon -ガロン《*counter for gallons; see Appendix 2*》

-garu -がる *to come to show signs of,* *to come to appear to* 《This suffix is typically added to bases of adjectives expressing internal feelings. Forms with –**garu** are used to assert that a third person has such feelings.》
¶Yamane-san wa ongaku o narai-ta-gatte imasu.
山根さんは音楽を習いたがっています。
Mr. Yamane wants to study music.

gārufuréndo ガールフレンド *casual girlfriend* 《as opposed to a steady girlfriend or lover》[→**bōifurendo** ボーイフレンド]

gārusukáuto ガールスカウト ① *the Girl Scouts*
  ② *girl scout*

gasorin ガソリン <*US*>*gasoline,* <*UK*>*petrol*
- gasorin-sutando ガソリンスタンド <*US*>*gas station,* <*UK*>*petrol station*

gasshō 合唱 *singing in chorus; choral music, chorus*
- gasshō suru 合唱する *to sing in chorus*
¶Seito-tachi wa sono uta o gasshō shimashita.
生徒たちはその歌を合唱しました。
The students sang that song in chorus.
- gasshō-dan 合唱団 *chorus, choral group, choir*
- gasshō-kyoku 合唱曲 *choral piece*
- dansei-gasshō 男声合唱 *chorus of male voices*
- josei-gasshō 女声合唱 *chorus of female voices*
- konsei-gasshō 混声合唱 *mixed chorus*
- ni-bu-gasshō 二部合唱 *two-part chorus*

gasshúkoku 合衆国 *country of united states*
- Amerika-gasshūkoku アメリカ合衆国 *the United States of America*

gassō 合奏 *musical instrument ensemble performance*
- gassō suru 合奏する *to play in ensemble*

gásu ガス *gas, substance in a gaseous state* 《This word ordinarily refers to gas used as fuel.》[→**kitai** 気体]

- gasu o tsukeru〔kesu〕ガスをつける〔消す〕*to turn on*〔*off*〕*the gas*
- gasu-chūdoku ガス中毒 *gas poisoning*
- gasu-sutōbu ガスストーブ *gas heater*
- haiki-gasu 排気ガス *exhaust fumes*
- puropan-gasu プロパンガス *propane gas*
- tennen-gasu 天然ガス *natural gas*

-gatai －難い *difficult, hard* 《Added to verb bases.》〔→**-nikui** －にくい〕

- shinji-gatai 信じ難い *difficult to believe*

gáttsu ガッツ *guts, pluck, spirit* 〔→**konjō** 根性②〕

¶Ken wa gattsu ga aru nā.
健はガッツがあるなあ。
Boy, Ken has guts!

- gattsu-pōzu ガッツポーズ *holding up both fists in exultation*

gáun ガウン ① *housedress; dressing gown*

② *gown* 《of the type worn by judges, clergymen, etc.》

gawa 側 *side*

- hidari-gawa 左側 *the left side*
- migi-gawa 右側 *the right side*
- mukō-gawa 向こう側 *the other side, the far side*

¶Hoteru wa yūbin-kyoku no mukō-gawa ni arimasu.
ホテルは郵便局の向こう側にあります。
The hotel is on the other side of the post office.

- soto-gawa 外側 *the outside*

¶Sono hako no soto-gawa wa akaku nutte arimasu.
その箱の外側は赤く塗ってあります。
The outside of that box has been painted red.

- uchi-gawa 内側 *the inside*

gayóshi 画用紙 *drawing paper*

gāze ガーゼ *gauze*

gehín 下品 ～**na** ～な *coarse, vulgar, unrefined* 〔⇔**jōhin na** 上品な〕

géi 芸 ① *accomplishment, acquired art or skill*

② *trick, stunt*

geijutsu 芸術 *an art; art, the arts*

¶Geijutsu wa nagaku, jinsei wa mijikai.

芸術は長く、人生は短い。《proverb》
Art is long; life is short.

- geijutsu-ka 芸術家 *artist*
- geijutsu-sakuhin 芸術作品 *work of art*
- geijutsu-teki na 芸術的な *artistic*

geinōjin 芸能人 *entertainer, show business personality*

geinōkai 芸能界 *the world of show business*

gejigejí げじげじ *millipede*

gejun 下旬 *last third of a month* 〔⇔**chūjun** 中旬; **jōjun** 上旬〕

¶Shunō-kaidan wa Roku-gatsu no gejun ni hirakaremasu.
首脳会談は6月の下旬に開かれます。
The summit conference will be held in late June.

geka 外科 *surgery* 《as a specialty》 〔⇔**naika** 内科〕

- geka-i 外科医 *surgeon*

géki 劇 *play, drama* 〔→**engeki** 演劇, **shibai** 芝居〕

- geki-dan 劇団 *dramatic troupe, theatrical company*
- geki-sakka 劇作家 *dramatist, playwright*
- geki-teki na 劇的な *dramatic*

gekijō 劇場 *theater, playhouse*

- yagai-gekijō 野外劇場 *open-air theater*

gekirei 激励 *encouragement*

- gekirei suru 激励する *to encourage, to cheer up* 〔→**hagemasu** 励ます〕

gekkan 月刊 ～**no** ～の (*published*) *monthly*

- gekkan-zasshi 月刊雑誌 *monthly magazine*

gekkei 月経 *mensuration* 〔→**seiri** 生理②, **mensu** メンス〕

gekkyū 月給 *monthly salary*

gēmu ゲーム ① *game, competitive pastime* 《This meaning does not include sports.》

¶Kono gēmu wa kodomo-muki desu ne.
このゲームは子供向きですね。
This game is intended for children, isn't it.

② *game* 《i.e., a single contest in a game

or sport》[→**shiai** 試合]
- yakyū no gēmu 野球のゲーム *baseball game*
- gēmu-sentā ゲームセンター *amusement arcade*
- gēmu-setto ゲームセット *end of the game*
- terebi-gēmu テレビゲーム *video game*

gén 弦 *string* 《on a musical instrument》
- gen-gakki 弦楽器 *stringed instrument*

genba 現場 *site, scene* 《where something takes place》

genbun 原文 *original text* 《i.e., a text which has not been revised, edited, translated, etc.》

géndai 現代 *the present age, modern times, today*
¶Gendai no wakamono wa aruku koto o konomimasen.
現代の若者は歩くことを好みません。
Today's young people don't like walking.
¶Gendai wa konpyūtā no jidai desu.
現代はコンピューターの時代です。
The present age is the computer age.
- gendai no Nihon 現代の日本 *present-day Japan, modern Japan*
- gendai-Eigo 現代英語 *modern English*
- gendai-ongaku 現代音楽 *modern music*
- gendai-teki na 現代的な *modern, up-to-date*
¶Hirayama-san no ie wa gendai-teki desu.
平山さんの家は現代的です。
Mr. Hirayama's house is modern.

géndo 限度 *limit, bound*
¶Sore wa watashi no tairyoku no gendo o koete imasu.
それは私の体力の限度を越えています。
That exceeds the limit of my strength.
¶Nani-goto ni mo gendo ga arimasu.
何事にも限度があります。
There are limits to everything.
- gendo ni tassuru 限度に達する *to reach a limit*

gendō 言動 *speech and behavior, words and deeds*

géngo 言語 *language*
- gengo-gaku 言語学 *linguistics*

- gengo-shōgai 言語障害 *speech impediment*

gen'in 原因 *cause, source, origin* [⇔ **kekka** 結果]
¶Sono kaji no gen'in wa nan deshita ka.
その火事の原因はなんでしたか。
What was the cause of the fire ?

genjitsu 現実 *reality, actuality*
- genjitsu no 現実の *real, actual*
- genjitsu-teki na 現実的な *realistic, practical*
¶Sono kangae wa genjitsu-teki de wa arimasen.
その考えは現実的ではありません。
That idea is not realistic.

genjō 現状 *present conditions, present situation*
¶Genjō de wa watashi wa minna ni dōi dekimasen.
現状では私はみんなに同意できません。
Under the present conditions I cannot agree with everyone.

genjū 厳重 〜**na** 〜な *strict* [→**kibishii** 厳しい①]
- genjū na kisoku 厳重な規則 *strict rule*

genkai 限界 *limit, limitation* [→**gendo** 限度]

génkan 玄関 *entryway, vestibule* 《the part of a Japanese dwelling, just inside the front door, where shoes are removed》
¶Dōzo genkan kara haitte kudasai.
どうぞ玄関から入ってください。
Please come in from the entryway.

génki 元気 ① *vigor, liveliness; health*
- genki na 元気な *vigorous, lively; healthy, well* [→**kenkō na** 健康な]
¶O-genki desu ka.
お元気ですか。
How are you?
¶Sobo wa dandan genki ni natte kite imasu.
祖母はだんだん元気になってきています。
My grandmother has gradually gotten better.
　② *good spirits, cheerfulness*
- genki ga ii 元気がいい *to be in good spirits, to be cheerful*

- genki ga nai 元気がない *to be in low spirits, to be downhearted*
- genki o dasu 元気を出す *to cheer up, to become cheerful*
- genki na 元気な *spirited, cheerful*

¶Otōto wa totemo genki na ko desu.
弟はとても元気な子です。
My younger brother is a very spirited child.

- genki-naku 元気なく *spiritlessly, cheerlessly*
- genki-yoku 元気よく *spiritedly, cheerfully*

genkín 現金 *cash*

¶Kono sutereo wa genkin de katta yo.
このステレオは現金で買ったよ。
I bought this stereo with cash!

¶Yubiwa no daikin o genkin de haraimashita.
指輪の代金を現金で払いました。
I paid for the ring in cash.

- genkin-kakitome 現金書留 *cash sent by registered mail*

genkin 厳禁 ～**da** ～だ *to be strictly prohibited*

- genkin suru 厳禁する *to prohibit strictly*

genkō 原稿 *manuscript, (preliminary) draft*

- genkō-yōshi 原稿用紙 *manuscript paper* 《divided into small squares, each of which is to be filled by one handwritten character》

genkoku 原告 *plaintiff* [⇔**hikoku** 被告]

genkotsu 拳骨 *fist*

¶Ano yakuza wa keikan o genkotsu de nagutta yo.
あのやくざは警官をげんこつで殴ったよ。
That gangster hit the police officer with his fist!

génmai 玄米 *brown rice, unpolished rice*

genmitsu 厳密 ～**na** ～な *strict, exact, precise*

¶Genmitsu ni ieba, sore wa kisoku-ihan desu.
厳密に言えば、それは規則違反だ。
Strictly speaking, that's a rule violation.

génri 原理 *(basic)principle*

genron 言論 *expressing one's ideas*

- genron no jiyū 言論の自由 *freedom of speech, freedom of expression*

genryō 原料 *raw materials*

¶Chīzu no genryō wa nan desu ka.
チーズの原料は何ですか。
What are the raw materials of cheese?

gensaku 原作 *the original (written work)* 《the work on which a movie, translation, etc., is based》

- gensaku-sha 原作者 *author of the original*

génshi 原子 *atom*

- genshi-bakudan 原子爆弾 *atomic bomb*

génshi 原始 ～**no** ～の *primitive, primeval*

- genshi-jidai 原始時代 *the primitive ages*
- genshi-jin 原始人 *a primitive human*

genshíryoku 原子力 *atomic energy, nuclear power*

- genshiryoku-hatsuden 原子力発電 *nuclear power generation*
- genshiryoku-hatsuden-sho 原子力発電所 *nuclear power plant*

genshō 現象 *phenomenon*

- shizen-genshō 自然現象 *natural phenomenon*

genshō 減少 *decrease* [⇔**zōka** 増加]

- genshō suru 減少する *to decrease* 《intransitive》 [→**heru** 減る]
- genshō-ritsu 減少率 *rate of decrease*

genshoku 原色 *primary color*

génso 元素 *(chemical)element*

- genso-kigō 元素記号 *symbol for an element*

gensoku 原則 *principle, general rule*

¶Gensoku to shite wa sore wa tadashii desu.
原則としてはそれは正しいです。
As a general rule, that is correct.

gensoku 減速 *deceleration* [⇔**kasoku** 加速]

- gensoku suru 減速する *to decelerate* 《transitive or intransitive》

génzai 現在 ① *the present* (*time*)
- genzai no 現在の *present, current*
¶Kore ga genzai no jūsho desu.
これが現在の住所です。
This is my present address.
　② *at present, now*
¶Daitōryō wa genzai nyūin shite imasu.
大統領は現在入院しています。
The President is in the hospital at present.

geppu げっぷ【COL.】*burp, belch*
- geppu ga deru げっぷが出る *a burp comes out*

geppu 月賦 *monthly installment payment*
- geppu de kau 月賦で買う *to buy on monthly installments*

gerende ゲレンデ (*ski*)*slope*

geri 下痢 *diarrhea*
- geri suru 下痢する *to have diarrhea*

gérira ゲリラ *guerrilla*

gesha 下車 *getting off*／*out of* 《a train, bus, car, etc.》[⇔**jōsha** 乗車]
- gesha suru 下車する *to get* 《off／out of a train, bus, car, etc.》

geshi 夏至 *summer solstice* [⇔**tōji** 冬至]

geshuku 下宿 ① *rooming, boarding, lodging* 《in someone's house》
- geshuku suru 下宿する *to room, to board, to lodge*
　② *rented room* 《in someone's house》
- geshuku-nin 下宿人 *roomer, boarder*

gessha 月謝 *monthly payment for lessons*

gesshoku 月食 *lunar eclipse*
- bubun-gesshoku 部分月食 *partial lunar eclipse*
- kaiki-gesshoku 皆既月食 *total lunar eclipse*

gesui 下水 ① *waste water, sewage*
　② (*waste-water*)*drains, drain system*
¶Gesui ga tsumatte imasu.
下水が詰まっています。
The drains are blocked.
- gesui-kan 下水管 *drainpipe, sewer pipe*

gésuto ゲスト (*television program*)*guest*

geta 下駄 *geta, Japanese wooden clogs*
- geta-baki 下駄履き *wearing clogs*
- geta-bako 下駄箱 *footwear cupboard*

gḗto ゲート *gate, gateway*
- kūkō no gēto 空港のゲート *airport gate*

gētobóru ゲートボール *gateball* 《a version of croquet popular among senior citizens in Japan》

Getsuyō 月曜 [☞**Getsuyōbi** 月曜日]

Getsuyóbi 月曜日 *Monday*

gía ギア *gear*

gíbo 義母 *mother-in-law*

gíchō 議長 *chairperson* 《of a meeting, conference, etc.》
¶Taguchi-san ga gichō ni erabaremashita.
田口さんが議長に選ばれました。
Mr. Taguchi was elected chairperson.

gífu 義父 *father-in-law*

gífuto ギフト *gift* [→**okurimono** 贈り物]
- gifuto-shoppu ギフトショップ *gift shop*

gíin 議員 *member of a legislative assembly*
- Shūgiin-giin 衆議院議員 *member of the House of Representatives* 《in the Japanese Diet》
- Sangiin-giin 参議院議員 *member of the House of Councilors* 《in the Japanese Diet》

gíjutsu 技術 *technique of applying learning, technical skill*
- gijutsu-sha 技術者 *engineer; technologist*
- gijutsu-teki na 技術的な *technical*
- kagaku-gijutsu 科学技術 *technology*

gíkai 議会 (*legislative*)*assembly, congress, parliament*
- gikai-seido 議会制度 *parliamentary system*
- gikai-seiji 議会政治 *parliamentary government*
- ken-gikai 県議会 *prefectural assembly*
- shi-gikai 市議会 *city assembly*

gikochinái ぎこちない *awkward, clumsy*

gimon 疑問 *doubt, uncertainty* [→**utagai** 疑い①]

¶Nani-ka gimon no ten ga arimasu ka.
何か疑問の点がありますか。
Do you have any doubts?

• gimon no yochi ga nai 疑問の余地がない *there is no doubt*

• gimon-bun 疑問文 *interrogative sentence*

• gimon-fu 疑問符 *question mark*

gímu 義務 *duty, obligation*

• gimu o okotaru 義務を怠る *to neglect one's duty*

• gimu o hatasu 義務を果たす *to carry out one's duty*

• gimu-kyōiku 義務教育 *compulsory education*

gín 銀 *silver*

• gin-ka 銀貨 *silver coin*

• gin-medaru 銀メダル *silver medal*

Gínga 銀河 *the Milky Way, the Galaxy*
[→**Ama-no-gawa** 天の川]

ginkō 銀行 *bank* 《i.e., a financial institution》

¶Ginkō kara o-kane o sukoshi hikidashimasu.
銀行からお金を少し引き出します。
I'm going to withdraw a little money from the bank.

¶Ani wa ginkō ni niman-en yokin shimashita.
兄は銀行に2万円預金しました。
My older brother deposited 20,000 yen in the bank.

• ginkō-in 銀行員 *bank clerk; bank employee*

• ginkō-ka 銀行家 *banker*

ginmí 吟味 *scrutiny*

• ginmi suru 吟味する *to scrutinize*

ginnán 銀杏 *ginkgo nut*

gípusu ギプス *cast* 《for an injury》

girí 義理 *duty, obligation* 《toward another person as a result of social interaction》

¶Ano hito ni wa giri ga arimasu.
あの人には義理があります。
I have an obligation to that person.

• giri no 義理の *-in-law; step-*

• giri no haha 義理の母 *mother-in-law; stepmother*

girigiri ぎりぎり *just barely* (*within the limit*)

¶Jikan girigiri de dēto ni ma ni atta.
時間ぎりぎりでデートに間に合った。
I just barely made it on time for the date.

• girigiri no ぎりぎりの *just-within-the-limit*

gíron 議論 *argument, debate; discussion*

• giron suru 議論する *to have an argument, to have a debate; to have a discussion*

¶Shōrai no shinro ni tsuite haha to giron shimashita.
将来の進路について母と議論しました。
I had a discussion about my future course with my mother.

gisei 犠牲 *sacrifice*

• gisei o harau 犠牲を払う *to make a sacrifice*

• gisei-banto 犠牲バント *sacrifice bunt*

• gisei-furai 犠牲フライ *sacrifice fly*

• gisei-sha 犠牲者 *casualty*

gíshi 技師 *engineer, engineering specialist*

• denki-gishi 電気技師 *electrical engineer*

gíshiki 儀式 *ceremony*

gitā ギター *guitar*

• gitā o hiku ギターを弾く *to play a guitar*

giwaku 疑惑 *suspicion, misgivings*

gizō 偽造 *counterfeiting*

• gizō suru 偽造する *to counterfeit*

gó 五 *five* 《see Appendix 2》

• Go-gatsu 五月 *May*

gó 語 *word* [→**tango** 単語]

¶Kono go wa dō hatsuon shimasu ka.
この語はどう発音しますか。
How do you pronounce this word?

• -go 一語《counter for words; see Appendix 2》

-go 一語 *language* 《Added to bases denoting the names of countries, tribes, etc.》

¶Mekishiko de wa Supein-go o hanashimasu ka.
メキシコではスペイン語を話しますか。

Do they speak Spanish in Mexico?
- Chūgoku-go 中国語 *the Chinese language*
- nani-go 何語 *what language*
- Suwahiri-go スワヒリ語 *the Swahili language*

-go －後 *after, later, since* 《Added to noun bases, often numbers denoting periods of time.》[⇔**-mae** －前]
- sono go その後 *after that, since then* 《In this one combination, **go** behaves like an independent word rather than a suffix.》
¶Sono go sono hito ni wa atte imasen.
その後その人には会っていません。
I haven't seen that person since then.
¶Kimi-san wa ichi-jikan-go ni denwa shimashita.
喜美さんは1時間後に電話しました。
Kimi telephoned one hour later.
¶Futsuka-go ni mokuteki-chi ni mukete shuppatsu shimashita.
2日後に目的地に向けて出発しました。
Two days later I set out for my destination.
- kikoku-go 帰国後 *after returning home* (*to one's own country*)

go- 御－《This prefix is typically honorific, but in some words it has lost its honorific force. It also appears in some humble forms.》

gó 碁 (*the game of*)*go*
- go-ishi 碁石 *go stone*
- go-ban 碁盤 *go board*

-gō －号《counter for train numbers, issues of magazines, etc.; see Appendix 2》

gobō ごぼう *burdock*

gobusata ご無沙汰 【HUM.】 *hiatus in contact* 《with someone》
- gobusata suru ごぶさたする *to fail to get in contact, to fail to get in touch*
¶Gobusata shite orimasu.
ごぶさたしております。
I'm sorry for not having been in touch for so long. 《Literally: *I have failed to get in touch.*》

gochisō ご馳走 *good food, feast*

¶Ane wa watashi no tanjōbi no o-iwai ni gochisō o tsukutte kureta yo.
姉は私の誕生日のお祝いにごちそうを作ってくれたよ。
My older sister cooked a feast for my birthday.
- gochisō suru ごちそうする *to treat* 《a person to food and／or drink》[→**ogoru** 奢る]
¶Kyō wa watashi ga gochisō shimasu.
きょうは私がごちそうします。
Today I'll treat.
- A ni B o gochisō suru AにBをごちそうする *to treat A to B*
¶Senpai no hitori ga chūshoku o gochisō shite kuremashita.
先輩の一人が昼食をごちそうしてくれました。
One of my seniors treated me to lunch.
- gochisō ni naru ごちそうになる *to be treated to* 《food and／or drink》
- A ni B o gochisō ni naru AにBをごちそうになる *to be treated by A to B*
¶Hayashi-san ni o-sushi o gochisō ni narimashita.
林さんにおすしをごちそうになりました。
I was treated to sushi by Ms. Hayashi.
- Gochisō-sama (deshita) ご馳走さま (でした) *Everything was delicious* 《This is the required expression of thanks after eating. It is typically said to one's host at a meal or to the person who prepared the food, but it can also be addressed to no one in particular as an indication that one has finished eating.》

gofuku 呉服 *cloth for traditional Japanese clothing*

gogen 語源 *word origin, etymology*

gógo 午後 [[⇔**gozen** 午前]] *p. m.; afternoon*
¶Gakkō wa gogo san-ji ni owarimasu.
学校は午後3時に終わります。
School ends at 3:00 p. m.
¶Doyōbi no gogo wa hima desu.
土曜日の午後は暇です。
On Saturday afternoon I'm free.
¶Kyō no gogo sensei o tazuneru

tsumori desu.

きょうの午後先生を訪ねるつもりです。

I intend to visit the teacher this afternoon.

¶Ashita no gogo yo-ji no ressha de shuppatsu shimasu.

あしたの午後4時の列車で出発します。

I'm going to leave on the 4:00 p.m. train tomorrow.

góhan ご飯 ① (*cooked*)*rice* [⇔**kome** 米]

¶Kesa wa gohan o ni-hai tabemashita.

けさはご飯を2杯食べました。

This morning I ate two bowls of rice.

• gohan o taku ご飯を炊く *to cook rice, to boil rice*

② *meal* [→**shokuji** 食事]

• gohan no shitaku o suru ご飯の支度をする *to prepare a meal*

gói 語彙 *vocabulary*

gói 合意 *agreement* (*of opinion*)

• gói ni tassuru 合意に達する *to reach agreement*

gójō 強情 *obstinacy, stubbornness*

• gójō o haru 強情を張る *to be obstinate, to be stubborn*

• gójō na 強情な *obstinate, stubborn* [→**ganko na** 頑固な]

gojúon 五十音 *the Japanese kana syllabary* 《This word literally means *50 sounds* and reflects the traditional arrangement of **kana** symbols into a table with 10 columns and 5 rows. There are, however, only 46 distinct basic symbols in modern **kana**.》 [→**kana** 仮名]

• gojūon-zu 五十音図 *table of kana* 《in the traditional arrangement》

góka 豪華 ～**na** ～な *luxurious, deluxe, magnificent*

¶Ano góka na fune o mimashita ka.

あの豪華な船を見ましたか。

Did you see that luxurious ship?

¶Sono kashu wa góka na doresu o kite imashita.

その歌手は豪華なドレスを着ていました。

The singer was wearing a magnificent dress.

gokai 誤解 *misunderstanding*

¶Sore wa Nozaki-san no gokai desu.

それは野崎さんの誤解です。

That is a misunderstanding on Mr. Nozaki's part. 《Literally: *That is Mr. Nozaki's misunderstanding.*》

¶Sono hanashi-kata wa gokai o maneku to omoimasu.

その話し方は誤解を招くと思います。

I think that way of talking invites misunderstanding.

• gokai suru 誤解する *to misunderstand*

¶Mariko-san wa watashi o gokai shite imasu.

真理子さんは私を誤解しています。

Mariko misunderstands me.

gōkaku 合格 *meeting* 《a standard》, *passing* 《a test》 [⇔**fugōkaku** 不合格]

¶Gōkaku omedetō!

合格おめでとう!

Congratulations on passing!

• gōkaku suru 合格する *to achieve a passing result, to succeed*

• A ni gōkaku suru Aに合格する *to pass A, to succeed on A*

¶Satō-san mo nyūgaku-shiken ni gōkaku shimashita.

佐藤さんも入学試験に合格しました。

Ms. Sato also passed the entrance examination.

• gōkaku-ten 合格点 *passing mark, passing score*

gokan 五感 *the five senses*

gōkáto ゴーカート *go-cart*

gōkei 合計 ① *sum, total*

• gōkei de 合計で *in total, all together*

¶Gōkei de ikura desu ka.

合計でいくらですか。

How much is it all together?

• gōkei suru 合計する *to add up, to total*

② [☞**gōkei de** 合計で (*above*)]

¶Kutsu to bōshi wa gōkei ichiman-en kakarimashita.

靴と帽子は合計1万円かかりました。

The shoes and the hat cost 10,000 yen all together.

gokiburi ごきぶり *cockroach*

-gokko －ごっこ *imitative playing*
《Added to noun bases.》
• densha-gokko 電車ごっこ *playing train*
• gakkō-gokko 学校ごっこ *playing school*
• kaubōi-gokko カウボーイごっこ *playing cowboy*
• oni-gokko 鬼ごっこ *(the game of)tag*

go-kúrō-sama ご苦労さま《The addition of **deshita** でした makes this expression more polite. The less polite form **go-kurō-san** ご苦労さん is sometimes used as well.》 ① *Thank you for your trouble.* 《Used to thank subordinates and people who perform services as an occupation (e.g., a person who makes a delivery).》
② *That was hard work.* 《Used to comment on how hard another person worked at something. This use is appropriate even toward superiors.》

goma 胡麻 *sesame seed*
• goma-abura 胡麻油 *sesame oil*

gomakásu ごまかす ① *to deceive* [→ **damasu** 騙す]
¶Naite watashi o gomakasanai de kudasai.
泣いて私をごまかさないでください。
Don't deceive me by crying.
② *to cheat out of; to embezzle*
¶Shihai-nin wa watashi-tachi no toribun o gomakashita yo.
支配人は私たちの取り分をごまかしたよ。
The manager cheated us out of our share!
③ **to** *lie about, to misrepresent*
• toshi o gomakasu 年をごまかす *to lie about one's age*
④ *to gloss over, to cover up*
• kashitsu o gomakasu 過失をごまかす *to cover up an error*

gomen ご免 ～**da** ～だ *to be something one wants no part of*
¶Kaigai-ryokō wa gomen da yo.
海外旅行はご免だよ。
I want no part of traveling abroad!

gomen-kudasai ご免ください ① *Excuse me, is anyone here?* 《Used upon entering a store or home when no one is in sight.》
② *Good-by* 《on the telephone》

gomen-nasai ご免なさい [[→**sumimasen** すみません]] *I'm sorry; Excuse me*
¶Okurete gomen-nasai.
遅れてごめんなさい。
I'm sorry for being late.

gomi ごみ ① *trash, garbage; litter*
• gomi o suteru ごみを捨てる *to throw out trash; to litter*
② [[→**chiri** 塵]] *dust; bits of trash*
• gomi-bako ごみ箱 *trash can, garbage can*

gōmon 拷問 *torture*
• gōmon suru 拷問する *to torture*

gómu ゴム *rubber*
• gomu no ki ゴムの木 *rubber tree*
• keshi-gomu 消しゴム *(rubber)eraser*
• wa-gomu 輪ゴム *rubber band*

gondora ゴンドラ ① *gondola* 《(boat)》
② *gondola* 《on a balloon, aerial cableway, etc.》

goraku 娯楽 *amusement, entertainment*
• goraku-bangumi 娯楽番組 *entertainment program*
• goraku-shisetsu 娯楽施設 *amusement facilities*

goran ご覧 ～**ni naru** ～になる 【HON. for **miru** 見る】
¶Goran kudasai.
ごらんください。
Please look.

gōrei 号令 *command, order* 《spoken to a group》
• gōrei o kakeru 号令を掛ける *to give a command, to give an order*
¶Kōchō wa seito ni "chakuseki" to gōrei o kaketa.
校長は生徒に「着席」と号令をかけた。
The principal gave the students the command "sit down."
• gōrei suru 号令する *to give a command, to give an order*

Gorin 五輪 *the Olympics* [→**Orinpikku** オリンピック]

górira ゴリラ *gorilla*

góriteki 合理的 〜**na** 〜な *rational, reasonable, logical*

¶Ani wa itsu-mo gōriteki na kangae-kata o shimasu.

兄はいつも合理的な考え方をします。

My older brother always thinks logically.

-goro 〜ごろ *about* 《Added to bases referring to specific times.》

¶Yōko-chan wa go-ji-goro ni kaette kuru yo.

洋子ちゃんは5時ごろに帰って来るよ。

Yoko will come home around five.

¶Rainen no ima-goro mata kimasu.

来年の今ごろまた来ます。

I'll come again about this time next year.

góro ゴロ *grounder* 《in baseball》

• goro o utsu ゴロを打つ *to hit a grounder*

góru ゴール ① *(scored)goal* 《in sports》 ② *finish line*

• gōru-in ゴールイン *crossing the finish line*

• gōru-in suru ゴールインする *to cross the finish line*

¶Ken-chan wa it-chaku de gōru-in shita yo.

健ちゃんは1着でゴールインしたよ。

Ken crossed the finish line in first place!

• gōru-kīpā ゴールキーパー *goalkeeper* [→**kīpā** キーパー]

Gōruden'uīku ゴールデンウィーク *Golden Week* 《the period of April 29 through May 5 when three Japanese national holidays fall in close succession: **Midori no hi** みどりの日 (April 29), **Kenpō-kinen-bi** 憲法記念日 (May 3), and **Kodomo no hi** 子供の日 (May 5)》

górufu ゴルフ *golf*

• gorufu-jō ゴルフ場 *golf course*

go-ryōshin ご両親 【HON. for **ryōshin** 両親】 *parents*

goshíppu ゴシップ *gossip* [→**uwasa-banashi** 噂話 (s.v. **uwasa** 噂)]

goshoku 誤植 *misprint*

go-shújin ご主人 【HON. for **shujin** 主人】

gōtō 強盗 ① *robbery* ② *robber*

-goto 〜毎 *every, each* 《Added to noun bases, often numbers denoting time periods.》

¶Nichiyōbi-goto ni chichi to sakana-tsuri ni ikimasu.

日曜日ごとに父と魚釣りに行きます。

Every Sunday I go fishing with my father.

¶Orinpikku wa yo-nen-goto ni hirakaremasu.

オリンピックは4年ごとに開かれます。

The Olympics are held every four years.

gottagáesu ごった返す *to become chaotically crowded, to become thronged*

go-yō ご用 【HON. for **yō** 用】 *business, matter to attend to*

¶Nani-ka go-yō desu ka.

何かご用ですか。

Is there something I can do for you? 《Literally: *Is it some kind of business?*》

gozá ござ *straw mat*

gozaimásu ございます 【FORMAL for **aru** ある】 《more polite than **arimasu** あります》《This word is a verb with the semi-formal -**masu** ending. The informal nonpast (the form of a verb that ordinarily appears in a dictionary)is **gozaru** ござる, but such informal forms are not used in modern Japanese.》

• de gozaimsu でございます [☞**de gozaimasu** でございます]

gozaru ござる{Irreg.}[☞**gozaimasu** ございます]

gózen 午前 [[⇔**gogo** 午後]] *a. m.; morning*

¶Shi-gatsu itsuka no gozen ni umaremashita.

4月5日の午前に生まれました。

I was born on the morning of April 5.

¶Kesshō-sen wa gozen jū-ji ni hajimarimasu.

決勝戦は午前10時に始まります。

The championship game begins at 10:00 a.m.

• gozen-chū 午前中 *during the morning,*

before noon

¶Gozen-chū wa zutto ame ga futte imashita.

午前中はずっと雨が降っていました。

It rained all morning.

¶Kinō no gozen-chū wa uchi ni imashita.

きのうの午前中はうちにいました。

Yesterday morning I was at home.

¶Gozen-chū ni jugyō ga aru yo.

午前中に授業があるよ。

In the morning I have class!

gozónji ご存じ 〜da 〜だ 【HON. for **shitte iru** 知っている(s.v. **shiru** 知る)】

guai 具合 ① *condition, state* [→**chōshi** 調子①]

• karada no guai 体の具合 *state of health, how one feels*

② *way (of doing)* [→**chōshi** 調子②]

¶Konna guai ni yatte kudasai.

こんな具合にやってください。

Please do it this way.

guchi 愚痴 *complaining, grumbling*

• guchi o iu ぐちを言う *to complain, to grumble*

gun 軍 ① *troops, forces*

② *the military*

gún 郡 *rural district, rural county* 《an administrative subdivision of a prefecture in Japan》

gúnbi 軍備 *armaments, military preparations*

• gunbi-shukushō 軍備縮小 *reduction of armaments*

gúnji 軍事 *military affairs*

gunjin 軍人 *person in the military*

gunkaɲ 軍艦 *warship*

gunshū 群衆 *crowd, multitude* 《of people or animals》

¶Kōen ni wa ōzei no gunshū ga imashita.

公園には大勢の群衆がいました。

There was a large crowd in the park.

gúntai 軍隊 *armed forces, the military*

guntō 群島 *group of islands*

gurabia グラビア *(photo-)gravure*

gurafikkudezáinā グラフィックデザイナー *graphic designer*

gúrafu グラフ *graph* [→**zuhyō** 図表]

¶Seito wa kono gurafu o kakimashita.

生徒はこのグラフを書きました。

A student drew this graph.

• gurafu-yōshi グラフ用紙 *graph paper*

• bō-gurafu 棒グラフ *bar graph*

• en-gurafu 円グラフ *circle graph, pie chart*

• ore-sen-gurafu 折れ線グラフ *line graph*

gúrai 位 ① *extent, degree* 《following a predicate in the nonpast tense》 [→**hodo** 程②]

¶Nichiyōbi mo yasumenai gurai isogashii desu.

日曜日も休めないぐらい忙しいです。

I'm so busy that I can't even take Sunday off. 《Literally: I'm busy to the extent that I cannot take off even Sunday.》

¶Gaman dekinai gurai no itami desu.

我慢できないぐらいの痛みです。

It's unbearable pain. 《Literally: It's pain of a degree that one cannot stand.》

② *approximate amount, approximate extent, approximate degree*

¶Eki made dono gurai arimasu ka.

駅までどのぐらいありますか。

About how far is it to the station?

¶Tomodachi no shinchō wa boku to onaji gurai desu.

友達の身長は僕と同じぐらいです。

My friend is about the same height as I am.

-gurai −位 ① *about, <US>around, or so* 《Added to number bases.》

¶Tsuki ni ni-do-gurai ryōshin ni tegami o dashimasu.

月に2度ぐらい両親に手紙を出します。

I send a letter to my parents about twice a month.

② 《Added to noun bases.》 *about the same extent as; at least the same extent as; at least*

¶Techō-gurai no ōkisa ga chōdo ii.

手帳ぐらいの大きさがちょうどいい。

A size about the same as a pocket-book is just right.

¶Tomoko-chan ni enpitsu-gurai

agenasai.
友子ちゃんに鉛筆ぐらいあげなさい。
Give Tomoko a pencil at least.

guráidā グライダー *glider*
 • hangu-guraidā ハンググライダー *hang glider*

gúramu グラム *gram*
 • -guramu –グラム《counter for grams; see Appendix 2》

guránpuri グランプリ *grand prix, grand prize*

gúrasu グラス (*drinking*)*glass*

guratan グラタン *gratin*
 • chikin-guratan チキングラタン *chicken au gratin*

guraundo グラウンド *playground* [→ **undō-jō** 運動場 (s.v. **undō** 運動)]; *playing field* [→**kyōgi-jō** 競技場 (s.v. **kyōgi** 競技)]

gurḗ グレー *gray* 《as a noun》 [→**haiiro** 灰色]
 ¶Tomodachi wa gurē no jaketto o kite imasu.
友達はグレーのジャケットを着ています。
My friend is wearing a gray jacket.

gurḗpufurū́tsu グレープフルーツ *grapefruit*

gurḗpujū́su グレープジュース *grape juice*

gurī́npīsu グリーンピース *green peas*

gurṓbu グローブ (*sports*)*glove*
 • bokushingu-yō-gurōbu ボクシング用グローブ *boxing gloves*

gurotésuku グロテスク 〜**na** 〜な *grotesque*

gurū́pu グループ *group* (*of people*)
 • gurūpu de グループで *in a group, in groups*
 • gurūpu-katsudō グループ活動 *group activities*

gussúri ぐっすり 〜**nemuru** 〜眠る *to sleep soundly*

gū́sū 偶数 *even number* [⇔**kisū** 奇数]

gutaiteki 具体的 〜**na** 〜な *concrete* 《i.e., not abstract》 [⇔**chūshōteki na** 抽象的な]

gū́zen 偶然 ① *chance, accident, coincidence*
 • gūzen no 偶然の *accidental, coincidental*
 ② (〜**ni** 〜に) *by chance, by accident*
 ¶Kinō gūzen tomodachi ni atta.
きのう偶然友達に会った。
Yesterday I ran into a friend by chance.

gúzuguzu ぐずぐず ① 〜**suru** 〜する *to dawdle, to delay, to waste time*
 ¶Guzuguzu shite wa ikemasen.
ぐずぐずしてはいけません。
You mustn't delay.
 ② 〜**iu** 〜言う *to complain, to grumble*
 ¶Guzuguzu iwazu ni, sassa to shokki o arae.
ぐずぐず言わずに、さっさと食器を洗え。
Stop grumbling and wash the dishes quickly.

gyágu ギャグ *gag* ((joke))

gyaku 逆 *the reverse, the opposite* [→ **hantai** 反対①]
 ¶"Takai" wa "hikui" no gyaku desu.
「高い」は「低い」の逆です。
"High" is the opposite of "low."
 • gyaku no 逆の *reverse, contrary, opposite*
 ¶Kodomo-tachi wa gyaku no hōkō ni ikimashita.
子供たちは逆の方向に行きました。
The children went in the opposite direction.
 • gyaku-kōka 逆効果 *opposite effect*
 • gyaku-kōsu 逆コース *reverse course*

gyakusatsu 虐殺 *massacre, slaughter*
 • gyakusatsu suru 虐殺する *to massacre, to slaughter*

gyakutai 虐待 *cruel treatment*
 • gyakutai suru 虐待する *to treat cruelly*
 ¶Dōbutsu o gyakutai shite wa ikemasen.
動物を虐待してはいけません。
You must not be cruel to animals.

gyakuten 逆転 *reversal, inversion*
 • gyakuten suru 逆転する *to become reversed, to become inverted*
 • keisei ga gyakuten suru 形勢が逆転する *the situation reverses, the tables get turned*

gyángu ギャング ① *gangster*

② *mob (of gangsters)*

• gyangu-eiga ギャング映画 *gangster movie*

gyáppu ギャップ *gap, difference*

¶Watashi to chichi no kangae-kata ni wa ōki na gyappu ga aru.

私と父の考え方には大きなギャップがある。

There is a big gap between my way of thinking and my father's.

gyára ギャラ *guaranteed payment to a performer for appearing*

gyō 行 *line (of text)*

• -gyō 一行《*counter for lines; see Appendix 2*》

¶Jūhachi-pēji no san-gyō-me o minasai.

18ページの3行目を見なさい。

Look at line three on page 18.

• ichi-gyo-oki ni 1行おきに *on every other line*

gyōgi 行儀 *manners*

¶Yumiko-chan wa gyōgi ga ii desu.

由美子ちゃんは行儀がいいです。

Yumiko is well mannered.

• gyōgi-yoku 行儀よく *in a well-mannered fashion*

• gyōgi-yoku suru 行儀よくする *to behave oneself*

gyógyō 漁業 *fishery, fishing industry*

• engan-gyogyō 沿岸漁業 *coastal fishery*

• en'yō-gyogyō 遠洋漁業 *deep-sea fishery*

gyōji 行事 *planned event, function*

• gakkō-gyōji 学校行事 *school event*

• nenjū-gyōji 年中行事 *annual event*

gyōkai 業界 *the business world, business circles*

gyōretsu 行列 ① <*US*>*line,* <*UK*>*queue* 《*i.e., entities arranged in a line*》

¶Gekijō no mae ni nagai gyōretsu ga dekite imasu.

劇場の前に長い行列が出来ています。

A long line has formed in front of the theater.

② <*US*>*lining up,* <*UK*>*queueing up*

• gyōretsu suru 行列する <*US*>*to line up,* <*UK*>*to queue up* 《*intransitive*》

¶Hitobito wa kippu o kau tame ni gyōretsu shite matte imasu.

人々は切符を買うために行列して待っています。

People are waiting in line to buy tickets. 《*Literally: People are lining up and waiting to buy tickets.*》

• kasō-gyōretsu 仮装行列 *fancy-dress parade*

gyōsho 行書 *running style* 《*of Japanese calligraphy*》[⇔**kaisho** 楷書; **sōsho** 草書]

gyoson 漁村 *fishing village*

gyōza 餃子 *jiao-zi* 《*a kind of Chinese stuffed dumpling*》

gyūniku 牛肉 *beef*

gyūnyū 牛乳 *(cow's)milk*

• gyūnyū-bin 牛乳瓶 *milk bottle*

H

há 刃 *blade; blade edge*

¶Kono hōchō no ha wa surudoi yo.

この包丁の刃は鋭いよ。

The blade of this kitchen knife is sharp!

há 歯 *tooth*

¶Otona ni wa ha ga sanjūni-hon arimasu.

大人は歯が32本あります。

Adults have 32 teeth.

¶Kinō kono ha o chiryō shite moraimashita.

きのうこの歯を治療してもらいました。

I had treatment on this tooth yesterday.

¶Ha o ip-pon nuite moraimashita.

歯を1本抜いてもらいました。

I had one tooth taken out.

• ha ga itai 歯が痛い *a tooth aches*

• ha o migaku 歯を磨く *to brush one's teeth*

• ha-burashi 歯ブラシ *toothbrush*

• ha-guki 歯茎 *gums*

- ha-isha 歯医者 *dentist*
- ha-migaki 歯磨き *brushing one's teeth; toothpaste*
- ire-ba 入れ歯 *false tooth*
- mae-ba 前歯 *front tooth*
- oku-ba 奥歯 *back tooth*

ha 葉 [[→**happa** 葉っぱ]] *leaf; blade ⟪of grass⟫*
- kare-ha 枯れ葉 *dead leaves*
- ochi-ba 落ち葉 *fallen leaves*
- waka-ba 若葉 *young leaves*

haba 幅 *width*
¶Kono kawa no haba wa dono gurai desu ka.
この川の幅はどのぐらいですか。
How wide is this river?
¶Kono tōri wa haba ga semai desu.
この通りは幅が狭いです。
This street is narrow. ⟪Literally: As for this street, the width is narrow.⟫
- haba-tobi 幅跳び ＜US＞ *broad jump, long jump*

habúku 省く ① *to leave out, to omit, to exclude*
¶Kono bunshō o habukinasai.
この文章を省きなさい。
Leave out this text.
¶Kono hito no namae o meibo kara habuite shimatta.
この人の名前を名簿から省いてしまった。
I omitted this person's name from the list.
② *to curtail, to reduce, to save, to make it possible to do with less of*
- jikan o habuku 時間を省く *to save time*

hachí 八 *eight* ⟪see Appendix 2⟫
- Hachi-gatsu 八月 *August*

hachí 鉢 ① *bowl*
② *flowerpot* [→**ueki-bachi** 植木鉢 (s.v. **ueki** 植木)]

hachi 蜂 *bee*
¶Ōki na hachi ga bunbun tobi-mawatte iru yo.
大きなはちがぶんぶん飛び回っているよ。
A big bee is buzzing around!
- hachi no su はちの巣 *beehive; honeycomb*

- hachi ni sasareru はちに刺される *to be stung by a bee*
- hachi-mitsu 蜂蜜 *honey*

háda 肌 ① (*person's*)*skin*
¶Kyōko-san wa hada ga shiroi desu ne.
京子さんは肌が白いですね。
Kyoko's skin is fair, isn't it.
- asaguroi hada 浅黒い肌 *dark skin*
② *outer surface* [→**hyōmen** 表面]
- yama-hada 山肌 *surface of a mountain*

hadaka 裸 *nakedness, nudity*
- hadaka no 裸の *naked*
- hadaka ni naru 裸になる *to become naked, take off one's clothes*

hadashi 裸足 *bare feet*
- hadashi de はだしで *with bare feet, barefoot*
¶Kono ko wa hadashi de aruku no ga suki desu.
この子ははだしで歩くのが好きです。
This child likes to walk barefoot.

hadé 派手 ～**na** ～な *gaudy, showy*
¶Ani no nekutai wa hade desu.
兄のネクタイは派手です。
My older brother's tie is gaudy.
¶Kashu wa hade na doresu o kite imasu.
歌手は派手なドレスを着ています。
The singer is wearing a showy dress.

hádo ハード ～**na** ～な *hard, severe* [→**kibishii** 厳しい②]; *hard, intense* [→**hageshii** 激しい]

hádobóirudo ハードボイルド ～**na** ～な *hard-boiled, emotionally tough*

hādoru ハードル ① *hurdle* ⟪in track events⟫
- hādoru o tobikoeru ハードルを飛び越える *to clear a hurdle*
② *hurdle race*

hādouéa ハードウエア (*computer*)*hardware* [⇔**sofutouea** ソフトウエア]

hae 蝿 *fly* ⟪(insect)⟫

haéru 生える *to sprout, to appear*
¶Zassō ga hana no aida ni haete imasu.
雑草が花の間に生えています。
Weeds are sprouting among the flowers.
- hige ga haeru ひげが生える *a beard grows*
- ha ga haeru 歯が生える *a tooth comes*

in

háfu ハーフ ① *person of racially mixed parentage*

② *half* [→**hanbun** 半分]

hagaki 葉書 *postcard*

• kansei-hagaki 官製葉書 *government-printed postcard*

hagásu 剝がす *to peel off, to tear off* [→**hagu** 剝ぐ]

¶Posutā o zenbu hagashinasai.

ポスターを全部はがしなさい。

Take down all the posters.

háge 禿げ *baldness; bald spot*

• hage-atama 禿げ頭 *bald head*

• hage-yama 禿げ山 *bare mountain*

hagemásu 励ます *to encourage, to cheer up*

¶Tomodachi ga yasashii kotoba de hagemashite kureta.

友達がやさしい言葉で励ましてくれた。

My friend encouraged me with kind words.

hagému 励む *to work hard, to become diligent*

¶Imōto wa benkyō ni hagende imasu.

妹は勉強に励んでいます。

My younger sister is working hard at her studies.

hagéru 剝げる ① *to peel off, to wear off* 《intransitive》

¶Hei no penki ga hagemashita.

塀のペンキがはげました。

The paint on the fence has peeled off.

② *to fade* 《when the subject is a color》

hagéru 禿る *to become bald*

¶Chichi wa dandan atama ga hagete kimashita.

父はだんだん頭がはげてきました。

My father has gradually become bald.

《Literally: As for my father, his head has gradually become bald.》

hageshíi 激しい *intense, hard, heavy, violent*

¶Kaze ga hageshiku fuite iru yo.

風が激しく吹いているよ。

The wind is blowing hard!

• hageshii samusa 激しい寒さ *intense cold*

• hageshii renshū 激しい練習 *hard training*

• hageshii ame 激しい雨 *heavy rain*

• hageshii arashi 激しいあらし *violent storm*

hágu 剝ぐ *to peel off, to tear off* [→**hagasu** 剝がす]

hagúruma 歯車 *gear (-wheel), cogwheel*

háha 母 *mother* [⇔**okāsan** お母さん; ⇔**chichi** 父]

¶Haha wa ryōri ga dai-suki desu.

母は料理が大好きです。

My mother loves cooking.

¶Haha wa ima isogashii no desu.

母は今忙しいのです。

My mother is busy now.

¶Shippai wa seikō no haha.

失敗は成功の母。《proverb》

Failure teaches success. 《Literally: Failure is the mother of success.》

• Haha no hi 母の日 *Mother's Day*

• haha-oya 母親 *mother, female parent* [⇔**chichi-oya** 父親 (s.v. **chichi** 父)]

hai 灰 *ash*

hai 肺 *lung*

• hai-en 肺炎 *pneumonia*

• hai-gan 肺癌 *lung cancer*

• hai-katsuryō 肺活量 *lung capacity*

hai はい ① 【FORMAL for **ē** ええ】 *yes* [⇔**iie** いいえ]

¶"Itō-san desu ka." "Hai, sō desu."

「伊藤さんですか」「はい、そうです」

"Are you Mr. Ito?" "Yes, that's right."

¶"Yuasa-san wa sakkā wa shinai no desu ne." "Hai, shimasen."

「湯浅さんはサッカーはしないのですね」「はい、しません」

"Mr. Yuasa doesn't play soccer, does he." "No, he doesn't". 《In response to a question that presumes a negative answer, **hai** is used to mean *Yes, your presumption is correct.* A natural English translation will often have *no* rather than *yes* .》

② *I will comply, OK, all right*

¶"Ki o tsukete kudasai." "Hai."

「気をつけてください」「はい」

"Please be careful." "All right."

③ 《in response to hearing one's name called》 *Here, Present; Yes?*

¶ "Tanaka-san." "Hai."

「田中さん」「はい」

"Miss Tanaka." "Here."

④ *Here, Here you are* 《when offering something》

¶ Hai, kore o tabete kudasai.

はい、これを食べてください。

Here, please eat this.

hái 杯 *sake cup*

• -hai －杯《counter for cupfuls, glassfuls, bowlfuls, spoonfuls; see Appendix 2》

¶ O-cha o ip-pai kudasai.

お茶を１杯ください。

Please give me a cup of tea.

• yūshō-hai 優勝杯 *championship cup*

haiboku 敗北 *defeat* [⇔**shōri** 勝利]

• haiboku suru 敗北する *to be defeated* [→**makeru** 負ける①]

haiei 背泳 *backstroke* [→**seoyogi** 背泳ぎ]

haiena ハイエナ *hyena*

haifai ハイファイ *hi-fi*

háifun ハイフン *hyphen*

haihíru ハイヒール *high-heeled shoes*

haiiro 灰色 *gray* 《as a noun》

¶ Kyō wa haiiro no sora desu ne.

きょうは灰色の空ですね。

Today the sky is gray, isn't it. 《Literally: *Today it's a gray sky, isn't it.*》

haijákku ハイジャック *hijacking*

• haijakku suru ハイジャックする *to hijack*

haijánpu ハイジャンプ *high jump* 《(athletic event)》 [→**hashiritakatobi** 走り高跳び]

haikara ハイカラ 【COL.】 ～**na** ～な *fashionable, stylish*

haikei 背景 ① *background, backdrop*

¶ Tōkyō-tawā o haikei ni shashin o torimashō.

東京タワーを背景に写真を撮りましょう。

Let's take a picture with Tokyo Tower in the background.

② *backing, support*

¶ Sono kōho-sha no haikei ni yūryoku na seiji-ka ga iru.

その候補者の背景に有力な政治家がいる。

That candidate has support from a powerful politician.

háikei 拝啓 【FORMAL】 《opening phrase used in formal letters》 [⇔**keigu** 敬具]

haiken 拝見 ～**suru** ～する 【HUM. for **miru** 見る】

haikigásu 排気ガス *exhaust (gas)*

háikingu ハイキング *hiking, hike*

¶ Mori e haikingu ni ikimashō.

森へハイキングに行きましょう。

Let's go hiking in the woods.

• haikingu o suru ハイキングをする *to hike*

haiku 俳句 *haiku* 《a kind of traditional Japanese three-line poem》

hairáito ハイライト ① *highlight, outstanding part*

② *highlight, brightest part*

háiru 入る{5}① *to enter, to go in, to come in* [⇔**deru** 出る①]

¶ Ura-guchi kara ie ni hairimashita.

裏口から家に入りました。

I entered the house from the back door.

¶ Haitte mo yoroshii desu ka.

入ってもよろしいですか。

May I come in?

• furo ni hairu ふろに入る *to take a bath*

• haitte iru 入っている *to be inside*

② *to enter, to join, to become a participant* [⇔**yameru** 辞める]

¶ Otōto wa rainen sono chūgakkō ni hairimasu.

弟は来年その中学校に入ります。

My younger brother will enter that junior high school next year.

¶ Jirō wa basukettobōru-bu ni haitta yo.

次郎はバスケットボール部に入ったよ。

Jiro joined the basketball club!

¶ Kurabu ni haitte imasu ka.

クラブに入っていますか。

Are you in a club?

③ *to fit (inside)*

¶ Kono hōru ni wa nan-nin hairu deshō ka.

このホールには何人入るでしょうか。

How many people will fit in this hall?

háisha 歯医者 *dentist*

haishaku 拝借 〜**suru** 〜する 【HUM. for **kariru** 借りる①】

haishi 廃止 *abolition, repeal*
- haishi suru 廃止する *to abolish, to repeal*

haitatsu 配達 *delivery, distribution*
- haitatsu suru 配達する *to deliver, to distribute*
¶Yūbin wa ichi-nichi ni ni-kai haitatsu saremasu.
郵便は 1 日に 2 回配達されます。
Mail is delivered twice a day.
- haitatsu-ryō 配達料 *delivery charge*

haiuē ハイウェー <*US*>*expressway*, <*UK*>*motorway* [→**kōsoku–dōro** 高速道路 (s.v. **kōsoku** 高速)]

háiyā ハイヤー *taxi hired for a fixed period*

haiyū 俳優 *actor, actress* [→**yakusha** 役者]
- eiga–haiyū 映画俳優 *movie actor*

haizara 灰皿 *ashtray*

hají 恥 *shame, disgrace*
- haji o kaku 恥をかく *to disgrace oneself, to be put to shame*
¶Akira–san wa minna no mae de haji o kakimashita.
明さんはみんなの前で恥をかきました。
Akira was put to shame in front of everyone.
- haji–shirazu 恥知らず *shamelessness; shameless person*

hajimari 始まり *beginning, start* [→**hajime** 初め]

hajimaru 始まる *to begin, to start* 《intransitive》《The time at which something begins can be marked with either **ni** に or **kara** から.》
¶Gakkō wa nan-ji ni hajimaru no desu ka.
学校は何時に始まるのですか。
What time does school begin?
¶Tenisu no shiai wa sugu ni hajimarimasu.
テニスの試合はすぐに始まります。

The tennis match will start right away.
¶Yakyū no shīzun wa kongetsu kara hajimarimasu.
野球のシーズンは今月から始まります。
The baseball season begins this month.

hajime 初め *beginning, start* [⇔**owari** 終わり]
¶Hiroshi wa hajime kara sono jijitsu o shitte ita yo.
浩は初めからその事実を知っていたよ。
Hiroshi knew that fact from the beginning!
¶Ten'in wa hajime kara owari made damatte ita.
店員は初めから終わりまで黙っていた。
The salesclerk kept silent from beginning to end.
¶Raigetsu no hajime ni Besu–san ga Nihon ni kimasu.
来月の初めにベスさんが日本に来ます。
Beth will come to Japan at the beginning of next month.
- hajime no 初めの *first; original*
¶Ryokō no hajime no mikka-kan wa ame deshita.
旅行の初めの 3 日間は雨でした。
It rained for the first three days of the trip.
- hajime wa 初めは *at first*
¶Yumi–san wa hajime wa hazukashi-sō deshita.
由美さんは初めは恥ずかしそうでした。
Yumi looked shy at first.

hajimemáshite 初めまして *How do you do?* 《a polite greeting used when meeting a person for the first time》

hajimeru 始める *to begin, to start* 《transitive》《The time at which something is begun can be marked with either **ni** に or **kara** から.》
¶Hachi-ji kara shukudai o hajimemasu.
8 時から宿題を始めます。
I'll start my homework at 8:00.
¶Go–pēji kara hajimemashō ka.
5 ページから始めましょうか。
Shall we begin at page 5?

–hajimeru −始める *to begin to, to start*

to 《Added to both transitive and intransitive verb bases.》

¶Ani wa Furansu-go o benkyō shi-hajimemashita.

兄はフランス語を勉強し始めました。

My older brother began studying French.

¶Ame ga furi-hajimemashita.

雨が降り始めました。

It began to rain.

hajímete 初めて *for the first time*

¶Hajimete Kyōko-san ni atta no wa itsu desu ka.

初めて京子さんに会ったのはいつですか。

When did you meet Kyoko for the first time?

¶Kotoshi hajimete Shikoku o otozuremasu.

今年初めて四国を訪れます。

I will visit Shikoku this year for the first time.

• hajimete no 初めての *first, not experienced previously*

hajíru 恥じる *be ashamed of, to feel humiliated by*

¶Sensei wa jibun no machigai o hajimashita.

先生は自分のまちがいを恥じました。

The teacher was ashamed of her mistake.

haká 墓 *a grave*

• haka-mairi 墓参り *visiting a grave*

hakai 破壊 *destruction*

• hakai suru 破壊する *to destroy*

¶Ōku no ie ga taifū de hakai saremashita.

多くの家が台風で破壊されました。

Many houses were destroyed by the typhoon.

hakarí 秤 *scale(s), weighing device*

¶Sakana-ya-san wa sono sakana o hakari ni kakemashita.

魚屋さんはその魚をはかりにかけました。

The fish store proprietor put the fish on those scales.

hakáru 計る; 測る; 量る *to measure*

¶Kangofu wa watashi no taion o hakarimashita.

看護婦は私の体温を計りました。

The nurse took my temperature.

¶Taiiku no sensei wa watashi no shinchō o hakarimashita.

体育の先生は私の身長を測りました。

The physical education teacher measured my height.

¶Ane wa shū ni ik-kai taijū o hakarimasu.

姉は週に１回体重を量ります。

My older sister weighs herself once a week.

hakáru 図る [[→**kuwadateru** 企てる]]

① *to attempt*

• jisatsu o hakaru 自殺を図る *to attempt suicide*

② *to plan*

hákase 博士 ① *knowledgeable person, expert*

② *person with a doctorate*

• -hakase −博士《Sometimes added to the surname of a person with a doctoral degree instead of -sensei −先生 as a title of respect roughly equivalent to *Dr.*》

¶Narita-hakase mo shusseki nasaimashita.

成田博士も出席なさいました。

Dr. Narita also attended.

• hakase-gō 博士号 *doctoral degree*

• hakase-ronbun 博士論文 *doctoral thesis*

haké 刷毛 *brush* ((implement))

¶Kono hake de penki o nutte kudasai.

このはけでペンキを塗ってください。

Please apply the paint with this brush.

hakiké 吐き気 *nausea*

• hakike ga suru 吐き気がする *to feel sick in one's stomach*

hakimono 履物 *footwear*

hakka 薄荷 *mint* ((plant))

hakken 発見 *discovery*

• hakken suru 発見する *to discover*

¶Dare ga ekkusu-sen o hakken shimashita ka.

だれがエックス線を発見しましたか。

Who discovered X-rays?

• hakken-sha 発見者 *discoverer*

hakketsubyō 白血病 *leukemia*

hakki 発揮 *display, exhibition, making full use* 《*of an ability or power*》
• hakki suru 発揮する *to display, to exhibit, to make full use of*

hakkíri はっきり *clearly*
¶Kono megane o kakeru to, hakkiri miemasu.
この眼鏡をかけると、はっきり見えます。
When I put on these glasses, I can see clearly.
• hakkiri suru はっきりする *to become clear*
¶Sono setsumei wa hakkiri shite imasu.
その説明ははっきりしています。
That explanation is clear.

hakkō 発行 *publication, issuing*
• hakkō suru 発行する *to publish, to issue*
¶Kono hon wa zehi hakkō shimashō.
この本はぜひ発行しましょう。
Let's publish this book by all means.
• hakkō-bu-sū 発行部数 *the number of copies printed*
• hakkō-sha 発行者 *publisher*

hako 箱 *box, case*
¶Sono hako no naka ni tenisu-bōru ga haitte iru.
その箱の中にテニスボールが入っている。
There are tennis balls in that box.
• –hako ー箱《*counter for boxes, boxfuls; see Appendix 2*》
¶Budō o hito-hako kaimasu.
ぶどうを1箱買います。
I'll buy one box of grapes.
• bentō-bako 弁当箱 *lunch box*
• e-no-gu-bako 絵の具箱 *paintbox*
• hon-bako 本箱 *bookcase*
• hōseki-bako 宝石箱 *jewel case*

hakobu 運ぶ ① *to carry, to convey, to transport*
¶Kono nimotsu o heya made hakonde kudasai.
この荷物を部屋まで運んでください。
Please carry this baggage to the room.
¶O-sara o daidokoro ni hakobinasai.
お皿を台所に運びなさい。
Carry the dishes to the kitchen.

② *to progress, to continue*
¶Kensetsu wa umaku hakobimashita.
建設はうまく運びました。
The construction progressed well.

háku 吐く ① *to vomit, to throw up* 《*transitive or intransitive*》
¶Yūbe sukoshi hakimashita ga, mō heiki desu.
ゆうべ少し吐きましたが、もう平気です。
Last night I vomitted a little, but I'm all right now.
② *to spit out, to expel*
• iki o haku 息を吐く *to breathe out*

háku 掃く *to sweep* 《*with a broom, etc.*》

haku 履く *to put on* 《*The direct object of* **haku** *is generally an article of clothing that goes below the waist. Compare* **kiru** 着る *and* **kaburu** 被る. *Like other verbs for putting on clothing,* **haku** *in the* -te iru *form can express the meaning* be wearing, have on.*》 [⇔**nugu** 脱ぐ]
¶Chichi wa atarashii kutsu o hakimashita.
父は新しい靴をはきました。
My father put on his new shoes.
¶Ani wa itsu-mo jīpan o haite iru yo.
兄はいつもジーパンをはいているよ。
My older brother always wears jeans!

–haku ー泊《*counter for nights of a stayover; see Appendix 2*》

hakuboku 白墨 *chalk* [→**chōku** チョーク]

hakubutsúkan 博物館 *museum*

hakuchō 白鳥 *swan*

hakujin 白人 *white person*

hákujō 白状 *confession*
• hakujō suru 白状する *to confess*
¶Hannin wa yatto hakujō shimashita.
犯人はやっと白状しました。
The criminal finally confessed.

hakujō 薄情 ~**na** ~な *cold-hearted, cold, unkind* [→**reitan na** 冷淡な]

hakuránkai 博覧会 *exposition, fair*
• bankoku-hakurankai 万国博覧会 *world exposition, world's fair*

hakusái 白菜 *Chinese cabbage, bok-choi*

hakushi 白紙 *blank paper*
- A o hakushi ni modosu Aを白紙に戻す *to start A afresh*

hákushi 博士 [☞**hakase** 博士②]

hákushu 拍手 *clapping, applause*
- hakushu suru 拍手する *to clap*
¶Sensei no teian ni seito zenin ga hakushu shimashita.
先生の提案に生徒全員が拍手しました。
All the students clapped at their teacher's proposal.
- hakushu-kassai 拍手喝采 *clapping and cheering, a big hand*

hamá 浜 *beach*
¶Hama o sanpo shimashō.
浜を散歩しましょう。
Let's walk along the beach.
- hama-be 浜辺 [☞**hama** 浜 (above)]

hamáguri 蛤 *clam*

hamaru 嵌まる, 填まる ① *to fit in place* 《intransitive》
¶To ga umaku hamarimasen ne.
戸がうまくはまりませんね。
The door doesn't close properly, does it.
- kata ni hamaru 型にはまる *to fit a mold, to be stereotypical*
 ② *to fall into, to get trapped*
¶Chichi no kuruma ga doro-michi ni hamarimashita.
父の車は泥道にはまりました。
My father's car got stuck in the muddy road.

hameru 嵌める, 填める ① *to fit in place* 《transitive》
¶Daiku-san wa mado ni sutendogurasu o hameta.
大工さんは窓にステンドグラスをはめた。
The carpenter fitted stained glass into the window.
 ② *to put on, to slip on* 《The direct object is ordinarily something that fits snugly on a hand, finger, etc. Like other verbs for putting on clothing, **hameru** in the -**te iru** form can express the meaning *be wearing, have on.*》
¶Unten-shu wa tebukuro o hamemashita.

運転手は手袋をはめました。
The driver put on gloves.
¶Yumi wa itsu-mo kekkon-yubiwa o hamete imasu.
由美はいつも結婚指輪をはめています。
Yumi is always wearing a wedding ring.
 ③ 【CRUDE】 *to ensnare; to take in, to deceive* [→**damasu** 騙す]

hametsu 破滅 *ruin, ruination*
- hametsu suru 破滅する *to be ruined*

hamon 波紋 ① *concentric ripples*
 ② *repercussion, subsequent effect*
- A ni hamon o tōjiru Aに波紋を投じる *to have repercussions on A*

hámonī ハーモニー (*musical*)*harmony*

hāmonika ハーモニカ *harmonica*

hámu ハム *ham* ((*meat*))

hámu ハム *ham radio operator*

hamuéggu ハムエッグ *ham and eggs*

han- 半- 《Added to noun bases.》
- han-gaku 半額 *half price*
- han-seiki 半世紀 *half a century*
- han-sode 半袖 *short sleeves*
- han-toshi 半年 *half a year*
- han-zubon 半ズボン *shorts, short pants*

-han -半 *and a half* 《Added to number bases.》
¶Jugyō wa ni-jikan-han desu.
授業は2時間半です。
The class is two and a half hours.
¶Ima jū-ji-han desu.
今10時半です。
It's 10:30 now.

hán 判 *signature seal* 《Documents are ordinarily stamped with a seal rather than signed in Japan.》 [→**inkan** 印鑑]
- A ni han o osu Aに判を押す *to stamp one's seal on A, to stamp A with one's seal*
¶Kono yōshi ni han o oshite kudasai.
この用紙に判を押してください。
Please put your seal on this form.

haná 花 *flower, blossom*
¶Haru ni wa ōku no hana ga sakimasu.
春には多くの花が咲きます。
Many flowers bloom in spring.
¶Mai-asa hana ni mizu o yarimasu.

毎朝花に水をやります。
I water the flowers every morning.
¶Haha wa niwa no hana o tsumimashita.
母は庭の花を摘みました。
My mother picked a flower from the garden.
• hana-batake 花畑 *flower field*
• hana-mi 花見 cherry-blossom viewing 《*a popular springtime activity in Japan*》
• hana-niwa 花園 *flower garden*
• hana-ya 花屋 *flower shop; florist*
• hana-zakari 花盛り *full bloom*
• o-hana お花 (*traditional Japanese*)*flower arranging* 《This word contains the honorific prefix **o**– and can also be used simply as an honorific form of **hana.**》[→**ikebana** 生け花]

hana 鼻 *nose*
• hana no ana 鼻の穴 *nostril*
• hana ga takai 鼻が高い *to have a prominent nose; to be proud*
• hana ga hikui 鼻が低い *to have a flat nose*
• hana ga kiku 鼻が利く *to have a keen nose*
• hana ga tsumaru 鼻がつまる *one's nose gets stuffed up*
• hana-ji 鼻血 *nosebleed*
• hana-ji o dasu 鼻血を出す *to have a nosebleed*
• hana-uta 鼻歌 *humming* 《i.e., a kind of singing》
• hana-uta o utau 鼻歌を歌う *to hum a tune*

hana 洟 *nasal mucus, snivel*
• hana ga deru はなが出る *one's nose runs*
• hana o kamu はなをかむ *to blow one's nose*

hánabi 花火 *fireworks*
• hanabi o ageru 花火を上げる *to set off fireworks*
• hanabi-taikai 花火大会 *fireworks display*

hanabíra 花びら *petal*

hanamúko 花婿 *bridegroom* [⇔**hana-yome** 花嫁]

hanaréru 離れる *to become separate; to move away, to leave* 《the place away from which the movement occurs can be marked either with **kara** から or with **o** を.》
¶Chichi wa chōshoku ga owaru to sugu shokutaku o hanaremasu.
父は朝食が終わるとすぐ食卓を離れます。
As soon as he finishes breakfast, my father leaves the table.
• retsu o／kara hanareru 列を／から離れる *to get out of line*
• hanarete iru 離れている *to be located at a distance, to be distant*
¶Shōgakkō wa eki kara yon-kiro hanarete imasu.
小学校は駅から4キロ離れています。
The elementary school is four kilometers from the station.
¶Kono inu kara hanarete inasai.
この犬から離れていなさい。
Stay away from this dog.

hanashí 話 ① *talking; conversation* [→**kaiwa** 会話]
¶Hanashi ni kuwawarimasen ka.
話に加わりませんか。
Won't you join in the conversation?
¶Nan no hanashi desu ka.
何の話ですか。
What are you talking about?
• hanashi o suru 話をする *to have a talk, to talk*
¶Kinō Yoneyama-san to nagai aida hanashi o shimashita.
きのう米山さんと長い間話をしました。
Yesterday I had a long talk with Mr. Yoneyama.
• hanashi o kaeru 話を変える *to change the subject*
② *story, report, account*
¶Masako-san wa omoshiroi hanashi o shite kureta yo.
正子さんはおもしろい話をしてくれたよ。
Masako told me an interesting story!
• to iu hanashi da という話だ *they say that, I hear that* 《following a clause》[→**sō da** そうだ]

¶Hayashi-sensei ga Kōchi ni o-kaeri ni naru to iu hanashi da.

林先生が高知にお帰りになるという話だ。

They say Mr. Hayashi will return home to Kochi.

• hanashi-chū no 話中の <*US*>*busy*, <*UK*>*engaged* 《*describing a telephone line or number*》

• hanashi-zuki no 話好きの *fond of talking, talkative*

hanashiáu 話し合う ① *to talk with each other*

¶Tomodachi to shōrai ni tsuite hanashi-aimashita.

友達と将来について話し合いました。

I talked with my friend about the future.

② *to discuss*

¶Kachō to sono keikaku o hanashi-aimasu.

課長とその計画を話し合います。

I'll discuss that plan with the section chief.

hanashikakéru 話しかける *to start talking, to initiate a conversation*

¶Shiranai hito ga watashi ni hanashi-kakete kimashita.

知らない人が私に話しかけてきました。

A person I don't know started talking to me.

hanásu 放す ① *to let go, to release one's grasp on*

¶Shujin wa inu o hanashimashita.

主人は犬を放しました。

The master let the dog go.

• A kara te o hanasu Aから手を放す *to release one's hold on A, to let go of A*

¶Tetsubō kara te o hanasanai de.

鉄棒から手を放さないで。

Don't let go of the bar.

② *to set free, to release*

¶Haha wa sono tori o hanashite yarimashita.

母はその鳥を放してやりました。

My mother set that bird free.

hanásu 話す ① *to speak, to talk*

¶Ane wa sono tomodachi to Furansu-go de hanashimasu.

姉はその友達とフランス語で話します。

My older sister speaks to her friend in French.

¶Motto yukkuri hanashite kudasaimasen ka.

もっとゆっくり話してくださいませんか。

Won't you please speak more slowly?

¶Ato de kōchō-sensei to hanashimasu.

あとで校長先生と話します。

I will talk with the principal later.

¶Mazu konpyūtā ni tsuite hanashimashō.

まずコンピューターについて話しましょう。

First, let's talk about the computer.

② *to talk about, to tell about*

¶Go-kazoku no koto o sukoshi hanashite kudasai.

ご家族のことを少し話してください。

Please tell me a little about your family.

¶Nishioka-san ni hanashitai koto ga arimasu.

西岡さんに話したいことがあります。

There is something I want to tell Ms. Nishioka.

hanásu 離す *to part, to separate* 《*transitive*》

¶Ani wa kenka shite iru futari o hana-shimashita.

兄はけんかしている二人を離しました。

My older brother separated two people fighting.

hanátaba 花束 *bouquet*

hanawa 花輪 *flower wreath*

hanáyaka 華やか 〜**na** 〜な *gorgeous, brilliant, splendid*

• hanayaka na iro 華やかな色 *brilliant colors*

• hanayaka na pātī 華やかなパーティー *splendid party*

hanáyome 花嫁 *bride* [⇔**hanamuko** 花婿]

• hanayome-ishō 花嫁衣装 *wedding dress*

hanbágā ハンバーガー *hamburger*

hanbágu ハンバーグ *hamburger steak*

hanbai 販売 *selling* (*merchandise*)

• hanbai suru 販売する *to sell, to deal in*

• hanbai-bu 販売部 *sales department*

- hanbai-in 販売員 *salesperson* [→**sēru-suman** セールスマン]
- jidō-hanbai-ki 自動販売機 *vending machine*

hanbún 半分 *half*
¶Hachi no hanbun wa yon desu.
8の半分は4です。
Half of eight is four.
¶Watashi no furui kitte no hanbun wa gaikoku no mono desu.
私の古い切手の半分は外国のものです。
Half of my old stamps are foreign ones.
¶Kono kēki o hanbun ni kitte kudasai.
このケーキを半分に切ってください。
Cut the cake in half, please.
¶Kono shigoto wa mō hanbun owarimashita.
この仕事はもう半分終わりました。
I've already finished half this work.

hándan 判断 *a judgment, assessment*
¶Jibun-jishin no handan ni shitagatte kōdō su-beki desu.
自分自身の判断に従って行動すべきです。
You have to act according to your own judgment.
- handan suru 判断する *to judge, to form a judgment about*
¶Hito o gaiken de handan shite wa ikenai yo.
人を外見で判断してはいけないよ。
You mustn't judge a person by outward appearances!

handikyáppu ハンディキャップ ① *handicap, disadvantage*
② *handicap* 《in golf》

handobággu ハンドバッグ *handbag, purse*

handobóru ハンドボール ① 《the game of》*handball*
② *a handball*

handoru ハンドル ① *steering wheel*
¶Unten-shu wa handoru o hidari ni kirimashita.
運転手はハンドルを左に切りました。
The driver cut the steering wheel to the left.
② *handlebars*

- hidari-handoru 左ハンドル *left-side steering wheel*
- migi-handoru 右ハンドル *right-side steering wheel*

hane 羽 ① *feather*
② *wing* [→**tsubasa** 翼]

han'ei 繁栄 *prosperity, flourishing*
- han'ei suru 繁栄する *to prosper, to flourish, to thrive*

hanemún ハネムーン *honeymoon* [→**shinkon-ryokō** 新婚旅行 (s.v. **shinkon** 新婚)]
¶Futari wa hanemūn ni Kanada ni ikimasu.
二人はハネムーンにカナダに行きます。
The couple will go to Canada on their honeymoon.

hanéru 跳ねる ① *to jump* 《upward》 [→**tobiagaru** 跳び上がる]; *to bounce*
¶Kono kaeru wa yoku haneru ne.
このかえるはよく跳ねるね。
This frog jumps well, doesn't it.
② *to splash, to spatter* 《transitive or intransitive》
¶Epuron ni abura ga hanemashita.
エプロンに油が跳ねました。
Oil spattered on my apron.
¶Kuruma ga doresu ni doro-mizu o haneta yo.
車がドレスに泥水を跳ねたよ。
A car splashed muddy water on my dress!

hanga 版画 *woodblock print; etching*
hángā ハンガー 《clothes》*hanger*
hangeki 反撃 *counterattack*
- hangeki suru 反撃する *to counterattack*
hanguguráidā ハンググライダー *hang glider*
hán'i 範囲 *range, extent, scope*
¶Chichi wa dokusho no han'i ga hiroi desu.
父は読書の範囲が広いです。
My father reads widely. 《Literally: As for my father, the range of reading is wide.》

hánji 判事 *judge, magistrate* [→**saiban-kan** 裁判官 (s.v. **saiban** 裁判)]

hankachi ハンカチ *handkerchief*
¶Kono hankachi de ase o fukinasai.
このハンカチで汗をふきなさい。
Wipe the sweat with this handkerchief.

hánkei 半径 *radius* 《of a circle or sphere》
¶Kono chikyū-gi no hankei wa nijūgo-senchi desu.
この地球儀の半径は25センチです。
The radius of this globe is 25 centimeters.

hánketsu 判決 *judicial decision, court judgment*
• hanketsu o kudasu 判決を下す *to hand down a decision, to make a ruling*

hankō 反抗 *resistance, opposition* [⇔**fukujū** 服従]
• hankō suru 反抗する *to resist, to oppose*

hankó 判子 【COL. for **han** 判, **in** 印】 *signature seal*

hankyū 半球 *hemisphere*

hánmā ハンマー *hammer* [→**kanazuchi** 金槌①]
• hanmā-nage ハンマー投げ *hammer throw* 《athletic event》

hánnin 犯人 *criminal, culprit*

hannō 反応 *response, reaction*
¶Shimin wa atarashii keikaku ni hannō o shimesanakatta.
市民は新しい計画に反応を示さなかった。
The citizens showed no reaction to the new plan.
• hannō suru 反応する *to respond, to react*
• kagaku-hannō 化学反応 *chemical reaction*
• rensa-hannō 連鎖反応 *chain reaction*

hanpatsu 反発 ① *repelling, repulsion*
• hanpatsu suru 反発する *to repel*
② *rebounding, springing back*
• hanpatsu suru 反発する *to rebound, to spring back*
③ *resistance, opposition* [→**hankō** 反抗]
• hanpatsu suru 反発する *to resist, to oppose*

hanran 反乱 *revolt, rebellion*
• hanran suru 反乱する *to revolt, to rebel*
• hanran o okosu 反乱を起こす *to revolt, to rebel*
• hanran-gun 反乱軍 *rebel army, rebel forces*

hanran 氾濫 *overflowing, flood*
• hanran suru はんらんする *to overflow its banks, to flood*
¶Kono kawa wa maitoshi hanran shimasu.
この川は毎年はんらんします。
The river overflows its banks every year.

hanrei 凡例 *introductory explanatory notes*
• chizu no hanrei 地図の凡例 *map legend*

hánsamu ハンサム 〜**na** 〜な *handsome*

hansei 反省 *reflection, thinking back* 《on something one has done》
¶Yari-naosu mae ni motto hansei ga hitsuyō desu.
やり直す前にもっと反省が必要です。
Before doing it over, more reflection is necessary.
• hansei suru 反省する *to reflect on, to think back on*
¶Jibun no kotoba o hansei shimashita.
自分の言葉を反省しました。
I thought back on my own words.

hansha 反射 *refrection* 《back from a surface》
• hansha suru 反射する *to reflect* 《transitive or intransitive》
• A ga B ni hansha suru A が B に反射する *A reflects off B*
¶Hikari ga okujō ni hansha shite imashita.
光が屋上に反射していました。
Light was reflecting off the rooftop.

Hánshin 阪神 *the Osaka-Kobe area*

hansoku 反則 *foul* 《in sports》 [→**fauru** ファウル②]
• hansoku suru 反則する *to commit a foul*

hansúru 反する 《Irreg.》 *to go against, to be contrary*

¶Sono kōi wa hōritsu ni hanshite imasu.

その行為は法律に反しています。

That act is against the law.

hansuto ハンスト *hunger strike*

hántā ハンター *hunter* [→**ryō-shi** 猟師 (s.v. **ryō** 猟)]

hantai 反対 ① *the opposite, the contrary* [→**gyaku** 逆]

¶"Hidari" no hantai wa nan desu ka.

「左」の反対は何ですか。

What is the opposite of "left"?

¶Ishigami-san wa hantai no hōkō ni aruite imasu.

石上さんは反対の方向に歩いています。

Mr. Ishigami is walking in the opposite direction.

② *opposition, objection* [⇔**sansei** 賛成]

¶Daitōryō no hantai de sono hōan wa tōranakatta.

大統領の反対でその法案は通らなかった。

Due to the president's opposition that bill did not pass.

• hantai no hito 反対の人 *a person who is opposed*

• hantai suru 反対する *to be opposed, to object*

¶Kono keikaku ni wa tsuyoku hantai shimasu.

この計画には強く反対します。

I am strongly opposed to this plan.

• hantai-gawa 反対側 *opposite side*

hantei 判定 *judgment, decision*

hantō 半島 *peninsula*

hanzai 犯罪 *crime*

• hanzai-sha 犯罪者 *a criminal*

happa 葉っぱ [[→**ha** 葉]] *leaf; blade* 《of grass》

happyō 発表 *announcement; public presentation*

• happyō suru 発表する *to announce; to present publicly*

hāpu ハープ *harp*

hápuningu ハプニング *a happening*

hará 腹 ① 【CRUDE for **onaka** お腹】 *stomach, belly*

• hara ga heru 腹が減る *to get hungry*

• hara ga itai 腹が痛い *one's stomach aches*

② *mind, heart*

• hara ga tatsu 腹が立つ *to get angry*

• hara o tateru 腹を立てる *to get angry*

harabai 腹這い 〜**ni naru** 〜になる *to lie on one's stomach*

hárahara はらはら 〜**suru** 〜する *to become uneasy, to get anxious*

¶Fāsuto no purē ni harahara shita yo.

ファーストのプレーにははらはらしたよ。

I became uneasy about the first baseman's play!

haráu 払う ① *to pay* 《The direct object is the money, charge, expense, etc.》

¶Kyō wa watashi ga kanjō o haraimasu.

きょうは私が勘定を払います。

Today I will pay the bill.

• A ni B o harau AにBを払う *to pay B to A*

¶Ashita ōya-san ni goman-en haraimasu.

あした大家さんに5万円払います。

I will pay 50,000 yen to the landlord tomorrow.

• chūi o harau 注意を払う *to pay attention*

② *to sweep away, to wipe away, to clean away*

• hokori o harau ほこりを払う *to clean away dust*

haré 晴れ 〜**no** 〜の *cloudless, fair, clear*

¶Ashita wa hare deshō.

あしたは晴れでしょう。

It will probably be fine tomorrow.

¶Hare nochi kumori.

晴れのち曇り。《a weather forecast》

Fair, cloudy later.

haréru 晴れる ① *to clear up, to become cloudless*

¶Gogo ni wa hareru deshō.

午後には晴れるでしょう。

It will probably clear up in the afternoon.

¶Hareta sora o hibari ga tonde imasu.

晴れた空をひばりが飛んでいます。

Skylarks are flying in the clear sky.

• kibun ga hareru 気分が晴れる *to feel*

better, to recover one's spirits

② *to clear up, to clear away* 《when the subject is clouds, etc.》

¶Kiri wa sugu hareru sō desu.

霧はすぐ晴れるそうです。

I hear the fog will clear up right away.

• utagai ga hareru 疑いが晴れる *suspicion becomes cleared up*

hareru 腫れる *to swell, to become swollen* 《The subject is part of the body.》

¶Kega o shita yubi wa hareru ni chigai nai yo.

けがをした指ははれるに違いないよ。

An injured finger will certainly swell!

haretsu 破裂 *bursting, rupture*

• haretsu suru 破裂する *to burst, to rupture*

¶Chika no boirā ga haretsu shimashita yo.

地階のボイラーが破裂しましたよ。

The boiler in the basement burst!

hári 針 ① *needle*

• hari ni ito o tōsu 針に糸を通す *to thread a needle*

② *hand* 《of a clock》

¶Tokei no hari ga jūni-ji o sashite imasu.

時計の針が12時を指しています。

The hands of the clock are pointing to 12:00.

harigane 針金 *(metal)wire*

harikḗn ハリケーン *hurricane*

háru 春 *spring* 《(season)》 [⇔**aki** 秋]

¶Mō sugu haru desu.

もうすぐ春です。

It will soon be spring.

¶Haru ni wa hana-mi ni dekakemasu.

春には花見に出かけます。

In the spring we go out cherry-blossom viewing.

¶Kono haru kazoku de haikingu ni ikimashita.

この春家族でハイキングに行きました。

We went hiking as a family this spring.

• haru-kaze 春風 *spring wind*

• haru-same 春雨 *spring rain*

• haru-yasumi 春休み <US>*spring vacation,* <UK>*the spring holidays*

haru 張る ① *to spread out, to stretch out* 《transitive or intransitive》

¶Sono ni-hon no ki no aida ni rōpu o harō.

その2本の木の間にロープを張ろう。

Let's stretch a rope between those two trees.

¶Kono ki wa eda ga hiroku hatte imasu ne.

この木は枝が広く張っていますね。

The branches of this tree are spread out wide, aren't they.

• tento o haru テントを張る *to put up a tent*

• ho o haru 帆を張る *to put up a sail*

• mune o haru 胸を張る *to throw out one's chest*

• ne ga haru 根が張る *roots spread out*

• nedan ga haru 値段が張る *a price is expensive*

② *to tauten* 《transitive or intransitive》

• ito ga haru 糸が張る *a thread becomes taut*

• tsuna o haru 綱を張る *to pull a rope taut*

• ki ga haru 気が張る *to become nervous, to become strained*

• ki o haru 気を張る *to strain one's nerves*

• kata ga haru 肩が張る *one's shoulder becomes stiff*

③ *to spread over the entire surface* 《transitive or intransitive》

• tanbo ni mizu o haru 田んぼに水を張る *to flood a paddy*

• ike ni kōri ga haru 池に氷が張る *ice forms on a pond*

④ *to slap, to hit with an open hand*

haru 貼る *to affix, to stick* 《on a flat surface》

¶Kono fūtō ni rokujūni-en kitte o hatte kudasai.

この封筒に62円切手をはってください。

Please stick a 62-yen stamp on this envelope.

¶Keiji-ban ni kono posutā o harimashō.

掲示板にこのポスターをはりましょう。

Let's put this poster on the bulletin board.

harubáru はるばる（〜to 〜と）*all the way, covering a great distance*
¶Sono yakusha wa harubaru Mosukuwa kara kita.
その役者ははるばるモスクワからきた。
That actor came all the way from Moscow.

háruka 遥か ① 〜na 〜な *distant, faraway*
• haruka na mirai はるかな未来 *distant future*
• haruka ni はるかに *distantly, in the distance*
¶Haruka ni akari ga miemasu.
はるかに明かりが見えます。
A light is visible in the distance.
② 〜ni 〜に *by far, much*［→**zutto** ずっと③］
¶Kono gitā wa watashi no yori haruka ni ii desu.
このギターは私のよりはるかにいいです。
This guitar is much better than mine.

hasamáru 挟まる *to get caught, to become sandwiched*
¶Sukāto ga doa ni hasamarimashita.
スカートがドアに挟まりました。
My skirt got caught in the door.

hasamí 鋏 *scissors*
¶Kono hasami wa yoku kiremasu ne.
このはさみはよく切れますね。
These scissors cut well, don't they.
• it-chō no hasami 1丁のはさみ *one pair of scissors*

hasámu 挟む ① *to insert, to sandwich* 《between two things》
¶Watashi wa hon no pēji no aida ni memo o hasanda.
私は本のページの間にメモを挟んだ。
I put a note between the pages of the book.
② *to insert and have pinched*
¶Akiko-chan wa kuruma no doa ni ko-yubi o hasanda.
明子ちゃんは車のドアに小指を挟んだ。
Akiko got her little finger pinched

in the car door.

hasan 破産 *bankruptcy*
• hasan suru 破産する *to go bankrupt*
¶Hasegawa-san wa jigyō ni shippai shite hasan shita.
長谷川さんは事業に失敗して破産した。
Mr. Hasegawa failed in business and went bankrupt.

hashi 端 *end, tip*［→**saki** 先①］; *edge*［→**fuchi** 縁］
¶Koppu o tēburu no hashi ni okanai de.
コップをテーブルの端に置かないで。
Don't put the glass on the edge of the table.

háshi 箸 *chopsticks*
• ichi-zen no hashi 1ぜんのはし *one pair of chopsticks*

hashí 橋 *bridge* 《spanning a river, etc.》
¶Sono hashi o kakeru no ni go-nen kakarimasu.
その橋を架けるのに5年かかります。
It will take five years to build that bridge.
¶Kono kawa ni wa ikutsu-ka no hashi ga kakatte iru.
この川にはいくつかの橋が架かっている。
There are several bridges spanning this river.
• hashi o wataru 橋を渡る *to cross a bridge*

hashigo 梯子 *ladder*
¶Kabe ni hashigo o kakemashō.
壁にはしごをかけましょう。
Let's set up a ladder against the wall.
• hashigo o noboru はしごを登る *to climb a ladder*

hashiká 麻疹 *measles*
• hashika ni kakaru はしかにかかる *to catch measles*

hashira 柱 *post, pillar*
• hashira-dokei 柱時計 *wall clock*

hashirihábatobi 走り幅跳び（*running*)*long jump* 《athletic event》

hashimawáru 走り回る *to run around* 《intransitive》

hashirisaru 走り去る *to run away, to run off*

hashiritákatobi 走り高跳び (*running*)*high jump* ((athletic event))

hashíru 走る{5} ① *to run* «when the subject is a person or animal» [→**kakeru** 駆ける]

¶Shinji-san wa hashiru no ga totemo hayai ne.

信次さんは走るのがとても速いね。

Shinji runs very fast, doesn't he. «Literally: *As for Shinji, running is very fast, isn't it.*»

¶Otōto wa watashi no tokoro e hashitte kimashita.

弟は私のところへ走ってきました。

My younger brother came running to me.

¶Watashi-tachi wa eki made zutto hashirimashita.

私たちは駅までずっと走りました。

We ran all the way to the station.

② *to run* «when the subject is a vehicle»

¶Sono basu wa Tōkyō-Nagoya-kan o hashirimasu.

そのバスは東京・名古屋間を走ります。

That bus runs between Tokyo and Nagoya.

hassei 発生 *occurrence, outbreak; coming into existence*

• jishin no hassei 地震の発生 *occurrence of an earthquake*

• korera no hassei コレラの発生 *outbreak of cholera*

• hassei suru 発生する *to occur, to break out; to come into existence*

hassha 発車 *departure, starting off* «of a train, bus, etc.»

• hassha suru 発車する *to depart, to start off*

¶Tsugi no densha wa jū-ji ni hassha shimasu.

次の電車は10時に発車します。

The next train will depart at 10:00.

¶Nagano-yuki no kyūkō wa roku-ban-sen kara hassha shimasu.

長野行きの急行は6番線から発車します。

The express for Nagano leaves from Track No. 6.

hassha 発射 ① *firing, shooting* «of a gun»

• hassha suru 発射する *to fire, to shoot* «transitive or intransitive»

• pisutoru o hassha suru ピストルを発射する *to fire a pistol*

② *launch* «of a rocket»

• hassha suru 発射する *to launch*

• hassha-dai 発射台 *launching pad*

hasshin 発信 [[⇔**jushin** 受信]] *transmission of a message; transmission of a broadcast*

• hasshin suru 発信する *to transmit*

• hasshin-ki 発信機 *transmitter* ((machiine))

hasu 蓮 *lotus*

hatá 旗 *flag*

¶Hata wa kaze ni hirugaette imasu.

旗は風に翻っています。

The flag is fluttering in the wind.

• hata-zao 旗竿 *flagpole*

hátachi 二十歳 *20 years old* «see Appendix 2»

hatake 畑 (*non-paddy, farm*)*field*

• hatake o tagayasu 畑を耕やす *to plow a field*

hataraki 働き ① *work, working*

¶Chichi wa kaisha no tame ni mezamashii hataraki o shita.

父は会社のために目覚ましい働きをした。

Father did outstanding work for the company.

② *ability, talent* [→**sainō** 才能]

• hataraki no aru hito 働きのある人 *able person*

③ *function* [→**kinō** 機能]; *action, activity* [→**sayō** 作用]

• shinzō no hataraki 心臓の働き *the function of the heart*

• hataraki-guchi 働き口 *job, employment*

• hataraki-mono 働き者 *hard worker*

• hataraki-zakari 働き盛り *the prime of one's working life*

hataraku 働く *to work, to labor*

¶Ano hito wa yoku hatarakimasu.

あの人はよく働きます。

That person works hard.

¶Ane wa pāto de hataraite imasu.

姉はパートで働いています。
My older sister works part-time.

¶ Oji wa kōjō de hataraite imasu.
叔父は工場で働いています。
My uncle works in a factory.

¶ Toda-san wa kangofu to shite hataraku tsumori desu.
戸田さんは看護婦として働くつもりです。
Miss Toda intends to work as a nurse.

hatásu 果たす *to carry out, to fulfill; to achieve, to accomplish*

¶ Satoshi wa kyaputen to shite no gimu o hatashita.
聡はキャプテンとしての義務を果たした。
Satoshi carried out his duty as captain.

• yakusoku o hatasu 約束を果たす *to fulfill a promise*
• mokuteki o hatasu 目的を果たす *to achieve a purpose*
• yakuwari o hatasu 役割を果たす *to play a role, to play a part*

hāto ハート ① *heart* ((bodily organ)) [→**shinzō** 心臓]
② *heart, feelings* [→**kokoro** 心②]
③ *hearts* ((playing-card suit))
• hāto no ēsu ハートのエース *ace of hearts*
• hāto-gata no ハート型の *heart-shaped*

háto 鳩 *pigeon; dove*
• hato-dokei 鳩時計 *cuckoo clock*
• hato-goya 鳩小屋 *pigeon house*
• densho-bato 伝書鳩 *carrier pigeon*

hatsú 初 〜**no** 〜の *first (–time)*
• hatsu-mago 初孫 *first grandchild*
• hatsu-mimi 初耳 *the first one has heard of something*
• hatsu-mōde 初詣で *first visit to a Shinto shrine after New Year's* ((a popular traditional activity in the first few days of a new year in Japan))

hatsubai 発売 *putting on sale, putting on the market* [→**uridashi** 売り出し①]
• hatsubai suru 発売する *to put on sale, to put on the market* [→**uridasu** 売り出す]

¶ Kono shūkan-shi wa Kin'yōbi ni hatsubai saremasu.
この週刊誌は金曜日に発売されます。

This weekly magazine is put on sale on Friday.

hatsuden 発電 *electricity generation*
• hatsuden suru 発電する *to generate electricity*
• hatsuden-ki 発電機 *generator*
• hatsuden-sho 発電所 *power plant, generating station*

hatsugen 発言 *speaking; statement, utterance*
• hatsugen suru 発言する *to speak, to say something*

¶ Kachō wa kaigi de hitokoto mo hatsugen shimasen deshita.
課長は会議で一言も発言しませんでした。
The section chief didn't say a word at the meeting.

• hatsugen-ken 発言権 *the right to speak*

hatsuka 二十日 ((see Appendix 2))
① *twenty days*
② *the twentieth* ((day of a month))

hatsukanézumi 二十日鼠 (*house)mouse*

hatsukoi 初恋 *one's first love*

hatsumei 発明 *inventing, invention*
• hatsumei suru 発明する *to invent*

¶ Dare ga denshin-ki o hatsumei shimashita ka.
だれが電信機を発明しましたか。
Who invented the telegraph?

¶ Hitsuyō wa hatsumei no haha.
必要は発明の母。((proverb))
Necessity is the mother of invention.

• hatsumei-hin 発明品 *an invention*
• hatsumei-ka 発明家 *inventor*

hatsuon 発音 *pronunciation*

¶ Sono tango ni wa futatsu no kotonatta hatsuon ga aru.
その単語には二つの異なった発音がある。
That word has two different pronunciations.

• hatsuon suru 発音する *to pronounce*

¶ Kono tango wa dō hatsuon shimasu ka.
この単語はどう発音しますか。
How do you pronounce this word?

• hatsuon-kigō 発音記号 *pronunciation symbol*

hattatsu 発達 *development, advancement* [→**hatten** 発展]

• hattatsu suru 発達する *to develop, to advance* 《intransitive》

¶Amerika de wa uchū-kagaku ga hattatsu shite iru.

アメリカでは宇宙科学が発達している。

Space science is developed in the United States.

¶Tei-kiatsu ga hattatsu shite, taifū ni narimashita.

低気圧が発達して、台風になりました。

The low pressure developed into a typhoon.

hatten 発展 *development, expansion* [→**hattatsu** 発達]

• hatten suru 発展する *to develop, to expand* 《intransitive》

¶Kono toshi wa kyūsoku ni hatten shimashita.

この都市は急速に発展しました。

This city developed rapidly.

• hatten-tojō-koku 発展途上国 *developing country* [⇔**senshin-koku** 先進国 (s.v. **senshin** 先進)]

háu 這う *to crawl, to creep*

¶Akachan wa tonari no heya ni hatte ikimashita.

赤ちゃんは隣の部屋にはっていきました。

The baby crawled into the next room.

hayagáten 早合点 *hasty conclusion, premature conclusion*

• hayagaten suru 早合点する *to jump to a conclusion*

hayái 早い *early* [⇔**osoi** 遅い①]

¶Kinō wa hayai chūshoku o torimashita.

きのうは早い昼食をとりました。

Today I took an early lunch.

¶Kyō wa hayai desu ne.

きょうは早いですね。

You're early today, aren't you.

¶Sofu wa itsu-mo hayaku okimasu.

祖父はいつも早く起きます。

My grandfather always gets up early.

¶Otōto wa itsu-mo yori hayaku gakkō e dekakemashita.

弟はいつもより早く学校へ出かけました。

My younger brother left for school earlier than usual.

¶Dekiru dake hayaku kaette kite ne.

できるだけ早く帰ってきてね。

Come home as soon you can, OK?

hayái 速い *fast, quick* [⇔**osoi** 遅い②]

¶Yamamoto-senshu wa hashiru no ga hayai ne.

山本選手は走るのが速いね。

Yamamoto runs fast, doesn't he. 《Literally: As for Yamamoto, running is fast, isn't it.》

¶Nagare no hayai kawa o wataranakereba narimasen.

流れの速い川を渡らなければなりません。

We have to cross a fast-flowing river.

¶Takahashi-kun wa keisan ga hayai yo.

高橋君は計算が速いよ。

Takahashi is quick at calculation!

¶Motto hayaku aruite kudasai.

もっと速く歩いてください。

Please walk faster.

hayákuchi 早口 *rapid talking*

• hayakuchi-kotoba 早口言葉 *tongue twister*

hayame-ni 早めに *earlier than the appointed time, ahead of schedule*

hayarí はやり [[→**ryūkō** 流行]]

① *fashion, vogue, popularity, popular trend*

② *going around, prevalance* 《of a disease》

hayáru はやる ① *to become fashionable, to become popular*

¶Ima kono heasutairu ga hayatte iru yo.

今このヘアスタイルがはやっているよ。

This hair style is in fashion now!

¶Kono uta ga daigaku-sei no aida de wa hayatte imasu.

この歌が大学生の間ではやっています。

This song is popular among college students.

② *to go around, to become prevalent, to become widespread* 《when the subject is a disease》

¶Kono gakkō de wa ryūkan ga hayatte imasu.

この学校では流感がはやっています。
'Flu is going around at this school.

hayashi 林 *a woods*

hayásu 生やす *to let grow, to cultivate*
• hige o hayasu ひげを生やす *to grow a beard*

hazu 筈 *likelihood, good reason to think something*
• hazu da はずだ *it must be that, it should be the case that, I am almost sure that《following a clause》*
¶Senshu-tachi wa nodo ga kawaite iru hazu da yo.
選手たちはのどがかわいているはずだよ。
The players must be thirsty!
¶Yōko wa watashi no denwa-bangō o shitte iru hazu da.
洋子は私の電話番号を知っているはずだ。
Yoko should know my telephone number.
¶Imōto wa haha to issho ni kaimono ni iku hazu desu.
妹は母といっしょに買物に行くはずです。
I am almost sure my younger sister is going shopping with my mother.
• hazu ga nai はずがない *there is no reason to think that, it is very unlikely that 《following a clause》*
¶Akira ga nyūshi ni ochiru hazu ga nai yo.
明が入試に落ちるはずがないよ。
It is very unlikely that Akira will fail on the entrance examination!

hazukashíi 恥ずかしい《This adjective is used to describe both people who are embarrassed or ashamed and the things they are embarrassed or ashamed about.》*embarrassed; ashamed*
¶Misa wa hazukashikute, nani mo dekinakatta.
美砂は恥ずかしくて、何もできなかった。
Misa was so embarrassed, she couldn't do anything.
¶Yogoreta fuku ga hazukashikatta yo.
汚れた服が恥ずかしかったよ。
I was ashamed of my dirty clothes!

hazumi 弾み ① *bounce, rebound*

② *momentum; impetus, stimulus*
• hazumi ga tsuku はずみがつく *momentum gathers; stimulus acts*
• hazumi-guruma 弾み車 *flywheel*

hazumu 弾む ① *to bounce, to rebound*
¶Bōru wa hazunde, kakine o koemashita.
ボールは弾んで、垣根を越えました。
The ball bounced over the fence.
② *to become lively, to become animated; to be stimulated*
• hanashi ga hazumu 話が弾む *talk gets lively*

hazure 外れ ① *miss, failed attempt* [⇔ **atari** 当たり②]
¶Senshū hiita kuji mo hazure deshita.
先週引いたくじも外れでした。
The lot I drew last week was also a miss.
② [[→**hashi** 端]] *end; edge*
¶Mise wa tōri no hazure ni arimasu.
店は通りの外れにあります。
The store is at the end of the street.
¶Mizuumi no higashi no hazure ni hoteru ga arimasu.
湖の東の外れにホテルがあります。
There is a hotel on the eastern edge of the lake.

hazureru 外れる ① *to come off, to become detached; to come undone, to come unfastened*
¶Botan ga hitotsu hazurete imasu.
ボタンが一つ外れています。
One of my buttons has come undone.
¶Kikai no beruto ga hazuremashita.
機械のベルトが外れました。
The machine belt came off.
② *to miss 《a target or aim》《The subject is inanimate.》*[⇔**ataru** 当たる②]
¶Sono tama wa mato o hazuremashita.
その弾は的を外れました。
That bullet missed the target.
③ *to prove incorrect* [⇔**ataru** 当たる④]
¶Tenki-yohō wa yoku hazuremasu.
天気予報はよく外れます。
The weather forecast is often incorrect.

hazusu 外す ① *to take off, to remove; to undo, to unfasten*

¶Haha wa tokei o hazushimashita.
母は時計を外しました。
My mother took off her watch.

¶Botan o hazushita hō ga ii deshō.
ボタンを外したほうがいいでしょう。
It's probably better to undo your buttons.

② *to evade, to avoid* [→**sakeru** 避ける]
• shitsumon o hazusu 質問を外す *to evade a question*

③ *to miss* 《what one is aiming at》
• mato o hazusu 的を外す *to miss a target*

④ *to go away from temporarily* 《The direct object is a place.》
• seki o hazusu 席を外す *to leave one's seat*

hē へえ *No kidding!, Really?!* 《an interjection used to indicate that one is surprised or impressed》

¶Hē, odoroita.
へえ、驚いた。
Really?! I'm surprised!

¶Hē, sore wa sugoi ne.
へえ、それはすごいね。
No kidding! That's amazing, isn't it.

heasutáiru ヘアスタイル *hairstyle*

hébi 蛇 *snake*
• doku-hebi 毒蛇 *poisonous snake*

heddoráito ヘッドライト *headlight*

hei 塀 *wall, fence* 《surrounding a house or piece of land》

¶Daiku-san wa ie no shūi ni hei o tatemashita.
大工さんは家の周囲に塀を建てました。
The carpenter built a fence around the house.

• burokku-bei ブロック塀 *concrete-block wall*
• ita-bei 板塀 *board fence*
• renga-bei 煉瓦塀 *brick wall*

heibon 平凡 〜**na** 〜な *ordinary, commonplace* [⇔**hibon na** 非凡な]

¶Heibon na shufu ni wa nari-taku nai wa.
平凡な主婦にはなりたくないわ。
I don't want to become an ordinary housewife!

• heibon na hitobito 平凡な人々 *ordinary people*
• heibon na dekigoto 平凡な出来事 *an everyday event*

heihō 平方 *square* 《of a number》

¶Jū no heihō wa hyaku desu.
10の平方は100です。
The square of 10 is 100.

• heihō- 平方- *square* 《Added to bases denoting units of length.》
• heihō-mētoru 平方メートル *square meter*
• -heihō-mētoru 一平方メートル《counter for square meters; see Appendix 2》

¶Kono kyōshitsu wa hyakun-ijū-heihō-mētoru arimasu.
この教室は120平方メートルあります。
This classroom is 120 square meters.

• heihō-kon 平方根 *square root*

heijitsu 平日 *weekday*

heikai 閉会 *close* 《of a meeting, gathering, conference, etc.》[⇔**kaikai** 開会]
• heikai suru 閉会する *to close* 《transitive》
• heikai-shiki 閉会式 *closing ceremony*

heiki 平気 *composure, calmness; nonchalance, indifference*
• heiki na 平気な *composed, calm; nonchalant, indifferent, unbothered* 《This adjectival noun is used to describe both the people who are unbothered and the things they are unbothered by.》

¶Yuki wa heiki desu.
雪は平気です。
I'm not bothered by snow.

¶Kaminari ga natte mo heiki desu.
雷が鳴っても平気です。
Thunder doesn't bother me. 《Literally: Even if thunder sounds, I'm unbothered.》

héiki 兵器 *weapon, arms* [→**buki** 武器]
• kaku-heiki 核兵器 *nuclear weapon*

heikin 平均 ① *an average*
• heikin no 平均の *average*

¶Musume no seiseki wa daitai heikin desu.
娘の成績はだいたい平均です。

My daughter's grades are about average.

• heikin suru 平均する *to average, to take the average*

• heikin shite 平均して *on average*

¶Watashi wa heikin shite ichi-nichi ni-ji-kan benkyō shimasu.

私は平均して1日2時間勉強します。

I study two hours a day on average.

② *balance, equilibrium* [→**tsuriai** 釣り合い]

• heikin o toru 平均を取る *to gain one's balance*

• heikin o ushinau 平均を失う *to lose one's balance*

• heikin-dai 平均台 *balance beam*

• heikin-ijō no 平均以上の *above-average*

• heikin-ika no 平均以下の *below-average*

• heikin-jumyō 平均寿命 *average life-span*

• heikin-nenrei 平均年齢 *average age*

• heikin-ten 平均点 *average score, average number of points*

heikō 平行 ～**no** ～の *parallel*

• heikō suru 平行する *to become parallel*

¶Dōro wa tetsudō ni heikō shite imasu.

道路は鉄道に平行しています。

The road is parallel to the railroad.

• heikō-bō 平行棒 *parallel bars* 《in gymnastics》

• heikō-sen 平行線 *parallel line*

heiko 閉口 ～**da** ～だ *to be at a loss, to be unable to stand*

¶Kono samusa ni wa heikō desu.

この寒さには閉口です。

I can't stand this cold.

• heikō suru 閉口する *to be at a loss, to be unable to stand*

¶Sono hito ni wa heikō shimasu.

その人には閉口します。

I can't stand that person.

heimen 平面 *plane* (*surface*)

• heimen-zu 平面図 *plane figure*

heinen 平年 *typical year, average year*

Heisei 平成《Japanese imperial era name for the period beginning 1989》

heitai 兵隊 *soldier; sailor*

heiten 閉店 [[⇔**kaiten** 開店]]

① *closing* 《of a store, restaurant, etc., for the business day》

• heiten suru 閉店する *to close* 《intransitive》

¶Kono mise wa shichi-ji ni heiten shimasu.

この店は7時に閉店します。

This store closes at 7:00.

② *closing, going out of business* 《of a store, restaurant, etc.》

• heiten suru 閉店する *to close, to go out of business*

¶Tonari no hon-ya wa raishū heiten shimasu.

隣の本屋は来週閉店します。

The bookstore next-door will close down next week.

heiwa 平和 *peace, tranquility* [⇔**sensō** 戦争]

¶Minna heiwa o nozonde imasu.

みんな平和を望んでいます。

Everyone wants peace.

• heiwa na 平和な *peaceful, tranquil*

¶Watashi-tachi wa heiwa na seikatsu o okutte imasu.

私たちは平和な生活を送っています。

We are leading a peaceful life.

• heiwa-jōyaku 平和条約 *peace treaty*

• heiwa-undō 平和運動 *peace movement*

heiya 平野 *a plain*

hekomu 凹む *to become dented, to become sunken, to cave in*

hekutāru ヘクタール *hectare*

• -hekutāru －ヘクタール《counter for hectares; see Appendix 2》

héma へま 【COL.】 *blunder, goof*

• hema o suru へまをする *to make a blunder, to make a goof*

• hema na へまな *bungling, stupid*

hen 辺 ① *area around, vicinity* [→**atari** 辺り]

¶Kono hen ni yūbin-kyoku wa arimasu ka.

この辺に郵便局はありますか。

Is there a post office around here?

② *side* 《of a polygon》
• sankaku-kei no hen 三角形の辺 *side of a triangle*
• -hen −辺《counter for sides; see Appendix 2》

−**hen** −遍《counter for number of times, occasions, see Appendix 2》[→**kai** −回②]

hén 変 ～**na** ～な *strange, curious, odd*
¶ Daidokoro de hen na oto ga shimashita.
台所で変な音がしました。
There was a strange sound in the kitchen.
¶ Hen na uwasa ga tatte imasu.
変なうわさが立っています。
A strange rumor is going around.
¶ Yoshiko-san wa hen na shaberi-kata o shimasu.
良子さんは変なしゃべり方をします。
Yoshiko has an odd way of talking.

hen'atsúki 変圧器 *(electrical)transformer*

hendensho 変電所 *(electrical)transformer substation*

hénji 返事 *answer, reply, response*
《This word is not used to mean an answer to a question (cf. **kotae** 答え).》
¶ Yōko-san kara henji o uketorimashita.
洋子さんから返事を受け取りました。
I received an answer from Yoko.
¶ Sono tegami ni henji o dashimasu.
その手紙に返事を出します。
I will send an answer to that letter.
• henji suru 返事する *to reply, to respond*
¶ Namae o yobimasu node, henji shite kudasai.
名前を呼びますので、返事してください。
I will call your names, so please respond.

hénka 変化 *change, alteration*
• henka suru 変化する *to change* 《intransitive》[→**kawaru** 変わる]
¶ Kono chiiki de wa kion no henka ga kyū desu.
この地域では気温の変化が急です。
In this area temperature changes are sudden.

• henka no aru seikatsu 変化のある生活 *a lifestyle with variety*
• henka no nai shigoto 変化のない仕事 *monotonous job*

henken 偏見 *prejudice, bias*

henkō 変更 *change, alteration, modification*
¶ Jikan-wari ni nani-ka henkō ga arimasu ka.
時間割に何か変更がありますか。
Is there some kind of change in the class schedule?
• henkō suru 変更する *to change, to alter, to modify*
¶ Keikaku o henkō shinakereba narimasen.
計画を変更しなければなりません。
We have to change our plans.

henkyoku 編曲 *arrangement* 《of a musical piece》
• henkyoku suru 編曲する *to arrange*

hensai 返済 *repayment* 《of a loan》; *return* 《of something borrowed》
• hensai suru 返済する *to repay; to return*

hensei 編成 *formation, organization, composition*
• hensei suru 編成する *to form, to organize, to make up*

henshū 編集 *editing*
¶ Gakkō-shinbun no henshū de isogashii desu.
学校新聞の編集で忙しいです。
I'm busy with the editing the school newspaper.
• henshū suru 編集する *to edit*
• henshū-bu 編集部 *editorial department*
• henshū-bu-in 編集部員 *editorial staff member*
• henshū-chō 編集長 *chief editor*
• henshū-sha 編集者 *editor*

hensō 変装 *disguising oneself; disguise*
• hensō suru 変装する *to disguise oneself*
¶ Hannin wa rōjin ni hensō shimashita.
犯人は老人に変装しました。
The criminal disguised himself as an elderly person.

hentōsen 扁桃腺 *tonsils*

herasu 減らす *to reduce, to decrease* 《transitive》 [⇔**fuyasu** 増やす]

¶Ane wa taijū o herashimashita.

姉は体重を減らしました。

My older sister lost weight.

herikóputā ヘリコプター *helicopter*

herikudaru 謙る *to humble oneself, to be modest*

heru 減る{5} *to decrease, to lessen* 《intransitive》 [⇔**fueru** 増える]

¶Kōtsū-jiko no kazu ga kyū ni herimashita.

交通事故の数が急に減りました。

The number of traffic accidents suddenly decreased.

¶Chichi wa taijū ga san-kiro herimashita.

父は体重が3キロ減りました。

My father lost three kilograms.

hérumetto ヘルメット *helmet, hard hat*

heso へそ *navel, belly button*

• heso-kuri へそくり *secretly saved money*

hetá 下手 ～**na** ～な *unskillful, poor at* 《This adjectival noun is used to describe both the people who are unskillful and the things they are unskillful at.》 [⇔**jōzu na** 上手な]

¶Ane wa sukī ga heta desu.

姉はスキーが下手です。

My older sister is poor at skiing.

¶Nakagawa-san wa ji ga heta desu ne.

中川さんは字が下手ですね。

Mr. Nakagawa's handwriting is poor, isn't it.

• heta-kuso na 下手くそな 【CRUDE for **heta na** 下手な (above)】

heyá 部屋 *a room*

¶Kore wa roku-jō no heya desu.

これは6畳の部屋です。

This is a six-mat room.

¶Kyō heya o sōji suru tsumori desu.

きょう部屋を掃除するつもりです。

I'm planning to clean my room today.

• hiroi 〔semai〕 heya 広い〔狭い〕部屋 *large* 〔*small*〕 *room*

hí 火 *fire*

¶Hi no nai tokoro ni kemuri wa tatanai.

火のない所に煙は立たない。《proverb》

Where there's smoke there's fire. 《Literally: In a place where there is no fire, smoke does not rise.》

• A ni hi o tsukeru Aに火をつける *to set fire to A, to light A on fire*

¶Dare ga sono ie ni hi o tsuketa no desu ka.

だれがその家に火をつけたのですか。

Who set fire to that house?

• hi o okosu 火を起こす *to build a fire, to get a fire going*

• hi o kesu 火を消す *to put out a fire*

• hi ni ataru 火に当たる *to warm oneself at a fire*

• hi no yōjin o suru 火の用心をする *to look out for fire*

hi 日 ① *the sun* [→**taiyō** 太陽]; *sunshine* [→**nikkō** 日光]

• hi ga noboru 日が昇る *the sun rises*

• hi ga shizumu 日が沈む *the sun sets*

• A ni hi ga ataru Aに日が当たる *the sun shines on A, the sun shines into A*

• A ni hi ga sashikomu Aに日が差し込む *the sun shines into A*

• hi ni yakeru 日に焼ける *to become suntanned; to become sunburned*

② *day*

¶Hi ga mijikaku natte kimashita.

日が短くなってきました。

The days have become shorter.

¶Sono hi ni eiga o mi ni ikimashita.

その日に映画を見に行きました。

On that day I went to see a movie.

¶Kyanpu no hi o kimemashō.

キャンプの日を決めましょう。

Let's decide the day for camping.

• hi-atari 日当たり *the degree to which sunshine strikes*

¶Kono kyōshitsu wa hi-atari ga ii desu ne.

この教室は日当たりがいいですね。

This classroom is nice and sunny, isn't it.

• hi-gasa 日傘 *parasol*

• hi-mashi ni 日増しに *day by day,*

as each day goes by
- hi-no-de 日の出 *sunrise*
- hi-no-iri 日の入り *sunset*
- hi-yatoi 日雇い *hiring as day labor*
- hi-zashi 日差し *sunshine, sunlight*

hi- 非- *non-, un-* 《Added to noun and adjectival noun bases.》
- hi-bunmei no 非文明の *uncivilized*
- hi-jōshiki na 非常識な *lacking in common sense*
- hi-kagaku-teki na 非科学的な *unscientific* [⇔**kagaku-teki na** 科学的な (s.v. **kagaku** 科学)]

híbachi 火鉢 *charcoal brazier*

híbana 火花 *spark*
- hibana ga chiru 火花が散る *sparks fly*

hibari 雲雀 *skylark*

hibi ひび *crack, small fissure*
¶Kono koppu ni wa hibi ga haitte iru yo.
このコップにはひびが入っているよ。
There is a crack in this glass!

hibíku 響く ① *to sound, to ring out, to be widely audible*
¶Kachō no koe ga rōka ni hibikimashita.
課長の声が廊下に響きました。
The section chief's voice rang out in the hall.
　② *to resound, to reverberate, to echo*
　③ *to have an effect* [→**eikyō suru** 影響する]
¶Nomi-sugi wa kenkō ni hibikimasu.
飲みすぎは健康に響きます。
Drinking too much affects one's health.

hibon 非凡 ~**na** ~な *extraordinary* [⇔**heibon na** 平凡な]

hidari 左 *the left* [⇔**migi** 右]
¶Hidari ni ginkō ga miemasu.
左に銀行が見えます。
You can see a bank on the left.
¶Tsugi no kado o hidari ni magatte kudasai.
次の角を左に曲がってください。
Turn left at the next corner.
- hidari-gawa 左側 *left side*
- hidari-gawa-tsūkō 左側通行 *left-side traffic* 《Typically used on signs to mean *Keep left.*》

- hidari-kiki no 左利きの *left-handed*
- hidari-te 左手 *left hand*

hidói 酷い *terrible, awful, severe, cruel*
¶Hidoi arashi ga sono chihō o osoimashita.
ひどいあらしがその地方を襲いました。
A terrible storm hit that region.
¶Senaka ni hidoi itami o kanjimashita.
背中にひどい痛みを感じました。
I felt terrible pain in my back.
- hidoi me ni au ひどい目にあう *to have a terrible experience*

hiéru 冷える *to get cold, to get chilly* [⇔**atatamaru** 暖まる, 温まる]
¶Yoru ni naru to, hiemasu ne.
夜になると、冷えますね。
It gets cold at night, doesn't it? 《Literally: When it becomes night, it gets cold, doesn't it.》
¶Bīru wa mada hiete imasen ne.
ビールはまだ冷えていませんね。
The beer has not gotten cold yet, has it.

hífu 皮膚 *skin* 《of a person or animal》
¶Ane wa hifu ga nameraka desu.
姉は皮膚が滑らかです。
My older sister's skin is smooth.
- tsuyoi 〔yowai〕 hifu 強い〔弱い〕皮膚 *strong* 〔*delicate*〕 *skin*
- hifu-byō 皮膚病 *skin disease*

hígai 被害 *damage, harm*
- higai o ataeru 被害を与える *to do damage, to harm*
- higai o ukeru 被害を受ける *to suffer damage, to be harmed*
¶Taifū de sakumotsu wa ōki na higai o ukemashita.
台風で作物は大きな被害を受けました。
The crops suffered great damage in the typhoon.
- higai-sha 被害者 *victim*

higashi 東 *the east* [⇔**nishi** 西]
- Higashi-Ajia 東アジア *East Asia*
- higashi-kaze 東風 *east wind*
- Higashi-Nihon 東日本 *Eastern Japan*

hige 髭 *whiskers; beard; mustache*
- hige o nobasu ひげを伸ばす *to let one's whiskers grow*

• hige o soru ひげをそる *to shave (one's whiskers)*

¶Chichi wa mai-asa hige o sorimasu.

父は毎朝ひげをそります。

My father shaves every morning.

• hige o hayasu ひげを生やす *to grow a beard / mustache*

¶Sono gaka wa hige o hayashite imasu.

その画家はひげを生やしています。

That painter has a beard.

• ago-hige 顎髭 *beard*

• kuchi-hige 口髭 *mustache*

hígeki 悲劇 *tragedy* [⇔**kigeki** 喜劇]

• higeki-teki na 悲劇的な *tragic*

higoro 日頃 *usually, habitually, all the time* [→**fudan** (**ni**) 普段 (に)]

• higoro no 日ごろの *usual, habitual, everyday*

higure 日暮れ *nightfall, sunset* [→**nichibotsu** 日没]*; early evening*

¶Higure ni modotte ikimashita.

日暮れに戻っていきました。

I went back at sunset.

hihan 批判 *criticism, critical assessment*

• hihan suru 批判する *to criticize, to assess critically*

¶Sensei wa sono tetsugaku-sha no kangae o hihan shimashita.

先生はその哲学者の考えを批判しました。

The teacher criticized that philosopher's ideas.

• hihan-teki na 批判的な *critical*

hihyō 批評 *criticism, comment, review*

• hihyō suru 批評する *to criticize, to comment on, to review*

¶Yano-kyōju wa sono hon o hihyō shimashita.

矢野教授はその本を批評しました。

Professor Yano reviewed that book.

• hihyō-ka 批評家 *critic, reviewer*

hijí 肘 *elbow*

• hiji-kake 肘掛け *armrest*

hijō 非常 ① *emergency*

¶Hijō no baai wa buzā o oshite kudasai.

非常の場合はブザーを押してください。

In case of an emergency please push this buzzer.

② ~**na** ~な *extraordinary, extreme*

• hijō ni 非常に *very, extremely*

¶Yamaguchi-san wa hijō ni yukkuri arukimashita.

山口さんは非常にゆっくりと歩きました。

Ms. Yamaguchi walked very slowly.

¶Sono shiai wa hijō ni omoshirokatta yo.

その試合は非常におもしろかったよ。

That game was very interesting!

¶Sono shirase o kiite hijō ni odorokimashita.

その知らせを聞いて非常に驚きました。

I heard that news and was really surprised.

¶Watashi wa ongaku ni hijō ni kyōmi ga arimasu.

私は音楽に非常に興味があります。

I am very interested in music.

• hijō-beru 非常ベル *emergency bell*

• hijō-guchi 非常口 *emergency exit*

• hijō-kaidan 非常階段 *emergency stairs, fire escape*

hikage 日陰 *shade, place shaded from sunlight* [⇔**hinata** 日向]

¶Hikage de yasumimashō.

日陰で休みましょう。

Let's rest in the shade.

hikaku 比較 *comparison*

• hikaku suru 比較する *to compare* [→**kuraberu** 比べる]

¶Jibun no kotae o seikai to hikaku shite kudasai.

自分の答えを正解と比較してください。

Please compare your own answers with the correct answers.

• hikaku-teki (ni) 比較的 (に) *comparatively, relatively* [→**wariai ni** 割合に]

hikan 悲観 *pessimism* [⇔**rakuten** 楽天, **rakkan** 楽観]

• hikan suru 悲観する *to be pessimistic*

• hikan-teki na 悲観的な *pessimistic*

• hikan-teki na mikata 悲観的な見方 *pessimistic view*

hikarí 光 *light, illumination*

• hikari no hayasa 光の速さ *the speed of light*

• hoshi no hikari 星の光 *starlight*

hikáru 光る *to emit light, to shine, to flash*

¶Tsuki ga akaruku hikatte iru ne.
月が明るく光っているね。
The moon is shining brightly, isn't it.

¶Kon'ya wa hoshi ga ippai hikatte iru yo.
今夜は星がいっぱい光っているよ。
A lot of stars are shining tonight!

¶Kurai sora ni inazuma ga hikarimashita.
暗い空に稲妻が光りました。
Lightning flashed in the dark sky.

hiketsu 秘訣 *secret, key, trick*

híki 晶屓 *favor, partiality*

• híki suru ひいきする *to favor, to be partial to*

¶Haha wa otōto o híki shite imasu.
母は弟をひいきしています。
My mother favors my younger brother.

–hiki 一匹 《counter for animals; see Appendix 2》

hikiagéru 引き上げる ① *to pull up, to raise by pulling*

¶Shizunda fune o hikiageru no wa jikan ga kakaru.
沈んだ船を引き上げるのは時間がかかる。
Raising a sunken ship takes time.

② *to raise 《a price》*

¶Basu-gaisha wa unchin o sukoshi hikiageru darō.
バス会社は運賃を少し引き上げるだろう。
The bus company will probably raise fares a little.

hikidashi 引き出し *drawer*

¶Haha wa hikidashi o akete, kutsushita o dashimashita.
母は引き出しを開けて、靴下を出しました。
My mother opened a drawer and took out some socks.

hikidásu 引き出す ① *to pull out, to draw out*

② *to withdraw 《money》* [→**orosu** 下ろす②]

¶Kesa ginkō kara gosen-en hikidashimashita.
けさ銀行から5000円引き出しました。

This morning I withdrew 5,000 yen from the bank.

hikigane 引き金 *trigger*

hikikáesu 引き返す *to turn back; to return to where one started*

¶Tozan-ka wa chōten ni tsuku to sugu ni hikikaeshiita.
登山家は頂点に着くとすぐに引き返した。
The mountain climber turned back as soon as he reached the summit.

hikinige 轢き逃げ *hit and run 《(traffic accident)》*

• hikinige suru ひき逃げする *to hit and run*

• hikinige-jiken 轢き逃げ事件 *hit-and-run accident*

hikiniku 挽肉 *ground meat*

hikinobashi 引き伸ばし *enlargement 《(photograph)》*

hikinobásu 引き伸ばす ① *to stretch out by pulling*

② *to enlarge 《a photograph》*

¶Kono shashin o ōkiku hikinobashite kudasai.
この写真を大きく引き伸ばしてください。
Please enlarge this photograph.

hikiokósu 引き起こす *to cause, to bring about, to give rise to*

¶Basu no unten-shu wa kōtsū-jiko o hikiokoshita.
バスの運転手は交通事故を引き起こした。
The bus driver caused a traffic accident.

hikitsúgu 引き継ぐ *to take over, to succeed to* [→**tsugu** 継ぐ]

hikiukéru 引き受ける *to undertake, to take, to agree to do*

¶Sono shigoto o hikiukemasu.
その仕事を引き受けます。
I will take on that job.

hikiwake 引き分け *tie, draw*

¶Shiai wa hikiwake ni owarimashita.
試合は引き分けに終わりました。
The game ended in a tie.

hikiwakéru 引き分ける ① *to pull apart, to separate by pulling*

② *to tie, to draw 《in a contest》*

hikízan 引き算 *subtraction 《in*

arithmetic》[⇔**tashizan** 足し算]

• hikizan suru 引き算する *to subtract* [→ **hiku** 引く④]

hikizuru 引きずる *to drag* 《transitive》

¶Kodomo-tachi wa ōki na hako o hikizutte imasu.

子供たちは大きな箱を引きずっています。

The children are dragging a large box.

hikkáku 引っ掻く *to scratch, to claw*

¶Neko ga otōto no kao o hikkakimashita.

猫が弟の顔を引っかきました。

A cat scratched my younger brother's face.

hikki 筆記 ① *writing down; note taking*

• hikki suru 筆記する *write down; to take notes*

② *transcript; notes*

• hikki-shiken 筆記試験 *written examination*

• hikki-yōgu 筆記用具 *writing materials*

hikkoméru 引っ込める *to put back, to return to a container*

hikkósu 引っ越す *to move* 《to a new residence》

¶Hirota-san wa Tōkyō kara Kyōto ni hikkoshita.

広田さんは東京から京都に引っ越した。

Mr. Hirota moved from Tokyo to Kyoto.

hikkurikáesu ひっくり返す ① *to turn upside down* 《transitive》

② *to upset, to tip over* [→**taosu** 倒す①]

¶Koppu o hikkurikaeshite mizu o koboshita.

コップをひっくり返して水をこぼした。

I tipped over a glass and spilled some water.

hikkurikáeru ひっくり返る{5} ① *to turn upside down* 《intransitive》

¶Yotto ga kaze de hikkurikaetta yo.

ヨットが風でひっくり返ったよ。

The sailboat turned over in the wind!

② *to fall over, to tip over* [→**taoreru** 倒れる①]

hikō 飛行 *flight*

• hikō suru 飛行する *to fly,*

to make a flight

• hikō-shi 飛行士 *aviator, flyer*

• yakan-hikō 夜間飛行 *night flight*

hikōjō 飛行場 *airfield; airport* [→**kūkō** 空港]

hikōki 飛行機 *airplane*

¶Chichi wa Chitose de Tōkyō-yuki no hikōki ni notta.

父は千歳で東京行きの飛行機に乗った。

My father boarded a plane for Tokyo at Chitose.

¶Souru de kono hikōki o orimasu.

ソウルでこの飛行機を降ります。

We'll get off this plane at Seoul.

¶Oba wa Fukuoka ni hikōki de ikimasu.

伯母は福岡に飛行機で行きます。

My aunt will go to Fukuoka by plane.

hikoku 被告 *defendant* [⇔**genkoku** 原告]

hikōsen 飛行船 *airship, dirigible*

hiku 引く ① *to pull, to tug, to draw* [→ **hipparu** 引っ張る①] [⇔**osu** 押す①]

¶Kāten o hiite kudasai.

カーテンを引いてください。

Please draw the curtain.

¶Rōpu o isshōkenmei hikimashita.

ロープを一生懸命引きました。

I pulled the rope as hard as I could.

• kuji o hiku くじを引く *to draw lots*

• jisho o hiku 辞書を引く *to consult a dictionary*

② *to draw* 《a line》

¶Pen to monosashi de chokusen o hikimasu.

ペンと物差しで直線を引きます。

I draw a straight line with a pen and a ruler.

③ *to attract, to draw*

• chūi o hiku 注意を引く *to attract attention*

• kaze o hiku かぜを引く *to catch a cold*

④ *to subtract, to deduct* [⇔**tasu** 足す②]

¶Roku hiku ni wa yon.

6引く2は4。

Six minus two is four. 《Although odd grammatically, this kind of sentence is a typical way of stating a fact of arithmetic.》

⑤ **nedan o**~ 値段を~ *to lower a price*

hiku 弾く *to play* 《*a stringed instrument*》; *to play* 《*music on a stringed instrument*》

¶Baiorin o hiku no wa muzukashii desu.
バイオリンを弾くのは難しいです。
Playing the violin is difficult.

hiku 轢く *to run over* 《*The subject can be a vehicle or a person driving.*》

¶Sono kuruma wa neko o hikimashita.
その車は猫をひきました。
That car ran over a cat.

hikúi 低い ① [[⇔**takai** 高い①]] *low; short* 《*vertically*》

¶Kyōko wa san-nin no uchi de ichiban se ga hikui.
京子は3人のうちでいちばん背が低い。
Kyoko is the shortest of the three.

¶Sono hikui isu ni suwatte kudasai.
その低いいすに座ってください。
Please sit on that low chair.

• hikui oka 低い丘 *low hill*

• hikui hana 低い鼻 *flat nose*

② *low, not loud* [⇔**takai** 高い②]

¶Rajio no oto o hikuku shimashō.
ラジオの音を低くしましょう。
Let's turn down the sound on the radio.

¶Motto hikui koe de hanashite kudasai.
もっと低い声で話してください。
Please speak in a lower voice.

• koe o hikuku suru 声を低くする *to lower one's voice*

hikyṓ 卑怯 ~**na** ~な ① *cowardly* [→**okubyō na** 臆病な]

¶Nigeru no wa hikyō desu yo.
逃げるのはひきょうですよ。
Running away is cowardly!

② *unfair, mean, base*

¶Sore wa hikyō na yari-kata desu yo.
それはひきょうなやり方ですよ。
That's an unfair way to do it!

• hikyō-mono 卑怯者 *coward*

hima 暇 ① (*amount of*)*time* [→**jikan** 時間②]

¶Tegami o kaku hima ga nai desu.
手紙を書く暇がないです。
I don't have time to write letters.

• hima o tsubusu 暇をつぶす *to kill time*

② *spare time, free time, leisure time* [→**yoka** 余暇]

• hima na 暇な *free, not busy* [⇔**isogashii** 忙しい]

¶Watashi wa hima na toki, ongaku o kikimasu.
私は暇なとき、音楽を聴きます。
I listen to music when I have spare time.

¶Ima o–hima desu ka.
今お暇ですか。
Are you free now?

• hima-tsubushi 暇潰し *killing time*

himáwari ひまわり *sunflower*

himei 悲鳴 *scream, cry*

• himei o ageru 悲鳴をあげる *to scream, to cry out*

¶Shōnen wa himei o agete tasuke o motomemashita.
少年は悲鳴をあげて助けを求めました。
The boy cried out for help.

himitsu 秘密 *secret, confidential matter; secrecy, confidentiality*

¶Kore wa himitsu ni shimashō.
これは秘密にしましょう。
Let's keep this a secret.

• himitsu o mamoru 秘密を守る *to keep a secret; to maintain secrecy*

• himitsu o uchiakeru 秘密を打ち明ける *to confide a secret*

• himitsu no 秘密の *secret, confidential*

¶Dorobō wa himitsu no basho ni o-kane o kakushimashita.
泥棒は秘密の場所にお金を隠しました。
The thief hid the money in a secret place.

himo 紐 *string, cord, thin strap*

¶Furu-zasshi o himo de shibatte kudasai.
古雑誌をひもで縛ってください。
Please tie up the old magazines with string.

• kutsu-himo 靴紐 *shoelace*

hína 雛 ① *newly hatched bird, chick* [→**hiyoko** ひよこ]

② [☞**hina-ningyō** 雛人形 (below)]

- hina-dori 雛鳥 [☞**hina** 雛① (above)]
- hina-ningyō 雛人形 *doll displayed for Hinamatsuri (the Doll Festival)*

hinágiku ひなぎく *daisy*

Hinamátsuri 雛祭り *the Girls' Festival, the Doll Festival* 《March 3rd》

hínan 非難 *criticism, reproach*
- hinan suru 非難する *to criticize, to reproach*

¶Kokumin wa seifu no sochi o hinan shimashita.
国民は政府の措置を非難しました。
The people criticized the steps taken by the government.

hínan 避難 *taking refuge, taking shelter; evacuation*
- hinan suru 避難する *to take refuge, to take shelter; to evacuate*

¶Ikkō wa koya ni hinan shimashita.
一行は小屋に避難しました。
The party took refuge in a hut.

- hinan-kunren 避難訓練 *evacuation practice, fire drill*
- hinan-min 避難民 *refugee*

hinata 日向 *place where the sun is shining* [⇔**hikage** 日陰]
- hinata ni deru ひなたに出る *to go out into the sun*

hinéru 捻る {5} ① *to twist, to turn* 《with one's fingers》

¶Sen o hinette gasu o keshimashita.
栓をひねってガスを消しました。
I twisted the stopper and turned off the gas.

② *to turn, to twist* 《one's body (at the waist)or neck so as to face another direction》

¶Karada o hidari ni hinette kudasai.
体を左にひねってください。
Please twist your body to the left.

- atama o hineru 頭をひねる *to think hard*

hinichi 日にち ① *date, day on which something takes place*

¶Pātī no hinichi o kimemashō.
パーティーの日にちを決めましょう。
Let's decide the date for the party.

② *the number of days; a number of days, several days*

¶Shimekiri made mada hinichi ga arimasu.
締め切りまでまだ日にちがあります。
There are still several days until the deadline.

hiniku 皮肉 *irony; sarcasm*
- hiniku na 皮肉な *ironic; sarcastic*

¶Sensei no kotoba ni wa tashō no hiniku ga arimashita.
先生の言葉には多少の皮肉がありました。
There was some irony in the teacher's words.

hinjaku 貧弱 〜na 〜な *poor, scanty, meager* [⇔**hōfu na** 豊富な]

hinketsu 貧血 *anemia*

hinoki 檜 *Japanese cypress*

Hi-no-maru 日の丸 *the Japanese national flag* 《Literally: *the Circle of the Sun*》

hinshi 品詞 *part of speech*

hinshitsu 品質 *quality* 《of goods》
- hinshitsu-kanri 品質管理 *quality control*

hínto ヒント *hint, suggestion*

¶Sono mondai no hinto o agemashō.
その問題のヒントをあげましょう。
I'll give you a hint to that question.

Hinzūkyō ヒンズー教 *Hinduism*

hippáru 引っ張る ① *to pull, to tug*

¶Tozan-sha wa tsuna o hippatte imasu.
登山者は綱を引っ張っています。
The mountain climber is pulling on a rope.

¶Uma wa basha o hippatte imashita.
馬は馬車を引っ張っていました。
The horse was pulling a carriage.

② *to take, to bring, to drag along* 《The direct object is a person.》

¶Keikan wa hannin o keisatsu-sho ni hippatte itta.
警官は犯人を警察署に引っ張っていった。
The police officer took the criminal to the police station.

híppu ヒップ *portion of the body from hip to hip; hip circumference*

hiragána 平仮名 *hiragana* «i.e., the cursive variety of the Japanese **kana** syllabary»

hirakéru 開ける *to develop, to become developed*
¶Kono chiiki wa jojo ni hirakete kimashita.
この地域は徐々に開けてきました。
This area has gradually developed.

hiráku 開く ① *to open, to unclose* «transitive or intransitive» [⇔**tojiru** 閉じる]
¶To ga totsuzen hirakimashita.
戸が突然開きました。
The door opened suddenly.
¶Niwa no bara ga hirakimashita.
庭のばらが開きました。
The roses in the yard have bloomed.
¶Hon no go-pēji o hirakinasai.
本の5ページを開きなさい。
Open the book to page 5.
② *to give, to have, to hold* «an event»
¶Ashita pātī o hirakimashō ka.
あしたパーティーを開きましょうか。
Shall we have a party tomorrow?

hirame 鮃 «a kind of flounder»

hiraóyogi 平泳ぎ *breaststroke*

hiratai 平たい *flat, level* [→**taira na** 平らな]

hiré 鰭 *fin*

hirei 比例 *proportion, proportionality*
• hirei no 比例の *proportional*
• hirei suru 比例する *to be proportional*
• A ga B ni hirei suru AがBに比例する
A is proportional to B

hiritsu 比率 *ratio*
¶Kono kurasu no danjo no hiritsu wa yon tai go desu.
このクラスの男女の比率は4対5です。
The ratio of boys to girls in this class is four to five.

hīrō ヒーロー ① *hero, heroic man* [→**eiyū** 英雄] [⇔**hiroin** ヒロイン]
② *hero, protagonist* «of a story» [→**shujin-kō** 主人公 (s.v. **shujin** 主人)]

hírō 疲労 *fatigue* [→**tsukare** 疲れ]

híroba 広場 *open space, square, plaza*
¶Eki-mae no hiroba ni minna ga atsumarimashita.
駅前の広場にみんなが集まりました。
Everyone gathered in the square in front of the station.

hirogaru 広がる ① *to widen, to become more spacious*
¶Mō sukoshi iku to, kawa ga hirogarimasu.
もう少し行くと、川が広がります。
If you go a little further, the river will widen.
② *to spread, to become widespread* [→**hiromaru** 広まる]
¶Sono nyūsu wa sekai-jū ni hirogarimashita.
そのニュースは世界中に広がりました。
That news spread throughout the world.
③ *to stretch out as a large expanse*
¶Me no mae ni aoi umi ga hirogatte imasu.
目の前に青い海が広がっています。
The blue sea is stretching out before our eyes.

hirogeru 広げる ① *to widen, to make more spacious*
¶Sono dōro o hirogeru hitsuyō ga arimasu.
その道路を広げる必要があります。
It is necessary to widen that road.
② *to spread out, to lay out, to unfold* «transitive»
¶Seito wa tsukue no ue ni sekai-chizu o hirogemashita.
生徒は机の上に世界地図を広げました。
The student spread out a world map on the desk.

hirói 広い [[⇔**semai** 狭い]] ① *wide, broad*
¶Shinano-gawa wa kawa haba ga totemo hiroi desu.
信濃川は川幅がとても広いです。
The Shinano River is very wide. «Literally: As for the Shinano River, the width of the river is very wide.»
¶Torakku wa hiroi tōri ni demashita.
トラックは広い通りに出ました。
The truck went out onto a broad street.

¶Sono gaka wa hiroku shirarete imasu.
その画家は広く知られています。
The painter is widely known.

• kao ga hiroi 顔が広い *one's circle of acquaintances is wide*

② *large (in area), spacious*
¶Kono heya wa watashi no yori hiroi yo.
この部屋は私のより広いよ。
This room is more spacious than mine!

• kokoro ga hiroi 心が広い *generous; broad-minded*

hiróin ヒロイン *heroine* [→**eiyū** 英雄]
[⇔**hīrō** ヒーロー]

hiromáru 広まる *to spread, to become widespread*
¶Sono hanashi wa kyūsoku ni hiromarimashita.
その話は急速に広まりました。
That story spread quickly.

hироméru 広める *to spread, to make widespread, to propagate*
¶Jūgyōin ga sono uwasa o hiromemashita.
従業員がそのうわさを広めました。
The employees spread that rumor.

hírosa 広さ ① *width, breadth* [→**haba** 幅]

② *area, spaciousness* [→**menseki** 面積]
¶Kono niwa no hirosa wa nijū-heihō-mētoru-gurai da.
この庭の広さは20平方メートルぐらいだ。
The area of this garden is about 20 square meters.

hirou 拾う ① *to pick up* «something that has fallen or been scattered»
¶Kōen no gomi o hiroimashō.
公園のごみを拾いましょう。
Let's pick up the trash in the park.
¶Undō-jō de kono bōrupen o hirotta yo.
運動場でこのボールペンを拾ったよ。
I picked up this ballpoint pen on the playground!

• inochi o hirou 命を拾う *to narrowly escape with one's life*

• takushī o hirou タクシーを拾う *to catch a taxi*

② *to pick out, to select and take*

hirú 昼 ① *noon* [→**shōgo** 正午]
¶Hiru made ni denwa shite kudasai.
昼までに電話してください。
Please telephone by noon.

② *daytime, the daylight hours, day* [→**nitchū** 日中, **hiruma** 昼間]
¶Hiru wa atatakakatta desu ne.
昼は暖かかったですね。
It was warm during the day, wasn't it.
¶Natsu wa hiru ga nagai desu.
夏は昼が長いです。
The days are long in summer.
¶Chichi wa hiru mo yoru mo isogashikatta desu.
父は昼も夜も忙しかったです。
My father was busy both day and night.

• hiru-gohan 昼ご飯 *lunch* [→**chūshoku** 昼食]

• hiru-ne 昼寝 *nap*

• hiru-yasumi 昼休み *lunch break*

hirumá 昼間 *daytime, the daylight hours* [→**nitchū** 日中] [⇔**yakan** 夜間]

hisan 悲惨 ~**na** ~な *miserable, wretched, tragic*

hisashiburi 久し振り ~**no** ~の *the first in a long while*
¶Hisashiburi no sāfin wa tanoshikatta yo.
久しぶりのサーフィンは楽しかったよ。
It was fun surfing again after such a long time! «Literally: The first surfing in a long while was fun.»
¶Hisashiburi desu ne.
久しぶりですね。
It's been a long time, hasn't it. «Literally: It's the first time (that I've seen you)in a long while.»

• hisashiburi ni／de 久しぶりに／で *for the first time in a long while*
¶Oji wa hisashiburi ni kikoku shimasu.
叔父は久しぶりに帰国します。
My uncle will return to his home country for the first time in a long while.

hishó 秘書 *(private)secretary*
¶Nishizawa-san wa shachō no hisho desu.

西沢さんは社長の秘書です。
Ms. Nishizawa is the company president's secretary.

hishó 避暑 *escaping the heat of summer* 《*by going to a cool location*》
¶Karuizawa e hisho ni iku tsumori desu.
軽井沢へ避暑に行くつもりです。
I am planning to go to Karuizawa to avoid the heat of summer.
• hisho-chi 避暑地 *summer resort area*

hisóka 密か ～**na** ～な *secret, covert*
¶Tantei wa hisoka ni jimu-sho ni hairimashita.
探偵は密かに事務所に入りました。
The detective secretly entered the office.

hisshi 必死 ～**no** ～の *desperate, frantic, furious*
¶Gakusei-tachi wa hisshi no doryoku o shimashita.
学生たちは必死の努力をしました。
The students made desperate efforts.
• hisshi ni natte 必死になって *desperately, frantically, furiously*

hisshō 必勝 *certain victory*

hítā ヒーター *heater*

hitai 額 *forehead*
• hiroi 〔semai〕 hitai 広い〔狭い〕額 *broad/high 〔narrow/low〕forehead*

hitchiháiku ヒッチハイク *hitchhiking*
• hitchihaiku suru ヒッチハイクする *to hitchhike*

hitei 否定 *denial* [⇔**kōtei** 肯定]
• hitei suru 否定する *to deny*
¶Seiji-ka wa sono jijitsu o hitei shimashita.
政治家はその事実を否定しました。
The politician denied that fact.
• hitei-bun 否定文 *negative sentence*
• hitei-teki na 否定的な *contradictory, negative*

hito 人 ① *person*
¶Kishi-san wa donna hito desu ka.
岸さんはどんな人ですか。
What kind of person is Mr. Kishi?
¶Hito wa yakusoku o mamoru-beki desu.
人は約束を守るべきです。
A person should keep promises.

¶Ano hito wa Terada-san desu.
あの人は寺田さんです。
That person is Ms. Terada.
¶Sō kangaeru hito mo imasu.
そう考える人もいます。
There are also people who think so.
¶Takusan no hito ga ume de oyoide imasu.
たくさんの人が海で泳いでいます。
A lot of people are swimming in the ocean.
② *another person, others*
¶Hito ni wa shinsetsu ni shinasai.
人には親切にしなさい。
Be kind to others.
¶Mudan de hito no jitensha ni notte wa ikenai yo.
無断で人の自転車に乗ってはいけないよ。
You mustn't ride someone else's bicycle without their permission.
• hito-gara 人柄 *personal character, personality*
• hito-nami no 人並みの *the same as other people*

hito- 一一 *one, a* 《*Added to noun bases, in many cases those derived from verbs.*》
• hito-kuchi 一口 *one mouthful, one drink, one bite; a word, a few words*
• hito-kuchi ni iu 一口に言う *to say in a word, to say in a few words*
• hito-shigoto 一仕事 *a considerable task, quite a job*
• hito-oyogi 一泳ぎ *a swim*
• hito-oyogi suru 一泳ぎする *to take a swim*
• hito-nemuri 一眠り *a nap, a sleep*
• hito-nemuri suru 一眠りする *to take a nap*

hitóbito 人々 *people, persons*

hitode ひとで *starfish*

hitode 人手 *workers, help*
• hitode-busoku 人手不足 *shortage of workers*

hitogomi 人込み *crowd of people*

hitogoroshi 人殺し ① *murder* [→**satsujin** 殺人]
② *murderer*

hitojichi 人質 ① *hostage*

¶Terorisuto wa shinbun-kisha o hitojichi ni totta.

テロリストは新聞記者を人質に取った。

Terrorists took the newspaper reporter hostage.

② *hostage taking*

hitokoto 一言 *a word, a few words*

• hitokoto de iu 一言で言う *to say in a word, to say in a few words*

hitomi 瞳 *pupil «of the eye»*

hitóri 一人 ① *one «when counting people; see Appendix 2»*

¶Ken-san wa watashi no tomodachi no hitori desu.

健さんは私の友達の一人です。

Ken is one of my friends.

¶Furansu-go ga dekiru hito wa hitori mo imasen.

フランス語ができる人は一人もいません。

There isn't even one person who can speak French.

② *oneself alone «often written 独り»*

¶Hitori ni shite oite kudasai.

一人にしておいてください。

Please leave me alone.

• hitori de 一人で, 独りで *alone, by oneself*

¶Sobo wa hitori de sunde imasu.

祖母は独りで住んでいます。

My grandmother lives by herself.

¶Watashi wa hitori de sono shigoto o shimashita.

私は一人でその仕事をしました。

I did that work by myself.

• hitori no 独りの *unmarried, single* [→ **dokushin no** 独身の]

• hitori-botchi no 独りぼっちの *solitary, all alone*

• hitori-de ni 独りでに *spontaneously, by itself*

• hitori-kko 一人っ子 *only child*

• hitori-musuko 一人息子 *only son*

• hitori-musume 一人娘 *only daughter*

hitorigotó 独り言 *talking to oneself; words directed at oneself*

• hitorigoto o iu 独り言を言う *to*

talk to oneself

hitosashíyubi 人指し指 *forefinger, index finger*

hitoshíi 等しい *equal, equivalent, identical* [→**onaji** 同じ]

¶Kono nawa to sono sao wa nagasa ga hitoshii desu.

この縄とその竿は長さが等しいです。

This rope and that pole are equal in length. «Literally: As for this rope and that pole, the length is equal.»

hitótsu 一つ *one «see Appendix 2»*

¶Sakkā wa boku no suki na supōtsu no hitotsu desu.

サッカーは僕の好きなスポーツの一つです。

Soccer is one of the sports I like.

• hitotsu-hitotsu 一つ一つ *one by one*

¶Kodomo wa hako ni omocha o hitotsu-hitotsu ireta.

子供は箱におもちゃを一つ一つ入れた。

The child put the toys into the box one by one.

hitsuji 羊 *sheep*

• hitsuji-kai 羊飼い *shepherd*

• ko-hitsuji 子羊 *lamb*

hitsujun 筆順 *stroke order «in Japanese writing»*

hitsuyō 必要 *necessity, need*

¶Kono hon o yomu hitsuyō wa nai desu.

この本を読む必要はないです。

There is no need to read this book.

¶Daitōryō mo iku hitsuyō ga arimasu.

大統領も行く必要があります。

It is necessary for the president to go too.

• A o hitsuyō to suru A を必要とする *to come to need A*

¶Ima enjo o hitsuyō to shite imasu.

今援助を必要としています。

I need help now.

• hitsuyō na 必要な *necessary*

¶Undō wa kenkō ni hitsuyō desu.

運動は健康に必要です。

Exercise is necessary for health.

hitsuzen 必然 ～**no** ～の *inevitable, certain*

hittakúru ひったくる 【COL.】 *to steal*

by snatching

hitteki 匹敵 ～**suru** ～する *to be a match, to equal*

hítto ヒット ① *hit* 《in baseball》 [→**anda** 安打]

¶Pitchā wa hitto o ni-hon dake yurushita.

ピッチャーはヒットを2本だけ許した。

The pitcher only allowed two hits.

• hitto o utsu ヒットを打つ *to get a hit*

② *hit, success* [→**atari** 当たり③]

• hitto suru ヒットする *to become a hit*

¶Sono eiga wa hitto suru to omoimasu.

その映画はヒットすると思います。

I think the movie will become a hit.

• hitto-kyoku ヒット曲 *hit song*

• dai-hitto 大ヒット *big hit, great success* [→**ō-atari** 大当たり(s.v. **atari** 当たり)]

hiyakásu 冷やかす *to make fun of, to tease* [→**karakau** からかう]

hiyake 日焼け *suntan; sunburn*

• hiyake suru 日焼けする *to become suntanned; to become sunburned*

• hiyake-dome-kurīmu 日焼け止めクリーム *sunscreen*

hiyásu 冷やす *to cool, to chill* 《transitive》

¶Suika o reizōko de hiyashimashō.

すいかを冷蔵庫で冷やしましょう。

Let's chill the watermelon in the refrigerator.

• atama o hiyasu 頭を冷やす *to calm down, to regain one's composure*

híyō 費用 *expense, expenditure, cost*

¶Ryokō no hiyō wa nijū-man-en kurai ni narimasu.

旅行の費用は20万円くらいになります。

Travel expenses come to about 200,000 yen.

hiyoko ひよこ *newly hatched bird, chick* 《Most commonly used for chickens.》 [→**hina** 雛①]

híyu 比喩 *metaphor, simile*

• hiyu-teki na 比喩的な *metaphorical, figurative*

hiza 膝 ① *knee*

¶Bōru ga hiza ni atarimashita.

ボールがひざに当たりました。

A ball hit my knee.

② *lap* 《portion of a person's body》

¶Kodomo wa haha-oya no hiza no ue ni suwatte imashita.

子供は母親のひざの上に座っていました。

The child was sitting on her mother's lap.

• hiza-kozō 膝小僧 *kneecap*

hizamazúku 跪く *to kneel*

hizuke 日付 *date* 《written on something》

• A ni hizuke o kaku Aに日付を書く *to date A, to write the date on A*

¶Hirano-san no tegami wa Jū-gatsu tōka no hizuke deshita.

平野さんの手紙は10月10日の日付でした。

Mr. Hirano's letter was dated October 10.

• Hizuke-henkō-sen 日付変更線 *the International Date Line*

ho 帆 *sail* 《on a boat》

¶Yotto wa ho o ippai ni hatte imasu.

ヨットは帆をいっぱいに張っています。

The sailboat is in full sail.

• ho-bashira 帆柱 *mast*

hó 穂 (*grain*)*ear*

–ho －歩 《counter for steps, paces; see Appendix 2》

¶Ip-po mae e susuminasai.

1歩前へ進みなさい。

Move forward one step.

¶Mō ip-po mo arukenai yo.

もう1歩も歩けないよ。

I can't walk another step!

¶Ni- san-po sagarimashita.

2、3歩下がりました。

I moved back two or three steps.

hō 方 ① *way, direction* [→**hōkō** 方向]

¶Kochira no hō e oide kudasai.

こちらのほうへおいでください。

Please come this way.

¶Keikan wa kōen no hō e aruite ikimashita.

警官は公園のほうへ歩いていきました。

The police officer walked in the direction of the park.

¶Sono shōnen wa mon no hō e hashirimashita.

その少年は門のほうへ走りました。

That boy ran toward the gate.

② *side, type; the one* 《*of a set of alternatives*》

¶Chichi wa hoshu-teki na hō desu.

父は保守的なほうです。

My father is on the conservative side.

¶Ōkii hō o kaimashō.

大きいほうを買いましょう。

Let's buy the big one.

③ *side* 《This is a figurative use in which **hō** marks which of two alternatives is more so in terms of a criterion of comparison. This **hō** can follow a noun plus **no** の or a clause. When it follows a clause ending in an affirmative verb, the verb is typically in the past tense.》

¶Watashi no heya no hō ga ani no yori semai.

私の部屋のほうが兄のより狭い。

My room is smaller than my older brother's.

¶Fuyu yori natsu no hō ga suki desu.

冬より夏のほうが好きです。

I like summer better than winter.

¶Okāsan to sōdan shita hō ga ii deshō.

お母さんと相談したほうがいいでしょう。

It would be better to talk it over with your mother.

¶Hitori de soko e ikanai hō ga ii yo.

一人でそこへ行かないほうがいいよ。

It would be better not to go there alone!

hō 法 *law* [→**hōritsu** 法律]

• hō o mamoru 法を守る *to obey the law*
• hō o yaburu 法を破る *to break the law*

-hō －法 *way, method* 《Added to noun bases denoting activities.》

• chiryō-hō 治療法 *medical treatment method*
• yobō-hō 予防法 *prevention method*

hố 頬 *cheek*

¶Kyōko-chan wa bara-iro no hō o shite imasu.

京子ちゃんはばら色のほおをしています。

Kyoko has rosy cheeks.

¶Hazukashikute hō ga akaku narimashita.

恥ずかしくてほおが赤くなりました。

I was embarrassed and my cheeks turned red.

hobākuráfuto ホバークラフト *hovercraft*

hōbi 褒美 *reward; prize* [→**shō** 賞]

¶Chichi wa hōbi ni kono pen o kureta yo.

父は褒美にこのペンをくれたよ。

My father gave me this pen as a reward!

¶Yōko-chan wa e de hōbi o moratta yo.

洋子ちゃんは絵で褒美をもらったよ。

Yoko got a prize for her painting!

hōbō 方々 *here and there, all over* [→**achikochi** あちこち]

hóbo 保母 *nursery school teacher*

hóbo ほぼ *nearly, almost* [→**hotondo** 殆ど①]

hóchikisu ホチキス *stapler*

• hochikisu de tomeru ホチキスで留める *to fasten with a stapler*

¶Sensei wa kopī o hochikisu de tomemashita.

先生はコピーをホチキスで留めました。

The teacher stapled the copies together.

hōchō 包丁 *kitchen knife*

hochō 歩調 *pace, step, walking tempo*

• hochō o awaseru 歩調を合わせる *to keep pace, to match walking tempo*

¶Hoka no hito to hochō o awasete arukinasai.

ほかの人と歩調を合わせて歩きなさい。

Walk in pace with the other people.

hōdō 報道 *news report; reporting the news*

• hōdō suru 報道する *to report*

¶Sono jiko wa shinbun de hōdō sarete imasu.

その事故は新聞で報道されています。

That accident is reported in the newspaper.

• hōdō-jin 報道陣 *reporters, the press*
• hōdō-kikan 報道機関 *the press, the news media*

hodo 程 ① *limit, bound* [→**gendo** 限度]

¶Yūjō ni mo hodo ga aru yo.

友情にも程があるよ。
There's a limit even to friendship!

• hodo o kosu 程を越す *to exceed the limits, to go to far*

② *extent, degree* 《following a predicate in the nonpast tense》 [→**gurai** 位①]

¶Kono mondai wa shinjirarenai hodo muzukashii yo.
この問題は信じられないほど難しいよ。
This problem is unbelievably hard!
《*Literally: This problem is hard to a degree that one can't believe!*》

¶Arukenai hodo ashi ga itai desu.
歩けないほど足が痛いです。
My leg hurts so much that I can't walk.
《*Literally: My leg is painful to the degree that I can't walk.*》

③ *the more* 《following a predicate first in the conditional (–**ba** form) and then in the nonpast form》

¶Nomeba nomu hodo oishiku narimasu.
飲めば飲むほどおいしくなります。
The more you drink, the better it tastes.

¶Hayakereba hayai hodo ii yo.
早ければ早いほどいいよ。
The sooner, the better!

④ 〈*not*〉 *as much as,* 〈*not*〉 *to the same extent as* 《In this use **hodo** functions as a noun-following particle or follows a verb in the nonpast tense. A negative predicate must follow **hodo**.》

¶Tarō wa Akimoto-san hodo Eigo ga hanasemasen.
太郎は秋元さんほど英語が話せません。
Taro can't speak English as well as Ms. Akimoto.

¶Kono kaban wa watashi no hodo omoku nai desu yo.
このかばんは私のほど重くないですよ。
This bag is not as heavy as mine!

¶Hokkaidō hodo ii tokoro wa nai desu.
北海道ほどいい所はないです。
There's no place as nice as Hokkaido.

¶Hon wa eiga hodo omoshiroku arimasen.
本は映画ほどおもしろくありません。
Books are not as interesting as movies.

–**hodo** －程 *about, or so* 《Added to number bases.》 [→–**gurai** －ぐらい①]

¶Jup-pun-hodo shite modotte kimasu.
10分ほどして戻ってきます。
I'll come back in ten minutes or so.

¶Nijū-nin-hodo no seito ga sono kai ni shusseki shite ita.
20人ほどの生徒がその会に出席していた。
About twenty students were attending that party.

hodō 歩道 ＜*US*＞*sidewalk,* ＜*UK*＞*pavement*

¶Watashi-tachi wa hodō o aruite imashita.
私たちは歩道を歩いていました。
We were walking along the sidewalk.

• hodō-kyō 歩道橋 *pedestrian overpass*
• ōdan-hodō 横断歩道 *crosswalk*

hodóku 解く *to undo, to untie* [⇔**musubu** 結ぶ①]

¶Kono tsutsumi o hodoite kudasaimasen ka.
この包みをほどいてくださいませんか。
Won't you please untie this package?

¶Chichi wa nekutai o hodokimashita.
父はネクタイをほどきました。
My father untied his tie.

hoéru 吠る《a generic verb for loud cries of animals》 *to bark; to roar; to howl*

¶Ano inu wa Yumi-chan ni hoeta ne.
あの犬は由美ちゃんにほえたね。
That dog barked at Yumi, didn't it.

¶Raion ga ori no naka de hoete imasu.
ライオンがおりの中でほえています。
The lion is roaring in the cage.

hōfu 豊富 ～**na** ～な *abundant, plentiful* [⇔**hinjaku na** 貧弱な]

¶Ano terebi-tarento wa wadai no hōfu na hito da.
あのテレビタレントは話題の豊富な人だ。
That TV star has plenty to talk about.
《*Literally: That TV star is a person whose topics of conversation are plentiful.*》

¶Ōhashi-san no hoshi no chishiki wa hōfu desu.
大橋さんの星の知識は豊富です。
Ms. Ohashi knows a great deal about

the stars. 《Literally: Ms. Ohashi's knowledge of the stars is abundant.》

hōgaku 方角 *direction, way, bearings*
[→**hōkō** 方向]

¶Basu-tei wa achira no hōgaku desu.

バス停はあちらの方角です。

The bus stop is in that direction.

¶Watashi-tachi wa machigatta hōgaku e ikimashita.

私たちはまちがった方角へ行きました。

We went in the wrong direction.

hōgannage 砲丸投げ *the shot put*

hogáraka 朗らか ~**na** ~な *cheerful*
[→**akarui** 明るい②]

¶Ojōsan wa hogaraka na seito desu.

お嬢さんは朗らかな生徒です。

Your daughter is a cheerful student.

¶Minna hogaraka ni waratte imashita.

みんな朗らかに笑っていました。

They were all laughing cheerfully.

hogei 捕鯨 *whaling*

• hogei-sen 捕鯨船 *whaling ship*

hōgén 方言 *dialect*

hógo 保護 *protection*

• hogo suru 保護する *to protect, to safeguard* [→**mamoru** 守る①]

¶Natsu no tsuyoi hizashi kara me o hogo suru tame ni sangurasu o kakemasu.

夏の強い日ざしから目を保護するためにサングラスをかけます。

I wear sunglasses to protect my eyes from the strong summer sun.

• hogo-chō 保護鳥 *protected bird*

• hogo-sha 保護者 *protector, guardian*

hōhō 方法 *method, way*

¶Tango o oboeru ii hōhō o oshiete kudasai.

単語を覚えるいい方法を教えてください。

Please tell me a good method for learning words.

¶Kono keikaku o jikkō suru hōhō ga shiri-tai desu.

この計画を実行する方法が知りたいです。

I want to know a way to put this plan into practice.

hóho 頬 [☞**hō** 頬]

hohoemashíi 微笑ましい *pleasant,*

smile-provoking

¶Hohoemashii kōkei desu ne.

ほほえましい光景ですね。

It's a pleasant sight, isn't it.

hohoemí 微笑み *smile*

hohoému 微笑む *to smile*

¶Sono akachan wa watashi ni hohoemimashita.

その赤ちゃんは私にほほえみました。

That baby smiled at me.

¶Ikeda-san ga hohoemi-nagara kochira ni kita.

池田さんがほほえみながらこちらに来た。

Ms. Ikeda came over to us smiling.

hoikúen 保育園 *nursery school*

hoíssuru ホイッスル *whistle* ((device))

• hoissuru o narasu ホイッスルを鳴らす *to sound a whistle*

hōji 法事 *Buddhist memorial service*

hójo 補助 *help, assistance*

• hojo suru 補助する *to help with*

¶Keiko-san mo sono shigoto o hojo shimashita.

恵子さんもその仕事を補助しました。

Keiko also helped with that work.

hoka 他, 外 ~**no** ~の *other, another*

¶Hoka no seito wa kaette yoroshii.

ほかの生徒は帰ってよろしい。

The other students may go home.

¶Hoka no dono supōtsu yori mo yakyū ga suki da.

ほかのどのスポーツよりも野球が好きだ。

I like baseball better than any other sport.

¶Kono sētā wa chotto ki ni iranai n desu. Hoka no o misete kudasai.

このセーターはちょっと気に入らないんです。ほかのを見せてください。

This sweater doesn't really appeal to me. Please show me another one.

¶Hoka no hito wa dare-mo sono shirase o shiranai.

ほかの人はだれもその知らせを知らない。

Nobody else knows that news.

• hoka ni ほかに *besides, in addition, else*

¶Hoka ni nani-ka ossharu koto wa

arimasu ka.
ほかに何かおっしゃることはありますか。
Do you have something else to say?

¶Kyōko wa Eigo no hoka ni Furansu-go mo hanasu yo.
京子は英語のほかにフランス語も話すよ。
Kyoko can speak French in addition to English!

¶Akira no hoka ni wa dare-mo kesseki shinakatta yo.
明のほかにはだれも欠席しなかったよ。
Nobody was absent besides Akira!

hóka 放火 *arson*
• hōka suru 放火する *to deliberately set a fire*
• hōka-hannin 放火犯人 *arsonist*

hōkago 放課後 *after school*
¶Hōkago yakyū o shiyō.
放課後野球をしよう。
Let's play baseball after school.

hokan 保管 *safekeeping*
• hokan suru 保管する *to keep safely*

hoken 保健 *health preservation*
• hoken-fu 保健婦 *(female)public health nurse*
• hoken-jo 保健所 *health center, public health clinic*
• hoken-taiiku 保健体育 *health and physical education*

hoken 保険 *insurance*
• A ni hoken o kakeru Aに保険をかける *to get insurance on A, to insure A*
¶Haha mo kuruma ni hoken o kakete imasu.
母も車に保険をかけています。
My mother also has insurance on her car.
• hoken ni hairu 保険に入る *to get insurance, to become insured*
• hoken-gaisha 保険会社 *insurance company*
• hoken-kin 保険金 *insurance money*
• kenkō-hoken 健康保険 *health insurance*
• seimei-hoken 生命保険 *life insurance*
• shōgai-hoken 傷害保険 *accident insurance*

hoketsu 補欠 ① *filling a vacancy, substitution*
② *person who fills a vacancy, substitute*
¶Jirō wa hoketsu de sono yakyū no shiai ni demashita.
次郎は補欠でその野球の試合に出ました。
Jiro played in that baseball game as a substitute.
• hoketsu-senkyo 補欠選挙 *special election (to fill a vacancy)*
• hoketsu-senshu 補欠選手 *substitute player* [⇔**regyurā** レギュラー①]

hōki ほうき *broom*

hókkē ホッケー *(field)hockey*
• aisu-hokkē アイスホッケー *ice hockey*

hókku ホック *hook ((clothing fastener))*
• hokku de tomeru ホックで留める *to fasten with a hook*
• hokku o kakeru ホックをかける *to hook a hook*
• hokku o hazusu ホックを外す *to undo a hook*

Hokkyoku 北極 *the North Pole* [⇔**Nankyoku** 南極]
• Hokkyoku-kai 北極海 *the Arctic Ocean*
• Hokkyoku-sei 北極星 *the Polestar, the North Star*

hōkō 方向 *direction, way, bearings* [→**hōgaku** 方角]
• hōkō-onchi no 方向音痴の *having no sense of direction*

hōkoku 報告 *report, account, briefing*
¶Watashi-tachi wa sensei ni ryokō no hōkoku o shimasu.
私たちは先生に旅行の報告をします。
We will make a report of our trip to our teacher.
• hōkoku suru 報告する *to report*
• hōkoku-kai 報告会 *briefing session*
• hōkoku-sho 報告書 *(written)report*

hokori 埃 *dust ((i.e., fine particles of dirt))*
¶Tokidoki hondana no hokori o haraimasu.
時々本棚のほこりを払います。

I sometimes brush off the dust on the bookshelf.

• hokori-darake no 埃だらけの *covered with dust*

• hokori-ppoi 埃っぽい *dusty*

hokorí 誇り ① *pride, thing to be proud of*

¶ Kono hakubutsukan wa shi no hokori desu.

この博物館は市の誇りです。

This museum is the pride of the city.

② *pride, self-esteem*

¶ Chichi wa jibun no shigoto ni hokori o motte imasu.

父は自分の仕事に誇りを持っています。

My father takes pride in his work.

hokóru 誇る *to be proud of, to take pride in*

hokósha 歩行者 *pedestrian*

• hōkosha-tengoku 歩行者天国 *street on which vehicular traffic has been temporarily suspended* 《*typically on a Sunday or holiday*》

Hokubei 北米 *North America* [⇔**Nanbei** 南米]

hókubu 北部 *northern part* [⇔**nanbu** 南部]

Hokuriku-chíhō 北陸地方 *the Hokuriku region of Japan* 《*Niigata, Toyama, Ishikawa, and Fukui Prefectures*》

hokuro ほくろ *mole* 《*on the skin*》

hokusei 北西 *the northwest* [→**seihoku** 西北]

• hokusei no kaze 北西の風 *northwest wind*

hokutō 北東 *the northeast* [→**tōhoku** 東北]

• hokutō no kaze 北東の風 *northeast wind*

Hokutoshichísei 北斗七星 *the Big Dipper*

hokyū 補給 *supply; replenishment*

• hokyū suru 補給する *to supply; to replenish*

¶ Nanmin ni shokuryō o hokyū shimasu.

難民に食糧を補給します。

We supply food to the refugees.

hōmén 方面 ① *direction, way* [→**hōkō** 方向]

• -hōmen -方面 *the direction of* 《Added to bases denoting places.》

¶ Sendai-hōmen ni iku basu wa dore desu ka.

仙台方面に行くバスはどれですか。

Which one is the bus going in the Sendai direction?

② *district, area* [→**chiiki** 地域]

③ *field* (*of endeavor*) [→**bun'ya** 分野]

¶ Chichi wa kono hōmen no kenkyū de wa yūmei na kagaku-sha da.

父はこの方面の研究では有名な科学者だ。

My father is a famous scientist in this field of research.

homéru 褒める *to praise, to commend* [⇔**kenasu** 貶す]

¶ Nakano-san no yūki o homemashita.

中野さんの勇気を褒めました。

We praised Mr. Nakano's courage.

¶ Masako wa Noriko no atarashii doresu o hometa yo.

正子は典子の新しいドレスを褒めたよ。

Masako praised Noriko's new dress!

hōmon 訪問 *visit, call*

• hōmon suru 訪問する *to visit, to call on* [→**otozureru** 訪れる]

¶ Watashi-tachi wa Shimoda-sensei no otaku o hōmon shimasu.

私たちは下田先生のお宅を訪問します。

We will visit Mr. Shimoda's house.

• hōmon-kyaku 訪問客 *visitor*

• katei-hōmon 家庭訪問 *home visit* (*by a child's teacher*)

hốmu ホーム ① *home, household* [→**katei** 家庭①]

② *home base, home plate* [→**honrui** 本塁] 《*in baseball*》

• hōmu-dorama ホームドラマ *soap opera*

• hōmu-guraundo ホームグラウンド *home field*

• hōmu-in ホームイン *scoring a run, reaching home*

• hōmu-sutei ホームステイ *homestay*

• rōjin-hōmu 老人ホーム

old people's home

hōmu 法務 *judicial affairs*
• Hōmu-shō 法務省 *the Ministry of Justice*

hōmu ホーム *train platform*

hōmúran ホームラン *home run*
• hōmuran o utsu ホームランを打つ *to hit a home run*
• hōmuran-ō ホームラン王 *home-run king*

hōmúru 葬る *to bury, to put in a grave*

hōmurū̆mu ホームルーム *homeroom*

hōmushíkku ホームシック *homesickness*
¶Michiko wa hōmushikku ni kakatte iru ne.
美知子はホームシックにかかっているね。
Michiko is suffering from homesickness, isn't she?

hón 本 *book*
¶Ani wa hikōki no hon o kai-ta-gatte imasu.
兄は飛行機の本を買いたがっています。
My older brother wants to buy a book about airplanes.
¶Hon no jūhachi-pēji o hiraite kudasai.
本の18ページを開いてください。
Please open the book to page 18.
¶Kono tosho-kan wa hon ga nan-satsu kariraremasu ka.
この図書館は本が何冊借りられますか。
How many books can one borrow from this library?
• atsui〔usui〕hon 厚い〔薄い〕本 *thick〔thin〕book*
• hon-bako 本箱 *bookcase*
• hon-dana 本棚 *bookshelf*
• hon-tate 本立て *bookstand*
• hon-ya 本屋 <US>*bookstore*, <UK>*bookshop; bookseller*
• e-hon 絵本 *picture book*
• furu-hon 古本 *used book, secondhand book*

–hon 一本《counter for long objects; see Appendix 2》

hónbu 本部 *main office, headquarters; administration building*

honé 骨 *bone*
¶Kono sakana wa chīsa na hone ga

takusan aru yo.
この魚は小さな骨がたくさんあるよ。
This fish has a lot of small bones!
• hone o oru 骨を折る *to break a bone; to take pains, to make efforts*
¶Yumi wa sukēto de migi-ashi no hone o orimashita.
由美はスケートで右足の骨を折りました。
Yumi broke a bone in her right leg while skating.
• hone ga oreru 骨が折れる *a bone breaks; to be difficult, to be laborious*
¶Eigo de tegami o kaku no wa hone no oreru shigoto da.
英語で手紙を書くのは骨の折れる仕事だ。
Writing letters in English is laborious work.
• hone-ori 骨折り *efforts, pains* [→**doryoku** 努力]
• hone-oru 骨折る *to make efforts, to take pains* [→**doryoku suru** 努力する]
¶Sono sakuhin o shiageru noni hijō ni hone-otta.
その作品を仕上げるのに非常に骨折った。
I took great pains to finish that work.

hónjitsu 本日 【FORMAL for **kyō** 今日】 *today*

honkakuteki 本格的 ～**na** ～な *full-scale, full-fledged, serious*

honki 本気 *seriousness, earnestness*
• honki no 本気の *serious, earnest* [→**shinken na** 真剣な]
¶Honki desu ka.
本気ですか。
Are you serious?
¶Masaka honki ja nai deshō?
まさか本気じゃないでしょう？
You can't possibly be serious, right?
• honki de 本気で *seriously, earnestly*
• honki ni suru 本気にする *to take seriously*
¶Sonna jōdan o honki ni shite wa ikenai yo.
そんな冗談を本気にしてはいけないよ。
You mustn't take such jokes seriously!

honmono 本物 *real thing* [⇔**nise-mono** 偽物 (s.v. **nise** 偽)]

• honmono no 本物の *real, genuine* [⇔ **nise no** 偽の]

¶Kore wa honmono no daiya desu.

これは本物のダイヤです。

This is a real diamond.

honne 本音 *true feelings, real motivation* [→**honshin** 本心] [⇔**tatemae** 立て前]

hónnin 本人 *the person himself／herself, the person in question*

hon-no ほんの *only a, just a, a mere*

¶Tarō wa mada hon-no kodomo desu.

太郎はまだほんの子供です。

Taro is still only a child.

¶Chichi wa hon-no sukoshi Furansu-go ga dekimasu.

父はほんの少しフランス語ができます。

My father can speak French just a little.

¶Akira wa hon-no sūjitsu-mae ni hikkoshimashita.

明はほんの数日前に引っ越しました。

Akira moved out only a few days ago.

¶Sore o hon-no jōdan de iimashita.

それをほんの冗談で言いました。

I said that as a mere joke.

hónnō 本能 *instinct*

• honnō-teki na 本能的な *instinctive*

honomekásu 仄めかす *to hint at*

¶Imōto wa ryūgaku suru tsumori da to honomekashita.

妹は留学するつもりだとほのめかした。

My younger sister hinted that she intends to study abroad.

honóo 炎 *flame*

¶Gasu no honoo wa nani-iro desu ka.

ガスの炎は何色ですか。

What color is a gas flame?

¶Kaidan wa honoo ni tsutsumarete imashita.

階段は炎に包まれていました。

The stairs were enveloped in flames.

hónrai 本来 *originally* [→**ganrai** 元来]; *by nature* [→**umaretsuki** 生まれつき]

¶Kore wa honrai wa Chūgoku no shokubutsu desu.

これは本来は中国の植物です。

This is originally a plant from China.

• honrai no 本来の *original; inborn*

hónrui 本塁 *home base, home plate* [→ **hōmu** ホーム②] 《in baseball》

• honrui-da 本塁打 *home run* [→**hōmuran** ホームラン]

hónshin 本心 *true feelings; real intentions*

¶Hoshino-kun wa watashi ni honshin o uchiakete kureta.

星野君は私に本心を打ち明けてくれた。

Hoshino confided his real feelings to me.

honshitsu 本質 *essence, true nature*

honten 本店 *head office, main store* [⇔**shiten** 支店]

hontō 本当 ～no ～の *true, real*

¶Kore wa hontō no hanashi desu ka.

これはほんとうの話ですか。

Is this is a true story?

¶Sono yume wa hontō ni narimashita.

その夢はほんとうになりました。

That dream came true.

¶Chichi ga hasan shita to iu no wa hontō desu ka.

父が破産したというのはほんとうですか。

Is it true that Father has gone bankrupt?

¶Issho ni ite hontō ni tanoshii desu.

いっしょにいてほんとうに楽しいです。

It's really fun being with you.

¶Sano-san wa hontō ni ii hito desu.

佐野さんはほんとうにいい人です。

Ms. Sano is a really good person.

¶Hontō ni sō omoimasu ka.

ほんとうにそう思いますか。

Do you really think so?

¶"Raishū Hawai ni ikimasu yo." "Ě, hontō desu ka."

「来週ハワイに行きますよ」「えっ、ほんとうですか」

"I'm going to go to Hawaii next week!" "What! Really?"

¶Hontō ni arigatō gozaimasu.

ほんとうにありがとうございます。

Thank you very much indeed. 《Literally: Truly thank you.》

honto ほんと [☞**hontō** 本当]

hon'yaku 翻訳 *translation*

• hon'yaku suru 翻訳する *to translate* [→**yakusu** 訳す]

¶Shēkusupia o hon'yaku de yomimashita.
シェークスピアを翻訳で読みました。
I read Shakespeare in translation.

• hon'yaku-sha 翻訳者 *translator*

honyūdōbutsu 哺乳動物 *mammal*

hoppéta ほっぺた【COL. for **hō** 頬】 *cheek*

hṓpu ホープ *hope* ((person))

¶Sakurai-senshu wa kono chīmu no hōpu desu.
桜井選手はこのチームのホープです。
Sakurai is the hope of this team.

hóra ほら *Look!, Listen!* «an interjection used to call a person's attention to something»

¶Hora, densha ga kita yo.
ほら、電車が来たよ。
Look! The train has come!

¶Hora, kanaria ga naite iru yo.
ほら、カナリアが鳴いているよ。
Listen! A canary is singing!

horaana 洞穴 *cave* [→**dōkutsu** 洞窟]

hōrénsō ホウレン草 *spinach*

hōridásu 放り出す ① *to throw outside*

¶Otōto wa neko o doa kara hōridashimashita.
弟は猫をドアからほうり出しました。
My younger brother threw the cat out the door.

② ‹US›*to fire*, ‹UK›*to sack, to dismiss* [→**kubi ni suru** 首にする]

③ *to give up, to quit, to abandon*

¶Shigoto o tochū de hōridashite wa ikenai yo.
仕事を途中でほうり出してはいけないよ。
You mustn't give up your work in the middle!

hōritsu 法律 *law, statute*

¶Sono kōi wa hōritsu de kinshi sarete imasu.
その行為は法律で禁止されています。
That action is prohibited by law.

• hōritsu o mamoru 法律を守る *to obey the law*

• hōritsu ni shitagau 法律に従う *to follow the law*

• hōritsu o yaburu 法律を破る *to break the law*

• hōritsu-ka 法律家 *jurist*

horobíru 滅びる *to be destroyed, to fall, to cease to exist*

¶Rōma-teikoku ga itsu horobita ka wakarimasu ka.
ローマ帝国がいつ滅びたかわかりますか。
Do you know when the Roman Empire fell?

horobósu 滅ぼす *to ruin, to destroy, to wipe out*

• mi o horobosu 身を滅ぼす *to ruin oneself, to bring oneself to ruin*

hōru 放る [[→**nageru** 投げる]]
① *to throw*
② *to give up on and quit*

hōru ホール *large room, hall*

• bia-hōru ビアホール *beer hall*

hōru ホール (golf)*hole*

• hōru-in-wan ホールインワン *hole in one*

hóru 掘る *to dig; to dig up, to dig for*

¶Asoko de nani o hotte iru no desu ka.
あそこで何を掘っているのですか。
What are they digging for over there?

¶Kono shaberu de ana o horimashita.
このシャベルで穴を掘りました。
I dug a hole with this shovel.

hóru 彫る *to carve, to engrave* [→**kizamu** 刻む②]

• A ni B o horu AにBを彫る *to carve A in／on B, to engrave A on B*

hórumon ホルモン ① *hormone*
② [☞**holumon-yaki** ホルモン焼き]

• horumon-yaki ホルモン焼き *grilled organ meats*

hóryo 捕虜 *prisoner of war*

hōsaku 豊作 *good harvest, good crop* [⇔**fusaku** 不作]

¶Kotoshi wa kome ga hōsaku desu.
今年は米が豊作です。
This year the rice crop is good. «Literally: This year rice is a good crop.»

hōseki 宝石 *jewel, gem*

• hōseki-bako 宝石箱 *jewel box*

• hōseki-shō 宝石商 *jeweler*

hōsha 放射 ～**suru** ～する *to emit, to radiate*
- hōsha-nō 放射能 *radioactivity*
- hōsha-sei no 放射性の *radioactive*
- hōsha-sen 放射線 *radiation, rays*

hoshi 星 *star; planet* [→**wakusei** 惑星]
¶Kon'ya wa sora ni hoshi ga kagayaite imasu.
今夜は空に星が輝いています。
Tonight stars are shining in the sky.
¶Kon'ya wa hoshi ga takusan mieru yo.
今夜は星がたくさん見えるよ。
Tonight you can see a lot of stars!
- hoshi-akari 星明かり *starlight*
- hoshi-kuzu 星屑 *stardust*
- hoshi-uranai 星占い *astrological fortunetelling*
- hoshi-zora 星空 *starry sky*
- nagare-boshi 流れ星 *shooting star*

hoshigaru 欲しがる *to come to want*
《Used instead of **hosii** 欲しいwhen the person who wants is a third person.》
¶Otōto wa atarashii jitensha o hoshigatte imasu.
弟は新しい自転車を欲しがっています。
My younger brother wants a new bicycle.

hoshíi 欲しい ① *to want, to desire* 《This word is an adjective, and what is wanted is treated as a grammatical subject and marked with **ga** が. The word **hoshii** is not used to describe the wants of a third person; see **hoshigaru** 欲しがる.》
¶Atarashii doresu ga hoshii.
新しいドレスが欲しい。
I want a new dress.
¶Ima watashi wa nani-mo hoshiku arimasen.
今私は何も欲しくありません。
I don't want anything now.
¶Kore wa watashi ga nagai aida hoshikatta sutereo da.
これは私が長い間欲しかったステレオだ。
This is the stereo I wanted for a long time.
② *to want* ⟨*someone*⟩ *to* 《following the gerund (-**te** form) of a verb》
¶Chichi ni Okinawa ni tsurete itte hoshii desu.
父に沖縄に連れていってほしいです。
I want my father to take me to Okinawa.

hōshin 方針 *course* (*of action*), *policy, plan*
¶Mō shōrai no hōshin o tatemashita ka.
もう将来の方針を立てましたか。
Have you already made plans for the future?

hoshō 保証 *guarantee, warranty*
¶Watashi no tokei wa ni-nen-kan no hoshō ga tsuite imasu.
私の時計は2年間の保証がついています。
My watch has a two-year guarantee.
- hoshō suru 保証する *to guarantee*
¶Unten-sha no anzen wa hoshō dekimasen.
運転者の安全は保証できません。
I cannot guarantee the driver's safety.
- hoshō-kikan 保証期間 *warranty period*
- hoshō-kin 保証金 *security money, security deposit*
- hoshō-nin 保証人 *guarantor; sponsor*
- hoshō-sho 保証書 (*written*)*guarantee*
- hoshō-tsuki no 保証つきの *guaranteed, with a guarantee*

hóshu 捕手 (*baseball*)*catcher* [→ **kyatchā** キャッチャー]

hóshu 保守 *conservatism*
- hoshu-teki na 保守的な *conservative*

hōsō 包装 *packing, wrapping*
- hōsō suru 包装する *to wrap, to pack* [→**tsutsumu** 包む]
- hōsō-shi 包装紙 *wrapping paper, packing paper*

hōsō 放送 *broadcasting; broadcast*
- hōsō suru 放送する *to broadcast*
¶Sono jiken wa terebi de Nihon-jū ni hōsō sareta.
その事件はテレビで日本中に放送された。
That incident was broadcast on TV all over Japan.
- hōsō-kyoku 放送局 *broadcasting station*
- kaigai-hōsō 海外放送 *overseas broadcasting*
- nama-hōsō 生放送 *live broadcast*

• ni-kakokugo-hōsō 2ヵ国語放送 *bilingual broadcasting*

• onsei-tajū-hōsō 音声多重放送 *multiplex broadcasting*

• sai-hōsō 再放送 *rerun, rebroadcast* <UK>*repeat*

• terebi-hōsō テレビ放送 *television broadcast*

hosō 舗装 *pavement; paving*

• hosō suru 舗装する *to pave*

• hosō-dōro 舗装道路 *paved road*

hosói 細い *thin, slender, slim, small in diameter* [⇔futoi 太い]*; narrow* [→ **semai** 狭い①]

¶Tanimoto-san no yubi wa hosoi desu ne.

谷本さんの指は細いですね。

Ms. Tanimoto's fingers are slender, aren't they?

¶Ane wa hosoi karada o shite imasu.

姉は細い体をしています。

My older sister is slim. 《*Literally: My older sister has a slim body.*》

¶Kono hosoi himo o tsukatte mo ii desu ka.

この細いひもを使ってもいいですか。

Is it all right to use this thin string?

¶Kono hosoi michi o ikeba, kōen ni demasu.

この細い道を行けば、公園に出ます。

If you go along this narrow road, you'll come to the park.

• hosoi koe 細い声 *weak voice, small voice*

hōsoku 法則 (*scientific*)*law, principle, rule*

• shizen no hōsoku 自然の法則 *a law of nature*

hosonagái 細長い *long and slender*

hossa 発作 *fit, attack, spasm*

hossóri ほっそり 〜**shita** 〜した *slender, slim*

hósu ホース *a hose*

hósu 干す *to put out to dry*

¶Nureta uwagi o hinata ni hoshimashita.

ぬれた上着を日なたに干しました。

I put my wet jacket out to dry in

the sun.

¶Haha wa sentaku-mono o hoshimashita.

母は洗濯物を干しました。

My mother hung the washing out to dry.

hōtai 包帯 *bandage*

¶Haha wa watashi no yubi ni hōtai o shite kuremashita.

母は私の指に包帯をしてくれました。

My mother put a bandage on my finger.

• hōtai suru 包帯する *to bandage*

hótaru 蛍 *firefly*

hōtei 法廷 *court* (*of law*)

hōtéishiki 方程式 *equation*

hóteru ホテル *hotel*

¶Watashi-tachi wa Hiroshima no hoteru ni tomarimashita.

私たちは広島のホテルに泊まりました。

We stayed at a hotel in Hiroshima.

¶Imagawa-san wa ima hoteru ni tsukimashita.

今川さんは今ホテルに着きました。

Ms. Imagawa just now arrived at the hotel.

¶Hachi-ji ni hoteru o demasu.

8時にホテルを出ます。

We will leave the hotel at 8:00.

Hotoké 仏 ① *Buddha*

• Hotoke no yō na hito 仏のような人 *saintly person*

② *deceased person* 《This use is a reflection of the traditional religious belief that a person becomes an enlightened being like Buddha after death.》

• Hotoke ni naru 仏になる *to pass on, to pass away*

hotóndo 殆ど ① *almost, nearly, almost completely*

¶Shukudai wa hotondo owatta yo.

宿題はほとんど終わったよ。

I've almost finished my homework!

¶Ayamari wa hotondo arimasen deshita.

誤りはほとんどありませんでした。

There were almost no mistakes.

¶Baketsu ni wa hotondo mizu ga nokotte imasen.

バケツにはほとんど水が残っていません。

In the bucket there's almost

no water left.
　② *almost all, the greater part*
¶Hotondo no seito ga kono shūkai ni
sanka shita.
ほとんどの生徒がこの集会に参加した。
*Almost all the students took part in this
meeting.*
¶Kankō-kyaku no hotondo wa gakusei
desu.
観光客のほとんどは学生です。
Almost all of the tourists are students.

hototógisu 時鳥, 子規, 不如帰
common cuckoo

hotte-oku ほっておく ① *to leave alone,
to let alone*
¶Boku no koto wa hotte-oite kudasai.
僕のことはほっておいてください。
Please leave me alone.
　② *to leave undone, to set aside*
¶Sono mondai o hotte-okimashō.
その問題をほっておきましょう。
Let's set that problem aside.

hōtte-oku ほうっておく [☞**hotte-oku**
ほっておく]

hotto ほっと 〜**suru** 〜する *to be
relieved, to feel relief* [→**anshin suru**
安心する]
¶Minna ga buji da to kiite hotto shimashita.
みんなが無事だと聞いてほっとしました。
*I heard that everyone is safe and felt
relieved.*

hottokḗki ホットケーキ *hot cake,
pancake*

hottonyū́su ホットニュース *hot news*

hottoráin ホットライン *hotline*

hozon 保存 *preservation; storage*
・hozon suru 保存する *to preserve; to
store*
¶Kono firumu wa suzushii tokoro ni hozon shinasai.
このフィルムは涼しい所に保存しなさい。
Store this film in a cool place.

hyakkajíten 百科事典 *encyclopedia*

hyakkáten 百貨店 *department store*
[→**depāto** デパート]

hyakú 百 *hundred* 《see Appendix 2》

・hyaku-man 百万 *one million*
・hyaku-pāsento １００パーセント *100 percent*

hyō 表 *chart, table; list* [→**ichiranhyō**
一覧表]
・hyō ni suru 表にする *to make into a
table; to make into a list*
¶Sensei wa shiken no kekka o hyō ni
shimashita.
先生は試験の結果を表にしました。
*The teacher made the examination
results into a table.*
・jikan-hyō 時間表 *timetable*
・yotei-hyō 予定表 *chart of one's schedule*

hyṓ 豹 *leopard; panther*

hyō 票 *vote; ballot*
・-hyō －票《counter for votes; see Appendix 2》
¶Hirata-san wa nijūgo-hyō o kakutoku
shimashita.
平田さんは25票を獲得しました。
Ms. Hirata got 25 votes.

hyṓ 雹 *hail* ((precipitation))
・hyō ga furu ひょうが降る *hail falls*

hyōban 評判 ① *reputation*
¶Sono isha wa hyōban ga ii desu.
その医者は評判がいいです。
That doctor's reputation is good.
　② *fame, popularity, notoriety*
・hyōban no 評判の *famous, popular,
notorious*
¶Ano haiyū wa Nihon de mo hyōban
desu.
あの俳優は日本でも評判です。
That actor is popular in Japan too.

hyṓga 氷河 *glacier*
・hyōga-jidai 氷河時代 *ice age*

hyōgén 表現 *expression, manifestation*
・hyōgen suru 表現する *to express*
・hyōgen no jiyū 表現の自由 *freedom of
expression*

hyōjṓ 表情 *facial expression, look* (*on
one's face*) [→**metsuki** 目付き]
¶Yumi-san wa kanashi-sō na hyōjō
deshita.
由美さんは悲しそうな表情でした。

Yumi had a sad look on her face.

¶Kōchi no kao ni wa ikari no hyōjō ga ukande ita.

コーチの顔には怒りの表情が浮んでいた。

An expression of anger appeared on the coach's face.

hyōjun 標準 *standard, norm*

¶Kono sakuhin wa hyōjun ni tasshite imasen.

この作品は標準に達していません。

This work does not come up to the standard.

• hyōjun-go 標準語 *standard language*

• hyōjun-ji 標準時 *standard time*

hyōka 評価 *evaluation, appraisal, assessment*

• hyōka suru 評価する *to evaluate, to appraise, to assess*

¶Buchō wa Ichiyama-san no nōryoku o takaku hyōka shita.

部長は市山さんの能力を高く評価した。

The department head evaluated Ms. Ichiyama's ability highly.

• kadai-hyōka suru 過大評価する *to overestimate, to overrate*

• kashō-hyōka suru 過小評価する *to underestimate, to underrate*

hyōkin 剽軽 **~na** ~な *funny, comical*

¶Onīsan wa hyōkin desu ne.

お兄さんはひょうきんですね。

Your older brother is funny, isn't he.

hyōmen 表面 *surface*

hyōsatsu 表札 *nameplate* 《displayed near the entrance of a home in Japan》

hyōshi 表紙 *cover* 《i.e., the outermost part of a book, etc.》

hyōshi 拍子 *(musical)time, (musical)rhythm*

¶Tamura-san wa pen de hyōshi o totte imasu.

田村さんはペンで拍子を取っています。

Mr. Tamura is keeping time with his pen.

• ni-hyōshi 2拍子 *double time*

hyōshiki 標識 *marker, sign*

hyōshō 表彰 *official commendation, public honoring*

• hyōshō suru 表彰する *to officially commend, to honor publicly*

¶Keikan wa jinmei-kyūjo de hyōshō saremashita.

警官は人命救助で表彰されました。

The police officer was honored for saving a life.

• hyōshō-dai 表彰台 *commendation award platform*

• hyōshō-jō 表彰状 *certificate of commendation*

• hyōshō-shiki 表彰式 *commendation award ceremony*

hyōtan 瓢箪 *gourd*

hyōten 氷点 *the freezing point*

• hyōten-ka 氷点下 *(the temperature range)below the freezing point*

¶Ima hyōten-ka nijūgo-do desu.

今氷点下25度です。

It's 25 degrees below freezing now.

hyotto ひょっと **~shitara** ~したら *just maybe, by some chance* 《This expression typically occurs in sentences ending with an expression of possibility (usually **ka mo shirenai** かもしれない). Since such a sentence has virtually the same meaning whether or not **hyotto shitara** is present, **hyotto shitara** is redundant in a sense, but it serves as a signal of how a sentence will end.》

• hyotto suru to ひょっとすると [☞**hyotto** ひょっと (above)]

• hyotto shite ひょっとして [☞**hyotto** ひょっと (above)]

hyōzan 氷山 *iceberg*

• hyōzan no ikkaku 氷山の一角 *the tip of an iceberg*

hyūmanizumu ヒューマニズム *humanitarianism*

hyūzu ヒューズ *(electrical)fuse*

I

i 胃 *stomach* «the internal organ»

¶I ga jōbu desu.

胃が丈夫です。

My stomach is strong.

¶Chichi wa nani-ka i no byōki desu.

父は何か胃の病気です。

My father has some kind of stomach trouble.

ibara 茨 *thorn bush, bramble*

ibáru 威張る *to become arrogant, to act high and mighty*

¶Ano isha wa ibatte iru yo.

あの医者は威張っているよ。

That doctor is arrogant!

ibento イベント ① *special event*

② *event* «in a competition»

ibikí いびき *snore, snoring*

• ibiki o kaku いびきをかく *to snore*

ibo いぼ *wart*

ibuningudóresu イブニングドレス *evening dress*

ichí 一 *one* «see Appendix 2»

• Ichi-gatsu 一月 *January*

íchi 市 *market, marketplace*

• kokusai-mihon-ichi 国際見本市 *international trade fair*

íchi 位置 *position, place, location*

¶Kono tēburu no ichi o kaete kureru?

このテーブルの位置を変えてくれる？

Will you change the location of this table?

¶Senshu-tachi wa sorezore no ichi ni tsukimashita.

選手たちはそれぞれの位置につきました。

Each player took her position.

¶Ichi ni tsuite, yōi, don!

位置について、用意、どん！

On your mark, get set, go!

íchiba 市場 *market, marketplace*

¶Kaimono ni ichiba e ikimasu.

買い物に市場へ行きます

I'll go to the marketplace for shopping.

ichí-ban 一番 ① *(the)number 1* «see –ban –番 ① and Appendix 2»

¶Pitchā no se-bangō wa ichi-ban desu.

ピッチャーの背番号は１番です。

The pitcher's number is number 1.

② *first place, the first one* «see –ban –番 ② and Appendix 2»

¶Musume wa kontesuto de ichi-ban ni narimashita.

娘はコンテストで１番になりました。

My daughter was first in the contest.

ichiban 一番 *the most* «indicating a superlative» [→**mottomo** 最も]

¶Nihon de ichiban takai yama wa Fuji-san desu.

日本でいちばん高い山は富士山です。

The highest mountain in Japan is Mt. Fuji.

¶Fumiko wa kurasu de ichiban yūshū na seito desu.

文子はクラスでいちばん優秀な生徒です。

Fumiko is the most outstanding student in the class.

¶Taira-san wa ichiban nesshin ni benkyō shimashita.

平さんはいちばん熱心に勉強しました。

Ms. Taira studied the hardest.

¶Kamoku no naka de rekishi ga ichiban suki desu.

科目の中で歴史がいちばん好きです。

Among school subjects I like history the most.

ichíbu 一部 ① *a part, a portion*

¶Sono hanashi wa hon-no ichibu dake ga hontō desu.

その話はほんの一部だけがほんとうです。

Only a part of that story is true.

¶Ichibu no hito-tachi wa kono an ni hantai desu.

一部の人たちはこの案に反対です。

Some of the people are against this plan.

② *one copy* «see –**bu** –部 and Appendix 2»

• ichibu-shijū 一部始終 *the whole story, all the details*

¶Sono jiken no ichibu-shijū o hanashite kudasai.

その事件の一部始終を話してください。

Please tell me all the details of that incident.

ichi-do 一度 *once, one time* 《see **-do** −度and Appendix 2》

¶Mō ichi-do yatte minasai.

もう一度やってみなさい。

Try doing it one more time.

• ichi-do ni 一度に *at the same time, at once* [→**dōji ni** 同時に]

¶Ichi-do ni futatsu no koto wa dekimasen.

一度に二つの事はできなません。

I can't do two things at once.

• ichi-do mo 一度も *ever, even once* 《in combination with a negative predicate》

¶Ichirō wa ichi-do mo Tōkyō ni itta koto ga nai.

一郎は一度も東京に行ったことがない。

Ichiro has never once been to Tokyo.

ichigo 苺 *strawberry*

ichiichi 一々 ① *one by one, one after another* [→**hitotsu-hitotsu** 一つ一つ (s.v. **hitotsu** 一つ)]

② *all, every single one*

¶Watashi no suru koto ni ichiichi monku o iwanai de.

私のする事にいちいち文句を言わないで。

Don't complain about every single thing I do.

ichiji 一時 ① *once, at one time, before*

¶Watashi-tachi wa ichiji Fukushima ni sunde imashita.

私たちは一時福島に住んでいました。

We once lived in Fukushima.

② *for a while, for a time, temporarily* [→**shibaraku** しばらく]

¶Ichiji kyūkei shimashō.

一時休憩しましょう。

Let's rest for a while.

¶Shiai wa ame de ichiji chūdan saremashita.

試合は雨で一時中断されました。

The game was stopped for a while because of rain.

③ *one o'clock* 《see **-ji** −時 and Appendix 2》

ichijirushíi 著しい *remarkable, notable, striking*

¶Kon-gakki Miyamoto-kun no benkyō no shinpo wa ichijirushii desu.

今学期宮本君の勉強の進歩は著しいです。

This term the progress in Miyamoto's studies is remarkable.

¶Jiko no kazu ga ichijirushiku fuemashita.

事故の数が著しく増えました。

The number of accidents has increased notably.

ichimen 一面 ① *the whole surface; an unbroken expanse*

¶Nohara wa ichimen no yuki deshita.

野原は一面の雪でした。

The fields were an unbroken expanse of snow.

• ichimen ni 一面に *all over (the whole surface)*

¶Sora wa kuroi kumo de ichimen ni ōwarete imasu.

空は黒い雲で一面に覆われています。

The sky is covered all over with black clouds.

② *one facet, one side, one aspect* 《see **-men** −面 and Appendix 2》

¶Jiken no ichimen shika shirimasen.

事件の一面しか知りません。

I know only one aspect of the incident.

ichí-nen 一年 *one year* 《see **-nen** −年 and Appendix 2》

• ichi-nen-jū 一年中 *all year round*

¶Arasuka wa ichi-nen-jū samui desu ka.

アラスカは一年中寒いですか。

Is it cold in Alaska all year round?

ichi-nichí 一日 *one day* 《see **-nichi** −日and Appendix 2》

¶Rōma wa ichi-nichi ni shite narazu.

ローマは1日にして成らず。《proverb》

Rome was not built in a day. 《Literally: Rome does not come into existence in one day.》

• ichi-nichi-jū 一日中 *all day long*

• ichi-nichi-ichi-nichi to 一日一日と *day*

by day; day after day

¶Ichi-nichi-ichi-nichi to haru ga chika-zuite imasu.

一日一日と春が近づいています。

Spring is getting closer everyday.

ichininmae 一人前 ① *a full-fledged adult*

② *a portion of food for one person* 《see **-nin-mae** 人前 and Appendix 2》

ichiō 一応 *provisionally, for the time being*

ichiranhyō 一覧表 *list, listing*

ichírui 一塁 *first base* [→**fāsuto** ファースト①]

• ichirui-shu 一塁手 *first baseman* [→**fāsuto** ファースト②] 《in baseball》

ichiryū 一流 ～**no** ～の *first-class, top-rank*

¶Hayashi-san wa ichiryū no pianisuto desu.

林さんは一流のピアニストです。

Miss Hayashi is a top-rank pianist.

• ichiryū-hoteru 一流ホテル *first-class hotel*

ichō いちょう *ginkgo*

ichō 胃腸 *stomach and intestines, digestive system*

idai 偉大 ～**na** ～な *great, mighty, grand*

¶Pikaso wa idai na geijutsu-ka deshita.

ピカソは偉大な芸術家でした。

Picasso was a great artist.

ideórogī イデオロギー *ideology*

ído 井戸 *a well*

ído 緯度 *latitude* 《on the earth's surface》[⇔**keido** 経度]

¶Tōkyō no ido wa hokui sanjūgo-do yon-jūgo-fun desu.

東京の緯度は北緯35度45分です。

Tokyo's latitude is 35 degrees 45 minutes north latitude.

idō 移動 *movement* 《from one place to another》

• idō suru 移動する *to move* 《transitive or intransitive》

¶Tēburu o migi e idō shite kuremashita.

テーブルを右へ移動してくれました。

They moved the table to the right for me.

īe いいえ *no* 《negative response to a question》[⇔**ē** ええ]

¶"Tanaka-san desu ka." "Iie, chigai-masu."

「田中さんですか」「いいえ、違います」

"Are you Mr. Tanaka?" "No, I'm not."

¶"Sukī wa dekinai no desu ne." "Iie, deki-masu."

「スキーはできないのですね。」「いいえ、できます。」

"You can't ski, can you." "Yes, I can."

《In response to a question that presumes a negative answer, **iie** is used to mean *No, your presumption is incorrect.* A natural English translation will often have *yes* rather than *no.*》

ié 家 ① *house, home* [→**uchi** 家①]

¶Oji wa ōki na ie ni sunde imasu.

伯父は大きな家に住んでいます。

My uncle lives in a large house.

¶Ane no ie wa kōen no chikaku ni arimasu.

姉の家は公園の近くにあります。

My older sister's home is near the park.

¶Watashi-tachi wa shichi-ji ni ie o demasu.

私たちは7時に家を出ます。

We leave home at 7:00.

¶Go-ji ni ie ni tsukimashita.

5時に家に着きました。

I arrived home at 5:00.

¶Roku-ji-mae ni wa ie ni modorimasu.

6時前には家に戻ります。

I will return home before 6:00.

¶Ken-san wa ie ni imasu ka.

健さんは家にいますか。

Is Ken at home?

② *household* [→**katei** 家庭②]; *family* [→**kazoku** 家族]

iedé 家出 *running away from home*

• iede suru 家出する *to run away from home*

¶Jūyon-sai no toki iede shimashita.

14歳の時家出しました。

I ran away from home when I was 14.

• iede-nin 家出人 *a runaway*

ífuku 衣服 *clothing* [→**fuku** 服]

igai 意外 ～**na** ～な *unexpected*
¶Watashi-tachi no geki wa igai na seikō o osamemashita.
私たちの劇は意外な成功を収めました。
Our play had unexpected success.
¶Tsuma no kotoba wa mattaku igai deshita.
妻の言葉はまったく意外でした。
My wife's words were completely unexpected.
¶Kono hon wa igai ni yomiyasui ne.
この本は意外に読みやすいね。
This book is unexpectedly easy to read, isn't it.

-igai －以外 *except, other than* 《Added to noun bases.》
¶Chichi wa Nichiyōbi-igai wa mainichi shigoto ni ikimasu.
父は日曜日以外は毎日仕事に行きます。
My father goes to work every day except Sunday.

ígaku 医学 (*the study of*)*medicine, medical science*
• igaku-bu 医学部 *medical department*
• igaku-hakushi 医学博士 *Doctor of Medicine*

igen 威厳 *dignity*
• igen no aru hito 威厳のある人 *dignified person*

ígo 以後 *from now on* [→**izen** 以前①]
¶Igo ganbarimasu.
以後頑張ります。
I will do my best from now on.

-igo －以後 *after, since* 《Added to noun bases referring to points in time.》
¶Hachi-ji-igo ni denwa shite kudasai.
8時以後に電話してください。
Please phone after 8:00.
¶Watashi mo sore-igo Wada-san ni atte imasen.
私もそれ以後和田さんに会っていません。
I haven't seen Mr. Wada since then either.

ígo 囲碁 [☞**go** 碁]

igokochi 居心地 *feeling about living, feeling about being*

《that a place gives one》
• igokochi ga ii 居心地がいい *comfortable to live in, pleasant to be in*
¶Kono heya wa igokochi ga ii desu ne.
この部屋は居心地がいいですね。
This room is comfortable, isn't it.
• igokochi-yoku 居心地よく *comfortably*

ihan 違反 *violation*
• A ni ihan suru Aに違反する *to violate A*
¶Kōsoku ni ihan shite wa ikenai yo.
校則に違反してはいけないよ。
You mustn't violate the school rules!
• chūsha-ihan 駐車違反 *parking violation*
• kōtsū-ihan 交通違反 *traffic violation*
• senkyo-ihan 選挙違反 *election irregularities*
• supīdo-ihan スピード違反 *speeding violation*

ii いい{Irreg.} ① *good* [⇔**warui** 悪い]
¶Ii shirase ga aru yo.
いい知らせがあるよ。
I have good news!
¶Ii tenki desu ne.
いい天気ですね。
It's good weather, isn't it?
¶Chichi no taichō wa totemo ii desu.
父の体調はとてもいいです。
Father is very fit.
¶Undō wa kenkō ni ii desu.
運動は健康にいいです。
Exercise is good for the health.
¶Kono kamera wa are yori ii desu.
このカメラはあれよりいいです。
This camera is better than that one.
¶Kore wa mottomo ii hon desu.
これは最もいい本です。
This is the best book.
• hō ga ii ほうがいい *you had better, it would be better to*
《following a verb》《If the verb is affirmative, it may be in either the past tense or the nonpast tense.》
¶Sugu itta hō ga ii desu.
すぐ行ったほうがいいです。

You had better go right away.

② *all right, OK, appropriate*

¶Ii to shinjiru koto o yarinasai.

いいと信じることをやりなさい。

Do what you believe is appropriate.

¶Suwatte mo ii desu ka.

座ってもいいですか。

May I sit down? 《A form of **ii** following a clause that ends in a gerund (-**te** form) optionally followed by **mo** is the typical way of expressing permission or approval in Japanese. Translations into English ordinarily use *may* rather than *all right even if* and *do not have to* rather than *all right even if not.*》

¶Sono shigoto wa yaranakute mo ii yo.

その仕事はやらなくてもいいよ。

You don't have to do that work!

¶Eki e iku ni wa kono basu de ii no desu ka.

駅へ行くにはこのバスでいいのですか。

Is this bus all right to go to the station?

iiarawásu 言い表す *to express (in words)*

¶Kansha no kimochi o iiarawasu no wa muzukashii desu.

感謝の気持ちを言い表すのは難しいです。

To express a feeling of gratitude is difficult.

iidásu 言い出す ① *to bring up, to broach* 《a subject》

¶Fujita-kun ga saisho ni iidashita n da yo.

藤田君が最初に言い出したんだよ。

Fujita brought it up first!

② *to propose, to suggest* [→**teian suru** 提案する]

¶Keiko-san wa haikingu ni ikō to iidashimashita.

恵子さんはハイキングに行こうと言い出しました。

Keiko proposed going on a hike.

iiháru 言い張る *to keep saying; to insist* [→**shuchō suru** 主張する]

¶Otōto wa eiga ni iku to iihatta.

弟は映画に行くと言い張った。

My younger brother insisted on going to the movies.

ii-kagen いい加減 ～**na** ～な ① *irresponsible* [→**musekinin na** 無責任な]; *sloppy, haphazard; vague* [→**aimai na** 曖昧な]

¶Ii-kagen na henji o shimashita.

いいかげんな返事をしました。

I made a vague answer.

¶Sono hito wa ii-kagen na shigoto o shimashita.

その人はいいかげんな仕事をしました。

That person did a sloppy job.

② *moderate, appropriate* 《especially when used in an imperative like the following example》

¶Ii-kagen ni shinasai.

いいかげんにしなさい。

Start behaving appropriately.

iikata 言い方 *way of saying, way of speaking*

¶Yōko-san wa tekisetsu na iikata o shiranai ne.

洋子さんは適切な言い方を知らないね。

Yoko doesn't know the proper way of saying it, does she.

íin 委員 *committee member; committee*

¶Iin-tachi wa zen'in shusseki shite imasu.

委員たちは全員出席しています。

The committee members are all present.

• iin-chō 委員長 *committee chairperson*

• iin-kai 委員会 *committee; committee meeting*

iisugi 言い過ぎ *overstatement, exaggeration*

iisugíru 言い過ぎる *to say too much; to exaggerate, to go too far*

iitsukéru 言いつける ① *to tell to do, to order to do*

¶Chichi wa watashi ni kono shigoto o iitsukemashita.

父は私にこの仕事を言いつけました。

My father told me to do this work.

② *to tattle about*

¶Gotō-kun no koto wa sensei ni iitsukenai yo.

後藤君のことは先生に言いつけないよ。

I won't tattle to the teacher about Goto!

iitsutae 言い伝え *tradition, legend* [→ **densetsu** 伝説]

iiwake 言い訳 *excuse, exculpatory explanation*
¶Sore wa iiwake ni naranai yo.
それは言い訳にならないよ。
That is no excuse!
•iiwake o suru 言い訳をする *to make an excuse*
¶Akira-san wa chikoku no iiwake o shimashita.
明さんは遅刻の言い訳をしました。
Akira made an excuse for being late.

ijí 意地 ① *will power, backbone* ② *stubbornness, obstinacy* [→**ijippari** 意地っ張り①]
•iji ni naru 意地になる *to become stubborn*
•iji o haru 意地を張る *to become stubborn*

ijime いじめ *bullying, cruel treatment*
•ijime-kko いじめっ子 *child who bullies others*
•yowai-mono-ijime 弱い者いじめ *bullying weaker people*

ijimeru いじめる *to bully, to pick on, to treat cruelly*
¶Otōto wa tokidoki imōto o ijimemasu.
弟は時々妹をいじめます。
My younger brother sometimes picks on my younger sister.
¶Dōbutsu o ijimete wa ikenai yo.
動物をいじめてはいけないよ。
You mustn't treat animals cruelly.

ijippari 意地っ張り ① *stubbornness, obstinacy* [→**gōjō** 強情]
•ijippari na 意地っ張りな *stubborn* ② *stubborn person*

ijíru いじる{5} *to handle; to play with; to fiddle with, to tamper with*
¶Watashi no tsukue no mono o ijiranai de kudasai.
私の机の物をいじらないでください。
Don't fiddle with the things on my desk.
¶Bōya wa omocha o ijitte imasu.
坊やはおもちゃをいじっています。
The little boy is playing with a toy.

ijiwáru 意地悪 *meanness, spitefulness, ill-naturedness*
•ijiwaru na 意地悪な *mean, spiteful, ill-natured*
¶Hito ni ijiwaru na koto o shinai de.
人に意地悪な事をしないで。
Don't do mean things to people.

ijō 異状 *something wrong*
¶Kono kamera wa doko-ka ijō ga arimasu.
このカメラはどこか異状があります。
There's something wrong with this camera.
¶Enjin ni wa ijō wa arimasen.
エンジンには異状はありません。
There is nothing wrong with the engine.

ijō 異常 〜**na** 〜な *unusual, abnormal* [⇔**seijō na** 正常な]
¶Kono samusa wa aki ni shite wa ijō desu.
この寒さは秋にしては異常です。
This cold is unusual for autumn.

ijō 以上 ① *what precedes, what is above* [⇔**ika** 以下] ② *now that, since*
¶Sotsugyō shita ijō, shūshoku shinakereba naranai.
卒業した以上、就職しなければならない。
Now that I've graduated, I have to get a job.

-ijō －以上 《Added to noun bases, especially numbers. When -ijō is added to a specific number, the combination is understood to include that number as a lower limit. For example, **itsutsu-ijō** 五つ以上 means *five or more*, not *more than five*.》 [[⇔**-ika** －以下]] *more than; or more*
¶Heya ni wa go-nin-ijō no seito ga imasu.
部屋には5人以上の生徒がいます。
There are five or more students in the room.
¶Kore-ijō iu koto wa arimasen.
これ以上言う事はありません。
I have nothing more than this to say.
¶Eigo no seiseki wa heikin-ijō desu.
英語の成績は平均以上です。

英語の成績は平均以上です。
My English grades are above average.

ijū 移住 *migration; emigration; immigration*

•ijū suru 移住する *to migrate; to emigrate; to immigrate*

¶Ani wa kyonen Kanada e ijū shimashita.
兄は去年カナダへ移住しました。
My older brother emigrated to Canada last year.

ika いか *cuttlefish; squid*

íka 以下 *what is below, what follows* [⇔**ijō** 以上①]

¶Dēta wa ika no tōri desu.
データは以下のとおりです。
The data are as follows.

-ika 一以下《Added to noun bases, especially numbers. When **-ika** is added to a specific number, the combination is understood to include that number as an upper limit. For example, **itsutsu-ika** 五つ以下 means *five or fewer*, not *fewer than five*.》[[⇔**-ijō** -以上]] *less than; or less, or fewer*

¶Kono kaban wa gosen-en-ika de kaeru yo.
このかばんは5000円以下で買えるよ。
You can buy this bag for 5,000 yen or less!

¶Go-sai-ika no kodomo wa hairemasen.
5歳以下の子供は入れません。
Children five or under can't enter.

¶Sono seito no seiseki wa heikin-ika desu
その生徒の成績は平均以下です。
That student's grades are below average.

ikada 筏 *raft*

ikága いかが 【FORMAL for **dō** どう】 *how*

¶Nishimoto-san, go-kigen ikaga desu ka.
西本さん、ご機嫌いかがですか。
How are you, Nr. Nishimoto?

¶Ikaga o-sugoshi desu ka.
いかがお過ごしですか。
How are you doing?

¶Kyō wa go-kibun wa ikaga desu ka.
きょうはご気分はいかがですか。

How do you feel today?

¶Kōhī o mō ip-pai ikaga desu ka.
コーヒーをもう1杯いかがですか。
How about another cup of coffee?

ikan 遺憾 *regret*

•ikan na 遺憾な *regrettable*

ikari 錨 *anchor* 《*of a ship, etc.*》

ikarí 怒り *anger*

¶Sono otoko ni taishite ikari o kanjimasu.
その男に対して怒りを感じます。
I feel anger at that man.

¶Ikari ni ware o wasuremashita.
怒りにわれを忘れました。
I forgot myself in anger.

ikásu 生かす *to make good use of, to make the most of* [→**katsuyō suru** 活用する①]

¶O-kane o ikashite tsukau yō ni shinasai.
お金を生かして使うようにしなさい。
Try to make good use of your money.

¶Watashi-tachi wa jikan o ikasanakereba naranai.
私たちは時間を生かさなければならない。
We have to make the most of our time.

iké 池 *pond*

ikébana 生け花 (*traditional Japanese*)*flower arranging*

íken 意見 ① *opinion* [→**kangae** 考え③]

¶Matsumoto-san no iken wa dō desu ka.
松本さんの意見はどうですか。
What is Ms. Matsumoto's opinion?

¶Sono mondai ni tsuite iken o nobemashita.
その問題について意見を述べました。
I expressed my opinion on that subject.

¶Watashi no iken de wa Yano-san ga tadashii desu.
私の意見では矢野さんが正しいです。
In my opinion, Mr. Yano is right.

¶Sono koto ni tsuite buchō to iken ga aimashita.
その事について部長と意見が合いました。
My opinion was the same as the department head on that matter.

② *advice* [→**jogen** 助言]

¶Watashi-tachi wa sensei no iken ni

shitagaimashita.

私たちは先生の意見に従いました。

We followed our teacher's advice.

- shōsū-iken 少数意見 *minority opinion*
- tasū-iken 多数意見 *majority opinion*

ikenai いけない《This word is the regular negative of the potential form of the verb **iku** 行く and has the predictable meanings as well.》

① *bad, unacceptable* 《This meaning is particularly common in combination with a conditional clause of some kind. Translations of such combinations into English ordinarily use *must not* or *may not* rather than *unacceptable if*, and *must* or *have to* rather than *unacceptable if not*.》

¶Uso o tsuku koto wa ikenai yo.

うそをつくことはいけないよ。

You must not tell lies!

¶Kono keikaku no doko ga ikenai no desu ka.

この計画のどこがいけないのですか。

What's unacceptable in this plan?

¶Dōro de kyatchibōru o shite wa ikenai.

道路でキャッチボールをしてはいけない。

You mustn't play catch in the street.

¶Jisho o mite wa ikemasen.

辞書を見てはいけません。

You may not look at a dictionary.

¶Shibafu ni haitte wa ikenai.

芝生に入ってはいけない。

Keep off the grass. 《Literally: *You must not come on the grass.*》

¶Sugu sore o shinakereba ikemasen.

すぐそれをしなければいけません。

You must do that at once.

¶Motto benkyō shinakereba ikenai yo.

もっと勉強しなければいけないよ。

You have to study harder!

② *unfortunate, too bad*

¶"Haha wa byōki de nete imasu." "Sore wa ikemasen."

「母は病気で寝ています」「それはいけません」

"My mother is sick in bed." "That's too bad."

íki 息 *breath*

¶Odoroite iki o nomimashita.

驚いて息をのみました。

I caught my breath in surprise.

¶Sono onna no ko wa totemo hayaku hashitta node, iki o kirashite imasu.

その女の子はとても速く走ったので、息を切らしています。

That girl ran very fast, so she is out of breath.

- iki o suru 息をする *to breathe*
- iki o suu 〔haku〕息を吸う〔吐く〕 *to breathe in 〔out〕*

¶Fukaku iki o suinasai.

深く息を吸いなさい。

Breathe in deeply.

- iki o tsumeru 息を詰める *to hold one's breath*

iki 行き *going, outbound trip* 〔⇔**kaeri** 帰り〕

¶Iki wa densha de, kaeri wa takushī desu.

行きは電車で、帰りはタクシーです。

We will go by train, and return by taxi.

-iki －行き〔☞**-yuki** 行き〕

ikigai 生き甲斐 *reason for living, what one lives for*

ikiíki 生き生き ～**to** ～と *animatedly, in a lively manner; vividly*

¶Akio-san wa sono shiai no yōsu o ikiiki to setsumei shimashita.

明夫さんはその試合の様子を生き生きと説明しました。

Akio vividly described the game.

- ikiiki-to-suru 生き生きとする *to become lively; to become vivid*

¶Kyōko-chan wa ikiiki to shita onna no ko desu.

京子ちゃんは生き生きとした女の子です。

Kyoko is a lively girl.

ikikaeru 生き返る{5} *to come back to life; to revive, to return to consciousness*

¶Kingyo wa mizu ni iretara ikikaetta yo.

金魚は水に入れたら生き返ったよ。

The goldfish revived when I put it in water!

ikímono 生き物 ① *living thing* 〔→**seibutsu** 生物〕

② *animal, creature* [→**dōbutsu** 動物]

ikinari いきなり *suddenly; abruptly* [→ **totsuzen** 突然]

ikinokóru 生き残る *to survive*

¶Sono jiko de ikinokotta hito ga sū-nin imashita.

その事故で生き残った人が数人いました。

There were several people who survived the accident.

ikiói 勢い ① *force, power*

¶Taifū no ikioi ga otoroemashita.

台風の勢いが衰えました。

The force of the typhoon weakened.

② *vigor, spirit*

ikíru 生きる *to live, to stay alive*

¶Ningen wa mizu ga nai to ikiraremasen.

人間は水がないと生きられません。

A human being cannot live if there is no water.

¶Sobo wa hachijus-sai made ikimashita.

祖母は80歳まで生きました。

My grandmother lived to 80.

• ikite iru 生きている *to be alive*

¶Kono ise-ebi wa mada ikite iru yo.

この伊勢海老はまだ生きているよ。

This lobster is still alive!

ikisaki 行き先 [☞**yukisaki** 行き先]

ikisatsu いきさつ *circumstances, details, particulars*

íkka 一家 (*one entire*)*family*, (*one entire*)*household*

¶Haha ga ikka o sasaete imasu.

母が一家を支えています。

Mother supports the family.

• -ikka ――家 *and the entire family*

《Added to bases that refer to persons.》

¶Doi-san-ikka wa Fukuoka e hikko-shimashita.

土井さん一家は福岡へ引っ越しました。

The Doi family moved to Fukuoka.

ikkén'ya 一軒家 *single-family house*

íkki 一気 ～**ni** ～に *without pause*

• ikki ni nomu 一気に飲む *to drink in one gulp*

ikkō 一行 *party* 《i.e., a group of people》

¶Ikkō wa jūni-mei desu.

一行は12名です。

The party is twelve people.

ikṓru イコール *equals* 《Used in giving arithmetic problems or mathematical equations.》

¶San purasu ni ikōru go.

$3 + 2 = 5$

Three plus two equals five.

iku 行く{Irreg.} *to go* [⇔**kuru** 来る①]

¶Kono basu wa eki e ikimasu ka.

このバスは駅へ行きますか。

Does this bus go to the station?

¶Kondo no fuyu-yasumi ni sukī ni iku tsumori desu.

今度の冬休みにスキーに行くつもりです。

During this coming winter vacation I plan to go skiing.

¶Chikatetsu de ikimashō yo.

地下鉄で行きましょうよ。

Let's go by subway!

¶Jēn-san wa Kanada ni ikimashita.

ジェーンさんはカナダに行きました。

Jane went to Canada.

¶Kyōto ni wa ni-do itta koto ga arimasu.

京都には2度行ったことがあります。

I have gone to Kyoto twice.

¶"Ken-chan, doko ni iru no?" "Ima iku yo."

「健ちゃん、どこにいるの？」「今行くよ」

"Where are you, Ken?" "I'm coming."

《In general, Japanese requires **iku** rather than **kuru** 来る for movement away from the speaker's current location.》

• asobi ni iku 遊びに行く *to go and visit, to go for a visit*

¶Kondo no Nichiyōbi ni asobi ni iku yo.

今度の日曜日に遊びに行くよ。

I'll go and visit next Sunday.

• umaku iku うまく行く *to go well*

¶Subete umaku itte imasu.

すべてうまく行っています。

Everything is going well.

¶Itte kimasu.

行ってきます。

I'll be back. 《Literally: *I'll go and come (back).*》《This is the standard expression for announcing one's departure and temporary absence from home or a home base of some kind. Typical occasions of calling for its use are leaving the house in the morning, leaving on a trip, and leaving the office on an errand.»

¶Itte irasshai.

行っていらっしゃい。

See you later. «Literally: *Go and come (back).*» «This is the standard expression for acknowledging another's departure and temporary absence from home or a home base of some kind.»

íkura いくら *how much*

¶Kono tokei wa ikura desu ka.

この時計はいくらですか。

How much is this watch?

¶O-kane wa ikura motte imasu ka.

お金はいくら持っていますか

How much money do you have?

• ikura demo いくらでも *any amount, as much as you like, a lot*

¶Ikura demo tabete ii desu yo.

いくらでも食べていいですよ。

You may eat as much as you like!

• ikura-ka いくらか *some, a little*

¶"Gyūnyū wa arimasu ka." "Ē, ikura-ka arimasu."

「牛乳はありますか」「ええ、いくらかあります」

"Do you have any milk?" "Yes, I have some."

¶Oji wa Supein-go ga ikura-ka hanasemasu.

叔父はスペイン語がいくらか話せます。

My uncle can speak a little Spanish.

íkutsu 幾つ ① *how many* «for things that are counted using **hitotsu** 一つ, **futatsu** 二つ, etc.; see Appendix 2»

¶Tēburu no ue ni momo ga ikutsu arimasu ka.

テーブルの上に桃がいくつありますか。

How many peaches are there on the table?

② *how old* «because ages can be counted using **hitotsu** 一つ, **futatsu** 二つ, etc.; see Appendix 2»

¶Imōto-san wa ikutsu desu ka.

妹さんはいくつですか。

How old is your younger sister?

• ikutsu demo いくつでも *any number, as many as you like*

¶Ikutsu demo totte ii yo.

いくつでも取っていいよ。

You may take as many as you want!

• ikutsu-ka 幾つか *some, several*

¶Shiken de ikutsu-ka no machigai o shimashita.

試験でいくつかのまちがいをしました。

I made some mistakes on the examination.

¶Kono tango wa ikutsu-ka no imi ga arimasu.

この単語はいくつかの意味があります。

This word has several meanings.

• ikutsu-mo 幾つも *many*

íma 今 *now; just now* «in combination with a past-tense verb»

¶Ima totemo isogashii desu.

今とても忙しいです。

I am very busy now.

¶Ima no wakai hito wa aruku koto o konomimasen.

今の若い人は歩くことを好みません。

Today's young people don't like to walk.

¶Densha wa ima demashita.

電車は今出ました。

The train left just now.

¶Ima made nani o shite imashita ka.

今まで何をしていましたか。

What have you been doing until now?

• ima-goro 今ごろ *about now, about this time*

¶Rainen no ima-goro wa Kyūshū ni iru deshō.

来年の今ごろは九州にいるでしょう。

I will be in Kyushu about this time next year.

¶Kazuko wa ima-goro wa mō uchi ni iru deshō.

和子は今ごろはもううちにいるでしょう。

Kazuko is probably already at home about now.

imá 居間 *living room,* <UK>*sitting room*

imada-ni 未だに *still,* 〈*not*〉 *yet* [→ **mada** まだ①]

¶Imada-ni Michio-san wa sugata o misemasen.

いまだに道夫さんは姿を見せません。

Michio has not shown up yet.

íma-ni 今に *soon, before long, by and by* [→**ma-mo-naku** 間も無く, **yagate** やがて]

¶O-isha-san wa ima-ni koko e kimasu yo.

お医者さんは今にここへ来ますよ。

The doctor will come here soon!

¶Ima-ni wakaru to omoimasu.

今にわかると思います。

I think you'll understand by and by.

• ima-ni mo 今にも *at any moment*

¶Ima-ni mo ame ga furi-sō desu.

今にも雨が降りそうです。

It looks as if it's going to rain at any moment.

¶Ano ko wa ima-ni mo nakidashi-sō desu.

あの子は今にも泣き出しそうです。

That child looks as if she's going to start crying at any moment.

imasara 今更 *at this (belated)point, now (when it's too late)*

¶Imasara kōkai shite mo osoi yo.

いまさら後悔しても遅いよ。

At this point it's too late to be sorry about it!

iméji イメージ ① *image, conception, mental picture*

② *image, impression on people*

¶Shiro wa seiketsu na imēji o rensō saseru iro da.

白は清潔なイメージを連想させる色だ。

White is a color with a clean image.

• imēji-appu イメージアップ *improvement in image*

• imēji-daun イメージダウン *deterioration in image*

ími 意味 *meaning, sense*

¶Kono tango wa dō iu imi desu ka.

この単語はどういう意味ですか。

What is the meaning of this word?

¶Aru imi de wa sore wa jijitsu desu.

ある意味ではそれは事実です。

In a sense that's true.

¶Haha wa imi no nai koto bakari itte imasu.

母は意味のないことばかり言っています。

My mother is saying nothing but meaningless things.

• imi suru 意味する *to mean, to signify*

¶Sono māku wa kiken o imi shimasu.

そのマークは危険を意味します。

That mark means danger.

imin 移民 *immigrant; emigrant*

• imin suru 移民する *to immigrate; to emigrate*

imitēshon イミテーション *an imitation* ((object))

imó 芋 *potato* [→**jagaimo** じゃがいも]; *sweet potato*

[→**satsumaimo** 薩摩芋]; *taro* [→**satoimo** 里芋]

ímori 井守 *newt*

imótó 妹 *younger sister* [⇔**ane** 姉; **otōto** 弟]

• sue no imōto 末の妹 *youngest sister*

• imōto-san 妹さん 【HON. for **imōto** 妹 (above)】

inabíkari 稲光 *lightning* [→**inazuma** 稲妻]

inago いなご *locust*

-inai 一以内 *within, or less* 《Added to bases denoting quantities.》[→ **-ika** 一以下]

¶Morimoto-san wa is-shūkan-inai ni kaette kimasu.

森本さんは1週間以内に帰ってきます。

Mr. Morimoto will come back within a week.

¶Eki wa kuruma de go-fun-inai no tokoro ni arimasu.

駅は車で5分以内の所にあります。

The station is in a place that's five minutes or less by car.

inaka 田舎 ① *the country, rural area*

② *hometown, birthplace* [→**kyōri** 郷里]

• inaka-mono 田舎者 *country bumpkin*

- inaka-ryōri 田舎料理 *country cooking*

inazuma 稲妻 *lightning* [→**inabikari** 稲光]

- inazuma ga hikaru 稲妻が光る *lightning flashes*

ínchi インチ *inch*

- -inchi －インチ《*counter for inches; see Appendix 2*》

Índian インディアン *Native American, Indian* [→**Amerika-Indian** アメリカインディアン (s.v. **Amerika** アメリカ)]

íne 稲 *rice plant*

- ine-kari 稲刈り *rice reaping*

inemúri 居眠り *dozing off, inadvertenly falling asleep*

- inemuri suru 居眠りする *to doze off*
- inemuri-unten 居眠り運転 *dozing off while driving*

infoméshon インフォメーション *information* [→**jōhō** 情報]

infure インフレ（*monetary*）*inflation* [⇔**defure** デフレ]

¶Infure de bukka ga agatte imasu.
インフレで物価が上がっています。
Prices are going up because of inflation.

infuréshon インフレーション [☞**infure** インフレ]

infuruénza インフルエンザ *influenza*

¶Sensei wa infuruenza ni kakatta sōda.
先生はインフルエンザにかかったそうだ。
I hear the teacher caught influenza.

ínga 因果 *cause and effect*

- inga-kankei 因果関係 *causal relation*

íningu イニング *inning* [→**kai** 回①]《*in baseball*》

inishiáchibu イニシアチブ *the initiative, leadership role*

- inishiachibu o toru イニシアチブを取る *to take the initiative*

¶Sano-san wa keikaku no inishiachibu o totta.
佐野さんは企画のイニシアチブを取った。
Ms. Sano took the planning initiative.

iníshiaru イニシアル *initial* (*letter*) [→**kashira-moji** 頭文字①]

inkan 印鑑 *signature seal* 《Documents are ordinarily stamped with a seal rather than signed in Japan.》 [→**han** 判]

inken 陰険 ～**na** ～な *cunning, crafty, sly*

¶Ano yakuza wa inken desu.
あのやくざは陰険です。
That gangster is sly.

inki 陰気 ～**na** ～な *gloomy, dreary, melancholy* [⇔**yōki na** 陽気な①]

¶Sono onna no hito wa inki na kao o shite imashita.
その女の人は陰気な顔をしていました。
That woman had a gloomy face.

ínku インク *ink*

- inku-keshi インク消し *ink eraser*

ínochi 命 *life, animate existence* [→**seimei** 生命]

¶Gorō-san wa sono onna no ko no inochi o sukutta yo.
五郎さんはその女の子の命を救ったよ。
Goro saved that girl's life!

- inochi-biroi 命拾い *narrow escape from death*
- inochi-zuna 命綱 *lifeline*

inorí 祈り *prayer*

- inori o sasageru 祈りを捧げる *to offer a prayer*
- inori o suru 祈りをする *to say a prayer, to say one's prayers*

¶Haha wa shokuji no mae ni o-inori o shimasu.
母は食事の前にお祈りをします。
My mother says a prayer before meals.

inóru 祈る ① *to pray; to pray for*

¶Mura-bito wa kami ni inorimashita.
村人は神に祈りました。
The villagers prayed to the god.

② *to wish for, to hope for* 《*for someone else's sake*》

¶Go-seikō o inorimasu.
ご成功を祈ります。
I wish you success.

¶Kōun o inoru yo.
幸運を祈るよ。
I wish you good luck!

inoshíshi 猪 *wild boar*

inpútto インプット（*computer*）*input* [→

nyūryoku 入力 [⇔**autoputto** アウトプット]

inryō 飲料 *beverage, drink*
- inryō-sui 飲料水 *drinking water*

ínryoku 引力 ① *gravitational attraction, gravitation*
- inryoku no hōsoku 引力の法則 *the law of gravitation*
  ② *magnetic attraction*

insatsu 印刷 *printing* «of books, newspapers, etc.»
- insatsu suru 印刷する *to print*
- insatsu-butsu 印刷物 *printed matter*
- insatsu-ki 印刷機 *printing press*
- insatsu-sho 印刷所 *printing office, print shop*
- karā-insatsu カラー印刷 *color printing*

inshi 印紙 *revenue stamp*

inshō 印象 *impression* «on a person»
¶Kyōto no inshō wa ikaga desu ka.
京都の印象はいかがですか。
What is your impression of Kyoto?
- inshō o ataeru 印象を与える *to make an impression*
- inshō o ukeru 印象を受ける *to get an impression*
- inshō-teki na 印象的な *impressive*
¶Sono myūjikaru wa totemo inshō-teki deshita.
そのミュージカルはとても印象的でした。
That musical was very impressive.

insupirēshon インスピレーション *inspiration, sudden idea*
¶Totsuzen insupirēshon ga wakimashita.
突然インスピレーションがわきました。
Suddenly an inspiration came to me.

insutanto- インスタント- *instant*
«Added to bases denoting things to eat or drink.»
- insutanto-kōhī インスタントコーヒー *instant coffee*
- insutanto-rāmen インスタントラーメン *instant noodles*

íntabyū インタビュー *interview* «by a reporter»
- intabyū suru インタビューする *to do an interview*

¶Ano kisha wa daitōryō ni intabyū shita.
あの記者は大統領にインタビューした。
That reporter did an interview with the president.

intāchénji インターチェンジ *(highway) interchange*

intáhon インターホン *intercom*

intai 引退 *going into retirement*
- intai suru 引退する *to retire, to go into retirement*
¶Oji wa rokujus-sai de intai shimashita.
叔父は60歳で引退しました。
My uncle retired at 60.

interi インテリ *an intellectual; the intelligentsia*

interiadezáin インテリアデザイン *interior design*

interiadezáinā インテリアデザイナー *interior designer*

intonḗshon イントネーション *intonation*

inú 犬 *dog*
¶Sono inu wa wanwan to hoemashita.
その犬はわんわんとほえました。
That dog barked bow-wow.
- inu-goya 犬小屋 *doghouse*
- inu-kaki 犬搔き *dog-paddling*
- ko-inu 子犬 *puppy*

in'yō 引用 *quotation, citation*
- in'yō suru 引用する *to quote, to cite*
¶"Toki wa kane nari" wa Furankurin no kotoba kara in'yō sarete imasu.
「時は金なり」はフランクリンの言葉から引用されています。
"Time is money" is quoted from the words of Franklin.
- in'yō-bun 引用文 *quoted passage*
- in'yō-fu 引用符 *quotation marks*

iō 硫黄 *sulfur*

íon イオン *ion*

íp-pai 一杯 ① *one cupful, one glassful, one bowlful, one spoonful* «see -**hai** -杯 and Appendix 2»
  ② 【COL.】 *drinking a little* «alcohol»
- ip-pai-kigen 一杯機嫌 *good feeling from being a little drunk*

ippai 一杯 ① *fully, to full capacity*

¶Kago ni wa ringo ga ippai haitte imasu.
かごにはりんごがいっぱい入っています。
The basket is full of apples. 《Literally:
In the basket there are apples to full capacity.》

• ippai no いっぱいの *full, filled*
¶Aiko-chan no me wa namida de ippai
desu.
愛子ちゃんの目は涙でいっぱいです。
Aiko's eyes are filled with tears.
¶Mō onaka ga ippai desu.
もうおなかがいっぱいです。
My stomach is already full.

② *many, much, lots* [→**takusan**
たくさん]
¶Heya ni wa omocha ga ippai arimasu.
部屋にはおもちゃがいっぱいあります。
There are lots of toys in that room.

–**ippai** －いっぱい *entire, whole* 《Most
commonly added to bases denoting particular time periods.》
¶Konshū-ippai wa koko ni imasu.
今週いっぱいはここにいます。
I'll be here the whole week.

ippan 一般 〜**no** 〜の ① *general, uni-
versal*

② *common, ordinary*
• ippan-gensoku 一般原則 *general principle*
• ippan-jin 一般人 *ordinary person;
commoner*
• ippan-teki na 一般的な [☞**ippan no**
一般の (above)]

íp–po 1歩 *one step* 《see –**ho** －歩 and
Appendix 2》
• ip-po-ip-po 一歩一歩 *step by step*

ippō 一方 ① [[→**katahō** 片方]] *one
side (of two); one (of two), one (of a
pair)*
¶Kyō hon o ni-satsu kaimashita. Ippō
wa shōsetsu de, mō ippō wa jisho desu.
きょう本を2冊買いました。一方は小説で、
もう一方は辞書です。
*I bought two books today. One is a
novel, and the other is a dictionary.*

② (〜**de wa** 〜では) *on the one hand;
on the other hand*

¶Niku no suki na hito mo imasu ga, ippō
sakana no suki na hito mo imasu.
肉の好きな人もいますが、一方魚の好きな
人もいます。
*There are people who like meat, but on
the other hand there are people who like
fish.*

③ *to keep on, to do nothing but* 《in
combination with a preceding verb in the
nonpast tense》
¶Bukka wa agaru ippō desu.
物価は上がる一方です。
Prices keep going up.

• ippō-teki na 一方的な *one-sided*
¶Shachō no iken wa ippō-teki desu.
社長の意見は一方的です。
*The company president's opinion is
one-sided.*

• ippō-tsūkō 一方通行 *one-way traffic*
¶Kono tōri wa ippō-tsūkō desu.
この通りは一方通行です。
This street is one-way.

irai 依頼 *request, favor (to ask)* [→
tanomi 頼み①]
¶Katō-san wa kaisha no irai ni ōjite
sanka shita.
加藤さんは会社の依頼に応じて参加した。
*Ms. Kato participated at the company's
request.*

• irai suru 依頼する [[→**tanomu** 頼む]]
*to request, to ask for; to importune to
handle*

–**irai** －以来 *since* 《Added to bases
denoting past events or past times.》
¶Watashi wa sen-kyūhyaku-nanajū-
hachi-nen-irai koko ni sunde imasu.
私は1978年以来ここに住んでいます。
I have lived here since 1978.
¶Sotsugyō-irai jū-nen ni narimasu.
卒業以来10年になります。
It's ten years since graduation.

íraira いらいら 〜**suru** 〜する *to become
irritated, to get impatient*
¶Sono sōon ni iraira shite imashita.
その騒音にいらいらしていました。
I was irritated by the noise.

irassháru いらっしゃる {Irreg.}

① 【HON. for **iru** 居る】
② 【HON. for **iku** 行く】 *to go*
③ 【HON. for **kuru** 来る①】
to come
¶Irasshai.
いらっしゃい。
Welcome! 《Literally: *Come.*》《the imperative form of **irassharu**》
¶Irasshaimase.
いらっしゃいませ。
Welcome! 《Literally: *Come.*》《This is a more formal imperative form of **irassharu**. In Japanese stores, restaurants, etc., it is the standard expression used by employees to greet customers.》

irasuto イラスト *illustration* 《in a book, newspaper, etc.》[→**sashie** 挿絵]
¶Kono hon ni wa irasuto ga takusan arimasu.
この本にはイラストがたくさんあります。
There are a lot of illustrations in this book.

irasutorētā イラストレーター *illustrator*

ireba 入れ歯 *false tooth*

iregyurābáundo イレギュラーバウンド *strange bounce, bad hop* 《in baseball, tennis, etc.》

irekaéru 入れ替える *to replace* 《one thing with another》
•A o B to irekaeru AをBと入れ替える *to replace A with B, to substitute B for A*
¶Furui kikai o atarashii no to irekaemashō.
古い機械を新しいのと入れ替えましょう。
Let's replace the old machines with new ones.
¶Enjin no oiru o irekaemashita.
エンジンのオイルを入れ替えました。
I replaced the engine oil.

iremono 入れ物 *container, box, case*

ireru 入れる ① *to put into, to insert*
¶Kabin ni mizu o irenasai.
花瓶に水を入れなさい。
Put water into the vase.
¶Kōhī ni kurīmu o iremasu ka.
コーヒーにクリームを入れますか。
Do you put cream in your coffee?

② *to let in*
¶Inu o irete kudasai.
犬を入れてください。
Please let the dog in.
¶Mado o akete, kirei na kūki o iremashita.
窓を開けて、きれいな空気を入れました。
I opened the window and let in some clean air.
¶Tenisu-bu ni irete kudasai.
テニス部に入れてください。
Please let me into the tennis club.
　③ *to make* 《tea or coffee》
¶O-kyaku-san ni o-cha o iremashita.
お客さんにお茶を入れました。
I made tea for the guest.

irezumi 入れ墨 *tattoo*

iriguchi 入り口 *entrance*, (*entry*)*doorway* [⇔**deguchi** 出口]
¶Shōmen no iriguchi kara haitte kudasai.
正面の入り口から入ってください。
Please come in through the front entrance.
¶Iriguchi ni onna no ko ga tatte imasu.
入り口に女の子が立っています。
There is a girl standing at the door.

iró 色 *color*
¶Uwagi no iro wa hade desu ne.
上着の色は派手ですね。
The color of the coat is loud, isn't it?
¶Ko-no-ha wa aki ni iro ga kawarimasu.
木の葉は秋に色が変わります。
The color of leaves changes in autumn.
•akarui〔kurai〕iro 明るい〔暗い〕色 *bright* 〔*dark*〕 *color*
•usui〔koi〕iro 薄い〔濃い〕色 *pale* 〔*deep*〕 *color*
•iro-enpitsu 色鉛筆 *colored pencil*

iróha いろは ① *the Japanese kana syllabary* [→**gojūon** 五十音]《This name refers to the first three letters in a traditional arrangement of the the kana syllabary based on a poem in which each letter occurs once.》
　② *rudiments, ABC's* [→**shoho** 初歩]

iroiro 色々 (〜**to**/**ni** 〜と/に) *variously, in various ways,* *in great variety*

¶Iroiro hanashi-tai koto ga arimasu.

いろいろ話したい事があります。

There is a great variety of things I want to talk about.

¶Iroiro arigatō gozaimashita.

いろいろありがとうございました。

Thank you for everything. 《*Literally: Thank you in various ways.*》

• iroiro na いろいろな *various* [→**shuju no** 種々の]

¶Iroiro na riyū de sono kaigō ni denakatta.

いろいろな理由でその会合に出なかった。

For various reasons I was absent from the meeting.

iron-na いろんな 【COL. for **iroiro na** 色々な】

iru 居る ① 《*The subject ordinarily must be animate.*》 *there is / are; to be (located); to exist* [→**sonzai suru** 存在する]

¶Genkan ni dare-ka imasu.

玄関にだれかいます。

There is somebody in the entryway.

¶Kono gakkō ni wa seito ga nan-nin imasu ka.

この学校には生徒が何人いますか。

How many students are there in this school?

¶Ashita wa uchi ni imasen.

あしたはうちにいません。

I will not be home tomorrow.

¶Watashi wa shibaraku oba no tokoro ni imasu.

私はしばらく伯母の所にいます。

I'm going to be at my aunt's place for a while.

② *to have* 《a person in some relationship to oneself》 《A person that someone has in this sense is treated as a grammatical subject and marked with **ga** が rather than with **o** を.》

¶Watashi ni wa kyōdai ga futari imasu.

私には兄弟が二人います。

I have two siblings.

③ *to be ⟨doing⟩* 《in combination with

the gerund (**-te** form)of another verb》 《When **iru** is used as an auxiliary following a gerund, there is no requirement that the subject of the clause be animate.》

¶Hideo-san to Akemi-san wa hanashiatte imasu.

英男さんと明美さんは話し合っています。

Hideo and Akemi are talking to each other.

④ *to have ⟨done⟩* 《in combination with the gerund (**-te** form)of another verb》 《When **iru** is used as an auxiliary following a gerund, there is no requirement that the subject of the clause be animate.》

¶Erebētā ga kowarete iru yo.

エレベーターが壊れているよ。

The elevator has broken!

¶Hikōki wa mada ugoite imasen.

飛行機はまだ動いていません。

The plane hasn't moved yet.

iru 要る｛5｝《What is needed is treated as a grammatical subject and marked with **ga** が rather than with **o** を.》 *to need; to be necessary*

¶O-kane ga iru yo.

お金が要るよ。

I need money!

¶Ima nani ga irimasu ka.

今何が要りますか。

What do you need now?

¶Kono konma wa irimasen.

このコンマは要りません。

This comma is not necessary.

iruka いるか *dolphin; porpoise*

iryoku 威力 *power, force*

¶Chanpion no panchi wa iryoku ga aru yo.

チャンピオンのパンチは威力があるよ。

The champion's punch has power!

isamashíi 勇ましい *brave*

isan 遺産 *inheritance, estate, legacy*

¶Gosenman-en no isan o sōzoku shimashita.

5000万円の遺産を相続しました。

I received an inheritance of 50 million yen.

isei 威勢 [[→**ikioi** 勢い]] ① *vigor, spirit*

　② *force, power*

• isei-yoku 威勢よく *in high spirits*

isei 異性 *the opposite sex*

íseki 遺跡 *ruins, remains, relics*

isha 医者 *doctor, physician*

¶Isha o yobimashō ka.

医者を呼びましょうか。

Shall I summon a doctor?

¶Isha ni mite moratta hō ga ii desu yo.

医者に見てもらったほうがいいですよ。

You'd better have a doctor look at it!

• kakaritsuke no isha 掛かりつけの医者 *the doctor one usually sees*

• ha-isha 歯医者 *dentist*

• me-isha 目医者 *eye doctor*

ishí 石 *stone, rock*

¶Kono mon wa ishi de dekite imasu.

この門は石でできています。

This gate is made of stone.

¶Ishi o nagenai de ne.

石を投げないでね。

Don't throw stones, OK?

• ishi-dan 石段 *stone steps*

• ishi-datami 石畳 *stone pavement*

íshi 意志 *will, volition*

¶Haraguchi-san wa ishi ga tsuyoi desu.

原口さんは意志が強いです。

Mr. Haraguchi's will is strong.

¶Jibun no ishi de kōchō-sensei ni ai ni itta.

自分の意志で校長先生に会いに行った。

I went to see the principal of my own volition.

íshiki 意識 *consciousness, one's senses; awareness*

¶Sono chīsai onna no ko wa ishiki o ushinaimashita.

その小さい女の子は意識を失いました。

That little girl lost consciousness.

• ishiki shite 意識して *consciously; intentionally* [→**waza-to** わざと]

• ishiki suru 意識する *to become conscious of, to become aware of*

• ishiki-teki na 意識的な *conscious; intentional*

¶Yumiko-san ni ishiki-teki ni tsumetaku shimashita.

由美子さんに意識的に冷たくしました。

I intentionally treated Yumiko coldly.

ísho 遺書 *note left behind by a dead person; will* [→**yuigon-jō** 遺言状 (s.v. **yuigon** 遺言)]

íshō 衣装 ① *clothes, clothing* [→**ifuku** 衣服]

¶Mago ni mo ishō.

馬子にも衣装。《proverb》

Clothes make the man. 《Literally: *Even for a horse driver, clothes.*》

　② *costume* 《for a play, etc.》

• hanayome-ishō 花嫁衣装 *wedding dress*

• minzoku-ishō 民族衣装 *national costume*

iso 磯 *rocky beach, rocky shore*

isogashíi 忙しい *busy* [⇔**hima na** 暇な]

¶Kyō wa isogashii desu ga, ashita wa hima desu.

きょうは忙しいですが、あしたは暇です。

Today I'm busy, but tomorrow I'll be free.

¶Kinō no yoru wa shukudai de isogashikatta desu.

きのうの夜は宿題で忙しかったです。

I was busy with my homework last night.

¶Chichi wa itsu-mo isogashiku hataraite imasu.

父はいつも忙しく働いています。

My father is always working busily.

isógu 急ぐ *to hurry*

¶Isoganai to densha ni okuremasu yo.

急がないと電車に遅れますよ。

If you don't hurry, you'll be late for the train!

• isoide 急いで *in a hurry, hurriedly* 《This form is the gerund (-te form) of **isogu**, and it has the predictable range of meanings as well.》

¶Kodomo-tachi wa isoide gakkō ni ikimashita.

子供たちは急いで学校に行きました。

The children went hurriedly to school.

¶Isoide ie o demashita.

急いで家を出ました。

I left the house in a hurry.

íssai 一切 ① *everything* [→**zenbu** 全部]

• issai no 一切の *whole, entire, every*

② *completely*

issei 一斉 〜**ni** 〜に *everyone at the same time, all together*

¶Mura no hito-tachi wa issei ni tachi-agarimashita.

村の人たちは一斉に立ち上がりました。

The people of the village all stood up together.

¶Roku-nin no sōsha ga issei ni sutāto shimashita.

6人の走者が一斉にスタートしました。

Six runners started off all together.

¶Seito wa minna issei ni "Ohayō goza-imasu" to iimashita.

生徒はみんな一斉に「おはようございます」と言いました。

The pupils said all together, "Good morning."

issho 一緒 〜**no** 〜の ① *accompanying* 《as an adjective》

• issho ni いっしょに *together* [→**tomo-ni** 共に]

¶Issho ni sanpo ni ikimasu ka.

いっしょに散歩に行きますか。

Are you going to go for a walk together?

¶Minna issho ni yarinasai.

みんないっしょにやりなさい。

Everyone do it together.

¶Watashi wa Hiroshi-san to issho ni ten-isu o shita.

私は浩さんといっしょにテニスをした。

I played tennis with Hiroshi.

¶Minna haikingu ni ikimasu ga, issho ni ikimasen ka.

みんなハイキングに行きますが、いっしょに行きませんか。

We're all going hiking; won't you go with us?

• issho ni naru いっしょになる *to join together, to unite* 《intransitive》

② *simultaneous* [→**dōji no** 同時の]

• issho ni いっしょに *simultaneously,*

at once

③ *same* [→**onaji** 同じ]

¶Boku-tachi wa kurasu ga issho desu.

僕たちはクラスがいっしょです。

We're in the same class. 《Literally: Our class is the same.》

isshō 一生 [[→**shōgai** 生涯]] ① *throughout one's lifetime, all one's life*

¶Sobo wa isshō Aomori de kurashima-shita.

祖母は一生青森で暮らしました。

My grandmother lived in Aomori all her life.

② *lifetime, one's whole life*

¶Chichi wa kōfuku na isshō o okurima-shita.

父は幸福な一生を送りました。

My father lived a happy life.

¶Sono yō na jiken wa isshō no uchi ni wa ni-do to okoranai deshō.

そのような事件は一生のうちには二度と起こらないでしょう。

That kind of event will probably not happen twice in a lifetime.

isshōkénmei 一生懸命 (〜**ni** 〜に) *as hard as one can, with all one's might*

¶Michiko-san wa isshōkenmei benkyō shite imasu.

美知子さんは一生懸命勉強しています。

Michiko is studying as hard as she can.

¶Isshōkenmei ni hashirinasai.

一生懸命に走りなさい。

Run as fast as you can.

ísshu 一種 *one kind, one sort*

¶Sore wa orenji no isshu desu.

それはオレンジの一種です。

That's a kind of orange.

¶Kore wa, mā, isshu no kaban desu.

これは、まあ、一種のかばんです。

This is, well, a kind of bag.

is-shū 一周 *one trip around, one lap* 《see **-shū** 周 and Appendix 2》

¶Kono kōen wa ish-shū go-kiro-gurai arimasu.

この公園は1周5キロぐらいあります。

This park is about five kilometers once around.

- is-shū suru 一周する *to make one trip around*

¶Ike no mawari o is-shū shimashita.

池の周りを1周しました。

I made one trip around the pond.

- sekai-is-shū-ryokō 世界一周旅行 *a trip around the world*

isshun 一瞬 *a moment, an instant*

¶Isshun tachidomarimashita.

一瞬立ち止まりました。

I stood still for a moment.

issō 一層 *even more, all the more*

¶Issō doryoku shinakereba narimasen.

いっそう努力しなければなりません。

You must strive even more.

isu 椅子 *chair; stool*

¶Dōzo isu ni koshikakete kudasai.

どうぞいすに腰掛けてください。

Please sit down on the chair.

¶Sensei wa isu kara tachiagarimashita.

先生はいすから立ち上がりました。

The teacher rose from the chair.

íta 板 *board; plate* «i.e., a thin, flat sheet of metal, etc.»

- yuka-ita 床板 *floor board*

itabásami 板ばさみ *dilemma*

- itabasami ni natte iru 板ばさみになっている *to be in a dilemma*

itachi いたち *weasel*

itadaku 頂く ① 【HUM. for **morau** 貰う①】 *to receive, to get*

¶Yamamoto-san kara kono tokei o itadakimashita.

山本さんからこの時計をいただきました。

I got this watch from Mr. Yamamoto.

¶Kono hon o itadaite mo yoroshii desu ka.

この本をいただいてもよろしいですか。

May I have this book?

② 【HUM. for **morau** 貰う②】 *to receive the favor of* «following the gerund (-te form)of another verb»

¶Kyōju ni mō sukoshi yukkuri hanashite itadakō.

教授にもう少しゆっくり話していただこう。

Lets have the professor speak a little more slowly.

¶O–name o oshiete itadakemasen ka.

お名前を教えていただけませんか。

Could you please tell me your name?

«Literally: *Can't I have you tell me your name?*»

③ 【HUM. for **taberu** 食べる; **nomu** 飲む①】 *to eat; to drink*

¶"Motto kēki o meshiagarimasen ka."
"Mō jūbun itadakimashita."

「もっとケーキを召し上がりませんか」「もう十分いただきました」

"Won't you have some more cake?" "I've already had plenty."

¶Itadakimasu.

いただきます。

I'm going to begin. «Literally: *I will eat╱drink*» «This expression of deference is required before beginning a meal.»

itadaku 頂く *to put on a crown of, to become covered with*

¶Fuji-san wa yuki o itadaite imasu.

富士山は雪を頂いています。

Mt. Fuji is covered with snow.

itái 痛い *painful, sore, hurting*

¶Itai!

痛い！

Ouch!

¶Doko ga itai no desu ka.

どこが痛いのですか。

Where does it hurt?

¶Senaka ga itakute tamarimasen.

背中が痛くてたまりません。

My back is so painful I can't stand it.

- atama ga itai 頭が痛い *one's head aches*

- nodo ga itai のどが痛い *one's throat is sore*

- onaka ga itai おなかが痛い *one's stomach aches*

itai 遺体 *corpse,* (*dead person's*) *remains*

itamae 板前 *cook, chef* «in a Japanese-style restaurant»

itaméru 痛める *to injure, to hurt*

¶Koronde hiza o itamemashita.

転んでひざを痛めました。

I fell down and hurt my knee.

• kokoro o itameru 心を痛める *to become worried*

¶ Otōto wa shōrai no shinro no koto de kokoro o itamete iru.

弟は将来の進路のことで心を痛めている。

My brother is worried about his future course.

itaméru 炒める *to fry* «in oil in a frying pan»

itamí 痛み *pain*

¶ Senaka ni hageshii itami o oboemashita.

背中に激しい痛みを覚えました。

I felt a severe pain in my back.

¶ Mattaku itami o kanjimasen.

まったく痛みを感じません。

I don't feel any pain at all.

• itami-dome 痛み止め *painkiller*

itámu 痛む *to ache, to hurt*

¶ Kizu ga mada itamimasu.

傷がまだ痛みます。

The wound still hurts.

¶ Ano kawaisō na kodomo no koto o omou to kokoro ga itamimasu.

あのかわいそうな子供のことを思うと心が痛みます。

When I think of that poor child, my heart aches.

itámu 傷む ① *to go bad, to spoil*

¶ Kono momo wa itande imasu.

この桃は傷んでいます。

This peach is spoiled.

② *to become damaged, to wear out*

¶ Sono jitensha wa daibu itande iru ne.

その自転車はだいぶ傷んでいるね。

That bicycle is badly damaged, isn't it.

itáru tokoro いたる所 *everywhere*

¶ Kono hon wa sekai-jū itaru tokoro de yomarete iru.

この本は世界中いたる所で読まれている。

This book is being read everywhere all over the world.

itasu 致す 【HUM. for **suru** する】

itawáru 労る *to take good care of; to be kind to*

¶ Toshiyori o itawaru yō ni shinasai.

年寄りをいたわるようにしなさい。

Make sure to be kind to old people.

¶ Dōzo o-karada o itawatte kudasai.

どうぞお体をいたわってください。

Please take care of yourself.

itazura いたずら *mischief, prank, trick*

• itazura na いたずらな *mischievous, prankish*

• itazura o suru いたずらをする *to do mischief, to play a trick*

¶ Ken-chan wa yoku watashi ni itazura o suru yo.

健ちゃんはよく私にいたずらをするよ。

Ken often plays tricks on me!

• itazura-kko いたずらっ子 *mischievous child*

itazura ni 徒に *in vain, to no purpose*

itchi 一致 *agreement, match, correspondence*

• itchi suru 一致する *to come to agree, to come to coincide, to come to match*

¶ Watashi wa Fusako-san to iken ga itchi shite imasu.

私は房子さんと意見が一致しています。

My opinion coincides with Fusako's.

itchókusen 一直線 〜**ni** 〜に *in a straight line, straight*

íto 糸 *thread*

• hari to ito 針と糸 *needle and thread*

• ito ga kireru 糸が切れる *a thread breaks*

• tsuri-ito 釣り糸 *fishing line*

itóko いとこ *cousin*

• o-itoko-san おいとこさん 【HON. for **itoko** いとこ (above)】

ítsu いつ *when* «as a question word»

¶ O-tanjōbi wa itsu desu ka.

お誕生日はいつですか。

When is your birthday?

¶ Itsu shuppatsu shimasu ka.

いつ出発しますか。

When will you depart?

• itsu kara いつから *since when, how long, beginning when*

¶ Itsu kara matte imasu ka.

いつから待っていますか。

How long have you been waiting?

¶ Shiken wa itsu kara hajimarimasu ka.

試験はいつから始まりますか。

When do the examinations begin?

• itsu made いつまで *until when, how long*

¶ Koko ni itsu made taizai shimasu ka.

ここにいつまで滞在しますか。

How long will you stay here?

• itsu made ni いつまでに *by when*

¶ Kono shigoto wa itsu made ni shiage-rare masu ka.

この仕事はいつまでに仕上げられますか。

By when must I finish this work?

• itsu made mo いつまでも *forever; as long as you like*

¶ Itsu made mo wasurenai deshō.

いつまでも忘れないでしょう。

I will probably never forget.

• itsu demo いつでも *any time, no matter when, always*

¶ Itsu demo asobi ni irasshai.

いつでも遊びにいらっしゃい。

Come and visit any time.

¶ "Itsu o-denwa shimashō ka." "Itsu demo ii desu yo."

「いつお電話しましょうか」「いつでもいいですよ」

"When shall I phone you?" "Any time is all right!"

¶ Sofu wa itsu demo terebi o mite imasu.

祖父はいつでもテレビを見ています。

My grandfather is always watching television.

• itsu-ka いつか *sometime, some day* «i.e., some time in the future»; *once, before* «i.e., some time in the past»

¶ Itsu-ka Pari ni ikitai yo.

いつかパリに行きたいよ。

I want to visit Paris some day!

¶ Ano hito ni itsu-ka atta koto ga arimasu.

あの人にいつか会ったことがあります。

I have met that person before.

• itsu-mo いつも *always* [→**tsune ni** 常に]; *usually* [→**taitei** 大抵]

¶ Ani wa itsu-mo isogashii desu.

兄はいつも忙しいです。

My older brother is always busy.

¶ Itsu-mo shichi-ji ni okimasu.

いつも7時に起きます。

I always get up at 7:00.

¶ Itsu-mo yori osoku tsukimashita.

いつもより遅く着きました。

I arrived later than usual.

itsuka 五日 «see Appendix 2» ① *five days*

② *the fifth* «day of a month»

itsu-no-ma-ní-ka いつの間にか *before one realizes, before one knows it*

¶ Itsu-no-ma-ni-ka kuraku natte ima-shita.

いつの間にか暗くなっていました。

Before I knew it it had gotten dark.

itsútsu 五つ *five* «see Appendix 2»

ittai 一体 *on earth* «in combination with a question word»

¶ Ittai nani o hanashite iru n desu ka.

いったい何を話しているんですか。

What on earth are you talking about?

ittan 一旦 *once* «typically in combination with a conditional»

¶ Ittan yakusoku shitara, mamoru-beki desu.

いったん約束したら、守るべきです。

Once you make a promise, you must keep it.

iu 言う «In spite of the hiragana spelling いう, this word is pronounced **yū** except in unnaturally precise speech.» *to say; to tell* [→**tsugeru** 告げる]

¶ Asano-san wa nan to iimashita ka.

浅野さんは何と言いましたか。

What did Mr. Asano say?

¶ "Nodo ga kawaita" to Yōko-san wa itta.

「のどが渇いた」と洋子さんは言った。

"I'm thirsty," said Yoko.

¶ Kyōko-san wa otōsan ga pairotto da to sensei ni itta yo.

京子さんはお父さんがパイロットだと先生に言ったよ。

Kyoko told the teacher that her father is a pilot!

¶ Itta tōri ni shinasai.

言ったとおりにしなさい。

Do as I said.

¶Watashi no iu koto ga kikoemasu ka.

私の言うことが聞こえますか。

Can you hear what I say?

• mono o iu 物を言う *to talk, to speak*

• mono ga ieru 物が言える *to be able to talk*

¶Ano akachan wa mada mono ga iemasen.

あの赤ちゃんはまだ物が言えません。

That baby cannot speak yet.

• negoto o iu 寝言を言う *to talk in one's sleep*

• A to iu B AというB *a B called A*

¶Komori-san to iu hito mo kimashita.

小森さんという人も来ました。

A person called Mr. Komori also came.

¶Nakao-san wa Maui to iu utsukusii shima ni bessō ga arimasu.

中尾さんはマウイという美しい島に別荘があります。

Mr. Nakao has a villa on a beautiful island called Maui.

iwá 岩 (*very large*)*rock*

¶Iwa no ōi yama ni noborimashita.

岩の多い山に登りました。

We climbed a mountain with many rocks.

¶Bōto wa iwa ni butsukarimashita.

ボートは岩にぶつかりました。

The boat ran against a rock.

• iwa-nobori 岩登り *rock-climbing*

iwába 言わば *so to speak, as it were, one might say*

¶Otto wa iwaba ōki na akanbō desu.

夫はいわば大きな赤ん坊です。

My husband is, one might say, a big baby.

iwái 祝い ① *congratulations; congratulatory celebration*

¶Kokoro kara o-iwai o mōshiagemasu.

心からお祝いを申し上げます。

I offer my hearty congratulations. «Literally: From my heart I (humbly)say congratulations.»

• shinnen no o-iwai 新年のお祝い *New Year's congratulations*

② *congratulatory gift*

¶Mago ni nyūgaku no o-iwai o okurimashita.

孫に入学のお祝いを送りました。

I sent a congratulatory gift for entering school to my grandchild.

• iwai-goto 祝い事 *happy event; celebration*

• iwai-mono 祝い物 [☞**iwai** 祝い② (above)]

iwashi 鰯 *sardine*

iwáu 祝う ① *to celebrate «an event»*

¶Watashi-tachi wa Kurisumasu o iwaimasu.

私たちはクリスマスを祝います。

We celebrate Christmas.

② *to congratulate; to offer congratulations on*

• hito o iwau 人を祝う *to congratulate a person*

• seikō o iwau 成功を祝う *to offer congratulations on a success*

iwayúru いわゆる *what is called; so-called*

¶Ano kata wa iwayuru shin no geijutsuka desu.

あの方はいわゆる真の芸術家です。

That person is what is called a true artist.

iyá 嫌 ～**na** ～な《This adjectival noun is used to describe both the people who find things distasteful and the people or things that are distasteful.》 *distasteful, unpleasant, hateful; unfond, averse, unwilling*

¶Murakami wa iya na yatsu da ne.

村上は嫌なやつだね。

Murakami is an unpleasant guy, isn't he.

¶Hitori de iku no wa iya desu.

一人で行くのは嫌です。

I don't want to go alone. «Literally: Going alone is distasteful.»

¶"O-yasai mo tabenasai." "Iya da."

「お野菜も食べなさい」「嫌だ」

"Eat the vegetables too." "No!" «Literally: It's undesirable.»

iyagáru 嫌がる *to show distaste for, to show aversion to* 《Used instead of **iya da** 嫌だ *when the subject is a third person.*》

¶Yōko-chan wa kusuri o nomu no o iyagaru ne.

洋子ちゃんは薬を飲むのを嫌がるね。

Yoko doesn't like taking medicine, does she?

iyahōn イヤホーン *earphone*

iyaiya 嫌々 *against one's will, unwillingly, grudgingly*

¶Watashi wa iyaiya uchi ni nokorimashita.

私はいやいやうちに残りました。

I stayed at home unwillingly.

¶Iyaiya sara o araimashita.

いやいや皿を洗いました。

I washed the dishes grudgingly.

iyarashíi 嫌らしい ① *distasteful, unpleasant* [→**fukai na** 不快な]

② *indecent, lewd, dirty*

¶Iyarashii kotoba o tsukau no wa yoku nai yo.

嫌らしい言葉を使うのはよくないよ。

It's not good to use dirty words!

¶Ano hito wa totemo iyarashii desu.

あの人はとても嫌らしいです。

That person is very lewd.

íyaringu イヤリング *earring*

¶Haha wa shinju no iyaringu o shite imashita.

母は真珠のイヤリングをしていました。

My mother was wearing pearl earrings.

iyóiyo いよいよ ① *at last, finally* [→**tsui-ni** 遂に①]

¶Iyoiyo tsuyu ni hairimashita ne.

いよいよ梅雨に入りましたね。

We've entered the rainy season at last, haven't we.

② *more and more* [→**masumasu** 益々]

¶Monogatari wa iyoiyo omoshiroku narimashita.

物語はいよいよおもしろくなりました。

The tale became more and more interesting.

¶Kaze wa iyoiyo hageshiku natte imasu.

風はいよいよ激しくなっています。

The wind has become more and more intense.

íza いざ ～**to naru to** ～となると *when push comes to shove, in a crisis*

• iza to iu toki いざという時 *time of emergency, time of need*

ízen 以前 ① *before, previously, formerly*

¶Izen sono eiga o mita koto ga arimasu.

以前その映画を見たことがあります。

I've seen that movie before.

¶Tada-san wa izen Kyōto ni sunde imashita.

多田さんは以前京都に住んでいました。

Mr. Tada formerly lived in Kyoto.

② *former times, the past*

¶Chichi wa zutto izen ni Rōma o otozuremashita.

父はずっと以前にローマを訪れました。

My father visited Rome long ago.

• izen no 以前の *previous, former*

-izen －以前 ① *or earlier* 《Added to a word denoting a point in time.》

¶Ishibashi-san wa san-ji-izen ni tsuku deshō.

石橋さんは3時以前に着くでしょう。

Mr. Ishibashi will probably arrive at 3:00 or earlier.

② *ago, earlier* [→**mae** －前] 《Added to a word denoting a period of time.》

¶Sen-nen-izen wa sabaku deshita.

千年以前は砂漠でした。

A thousand years ago it was a desert.

izen 依然 ～**to shite** ～として *as ever, as before, still*

[→**aikawarazu** 相変らず]

izumi 泉 *spring* 《water source》

izure いずれ ① *sometime soon; sooner or later*

② ～**ni shite mo** ～にしても *either way, in any case*

J

já ジャー *thermos bottle* [→**mahō-bin** 魔法瓶 (s.v. **mahō** 魔法)]

jagaimo じゃがいも *potato*

jaguchi 蛇口 ＜*US*＞*faucet*, (*water*) *tap*
• jaguchi o akeru〔shimeru〕蛇口を開ける〔閉める〕*to turn on*〔*off*〕*a faucet*

jájī ジャージー ① *jersey cloth*
② *a jersey* ((*shirt*))

jájji ジャッジ ① *judge* 《for a competition》
② *judgment* 《given by a judge for a competition》
• jajji suru ジャッジする *to judge*

jáketto ジャケット ① *jacket* ((*article of clothing*))
② (*record*)*jacket*

jakkan 若干 *a small amount, some* [→**sukoshī** 少し]

-jáku －弱 *a little less than* 《Added to number bases.》[⇔**-kyō** －強]
¶Sore wa gojū-nen-jaku kakarimashita.
それは50年弱かかりました。
That took a little less than 50 years.

jakutén 弱点 *weak point, shortcoming* [→**yowami** 弱み]
¶Jibun no jakuten o kokufuku shiyō to doryoku shimasu.
自分の弱点を克服しようと努力します。
I will work hard to overcome my own weak points.

jama 邪魔 *obstruction, hindrance, obstacle*
• jama na 邪魔な *burdensome, obstructive, in-the-way*
• jama suru 邪魔する *to disturb, to interrupt, to obstruct, to hinder*
• A no jama o suru Aの邪魔をする *to disturb A, to obstruct A, to hinder A*
¶Benkyō no jama o shinai de kudasai.

勉強の邪魔をしないでください。
Please don't disturb my studying.
• A no jama ni naru Aの邪魔になる *to interfere with A, to get in the way of A*
¶Gitā no oto ga dokusho no jama ni narimasu.
ギターの音が読書の邪魔になります。
The sound of the guitar interferes with my reading.
• o-jama suru お邪魔する 【HUM.】 *to intrude* 《This expression is used as a polite way of describing a visit by labeling it an intrusion.》
¶O-jama shimasu.
お邪魔します。《when entering another person's home, office, etc.》
Pardon me for intruding. 《Literally: I will intrude.》
¶Dewa, raishū no Suiyōbi ni o-jama shimasu.
では、来週の水曜日にお邪魔します。
Well then, I'll visit you on Wednesday of next week.
¶O-jama shimashita.
お邪魔しました。《when leaving another person's home, office, etc.》
Sorry to have intruded. 《Literally: I have intruded.》

jámu ジャム *jam* ((*food*))
¶Pan ni jamu o nurimashita.
パンにジャムを塗りました。
I spread jam on the bread.
• ichigo-jamu 苺ジャム *strawberry jam*

jānarísuto ジャーナリスト *journalist*

jánbo ジャンボ *jumbo jet*

jánguru ジャングル *jungle*
• janguru-jimu ジャングルジム *jungle gym*

janken じゃん拳 *"scissors-paper-rock" game* 《Used to determine the order of turn-taking, etc.》
• janken suru じゃんけんする *to do "scissors-paper-rock"*
• janken de kimeru じゃんけんで決める *to decide by doing "scissors-paper-rock"*

jánpā ジャンパー *windbreaker*

jánpu ジャンプ (*upward*)*jump* [→**chōyaku** 跳躍]

• janpu suru ジャンプする *to jump* [→ **tobu** 跳ぶ]

jari 砂利 *gravel, small pebbles*
• jari-michi 砂利道 *gravel road*

jázu ジャズ *jazz*

Jéaru JR 《Generally not written out in katakana.》 *Japanese Railways* 《collective name for the six passenger railway companies formed when the Japanese National Railways was broken up in 1987.》

jésuchā ジェスチャー ① *gesture* [→ **miburi** 身ぶり]
② *charades* ((game))

jésuchua ジェスチュア [☞**jesuchā** ジェスチャー]

jettokŏsutā ジェットコースター *roller coaster*

jí 字 *letter, character* 《in a writing system》 [→**moji** 文字]
¶Ōtsuka-san wa ji ga jōzu desu.
大塚さんは字が上手です。
Ms. Otsuka has nice handwriting. 《Literally: Ms. Otsuka's characters are skillfull.》
• rōma-ji ローマ字 *Roman letters*

-ji －時《counter for o'clock; see Appendix 2》
¶Watashi wa mai-asa roku-ji ni okimasu.
私は毎朝6時に起きます。
I get up at 6:00 every morning.
¶"Ima nan-ji desu ka" "Chōdo san-ji desu."
「今何時ですか」「ちょうど3時です」
"What time is it now?" "It's exactly 3:00."

ji 痔 *hemorrhoids*

jibikí 字引き *dictionary* [→**jisho** 辞書]
• iki-jibiki 生き字引き *walking dictionary, walking encyclopedia*

jibun 自分 *oneself*
¶Hajimete jibun o terebi de mimashita.
初めて自分をテレビで見ました。
I saw myself for the first time on TV.
• jibun de 自分で *by oneself, on one's own*
¶Sono shukudai o jibun de yarinasai.
その宿題を自分でやりなさい。

Do that homework yourself.
• jibun no 自分の *one's own*
¶Jibun no keshigomu o tsukainasai.
自分の消しゴムを使いなさい。
Use your own eraser.
¶Watashi wa jibun no ie o motte imasu.
私は自分の家を持っています。
I have my own house.
• jibun-jishin 自分自身 *oneself* 《emphatic》
• jibun-katte na 自分勝手な *selfish*

jíchi 自治 *self-government, home rule*
• jichi-kai 自治会 *self-government association; student council*
• Jichi-shō 自治省 *the Ministry of Home Affairs*
• jichi-tai 自治体 *self-governing body*

jidai 時代 ① *period, era, age*
¶Nihon de wa jūkyū-seiki wa keizai-seichō no jidai deshita.
日本では19世紀は経済成長の時代でした。
In Japan the 19th century was an age of economic growth.
② *the times*
¶Jidai ga kawarimashita.
時代が変わりました。
Times have changed.
• jidai-geki 時代劇 *samurai drama, historical drama*
• jidai-okure no 時代遅れ *behind-the-times, out-of-date*
• gakusei-jidai 学生時代 *one's student days*
• Meiji-jidai 明治時代 *the Meiji Period*
• uchū-jidai 宇宙時代 *the space age*

jidō 自動 ～**no** ～の *automatic*
• jidō-doa 自動ドア *automatic door*
• jidō-hanbai-ki 自動販売機 *vending machine*
• jidō-teki na 自動的な [☞**jidō no** 自動の (above)]

jidō 児童 ① *child* [→**kodomo** 子供]
② *elementary-school pupil* [→**shōgakusei** 小学生]
• jidō-bungaku 児童文学 *children's*

literature

jidṓsha 自動車 [[→**kuruma** 車①]]
<*US*>*automobile*, <*UK*>*motorcar*;
<*US*>*truck*, <*UK*>*lorry* [→**torakku**
トラック]
• jidōsha-jiko 自動車事故 *automobile
accident*
• jidōsha-kyōshū-jo 自動車教習所 *driving school*
• jidōsha-rēsu 自動車レース *auto race*
• jidōsha-shō 自動車ショー *auto show*

jidṓshi 自動詞 *intransitive verb* [⇔
tadōshi 他動詞]

jiei 自衛 *self-defense, self-preservation*
• Jiei-tai 自衛隊 *the (Japanese)Self-
Defense Forces*
• Jiei-tai-in 自衛隊員 *Self-Defense
Forces member*

jīenupí ＧＮＰ《*Generally not written out
in katakana.*》 *GNP* [→**kokumin-sō-seisan** 国民総生産 (s.v. **kokumin** 国民)]

jigokú 地獄 *hell* [⇔**tengoku** 天国]

jigusōpázuru ジグソーパズル *jigsaw puzzle*

jíguzagu ジグザグ *a zigzag*

jígyō 事業 *work, business, undertaking, enterprise*
¶Chichi wa nijuis-sai de jigyō o okoshimashita.
父は21歳で事業を起こしました。
*My father started a business at the age
of twenty-one.*
• kōkyō-jigyō 公共事業 *public works*
• kyōiku-jigyō 教育事業 *educational
work*

jihatsuteki 自発的 ～**na**～な *spontane-
ous, voluntary*

jihéishō 自閉症 *autism*

jihi 慈悲 *mercy*
• jihi-bukai 慈悲深い *merciful*

jíin 寺院 *Buddhist temple* [→**tera** 寺]

jíji 時事 *current events, current affairs*

jíjitsu 事実 *fact, actuality, reality, truth*
¶Sono uwasa wa jijitsu desu ka.
そのうわさは事実ですか。
Is that rumor true?
¶Jijitsu wa shōsetsu yori mo ki nari.

事実は小説よりも奇なり。《*proverb*》
Fact is stranger than fiction.
• jijitsu no 事実の *actual, real, true*
• jijitsu ni hansuru 事実に反する *to be
contrary to the facts*

jijō 事情 *circumstances, conditions,
situation* [→**jōkyō** 状況]
¶Donna jijō ga atte mo kanarazu kite
kudasai.
どんな事情があっても必ず来てください。
*You must come no matter what the
circumstances!*
¶Ano ko wa katei no jijō de tenkō shimashita.
あの子は家庭の事情で転校しました。
*That child changed schools because of
family circumstances.*

jíjo 次女 *second-born daughter*

jijóden 自叙伝 *autobiography* [→**jiden**
自伝]

jikaku 自覚 *self-awareness, self-knowl-
edge; awakening, realization*
• jikaku suru 自覚する *to become aware
of, to realize*
¶Jibun no jakuten o jikaku shite imasu.
自分の弱点を自覚しています。
I am aware of my own weak points.

jikan 時間 ① (*point in*)*time* [→**jikoku**
時刻]
¶Neru jikan desu yo.
寝る時間ですよ。
It's time for bed!
¶Yakusoku no jikan ni okurete shimaimashita.
約束の時間に遅れてしまいました。
*I was late for the time of my appoint-
ment.*
• jikan o mamoru 時間を守る *to be punctual*
② (*amount of*)*time*
¶Mō jikan ga amari nai desu.
もう時間があまりないです。
There's not much time left.
③ *fixed period of time for a certain
activity; class* (*period*)
¶Rekishi no jikan ga ichiban suki desu.
歴史の時間がいちばん好きです。

I like history class best.
- jikan-dōri no 時間通りの *on-time*
- jikan-hyō 時間表 *timetable,* <*US*>*schedule*
- jikan-wari 時間割り <*US*>*class schedule,* <*UK*>*class timetable*
- eigyō-jikan 営業時間 *business hours*
- jugyō-jikan 授業時間 *time in class*
- kinmu-jikan 勤務時間 *time spent at work, working hours*

-jikan －時間《counter for hours; see Appendix 2》
¶Tomodachi o ni-jikan machimashita.
友達を2時間待ちました。
I waited for my friend for two hours.
¶Okayama made densha de nan-jikan kakarimasu ka.
岡山まで電車で何時間かかりますか。
How many hours does it take to Okayama by train?
¶Koko kara aruite ni-jikan-gurai desu.
ここから歩いて2時間ぐらいです。
It's about two hours on foot from here.

jíka-ni 直に ① *directly, with nothing intervening*
② *directly, personally, in person*

jikayṓsha 自家用車 *personal car, family car*

jíken 事件 *event, incident* [→**dekigoto** 出来事]
¶Sore wa osoroshii jiken deshita.
それは恐ろしい事件でした。
That was a frightening incident.
- satsujin-jiken 殺人事件 *a murder (incident)*

jíki 時期 *time period, season*
¶Maitoshi kono jiki ni wa yoku ame ga furimasu.
毎年この時期にはよく雨が降ります。
Every year at this time it rains a lot.
¶Ima ga sakana-tsuri ni wa ichiban ii jiki da yo.
今が魚釣りにはいちばんいい時期だよ。
Now is the best season for fishing!

jíki 磁気 *magnetism*
- jiki-tēpu 磁気テープ *magnetic tape*

jiki 直 ① (～**ni** ～に) *at once,*

<*US*>*right away,* <*UK*>*straight away* [→**sugu** (**ni**) すぐ（に）①]
② *right, directly* [→**sugu** すぐ②]

jikka 実家 *one's parents' home; family into which one was born*

jikken 実験 *experiment, test*
¶Kyō wa kagaku no jikken o shimasu.
きょうは化学の実験をします。
Today we will do a chemistry experiment.
- jikken-dai 実験台 *experimental subject, guinea pig*
- jikken-shitsu 実験室 *laboratory*
- kaku-jikken 核実験 *nuclear test*

jikkō 実行 *putting into practice, carrying out, execution*
- jikkō suru 実行する *to carry out, to put into practice*
¶Seito-tachi wa sono keikaku o jikkōshimashita.
生徒たちはその計画を実行しました。
The students carried out that plan.
- jikkō-iin-kai 実行委員会 *executive committee*
- jikkō-ryoku 実行力 *ability to put things into practice*

jikkyō 実況 *actual state of affairs; actual scene*
¶Kore wa Nyūyōku kara no jikkyō desu.
これはニューヨークからの実況です。
This is the actual scene from New York.
- jikkyō-hōsō 実況放送 *on-the-scene broadcast*

jíko 自己 *self, oneself*
¶Jiko o shiru koto ga taisetsu desu.
自己を知ることが大切です。
It is important to know oneself.
- jiko-shōkai 自己紹介 *introducing oneself*
- jiko-ryū no 自己流の *in one's own style, of one's own style*

jíko 事故 *accident, unfortunate incident*
¶Murata-san wa kesa no jiko de kega o shimashita.
村田さんはけさの事故でけがをしました。

Mr. Murata was injured in this morning's accident.

- kōtsū–jiko 交通事故 *traffic accident*

jíkoku 時刻 (*point in*)*time* [→**jikan** 時間①]

¶Jikoku wa tadaima shichi-ji desu.

時刻はただいま7時です。

The time is now 7:00.

- jikoku-hyō 時刻表 *schedule, timetable*

jikú 軸 ① *axis; axle, shaft*
    ② *roller* 《*of a scroll*》
    ③ [☞**kake-jiku** 掛け軸 (below)]

- kake-jiku 掛け軸 *decorative hanging scroll* [→**kakemono** 掛け物]

jiman 自慢 *showing pride; boasting*

- jiman suru 自慢する *to show pride in; to boast about*

¶Miyamura-san wa musume-san o jiman shite imasu.

宮村さんは娘さんを自慢しています。

Ms. Miyamura is showing pride in her daughter.

¶Yagi-san wa uta ga umai koto o jiman shimasu.

八木さんは歌がうまいことを自慢します。

Mr. Yagi boasts that he is good at singing.

jímen 地面 *ground, surface of the ground*

jimí 地味 ～**na** ～な *plain, quiet, not flashy, not gaudy* [⇔**hade na** 派手な]

¶Kono doresu wa kodomo ni wa chotto jimi desu.

このドレスは子供にはちょっと地味です。

This dress is a little plain for a child.

Jimintō 自民党 *the Liberal Democratic Party* 《*an abbreviation of* **Jiyū–minshu–tō** 自由民主党(s.v. **jiyū** 自由)》

jimotó 地元 *local area, area directly involved*

jímu 事務 *office work, clerical work*

- jimu-in 事務員 *clerical worker*
- jimu-shitsu 事務室 *office* 《*single room*》
- jimu-sho 事務所 *office* 《*more than one room*》

- jimu–sōchō 事務総長 *secretary-general*

jínan 次男 *second-born son*

jínbutsu 人物 *person, character, figure*

¶Ieyasu wa rekishi-jō no idai na jinbutsu desu.

家康は歴史上の偉大な人物です。

Ieyasu is a great figure in history.

- kiken-jinbutsu 危険人物 *dangerous character*

jinin 辞任 *resignation* 《*from a job*》

- jinin suru 辞任する *to resign from*

jínja 神社 *Shinto shrine*

jínji 人事 ① *personnel matters*
    ② *human affairs*

jinkaku 人格 *personal character, personality*

- jinkaku-sha 人格者 *person of fine character*
- nijū–jinkaku 二重人格 *dual personality*

jinken 人権 *human rights*

- jinken-mondai 人権問題 *human rights question*
- Jinken-sengen 人権宣言 *the Declaration of Human Rights*
- kihon-teki-jinken 基本的人権 *fundamental human rights*

jinkō 人口 *population*

¶Tōkyō no jinkō wa dore-gurai desu ka.

東京の人口はどれぐらいですか。

About how much is the population of Tokyo?

¶Nihon wa sekai de nana-ban-me ni jinkō ga ōi desu.

日本は世界で7番目に人口が多いです。

Japan has the seventh largest population in the world.

- jinkō-mitsudo 人口密度 *population density*

jinkō 人工 *human skill, human work*

- jinkō no 人工の *artificial*
- jinkō-eisei 人工衛星 *artificial satellite*
- jinkō-kokyū 人工呼吸 *artificial respiration*
- jinkō-shiba 人工芝 *artificial grass*

jínkusu ジンクス *jinx*

jinmei 人名 *person's name*

jinmín 人民 *people* (*of a country*) [→

kokumin 国民〕
•jinmin–kyōwakoku 人民共和国 *people's republic*

jinmon 訊問 *interrogation, questioning*
•jinmon suru 訊問する *to interrogate, to question*

jinrikísha 人力車 *rickshaw*

jínrui 人類 *humankind*
•jinrui–gaku 人類学 *anthropology*

jínsei 人生 (*a person's*)*life, human existence*
¶Yume no nai jinsei wa mijime desu.
夢のない人生は惨めです。
A life without dreams is pitiful.
¶Jinsei wa ichi–do shika nai desu yo.
人生は1度しかないですよ。
One has only one life!
•jinsei o rakkan– 〔hikan–〕 teki ni miru 人生を楽観〔悲観〕的に見る *to look on the bright* 〔*dark*〕 *side of life*
•jinsei–kan 人生観 *view of life*

jinshu 人種 *race* (*of people*)
•jinshu–mondai 人種問題 *race problem*
•jinshu–sabetsu 人種差別 *racial discrimination*

jinzai 人材 *talented person, person who will make a contribution*

jinzō 人造 **no** ～の *man–made, artificial, synthetic*
•jinzō–ko 人造湖 *artificial lake*
•jinzō–ningen 人造人間 *android, cyborg*

jinzō 腎臓 *kidney*

jínzu ジーンズ *jeans* [→**jīpan** ジーパン]
•burū–jīnzu ブルージーンズ *blue jeans*

jīpan ジーパン *jeans* [→**jīnzu** ジーンズ]

jippā ジッパー *zipper,* <*UK*>*zip fastener* [→**fasunā** ファスナー]

jīpu ジープ *jeep*

Jípushī ジプシー *Gypsy*

jirettái じれったい ① *irritating, aggravating, provoking*
② *irritated, impatient*

jírojiro じろじろ (**to** ～と) *repeatedly and staringly*
•jirojiro miru じろじろ見る *to stare repeatedly at*

jísa 時差 ① *time difference* 《between different time zones》
② *time staggering*
•jisa–boke 時差惚け *jet lag*
•jisa–shukkin 時差出勤 *staggered work hours*

jisan 持参 ～**suru** ～する *to bring along, to take along* 《The direct object must be a thing.》
¶Suitō o jisan shinasai.
水筒を持参しなさい。
Bring along a canteen.
•jisan–kin 持参金 *dowry*

jisatsu 自殺 *suicide*
•jisatsu suru 自殺する *to commit suicide*

jisei 自制 *self–control, self–restraint*
•jisei suru 自制する *to control oneself, to restrain oneself*

jíshaku 磁石 ① *magnet*
② (*magnetic*)*compass*

jishin 自信 *confidence, self–assurance*
¶Sūgaku ni wa amari jishin ga nai yo.
数学にはあまり自信がないよ。
I don't have much self–confidence in math!
¶Senshu–tachi wa yūshō suru jishin ga aru yō da.
選手たちは優勝する自信があるようだ。
The players seem to have confidence that they will win the championship.
•jishin o ushinau 自信を失う *to lose one's confidence*
•jishin–manman no 自信満々の *very confident, full of confidence*

jishin 地震 *earthquake*
¶Yūbe tsuyoi jishin ga arimashita.
ゆうべ強い地震がありました。
There was a strong earthquake last night.

–jishin –自身 *oneself* 《Added to noun or pronoun bases.》
¶Jibun–jishin de yarinasai.
自分自身でやりなさい。
Do it yourself.
¶Sore wa Nomoto–san–jishin no mondai desu yo.
それは野本さん自身の問題ですよ。
That's Mr. Nomoto's own problem.

jísho 辞書 *dictionary*
¶Sono tango o jisho de shirabete kudasai.
その単語を辞書で調べてください。
Please check that word in a dictionary.
•jisho o hiku 辞書を引く *to consult a dictionary*

jishoku 辞職 *resignation, quitting one's job*
•jishoku suru 辞職する *to resign*
¶Takahashi-san wa kaisha ni shitsubō shite jishoku shimashita.
高橋さんは会社に失望して辞職しました。
Mr. Takahashi got discouraged with work and resigned.

jishū 自習 *self-study, studying by oneself*
•jishū suru 自習する *to study by oneself*
¶Doyōbi no gogo wa tosho-kan de jishū shimasu.
土曜日の午後は図書館で自習します。
On Saturday afternoons I study by myself in the library.

jísoku 時速 *speed per hour*
¶Kono tokkyū wa jisoku nihyaku-hachi-juk-kiro de hashiru yo.
この特急は時速280キロで走るよ。
This special express runs at a speed of 280 kilometers per hour!

jisónshin 自尊心 *self-respect, pride*
¶Shachō wa jisonshin ga tsuyoi desu ne.
社長は自尊心が強いですね。
The company president's self-respect is strong, isn't it.
¶Sono kotoba de jisonshin ga kizu-tsuita yo.
その言葉で自尊心が傷ついたよ。
My pride was hurt by those words!

jissai 実際 *truth, reality, actuality*
¶Kono ko wa jissai yori toshiue ni miemasu.
この子は実際より年上に見えます。
This child looks older than he really is.
•jissai no 実際の *real, actual, true* [→hontō no 本当の]
•jissai ni 実際に *really, actually, truly*
¶Kore wa jissai ni atta hanashi desu.
これは実際にあった話です。

This is a story that really happened.

jissen 実践 *(actual)practice, putting into practice*
•jissen suru 実践する *to put into practice*

jisshínhō 十進法 *the decimal system*

jisúberi 地滑り *landslide*

jisui 自炊 *doing one's own cooking*
•jisui suru 自炊する *to do one's own cooking*

jítai 事態 *the situation*
•jitai ga kōten suru 事態が好転する *the situation takes a favorable turn*

jítai 辞退 *modest refusal, nonacceptance*
•jitai suru 辞退する *to decline, to modestly refuse*

jitaku 自宅 *one's house, one's home*
¶Hamaguchi-san wa jitaku ni imasu.
浜口さんは自宅にいます。
Ms. Hamaguchi is at home.

jiten 辞典 *dictionary* [→jisho 辞書]
•Ei-Wa-jiten 英和辞典 *English-Japanese dictionary*
•kokugo-jiten 国語辞典 *Japanese dictionary*
•Wa-Ei-jiten 和英辞典 *Japanese-English dictionary*

jiténsha 自転車 *bicycle*
¶Eki made jitensha de ikimashita.
駅まで自転車で行きました。
I went as far as the station by bicycle.
¶Junko-chan wa jitensha ni noreru?
順子ちゃんは自転車に乗れる？
Can Junko ride a bicycle?
•jitensha-ryokō 自転車旅行 *bicycle trip, cycling tour*

jitsú 実 ① *truth, reality* [→shinjitsu 真実]
•jitsu no 実の *true, real* [→hontō no 本当の]
•jitsu wa 実は *actually, in fact*
¶Jitsu wa ano hanashi wa uso deshita.
実はあの話はうそでした。
In fact, that story was a lie.
•jitsu o iu to 実を言うと *to tell the truth*
•jitsu ni 実に *really, truly, very*
② *sincerity* [→seii 誠意]

¶Noguchi-san wa jitsu no aru hito desu.
野口さんは実のある人です。
Ms. Noguchi is a person of sincerity.

jitsubutsu 実物 *the real thing* [→**honmono** 本物]; *the actual person*
¶Kono shōzō-ga wa jitsubutsu ni sokkuri desu.
この肖像画は実物にそっくりです。
This portrait looks just like the actual person.
• jitsubutsu-dai 実物大 *life size, actual size*

jitsugen 実現 *realization, coming true*
• jitsugen suru 実現する *to be realized, to come true; to realize, to actualize*
¶Daitōryō wa jibun no risō o jitsugen shimashita.
大統領は自分の理想を実現しました。
The president realized his own ideals.
¶Sono yume wa jū-nen-go ni jitsugen shimashita.
その夢は10年後に実現しました。
That dream came true ten years later.

jitsugyō 実業 *business, production and commerce*
• jitsugyō-ka 実業家 *businessman, businesswoman*

jitsuin 実印 *registered signature seal*
《Documents are ordinarily stamped with a seal rather than signed in Japan.》

jitsujō 実情 *actual circumstances, actual state of affairs*

jitsuryoku 実力 *real ability, capability, competence*
¶Hayashi-sensei wa jitsuryoku no aru sensei desu.
林先生は実力のある先生です。
Mr. Hayashi is a capable teacher.
¶Kikuchi-san wa Eigo no jitsuryoku ga arimasu.
菊池さんは英語の実力があります。
Ms. Kikuchi has real ability in English.
• jitsuryoku o tsukeru 実力を付ける *to attain competence, to cultivate one's ability*
¶Sūgaku no jitsuryoku o tsuke-tai n desu.
数学の実力をつけたいんです。

I want to improve my competence in math.
• jitsuryoku-sha 実力者 *influential person*
• jitsuryoku-tesuto 実力テスト *proficiency test*

jitsuyō 実用 *practical use*
• jitsuyō-Eigo 実用英語 *practical English*
• jitsuyō-hin 実用品 *daily necessities, useful articles*
• jitsuyō-sei 実用性 *practical usefulness, utility*
• jitsuyō-teki na 実用的な *practical, of practical use*
¶Kono shin-seihin wa amari jitsuyō-teki de wa nai.
この新製品はあまり実用的ではない。
This new product is of little practical use.

jitto じっと ① *still, motionlessly; steadily, fixedly*
¶Keikan wa jitto tatte imasu.
警官はじっと立っています。
The police officer is standing still.
¶Henshū-sha wa shashin o jitto mitsumete imashita.
編集者は写真をじっと見つめていました。
The editor was staring steadily at the photograph.
② *patiently, uncomplainingly*
¶Shōnen wa itami o jitto gaman shimashita.
少年は痛みをじっと我慢しました。
The boy put up with the pain uncomplainingly.

jiyū 自由 *freedom, liberty*
¶Kojin no jiyū o sonchō shinakute wa narimasen.
個人の自由を尊重しなくてはなりません。
We must respect individual liberty.
• genron no jiyū 言論の自由 *freedom of speech*
• jiyū na 自由な *free, unrestrained*
¶Jiyū na jikan ga hotonodo nai desu.
自由な時間がほとんどないです。
I have almost no free time.
¶Kono jisho o jiyū ni tsukatte kudasai.

この辞書を自由に使ってください。
Please use this dictionary freely.
¶Ōishi-san wa Eigo o jiyū ni hanashimasu.
大石さんは英語を自由に話します。
Mr. Oishi speaks English fluently.
•Jiyū-minshu-tō　自由民主党　*the Liberal Democratic Party*　[→**Jimintō**　自民党]
•jiyū-seki　自由席　*unreserved seat*　[⇔**shitei-seki**　指定席　(s.v. **shitei**　指定)]
•jiyū-shijō　自由市場　*free market*
•jiyū-shugi　自由主義　*liberalism*
•jiyū-shugi-koku　自由主義国　*free nation*
•jiyū-shugi-sha　自由主義者　*liberalist*
•Jiyū no megami-zō　自由の女神像　*the Statue of Liberty*

jizen　慈善　*charity, benevolence, philanthropy*
•jizen-jigyō　慈善事業　*charitable work; charities*

Jizō　地蔵　*Jizo*　《*the Buddhist guardian deity of children and travelers*》

jō　錠　*lock*
¶Kagi de doa no jō o akemashita.
かぎでドアの錠を開けました。
I opened the lock on the door with the key.
•jō ga kakaru　錠が掛かる　*a lock becomes locked*
¶Kono sūtsukēsu wa jō ga kakatte imasu.
このスーツケースは錠がかかっています。
This suitcase's lock is locked.
•jō o kakeru　錠を掛ける　*to lock a lock*

–**jō**　–畳　《*counter for mats (i.e., **tatami**), the traditional units of measure for room size; see Appendix 2*》

jōba　乗馬　① *horse riding* ② *riding horse*
•jōba-kurabu　乗馬クラブ　*horse-riding club*

jōbu　丈夫　～**na**　～な　① *strong, healthy, robust*
¶Sofu wa hachijus-sai desu ga, totemo jōbu desu.
祖父は80歳ですが、とても丈夫です。
My grandfather is 80, but he's

very healthy.
② *solid, strong, durable*
¶Jōbu na nawa o tsukatte kudasai.
丈夫な縄を使ってください。
Please use a strong rope.

jōdan　冗談　*joke, jest*
¶Sono jōdan ga wakaranatta.
その冗談がわからなかった。
I didn't understand that joke.
¶Jōdan ja nai yo.
冗談じゃないよ。
Get serious! 《*Literally: It's not a joke!*》
•jōdan ni　冗談に　*jokingly, in jest*
•jōdan o iu　冗談を言う　*to joke, to tell a joke, to make a joke*
¶Ano sensei wa jugyō-chū ni yoku jōdan o iimasu.
あの先生は授業中によく冗談を言います。
That teacher often tells jokes during class.
•jōdan-hanbun ni　冗談半分に　*half in jest*

jodōshi　助動詞　*inflected auxiliary suffix*　《*a part of speech in some versions of Japanese grammar*》

jōei　上映　*showing*　《*of a movie*》
•jōei suru　上映する　*to show*

jōen　上演　*staging, performance*
•jōen suru　上演する　*to stage, to put on*
¶Raigetsu sono geki o jōen shimasu.
来月その劇を上演します。
They will stage that play next month.

jōge　上下　*top and bottom; high and low*
¶Gondora wa jōge ni ugokimasu.
ゴンドラは上下に動きます。
The gondolas move up and down.
•jōge suru　上下する　*to go up and down, to rise and fall*

jogen　助言　*advice, helpful suggestion*
¶Isha no jogen ni shitagaimashita.
医者の助言に従いました。
I followed the doctor's advice.
•jogen suru　助言する　*to advise*
¶Watashi wa Yumi ni hayame ni deru yō jogen shimashita.
私は由美に早めに出るよう助言しました。

I advised Yumi to leave early.

jōgi 定規 *drafting tool; ruler*
- sankaku-jōgi 三角定規 *drafting triangle*
- tī-jōgi T定規 *T-square*

jogingu ジョギング *jogging*
- jogingu suru ジョギングする *to jog*

jōgo 漏斗 *funnel*

jōhánshin 上半身 *upper half of the body* [⇔**kahanshin** 下半身]

jōhatsu 蒸発 *evaporation, vaporization*
- jōhatsu suru 蒸発する *to evaporate, to become vaporized*
  ¶Mizu wa nessuru to, jōhatsu shimasu.
  水は熱すると、蒸発します。
  Water evaporates when it heats up.

jōhín 上品 〜**na** 〜な *genteel, elegant, refined* [⇔**gehin na** 下品な]
  ¶Jirō-san no okāsan wa jōhin na kata desu.
  次郎さんのお母さんは上品な方です。
  Jiro's mother is a refined person.
  ¶Takauchi-san wa jōhin na doresu o kite imasu.
  高内さんは上品なドレスを着ています。
  Ms. Takauchi is wearing an elegant dress.

jōho 譲歩 *concession, yielding*
- jōho suru 譲歩する *to make a concession, to yield*

jōhō 情報 *information, piece of information*
  ¶Sono jōhō wa ima hairimashita.
  その情報は今入りました。
  That information came in just now.
- jōhō o eru 情報を得る *to obtain information*
- jōhō-ka-shakai 情報化社会 *information-oriented society*
- jōhō-sangyō 情報産業 *information industry*
- saishin-jōhō 最新情報 *the latest information*

Jōin 上院 [[⇔**Kain** 下院]] *upper house* 《of a legislature》; *the Senate* 《in the United States Congress》; *the House of Lords* 《in the British Parliament》
- Jōin-giin 上院議員 *upper-house member*

jójo-ni 徐々に *gradually, slowly, little by little* [→**dandan** 段々]
  ¶Teshima-san no kenkō wa jojo-ni kaifuku shite imasu.
  手島さんの健康は徐々に回復しています。
  Mr. Teshima's health is gradually improving.

jōjun 上旬 *the first third of a month* [→**shojun** 初旬] [⇔**chūjun** 中旬; **gejun** 下旬]
  ¶Shi-gatsu no jōjun ni wa sakura ga mankai deshō.
  4月の上旬には桜が満開でしょう。
  In early April the cherry trees will probably be in full bloom.

jōkā ジョーカー *joker* ((playing card))

jōkén 条件 *condition, prerequisite*
  ¶Isshōkenmei benkyō suru koto ga gōkaku no jōken desu.
  一生懸命勉強することが合格の条件です。
  Studying hard is a condition of success.
  ¶Hikōki ni noranai to iu jōken de ikimasu.
  飛行機に乗らないという条件で行きます。
  I will go on condition that we will not board a plane.
- jōken-tsuki no 条件付きの *conditional*

jóki 蒸気 *steam, vapor*
- jōki-kikan-sha 蒸気機関車 *steam locomotive*

jókki ジョッキ *beer mug, stein*

jókkī ジョッキー *jockey*

jokō 徐行 〜**suru** 〜する *to go slow*
  ¶Kōji no tame densha wa jokō shite imasu.
  工事のため電車は徐行しています。
  The train is going slow because of construction work.

jóku ジョーク *joke* [→**jōdan** 冗談]

jōkyaku 乗客 *(paying)passenger*
  ¶Densha ni wa takusan no jōkyaku ga notte imashita.
  電車にはたくさんの乗客が乗っていました。
  A lot of passengers were riding

on the train.

jōkyō 状況 *circumstances, state of affairs*
¶Jōkyō o setsumei shite kudasai.
状況を説明してください。
Please explain the circumstances.

jōkyō 上京 *going to Tokyo «from elsewhere in Japan»*
• jōkyō suru 上京する *to go to Tokyo*

jokyōju 助教授 *assistant professor*

jōkyū 上級 *high rank, upper class* [⇔ **kakyū** 下級; **shokyū** 初級]
• jōkyū no 上級の *high-ranking, advanced*
• jōkyū-kōsu 上級コース *advanced course*
• jōkyū-sei 上級生 *student in one of the upper grades,* <*US*>*upperclassman*

jōmyaku 静脈 *vein ((blood vessel))* [⇔**dōmyaku** 動脈]

jōnetsu 情熱 *passion, enthusiasm*
• jōnetsu-teki na 情熱的な *passionate, enthusiastic*

joō 女王 *queen* [⇔**ō** 王]
• joō-bachi 女王蜂 *queen bee*
• Erizabesu-joō エリザベス女王 *Queen Elizabeth*

jōriku 上陸 *coming ashore, landing*
• jōriku suru 上陸する *to come ashore, to land*
¶Hinan-min wa Sanfuranshisuko ni jōriku shita.
避難民はサンフランシスコに上陸した。
The refugees landed at San Francisco.

jōro じょうろ *watering can, sprinkling can*

jōryū 上流 [[⇔**karyū** 下流]] ① *the area upriver; upper portion of a river*
¶Kono hashi no jōryū ni damu ga arimasu.
この橋の上流にダムがあります。
There is a dam upriver from this bridge.
② *upper social stratum*
• jōryū-kaikyū 上流階級 *upper class* [⇔ **chūryūkaikyū** 中流階級]

jōryū 蒸留 *distillation*
• jōryū suru 蒸留する *to distill*
• jōryū-sui 蒸留水 *distilled water*

josei 女性 *woman* [⇔**dansei** 男性]
• josei-kaihō 女性解放 *women's liberation*

jōsha 乗車 *boarding, getting on／in «a train, bus, car, etc.»* [⇔**gesha** 下車]
• jōsha suru 乗車する *to get «on／in a train, bus, car, etc.»*
• jōsha-ken 乗車券 *ticket «for a ride»*

jōshi 女子 [[⇔**danshi** 男子]] *girl; woman* [→**josei** 女性]
• joshi-daigaku 女子大学 *women's college*
• joshi-daisei 女子大生 *woman college student*
• joshi-kōkō 女子高校 *girls' high school*
• joshi-seito 女子生徒 *girl pupil*

joshi 助詞 *particle «a part of speech in traditional Japanese grammar»*

jōshiki 常識 *common sense, common knowledge*
¶Ano hito wa jōshiki ga nai ne.
あの人は常識がないね。
That person has no common sense, does he.

joshu 助手 *assistant, helper*
• unten-joshu 運転助手 *assistant driver*

jōtai 状態 *condition, state*
¶Genzai no jōtai de wa, shuppatsu dekimasen.
現在の状態では、出発できません。
We cannot leave under present conditions.
• kenkō-jōtai 健康状態 *state of health*
• seishin-jōtai 精神状態 *mental state*

jōtatsu 上達 *improvement, progress*
• jōtatsu suru 上達する *to improve, to make progress*
¶Yōko-san wa sukēto ga ōi-ni jōtatsu shita.
洋子さんはスケートが大いに上達した。
Yoko's skating greatly improved.

jōtō 上等 〜の〜 *first-class, excellent, high-quality*
¶O-miyage ni jōtō no wain o moraimashita.
お土産に上等のワインをもらいました。
I received first-class wine as a gift.

• jōtō-hin 上等品 *high-quality item*

jōyaku 条約 *treaty*

¶Shushō wa sono jōyaku ni chōin shimashita.

首相はその条約に調印しました。

The prime minister signed the treaty.

• heiwa-jōyaku 平和条約 *peace treaty*

• Nichi-Bei-anzen-hoshō-jōyaku 日米安全保障条約 *the Japan–US Security Treaty*

jōyō 常用 *common use, general use, everday use*

• jōyō suru 常用する *to use commonly, to use regularly, to use generally*

• Jōyō-kanji 常用漢字 *Characters for General Use* 《the 1,945 kanji (Chinese characters)designated by the Japanese Ministry of Education in 1981 to be taught in the first nine years of schooling》

jōyōsha 乗用車 *(passenger)car, (passenger)automobile*

joyū 女優 *actress*

jōzai 錠剤 *tablet* ((medicine))

jōzú 上手 〜**na** 〜な *skillful, good (at)* 《This adjectival noun is used to describe both the people who are skillful and the things they are skillful at.》 [⇔**heta na** 下手な]

¶Kyōko-san wa Eigo ga jōzu desu.

京子さんは英語が上手です。

Kyoko is good at English.

¶Haha wa chichi yori tenisu ga jōzu desu.

母は父よりテニスが上手です。

My mother is better at tennis than my father.

¶Tokubetsu ni hanashi-jōzu na hito wa imasen.

特別に話し上手な人はいません。

There is nobody especially good at talking.

jú 十 *ten* 《see Appendix 2》

• Jū-gatsu 十月 *October*

jú 銃 *gun* 《of a type small enough to be portable》

• ken-jū 拳銃 *pistol*

• kikan-jū 機関銃 *machine gun*

• raifuru-jū ライフル銃 *rifle*

-jū 　-中 ① *throughout, all through* 《Added to bases denoting time periods.》

¶Watashi wa natsu-yasumi-jū shinseki no bessō ni imashita.

私は夏休み中親せきの別荘にいました。

I was at my relatives' villa all through the summer vacation.

② *all over, throughout* 《Added to bases denoting places.》

¶Ano hito wa Nihon-jū ni shirarete imasu.

あの人は日本中に知られています。

That person is known all over Japan.

¶Machi-jū ga ō-sawagi ni natte imashita.

町中が大騒ぎになっていました。

The whole town was in a great uproar.

• hito-ban-jū 一晩中 *throughout the night, all night long*

• ichi-nen-jū 一年中 *throughout the year, all year round*

• ichi-nichi-jū 一日中 *throughout the day, all day long*

¶Kinō wa ichi-nichi-jū mokei o tsukutte imashita.

きのうは一日中模型を作っていました。

I was making a model all day yesterday.

• sekai-jū 世界中 *all over the world*

jūbako 重箱 *stacked square lacquered boxes* 《for carrying food》

jūbún 十分 （〜**ni** 〜に） *enough, sufficiently; plenty, fully*

¶Kippu o kau o-kane wa jūbun ni motte imasu.

切符を買うお金は十分に持っています。

I have plenty of money to buy the ticket.

¶Hako wa jūbun ni ōkii desu.

箱は十分に大きいです。

The box is large enough.

¶Mō jūbun itadakimashita.

もう十分いただきました。

I've already had plenty.

¶Kono shigoto wa tōka wa jūbun ni kakaru deshō.

この仕事は10日は十分にかかるでしょう。

This work will probably take a

full ten days.

•jūbun na 十分な *sufficient, ample*

¶Sanjup-pun areba jūbun desu.

30分あれば十分です。

Thirty minutes will be enough.

jūbyō 重病 *serious illness*

¶Ishiyama-san no otōsan wa jūbyō desu.

石山さんのお父さんは重病です。

Ms. Ishiyama's father is seriously ill.

júdai 十代 *the 10–19 age range, the teen years*

¶Gakusei-tachi wa mada zen'in jūdai desu.

学生たちはまだ全員十代です。

The students are all still in their teens.

•jūdai no shōnen〔shōjo〕十代の少年〔少女〕*teenage boy〔girl〕*

jūdai 重大 ～**na** ～な ① *important* [→**jūyō na** 重要な]

② *serious, critical* [→**shinkoku na** 深刻な]

¶Kore wa jūdai na mondai desu.

これは重大な問題です。

This is a serious problem.

júdō 柔道 *judo*

•jūdō-bu 柔道部 *judo club, judo team*

jūgoya 十五夜 *full-moon night*

júgyō 授業 *class, lessons at school*

¶Is-shūkan ni sanjūyo-jikan no jugyō ga arimasu.

1週間に34時間の授業があります。

There are 34 hours of classes a week.

¶Ichi-jikan-me ni Eigo no jugyō ga arimasu.

1時間目に英語の授業があります。

We have an English class first period.

¶Jugyō wa san-ji ni owarimasu.

授業は3時に終わります。

Class ends at 3:00.

•jugyō-ryō 授業料 *school fee, tuition*

•jugyō-sankan 授業参観 *class visit, parent's day*

jūgyóin 従業員 *employee*

júi 獣医 *veterinarian*

júichí 十一 *eleven*《see Appendix 2》

•Jūichi-gatsu 十一月 *November*

júji 十字 *cross shape, the shape of the*

character for **jū** *"ten"*《十》

•jūji-ka 十字架 *cross for crucifiction*

jūjitsu 充実 *substantialness, repleteness; enrichment*

•jūjitsu suru 充実する *to become more substantial, to become replete; to become enriched*

jūjun 従順 ～**na** ～な *obedient; docile*

¶Hanako-chan wa ojīsan ni totemo jūjun da.

花子ちゃんはおじいさんにとても従順だ。

Hanako is very obedient to her grandfather.

juken 受験 *taking an entrance examination*

•juken suru 受験する *to take the entrance examination for*

¶Watashi mo Minami-kōkō o juken suru tsumori desu.

私も南高校を受験するつもりです。

I, too, intend to take the entrance examination for Minami High School.

•juken-bangō 受験番号 *examinee's number*

•juken-benkyō 受験勉強 *studying for an entrance examination*

•juken-hyō 受験票 *admission ticket for an examination*

•juken-kamoku 受験科目 *entrance examination subjects*

•juken-sei 受験生 *student preparing for an entrance examination*

jūkógyō 重工業 *heavy industry*

júku 塾 *after-school tutoring school*

jukugo 熟語 ① *compound word written with two or more Chinese characters*

② *compound word* [→**fukugōgo** 複合語]

jukuren 熟練 *expert skill*

•jukuren suru 熟練する *to become skilled*

•jukuren-kō 熟練工 *skilled worker*

jukusúru 熟する{Irreg.} *to ripen*

¶Budō wa aki ni jukushimasu.

ぶどうは秋に熟します。

Grapes ripen in fall.

¶Tomato wa mada jukushite inai ne.

トマトはまだ熟していないね。
The tomatoes are not ripe yet, are they.
• ki ga jukusuru 機が熟する *the time becomes ripe*

Júkyō 儒教 *Confucianism*

jūmin 住民 *resident, inhabitant*
• jūmin-tōroku 住民登録 *resident registration*
• gen-jūmin 原住民 *original inhabitant*

jumyō 寿命 *life span*
¶Zō wa jumyō ga nagai desu ne.
象は寿命が長いですね。
An elephant's life-span is long, isn't it.
• heikin—jumyō 平均寿命 *average life-span*
¶Nihon-jin-josei no heikin-jumyō wa hachijus-sai o koeta.
日本人女性の平均寿命は80歳を越えた。
The average life span of Japanese women has exceeded 80 years.

jun 順 *order, sequence* [→**junjo** 順序]
• jun ni 順に *in order, in sequence, by turns*
¶Se no jun ni narande kudasai.
背の順に並んでください。
Please line up in order of height.
¶Kodomo-tachi wa jun ni basu ni norimashita.
子供たちは順にバスに乗りました。
The children got on the bus in order.
• jun-jun ni 順々に *one by one, each in turn; one step at a time*
¶Seito-tachi wa jun-jun ni uta o utaimashita.
生徒たちは順々に歌を歌いました。
The students each sang a song in turn.
• bangō-jun 番号順 *numerical order*
• ēbīshī-jun ＡＢＣ順 *alphabetical order*
• senchaku-jun 先着順 *order of arrival*

jun- 準－ *semi-, quasi-* 《Added to noun bases.》
• jun-kesshō 準決勝 *championship semifinal*
• jun-jun-kesshō 準々決勝 *championship quarterfinal*

jūnan 柔軟 ～**na** ～な *flexible, pliant, supple*

¶Daitōryō no kangae-kata wa jūnan desu.
大統領の考え方は柔軟です。
The president's way of thinking is flexible.

junban 順番 ① *order, sequence* [→**junjo** 順序]
• junban ni 順番に *in order, in sequence, by turns*
② *one's turn* [→**ban** 番①]
¶Koko de junban o matte kudasai.
ここで順番を待ってください。
Please wait for your turn here.

júnbi 準備 *preparations* [→**yōi** 用意]
¶Chichi wa shutchō no junbi de isogashii desu.
父は出張の準備で忙しいです。
My father is busy with preparations for a business trip.
¶Watashi-tachi wa shūgakuryokō no junbi o shite imasu.
私たちは修学旅行の準備をしています。
We are making preparations for the school excursion.
• junbi suru 準備する *to prepare, to make ready*
• junbi-undō 準備運動 *warm-up exercise*

junchō 順調 ～**na** ～な *smooth, free from difficulties*
¶Shujutsu-go no keika wa junchō desu.
手術後の経過は順調です。
My progress has been smooth since the operation.
¶Subete junchō ni shinkō shimashita.
すべて順調に進行しました。
Everything went smoothly.

jūni 十二 *twelve* 《see Appendix 2》
• Jūni-gatsu 十二月 *December*
• jūni-shi 十二支 *the twelve signs of the Chinese zodiac*

jún'i 順位 *order, ranking*
¶Jun'i o kimeru no ni jikan ga kakarimashita.
順位を決めるのに時間がかかりました。
It took time to decide the ranking.

jūnibun 十二分 （～**ni** ～に） *more than*

fully, to the fullest

júnjo 順序 *order, sequence* [→**jun** 順]
¶Pēji no junjo ga chigau yo.
ページの順序が違うよ。
The page order is wrong!
•junjo-tadashii 順序正しい *orderly, systematic*
•junjo-yoku 順序よく *in appropriate sequence, in orderly fashion*

junkan 循環 *circulation; rotation; cycle*
•junkan suru 循環する *to circulate; to rotate; to move in a circular path*

júnro 順路 *usual route*

júnsa 巡査 *police patrol officer*
•kōtsū-junsa 交通巡査 *traffic police officer*

junshin 純真 ～**na** ～な *pure-hearted, innocent*

junsui 純粋 ～**na**／**no** ～な／の *pure*
•junsui na kokoro 純粋な心 *pure heart*

júrai 従来 *until now, heretofore*

jūryō 重量 *weight* 《of an object》
•jūryō-age 重量挙げ *weight lifting*
•jūryō-age-senshu 重量挙げ選手 *weight lifter*

jūryoku 重力 *gravity* 《in physics》
¶Sensei wa jūryoku no hōsoku o setsumei shite kudasatta.
先生は重力の法則を説明してくださった。
The teacher explained the law of gravity to us.
•mu-jūryoku-jōtai 無重力状態 *weightlessness*

jushin 受信 [[⇔**hasshin** 発信]]
receipt of a message; reception of a broadcast
•jushin suru 受信する *to receive*
•jushin-ki 受信機 *receiver* ((machine))

jūsho 住所 *address*
¶Namae to jūsho o kinyū shimashita.
名前と住所を記入しました。
I filled in my name and address.
•jūsho-roku 住所録 *address book, list of addresses*

jūshō 重傷 *serious injury*
¶Unten-shu wa jiko de jūshō o oimashita.
運転手は事故で重傷を負いました。
The driver suffered a serious injury in the accident.

jushō 受賞 ～**suru** ～する *to win a prize*
¶Aoyama-san wa benron-taikai de ittō-shō o jushō shita.
青山さんは弁論大会で1等賞を受賞した。
Ms. Aoyama won first prize in the debating contest.
•jushō-sha 受賞者 *prize winner*

jūsu ジュース ① *juice*
② *fruit-flavored soft drink*

jūtai 重態, 重体 *serious condition* 《due to illness》
¶Kanja-san wa jūtai desu.
患者さんは重態です。
The patient is in a serious condition.

jūtai 渋滞 *delay, lack of progress, bogging down* 《most commonly used in reference to traffic》
•jūtai suru 渋滞する *to become delayed, to bog down*

jūtaku 住宅 *house, dwelling, residence*
•jūtaku-chi 住宅地 *residential area*
•jūtaku-mondai 住宅問題 *housing problem*
•Kōdan-jūtaku 公団住宅 *Japan Housing Corporation apartment*
•mokuzō-jūtaku 木造住宅 *wooden house*

jūtan 絨毯 *carpet; rug*
¶Kono heya ni jūtan o shiku tsumori desu.
この部屋にじゅうたんを敷くつもりです。
I plan to lay a carpet in this room.
•Perusha-jūtan ペルシャじゅうたん *Persian rug*

jūten 重点 *importance, emphasis, stress*
•A ni jūten o oku Aに重点を置く *to put emphasis on A*
¶Kono gakkō wa ongaku-kyōiku ni jūten o oite iru.
この学校は音楽教育に重点を置いている。
This school is putting emphasis on music education.

- jūten-teki na 重点的な *high-priority*

jutsugo 述語 *predicate* [⇔**shugo** 主語]

juwáki 受話器 *receiver* 《i.e., the part of a telephone or other device held to the ear to hear a transmission》

jūyaku 重役 *company executive, company director*

jūyō 重要 〜**na** 〜な *important* [→**taisetsu na** 大切な]
- jūyō-bunka-zai 重要文化財 *important cultural property*
- jūyō-jinbutsu 重要人物 *very important person*

juyō 需要 *demand, desire to obtain* [⇔**kyōkyū** 供給]
- juyō-kyōkyū 需要供給 *supply and demand*

juzú 数珠 *rosary, string of rosary beads*

K

ká 科 ① *family* 《in biological taxonomy》
② *department* 《of a university, hospital, etc.》
③ *course of study*
- Eigo-ka 英語科 *English department*
- futsū-ka 普通科 *the general course of study*
- neko-ka ネコ科 *the cat family*

ká 課 ① *lesson* 《in a textbook》
- dai-ik-ka 第1課 *Lesson 1*
② *section* 《of a company, government bureau, etc.》
- ka-chō 課長 *section chief*
- hanbai-ka 販売課 *sales section*

ka 蚊 *mosquito*
¶Akanbō ga ka ni sasareta yo.
赤ん坊が蚊に刺されたよ。
The baby was bitten by a mosquito!
- ka-tori-senkō 蚊取り線香 *mosquito coil*

ka か ① 《As a clause-final particle **ka** marks a clause as a question. The copula

form **da** だ is optionally omitted before **ka** in non-final clauses. When **ka** is sentence-final, **da** cannot appear before it. Question sentences in the informal style are ordinarily marked only with rising intonation, and using **ka** at the end of such sentences sounds quite rough.》
¶Kore wa nan desu ka.
これは何ですか。
What is this?
¶Onīsan wa gitā ga hikemasu ka.
お兄さんはギターが弾けますか。
Can your older brother play the guitar?
¶Kyatchibōru o shiyō ka.
キャッチボールをしようか。
Shall we play catch?
¶Ano hito wa dare (da)ka shirimasen.
あの人はだれ(だ)か知りません。
I don't know who that person is.
② *or* 《noun-conjoining particle》
¶Chichi ka haha ga soko e ikanakereba narimasen.
父か母がそこへ行かなければなりません。
My father or mother has to go there.

kába 河馬 *hippopotamus*

kábā カバー ① *cover, covering*
- hon no kabā 本のカバー *book cover* 《of the type added over the binding or jacket for protection》
- beddo-kabā ベッドカバー *bedspread*
- makura-kabā 枕カバー *pillowcase*
② *covering* 《an insufficiency of some kind》
- kabā suru カバーする *to cover*

kaban 鞄 *satchel, bag; briefcase; suitcase* [→**sūtsukēsu** スーツケース]
- ryokō-kaban 旅行鞄 *traveling bag*

kabáu 庇う *to protect, to defend, to stick up for* 《a person》
¶Sono hito wa musume-san o inu kara kabau tame ni mae ni demashita.
その人は娘さんを犬からかばうために前に出ました。
That person stepped in front to protect his daughter from the dog.
¶Mori-sensei wa watashi o kabatte kudasaimashita.

森先生は私をかばってくださいました。
Mr. Mori stuck up for me.

kabe 壁 *wall*
  ¶Kabe ni mimi ari.
  壁に耳あり。《*proverb*》
  The walls have ears.
  • kabe-gami 壁紙 *wallpaper*

kabi 黴 *mold* ((organism))
  ¶Pan ni kabi ga haete shimatta yo.
  パンにかびが生えてしまったよ。
  Mold appeared on that bread!

kabin 花瓶 (*flower*)*vase*

kabocha カボチャ *pumpkin; squash*

kābu カーブ ① *curve, bend*
  ¶Kono michi wa kyū na kābu ga ōi desu.
  この道は急なカーブが多いです。
  This road has a lot of sharp curves.
  ② *curve* (-*ball*)
  ¶Pitchā wa kābu o nagemashita.
  ピッチャーはカーブを投げました。
  The pitcher threw a curve.

kabu かぶ *turnip*

kabu 株 *stock* 《i.e., shares in a company》
  • kabu-ken 株券 *stock certificate*
  • kabu-nushi 株主 *stockholder*
  • kabu-shiki 株式 *shares*
  • kabu-shiki-gaisha 株式会社 *joint-stock corporation*
  • -kabu －株《counter for shares of stock; see Appendix 2》

kabúru 被る ① *to put on* 《The direct object of **kaburu** is generally an article of clothing that goes on the head. Compare **kiru** 着る and **haku** 履く. Like other verbs for putting on clothing, **kaburu** in the -**te iru** form can express the meaning *be wearing, have on*.》［⇔**nugu** 脱ぐ］
  ¶Herumetto o kabutta hō ga ii desu.
  ヘルメットをかぶったほうがいいです。
  It would be better to put on a helmet.
  ¶Yukari-chan wa bōshi o kabutte inai yo.
  ゆかりちゃんは帽子をかぶっていないよ。
  Yukari isn't wearing a hat!
  ② *to become covered with*
  ¶Danbōru-bako wa hokori o kabutte imasu.

段ボール箱はほこりをかぶっています。
The cardboard box is covered with dust.

kabuséru 被せる ① *to put on* 《a hat on someone else's head》
  ¶Otōto ni bōshi o kabusemashita.
  弟に帽子をかぶせました。
  I put a hat on my younger brother's head.
  • A ni tsumi o kabuseru Aに罪をかぶせる *to blame a sin ∕ crime on* A 《A is a person.》
  ② *to put as a covering, to put to cover up*
  ¶Shinda kanaria ni tsuchi o kabusemashita.
  死んだカナリアに土をかぶせました。
  I covered the dead canary with earth.

kábuto 兜 *warrior's helmet*

kabutómushi 甲虫 *beetle*

káchi 価値 *value, worth*
  ¶Kono kitte wa hijō ni kachi ga arimasu.
  この切手は非常に価値があります。
  This stamp has great value.
  ¶Ano ie wa amari kachi ga nai desu.
  あの家はあまり価値がないです。
  That house is not worth very much.
  ¶Kono shinamono wa sanzen-en no kachi ga arimasu.
  この品物は 3,000 円の価値があります。
  This item has a value of 3,000 yen.
  ¶Kono hon wa yomu kachi ga aru sō desu.
  この本は読む価値があるそうです。
  They say this book is worth reading.

kachí 勝ち *victory, win* ［⇔**make** 負け］
  ¶Hiroshima no kachi desu.
  広島の勝ちです。
  It's a win for Hiroshima.

kachikoshi 勝ち越し *having more wins than losses*

kachiku 家畜 *domestic animal*

kachō 課長 *section chief*

kadai 課題 ① *assigned topic, assigned theme*
  ② *problem, difficult matter* ［→**mondai** 問題②］

kádan 花壇 *flower bed*

kǎdigan カーディガン *a cardigan*
kādo カード *card* 《made of thin, stiff material》
- bāsudē-kādo バースデーカード *birthday card*
- kurejitto-kādo クレジットカード *credit card*
- Kurisumasu-kādo クリスマスカード *Christmas card*
- kyasshu-kādo キャッシュカード *automatic teller card*

kǎdo 角 *corner* 《When an enclosed or delimited area has a corner, **kado** refers to the outside of the corner.》
¶ Tōri no kado ni ginkō ga arimasu.
通りの角に銀行があります。
There is a bank on the street corner.
¶ Tsugi no kado o sasetsu shite kudasai.
次の角を左折してください。
Please turn left at the next corner.

kaede 楓 *maple* ((tree))

kaerí 帰り *return* (*home*), *returning home*
¶ Haha-oya wa kodomo no kaeri o matte imasu.
母親は子供の帰りを待っています。
The mother is waiting for her child's return.
¶ Chichi wa itsu-mo kaeri ga osoi desu.
父はいつも帰りが遅いです。
My father's return home is always late.
¶ Gakkō no kaeri ni tomodachi no okā-san ni aimashita.
学校の帰りに友達のお母さんに会いました。
I met my friend's mother on my way home from school.
- kaeri-michi 帰り道 *way home*

kaerimíru 顧みる ① *to look back on* 《a past event》
② *to take into consideration, to pay heed to*
③ *to turn around and look at*

kaeru 蛙 *frog*

káeru 帰る{5} *to return home*
¶ Yamamoto-san wa itsu kaeri masu ka.
山本さんはいつ帰りますか
When will Mr. Yamamoto return home?

- kaette kuru 帰ってくる *to come home*
¶ Tomoko-san wa raishū Kanada kara kaette kimasu.
友子さんは来週カナダから帰ってきます。
Tomoko will come home from Canada next week.
- kaette iku 帰っていく *to go home*
¶ Kodomo-tachi wa roku-ji-goro kaette ikimashita.
子供たちは6時ごろ帰っていきました。
The children went home about 6:00.

káeru 返る{5} ① *to return* 《to a place of origin》《The subject is inanimate.》
¶ Senshū dashita tegami ga kaette kimashita.
先週出した手紙が返ってきました。
A letter I mailed last week came back.
② *to return* 《to an earlier state》
- wadai ni kaeru 話題に返る *to return to a topic*
- kodomo ni kaeru 子供に返る *to return to childish behaviour*

káeru 孵る{5} *to hatch* 《The subject may be either an egg or a baby bird.》
¶ Hina ga kaetta yo.
ひながかえったよ。
The chick hatched!

kaeru 変える *to change, to alter* 《transitive》
¶ Watashi-tachi wa sono keikaku o kaemashita.
私たちはその計画を変えました。
We changed that plan.

kaeru 換える, 替える *to exchange, to convert, to replace* [→**kōkan suru** 交換する]
- A o B to kaeru AをBと換える *to exchange A for B*
¶ Kore o eru-saizu to kaete mo ii desu ka.
これをLサイズと換えてもいいですか。
May I exchange this for a size L?
- A o B ni kaeru AをBに替える *to convert A into B*
¶ Kono o-kane o doru ni kaete kudasai.
このお金をドルに替えてください。
Please convert this money into dollars.

káesu 返す *to give back, to return*
¶Sono hon o tosho-kan ni kaeshinasai.
その本を図書館に返しなさい。
Return that book to the library.
¶Sono nōto o ashita kaeshite ne.
そのノートをあした返してね。
Give that notebook back tomorrow, OK?
¶O-kane wa kondo no Getsuyōbi ni
kaeshimasu.
お金は今度の月曜日に返します。
I will return the money next Monday.

káette 却って *on the contrary*

kāférī カーフェリー *car ferry*

kafun 花粉 *pollen*
• kafun-shō 花粉症 *pollinosis, hay fever*

kágaku 化学 *chemistry*
• kagaku-hannō 化学反応 *chemical reaction*
• kagaku-hōteishiki 化学方程式 *chemical equation*
• kagaku-sha 化学者 *chemist*
• kagaku-shiki 化学式 *chemical formula*
• kagaku-teki na 化学的な *chemical, pertaining to chemistry*

kágaku 科学 *science*
• kagaku-gijutsu 科学技術 *technology*
• kagaku-hakubutsukan 科学博物館 *science museum*
• kagaku-sha 科学者 *scientist*
• kagaku-teki na 科学的な *scientific*
• jinbun-kagaku 人文科学 *cultural science*
• shakai-kagaku 社会科学 *social science*
• shizen-kagaku 自然科学 *natural science*

kagamí 鏡 *mirror*

kagamu 屈む *to bend over, to stoop down*
¶Kagande, bōru o hiroimashita.
かがんで、ボールを拾いました。
I bent over and picked up the ball.

kagayakashíi 輝かしい *bright, brilliant*
¶Gaka wa sono sakuhin de kagayakashii meisei o eta.
画家はその作品で輝かしい名声を得た。
The artist gained a brilliant reputation because of that work.

• kagayakashii mirai 輝かしい未来 *bright future*

kagayáku 輝く *to shine (strongly)*
¶Taiyō wa akaruku kagayaite imasu.
太陽は明るく輝いています。
The sun is shining brightly.
¶Hoshi wa yoru kagayakimasu.
星は夜輝きます。
Stars shine at night.
¶Shōnen no kao ga patto kagayakimashita.
少年の顔がぱっと輝きました。
The boy's face suddenly brightened.

káge 陰 ① *shade* «i.e., place where light is blocked»
¶Ano ki no kage ni suwarimashō.
あの木の陰に座りましょう。
Let's sit in the shade of that tree.
② *the area out of sight behind*
¶Kabe no kage ni kakuremashita.
壁の陰に隠れました。
We hid behind the wall.
③ *the area behind a person's back* «figurative»
¶Kage de nani o kossori shite iru no da.
陰で何をこっそりしているのだ。
What are you doing behind my back?

káge 影 ① *shadow*
¶Sono ko wa jibun no kage o kowagatte imasu.
その子は自分の影を怖がっています。
That child is afraid of his own shadow.
② *reflection, reflected image*
¶Kagami ni kao no kage ga utsutte imashita.
鏡に顔の影が映っていました。
My face was reflected in the mirror.
• kage-e 影絵 *shadow picture*

kagen 加減 [☞ii-kagen いい加減]

-kagetsu ーか月 «counter for number of months; see Appendix 2»

kagí 鍵 ① *key* «to a lock»
¶Kore wa omote no doa no kagi desu.
これは表のドアのかぎです。
This is the key to the front door.
• kagi ga kakaru かぎがかかる *a key is used* «on something to lock it»

• kagi o kakeru かぎをかける *to use a key* 《on something to lock it》

¶ Doa ni kagi o kakete kudasai.
ドアにかぎをかけてください。
Please lock the door.

② *key, essential means*

¶ Kore ga mondai o toku kagi desu.
これが問題を解くかぎです。
This is the key to solving the problem.

③ *lock* [→**jō** 錠]

• kagi-ana 鍵穴 *keyhole*
• kagi-kko 鍵っ子 *latchkey child*
• ai-kagi 合い鍵 *duplicate key*

kagiránai 限らない **to wa**～ とは～
《The word **kagiranai** is the negative form of the verb **kagiru** 限る and has the predictable meanings as well.》 *is / are not necessarily* 《following a noun》; *it is not necessarily the case that* 《following a predicate》

¶ Kono gakkō no seito wa yūtōsei to wa kagirimasen.
この学校の生徒は優等生とは限りません。
The students at this school are not necessarily honor students.

¶ Ueda-san wa Nichiyōbi ni itsu-mo uchi ni iru to wa kagirimasen.
上田さんは、日曜日にいつもうちにいるとは限りません。
Mr. Ueda is not necessarily always at home on Sunday.

kágiri 限り ① *limit, bound* [→**gendo** 限度]

¶ Hito no chikara ni wa kagiri ga arimasu.
人の力には限りがあります。
There is a limit to a person's power.

② *to the extent that, as far as, as much as* 《following a predicate》

¶ Watashi no shitte iru kagiri, Michio-san wa kinben desu.
私の知っている限り道夫さんは勤勉です。
As far as I know, Michio is diligent.

¶ Dekiru kagiri tetsudaimashō.
できる限り手伝いましょう。
I'll help you as much as I can.

③ *as long as, provided that* 《following a predicate》

¶ Ame ga furanai kagiri daijōbu desu.
雨が降らない限り大丈夫です。
As long as it doesn't rain, it'll be all right.

kagíru 限る {5} ① *to limit* [→**seigen suru** 制限する]

¶ Supīchi wa jup-pun-kan ni kagirimasu.
スピーチは10分間に限ります。
We will limit the speeches to ten minutes.

• kagitte 限って [☞**ni kagitte** に限って]

② **ni**～ に～ *to be the best* 《following a noun》; *it is best to* 《following a verb in the non-past tense》

¶ Ryokō wa aki ni kagirimasu.
旅行は秋に限ります。
For traveling autumn is the best.

¶ Konna toki wa nigeru ni kagiru yo.
こんなときは逃げるに限るよ。
At a time like this it's best to run away!

kagítte 限って [☞**ni kagitte** に限って]

kago 籠 *basket; (bird-)cage*

• kaimono-kago 買い物籠 *shopping basket*

kagō 化合 *chemical combination*

• kagō suru 化合する *to combine chemically* 《intransitive》
• kagō-butsu 化合物 *(chemical)compound*

kágu 家具 *furniture*

• kagu-ten 家具店 *furniture store*

kagu 嗅ぐ *to smell, to sniff*

¶ Sono hana no nioi o kaide kudasai.
その花のにおいをかいでください。
Please smell the scent of the flower.

kahanshin 下半身 *lower half of a person's body* [⇔**jōhanshin** 上半身]

káhei 貨幣 *money, currency*

kái 会 ① *meeting, gathering* [→**kaigō** 会合]; *party*

¶ Sono kai ni shusseki shimasu.
その会に出席します。
I will attend that meeting.

② *club* [→**kurabu** クラブ]; *association, society* [→**kyōkai** 協会]

• kai ni hairu 会に入る *to join a club;*

to join an association
- kai o nukeru 会を抜ける *to leave a club; to leave an association*
- kangei-kai 歓迎会 *welcome party*
- sōbetsu-kai 送別会 *farewell party*
¶Sotsugyō-sei no sōbetsu-kai wa raishū hirakaremasu.
卒業生の送別会は来週開かれます。
A farewell party for graduates will be held next week.

kái 貝 *shellfish*
- kai-gara 貝殻 *seashell, (shellfish)shell*

kái 回 ① *inning; (boxing)round*
- -kai 一回《counter for innings or rounds; see Appendix 2》
② -kai 一回《counter for number of times; see Appendix 2》[→ -do 一度]
¶Mō ik-kai itte kudasai.
もう1回言ってください。
Please say it one more time.
¶Tsuki ni ni-kai musume kara tayori ga arimasu.
月に2回、娘から便りがあります。
Twice a month there is a letter from my daughter.
¶Kanri-nin ni wa nan-kai aimashita ka.
管理人には何回会いましたか。
How many times did you see the manager?

kái 階 *floor, story* 《of a building》
- ue 〔shita〕 no kai 上〔下〕の階 *the floor above 〔below〕*
- -kai 一階《counter for floor numbers; see Appendix 2》;《counter for number of floors; see Appendix 2》
¶Jimu-sho wa rok-kai ni arimasu.
事務所は6階にあります。
The office is on the sixth floor.
- A-kai-date no A階建ての *A-story, having A floors*
¶Kono biru wa rokujuk-kai-date desu.
このビルは60階建てです。
This building has 60 floors.

kaibáshira 貝柱 *scallop ((shellfish))*

kaibatsu 海抜 *elevation above sea level*
¶Fuji-san wa kaibatsu sanzen-nana-hyaku-nanajūroku-mētoru desu.

富士山は海抜3776メートルです。
Mt. Fuji is 3,776 meters above sea level.

kaibō 解剖 *dissection; autopsy*
- kaibō suru 解剖する *to dissect; to perform an autopsy on*
- kaibō-gaku 解剖学 *(the study of)anatomy*

kaibutsu 怪物 ① *monster, apparition* ② *enigmatic person*

kaichō 会長 *chairperson, president* 《of an association, society, club, etc.》
¶Hirose-kun wa seito-kai no kaichō desu.
広瀬君は生徒会の会長です。
Hirose is president of the student council.

kaichūdéntō 懐中電灯 <US>*flashlight*, <UK>*torch*

kaidan 会談 *talks, conference*
- shunō-kaidan 首脳会談 *summit conference*

kaidan 階段 *stairs, stairway*
- kaidan o noboru 〔oriru〕 階段を上る〔降りる〕 *to go up 〔down〕 the stairs*

kaidō 街道 *highway*

kaien 開演 *beginning of a performance*
¶Kaien wa gogo roku-ji desu.
開演は午後6時です。
The beginning of the performance is 6:00 p.m.

kaifuku 回復 *recovery, restoration*
- kaifuku suru 回復する *to recover* 《transitive or intransitive》
¶Fukui-san wa kenkō o kaifuku shimashita.
福井さんは健康を回復しました。
Mr. Fukui recovered his health.
¶Haha wa byōki kara kaifuku shimashita.
母は病気から回復しました。
My mother has recovered from her sickness.
- tenkō ga kaifuku suru 天候が回復する *the weather improves*

káigai 海外 *overseas, foreign countries*
- kaigai-nyūsu 海外ニュース *foreign news*
- kaigai-ryokō 海外旅行 *overseas travel,*

traveling abroad

¶Tanaka-san wa maitoshi kaigai-ryokō o shimasu.

田中さんは毎年海外旅行をします。

Ms. Tanaka takes a trip overseas every year.

kaigan 海岸 *seashore, seaside; beach; coast*

¶Mai-asa kaigan o sanpo shimasu.

毎朝海岸を散歩します。

I walk along the seashore every morning.

¶Kaigan wa bīchi-parasoru de ippai desu.

海岸はビーチパラソルでいっぱいです。

The beach is full of beach umbrellas.

¶Ishii-san wa natsu-yasumi ni kaigan e ikimasu.

石井さんは夏休みに海岸へ行きます。

Mr. Ishii goes to the seaside for the summer vacation.

• higashi-kaigan 東海岸 *east coast*

• nishi-kaigan 西海岸 *west coast*

káigi 会議 *meeting, conference*

• kaigi-chu no 会議中の *in conference, in a meeting*

¶Toda-san wa ima kaigi-chū desu.

戸田さんは今会議中です。

Mr. Toda is in a meeting now.

• kaigi-shitsu 会議室 *conference room*

• kokusai-kaigi 国際会議 *international conference*

kaigō 会合 *meeting, gathering*

káigun 海軍 *navy*

kaigyō 開業 *starting a business; starting a practice* «in the case of a doctor, lawyer, etc.»

• kaigyō suru 開業する *to start a business; to start a practice*

kaihatsu 開発 *development, exploitation* «for human use»

• kaihatsu suru 開発する *to develop, to exploit*

• kaihatsu-tojō-koku 開発途上国 *developing country*

kaihi 会費 *membership fee, dues; party participation fee*

¶Kyō no pātī no kaihi wa nisen-en desu.

きょうのパーティーの会費は2000円です。

The fee for today's party is 2,000 yen.

kaihō 開放 ～**suru** ～する *to open, to leave open*

¶Sono pūru wa ippan ni kaihō sarete imasu.

そのプールは一般に開放されています。

That pool is open to the general public.

¶Kaihō kinshi

「開放厳禁」《sign on a door》

Keep closed «Literally: *Leaving Open Forbidden*»

kaihō 解放 *liberation*

• kaihō suru 解放する *to liberate, to set free*

¶Heishi-tachi wa horyo o kaihō shimashita.

兵士たちは捕虜を解放しました。

The soldiers set the prisoners free.

¶Yatto shukudai kara kaihō sareta yo.

やっと宿題から解放されたよ。

Finally I was set free from homework!

kaiin 会員 *member* «of an association, society, club, etc.»

• kaiin-shō 会員証 *membership card*

kaijō 会場 *place where a meeting or gathering takes place, meeting hall*

¶Kaijō wa wakai hito-tachi de ippai desu.

会場は若い人たちでいっぱいです。

The meeting hall is full of young people.

kaijō 海上 *the sea (surface)*

¶Kyūmei-bōto wa kaijō o go-jikan mo tadayotte ita.

救命ボートは海上で5時間も漂っていた。

The lifeboat was floating on the sea for five hours.

• kaijō-hoken 海上保険 *marine insurance*

• kaijō-kōtsū 海上交通 *sea traffic*

kaijū 怪獣 *monster, monstrous animal*

• kaijū-eiga 怪獣映画 *monster movie*

kaikai 開会 *opening* «of a meeting, gathering, conference, etc.» [⇔**heikai** 閉会]

• kaikai suru 開会する *to open* «transitive»

• kaikai no ji o noberu 開会の辞を述べる

to give an opening address
- kaikai-shiki 開会式 *opening ceremony*

kaikaku 改革 *reform, improvement*
- kaikaku suru 改革する *to reform, to improve* 《transitive》

kaikan 会館 *assembly hall*

kaikatsu 快活 〜**na** 〜な *cheerful, jovial* [⇔**yūutsu na** 憂鬱な]

kaikei 会計 ① *accounts, accounting* ② *bill, check* 《to pay》
¶Kaikei o o-negai shimasu.
会計をお願いします。《in a restaurant》
Check, please.
- kaikei-gakari 会計係 *accountant, treasurer* 《in an organization》; *cashier* 《in a hotel, restaurant, etc.》
- kaikei-nendo 会計年度 *fiscal year*
- kaikei-shi 会計士 (*professional*) *accountant*

kaiketsu 解決 *solution* 《of a problem》; *settlement* 《of a dispute》
- kaiketsu suru 解決する *to solve, to settle*
¶Keisatsukan wa sono mondai o kaiketsu shimashita.
警察官はその問題を解決しました。
The police officer solved that problem.

kaikisen 回帰線 *tropic*
- Kita-kaikisen 北回帰線 *the Tropic of Cancer*
- Minami-kaikisen 南回帰線 *the Tropic of Capricorn*

káiko 蚕 *silkworm*

Kaikyō 回教 *Islam*

kaikyō 海峡 *strait, channel*
- Igirisu-kaikyō イギリス海峡 *the English Channel*
- Tsugaru-kaikyō 津軽海峡 *the Tsugaru Strait*

kaikyū 階級 ① (*social*)*class* ② *rank* 《in an organization》 [→**chii** 地位]
- chūryū-kaikyū 中流階級 *the middle class*
- jōryū-kaikyū 上流階級 *the upper class*
- rōdō-sha-kaikyū 労働者階級 *the working class*

kaimaku 開幕 *curtain raising; beginning, opening*

kaimono 買い物 *shopping*
¶Depāto e kaimono ni dekakemashita.
デパートへ買い物に出かけました。
I went out at a department store shopping.
¶Kore wa ii kaimono desu.
これはいい買い物です。
This is a good buy. 《Literally: *This is good shopping.*》
- kaimono o suru 買い物をする *to do shopping, to shop*
¶Ginza de sukoshi kaimono o shimashita.
銀座で少し買い物をしました。
I did a little shopping in Ginza.
- kaimono-bukuro 買い物袋 *shopping bag*
- kaimono-kyaku 買い物客 *shopper*

Káin 下院 [[⇔**Jōin** 上院]] *lower house* 《of a legislature》; *the House of Representatives* 《in the United States Congress》; *the House of Commons* 《in the British Parliament》
- Kain-giin 下院議員 *lower-house member*

Kaiōsei 海王星 (*the planet*)*Neptune*

káiri 海里 *nautical mile*
- -kairi 〜海里《*counter for nautical miles; see Appendix 2*》

káiro 回路 (*electrical*)*circuit*

kairyō 改良 *improvement* [→**kaizen** 改善]
- kairyō suru 改良する *to improve* 《transitive》
- hinshu-kairyō 品種改良 *breed improvement*

kairyū 海流 *ocean current*

kaisai 開催 〜**suru** 〜する *to hold* 《an event》
¶Nanajūni-nen no tōki-Orinpikku wa Sapporo de kaisai saremashita.
72年の冬季オリンピックは札幌で開催されました。
The '72 Winter Olympics were held in Sapporo.

kaisan 解散 *break-up, dissolution, dispersing*
• kaisan suru 解散する *to break up, to disperse* «transitive or intransitive»
¶Kai wa gogo ku-ji ni kaisan shimasu.
会は午後9時に解散します。
The meeting will break up at 9:00 p.m.

kaisatsúguchi 改札口 *ticket gate* «in a train station»

kaisei 快晴 *very fine weather*
¶Kyō wa kaisei desu ne.
今日は快晴ですね。
Today it's very fine weather, isn't it.

kaisei 改正 *revision, amendment, improvement*
• kaisei suru 改正する *to revise, to amend, to improve*

kaisen 開戦 *beginning of a war*
• kaisen suru 開戦する *to go to war*

kaisetsu 解説 *explanation, commentary, interpretation*
• kaisetsu suru 解説する *to explain, to comment on, to interpret*
• kaisetsu-sha 解説者 *commentator*
• nyūsu-kaisetsu ニュース解説 *news commentary*
• yakyū-kaisetsu-sha 野球解説者 *baseball commentator*

kaisha 会社 *company, firm*
¶Dochira no kaisha ni tsutomete irasshaimasu ka.
どちらの会社に勤めていらっしゃいますか。
Which company do you work for?
¶Chichi wa basu de kaisha e ikimasu.
父はバスで会社へ行きます。
My father goes to his company by bus.
• kaisha-in 会社員 *office worker, company employee*

káishaku 解釈 *interpretation, construal*
• kaishaku suru 解釈する *to interpret, to construe*

kaishi 開始 *beginning, start*
• kaishi suru 開始する *to begin, to start* «transitive» [→**hajimeru** 始める]

kaishiméru 買い占める *to buy up, to corner the market in*

kaisho 楷書 *block style* «of Japanese calligraphy» [⇔**gyōsho** 行書; **sōsho** 草書]

kaisō 海草 *seaweed*

kaisō 回送 *sending on, forwarding; Out of Service* «when displayed on a bus or train»
• kaisō suru 回送する *to send on, to forward*
¶Yūbin-butsu o kono jūsho ni kaisō shite kudasai.
郵便物をこの住所に回送してください。
Please forward the mail to this address.

kaisō 階層 *social stratum*

kaisoku 快速 *wonderfully high speed*
¶Ressha wa jisoku hyaku-rokujuk-kiro no kaisoku de hashitte iru.
列車は時速160キロの快速で走っている。
The train is going at a high speed of 160 kilometers an hour.
• kaisoku-densha 快速電車 *high-speed train*

kaisū 回数 *the number of times*
¶Yokota-kun no chikoku no kaisū o kazoete kudasai.
横田君の遅刻の回数を数えてください。
Please count the number of times Yokota has been late.
• kaisū-ken 回数券 *coupon ticket*

kaisui 海水 *seawater*
• kaisui-pantsu 海水パンツ *swimming trunks* [→**suiei-pantsu** 水泳パンツ (s.v. **suiei** 水泳)]

kaisúiyoku 海水浴 *swimming in the sea*
¶Kaisuiyoku wa tanoshii desu ne.
海水浴は楽しいですね。
Swimming in the sea is fun, isn't it.
• kaisuiyoku-jō 海水浴場 *swimming beach*

kaitaku 開拓 ① *reclamation, bringing under cultivation*
• kaitaku suru 開拓する *to reclaim, to bring under cultivation*
¶Nōson no hito-tachi wa arechi o kaitaku shimashita.
農村の人たちは荒れ地を開拓しました。
The people of the farming village reclaimed the wasteland.

② *opening up* 《a new place or a new area of endeavor》

• kaitaku suru 開拓する *to open up*
• kaitaku-sha 開拓者 *pioneer, settler*

kaitei 海底 *sea bottom*

• kaitei-kazan 海底火山 *submarine volcano*
• kaitei-tonneru 海底トンネル *undersea tunnel*

kaitei 改訂 *revision* 《of a book, etc.》

• kaitei suru 改訂する *to revise*
• kaitei-ban 改訂版 *revised edition*

kaiteki 快適 ～**na** ～な *comfortable; pleasant* [→**yukai na** 愉快な]

¶Hontō ni kaiteki na ryokō deshita.
ほんとうに快適な旅行でした。
It was a really pleasant trip.

kaiten 回転 *rotation, revolution, turning*

• kaiten suru 回転する *to rotate, to revolve, to turn* [→**mawaru** 回る①]
• kaiten-doa 回転ドア *revolving door*
• kaiten-kyōgi 回転競技 *slalom*
• kaiten-mokuba 回転木馬 *merry-go-round* [→**merīgōraundo** メリーゴーラウンド]

kaiten 開店 [[⇔**heiten** 閉店]]

① *opening* 《of a store, restaurant, etc., for the business day》

• kaiten suru 開店する *to open* 《transitive or intransitive》

¶Sono hon-ya wa gozen ku-ji ni kaiten shimasu.
その本屋は午前9時に開店します。
That bookstore opens at 9:00 a.m.

② *opening* 《of a newly established store, restaurant, etc.》

• kaiten suru 開店する *to open* 《transitive or intransitive》

kaitō 解答 *answer, solution* 《to a test question or study problem》

• tadashii kaitō 正しい解答 *right answer, right solution*
• machigatta kaitō まちがった解答 *wrong answer, wrong solution*
• kaitō suru 解答する *to answer, to solve*

kaitsū 開通 *opening to traffic*

• kaitsū suru 開通する *to be opened to traffic*

¶Kono tonneru wa San-gatsu ni kaitsū shimasu.
このトンネルは3月に開通します。
This tunnel will be opened to traffic in March.

• kaitsū-shiki 開通式 *opening ceremony*

kaiwa 会話 *conversation*

• kaiwa suru 会話する *to converse, to have a conversation*

¶Gaijin to Eigo de kaiwa shita koto ga arimasu ka.
外人と英語で会話したことがありますか。
Have you ever had a conversation with a foreigner in English?

• Ei-kaiwa 英会話 *English conversation*

kaizen 改善 *improvement*

• kaizen suru 改善する *to improve* 《transitive》

¶Sakurai-san wa seikatsu o kaizen shiyō to shimashita.
桜井さんは生活を改善しようとしました。
Mr. Sakurai tried to improve his life.

kaizoku 海賊 *pirate*

• kaizoku-sen 海賊船 *pirate ship*

káji 舵 *rudder*

• kaji o toru かじを取る *to take the rudder, to steer*

káji 火事 (*destructive*)*fire*

¶Uchi no chikaku de kaji ga arimashita.
うちの近くで火事がありました。
There was a fire near my house.

¶Ano biru wa kaji da yo.
あのビルは火事だよ。
That building is on fire!

¶Kaji wa ma-mo-naku kiemashita.
火事はまもなく消えました。
The fire soon went out.

káji 家事 *housework*

kájino カジノ *casino*

kajíru かじる {5} *to bite, to gnaw on, to nibble on*

¶Nezumi ga hako o kajitte ana o aketa.
ねずみが箱をかじって穴をあけた。
The rat gnawled a hole in the box.

kajō 過剰 *an excess, a surplus*

kakaeru 抱える *to hold* 《under one arm or in both arms》
• kowaki ni kakaeru 小わきに抱える *to hold under one's arm*
¶Sono gakusei wa jisho o kowaki ni kakaete imasu.
その学生は辞書を小わきに抱えています。
That student is holding a dictionary under her arm.

kakageru 掲げる ① *to put up, to hoist, to post* 《so that people will notice》
② *to carry, to print* 《in a newspaper, magazine, etc.》

kakaku 価格 *price* [→**nedan** 値段]
• kakaku-chōsei 価格調整 *price adjustment*
• kakaku-suijun 価格水準 *price level*

kakarichō 係長 *chief clerk*

kakariin 係員 *clerk in charge, attendant*

kakáru 掛かる ① *to hang, to be suspended*
¶Kabe ni e ga kakatte imasu.
壁に絵がかかっています。
A picture is hanging on the wall.
② *to take, to require, to cost*
¶Eki made aruite jup-pun-gurai kakarimasu.
駅まで歩いて10分ぐらいかかります。
It takes about 10 minutes to the station on foot.
¶Sono ryokō wa totemo o-kane ga kakaru deshō.
その旅行はとてもお金がかかるでしょう。
That trip will probably cost a lot of money.
③ *to fall on, to be put on* 《The subject is a liquid or powder.》
¶Ichigo ni kurīmu ga kakatte imasu.
いちごにクリームがかかっています。
There's cream on the strawberries.
¶Sore ni ame ga kakaranai yō ni shinasai.
それに雨がかからないようにしなさい。
Make sure the rain does not fall on that.
④ *to come to depend, to become contingent*
¶Kono shigoto wa Akatsuka-kun no shuwan ni kakatte iru.
この仕事は赤塚君の手腕にかかっている。
This job depends on Akatsuka's ability.
⑤ *to start to run* 《The subject is a machine.》
• enjin ga kakaru エンジンがかかる *an engine starts*
⑥ isha ni〜 医者に〜 *to consult a doctor*
¶Sugu isha ni kakaranakereba ikemasen.
すぐ医者にかからなければいけません。
You must consult a doctor right away.
⑦ kagi ga〜 かぎが〜 *a key is used* 《on something to lock it》
¶Doa ni kagi ga kakatte imasu.
ドアにかぎがかかっています。
The door is locked.
⑧ denwa ga〜 電話が〜 *a telephone call arrives*
¶O-rusu ni Keiko-san kara no denwa ga kakatte kimashita.
お留守に恵子さんからの電話がかかってきました。
A telephone call came from Keiko while you were out.

kakáru 架かる *to be built* 《so as to span something from one side to the other》
¶Koko ni hashi ga kakarimasu.
ここに橋が架かります。
A bridge is going to be built here.

kakáru 罹る *to fall victim* 《to an illness》
¶Sono akachan wa hashika ni kakatte imasu.
その赤ちゃんははしかにかかっています。
That baby has caught measles.

kakashi かかし *scarecrow*

kakato 踵 ① *heel* 《of a foot》
② *heel* 《of a shoe》
¶Hayashi-san wa kakato no hikui kutsu o haite imasu.
林さんはかかとの低い靴をはいています。
Ms. Hayashi is wearing low-heeled shoes.

kakawárazu かかわらず [☞**ni kakawarazu** にかかわらず; **ni mo kakawarazu** にもかかわらず]

kaké 賭 *bet*

¶Sono kake ni katsu deshō.

そのかけに勝つでしょう。

I will probably win that bet.

• kake-goto 賭事 *wagering, gambling*

kakéashi 駆け足 *running* 《done by a person or animal》

¶Hirano-san wa kakeashi de yatte kimashita.

平野さんは駆け足でやってきました。

Mr. Hirano came running.

kakebúton 掛け布団 *upper futon, quilt-type futon* 《The word **futon** 布団 refers to traditional Japanese bedding, which is folded up an put in closets during the day and laid out on the floor at night.》［⇔**shikibuton** 敷布団］

kakegóe 掛け声 *shout of encouragment; cheer*

• kakegoe o kakeru 掛け声をかける *to shout encouragingly; to cheer*

¶Kodomo-tachi wa "yoisho" to kakegoe o kakemashita

子供たちは「よいしょ」と掛け声をかけました。

The children shouted, "Heave-ho!"

kakei 家計 *household accounts, family budget*

• kakei-bo 家計簿 *household account book*

kakera 欠片 *broken piece, fragment, crumb*

kakeru 欠ける ① *to become partially broken, to become chipped*

¶Chawan ga kakete iru yo.

茶わんが欠けているよ。

The teacup is chipped!

② *to become lacking, to become insufficient* ［→**fusoku suru** 不足する］

¶Otōto ni wa yūki ga kakete imasu.

弟には勇気が欠けている。

Courage is lacking in my younger brother.

③ *to wane* 《when the subject is the moon》

kakéru 掛ける ① *to hang, to suspend* ［→**tsurusu** 吊す］

¶Uwagi o yōfuku-kake ni kakete kudasai.

上着を洋服掛けにかけてください。

Please hang your coat on the hook.

• megane o kakeru 眼鏡をかける *to put on glasses* 《In the **-te iru** form, this expression can mean *be wearing glasses, have glasses on.*》

¶Kyōko-san wa megane o kakete imasu.

京子さんは眼鏡をかけています。

Kyoko is wearing glasses.

② *to put as a covering*

• A ni B o kakeru AにBを掛ける *to put B on A as a covering, to cover A with B*

¶Tēburu ni tēburu-kake o kakete kudasai.

テーブルにテーブル掛けをかけてください。

Please put a tablecloth on the table.

③ *to sit* 《Used only for sitting on a chair, etc., not for sitting on the floor.》 ［→**koshikakeru** 腰掛ける］

¶Dōzo kakete kudasai.

どうぞかけてください。

Please sit down.

④ *to start* 《a machine》

• enjin o kakeru エンジンをかける *to start an engine*

⑤ *to spend, to expend* ［→**tsuiyasu** 費やす］

¶Ane wa kiru mono ni o-kane o kakemasu.

姉は着る物にお金をかけます。

My older sister spends money on things to wear.

⑥ *to multiply* 《in arithmetic》

¶Ni ni yon o kakaeru to, hachi ni naru deshō?

2に4をかけると、8になるでしょう？

When you multiply 4 times 2, it's 8, right?

¶San kakeru go wa jūgo.

3かける5は15。

3 times 5 is 15. 《Although odd grammatically, this kind of sentence is a typical way of stating a fact of arithmetic.》

⑦ *to pour, to sprinkle*

¶Sore ni sōsu o kakete kudasai.

それにソースをかけてください。

Please pour sauce on that.

⑧ **kagi o**～ かぎを～ *to use a key* 《on something to lock it》

¶Doa ni kagi o kakete kudasai.

ドアにかぎをかけてください。

Please lock the door.

⑨ **denwa o**～ 電話を～ *to make a telephone call, to telephone*

¶Konban denwa o kakete kudasai.

今晩電話をかけてください。

Please telephone tonight.

kakéru 架ける *to build* 《so as to span something from one side to the other》

¶Sono kawa ni atarashii hashi o kakemashita.

その川に新しい橋を架けました。

They built a new bridge over that river.

kakéru 駆ける *to run* 《The subject is a person or animal.》[→**hashiru** 走る①]

¶Densha ni noru noni isoide kakemashita.

電車に乗るのに急いで駆けました。

I ran hurriedly to board the train.

kakéru 賭ける *to bet, to wager*

¶Chichi wa sono rēsu ni gosen-en kakemashita.

父はそのレースに5000円かけました。

My father bet 5,000 yen on that race.

• inochi o kakeru 命をかける *to stake one's life, to risk one's life*

kákete かけて [☞**ni kakete** にかけて]

kakézan 掛け算 *multiplication* 《in arithmetic》[⇔**warizan** 割り算]

• kakezan o suru 掛け算をする *to multiply* [→**kakeru** 掛ける⑥]; *to do multiplication*

kaki 柿 *persimmon*

káki 夏季 *summertime, the summer season* [⇔**tōki** 冬季]

• kaki-Orinpikku 夏季オリンピック *the Summer Olympics*

káki 夏期 *summer, the period during summer*

• kaki-kyūka 夏期休暇 *summer vacation, <UK>summer holidays*

• kaki-kōshū 夏期講習 *summer course, summer school*

káki 牡蛎 *oyster*

• kaki-furai かきフライ *deep-fried oysters*

• nama-gaki 生がき *raw oyster*

kakimawasu 掻き回す ① *to stir* 《transitive》

¶Makiko-san wa kōcha o supūn de kakimawashite imasu.

真紀子さんは紅茶をスプーンでかき回しています。

Makiko is stirring her tea with a spoon.

② *to rummage through* 《with one's hands》

③ *to throw into confusion, to disrupt* [→**midasu** 乱す]

kakinaosu 書き直す *to rewrite*

kakíne 垣根 *fence; hedge*

kakitome 書留 *registered mail*

¶Kono tegami o kakitome de dashite kudasai.

この手紙を書留で出してください。

Please send this letter by registered mail.

• tegami o kakitome ni suru 手紙を書留にする *to register a letter*

• kakitome-ryō 書留料 *registered mail fee*

kakitori 書き取り *writing down* 《what is said》

kakitoru 書き取る *to write down* 《what is said》

kakki 活気 *liveliness, vigor, spirit*

¶Kono machi wa kakki ga arimasu.

この町は活気があります。

This town is lively.

kakkiteki 画期的 ～**na** ～な *epoch-making*

kákko 括弧 *parentheses*

¶Sono sūji o kakko de kakominasai.

その数字をかっこで囲みなさい。

Enclose that number in parentheses.

• kaku-kakko 角括弧 *square brackets*

• nijū-kakko 二重括弧 *double parentheses*

kakko 格好 【COL. for **kakkō** 格好】

• kakko-ii 格好いい *stylish, chic; impressive, attractive, cool*

¶Kono kōto wa kakko-ii ne.

このコートは格好いいね。

This coat is stylish, isn't it.

• kakko-warui 格好悪い *unstylish, unchic; wretched, unattractive, uncool*
¶Sonna koto o suru no wa kakko-warui yo.
そんなことをするのは格好悪いよ。
Doing such a thing is uncool!

kakkō 格好 ① *shape, form, appearance* [→**sugata** 姿]
  ② *garb, dress, attire* [→**minari** 身なり]
¶Kono gakkō no seito wa minna hen na kakkō o shite imasu.
この学校の生徒はみんな変な格好をしています。
The students at this school all wear weird clothes.
  ③ ～**na** ～な *suitable, appropriate* [→**tekitō na** 適当な]
• kakkō na nedan 格好な値段 *reasonable price*

kákkō 郭公 *cuckoo*

káko 過去 ① *the past*
¶Kako no higeki o wasuremashō.
過去の悲劇を忘れましょう。
Let's forget the tragedies of the past.
  ② *for the past, during the past* 《preceding a word specifying a length of time》
¶Kako san-nen-kan kesseki shita koto ga nai yo.
過去3年間欠席したことがないよ。
I have not been absent during the past three years!
• kako-kei 過去形 *past-tense form*

kakō 加工 *manufacturing; processing, treatment*
• kakō suru 加工する *to manufacture; to process, to treat*
• kakō-shokuhin 加工食品 *processed food*

kakoi 囲い *enclosing wall; fence* [→**saku** 柵]

kakomu 囲む *to surround, to encircle, to enclose*
¶Nihon wa umi ni kakomarete imasu.
日本は海に囲まれています。
Japan is surrounded by sea.
¶Watashi-tachi wa hi o kakonde

suwarimashita.
私たちは火を囲んで座りました。
We sat down around the fire. 《Literally: We encircled the fire and sat down.》

káku 角 *(geometric)angle*
• chok-kaku 直角 *right angle*
• don-kaku 鈍角 *obtuse angle*
• ei-kaku 鋭角 *acute angle*

káku 核 *nucleus; kernel; core*
• kaku-heiki 核兵器 *nuclear weapon*
• kaku-hoyū-koku 核保有国 *country with nuclear weapons*
• kaku-jikken 核実験 *nuclear test*
• kaku-kazoku 核家族 *nuclear family*
• kaku-sensō 核戦争 *nuclear war*

kaku 欠く ① *to lack*
¶Kyōju wa jōshiki o kaite imasu.
教授は常識を欠いています。
The professor lacks common sense.
  ② *to break a piece off, to chip*
• kōri o kaku 氷を欠く *to chip ice*
• sara o kaku 皿を欠く *to chip a dish*
• ha o kaku 歯を欠く *to chip a tooth*

káku 書く *to write*
¶Kotae wa enpitsu de kakinasai.
答えは鉛筆で書きなさい。
Write your answers with a pencil.
¶Konban kazoku ni tegami o kakimasu.
今晩家族に手紙を書きます。
I'm going to write a letter to my family tonight.

káku 描く *to draw; to paint*
¶Chizu o kaite agemashō.
地図をかいてあげましょう。
I'll draw you a map.
¶Ano hito wa abura-e o kaite imasu.
あの人は油絵をかいています。
That person is painting an oil painting.

káku 掻く *to scratch* 《The subject is animate.》
¶Tsume de atama o kakimashita.
つめで頭をかきました。
I scratched my head with my fingernails.

kaku- 各― *each, every* 《Added to noun bases.》
• kaku-kyōshitsu 各教室 *each classroom*

kakū 架空 ～**no** ～の *imaginary*

- kakū no jinbutsu 架空の人物 *imaginary character, fictional person*

kakudai 拡大 *magnification; expansion, extension*

- kakudai suru 拡大する *to magnify; to expand, to extend* 《transitive or intransitive》

¶Kono chizu o go-bai ni kakudai shite kudasai.
この地図を5倍に拡大してください。
Please magnify this map five times.

- kakudai-kyō 拡大鏡 *magnifying glass* [→**mushimegane** 虫眼鏡]

kákudo 角度 ① *(the size of an)angle*

- kakudo o hakaru 角度を測る *to measure an angle*
- kyūjū-do no kakudo 90度の角度 *90-degree angle*

② *angle, viewpoint*

¶Watashi-tachi wa sono mondai o samazama na kakudo kara kōsatsu shimashita.
私たちはその問題をさまざまな角度から考察しました。
We viewed that problem from different angles.

kakuekitéisha 各駅停車 *train which stops at every station*

¶Kono densha wa kakuekiteisha desu ka.
この電車は各駅停車ですか。
Is this a train that stops at every station?

kakugen 格言 *proverb, adage, maxim* [→**kotowaza** 諺]

kákugo 覚悟 *resignation* 《to what may happen》, *preparation* 《to accept an undesirable outcome》

- kakugo suru 覚悟する *to resign oneself to, to prepare for*

¶Shippai wa kakugo shite imasu.
失敗は覚悟しています。
I am resigned to failure.

kakujitsu 確実 ~na ~な *sure, certain, beyond doubt* [→**tashika na** 確かな]

¶Miyamoto-san ga kuru no wa kakujitsu desu.
宮本さんが来るのは確実です。
It is certain that Mr. Miyamoto

will come.

kakumei 革命 *revolution, revolutional upheaval*

- kakumei-ka 革命家 *a revolutionary*
- Furansu-kakumei フランス革命 *the French Revolution*
- Sangyō-kakumei 産業革命 *the Industrial Revolution*

kakunin 確認 *confirmation, verification*

- kakunin suru 確認する *to confirm, to verify*

kakurénbō かくれんぼう *hide-and-seek*

- kakurenbō o suru かくれんぼうをする *to play hide-and-seek*

kakuréru 隠れる *to hide, to conceal oneself*

¶Doko ni kakurete iru no?
どこに隠れているの？
Where are you hiding?

¶Oshiire no naka ni kakuremashita.
押し入れの中に隠れました。
I hid in the closet.

- kakureta sainō 隠れた才能 *hidden talent*

kakuryō 閣僚 *cabinet minister*

kakuséizai 覚醒剤 *amphetamine, pep pill*

kakushin 確信 *conviction, certainty, confidence*

- kakushin suru 確信する *to become certain of, to come to really believe*

¶Otto ga muzai da to kakushin shite imasu.
夫が無罪だと確信しています。
I really believe that my husband is innocent.

kakúsu 隠す *to hide, to conceal*

¶O-kane o doko ni kakushita no?
お金をどこに隠したの？
Where did you hide the money?

¶Kono keikaku wa Akira ni wa kakushite oite kudasai.
この計画は明には隠しておいてください。
Please conceal this plan from Akira.

kákuteru カクテル *cocktail*

kakutoku 獲得 *acquisition*

- kakutoku suru 獲得する *to acquire,*

to obtain [→**eru** 得る]

kakyū 下級 *low class, low grade* [⇔**jō-kyū** 上級]
- kakyū-sei 下級生 *student in one of the lower grades,* <*US*>*underclassman*

kama 釜 *kettle, cauldron*

kama 窯 *kiln; oven; furnace*

káma 鎌 *sickle*

kamaboko かまぼこ *steamed fish paste* 《*a popular Japanese food typically formed into a semicylinder on a small board for sale*》

kámakiri かまきり *(praying)mantis*

kamáu 構う *to mind, to care, to concern oneself*
¶Chichi wa fukusō ni wa kamaimasen.
父は服装には構いません。
My father doesn't care about his attire.
- kamawanai 構わない *I don't mind, it's all right* 《This word is the negative form of **kamau** and has the predictable meanings as well. Following a clause that ends in a gerund (-te form)optionally followed by **mo** も, a negative form of **kamau** expresses permission or approval. Translations into English ordinarily use *may* rather than *all right even if* and *do not have to* rather than *all right even if not.*》
¶Koko ni suwatte mo kamaimasen.
ここに座っても構いません
You may sit down here.

káme 亀 *turtle; tortoise*

kamen 仮面 *mask, false face*
- kamen o kaburu 仮面をかぶる *to put on a mask*

kámera カメラ *camera*
- kamera no shattā o osu カメラのシャッターを押す *to press a camera's shutter (button), to take a picture with a camera*
- kamera-man カメラマン *photographer* [→**shashin-ka** 写真家 (s.v. **shashin** 写真)]; *camera operator* 《*for television, movies, etc.*》
- ichigan-refu-kamera 1眼レフカメラ *single-lens reflex camera*

kameréon カメレオン *chameleon*

kámi 神 *god; God*
¶Kami o shinjimasu ka.
神を信じますか。
Do you believe in God?
¶Kami ni inorimashō.
神に祈りましょう。
Let's pray to God.
- kami-dana 神棚 *household Shinto altar*

kamí 紙 *paper*
¶Kami o ichi-mai kudasai.
紙を1枚ください。
Give me one sheet of paper.
- kami-bukuro 紙袋 *paper bag*
- kami-kuzu 紙屑 *wastepaper*
- kami-taoru 紙タオル *paper towel*
- kami-yasuri 紙やすり *sandpaper*

kamí 髪 *hair* 《*on a person's head*》
¶Yōko-san wa nagaku utsukushii kami o shite imasu.
洋子さんは長く美しい髪をしています。
Yoko has long beautiful hair.
¶Kami o setto shite moraimashita.
髪をセットしてもらいました。
I had my hair set.

kaminári 雷 ① *thunder*
¶Tōku de kaminari no oto ga shimashita.
遠くで雷の音がしました。
In the distance there was the sound of thunder.
- kaminari ga naru 雷が鳴る *thunder sounds*
② *lightning* [→**inazuma** 稲妻]
- kaminari ga A ni ochiru 雷がAに落ちる *lightning strikes A*
¶Kaminari ga sono ki ni ochita yo.
雷がその木に落ちたよ。
Lightning struck that tree!

kami-nó-ke 髪の毛 *hair (on a person's head)* [→**kami** 髪]

kamisorí 剃刀 *razor*
- kamisori no ha かみそりの刃 *razor blade*
- denki-kamisori 電気剃刀 *electric razor*

kámo 鴨 *wild duck*

kamoku 科目 *(school)subject* [→**gakka** 学科]

• hisshū-kamoku 必修科目 *required subject*

• sentaku-kamoku 選択科目 *elective subject*

kamome 鷗 *sea gull*

kamoshika かもしか *antelope*

ká-mo-shirenai かも知れない *it may be that, it might be that* 《This expression generally follows an informal-style predicate, but the word preceding **ka-mo-shirenai** cannot be the copula form **da** だ. When **ka-mo-shirenai** is added to a clause that would end with **da**, the **da** does not appear.》

¶Ichirō-san wa kyō wa konai ka-mo-shiremasen.

一郎さんはきょうは来ないかもしれません。

Ichiro might not come today.

¶Sore wa hontō ka-mo-shirenai.

それはほんとうかもしれない。

That may be true.

kámotsu 貨物 *freight,* <*UK*>*goods*

• kamotsu-ressha 貨物列車 *freight train,* <*UK*>*goods train*

• kamotsu-sen 貨物船 *freighter (ship)*

kámu 嚙む ① *to chew*

¶Tabemono wa yoku kaminasai.

食べ物はよくかみなさい。

Chew your food well.

② *to bite*

¶Inu wa kodomo no ashi o kamimashita.

犬は子供の足をかみました。

The dog bit the child's leg.

kamufurāju カムフラージュ *camouflage*

• kamufurāju suru カムフラージュする *to camouflage*

kán 缶 <*US*>*can,* <*UK*>*tin* ((container))

• kan-bīru 缶ビール *canned beer*

• kan-jūsu 缶ジュース *canned juice*

• kan-kiri 缶切り <*US*>*can opener,* <*UK*>*tin opener*

kan 勘 *intuition, perceptiveness*

• kan ga ii 勘がいい *one's intuition is good*

kán 管 *pipe, tube* [→kuda 管]

• shiken-kan 試験管 *test tube*

• suidō-kan 水道管 *water pipe*

-kan －感 *feeling, sense* 《Added to noun bases.》

• kōfuku-kan 幸福感 *feeling of happiness*

• sekinin-kan 責任感 *sense of responsibility*

kán 巻 *volume (in a set of books)*

• -kan －巻《counter for volumes; see Appendix 2》

• dai-san-kan 第3巻 *the third volume, vol. 3*

• zen-san-kan no 全3巻の *three-volume*

-kan －間 ① *period, interval (of time)* 《Added optionally to numbers referring to time spans.》

¶Ame ga mikka-kan furimashita.

雨が3日間降りました。

It rained for three days.

② *the area between* 《Added to noun bases denoting two or more places. The base often consists of a combination of the names of two places.》

¶Ueno-Sendai-kan ni eki wa ikutsu arimasu ka.

上野—仙台間に駅はいくつありますか。

How many stations are there between Ueno and Sendai?

③ *relation between／among* 《Added to noun bases denoting two or more entities.》

• kokka-kan no kyōtei 国家間の協定 *pact among nations*

kana 仮名 *kana* 《This term refers to Japanese syllabic writing in general and covers both **hiragana** and **katakana**.》

• kana-zukai 仮名遣い *kana spelling*

kanabō 金棒 *metal rod*

kanagu 金具 *metal fittings, metal parts*

kánai 家内 *wife* 《This word is used only to refer to one's own wife or to refer to oneself as a person's wife.》

kaname 要 ① *pivot, rivet* 《holding a folding fan together》

② *key point, most important point*

kanamono 金物 *hardware*

• kanamono-ya 金物屋 *hardware store;*

hardware dealer

kanarazu 必ず *surely, certainly, without fail* [→**kitto** きっと]; *always* [→**tsune ni** 常に]

¶Kanarazu kuru yo.

必ず来るよ。

I will certainly come!

¶Ikeda-san wa kanarazu seikō suru to shinjite imasu.

池田さんは必ず成功すると信じています。

Mr. Ikeda believes that he will surely succeed.

¶Shokuji no mae ni wa kanarazu te o araimasu.

食事の前にはかならず手を洗います。

I always wash my hands before meals.

kanarazú-shimo 必ずしも 〈*not*〉 *necessarily,* 〈*not*〉 *always*

《Always occurs in combination with a negative predicate.》

¶Nihon-jin wa kanarazu-shimo unagi ga suki na wake de wa arimasen.

日本人は必ずしもうなぎが好きなわけではありません。

A Japanese person doesn't necessarily like eel.

kánari かなり *pretty, rather, quite, quite a lot*

¶Aki-san wa Eigo o kanari umaku hanashimasu.

亜紀さんは英語をかなりうまく話します。

Aki speaks English fairly well.

¶Tenkō wa kanari atsukatta desu.

気候はかなり暑かったです。

The weather was quite hot.

•kanari no かなりの *considerable, fair*

¶Kanari no kingaku deshita.

かなりの金額でした。

It was a considerable sum of money.

kanaria カナリア *canary*

kanashii 悲しい *sad, sorrowful* 《This adjective is ordinarily restricted to describing the speaker's sadness. To describe another person's (apparent)sadness requires a form such as **kanashi-sō** (below).》 [⇔ **ureshii** 嬉しい]

•kanashii koto ni 悲しいことに *sadly,*

unfortunately

¶Kanashii koto ni sono hanashi wa hontō desu.

悲しいことにその話はほんとうです。

Sadly, that story is true.

•kanashi-sō na 悲しそうな *sad-looking, sad-seeming*

¶Sono toki Akiko wa totemo kanashi-sō deshita.

そのとき明子はとても悲しそうでした。

Akiko looked very sad then.

kanashimi 悲しみ *sorrow, sadness*

¶Haha no kanashimi wa fukai desu.

母の悲しみは深いです。

My mother's sorrow is deep.

kanashímu 悲しむ *to come to feel sad, to become saddened*

¶Sono shirase o kiite kanashimimashita.

その知らせを聞いて悲しみました。

I heard that news and felt sad.

¶Tamura-san wa fukaku kanashinde imasu.

田村さんは深く悲しんでいます。

Ms. Tamura is deeply saddened.

kanatoko 金床 *anvil*

kanáu 敵う *to be a match, to equal* [→**hitteki suru** 匹敵する]

¶Suiei de wa Yamamoto-san ni kanau mono wa imasen.

水泳では山本さんにかなう者はいません。

In swimming, there's no one who is a match for Yamamoto.

kanáu 適う *to be suitable, to accord, to match*

•mokuteki ni kanau 目的にかなう *to suit the purpose*

kanáu 叶う *to come true, to be fulfilled*

¶Sono yume ga kanatta yo.

その夢がかなったよ。

That dream came true!

kanazúchi 金槌 ① *hammer*

② *person who cannot swim*

¶Boku wa kanazuchi desu.

僕は金づちです。

I can't swim.

kanban 看板 (*storefront*)*sign, signboard*

kánbasu カンバス *a canvas* «for an oil painting»

kánben 勘弁 ～**suru** ～する *to forgive, to pardon* [→**yurusu** 許す②]

kanbun 漢文 *classical Chinese writings; writings by Japanese in classical Chinese*

kánbyō 看病 *nursing* «a sick person»
• kanbyō suru 看病する *to nurse*
¶Sachiko-san wa byōki no okāsan o kanbyō shimashita.
幸子さんは病気のお母さんを看病しました。
Sachiko nursed her sick mother.

kanchígai 勘違い *misunderstanding, misapprehension*
• kanchigai suru 勘違いする *to misunderstand, to mistake*
¶Sensei wa watashi o ane to kanchigai shimashita.
先生は私を姉と勘違いしました。
The teacher mistook me for my older sister.

kandai 寛大 ～**na** ～な *generous; magnanimous*
¶Hoshino-san wa yūjin ni kandai desu.
星野さんは友人に寛大です。
Mr. Hoshino is generous to his friends.

kandō 感動 *deep emotion, emotional impression* [→**kangeki** 感激]
• kandō suru 感動する *to be moved, to be impressed*
¶Sono hanashi ni wa fukaku kandō shimashita.
その話には深く感動しました。
I was deeply moved by that story.
• kandō-teki na 感動的な *moving, impressive*

kane 金 ① *money* [☞**o-kane** お金]
¶Toki wa kane nari.
時は金なり。《proverb》
Time is money.
② *metal* [→**kinzoku** 金属]

kane 鐘 *bell* «of the type that hangs in a bell tower, etc.»
• kane o narasu 鐘を鳴らす *to ring a bell*
• kane ga naru 鐘が鳴る *a bell rings*

kanemóchi 金持ち *rich person*

¶Kanemochi ga kanarazu-shimo kōfuku to wa kagirimasen.
金持ちが必ずしも幸福とは限りません。
Rich people are not necessarily happy.
• kanemochi no 金持ちの *rich* [⇔**binbō na** 貧乏な]
¶Jirō-san wa kanemochi no katei ni umaremashita.
次郎さんは金持ちの家庭に生まれました。
Jiro was born into a rich family.

kānéshon カーネーション *carnation*

kangáe 考え ① *thought, thinking* [→**shikō** 思考]
¶Kimura-san wa kangae ni fukette imasu.
木村さんは考えにふけっています。
Ms. Kimura is lost in thought.
② *idea*
¶Sumida-san wa ii kangae o omoitsuku hito desu.
隅田さんはいい考えを思いつく人です。
Mr. Sumida is a person who thinks of good ideas.
③ *opinion* [→**iken** 意見]
¶Watashi no kangae de wa, kono hito ga warui no de wa arimasen.
私の考えでは、この人が悪いのではありません。
In my opinion, this man is not to blame.
④ *intention* [→**ito** 意図]
¶Kaigai-ryokō o suru kangae wa arimasen.
海外旅行をする考えはありません。
I have no intention of taking a trip abroad.

kangaenaósu 考え直す *to reconsider*
¶Sono kesshin o kangaenaoshita hō ga ii desu.
その決心を考え直したほうがいいです。
It would be better to reconsider that resolution.

kangaéru 考える ① *to think, to have the idea* [→**omou** 思う]
¶Watashi wa sō wa kangaemasen.
私はそうは考えません。
I don't think so.
¶Sore ni tsuite wa dō kangaemasu ka.

それについてはどう考えますか。
What do you think about that?
¶Kono natsu Yōroppa ni ikō to kangaete imasu.
この夏ヨーロッパに行こうと考えています。
I'm thinking of going to Europe this summer.
¶Nomura-sensei wa minna ga kangaeru yō na ii isha ja nai yo.
野村先生はみんなが考えるようないい医者じゃないよ。
Dr. Nomura is not the good doctor everyone thinks he is!
② *to think about, to consider*
¶Sono mondai o yoku kangaete kudasai.
その問題をよく考えてください。
Please think about that problem carefully.

kangárū カンガルー *kangaroo*

kangei 歓迎 *a welcome*
• kangei suru 歓迎する *to welcome*
¶Mura-bito wa watashi o kangei shite kuremashita.
村人は私を歓迎してくれました。
The villagers welcomed me.
• kangei-kai 歓迎会 *welcome party*

kangeki 感激 *deep emotion, emotional impression* [→**kandō** 感動]
• kangeki suru 感激する *to be deeply moved, to be touched*
¶Tomodachi no seien ni totemo kangeki shimashita.
友達の声援にとても感激しました。
I was deeply moved by the cheers of my friends.

kangéngaku 管弦楽 *orchestral music*
• kangengaku-dan 管弦楽団 *orchestra*

kango 漢語 *word of Chinese origin* [⇔ **gairaigo** 外来語; **wago** 和語]

kangófu 看護婦 *(female)nurse*

kani 蟹 *crab* ((animal))

kánibaru カーニバル *carnival*

kanja 患者 *(medical)patient*

kanji 感じ ① *sensation, feeling* «ascribed to the perceiver»
• sabishii kanji 寂しい感じ *a lonely feeling*

• kanji ga suru 感じがする *to have a feeling* «Always preceded by a modifier.»
¶Nani-ka ga okori-sō na kanji ga shimasu.
何かが起こりそうな感じがします。
I have a feeling that something is going to happen.
② *impression, feeling* «ascribed to what induces the feeling in the perceiver» [→ **inshō** 印象]
• kanji ga suru 感じがする *to give a feeling, to feel* «Always preceded by a modifier.»
• kanji ga ii 感じがいい *giving a good impression, appealing, pleasant*
¶Yumi-chan wa totemo kanji no ii ko desu yo.
由美ちゃんはとても感じのいい子ですよ。
Yumi is a very pleasant child!
• kanji ga warui 感じが悪い *giving a bad impression, unappealing, unpleasant*

kanji 漢字 *Chinese character, kanji*

kanjin 肝心 ～**na** ～な *important* [→ **jūyō na** 重要な]; *essential* [→**hitsuyō na** 必要な]
¶Yoku nemuru koto ga kanjin desu.
よく眠ることが肝心です。
Sleeping well is essential.

kanjiru 感じる *to feel, to sense*
¶Haru ga chikai no o kanjimasu.
春が近いのを感じます。
I feel that spring is near.
¶Namida ga koboreru no o kanjimashita.
涙がこぼれるのを感じました。
I felt tears overflowing.
¶Itami wa kanjimasen.
痛みは感じません。
I don't feel pain.
• tsukare o kanjiru 疲れを感じる *to feel fatigue*

kanjō 勘定 ① *calculation, computation* [→**keisan** 計算]
• kanjō suru 勘定する *to calculate*
② *check, bill, account* [→**kaikei** 会計②]
¶O-kanjō o o-negai shimasu.
お勘定をお願いします。《in a restaurant》

Check, please.

¶Kanjō wa watashi ga haraimasu.

勘定は私が払います。

I'll pay the bill.

kanjō 感情 *feelings, emotion*

¶Chichi wa metta ni kanjō o arawashimasen.

父はめったに感情を表しません。

My father seldom shows his feelings.

¶Tanin no kanjō o gaisanai yō ni ki o tsukete kudasai.

他人の感情を害さないように気をつけてください。

Please be careful not to hurt the feelings of others.

kankaku 間隔 *interval* 《or time or space》

¶Basu wa jup-pun-kankaku de kimasu.

バスは10分間隔で来ます。

The buses come at ten-minute intervals.

¶Tsukue to tsukue no aida wa ikura-ka kankaku o akenasai.

机と机の間はいくらか間隔を空けなさい。

Leave some space between the desks.

kankaku 感覚 ① *ability to sense, sensation* 《involving one of the five senses》

¶Samusa de yubi no kankaku ga nakatta desu.

寒さで指の感覚がなかったです。

Because of the cold I had no sensation in my fingers.

② *sense, sensitivity, capacity for appreciation*

•kankaku ga surudoi 感覚が鋭い *one's sensitivity is keen*

•shikisai-kankaku 色彩感覚 *sense of color*

kankei 関係 *relation, relationship, connection*

¶Watashi mo kono gakkō to kankei ga arimasu.

私もこの学校と関係があります。

I also have a connection with this school.

¶Chichi wa shigoto no kankei de Nyūyōku ni imasu.

父は仕事の関係でニューヨークにいます。

My father is in New York in connection

with his work.

¶Igirisu to Nihon to no kankei wa jūyō desu.

イギリスと日本との関係は重要です。

Relations between England and Japan are important.

•kankei suru 関係する *to come to have a relationship*

¶Hinshitsu-kanri wa rieki to missetsu ni kankei shite imasu.

品質管理は利益と密接に関係しています。

Quality control is closely related to profits.

•kokusai-kankei 国際関係 *international relations*

•ningen-kankei 人間関係 *human relations*

kanketsu 簡潔 〜na 〜な *concise, brief*

kanki 換気 *ventilation, ventilating*

•kanki suru 換気する *to ventilate*

•kanki-sen 換気扇 *ventilating fan*

kankō 観光 *sightseeing*

¶Guamu e kankō ni dekakemasu.

グアムへ観光に出かけます。

I'm going to go to Guam for sightseeing.

•kankō-annai-jo 観光案内所 *sightseeing information office／booth*

•kankō-basu 観光バス *sightseeing bus*

•kankō-chi 観光地 *tourist resort, sightseeing spot, place of interest*

•kankō-kyaku 観光客 *sightseer, tourist*

•kankō-ryokō 観光旅行 *sightseeing trip*

kankonsōsai 冠婚葬祭 *ceremonial occasions* 《specifically, coming of age ceremonies, weddings, funerals, and ceremonies venerating ancestors》

kankyaku 観客 *audience member, spectator*

¶Futtobōru no shiai wa ōzei no kankyaku o atsumemashita.

フットボールの試合は大勢の観客を集めました。

The football game drew many spectators.

¶Kankyaku wa sukunakatta desu ne.

観客は少なかったですね。

The audience was small, wasn't it.

•kankyaku-seki 観客席 *audience seat;*

stands

kankyō 環境 *environment, surroundings*
- kankyō ni junnō suru 環境に順応する *to adapt to an environment*
- kankyō-hakai 環境破壊 *environmental destruction*
- kankyō-hogo 環境保護 *environmental protection*
- kankyō-osen 環境汚染 *environmental pollution*
- katei-kankyō 家庭環境 *home environment*
- shakai-kankyō 社会環境 *social environment*
- shizen-kankyō 自然環境 *natural environment*

kanná 鉋 *plane* ((tool))
- ita ni kanna o kakeru 板にかんなをかける *to plane a board*
- kanna-kuzu 鉋屑 *plane shavings*

kánnen 観念 ① *idea, concept* [→**kangae** 考え②]
   ② *sense, conception*
   ¶Ani wa jikan no kannen ga nai yo.
   兄は時間の観念がないよ。
   My older brother has no sense of time!
- keizai-kannen 経済観念 *sense of frugality*
- kotei-kannen 固定観念 *fixed idea*

kanningu カンニング【COL.】 *cheating, cribbing* 《on a test》
- kanningu suru カンニングする *to cheat*
   ¶Ueda-kun wa rika no shiken de kanningu shita yo.
   上田君は理科の試験でカンニングしたよ。
   Ueda cheated on the science exam!

Kannon 観音 *Kannon* 《a goddess of mercy》

kanō 可能 ～**na** ～な *possible* [⇔**fukanō na** 不可能な]
   ¶Jikan made ni soko ni tsuku no wa kanō desu ka.
   時間までにそこに着くのは可能ですか。
   Is it possible to arrive there in time?
- kanō-sei 可能性 *possibility*

kánojo 彼女 ① *she, her*

¶Yumi-chan wa watashi no tomodachi desu. Kanojo mo Higashi-chūgaku ni kayotte imasu.
由美ちゃんは私の友達です。彼女も東中学に通っています。
Yumi is my friend. She also goes to Higashi Junior High School.
   ② *girlfriend*

kan'óke 棺桶 *coffin*

kánpa 寒波 *cold wave* ((weather phenomenon))

kánpa カンパ *fund-raising campaign*
- kanpa suru カンパする *to campaign to raise funds*

kanpai 乾杯 *drinking a toast, ceremonial drink in celebration*
   ¶Kanpai!
   乾杯！
   Cheers!
- kanpai suru 乾杯する *to drink a toast*
   ¶Oda-sensei no tame ni kanpai shimashō.
   小田先生のために乾杯しましょう。
   Let's drink a toast to Dr. Oda.

kanpan 甲板 《ship's》*deck*

kanpeki 完璧 *perfection, flawlessness* [→**kanzen** 完全①]
- kanpeki na 完ぺきな *perfect, flawless*
   ¶Keiko-san no Eigo wa hobo kanpeki desu.
   恵子さんの英語はほぼ完ぺきです。
   Keiko's English is almost perfect.

kanpóyaku 漢方薬 *Chinese herbal medicine*

kanpū 完封 *shutout* 《in baseball》

kanpyō 干瓢 *dried gourd shavings*

kanreki 還暦 *60th birthday* 《This birthday is traditionally a special occasion because the ancient Japanese calendar went in 60-year cycles.》

kanren 関連 *relation, connection* [→**kankei** 関係]

kánri 管理 *management, supervision*
- kanri suru 管理する *to manage, to supervise*
- kanri-nin 管理人 *manager;* <US> *janitor,* <UK> *caretaker*
- kanri-sha 管理者 *manager*

kanroku 貫禄 *dignity, weight of character* [→**igen** 威厳]

¶Sofu wa kanroku no aru hito deshita.
祖父は貫禄のある人でした。
My grandfather was a person of dignity.

kanryō 完了 *completion, finishing*

• kanryō suru 完了する *to complete; to be completed*

¶Ryokō no junbi ga kanryō shimashita.
旅行の準備が完了しました。
The preparations for the trip were completed.

kanryū 寒流 *cold (ocean)current* [⇔ **danryū** 暖流]

Kánsai 関西 *the Kansai (Region of Japan)* 《Kyoto, Osaka, Shiga, Nara, Mie, Wakayama, and Hyogo Prefectures》[→ **Kinki-chihō** 近畿地方] [⇔**Kantō** 関東]

• Kansai-ben 関西弁 *Kansai dialect*

kansatsu 観察 *observing, observation*

• kansatsu suru 観察する *to observe, to watch*

¶Maiban hoshi o kansatsu shite imasu.
毎晩星を観察しています。
I observe the stars every night.

¶Yachō o kansatsu suru no ga watashi no shumi desu.
野鳥を観察するのが私の趣味です。
Watching wild birds is my hobby.

• kansatsu-sha 観察者 *observer*

kansei 完成 *completion* 《of a tangible object》

• kansei suru 完成する *to complete; to be completed*

¶Sono biru wa raigetsu kansei shimasu.
そのビルは来月完成します。
The building will be completed next month.

kansei 歓声 *shout of joy, cheer*

¶Seito-tachi wa kansei o agemashita.
生徒たちは歓声を上げました。
The students gave shouts of joy.

kansetsu 間接 ～**no** ～の *indirect* [⇔ **chokusetsu no** 直接の]

• kansetsu-teki na 間接的な *indirect*

• kansetsu-zei 間接税 *indirect tax*

kansetsu 関節 *joint* 《where two bones come together》[→**fushi** 節②]

• kansetsu-en 関節炎 *arthritis*

kánsha 感謝 *thanks, gratitude*

• kansha suru 感謝する *to give one's thanks for, to express gratitude for*

¶Go-shinsetsu o kokoro kara kansha shimasu.
ご親切を心から感謝します。
I am very grateful for your kindness.
《Literally: *I give thanks from the heart for your kindness.*》

• Kansha-sai 感謝祭 *Thanksgiving Day*

kanshin 感心 ～**na** ～な *admirable, laudable*

• kanshin suru 感心する *to be impressed, to be struck with admiration*

¶Akiko-san no yūki ni kanshin shimashita.
明子さんの勇気に感心しました。
I was impressed by Akiko's courage.

kanshin 関心 *(feeling of)interest* [→ **kyōmi** 興味]

¶Wakamono wa Nihon no ongaku ni kanshin o shimeshimasen.
若者は日本の音楽に関心を示しません。
Young people do not show any interest in Japanese music.

• A ga B ni kanshin ga aru AがBに関心がある *A is interested in B*

¶Rekishi ni taihen kanshin ga arimasu.
歴史にたいへん関心があります。
I am very interested in history.

kánshite 関して [☞**ni kanshite** に関して]

kanshō 干渉 *interference, meddling*

• kanshō suru 干渉する *to interfere, to meddle*

kanshō 感傷 *sentimentality*

• kanshōteki na 感傷的な *sentimental*

kanshō 観賞 *admiration, enjoyment* 《of something beautiful》

• kanshō suru 観賞する *to admire, to enjoy*

• kanshō-yō-shokubutsu 観賞用植物 *decorative plant*

kanshō 鑑賞 *appreciation* 《of a work of art》

• kanshō suru 鑑賞する *to appreciate*

¶Ishikawa-san wa shi o kanshō shimasu.

石川さんは詩を鑑賞します。

Ms. Ishikawa appreciates poetry.

kanshoku 間食 *eating between meals; between-meals snack*

• kanshoku suru 間食する *to eat between meals*

kanshū 観衆 *audience, spectators*

¶Kanshū wa kijutsu o tanoshimimashita.

観衆は奇術を楽しみました。

The audience enjoyed the magic tricks.

¶Kanshū wa shiai ni kōfun shimashita.

観衆は試合に興奮しました。

The spectators got excited about the game.

kansō 乾燥 *dryness, dessication*

• kansō suru 乾燥する *to dry* 《transitive or intransitive》

¶Kūki ga kansō shite masu ne.

空気が乾燥してますね。

The air is dry, isn't it.

• kansō-ki 乾燥機 *drying machine, drier*

kansō 感想 *impression(s), thoughts*

¶Kono hon ni tsuite no kansō o kikasete kudasai.

この本についての感想を聞かせてください。

Please tell me your thoughts about this book.

kansoku 観測 *observation and measurement* 《of natural phenomena》

• kansoku suru 観測する *to observe and measure*

• kansoku-jo 観測所 *observatory, observation station*

• kishō-kansoku 気象観測 *weather observation*

kansúru 関する [☞**ni kansuru** に関する]

kantai 寒帯 *frigid zone* [⇔**nettai** 熱帯]

kantan 感嘆 *admiration; wonder*

• kantan suru 感嘆する *to be struck with admiration; to marvel*

• kantan-bun 感嘆文 *exclamatory sentence*

• kantan-fu 感嘆符 *exclamation mark*

kantan 簡単 〜**na** 〜な ① *easy, simple*

[→**yasashii** 易しい] [⇔**muzukashii** 難しい]

• kantan na shitsumon 簡単な質問 *easy question, simple question*

② *simple, uncomplicated* [→**tanjun na** 単純な①] [⇔**fukuzatsu na** 複雑な]

¶Kantan na hōkoku o dashimashita.

簡単な報告を出しました。

I turned in a simple report.

• kantan na shokuji 簡単な食事 *simple meal*

Kántō 関東 *the Kanto* (*region of Japan*) 《Tokyo, Kanagawa, Saitama, Chiba, Ibaraki, Tochigi, and Gunma Prefectures》 [⇔**Kansai** 関西]

• Kantō-heiya 関東平野 *the Kanto Plain*

kantoku 監督 ① *superintendent, supervisor; director* 《in movies, television, etc.》; *manager* 《of a baseball team》 ② *supervision, superintendency*

• kantoku suru 監督する *to supervise, to superintend*

kantorī-kurabu カントリークラブ *country club*

kantóshi 間投詞 *interjection* ((part of speech))

kánū カヌー *canoe*

kanwa 緩和 *mitigation, alleviation*

• kanwa suru 緩和する *to alleviate, to mitigate, to ease*

Kanwajíten 漢和辞典 *Japanese dictionary for looking up Chinese characters*

kanzei 関税 *customs duty*

kanzen 完全 ① *perfection* [→**kanpeki** 完璧]

• kanzen na 完全な *perfect*

② *completeness*

• kanzen na 完全な *complete*

• kanzen-shiai 完全試合 *perfect game* 《in baseball》

kanzō 肝臓 *liver* ((organ))

• kanzō-byō 肝臓病 *liver disease*

• kanzō-gan 肝臓癌 *liver cancer*

kanzumé 缶詰 <*US*>*canned food,* <*UK*>*tinned food*

• kanzume no sake 缶詰の鮭 *canned salmon*

- painappuru no kanzume パイナップルの缶詰 *can of pineapple*

kao 顔 ① *face* 《of a person or animal》

¶Kono ko wa kawaii kao o shite imasu ne.

この子はかわいい顔をしていますね。

This child has a cute face, doesn't she.

- kao o miawaseru 顔を見合わせる *to look at each other's faces*

- kao o arau 顔を洗う *to wash one's face*

② *look* (*on a face*), *expression* (*on a face*) [→**hyōjō** 表情]

- kao o suru 顔をする *to get a look on one's face* 《Always preceded by a modifier.》

¶Kawamura-san wa sono toki kanashi-sō na kao o shite imashita.

川村さんはそのとき悲しそうな顔をしていました。

Mr. Kawamura had a sad look on his face then.

kaoiro 顔色 ① *color* (*of a face*), *complexion*

¶Dō shimashita ka. Kaoiro ga warui desu yo.

どうしましたか。顔色が悪いですよ。

What's the matter? Your color is bad!

¶Sono shirase ni buchō wa kaoiro o kaemashita.

その知らせに部長は顔色を変えました。

The department head changed color at that news.

② *look* (*on a face*), *expression* (*on a face*) [→**hyōjō** 表情]

- kaoiro ni deru 顔色に出る *to appear in one's expression*

káoku 家屋 *house, residential building*

kaomake 顔負け *being put to shame*

- kaomake suru 顔負けする *to be put to shame*

kaori 香り *fragrance*

¶Kono hana wa kaori ga ii desu.

この花は香りがいいです。

This flower's fragrance is nice.

kaoru 香る *to be fragrant*

kápetto カーペット *carpet* [→**jūtan** 絨毯]

kappa 河童 *water imp* 《a Japanese mythological creature》

kappatsu 活発 ～**na** ～な *active, lively*

¶Eiko-chan wa kappatsu na kodomo desu ne.

英子ちゃんは活発な子供ですね。

Eiko is a lively child, isn't she.

- kappatsu na rongi 活発な議論 *lively discussion*

káppu カップ ① *cup* ((trophy))

② *cup with a handle* 《for drinks》

káppuru カップル *couple* 《man and woman》

kápuseru カプセル *capsule*

- kapuseru-hoteru カプセルホテル *capsule hotel*

- taimu-kapuseru タイムカプセル *time capsule*

kará 空 ～**no** ～の *empty*

¶Kara no hako wa mō nai desu.

空の箱はもうないです。

There are no more empty boxes.

- kara ni suru 空にする *to make empty, to empty*

¶Akira-chan wa gurasu o kara ni shita ne.

明ちゃんはグラスを空にしたね。

Akira emptied the glass, didn't he.

kará 殻 *shell, husk*

- tamago no kara 卵の殻 *eggshell*

kara から ① *from, out of, off of* 《noun-following particle》

¶Ōsaka kara Kyōto made densha de ikimashita.

大阪から京都まで電車で行きました。

I went from Osaka to Kyoto by train.

¶Taiyō wa higashi kara noborimasu.

太陽は東から昇ります。

The sun rises from the east.

¶Mado kara hi ga sashikonde imasu.

窓から日が差し込んでいます。

The sun is shining in from the window.

¶Batā wa gyūnyū kara tsukuraremasu.

バターは牛乳から造られます。

Butter is made from milk.

¶Sore wa nani kara dekite imasu ka.

それは何からできていますか。

What is that made out of?

¶Atarashii hatsumei wa hitsuyō kara umaremasu.

新しい発明は必要から生まれます。

New inventions come from necessity.

•kuruma kara oriru 車から降りる *to get out of a car*

•jitensha kara ochiru 自転車から落ちる *to fall off a bicycle*

② *from, since,* ⟨*beginning*⟩ *at,* ⟨*beginning*⟩ *on* «noun-following particle»

¶Jup-pēji kara hajimemashō.

10ページから始めましょう。

Let's begin at page 10.

¶Gakkō wa Getsuyōbi kara Kinyōbi made arimasu.

学校は月曜日から金曜日まであります。

There is school from Monday through Friday.

¶Kesa kara zutto koko ni imasu.

けさからずっとここにいます。

I have been here ever since this morning.

¶Natsu-yasumi wa Shichi-gatsu ni-jūichi-nichi kara hajimarimasu.

夏休みは7月21日から始まります。

Summer vacation begins on July 21.

③ *after, since* «following the gerund (-**te** form) of a verb»

¶Koko e kite kara dono kurai ni narimasu ka.

ここへ来てから、どのくらいになりますか。

About how long is it since you came here?

¶Shawā o abite kara dekakemashita.

シャワーを浴びてから出かけました。

I went out after taking a shower.

④ *because, since* «clause-conjoining particle»

¶Kibun ga warui kara, issho ni ikemasen.

気分が悪いから、いっしょに行けません。

Since I feel unwell, I can't go with you.

¶"Naze konakatta n desu ka." "Isogashi-katta kara desu."

「なぜ来なかったんですか」「忙しかったからです」

"Why didn't you come?" "Because

I was busy."

kárā カラー *color* [→**iro** 色]

¶Sono eiga wa karā de wa arimasen.

その映画はカラーではありません。

That movie isn't color.

•karā-firumu カラーフィルム *color film*

•karā-shashin カラー写真 *color photograph*

•karā-terebi カラーテレビ *color TV*

kárā カラー *collar* «on an article of clothing» [→**eri** 襟]

karada 体 *body* «of a living creature» [→**shintai** 身体]

¶Ano hito wa karada ga jōbu desu.

あの人は体が丈夫です。

That person is healthy. «Literally: *That person's body is strong.*»

¶Jirō-chan wa karada ga gasshiri shite iru ne.

次郎ちゃんは体ががっしりしているね。

Jiro's body is sturdily-built, isn't it.

¶Dōzo o-karada o o-daiji ni.

どうぞお体をお大事に。《to a person who is ill》

Please take good care of yourself. «Literally: *Please, your body carefully.*»

•karada o arau 体を洗う *to wash oneself* «Literally: *to wash the body*»

•karada no chōshi ga ii〔warui〕体の調子がいい〔悪い〕*to be in good*〔*bad*〕*health* «Literally: *the body's condition is good*〔*bad*〕»

•karada ni ii〔warui〕体にいい〔悪い〕*good*〔*bad*〕*for one's health* «Literally: *good*〔*bad*〕*for the body*»

kárafuru カラフル ～**na** ～な *colorful*

Karafuto 樺太 *Sakhalin*

karái 辛い ① (*spicy-*)*hot*

•karai karē 辛いカレー *hot curry*

② *salty* «In this meaning, normally written in hiragana.» [→**shio-karai** 塩辛い (s.v. **shio** 塩)]

¶Kono sūpu wa karai desu yo.

このスープはからいですよ。

This soup is salty!

③ *severe* «describing how a person deals with or evaluates something»

• ten ga karai 点が辛い *one's grading is severe*

karakáu からかう *to tease, to make fun of*

karaoke カラオケ ① *recordings of songs with the vocals left out* ② *singing with such recordings as background*

karappo 空っぽ ～**no** ～の 【COL. for **kara no** 空の】

karashi 芥子 *mustard*

kárasu 烏 *crow*

¶Karasu ga kākā naku koe ga kikoemashita.
からすがかあかあ鳴く声が聞こえました。
I heard the voice of a crow calling caw-caw.

karate 空手 *karate*

karatto カラット *carat*

• -karatto －カラット《*counter for carats; see Appendix 2*》

káre 彼 ① *he, him* ② *boyfriend*

¶Kare ni yoroshiku.
彼によろしく。
My best to your boyfriend.

• kare-ra 彼ら *they, them*

kareha 枯れ葉 *dead leaf*

karéndā カレンダー *calendar* [→**koyomi** 暦]

karēráisu カレーライス *curry and rice*

kareru 枯れる ① *to die, to wither* 《*The subject is a plant.*》

¶Kono hana wa jiki ni kareru deshō.
この花はじきに枯れるでしょう。
This flower will probably die soon.

• karete iru 枯れている *to be dead, to be withered*

¶Kono ki wa karete imasu.
この木は枯れています。
This tree is dead.

② *to become seasoned, to become mature* 《*The subject is a person's character or art.*》

kari 仮 ～**no** ～な *temporary, provisional, tentative*

• kari ni 仮に *on the assumption, suppos-*

ing 《*a lead-in for a conditional clause*》

¶Kari ni sonna koto ga okotta to shitara, dō shimasu ka.
仮にそんなことが起こったとしたら、どうしますか。
Supposing such a thing happened, what would you do?

• kari-menkyo 仮免許 *temporary license*

kári 狩り *hunting, hunt*

• kari o suru 狩りをする *to hunt*

• kari ni iku 狩りに行く *to go hunting*

kari 借り ① *debt* 《(*money*)》, *borrowed item*

• A ni kari ga aru Aに借りがある *to have a debt to A, to owe A*

¶Okada-san ni goman-en no kari ga arimasu.
岡田さんに5万円の借りがあります。
I have a 50,000-yen debt to Ms. Okada.

② *borrowing* ③ *renting* 《*from someone*》

karifuráwā カリフラワー *cauliflower*

kariiréru 刈り入れる *to reap, to harvest*

¶Sono mura no hito-tachi wa, ima, ine o kariirete imasu.
その村の人たちは、今、稲を刈り入れています。
The people of that village are now reaping the rice.

karíkyuramu カリキュラム *curriculum*

kariru 借りる [[⇔**kasu** 貸す]] ① *to borrow, to use* (*temporarily*)

¶Imōto wa tosho-kan kara kono hon o karimashita.
妹は図書館からこの本を借りました。
My younger sister borrowed this book from the library.

¶Denwa o karite ii desu ka.
電話を借りていいですか。
May I use your telephone?

• chikara o kariru 力を借りる *to get assistance*

② *to rent* 《*from someone*》

¶Oji wa ōki na ie o karite imasu.
伯父は大きな家を借りています。
My uncle is renting a big house.

karō 過労 *overwork*
- karō-shi 過労死 *death from overwork*

karójite 辛うじて *just barely*

károrī カロリー *calorie*
- -karorī －カロリー《counter for calories; see Appendix 2》

kāru カール (*hair*)*curl*
- kāru suru カールする *to curl* 《transitive or intransitive》

¶Michiko-san wa kami o kāru shite imasu.

美知子さんは髪をカールしています。

Michiko has curled her hair.

¶Imōto no kami wa umaretsuki kāru shite imasu.

妹の髪は生まれつきカールしています。

My younger sister's hair is naturally curly.

karu 刈る *to mow, to cut* 《grass, hair, etc.》*; to reap* [→**kariireru** 刈り入れる]

¶Ken-chan wa kusa o katte imasu.

健ちゃんは草を刈っています。

Ken is mowing the grass.

¶Boku mo kami o katte moratta yo.

僕も髪を刈ってもらったよ。

I also had my hair cut!

karui 軽い ① *light (-weight)* [⇔**omoi** 重い]

¶Kono isu wa zuibun karui desu.

このいすはずいぶん軽いです。

This chair is very light.

② *slight, light, minor*

¶Akira-san wa karui kaze o hiite imasu.

明さんは軽いかぜをひいています。

Akira has a slight cold.

- karui shokuji 軽い食事 *light meal*
- kuchi ga karui 口が軽い *glib; unable to keep a secret*

karushūmu カルシウム《Note the mismatch between the katakana spelling and the pronunciation.》*calcium*

káruta カルタ ① *playing cards* 《ordinarily any of several types used in traditional Japanese card games》

② *card game*

kárute カルテ *medical record, patient's chart*

karyū 下流 [[⇔**jōryū** 上流]] ① *the area downriver; the lower part of a river*

¶Sono kawa no karyū ni wa sakana ga imasen.

その川の下流には魚がいません。

In the lower part of that river there are no fish.

¶Yaku hyaku-mētoru karyū ni hashi ga arimasu.

約100メートル下流に橋があります。

About 100 meters down river there is a bridge.

② *lower social stratum*

karyūmu カリウム《Note the mismatch between the katakana spelling and the pronunciation.》*potassium*

kása 傘 *umbrella; parasol* [→**hi-gasa** 日傘 (s.v. **hi** 日)]
- kasa o sasu 傘を差す *to put an umbrella over one's head*
- oritatami no kasa 折り畳みの傘 *folding umbrella*
- kasa-tate 傘立て *umbrella stand, umbrella holder*

kasai 火災 (*destructive*)*fire* [→**kaji** 火事]
- kasai-hōchi-ki 火災報知器 *fire alarm*

kasanaru 重なる ① *to pile up, to become piled up*

② *to come to overlap; to fall on the same day*

¶Kotoshi wa Kurisumasu ga Nichiyōbi ni kasanarimasu.

今年はクリスマスが日曜日に重なります。

Christmas falls on Sunday this year.

③ *to happen one after another, to happen repeatedly*

¶Futatsu no jiko ga kasanarimashita.

二つの事故が重なりました。

Two accidents happened one after another.

kasaneru 重ねる ① *to pile up* 《transitive》

¶Soko ni hon o kasanenai de kudasai.

そこに本を重ねないでください。

Don't pile up books there.

② *to do repeatedly, to undergo repeatedly*
• kurō o kasaneru 苦労を重ねる *to suffer hardships repeatedly*

kaségu 稼ぐ ① *to work and earn money*
¶Ani wa arubaito de kaseide imasu.
兄はアルバイトで稼いでいます。
My older brother is earning money with a part-time job.
② *to earn by working* 《Except in figurative uses, the direct object is a word that refers to money.》
¶Oba wa Eigo o oshiete o-kane o kaseide imasu.
伯母は英語を教えてお金を稼いでいます。
My aunt is earning money by teaching English.
• ten o kasegu 点を稼ぐ *to earn a point, to score a point*

Kasei 火星 (*the planet*) *Mars*
• Kasei-jin 火星人 *a Martian*

kaséifu 家政婦 *housekeeper*

kaseki 化石 *fossil*

kásen 河川 *rivers*

kasetsu 仮説 *hypothesis*

kasétto カセット *cassette*
• kasetto-dekki カセットデッキ *cassette deck*
• kasetto-tēpu カセットテープ *cassette tape*

káshi 樫 *oak*

káshi 菓子 *sweets; cake* [→**kēki** ケーキ]; *candy* [→**kyandē** キャンデー]; *cookie* [→**kukkī** クッキー]
• kashi-ya 菓子屋 *confectionery; confectioner*

káshi 歌詞 *words of a song, lyrics*

kashi 貸し ① *loan* ((*money*)), *loaned item*
• A ni kashi ga aru Aに貸しがある *to have a loan to A, to be owed by A*
¶Suzuki-san ni wa kashi ga gosen-en arimasu.
鈴木さんには貸しが5000円あります。
I have a loan to Ms. Suzuki of 5,000 yen.
② *lending*
③ *renting* 《to someone》

• kashi-bideo 貸しビデオ *rental video*
• kashi-hon 貸本 *rental book*
• kashi-hon-ya 貸本屋 *rental library*
• kashi-jitensha 貸し自転車 *rental bicycle*
• kashi-ya 貸家 *rental house*

Káshi カ氏, 華氏 *Fahrenheit* [⇔**Seshi** セ氏]
¶Kion wa Kashi rokujū-do desu.
気温はカ氏60度です。
The temperature is 60 degrees Fahrenheit.

kashigéru 傾げる *to lean, to tilt* 《transitive》 [→**katamukeru** 傾ける]
• atama o kashigeru 頭を傾げる *to tilt one's head to the side* 《as an expression of doubt》

kashikói 賢い *wise, clever, intelligent* [⇔**baka na** 馬鹿な]

kashimiya カシミヤ *cashmere fabric*

káshira かしら *I wonder* 《This sentence-final particle expresses uncertainty and is typically used by female speakers. The word preceding **kashira** cannot be the copula form da だ. When **kashira** is added to a sentence that would end with **da**, the **da** does not appear.》
¶Ano hito wa ittai dare kashira.
あの人はいったいだれかしら。
I wonder who in the world that person is.
¶Kore de ii no kashira.
これでいいのかしら。
I wonder if this will do.
¶Hayaku ame ga yamanai kashira.
早く雨がやまないかしら。
I wonder if the rain won't stop soon.

kashiramóji 頭文字 ① *initial* (*letter*)
② *capital letter* [→**ōmoji** 大文字]

kashitsu 過失 ① *mistake, error* 《due to negligence》
② *fault, defect* [→**ketten** 欠点]

kásho 箇所, 個所 *place* 《within something larger》
• itami no kasho 痛みの箇所 *place where it hurts*
• -kasho 一箇所 《counter for places; see Appendix 2》
¶Dōro no migi-gawa ni kōji-chū no

basho ga san-kasho arimasu.
道路の右側に工事中の場所が３箇所
あります。
*On the right side of the road there are
three places under construction.*

káshu 歌手 （*professional*)*singer*
• ryūkō-kashu 流行歌手 *pop singer*

kasō 仮装 *disguise, masquerade*
• kasō suru 仮装する *to disquise oneself,
to dress up*
¶Musume wa rokku-kashu ni kasō shimashita.
娘はロック歌手に仮装しました。
*My daughter dressed up as a rock
singer.*

kasō 火葬 *cremation* [⇔**dosō** 土葬,
maisō 埋葬]

kasoku 加速 *acceleration* [⇔**gensoku**
減速]
• kasoku suru 加速する *to accelerate*
《*transitive or intransitive*》

kassha 滑車 *pulley*

kasshoku 褐色 *dark brown* 《*as a noun*》

kassōro 滑走路 （*airport*)*runway*

kasu 貸す [[⇔**kariru** 借りる]] ① *to
lend*
¶Kazuo-san ni sono hon o kashimashita.
和夫さんにその本を貸しました。
I lent that book to Kazuo.
¶Denwa o kashite itadakemasu ka.
電話を貸していただけますか。
May I use your telephone? 《*Literally:
Can I have you lend me the telephone?*》
② *to rent* 《*to someone*》
¶Haha wa sono heya o gakusei ni kashite
imasu.
母はその部屋を学生に貸しています。
*My mother is renting that room to a stu-
dent.*

kásu 粕 *dregs; scum*
• kōhī-kasu コーヒー粕 *coffee grounds*

kásuka 微か ～**na** ～な *faint, dim,
slight*
¶Sono onna no ko no koto wa kasuka ni
oboete imasu.
その女の子のことはかすかに覚えています。
I remember that girl slightly.

• kasuka na oto かすかな音 *faint sound*

kasumi 霞 *haze, mist*

kasuríkizu かすり傷 *scratch, abrasion*
《《*injury*》》

kasutanétto カスタネット *castanets*

kasutera カステラ *sponge cake*

katá 方 【HON. for **hito** 人】 *person*
¶Ano kata wa donata desu ka.
あの方はどなたですか。
Who is that person over there?

-kata －方 *way of, how to* 《Added to
verb bases.》
¶Ano hito no kangae-kata wa okashii
desu.
あの人の考え方はおかしいです。
That person's way of thinking is strange.
¶Konpyūta no tsukai-kata o oshiete
kudasai.
コンピューターの使い方を教えてください。
Please teach me how to use a computer.

-kata －方 *in care of* 《Added to names
and used in addresses.》
¶Ono-sama-kata, Yamada Kyōko-sama
小野様方、山田京子様
Ms. Kyoko Yamada c/o Mr. Ono

káta 肩 *shoulder*
¶Kimura-san wa watashi no kata o
karuku tatakimashita.
木村さんは私の肩を軽くたたきました。
*Mr. Kimura tapped me lightly on the
shoulder.*
¶Kodomo-tachi wa kata o narabete
aruite imasu.
子供たちは肩を並べて歩いています。
*The children are walking shoulder to
shoulder.*
• kata o sukumeru 肩をすくめる *to shrug
one's shoulders*
¶Sensei wa kata o sukumete, watashi no
shitsumon o mushi shita.
先生は肩をすくめて私の質問を無視した。
*The teacher shrugged her shoulders and
ignored my question.*
• kata-guruma 肩車 *carrying piggyback*
• kata-guruma ni noru 肩車に乗る *to get
on for a piggyback ride*

katá 型 ① *type, style, model*

• atarashii kata no kuruma 新しい型の車 *new model car*

② *pattern, model, mold* «for making something»

• yōfuku no kata 洋服の型 *pattern for making clothing*

• kata ni hamaru 型にはまる *to fit a mold, to be stereotypical*

③ *form, model way of doing something* «in a peforming art or martial art»

• jūdō no kata 柔道の型 *judo forms*

• kata-gami 型紙 *paper pattern* «for making cothing»

kata- 片－ *one（of two）*«Added to noun bases.»

• kata-ashi 片足 *one leg; one foot*

• kata-me 片目 *one eye*

katachi 形 *shape, form*

¶ Sore wa donna katachi desu ka.
それはどんな形ですか。
What kind of shape is that?

¶ Sono pan wa dōbutsu no katachi o shite imasu.
そのパンは動物の形をしています。
That bread is in the shape of an animal.

katagaki 肩書き *title（of rank）;（academic）degree* [→**gakui** 学位]

katáhō 片方 *one side（of two）; one（of two, of a pair）*

¶ Kutsu no mō katahō wa doko ni aru no?
靴のもう片方はどこにあるの？
Where's the other shoe?

• michi no katahō 道の片方 *one side of the street*

katai 固い、堅い、硬い ①[[⇔**yawarakai** 柔らかい①]] *hard, solid, rigid; tough* «describing meat»

¶ Kono niku wa katai desu ne.
この肉は堅いですね。
This meat is tough, isn't it.

¶ Katai ki o tsukatta hō ga ii desu.
堅い木を使ったほうがいいです。
It would be better to use hard wood.

¶ Tamago o kataku yudete kudasai.
卵を堅くゆでてください。
Please boil the egg hard.

② *firm, strong, tight, unalterable*

¶ Daitōryō wa ishi ga katai desu ne.
大統領は意志が固いですね。
The president's will is strong, isn't it.

¶ Kutsu-himo o kataku musunda yo.
靴ひもを固く結んだよ。
I tied my shoelaces tightly!

• katai yūjō 固い友情 *firm friendship*

• A wa atama ga katai Aは頭が固い A is stubborn, A's thinking is rigid

③ *sound, solid, reliable*

• katai kaisha 堅い会社 *solid company*

④ *overly serious*

• katai hanashi 堅い話 *overly serious talk*

⑤ *tense, nervous*

¶ Sonna ni kataku naranai de.
そんなに固くならないで。
Don't get so tense.

katákana 片仮名 *katakana* «the squarish Japanese syllabary»

katakoto 片言 *imperfect language, broken language* «of children or foreigners»

• katakoto no Nihongo 片言の日本語 *broken Japanese*

katamari 塊; 固まり *lump; mass*

• nendo no katamari ねん土のかたまり *lump of clay*

• kumo no katamari 雲のかたまり *mass of clouds*

katamaru 固まる *to harden* «intransitive»

¶ Mō nori ga katamatta deshō.
もうのりが固まったでしょう。
The paste has probably hardened already.

katameru 固める *to harden* «transitive»

katamichi 片道 *one way* «of a trip» [⇔**ōfuku** 往復]

• katamichi-kippu 片道切符
<US>one-way ticket, <UK>single ticket

• katamichi-ryōkin 片道料金
<US>one-way fare, <UK>single fare

katamukéru 傾ける *to lean, to slant, to tilt* «transitive»

¶ Aiko-san wa kubi o migi ni

katamukemashita.

愛子さんは首を右に傾けました。

Aiko tilted her head to the right.

¶Ojīsan no hanashi ni mimi o katamukemashita.

おじいさんの話に耳を傾けました。

We listened to grandfather's story.

《*Literally: We tilted our ears to grandfather's story.*》

katamúku 傾く *to lean, to slant, to tilt* 《*intransitive*》

¶Pisa no shatō wa zuibun katamuite imasu ne.

ピサの斜塔はずいぶん傾いていますね。

The Leaning Tower of Pisa leans a lot, doesn't it.

• hi ga katamuku 日が傾く *the sun sets*

kataná 刀 *sword*

kataómoi 片思い *one-sided love*

katarogu カタログ *catalog*

kataru 語る *to talk about, to give a narration of, to tell* [→**hanasu** 話す②]

¶Takahashi-san wa jibun no shōrai no yume o katarimashita.

高橋さんは自分の将来の夢を語りました。

Mr. Takahashi talked about his dreams for his own future.

• shinjitsu o kataru 真実を語る *to tell the truth*

katatsúmuri かたつむり *snail*

katazukéru 片づける ① *to put in order, to tidy up, to put in the proper place* [→**seiri suru** 整理する (s.v. **seiri** 整理)]

¶Mazu kono heya o katazukemashita.

まずこの部屋を片づけました。

I tidied up this room first.

¶Chawan o katazukemashō ka.

茶わんを片づけましょうか。

Shall I clear away the tea cups?

② *to finish, to settle, to take care of* [→**shori suru** 処理する (s.v. **shori** 処理)]

¶Yamamoto-san wa shigoto o tekipaki to katazukemashita.

山本さんは仕事をてきぱきと片づけました。

Mr. Yamamoto finished his work

quickly.

¶Kono nanmon o katazukenakute wa narimasen.

この難問を片づけなくてはなりません。

We must settle this difficult problem.

katazúku 片づく ① *to be put in order, to be tidied up*

¶Kono heya wa mō katazuite imasu.

この部屋はもう片づいています。

The room has already been tidied up.

② *to be finished, to be taken care of, to be settled*

¶Shukudai wa ku-ji made ni wa katazuku deshō.

宿題は9時までには片づくでしょう。

My homework will probably be finished by 9:00.

katei 仮定 *supposition, assumption*

• katei suru 仮定する *to suppose, to assume*

katei 家庭 ① *home, household* ② *family (in a household)*

¶Mori-san wa katei no jijō de shigoto o yamemashita.

森さんは家庭の事情で仕事を辞めました。

Mr. Mori left his job for family reasons.

• katei-hōmon 家庭訪問 *home visit* 《*by a child's teacher*》

• katei-ka 家庭科 *homemaking, domestic science* 《*as a school subject*》

• katei-kankyō 家庭環境 *home environment*

• katei-kyōshi 家庭教師 *home tutor*

• katei-saiban-sho 家庭裁判所 *family court*

• katei-seikatsu 家庭生活 *home life, family life*

• katei-yōhin 家庭用品 *household articles*

kâten カーテン *curtain*

• kâten o akeru 〔shimeru〕 カーテンを開ける 〔閉める〕 *to open 〔close〕 a curtain*

katō 下等 〜**na** 〜な ① *low, inferior* ② *coarse, vulgar, unrefined* [→**gehin na** 下品な]

• katō-dōbutsu 下等動物 *lower animal*

kâtorijji カートリッジ *cartridge*

Katoríkku カトリック *Catholicism*
- Katorikku-kyō カトリック教［☞**Kato-rikku** カトリック（above）］
- Katorikku-kyō-to カトリック教徒 *a Catholic*

kátsu 勝つ *to win, to be victorious*［⇔ **makeru** 負ける①］
- A ga B ni katsu AがBに勝つ *A wins B, A is victorious in B*《when B denotes a contest or competition》
¶Boku-tachi no chīmu wa sono shiai ni go tai san de katta yo.
僕たちのチームはその試合に5対3で勝ったよ。
Our team won that game 5 to 3!
- sensō ni katsu 戦争に勝つ *to win a war*
- A ga B ni katsu AがBに勝つ *A is victorious over B, A beats B, A defeats B*《when B denotes an opponent.》
¶Rēsu de Hirata-kun ni katta yo.
レースで平田君に勝ったよ。
I beat Hirata in the race!

katsudō 活動 *activity, activeness*
- kazan no katsudō 火山の活動 *volcanic activity*
- katsudō suru 活動する *to become active*
- katsudō-teki na 活動的な *active, energetic*
- kurabu-katsudō クラブ活動 *club activities*

katsúgu 担ぐ ① *to carry on one's shoulder*［→**ninau** 担う］
¶Kazuko-san wa sukī o katsuide imasu.
和子さんはスキーを担いでいます。
Kazuko is carrying skis on her shoulder.
　② *to play a trick on, to deceive*［→**damasu** 騙す］
¶Katō-kun wa mata onīsan o katsuida yo.
加藤君はまたお兄さんを担いだよ。
Kato played a trick on his older brother again!

katsuji 活字 *(printer's)type*
- katsuji-tai 活字体 *typeface, type style*

katsuo 鰹 *bonito*《fish》

katsura 鬘 *wig; hairpiece*

katsura 桂 *Japanese Judas (tree)*

katsuyaku 活躍 *activity, activeness*
- katsuyaku suru 活躍する *to become active, to become an active participant*《The subject must be human.》
¶Takako-san wa ongaku-bu de katsuyaku shite iru yo.
高子さんは音楽部で活躍しているよ。
Takako is active in the music club!

katsuyō 活用 ① *practical use*
- katsuyō suru 活用する *to put to practical use, to make good use of*
¶Kono wākubukku o ōi-ni katsuyō shinasai.
このワークブックを大いに活用しなさい。
Make good use of this workbook.
　② *inflection*《in grammar》
- katsuyō suru 活用する *to inflect*《intransitive》

katte 勝手 *selfishness, doing as one pleases without consideration for others*［→**wagamama** わがまま］
¶Sore wa boku no katte deshō?.
それは僕の勝手でしょう？
It's up to me to do as I please, right?《Literally: That's my selfishness, right?》
- katte na 勝手な *selfish*
¶Sonna katte na koto o iwanai de kudasai.
そんな勝手なことを言わないでください。
Please don't say such selfish things.
- katte ni 勝手に *as one (selfishly) pleases; without permission*
¶Katte ni shinasai.
勝手にしなさい。
Do as you like.《a rebuke》
¶Kore o katte ni tsukatte wa ikenai yo.
これを勝手に使ってはいけないよ。
You shouldn't use this without permission!

kátto カット *cutting away a portion*
- chingin no katto 賃金のカット *cut in wages*
- katto suru カットする *to cut away a portion*
¶Kami-no-ke o chotto katto shimashō ka.
髪の毛をちょっとカットしましょうか。

Shall I cut my hair a little?

¶Sono eiga o katto suru sō desu.

その映画をカットするそうです。

I hear they're going to cut that movie.

kátto カット *cut, illustration «on a printed page»* [→**sashie** 挿絵]

kau 買う *to buy* [⇔**uru** 売る]

¶Jitensha o katte kudasai.

自転車を買ってください。

Please buy a bicycle.

¶Sono kamera o goman-en de kaimashita.

そのカメラを5万円で買いました。

I bought that camera for 50,000 yen.

káu 飼う *to keep as a pet; to raise «animals»*

¶Boku mo inu o katte iru yo.

僕も犬を飼っているよ。

I also keep a pet dog!

¶Sono nōjō de ushi o sanjut-tō o katte imasu.

その農場では牛を30頭飼っています。

They're raising 30 cows on that farm.

kaubōi カウボーイ *cowboy*

káunserā カウンセラー *psychological counselor*

kauntā カウンター ① *counter «in a store, restaurant, etc.»*

② *counter, counting device*

kawá 川 *river, stream*

¶Kawa ni sotte aruku no wa kimochi ga ii desu.

川に沿って歩くのは気持ちがいいです。

Walking along the river is pleasant.

¶Sono kawa o oyoide watarimashita.

その川を泳いで渡りました。

I swam across that river.

• kawa-bata 川端 *riverside*

• kawa-gishi 川岸 *riverbank*

• kawa-guchi 川口 *river mouth*

kawá 皮 *skin «of an animal»; skin, peel, rind; (tree)bark*

¶Ringo no kawa o muite kureru?

りんごの皮をむいてくれる？

Will you peel the apple for me?

• banana no kawa バナナの皮 *banana peel*

kawá 革 *leather*

¶Kono kaban wa kawa desu ka.

このかばんは革ですか。

Is this bag leather?

• kawa-gutsu 革靴 *leather shoes*

• kawa-janpā 革ジャンパー *leather jacket*

• kawa-seihin 革製品 *leather products*

kawaigáru 可愛がる *to treat with affection, to love*

¶Otōto wa sono inu o totemo kawaigatte imasu.

弟はその犬をとてもかわいがっています。

My younger brother loves that dog very much.

kawaii 可愛い *cute, darling*

¶Kono ko wa kawaii desu ne.

この子はかわいいですね。

This child is cute, isn't he.

kawairashíi 可愛らしい *cute, darling* [→**kawaii** 可愛い]

kawaisō かわいそう ～**na** ～な *pitiable, unfortunate, pathetic*

¶Oda-san wa hontō ni kawaisō na hito desu.

小田さんはほんとうにかわいそうな人です。

Mr. Oda is really an unfortunate person.

¶Sono ko no kawaisō na hanashi o kikimashita ka.

その子のかわいそうな話を聞きましたか。

Did you hear that child's pathetic story?

• kawaisō ni かわいそうに *unfortunately* «expressing sympathy for a victim»

¶Kawaisō ni sono kotori wa shinimashita.

かわいそうにその小鳥は死にました。

Unfortunately, that bird died.

¶Kawaisō ni!

かわいそうに！

Poor thing! «Literally: Unfortunately!»

• kawaisō ni omou かわいそうに思う *to feel pity for, to consider pitiable*

¶Sono nora-neko o kawaisō ni omoimashita.

その野良猫をかわいそうに思いました。

I felt pity for that stray cat.

kawakásu 乾かす *to dry «transitive»*

¶Shatsu o hi de kawakashita yo.

シャツを火で乾かしたよ。
I dried my shirt at the fire!

kawáku 乾く *to dry* 《intransitive》
¶Kutsushita wa mada kawaite imasen.
靴下はまだ乾いていません。
The socks haven't dried yet.

kawáku 渇く **nodo ga**〜 のどが〜 *to get thirsty*
¶Atsui ne. Nodo ga kawaita yo.
暑いね。のどが渇いたよ。
It's hot, isn't it. I'm thirsty!

kawara 瓦 *tile* 《for exterior use, typically on roofs》
• kawara-buki 瓦葺き *covering a roof with tiles*

kawari 代わり *substitute, replacement*
¶Kawari no hito o sagashite imasu.
代わりの人を探しています。
I'm looking for a replacement person.
• A no kawari ni Aの代わりに *instead of A, in place of A*
¶Ani no kawari ni watashi ga ikimasu.
兄の代わりに私が行きます。
I'll go in place of my older brother.
• kawari ni 代わりに《following a predicate》 *instead of; in return for*
¶Jēn-san ni Eigo o oshiete morau kawari ni, Nihon-go o oshiemasu.
ジェーンさんに英語を教えてもらう代わりに、日本語を教えます。
In return for having Jane teach me English, I'll teach her Japanese.

kawari 変わり ① *change, alteration* [→ **henka** 変化]
¶O-kawari arimasen ka.
お変わりありませんか。
How is everything with you? 《Literally: There aren't any changes?》
② *difference, distinction* [→**chigai** 違い]

kawaru 代わる *to trade places, to substitute*
• A ga B to kawaru AがBと代わる *A trades places with B, A takes the place of B, A substitutes for B*
¶Kono hito to kawatte kudasai.
この人と代わってください。

Please take this person's place.
¶Shōshō o-machi kudasai. Ima haha to kawarimasu
少々お待ちください。今母と代わります。
《on the telephone》
Just a moment, please. I'll put my mother on. 《Literally: *Please wait a little. I'll trade places with with mother now.*》

kawaru 変わる *to change* 《intransitive》
¶Ame ga yuki ni kawarimashita.
雨が雪に変わりました。
The rain changed to snow.
¶Shingō ga aka ni kawarimashita.
信号が赤に変わりました。
The traffic light turned red.
• ki ga kawaru 気が変わる *one's mind changes*

kawarugáwaru 代わる代わる *by turns, alternately*
¶Imōto to watashi ga kawarugawaru heya no sōji o shimasu.
妹と私がかわるがわる部屋の掃除をします。
My younger sister and I take turns cleaning the room.

kawase 為替 ① *money order* ② *(monetary)exchange*
• gaikoku-kawase 外国為替 *foreign exchange*
• yūbin-kawase 郵便為替 *postal money order*

kawasemi 川蝉 *kingfisher*

kawauso 獺 *river otter*

kayaku 火薬 *gunpowder*

Kayō 火曜 [☞**Kayōbi** 火曜日]

Kayōbi 火曜日 *Tuesday*

kayōkyoku 歌謡曲 *popular song*

kayou 通う *to commute (back and forth); to attend* 《school》
¶Shiritsu-kōkō ni kayotte imasu.
私立高校に通っています。
I'm attending a private high school.
¶Chichi wa basu de kaisha ni kayotte imasu.
父はバスで会社に通っています。
My father commutes to his office by bus.
¶Otōto wa aruite gakkō ni

kayotte imasu.
弟は歩いて学校に通っています。
My younger brother goes to school on foot.

kayu 粥 *rice gruel*

kayúi 痒い *itchy*
¶Senaka ga kayui desu.
背中がかゆいです。
My back is itchy.

kazagúruma 風車 ① *windmill* [→**fūsha** 風車]
② (*toy*)*pinwheel*

kazamuki 風向き *wind direction*

kázan 火山 *volcano*
• kazan ga funka suru 火山が噴火する *a vocano erupts*
• kazan-bai 火山灰 *volcanic ash*
• kazan-gan 火山岩 *volcanic rock, igneous rock*
• kazan-tai 火山帯 *volcanic zone*
• kak-kazan 活火山 *active volcano*
• kyū-kazan 休火山 *dormant volcano*
• shi-kazan 死火山 *extinct volcano*

kazari 飾り *decoration, ornament*
• Kurisumasu no kazari クリスマスの飾り *Christmas decoration*

kazaru 飾る ① *to decorate, to adorn*
¶Sono heya o e de kazarimashita.
その部屋を絵で飾りました。
We decorated that room with pictures.
② *to put on display*
¶Kabe ni kono karendā o kazarimashō.
壁にこのカレンダーを飾りましょう。
Let's display this calendar on the wall.

kaze 風 *wind, breeze*
¶Kaze ga minami kara soyosoyo to fuite imasu.
風が南からそよそよと吹いています。
The wind is blowing gently from the south.
¶Kaze ga dete kita ne.
風が出てきたね。
The wind has risen, hasn't it.
• kimochi no ii kaze 気持ちのいい風 *pleasant breeze*
• kaze no tsuyoi hi 風の強い日 *windy day*

• kaze ga yamu 風がやむ *the wind dies down*
• kita-kaze 北風 *north wind*
• soyo-kaze そよ風 *gentle breeze*

kaze 風邪 *a cold*
¶Yōko-chan wa kaze de yasunde iru yo.
洋子ちゃんはかぜで休んでいるよ。
Yoko is absent because of a cold!
¶Kaze ga hayatte imasu ne.
かぜがはやっていますね。
Colds are going around, aren't they.
• kaze o hiku かぜをひく *to catch a cold*
¶Sensei mo hidoi kaze o hiite imasu.
先生もひどいかぜをひいています。
The teacher has a terrible cold, too.
• kaze-gimi 風邪気味 *feeling of having a slight cold*
• kaze-gusuri 風邪薬 *cold medicine*

kazoéru 数える *to count, to reckon the number of*
¶Shusseki-sha o kazoete kudasai.
出席者を数えてください。
Please count the people present.

kázoku 家族 *family*
¶Sono ko no kazoku wa nan-nin desu ka.
その子の家族は何人ですか。
How many people are there in that child's family?
• go-kazoku ご家族 【HON. for **kazoku** (above)】
¶Go-kazoku no mina-san wa o-genki desu ka.
ご家族の皆さんはお元気ですか。
Is everyone in your family well?
• dai-kazoku 大家族 *large family*

kázu 数 *number*
¶Seito no kazu wa gohyaku-nin desu.
生徒の数は500人です。
The number of students is five hundred.
¶Ike no ahiru no kazu o kazoenasai.
池のあひるの数を数えなさい。
Count the number of ducks in the pond.
• kazu-ōku 数多く *many*
¶Hiroba ni kazu-ōku no hito ga imasu.
広場に数多くの人がいます。
There are a lot of people in the square.

kazu-no-ko 数の子 *herring roe*
ke 毛 *hair; fur* [→**kegawa** 毛皮]*;*
wool [→**yōmō** 羊毛]
¶Kono inu wa ke ga usuku natte kima-shita.
この犬は毛が薄くなってきました。
This dog's hair has become thin.
• katai [yawarakai] ke 堅い〔柔らかい〕
毛 *stiff* [*soft*] *hair*
• ke-bukai 毛深い *hairy, shaggy*
• chijire-ge 縮れ毛 *curly hair*
kēburu ケーブル *cable*
• kēburu-kā ケーブルカー *cable car*
kecháppu ケチャップ *ketchup*
kéchi けち ① ~**na** ~な *stingy*
② 【COL.】 ~**o tsukeru** ~を付ける
to find fault
• A ni kechi o tsukeru Aにけちをつける
to find fault with A, to criticize A
• kechi-nbō けちん坊 【COL.】 *miser,*
tightwad
kéchikechi けちけち 【COL.】 ~**suru**
~する *to be stingy*
kedamono 獣 *beast* [→**kemono** 獣]
kédo けど 【COL. for **keredomo**
けれども】
kédomo けども [☞**keredomo** けれども]
kegá 怪我 *injury, wound*
• kega o suru けがをする *to get hurt, to*
get injured, to get wounded
¶Naifu de ude ni kega o shimashita.
ナイフで腕にけがをしました。
I got wounded in the arm with a knife.
¶Sono jiko de kega o shimashita.
その事故でけがをしました。
I got injured in that accident.
• kega suru けがする *to get injured; to in-*
jure «a part of one's body»
¶Ueda-san wa ashi o kega shimashita.
上田さんは足をけがしました。
Mr. Ueda injured his foot.
• kega-nin 怪我人 *injured person*
kegawa 毛皮 *fur*
• kegawa-seihin 毛皮製品 *product made*
of fur
kehai 気配 *indication, sign* «that a
person senses in the surroundings»

keiba 競馬 *horse racing*
• keiba-jō 競馬場 *racetrack,* <*UK*>*rac-*
ecourse
keibetsu 軽蔑 *contempt, scorn, disdain*
«for a person»
• keibetsu suru 軽べつする *to look down*
on, to scorn, to disdain
¶Minna wa Yukio-san o keibetsu shite
imasu.
みんなは幸夫さんを軽べつしています。
Everybody looks down on Yukio.
¶Anna hito wa keibetsu suru wa.
あんな人は軽べつするわ。
I disdain such a person!
kéibi 警備 *guarding*
• keibi suru 警備する *to guard*
• keibi-in 警備員 *guard; watchman*
keido 経度 *longitude* [⇔**ido** 緯度]
keiei 経営 *running, management* «of an
organization, typically a business»
• keiei suru 経営する *to manage, to run*
¶Chichi wa resutoran o keiei shite imasu.
父はレストランを経営しています。
My father is running a restaurant.
• keiei-sha 経営者 *proprietor, manager*
keigo 敬語 *respectful word* «Japanese respectful vocabulary is usually classified
into three types: honorific, humble, and
polite.»
kéigu 敬具 【FORMAL】 *Sincerely*
yours «Used as a closing phrase in
formal letters.» [⇔**haikei** 拝啓]
kéihi 経費 *expense(s), cost* [→**hiyō**
費用]
¶Sore wa keihi ga kakari-sugimasu.
それは経費がかかりすぎます。
That involves too much cost.
keihin 景品 ① *free gift, giveaway,*
premium «accompanying something one
buys» [→**omake** お負け]
② *prize item* [→**shōhin** 賞品]
Keihin 京浜 *Tokyo and Yokohama*
keihō 警報 *warning, alarm*
• keihō-sōchi 警報装置 *alarm system*
• bōfū-u-keihō 暴風雨警報 *storm warn-*
ing
• kasai-keihō 火災警報 *fire alarm*

kéiji 刑事 (*police*)*detective*

keiji 掲示 *notice, bulletin*
- keiji-ban 掲示板 *bulletin board, notice board*

keika 経過 ① *progress, course* 《of events》
¶Kanja no shujutsu-go no keika wa ryōkō desu.
患者の手術後の経過は良好です。
The patient's post-operation progress is good.
 ② *passage* 《of time》
- keika suru 経過する *to pass, to elapse* [→**tatsu** 経つ]
¶Shiai-kaishi-go, jup-pun ga keika shimashita.
試合開始後、10分が経過しました。
Ten minutes have passed since the game started.

keikai 警戒 ① *caution, precaution* [→**yōjin** 用心]
- keikai suru 警戒する *to exercise caution against*
 ② *lookout, guarding* [→**mihari** 見張り]
- keikai suru 警戒する *to look out for, to watch out for* [→**miharu** 見張る]
- keikai-shingō 警戒信号 *warning signal*

keikai 軽快 ~**na** ~な ① *light, nimble*
¶Sono shōjo wa keikai na ashi-dori de odotte imasu.
その少女は軽快な足どりで踊っています。
That girl is dancing with light steps.
 ② *light-hearted, cheerful*
¶Kashu wa keikai na rizumu de utaimashita.
歌手は軽快なリズムで歌いました。
The singer sang in cheerful rhythm.

keikaku 計画 *plan* (*of action*)
- keikaku suru 計画する *to plan*
- keikaku o jikkō suru 計画を実行する *to carry out a plan*
- keikaku o tateru 計画を立てる *to make a plan, to make plans*
¶Natsu-yasumi no keikaku o tatete imasu.
夏休みの計画を立てています。

I am making plans for the summer vacation.
¶Pikunikku ni iku keikaku o tatemashita.
ピクニックに行く計画を立てました。
We planned to go on a picnic.
- toshi-keikaku 都市計画 *city planning*

keikan 警官 *police officer*
- fujin-keikan 婦人警官 *policewoman*

keiken 経験 *experience*
¶Sono hito wa mattaku keiken ga nai.
その人はまったく経験がない。
That person has absolutely no experience.
- tanoshii 〔kurushii〕 keiken 楽しい〔苦しい〕経験 *pleasant* 〔*bitter*〕 *experience*
- keiken suru 経験する *to experience*
¶Konna atsusa wa keiken shita koto ga nai desu.
こんな暑さは経験したことがないです。
I have never experienced such heat.

keiki 景気 ① *business* (*conditions*); *the times, the economy*
¶Keiki wa dō desu ka.
景気はどうですか。
How's business?
¶San-nen-mae kara zutto keiki ga ii desu.
3年前からずっと景気がいいです。
Business has been good for the past three years.
 ② *liveliness, vitality* [→**kakki** 活気]

kéiko 稽古 *practice, training, rehearsal*
¶Maishū Nichiyōbi o-hana no keiko o shimasu.
毎週日曜日お花のけいこをします。
I take flower arranging lessons every Sunday.
- keiko suru 稽古する *to practice, to take lessons in*

keikō 傾向 *tendency; trend*
¶Fasshon wa gojū-nendai ni modoru keikō ni aru.
ファッションは50年代に戻る傾向にある。
The trend in fashion is a return to the 50's.

keikoku 警告 *warning*
- keikoku o ukeru 警告を受ける *to receive*

a warning

• keikoku suru 警告する *to warn, to give a warning*

¶Keikan wa watashi-tachi ni sono hashi o wataranai yō ni keikoku shimashita.
警官は私たちにその橋を渡らないように警告しました。
The police officer warned us not to cross that bridge.

keikōtō 蛍光灯 *fluorescent light*

keimúsho 刑務所 *prison*

keireki 経歴 *educational and employment history, career background*

¶Kimura-san wa donna keireki no kata desu ka.
木村さんはどんな経歴の方ですか。
What is Ms.Kimura's career background? 《*Literally: Ms.Kimura is a person of what kind of career background?*》

keirin 競輪 *professional bicycle racing* 《on which betting is legal in Japan》

Keirō no hi 敬老の日 *Respect for the Aged Day* 《a Japanese national holiday on September 15》

keisan 計算 *calculation, computation*

¶Imōto wa keisan ga hayai desu.
妹は計算が速いです。
My younger sister is quick at calculation.

• keisan suru 計算する *to calculate, to compute*

• keisan-ki 計算器 *calculator*

• keisan-machigai 計算間違い *mistake in calculation*

• denshi-keisan-ki 電子計算機 (*electronic*)*computer* [→konpyūtā コンピューター]

keisatsu 警察 *police, police force*

• keisatsu-kan 警察官 *police officer* [→ keikan 警官]

• keisatsu-ken 警察犬 *police dog*

• keisatsu-sho 警察署 *police station*

Keishíchō 警視庁 *the* (*Tokyo*)*Metropolitan Police Department*

keishiki 形式 ① (*outward*)*form* [⇔ naiyō 内容①]

② *a formality*

• keishiki-teki na 形式的な *formal,*

perfunctory

keisotsu 軽率 〜na 〜な *rash, reckless, careless*

keitai 携帯 *carrying* (*along with one*)

• keitai suru 携帯する *to carry*

• keitai-yō no 携帯用の *portable*

• keitai-denwa 携帯電話 *portable telephone*

¶Keitai-denwa o motte itte kudasai.
携帯電話を持っていってください。
Please take a portable telephone.

keitai 形態 *form, shape*

• seiji no keitai 政治の形態 *form of government*

keiteki 警笛 *warning horn, warning whistle*

• keiteki o narasu 警笛を鳴らす *to sound a warning horn╱whistle*

keito 毛糸 *woolen yarn*

• keito no tebukuro 毛糸の手袋 *woolen gloves; woolen mittens*

keiyaku 契約 *contract*

• keiyaku suru 契約する *to contract, to enter into a contract*

• keiyaku-kikan 契約期間 *contract period*

• keiyaku-sho 契約書 *written contract*

keiyōdóshi 形容動詞 *adjectival noun* 《This term refers to the type of word that is followed by **na** when modifying a following noun. This is one of the parts of speech in traditional Japanese grammar.》

keiyōshi 形容詞 *adjective*

-keiyu 〜経由 *by way of, via* 《Added to bases denoting a place where an intermediate stop is made.》

¶Hachijūsan-bin wa Honoruru-keiyu desu.
83便はホノルル経由です。
Flight 83 is via Honolulu.

¶Ōsaka-keiyu de Fukuoka ni ikimasu.
大阪経由で福岡に行きます。
I'll go to Fukuoka by way of Osaka.

kéizai 経済 ① *economy* 《of a country, etc.》

• Nihon no keizai 日本の経済 *Japan's economy*

• keizai-enjo 経済援助 *economic aid*

- keizai-gaku 経済学 *(the study of)*
economics
- keizai-gaku-sha 経済学者 *economist*
② *economy, thrift, frugality*
- keizai-teki na 経済的な *economical,
thrifty, frugal*
¶Kono sutōbu wa achira no yori keizai-
teki desu.
このストーブはあちらのより経済的です。
*This heater is more economical than that
one over there.*

keizoku 継続 *continuation*
- keizoku suru 継続する *to continue*
《*transitive or intransitive*》

keizu 系図 *family tree, genealogical
chart*

kejimé けじめ *distinction, difference*
《*especially involving morality or social
norms*》
- kejime o tsukeru けじめを付ける *to
draw a distinction*

kéki ケーキ *cake*
¶Kyōko-san wa kēki o yaite kuremashita.
京子さんはケーキを焼いてくれました。
Kyoko baked a cake for me.
¶Kēki o hito-kire kudasai.
ケーキを一切れください。
Please give me one slice of cake.
- bāsudē-kēki バースデーケーキ *birthday
cake*
- dekorēshon-kēki デコレーションケーキ
decorated cake
- shōto-kēki ショートケーキ *shortcake*

kekka 結果 *result, effect* [⇔**gen'in**
原因]
¶Tesuto no kekka wa dō deshita ka.
テストの結果はどうでしたか。
How were the test results?
- gen'in to kekka 原因と結果 *cause and
effect*

kekkaku 結核 *tuberculosis*

kekkan 欠陥 *defect, shortcoming, defi-
ciency* 《*i.e., the lack of something necessary*》
¶Kono kikai ni wa kekkan ga arimasu.
この機械には欠陥があります。
There is a defect in this machine.

- kekkan-shōhin 欠陥商品 *defective
merchandise*

kekkan 血管 *blood vessel*

kékkō 結構 ① ～**na** ～な *good, fine,
nice* [→**rippa na** 立派な]
¶Kekkō na okurimono o dōmo arigatō.
結構な贈り物をどうもありがとう。
Thank you for the nice present.
② ～**da** ～だ *all right, fine* [→**ii**②]
¶"Sumimasen ga pen wa arimasen." "Enpitsu de kekkō desu."
「すみませんが、ペンはありません」「鉛筆
で結構です」
*"I'm sorry, but I don't have a pen." "A
pencil will be fine."*
¶"Kōhī o mō ip-pai ikaga desu ka." "Iie,
mō kekkō desu."
「コーヒーをもう1杯いかがですか」「いい
え、もう結構です」
"How about another cup of coffee?"
"No, thank you." 《*Literally: No, it's already fine.*》
③ *quite, rather, considerably* [→**kanari** かなり]

kekkon 結婚 *marriage*
- kekkon suru 結婚する *to marry, to get
married*
¶Ani wa Yōko-san to kekkon shimashita.
兄は洋子さんと結婚しました。
My older brother got married to Yoko.
¶Kimura-san wa kekkon shite imasu.
木村さんは結婚しています。
Mr. Kimura is married.
- kekkon-kinen-bi 結婚記念日 *wedding
anniversary*
- kekkon-shiki 結婚式 *wedding*
¶Kyōkai de kekkon-shiki o ageru yotei
desu.
教会で結婚式をあげる予定です。
*We plan to hold the wedding ceremony
at church.*
- miai-kekkon 見合い結婚 *marriage
resulting from an arranged meeting*
- ren'ai-kekkon 恋愛結婚 *love marriage*

kekkyoku 結局 *after all, in the end*

¶Kekkyoku, Eiko-san wa kimasen
deshita.
結局、英子さんは来ませんでした。
In the end, Eiko didn't come.

kemono 獣 *beast*

kemui 煙い *smoky*

kemuri 煙 *smoke*

¶Hora, kemuri ga dete iru yo.
ほら、煙が出ているよ。
Look, smoke is coming out!

¶Hi no nai tokoro ni kemuri wa tatanai.
火のない所に煙は立たない。《proverb》
Where there's smoke, there's fire. 《Literally: *In a place where there is no fire,
smoke does not rise.*》

kemushí 毛虫 *hairy caterpillar*

kén 券 *ticket* [→**kippu** 切符]
• nyūjō-ken 入場券 *admission ticket*
• shōtai-ken 招待券 *invitation ticket*

kén 県 *prefecture* 《Japan has 47 prefectures, and all except Tokyo, Osaka,
Kyoto, and Hokkaido are called **ken**.》
• ken-chiji 県知事 *prefectural governor*
• ken-chō 県庁 *prefectural office*
• Aomori-ken 青森県 *Aomori Prefecture*

kén 剣 *double-edged sword*

kén 件 *matter, incident*
• -ken －件《counter for incidents; see
Appendix 2》

-ken －軒《counter for houses and small
buildings; see Appendix 2》

kenasu 貶す *to speak ill of, to criticize*
[⇔**homeru** 褒める]

¶Hideko-san wa tokidoki watashi no hanashi-kata o kenasu ne.
秀子さんは時々私の話し方をけなすね。
*Hideko sometimes criticizes my way of
speaking, doesn't she*

kenbikyō 顕微鏡 *microscope*

kenbutsu 見物 *seeing, watching, visiting* 《a famous place, an event, etc.》
• kenbutsu suru 見物する *to see, to
watch, to visit*

¶Kegon-no-taki o kenbutsu ni ikimasu.
華厳の滝を見物に行きます。
I'm going to go to see the Kegon Falls.

¶Ashita wa bijutsu-kan o kenbutsu suru

yotei desu.
あしたは美術館を見物する予定です。
*Tomorrow I'm planning to visit the art
museum.*

• kenbutsu-nin 見物人 *sightseer* [→
kankō-kyaku 観光客 (s.v. **kankō**
観光)]; *spectator* [→**kankyaku** 観客]
• kenbutsu-seki 見物席 (*spectator*)*seat*
• Tōkyō-kenbutsu 東京見物 *Tokyo sightseeing*

kenchiku 建築 ① *a building* [→**tatemono** 建物]

¶Kono ie wa kono machi de mottomo
furui kenchiku desu.
この家はこの町で最も古い建築です。
*This house is the oldest building in this
town.*

② *construction, building* [→**kensetsu**
建設]
• kenchiku suru 建築する *to build, to
construct*

¶Watashi-tachi wa atarashii ie o kenchiku shite imasu.
私たちは新しい家を建築しています。
We are building a new house.

• kenchiku-gaku 建築学 *the study of
architecture*
• kenchiku-ka 建築家 *architect*
• mokuzō-kenchiku 木造建築 *wooden
building*

kéndō 剣道 *kendo* 《traditional Japanese
fencing》

¶Mainichi kendō no keiko o shimasu.
毎日剣道のけいこをします。
I do kendo practice every day.

kengaku 見学 *study by observation,
field trip*
• kengaku suru 見学する *to study by
observing, to make a field trip to*

¶Watashi-tachi wa yūbin-kyoku o
kengaku shimashita.
私たちは郵便局を見学しました。
We made a field trip to the post office.

kén'i 権威 ① *power, authority* [→**ken-
ryoku** 権力]
• ken'i o furuu 権威をふるう *to exercise
authority*

② *expert, authority*

¶Ōno-hakase wa seibutsu-gaku no ken'i desu.

大野博士は生物学の権威です。

Dr. Ono is an authority on biology.

kénji 検事 *public prosecutor*

kenjō 謙譲 *humility, modesty* [→**kenson** 謙遜]

• kenjō-go 謙譲語 *humble word* 《one type of respectful vocabulary in Japanese》 [⇔**sonkei-go** 尊敬語 (s.v. **sonkei** 尊敬)]

kenjū 拳銃 *pistol, handgun*

kenka 喧嘩 *quarrel; fight*

• kenka suru けんかする *to quarrel; to fight*

¶Ikegami-kun wa Nakao-kun to kenka shita yo.

池上君は中尾君とけんかしたよ。

Ikegami fought with Nakao!

¶Imōto to otōto wa terebi no koto de kenka shite imasu.

妹と弟はテレビのことでけんかしています。

My younger sister and younger brother are quarreling about the TV.

kenkō 健康 *health* [⇔**byōki** 病気]

¶Sanpo o suru no wa kenkō ni ii desu.

散歩をするのは健康にいいです。

Taking a walk is good for your health.

¶Kenkō wa tomi ni masaru.

健康は富にまさる。《proverb》

Health is better than wealth. 《Literally: Health surpasses wealth.》

• kenkō o gaisuru 健康を害する *to injure one's health, to ruin one's health*

• kenkō o kaifuku suru 健康を回復する *to recover one's health*

• kenkō na 健康な *healthy, well, fine*

¶Kazoku wa minna kenkō desu.

家族はみな健康です。

Everyone in my family is healthy.

• kenkō-hoken 健康保険 *health insurance*

• kenkō-jōtai 健康状態 *state of health*

• kenkō-shindan 健康診断 *physical examination, <US>health checkup*

Kenkoku-kínen no hi 建国記念の日

National Founding Day 《a Japanese national holiday on February 11th》

kenkyū 研究 *study; research*

¶Yagi-sensei wa Nihon-shi no kenkyū o tsuzukete iru.

八木先生は日本史の研究を続けている。

Prof. Yagi is continuing research on Japanese history.

• kenkyū suru 研究する *to study; to do research on*

¶Shinri-gaku o kenkyū shite imasu.

心理学を研究しています。

I am studying psychology.

• kenkyū-happyō 研究発表 *presentation of research results*

• kenkyū-hi 研究費 *reserarch funds*

• kenkyū-jo 研究所 *laboratory, research institute*

kenmei 賢明 ～**na** ～な *wise*

¶Sensei ni sōdan shita no wa kenmei deshita.

先生に相談したのは賢明でした。

It was wise to consult with the teacher.

kénpō 憲法 *constitution* 《of a country》

• Kenpō-kinen-bi 憲法記念日 *Constitution Memorial Day* 《a Japanese national holiday on May 3》

• Nihon-koku-kenpō 日本国憲法 *the Constitution of Japan*

kénri 権利 *a right*

¶Ano hito ni hatsugen suru kenri wa nai yo.

あの人に発言する権利はないよ。

That person has no right to speak.

• kenri to gimu 権利と義務 *rights and obligations*

kenritsu 県立 ～**no** ～の *prefectural, administered by a prefecture*

• kenritsu-kōkō 県立高校 *prefectural high school*

kénryoku 権力 *power, authority* [→**ken'i** 権威, **seiryoku** 勢力]

• kenryoku-sha 権力者 *person of power*

kénsa 検査 *inspection, examination*

• kensa suru 検査する *to inspect, to examine*

¶Haisha ga watashi no ha o kensa

shimashita.
歯医者が私の歯を検査しました。
The dentist examined my teeth.
¶Haha wa byōin de kensa o ukemashita.
母は病院で検査を受けました。
My mother underwent an examination at the hospital.
• kensa-kan 検査官 *(government)inspector*
• gakuryoku-kensa 学力検査 *scholastic achievement test* [→**gakuryoku-tesuto** 学力テスト (s.v. **gakuryoku** 学力)]
• shintai-kensa 身体検査 *physical examination*

kensetsu 建設 *construction, erecting, building*
• kensetsu suru 建設する *to build, to construct, to erect*
¶Uchū-sutēshon o kensetsu shimashita.
宇宙ステーションを建設しました。
They built a space station.
• kensetsu-chū no 建設中の *under-construction*
¶Shin-taiiku-kan wa mada kensetsu-chū desu.
新体育館はまだ建設中です。
The new gym is still under construction.
• kensetsu-gaisha 建設会社 *construction company*
• Kensetsu-shō 建設省 *the Ministry of Construction*

kenshō 懸賞 ① *contest with a prize*
② *contest prize; reward* 《for finding a criminal》

kenson 謙遜 *modesty, humility*
• kenson na けんそんな *modest, humble*
• kenson na taido けんそんな態度 *humble attitude*
• kenson suru けんそんする *to be modest, to be humble*

kentō 見当 ① *guess, conjecture, estimate*
¶Watashi no kentō wa atarimashita.
私の見当は当たりました。
My guess proved right.
• kentō o tsukeru 見当を付ける *to make a guess, to make an estimate*

• kentō ga tsuku 見当が付く *to have some idea, to be able to imagine*
¶Sore ga nan da ka kentō ga tsukanai yo.
それが何だか見当がつかないよ。
I can't imagine what that is!
② *general direction*
-**kentō** -見当 *about, <US>around* 《Added to number bases.》 [→-**gurai** -ぐらい]
¶Ano hito wa gojus-sai-kentō desu.
あの人は50歳見当です。
That person is about 50 years old.

kentō 検討 *examination, investigation, inquiry*
• kentō suru 検討する *to examine, to investigate, to inquire into*
¶Kono mondai o kentō shite mimashō.
この問題を検討してみましょう。
Let's examine this problem and see.

ken'yaku 倹約 *economy, thrift, frugality* [→**setsuyaku** 節約]
• ken'yaku suru 倹約する *to be thrifty, to economize; to save, to avoid using*
¶Ken'yaku shite o-kane o tamemashita.
倹約してお金をためました。
I was thrifty and saved money.
¶Basu-dai o ken'yaku shite aruite kaerimashita.
バス代を倹約して歩いて帰りました。
I saved the bus fare and walked home.
• ken'yaku-ka 倹約家 *frugal person*
• ken'yaku-teki na 倹約的な *frugal, thrifty*

kenzen 健全 ～**na** ～な *healthy, sound* [→**kenkō na** 健康な]

kéredo けれど [☞**keredomo** けれども]

kéredomo けれども *but* [→**ga** が]; *however* [→**shikashi** しかし]
¶Fuyu wa samui keredomo, watashi wa suki desu.
冬は寒いけれども、私は好きです。
Winter is cold, but I like it.
¶Yuki ga futte ita keredomo, kaimono ni deta.
雪が降っていたけれども、買い物に出た。
It was snowing, but we went out shopping.

¶Keredomo, anzen wa hoshō dekimasen.
けれども、安全は保証できません。
However, I cannot guarantee safety.

kéru 蹴る{5}*to kick*
¶Bōru o omoikiri kerinasai.
ボールを思い切りけりなさい。
Kick the ball hard.

késa 今朝 *this morning*
¶Kesa no nyūsu o mimashita ka.
けさのニュースを見ましたか。
Did you watch this morning's news?
¶Kesa shichi-ji ni okimashita.
けさ7時に起きました。
I got up at 7:00 this morning.

keshigomu 消しゴム *(rubber)eraser*
¶Keshigomu de machigai o keshimashita.
消しゴムでまちがいを消しました。
I erased the error with an eraser.

keshikarán 怪しからん *disgraceful, unpardonable, outrageous* 《Used either as a noun modifier or as a predicate.》

késhiki 景色 *scenery, view*
¶Yama no keshiki ga suki desu.
山の景色が好きです。
I like mountain scenery.
¶Utsukushii keshiki desu ne.
美しい景色ですね。
It's beautiful scenery, isn't it.
¶Oka kara miru keshiki wa subarashii yo.
丘から見る景色はすばらしいよ。
The view one sees from the hill is wonderful!

keshō 化粧 *make-up*
• keshō suru 化粧する *to put on make-up*
• keshō-hin 化粧品 *cosmetic product*
• keshō-sekken 化粧石鹸 *toilet soap*
• keshō-shitsu 化粧室 *powder room, bathroom* [→**toire** トイレ]

kessaku 傑作 ① *masterpiece*
② *big and humorous blunder*

kesseki 欠席 *absence, nonattendance* [⇔**shusseki** 出席]
• kesseki suru 欠席する *to be absent, to fail to attend*
¶Naze kinō kesseki shita no?

なぜきのう欠席したの？
Why were you absent yesterday?
• gakkō o kesseki suru 学校を欠席する *to be absent from school*
• kesseki-sha 欠席者 *absentee, person not in attendance*
• kesseki-todoke 欠席届 *report of absence*
• chōki-kesseki 長期欠席 *long absence*

késshin 決心 *determination, resolution* [→**ketsui** 決意]
• kesshin suru 決心する *to resolve, to make up one's mind*
¶Akira-san wa pairotto ni narō to kesshin shita.
明さんはパイロットになろうと決心した。
Akira made up his mind to become a pilot.

kesshite 決して 〈*not*〉 *ever, certainly* 〈*not*〉 《Always occurs in combination with a negative predicate.》
¶Harumi-san wa kesshite yakusoku o yaburimasen.
春美さんは決して約束を破りません。
Harumi never breaks a promise.
¶Yutaka-chan wa kesshite gakkō ni chikoku shimasen.
豊ちゃんは決して学校に遅刻しません。
Yutaka is never late for school.
¶Kesshite kibō wa sutemasen.
決して希望は捨てません。
I certainly won't give up hope.

kesshō 決勝 ① *deciding the champion* ② *finals, championship game, title match*
• kesshō-sen 決勝戦 [☞**kesshō** 決勝② (above)]
• jun-kesshō 準決勝 *semifinals*
• jun-jun-kesshō 準々決勝 *quarterfinals*

kesshō 結晶 ① *a crystal*
• yuki no kesshō 雪の結晶 *snow crystal*
• doryoku no kesshō 努力の結晶 *result of effort*
② *crystallization*
• kesshō suru 結晶する *to crystallize*

kēsu ケース *case* ((container))

kēsu ケース *case, instance*

• kēsu–bai–kēsu de ケースバイケースで
case by case, on a case-by-case basis

kesu 消す ① *to put out* 《a fire》[⇔**tsu-keru** 点ける①]

¶Mizu o kakete hi o keshinasai.
水をかけて火を消しなさい。
Pour water on it and put out the fire.

② *to turn off* 《a device》[⇔**tsukeru** 点ける②]

¶Neru mae ni terebi o keshite kudasai.
寝る前にテレビを消してください。
Please turn off the TV before going to bed.

¶Denki o kesu no o wasuremashita.
電気を消すのを忘れました。
I forgot to turn off the light.

③ *to erase*

¶Kokuban o keshite kudasai.
黒板を消してください。
Please erase the blackboard.

keta 桁 ① *digit, figure* 《in a number written in Arabic numerals》

• –keta −桁《counter for digits; see Appendix 2》

• san–keta no kazu 3けたの数
three–digit number

② *beam, girder; bead rod* 《on an abacus》

ketsu けつ 【CRUDE for **shiri** 尻】
<US>*ass*, <UK>*arse*

ketsudan 決断 *decision, deciding*

¶Ano hito wa ketsudan ga hayai desu.
あの人は決断が早いです。
That person is quick at deciding.

• ketsudan suru 決断する *to decide, to make up one's mind*

• ketsudan–ryoku 決断力 *decisiveness*

ketsúeki 血液 *blood* [→**chi** 血] 《The ordinary word for blood is **chi**; **ketsueki** has a scientifc or medical nuance.》

• ketsueki–gata 血液型 *blood type*

¶Watashi no ketsueki–gata wa ō–gata desu.
私の血液型はO型です。
My blood type is type O.

• ketsueki–ginkō 血液銀行 *blood bank*

kétsui 決意 *determination, resolution*

[→**kesshin** 決心]

• ketsui suru 決意する *to resolve, to make up one's mind*

ketsumakúen 結膜炎 *conjunctivitis, pinkeye*

ketsumatsu 結末 *ending, conclusion, outcome*

¶Kore wa kanashii ketsumatsu no monogatari desu.
これは悲しい結末の物語です。
This is a story with a sad ending.

ketsuron 結論 *conclusion* ((idea))

¶Yatto kono ketsuron ni tasshimashita.
やっとこの結論に達しました。
At last we reached this conclusion.

• ketsuron to shite 結論として *in conclusion*

kettei 決定 *decision, determination*

• kettei suru 決定する *to decide, to determine, to set* [→**kimeru** 決める]

• kettei–teki na 決定的な *decisive, conclusive*

kettén 欠点 *fault, defect, weak point*
[→**tansho** 短所]

¶Dare ni demo ketten ga arimasu.
だれにでも欠点があります。
Everyone has weak points.

¶Jibun no ketten o naoshitai desu.
自分の欠点を直したいです。
I want to correct my own faults.

kewashíi 険しい ① *steep, precipitous*

¶Nihon ni wa kewashii yama ga takusan arimasu.
日本には険しい山がたくさんあります。
In Japan there are a lot of steep mountains.

② *grim, difficult* 《describing future conditions》

¶Mitōshi wa kewashii desu ne.
見通しは険しいですね。
The prospects are grim, aren't they.

③ *stern, angry–seeming*

• kewashii koe 険しい声 *stern voice*

kezuru 削る ① *to shave, to scrape*

¶Kono ita o kanna de kezutte kureru?
この板をかんなで削ってくれる？
Will you plane this board for me?

《Literally: *Will you shave this board for me with a plane?*》

•enpitsu o kezuru 鉛筆を削る *to sharpen a pencil*

② *to cut down, to reduce, to curtail*

•keihi o kezuru 経費を削る *to cut down expenses*

③ *to delete, to cut out*

kí 木 ① *tree*

•ki o ueru 木を植える *to plant a tree*

•ki ni noboru 木に登る *to climb a tree*

② *wood*

¶Kore wa ki no tēburu desu.

これは木のテーブルです。

This is a wooden table.

ki 気 ① *heart, mind, feeling*

•ki ga omoi 気が重い *to feel depressed, to feel gloomy*

¶Atarashii shigoto no koto o kangaeru to, ki ga omoi.

新しい仕事のことを考えると、気が重い。

When I think about my new job, I feel depressed.

•ki ga kawaru 気が変わる *to have a change of heart, one's mind changes*

② *care, concern*

•A ni ki ga tsuku Aに気がつく *to notice A, to become aware of A*

¶Watashi mo sono machigai ni ki ga tsukimashita.

私もその間違いに気がつきました。

I noticed that mistake too.

•ki o tsukeru 気をつける *to be careful, to take care, to watch out*

¶Kuruma ni ki o tsukenasai.

車に気をつけなさい。

Watch out for cars.

¶O-karada ni ki o tsukete kudasai.

お体に気をつけてください。

Please take care of yourself. 《Literally: *Please take care of your body.*》

•ki ni naru 気になる *to weigh on one's mind, to be troubling*

¶Ashita no shiken wa ki ni natte imasu.

あしたの試験は気になっています。

Tomorrow's exam is weighing on my mind.

•ki ni suru 気にする *to be concerned about, to worry about, to mind*

¶Sonna koto o ki ni shinai de kudasai.

そんなことを気にしないでください。

Please don't worry about such a thing.

③ *intention, inclination*

•ki ga suru 気がする *to feel like doing* 《following a verb》

¶Kyō wa hataraku ki ga shinai yo.

きょうは働く気がしないよ。

Today I don't feel like working!

•ki ni iru 気に入る *to be pleasing, to strike one's fancy*

¶Sono kuruma ga ki ni irimashita.

その車が気に入りました。

That car struck my fancy.

④ *temper, disposition*

•ki ga mijikai 気が短い *to be short-tempered*

•ki ga tsuyoi 気が強い *to be strong-minded, to have a strong will*

•ki ga chīsai 気が小さい *to be timid*

⑤ *consciousness, one's senses* [→ **ishiki** 意識]

•ki ga tsuku 気がつく *to regain consciousness, to come to one's senses*

¶Ni- san-pun shite kara ki ga tsukimashita.

２、３分してから気がつきました。

I came to my senses after two or three minutes.

•ki o ushinau 気を失う *to lose consciousness, to faint* [→**kizetsu suru** 気絶する]

¶Keiko-san wa sono shirase o kiite ki o ushinatta.

恵子さんはその知らせを聞いて気を失った。

Keiko heard that news and fainted.

kí キー ① *key* 《on a piano, typewriter, etc.》

② *key* 《to a lock》 [→**kagi** 鍵①]

•kī-horudā キーホルダー *key ring; key case*

kiatsu 気圧 *atmospheric pressure; air pressure*

•kiatsu-kei 気圧計 *barometer*

•kō-kiatsu 高気圧 *high atmospheric pressure*

• tei–kiatsu 低気圧 *low atmospheric pressure*

kíba 牙 *tusk; fang*
• it–tsui no kiba 1対のきば *one pair of tusks*

kibarashi 気晴らし *recreation, pastime, diversion*
¶Kibarashi ni sanpo o shimashō.
気晴らしに散歩をしましょう。
Let's take a walk for recreation.
¶Chichi no kibarashi wa engei desu.
父の気晴らしは園芸です。
My father's pastime is gardening.

kíbi きび *millet*

kibishíi 厳しい ① *stern, strict*
¶Watashi–tachi no sensei wa totemo kibishii desu.
私たちの先生はとても厳しいです。
Our teacher is very strict.
② *severe, harsh, bitter*
¶Kyonen no fuyu wa samusa ga kibishikatta desu.
去年の冬は寒さが厳しかったです。
Last winter the cold was severe.

kíbo 規模 *scale, extent, proportionate size*
¶Oji wa shōbai no kibo o shukushō shimashita.
伯父は商売の規模を縮小しました。
My uncle reduced the scale of his business.
• dai–kibo na／no 大規模な／の *large-scale*
• shō–kibo no 小規模の *small-scale*

kibō 希望 [[→**nozomi** 望み]] *hope; wish*
¶Isha ni naru no ga boku no kibō desu.
医者になるのが僕の希望です。
I hope to become a doctor. 《*Literally: Becoming a doctor is my wish.*》
• kibō suru 希望する [[→**nozomu** 望む]] *to hope for; to wish for*
• kibō o ushinau 希望を失う *to lose hope*
¶Zen–sekai ga heiwa o kibō shite imasu.
全世界が平和を希望しています。
The whole world is hoping for peace.

kībódo キーボード *keyboard; keyboard*

(*musical*)*instrument*

kíbun 気分 *feeling, mood, frame of mind*
¶Ima wa uta o utau kibun ja nai yo.
今は歌を歌う気分じゃないよ。
I am not in the mood for singing songs now!
• kibun ni naru 気分になる *to come to feel like, to get in the mood for* 《*following a verb*》
¶Benkyō suru kibun ni naremasen.
勉強する気分になれません。
I can't get in the mood for studying.
• kibun–tenkan 気分転換 *something to change one's mood*
• kibun–ya 気分屋 *moody person*

kíchi 基地 *base* (*of operations*)
• kūgun–kichi 空軍基地 *air-force base*

kichigái 気違い *crazy person*

kichín–to きちんと ① *neatly*
¶Kyōshitsu wa kichin–to katazuite imasu.
教室はきちんと片づいています。
The classroom has been neatly tidied up.
• kichin to shita きちんとした *neat*
¶Ueda–sensei wa itsu–mo kichin–to shita fukusō o shite imasu.
上田先生はいつもきちんとした服装をしています。
Dr. Ueda always wears neat clothes.
② *regularly; punctually*
¶Eigo wa mainichi kichin–to benkyō shinasai.
英語は毎日きちんと勉強しなさい。
Study English regularly every day.

kichō 貴重 ～**na** ～な *precious, valuable*
• kichō na jikan 貴重な時間 *precious time*
• kichō na keiken 貴重な体験 *valuable experience*
• kichō–hin 貴重品 *valuable item*

kichōmen 几帳面 ～**na** ～な *punctilious*
• A ni kichōmen na Aにきちょうめんな *punctilious about A*
¶Harada–san wa jikan ni kichōmen desu.

原田さんは時間にきちょうめんです。
Ms. Harada is punctual.

kidō 軌道 *orbit*

kidoru 気取る *to put on airs*
　¶Yukari-san wa itsu-mo kidotte imasu.
ゆかりさんはいつも気取っています。
Yukari is always putting on airs.
　•kidotta hito 気取った人 *affected person, conceited person*

kieru 消える ① *to go out* 《when the subject is something burning or turned on》 [⇔**tsuku** 点く]
　¶Denki ga patto kiemashita.
電気がぱっと消えました。
The lights suddenly went out.
　¶Kaji wa ma-mo-naku kieru deshō.
火事はまもなく消えるでしょう。
The fire will probably go out soon.
　② *to disappear* [⇔**arawareru** 表れる, 現れる]
　¶Sono hito wa hitogomi no naka ni kiemashita.
その人は人込みの中に消えました。
That person disappeared in the crowd.

kifu 寄付 *donation*
　•kifu suru 寄付する *to make a donation*
　•kifu-kin 寄付金 *monetary donation*

kigae 着替え ① *changing one's clothes*
　② *a change of clothes*
　¶Kigae o motte ikinasai.
着替えを持って行きなさい。
Take a change of clothes.

kigaeru 着替える *to change one's clothes*
　•A ni kigaeru Aに着替える *to change into A*
　¶Jirō-san wa gakusei-fuku ni kigaemashita.
次郎さんは学生服に着替えました。
Jiro changed into his school uniform.

kigákari 気掛り *anxiety, concern* [→**shinpai** 心配]

kigaru 気軽 ～**na** ～な *light-hearted, cheerful, unceremonious*

kígeki 喜劇 *comedy* [⇔**higeki** 悲劇]
　•kigeki-haiyū 喜劇俳優 *comic actor*
　•kigeki-teki na 喜劇的な *comic, comical*

kígen 紀元 ① *first year of a historical era*
　② *the first year of the Christian era* 《Typically used to mark years as A. D. by the Gregorian calendar.》 [→**Seireki** 西暦]
　•kigen-zen 紀元前 *B.C.*
　¶Sono tetsugaku-sha wa kigen-zen rokujū-nen ni umareta.
その哲学者は紀元前60年に生まれた。
That philosopher was born in 60 B. C.
　•shin-kigen 新紀元 *beginning of a new era*

kígen 起源 *origin, genesis*
　•bunmei no kigen 文明の起源 *the origin of civilization*

kígen 期限 *time limit*
　¶Shukudai wa kigen made ni teishutsu shinasai.
宿題は期限までに提出しなさい。
Hand in your homework by the time limit.

kigen 機嫌 ① *mood, humor*
　¶Chichi wa kyō wa kigen ga ii desu.
父はきょうは機嫌がいいです。
My father's mood is good today.
　② *a person's health, a person's welfare*
　¶Go-kigen ikaga desu ka.
ご機嫌いかがですか。
How are you?

kigō 記号 *symbol, sign, mark*
　•hatsuon-kigō 発音記号 *pronunciation symbol*
　•kagaku-kigō 化学記号 *chemical symbol*

kígyō 企業 *business, company, enterprise*
　•chū-shō-kigyō 中小企業 *medium- and small-sized enterprises*
　•dai-kigyō 大企業 *large company, large enterprise*
　•kōei-kigyō 公営企業 *a public enterprise, a government enterprise*
　•minkan-kigyō 民間企業 *a private enterprise, a private company*

kihon 基本 *basis, foundation* 《only in an abstract sense, not as a concrete object》

¶Kore ga kendō no kihon desu.
これが剣道の基本です。
This is the foundation of kendo.
• kihon-teki na 基本的な *basic, fundamental*
• kihon-teki-jinken 基本的人権 *fundamental human rights*

kiiro 黄色 *yellow* 《as a noun》
¶Shingō ga kiiro ni kawarimashita.
信号が黄色に変わりました。
The traffic light turned yellow.

kiiroi 黄色い *yellow* 《as an adjective》

kíji 記事 *(news)article*

kiji 雉 *pheasant*

kijitsu 期日 *appointed day, date*
¶Sono shiken no kijitsu o oshiete kudasai.
その試験の期日を教えてください。
Please tell me the date of that examination.
¶Kijitsu made ni shiharaemasu ka.
期日までに支払えますか。
Can you pay by the appointed day?

kijun 基準 *criterion, standard, basis*

kijutsu 記述 *description*
• kijutsu suru 記述する *to describe*

kiká 帰化 *naturalization* 《i.e., obtaining citizenship》
• kika suru 帰化する *to become a naturalized citizen*

kikágaku 幾何学 *(the study of)geometry*

kikái 機会 *chance, opportunity*
¶Musume wa Rondon o tazuneru kikai ga arimashita.
娘はロンドンを訪ねる機会がありました。
My daughter had a chance to visit London.
¶Masuda-san to au kikai ga nakatta desu.
増田さんと会う機会がなかったです。
I didn't have an opportunity to see Mr. Masuda.
¶Ima ga zekkō no kikai desu yo.
今が絶好の機会ですよ。
Now is the best opportunity!
• kikai o nogasu 機会を逃す *to miss a chance, to let an opportunity get away*

kikái 機械 *machine*
¶Kono kikai wa umaku hatarakimasen.
この機械はうまく働きません。
This machine doesn't run well.
• kikai-ka 機械化 *mechanization*
• kikai-kōgaku 機械工学 *mechanical engineering*
• kikai-teki na 機械的な *mechanical*

kikaku 企画 *plan (of action)* [→**keikaku** 計画]; *planning*
• kikaku suru 企画する *to plan*

kikán 期間 *(time)period*
• chō-kikan 長期間 *long period*
• tan-kikan 短期間 *short period*

kikán 器官 *(bodily)organ*
• kokyū-kikan 呼吸器官 *respiratory organs*
• shōka-kikan 消化器官 *digestive organs*

kikán 機関 ① *engine* [→**enjin** エンジン] ② *institution, facility; mechanism, set-up, means*
• kikan-sha 機関車 *locomotive*
• jōki-kikan 蒸気機関 *steam engine*
• kōtsū-kikan 交通機関 *means of transportation*
• kinyū-kikan 金融機関 *financial institution*
• kyōiku-kikan 教育機関 *educational institution*

kikaseru 聞かせる *to tell, to tell about* 《This word is the causative form of **kiku** 聞く and has the predictable range of meanings in addition to the definition given here.》
¶Ryokō no hanashi o kikasete kudasai.
旅行の話を聞かせてください。
Please tell us about your trip.

kikazáru 着飾る *to get dressed up*
¶Ōta-san wa pātī no tame ni kikazatta.
大田さんはパーティーのために着飾った。
Ms. Ota was dressed up for the party.

kiken 危険 *danger*
• kiken na 危険な *dangerous* [⇔**anzen na** 安全な]
¶Sono kanja no seimei wa kiken na jōtai ni arimasu.

その患者の生命は危険な状態にあります。
That patient's life is in danger.

¶Koko de oyogu no wa kiken desu.
ここで泳ぐのは危険です。
It is dangerous to swim here.

•kiken-shingō 危険信号 *danger signal*

kiken 棄権 *abstention* «from voting»;
renunciation «of a right»; *withdrawal*
«from a competition»

•kiken suru 棄権する *to abstain from; to
renounce; to withdraw*

•tōhyō o kiken suru 投票を棄権する *to
abstain from voting*

•kyōgi o kiken suru 競技を棄権する *to
withdraw from an athletic competition*

kíki 危機 *crisis*

•kiki ni chokumen suru 危機に直面する
to face a crisis

•kiki o norikoeru 危機を乗り越える *to
get through a crisis*

•kiki-ippatsu no tokorode 危機一髪のと
ころで *by a hair's breadth, by the skin of
one's teeth*

•sekiyu-kiki 石油危機 *oil crisis*

kikime 効き目 *effect, efficacy* [→**kōka**
効果]

¶Chichi no chūkoku wa otōto ni wa nan
no kikime mo nai.
父の忠告は弟にはなんの効き目もない。
*My father's advice has no effect on my
younger brother.*

kikín 飢饉 *famine*

kikín 基金 *fund, endowment*

kikitori 聞き取り *catching* (*what is
said*)

kikitóru 聞き取る *to catch* «what is
said»

kikkake きっかけ ① *opportunity,* (*favorable*)*occasion* [→**kikai** 機会]

② *motive, motivation* [→**dōki** 動機]

kíkku キック *kick* «Ordinarily refers to
kicking a ball in sports.»

•kikku suru キックする *to kick*

•kikku-ofu キックオフ *kickoff*

•kōnā-kikku コーナーキック *corner kick*

kikō 気候 *climate*

¶Nihon wa kikō ga odayaka desu.

日本は気候が穏やかです。
Japan's climate is mild.

•kikō no kawari-me 気候の変わり目
change from one season to the next

kikoeru 聞こえる ① *to be able to hear;
to be audible* «What is heard is treated
as a grammatical subject and marked
with **ga** が rather than with **o** を.»

¶Moshimoshi, kikoemasu ka.
もしもし、聞こえますか。
Hello, can you hear me?

¶Tori ga naite iru no ga kikoemasu.
鳥が鳴いているのが聞こえます。
I can hear birds singing.

② *to sound, to give an auditory impression*

¶Sono ongaku wa mimi ni kokoroyoku
kikoemasu ne.
その音楽は耳に快く聞こえますね。
*That music sounds pleasant to the ears,
doesn't it?*

kikoku 帰国 *returning home* (*to one's
own country*)

•kikoku suru 帰国する *to return home*

¶Sono gakusei wa raigetsu Amerika kara
kikoku shimasu.
その学生は来月アメリカから帰国します。
*That student will come home from the
United States next month.*

kikú 菊 *chrysanthemum*

kiku 効く *to take effect, to work*

¶Kono kusuri wa zutsū ni yoku kikimasu.
この薬は頭痛によく効きます。
This medicine works well for headaches.

kiku 利く ① *to work, to function well*

¶Kono kuruma wa burēki ga kikanai yo.
この車はブレーキが利かないよ。
This car's brakes don't work!

•hana ga kiku 鼻が利く *to have a keen
nose*

② *to be possible; to be available for
use*

•sentaku ga kiku 洗濯が利く *laundering
is possible*

③ **kuchi o**~ 口を~ *to speak, to say
something*

kiku 聞く, 聴く ① *to hear*
¶Arisutoteresu ni tsuite kiita koto ga aru ka.
アリストテレスについて聞いたことがあるか。
Have you ever heard about Aristotle?
　② *to listen to*
¶Sono setsumei o kiite kudasai.
その説明を聞いてください。
Please listen to that explanation.
¶Watashi-tachi wa Nichiyōbi ni ongaku o kikimasu.
私たちは日曜日に音楽を聴きます。
We listen to music on Sundays.
¶Rajio o kiki-nagara, benkyō shimasu.
ラジオを聞きながら勉強します。
I study while listening to the radio.
¶Sono shōnen wa watashi no iu koto o kiite, kaetta.
その少年は私の言うことを聞いて、帰った。
That boy listened to what I said and went home.
　③ *to ask, to inquire* [→**tazuneru** 尋ねる]
・A ni B o kiku　AにBを聞く *to ask A about B*
¶Eki e no michi o sono hito ni kikimashita.
駅への道をその人に聞きました。
I asked that person the way to the station.
¶"Dekimasu ka" to Kaneda-san ni kikimashita.
「できますか」と金田さんに聞きました。
"Can you do it?" I asked Mr. Kaneda.

kikúbari 気配り *attentiveness, caring*
・kikubari suru 気配りする *to be attentive, to show caring*

kikyū 気球 *balloon* «i.e., a device designed to rise into the atmosphere»

kimae 気前 ～**ga ii** ～がいい *generous*
・kimae-yoku 気前よく *generously*

kimagure 気まぐれ *caprice, whim*
・kimagure na 気まぐれな *capricious, changeable*

kimari 決まり ① *rule* [→**kisoku** 規則]
¶Bōshi o kaburu no ga gakkō no kimari desu.
帽子をかぶるのが学校の決まりです。
Wearing a cap is a school rule.
　② *settlement, conclusion*
・A no kimari ga tsuku　Aの決まりが付く
A is settled, A is brought to a conclusion
・A no kimari o tsukeru　Aの決まりを付ける *to settle A, to bring A to a conclusion*
　③ ～**ga warui** ～が悪い *to feel awkward, to feel embarrassed*

kimarimónku 決まり文句 *set phrase, stereotyped expression*

kimaru 決まる *to be decided, to be set*
・A ga B ni kimaru　AがBに決まる *A is set for B, B is chosen as A*
¶Ane no kekkon-shiki wa Jūichi-gatsu tōka ni kimatta.
姉の結婚式は11月10日に決まった。
My older sister's wedding was set for November 10.
¶Kaigi no basho ga Sendai ni kimarimashita.
会議の場所が仙台に決まりました。
Sendai was chosen as the conference venue.
・A ni kimatte iru　Aに決まっている *it's certain that it's A* «In this pattern, A can be a clause as well as a noun.»
¶Akira-kun ga shiken ni ukaru ni kimatte iru yo.
明君は試験に受かるに決まっているよ。
Akira is certain to pass the exam!

kimatte 決まって *regularly, invariably, always* «This word is the gerund (-te form) of **kimaru** 決まる and has the predictable meanings as well.»

kimeru 決める *to decide, to set*
¶Kaigō no jikan to basho o kimemashō.
会合の時間と場所を決めましょう。
Let's set the time and place for our meeting.
・A o B ni kimeru　AをBに決める *to decide on B for A, to decide on B as A*
¶Atarashii dezain o kore ni kimemashita.
新しいデザインをこれに決めました。
I decided on this for the new design.
・koto ni kimeru ことに決める *to decide*

to 《following a nonpast-tense verb》

¶Watashi-tachi wa sugu iku koto ni kime-mashita.

私たちはすぐ行くことに決めました。

We decided to go at once.

kimi 君 *you* 《There are several Japanese words for *you*, but in general, Japanese speakers prefer to use names or titles instead. The use of **kimi** is typical of a male speaker addressing a younger person or an intimate equal. Female speakers typically use **kimi** only to address a child. Other words for *you* include **anata** あなた, **omae** お前, and **kisama** 貴様.》

¶Oi, kimi, mado kara haitte wa ikenai yo.

おい、君、窓から入ってはいけないよ。

Hey, you! You mustn't go in through the window!

kimi 黄身 *yolk, yellow* 《of an egg》 [⇔ **shiromi** 白身①]

Kimi-ga-yo 君が代 *Kimi-ga-yo* 《the Japanese national anthem》

kimó 肝 ① *liver* 《bodily organ》 [→ **kanzō** 肝臓]

② *courage, nerve* [→**dokyō** 度胸]

kimochi 気持ち *feeling, how a person feels*

¶Ano hito no kimochi ga yoku wakaru yo.

あの人の気持ちがよくわかるよ。

I understand very well how that person feels!

•kimochi ga ii 気持ちがいい *to feel good* 《when describing a person》; *to be pleasant, to be comfortable* 《when describing a thing》

¶Kore wa kimochi no ii heya desu ne.

これは気持ちのいい部屋ですね。

This is a comfortable room, isn't it.

•kimochi ga warui 気持ちが悪い *to feel bad, to feel sick* 《when describing a person》; *to be unpleasant, to be disgusting* 《when describing a thing》

kimono 着物 ① *kimono*

¶Keiko-san wa kimono ga yoku niai-masu.

恵子さんは着物がよく似合います。

Keiko looks nice in a kimono.

② *clothes* [→**fuku** 服]

kimuzukashii 気難しい *hard to please*

kímyō 奇妙 ~**na** ~な *odd, peculiar, strange* [→**myō na** 妙な]

•kimyō na fūshū 奇妙な風習 *odd customs*

kín 金 *gold*

¶Takayama-san wa kin no yubiwa o shite imasu.

高山さんは金の指輪をしています。

Ms. Takayama is wearing a gold ring.

•kin-iro 金色 *gold color*

•kin-ka 金貨 *gold coin*

•kin-medaru 金メダル *gold medal*

kínako きな粉 *parched soybean flour*

kinben 勤勉 *diligence*

•kinben na 勤勉な *diligent, hardworking*

¶Hiroshi-kun wa kinben na seito desu.

弘君は勤勉な生徒です。

Hiroshi is a diligent pupil.

kinchō 緊張 《*mental*》*tension*

•kinchō suru 緊張する *to become tense*

¶Shiken no mae wa kinchō shimasu.

試験の前は緊張します。

I become tense before an exam.

kíndai 近代 *the modern age, modern times* 《In Japanese history, this word is ordinarily used to mean specifically the period from the beginning of the Meiji period (1868) until the end of the Second World War.》

•kindai-shi 近代史 *modern history*

•kindai-teki na 近代的な *modern, contemporary*

kinen 記念 *commemoration, remembrance*

¶Sotsugyō no kinen ni kōtei ni taimu-kapuseru o umemashita.

卒業の記念に校庭にタイムカプセルを埋めました。

We buried a time capsule on the school grounds in commemoration our graduation.

•kinen-bi 記念日 *anniversary, day of commemoration*

•kinen-hi 記念碑 *monument*

- kinen-hin 記念品 *souvenir, memento*
- kinen-kitte 記念切手 *commemorative stamp*
- kinen-shashin 記念写真 *souvenir photo*

kin'en 禁煙 ① *prohibition of smoking* ② *giving up smoking, abstaining from smoking*

- kin'en suru 禁煙する *to give up smoking, to abstain from smoking*

¶Oji wa kyonen kara kin'en shite imasu.

伯父は去年から禁煙しています。

My uncle has been abstaining from smoking since last year.

- kin'en-sha 禁煙車 *no-smoking car*

kingaku 金額 *amount of money*

¶Sono kashu wa kanari no kingaku no hōseki o katta.

その歌手はかなりの金額の宝石を買った。

The singer bought some very expensive jewels.

kingan 近眼 *near-sightedness* [→**kinshi** 近視]

kíngyo 金魚 *goldfish*

- kingyo-bachi 金魚鉢 *goldfish bowl*

kinjiru 禁じる *to forbid, to prohibit*

¶Isha wa chichi ni gaishutsu o kinjimashita.

医者は父に外出を禁じました。

The doctor forbade my father to go out.

¶Kono kawa de no suiei wa kinjirarete imasu.

この川での水泳は禁じられています。

Swimming in this river is prohibited.

kínjo 近所 *neighborhood, vicinity* [→**fukin** 付近]

¶Kore wa kinjo no mise de kaimashita.

これは近所の店で買いました。

I bought this in a neighborhood store.

¶Kinō, uchi no kinjo de jiko ga atta yo.

きのう、うちの近所で事故があったよ。

Yesterday, there was an accident in my neighborhood!

¶Kono kinjo ni yūbin-kyoku wa arimasu ka.

この近所に郵便局はありますか。

Is there a post office near here?

- kinjo no hito 近所の人 *neighbor*

Kinki-chíhō 近畿地方 *the Kinki Region of Japan* [→**Kansai** 関西]

kínko 金庫 *a safe*

kinkō 均衡 *balance, equilibrium* [→**tsuriai** 釣り合い]

kinkyū 緊急 *urgency; emergency*

¶Kinkyū no baai wa kono denwa o tsukatte kudasai.

緊急の場合はこの電話を使ってください。

In an emergency, please use this telephone.

- kinkyu na／no 緊急な／の *urgent, critical*

¶Sakamoto-san wa kinkyū na yōji de Miyazaki ni itta.

坂本さんは緊急な用事で宮崎に行った。

Mr. Sakamoto went to Miyazaki on urgent business.

kínmu 勤務 *work, (job)duty* «for an organization»

- kinmu suru 勤務する *to work* [→**hataraku** 働く]
- kinmu-chū no 勤務中の *on-duty*
- kinmu-jikan 勤務時間 *office hours, working hours*
- kinmu-jōken 勤務条件 *working conditions*
- kinmu-saki 勤務先 *one's place of employment, one's office*

kínniku 筋肉 *muscle*

kinō 昨日 *yesterday*

¶Kinō wa Nichiyōbi deshita.

きのうは日曜日でした。

Yesterday was Sunday.

¶Onēsan wa kinō koko ni imashita ka.

お姉さんはきのうここにいましたか。

Was your older sister here yesterday?

kínō 機能 *function*

¶Shinzō no kinō wa ketsueki o okuridasu koto desu.

心臓の機能は血液を送り出すことです。

The function of the heart is to send out blood.

ki-no-dokú 気の毒 ～**na** ～な *pitiable, unfortunate* [→**kawaisō na** かわいそうな]

¶Sono ki-no-doku na hito-tachi

o tasukemashō.
その気の毒な人たちを助けましょう。
Let's help those unfortunate people.
¶Tomoko-chan no onīsan wa,
ki-no-doku ni shiken ni ochimashita.
友子ちゃんのお兄さんは、気の毒に試験に
落ちました。
Tomoko's older brother unfortunately failed the exam.
• A o ki-no-doku ni omou Aを気の毒に
思う *to feel sorry for A*

kínoko きのこ *mushroom*
• kinoko-gari 茸狩り *mushroom gathering*

kinpatsu 金髪 *blond hair*
• kinpatsu no 金髪の *blond, blond-haired*
¶Monika-san wa kinpatsu desu.
モニカさんは金髪です。
Monica is blond.

kinrō 勤労 *labor, work, service* [→**rōdō** 労働]
• Kinrō-kansha no hi 勤労感謝の日 *Labor Thanksgiving Day* 《a Japanese national holiday on November 23rd》

Kinsei 金星 *(the planet) Venus*

kínsei 近世 *early modern times* 《In Japanese history, this word is ordinarily used to mean specifically the period from the beginning of the Azuchi-Momoyama period (1568) until the end of the Edo period (1868).》

kinshi 近視 *near-sightedness,* <*UK*>*short-sightedness* [⇔**enshi** 遠視]
¶Chichi mo haha mo kinshi desu.
父も母も近視です。
Both my father and my mother are near-sighted.

kinshi 禁止 *prohibition, ban*
• kinshi suru 禁止する *to prohibit, to ban* [→**kinjiru** 禁じる]
¶Chūsha kinshi
「駐車禁止」《on a sign》
No Parking
¶Tachiiri kinshi
「立入禁止」《on a sign》
Keep Out 《Literally: *Entry prohibited*》

Kintō 近東 *the Near East*

kínu 絹 *silk* .

Kin'yō 金曜 [☞**Kin'yōbi** 金曜日]

Kin'yōbi 金曜日 *Friday*

kinyū 記入 ① *writing in, filling in, writing as an entry*
• kinyū suru 記入する *to fill in, to write as an entry*
¶Kono kādo ni o-namae o kinyū shite kudasai.
このカードにお名前を記入してください。
Please fill in your name on this card.
② *written entry*

kínzoku 金属 *metal*
• kinzoku-batto 金属バット *metal (baseball) bat*
• kinzoku-seihin 金属製品 *metal manufactured article*

kioku 記憶 *memory*
¶Sono hito ni wa izen atta kioku ga arimasu.
その人には以前会った記憶があります。
I have a memory of having met that person before.
• kioku suru 記憶する *to commit to memory* [→**oboeru** 覚える①]
¶Kono koto o kioku shite oite kudasai.
この事を記憶しておいてください。
Please remember this fact.
• kioku-ryoku 記憶力 *ability to remember*
• kioku-sōshitsu 記憶喪失 *amnesia*

kion 気温 *(atmospheric) temperature*

kípā キーパー *goalkeeper*

kippári きっぱり（～**to** ～と）*flatly, definitely, clearly*
¶Yamada-kun no yōkyū o kippari kotowatta yo.
山田君の要求をきっぱり断ったよ。
I flatly refused Yamada's request!

kippu 切符 *ticket*
¶Eiga no kippu o kaimashita ka.
映画の切符を買いましたか。
Did you buy the movie tickets?
¶Kyōto made no kippu o san-mai kudasai.
京都までの切符を3枚ください。

Three tickets to Kyoto, please.
• kippu-uriba 切符売り場 *ticket office, box office, <UK>booking office*
• katamichi-kippu 片道切符 *one-way ticket*
• ōfuku-kippu 往復切符 *round-trip ticket*

kirai 嫌い ～**na** ～な《This adjectival noun is used to describe both the people who dislike and the people or things that are disliked.》[[⇔**suki na** 好きな]] *disliked; unfond*
¶Sūgaku ga kirai na node, enjinia ni wa naremasen.
数学が嫌いなので、エンジニアにはなれません。
Since I dislike math, I can't become an engineer.
¶Watashi wa sakana ga suki desu ga, musuko wa kirai desu.
私は魚が好きですが、息子は嫌いです。
I like fish, but my son dislikes it.

kírakira きらきら *twinklingly, glitteringly, sparklingly*
¶Kon'ya wa hoshi ga kirakira kagayaite imasu.
今夜は星がきらきら輝いています。
Tonight the stars are shining glitteringly.
• kirakira suru きらきらする *to twinkle, to glitter, to sparkle*

kiraku 気楽 ～**na** ～な *easygoing, carefree*
¶Haha wa ima wa kiraku na kurashi o shite imasu.
母は今は気楽な暮らしをしています。
My mother now leads a carefree life.

kiré 切れ *piece of cloth*

-**kire** －切れ ① *piece, slice* 《Added to noun bases denoting things that can be sliced or cut》
• kami-kire 紙切れ (*cut*)*piece of paper*
② 《counter for slices; see Appendix 2》

kírei 奇麗 ① ～**na** ～な *pretty, beautiful* [→**utsukushii** 美しい]
¶Haru ni naru to, kirei na hana ga sakimasu.
春になると、きれいな花が咲きます。

Beautiful flowers bloom in spring. 《Literally: When it becomes spring, beautiful flowers bloom.》
¶Junko-chan wa kirei na shōjo desu ne.
順子ちゃんはきれいな少女ですね。
Junko is a pretty girl, isn't she.
② ～**na** ～な *clean* [→**seiketsu na** 清潔な] [⇔**kitanai** 汚い]
¶Te o kirei ni shite okinasai.
手をきれいにしておきなさい。
Keep your hands clean.
¶Kono mizuumi no mizu wa totemo kirei desu.
この湖の水はとてもきれいです。
The water in this lake is very clear.
③ ～**ni** ～に *completely* [→**sukkari** すっかり]
¶Angō o kirei ni wasurete shimatta yo.
暗号をきれいに忘れてしまったよ。
I've completely forgotten the code!

kiréru 切れる ① *to cut* 《intransitive》《The subject is a cutting tool.》
¶Kono naifu wa yoku kiremasu.
このナイフはよく切れます。
This knife cuts well.
② *to get cut*
¶Haha no te wa samusa de hibi ga kirete ita.
母の手は寒さでひびが切れていた。
Mother's hands are chapped from the cold.
• en ga kireru 縁が切れる *a relationship is broken off*
• denwa ga kireru 電話が切れる *a phone call is cut off*
③ *to break* 《The subject is a string, rope, etc.》
¶Kutsu no himo ga kireta.
靴のひもが切れた。
My shoe lace broke.
④ *to run out, to be used up* [→**tsukiru** 尽きる]
¶Satō ga kirete shimatta yo.
砂糖が切れてしまったよ。
The sugar has run out!
¶Hōkokusho no teishutsu-kigen ga kirete imasu.
報告書の提出期限が切れています。

報告書の提出期限が切れています。
Time has run out for submitting reports.
⑤ *to be shrewd, to be sharp*
¶Masao-san wa kireru hito desu ne.
正雄さんは切れる人ですね。
Masao is a shrewd person, isn't he.

kíri 錐 *drill; awl; gimlet*

kiri 霧 ① *fog; mist*
¶Mada hayai desu ga, kiri wa harema-shita.
まだ早いですが、霧は晴れました。
It's still early, but the fog has cleared up.
¶Kesa wa kiri ga fukakatta desu.
けさは霧が深かったです。
This morning the fog was thick.
② *spray, atomized liquid*
• kiri o fuku 霧を吹く *to spray atomized liquid*
• kiri-same 霧雨 *misty rain, drizzle*

kirí 切り *end* [→**owari** 終わり]*; limit* [→**gendo** 限度]
¶Sobo wa hanashi-hajimetara, kiri ga nai desu.
祖母は話し始めたら、切りがないです。
If my grandmother starts talking, there's no end.
¶Mukō no yōkyū wa kiri ga nai desu.
向こうの要求は切りがないです。
The other side's demands have no limits.

kiri 桐 *paulownia*

kirigírisu きりぎりす *katydid* ((insect))

kirin きりん *giraffe*

kirinuki 切り抜き <*US*> <*newspaper*> *clipping,* <*UK*> <*newspaper*> *cutting*

kirinuku 切り抜く *to cut out, to clip* 《from a newspaper, magazine, etc.》
¶Ani wa sono shashin o shinbun kara kirinukimashita.
兄はその写真を新聞から切り抜きました。
My older brother cut out that picture from the newspaper.

Kirisuto キリスト（*Jesus*）*Christ*
• Kirisuto-kyō キリスト教 *Christianity*
• Kirisuto-kyō-to キリスト教徒 *a Christian*

kiritaosu 切り倒す *to cut down, to fell*
¶Ōno-san wa sono ki o ono de kiritaoshita.
大野さんはその木をおので切り倒した。
Mr. Ono cut down that tree with an ax.

kiritsu 起立 ～**suru** ～する *to stand up, to rise (to one's feet)*
¶Kiritsu!
起立！
Stand up! 《This use as a command is typical when ordering an assembled group of people to stand.》

kiritsu 規律 ① *order, discipline* [→**chitsujo** 秩序]
② *rules, regulations*

kíro キロ [☞**kiroguramu** キログラム; **kiromētoru** キロメートル]
• -kiro －キロ《counter for kilograms or kilometers; see Appendix 2》

kirogúramu キログラム *kilogram*
• -kiroguramu －キログラム《counter for kilograms; see Appendix 2》

kiroku 記録 ① *record, chronicle, document*
• kiroku suru 記録する *to record, to chronicle, to document*
② 〈*world*〉 *record*
¶Mori-senshu wa jūryōage no kiroku o motte iru.
森選手は重量挙げの記録を持っている。
Mori holds the weightlifting record.
• kiroku o yaburu 記録を破る *to break a record*
• kiroku-eiga 記録映画 *documentary film*
• kiroku-gakari 記録係 *recorder; scorer*
• kiroku-hoji-sha 記録保持者 *record holder*
• sekai-kiroku 世界記録 *world record*

kiromḗtoru キロメートル *kilometer*
• -kiromētoru －キロメートル《counter for kilometers; see Appendix 2》

kirowátto キロワット *kilowatt*
• -kirowatto －キロワット《counter for kilowatts; see Appendix 2》

kíru 切る{5} ① *to cut* 《transitive》
¶Sono kēki o muttsu ni kitte kudasai.

そのケーキを六つに切ってください。
Please cut that cake into six.
¶Pan o kitte kureru?
パンを切ってくれる？
Will you cut the bread for me?
• toranpu o kiru トランプを切る *to shuffle cards; to cut (a deck of)cards*
• hanashi o kiru 話を切る *to stop talking, to break off what one is saying*
• en o kiru 縁を切る *to break off a relationship*
• denwa o kiru 電話を切る *to cut off a telephone call «ordinarily by hanging up»*
¶Denwa o kiranai de kudasai.
電話を切らないでください。
Please don't hang up the phone.
  ② *to turn off «a device»*
¶Neru mae ni terebi o kirinasai.
寝る前にテレビを切りなさい。
Before you go to bed turn off the TV.

kiru 着る *to put on* «The direct object of **kiru** is generally an article of clothing that goes at least in part on the torso. Compare **haku** 履く and **kaburu** 被る. Like other verbs for putting on clothing, **kiru** in the -**te iru** form can express the meaning *be wearing, have on*.» [⇔**nugu** 脱ぐ]
¶Kōto o kinasai.
コートを着なさい。
Put on your coat.
¶Kazuko-san wa atarashii sētā o kite imasu.
和子さんは新しいセーターを着ています。
Kazuko is wearing a new sweater.
¶Ōbā o kita mama de haitte kudasai.
オーバーを着たままで入ってください。
Please come in with your overcoat on.

kiryoku 気力 *energy, spirit, vigor*
¶Ano hito wa kiryoku ni michite imasu.
あの人は気力に満ちています。
That person is full of energy.
¶Imōto wa kiryoku ga mattaku nai desu.
妹は気力がまったくないです。
My younger sister has absolutely no energy.

kiryū 気流 *air current*
• jōshō-kiryū 上昇気流 *ascending air current*

• kakō-kiryū 下降気流 *descending air current*
• ran-kiryū 乱気流 *turbulent air currents, turbulence*

kisama 貴様 【CRUDE】 *you*
《There are several Japanese words for *you*, but in general, Japanese speakers prefer to use names or titles instead. The word **kisama** is very insulting. Other words for *you* include **anata** あなた, **kimi** 君, and **omae** お前.》

kisei 帰省 *returning to one's hometown*
• kisei suru 帰省する *to return to one's hometown*

kiseki 奇跡 *miracle*
• kiseki-teki na 奇跡的な *miraculous*

kiseru 着せる *to put on* «The direct object must be clothing that goes on someone else. Like **kiru** 着る, this verb is used for articles of clothing that go at least in part on the torso.»
¶Kono ningyō ni fuku o kisete chōdai.
この人形に服を着せてちょうだい。
Please put clothes on this doll.

kisétsu 季節 *season*
¶Dono kisetsu ga ichiban suki desu ka.
どの季節がいちばん好きですか。
Which season do you like best?
¶Maitoshi kono kisetsu ni wa ame ga ōi desu.
毎年この季節には雨が多いです。
Every year in this season there is a lot of rain.
• kisetsu-hazure no 季節外れの *out-of-season*
¶Kaki wa mō kisetsu-hazure desu.
かきはもう季節外れです。
Oysters are already out of season.

kishá 汽車 *(non-electric)train*
kishá 記者 *(press)reporter*
• kisha-kaiken 記者会見 *press conference, news conference*
• shinbun-kisha 新聞記者 *newspaper reporter*

kishí 岸 *(river)bank; shore; coast* [→ **kaigan** 海岸]

¶Kawa no kishi ni hodō ga arimasu.
川の岸に歩道があります。
There is a sidewalk on the river bank.

¶Nami ga kishi ni uchi-yosete imasu.
波が岸に打ち寄せています。
Waves are washing against the shore.

kishō 気象 *weather, metereological phenomena*
- Kishō-chō 気象庁 *the Meteorological Agency* 《of the Japanese government》
- kishō-dai 気象台 *weather station*
- kishō-eisei 気象衛星 *weather satellite*
- kishō-kansoku 気象観測 *weather observation*

kisó 基礎 *base, basis, foundation*
- tatemono no kiso 建物の基礎 *foundation of a building*
- sūgaku no kiso 数学の基礎 *the basis of mathematics*
- kiso-kōji 基礎工事 *foundation work* 《on a building》
- kiso-teki na 基礎的な *basic, fundamental*

kisó 起訴 *indictment*
- kiso suru 起訴する *to indict*

kisóku 規則 *rule, regulation*
- kisoku ni shitagau 規則に従う *to follow a rule*
- kisoku o yaburu 規則を破る *to break a rule*
- kisoku-tadashii 規則正しい *regular, systematic, orderly* [⇔**fukisoku na** 不規則な]

¶Megumi-san wa kisoku-tadashii seikatsu o okutte imasu.
恵さんは規則正しい生活を送っています。
Megumi leads an orderly life.
- kisoku-teki na 規則的 *regular, systematic, orderly*

kissaten 喫茶店 *tearoom, coffee shop*

kisū 奇数 *odd number* [⇔**gūsū** 偶数]

kísu キス *kiss*
- kisu suru キスする *to give a kiss*

¶Jēn-san wa Jirō-san ni kisu shimashita.
ジェインさんは次郎さんにキスしました。
Jane gave Jiro a kiss.

kita 北 *the north* [⇔**minami** 南]

¶Gakkō wa machi no kita ni arimasu.
学校は町の北にあります。
The school is in the north of the town.

¶Sono mizuumi wa machi no kita no hazure ni arimasu.
その湖は町の北の外れにあります。
That lake is on the north edge of the town.

¶Nikkō wa Tōkyō no kita ni arimasu.
日光は東京の北にあります。
Nikko is north of Tokyo.

¶Uchi wa Nara no kita nijuk-kiro no tokoro ni arimasu.
うちは奈良の北20キロのところにあります。
My house is in a place 20 kilometers north of Nara.
- kita-kaze 北風 *north wind*
- kita-muki no 北向きの *north-facing*

¶Watashi no heya wa kita-muki desu.
私の部屋は北向きです。
My room is north-facing.

kitaéru 鍛える ① *to forge* 《metal》 ② *to build up through training*
- karada o kitaeru 体を鍛える *to build up one's body*

¶Jogingu wa karada o kitaeru ni wa ii yo.
ジョギングは体を鍛えるにはいいよ。
Jogging is good for building up one's body!

kitai 気体 *gas, substance in a gaseous state* [⇔**ekitai** 液体; **kotai** 固体]

kitai 期待 *hopeful expectation*
- kitai suru 期待する *to expect, to count on*
- A no kitai ni sou Aの期待に添う *to meet A's expectations*

kitaku 帰宅 *returning home (to one's house)*

¶Kitaku no tochū de sensei ni aimashita.
帰宅の途中で先生に会いました。
I met the teacher on my way home.
- kitaku suru 帰宅する *to return home*

¶Go-ji ni kitaku shimashita.
5時に帰宅しました。
I returned home at 5:00.

kitanái 汚い ① *dirty, filthy* [⇔**kirei na**

奇麗な②〕

¶Kitanai te de sawaranai de.

汚い手で触らないで。

Don't touch it with dirty hands.

② *mean, nasty, dirty*

¶Aite wa kitanai te o tsukatta yo.

相手は汚い手を使ったよ。

My opponent used a dirty trick!

kítchin キッチン *kitchen* [→**daidokoro** 台所]

• dainingu-kitchin ダイニングキッチン *combined dining room and kitchen*

kitsui きつい ① *tight-fitting* [→**kyūkutsu na** 窮屈な①] [⇔**yurui** 緩い①]

¶Kono kutsu wa kitsui desu.

この靴はきついです。

These shoes are tight.

• kitsui sukejūru きついスケジュール *tight schedule*

② *severe, hard, harsh* [→**kibishii** 厳しい②]

¶Kono shigoto wa watashi ni wa kitsui desu.

この仕事は私にはきついです。

This work is hard for me.

③ *intense, strong* [→**kyōretsu na** 強烈な]

• kitsui hizashi きつい日差し *strong sunshine*

④ *strong-minded*

¶Akira-chan wa kitsui kodomo desu ne.

明ちゃんはきつい子供ですね。

Akira is a strong-minded child, isn't he.

kitsune 狐 *fox*

kitsútsuki 啄木鳥 *woodpecker*

kitte 切手 (*postage*)*stamp*

• kitte-arubamu 切手アルバム *stamp album*

kitto きっと *surely, for sure*

kíui キーウィ *kiwi fruit*

kiwámete 極めて 【FORMAL for **hijō ni** 非常に】 *extremely*

kíyō 器用 ～**na** ～な *skillful, adroit, dexterous*

¶Haha wa tesaki ga kiyō desu.

母は手先が器用です。

My mother is good with her hands.

kiyói 清い *clean, pure*

kizamu 刻む ① *to cut, to chop, to slice* 《*into small pieces*》

¶Tamanegi o komakaku kizande kudasai.

たまねぎを細かく刻んでください。

Please chop the onion finely.

② *to carve, to engrave* [→**horu** 彫る]

• A ni B o kizamu AにBを刻む *to carve A in／on B, to engrave A on B*

¶Makino-kun wa kono ki ni namae o kizanda yo.

牧野君はこの木に名前を刻んだよ。

Makino carved his name on this tree!

kizetsu 気絶 *fainting, loss of consciousness*

• kizetsu suru 気絶する *to faint, to lose consciousness*

¶Shōjo wa sono shirase o kiite kizetsu shimashita.

少女はその知らせを聞いて気絶しました。

The girl heard that news and fainted.

kízoku 貴族 *aristocrat*

kizu 傷 ① *wound, visible injury*

¶Sono heishi wa sensō de atama ni hidoi kizu o uketa.

その兵士は戦争で頭にひどい傷を受けた。

The soldier received a severe injury to the head in the war.

• omoi kizu 重い傷 *serious wound*

② *flaw, defect, blemish*

• kizu-tsukeru 傷つける *to wound, to injure, to hurt*

¶Hito no kanjō o kizu-tsukenai yō ni ki o tsukero.

人の感情を傷つけないように気をつけろ。

Be careful not to hurt people's feelings.

• kizu-tsuku 傷つく *to be wounded, to get injured, to get hurt*

kizúku 築く *to build, to construct*

¶Toyotomi Hideyoshi ga Ōsaka-jō o kizukimashita.

豊臣秀吉が大阪城を築きました。

Hideyoshi Toyotomi built Osaka Castle.

kizúku 気付く *to become aware, to notice*

• A ga B ni kizuku AがBに気づく *A becomes aware of B, A notices B*

¶Hito ga haitte kuru no ni kizukimashita.
人が入って来るのに気づきました。
I noticed someone coming in.

kízuna 絆 (emotional)bonds, (emotional)ties

ko 子 ① *child* [→**kodomo** 子供]
• otoko no ko 男の子 *boy*
• onna no ko 女の子 *girl*
② *the young* «of an animal»
• raion no ko ライオンの子 *lion cub*

kō こう *like this, in this way* [⇔**sō** そう; **ā** ああ]
¶Kayoko-san wa kō itte watashi o mitsumeta yo.
加代子さんはこう言って私を見つめたよ。
Kayoko said it in this way and looked at me!
• kō iu こういう *this kind of* [→**konna** こんな]
¶Kō iu kōto ga hoshii desu.
こういうコートが欲しいです。
I want this kind of coat.

-ko 一個 «counter for objects, especially spherical or cube-shaped objects; see Appendix 2»

kóara コアラ *koala*

kōbá 工場 *factory, plant* [→**kōjō** 工場]

kobámu 拒む *to refuse, to reject* [→**kotowaru** 断る]
¶Otōto wa watashi-tachi to iku koto o kobamimashita.
弟は私たちと行くことを拒みました。
Our younger brother refused to go with us.

kōban 交番 *police box, police stand*

kōboku 公僕 *public servant*

koboréru 零れる *to spill, to overflow*
¶Haha no me kara namida ga koboremashita.
母の目から涙がこぼれました。
Tears spilled from my mother's eyes.
¶Mizu ga baketsu kara koboremashita.
水がバケツからこぼれました。
Water spilled from the bucket.

kobósu 零す ① *to spill* «transitive»; *to shed* «tears»

¶Koko ni gyūnyū o koboshita no wa dare desu ka.
ここに牛乳をこぼしたのはだれですか。
Who is the one who spilled milk here?
¶Kyōko-san wa eiga o mite namida o koboshimashita.
京子さんは映画を見て涙をこぼしました。
Kyoko saw the movie and shed tears.
② *to complain about, to grumble about*
¶Ano hito wa itsu-mo fuun o koboshite imasu.
あの人はいつも不運をこぼしています。
That person is always grumbling about his bad luck.

kobú 瘤 *swelling, lump, bump* «on a person's or animal's body»
¶Kono ko wa atama ni ōki na kobu ga dekite imasu.
この子は頭に大きなこぶができています。
A large bump has developed on this child's head.
• rakuda no kobu らくだのこぶ *camel's hump*

kóbun 子分 *henchman, follower* [⇔**oyabun** 親分]

kóbura コブラ *cobra*

kobushi 拳 *fist* [→**genkotsu** 拳骨]

kóbutsu 好物 *favorite food／drink; favorite thing to eat／drink*
¶Watashi no kōbutsu wa chokorēto desu.
私の好物はチョコレートです。
My favorite food is chocolate.

kóbutsu 鉱物 *mineral*
• kōbutsu-shigen 鉱物資源 *mineral resources*

kōcha 紅茶 *black tea* [⇔**o-cha** お茶②]

kóchi コーチ ① (athletic)coach
¶Aoki-sensei wa watashi-tachi no chīmu no kōchi desu.
青木先生は私たちのチームのコーチです。
Mr. Aoki is the coach of our team.
② (athletic)coaching
• kōchi suru コーチする *to coach*

kochira こちら 【FORMAL for kotchi こっち】 ① [[⇔**sochira** そちら①; **achira** あちら①]] *this way; here*

¶Deguchi wa kochira desu.
出口はこちらです。
The exit is this way.
¶Kochira e dōzo.
こちらへどうぞ。
This way, please.
¶Kochira e mo tokidoki kimasu.
こちらへも時々来ます。
We sometimes come here also.
  ② *this person* [⇔**achira** あちら②]
¶Itō-sensei, kochira ga tomodachi no Kimura-kun desu.
伊藤先生、こちらが友達の木村君です。
Prof. Ito, this is my friend Kimura.
  ③ [[⇔**sochira** そちら②]] *I, me; my family*
¶Moshimoshi, kochira wa Katō desu.
もしもし、こちらは加藤です。
Hello, this is Kato.

kōchō 好調 ～**na** ～な *satisfactory, in good condition, favorable*
¶Ano tōshu wa kōchō desu.
あの投手は好調です。
That pitcher is in good condition.
¶Subete kōchō ni susunde imasu.
すべて好調に進んでいます。
It's all progressing satisfactorily.

kōchō 校長 (*school*)*principal, headmaster*

kochō 誇張 *exaggeration, overstatement* [→**ōgesa** 大袈裟]
• kochō suru 誇張する *to exaggerate, to overstate*

kódachi 木立 *cluster of trees*

kōdai 広大 ～**na** ～な *immense, vast*

kódai 古代 *ancient times, antiquity*
• kodai-shi 古代史 *ancient history*

kodama こだま *echo* [→**yamabiko** 山彦]
• kodama suru こだまする *to echo, to reverberate*

kodawáru こだわる *to worry about, to be a stickler for*

kōdō 行動 *act, action; behavior, conduct*
¶Sore wa keisotsu na kōdō desu.
それは軽率な行動です。
That is a careless act.

¶Uemura-hakase no kimyō na kōdō wa rikai dekimasen.
上村博士の奇妙な行動は理解できません。
We cannot understand Dr. Uemura's strange behavior.
• kōdo suru 行動する *to act; to behave*
¶Ano hito-tachi wa itsu-mo dantai de kōdō shimasu.
あの人たちはいつも団体で行動します。
Those people always act in a group.
• kōdō-shugi 行動主義 *behaviorism*

kōdō 講堂 *lecture hall, assembly hall,* <*US*>*auditorium*

kódo コード (*electrical*)*cord*

kodō 鼓動 *beat, pulsation*
¶Shinzō no kodō ga hageshiku narimashita.
心臓の鼓動が激しくなりました。
My heart began to beat faster. 《Literally: My heartbeat became intense.》
• kōdō suru 鼓動する *to beat, to pulse*

kodoku 孤独 *loneliness; solitude*
¶Watashi mo kodoku wa suki de wa arimasen.
私も孤独は好きではありません。
I don't like solitude either.
¶Tōkyō de kodoku o kanjite imasu.
東京で孤独を感じています。
I feel lonely in Tokyo.
• kodoku na 孤独な *lonely; solitary*

kodomo 子供 *child*
¶Keiko to Akira o kodomo no koro kara shitte iru yo.
恵子と明を子供のころから知っているよ。
I have known Keiko and Akira since they were children!
• Kodomo no hi 子供の日 *Children's Day* 《a Japanese national holiday on May 5》
• kodomo-atsukai 子供扱い *treating like a child*
• kodomo-ppoi 子供っぽい *childish*

kóe 声 *voice*
¶Yōko-san wa yasashii koe o shite imasu.
洋子さんは優しい声をしています。
Yoko has a gentle voice.

¶Tagami-kun wa chīsa na koe de shaberu ne.

田上君は小さな声でしゃべるね。

Tagami talks in a soft voice, doesn't he.

¶Sensei no koe ga yoku tōrimasu.

先生の声がよく通ります。

The teacher's voice carries well.

¶Kodomo-tachi wa koe o soroete sakebimashita.

子供たちは声をそろえて叫びました。

The children joined their voices and shouted.

¶Mō sukoshi ōki na koe de itte kudasai.

もう少し大きな声で言ってください。

Please say it in a little louder voice.

• koe o dasu 声を出す *to talk aloud*

¶Koe o dashite hon o yomimashita.

声を出して本を読みました。

I read the book aloud.

• koe-gawari 声変わり *voice change* 《in an adolescent boy》

¶Uchi no Tarō wa ima koe-gawari no jiki desu.

うちの太郎は今声変わりの時期です。

Our Taro's voice is changing now.

kōei 光栄 *honor, glory*

¶O-me ni kakarete kōei desu.

お目にかかれて光栄です。

It is an honor to be able meet you.

kōen 公園 *park*

• kokuritsu-kōen 国立公園 *national park*

• Ueno-kōen 上野公園 *Ueno Park*

kōen 講演 *lecture, talk*

• kōen suru 講演する *to lecture, to give a lecture*

¶Omocha no rekishi ni tsuite kōen shimasu.

おもちゃの歴史について講演します。

I will give a lecture on the history of toys.

• kōen-kai 講演会 *lecture meeting*

koeru 越える, 超える ① *to cross over, to go over* 《a distance or boundary》 [→kosu 越す, 超す①]

¶Jitensha de Rokkī-sanmyaku o koemasu.

自転車でロッキー山脈を越えます。

I will cross the Rocky Mountains by bicycle.

② *to exceed, to go over* [→kosu 越す, 超す②, uwamawaru 上回る]

¶Kono ko wa jus-sai o koete imasu.

この子は10歳を越えています。

This child is over ten.

kōfū 校風 *school traditions* 《unique to a particular school》

kōfuku 幸福 [[→shiawase 幸せ]] *happiness; good fortune*

• kōfuku na 幸福な *happy; fortunate*

kōfun 興奮 *excitement, excitation, agitation*

• kōfun suru 興奮する *to get excited, to become agitated*

¶Kōfun shite tobiagatta yo.

興奮して跳び上がった。

I got excited and jumped up.

¶Sono enzetsu o kiite kōfun shite shimaimashita.

その演説を聞いて興奮してしまいました。

We heard that speech and got excited.

kofun 古墳 *ancient burial mound*

kōgai 公害 *environmental pollution*

¶Wareware wa kōgai ni nayande imasu.

われわれは公害に悩んでいます。

We are afflicted by environmental pollution.

• kōgai-taisaku 公害対策 *measures against pollution*

• sōon-kōgai 騒音公害 *noise pollution*

kōgai 郊外 *suburbs*

¶Watashi-tachi wa Sapporo no kōgai ni sunde imasu.

私たちは札幌の郊外に住んでいます。

We live in the suburbs of Sapporo.

kōgai 戸外 *the outdoors, the open air*

¶Sensei wa kogai de jugyō o okonaimashita.

先生は戸外で授業を行ないました。

The teacher held class outside.

kogasu 焦がす *to scorch, to burn* 《transitive》

¶Haha wa airon o kaketa toki ni shatsu o chotto kogashite shimatta.

母はアイロンをかけたときに、シャツをちょっ

と焦がしてしまった。
My mother scorched the shirt a little when she ironed it.

kogata 小型 〜**no** 〜の *miniature, small-sized* [⇔**ōgata no** 大型の]
• kogata no jisho 小型の辞書 *pocket-sized dictionary*

kōgeki 攻撃 *attack, assault, offensive*
• kōgeki suru 攻撃する *to attack*
• kōgeki-teki na 攻撃的な *offensive, attack-like*

kōgen 高原 *high plain, plateau*

kogéru 焦げる *to scorch, to burn* 《intransitive》
¶Nani-ka kogete imasu yo.
何か焦げていますよ。
Something's burning!

kōgi 抗議 *protest*
• kōgi suru 抗議する *to make a protest, to protest*
¶Senshu wa shinpan no hantei ni kōgi shimashita.
選手は審判の判定に抗議しました。
The player protested against the umpire's decision.
¶Watashi-tachi wa sono atarashii keikaku ni kōgi shimashita.
私たちはその新しい計画に抗議しました。
We protested against that new plan.

kōgí 講義 (*academic*)*lecture*
• kōgi suru 講義する *to lecture*

kogítte 小切手 〈*bank*〉*check*
¶Hoteru-dai o kogitte de haraimashita.
ホテル代を小切手で払いました。
I paid my hotel bill by check.
• ryokō-kogitte 旅行小切手 *traveler's check* [→**toraberāzuchekku** トラベラーズチェック]

kōgo 口語 *spoken language, colloquial language* [⇔**bungo** 文語]
• kōgo-Eigo 口語英語 *spoken English*

kōgo 交互 〜**no** 〜の *mutual, reciprocal* [→**tagai no** 互いの]; *alternating* [→**kōtai no** 交代の]
¶Ryōshin wa kōgo ni unten shimashita.
両親は交互に運転しました。
My parents drove alternately.

Kōgō 皇后 *the Empress* (*of Japan*)
• Kōgō-heika 皇后陛下 *Her Majesty the Empress*

kogoéru 凍える *to become numb* (*from the cold*)
¶Kesa wa samukute kogoe-sō desu.
けさは寒くて凍えそうです。
This morning it's cold, and it seems likely that I'll get numb.
¶Sono tsubame wa kogoete shinimashita.
そのつばめは凍えて死にました。
That swallow became numb from the cold and died.

kogoto 小言 *scolding, rebuke*
• A ni kogoto o iu Aに小言を言う *to scold A, to nag A*
¶Haha wa itsu-mo otōto ni kogoto o itte imasu.
母はいつも弟に小言を言っています。
My mother is always scolding my younger brother.

kógu 漕ぐ *to row; to pedal; to pump* 《*a swing*》
¶Mizuumi de bōto o koide asobimashita.
湖でボートをこいで遊びました。
We had a good time rowing a boat on the lake.

kōgyō 工業 *industry, manufacturing*
• kōgyō-chitai 工業地帯 *industrial district*
• kōgyō-kōkō 工業高校 *technical high school*
• kōgyō-robotto 工業ロボット *industrial robot*
• kōgyō-toshi 工業都市 *industrial city*
• jū-kōgyō 重工業 *heavy industry*
• kei-kōgyō 軽工業 *light industry*

kōgyō 鉱業 *mining industry*

kōhai 後輩 *one's junior* 《a person who entered the same organization later》 [⇔**senpai** 先輩]
¶Ueda-kun wa boku no kōhai desu.
上田君は僕の後輩です。
Ueda is my junior.

kōhan 後半 *the second half* [⇔**zenhan** 前半]

kōhei 公平 *fairness, impartiality* [→

kōsei 公正［⇔**fukōhei** 不公平］
- kōhei na 公平な *fair, impartial*

kōhī コーヒー *coffee*
¶Chōshoku wa kōhī ip-pai de kekkō desu.
朝食はコーヒー1杯で結構です。
A cup of coffee is fine for breakfast.
¶Kōhī o futatsu o-negai shimasu.
コーヒーを二つお願いします。
Two coffees, please.
- kōhī o ireru コーヒーを入れる *to make coffee, to brew coffee*
¶Sensei wa watashi-tachi ni kōhī o irete kudasaimashita.
先生は私たちにコーヒーを入れてください
ました。
Our teacher made coffee for us.
- koi〔usui〕kōhī 濃い〔薄い〕コーヒー *strong〔weak〕coffee*

kōho 候補 ① *candidacy*［→**rikkōho** 立候補］
- kōho ni tatsu 候補に立つ *to become a candidate, to run*
　② *candidate*
¶Maeda-san wa kaichō no kōho desu.
前田さんは会長の候補です。
Ms. Maeda is a candidate for chairperson.
- kōho-sha 候補者［☞**kōho** 候補② (above)]
- yūshō-kōho 優勝候補 *one of the favorites for the championship*

kōhyō 好評 *public favor, favorable reception, popularity*
- kōhyō no 好評の *well-received, popular*
¶Sono eiga wa wakamono no aida de taihen kōhyō desu.
その映画は若者の間でたいへん好評です。
That movie is very popular among young people.

kói 恋 *(romantic)love*［→**ren'ai** 恋愛］
- A ni koi o suru Aに恋をする *to love A; to fall in love with A*
¶Ōji wa sono shōjo ni koi o shite imashita.
王子はその少女に恋をしていました。
The prince was in love with that girl.

- koi-bito 恋人 *lover*
- koi-suru 恋する｛Irreg.｝*to love; to fall in love with*
- hatsu-koi 初恋 *first time in love*

kói 鯉 *carp*
- koi-nobori 鯉幟 *carp streamer 《traditional decorations for Children's Day (May 5)》*
- koi-nobiri o tateru こいのぼりを立てる *to put up carp streamers*

kói 濃い［[⇔**usui** 薄い②]] *deep, dark 《describing a color》; thick, dense, heavy 《describing liquid, hair, etc.》; strong 《describing coffee, tea, etc.》*
¶Fumiko-san wa koi aka no sētā o kite iru.
文子さんは濃い赤のセーターを着ている。
Fumiko is wearing a deep red sweater.
¶O-cha o koku shita hō ga suki desu.
お茶は濃くしたほうが好きです。
I like strong tea better.
¶Komatsu-sensei wa hige ga koi desu ne.
小松先生はひげが濃いですね。
Prof. Komatsu's beard is thick, isn't it.
- koi sūpu 濃いスープ *thick soup*
- koi kiri 濃い霧 *dense fog*
- koi kōhī 濃いコーヒー *strong coffee*

kói 好意 *kindness, goodwill, friendliness*
¶Go-kōi ni kansha shimasu.
ご好意に感謝します。
I thank you for your kindness.
- kōi-teki na 好意的な *kind, friendly*
¶Ōya-san wa watashi-tachi ni totemo kōi-teki desu.
大家さんは私たちにとても好意的です。
The landlady is very kind to us.

kói 行為 *intentional action, behavior, conduct*

kóin コイン *coin*［→**kōka** 硬貨］
- koin-randorī コインランドリー <US>*laundromat*, <UK>*launderette*
- koin-rokkā コインロッカー *coin-operated locker*

kóiru コイル *(electrical)coil*

koitsu こいつ【CRUDE】*this person*

kōji 工事 *construction work; repair work* «on major construction projects»
- kōji-chū no 工事中の *under construction; under repair*
¶Tetsudō wa mada kōji-chū desu.
鉄道はまだ工事中です。
The railroad is still under construction.
- dōro-kōji 道路工事 *road building; road repairs*

kóji 孤児 *orphan*
- koji-in 孤児院 *orphanage*

kojikí 乞食 *beggar*

kójin 個人 *an individual* (*person*)
- kojin-jugyō 個人教授 *private lessons*
- kojin-sa 個人差 *difference among individuals*
- kojin-shugi 個人主義 *individualism*
- kojin-teki na 個人的な *personal, individual*
¶Kore wa watashi no kojin-teki na iken desu.
これは私の個人的な意見です。
This is my personal opinion.

kōjitsu 口実 *excuse, pretext*

kōjō 工場 *factory, plant, mill*
- kōjō-chitai 工場地帯 *factory district*
- kōjō-chō 工場長 *factory manager*
- gasu-kōjō ガス工場 *gasworks*
- jidōsha-kōjō 自動車工場 *automobile plant*
- jidōsha-shūri-kōjō 自動車修理工場 *auto repair shop*
- kikai-kōjō 機械工場 *machine shop*
- seishi-kōjō 製紙工場 *paper mill*
- sekiyu-kagaku-kōjō 石油化学工場 *petrochemical plant*

kōjōsen 甲状腺 *thyroid gland*

kōka 効果 *effectiveness, effect* [→**kikime** 効き目]
¶Kono kusuri wa zutsū ni wa nan no kōka mo nai yo.
この薬は頭痛には何の効果もないよ。
This medicine has no effect on headaches!
- kōka-teki na 効果的な *effective*
¶Eigo no kōka-teki na gakushū-hō o oshiete kudasai.

英語の効果的な学習法を教えてください。
Please teach me an effective study method for English.
- onkyō-kōka 音響効果 *sound effect*

kōka 高価 *high price*
- kōka na 高価な *expensive* [→**takai** 高い③]

kōka 校歌 *school song*

kōka 硬貨 *coin*

kokage 木陰 *shade of a tree*

kōkai 公開 *making open to the public; making public*
- kōkai suru 公開する *to open to the public; to make public*
¶Sono pūru wa ippan ni kōkai sarete imasu
そのプールは一般に公開されています。
That pool is open to the general public.
- kōkai no 公開の *open-to-the-public; in-public*
- kōkai-kōza 公開講座 *open class; extension course*
- kōkai-tōron 公開討論 *public debate*

kōkai 後悔 *regret, remorse*
¶Kōkai saki nitatazu.
後悔先に立たず。《*proverb*》
There's no use crying over spilled milk.
《*Literally: Remorse does not arise beforehand.*》
- kōkai suru 後悔する *to come to regret*
¶Kinben de nakatta koto o kōkai shite imasu.
勤勉でなかったことを後悔しています。
I regret that I was not diligent.
¶Ayamachi o totemo kōkai shite imasu.
過ちをとても後悔しています。
I very much regret my mistake.

kōkai 航海 (*sea*)*voyage*, (*ocean*)*cruise*, (*ocean*)*sailing*
- kōkai suru 航海する *to voyage, to sail*
¶Yotto de Taiheiyō o kōkai shimashita.
ヨットで太平洋を航海しました。
I sailed the Pacific in a sailboat.
- shojo-kōkai 処女航海 *maiden voyage*

kōkaidō 公会堂 *public meeting hall* «in a city or town»

kokáin コカイン *cocaine*

kōkan 交換 *exchange, trade*
- kōkan suru 交換する *to exchange, to trade* [→**torikaeru** 取り替える]
- A o B to kōkan suru AをBと交換する *to exchange A for B, to trade A for B*
¶Kono bōshi o motto ōkī no to kōkan shi-tai.
この帽子をもっと大きいのと交換したい。
I want to exchange this hat for a bigger one.
¶Yōko-san to kippu o kōkan shimashita.
洋子さんと切符を交換しました。
I exchanged tickets with Yoko.
- kōkan-dai 交換台 *switchboard*
- kōkan-gakusei 交換学生 *exchange student*
- kōkan-shu 交換手 *(telephone)operator*

koké 苔 *moss*
¶Korogaru ishi ni koke wa haenai.
転がる石にこけは生えない。《*proverb*》
A rolling stone gathers no moss. 《*Literally: No moss grows on a rolling stone.*》

kōkei 光景 *sight, spectacle; scene, view* [→**keshiki** 景色]
¶Watashi-tachi wa minna sono kōkei ni bikkuri shita yo.
私たちはみんなその光景にびっくりしたよ。
We were all surprised at that sight!

kōken 貢献 *contribution*
- kōken suru 貢献する *to make a contribution, to contribute*
¶Shushō wa sekai-heiwa ni ōi ni kōken shimashita.
首相は世界平和に大いに貢献しました。
The prime minister contributed greatly to world peace.

kokeshi こけし *kokeshi (doll)* 《*made of painted wood with a round head and cylindrical body*》

kōkíatsu 高気圧 [[⇔**teikiatsu** 低気圧]] ① *high atmospheric pressure*
② *high pressure (weather) system*

kōkíshin 好奇心 *curiosity*
¶Kōkishin kara sono hako o akemashita.
好奇心からその箱を開けました。
I opened that box out of curiosity.

¶Shinji-chan wa kōkishin no tsuyoi shōnen desu.
信次ちゃんは好奇心の強い少年です。
Shinji is a very curious boy.

kókka 国家 *nation state, nation, country* [→**kuni** 国①]
- kokka-shiken 国家試験 *state examination*

kokka 国歌 *national anthem*

kokkai 国会 *national legislature; the (Japanese)Diet; (United States)Congress; (British)Parliament*
- kokkai-giin 国会議員 *member of a national legislature*
- Kokkai-giji-dō 国会議事堂 *the Diet Building*
- Kokkai-tosho-kan 国会図書館 *the Diet Library*

kokkei 滑稽 ～**na** ～な *funny, humorous, comical*
¶Watashi-tachi wa sono kokkei na deki-goto ni waratte shimatta.
私たちはそのこっけいなできごとに笑ってしまった。
We laughed at that comical happening.

kokki 国旗 *national flag*

kokkō 国交 *diplomatic relations*
- kokkō-danzetsu 国交断絶 *breaking off of diplomatic relations*
- kokkō-kaifuku 国交回復 *restoration of diplomatic relations*

kókku コック *cook* 《*in a restaurant serving non-Japanese food*》

kokkyō 国境 *border between countries, national boundary*
- kokkyō-sen 国境線 *borderline between countries*

kókō 孝行 *filial piety, devotion to one's parents* [→**oyakōkō** 親孝行]
- kōkō suru 孝行する *to be filial, to show devotion to one's parents*

kōkō 高校 *high school* 《*an abbreviation of kōtō-gakkō* 高等学校《s.v. **kōtō** 高等)》
- kōkō-nyūshi 高校入試 *high-school entrance examination*
- kōkō-sei 高校生 *high-school student*
- Zenkoku-kōkō-yakyū-taikai 全国高校

野球大会 *National Senior High School Baseball Tournament*

koko ここ *this place, here* [⇔**soko** そこ; **asoko** あそこ]

¶Koko ni kite kudasai.

ここに来てください。

Please come here.

¶Koko ni Nyūyōku no chizu ga arimasu.

ここにニューヨークの地図があります。

There's a map of New York here.

¶Koko kara hoteru made dono kurai desu ka.

ここからホテルまでどのくらいですか。

About how far is it from here to the hotel?

¶Koko ga Satō-san no otaku desu.

ここが佐藤さんのお宅です。

This is Mr. Sato's house.

¶Koko wa doko desu ka.

ここはどこですか。

Where am I? 《*Literally: Where is this place?*》

kókoa ココア *cocoa*

¶Atsui kokoa o ip-pai nomimashita.

熱いココアを１杯飲みました。

I drank one cup of hot cocoa.

kōkógaku 考古学 *archaeology*

kōkoku 広告 ① *advertisement*

¶Sono kaisha wa shinbun ni kōkoku o dashite imasu.

その会社は新聞に広告を出しています。

The company places advertisements in the newspaper.

• kōkoku suru 広告する *to advertise*

② *notice, announcement* 《in the mass media, etc.》

• kōkoku suru 広告する *to announce, to make widely known*

• kōkoku-nushi 広告主 *sponsoring advertiser, sponsor* [→**suponsā** スポンサー]

• kyūjin-kōkoku 求人広告 *help-wanted ad*

• shibō-kōkoku 死亡広告 *obituary notice*

• terebi-kōkoku テレビ広告 *TV commercial* [→**komāsharu** コマーシャル]

kokonatsu ココナツ *coconut*

kokonoká 九日 《see Appendix 2》

① *nine days*

② *the ninth* 《day of a month》

kokónotsu 九つ *nine* 《see Appendix 2》

kokóro 心 ① *mind, mentality*

• kokoro ni kakaru 心に掛かる *to weigh on one's mind*

• kokoro ni tomeru 心に留める *to keep in mind*

• kokoro o komete 心をこめて *with one's whole heart, whole-heartedly*

¶Kokoro o komete shigoto o shimasu.

心をこめて仕事をします。

I do my work wholeheartedly.

• kokoro ga hiroi 〔semai〕 心が広い〔狭い〕 *one's mind is broad* 〔*narrow*〕

¶Katō-san wa kokoro no hiroi hito desu.

加藤さんは心の広い人です。

Mr. Kato is a broad-minded person.

② *heart, feelings*

¶Yōko-san wa kokoro no yasashii hito desu.

洋子さんは心の優しい人です。

Yoko is a kindhearted person.

¶Kokoro kara kansha shimasu.

心から感謝します。

I thank you from my heart.

• A ga B no kokoro o utsu AがBの心を打つ *A touches B's heart*

¶Michiko-san no kotoba wa watashi no kokoro o utta yo.

美知子さんの言葉は私の心を打ったよ。

Michiko's words touched my heart!

• kokoro o irekaeru 心を入れ替える *to turn over a new leaf, to reform oneself*

• kokoro kara no kangei 心からの歓迎 *hearty welcome*

kokoroátari 心当たり *inkling, idea*

¶Dare ga kono tegami o okutta ka kokoroatari wa nai no desu ka.

だれがこの手紙を送ったか心当たりはないのですか。

Don't you have any idea who sent this letter?

kokorobosói 心細い [[⇔**kokorozuyoi** 心強い]] ① *forlorn, discouraged, helpless-feeling, uneasy*

¶Ane ga inai to kokorobosoi desu.

姉がいないと心細いです。
When my older sister isn't here, I feel helpless.
② *discouraging, disheartening*

kokorogakéru 心掛ける ① *to keep striving for*
¶Motto hayaku okiru yō ni kokorogake-mashō.
もっと早く起きるように心がけましょう。
Let's keep striving to get up earlier.
② *to keep in mind*

kokoromíru 試みる *to try, to attempt*
¶Atarashii hōhō o kokoromimashō.
新しい方法を試みましょう。
Let's try a new method.
¶Shōnen wa ki ni noborō to kokoromima-shita.
少年は木に登ろうと試みました。
The boy tried to climb the tree.

kokoroyói 快い *nice, pleasant*
¶Kyō wa kokoroyoi tenki desu.
きょうは快い天気です。
Today it's pleasant weather.

kokorozásu 志す ① *to aspire, to set one's mind*
• gakumon ni kokorozasu 学問に志す *to set one's mind on scholarship*
② *to set one's mind on becoming, to aspire to become*
¶Honda-san wa gaikō-kan o kokorozashi-mashita.
本多さんは外交官を志しました。
Mr. Honda has set his mind on becoming a diplomat.

kokorozuyói 心強い [[⇔**kokorobosoi** 心細い]] ① *reassured, secure, encouraged*
② *reassuring, encouraging*

kōkū 航空 *aviation*
• kōkū-bin 航空便 *airmail*
• kōkū-gaisha 航空会社 *airline (company)*
• kōkū-ken 航空券 *airline ticket*

kokuban 黒板 *blackboard, chalkboard*
¶Keiko-chan, kokuban o keshite chōdai.
恵子ちゃん、黒板を消してちょうだい。
Keiko, please erase the blackboard.

• kokuban-fuki 黒板拭き *blackboard eraser*

kokubetsúshiki 告別式 *funeral service*

kokudō 国道 *national highway*

kókudo 国土 *national territory, country's land*

kokufuku 克服 *conquest*
• kokufuku suru 克服する *to conquer*

kokúgai 国外 *outside of a country, abroad* 《as a noun》 [⇔**kokunai** 国内]

kókugi 国技 *national sport* 《**sumō** 相撲 in the case of Japan》

kokugo 国語 ① *the language of a country*
② *the Japanese language* [→ **Nihon-go** 日本語 (s.v. **Nihon** 日本)]
• kokugo-jiten 国語辞典 *Japanese dictionary*

kokuhaku 告白 *confession*
• kokuhaku suru 告白する *to confess*

kokuhō 国宝 *national treasure*

kokujin 黒人 *black person*

kokumin 国民 *people (of a country)*
¶Nihon-jin wa kinben na kokumin da sō desu.
日本人は勤勉な国民だそうです。
I hear that the Japanese are a hardwork-ing people.
• kokumin no shukujitsu 国民の祝日 *national holiday*
• kokumin-sō-seisan 国民総生産 *gross national product* [→**jìenupī** GNP]
• Kokumin-taiiku-taikai 国民体育大会 *the National Athletic Meet*

kokúmotsu 穀物 <US>*grain*, <UK>*cereal*

kokúnai 国内 *inside of a country* 《as a noun》 [⇔**kokugai** 国外]
¶Sono opera kashu wa kokunai de mo kokugai de mo ninki ga arimasu.
そのオペラ歌手は国内でも国外でも人気があります。
The opera singer is popular both at home and abroad.
• kokunai no 国内の *internal, domestic*
• kokunai-jijō 国内事情 *internal affairs, domestic affairs*

- kokunai-sen 国内線 *domestic flight*

kokuō 国王 *king of a country*

Kokuren 国連 *the United Nations* 《an abbreviation of **Kokusai-rengō** 国際連合(s.v. **kokusai-** 国際－)》
- Kokuren-jimusōcho 国連事務総長 *Secretary General of the UN*
- Kokuren-sōkai 国連総会 *UN General Assembly*
- Kokuren-taishi 国連大使 *ambassador to the UN*

kokuritsu 国立 ～**no** ～の *national, nationally administered*
- kokuritsu-daigaku 国立大学 *national university*
- kokuritsu-kōen 国立公園 *national park*

kokusai- 国際－ *international* 《Added to noun bases.》
- kokusai-denwa 国際電話 *international telephone call*
- kokusai-kaigi 国際会議 *international conference*
- kokusai-kekkon 国際結婚 *marriage between people from different countries*
- kokusai-kūkō 国際空港 *international airport*
- Kokusai-rengō 国際連合 *the United Nations* [→**Kokuren** 国連]
- kokusai-shinzen 国際親善 *international goodwill*

kokusai-teki 国際的 ～**na**～な *international*

kokusan 国産 ～**no** ～の ① *domestically produced, made in-country* ② *Japanese-made, made in Japan* [→**Nihon-sei no** 日本製の (s.v. **Nihon** 日本)]
¶Kore wa kokusan no kuruma desu ka.
これは国産の車ですか。
Is this a Japanese-made car?
- kokusan-hin 国産品 *domestic product; Japanese-made product*
¶Kono tokei wa kokusan-hin desu.
この時計は国産品です。
This watch is a Japanese-made product.

kokuseichōsa 国勢調査 *national census*

kokuseki 国籍 *nationality, citizenship*
¶Ano hito no kokuseki wa doko desu ka.
あの人の国籍はどこですか。
What is that person's nationality?

kokutei-kōen 国定公園 *quasi-national park*

Kokutetsu 国鉄 *the Japanese National Railways* 《an abbreviation of **Nihon-kokuyū-tetsudō** 日本国有鉄道》《The Japanese National Railways was broken up into several private companies in 1987.》

kōkyō 公共 ～**no** ～の *public, communal*
- kōkyō-setsubi 公共施設 *public facilities*

kókyō 故郷 *hometown, birthplace*
¶Kokyō wa doko desu ka.
故郷はどこですか。
Where is your hometown?

Kốkyo 皇居 *the Imperial Palace*

kōkyốkyoku 交響曲 *symphony* ((musical piece)) [→**shinfonī** シンフォニー]
¶Ani wa Bētōben no kōkyōkyoku ga dai-suki desu.
兄はベートーベンの交響曲が大好きです。
My older brother really likes Beethoven's symphonies.

kōkyū 高級 ～**no** ～の *high-class, high-grade*
- kōkyū-hin 高級品 *high-quality item*

kokyū 呼吸 ① *breathing, respiration*
¶Sofu wa kokyū ga arai desu.
祖父は呼吸が荒いです。
My grandfather's breathing is hard.
- kokyū suru 呼吸する *to breathe*
② *knack, trick* [→**kotsu** こつ]
- jinkō-kokyū 人工呼吸 *artificial respiration*
- shin-kokyū 深呼吸 *deep breathing, deep breath*

kóma こま *top* ((toy))
- koma o mawasu こまを回す *to spin a top*

komakái 細かい ① *very small, fine* 《describing a large number of things or something consisting of a large number of pieces》
¶Komakai ji o kakimasu ne.

細かい字を書きますね。
Your writing is very small, isn't it.

¶Kono kaigan wa suna ga totemo komakai desu.
この海岸は砂がとても細かいです。
The sand on this beach is very fine.

¶Tamanegi o komakaku kizaminasai.
たまねぎを細かく刻みなさい。
Chop the onions fine.

• komakai o-kane 細かいお金 *(small)change* [→**kozeni** 小銭]

② *minor, trivial* [→**sasai na** 些細な]

¶Komakai koto de kenka o shinai de.
細かい事でけんかをしないで。
Don't quarrel over trivial things.

• komakai ayamari 細かい誤り *minor error*

③ *detailed, minute*

• komakai bunseki 細かい分析 *detailed analysis*

• o-kane ni komakai お金に細かい *stingy; frugal*

komaraséru 困らせる *to annoy, to bother* 《This word is the regular causative form of **komaru** 困る.》

¶Hen na shitsumon de watashi o komarasenai de kudasai.
変な質問で私を困らせないでください。
Please don't bother me with strange questions.

¶Otōto wa itazura o shite yoku haha o komaraseru yo.
弟はいたずらをしてよく母を困らせるよ。
My younger brother plays pranks and often annoys my mother!

komáru 困る *to get into difficulty, to get into a quandary, to become troubled*

¶Shukudai ga owaranakute komatte iru yo.
宿題が終わらなくて困っているよ。
I'm having trouble because I can't finish my homework!

¶Okuda-san wa kippu o nakushite komatte imasu.
奥田さんは切符を無くして困っています。
Mr. Okuda has lost his ticket and is in a quandary.

• o-kane ni komaru お金に困る *to become hard up for money*

komásharu コマーシャル *a commercial*

• komāsharu-songu コマーシャルソング *song used in a commercial*

komé 米 *(uncooked)rice* [⇔ **gohan** ご飯]

¶Kono minzoku wa kome o shushoku ni shite imasu.
この民族は米を主食にしています。
This ethnic group makes rice their staple food.

kómedī コメディー *comedy* [→**kigeki** 喜劇]

komédian コメディアン *comedian*

Kōmeitō 公明党 *the Clean Government Party*

komekami こめかみ *temple* 《i.e., a part of the head》

komichi 小道 *path, lane*

kómikku コミック ① *comic (strip), comic (book)* [→**manga** 漫画]

② 〜**na** 〜な *comical* [→**kigeki-teki na** 喜劇的な (s.v. **kigeki** 喜劇)]

kōmin 公民 *citizen* [→**shimin** 市民]

• kōmin-kan 公民館 *community center, public hall*

komísshonā コミッショナー *commissioner*

komoji 小文字 *lower-case letter, small letter* [⇔**ōmoji** 大文字]

kōmon 校門 *school gate*

kómon 顧問 *adviser*

kómori 蝙蝠 *bat* ((animal))

komóri 子守 ① *childcare*

② *person doing childcare*

• komori-uta 子守歌 *lullaby*

kómu 込む *to become crowded, to become congested*

¶Basu wa gakusei de konde imashita.
バスは学生で込んでいました。
The bus was crowded with students.

¶Dōro ga konde ite okuremashita.
道路が込んでいて遅れました。
The road was congested, so we were late.

komúgi 小麦 *wheat*

• komugi-ko 小麦粉 *wheat flour*

kōmúin 公務員 *civil servant, government employee*

kōmyō 巧妙 〜**na** 〜な *clever, skillful*

komyunikēshon コミュニケーション *communication*

kón 紺 *dark blue, navy blue*

kōnā コーナー ① *department, counter* 《in a store》[→**uriba** 売り場]
② *corner* 《of a boxing ring, playing field, etc.》
③ *photo corner* 《for mounting photographs in an album》

koná 粉 ① *powder*
② *flour, meal*
• kona-gusuri 粉薬 *powdered medicine*
• kona-miruku 粉ミルク *powdered milk*
• kona-sekken 粉石鹸 *soap powder*
• kona-yuki 粉雪 *powdery snow*

konagona 粉々 〜**ni** 〜に *into small pieces, into bits, into smithereens*

kónban 今晩 *this evening, tonight* [→kon'ya 今夜]
¶Shiai wa konban shichi-ji ni hajimarimasu.
試合は今晩7時に始まります。
The game starts at 7:00 this evening.

konban-wá こんばんは *Good evening, Hello*

kónbi コンビ ① *combination, pair, duo* 《of people in some activity》
• konbi o kumu コンビを組む *to form a pair, to become partners*
② *article of clothing with a combination of different colors or materials*

konbífu コンビーフ *corned beef*

konbiniensusutóa コンビニエンスストア *convenience store*

kónbu 昆布 *kelp, sea tangle* 《Commonly used as food in Japan.》

kóncheruto コンチェルト *concerto* [→ **kyōsōkyoku** 協奏曲]

konchū 昆虫 *insect*
• konchū-gaku 昆虫学 *entomology*
• konchū-saishū 昆虫採集 *insect collecting*

kondan 懇談 *friendly talk, open conversation*

kondate 献立 *menu* [→**menyū** メニュー]

kondénsā コンデンサー *condenser*

kondíshon コンディション *condition, state of fitness*
• kondishon ga ii 〔warui〕 コンディションがいい〔悪い〕 *to be in good 〔bad〕 condition*

kóndo 今度 ① *this time* [→**konkai** 今回①]
¶Kondo wa umaku ikimashita.
今度はうまくいきました。
This time it went well.
¶Kondo wa kimi ga utau ban da yo.
今度は君が歌う番だよ。
This time it's your turn to sing!
② *next time, this coming time* [→**konkai** 今回②]
¶Kondo wa itsu kuru no desu ka.
今度はいつ来るのですか。
When are you next coming?
¶Kondo no Nichiyōbi wa yūenchi ni ikimasu.
今度の日曜日は遊園地に行きます。
This coming Sunday we're going to go to theme park.
③ *sometime soon* [→**sono uchi** そのうち]
¶Kondo mata tsuri ni ikimashō.
今度また釣りに行きましょう。
Let's go fishing again sometime soon.

kóne コネ *connections* 《with people who can further one's interests》
¶Chichi wa ano kaisha ni yūryoku na kone ga arimasu.
父はあの会社に有力なコネがあります。
My father has powerful connections in that company.

kōnen 光年 *light-year*
• -kōnen -光年《counter for light years; see Appendix 2》

kongetsu 今月 *this month*
¶Kongetsu no yōka ni undō-kai ga arimasu.
今月の8日に運動会があります。
There is a field day on the eighth of this month.

¶Imagawa-san wa kongetsu
kaette kimasu.
今川さんは今月帰ってきます。
*Ms. Imagawa will come home this
month.*

kóngo 今後 *after this, from now on, in
the future* [→**kore kara** これから]
¶Kongo no yotei wa nan desu ka.
今後の予定は何ですか。
What are your plans after this?
¶Kongo wa shukudai o wasuremasen.
今後は宿題を忘れません。
*From now on I won't forget my home-
work.*

kongō 混合 *mixing, blending*
• kongō suru 混合する *to mix, to blend*
《transitive or intransitive》
• kongō-butsu 混合物 *a mixture*
• kongō-daburusu 混合ダブルス *mixed
doubles*

koními motsu 小荷物 ① *small baggage,
small luggage*
② <US>*small package,*
<UK>*small parcel* 《shipped by rail-
way and not sent through the mail》

kónjō 根性 ① *nature, inborn disposition*
② *willpower, tenacity, spirit*
¶Ano hito wa konjō ga aru ne.
あの人は根性があるね。
That person has tenacity, doesn't she.

kónkai 今回 ① *this time* [→**kondo**
今度①]
② *this coming time, next time* [→
kondo 今度②]

konki 根気 *perseverance*
¶Eigo no benkyō wa konki ga irimasu.
英語の勉強は根気が要ります。
*For the study of English one needs
perseverance.*
• konki-yoku 根気よく *with perseverance,
perseveringly*

konkuríto コンクリート *concrete*
¶Kore wa konkurīto no tatemono desu.
これはコンクリートの建物です。
This is a concrete building.
• tekkin-konkurīto 鉄筋コンクリート

steel-reinforced concrete

konkűru コンクール *contest* 《in which
relative excellence is judged》 [→**kontesuto** コンテスト]
• shashin-konkūru 写真コンクール *photo
contest*

kónkyo 根拠 *basis, grounds*
• konkyo-chi 根拠地 *base* (*of operations*)

kónma コンマ *comma*

konna こんな *this kind of* [⇔ **sonna**
そんな; **anna** あんな]
¶Konna tenki no ii hi ni ie ni iru no wa
mottai-nai ne.
こんな天気のいい日に家にいるのはもった
いないね。
*It's a waste to stay in the house on such
a beautiful day, isn't it.*
¶Tango wa konna fū ni kakinasai.
単語はこんなふうに書きなさい。
Write the words this way.
• konna ni こんなに *to this extent, this
much*
¶Konna ni yuki ga furu to wa omoimasen deshita.
こんなに雪が降るとは思いませんでした。
I didn't think it would snow this much.
¶Konna ni osoku made nani o benkyō
shite iru no?
こんなに遅くまで何を勉強しているの？
What are you studying until so late?

kónnan 困難 *difficulty, hardship*
¶Ōku no konnan ni aimashita.
多くの困難にあいました。
I met with many difficulties.
¶Arayuru konnan ni taeru tsumori desu.
あらゆる困難に耐えるつもりです。
I intend to bear every hardship.
• konnan na 困難な *difficult, hard* [→
muzukashii 難しい]
¶Sakadachi de aruku no wa konnan na
koto desu.
逆立ちで歩くのは困難なことです。
*Walking on your hands is a difficult
thing.*

kónnichi 今日 *today, nowadays*
¶Konnichi de wa dare-mo sonna koto wa

shinjimasen.

今日ではだれもそんなことは信じません。

Nowadays nobody believes such things.

• konnichi no Nihon 今日の日本 *Japan today*

konnichi-wá こんにちは *Good day, Hello*

konnyakú こんにゃく ① *devil's tongue* 《a plant related to taro》

② *konnyaku* 《a gelatinous paste made from the starch of the devil's tongue root and typically formed in to cakes or strips》

kono この *this, these* 《as a noun modifier》 [⇔ **sono** その; **ano** あの]

¶Kono kutsu wa watashi no desu.

この靴は私のです。

These shoes are mine.

¶Chichi wa kono Shichi-gatsu ni kaette kimasu.

父はこの7月に帰って来ます。

My father will come home this July.

¶Kono chikaku ni sunde iru n desu ka.

この近くに住んでいるんですか。

Do you live near here?

• kono hen この辺 *the area near here, the area around here*

¶Kono hen ni basu-tei wa arimasu ka.

この辺にバス停はありますか。

Is there a bus stop around here?

¶Kono hen wa hajimete desu.

この辺は初めてです。

It's the first time I've been around here.

• kono mae この前 *previously, last*

¶Kono mae Tomoko-san ni atta no wa itsu desu ka.

この前友子さんに会ったのはいつですか。

When did you last see Tomoko?

• kono mae no この前の *previous, last*

¶Kono mae no Nichiyōbi wa nijūsan-nichi deshita.

この前の日曜日は23日でした。

Last Sunday was the 23rd.

¶Kono mae no shushō wa mada wakai desu.

この前の首相はまだ若いです。

The previous prime minister is still young.

• kono mama このまま *as is, like this*

¶Hon wa kono mama ni shite okinasai.

本はこのままにしておきなさい。

Leave the books like this.

kono-aida この間 ① *the other day* [→ **senjitsu** 先日]

¶Kono-aida michi de Yōko-san ni aimashita.

この間、道で洋子さんに会いました。

The other day I met Yoko on the street.

② *recently* [→**saikin** 最近]

¶Kono-aida made Kyūshū ni imashita.

この間まで九州にいました。

Until recently I was in Kyushu.

kono-goro このごろ *these days, recently, lately*

¶Kono-goro ane wa totemo isogashii desu.

このごろ姉はとても忙しいです。

My older sister is very busy these days.

¶Kono-goro Ken-san ni atte imasen.

このごろ健さんに会っていません。

I haven't seen Ken lately.

kó-no-ha 木の葉 *tree leaf*

konomí 好み *liking, taste, preference*

¶Kono kabin wa watashi no konomi ni aimasen.

この花瓶は私の好みに合いません。

This vase is not to my taste.

konómu 好む *to like, to have a preference for* 《The direct object cannot be a specific person that one is fond of.》

¶Hotondo no daigaku-sei wa rokku o konomimasu.

ほとんどの大学生はロックを好みます。

Almost all college students like rock.

kōnótori 鸛 *Japanese stork*

konpakutodísuku コンパクトディスク *compact disc*

kónpasu コンパス ① *compass* ((drawing tool))

¶Toshiko-san wa konpasu de en o kaite imasu.

敏子さんはコンパスで円をかいています。

Toshiko is drawing a circle with a compass.

② (*ship*)*compass*
③ *length of one's stride; length of one's legs*

• konpasu ga nagai コンパスが長い *one's stride is long; one's legs are long*
• konpasu ga mijikai コンパスが短い *one's stride is short; one's legs are short*

konpon 根本 *basis, foundation, essence*

• konpon-teki na 根本的な *basic, fundamental, essential*
¶ Sono keikaku o konpon-teki ni henkō shimashita.
その計画を根本的に変更しました。
I changed that plan fundamentally.

konpurékkusu コンプレックス (*psychological*)*complex*

konpyū́tā コンピューター *computer*
¶ Dēta o konpyūtā ni nyūryoku shinasai.
データをコンピューターに入力しなさい。
Please put the data into the computer.

konran 混乱 *confusion, disorder, chaos*

• konran suru 混乱する *to be thrown into disorder, to become chaotic*
• konran-jōtai 混乱状態 *state of confusion, chaotic state*

konsárutanto コンサルタント *consultant*

kónsāto コンサート *concert* [→**ongaku-kai** 音楽会 (s.v. **ongaku** 音楽)]
¶ Ashita no konsāto ni ikō yo.
あしたのコンサートに行こうよ。
Let's go to tomorrow's concert!

kónsento コンセント (*electrical*)*outlet*, (*electrical*)*socket*
¶ Sono eakon no puragu o konsento ni sashikonde kudasai.
そのエアコンのプラグをコンセントに差し込んでください。
Please push that air conditioner plug into the outlet.

konshū 今週 *this week*
¶ Konshūno Kinyōbi wa yasumi desu.
今週の金曜日は休みです。
Friday of this week is a day off.
¶ Masako-san wa konshū zutto kesseki shite imasu.
正子さんは今週ずっと欠席しています。

Masako has been absent all this week.

konsome コンソメ *consommé*

kontakutorénzu コンタクトレンズ *contact lens*
¶ Ano senshu wa kontakutorenzu o shite iru.
あの選手はコンタクトレンズをしている。
That player wears contact lenses.

kóntesuto コンテスト *contest* «*in which relative excellence is judged*» [→**konkūru** コンクール]
¶ Ane wa sono kontesuto de yūshō shimashita.
姉はそのコンテストで優勝しました。
My older sister was first in that contest.
• supīchi-kontesuto スピーチコンテスト *speech contest*

kontorórū コントロール *control, regulating*
¶ Sono pitchā wa kontorōru ga ii.
そのピッチャーはコントロールがいい。
That pitcher's control is good.
• konotorōru suru コントロールする *to control, to regulate*

kón'ya 今夜 *tonight, this evening* [→**konban** 今晩]
¶ Kon'ya wa tsuki ga totemo kirei desu.
今夜は月がとてもきれいです。
The moon is very beautiful tonight.

kon'yaku 婚約 *engagement* (*to be married*)
• kon'yaku suru 婚約する *to get engaged*
¶ Jirō-san to Yumi-san wa kon'yaku shite imasu.
次郎さんと由美さんは婚約しています。
Jiro and Yumi are engaged.
• kon'yaku-sha 婚約者 *fiancé, fiancée*
• kon'yaku-yubiwa 婚約指輪 *engagement ring* [→**engéjiringu** エンゲージリング]

kōnyū 購入 *purchasing, buying*
• kōnyū suru 購入する *to purchase*

kónzatsu 混雑 ① *crowding, congestion*
• konzatsu suru 混雑する *to become crowded, to become congested* [→**komu** 込む]
¶ Mise wa kyaku de konzatsu shite imashita.

店は客で混雑していました。
The store was crowded with customers.

② *confusion, disorder* [→**konran**
混乱]

•konzatsu suru 混雑する *to be thrown
into disorder, to become confused*

kópī コピー ① *copy, duplicate* [→**fukusha** 複写①]

•kopī suru コピーする *to copy*

•kopī o toru コピーを取る *to make a
copy*

¶Kono tegami no kopī o ni-tsū totte kudasai.
この手紙のコピーを2通取ってください。
Please make two copies of this letter.

② *(advertising)copy*

•kopī-raitā コピーライター *copywriter*

koppu コップ *(drinking)glass*

¶Mai-asa koppu ip-pai no gyūnyū o no-
mimasu.
毎朝コップ1杯の牛乳を飲みます。
Every morning I drink one glass of milk.

koraéru 怺える, 堪える ① *to endure,
to bear* [→**gaman suru** 我慢する]

② *to suppress, to control, to refrain
from* «an expression of one's emotions»

¶Watashi-tachi wa warai-tai no o kora-
emashita.
私たちは笑いたいのをこらえました。
We suppressed the urge to laugh.

•namida o koraeru 涙をこらえる *to suppress one's tears*

•ikari o koraeru 怒りをこらる *to control
one's anger*

kōrakubíyori 行楽日和 *ideal weather
for an outing*

kóramu コラム *short commentary
column* «in a newspaper, etc.»

kórasu コーラス ① *singing in chorus;
choral music, chorus* [→**gasshō** 合唱]

② *chorus, choral group* [→**gasshō-dan**
合唱団 (s.v. **gasshō** 合唱)]

kore これ *this (one)* [⇔ **sore** それ; *are*
あれ]

¶Kore o kudasai.
これをください。
Please give me this.

¶Kore wa watashi no megane desu.
これは私の眼鏡です。
These are my glasses.

•kore kara これから *after this, from this
point, in the future, from now on* [→
kongo 今後]

¶Shiai wa kore kara hajimarimasu.
試合はこれから始まります。
*The game is going to start from this
point.*

•kore hodo これほど *to this extent, this
much* [→**konna ni** こんなに]

•kore made これまで *until now, so far*
[→**ima made** 今まで]

¶Kore made wa subete umaku itte imasu.
これまではすべてうまく行っています。
So far, it's all going well.

•kore-ra これら *these (ones)*

kōrei 高齢 *advanced age, elderliness*

•kōrei-sha 高齢者 *elderly person*

korékushon コレクション ① *collection*
«of items as a hobby»

¶Tomodachi no kitte no korekushon wa
subarashii.
友達の切手のコレクションはすばらしい。
*My friend's collection of stamps is won-
derful.*

② *collection* «of a high-fashion clothing
designer»

kōri 氷 *ice*

¶Kōri o sukoshi kudasai.
氷を少しください。
Please give me a little ice.

¶Uchi e kaeru tochū kōri de subette
shimatta.
うちへ帰る途中氷で滑ってしまった。
I slipped on the ice on my way home.

¶Ike ni kōri ga harimashita.
池に氷が張りました。
Ice formed on the pond.

¶Wain o kōri de hiyashimashita.
ワインを氷で冷やしました。
I chilled the wine with ice.

koríru 懲りる *to learn one's lesson*
«from a bad experience»

¶Kono shippai de otōto mo koriru deshō.
この失敗で弟も懲りるでしょう。

My younger brother also will probably learn his lesson from this failure.

kōritsu 公立 ～**no** ～の *public, publicly administered* [⇔**shiritsu no** 私立の]
• kōritsu-gakkō 公立学校 <*US*>*public school*, <*UK*>*state school*

kōritsu 効率 *efficiency* [→**nōritsu** 能率]
• kōritsu-teki na 効率的な *efficient*

koritsu 孤立 *isolation*
• koritsu suru 孤立する *to become isolated*

kóro 頃 [[→**toki** 時②]] *time, occasion; (time)when*
¶Sorosoro benkyō o hajimete mo ii koro desu yo.
そろそろ勉強を始めてもいいころですよ。
It's almost time for you to start studying!
¶Osanai koro wa basu no unten-shu ni nari-takatta.
幼いころはバスの運転手になりたかった。
When I was young I wanted to become a bus driver.

korobu 転ぶ *to fall over, to fall down* 《The subject is a person.》
¶Kōtta michi de subette koronde shimatta yo.
凍った道で滑って転んでしまったよ。
I slipped and fell down on the frozen road!

korogaru 転がる ① *to roll* 《intransitive》
¶Ringo ga fukuro kara korogatte demashita.
りんごが袋から転がって出ました。
An apple rolled out of the bag.
② *to fall over, to fall down* 《The subject is a person.》 [→**korobu** 転ぶ]
¶Ishi ni tsumazuite korogarimashita.
石につまずいて転がりました。
I tripped on a stone and fell down.
③ *to lie down* [→**yokotawaru** 横たわる]

kōrogi こうろぎ *cricket* ((insect))
kórokke コロッケ *croquette*
korosu 殺す ① *to kill*
¶Nezumi o korosu tsumori desu ka.

ねずみを殺すつもりですか。
Do you intend to kill the mouse?
② *to suppress, to stifle* 《one's own breathing, feelings, etc.》
• iki o korosu 息を殺す *to suppress one's breathing*
• ikari o korosu 怒りを殺す *to suppress one's anger*
• akubi o korosu あくびを殺す *to stifle a yawn*
③ *to let go to waste, to make poor use of*
• sainō o korosu 才能を殺す *to make poor use of talent*

kōru 凍る *to freeze* 《intransitive》
¶Senmen-ki no mizu ga kōtte imasu.
洗面器の水が凍っています。
The water in the wash basin has frozen.

kóru 凝る ① *to become ardent, to become absorbed* [→**netchū suru** 熱中する]
¶Musuko wa sukī ni kotte imasu.
息子はスキーに凝っています。
My son is ardent about skiing.
② *to become elaborate*
¶Kono hoteru wa kotte imasu ne.
このホテルは凝っていますね。
This hotel is elaborate, isn't it.
③ *to get stiff* 《The subject is a part of the body in which the muscles become stiff.》
¶Kata ga kotte, kubi ga mawaranai yo.
肩が凝って、首が回らないよ。
My shoulders got stiff and my neck won't turn!

kōrudogému コールドゲーム *called game*
¶Tenisu no shiai wa niwaka-ame de kōrudogému ni narimashita.
テニスの試合は、にわか雨でコールドゲームになりました。
The tennis match was a called game because of a rain shower.

kóruku コルク *cork*
kóryo 考慮 *consideration, thought*
• kōryo ni ireru 考慮に入れる *to take into consideration*
¶Dōzo sono jijitsu o kōryo ni irete ku-

dasai.
どうぞその事実を考慮に入れてください。
Please take that fact into consideration.

• kōryo suru 考慮する *to consider, to think over*

kōryū 交流 ① *exchange, interchange* «between people of different areas, organizations, cultures, etc.»

• kōryū suru 交流する *to exchange, to interchange* «transitive or intransitive»

② *alternating（electrical）current*

kōsa 交差 *intersecting, crossing*

• kōsa suru 交差する *to intersect, to cross* «intransitive»

¶Kono tōri wa tetsudō to kōsa shite imasu.
この通りは鉄道と交差しています。
This street crosses the railroad.

• kōsa-ten 交差点 *(point of)intersection*

kōsai 交際 *association, intercourse, companionship*

¶Nakamura-san wa kōsai ga hiroi desu.
中村さんは交際が広いです。
Mr. Nakamura has a wide circle of acquaintances. «Literally: Mr. Nakamura's association is wide.»

• kōsai suru 交際する *to associate, to have contact, to keep company*

¶Keiko-san to shitashiku kōsai shite imasu.
恵子さんと親しく交際しています。
I am very close to Keiko.

kōsaku 工作 ① *building, construction work*

• kōsaku suru 工作する *to build, to construct*

② *handcrafting*

• kōsaku suru 工作する *to handcraft*

③ *operations, activities, maneuvering* «to achieve some goal»

• kōsaku suru 工作する *to operate, to maneuver*

• kōsaku-kikai 工作機械 *machine tool*

• seiji-kōsaku 政治工作 *political maneuvering*

kōsan 降参 *surrender, submission, yielding*

• kōsan suru 降参する *to surrender, to give up, to yield*

¶Wakatta, wakatta, kōsan suru yo.
わかった、わかった、降参するよ。
All right, all right, I give up!

kōsei 公正 *fairness, impartiality, justice* [→kōhei 公平]

• kōsei na 公正な *fair, impartial, just*

¶Hō wa nani-goto ni mo kōsei de nakereba narimasen.
法は何事にも公正でなければなりません。
The law must be fair in everything.

kōsei 厚生 *public welfare*

• kōsei-shisetsu 厚生施設 *welfare facilities*

• Kōsei-shō 厚生省 *the Ministry of Health and Welfare*

kōsei 恒星 *fixed star*

kōsei 構成 *composition, make-up, organization*

• kōsei suru 構成する *to make up, to compose*

¶Amerika-gasshūkoku wa gojus-shū de kōsei sarete iru.
アメリカ合衆国は50州で構成されている。
The United states of America is made up of fifty states.

kósei 個性 *individual character, individuality*

¶Ano hito wa kosei ga tsuyoi desu.
あの人は個性が強いです。
That person is highly individual.

kōseibússhitsu 抗生物質 *an antibiotic*

koseki 戸籍 *family register* «This word refers to an official document which is kept in a municipal government office and which records the names, birthdates, etc., of a married couple and their unmarried children. Every Japanese citizen is listed on a **koseki**.»

kōsen 光線 *light ray, light beam*

• kōsen-jū 光線銃 *ray gun*

• rēzā-kōsen レーザー光線 *laser beam*

• taiyō-kōsen 太陽光線 *sunlight, rays of the sun*

kósha 校舎 *school building, schoolhouse*

kōshi 講師 ① (*college*)*lecturer, instructor*
② *speaker, lecturer*

koshi 腰 *lower back* 《i.e., the back side of the body between the waistline and the widest part of the pelvis》
¶Kyō wa koshi ga itai desu.
きょうは腰が痛いです。
My lower back hurts today.
¶Sono onna no hito wa toshi de koshi ga magatte imasu.
その女の人は年で腰が曲がっています。
That woman's back is bent with age.
• koshi o kakeru 腰を掛ける [☞**koshikakeru** 腰掛ける]

koshikakéru 腰掛ける *to sit, to take a seat* 《Used only for sitting on a chair, etc., not for sitting on the floor.》 [→**suwaru** 座る①]

kōshiki 公式 ① (*mathematical*)*formula*
② ～**no** ～の *official, formal* [→**seishiki na** 正式な]
• kōshiki-hōmon 公式訪問 *formal visit, official visit*
• kōshiki-sen 公式戦 *official game, regular-season game*

kōshin 行進 *march, parade; marching, parading*
• kōshin suru 行進する *to march, to parade*
• kōshin-kyoku 行進曲 *march* ((musical piece)) [→**māchi** マーチ]

koshiraeru 拵える *to make; to prepare; to build*
• bentō o koshiraeru 弁当をこしらえる *to pack a lunch*
• kao o koshiraeru 顔をこしらえる *to put on one's make-up*
• o-kane o koshiraeru お金をこしらえる *to raise money, to get money together*

kōshō 交渉 ① *negotiation(s)*
• kōshō suru 交渉する *to negotiate; to negotiate about*
¶Sono jigyō ni tsuite shichō to kōshō shimashita.
その事業について市長と交渉しました。
I negotiated with the mayor about that enterprise.
② *connection, dealings* 《between people》
• dantai-kōshō 団体交渉 *collective bargaining*

koshō 故障 (*mechanical*)*trouble, breakdown*
• koshō suru 故障する *to break down*
¶Sono kikai ga mata koshō shimashita.
その機械がまた故障しました。
That machine broke down again.
• koshō-chū no 故障中の *out-of-order*

koshó こしょう *pepper* 《of the hard, round variety》
¶Kono sarada ni koshō o kakete kudasai.
このサラダにこしょうをかけてください。
Please put pepper on this salad.
• koshō-ire 胡椒入れ *pepper shaker, pepper container*

kōshū 公衆 *the public*
• kōshū no menzen de 公衆の面前で *in public*
• kōshū-benjo 公衆便所 *public lavatory*
• kōshū-denwa 公衆電話 *public telephone*
• kōshū-dōtoku 公衆道徳 *public morality*
• kōshū-eisei 公衆衛生 *public health*
• kōshū-yokujō 公衆浴場 *public bathhouse*

kōshū 講習 *course, class*

koso こそ *indeed, precisely* 《This particle emphasizes the preceding phrase. The phrase preceding **koso** frequently ends in a noun or another particle, but **koso** can also appear after a clause ending in **kara** から *because*.》
¶Kore koso tenkei-teki na rei desu.
これこそ典型的な例です。
This is indeed a typical example.
¶Dekinai kara koso renshū ga hitsuyō nano desu.
できないからこそ練習が必要なのです。
It's precisely because you can't do it that you have to practice.

kōsōbíru 高層ビル *high-rise building*

kōsoku 校則 *school regulations, school*

rules

¶Kōsoku o mamoranakereba naranai yo.

校則を守らなければならないよ。

We must obey the school regulations!

kōsoku 高速 *high speed*

• kōsoku-dōro 高速道路 <*US*>*expressway*, <*UK*>*motorway*

kossetsu 骨折 (*bone*)*fracture*

• kossetsu suru 骨折する *to suffer a fracture, to break a bone*

kossóri こっそり (～to ～と) *secretly, in secret*

¶Keiko-san wa kossori to watashi ni sono nyūsu o hanashite kuremashita.

恵子さんはこっそりと私にそのニュースを話してくれました。

Keiko told me that news secretly.

kōsu コース ① *course, itinerary*
② (*race*)*lane*

kosu 越す, 超す ① *to cross, to go over* 《*a distance or boundary*》[→**koeru** 越える, 超える①]

¶Bōru wa fensu o koshita yo.

ボールはフェンスを越したよ。

The ball went over the fence!

② *to exceed, to go over* [→**koeru** 超える, 超える②, uwamawaru 上回る]

¶Nedan wa gosen-en o koshite imashita.

値段は5000円を越していました。

The price was over 5,000 yen.

③ *to move* 《*to a new residence*》[→**hikkosu** 引っ越す]

¶Watashi wa ni-nen-mae ni kono machi ni koshite kimashita.

私は2年前にこの町に越してきました。

I moved to this city two years ago.

④ *to spend* 《*a period of time*》[→**sugosu** 過ごす]

¶Maitoshi Hawai de fuyu o koshimasu.

毎年ハワイで冬を越します。

I spend the winter in Hawaii every year.

kosuchūmu コスチューム (*stage*) *costume*

kōsui 香水 *perfume*

kósumosu コスモス *cosmos* ((*flower*))

kosúru 擦る *to rub* 《*transitive*》

• me o kosuru 目をこする *to rub one's*

eyes

kósuto コスト (*monetary*)*cost*

• seisan-kosuto 生産コスト *production cost*

kotae 答え *answer, reply*

¶Sono kotae wa tadashii desu.

その答えは正しいです。

That answer is correct.

kotaéru 応える ① *to respond as hoped, to respond appropriately* 《*to another person's thoughts or actions*》

• kitai ni kotaeru 期待にこたえる *to meet expectations*

• shinsetsu ni kotaeru 親切にこたえる *to repay kindness*

② *to affect strongly, to tell on*

¶Haha no kotoba ga kotaemashita.

母の言葉がこたえました。

My mother's words affected me strongly.

• mi ni kotaeru 身にこたえる *to affect one physically, to tell on one physically*

kotaéru 答える *to give an answer, to reply, to respond*

¶Shitsumon ni ōki na koe de kotaemashita.

質問に大きな声で答えました。

I gave an answer to the question in a loud voice.

kōtai 交代, 交替 *alternating, taking another's place; (work)shift*

• kōtai no 交代の *alternating*

• kōtai ni／de 交代に／で *by turns, alternately* [→**kawarugawaru** 代わる代わる]

• kōtai de hataraku 交代で働く *to work in shifts*

• kōtai suru 交代する *to alternate, to take another's place*

¶Kyōko-san wa imōto-san to kōtai shite, kabe ni penki o nurimashita.

京子さんは妹さんと交代して、壁にペンキを塗りました。

Kyoko took her younger sister's place and painted the walls.

kotai 固体 *a solid* (*substance*) [⇔**ekitai** 液体; **kitai** 気体]

kōtáishi 皇太子 *crown prince*

• kōtaishi-hi 皇太子妃 *crown prince's*

wife

kotatsu 炬燵 *kotatsu* 《This word refers to a low table covered with a quilt and equipped with a heater underneath. In modern Japan, the heater is electric and attached to the underside of the table. People sit on the floor with their legs under the **kotatsu** to keep warm in the winter.》

kotchi こっち 【COL. for **kochira** こちら】

kōtei 肯定 *affirmation* [⇔**hitei** 否定]
- kōtei suru 肯定する *to affirm*
¶Daitōryō wa shihon-shugi o zenmen-teki ni kōtei shimasu.
大統領は資本主義を全面的に肯定します。
The president fully affirms capitalism.
- kōtei-bun 肯定文 *affirmative sentence*
- kōtei-teki na 肯定的な *affirmative*

kōtei 皇帝 *emperor*

kōtei 校庭 *school grounds, schoolyard*

kotei 固定 ～**suru** ～する *to fix, to set, to make stationary*

kōtēji コテージ *cottage*

koten 古典 *classic work* 《of literature, art, etc.》
- koten-bungaku 古典文学 *classical literature*
- koten-teki na 古典的な *classical*

kōtetsu 鋼鉄 *steel* [→**tekkō** 鉄鋼]

kōtō 高等 ～**no** ～の *high-level, advanced*
- kōtō-dōbutsu 高等動物 *higher animal*
- kōtō-gakkō 高等学校 *high school* [→**kōkō** 高校]
- kōtō-senmon-gakkō 高等専門学校 *technical college*

kōto コート *court* 《for tennis, volleyball, etc.》

kōto コート *coat, overcoat*

kotó 事 ① *thing, matter, affair*
¶Kyō wa suru koto ga takusan arimasu.
きょうはする事がたくさんあります。
Today I have a lot of things to do.
¶Sono koto ni tsuite wa nani-mo shiri-masen.
その事については何も知りません。
I don't know anything about that matter.

② *to, –ing, that* 《Makes a preceding clause function as a noun.》
¶Eigo o manabu koto wa omoshiroi desu.
英語を学ぶことはおもしろいです。
It is interesting to study English.
¶Oyogu koto ga suki desu.
泳ぐことが好きです。
I like swimming.
¶Fujimoto-san ga uta ga jōzu da to iu koto wa shitte imasu.
藤本さんが歌が上手だということは知っています。
I know that Ms. Fujimoto is good at singing.
- koto ga aru ことがある *it sometimes happens that* 《following a clause with a predicate in the nonpast tense》; *it has happened that* 《following a clause with a predicate in the past tense》
¶Ano kazan wa funka suru koto ga arimasu.
あの火山は噴火することがあります。
That volcano sometimes erupts.
¶Yukiko-san to ichi-do hanashita koto ga arimasu.
由紀子さんと一度話したことがあります。
I have talked with Yukiko once.
¶Watashi wa Kamakura ni itta koto ga nai desu.
私は鎌倉に行ったことがないです。
I have never been to Kamakura.
- koto ni naru ことになる *to be decided that* 《following a verb in the nonpast tense》
¶Ani wa asatte shuppatsu suru koto ni narimashita.
兄はあさって出発することになりました。
It has been decided that my elder brother will leave the day after tomorrow.
- koto ni suru ことにする *to decide to* 《following a verb in the nonpast tense》
¶Ashita kaeru koto ni shimashita.
あした帰ることにしました。
I decided to return home tomorrow.

kóto 琴 *koto, Japanese harp*

kotobá 言葉 ① *language* [→**gengo**

言語]

¶ Eigo wa kokusaiteki na kotoba desu.

英語は国際的な言葉です。

English is an international language.

② *word* [→**tango** 単語]

• kotoba o kaete ieba 言葉を換えて言えば *in other words*

• kotoba de arawasu 言葉で表す *to express in words*

• kotoba-asobi 言葉遊び *word game*

kotobazúkai 言葉遣い *choice of words, (use of)language*

¶ Kotobazukai ni ki o tsukenasai.

言葉づかいに気をつけなさい。

Watch your language.

kotonáru 異なる *to differ* [→**chigau** 違う]

kóto-ni 殊に *especially* [→**toku-ni** 特に]

kotori 小鳥 *small bird* 《i.e., a bird about the size of a typical songbird》

¶ Petto to shite kotori o ni-wa katte imasu.

ペットとして小鳥を2羽飼っています。

I keep two small birds as pets.

kotoshi 今年 *this year*

¶ Ojīsan wa kotoshi kyūjus-sai ni naru ne.

おじいさんは今年90歳になるね。

Grandfather will be 90 this year, won't he.

¶ Kotoshi no natsu wa Eikaiwa no benkyō o shimasu.

今年の夏は英会話の勉強をします。

This summer I'm going to study English conversation.

kotowáru 断る ① *to refuse, to decline, to turn down*

¶ Yamashita-san no shōtai o kotowarimashita.

山下さんの招待を断りました。

I declined Mr. Yamashita's invitation.

② *to tell in advance, to give prior notice*

kotowaza 諺 *proverb, adage, maxim*

kotozuké 言付け [[→**dengon** 伝言]] *message* 《that someone asks one person to give to another person》; *giving a message*

¶ Sugiyama-san e no kotozuke ga arimasu.

杉山さんへの言づけがあります。

There is a message for Ms. Sugiyama.

¶ Kotozuke o o-negai dekimasu ka.

言づけをお願いできますか。

Can I leave a message?

kōtsū 交通 *traffic* 《along a transportation route》

¶ Kono dōro wa kōtsū ga hageshii desu.

この道路は交通が激しいです。

On this road the traffic is heavy.

• kōtsū-ihan 交通違反 *traffic violation*

• kōtsū-jiko 交通事故 *traffic accident*

• kōtsū-junsa 交通巡査 *traffic police officer*

• kōtsū-shingō 交通信号 *traffic signal*

kotsu こつ *knack, trick*

¶ Sukī no kotsu o oboemashita.

スキーのこつを覚えました。

I learned the knack skiing.

kōun 幸運 *good luck, good fortune*

¶ Kōun o inorimasu.

幸運を祈ります。

I wish you good luck.

• kōun na 幸運な *lucky, fortunate*

¶ Sono gaka ni aeta no wa kōun deshita.

その画家に会えたのは幸運でした。

We were fortunate to be able to meet that painter.

• kōun ni mo 幸運にも *fortunately, luckily*

¶ Kōun ni mo shiai ni kachimashita.

幸運にも試合に勝ちました。

Luckily, we won the game.

kouri 小売り *retailing, retail* [⇔ **oroshi–uri** 卸売り (s.v. **oroshi** 卸)]

• kouri suru 小売りする *to sell at retail*

• kouri-ne 小売り値 *retail price*

• kouri-ten 小売り店 *retail store*

kōwa 講和 *peace* 《concluding a war》

• kōwa suru 講和する *to make peace*

• kōwa-jōyaku 講和条約 *peace treaty*

• kōwa-kaigi 講和会議 *peace conference*

kowagáru 怖がる *to become afraid of,*

to get scared of 《Used instead of **kowai** 怖い when the subject is a third person.》

¶Kodomo-tachi wa kaminari o kowaga-rimasu.

子供たちは雷を怖がります。

The children get scared of thunder.

¶Imōto wa soko e iku no o kowagatte imasu.

妹はそこへ行くのを怖がっています。

My younger sister is afraid of going there.

kowái 怖い《This adjective is used to de-scribe both the people who are afraid and what they are afraid of. The word **kowai** is not used to describe the fears of a third person; see **kowagaru** 怖がる.》

　① *frightening, scary* [→**osoroshii** 恐ろしい]

¶Maiban kowai yume o miru yo.

毎晩怖い夢を見るよ。

Every night I have frightening dreams!

　② *afraid, frightened*

¶Watashi mo kowai desu.

私も怖いです。

I'm afraid too.

kowaréru 壊れる *to break, to get dam-aged*

¶Sono isu wa sugu kowareru deshō.

そのいすはすぐ壊れるでしょう。

That chair will probably break right away.

¶Kono tokei wa kowarete iru yo.

この時計は壊れているよ。

This watch is broken!

kowásu 壊す ① *to break, to damage*

¶Sono kikai o kowashite shimaimashita.

その機械を壊してしまいました。

I broke that machine.

¶O-sara o konagona ni kowashita yo.

お皿を粉々に壊したよ。

I broke the plate into smithereens!

• karada o kowasu 体を壊す *to damage one's health*

• onaka o kowasu おなかを壊す *to get an upset stomach*

• keikaku o kowasu 計画を壊す *to frus-trate a plan*

　② *to tear down, to demolish*

¶Furui tatemono o kowashita hō ga ii desu.

古い建物を壊したほうがいいです。

It would be better to tear down the old building.

koya 小屋 *hut, cabin*

• buta-goya 豚小屋 <US>*pigpen, pigsty*

• inu-goya 犬小屋 *doghouse*

• maruta-goya 丸太小屋 *log cabin*

• monooki-goya 物置小屋 *storage shed*

• tori-goya 鳥小屋 *chicken coop*

• yama-goya 山小屋 *mountain hut*

kōyō 紅葉 *autumn leaves*

• kōyō suru 紅葉する *to turn color* 《The subject is leaves.》

¶Ko-no-ha ga sukkari kōyō shite imasu.

木の葉がすっかり紅葉しています。

The leaves of the trees have completely turned color.

koyomí 暦 *calendar* [→**karendā** カレンダー]

• koyomi no ue de 暦の上で *according to the calendar*

koyū 固有 ～**no** ～の *peculiar* 〈*to*〉, *characteristic*

• koyū-meishi 固有名詞 *proper noun*

koyubi 小指 ① *little finger*

　② *little toe*

kōza 講座 ① (*university*)*chair, profes-sorship*

　② *course* (*of lessons*)

• Eigo-kōza 英語講座 *English course*

kōzan 高山 *high mountain*

• kōzan-byō 高山病 *mountain sickness*

• kōzan-shokubutsu 高山植物 *alpine plant*

kōzan 鉱山 *mine* 《in which something is dug up》

kōzen 公然 ～**no** ～の *open, public*

• kōzen to 公然と *openly, publicly*

¶Sore wa watashi-tachi no aida de wa kōzen no himitsu desu.

それは私たちの間では公然の秘密です。

That is an open secret among us.

kozeni 小銭 *small change, coins*

¶Kozeni no mochiawase ga arimasen.

小銭の持ち合せがありません。

I have no small change with me.

•kozeni-ire 小銭入れ *coin purse*

kōzō 構造 *structure, make-up*

kōzui 洪水 *flood*

¶Kono machi wa sakunen kōzui ni aimashita.

この町は昨年洪水にあいました。

This town met with a flood last year.

kózukai 小遣い *pocket money, allowance*

¶Tsuki ni sanzen-en no kozukai o moratte imasu.

月に3000円の小遣いをもらっています。

I get an allowance of 3,000 yen a month.

¶Kozukai ga agatta yo.

小遣いが上がったよ。

My allowance went up!

kozútsumi 小包 ① <*US*>*small package,* <*UK*>*small parcel, small bundle* ② *parcel post*

¶Kono omocha wa kozutsumi de okurimashō.

このおもちゃは小包で送りましょう。

I'll send this toy by parcel post.

kú 九 *nine* 《see Appendix 2》[→**kyū** 九]

•Ku-gatsu 九月 *September*

¶Amerika de wa shin-gakunen wa kugatsu ni hajimarimasu.

アメリカでは新学年は9月に始まります。

In the United States the new school year begins in September.

kú 区 *ward* 《part of a city》

¶Watashi-tachi no gakkō wa onaji ku ni arimasu.

私たちの学校は同じ区にあります。

Our school is in the same ward.

kubáru 配る *to distribute, to pass out, to deliver*

¶Yūbin-haitatsu wa ichinichi ni nikai tegami o kubarimasu.

郵便配達は1日に2回手紙を配ります。

The mail carrier delivers letters twice a day.

¶Sensei wa shiken-mondai o kubarimashita.

先生は試験問題を配りました。

The teacher passed out the test questions.

•kokoro o kubaru 心を配る *to keep watch, to be on guard*

•toranpu o kubaru トランプを配る *to deal cards*

kúbetsu 区別 *distinction, difference*

¶Wakusei to kōsei no kubetsu ga dekimasu ka.

惑星と恒星の区別ができますか。

Can you tell the difference between a planet and a fixed star?

•A to B o kubetsu suru AとBを区別する *to distinguish A from B*

kubi 首 ① *neck*

¶Ano senshu wa kubi ga futoi desu ne.

あの選手は首が太いですね。

That player's neck is thick, isn't it.

•kubi o nagaku shite 首を長くして *expectantly, eagerly*

¶Musume wa natsu-yasumi o kubi o nagaku shite matte imasu.

娘は夏休みを首を長くして待っています。

My daughter is waiting eagerly for summer vacation.

② *head* 《including the neck》

¶Shōjo wa kubi o yoko ni furimashita.

少女は首を横に振りました。

The girl shook her head (no).

•kubi o kashigeru 首をかしげる *to incline one's head to the side* 《as an expression of doubt》

③ <*US*>*firing,* <*UK*>*sacking* 《of an employee》

¶Kimi wa kubi da!

君は首だ！

You're fired!

•kubi ni naru 首になる <*US*>*to be fired,* <*UK*>*to be sacked*

•kubi ni suru 首にする <*US*>*to fire,* <*UK*>*to sack*

kubikázari 首飾り *necklace* [→**nekkuresu** ネックレス]

kubiwa 首輪 (*animal*)*collar*

kubomi 窪み *hollow, depression*

kuchi 口 ① *mouth*

• kuchi o ōkiku akeru 口を大きく開ける *to open one's mouth wide*

• kuchi ni au 口に合う *to suit one's taste, to have a flavor that one likes*

¶Gyūniku wa musume no kuchi ni awanai desu.

牛肉は娘の口に合わないです。

Beef does not suit my daughter's taste.

• kuchi ga omoi 口が重い *untalkative, uncommunicative*

• kuchi ga karui 口が軽い *talkative; unable to keep secrets*

• kuchi o kiku 口をきく *to talk, to converse*

¶Ano senshu wa ōki na kuchi o kiku taipu desu.

あの選手は大きな口をきくタイプです。

That player is the type that talks big.

• kuchi ni suru 口にする *to mention, to say; to eat; to drink*

¶Tomodachi wa daitōryō no namae o yoku kuchi ni shimasu.

友達は大統領の名前をよく口にします。

My friend often mentions the President's name.

② *job, job opening* [→**shūshoku–guchi** 就職口 (s.v. **shūshoku** 就職)]

• kuchi-beta na 口下手な *poor at talking, clumsy in the use of words*

• kuchi-hige 口髭 *moustache*

• kuchi-jōzu 口上手な *glib, facile-tongued*

• kuchi-kazu 口数 *how much one talks*

kuchibashi 嘴 *bill, beak* «of a bird»

kuchibeni 口紅 *lipstick*

kuchibiru 唇 *lip* «Unlike the English word *lip*, Japanese **kuchibiru** is not used to refer to the areas just above and below the actual lips themselves.»

• shita–kuchibiru 下唇 *lower lip*

• uwa–kuchibiru 上唇 *upper lip*

kuchibue 口笛 *whistling* «with one's mouth»

• kuchibue o fuku 口笛を吹く *to whistle*

kuchō 口調 *tone (of voice); tone, style* «of spoken or written expression»

¶Keikan wa okotta kuchō de hanashimashita.

警官は怒った口調で話しました。

The police officer spoke in an angry tone.

kūchū 空中 *the sky, the air* «as a location»

¶Fūsen ga takusan kūchū ni ukande imasu.

風船がたくさん空中に浮かんでいます。

Many balloons are floating in the air.

• kūchū–buranko 空中ブランコ *trapeze*

kúda 管 *tube, pipe*

kudakéru 砕ける *to break, to smash, to shatter* «intransitive»

¶Nami ga iwa ni atatte kudakemashita.

波が岩に当たって砕けました。

The waves struck the rocks and broke.

¶Koppu ga konagona ni kudaketa yo.

コップが粉々に砕けたよ。

The glass smashed to pieces!

kudáku 砕く *to break, to crush, to smash, to shatter* «transitive»

¶Kore de sono kōri o kudaite kudasai.

これでその氷を砕いてください。

Please crush that ice with this.

kudámono 果物 *fruit*

¶Shinsen na kudamono wa mattaku nai desu.

新鮮な果物はまったくないです。

There is absolutely no fresh fruit.

¶Tomato wa yasai desu ka, kudamono desu ka.

トマトは野菜ですか、果物ですか。

Is a tomato a vegetable or a fruit?

• kudamono-naifu 果物ナイフ *fruit knife*

• kudamono-ya 果物屋 *fruit store; fruit seller*

kudaranai くだらない ① *worthless, useless, trivial*

¶Konna kudaranai mono o okuru no wa shitsurei da.

こんなくだらない物を贈るのは失礼だ。

It's rude to give such a worthless thing.

② *silly, stupid, foolish*

¶Kudaranai koto o iwanai de kudasai.

くだらないことを言わないでください。

Please don't say stupid things.

kudari 下り ① *going down, descent* [⇔**nobori** 上り①]

¶Kōsoku-dōro wa koko kara kudari ni narimasu.

高速道路はここから下りになります。

The expressway is downhill from here on. 《Literally: *The expressway becomes a descent from here.*》

② *going down* 《a river, etc.》 [⇔**nobori** 上り②]

③ *going from a capital to a provincial area* [⇔**nobori** 上り③]

• kudari-densha 下り電車 *outbound train*
• kudari-zaka 下り坂 *downward slope*

kudaru 下る ① *to come down, to go down, to descend* [→**oriru** 下りる, 降りる①]

② *to go down* 《a river, etc.》 [⇔**noboru** 上る②]

¶Tanken-ka wa kobune de kawa o kudarimashita.

探検家は小船で川を下りました。

The explorer went down the river in a small boat.

③ *to go* 《from a capital to a provincial area》 [⇔**noboru** 上る③]

kudasáru 下さる {Irreg.} 【HON. for **kureru** 呉れる】 《In either use of this word the recipient must be the speaker, the speaker's group, or a person or group with whom the speaker is identifying.》

① *to give*

¶Kono hon wa sensei ga kudasaimashita.

この本は先生がくださいました。

The teacher gave me this book.

¶Nani-ka atatakai nomimono o kudasai.

何か温かい飲み物をください。

Please give me some kind of warm drink. 《Although **kudasai** is the imperative form of **kudasaru**, the use of **kudasai** still conveys an honorific tone that is conventionally reflected in English translations by the use of *please*.》

② *to do the favor of* 《following the gerund (-**te** form) of another verb》

¶Shachō wa yonde kudasaru sō desu.

社長は読んでくださるそうです。

I understand that the company president will read it for me.

¶Chotto doite kudasai.

ちょっとどいてください。

Please get out of the way. 《Literally: *Do me the favor of getting out of the way.*》

kūdétā クーデター *coup d'etat*

kufū 工夫 *strategem, device, contrivance, scheme*

¶Nani-ka ii kufū wa nai desu ka.

何かいい工夫はないですか。

Don't you have any good ideas?

• kufū suru 工夫する *to devise, to contrive*

kūfuku 空腹 *hunger, empty stomach*

• kūfuku no 空腹の *hungry*

¶Sono shōnen wa kūfuku deshita.

その少年は空腹でした。

That boy was hungry.

¶Kūfuku ni mazui mono nashi.

空腹にまずいものなし。《proverb》

Hunger is the best sauce. 《Literally: *To an empty stomach there is no bad-tasting thing.*》

kugi 釘 *nail*

• kugi o utsu 〔nuku〕 くぎを打つ〔抜く〕 *to drive* 〔*pull out*〕 *a nail*

• A ni kugi o sasu Aにくぎを刺す *to give A a reminder, to give A a warning*

• kugi-nuki 釘抜き *pincers for pulling out nails*

kugíru 区切る {5} ① *to divide, to partition*

¶Chūsha-jō o hakusen de itsutsu ni kugirimashō.

駐車場を白線で五つに区切りましょう。

Let's divide the parking lot into five parts with white lines.

② *to punctuate* 《a sentence, etc.》

kūgun 空軍 *air force*

kugúru 潜る ① *to pass through; to pass under*

¶Ressha wa tonneru o kugurimashita.

列車はトンネルをくぐりました。

The train passed through a tunnel.

¶Bōto wa hashi o kugurimashita.

ボートは橋をくぐりました。

The boat passed under a bridge.
　② *to dive* 《starting in the water》 [→
moguru 潜る①]

kúi 杭 *stake, post*

kuichigai 食い違い *disparity, discrepancy, discord*

kuichigau 食い違う *to become contrary, to become discordant*

kúiki 区域 （*delimited*）*area, zone*
　¶Kono kuiki wa kyanpu ni riyō sarete imasu.
　この区域はキャンプに利用されています。
　This area is being used for camping.
　•haitatsu-kuiki 配達区域 *delivery zone, delivery area*
　•kiken-kuiki 危険区域 *danger zone, dangerous area*

kúizu クイズ *quiz*
　•kuizu-bangumi クイズ番組 *quiz program, quiz show*

kujaku 孔雀 *peacock, peahen*

kúji くじ ① *lot, lottery ticket*
　•kuji o hiku くじを引く *to draw a lot*
　② *lottery* [→**chūsen** 抽選]
　•kuji-biki くじ引き *drawing lots*
　•atari-kuji 当たりくじ *winning lot, winning ticket*
　•kara-kuji 空くじ *losing lot, losing ticket*
　•takara-kuji 宝くじ *public lottery*

kujikéru 挫ける ① *to get sprained, to get strained*
　② *to be disappointed, to be dampened* 《The subject is a person's hope, enthusiasm, etc.》
　¶Sonna koto de yūki ga kujikeru hazu wa nai.
　そんなことで勇気がくじけるはずはない。
　There's no reason to expect his courage to be dampened by such a thing.

kujíku 挫く ① *to sprain, to strain*
　¶Aite wa ashi o kujikimashita.
　相手は足をくじきました。
　My opponent sprained his ankle.
　② *to frustrate* 《a plan, etc.》; *to disappoint, to dampen* 《a person's hope, enthusiasm, etc.》

kujira 鯨 *whale*

kujō 苦情 *complaint* [→**monku** 文句②]
　•kujō o iu 苦情を言う *to complain, to make a complaint*
　¶Watashi-tachi wa tonari no hito ni sōon no kujō o itta.
　私たちは隣の人に騒音の苦情を言った。
　We complained to our next-door neighbor about the noise.

kūkan 空間 *space, room*
　•jikan to kūkan 時間と空間 *time and space*
　•uchū-kūkan 宇宙空間 *outer space*

kúki 空気 ① *air*
　¶Jitensha no taiya ni kūki o iremashō.
　自転車のタイヤに空気を入れましょう。
　Let's put some air in the bicycle tires.
　② *atmosphere, ambience* [→**fun'iki** 雰囲気]
　¶Musuko wa atarashii kurasu no kūki ni najimenai.
　息子は新しいクラスの空気になじめない。
　My son can't get used to the atmosphere in his new class.
　•kūki-jū 空気銃 *air gun*

kukí 茎 *stem, stalk*

kúkkī クッキー ＜*US*＞*cookie*, ＜*UK*＞*biscuit*

kūkō 空港 *airport*
　•Haneda-kūkō 羽田空港 *Haneda Airport*
　•Shin-Tōkyō-kokusai-kūkō 新東京国際空港 *the New Tokyo International Airport* 《located in Narita》

kumá 熊 *bear*
　•shiro-kuma 白熊 *polar bear*

kumadé 熊手 *rake*

kumí 組 ① *class* 《i.e., one of several groups of pupils in the same year in school》 [→**kurasu** クラス①]
　¶Michiko-chan to Jirō-chan wa onaji kumi desu.
　美知子ちゃんと次郎ちゃんは同じ組です。
　Michiko and Jiro are in the same class.
　② *group, party, team, squad*
　¶Kodomo-tachi o mittsu no kumi ni wakemashita.
　子供たちを三つの組にわけました。

We divided the children into three groups.

-**kumi** 一組《counter for sets, pairs; see Appendix 2》

¶Toranpu o hito-kumi kudasai.

トランプを一組ください。

Please give me a deck of cards.

kumiai 組合 *union* ((organization))

• rōdō-kumiai 労働組合 *labor union*

• seikatsu-kyōdō-kumiai 生活協同組合 *cooperative society*

kumiawase 組み合わせ *combination*

¶Iro no kumiawase ga okashii desu.

色の組み合わせがおかしいです。

The combination of colors is odd.

¶Tenisu-tōnamento no kumiawase ga kimatta.

テニストーナメントの組み合わせが決まった。

The tennis tournament pairings were decided.

kumiawaseru 組み合わせる *to combine, to match* 《transitive》

¶Mittsu no gurūpu o kumiawasete, hitotsu ni shite kudasai.

三つのグループを組み合わせて、一つにしてください。

Please combine the three groups and make them into one.

¶Baggu to kutsu no iro o jōzu ni kumiawaseta.

バッグと靴の色を上手に組み合わせた。

I matched the color of the bag and shoes well.

kumitatéru 組み立てる *to put together, to assemble*

¶Koko de buhin o kumitatemasu.

ここで部品を組み立てます。

They put the parts together here.

¶Kono kōjō de wa terebi o kumitatemasu.

この工場ではテレビを組み立てます。

In this factory they assemble television sets.

kúmo 雲 *cloud*

¶Sora ni wa kumo ga hitotsu mo nai.

空には雲が１つもない。

There isn't a cloud in the sky.

¶Totsuzen kumo ga dete kimashita.

突然雲が出てきました。

All of a sudden clouds began to appear.

• atsui 〔usui〕 kumo 厚い〔薄い〕雲 *thick* 〔*thin*〕 *clouds*

• ama-gumo 雨雲 *rain cloud*

• kinoko-gumo 茸雲 *mushroom cloud*

• nyūdō-gumo 入道雲 *thunderhead*

kúmo 蜘蛛 *spider*

kumorí 曇り *cloudiness*

• kumori no 曇りの *cloudy*

¶Kumori, nochi hare.

曇り、後晴れ。《a weather forecast》

Cloudy, later fair.

¶Ashita wa kumori deshō.

あしたは曇りでしょう。

Tomorrow it will probably be cloudy.

• kumori-garasu 曇りガラス *frosted glass*

• kumori-zora 曇り空 *cloudy sky*

kumóru 曇る ① *to become cloudy, to cloud up*

② *to cloud* 《with anxiety, etc.》

¶Sono shirase o kiite, haha no kao ga kumorimashita.

その知らせを聞いて、母の顔が曇りました。

When she heard that news, my mother's face clouded.

③ *to fog up*

¶Yuge de megane ga kumotta yo.

湯気で眼鏡が曇ったよ。

My glasses fogged up with steam!

kumu 汲む *to draw* 《water, etc.》

¶Shōnen wa baketsu de kawa no mizu o kumimashita.

少年はバケツで川の水をくみました。

The boy drew water from the river with a bucket.

kúmu 組む ① *to put together*

② *to put together* 《long objects by crossing them over each other》, *to interlink*

• ude o kumu 腕を組む *to fold one's arms; to join arms* 《with another person》

¶Tarō to Yumi wa ude o kunde aruite imashita.

太郎と由美は腕を組んで歩いていました。

Taro and Yumi were walking arm in

arm.

• ashi o kumu 脚を組む *to cross one's legs*

③ *to become partners, to pair up*

¶Watashi wa tenisu de itsu-mo Keiko-chan to kumu yo.

私はテニスでいつも恵子ちゃんと組むよ。

I always pair up with Keiko in tennis!

Kunáichō 宮内庁 *the Imperial House-hold Agency* 《of the Japanese government》

kuni 国 ① *country, nation*

¶Sekai ni wa ōku no kuni ga arimasu.

世界には多くの国があります。

There are many countries in the world.

② *home country, home province, home-town* [→**kokyō** 故郷]

¶"O-kuni wa dochira desu ka" "Kanada desu."

「お国はどちらですか」「カナダです」

"Where is your home country?" "Can-ada."

¶Takahashi-san no kuni wa Toyama desu.

高橋さんの国は富山です。

Mr. Takahashi's hometown is Toyama.

• kuni-guni 国々 *countries*

kúnren 訓練 *training, drill*

¶Ano hito-tachi wa mada kunren o ukete imasu.

あの人たちはまだ訓練を受けています。

Those people are still undergoing train-ing.

• kunren suru 訓練する *to train, to drill* 《transitive or intransitive》

• hinan-kunren 避難訓練 *fire drill, emer-gency evacuation drill*

kunshō 勲章 *decoration* 《conferred as an honor》

kun'yomi 訓読み *Japanese reading* 《of a kanji》

kuótsu クオーツ *quartz*

kūrā クーラー ① *air conditioner* [→**ea-kon** エアコン]

② *(picnic)cooler*

kurá 倉, 蔵 *storehouse, warehouse*

kurá 鞍 *saddle*

kuraberu 比べる *to compare*

¶Kono e o sensei no to kurabemashō.

この絵を先生のと比べましょう。

Let's compare this picture with the teacher's.

kúrabu クラブ *club* 《(organization)》

¶Kurabu ni haitte imasu ka.

クラブに入っていますか。

Are you in a club?

• kurabu-katsudō クラブ活動 *club activi-ties*

kúrabu クラブ *(golf)club*

kúrabu クラブ *clubs* 《(playing-card suit)》

kurage くらげ *jellyfish*

kurai 暗い [[⇔**akarui** 明るい]]

① *dark* 《i.e., characterized by an absence of light》

¶Soto wa kuraku natta yo.

外は暗くなったよ。

It got dark outside!

¶Kōchi wa mada kurai uchi ni okimasu.

コーチはまだ暗いうちに起きます。

The coach gets up while it's still dark.

② *gloomy*

¶Shōrai no koto o kangaeru to, kurai kimochi ni naru.

将来のことを考えると、暗い気持ちになる。

Thinking about the future makes me gloomy.

kúrai 位 [☞**gurai** 位]

-kurai 一位 [☞**-gurai** 一位]

kuraimákkusu クライマックス *climax*

¶Monogatari wa kuraimakkusu ni tasshi-mashita.

物語はクライマックスに達しました。

The story reached its climax.

kurákkā クラッカー *cracker*

kurákushon クラクション *(automo-bile)horn*

kurarinétto クラリネット *clarinet*

kurashi 暮らし *life, livelihood, way of living*

• kurashi o suru 暮らしをする *to lead a life*

¶Mura no hito-tachi wa kōfuku na ku-rashi o shite imasu.

村の人たちは幸福な暮らしをしています。
The people of this village lead happy lives.

• kurashi o tateru 暮らしを立てる *to make a living, to earn a livelihood*

kurashíkku クラシック ① *classical music* ② *a classic* [→**koten** 古典]

• kurashikku na クラシックな *classical*

kurasu 暮らす *to live, to lead a life, to make a living* [→**seikatsu suru** 生活する]

¶Sofu wa Fukui de hitori de kurashite imasu.
祖父は福井で一人で暮らしています。
My grandfather lives alone in Fukui.

kúrasu クラス ① *class* 《i.e., one of several groups of pupils in the same year in school》 [→**kumi** 組①]

¶Tarō wa kurasu de ichiban ashi ga hayai ne.
太郎はクラスでいちばん足が速いね。
Taro is the fastest in the class, isn't he.

② *class, grade, rank* [→**kyū** 級①]

• kurasu-kai クラス会 *class meeting; class reunion*

• kurasu-mēto クラスメート *classmate*

kurátchi クラッチ *clutch* 《in an automobile, etc.》

kurayami 暗闇 *darkness, the dark*

¶Raion wa kurayami no naka o arukimashita.
ライオンは暗闇の中を歩きました。
The lion walked through the darkness.

kuréjitto クレジット *credit* 《as a purchasing method》

¶Kono baggu wa kurejitto de kaimashita.
このバッグはクレジットで買いました。
I bought this bag on credit.

• kurejitto-kādo クレジットカード *credit card*

kurén クレーン (*construction*)*crane*

• kurén-sha クレーン車 *crane truck*

kurépu クレープ ① *crepe* (*fabric*) ② (*dessert*)*crepe*

kureru 呉れる{Irreg.} 《In either use of this word the recipient must be the speaker, the speaker's group, or a person or group with whom the speaker is identifying.》 ① *to give*

¶Oji ga kono tokei o kureta yo.
伯父がこの時計をくれたよ。
My uncle gave me this watch!

② *to do the favor of* 《following the gerund (-te form)of another verb》

¶Gakusei wa shinsetsu ni nimotsu o hakonde kuremashita.
学生は親切に荷物を運んでくれました。
The student kindly carried my baggage for me.

¶Mado o akete kuremasen ka.
窓を開けてくれませんか。
Won't you you open the window for me?

kureru 暮れる ① **hi ga**~ 日が~ *it gets dark* (*outside*), *the sun goes down*

¶Mō sugu hi ga kureru yo.
もうすぐ日が暮れるよ。
It's going to get dark soon!

② *to end* 《The subject is a year or season.》

¶Kotoshi mo kuremashita.
今年も暮れました。
This year, too, has ended.

kurétā クレーター *crater* 《on the moon or other planets》

kuréyon クレヨン *crayon*

kurí 栗 *chestnut*

kurikáesu 繰り返す *to do again, to repeat*

¶Machigai o kurikaesanai yō ni shinasai.
間違いを繰り返さないようにしなさい。
Please be careful not to repeat the same mistake.

• kurikaeshite 繰り返して *repeatedly, again, over* 《This form is the gerund (-te form)of **kurikaesu**, and it has the predictable range of meanings as well.》

¶Sensei wa sono tango o nan-do mo kurikaeshite hatsuon shimashita.
先生はその単語を何度も繰り返して発音しました。
The teacher pronounced the word over and over many times.

kurímu クリーム ① *cream* ((dairy product))

② *cream* 《food made with milk, eggs, and sugar》

③ *cream* ((cosmetic))

• kurīmu-iro クリーム色 *cream color*

• kōrudo-kurīmu コールドクリーム *cold cream*

• nama-kurīmu 生クリーム *fresh cream*

kurínikku クリニック *clinic* [→**shinryōjo** 診療所]

kurīningu クリーニング *cleaning* 《of clothing by a professional cleaner》

• kurīningu ni dasu クリーニングに出す *to take to the cleaner's for cleaning*

¶Kinō kōto o kurīningu ni dashita.

昨日コートをクリーニングに出した。

Yesterday I took my coat to the cleaner's.

• kurīningu-ya クリーニング屋 *cleaner, launderer; cleaner's (shop)*

• dorai-kurīningu ドライクリーニング *dry cleaning*

kuríppu クリップ ① *paperclip*

② *hair curler, curling pin*

Kurisúmasu クリスマス *Christmas*

¶Kurisumasu omedetō!

クリスマスおめでとう！

Merry Christmas!

• Kurisumasu-ibu クリスマスイブ *Christmas Eve*

• Kurisumasu-kādo クリスマスカード *Christmas card*

• Kurisumasu-purezento クリスマスプレゼント *Christmas present*

• Kurisumasu-tsurī クリスマスツリー *Christmas tree*

kúro 黒 *black* 《as a noun》 [⇔**shiro** 白]

kúrō 苦労 *trouble, difficulty, hardship* [→**konnan** 困難]

¶Kaisha-setsuritsu-tōsho wa shachō mo kurō ga ōkatta.

会社設立当初は社長も苦労が多かった。

The company president had many difficulties at the beginning when he set up the firm.

• kurō suru 苦労する *to have difficulty, to suffer hardship*

¶Ane no ie o sagasu noni daibu kurō shimashita.

姉の家を探すのにだいぶ苦労しました。

I had great difficulty in looking for my older sister's house.

• go-kurō-sama ご苦労さま [☞**go-kurō-sama** ご苦労さま]

kuróbā クローバー *clover*

kurói 黒い ① *black* 《as an adjective》 [⇔**shiroi** 白い]

¶Hirano-san wa kuroi neko o katte imasu.

平野さんは黒い猫を飼っています。

Mr. Hirano keeps a black cat.

② *dark* 《describing a person's eyes or skin》

kuroji 黒字 *non-deficit, being in the black* [⇔**akaji** 赤字]

kurókkasu クロッカス *crocus* ((flower))

kuróru クロール *the crawl* ((swimming stroke))

Kuroshio 黒潮 *the Black Current, the Japan Current* [→**Nihon-kairyū** 日本海流 (s.v. **Nihon** 日本)]

kurosuwādopázuru クロスワードパズル *crossword puzzle*

¶Tsui-ni kurosuwādopazuru ga tokemashita.

ついにクロスワードパズルが解けました。

At last I was able to solve the crossword puzzle.

kúrōto 玄人 *a professional, an expert* [⇔**shirōto** 素人]

kurōzuáppu クローズアップ *a close-up*

• korōzuappu suru クローズアップする *to take a close-up of*

kúru 来る{Irreg.} ① *to come* [⇔**iku** 行く]

¶Basu ga kimashita yo.

バスが来ましたよ。

The bus is coming!

¶Pātī ni kimasu ka.

パーティーに来ますか。

Will you come to the party?

¶Tegami ga takusan kite iru yo.

手紙がたくさん来ているよ。

Many letters have come.

¶Yamada-san wa koko ni ni-do kita

koto ga aru ne.
山田さんはここに 2 度来たことがあるね。
Mr. Yamada has been here twice, hasn't she.

¶Kondo no Nichiyōbi asobi ni kite kudasai.
今度の日曜日遊びに来てください。
Please come and visit this coming Sunday.

¶"Arubaito" to iu kotoba wa Doitsu-go kara kimashita.
「アルバイト」という言葉はドイツ語から来ました。
The word "arubaito" came from German.

② *to begin to, to come to* 《following the gerund (-te form) of another verb》
¶Himashi ni atatakaku natte kimashita.
日増しに暖かくなってきました。
It has begun getting warmer day by day.
¶Yuki ga futte kita yo.
雪が降ってきたよ。
It's started snowing !

kurúbushi 踝 *the place on either side of the ankle where the bone protrudes*

kuruma 車 ① [[→**jidōsha** 自動車]]
car, <US>automobile, <UK>motorcar; taxi [→**takushī** タクシー];
<US>truck, <UK>lorry [→**torakku** トラック]
¶Kuruma wa unten dekimasen.
車は運転できません。
I can't drive a car.
¶Chichi wa kuruma de tsūkin shimasu.
父は車で通勤します。
My father commutes to work by car.
¶Uchi kara eki made kuruma de jup-pun desu.
家から駅まで車で10分です。
It's ten minutes by car from my house to the station.
¶Atarashii kuruma ni notte, umi ni ikimashita.
新しい車に乗って、海に行きました。
We got in the new car and went to the ocean.

② *wheel* [→**sharin** 車輪]

• kuruma-isu 車椅子 *wheelchair*

kurumi くるみ *walnut*
• kurumi-wari くるみ割り *nutcracker*

kurushíi 苦しい ① *painful, afflicting, tormenting*
• iki ga kurushii 息が苦しい *breathing is labored*
② *hard, difficult, trying* [→**konnan na** 困難な]
¶Kore wa kurushii shigoto desu yo.
これは苦しい仕事ですよ。
This is a hard job!
• kurushii tachiba 苦しい立場 *difficult position*
③ *farfetched, forced*
• kurushii iiwake 苦しい言い訳 *lame excuse*

kurushimí 苦しみ [[→**kutsū** 苦痛]]
① *pain*
¶Kanja wa mattaku kurushimi o kanjinakatta.
患者はまったく苦しみを感じなかった。
The patient did not feel any pain.
② *suffering, anguish*
¶Oji wa kurushimi ni taemashita.
伯父は苦しみに耐えました。
My uncle bore his suffering.

kurushímu 苦しむ ① *to suffer*
¶Yūbe wa hidoi zutsū de kurushimimashita.
ゆうべはひどい頭痛で苦しみました。
I suffered from a terrible headache last night.
② *to become troubled, to come to have difficulty*

kurúu 狂う ① *to go crazy, to become insane*
② *to go wrong; to go out of order*
¶Keikaku ga sukkari kurutta yo.
計画がすっかり狂ったよ。
The plan went completely wrong!
¶Ano tokei wa kurutte iru yo.
あの時計は狂っているよ。
That clock is out of order!

kusá 草 ① *grass*
¶Kusa no ue ni nekorobō.
草の上に寝転ぼう。

Let's lie down on the grass.
• kusa o karu 草を刈る *to cut grass, to mow grass*
② *weed* [→**zassō** 雑草]
• kusa o toru 草を取る *to remove weeds*
• kusa-bana 草花 *flower, flowering plant*
• kusa-kari-ki 草刈り機 *mower*
• kusa-tori 草取り *weeding; person who does weeding*
• kusa-yakyū 草野球 *sandlot baseball*

kusabi 楔 *wedge*

kusái 臭い *bad-smelling, smelly*
¶Kono heya wa kusai desu.
この部屋は臭いです。
This room is bad-smelling.

kusari 鎖 *chain* 《of metal links》

kusáru 腐る ① *to go bad, to spoil, to rot*
¶Sono kusatta niku o sutenasai.
その腐った肉を捨てなさい。
Throw out that rotten meat.
¶Natsu wa tabemono ga sugu kusar-imasu.
夏は食べ物がすぐ腐ります。
In summer food spoils easily.
② *to become dejected*

kusé 癖 ① *habit*
¶Ano daigaku-sei wa kami o ijiru kuse ga arimasu.
あの大学生は髪をいじる癖があります。
That college student has a habit of fiddling with her hair.
• warui kuse ga tsuku 悪い癖が付く *a bad habit develops*
• warui kuse o naosu 悪い癖を直す *to break a bad habit*
② *peculiarity, idiosyncrasy*
¶Sore ga haha no kuse desu.
それが母の癖です。
That's my mother's peculiarity.

kusé-ni くせに *even though* 《implying that the speaker regards what follows with disapproval as strange or inappropriate》《This expression follows a predicate, but the word preceding **kuse-ni** cannot be the copula form **da** だ. When **kuse-ni** is added to a clause that would end with **da**, **no** の (after a noun) or **na**

na (after an adjectival noun) appears instead.》
¶Musuko wa kodomo no kuse-ni opera ga suki desu.
息子は子供のくせにオペラが好きです。
Even though my son is a child, he likes opera.
¶Shitte iru kuse-ni oshiete kurenai yo.
知っているくせに教えてくれないよ。
Even though he knows, he won't tell me!

kūsha 空車 *empty taxi*

kushámi くしゃみ *sneeze*
• kushami o suru くしゃみをする *to sneeze*

kushí 串 *skewer, (roasting)spit*

kushí 櫛 *comb*
• kami ni kushi o ireru 髪にくしを入れる *to comb one's hair*

kushín 苦心 *effort, pains, hard work* [→**doryoku** 努力]
¶Isha no kushin wa muda deshita.
医者の苦心はむだでした。
The doctor's efforts were futile.
• kushin suru 苦心する *to make efforts, to take pains, to work hard*
¶Kono mondai o toku no ni kushin shimashita.
この問題を解くのに苦心しました。
I worked hard to solve this problem.

kushō 苦笑 *forced smile, bitter smile; strained laugh*
• kushō suru 苦笑する *to smile bitterly; to give a strained laugh*

kūshū 空襲 *air raid*
• kūshū suru 空襲する *to make an air raid*

kūsō 空想 *fantasy, reverie, daydream*
• kūsō suru 空想する *to fantasize about, to imagine, to daydream about*

kusó 糞 【CRUDE for **daiben** 大便】 *shit*

kússhon クッション ① *cushion* 《to sit on》
② *cushioning, support*

kusuguru くすぐる *to tickle* 《transitive》

kusuguttai くすぐったい *affected by a tickling sensation*
¶Ashi ga kusuguttai yo.

足がくすぐったいよ。
My foot tickles!

kusuri 薬 *medicine, drug*
¶Maiasa kono kusuri o nonde imasu.
毎朝この薬を飲んでいます。
I take this medicine every morning.
¶Kore wa kaze ni yoku kiku kusuri desu.
これはかぜによく効く薬です。
This is a medicine that works well for colds.
• kusuri-ya 薬屋 *pharmacy* ((store)); *druggist*

kusuríyubi 薬指 *third finger, ring finger*

kutabáru くたばる 【CRUDE for **shinu** 死ぬ】 *to die*

kutabiréru くたびれる ① *to get tired* [→ **tsukareru** 疲れる]
¶Undō suru to, sugu kutabireru.
運動すると、すぐくたびれる。
When I exercise, I get tired right away.
② *to wear out* «when the subject is a thing»
¶Kono kutsu wa mō kutabirete shimatta ne.
この靴はもうくたびれてしまったね。
These shoes have already worn out, haven't they.

kutóten 句読点 *punctuation mark*

kutsú 靴 *shoe*
¶Kono kutsu o mō issoku katte kudasai.
この靴をもう1足買ってください。
Please buy one more pair of these shoes.
¶Dekakeru mae ni kutsu o migakinasai.
出かける前に靴を磨きなさい。
Polish your shoes before you go out.
¶Kono kutsu wa watashi ni wa kyūkutsu desu.
この靴は私には窮屈です。
These shoes are tight for me.
• kutsu o haku 〔nugu〕 靴を履く〔脱ぐ〕 *to put on* 〔*take off*〕 *one's shoes*
• kutsu-bera 靴べら *shoehorn*
• kutsu-himo 靴紐 *shoestring, shoelace*
• kutsu-migaki 靴磨き *shoe polishing; shoe polish*
• kutsu-ya 靴屋 *shoe store; shoe dealer;*

shoemaker
• kutsu-zumi 靴墨 *shoe polish*

kutsū 苦痛 [[→**kurushimi** 苦しみ]]
① *pain* [→**itami** 痛み]
② *suffering, anguish*

kutsurógu 寛ぐ *to make oneself at home, to relax*
¶Dōzo kutsuroide kudasai.
どうぞ寛いでください。
Please make yourself at home.
¶Chichi wa terebi o mite kutsuroide imasu.
父はテレビを見て寛いでいます。
My father is watching television and relaxing.

kutsúshita 靴下 *sock; stocking*
¶Samui kara, kutsushita o hakinasai.
寒いから、靴下を履きなさい。
It's cold, so put on your socks.
¶Kutsushita ga uragaeshi da yo.
靴下が裏返しだよ。
Your socks are inside out!

kutsuwa くつわ *bit* «for a horse»

kuttsukéru くっつける 【COL.】 *to stick, to affix*

kuttsúku くっつく 【COL.】 *to stick, to become affixed* «intransitive»
¶Kyarameru ga ha ni kuttsuite shimatta yo.
キャラメルが歯にくっついてしまったよ。
The caramel stuck to my teeth!

kúu 食う ① 【CRUDE for **taberu** 食べる】 *to eat*
② 【COL.】 *to consume excessively, to use lots of*
¶Kono kuruma wa gasorin o kuu yo.
この車はガソリンを食うよ。
This car uses lots of gasoline!
③ 【COL.】 *to bite* «when the subject is an insect» «Ordinarily used in the passive.» [→**sasu** 刺す②]
¶Boku mo ka ni kuwareta yo.
僕も蚊に食われたよ。
I was bitten by a mosquito too!
④ 【COL.】 *to fall for* «a trick, etc.»
¶Sono te wa kuwanai yo.
その手は食わないよ。

I won't fall for that trick!

kúwa 桑 *mulberry*

kuwa 鍬 *hoe*

kuwadate 企て ① *attempt, undertaking*
② *plan, scheme, project* [→**keikaku** 計画]

kuwadateru 企てる ① *to attempt, to undertake*
② *to plan; to contemplate*

kuwaeru 加える ① *to add*
¶Kōshinryō o sukoshi kuwaete kudasai.
香辛料を少し加えてください。
Add a little spice, please.
¶Yon ni roku o kuwaenasai.
4に6を加えなさい。
Add six to four.
② *to let participate, to let join*
¶Watashi mo kuwaete kudasai.
私も加えてください。
Please let me join in too.
③ *to inflict*
¶Teki-gun ni dageki o kuwaemashita.
敵軍に打撃を加えました。
We inflicted a blow on the enemy force.

kuwaeru 銜える *to take between one's teeth, to take in one's mouth*
¶Neko ga sakana o kuwaete nigeta yo.
猫が魚をくわえて逃げたよ。
The cat ran away with a fish in its mouth!

kuwashíi 詳しい ① *detailed*
¶Kono chizu wa kuwashii ne.
この地図は詳しいね。
This map is detailed, isn't it.
¶Gaido wa rekishi o kuwashiku setsumei shite kureta.
ガイドは歴史を詳しく説明してくれた。
The guide explained the history in detail for us.
② *knowledgeable ⟨about⟩*
¶Okāsan wa Furansu ni kuwashii desu.
お母さんはフランスに詳しいです。
Your mother knows a lot about France.

kuwawaru 加わる ① *to be added*
② *to participate, to join*
¶Nakama ni kuwawarimasen ka.
仲間に加わりませんか。

Won't you join our group?
¶Gēmu ni kuwawatte mo ii desu ka.
ゲームに加わってもいいですか。
May I join in the game?

kuyámu 悔やむ *to be sorry about, to regret*
¶Yakyū-senshu wa erā o kuyamu ne.
野球選手はエラーを悔やむね。
Baseball players regret their errors, don't they.

kuyashíi 悔しい *vexing, disappointing*
• kuyashii koto ni 悔しいことに *to one's chagrin*

kúyokuyo くよくよ ~**suru** ~する *to worry; to brood*
¶Sonna koto de kuyokuyo shinai de.
そんなことでくよくよしないで。
Don't worry about such a thing.

kūzen 空前 ~**no** ~の *unprecedented*
• kūzen-zetsugo no 空前絶後の *unprecedented and likely never to be repeated, first and probably last*

kúzu 屑 ① *trash, rubbish* [→**gomi** ごみ①]
② *scrap, crumb*
• kuzu-kago 屑籠 *wastebasket*
• kami-kuzu 紙屑 *wastepaper*
• pan-kuzu パン屑 *bread crumbs*

kuzuréru 崩れる *to collapse, to disintegrate*
¶Jishin de hashi ga kuzuremashita.
地震で橋が崩れました。
The bridge collapsed because of the earthquake.

kuzúsu 崩す ① *to demolish, to tear down* [→**kowasu** 壊す②]
¶Kotoshi wa sono tatemono o kuzushimasu.
今年はその建物を崩します。
This year we're going to tear down that building.
② *to break, to change* «money from large denominations to small»
¶Kono o-satsu o kozeni ni kuzushite kudasai.
このお札を小銭に崩してください。
Please change this bill into small change.

kyábetsu キャベツ *cabbage*

kyakkanteki 客観的 ～**na** ～な *objective* 《i.e., not subjective》[⇔**shukanteki na** 主観的な]

kyaku 客 ① *visitor; guest*
¶Kinō wa kyaku ga futari kimashita.
きのうは客が二人来ました。
I had two visitors yesterday.
② *customer;* (*paying*)*passenger* [→**jō-kyaku** 乗客]
¶Kyō wa kyaku ga ōi desu ne.
今日は客が多いですね。
There are a lot of customers today, aren't there.
•o-kyaku-san お客さん 【HON. for kyaku (above)】
¶Konban wa shokuji ni o-kyaku-san o yo-nin manekimashita.
今晩は食事にお客さんを４人招きました。
Tonight we invited four guests to dinner.

kyakuhon 脚本 *script, play* (*in written form*)*; scenario, screenplay*
•kyakuhon-ka 脚本家 *dramatist, play-wright; screenplay writer*

kyakuma 客間 ① *room in a home where visitors are received* [→**ōsetsuma** 応接間]
② *guest room*

kyánbasu キャンバス [☞**kanbasu** カンバス]

kyándē キャンデー ＜US＞*candy,* ＜UK＞*sweets*

kyánpasu キャンパス *campus*

kyanpḗn キャンペーン (*publicity*) *campaign*

kyánpu キャンプ *camping*
¶Yama e kyanpu ni ikō.
山へキャンプに行こう。
Let's go camping in the mountains.
•kyanpu suru キャンプする *to camp*
•kyanpu-faiā キャンプファイアー *campfire*
•kyanpu-faia o suru キャンプファイアーをする *to make a campfire*
•kyanpu-jō キャンプ場 *campsite, camp-ground*
•kyanpu-mura キャンプ村 *camping village*

kyánseru キャンセル *cancellation*
•kyanseru suru キャンセルする *to cancel* [→**torikesu** 取り消す]
¶Hoteru no yoyaku o kyanseru shimasu.
ホテルの予約をキャンセルします。
I will cancel the hotel reservation.

kyáppu キャップ ① *cap* ((*hat*))
② *cap* 《on a pencil or pen》*; cap* 《on a bottle》

kyáputen キャプテン ① (*team*)*captain* [→**shushō** 主将]
② (*ship*)*captain* [→**senchō** 船長]

kyárakutā キャラクター ① *character, personality* [→**seikaku** 性格]
② *famous character* 《in a story, movie, etc.》
•kyarakutā-shōhin キャラクター商品 *item of merchandise incorporating a famous character in its design*

kyarameru キャラメル *caramel*

kyásuto キャスト *cast* 《of a play, movie, etc.》

kyatatsu きゃたつ *stepladder*

kyátchā キャッチャー (*baseball*)*catcher* [→**hoshu** 捕手]

kyátchi キャッチ ～**suru** ～する *to catch; to obtain, to pick up*

kyatchibṓru キャッチボール *playing catch*
¶Kyatchibōru o shiyō.
キャッチボールをしよう。
Let's play catch.

kyṓ 今日 *today*
¶Kyō wa nan'yōbi desu ka.
きょうは何曜日ですか
What day of the week is it today?
¶Nakayama-sensei wa kyō jugyō o yasu-mimashita.
中山先生はきょう授業を休みました。
Prof. Nakayama missed class today.
•senshū no kyō 先週のきょう *a week ago today*
•raishū no kyō 来週のきょう *a week from today*

-kyō －強 *a little more than* 《Added to number bases.》[⇔**-jaku** －弱]
¶Ano sumō-tori no taijū wa hyak-

kiro–kyō desu.
あの相撲取りの体重は100キロ強です。
That sumo wrestler's weight is a little more than 100 kilograms.

kyō 経 [☞**o–kyō** お経]

kyōchō 強調 *stress, emphasis*
• kyōchō suru 強調する *to stress, to emphasize*

kyōdai 兄弟 *siblings, brothers and／or sisters*
¶Kyōdai ga imasu ka.
兄弟がいますか。
Do you have any brothers or sisters?
¶Ken–chan to Yumi–chan wa kyōdai desu.
健ちゃんと由美ちゃんは兄弟です。
Ken and Yumi are brother and sister.
•–kyōdai －兄弟 *group of siblings*
《Added to bases consisting of a number for counting people.》
¶Watashi wa san–nin–kyōdai desu.
私は3人兄弟です。
I am one of three children.
• kyōdai–genka 兄弟喧嘩 *sibling quarrel*

kyodai 巨大 ～**na** ～な *huge, enormous, gigantic*

kyōdan 教壇 *teacher's platform* 《at the front of a classroom》

kyōdō 共同 *cooperation, collaboration*
¶Kono heya wa otōto to kyōdō de tsukatte imasu.
この部屋は弟と共同で使っています。
I share this room with my younger brother.
• kyōdō no 共同の *joint, united, common*
• kyōdō suru 共同する *to cooperate, to work together*
• kyōdō–bokin 共同募金 *community chest*
• kyōdō–seimei 共同声明 *joint statement*

kyōdō 協同 *cooperation* [→**kyōdō** 共同, **kyōryoku** 協力]
• kyōdō suru 協同する *to cooperate, to work cooperatively*
• kyōdō–kumiai 協同組合 *cooperative association*

kyōfu 恐怖 *fear, terror, horror*

• kyōfu–eiga 恐怖映画 *horror movie*

kyōgaku 共学 *coeducation*
• kyōgaku no daigaku 共学の大学 *coeducational college*
• danjo–kyōgaku 男女共学 [☞**kyōgaku** 共学 (above)]

kyōgen 狂言 *kyogen* 《a kind of traditional Japanese comic play》

kyōgi 競技 *competition, contest of skill; athletic contest, sporting event*
• kyōgi suru 競技する *to compete*
• kyōgi–jō 競技場 *athletic field; stadium*
• kyōgi–kai 競技会 *athletic meet; competition*
• rikujō–kyōgi 陸上競技 *track and field competition*

kyōhaku 脅迫 *intimidation*
• kyōhaku no 脅迫の *threatening, intimidating*
• kyōhaku suru 脅迫する *to threaten, to intimidate*
• kyōhaku–denwa 脅迫電話 *threatening telephone call*
• kyōhaku–jō 脅迫状 *threatening letter*

kyōhi 拒否 *refusal, rejection, veto*
• kyohi suru 拒否する *to refuse, to turn down, to veto* [→**kotowaru** 断る①]

kyōi 胸囲 *chest measurement, circumference of the chest*

kyōi 驚異 *wonder, marvel*
• kyōi no me o miharu 驚異の目をみはる *to open one's eyes wide in amazement*
• kyōi–teki na 驚異的な *wonderful, marvelous, amazing*

kyōiku 教育 *education*
¶Ane wa Igirisu de kyōiku o ukemashita.
姉はイギリスで教育を受けました。
My older sister was educated in England.
• kyōiku suru 教育する *to educate*
• kyōiku–iin–kai 教育委員会 *board of education*
• kyōiku–seido 教育制度 *educational system*
• kyōiku–terebi 教育テレビ *educational television*
• gakkō–kyōiku 学校教育 *school educa-*

tion

kyōin 教員 *teacher, faculty member*
[→**sensei** 先生①]
• kyōin-shitsu 教員室 *teachers' room*
kyojin 巨人 *giant* (*person*)
kyōju 教授 *professor*
• jo-kyōju 助教授 *assistant professor*
kyojū 居住 *residing, dwelling*
• kyojū suru 居住する *to take up
residence* [→**sumu** 住む]
kyōka 教科 (*school*)*subject*
kyóka 許可 *permission*
¶Kyoka-nashi ni sono heya e haitte wa
ikemasen.
許可なしにその部屋へ入ってはいけません。
*You mustn't enter that room without
permission.*
• kyoka suru 許可する *to permit*
¶Chichi wa watashi ga baiku ni noru no
o kyoka shinakatta.
父は私がバイクに乗るのを許可しなかった。
*My father didn't permit me to ride a
motorbike.*
• kyoka o eru 許可を得る *to get permission*
• kyoka-shō 許可証 *permit, license*
kyóka 強化 *strengthening, fortifying,
intensification*
• kyoka suru 強化する *to strengthen, to
fortify, to intensify*
kyōkai 教会 *church*
¶Maishū Nichiyōbi ni kyōkai ni ikimasu.
毎週日曜日に教会に行きます。
I go to church every Sunday.
kyōkai 境界 *border, boundary* [→**sakai**
境]
¶Sono takai sanmyaku ga ryōkoku no
kyōkai desu.
その高い山脈が両国の境界です。
*That high mountain range is the border
between the two countries.*
• kyōkai-sen 境界線 *borderline, boundary line*
kyōkai 協会 *association, society*
kyōkásho 教科書 *textbook*
kyóku 曲 *piece* (*of music*)
¶Kono kyoku wa Bētōben ga kaita mono

desu.
この曲はベートーベンが書いたものです。
This piece is one that Beethoven wrote.
¶Yōko-san wa sono kyoku o piano de
hikimashita.
洋子さんはその曲をピアノで弾きました。
Yoko played that piece on the piano.
• -kyoku −曲《counter for musical
pieces; see Appendix 2》
kyokugei 曲芸 *acrobatic trick, stunt,
feat*
• kyokugei-shi 曲芸師 *acrobat*
kyōkun 教訓 *lesson, teaching, precept*
kyokusen 曲線 *curve, curved line*
kyokután 極端 *an extreme, extremity*
• kyokutan ni hashiru 極端に走る *to go
to extremes*
• kyokutan na 極端な *extreme*
¶Sore wa kyokutan na rei desu.
それは極端な例です。
That is an extreme example.
Kyokutō 極東 *the Far East*
kyōkyū 供給 *supply* 《*of a commodity,
etc.*》[⇔**juyō** 需要]
• kyōkyū suru 供給する *to supply*
• kyōkyū-sha 供給者 *supplier*
kyómi 興味 (*feeling of*)*interest*
• A ni kyōmi o motsu Aに興味を持つ *to
take an interest in A*
• A ni kyōmi ga aru Aに興味がある *to
be interested in A*
¶Rekishi ni taihen kyōmi ga arimasu.
歴史にたいへん興味があります。
I am very interested in history.
• kyōmi-bukai 興味深い *very interesting*
¶Kono hon wa watashi ni wa totemo
kyōmi-bukai desu.
この本は私にはとても興味深いです。
This book is very interesting to me.
kyónen 去年 *last year*
¶Kyonen no ima-goro Saipan ni imashita.
去年の今ごろサイパンにいました。
*About this time last year I was in
Saipan.*
¶Buraun-san wa kyonen Nihon ni kimashita.

ブラウンさんは去年日本に来ました。
Miss Brown came to Japan last year.

kyōretsu 強烈 **〜na** 〜な *strong, intense, powerful, severe*

kyóri 距離 *distance*

¶Ueno–Sendai-kan no kyori wa yaku san-byaku–gojuk-kiro desu.
上野−仙台間の距離は約350キロです。
The distance between Ueno and Sendai is about 350 kilometers.

¶Eki made dono kurai no kyori ga arimasu ka.
駅までどのくらいの距離がありますか
About how far is it to the station?

kyōryoku 協力 *cooperation*

¶Go-kyōryoku o kansha shimasu.
ご協力を感謝します。
I am grateful for your cooperation.

• kyōryoku suru 協力する *to cooperate*

¶Sono shigoto wa tomodachi to kyō-ryoku shinasai.
その仕事は友達と協力しなさい。
Cooperate with your friends on that job.
《Literally: *As for that work, cooperate with friends.*》

kyōryoku 強力 *strength, power, might*

• kyōryoku na 強力な *strong, powerful, mighty*

¶Sono seisaku wa kyōryoku na shiji o ukete imasu.
その政策は強力な支持を受けています。
That policy is receiving strong support.

¶Kono kikai wa kyōryoku na mōtā de ugoku.
この機械は強力なモーターで動く。
This machine runs on a powerful motor.

kyōryū 恐竜 *dinosaur*

kyōsanshúgi 共産主義 *communism*

• kyōsanshugi-sha 共産主義者 *a communist*

Kyōsantō 共産党 *Communist Party*

kyōsei 強制 *force, compulsion, coercion*

• kyōsei suru 強制する *to force to do, to compel to accept, to coerce* [→**oshitsu-keru** 押しつける②]

¶Heya o deru yō ni kyōsei saremashita.
部屋を出るように強制されました。

I was forced to leave the room.

• kyōsei-teki na 強制的な *compulsory, forcible, coercive*

kyōshi 教師 *teacher, instructor* [→**sen-sei** 先生①]

kyōshitsu 教室 *classroom*

kyōsō 競争 *competition, contest*

• kyōsō suru 競争する *to compete*

• kyōsō ni katsu 〔makeru〕 競争に勝つ 〔負ける〕 *to win* 〔*lose*〕 *a competition*

• kyōsō-aite 競争相手 *rival, competitor, opponent*

• kyōsō-ishiki 競争意識 *competitive consciousness*

• kyōsō-ritsu 競争率 *degree of competition*

• kyōsō-shin 競争心 *competitive spirit*

kyōsō 競走 (*running*)*race*

• kyōsō ni katsu 〔makeru〕 競走に勝つ 〔負ける〕 *to win* 〔*lose*〕 *a race*

• kyōsō suru 競走する *to run a race*

¶Ano oka no fumoto made kyōsō shiyō.
あの丘のふもとまで競走しよう。
Let's race to the foot of that hill.

• hyaku–mētoru-kyōsō 100メートル競走 *100-meter dash*

• shōgai-butsu-kyōsō 障害物競走 *hurdle race*

kyōsókyoku 協奏曲 *concerto* [→**koncheruto** コンチェルト]

kyōson 共存 *co-existence*

• kyōson suru 共存する *to co-exist*

kyōtō 教頭 *head teacher* 《In a Japanese school this person ranks just below the principal.》

kyōtsū 共通 **〜no** 〜の *mutual, common, shared*

¶Sachiko-san wa watashi-tachi no kyōtsū no yūjin desu.
幸子さんは私たちの共通の友人です。
Sachiko is our mutual friend.

• kyōtsū-ten 共通点 *point in common, something in common*

¶Ano futari wa kyōtsū-ten ga arimasu.
あの二人には共通点があります。
Those two have something in common.

kyōwákoku 共和国 *republic*

kyōyō 教養 *culturedness, educatedness, refinement*

¶Shachō wa kyōyō no aru hito desu.

社長は教養のある人です。

The company president is a cultured person.

kyōzai 教材 *teaching materials*

kyozetsu 拒絶 *refusal, rejection*

• kyozetsu suru 拒絶する *to refuse, to reject* [→kotowaru 断る①]

kyū 九 *nine* 《see Appendix 2》 [→ku 九]

kyū 急 ① *emergency, crisis; urgent need*

• kyū na 急な *urgent, pressing*

¶Satō-san wa kyū na yōji de dekakemashita.

佐藤さんは急な用事で出かけました。

Mr. Sato went out on urgent business.

② ~na ~な *sudden, abrupt* [→totsuzen no 突然の]

¶Densha ga kyū ni tomarimashita.

電車が急に止まりました。

The train stopped suddenly.

¶Kyū ni ame ga furi-dashimashita.

急に雨が降りだしました。

Suddenly it began to rain.

③ ~na ~な [[⇔yuruyaka na 緩やかな①]] *steep; sharp* 《describing a curve》

• kyū na kaidan 急な階段 *steep stairs*

• kyū na kābu 急なカーブ *sharp curve*

④ ~na ~な *swift* 《describing a flow》 [⇔yuruyaka na 緩やかな②]

¶Kono kawa wa nagare ga kyū desu.

この川は流れが急です。

This river's current is swift.

kyū 級 ① *class, grade, rank*

② (*school*)*class*, (*school*)*grade* [→gakkyū 学級]

• -kyū 一級 《counter for classes, grades, ranks; see Appendix 2》

¶Akiko-chan wa watashi yori ik-kyū ue desu.

明子ちゃんは私より1級上です。

Akiko is one grade above me.

kyū- 旧- *old, former, ex-* 《Added to noun bases》 [⇔shin- 新-]

• kyū-seido 旧制度 *old system*

• kyū-shoyū-sha 旧所有者 *former owner*

kyūbyō 急病 *sudden illness*

¶Imōto ga kyūbyō ni kakarimashita.

妹が急病にかかりました。

My younger sister came down with a sudden illness.

kyūden 宮殿 *palace*

kyūgaku 休学 *absence from school*

• kyūgaku suru 休学する *to be absent from school*

¶Ichirō-kun wa nagai aida kyūgaku shite imasu.

一郎君は長い間休学しています。

Ichiro has been absent from school for a long time.

kyūgeki 急激 ~na ~な *rapid, sudden, abrupt*

¶Kono kuni no jinkō wa kyūgeki ni zōka shimashita.

この国の人口は急激に増加しました。

This country's population increased rapidly.

kyūgyō 休業 *temporary closing* 《of a business》

• kyūgyō suru 休業する *to close temporarily* 《intransitive》

¶Taitei no mise ga Nichiyōbi ni wa kyūgyō shimasu.

たいていの店が日曜日には休業します。

Most stores are closed on Sundays.

¶Honjitsu kyūgyō

「本日休業」《on a sign》

Closed Today

kyūjin 求人 *job offer*

• kyūjin-kōkoku 求人広告 *help-wanted ad*

kyūjitsu 休日 *holiday, day off*

¶Kyō wa kyūjitsu desu ne.

きょうは休日ですね。

Today is a holiday, isn't it.

¶Kyūjitsu wa taitei tenisu o shimasu

休日はたいていテニスをします。

On holidays I usually play tennis.

kyūjo 救助 *rescue, saving, help*

¶Shōnen-tachi wa sakende kyūjo o motomemashita.

少年たちは叫んで救助を求めました。
The boys cried out and asked for help.

• kyūjo suru 救助する *to rescue, to save* [→**tasukeru** 助ける]

• kyūjo-tai 救助隊 *rescue party, rescue team*

kyūjō 球場 *ballpark, stadium*

• Yokohama-kyūjō 横浜球場 *Yokohama Stadium*

kyūka 休暇 *time off,* <*US*>*vacation,* <*UK*>*holidays*

¶Chichi wa is-shūkan no kyūka o torimashita.
父は1週間の休暇を取りました。
My father took a one-week vacation.

¶Maeda-san wa ashita wa kyūka desu.
前田さんはあしたは休暇です。
Mr. Maeda will be off tomorrow.

• kyūka-chū no 休暇中の *on-vacation*

¶Jonson-san wa ima kyūka-chū desu.
ジョンソンさんは今休暇中です。
Ms. Johnson is on vacation now.

• kaki-kyūka 夏期休暇 *summer vacation*

kyūkei 休憩 *short rest, break*

• kyūkei suru 休憩する *to take a short rest, to take a break*

¶Koko de chotto kyūkei shiyō.
ここでちょっと休憩しよう。
Let's take a break here for a little while.

• kyūkei-jikan 休憩時間 *recess; intermission*

• kyūkei-shitsu 休憩室 *lounge; lobby*

kyūkō 休校 *temporary closing of a school*

¶Futsuka-kan kyūkō ni narimashita.
2日間休校になりました。
School was closed for two days.

kyūkō 急行 *an express*

¶Kono densha wa kyūkō desu ka.
この電車は急行ですか。
Is this train an express?

¶San-ji-nijup-pun-hatsu no Atami-yuki no kyūkō ni notte kudasai.
3時20分発の熱海行きの急行に乗ってください。
Please get on the 3:20 express for Atami.

• kyūkō-ken 急行券 *express ticket*

• kyūkō-ryōkin 急行料金 *express charge*

kyūkutsu 窮屈 ～**na** ～な ① *tight-fitting; cramped*

¶Sensei wa kyūkutsu na uwagi o kite imasu.
先生は窮屈な上着を着ています。
The teacher is wearing a tight coat.

② *awkward, ill-at-ease, constrained*

kyūkyū 救急 ～**no** ～の *for first-aid, for (medical)emergencies*

• kyūkyuī-bako 救急箱 *first-aid kit*

• kyūkyuī-byōin 救急病院 *emergency hospital*

• kyūkyū-sha 救急車 *ambulance*

• kyūkyū-shochi 救急処置 *first aid*

kyūmei 救命 *lifesaving, saving a person's life*

• kyūmei-gu 救命具 *life preserver; life jacket, life vest*

• kyūmei-bōto 救命ボート *lifeboat*

kyūri きゅうり *cucumber*

kyūryō 給料 *pay, salary, wages*

¶Ane no kyūryō wa tsuki ni jūroku-man-en desu.
姉の給料は月に16万円です。
My older sister's salary is 160,000 yen a month.

• kyūryō-bi 給料日 *payday*

kyūshífu 休止符 *(musical)rest*

kyūshoku 給食 *providing meals; provided meal, school lunch*

• kyūshoku-hi 給食費 *expense for school lunches*

kyūshū 吸収 *absorption*

• kyūshū suru 吸収する *to absorb*

kyūsoku 休息 *rest, break* [→**kyūkei** 休憩]

• kyūsoku suru 休息する *to rest, to take a break*

kyūsoku 急速 ～**na** ～な *rapid, quick, swift*

¶Konpyūtā-sangyō wa saikin kyūsoku na shinpo o togemashita.
コンピューター産業は最近急速な進歩を遂げました。
The computer industry has achieved rapid progress recently.

kyūsu 急須 *teapot*

kyūyō 休養 *rest, respite from work*
- kyūyō suru 休養する *to take a rest*

kyūyō 急用 *urgent business*
¶Chichi wa kyūyō de dekakete imasu.
父は急用で出かけています。
My father is away on urgent business.

M

ma 間 ① *a room* [→**heya** 部屋]
- –ma –間《counter for rooms; see Appendix 2》
② *space, room*
- ma o akeru 間を空ける *to leave space, to make room*
③ *time to spare; time interval*
¶Shiai ga hajimaru made sukoshi ma ga arimasu.
試合が始まるまで少し間があります。
There is some time to spare before the game starts.
- ǎ to iu ma ni あっという間に *in an instant*

mā まあ ① *Oh!, Oh, dear!, My!, Well!*
《This use, expressing surprise, is typically restricted to female speakers.》
¶Mā, nan-te omoshiroi n deshō.
まあ、何ておもしろいんでしょう。
My, how interesting!
② *Come on* 《in a request or suggestion》
¶Mā, shizuka ni shinasai.
まあ、静かにしなさい。
Come on, be quiet.
③ *Well* 《indicating partial agreement》
¶Mā, ii deshō.
まあ、いいでしょう。
Well, it's probably all right.

mabátaki 瞬き *(eye)blink*
- mabataki (o)suru まばたき(を)する *to blink* [→**matataku** 瞬く①]
¶Akachan wa mabataki mo sezu watashi o mite ita.

赤ちゃんはまばたきもせず私を見ていた。
The baby looked at me without even blinking.

maboroshi 幻 *phantom, illusion*

mabushíi 眩しい *blinding, dazzling, excessively bright*
¶Taiyō ga mabushikute, me ga kuranda.
太陽がまぶしくて、目がくらんだ。
The suns was blinding, and I was dazzled.

mábuta 瞼 *eyelid*

máchi マーチ *(musical)march* [→**kō-shin-kyoku** 行進曲 (s.v. **kōshin** 行進)]

machí 町 ① *town, city*
¶Chīsa na machi de umaremashita.
小さな町で生まれました。
I was born in a small town.
② *district* 《an officially designated subdivision of a city (**shi** 市) or a ward (**ku** 区)》

machí 街 ① *shopping district, bustling part of town*
¶Haha wa machi ni kaimono ni ikimashita.
母は街に買い物に行きました。
My mother went to the shopping district for shopping.
② *city street, building-lined street*
¶Machi de tomodachi ni deaimashita.
街で友達に出会いました。
I ran into a friend on the street.

machiáishitsu 待合室 *waiting room*

machiawaseru 待ち合わせる *to meet* 《at an agreed on place and time》
¶Hon-ya no mae de machiawasemashō.
本屋の前で待ち合わせましょう。
Let's meet in front of the bookstore.

machigaéru 間違える ① *to make a mistake involving, to do incorrectly*
¶Eigo no shiken de yon mon no kaitō o machigaeta yo.
英語の試験で4問の解答をまちがえたよ。
I did four incorrect answers on the English test!
¶Machigaete otōto no kutsu o haite dekakemashita.
まちがえて弟の靴をはいて出かけました。

I made a mistake and put on my younger brother's shoes and went out.

¶Ken-chan wa noru basu o machigaeta yo.

健ちゃんは乗るバスをまちがえたよ。

Ken made a mistake about which bus to take!

② *to mistake*

• A o B to machigaeru AをBとまちがえる *to mistake A for B*

¶Mika-san wa oba o haha to machigaemashita.

美香さんは叔母を母とまちがえました。

Mika mistook my aunt for my mother.

machigái 間違い *mistake, error*

¶Kono bun ni wa tsuzuri no machigai ga futatsu aru.

この文にはつづりのまちがいが二つある。

In this sentence there are two spelling mistakes.

¶Sono kotae wa machigai desu.

その答えはまちがいです。

That answer is wrong.

• machigai-denwa 間違い電話 *(telephoning a)wrong number*

• machigai-nai 間違いない *certain, beyond doubt, indisputable*

¶Machigai-naku kono hon wa kaeshimasu.

まちがいなくこの本は返します。

I will certainly return this book.

machikamaeru 待ち構える *to be ready and wait for, to wait eagerly for*

máda まだ ① *still,* 〈*not*〉 *yet* [→ **imada-ni** 未だに]

¶Mada Ken-san kara tayori ga arimasen.

まだ健さんから便りがありません。

There still isn't any word from Ken.

¶"Mō sumimashita ka." "Īe, mada desu."

「もう済みましたか」「いいえ、まだです」

"Have you finished yet?" "No, I haven't."

¶Shimada-san wa mada wakai desu.

島田さんはまだ若いです。

Ms. Shimada is still young.

¶Otōto wa mada yon-sai da yo.

弟はまだ4歳だよ。

My younger brother is still (only) four years old!

② *somewhat* 《modifying the predicate in a comparison between two unsatisfactory alternatives》

¶Kono hō ga mada ii yo.

このほうがまだいいよ。

This one is somewhat better.

máde まで ① *until* 《following either a noun referring to a point in time or verb in the nonpast tense》; *through* 《when a preceding noun refers to something longer than a point in time》

¶Watashi-tachi wa go-ji made tosho-kan de benkyō shimashita.

私たちは5時まで図書館で勉強しました。

We studied in the library until 5:00.

¶Ame ga yamu made koko ni imasu.

雨がやむまでここにいます。

I'm going to stay here until the rain stops.

¶Natsu matsuri wa Mokuyōbi made tsuzukimasu.

夏祭りは木曜日まで続きます。

The summer festival will continue through Thursday.

• made ni までに *by, not later than*

¶Yūshoku made ni kaette kinasai.

夕食までに帰ってきなさい。

Come home by supper.

¶Kayōbi made ni shukudai o dashite kudasai.

火曜日までに宿題を出してください。

Hand in your homework by Tuesday!

¶Go-ji made ni kono shigoto o owarimashō.

5時までにこの仕事を終わりましょう。

Let's finish this work by 5:00.

② *as far as, to* 《following a noun referring to a place》

¶Basu-tei made hashirimashō.

バス停まで走りましょう。

Let's run to the bus stop.

¶Chikatetsu no eki made issho ni ikimasu.

地下鉄の駅までいっしょに行きます。

I'll go with you as far as the subway

station.

③ *even* 《indicating that what precedes is extreme》 [→**sae** さえ①]

¶Okāsan made sonna koto o iu no?

お母さんまでそんなことを言うの？

Even your mother says that kind of thing?

mádo 窓 *window*

¶Mado o akete kudasai.

窓を開けてください。

Please open the window.

¶Naoko-san wa mado kara soto o mite imasu.

直子さんは窓から外を見ています。

Naoko is looking out the window.

• mado-garasu 窓ガラス *window pane*

• mado-giwa 窓際 *area right near a window*

• mado-guchi 窓口 *transaction window*

• mado-waku 窓枠 *window frame*

madori 間取り *room layout, floor plan*

máe 前 ① *time before, earlier in time, previous time* [⇔**ato** 後②]

¶Mae ni sono e o mita koto ga aru yo.

前にその絵を見たことがあるよ。

I've seen that picture before!

¶Chichi wa itsu-mo chōshoku no mae ni jogingu o suru.

父はいつも朝食の前にジョギングをする。

My father always jogs before breakfast.

¶Kuraku naru mae ni kaerimashō.

暗くなる前に帰りましょう。

Let's go home before it gets dark.

¶Nomu mae ni denshi-renji de atatamemashita.

飲む前に電子レンジで温めました。

I heated it up in the microwave oven before drinking it. 《A verb preceding **mae** is always in the nonpast tense.》

• mae no 前の *previous, former*

¶Kono mae no tesuto wa muzukashikatta desu ne.

この前のテストは難しかったですね。

The previous test was difficult, wasn't it.

② *the area in front, the front* [⇔ **ushiro** 後ろ]

¶Mae kara san-ban-me no seki ni suwari-

mashita.

前から3番目の席に座りました。

I sat in the third seat from the front.

¶Eki no mae ni ginkō ga arimasu.

駅の前に銀行があります。

There is a bank in front of the station.

¶Akiko-chan wa watashi no mae o aruite iru yo.

明子ちゃんは私の前を歩いているよ。

Akiko is walking ahead of me!

¶Mae ni tachimashō.

前に立ちましょう。

Let's stand in front!

• -mae －前 *ago, before* 《Added to noun bases, often numbers denoting periods of time.》 [⇔**-go** －後]

¶Sore wa go-nen-mae no dekigoto deshita.

それは5年前のできごとでした。

It happened five years ago. 《Literally: It's an event of five years ago.》

¶Haha wa jup-pun-mae ni kaimono ni dekakemashita.

母は10分前に買い物に出かけました。

My mother went out shopping ten minutes ago.

maegami 前髪 *bangs, hair hanging down over the forehead*

maekake 前掛け *apron* [→**epuron** エプロン]

maekin 前金 *(full)payment in advance; downpayment*

maemótte 前以て *beforehand, in advance* [→**arakajime** 予め]

maeuri 前売り *advance sale, selling in advance*

• maeuri-ken 前売り券 *advance ticket*

máfurā マフラー ① *muffler, scarf* ② <*US*>*muffler,* <*UK*>*silencer* 《on an automobile, etc.》

mafuyu 真冬 *the midwinter* [⇔**manatsu** 真夏]

mágajin マガジン *magazine* [→**zasshi** 雑誌]

magarikunéru 曲がりくねる *to become crooked, to become winding*

¶Ano eda wa magarikunette imasu.

あの枝は曲がりくねっています。
That branch is crooked.

• magarikunetta michi 曲がりくねった道
winding road

māgarin マーガリン *margarine*

magaru 曲がる ① *to turn, to make a turn* 《*at a corner, etc.*》

• A o magaru Aを曲がる *to turn at A, to make a turn along A*

¶Tsugi no kōsa-ten o migi ni magatte kudasai.
次の交差点を右に曲がってください。
Please turn right at the next intersection.

② *to become bent; to become curved*

¶Sono magatta kugi o tsukawanai de.
その曲がったくぎを使わないで。
Don't use that bent nail.

¶Dōro wa soko de migi ni magatte imasu.
道路はそこで右に曲がっています。
The road curves to the right there.

mageru 曲げる *to bend* 《*transitive*》

¶Se o magenai yō ni shinasai.
背を曲げないようにしなさい。
Make sure not to bend your back.

magirawashíi 紛らわしい *confusing, easily confused* (*with something else*)*; easily confused* (*with each other*)

¶Magirawashii dōro-hyōshiki ga ōi desu yo.
紛らわしい道路標識が多いですよ。
There are a lot of confusing road signs!

¶Kono ni-mai no shashin wa magirawashii desu ne.
この2枚の写真は紛らわしいですね。
These two photos are easily confused, aren't they.

magire-mo-nái 紛れもない *unquestionable, beyond doubt*

magiréru 紛れる ① *to get confused* 〈*with*〉*, to become indistinguishable* 〈*from*〉*, to be mistaken* 〈*for*〉

• A ga B to magireru AがBと紛れる *A gets confused with B, A becomes indistinguishable from B, A is mistaken for B*

② *to take advantage of by blending into*

¶Dorobō ga yami ni magirete nigemashita.
泥棒がやみに紛れて逃げました。
The thief blended into the darkness and escaped.

③ *to become diverted, to become distracted, to become absorbed*

• A ni magireru Aに紛れる *to become diverted by A, to become distracted by A, to become absorbed in A*

• ki ga magireru 気が紛れる *to become diverted from one's worries*

magó 孫 *grandchild*

magókoro 真心 *sincerity, true-heartendness* [→**seijitsu** 誠実]

• magokoro o komete 真心を込めて *with sincerity, with one's whole heart*

¶Kyōko-san wa magokoro o komete aisatsu o shita.
京子さんは真心を込めてあいさつをした。
Kyoko greeted with sincerity.

magotsuku まごつく *to become confused about what to do, to find onself at a loss*

• A ni magotsuku Aにまごつく *to find oneself at a loss because of A, to find oneself at a loss for A*

¶Shin-seihin no setsumei ni magotsuki-mashita.
新製品の説明にまごつきました。
I was at a loss for an explanation of the new product.

máguma マグマ *magma*

maguneshúmu マグネシウム《Note the mismatch between the pronunciation and the katakana spelling.》 *magnesium*

magunichúdo マグニチュード *magnitude* 《of an earthquake measured on the Richter scale》

¶Sono jishin wa magunichūdo ni deshita.
その地震はマグニチュード2でした。
That earthquake was magnitude 2.

mágure まぐれ (*lucky*)*fluke*

¶Magure de shiai ni katta yo.
まぐれで試合に勝ったよ。
We won the game by a fluke!

¶Magure no hitto deshita.

まぐれのヒットでした。
It was a lucky hit.

maguro 鮪 *tuna*

Máhha マッハ *Mach, Mach number*
¶Sono hikōki wa Mahha ni no sokudo de tobimasu.
その飛行機はマッハ2の速度で飛びます。
The plane flies at a speed of Mach 2.

máhi 麻痺 *paralysis; numbness*
•mahi suru まひする *to become paralyzed; to become numb*
¶Taifū de kōtsū ga mahi shite imasu.
台風で交通がまひしています。
Traffic is paralyzed by the typhoon.
¶Samusa de yubi ga mahi shite imasu.
寒さで指がまひしています。
My fingers are numb with the cold.

mahō 魔法 *magic, magic spell; witchcraft, sorcery* [→**majutsu** 魔術①]
¶Majo wa mahō o tsukau koto ga dekimasu.
魔女は魔法を使うことができます。
A witch can use witchcraft.
•mahō o kakeru 魔法をかける *to cast a spell*
¶Akuma wa akanbō ni mahō o kakemashita.
悪魔は赤ん坊に魔法をかけました。
The devil cast a spell on the baby.
•mahō-bin 魔法瓶 *vacuum bottle, thermos bottle*
•mahō-zukai 魔法使い *wizard, witch, sorcerer*

-mai 一枚《counter for flat, thin objects; see Appendix 2》
¶Kami ga go-mai hitsuyō desu.
紙が5枚必要です。
I need five sheets of paper.
¶Pan o ni-mai yaite kureru?
パンを2枚焼いてくれる？
Will you toast two slices of bread for me?
¶Yonjūichi-en no kitte o jū-mai kudasai.
41円の切手を10枚ください。
Please give me ten 41-yen stamps.

mai- 毎一 *every*《Added to bases denoting regularly recurring time spans.》

•mai-asa 毎朝 *every morning*
¶Chichi wa mai-asa inu o sanpo sasemasu.
父は毎朝犬を散歩させます。
My father walks the dog every morning.

-mai 一まい《Added to the informal affirmative nonpast-tense form of a verb (i.e., the form listed in dictionaries). Alternatively, if the verb is ichidan, -**mai** may be added to the base（see Appendix 1). Instead of **kuru** 来る and **suru** する, the forms **ku-** and **su-** may occur before -**mai**.》① *probably will not, probably does not*
¶Kodomo dakara, konna mondai wa wakaru-mai.
子供だから、こんな問題はわかるまい。
He's a child, so he probably won't understand this kind of problem.
② *will not, will make sure not to*《The subject must be first person.》
¶Ano mise ni wa nido-to iku-mai.
あの店には2度と行くまい。
I'll never go to that shop again.

máigo 迷子 *lost child*
•maigo ni naru 迷子になる *to get lost*《The subject is a person or animal.》
¶Sono bōya wa kyōgi-jō de maigo ni narimashita.
その坊やは競技場で迷子になりました。
That little boy got lost in the stadium.

maikon マイコン *microcomputer*

máiku マイク *microphone*
•kakushi-maiku 隠しマイク *hidden microphone*

maikuróhon マイクロホン [☞**maiku** マイク]

mainasu マイナス [[⇔**purasu** プラス]]
① *minus (sign)*
¶Hyaku mainasu san-jū wa nana-jū desu.
100マイナス30は70です。
Ten minus three is seven.
•mainasu no kazu マイナスの数 *negative number*
② *minus, loss, detriment*

mainen 毎年 *every year* [→**maitoshi**

毎年]

máinichi 毎日 *every day*

¶Kuruma no jiko wa mainichi okori-
masu.

車の事故は毎日起こります。

Car accidents happen every day.

¶Mainichi no shigoto ga chōdo owatta
tokoro da.

毎日の仕事がちょうど終わったところだ。

My everyday work has just ended.

maipēsu マイペース 〜**de** 〜で *at one's
own pace*

¶Kobayashi-san wa maipēsu de yukkuri
aruita.

小林さんはマイペースでゆっくり歩いた。

*Mr. Kobayashi walked slowly at his own
pace.*

máiru マイル *mile*

• -mairu 　-マイル 《counter for miles; see
Appendix 2》

máiru 参る {5} ① 【HUM. for **iku**
行く】

② 【HUM. for **kuru** 来る①】

③ 【FORMAL for **kuru** 来る②】

maishū 毎週 *every week*

¶Chichi wa maishū kuruma o araimasu.

父は毎週車を洗います。

My father washes the car every week.

¶Yamada-san wa maishū Nichiyōbi ni
kyōkai ni ikimasu.

山田さんは毎週日曜日に教会に行きます。

*Mr. Yamada goes to church every Sun-
day.*

maisō 埋葬 *burial, interment* 《of a dead
body or cremated ashes》

• maisō suru 埋葬する *to bury, to inter*

maitoshi 毎年 *every year*

¶Nakayama-san wa maitoshi Hawai ni
ikimasu.

中山さんは毎年ハワイに行きます。

*Ms. Nakayama goes to Hawaii every
year.*

¶Nihon no o-Bon wa maitoshi no gyōji
desu.

日本のお盆は毎年の行事です。

Japan's Bon Festival is a yearly event.

maitsuki 毎月 *every month*

¶Ani wa maitsuki ik-kai eiga o mi
ni ikimasu.

兄は毎月1回映画を見に行きます。

*My older brother goes to see a movie
once every month.*

májika 間近 ① *(the area)nearby*

¶Haha mo majika ni sunde imasu.

母も間近に住んでいます。

My mother is also living nearby.

② *(the time)near at hand*

• majika ni sematte iru 間近に迫っている
to be impending, to be very near at hand

májikku マジック ① *magic, magic spell*
[→**mahō** 魔法]

② *magic trick, conjuring* [→**tejina**
手品]

majime 真面目 〜**na** 〜な *serious, earnest* [→**shinken na** 真剣な]

¶Yōko-chan wa majime na seito desu.

洋子ちゃんはまじめな生徒です。

Yoko is a serious student.

¶Otōto wa sensei no mae de majime na
kao o shimasu.

弟は先生の前でまじめな顔をします。

*My younger brother puts on a serious
face in front of the teacher.*

¶Motto majime ni benkyō shinakereba
naranai.

もっとまじめに勉強しなければならない。

You have to study more seriously.

majíru 混じる {5} *to become mixed,
to mix*

¶Abura to mizu wa majirimasu ka.

油と水は混じりますか。

Do oil and water mix?

majiwáru 交わる ① *to associate, to
keep company* [→**kōsai suru** 交際する]

¶Haha wa kinjo no hito to majiwaru no
ga heta desu.

母は近所の人と交わるのが下手です。

*My mother is poor at associating with
the people in the neighborhood.*

② *to cross, to intersect* [→**kōsa suru**
交差する]

¶Futatsu no sen wa kono ten de majiwari-
masu.

2つの線はこの点で交わります。

The two lines cross at this point.

májo 魔女 *(female)witch*

májutsu 魔術 ① *magic, magic spell* [→
mahō 魔法]

② *large-scale magic trick, illusion*

• majutsu-shi 魔術師 *magician, illusionist*

makaroni マカロニ *macaroni*

• makaroni-guratan マカロニグラタン
macaroni au gratin

makaséru 任せる *to leave* 《up to someone or something else》

¶Zenbu watashi ni makasete kudasai.
全部私に任せてください。
Please leave everything to me.

¶Ryōshin wa sono kettei o boku ni makasemashita.
両親はその決定を僕に任せました。
My parents left that decision to me.

makasu 負かす *to beat, to defeat*

¶Ani o takkyū de makashita yo.
兄を卓球で負かしたよ。
I beat my older brother in table tennis!

make 負け *defeat, loss* [⇔**kachi** 勝ち]

¶Kurosaki-san wa yatto make o mitomemashita.
黒崎さんはやっと負けを認めました。
Mr. Kurosaki finally admitted his defeat.

¶Kono shōbu wa boku no make desu.
この勝負は僕の負けです。
This game is my loss.

makeoshimi 負け惜しみ *unhappiness at losing*

• makeoshimi o iu 負け惜しみを言う *to express unhappiness at losing, to be a bad loser*

makeru 負ける ① *to lose, to be defeated* [⇔**katsu** 勝つ]

• A ga B ni makeru AがBに負ける *A loses B, A is defeated in B* 《when B denotes a contest or competition》

¶Watashi-tachi wa sono shiai ni makemashita.
私たちはその試合に負けました。
We lost that game.

• sensō ni makeru 戦争に負ける *to lose a war*

• A ga B ni makeru AがBに負ける *A loses to B, A is defeated by B* 《when B denotes an opponent》

¶Go tai ichi de sono chīmu ni maketa yo.
5対1でそのチームに負けたよ。
We lost to that team by 5 to 1!

• aite ni makeru 相手に負ける *to lose to an opponent*

② *to come down, to give a discount on*

¶Sen-en ni makete kuremasen ka.
1000円に負けてくれませんか。
Can't you come down to 1,000 yen?

¶Kono kamera o sukoshi makete kudasai.
このカメラを少し負けてください。
Please give me a bit of a discount on this camera.

¶Ichi-wari makemashō.
1割負けましょう。
I'll come down ten percent.

máketto マーケット *market* [→**shijō** 市場]

¶Ane wa māketto ni kaimono ni ikimashita.
姉はマーケットに買い物に行きました。
My older sister went to the market for shopping.

maki 薪 *firewood* [→**takigi** 薪]

makiba 牧場 *stock farm,* <US>*ranch; pasture* 《where farm animals graze》 [→**bokujō** 牧場]

makijaku 巻き尺 *tape measure* [→**mejā** メジャー]

makikómu 巻き込む *to drag, to involve willy-nilly*

• A ni makikomareru Aに巻き込まれる *to get dragged into A, to get involved without wanting to in A*

makitsúku 巻き付く *to wind around, to coil around* 《intransitive》

¶Tsuta ga sono ki ni makitsuite imasu.
つたがその木に巻きついています。
Ivy has coiled itself around that tree.

makká 真っ赤 ～**na** ～な *deep red, bright red, very red*

¶Sensei wa okotte makka ni natta yo.
先生は怒って真っ赤になったよ。

The teacher got angry and turned bright red!

¶Makka na bōshi ga hoshii yo.

真っ赤な帽子が欲しいよ。

I want a bright red hat!

makkúra 真っ暗 〜**na** 〜な *very dark, pitch dark*

¶Soto wa makkura deshita.

外は真っ暗でした。

Outside it was pitch dark.

makkúro 真っ黒 〜**na** 〜な *deep black, very black; completely black*

makoto 誠 ① *sincerity, true-heartedness* [→**magokoro** 真心]

② 〜**ni** 〜に 【FORMAL for **hontō ni** 本当に】 *really, truly, very*

¶Makoto ni arigatō gozaimashita.

誠にありがとうございました。

Thank you very much indeed.

mā́ku マーク *mark, label; trademark*

¶Hako ni wa akai ya-jirushi no māku ga tsuite imasu.

箱には赤い矢印のマークがついています。

On that box there's a red arrow mark.

•kuesuchon-māku クエスチョンマーク *question mark* [→**gimon-fu** 疑問符 (s.v. **gimon** 疑問)]

mā́ku マーク 〜**suru** 〜する *to keep an eye on; to mark* 《an opposing player》

¶Nana-ban o māku shite ne.

7番をマークしてね。

Mark number 7, OK?

makú 幕 ① *curtain* 《used as a partition or on a stage》

¶Maku ga yukkuri to agarimashita.

幕がゆっくりと上がりました。

The curtain rose slowly.

② *act* 《of a play》

•-maku －幕《counter for acts; see Appendix 2》

maku 巻く ① *to wind; to roll up* 《transitive》

¶Mezamashi-dokei no neji o mada maite inai.

目覚まし時計のねじをまだ巻いていない。

I haven't wound the alarm clock up yet.

¶Jūtan o maite kuremasen ka.

じゅうたんを巻いてくれませんか。

Won't you roll up the carpet for me?

② *to tie around, to wrap around*

¶Hidari-te ni hōtai o makimashita.

左手に包帯を巻きました。

I wrapped a bandage on my left hand.

maku 撒く ① *to scatter; to sprinkle*

¶Haha wa mainichi shibafu ni mizu o makimasu.

母は毎日芝生に水をまきます。

My mother waters the lawn every day.

② *to elude, to shake off* 《a pursuer》

mā́ku 蒔く *to sow*

¶Chichi wa hatake ni tane o maite imasu.

父は畑に種をまいています。

My father is sowing seeds in the field.

mā́kura 枕 *pillow*

•makura-kabā 枕カバー *pillowcase*

makuru まくる *to roll up* 《sleeves, pant legs, etc.》

¶Sara o arau tame ni sode o makurimashita.

皿を洗うためにそでをまくりました。

I rolled up my sleeves to wash the dishes.

mamá まま 《This word is always preceded by a modifier of some kind.》 ① *unchanged state*

¶Tsukue no ue no hon wa sono mama ni shite okinasai.

机の上の本はそのままにしておきなさい。

Leave the books on the desk as they are.

•mama da ままだ *to be in the unchanged state of*

¶Tanaka-san wa Tōkyō ni itta mama desu.

田中さんは東京に行ったままです。

Mr. Tanaka is still in Tokyo. 《Literally: Mr. Tanaka is in the unchanged state of having gone to Tokyo.》

② 〜**de**／**ni** 〜で／に *in the unchanged state of*

¶Sono heya ni kutsu o haita mama hairimashita.

その部屋に靴をはいたまま入りました。

I entered that room with my shoes on. 《Literally: I entered that room in the un-*

changed state of having put on my shoes.》

máma ママ *mommy, mom*

mamagoto ままごと *playing house*
¶Kodomo-tachi wa mada mamagoto o shite imasu.
子供たちはまだままごとをしています。
The children are still playing house.

māmarédo マーマレード *marmalade*

mamé 豆 *bean; pea*

mamé まめ *blister* 《on the hand or foot caused by rubbing against something》

mamizu 真水 *fresh water* [→**tansui** 淡水] [⇔**shiomizu** 塩水]

ma-mó-naku 間も無く *soon, before long, in no time*
¶Ma-mo-naku sensei ga irassharu deshō.
まもなく先生がいらっしゃるでしょう。
The teacher will probably come soon.

mamóru 守る ① *to keep* 《a promise, etc.》; *to obey* 《a rule, etc.》
¶Keiko-san wa itsu-mo yakusoku o mamorimasu.
恵子さんはいつも約束を守ります。
Keiko always keeps her promises.
¶Kōsoku o mamoranakereba narimasen.
校則を守らなければなりません。
We must obey the school regulations.
② *to protect, to defend* [⇔**semeru** 攻める]
¶Chichi-oya wa musume o kiken kara mamorimashita.
父親は娘を危険から守りました。
The father protected his daughter from danger.

-man －万 *ten thousand*
¶Chichi wa san-man-en shiharaimashita.
父は3万円支払いました。
My father paid 30,000 yen.

man- 満－ *full* 《Added to number bases denoting ages or time periods.》
¶Ashita de man-jūyon-sai ni narimasu.
あしたで満14歳になります。
I will be a full fourteen years old as of tomorrow.

mánā マナー *manners*
•manā no ii hito マナーのいい人 *well-mannered person*

•tēburu-manā テーブルマナー *table manners*

manabu 学ぶ *to study, to (try to)learn, to take lessons in* [→**narau** 習う, **benkyō suru** 勉強する]
¶Watashi-tachi wa Seki-sensei kara Eigo o manande imasu.
私たちは関先生から英語を学んでいます。
We are learning English from Mrs. Seki.
¶Daigaku de shinri-gaku o manabi-tai desu.
大学で心理学を学びたいです。
I want to study psychology at college.

manaitá 俎板 *cutting board* 《used in cooking》

manatsu 真夏 *the midsummer* [⇔**mafuyu** 真冬]
•manatsu-bi 真夏日 *very hot day*

manbiki 万引き ① *shoplifting*
•manbiki suru 万引きする *to shoplift* 《transitive》
② *shoplifter*

mandorin マンドリン *mandolin*

mane 真似 ① *imitation, mimicry, copying*
¶Hiroshi-san wa ano kashu no mane ga jōzu desu.
弘さんはあの歌手のまねが上手です。
Hiroshi's imitation of that singer is skillful.
¶Yōko-san wa Tada-sensei no mane o shita yo.
洋子さんは多田先生のまねをしたよ。
Yoko did an imitation of Prof. Tada!
•mane suru まねする *to imitate, to mimic, to copy*
② *pretense, false show* [→**furi** 振り]
•mane o suru まねをする *to pretend, to make a pretense*
¶Ano hito wa shinda mane o shimashita.
あの人は死んだまねをしました。
That person pretended to be dead.
③ *behavior, action* 《Used to refer to behavior that is undesirable.》
¶Baka na mane wa yamete yo.
ばかなまねはやめてよ。
Stop your foolish behavior!

manējā マネージャー *manager, person in charge* [→**shihai-nin** 支配人（s.v. **shihai** 支配)]

manekí 招き *invitation* [→**shōtai** 招待]

manekin マネキン *mannequin*

manéku 招く ① *to invite* [→**shōtai suru** 招待する]

¶Ani wa Nishiyama fusai o kekkon-shiki ni manekimashita.

兄は西山夫妻を結婚式に招きました。

My older brother invited Mr. and Mrs. Nishiyama to his wedding.

• gokai o maneku 誤解を招く *to invite misunderstanding*

② *to beckon*

¶Watashi o maneita ten'in ni tsuite iku koto ni shita.

私を招いた店員についていくことにした。

I decided to go to the store clerk who was beckoning me.

maneru 真似る *to imitate, to mimic, to copy*

¶Yumi-san wa sono joyū no koe o manemashita.

由美さんはその女優の声をまねました。

Yumi imitated that actress's voice.

manga 漫画 *comic strip, cartoon; caricature*

¶Ane wa manga o kaku no ga umai yo.

姉は漫画をかくのがうまいよ。

My older sister is good at drawing cartoons!

• manga-bon 漫画本 *comic book*

• manga-eiga 漫画映画 *cartoon movie*

• manga-ka 漫画家 *cartoonist*

• manga-zasshi 漫画雑誌 *comic magazine*

mán–ga–ichi 万が一 [☞**man'ichi** 万一]

mángan マンガン *manganese*

mángetsu 満月 *full moon* [⇔**shingetsu** 新月]

¶Kon'ya wa mangetsu desu.

今夜は満月です。

Tonight there is a full moon.

manhōru マンホール *manhole*

mánia マニア *enthusiast, devotee*

¶Ani wa shashin no mania desu.

兄は写真のマニアです。

My older brother is a photo enthusiast.

• jazu-mania ジャズマニア *jazz devotee*

• kitte-mania 切手マニア *stamp enthusiast*

maniáu 間に合う ① *to make it in time*

• A ni maniau Aに間に合う *to make it in time for A, to make it to A in time*

¶Isoganai to, gakkō ni maniawanai yo.

急がないと、学校に間に合わないよ。

If you don't hurry, you won't make it to school in time!

② *to be able to make do, to be able to get by*

¶Kono naifu de maniaimasu.

このナイフで間に合います。

I can make do with this knife.

mán'ichi 万一 ① *by some remote chance*

② *unlikely event, remote possibility*

manikyua マニキュア *manicure*

• yubi ni manikyua o suru 指にマニキュアをする *to manicure one's fingernails*

man'in 満員 〜**no** 〜の *full to capacity, crowded to capacity* 《with people》

¶Kyōshitsu wa seito de man'in desu.

教室は生徒で満員です。

The classroom is full to capacity with students.

¶Basu wa kyō mo man'in deshita.

バスはきょうも満員でした。

The bus was crowded to capacity today too.

• man'in-densha 満員電車 *train crowded to capacity*

manjū 饅頭 *steamed bun filled with sweet bean paste*

mankai 満開 *full bloom*

¶Chūrippu ga mankai desu.

チューリップが満開です。

The tulips are in full bloom.

manmá まんま【COL. for **mama** まま】

mannaka 真ん中 *middle, center*

¶Heya no mannaka ni tēburu ga arimasu.

部屋の真ん中にテーブルがあります。

There is a table in the middle of the room.

mannénhitsu 万年筆 *fountain pen*

manpuku 満腹 〜**no** 〜の *full, satiated*
• manpuku suru 満腹する *to eat until one is full*

manriki 万力 *vise*

manrui 満塁 *loaded bases, full bases* 《in baseball》
¶Tsū-auto manrui desu.
ツーアウト満塁です。
It's two outs, bases loaded.
• manrui-hōmuran 満塁ホームラン *grand slam (homerun)*

mánshon マンション *condominium*

mantén 満点 ① ＜US＞*perfect score,* ＜UK＞*full marks* 《on a test》
¶Kyōko-san wa Eigo no tesuto de manten o totta.
京子さんは英語のテストで満点を取った。
Kyoko got a perfect score on the English test.
② 〜**no** 〜の *fully satisfactory, perfect*
¶Konban no ensō wa manten deshita.
今晩の演奏は満点でした。
Tonight's performance was perfect.

manuke 間抜け 【CRUDE】 〜**na** 〜な *stupid, foolish*
¶Sonna koto o suru nante manuke da yo.
そんなことをするなんてまぬけだよ。
It's stupid to do such a thing!

mánzoku 満足 *satisfaction, contentment*
• manzoku suru 満足する *to become satisfied*
¶Atarashii sutereo ni manzoku shite imasu.
新しいステレオに満足しています。
I am satisfied with the new stereo.
• manzoku na 満足な *satisfactory, adequate*

máppu マップ *map* [→**chizu** 地図]

mararia マラリア *malaria*

marason マラソン *marathon*
• marason-kyōsō マラソン競走 *marathon race*
• marason-senshu マラソン選手 *marathon runner*

maré 稀 〜**na** 〜な *rare*
• mare ni まれに *rarely, seldom* 《Always occurs in combination with a negative predicate.》

marifána マリファナ *marijuana*

maru 丸 *circle*
¶Koko ni maru o kaite kudasai.
ここに丸をかいてください。
Draw a circle here, please.
• maru de kakomu 丸で囲む *to draw a circle around, to circle*
¶Seikai o maru de kakominasai.
正解を丸で囲みなさい。
Circle the correct answer.
• maru-gao 丸顔 *round face*

maru– 丸－ *full, whole* 《Added to number bases periods of time.》
¶Imōto wa maru-mikka-kan byōki de nete imasu.
妹は丸3日間病気で寝ています。
My younger sister has been sick in bed for three whole days.

marude まるで [[→**mattaku** 全く]] *quite, utterly, really;* 〈*not*〉 *at all*
¶Marude sore o oboete imasen.
まるでそれを覚えていません。
I don't remember that at all.
• marude . . . yō na まるで…ような *just like*
¶Kyōko-san wa marude byōnin no yō desu.
京子さんはまるで病人のようです。
Kyoko looks just like a sick person.

marui 丸い、円い *round*
¶Kaigi-shitsu ni marui tēburu ga arimasu.
会議室に円いテーブルがあります。
There is a round table in the conference room.
• maruku natte suwaru 円くなって座る *to sit in a circle*

maruta 丸太 *log*
• maruta-goya 丸太小屋 *log cabin*

másaka まさか ① *You're kidding!, That can't be true!* 《when used as an exclamatory response》
¶"Keiko wa shiken ni ochita yo."

"Masaka!"

「恵子は試験に落ちたよ」「まさか」

"Keiko failed on the exam!" "You're kidding!"

② *surely* ⟨*not*⟩, ⟨*not*⟩ *possibly* 《Always occurs in combination with a negative predicate.》

¶Masaka dekiru to wa omoimasen deshita.

まさかできるとは思いませんでした。

I didn't think he could possibly do it.

mása-ni 正に 【FORMAL for **tashika ni** 確かに】 *certainly, undoubtedly*

¶Masa-ni ossharu tōri desu.

正におっしゃるとおりです。

It's just as you say.

masáru 勝る *to be ⁄ become better, to be ⁄ become superior* [⇔**otoru** 劣る]

• A ni ⁄ yori masaru A に ⁄ より勝る *to be better than A*

¶Kyōko wa Eigo de wa Tarō yori zutto masarimasu.

京子は英語では太郎よりずっと勝ります。

Kyoko is much better at English than Taro.

¶Kenkō wa tomi ni masaru.

健康は富に勝る。《proverb》

Health is better than wealth.

masatsu 摩擦 *friction, rubbing*

• masatsu suru 摩擦する *to rub* 《one thing with another》

• bōeki-masatsu 貿易摩擦 *trade friction*

massáji マッサージ *massage*

• massāji suru マッサージする *to massage*

massáo 真っ青 〜**na** 〜な ① *deep blue, very blue*

¶Sora wa massao desu yo.

空は真っ青ですよ。

The sky is deep blue!

② *very pale* 《because of illness or fear》

¶Hiroshi-san wa Yoshiko-san no kotoba o kiite, massao ni natta yo.

弘さんは良子さんの言葉を聞いて、真っ青になったよ。

Hiroshi listened to what Yoshiko said and turned very pale! 《Literally: Hiroshi listened to Yoshiko's words and became

very pale.》

masshígura まっしぐら (〜**ni** 〜に) *full speed ahead, at full forward speed*

masshíro 真っ白 〜**na** 〜な *snow-white; completely white*

¶Toda-sensei no kami wa masshiro desu.

戸田先生の髪は真っ白です。

Dr. Toda's hair is snow-white.

massúgu 真っすぐ (〜**ni** 〜に) *straight ahead, without turning; directly, straight, without detours*

¶Koko kara massugu itte kudasai.

ここからまっすぐ行ってください。

Please go straight ahead from here.

¶Kono basu wa massugu Shinjuku ni ikimasu.

このバスはまっすぐ新宿に行きます。

This bus goes directly to Shinjuku.

• massugu na まっすぐな *straight, unbent; direct, detour-free*

¶Kono massugu na michi no hō ga suki desu.

このまっすぐな道のほうが好きです。

I prefer this straight road.

masú 鱒 *trout*

masu 増す *to increase* 《transitive or intransitive》 [→**fueru** 増える; **fuyasu** 増やす]

¶Ni-koku-kan no kinchō ga mashite imasu.

2国間の緊張が増しています。

The tension between the two countries has increased.

¶Unten-shu ga sokudo o mashimashita.

運転手が速度を増しました。

The driver increased the speed.

masui 麻酔 *anesthesia*

• masui-yaku 麻酔薬 *an anesthetic*

• kyokubu-masui 局部麻酔 *local anesthesia*

• zenshin-masui 全身麻酔 *general anesthesia*

masukomi マスコミ ① *mass media*

¶Sono jiken wa masukomi de mo hōjiraremashita.

その事件はマスコミでも報じられました。

That incident was also reported in the

mass media.

② *mass communication*

masukótto マスコット *mascot*

másuku マスク ① *cloth surgical mask* 《covering the mouth and nose to prevent dust or germs from passing through》

¶Kaze o hiitara, masuku o shinasai.

かぜを引いたら、マスクをしなさい。

Since you've caught a cold, wear a cloth mask.

② *mask* 《of the type worn by baseball catchers and umpires》

¶Kyatchā wa masuku o tsukemashita.

キャッチャーはマスクを着けました。

The catcher put on the mask.

masúmasu 益々 *more and more, increasingly*

¶Shiai wa masumasu omoshiroku narimashita.

試合はますますおもしろくなりました。

The game became more and more exciting.

¶Saikin masumasu samuku natte kimashita.

最近ますます寒くなってきました。

It has gotten colder and colder recently.

másutā マスター ① *master; employer* [→**shujin** 主人②]

② *proprietor, shop owner* [→**shujin** 主人③]

③ *master degree holder* [→**shūshi** 修士]

④ ～**suru** ～する *to master*

másuto マスト (*ship's*)*mast* [→**hobashira** 帆柱]

mata また ① *again* [→**futatabi** 再び]

¶Raishū no Getsuyōbi mata aimashō.

来週の月曜日また会いましょう。

Let's meet again next Monday.

¶Dewa mata.

ではまた。

See you. 《Literally: *Well then, again.*》

② *in addition, moreover, also*

¶Miyuki wa kashu de, soshite mata haiyū de mo aru.

美幸は歌手で、そしてまた俳優でもある。

Miyuki is a singer, and in addition,

she's also an actress.

③ *similarly, in the same way* 《In this use, **mata** follows the particle **mo** も and is essentially redundant.》

¶Kono keiyaku ni wa watashi no tsuma mo mata dōi shite iru.

この契約には私の妻もまた同意している。

My wife also agrees with this contract.

¶Yūki ga ikanai nara, watashi mo mata ikanai.

雄城が行かないなら、私もまた行かない。

If Yuki is not going to go, then I'm not either.

matá 股 *crotch* 《where the legs join》

matágu 跨ぐ *to step over, to straddle*

¶Hōsu o matagimashita.

ホースをまたぎました。

I stepped over the hose.

¶Keibiin ga mizutamari o mataide tatte ita.

警備員が水たまりをまたいで立っていた。

The security officer was standing straddled over a puddle.

mataséru 待たせる *to keep* 〈*someone*〉 *waiting* 《This word is the regular causative form of **matsu** 待つ.》

¶O-matase shimashita.

お待たせしました。

Sorry to have kept you waiting. 《Literally: *I have kept you waiting.* (humble)》

matatáku 瞬く ① *to blink* 《ones eye(s)》

• matataku ma ni 瞬く間に *in the blink of an eye, in an instant*

② 《when the subject is a light source》 *to twinkle; to blink; to flicker*

¶Hoshi ga matataite imasu.

星が瞬いています。

The stars are twinkling.

matá-wa または *or* [→**aruiwa** 或いは①]

¶Tōkyō mata-wa Yokohama ni atarashii biru o tatemasu.

東京または横浜に新しいビルを建てます。

We will be constructing a new building in either Tokyo or Yokohama.

mátchi マッチ *match* (*-stick*)

• matchi o suru マッチをする *to strike a match*

- matchi-bako マッチ箱 *matchbox*

mato 的 *target, mark, object*

¶Yōko-san wa kurasu-zen'in no sonkei no mato desu.

洋子さんはクラス全員の尊敬の的です。

Yoko is the object of the entire class's respect.

matomaru まとまる ① *to come together into a unit*

② *to become orderly, to become coherent, to take shape*

③ *to be settled, to be completed, to come to a satisfactory conclusion*

matomeru まとめる ① *to bring together into a unit, to consolidate, to unify*

¶Kantoku wa chīmu o umaku matomemashita.

監督はチームをうまくまとめました。

The manager skillfully unified the team.

¶Nimotsu o sugu matomenasai.

荷物をすぐにまとめなさい。

Get the luggage together at once.

② *to put in order, to make coherent*

- kangae o matomeru 考えをまとめる *to put one's thoughts in order*

③ *to settle, to complete, to bring to a satisfactory conclusion*

¶Kōshō o matomeru no wa jikan ga kakaru darō.

交渉をまとめるのは時間がかかるだろう。

It will probably take time to complete the negotiations.

mátsu 松 *pine*

- matsu-bayashi 松林 *pine woods*
- matsu-bokkuri 松ぼっくり *pine cone*
- matsu-kasa 松笠 *pine cone*

mátsu 待つ *to wait for*

¶Dare o matte iru no desu ka.

だれを待っているのですか。

Who are you waiting for?

¶Ashita made henji o matanakereba naranai.

あしたまで返事を待たなければならない。

I'll have to wait until tomorrow for the answer.

¶Chotto matte kudasai.

ちょっと待ってください。

Please wait a little.

¶Yōko-san kara no tegami o matte imasu.

洋子さんからの手紙を待っています。

I am waiting for a letter from Yoko.

¶Saigetsu hito o matazu.

歳月人を待たず。《proverb》

Time and tide wait for no man. 《Literally: Time does not wait for a person.》

matsubazúe 松葉杖 *crutch*

mátsuge 睫毛 *eyelash*

¶Marī-san wa nagai matsuge o shite imasu ne.

マリーさんは長いまつ毛をしていますね。

Marie has long eyelashes, doesn't she.

matsuri 祭り ① *traditional Japanese festival 《typically held yearly at a Shinto shrine》*

② *festival, gala event*

- Yuki-matsuri 雪祭り *the Snow Festival* 《an annual event in Sapporo》

matsutake 松茸 *matsutake mushroom* 《highly prized for its flavor》

mattaku 全く *quite, really, completely, absolutely; 〈not〉 at all*

¶Sore wa mattaku betsu no koto da yo.

それはまったく別の事だよ。

That's a completely different matter!

¶Yumi-chan wa mattaku hashiru no ga hayai ne.

由美ちゃんはまったく走るのが速いね。

Yumi runs really fast, doesn' t she. 《Literally: As for Yumi, running really is fast, isn't it.》

¶Mattaku sukī ga dekimasen.

まったくスキーができません。

I can't ski at all.

mátto マット *mat* 《of the type used for gymnastics, etc.》

máttoresu マットレス *mattress*

mau 舞う ① *to dance* [→odoru 踊る]

② *to flutter about* 《in the air》

maué 真上 *the area directly above*

¶Tēburu no maue ni shanderia ga aru.

テーブルの真上にシャンデリアがある。

There is a chandelier directly above the table.

mawari 周り [[→**shūi** 周囲]] ① *the area around, surroundings, vicinity* [→**atari** 辺り]

¶Mawari ni wa dare-mo imasen deshita.
周りにはだれもいませんでした。
There was no one in the vicinity.

¶Sensei no mawari ni suwarimashō.
先生の周りに座りましょう。
Let's sit around the teacher.

② *circumference, distance around*

mawari 回り ① *going around, turning, spinning, rotating* [→**kaiten** 回転]

② *going from place to place in succession; traveling around, touring*

③ *spread, spreading, circulating*

¶Hi no mawari ga hayakatta desu.
火の回りが早かったです。
The fire spread quickly. «Literally: The spread of the fire was fast.»

• mawari-michi 回り道 *detour* [→**ukai** 迂回]; *roundabout way* [→**tōmawari** 遠回り]

−**mawari** −回り *by way of, via* «Added to bases denoting a place where an intermediate stop is made.» [→ −**keiyu** −経由]

¶Shinjuku-mawari de Shibuya ni ikimashita.
新宿回りで渋谷に行きました。
I went to Shibuya by way of Shinjuku.

mawaru 回る ① *to turn, to spin, to rotate* «intransitive» [→**kaiten suru** 回転する]

¶Tsuki wa chikyū no mawari o mawatte imasu.
月は地球の周りを回っています。
The moon revolves around the earth.

¶Sono koma wa yoku mawatte iru ne.
そのこまはよく回っているね。
That top is spinning well, isn't it?

② *to go from place to place in succession; to travel around, to tour*

¶Kyonen wa Kyūshū o mawarimashita.
去年は九州を回りました。
Last year I traveled around Kyushu.

③ *to spread, to circulate*

¶Doku wa sugu ni karada-jū ni mawari-

mashita.
毒はすぐに体中に回りました。
The poison soon spread throughout his body.

④ *to go via, to stop off at on the way, to make a detour through*

¶Ōsaka o mawatte kaerimashita.
大阪を回って帰りました。
I went home via Osaka.

⑤ *to turn, to go past* «a time on the clock»

¶Mō ku-ji o mawarimashita.
もう9時を回りました。
It has already gone past 9:00.

mawasu 回す ① *to turn, to spin, to rotate* «transitive»

¶Unten-shu wa handoru o migi ni mawashimashita.
運転手はハンドルを右に回しました。
The driver turned the steering wheel to the right.

② *to send around, to pass around; to send on, to pass on, to forward*

¶Shio o mawashite kudasai.
塩を回してください。
Please pass the salt around.

¶Kono tsūchi o shiten ni mawashimasu.
この通知を支店に回します。
I'll forward this communication to the branch office.

mayaku 麻薬 *drug, narcotic*

mayónaka 真夜中 *the middle of the night*

mayonézu マヨネーズ *mayonnaise*

mayóu 迷う ① *to become confused about which way to go*

• michi ni mayou 道に迷う *to lose one's way*

¶Ano chīsai otoko no ko wa michi ni mayotta yo.
あの小さい男の子は道に迷ったよ。
That little boy lost his way!

② *to become at a loss, to become perplexed*

• A ni mayou Aに迷う *to become at a loss for A, to become perplexed about A*

¶Sono toki wa kotoba ni mayotte ima-

shita.
その時は言葉に迷っていました。
At that time I was at a loss for words.

máyu 眉 *eyebrow*
• mayu-ge 眉毛 [☞**mayu** 眉 (above)]

máyu 繭 *cocoon*

mazáru 混ざる *to become mixed, to mix* [→**majiru** 混じる]

mazéru 混ぜる *to mix* «transitive»
¶Gyūnyū ni satō o mazemashita.
牛乳に砂糖を混ぜました。
I mixed sugar into the milk.

mázu 先ず *first, first of all*
¶Mazu genbun o yomimashō.
まず原文を読みましょう。
First let's read the original text.

mazúi まずい ① *bad-tasting* «Can be used to describe a restaurant, cafeteria, etc., as well as food itself.» [⇔**oishii** 美味しい]
¶Kono sūpu wa mazui yo.
このスープはまずいよ。
This soup is bad-tasting!
¶Kono pan-ya wa mazui ne.
このパン屋はまずいね。
This bakery is bad isn't it.
② *poor, unskilled, clumsy* «describing what someone does»
¶Ano kashu wa uta ga mazui ne.
あの歌手は歌がまずいね。
That singer isn't any good at singing, is she.
③ *ill-advised, inappropriate; embarrassing, awkward*
¶Sono himitsu ga bareta no wa mazui nā.
その秘密がばれたのはまずいなあ。
Boy, it's awkward that that secret was revealed.

mazushíi 貧しい [[⇔**yutaka na** 豊かな]] ① *poor, indigent* [→**binbō na** 貧乏な]
¶Kaneda-san wa mazushii ie ni umaremashita.
金田さんは貧しい家に生まれました。
Mr. Kaneda was born into a poor family.
¶Kurashi ga mazushii hito mo imasu.
暮らしが貧しい人もいます。

There are also people who live in poverty. «Literally: *There are also people whose lives are poor.*»
② *scanty, insufficient* [→**toboshii** 乏しい]
¶Ano hito wa keiken ga mazushii desu.
あの人は経験が貧しいです。
That person's experience is scanty.

mé 目 ① *eye*
¶Komatsu-kun wa me ga ii yo.
小松君は目がいいよ。
Komatsu's eyes are good!
¶Hanako-san wa ōki na me o shite imasu ne.
花子さんは大きな目をしていますね。
Hanako has large eyes, doesn't she.
¶Yōko wa itsumo nemusō na me o shite imasu.
洋子はいつも眠そうな目をしています。
Yoko always has sleepy-looking eyes!
• me o akeru 〔tojiru〕 目を開ける〔閉じる〕 *to open* 〔*close*〕 *one's eyes*
• me ga mienai 目が見えない *to be unable to see, to be blind*
• me o fuseru 目を伏せる *to drop one's eyes*
• me ga kuramu 目がくらむ *to become dizzy; to become dazzled*
• me ga sameru 目が覚める *to wake up* «intransitive» [→**mezameru** 目覚める]
• me o samasu 目を覚ます *to wake up* «intransitive»
• A ni me o tōsu Aに目を通す *to take a look at A, to look over A, to check A*
¶Eigo de kaita tegami ni me o tōshite kudasai.
英語で書いた手紙に目を通してください。
Please take a look at the letter written in English.
• A o miru me ga aru Aを見る目がある *to have a good eye for A*
¶Oji wa e o miru me ga arimasu.
叔父は絵を見る目があります。
My uncle has a good eye for pictures.
• A kara me o hanasu Aから目を離す *to take one's eyes off A*
• me ni tsuku 目につく *to catch one's eye*

② *empty space between something in a crisscross pattern*

¶Kono ami no me wa arai desu.

この網の目は粗いです。

The mesh of this net is coarse. 《Literally: The holes (between the cords) of this net are coarse.》

mé 芽 *bud; sprout, shoot*

• me o dasu 芽を出す *to put out buds/shoots, to bud/sprout*

¶Bara no hana ga me o dashite imasu.

ばらの花が芽を出しています。

The roses have budded.

• me ga deru 芽が出る *buds/shoots appear*

-me 一目《Added to cardinal numbers to form ordinal numbers; see Appendix 2.》

méate 目当て ① *purpose, objective, aim* [→**mokuteki** 目的]

¶Koko ni kita meate wa nan desu ka.

ここに来た目当ては何ですか。

What was your purpose in coming here?

② *guide* 《i.e., a thing to keep one's eyes on》

¶Ryōshi wa tōdai o meate ni fune o hashiraseta.

漁師は灯台を目当てに船を走らせた。

The fisherman sailed the boat with the lighthouse as a guide.

mechakucha 滅茶苦茶 【COL.】 ~**na**

~な ① *absurd, nonsensical* [→**mucha na** 無茶な①]

• mechakucha na koto o iu めちゃくちゃな事を言う *to talk nonsense*

② *rash, reckless* [→**mucha na** 無茶な②]

③ *very messy, in great disorder*

¶Endō-san no heya wa mechakucha desu.

遠藤さんの部屋はめちゃくちゃです。

Mr. Endo's room is very messy.

medamá 目玉 *eyeball*

• medama-yaki 目玉焼き *egg fried sunny side up*

medarisuto メダリスト *medalist*

medaru メダル *medal, medallion*

• dō-medaru 銅メダル *bronze medal*

• gin-medaru 銀メダル *silver medal*

• kin-medaru 金メダル *gold medal*

medátsu 目立つ *to be conspicuous, to stand out*

¶Kyō no barēbōru no shiai de wa Hamada-senshu no katsuyaku ga medachi-mashita.

きょうのバレーボールの試合では浜田選手の活躍が目立ちました。

Hamada stood out in today's volleyball game. 《Literally: In today's volleyball game, Hamada's activeness stood out.》

¶Kono posutā o medatsu basho ni hari-nasai.

このポスターを目立つ場所にはりなさい。

Put up this poster in a conspicuous place.

Médē メーデー *May Day*

medetái めでたい *auspicious, joyous, worthy of congratulations*

¶Sore wa medetai koto desu ne.

それはめでたい事ですね。

That's an auspicious event, isn't it.

médo 目処 *prospect(s), hope* [→**mi-tōshi** 見通し①]

• medo ga tsuku めどがつく *the prospects become hopeful, light appears at the end of the tunnel*

médorē メドレー ① *(musical) medley* ② *medley (race)*

• kojin-medorē 個人メドレー *individual medley*

mégahon メガホン *megaphone*

mégami 女神 *goddess*

mégane 眼鏡 *(eye-) glasses*

¶Chichi wa dokusho suru toki megane o kakemasu.

父は読書するとき眼鏡をかけます。

My father wears glasses when he reads.

megumareru 恵まれる *to come to be blessed, to come to be favored*

¶Sofu wa kenkō ni megumarete imasu.

祖父は健康に恵まれています。

My grandfather is blessed with good health.

megúsuri 目薬 *eye lotion, eye drops, eye medicine*

¶Haha wa tokidoki megusuri o sash-

imasu.

母は時々目薬を差します。

My mother sometimes applies eye drops.

méi 姪 *niece* [⇔**oi** 甥]

• mei-go-san 姪御さん 【HON. for mei (above)】

-mei －名 【FORMAL for **-nin** －人】

《counter for persons; see Appendix 2》

meian 名案 *excellent idea*

meibo 名簿 *name list, name register*

¶Watashi no namae wa meibo ni notte imasu.

私の名前は名簿に載っています。

My name appears on the name list.

¶Bu-in no meibo o tsukurimashō.

部員の名簿を作りましょう。

Let's make a name list of the club members.

méibutsu 名物 ① *well-known product* [→**meisan** 名産]

② *well-known feature, well-known attraction*

meichū 命中 *hit, on-target impact*

• meichū suru 命中する *to hit, to make an on-target impact*

¶Hannin ga nageta ishi ga keikan no atama ni meichū shita.

犯人が投げた石が警官の頭に命中した。

The stone that the criminal threw hit the police officer on the head.

meihaku 明白 ～**na** ～な *clear, plain, evident* [→**akiraka na** 明らかな]

Méiji 明治《Japanese imperial era name for the period 1868-1912》

• Meiji-ishin 明治維新 *the Meiji Restoration*

• Meiji-jidai 明治時代 *the Meiji Era*

• Meiji-tennō 明治天皇 *the Meiji Emperor*

meijín 名人 *master, skilled expert*

¶Okumura-san wa shōgi no meijin desu.

奥村さんは将棋の名人です。

Mr. Okumura is a master of shogi.

meijiru 命じる *to give an order for, to give a command for* [→**meirei suru** 命令する]

• A ni B o meijiru AにBを命じる *to give*

an order for B to A, to order A to do B

¶Shachō wa Kawasaki-san ni tenkin o meijita.

社長は川崎さんに転勤を命じた。

The company president ordered Mr. Kawasaki to change jobs.

¶Sensei wa seito-tachi ni shizuka ni suru yō meijita.

先生は生徒たちに静かにするよう命じた。

The teacher ordered the students to be quiet.

meikaku 明確 ～**na** ～な *clear, precise, definite*

meiméi 銘々 ① *each, each respectively* [→**sorezore** それぞれ]

¶Seito wa meimei chigatta iken o motte iru.

生徒はめいめい違った意見を持っている。

The students each have a different opinion.

② *each respective one*

• meimei no めいめいの *each, each respective*

mein'íbento メインイベント *main event*

méinichi 命日 *anniversary of a person's death*

meinsutándo メインスタンド *main stands* 《in a stadium, etc.》

meinsutoríto メインストリート *main street, major street* [→**ōdōri** 大通り]

Meiōsei 冥王星 (*the planet*)*Pluto*

meirei 命令 *command, order*

¶Watashi wa shachō no meirei ni shitagaimasu.

私は社長の命令に従います。

I follow the company president's orders.

• meirei suru 命令する *to give an order for* [→**meijiru** 命じる]

• A ni B o meirei suru AにBを命令する *to give an order for B to A, to order A to do B*

¶Sensei wa watashi-tachi ni shuppatsu o meirei shimashita.

先生は私たちに出発を命令しました。

Our teacher ordered us to depart.

• meirei-bun 命令文 *imperative sentence*

méiro 迷路 *maze*

¶Seinen wa sū-jikan meiro de mayotte imashita.

青年は数時間迷路で迷っていました。

The young man was lost in the maze for several hours.

meiryō 明瞭 〜**na** 〜な *clear, plain, evident* [→**akiraka na** 明らかな]

meisan 名産 *well-known product*

¶Momo wa Okayama no meisan desu.

桃は岡山の名産です。

Peaches are a well-known product of Okayama.

meisei 名声 *good reputation, renown, illustriousness*

meishi 名刺 *business card, calling card,* <*UK*>*visiting card*

• meishi o dasu 名刺を出す *to present one's card*

• meishi o kōkan suru 名刺を交換する *to exchange cards*

meishi 名詞 *noun*

meishin 迷信 *superstition*

¶Boku wa meishin o shinjinai yo.

僕は迷信を信じないよ。

I don't believe in superstitions!

meishó 名所 *famous place, sight*

¶Rondon-tō wa Rondon no meisho no hitotsu desu.

ロンドン塔はロンドンの名所の一つです。

The Tower of London is one of the sights of London.

¶Pari no meisho o kenbutsu shitai to omoimasu.

パリの名所を見物したいと思います。

I want to see the sights of Paris.

¶Sono teien wa sakura no meisho desu.

その庭園は桜の名所です。

That garden is famous for its cherry blossoms. 《Literally: That garden is a famous place of cherry blossoms.》

méiwaku 迷惑 *trouble, annoyance, inconvenience* [→**mendō** 面倒]

• A ni meiwaku o kakeru Aに迷惑をかける *to trouble A, to bother A, to put A to trouble*

¶Sono tomodachi ni wa taihen meiwaku o kakemashita.

その友達にはたいへん迷惑をかけました。

I really troubled that friend.

¶Go-meiwaku o o-kakeshite mōshiwake gozaimasen.

ご迷惑をおかけして申し訳ございません。

I am sorry for troubling you.

méiyo 名誉 *honor, credit, glory*

¶Ishikawa-san no shōshin wa watashi ni totte mo meiyo desu.

石川さんの昇進は私にとっても名誉です。

Ms. Ishikawa's promotion was a credit for me as well.

• meiyo na／no 名誉な／の *honorable, meritorious, glorious*

• A no meiyo o yogosu Aの名誉を汚す *to stain A's honor, to bring dishonor on A*

• meiyo-kyōju 名誉教授 *emeritus professor; honorary professor*

méjā メジャー *tape measure* [→**makijaku** 巻き尺]

mejírushi 目印 *(identification)mark*

¶Gaido-san wa chizu ni mejirushi o tsukemashita.

ガイドさんは地図に目印をつけました。

The guide put a mark on the map.

mékā メーカー *manufacturer, maker*

mekanízumu メカニズム *mechanism*

mekata 目方 *weight*

¶Kono maruta wa hyak-kiro no mekata ga arimasu.

この丸太は100キロの目方があります。

This log weighs 100 kilograms.

¶Kono hamu wa mekata de urimasu.

このハムは目方で売ります。

This ham is sold by weight.

• A no mekata o hakaru Aの目方を計る *to measure the weight of A, to weigh A*

mekki 鍍金 *plating 《i.e., a coating of one metal on another》*

• mekki suru めっきする *to apply as plating*

mekúbase 目配せ 〜**suru** 〜する *to signal with one's eyes; to signal with a wink*

¶Nani-mo iwanai de tomodachi ni mekubase shimashita.

何も言わないで友達に目くばせしました。
I didn't say anything and signaled my friend with my eyes.

mekuru 捲る ① *to turn* 《a page》
¶Emi wa jisho o mekutte tango o shirabe-mashita.
恵美は辞書をめくって単語を調べました。
Emi turned the pages of the dictionary, looking for a word.
② *to roll up* 《sleeves, pant legs, etc.》 [→**makuru** まくる]
③ *to peel off*

mēkyáppu メーキャップ *makeup* 《especially that worn by actors》
• mēkyappu suru メーキャップする *to put on makeup*

memái 眩暈 *dizziness, giddiness*
• memai ga suru 目まいがする *to feel giddy*

mémo メモ *memo, note*
• memo suru メモする *to note down, to make a note of*
¶Sono denwa-bangō o memo shimashita.
その電話番号をメモしました。
I made a note of that telephone number.
• memo-chō メモ帳 *memo pad, scratch pad*
• memo-yōshi メモ用紙 *memo paper, note paper, scratch paper*

memorí 目盛り *division, graduation* 《on a measuring device》
¶Kono monosashi ni wa miri no memori ga arimasu.
この物差しにはミリの目盛りがあります。
This ruler is marked with millimeter divisions.

mémorī メモリー *memory* 《especially in a computer》

mén 面 ① *surface* [→**hyōmen** 表面]
② *facet, side, face* 《of a polyhedron》
• -men ー面《counter for facets; see Appendix 2》
③ *aspect, phase, respect*
④ *page* 《of a newspaper》
• -men ー面《counter for pages; see Appendix 2》

men 面 ① *face* 《of a person or animal》
[→**kao** 顔]
• men to mukatte 面と向かって *face to face*
② *mask, false face* [→**kamen** 仮面]
③ *protective mask, face guard*

mén 綿 *cotton* (*fabric*) [→**momen** 木綿]
• men-ka 綿花 *raw cotton*
• men-shatsu 綿シャツ *cotton shirt*

ménbā メンバー (*group*)*member*

mendō 面倒 *trouble, annoyance, complication* [→**meiwaku** 迷惑]
• A ni mendō o kakeru Aに面倒をかける *to bother A, to put A to trouble*
¶Go-ryōshin ni amari mendō o kakenai de.
ご両親にあまり面倒をかけないで。
Don't put your parents to too much trouble.
• mendō na 面倒な *troublesome, complicated, annoying*
¶Hiroshi wa itsu-mo mendō na shigoto o watashi ni oshitsukeru.
浩はいつも面倒な仕事を私に押しつける。
Hiroshi always forces the troublesome work on to me.
• A no mendō o miru Aの面倒を見る *to look after A, to take care of A*
¶Dare ga akachan no mendō o miru n desu ka.
だれが赤ちゃんの面倒を見るんですか。
Who is looking after the baby?

mendōkusái 面倒臭い 【COL. for **mendō na** 面倒な】 *troublesome, annoying, bothersome*

men'eki 免疫 *immunity*

menkai 面会 *face-to-face meeting, seeing; interview* [→**mensetsu** 面接]
• menkai suru 面会する *to see, to meet; to have an interview*
• A ni／to menkai suru Aに／と面会する *to see A, to meet* (*with*)*A, to have an interview with A*
¶Nyūin-chū no Mori-san ni ashita men-kai shimasu.
入院中の森さんにあした面会します。
I will see Miss Mori, who is in the hospi-

tal tomorrow.
• menkai-jikan 面会時間 *visiting hours*
ménkyo 免許 ① *licensing, official permission*
　② [☞ **menkyo-shō** 免許証 (below)]
• menkyo-shō 免許証 *license, permit*
ménseki 面積 *area, amount of surface*
¶Kono tochi no menseki wa go-hyaku-heihō-mētoru da.
この土地の面積は500平方メートルだ。
The area of this land is 500 square meters.
mensetsu 面接 *interview*
• mensetsu suru 面接する *to interview* 《transitive》
• mensetsu-shiken 面接試験 *oral interview examination*
ménsu メンス *mensuration* [→**gekkei** 月経, **seiri** 生理②]
mensuru 面する{Irreg.} *to face* 《The subject is a stationary object》
• A ni mensuru Aに面する *to face (toward)A*
¶Kono mado wa minami ni menshite imasu.
この窓は南に面しています。
This window faces south.
méntsu メンツ *face, honor*
• mentsu o tamotsu メンツを保つ *to save face*
• mentsu o ushinau メンツを失う *to lose face*
ményū メニュー *menu*
¶Menyū o misete kudasai.
メニューを見せてください。
Please let me see a menu.
menzei 免税 ～**no** ～の *tax-free, tax-exempt, duty-free*
• menzei suru 免税する *to exempt from tax*
• menzei-ten 免税店 *duty-free shop*
méon メロン *melon*
• masuku-meron マスクメロン *muskmelon*
merīgóraundo メリーゴーラウンド *merry-go-round* [→**kaiten**-**mokuba** 回転木馬 (s.v. **kaiten** 回転)]
méritto メリット *merit, strong point* [→

chōsho 長所]
mérodī メロディー *melody* [→**fushi** 節④]
méruhen メルヘン *fairy tale* [→**dōwa** 童話]
meshí 飯 【CRUDE for gohan ご飯】
　① *boiled rice*
　② *meal*
meshiagaru 召し上がる 【HON. for taberu 食べる; nomu 飲む①】 *to eat; to drink*
meshitá 目下 *one's inferior* 《in status》 [⇔**meue** 目上]
mésséji メッセージ *message* 《that someone asks one person to give to another person》
mesú 雌 *a female* (*animal*) [⇔**osu** 雄]
¶Kono neko wa osu desu ka, mesu desu ka.
この猫は雄ですか、雌ですか。
Is this cat male or female?
mésu メス *scalpel*
mētā メーター *meter* 《device》
• denki-mētā 電気のメーター *electric meter*
• takushī-mētā タクシーのメーター *taxi meter*
mētā メーター *meter* 《unit of measure》 [→**mētoru** メートル]
• -mētā -メーター《counter for meters; see Appendix 2》
metoronómu メトロノーム *metronome*
mētoru メートル *meter* 《unit of measure》
• -mētoru -メートル《counter for meters; see Appendix 2》
¶Kono hashi no nagasa wa gojū-mētoru desu.
この橋の長さは50メートルです。
The length of this bridge is 50 meters.
• mētoru-hō メートル法 *the metric system*
• heihō-mētoru 平方メートル *square meter*
• -heihō-mētoru -平方メートル《counter for square meters; see Appendix 2》
• rippō-mētoru 立方メートル *cubic meter*
• -rippō-mētoru -立方メートル《counter for cubic meters; see Appendix 2》

métsuki 目つき *look (on one's face)*

¶Kangofu-san wa yasashii metsuki o shite imasu.

看護婦さんは優しい目つきをしています。

The nurse has a gentle look.

métta-ni 滅多に *seldom, rarely*

《Always occurs in combination with a negative predicate.》

¶Nobue-chan wa metta-ni chikoku shinai yo.

信枝ちゃんはめったに遅刻しないよ。

Nobue is seldom late!

¶Kono ko wa metta-ni nakimasen.

この子はめったに泣きません。

This child rarely cries.

meue 目上 *one's superior* 《in status》[⇔**meshita**]

mezamashíi 目覚ましい *remarkable, wonderful* [→**subarashii** すばらしい]

¶Okada-san no Eigo wa mezamashiku shinpo shita.

岡田さんの英語は目覚ましく進歩した。

Mr. Okada's English improved remarkably.

mezaméru 目覚める *to wake up* 《intransitive》

¶Mai-asa go-ji ni mezamemasu.

毎朝5時に目覚めます。

Every morning I wake up at 5:00.

mezásu 目指す *to make one's goal, to aim at, to set one's mind on*

¶Hanamura-kun wa pairotto o mezashite imasu.

花村君はパイロットを目指しています。

Hanamura is aiming to become a pilot. 《Literally: *Hanamura is aiming at a pilot.*》

mezurashíi 珍しい ① *rare, unusual, uncommon, novel*

¶Musuko wa mezurashii kotori o katte imasu.

息子は珍しい小鳥を飼っています。

My son is keeping an unusual bird.

¶Kinō mezurashii kōkei ni deaimashita.

きのう珍しい光景に出会いました。

Yesterday I came across a novel sight.

mi 身 《This word is used mostly in fixed, often idiomatic expressions.》 ① *one's body, one's person*

• mi o kagameru 身をかがめる *to bend over, to stoop*

• mi mo kokoro mo uchikomu 身も心も打ち込む *to devote oneself body and soul*

• mi ni tsukeru 身につける *to put on, to carry* 《as clothing, equipment, etc.》

② *one's self; one's heart*

• mi o ireru 身を入れる *to put one's heart* 《into something》

¶Motto mi o irete renshū shinasai.

もっと身を入れて練習しなさい。

Put your heart into it more and practice.

• mi ni tsukeru 身につける *to learn well*

③ *position, status*

• mi ni amaru 身に余る *to be more than one deserves*

• A no mi ni naru Aの身になる *to put oneself in a A's position*

¶Watashi no mi ni natte kangaete kudasai.

私の身になって考えてください。

Please put yourself in my position and think about it.

• mi-no-mawari 身の回り *one's person; one's clothing; one's appearance*

• mi-no-mawari no mono 身の回りの物 *one's belongings*

mi 実 ① *fruit; nut; berry*

¶Kono ringo no ki wa mi ga takusan narimasu.

このりんごの木は実がたくさんなります。

This apple tree bears a lot of fruit. 《Literally: *As for this apple tree, a lot of fruit grows.*》

• mi o musubu 実を結ぶ *to come to fruition*

② *substance, real content*

mi- 未- *not yet* 《Added to noun bases denoting actions.》

• mi-bunseki no 未分析の *not-yet-analyzed, unanalyzed*

• mi-kaiketsu no 未解決の *not-yet-solved, unresolved*

miageru 見上げる ① *to look up at* [⇔**miorosu** 見下ろす]

¶Jirō-chan wa sono se no takai hito o

miageta.
次郎ちゃんはその背の高い人を見上げた。
Jiro looked up at that tall man.
② *to look up to, to admire* [⇔**mi-sageru** 見下げる]

miai 見合い *arranged first meeting between prospective marriage partners*
• miai-kekkon 見合い結婚 *marriage resulting from an arranged meeting*

míbun 身分 *status, social standing*
• mibun-shōmei-sho 身分証明書 *identification card*

míburi 身振り *gesture*
¶Kantoku wa miburi de aizu o shimasu.
監督は身ぶりで合図をします。
The director signals with gestures.

michi 道 ① *road, street, path*
¶Kono semai michi o ikeba, kōen ni demasu ka.
この狭い道を行けば、公園に出ますか。
If I go along this narrow road, will I arrive at the park?
¶Kono massugu na michi o ikō.
このまっすぐな道を行こう。
Let's go along this straight road.
¶Michi de Sonoda-san ni atta yo.
道で園田さんに会ったよ。
I met Mr. Sonoda on the street!
¶Mori o nukeru michi o yatto mitsukemashita.
森を抜ける道をやっと見つけました。
We finally found a path that emerged from the woods.
② *way, route, course, path*
¶Dōmo michi o machigaeta rashii.
どうも道をまちがえたらしい。
It looks very much as if I've gone the wrong way.
¶Mottomo anzen na michi o erabimashō.
最も安全な道を選びましょう。
Let's choose the safest way.
¶Yūshō e no michi wa kewashii desu.
優勝への道は険しいです。
The path to the championship is steep.
• michi-bata 道端 *roadside*
• michi-shirube 道しるべ *roadside signpost*

michibíku 導く *to lead, to guide* [→ **shidō suru** 指導する]
¶Senchō wa sono shima ni kyūjo-tai o michibikimashita.
船長はその島に救助隊を導きました。
The captain led the rescue party to that island.

michikusa 道草 *fooling around on the way, wasting time on the way*
• michikusa o kuu 道草を食う *to fool around on the way, to waste time on the way*
¶Michikusa o kuwanai de, uchi ni kaerinasai.
道草を食わないで、うちに帰りなさい。
Go home without fooling around on the way.

michíru 満ちる ① *to become full, to become filled*
¶Fuyu no tozan wa kiken ni michite imasu.
冬の登山は危険に満ちています。
Winter mountain climbing is full of danger.
• tsuki ga michiru 月が満ちる *the moon becomes full, the moon waxes*
¶Tsuki wa michitari kaketari shimasu.
月は満ちたり欠けたりします。
The moon waxes and wanes.
② *to go until full* 《into a container》
• A ni B ga michiru AにBが満ちる *B fills A*
• shio ga michiru 潮が満ちる *the tide comes in, the tide becomes high*

midaréru 乱れる *to become disordered, to become disrupted*
¶Sono kuni wa tōji hijō ni midarete imashita.
その国は当時非常に乱れていました。
That country was very much in disorder at that time.
¶Ressha no jiko de daiya ga midaremashita.
列車の事故でダイヤが乱れました。
The timetable was disrupted because of a train accident.

midashi 見出し *headline; heading;*

caption

• midashi-go 見出し語 (*dictionary*)entry word

midashinami 身だしなみ *attentiveness to one's personal appearance*

¶Itō-sensei wa midashinami ga ii.
伊藤先生は身だしなみがいい。
Mr. Ito pays carefull attention to his personal appearance. «*Literally: As for Mr. Ito, his attentiveness to his personal appearance is good.*»

midásu 乱す *to put into disorder, to disrupt*

¶Chian o midashite wa ikenai yo.
治安を乱してはいけないよ。
You musn't disrupt the public peace!

• retsu o midasu 列を乱す *to break ranks, to get out of line*

mídori 緑 *green* «*as a noun*»

¶Sono midori no hon o tsukatte kudasai.
その緑の本を使ってください。
Please use that green book.

• Midori no hi みどりの日 *Greenery Day* «*a Japanese national holiday on April 29*»

mié 見え *appearances, show, outward display, pose*

• mie o haru 見えを張る *to show off, to be ostentatious*

miéru 見える ① «*What is seen is treated as a grammatical subject and marked with **ga** が rather than with **o** を.*» *to be able to see; to be visible*

¶Chīsa na shima ga miete kimashita.
小さな島が見えてきました。
A small island became visible.

¶Mukō ni shiroi tatemono ga mieru deshō.
向こうに白い建物が見えるでしょう。
You can probably see a white building over there.

¶Watashi-tachi no gakkō kara umi ga miemasu.
私たちの学校から海が見えます。
The ocean is visible from our school.

• me ga mienai 目が見えない *to be unable to see, to be blind*

② *to look, to appear* «*to be*»

¶Onīsan wa toshi yori wakaku miemasu.
お兄さんは年より若く見えます。
Your older brother looks younger than his age.

¶Oda-san wa gaka ni mieru ne.
小田さんは画家に見えるね。
Mr. Oda looks like a painter, doesn't he.

③ 【HON. for **kuru** 来る①】 *to come*

¶O-kyaku-san wa roku-ji ni mieru sō desu.
お客さんは6時に見えるそうです。
I understand the guests will come at 6:00.

migaku 磨く ① *to polish, to shine*

¶Boku wa mai-asa kutsu o migaku yo.
僕は毎朝靴を磨くよ。
I polish my shoes every morning!

• ha o migaku 歯を磨く *to brush one's teeth*

② *to polish, to improve, to cultivate*

• sainō o migaku 才能を磨く *to cultivate one's talent*

• ude o migaku 腕を磨く *to polish one's skill*

migi 右 *the right* «*as opposed to the left*» [⇔**hidari** 左]

¶Tsugi no kōsa-ten o migi ni magatte kudasai.
次の交差点を右に曲がってください。
Please turn right at the next intersection.

¶Kenji no migi ni iru onna no ko o shitte imasu ka.
健二の右にいる女の子を知っていますか。
Do you know the girl on Kenji's right?

• migi-gawa 右側 *right side*

• migi-gawa-tsūkō 右側通行 *right-side traffic* «*Typically used on signs to mean Keep right .*»

• migi-kiki no 右利きの *right-handed*

• migi-te 右手 *right hand*

mígoto 見事 ～**na** ～な *excellent, wonderful, splendid*

¶Sono shiai wa migoto na purē ga ōkatta.
その試合はみごとなプレーが多かった。
A lot of excellent plays were made in that game.

migurushíi 見苦しい ① *ugly, unsightly* [→**minikui** 醜い]; *shabby-looking* [→**misuborashii** みすぼらしい] ② *disgraceful, shameful*

miharashi 見晴らし *view, vista* [→**nagame** 眺め]
¶Kono hoteru kara wa Biwa-ko no miharashi ga yoi.
このホテルからは琵琶湖の見晴らしがよい。
The view of Lake Biwa from this hotel is good.

mihari 見張り ① *keeping watch, being on guard*
• mihari o suru 見張りをする *to keep watch, to be on guard*
¶Gādoman wa toguchi de mihari o shimashita.
ガードマンは戸口で見張りをしました。
The guard kept watch at the door.
② *guard, lookout* ((person))
¶Ie no soto ni mihari ga san-nin imasu.
家の外に見張りが３人います。
There are three guards outside the house.

miharu 見張る ① *to keep watch on, to keep under surveillance*
¶Keikan wa ano josei o mihatte imasu.
警官はあの女性を見張っています。
The policeman is keeping that woman under surveillance.
② me o~ 目を~ *to look wide-eyed*
¶Bōya wa sono mokei-hikōki ni me o mihatta yo.
坊やはその模型飛行機に目を見張ったよ。
The little boy looked wide-eyed at that model plane!

mihon 見本 *sample, specimen, model*
¶Mihon o ikutsu-ka misete kudasai.
見本をいくつか見せてください。
Please show me some samples.
• mihon-ichi 見本市 *trade fair*

mijikái 短い *short* (*in length*) [⇔**nagai** 長い]
¶Yōko-san wa mijikai sukāto o haite iru ne.
洋子さんは短いスカートをはいているね。
Yoko is wearing a short skirt, isn't she.

¶Kotoshi no natsu-yasumi wa mijikai desu ne.
今年の夏休みは短いですね。
This year's summer vacation is short, isn't it.
¶Kono doresu no suso o mijikaku shimashita.
このドレスのすそを短くしました。
I shortened hem of this dress. «Literally: I made the hem of this dress short.»

míjime 惨め ~na ~な *miserable, pitiful, wretched*

mijin 微塵 *small particle, bit*
• mijin-giri みじん切り *cutting into tiny pieces, mincing*
• mijin-giri ni suru みじん切りにする *to cut into tiny pieces, to mince*

mijuku 未熟 ~na ~な ① *unripe, immature*
¶Mijuku na banana wa mazui desu yo.
未熟なバナナはまずいですよ。
An unripe banana is bad-tasting!
② *inexperienced; not fully developed*
¶Uchi no musuko wa mijuku na doraibā desu.
うちの息子は未熟なドライバーです。
My son is an inexperienced driver.
• mijuku-ji 未熟児 *premature baby*

míkan みかん *mandarin orange*
• mikan-batake みかん畑 *mandarin orange orchard*

mikánsei 未完成 ~no ~の *unfinished, incomplete*

mikata 味方 *person on one's side, ally, friend* [⇔**teki** 敵]
¶Shichō wa yowai mono no mikata desu.
市長は弱い者の味方です。
The mayor is a friend of the weak.
• A ni mikata suru Aに味方する *to take A's side, to side with A*
• A no mikata o suru Aの味方をする *to take A's side, to side with A*
¶Haha wa itsu-mo imōto no mikata o shimasu.
母はいつも妹の味方をします。
My mother always takes my younger sister's side.

mikazuki 三日月 *crescent moon*

míki 幹 (*tree*)*trunk*
  ¶Kono ki no miki wa shūi ga san-mētoru desu.
  この木の幹は周囲が 3 メートルです。
  This tree trunk's diameter is three meters.

mikka 三日《See Appendix 2》 ① *three days*
  ② *the third*《day of a month》

míkkusu ミックス ① *mix, mixture*
  ② *mixing*
  • mikkusu suru ミックスする *to mix*《transitive》[→**mazeru** 混ぜる]
  • mikkusu-jūsu ミックスジュース *mixed juice*
  • hottokēki-mikkusu ホットケーキミックス *pancake mix*

mikomi 見込み ① *prospect(s), outlook, future possibility* [→**mitōshi** 見通し①]
  ¶Kaifuku suru mikomi wa hotondo arimasen.
  回復する見込みはほとんどありません。
  There is almost no prospect of recovering.
  ¶Kono shiai ni katsu mikomi wa jūbun arimasu.
  この試合に勝つ見込みは十分あります。
  There is ample prospect of winning this game.
  ② (*future*)*promise*
  ③ *expectation; estimation*
  ¶Kore kara nesagari suru mikomi desu.
  これから値下がりする見込みです。
  The expectation is that it will drop in price after this.

mikoshi 神輿 *portable Shinto shrine*
  《Carried through the streets on the shoulders by a group during a festival.》

mimai 見舞い ① *sympathetic inquiry*
  《about a person who is sick or has suffered a loss》
  ¶O-mimai no o-tegami o dōmo arigatō.
  お見舞いのお手紙をどうもありがとう。
  Thank you for your letter of sympathetic inquiry.
  ② *visit*《to a person who is sick or has suffered a loss》
  • mimai-jō 見舞い状 *letter of sympathetic inquiry*
  • mimai-kyaku 見舞い客 *visitor*

–**miman** －未満 *under*《Added to number bases.》
  ¶Jūhas-sai-miman no hito wa sanka dekimasen.
  18歳未満の人は参加できません。
  People under 18 years old cannot participate.

mimau 見舞う ① *to inquire sympathetically about*《a person who is sick or has suffered a loss》
  ② *to visit*《a person who is sick or has suffered a loss》
  ¶Ashita nyūin-chū no Kuniko-san o mimaimasu.
  あした入院中の邦子さんを見舞います。
  Tomorrow I will visit Kuniko, who is in the hospital.

mimawasu 見回す *to look around at*
  ¶Musume wa fushigi-sō ni atari o mimawashimashita.
  娘は不思議そうに辺りを見回しました。
  My daughter looked around at the vicinity in wonder.

mimei 未明 【FORMAL】 *the predawn*

mimí 耳 *ear*
  ¶Kono inu wa mimi ga ōkii ne.
  この犬は耳が大きいね。
  This dog's ears are big, aren't they.
  • mimi o kasu 耳を貸す *to lend an ear, to listen*《to what someone says》
  ¶Otōto wa watashi no chūkoku ni mimi o kashimasen.
  弟は私の忠告に耳を貸しません。
  My younger brother does not listen to my advice.
  • mimi o katamukeru 耳を傾ける *to listen attentively*
  • mimi ga tōi 耳が遠い *hard of hearing*
  • mimi-aka 耳垢 *earwax*
  • mimi-kaki 耳掻き *earpick, ear cleaner*
  • mimi-tabu 耳朶 *earlobe*

mimizu みみず *earthworm*

miná 皆 [☞**minna** みんな]
- mina-san 皆さん 【HON.】 *everyone, everybody*

minami 南 *the south* [⇔**kita** 北]
¶Kono fuyu wa kazoku de minami no shima ni ikimasu.
この冬は家族で南の島に行きます。
We are going to a southern island as a family this winter.
- Minami-hankyū 南半球 *the Southern Hemisphere*
- Minami-jūji-sei 南十字星 *the Southern Cross*
- minami-kaze 南風 *south wind*

minamoto 源 ① *source* 《of a river, etc.》 ② *source, origin* [→**kigen** 起源]

minaosu 見直す ① *to look at again, to reexamine*
¶Gakusei wa tōan o yoku minaoshimashita.
学生は答案をよく見直しました。
The student carefully reexamined the test paper.
② *to reevaluate and form a better opinion of*

minarau 見習う *to look at and follow as an example*
- A o/ni minarau Aを／に見習う *to follow A as an example*
¶Sensei o minaratte ji o kirei ni kakinasai.
先生を見習って字をきれいに書きなさい。
Follow your teacher's example and write neatly.

minareru 見慣れる *to become used to seeing, to become familiar with (from seeing frequently)*
¶Fuji-san wa shashin de minarete imasu.
富士山は写真で見慣れています。
I am familiar with Mt. Fuji from pictures.

mínari 身なり *attire, dress* [→**kakkō** 格好②]
¶Ano ko wa misuborashii minari o shite iru.
あの子はみすぼらしい身なりをしている。
That child is wearing shabby attire.

minashígo みなしご *orphan* [→**koji** 孤児]

minasu 見なす *to regard ⟨as⟩, to consider ⟨to be⟩*
¶Sore wa hansoku to minashimasu.
それは反則と見なします。
I consider that a foul.

minato 港 *harbor; port*
¶Fune ga minato o dete ikimashita.
船が港を出ていきました。
The boat went out of the port.
- minato-machi 港町 *port town*

mingeihin 民芸品 *folk-art object*

minichua ミニチュア ① *miniature version* 《of something that is typically larger》 ② *miniature scale model*

miniká ミニカー *sub-compact car*

minikúi 醜い *ugly* [⇔**utsukushii** 美しい]

minisukáto ミニスカート *miniskirt*

minkan 民間 *non-governmental circles, civilian society*
- minkan no 民間の *non-governmental, private, civilian*
- minkan-hōsō 民間放送 *commercial broadcasting*

mínku ミンク *mink*

minná みんな *all, each and every one; everyone involved*
¶Jūgyōin wa minna kōfuku-sō desu.
従業員はみんな幸福そうです。
The employees all look happy.
¶Minna ga sono nyūsu o shitte imasu.
みんながそのニュースを知っています。
Everyone knows that news.
¶Koko ni aru mono wa minna watashitachi no mono desu.
ここにある物はみんな私たちの物です。
The things that are here are all our things.
- minna de みんなで *all together, in all; all together, as a group*
¶Seito wa minna de nan-nin imasu ka.
生徒はみんなで何人いますか。
How many students are there in all?
¶Minna de utaimashō.

みんなで歌いましょう。
Let's sing all together.

minogasu 見逃がす ① *to fail to see, to miss, to overlook* [→**miotosu** 見落とす]
¶Yūbe dai-suki na terebi-bangumi o minogashita.
ゆうべ大好きなテレビ番組を見逃がした。
Last night I missed a TV program I really like.

② *to overlook, to disregard, to let go* [→**ōme ni miru** 大目に見る]
¶Kondo dake wa kono ayamari o minogashimasu.
今度だけはこの誤りを見逃がします。
I will overlook this mistake just this once.

minóru 実る ① *to bear fruit*
¶Kono ringo no ki wa maitoshi yoku minoru ne.
このりんごの木は毎年よく実るね。
This apple tree bears a lot of fruit every year, doesn't it.
¶Sono doryoku wa itsu-ka kitto minoru darō.
その努力はいつかきっと実るだろう。
Those efforts will surely bear fruit someday.

② 《The subject is a fruit, nut, etc., that appears on a tree or plant.》*to grow, to be produced* [→**naru** 実る]; *to become ripe* [→**jukusuru** 熟する]
¶Meron wa mō minotta yo.
メロンはもう実ったよ。
The melons have already ripened!

minshū 民衆 *the people, the masses*

minshushúgi 民主主義 *democracy*

minshuteki 民主的 ～**na** ～な *democratic*

minwa 民話 *folktale*

min'yō 民謡 (*traditional*)*folk song*

mínzoku 民族 *a people, ethnic group*
¶Ajia ni wa takusan no minzoku ga imasu.
アジアにはたくさんの民族がいます。
There are many peoples in Asia.
• minzoku-ishō 民族衣装 *native costume*

miokuru 見送る ① *to see off* [⇔**mu-kaeru** 迎える①]
¶Gakusei-tachi wa Sumisu-sensei o kūkō de miokutta.
学生たちはスミス先生を空港で見送った。
The students saw Dr. Smith off at the airport.

② *to let go by, to pass up*
¶Musuko wa ryūgaku o miokuru koto ni shimashita.
息子は留学を見送ることにしました。
My son decided to pass up studying abroad.

miorosu 見下ろす *to look down at* [⇔**miageru** 見上げる①]
¶Tō no chōjō kara machi o mioroshite imasu.
塔の頂上から町を見下ろしています。
We are looking down at the town from the top of the tower.

miotosu 見落とす *to overlook, to fail to see* [→**minogasu** 見逃す①]

míra ミイラ *mummy*

mírā ミラー *mirror* [→**kagami** 鏡]
• bakku-mirā バックミラー *rearview mirror*

mírai 未来 *the future* [→**shōrai** 将来①]
¶Mirai no jidōsha ni kyōmi ga arimasu.
未来の自動車に興味があります。
I am interested in cars of the future.
¶Kono kuni ni wa subarashii mirai ga arimasu.
この国にはすばらしい未来があります。
This country has a wonderful future.

míri ミリ [☞**mirimētoru** ミリメートル; **miriríttoru** ミリリットル]

mirimétoru ミリメートル *millimeter*
• -mirimētoru －ミリメートル《counter for millimeters; see Appendix 2》

mirin 味醂 *sweet sake used as a seasoning*

miriríttoru ミリリットル *milliliter*
• -miriríttoru －ミリリットル《counter for milliliters; see Appendix 2》

míru 見る ① *to look at, to watch*
¶Sā, kono suraido o mimashō.
さあ、このスライドを見ましょう。
All right now, let's look at these slides.
¶Watashi-tachi wa terebi de tenisu no

shiai o mimasu.

私たちはテレビでテニスの試合を見ます。

We watch a tennis match on TV.

② *to see*

¶Sonna ni ōki na mizuumi wa mita koto ga nai yo.

そんなに大きな湖は見たことがないよ。

I've never seen such a big lake!

¶Hannin ga hashi o wataru no o mimashita.

犯人が橋を渡るのを見ました。

I saw the culprit cross the bridge.

¶Ōtsubo-san ga pūru de oyoide iru no o mita.

大坪さんがプールで泳いでいるのを見た。

I saw Mr. Otsubo swimming in the pool.

③ *to do and see, to try doing* 《following the gerund (-**te** form) of another verb》

¶Sono sōda o nonde mite kudasai.

そのソーダを飲んでみてください。

Please try that soda.

míruku ミルク *milk* [→**gyūnyū** 牛乳]

• miruku-sēki ミルクセーキ *milk shake*

• kona-miruku 粉ミルク *powdered milk, dried milk*

miryoku 魅力 *charm, appeal*

¶Aono hohoemi wa Keiko no miryoku no hitotsu desu.

あのほほえみは桂子の魅力の一つです。

That smile is one of the Keiko's charms.

• miryoku-teki na 魅力的な *charming, attractive, appealing*

¶Onēsan wa totemo miryoku-teki desu ne.

お姉さんはとても魅力的ですね。

Your older sister is very attractive, isn't she.

mísa ミサ (*Catholic*) *mass*

• misa ni sanretsu suru ミサに参列する *to attend mass*

misageru 見下げる *to look down on, to regard with disdain* [⇔**miageru** 見上げる②]

misáiru ミサイル *missile*

¶Teki ga misairu o hassha suru osore mo arimasu.

敵がミサイルを発射する恐れもあります。

There is also a fear that the enemy will launch missiles.

misaki 岬 *cape, promontory*

misé 店 *store, shop*

《This word refers to restaurants, bars, etc., as well as to stores.》

¶Pan o kai ni mise ni ikimashita.

パンを買いに店に行きました。

I went to the store to buy some bread.

¶Ano mise de wa gyūnyū o utte imasu ka.

あの店では牛乳を売っていますか。

Do they sell milk at that store?

¶Sono mise wa hachi-ji ni akimasu.

その店は8時に開きます。

That store opens at 8:00.

miséinen 未成年 ① ～**no** ～の *under the legal age of adulthood, minor*
② [☞**miseinen-sha** 未成年者 (below)]

• miseinen-sha 未成年者 *a minor*

¶Miseinen-sha wa sake o kaemasen.

未成年者は酒を買えません。

Minors cannot buy liquor.

miséru 見せる *to show, to allow to see*

¶Shashō ni kippu o misemashita.

車掌に切符を見せました。

I showed my ticket to the conductor.

¶Kitte-arubamu o misete kuremasen ka.

切手アルバムを見せてくれませんか。

Won't you show me your stamp album?

¶Kore wa kirai desu. Hoka no o misete kudasai.

これは嫌いです。ほかのを見せてください。

I don't like this. Please show me another one.

míshin ミシン *sewing machine*

¶Mishin de nani o nutte iru n desu ka.

ミシンで何を縫っているんですか。

What are you sewing on the sewing machine?

míso 味噌 *miso* 《A traditional Japanese seasoning, miso is a paste of fermented soybeans or rice bran.》

• miso-shiru 味噌汁 *miso soup*

missetsu 密接 ～**na** ～な *close, intimate* 《describing a relationship》

• missetsu na kankei 密接な関係 *close relationship, intimate connection*

misshonsukūru ミッションスクール *missionary school*

mísu ミス *mistake* [→**machigai** まちがい]

misuborashíi みすぼらしい *shabby-looking, wretched-looking*

misui 未遂 〜の *unsuccessfully attempted* 《describing a crime, etc.》
• misui ni owaru 未遂に終わる *to end unsuccessfully, to end abortively*
• ansatsu-misui 暗殺未遂 *attempted assassination*
• jisatsu-misui 自殺未遂 *attempted suicide*

mísuterī ミステリー ① *mystery, something unexplained* [→**shinpi** 神秘]
② *mystery story* [→**suiri-shōsetsu** 推理小説 (s.v. **suiri** 推理)]

misuteru 見捨てる *to desert, to abandon, to forsake*
¶Ano hito ga yūjin o misuteru hazu wa nai.
あの人が友人を見捨てるはずはない。
There is no reason to think she would desert her friends.

mítai みたい 【COL.】 〜**na** 〜な *to be like, to appear to be, to looks as if* 《This word follows a predicate and functions grammatically as an adjectival noun. The word preceding **mitai** cannot be the copula form **da** だ. Where **da** would be the appropriate predicate, **mitai** follows a noun or adjectival noun directly.》
¶Uehara-kun wa kuruma no unten ga dekinai mitai da ne.
上原君は車の運転ができないみたいだね。
It looks as if Uehara can't drive, doesn't it.
¶Heya ni wa robotto mitai na mono ga atta.
部屋にはロボットみたいな物があった。
In the room there was a thing like a robot.
¶Yamada-sensei wa haha-oya mitai ni watashi ni hanashimasu.

山田先生は母親みたいに私に話します。
Ms. Yamada speaks to me like a mother.

mitásu 満たす ① *to fill* 《a container with something》
• A o B de mitasu AをBで満たす *to fill A with B*
¶Sono baketsu o mizu de mitashite kudasai.
そのバケツを水で満たしてください。
Please fill that bucket with water.
② *to put until full* 《into a container》
• A ni B o mitasu AにBを満たす *to put B into A until A is full, to fill A with B*
¶Yokusō ni mizu o mitashimashita.
浴槽に水を満たしました。
I filled the bathtub with cold water.
③ *to satisfy* 《a need or desire》
¶Ip-pai no kōra ga nodo no kawaki o mitashita.
1杯のコーラがのどの渇きを満たした。
One glass of cola satisfied my thirst.

mitei 未定 〜**no** 〜の *not yet decided, not yet settled*
¶Nichiji wa mitei desu.
日時は未定です。
The date and time are not fixed yet.
¶Keikaku wa mada mitei desu ne.
計画はまだ未定ですね。
The plan is not yet settled, is it.

mītingu ミーティング *meeting* [→**kaigō** 会合]

mitomeru 認める ① *to admit, to acknowledge*
¶Sono hanashi wa hontō da to mitomemasu.
その話はほんとうだと認めます。
I admit that that story is true.
② *to recognize* 〈as〉, *to regard* 〈as〉 [→**minasu** 見なす]
¶Kōichi wa ichiryū-pianisuto to shite mitomerareta.
光一は一流ピアニストとして認められた。
Koichi has been recognized as a first-rate pianist.
③ *to allow, to approve* [→**yurusu** 許す①]

④ *to detect, to find, to notice*
¶Isha wa kensa de ijō o mitomemashita.
医者は検査で異常を認めました。
The doctor detected an abnormality in the examination.

mitōshi 見通し ① *prospect(s), outlook, future possibility*
• mitōshi ga akarui 見通しが明るい *the prospects are bright*
② *insight, penetration, vision*
③ *visibility, unobstructed view*
• mitōshi ga kiku 見通しがきく *visibility is good, there is an unobstructed view*

mítsu 蜜 ① *honey* [→**hachi–mitsu** 蜂蜜 (s.v. **hachi** 蜂)]
② *(flower)nectar*

mitsúbachi 蜜蜂 *honeybee*

mítsudo 密度 *density*
• jinkō–mitsudo 人口密度 *population density*

mitsugo 三つ子 *triplets*

mitsukaru 見つかる *to be found, to turn up*
¶Kagi wa mitsukarimashita ka.
かぎは見つかりましたか。
Did the key turn up?

mitsukeru 見つける ① *to find, to locate, to discover*
¶Musuko ga watashi no yubiwa o mitsukete kuremashita.
息子が私の指輪を見つけてくれました。
My son found my ring for me.
¶Hon'yaku–sha wa Eigo no ayamari o mitsukemashita.
翻訳者は英語の誤りを見つけました。
The translator found a mistake in the English.
② *to become used to seeing* [→**mina-reru** 見慣れる]

mitsumeru 見つめる *to stare at*
¶Akira wa Shinobu no me o jitto mitsumeta.
明は忍の目をじっと見つめた。
Akira stared into Shinobu's eyes.
¶Watashi-tach wa hi–no–de o mitsumete imashita.
私たちは日の出を見つめていました。

We were gazing at the sunrise.
• jitto mitsumeru じっと見つめる *to stare steadily at*

mitsuyúnyū 密輸入 *smuggling in*
• mitsuyunyū suru 密輸入する *to smuggle in*

mitsuyúshutsu 密輸出 *smuggling out*
• mitsuyushutsu suru 密輸出する *to smuggle out*

mítto ミット *(baseball)mitt* «of the type used by a catcher or first baseman»
• kyatchā–mitto キャッチャーミット *catcher's mitt*

mittomonái みっともない 【COL. for **migurushii** 見苦しい】 ① *shameful, disgraceful*
② *unsightly; shabby–looking*

mittsú 三つ *three* «see Appendix 2»

miushinau 見失う *to lose sight of*
¶Hitogomi de sono otoko no hito o miushinaimashita.
人込みでその男の人を見失いました。
I lost sight of that man in the crowd.

miwakeru 見分ける *to tell apart, to distinguish (by looking)*
• A to B o miwakeru AとBを見分ける *to tell A and B apart, to distinguish A and B*
¶Taka to washi o miwakeraremasu ka.
たかとわしを見分けられますか。
Can you distinguish a hawk and an eagle?

miwatasu 見渡す *to look out over, to survey*
¶Hoteru kara mizuumi o miwatashima-shita.
ホテルから湖を見渡しました。
I looked out over the lake from the hotel.

miyage 土産 *souvenir; present* «brought back from a trip»
¶Chichi wa o–miyage o takusan motte kaetta yo.
父はお土産をたくさん持って帰ったよ。
My father brought home a lot of souve-nirs!
¶Araki-san ni Kyōto no o–miyage ga arimasu.

荒木さんに京都のお土産があります。
I have a souvenir from Kyoto for Mr. Araki.
- miyage-banashi 土産話 *story one tells about one's trip*
- miyage-mono-ten 土産物店 *souvenir shop*

mizo 溝 ① *ditch; gutter*
  ② *groove*
  ③ *gap, gulf* «in mutual understanding»

mizore 霙 *sleet*
- mizore ga furu みぞれが降る *sleet falls, it sleets*

mizu 水 ① *water*
  ¶Mizu o san-bai motte kite kudasai.
  水を3杯持ってきてください。
  Please bring three glasses of water.
  ¶Ani wa ima shibafu ni mizu o maite imasu.
  兄は今芝生に水をまいています。
  My older brother is watering the lawn now.
- mizu o dasu〔tomeru〕水を出す〔止める〕*to turn on*〔*off*〕*the water*
  ② *cold water* «in contrast to hot water»〔⇔**yu** 湯〕
- mizu-deppō 水鉄砲 *water pistol, squirt gun*
- mizu-ppoi 水っぽい *watery*
- mizu-shōbai 水商売 *the bar and entertainment business*

mizubōsō 水疱瘡 *chicken pox*

mizubúkure 水膨れ *blister* «on the skin»

mizugi 水着 *swimsuit; swimming trunks*〔→**suiei**-**pantsu** 水泳パンツ（s.v. **suiei** 水泳）〕

mizuhiki 水引き «This word refers to a kind of string made of stiff paper, which is tied in a bow around the wrapping on a formal gift. The **mizuhiki** for happy occasions is red for half its length and white for the other half. That for sad occasions is black or blue for half its length and white for the other half.»

mizuiro 水色 *light blue* «as a noun»

mizumushi 水虫 *athlete's foot*

mizutamari 水溜まり *puddle* (*of water*)

mizuúmi 湖 *lake*
  ¶Boku-tachi wa mizuumi de bōto o koide imashita.
  僕たちは湖でボートをこいでいました。
  We were rowing a boat on the lake.
  ¶Kodomo-tachi wa mizuumi de oyoide imasu.
  子供たちは湖で泳いでいます。
  The children are swimming in the lake.

mo も ① «noun-following particle» *too, also; either* «in combination with a negative predicate»
  ¶Yakyū mo suki desu.
  野球も好きです。
  I like baseball, too.
  ¶Anata ga ikanai nara, watashi mo ikanai yo.
  あなたが行かないなら、私も行かないよ。
  If you're not going, then I won't either!
  ¶Gaikoku kara mo tegami ga kimashita.
  外国からも手紙が来ました。
  Letters also came from foreign countries.
- A mo B mo ＡもＢも *both A and B; either A or B* «in combination with a negative predicate»
  ¶Ken-san mo Yōko-san mo Eigo ga hanasemasu.
  健さんも洋子さんも英語が話せます。
  Both Ken and Yoko can speak English.
  ¶Boku wa niku mo sakana mo tabemasen.
  僕は肉も魚も食べません。
  I don't eat either meat or fish.
  ② «noun-following particle» *even*〔→**sae** さえ①〕
  ¶Seito-tachi wa hōkago mo kyōshitsu de benkyō shite iru.
  生徒たちは放課後も教室で勉強している。
  The students are studying in the classroom even after school.
  ③ «Following a number, **mo** indicates that the speaker considers that number inordinately large.»
  ¶Tomodachi wa manga-bon o jus-satsu mo katta yo.
  友達は漫画本を10冊も買ったよ。

My friend bought TEN comic books!

④ 《in combination with the gerund (-**te** form)of a predicate》 *even if, even though*

¶Ame ga futte mo ikimashō.

雨が降っても行きましょう。

Let's go even if it rains.

¶Yasukute mo kawanai hō ga ii deshō.

安くても買わないほうがいいでしょう。

Even if it's inexpensive, it would probably be better not to buy it.

mō もう ① *already* [→**sude-ni** 既に①]

¶Mō shukudai wa owatta yo.

もう宿題は終わったよ。

I've already finished my homework!

¶Okāsan wa mō dekaketa no?

お母さんはもう出かけたの？

Has Mother already gone out?

¶Mō satō o tsukai kitte shimaimashita.

もう砂糖を使いきってしまいました。

I've already used up all the sugar.

② *any more, any longer* 《in combination with a negative predicate》 [→**sude-ni** 既に②]

¶Tenisu wa mō dekimasen.

テニスはもうできません。

I cannot play tennis any more.

③ *any time now, soon* [→**ma-mo-naku** 間も無く]

¶Chichi wa mō kaette kuru deshō.

父はもう帰ってくるでしょう。

My father will probably come home soon.

mō もう *another, an additional* 《Always precedes a word referring to a relatively small quantity.》

¶Mō ichi-do Nara e iki-tai desu.

もう一度奈良へ行きたいです。

I want to go to Nara one more time.

¶Gyūnyū o mō ip-pai kudasai.

牛乳をもう１杯ください。

Please give me one more glass of milk.

¶Mō sukoshi nomimasen ka.

もう少し飲みませんか。

Won't you drink a little more?

mochi 餅 *rice cake* 《Traditionally made by pounding cooked rice in a mortar.》

• mochi o tsuku もちをつく *to make rice cakes (by pounding)*

• mochi-tsuki 餅搗き *rice-cake making*

mochiageru 持ち上げる ① *to lift, to raise*

¶Sono hako o mochiagete kudasai.

その箱を持ち上げてください。

Please lift that box.

② *to flatter*

mochiawase 持ち合わせ *something on one, something on hand*

• A no mochiawase ga aru Aの持ち合わせがある *to have A one one, to have A with one, to have A on hand*

mochiawaseru 持ち合わせる *to come to have on one, to come to have with one, to come to have on hand*

mochidasu 持ち出す ① *to take out, to carry outside*

¶Jūyō shorui o mochidasu no wa yamete kudasai.

重要書類を持ち出すのはやめてください。

Refrain from taking out important documents.

② *to bring up, to propose, to offer*

mochihakobu 持ち運ぶ *to carry, to convey, to transport* [→**hakobu** 運ぶ]

mochinushi 持ち主 *owner* [→**shoyū-sha** 所有者 (s.v. **shoyū** 所有)]

¶Kono mise no mochinushi wa dare desu ka.

この店の持ち主はだれですか。

Who is the owner of this shop?

mochiron 勿論 *of course, certainly*

¶"Watashi to issho ni itte kureru?" "Mochiron, iku yo."

「私といっしょに行ってくれる？」「もちろん、行くよ」

"Will you go with me?" "Certainly, I'll go!"

¶Mochiron mi-tai keredo, kyō wa muri da.

もちろん見たいけれど、きょうは無理だ。

Of course I'd like to see it, but today it's impossible.

mochīru 用いる ① *to use* [→**tsukau** 使う]

② *to adopt, to accept* [→**saiyō suru**

採用する①]
③ *to hire, to employ* [→**yatou** 雇う]

mốchō 盲腸 (*veriform*)*appendix*
• mōchō-en 盲腸炎 *appendicitis*

modan モダン 〜**na** 〜な *modern,
up-to-date* [→**gendai-teki na** 現代的な
(s.v. **gendai** 現代)]
• modan-dansu モダンダンス *modern
dance*

móderu モデル ① *model, type* [→**kata**
型①]
② *model* (*of the real thing*) [→**mokei**
模型]
③ *model, sample, prototype* [→**mohan**
模範]
④ (*artist's*)*model*
⑤ (*fashion*)*model* [→**fasshon-moderu**
ファッションモデル (s.v. **fasshon**
ファッション)]
• moderu-chenji モデルチェンジ *model
change*
• moderu-gan モデルガン *model gun*
• moderu-kā モデルカー *model car*

mốdo モード ① *fashion* (*in clothing*)
¶Kore ga Pari no saishin no mōdo desu.
これがパリの最新のモードです。
This is the latest fashion in Paris.
② *mode, style, form* [→**yōshiki** 様式]

modóru 戻る *to return* 《*intransitive*》
¶Chotto matte ne. Sugu modotte kuru
yo.
ちょっと待ってね。すぐ戻ってくるよ。
*Wait a little while, OK? I'll come back
right away!*
¶Jibun no seki e modorinasai.
自分の席へ戻りなさい。
Return to your own seat.

modósu 戻す *to return, to put back, to
give back* [→**kaesu** 返す]
¶Kagi o modosu no o wasurenai de kudasai.
かぎを戻すのを忘れないでください。
Please don't forget to return the key.
¶Sono jisho o tsukue no ue ni modoshi-
nasai.
その辞書を机の上に戻しなさい。
Put the dictionary back on the desk.

moeru 燃える *to catch fire; to burn*
¶Eki-mae no sūpā ga moete imasu yo.
駅前のスーパーが燃えていますよ。
*The supermarket in front of the station
is on fire!*

mốfu 毛布 *blanket*

mogáku もがく *to struggle, to writhe,
to wriggle*
¶Taiho sareta hannin wa mada mogaite
imasu.
逮捕された犯人はまだもがいています。
The arrested criminal is still struggling.

mogishikén 模擬試験 *practice examination*

mogura もぐら *mole* 《*animal*》

mogúru 潜る ① *to dive* 《*starting in the
water*》
¶Yamanaka-san wa pūru no soko ni
mogurimashita.
山中さんはプールの底にもぐりました。
*Ms. Yamanaka dived to the bottom of
the pool.*
② *to burrow, to slip* 《*inside or under
something*》
¶Jishin no toki wa beddo no shita ni
mogurinasai.
地震のときはベッドの下にもぐりなさい。
*When there's an earthquake burrow
under your bed.*

mohan 模範 *example, model, pattern*
[→**tehon** 手本]
¶Imōto-san-tachi no mohan ni nari-
nasai.
妹さんたちの模範になりなさい。
Be an example to your younger sisters.
《*Literally: Become your younger sisters'
example.*》

móhaya 最早 [[→**sude-ni** 既に]]
① *already*
② 〈*no*〉 *longer,* 〈*not*〉 *any more* 《*in
combination with a negative predicate*》
¶Uchū-ryokō wa mohaya yume de wa
arimasen.
宇宙旅行はもはや夢ではありません。
Space travel is no longer a dream.

mój i 文字 *letter, character* 《*in a writing
system*》

- moji-hōsō 文字放送 *teletext*
- ko-moji 小文字 *small letter, lower-case letter*
- ō-moji 大文字 *capital letter, upper-case letter*

mōjū 猛獣 *fierce animal*

mōkáru 儲かる ① *to make money, to make a profit* 《when the subject is a person》
¶Taguchi-san wa kabu de mōkarimashita.
田口さんは株でもうかりました。
Mr. Taguchi made money in stocks.
② *to be lucrative, to make a profit, to pay* 《when the subject is an activity》
¶Kono pāto wa mōkaranai ne.
このパートはもうからないね。
This part-time job doesn't pay, does it.
¶Chichi no shōbai wa totemo mōkatte imasu.
父の商売はとてももうかっています。
My father's business is really making a profit.

mōké 儲け (*monetary*)*profit*
¶Nōgyō wa mōke ga sukunai sō desu.
農業は儲けが少ないそうです。
In agriculture the profits are small.
- ō-mōke 大儲け *big profit*

mokei 模型 *model* (*of the real thing*)
- mokei-hikōki 模型飛行機 *model plane*

mōkéru 設ける ① *to provide; to prepare* [→**yōi suru** 用意する]
¶Kono daigaku ni taiiku-kan o mōkeru koto ni natta.
この大学に体育館を設けることになった。
It's been decided to provide a gym for this college.
② *to establish, to set up*
¶Shichō wa atarashii gakkō o mōkemashita.
市長は新しい学校を設けました。
The mayor established a new school.
- kisoku o mōkeru 規則を設ける *to establish a rule*

mōkéru 儲ける (**kane o**〜 金を〜) *to make money, to make a profit* 《The subject must be a person.》 [→**mōkaru**

儲かる①]

mokkin 木琴 *xylophone*

mokugeki 目撃 〜**suru** 〜する *to witness*
¶Hokō-sha ga sono jiko o mokugeki shimashita.
歩行者がその事故を目撃しました。
A pedestrian witnessed that accident.
- mokugeki-sha 目撃者 (*eye-*)*witness*

mokuhyō 目標 ① *aim, goal, purpose* [→**mokuteki** 目的]
- mokuhyō o toppa suru 目標を突破する *to surpass a goal*
② *landmark; guide; sign* [→**mejirushi** 目印]
③ *target* [→**mato** 的]

mokuji 目次 *table of contents*
¶Mazu mokuji o mite kudasai.
まず目次を見てください。
Please look at the table of contents first.

mokuroku 目録 *list, catalog*

Mokusei 木星 (*the planet*)*Jupiter*

mokuteki 目的 *purpose, aim, goal*
¶Jitsugyō-ka wa tsui-ni mokuteki o hatashimashita.
実業家はついに目的を果たしました。
The businessman finally achieved his aim.
- mokuteki-chi 目的地 *destination*
- mokuteki-go 目的語 *object* 《in grammar》

Mokuyō 木曜 [☞**Mokuyōbi** 木曜日]
Mokuyōbi 木曜日 *Thursday*

mokuzai 木材 ＜*US*＞*lumber*, ＜*UK*＞*timber* [→**zaimoku** 材木]

mokuzō 木造 〜**no** 〜の *made-of-wood, wooden*
- mokuzō no ie 木造の家 *wooden house*

momen 木綿 *cotton* (*fabric*) [→**men** 綿]
- momen-ito 木綿糸 *cotton thread*

mómiji 紅葉 ① *autumn leaves* [→**kōyō** 紅葉]
② *maple* [→**kaede** 楓]

momo 桃 *peach*

mómo 股 *thigh*

momu 揉む ① *to rub between one's*

hands

② *to knead; to massage* [→**massāji suru** マッサージする]

¶Kata o monde kureru?

肩をもんでくれる？

Will you massage my shoulders?

③ *to debate thoroughly*

④ **ki o〜** 気を〜 *to get worried, to get anxious* [→**shinpai suru** 心配する]

¶Shiken no koto de ki o monde imasu.

試験のことで気をもんでいます。

I'm worried about the exams.

món 門 *gate; gateway*

• kō-mon 校門 *school gate*

món 紋 *family crest, family insignia*

Monbúshō 文部省 *the Ministry of Education*

mondai 問題 ① *question* 《on a test, etc.》, *problem* 《in arithmetic, etc.》

¶Kono mondai wa tokeru deshō.

この問題は解けるでしょう？

You can solve this problem, right?

¶Mori-sensei wa muzukashii mondai o dashimasu.

森先生は難しい問題を出します。

Dr. Mori sets difficult questions.

② *problem, difficult matter, issue*

¶Shitsugyō mo saikin mondai ni natte kimashita.

失業も最近問題になってきました。

Unemployment, too, has recently become a problem.

③ *matter, question, topic*

¶Sore wa jikan no mondai desu.

それは時間の問題です。

That's a matter of time.

• mondai-ji 問題児 *problem child*

• mondai-shū 問題集 *collection of (sample examination)questions*

mónku 文句 ① *(connected)words, phrase, expression*

¶Eigo no uta no monku ga kikitore-masen.

英語の歌の文句が聞き取れません。

I can't catch the words of English songs.

② *complaint*

• monku o iu 文句を言う *to complain*

¶Kozukai no koto de monku o itte wa ikenai.

小遣いのことで文句を言ってはいけない。

You mustn't complain about your allowance.

monmō 文盲 ① *illiteracy*

② *an illiterate*

monó 物 *thing, object*

¶Tejina-shi wa fukuro kara takusan no mono o dashita.

手品師は袋からたくさんの物を出した。

The magician took many things out of the bag.

¶Betsu no mono o misete kudasai.

別の物を見せてください。

Please show me a different one.

¶Donna mono demo ii desu.

どんな物でもいいです。

Any kind of thing is all right.

¶Kore wa watashi no mono desu.

これは私の物です。

This is mine.

monó 者 ① 【HUM. for **hito** 人】 *person*

¶Itaria-go no hanaseru mono mo orimasu.

イタリア語の話せる者もおります。

There is also someone who can speak Italian.

② 【FORMAL for **hito** 人】 *person* 《Always preceded by a modifier of some kind and not used to refer to a specific, known individual.》

¶Shin-daitōryō wa yowai mono no mikata desu.

新大統領は弱い者の味方です。

The new president is a friend of the weak.

monogátari 物語 *tale, story, narrative*

• "Heike-monogatari" 『平家物語』 *"The Tale of the Heike"*

• "Isoppu-monogatari" 『イソップ物語』 *"Aesop's Fables"*

monógoto 物事 *things, everything*

¶Samazama na kakudo kara monogoto o kentō shinasai.

さまざまな角度から物事を検討しなさい。

Examine things from different angles.

monomane 物真似 *mimicking, doing an impression* «*of people or animals*»
¶Ano terebi–tarento wa monomane ga umai ne.
あのテレビタレントは物まねがうまいね。
That TV star is good at doing impressions, isn't she.

• A no monomane o suru Aの物まねをする *to mimic A, to do an impression of A*

monooki 物置 *closet, storeroom; storage shed*

monorēru モノレール *monorail*

monosáshi 物差し *ruler* ((*measuring device*))
¶Monosashi de sen no nagasa o hakarinasai.
物差しで線の長さを計りなさい。
Measure the line with a ruler.

monosugói 物凄い *amazing, tremendous, astounding, startling* [→**sugoi** 凄い]
¶Monosugoi kōkei datta yo.
ものすごい光景だったよ。
It was an amazing sight.

monotarinai 物足りない *unsatisfactory, not good enough*

monózuki 物好き ① *overly strong curiosity; eccentric interest*
• monozuki na 物好きな *overly curious; interested in eccentric things*
② *overly curious person; person with eccentric interests*

monshō 紋章 *family crest, family insignia* [→**mon** 紋]

monsūn モンスーン *monsoon*
• monsūn–kikō モンスーン気候 *monsoon climate*

montáju モンタージュ *montage*

moppara 専ら«*describing the degree of involvement in an activity*» *mainly, chiefly; exclusively, enitrely, wholeheartedly*

móppu モップ *mop*
• A ni moppu o kakeru Aにモップをかける *to mop A*

móraru モラル *morals, sense of morali-*

ty [→**dōtoku** 道徳]
¶Ano seiji–ka wa moraru ni kakete iru.
あの政治家はモラルに欠けている。
That politician lacks a sense of morality.

morásu 漏らす *to let leak, to let out*
¶Dare ga himitsu o morashita no kashira.
だれが秘密を漏らしたのかしら。
I wonder who let the secret out.

morau 貰う«*In either use of this word the giver cannot be the speaker, the speaker's group,or a person or group with whom the speaker is identifying.*» ① *to receive, to get*
• A kara/ni B o morau Aから/にBをもらう *to receive B from A*
¶Reiko–san kara tegami o moratta yo.
玲子さんから手紙をもらったよ。
I received a letter from Reiko!
¶Ani wa shōgakukin o moratte imasu.
兄は奨学金をもらっています。
My older brother is receiving a scholarship.
② *to receive the favor of* «*following the gerund (-te form)of another verb*»
¶Itoko ni shashin o totte moraimashita.
いとこに写真を撮ってもらいました。
My cousin took a photograph for me.
«*Literally: I received the favor of taking a photograph from my cousin.*»

morēru 漏れる *to leak out, to escape*
¶Gasu ga morete iru yo.
ガスが漏れているよ。
The gas is leaking!

mōretsu 猛烈 ～**na** ～な *intense, severe, furious* [→**hageshii** 激しい]
¶Mōretsu na arashi ga Kantō–chihō o osoimashita.
猛烈なあらしが関東地方を襲いました。
A severe storm hit the Kanto region.

mori 森 *woods, forest*
¶Mori no naka de michi ni mayoimashita.
森の中で道に迷いました。
I lost my way in the forest.

morói 脆い *easily broken, fragile, brittle*

¶Kono renga wa morokute tsukai-nikui.
このれんがはもろくて使いにくい。
These bricks are brittle and hard to use.

moru 盛る ① *to pile up* 《transitive》
¶Niwa-shi wa niwa ni tsuchi o morimashita.
庭師は庭に土を盛りました。
The gardener piled up earth in the garden.

② *to serve* 《food onto a dish》
¶Okāsan ga sara ni niku o motte kuremashita.
お母さんが皿に肉を盛ってくれました。
His mother served the meat onto my plate.

morumótto モルモット *guinea pig*

morutaru モルタル *mortar* 《for holding bricks, etc., together》

móshi もし *if* 《Introduces a conditional clause.》
¶Moshi ashita tenki ga yokereba, dekakemasu.
もしあした天気がよければ、出かけます。
If the weather is good tomorrow, I'll go out.

¶Moshi todokanakattara, shirasete kudasai.
もし届かなかったら、知らせてください。
If it doesn't arrive, please let me know.

mōshiageru 申し上げる 【HUM. for **iu** 言う】

mōshíbun 申し分 ~**ga nai** ~がない *to be faultless, to be perfect; to be ideal*

móshi-ka-shitára もしかしたら 【COL. for **aruiwa** 或いは②】 *perhaps* 《This expression typically occurs in sentences ending with an expression of possibility (usually **ka-mo-shirenai** かもしれない). Since such a sentence has virtually the same meaning whether or not **moshi-ka-shitara** is present, **moshi-ka-shitara** is redundant in a sense, but it serves as a signal of how a sentence will end.》
¶Moshi-ka-shitara mō owatta ka-mo-shirenai.
もしかしたらもう終わったかもしれない。
It may, perhaps, have ended already.

móshi-ka-suru-to もしかすると
[☞**moshi-ka-shitara** もしかしたら]

mōshikomi 申し込み ① *request, proposal*
•kekkon no mōshikomi 結婚の申し込み *marriage proposal*

② *applying, application* 《for something》
¶Mōshikomi no uketsuke-kikan wa is-shūkan desu.
申し込みの受け付け期間は1週間です。
The acceptance period for applications is one week.

¶Mōshikomi no shimekiri wa Roku-gatsu mika desu.
申し込みの締め切りは6月3日です。
The deadline for applying is June 3rd.

•mōshikomi-sho 申し込み書 *written application*

•mōshikomi-yōshi 申し込み用紙 *application form*

mōshikomu 申し込む ① *to make a request for, to propose*
¶Kiyoshi wa Kazuko ni kekkon o mōshikomimashita.
清は和子に結婚を申し込みました。
Kiyoshi proposed marriage to Kazuko.

•A ni shiai o mōshikomu Aに試合を申し込む *to propose a game to A, to challenge A to a game*

② *to apply for*
¶Sono daigaku ni nyūgaku o mōshikomimasu.
その大学に入学を申し込みます。
I'm going to apply for admission to that college.

•A ni sanka o mōshikomu Aに参加を申し込む *to apply for participation in A, to enter A*

móshimoshi もしもし ① *Hello* 《on the telephone》
¶Moshimoshi, Tanabe-san desu ka.
もしもし、田辺さんですか。
Hello, is that Ms. Tanabe?

② *Excuse me, Say* 《Used to get a person's attention.》
¶Moshimoshi, kore wa anata no bōrupen

de wa arimasen ka.

もしもし、これはあなたのボールペンではありませんか。

Say, isn't this your ballpen?

mōshiwake 申し訳 *excuse, exculpatory explanation* [→**iiwake** 言い訳]

• mōshiwake-nai 申し訳ない *inexcusable*

¶Mōshiwake-nai koto o shite shimaimashita.

申し訳ない事をしてしまいました。

I did an inexcusable thing.

¶Osoku natte mōshiwake-arimasen.

遅くなって申し訳ありません。

I'm very sorry I'm late. «Literally: I'm late, and it's inexcusable.»

mōsu 申す 【HUM. for **iu** 言う】

mōtā モーター *motor; engine* [→**enjin** エンジン]

mōtābōto モーターボート *motorboat*

motarásu 齎す *to bring, to bring about, to produce*

motenashi 持て成し *hospitable treatment, hospitable reception*

motenasu 持て成す *to treat hospitably, to entertain «a guest»*

¶Okusan wa watashi-tachi o atatakaku motenashite kureta.

奥さんは私たちを温かくもてなしてくれた。

The wife entertained us warmly.

motéru 持てる *to be made much of, to be popular* «This word is the potential form of **motsu** 持つ and has the predictable meanings as well.»

¶Ken-chan wa onna no ko ni moteru ne.

健ちゃんは女の子にもてるね。

Ken is popular with the girls, isn't he.

móto 元, 本 ① *cause* [→**gen'in** 原因]*; origin, source* [→**kigen** 起源]

¶Shippai no moto wa nan deshita ka.

失敗の元は何でしたか。

What was the cause of the failure?

② *foundation, basis* [→**kiso** 基礎]

③ *materials, ingredients* [→**zairyō** 材料]

④ *once, formerly, previously* [→**izen** 以前①]

¶Kida-san wa moto wa Ōsaka ni sunde

imashita.

木田さんは元は大阪に住んでいました。

Mr. Kida once lived in Osaka.

• moto no 元の *former; original*

¶Harisu-shi wa moto no shushō desu.

ハリス氏は元の首相です。

Mr. Harris is a former prime minister.

⑤ *capital, funds* «for starting an enterprise»

• moto-de 元手 [☞**moto** 元⑤ (above)]

motó 下, 許 ① *the area under, the area below* [→**shita** 下②]

② *same place of residence, same roof*

¶Ano daigaku-sei wa oya no moto de kurashite imasu.

あの大学生は親のもとで暮らしています。

That college student lives with his parents.

③ *position of compliance*

• A no moto de Aの下で *under A*

¶Hashimoto-san wa Maruyama-sensei no moto de kenkyū shite iru.

橋本さんは丸山先生の下で研究している。

Mr. Hashimoto is doing research under Prof. Maruyama.

motoméru 求める ① *to ask for, to request* [→**yōkyūsuru** 要求する]

¶Tomodachi ni tasuke o motomemashita.

友達に助けを求めました。

I asked my friend for help.

② *to look for, to seek* [→**sagasu** 捜す, 探す]

¶Ane wa ima shoku o motomete imasu.

姉は今職を求めています。

My older sister is now looking for a job.

③ *to buy, to purchase* [→**kau** 買う]

motomoto 元々 *from the beginning, originally* [→**ganrai** 元来]*; by nature, as an inborn characteristic* [→**umaretsuki** 生まれつき]

¶Boku wa motomoto sono keikaku ni hantai deshita.

僕はもともとその計画に反対でした。

I was against the plan from the beginning.

¶Ichikawa-kun wa motomoto tenisu ga umai yo.

市川君はもともとテニスがうまいよ。
Ichikawa is naturally good at tennis!

motozúku 基づく *to be based* 〈*on*〉
¶Shōsetsu wa sakka-jishin no keiken ni motozuite imasu.
小説は作家自身の経験に基づいています。
The novel is based on the author's own experiences.

mótsu 持つ ① *to hold, to take hold of; to carry*
¶Te ni nani o motte iru no.
手に何を持っているの。
What are you holding in your hand?
¶Rōpu o shikkari motte kudasai.
ロープをしっかり持ってください。
Please hold the rope tightly.
¶Obāchan no nimotsu o motte agenasai.
おばあちゃんの荷物を持ってあげなさい。
Carry Grandma's baggage for her.
• motte iku 持っていく *to take* 《*from one place to another*》《*The direct object is ordinarily an inanimate object.*》
¶Kyō wa kasa o motte ikinasai.
きょうは傘を持っていきなさい。
Today take your umbrella.
¶Sore o bu-chō ni motte itte kudasai.
それを部長に持っていってください。
Please take that to the department head.
• motte kuru 持ってくる *to bring, to fetch* 《*The direct object is ordinarily an inanimate object.*》
¶Shinbun o motte kite kureru?
新聞を持ってきてくれる？
Will you bring me the newspaper?
② *to come to have, to come to possess; to come to own*
¶Chichi wa kuruma o san-dai motte imasu.
父は車を３台持っています。
My father has three cars.
¶Kono tochi wa dare ga motte iru n desu ka.
この土地はだれが持っているんですか。
Who owns this land?
③ *to last, to remain intact*
¶Kono kasa wa ato ichi-nen-gurai motsu deshō.

この傘はあと１年ぐらい持つでしょう。
This umbrella will probably last about one more year.

mottai-nái もったいない *wasted, regrettable* 《*because of a more appropriate alternative*》
¶Konna ii pen wa kodomo ni wa mottai-nai.
こんないいペンは子供にはもったいない。
Such a fine pen would be wasted on a child.

mótte iku 持っていく [☞**motsu** 持つ①]

motte kúru 持ってくる [☞**motsu** 持つ①]

mótto もっと *more, to a greater degree*
¶Motto o-cha wa ikaga desu ka.
もっとお茶はいかがですか。
How about some more tea?
¶Motto hon o yominasai.
もっと本を読みなさい。
Read more books.
¶Ryokō no koto o motto kikasete kudasai.
旅行のことをもっと聞かせてください。
Please tell me more about your trip.
¶Motto chūi-bukaku unten shite kudasai.
もっと注意深く運転してください。
Please drive more carefully.
¶Eiga wa sono gensaku yori motto omoshiroi.
映画はその原作よりもっとおもしろい。
The movie is much more interesting than the book.
¶Motto yasui no ga arimasu ka.
もっと安いのがありますか。
Do you have a cheaper one?

móttō モットー *motto*

mottómo 尤も ① ～**na** ～な *natural, unsurprising* [→**tōzen no** 当然の]; *reasonable, sensible, rational*
¶O-kyaku-san ga sō kangaeru no wa mottomo desu.
お客さんがそう考えるのはもっともです。
It is natural for the customer to think so.

¶Go-mottomo desu.
ごもっともです。
You are quite right. «Literally: It is reasonable. (honorific)»

② *of course (however)*
¶Sotsugyō-sei wa daigaku ni hairimasu. Mottomo, reigai mo arimasu.
卒業生は大学に入ります。もっとも、例外もあります。
The graduates enter college. Of course, there are also exceptions.

mottómo 最も *the most «indicating a superlative»* [→**ichiban** 一番]
¶Suiei wa mottomo omoshiroi supōtsu da to omou.
水泳は最もおもしろいスポーツだと思う。
I think swimming is the most interesting sport.
¶Eberesuto wa sekai de mottomo takai yama desu.
エベレストは世界で最も高い山です。
Everest is the highest mountain in the world.

moyasu 燃やす *to set on fire; to burn*
¶Kono tegami o moyashite kudasai.
この手紙を燃やしてください。
Please burn this letter.

moyō 模様 ① *(decorative)pattern, (decorative)design*
② *look, appearance* [→**yōsu** 様子②]
• shima-moyō 縞模様 *striped pattern*
• sora-moyō 空模様 *the look of the sky, the weather*

moyōshi 催し ① *gathering, meeting, social function* [→**kai** 会①]
② *auspices, sponsorship* [→**shusai** 主催]
¶Daigaku no moyōshi de ongaku-kai ga hirakaremasu.
大学の催しで音楽会が開かれます。
A concert will be held under the auspices of the college.

moyōsu 催す ① *to hold «an event»* [→**kaisai suru** 開催する]
② *to feel «an emotional or physical reaction»*
• namida o moyōsu 涙を催す *to be moved to tears*

mozáiku モザイク *mosaic*

mózu 百舌 *shrike*

mu- 無- *un-, without «Added to noun bases.»*
• mu-jōken no 無条件の *unconditional*
• mu-seigen na／no 無制限な／の *unlimited*

múcha 無茶 【COL.】① *absurdity, nonsense*
• mucha o iu むちゃを言う *to talk nonsense*
• mucha na むちゃな *absurd, nonsensical*
② *rashness, recklessness*
• mucha na むちゃな *rash, reckless*

múchi 鞭 *whip*
• muchi-uchi-shō 鞭打ち症 *whiplash (injury)*
• muchi-utsu 鞭打つ *to whip*

muchū 夢中 〜**no** 〜の *absorbed, engrossed, carried away* [→**netchū no** 熱中の]
¶Shachō wa sono josei ni muchū desu.
社長はその女性に夢中です。
The company president is carried away with that woman.
• muchū de 夢中で *absorbedly; dazedly; frantically*
¶Ani wa muchū de konpyūtā o tsukatte iru.
兄は夢中でコンピュータを使っている。
My older brother is absorbedly using the computer.

muda 無駄 ① *futility*
• muda na むだな *futile, vain* [→**munashii** 空しい]
¶Sensei no chūkoku wa sono seito ni wa muda deshita.
先生の忠告はその生徒にはむだでした。
The teacher's advice was futile for that student.
② *waste, wastefulness*
¶Sonna koto o suru no wa jikan no muda desu yo.
そんな事をするのは時間のむだですよ。
Doing such a thing is a waste of time!
• muda na むだな *wasteful*

• muda ni suru むだにする *to waste, to let go to waste*

¶ Jikan to o-kane o muda ni shinai de.
時間とお金をむだにしないで。
Don't waste your time and money.

• muda-banashi 無駄話 *idle talk, gossip*

• muda-zukai 無駄遣い *waste, wasteful use*

mudan 無断 ～**de** ～で *without permission*

¶ Otōto wa mudan de watashi no hon o motte itta yo.
弟は無断で私の本を持っていったよ。
My younger brother took my book without permission!

¶ Akemi-chan wa mudan de gakkō o kesseki shimashita.
明美ちゃんは無断で学校を欠席しました。
Akemi was absent from school without permission.

mūdo ムード *mood, atmosphere* [→ **fun'iki** 雰囲気]

¶ Sono resutoran wa mūdo ga aru ne.
そのレストランはムードがあるね。
That restaurant has atmosphere, doesn't it.

múgai 無害 ～**no** ～の *harmless, innocuous* [⇔**yūgai no** 有害の]

mugen 無限 ～**no** ～の *infinite, limitless, boundless*

múgi 麦 《a generic term for wheat, barley, oats, and rye》

• mugi-batake 麦畑 *wheat／barley／oat／rye field*

• mugi-cha 麦茶 *barley tea*

• mugi-wara-bōshi 麦藁帽子 *straw hat*

• karasu-mugi 烏麦 *oats*

• ko-mugi 小麦 *wheat*

• ō-mugi 大麦 *barley*

• rai-mugi ライ麦 *rye*

muika 六日 《see Appendix 2》 ① *six days*

② *the sixth* 《day of a month》

muími 無意味 ～**na** ～な *meaningless; pointless*

¶ Sono keikaku wa mattaku muimi desu.
その計画はまったく無意味です。
That plan is completely pointless.

muíshiki 無意識 ～**no** ～の ① *unconscious* 《i.e., having lost consciousness》

¶ Kega-nin wa ichi-jikan-hodo muishiki no jōtai deshita.
けが人は1時間ほど無意識の状態でした。
The injured person was in an unconscious state for about an hour.

② *unconscious* 《i.e., not involving conscious thought》

¶ Ishihara-san wa muishiki ni densha ni norimashita.
石原さんは無意識に電車に乗りました。
Ms. Ishihara unconsciously boarded the train.

mújaki 無邪気 ～**na** ～な *innocent, naive, artless*

¶ Otōto wa akanbō no yō ni mujaki da yo.
弟は赤ん坊のように無邪気だよ。
My younger brother is innocent like a baby!

mujun 矛盾 *contradiction, inconsistency*

• mujun suru 矛盾する *to come into contradiction, to become inconsistent*

¶ Higai-sha no hanashi wa mokugeki-sha no shōgen to mujun suru.
被害者の話は目撃者の証言と矛盾する。
The victim's story is inconsistent with the witness's testimony.

¶ Kōchi wa tokidoki mujun shita koto o iimasu.
コーチは時々矛盾した事を言います。
The coach sometimes says contradictory things.

mukade むかで *centipede*

mukaeru 迎える ① *to meet* 《an arriving person》 [⇔**miokuru** 見送る①]

¶ Kūkō de itoko o mukaemashita.
空港でいとこを迎えました。
I met my cousin at the airport.

② *to greet, to welcome, to receive* 《a guest》

¶ Go-ryōshin wa otōto o atatakaku mukaete kudasatta yo.
ご両親は弟を温かく迎えてくださったよ。
Your parents welcomed my younger

brother warmly!

③ *to greet, to mark the coming the coming of* 《*a new year, a season, a birthday, etc.*》

mukai 向かい *the area opposite, the area across from*

¶Takako-san wa Yōko-san no mukai ni suwatta.

孝子さんは洋子さんの向かいに座った。

Takako sat across from Yoko.

¶Yūbin-kyoku wa eki no mukai ni arimasu.

郵便局は駅の向かいにあります。

The post office is opposite the station.

• mukai-gawa 向かい側 *opposite side*
• mukai-kaze 向かい風 *head wind*

mukashi 昔 *long ago*

¶Nagai-san wa haha no mukashi kara no yūjin desu.

永井さんは母の昔からの友人だ。

Ms. Nagai is a friend of my mother's from long ago.

¶Mukashi kono dai-tokai wa nōson deshita.

昔この大都会は農村でした。

Long ago this big city was a farming village.

• mukashi-banashi 昔話 *tale of long ago, legend*
• mukashi-mukashi 昔々 *long long ago, once upon a time*

mukatte 向かって [☞**ni mukatte** に向かって]

mukau 向かう ① *to leave* 〈*for*〉; *to head* 〈*for*〉

¶Chichi wa konban kuruma de Ōsaka e mukaimasu.

父は今晩車で大阪へ向かいます。

My father will leave for Osaka this evening by car.

¶Fune wa Yokohama o dete, Honkon ni mukaimasu.

船は横浜を出て、ホンコンに向かいます。

The ship will leave Yokohama, and head for Hong Kong.

¶Taifū wa doko ni mukatte imasu ka.

台風はどこに向かっていますか。

Where is the typhoon heading for?

② *to face, to orient oneself, to direct oneself*

• A ni mukau Aに向かう *to face (toward)A, to direct oneself toward A*

¶Himawari wa taiyō ni mukaimasu.

ひまわりは太陽に向かいます。

Sunflowers face the sun.

• tsukue ni mukau 机に向かう *to sit at a desk*

-muke －向け 〜**no** 〜の《Added to noun bases.》 ① *directed to, to be sent to*

¶Gaikoku-muke no hōsō mo arimasu.

外国向けの放送もあります。

There are also broadcasts directed to foreign countries.

② *intended for, suitable for* [→**-muki no** －向きの]

¶Kore wa chūgaku-sei-muke no jisho desu.

これは中学生向けの辞書です。

This is a dictionary intended for junior-high-school students.

mukeru 向ける *to turn, to point, to direct* 《*one thing toward another*》

¶Kochira ni kao o mukete kudasai.

こちらに顔を向けてください。

Please turn your face this way.

¶Mō hitotsu no wadai ni chūi o muke-mashō.

もう一つの話題に注意を向けましょう。

Let's turn our attention to the other topic.

¶Kamera-man wa kamera o watashi-tachi ni muketa.

カメラマンはカメラを私たちに向けた。

The photographer pointed the camera at us.

múki 向き *direction*(*of movement*)*; facing direction* 《*i.e., the direction something faces*》

¶Kaze no muki wa kawatte imasen.

風の向きは変わっていません。

The direction of the wind hasn't changed.

¶Tsukue no muki o mado no hō e kaete kudasai.

机の向きを窓のほうへ変えてください。
Please move the desk so that it faces the window. «Literally: *Please change the way the desk faces to the direction of the window.*»

• higashi-muki no 東向きの *east-facing*

¶Uchi no daidokoro wa higashi-muki desu.

うちの台所は東向きです。
Our kitchen faces east.

-muki －向き ～**no** ～の *intended for, suitable for* «Added to noun bases.» [→ **-muke no** －向けの②]

mukō 向こう ① *the area on the opposite side, the area beyond*

¶Watashi-tachi no gakkō wa kawa no mukō ni arimasu.

私たちの学校は川の向こうにあります。
Our school is on the other side of the river.

¶Mori no mukō ni bessō ga arimasu.

森の向こうに別荘があります。
Beyond the woods there is a villa.

② (*the area*)*over there*

¶Mukō no ano mado-giwa ni suwari-mashō.

向こうのあの窓際に座りましょう。
Let's sit by that window over there.

③ *the other party* «in an interaction»

¶Konkai no shutchō keihi wa mukō ga haraimasu.

今回の出張経費は向こうが払います。
The other party will pay the expenses for the business trip this time.

• mukō-gawa 向こう側 *the opposite side; the other party*

múko 婿 *son-in-law* [⇔**yome** 嫁②]

mukō 無効 ～**no** ～の [[⇔**yūkō no** 有効の]] ① *ineffective, unfruitful, futile*

② *invalid, not in effect, void*

¶Kono pasupōto wa mukō ni natte imasu.

このパスポートは無効になっています。
This passport has expired.

mukōzune 向こう脛 *shin*

muku 向く ① *to turn to face, to turn*

toward; to look toward, to turn one's head toward

• A ni／o muku Aに／を向く *to turn toward A; to look toward A*

¶Kochira o muite kudasai.

こちらを向いてください。
Please look this way.

¶Yumi-chan wa watashi no hō o muite waratta.

由美ちゃんは私のほうを向いて笑った。
Yumi turned toward me and smiled.

• ushiro o muku 後ろを向く *to look back*

② *to face* (*toward*) «The subject is a stationary object» [→**mensuru** 面する]

• A ni／o muku Aに／を向く *to face* (*toward*)*A*

¶Kono ie wa nishi ni muite imasu.

この家は西に向いています。
This house faces toward the west.

③ *to be suited* [→**tekisuru** 適する]

¶Ane wa kyōshi ni muite imasu.

姉は教師に向いています。
My older sister is suited to being a teacher.

muku 剝く ① *to peel* «something with a covering»

¶Kyōko-san wa momo o muite kurema-shita.

京子さんは桃をむいてくれました。
Kyoko peeled a peach for me.

② *to peel off* «a covering»

¶Ki no kawa o muku no wa muzukashii desu.

木の皮をむくのは難しいです。
It's hard to peel off the bark of a tree.

múkuchi 無口 ～**na** ～な *taciturn, quiet, reticent* [⇔**oshaberi na** おしゃべりな②]

¶Ane wa oshaberi desu ga, imōto wa mukuchi desu.

姉はおしゃべりですが、妹は無口です。
My older sister is talkative, but my younger sister is taciturn.

mukuíru 報いる *to do something as appropriate reciprocation, to do something in return* «for a favor, a kindness, etc.»

¶Akiko-san no shinsetsu ni mukuinakereba naranai.

明子さんの親切に報いなければならない。

I must do something in return for Akiko's kindness.

munashíi 空しい *vain, fruitless, futile*

¶Wareware no doryoku wa munashikatta desu.

われわれの努力はむなしかったです。

Our efforts were futile.

muné 胸 ① *chest ((body part))*

¶Ano hito wa mune ga warui sō desu.

あの人は胸が悪いそうです。

That person's chest is bad.

¶Mune ga itakute tamarimasen.

胸が痛くてたまりません。

My chest hurts so much that I can't stand it.

¶Ima mune ga dokidoki shite imasu.

今胸がどきどきしています。

My chest is throbbing with a fast heartbeat now.

② *heart, feelings* [→**kokoro** 心②]

¶Okāsan no mune wa ai de ippai deshita.

お母さんの胸は愛でいっぱいでした。

Her mother's heart was filled with love.

murá 村 *village*

• mura-yakuba 村役場 *village office*

muragáru 群がる *to crowd, to flock, to swarm*

¶Shōjo-tachi ga kashu no mawari ni muragatte imasu.

少女たちが歌手の周りに群がっています。

The girls are crowding around the singer.

¶Mitsubachi wa hana no mawari ni muragarimasu.

みつばちは花の周りに群がります。

Honeybees swarm around flowers.

murásaki 紫 *purple* ((as a noun))

¶Ueda-san wa murasaki no doresu o kite imasu.

上田さんは紫のドレスを着ています。

Ms. Ueda is wearing a purple dress.

muré 群れ ((This word is a generic term for gathered groups of people or animals)) *crowd, gathered group; flock; herd*

• hito no mure 人の群れ *crowd of people*

• hitsuji no mure 羊の群れ *flock of sheep*

• ushi no mure 牛の群れ *herd of cows*

múri 無理 ① *unreasonableness, unjustifiability*

• muri na 無理な *unreasonable, unjustifiable*

• muri o iu 無理を言う *to make an unreasonable request*

② 〜**na** 〜な *impossible* [→**fukanō na** 不可能な]

¶Hachi-ji made ni soko ni iku no wa muri desu.

8時までにそこに行くのは無理です。

It's impossible to go there by 8:00.

③ 〜**na** 〜な *forcible, against a person's will*

④ *excess, strain, overwork*

• muri na 無理な *excessive, immoderate*

• muri o suru 無理をする *to do too much, to strain oneself, to overwork*

muriyari 無理やり (〜**ni** 〜に) *in spite of opposition, coercively*

muron 無論 *of course, certainly* [→**mochiron** 勿論]

múryō 無料 〜**no** 〜の *free (of charge)* [→**tada no** 唯の, 只の③]

¶Nyūjō muryō

「入場無料」((on a sign))

Admission Free

• muryō-haitatsu 無料配達 *free delivery*

músekinin 無責任 〜**na**〜な *irresponsible*

¶Akemi-san wa mattaku musekinin desu.

明美さんはまったく無責任です。

Akemi is completely irresponsible.

musen 無線 ① 〜**no** 〜の *wireless* ((i.e., not using electrical wires for transmitting and receiving))

② *wireless communication, radio communication*

¶Keikan wa musen de keisatsu-sho ni renraku shimashita.

警官は無線で警察署に連絡しました。

The police officer communicated with the police station by radio.

• musen-denwa 無線電話 *radiotelephone*

• musen-gishi 無線技師 *radio operator*

- musen-takushī 無線タクシー *taxi equipped with a radio*
- musen-tsūshin 無線通信 [☞**musen** 無線② (above)]

mushi 虫 *bug; insect* [→**konchū** 昆虫]; *worm* 《Refers to maggots, caterpillars, etc., but not to earthworms.》

¶Tōru-san wa mushi o atsumete iru yo.
徹さんは虫を集めているよ。
Toru collects bugs.

¶Yabu de mushi ga naite imasu.
やぶで虫が鳴いています。
Bugs are chirping in the thicket.

- mushi-kago 虫籠 *insect cage*

múshi 無視 ～**suru** ～する *to ignore, to disregard*

¶Shingō o mushi shite wa ikenai yo.
信号を無視してはいけないよ。
You mustn't ignore traffic lights.

mushiatsúi 蒸し暑い *hot and humid, sultry*

¶Kyō wa mushiatsui desu ne.
きょうは蒸し暑いですね。
Today is hot and humid, isn't it?

mushiba 虫歯 *decayed tooth, tooth with a cavity*

¶Mushiba wa nan-bon arimasu ka.
虫歯は何本ありますか。
How many cavities do you have?

¶Yūbe mushiba ga itamimashita.
ゆうべ虫歯が痛みました。
Last night my decayed tooth ached.

mushimégane 虫眼鏡 *magnifying glass*

múshiro むしろ *rather, more accurately, preferably*

¶Sore wa aka yori mo, mushiro pinku ni chikai.
それは赤よりも、むしろピンクに近い。
That's not red; more accurately, it's close to pink.

¶Koko ni iru yori wa mushiro dekake-tai desu.
ここにいるよりはむしろ出かけたいです。
I would rather go out than stay here.

musū 無数 ～**no** ～の *countless, numberless*

¶Sora ni wa musū no hoshi ga matataite imashita.
空には無数の星が瞬いていました。
Countless stars were twinkling in the sky.

músu 蒸す ① *to steam, to heat by steaming*
② *to be hot and muggy*

musubime 結び目 *knot* 《where something is tied》

musubitsúku 結び付く *to become linked, to become connected*

musubitsukéru 結び付ける *to link, to connect* 《transitive》

musubu 結ぶ ① *to tie, to bind* [⇔**hodoku** 解く]

¶Hiroshi wa kutsu-himo o musubu koto ga mada dekinai yo.
宏は靴ひもを結ぶことがまだできないよ。
Hiroshi still can't tie his shoelaces!

¶Sono okurimono o ribon de musunde kudasai.
その贈り物をリボンで結んでください。
Please tie that present with a ribbon.

② *to link, to connect*

¶Chūō-sen wa Tōkyō to Matsumoto o musunde imasu.
中央線は東京と松本を結んでいます。
The Chuo Line links Tokyo and Matsumoto.

③ *to conclude, to finish, to close* 《something spoken or written》

¶Shushō wa sono kotoba de enzetsu o musubimashita.
首相はその言葉で演説を結びました。
The prime minister concluded the speech with those words.

④ *to enter into* 《an agreement, etc.》; *to conclude* 《a treaty, etc.》

¶Kinō sono kaisha to keiyaku o musubimashita.
きのうその会社と契約を結びました。
Yesterday we entered into a contract with that company.

musuko 息子 *son* [⇔**musume** 娘]

¶Ano ko wa ichiban sue no musuko desu.
あの子はいちばん末の息子です。

That child is my youngest son.
• musuko-san 息子さん 【HON. for
musuko (above)】
musumé 娘 ① *daughter* [⇔musuko
息子]
¶Musume wa mada shōgaku-sei desu.
娘はまだ小学生です。
*My daughter is still an elementa-
ry-school pupil.*
② *girl* [→shōjo 少女]; *unmarried
young woman*
• musume-san 娘さん 【HON. for
musume (above)】
¶Shimada-sensei ni wa musume-san ga
irasshaimasu.
島田先生には娘さんがいらっしゃいます。
Mr. Shimada has a daughter.
mutsukashii 難しい [☞**muzukashii**
難しい]
muttsú 六つ *six* 《see Appendix 2》
múzai 無罪 *innocence (of a crime)* [⇔
yūzai 有罪]
• muzai no 無罪の *innocent*
• muzai ni naru 無罪になる *to be found
innocent, to be acquitted*
• muzai ni suru 無罪にする *to find innocent, to acquit*
muzukashii 難しい *difficult, hard* [⇔
yasashii 易しい]
¶Rika wa watashi ni wa totemo muzukashii yo.
理科は私にはとても難しいよ。
Science is very difficult for me!
¶Kore wa muzukashii mondai desu ne.
これは難しい問題ですね。
This is a difficult problem, isn't it?
¶Eigo o hanasu no wa muzukashii desu.
英語を話すのは難しいです。
Speaking English is hard.
myakú 脈 ① *pulse, heartbeat*
¶Ishi wa kanja no myaku o torimashita.
医師は患者の脈をとりました。
The doctor took the patient's pulse.
¶Myaku ga haya-sugiru ne.
脈が速すぎるね。
Her pulse is too fast, isn't it.
② *hope, expectation, prospect* [→no-

zomi 望み②]
myō 妙 ～na ～な *odd, curious,
strange* [→kimyō na 奇妙な]
myōgónichi 明後日 【FORMAL for
asatte 明後日】 *the day after tomorrow*
myōji 名字 *family name, surname* [→
sei 姓]
myónichi 明日 【FORMAL for ashita
明日】 *tomorrow*
myūjikaru ミュージカル *a musical*
• myūjikaru-eiga ミュージカル映画 *musical movie*

na 名 *name* [→namae 名前]
nā なあ *Oh!, Boy!, Man!* 《sentence-
final particle expressing emotional involve-
ment》
¶Kanemochi dattara ii nā.
金持ちだったらいいなあ。
Oh, it would be nice to be rich!
¶Imōto ga hoshii nā.
妹が欲しいなあ。
Boy, I want a little sister!
¶Kawaii onna no ko da nā.
かわいい女の子だなあ。
Boy, that's a cute girl!
nábe 鍋 *pan, pot* 《for cooking》
nabíku なびく *to extend out and flutter,
to bend over and waver* 《in the direction of a passing current》
¶Takusan no kokki ga kaze ni nabiite
imasu.
たくさんの国旗が風になびいて
います。
*A lot of national flags are fluttering in
the wind.*
¶Kusa ga kaze ni nabiite imasu.
草が風になびいています。
The grass is blowing in the wind.
nabúru 嬲る *to tease, to make sport of*
nadaméru 宥める *to soothe, to calm, to
pacify*

nadáraka なだらか 〜**na** 〜な *gentle, gently-sloping* [⇔**kewashii** 険しい①]
¶Kono saka wa nadaraka desu.
この坂はなだらかです。
This slope is gentle.
• nadaraka na oka なだらかな丘 *low hill, gently-sloping hill*

nadare 雪崩 *snowslide, avalanche*

nadéru 撫でる *to stroke* (*gently*)*; to pat*
¶Shōnen wa inu no atama o nadete imasu.
少年は犬の頭をなでています。
The boy is patting his dog on the head.

nádo など《This particle can follow a noun or a predicate.》 ① *and so on, etcetera*
¶Sono shōnen ni kēki ya pai nado o ageta.
その少年にケーキやパイなどをあげた。
I gave that boy cake, pie, and so on.
② *or such, the likes of* 《often pejorative》
¶Ani wa, raigetsu kaeru nado to itte imashita.
兄は、来月帰るなどと言っていました。
My older brother was saying that he'll go home next month or something like that.

náe 苗 *young plant, seedling*

nafutarin ナフタリン *naphthalene*

nagabíku 長引く *to be prolonged, to run overtime*
¶Kaigi ga nagabiite, yakusoku no jikan ni okureta.
会議が長引いて、約束の時間に遅れた。
The meeting ran overtime and I was late for an appointment.

nagagutsu 長靴 *knee-length boot*

nagái 長い *long* [⇔**mijikai** 短い]
¶Chichi ni nagai tegami o kakimashita.
父に長い手紙を書きました。
I wrote my father a long letter.
¶Hokkaidō no fuyu wa nagakute samui desu.
北海道の冬は長くて寒いです。
The Hokkaido winter is long and cold.
¶Zannen-nagara nagaku wa iraremasen.

残念ながら長くはいられません。
I'm sorry I can't stay long.
• nagai aida 長い間 *for a long time*
¶Yumi-san wa nagai aida damatte imashita.
由美さんは長い間黙っていました。
Yumi was silent for a long time.

nagaikí 長生き *long life, living long*
• nagaiki suru 長生きする *to live long*
¶Watashi mo nagaiki shitai to omoimasu.
私も長生きしたいと思います。
I think I'd like to live long too.

nagamé 眺め *view, vista*
¶Sanchō kara no nagame wa subarashii mono deshita.
山頂からの眺めはすばらしいものでした。
The view from the mountaintop was wonderful.

nagaméru 眺める *to gaze at, to look at, to view*
¶Yoshida-san wa mado no soto o nagamete imasu.
吉田さんは窓の外を眺めています。
Ms. Yoshida is gazing at the area outside the window.
¶Onna-no-ko ga odotte iru no o nagamemashita.
女の子が踊っているのを眺めました。
I watched the girl dancing.

nagamochí 長持ち *lasting a long time, durability*
• nagamochi suru 長持ちする *to last a long time*
¶Kono seiten wa nagamochi suru deshō.
この晴天は長持ちするでしょう。
This nice weather will probably last a long time.
¶Sono mannenhitsu wa nagamochi shimashita.
その万年筆は長持ちしました。
That fountain pen lasted a long time.

-nagara −ながら *while, as* 《Added to verb bases to join two clauses. The subject of both clauses must be the same.》
¶Otōto wa terebi o mi-nagara nemutte shimatta.

弟はテレビを見ながら眠ってしまった。
My younger brother fell asleep while watching TV.

¶Watashi-tachi wa kōra o nomi-nagara hanashimashita.

私たちはコーラを飲みながら話しました。
We chatted while drinking cola.

nagaré 流れ *stream, flow, current*

¶Kono kawa wa nagare ga yuruyaka desu ne.

この川は流れがゆるやかですね。
This is a gentle river, isn't it. «Literally: As for this river, the current is gentle, isn't it.»

• hito no nagare 人の流れ *stream of people, flow of people*
• nagare-boshi 流れ星 *shooting star*

nagaréru 流れる ① *to flow*

¶Ōki na kawa ga machi no naka o nagarete imasu.

大きな川が町の中を流れています。
A big river flows through the town.

¶Ase ga kao o nagaremashita.

汗が顔を流れました。
Sweat flowed down my face.

② *to be floated, to drift, to be taken by the current*

nágasa 長さ *length*

¶Kono kawa no nagasa wa dono gurai desu ka.

この川の長さはどのぐらいですか。
About how long is this river? «Literally: As for the length of this river, about how much is it?»

nagashí 流し *sink ((plumbing fixture))*

nagásu 流す ① *to let flow; to shed «tears»; to pour out*

¶Shichō wa sono shirase o kiite namida o nagashita.

市長はその知らせを聞いて涙を流した。
The mayor heard the news and shed tears.

② *to float, to set adrift, to let the current take*

¶Ani wa sono bōto o kawa ni nagashimashita.

兄はそのボートを川に流しました。

My older brother set that boat adrift on the river.

③ *to wash away «transitive»*
④ *to wash «a part of the body with water»*

¶Chichi no senaka o nagashimashita.

父の背中を流しました。
I washed my father's back.

nagekí 嘆き *sorrow, grief*

nagéku 嘆く *to lament, to grieve over*

nagéru 投げる ① *to throw, to toss, to hurl*

¶Akira-chan wa bōru o nagemashita.

明ちゃんはボールを投げました。
Akira threw the ball.

¶Tōku ni ishi o nagemashita.

遠くに石を投げました。
I threw a stone in the distance.

¶Inu ni hone o nagemashita.

犬に骨を投げました。
I threw a bone to the dog.

② *to give up on and quit*

• shiken o nageru 試験を投げる *to give up on a test*

nagorí 名残り ① *trace, vestige, relic*
② *sadness felt on parting*

• nagori-oshii 名残り惜しい *sad to part*

nagóyaka 和やか ～**na** ～な *harmonious, congenial, peaceful*

¶Nagoyaka na kai deshita ne.

和やかな会でしたね。
It was a congenial gathering wasn't it.

nagúru 殴る *to hit (intentionally), to strike (intentionally) «The subject and the direct object must both be animate.»*

¶Ani ga boku no atama o nagutta yo.

兄が僕の頭を殴ったよ。
My older brother hit me on the head!

¶Hannin wa sono keikan o nagutta sō desu.

犯人はその警官を殴ったそうです。
It seems that the criminal hit that police officer.

nagusame 慰め *comfort, consolation, solace*

nagusaméru 慰める *to comfort, to console*

¶Yōko-san wa kanashi-sō na kodomo o nagusameta.

洋子さんは悲しそうな子供を慰めた。

Yoko comforted the sad-looking child.

¶Nan-toka Itō-kun o nagusameyō to shimashita.

何とか伊藤君を慰めようとしました。

I tried to console Ito somehow.

nái ない《the irregular informal negative form of **aru** ある; see Appendix 1》

① *there is ╱ are no*

¶Baketsu ni wa mizu ga nai yo.

バケツには水がないよ。

There's no water in the bucket!

¶Kabin wa atta kedo, hana wa nakatta ne.

花瓶はあったけど、花はなかったね。

There was a vase, but there were no flowers, were there.

② *not to have, to have no*

¶Ano kojiki ni wa taberu mono ga nai ne.

あのこじきには食べる物がないね。

That beggar doesn't have anything to eat, does he.

nái ない 《negative marker for adjectives and for the copula **da**; see Appendix 1》

¶Kono mise wa sorehodo yasuku nai yo.

この店はそれほど安くないよ。

This shop isn't that cheap!

¶Ano hito wa Mori-san de wa nai ne.

あの人は森さんではないね。

That person isn't Ms. Mori, is she.

-nai －ない《negative marker for verbs; see Appendix 1》

¶Ikeda-san mo shira-nai deshō.

池田さんも知らないでしょう。

Ms. Ikeda probably doesn't know either.

náibu 内部 *the inside, inner part* [⇔**gaibu** 外部]

náifu ナイフ *knife*

naika 内科 *internal medicine* 《as a specialty》 [⇔**geka** 外科]

• naika-i 内科医 *internist*

náikaku 内閣 *(government)cabinet*

• Naikaku-Sōridaijin 内閣総理大臣 *the Prime Minister (of Japan)* [→**Sōridai-**

jin 総理大臣]

náiron ナイロン *nylon*

naisen 内戦 *civil war*

naishin 内心 ① *one's mind, one's heart, one inner thoughts*

② *in one's heart, inwardly*

¶Chichi wa naishin watashi no koto o shinpai shite kurete iru.

父は内心私のことを心配してくれている。

In his heart my father is worried about me.

naishinshó 内申書 *confidential report of one's record at a school*

naishó 内緒 *a secret* [→**himitsu** 秘密]

¶Kono an o shachō ni wa naisho ni shite okō.

この案を社長には内緒にしておこう。

Let's keep this plan a secret from the company president.

• naisho-banashi 内緒話 *confidential talk*

naishoku 内職 *side job*

náitā ナイター *night game* 《in sports》

naiya 内野 *infield* [⇔**gaiya** 外野]

• naiya-shu 内野手 *infielder*

naiyō 内容 ① *content, substance* [⇔**keishiki** 形式①]

¶Kaichō no enzetsu no naiyō wa subarashikatta desu.

会長の演説の内容はすばらしかったです。

The content of the chairperson's speech was excellent.

② *contents* [→**nakami** 中身]

naizō 内臓 *internal organ*

najímu 馴染む *to become familiar, to get used*

• A ni najimu Aになじむ *to become familiar with A, to get used to A*

náka 中 ① *the inside, the area inside*

¶Sono hako no naka o mitai desu.

その箱の中を見たいです。

I want to see inside that box.

¶Soto wa atsui desu ga, naka wa suzushii desu.

外は暑いですが、中は涼しいです。

It's hot outside, but it's cool inside.

¶Inu wa inu-goya no naka de nemutte imasu.

犬は犬小屋の中で眠っています。
The dog is asleep in the doghouse.

¶Enpitsu o fude-ire no naka ni shimai-nasai.

鉛筆を筆入れの中にしまいなさい。
Put the pencils into the pencil case.

¶Otōto ga ie no naka kara dete kimashita.

弟が家の中から出てきました。
My younger brother came out from inside the house.

¶Watashi-tachi wa kōen no naka o tōrimashita.

私たちは公園の中を通りました。
We passed through the park.

② *included membership, included range* [→**uchi** 内③]

• A no naka de　Aの中で *among A, of A* 《in combination with a superlative》

¶Akira wa san-nen-sei no naka de hashiru no ga ichiban hayai.

明は3年生の中で走るのがいちばん速い。
Akira is the fastest runner among the third graders. 《Literally: *As for Akira, among the third graders, his running is fastest.*

¶Kyōko-san wa san-nin no naka de ichiban se ga takai.

京子さんは3人の中でいちばん背が高い。
Kyoko is the tallest of the three.

náka 仲 *terms, relationship* 《with someone》

• A ga B to naka ga ii [warui]　AがBと仲がいい[悪い] *A is on good [bad] terms with B*

¶Yōko-chan wa Kyōko-chan to naka ga ii desu.

洋子ちゃんは京子ちゃんと仲がいいです。
Yoko is on good terms with Kyoko.

¶Suzuki-san to kachō wa naka ga warui nā.

鈴木さんと課長は仲が悪いなあ。
Mr. Suzuki and the section chief are on bad terms, right.

nakabá 半ば ① *half* 《as an adverb》

¶Sakubun wa nakaba dekite imasu.

作文は半ばできています。

The composition is half finished.

② *approximate middle* 《of a time span》

¶Kuroda-san wa Shi-gatsu no nakaba ni kimasu.

黒田さんは4月の半ばに来ます。
Mr. Kuroda will come in the middle of April.

¶Chichi wa gojū-dai no nakaba desu.

父は50代の半ばです。
My father is in his mid-fifties.

nakamá 仲間 *companion, colleague, fellow*

• ii [warui] nakama to tsukiau　いい[悪い]仲間と付き合う *to keep good [bad] company*

• nakama ni hairu　仲間に入る *to join in*

nakámi 中身 *contents*

¶Hako no nakami wa dare-mo shiranai yo.

箱の中身はだれも知らないよ。
Nobody knows the contents of the box!

nakanaka なかなか ① *rather, quite, pretty* [→**kanari** かなり]

¶Kono terebi-bangumi wa nakanaka omoshiroi.

このテレビ番組はなかなかおもしろい。
This TV program is pretty interesting.

¶Kono shitsumon wa nakanaka kotae-nikui yo.

この質問はなかなか答えにくいよ。
This question is quite hard to answer!

② *just, readily* 《in combination with a negative predicate》

¶Haru ga nakanaka konai ne.

春がなかなか来ないね。
Spring just won't come, will it.

nakanáori 仲直り *reconciliation, making up*

• nakanaori suru　仲直りする *to reconcile, to make up*

¶Midori to kuchi-genka o shita ga, sugu nakanaori shita.

緑と口げんかをしたが、すぐ仲直りした。
I had an argument with Midori, but I soon made up with her.

nakáyoshi 仲良し ① *person one is*

friends with, close friend
② *friendly terms*

nakáyubi 中指 *middle finger*

nakigóe 泣き声 *cry, crying voice* «*of a person*»

nakigóe 鳴き声«*This word is generic for the vocal sounds of animals.*» *song* «*of a bird, etc.*»; *cry* «*of an animal*»
¶Rokurō wa tori no nakigoe o rokuon suru no ga suki da.
六郎は鳥の鳴き声を録音するのが好きだ。
Rokuro likes to record bird songs.

nakimúshi 泣き虫 【COL.】 *crybaby*

nakódo 仲人 *matchmaker, go-between*

naku 泣く *to cry, to weep*
¶Akachan wa mada naite iru yo.
赤ちゃんはまだ泣いているよ。
The baby is still crying!
¶Haha wa watashi no gōkaku o kiite nakimashita.
母は私の合格を聞いて泣きました。
My mother cried when she heard I had passed.

naku 鳴く«*This word is the generic verb for the vocal sounds of animals.*» *to sing; to roar; to meow*
¶Kanaria ga utsukushii koe de naite imasu.
カナリアが美しい声で鳴いています。
The canary is singing in a beautiful voice.

nakunaru 無くなる«*The subject must be inanimate.*» ① *to become lost*
¶Keshigomu ga nakunatta yo.
消しゴムが無くなったよ。
The eraser's gone!
② *to run out, to be used up* [→**tsukiru** 尽きる]
¶Kozukai ga mō nakunatta yo.
小遣いがもう無くなったよ。
My pocket money has already run out!
③ *to disappear, to go away*
¶Ha no itami ga nakunarimashita.
歯の痛みが無くなりました。
My toothache has gone away.

nakunaru 亡くなる 【FORMAL for **shinu** 死ぬ】 *to die, to pass away*

nakusu 無くす *to lose, to come to be without* [→**ushinau** 失う]
¶Chichi wa kinō tokei o nakushimashita.
父はきのう時計を無くしました。
My father lost his watch yesterday.

náma 生 ～**no** ～の ① *raw*
¶Yasai o nama de taberu no wa kenkō ni ii desu yo.
野菜を生で食べるのは健康にいいですよ。
Eating vegetables raw is good for one's health!
② *live, not recorded*
• nama-bīru 生ビール *draft beer*
• nama-ensō 生演奏 *live (instrumental)musical performance*
• nama-hōsō 生放送 *live broadcast*
• nama-tamago 生卵 *raw egg*

namae 名前 *name*
¶Namae o oshiete kureru?
名前を教えてくれる？
Will you tell me your name?
¶Koko ni namae o kaite kudasai.
ここに名前を書いてください。
Please write your name here.
• A ni namae o tsukeru Aに名前を付ける *to give a name to A, to name A*
¶Sono inu ni Rizu to iu namae o tsukemashita.
その犬にリズという名前をつけました。
I named that dog Liz.

namaiki 生意気 *impudence, audacity*
• namaiki na 生意気な *impudent, audacious*

namakemonó 怠け者 *lazy person*

namakéru 怠ける ① *to be lazy, to be idle*
② *to neglect, to devote insufficient effort to*
• shigoto o namakeru 仕事を怠ける *to neglect one's job*

namari 鉛 *lead* ((metal))

namarí 訛り *accent* «*i.e., non-standard characteristics of pronunciation*»
¶Mearī-san no Nihon-go ni namari ga aru.
メアリーさんの日本語になまりがある。
Mary speaks Japanese with an accent.

namazu 鯰 *catfish*

namekúji なめくじ *slug* ((animal))

naméraka 滑らか 〜**na** 〜な ① *smooth (-surfaced)*
¶Akanbō no hada wa nameraka desu.
赤ん坊の肌は滑らかです。
The baby's skin is smooth.
② *smooth, free from difficulties*

naméru 舐める ① *to lick; to lap*
¶Inu wa watashi no te o namemashita.
犬は私の手をなめました。
The dog licked my hand.
¶Neko wa miruku o namete shimaimashita.
猫はミルクをなめてしまいました。
The cat lapped up the milk.
② *to take lightly, to look down on*
¶Ano hito o namete wa ikenai yo.
あの人をなめてはいけないよ。
You mustn't take that person lightly!

namí 波 *wave* ((on the surface of a body of water))
¶Kyō wa nami ga takai desu ne.
きょうは波が高いですね。
Today the waves are high, aren't they.
• arai 〔shizuka na〕 nami 荒い〔静かな〕波 *rough 〔calm〕 waves*

nami 並み 〜**no** 〜の *common, ordinary, average* [→**futsū no** 普通の]

námida 涙 *tear* ((from crying))
¶Okāsan no kao wa namida ni nurete imashita.
お母さんの顔は涙にぬれていました。
My mother's face was wet with tears.
¶Midori wa me ni namida o ukabete sayonara o itta.
緑は目に涙を浮かべてさよならを言った。
Midori said goodbye with tears in her eyes. ((Literally: *Midori showed tears in her eyes and said goodbye.*))
• namida o fuku 涙をふく *to wipe tears*
• namida o nagasu 涙を流す *to shed tears*
• namida-goe 涙声 *tearful voice*
• namida-gumu 涙ぐむ *to have tears well up in one's eyes*
• ureshi-namida 嬉し涙 *tears of joy*

namiki 並木 *row of trees*
¶Ano tōri ni wa popura no namiki ga arimasu.
あの通りにはポプラの並木があります。
There is a row of poplars on that street.
• namiki-michi 並木道 *tree-lined street*

nán 何 [☞**nani** 何]

nan- 何− ① *how many* ((when followed by a cardinal counter; see Appendix 2))
¶Tanaka-san wa nan-sai desu ka.
田中さんは何歳ですか。
How old is Ms. Tanaka?
¶Kono kurasu ni wa seito ga nan-nin imasu ka.
このクラスには生徒が何人いますか。
How many students are there in this class?
¶Nan-nichi Kōbe ni taizai suru no desu ka.
何日神戸に滞在するのですか。
How many days will you stay in Kobe?
¶Tsuki ni nan-kai gorufu o shimasu ka.
月に何回ゴルフをしますか。
How many times a month do you play golf?
• nan-A mo 何−Aも *many, any number of* ((A is a cardinal counter.))
¶Oji wa nan-do mo Honkon ni itta koto ga aru.
伯父は何度も香港に行ったことがある。
My uncle has been to Hong Kong many times.
② *which, what* ((when followed by an ordinal counter; see Appendix 2))
¶Kyō wa nan-nichi desu ka.
きょうは何日ですか。
What day of the month is it today?
¶Kono ko wa nan-nen ni umareta n desu ka.
この子は何年に生まれたんですか。
In what year was this child born?
• nan-ji 何時 *what time*
¶Ima nan-ji desu ka.
今何時ですか。
What time is it now?
¶Mai-asa nan-ji ni okimasu ka.
毎朝何時に起きますか。
What time do you get up every morning?

nána 七 *seven* 《see Appendix 2》[→ **shichi** 七]

nanáme 斜め 〜**no** 〜の *slanting, diagonal*

¶Saisho ni naname no sen o hikinasai.
最初に斜めの線を引きなさい。
First draw a diagonal line.

nanátsu 七つ *seven* 《see Appendix 2》

nánbā ナンバー *number* 《used as an identifier》[→**bangō** 番号]
• nanbā-purēto ナンバープレート
<*US*>*license plate*, <*UK*>*number plate*
• bakku-nanbā バックナンバー *back number* 《of a periodical》

Nanbei 南米 *South America* [⇔ **Hokubei** 北米]

nánboku 南北 *north and south* [⇔ **tōzai** 東西]
• Nanboku-sensō 南北戦争 *the (American) Civil War*

nánbu 南部 *southern part* [⇔**hokubu** 北部]

nán-da-ka 何だか *somehow, for some reason*
¶Nan-da-ka sabishii desu.
何だか寂しいです。
For some reason I'm lonely.

nán-de 何で *why, what for* [→**naze** なぜ]

náni 何 *what* 《The alternate form **nan** usually appears before a word beginning with **t-**, **d-** or **n-**.》
¶Kore wa nan desu ka.
これは何ですか。
What's this?
¶Ima nani o shite iru no desu ka.
今何をしているのですか。
What are you doing now?
¶Kono hana wa Eigo de nan to iimasu ka.
この花は英語で何と言いますか。
What do you call this flower in English?
• nan demo 何でも *anything, everything, whatever it is*
¶Suki na mono wa nan demo totte kekkō desu.

好きな物は何でも取って結構です。
You may take anything you like. 《Literally: As for the things you like, you may take anything.》
¶Musuko wa omocha nara nan demo hoshi-garu.
息子はおもちゃなら何でも欲しがる。
If it's a toy, then my son wants it.
• nan demo nai 何でもない *to be nothing, to be of no concern*
¶Pasokon nyūryoku kurai, nan demo arimasen.
パソコン入力くらい、なんでもありません。
Computer input is nothing.
¶"Dōka shita no?" "Nan demo nai yo."
「どうかしたの？」「何でもないよ」
"What's the matter?" "Nothing!"
• nani-goto 何事 *what kind of matter, what kind of affair, what kind of thing*
• nani-goto ni mo 何事にも *in all matters, in everything*
• nani-iro 何色 *what color*
¶Kimi no kuruma wa nani-iro desu ka.
君の車は何色ですか。
What color is your car?
• nani-ka 何か *something*
¶Kono fukuro no naka ni nani-ka haitte imasu ka.
この袋の中に何か入っていますか。
Is there something inside this bag?
• nani-ka A 何かA *some kind of A*
¶Nani-ka nomimono o kudasai.
何か飲み物をください。
Please give me something to drink.
• nani-mo 何も *nothing, <not> anything* 《Always occurs in combination with a negative predicate》
¶Nani-mo hoshiku arimasen.
何も欲しくありません。
I don't want anything.
• nani-yori (mo) 何より (も) *above all, more than anything*
¶Otōto wa nani yori mo karēraisu ga suki desu.
弟は何よりもカレーライスが好きです。
My younger brother likes curry and rice better than anything else.

• nani-yori no 何よりの *better-than-any-thing, best*

nánishiro 何しろ *anyway, at any rate* [→**tonikaku** とにかく]

nán-ka 何か ① 【COL. for nado など】
② 【COL. for **nani-ka** 何か (s.v. **nani** 何)】
③ 【COL. for **nan-da-ka** 何だか】

nankotsu 軟骨 *cartilage*

Nankyoku 南極 *the South Pole* [⇔ **Hokkyoku** 北極]
• Nankyoku-tairiku 南極大陸 *Antarctica, the Antarctic Continent*

nanmin 難民 ① *people left destitute* 《by war, natural disaster, etc.》
② *refugees* [→**hinan-min** 避難民 (s.v. **hinan** 避難)]

nanoka 七日《see Appendix 2》 ① *seven days*
② *the seventh* 《day of a month》

nanpa 難破 *shipwreck*
• nanpa suru 難破する *to be wrecked* 《The subject must be a ship》
¶Fune wa anshō ni noriagete nanpa shimashita.
船は暗礁に乗り上げて難破した。
The ship struck a reef and was wrecked.

nansei 南西 *the southwest* [→**seinan** 西南]

nánsensu ナンセンス 〜na〜な *nonsensical, absurd*

nán-te 何て ① 【COL. for nan-to 何と】
② 【COL. for **nado** など②】

nán-to 何と *how, what* 《Used as an exclamatory modifier of an adjective, adjectival noun, or adverb in a sentence ending combination with **darō** だろう(or the semi-formal equivalent **deshō** でしょう).》
¶Nan-to samui n darō.
何と寒いんだろう。
How cold it is!
¶Eigo o nan-to jōzu ni shaberu no darō.
英語を何と上手にしゃべるのだろう。
How well you speak English!
¶Nan-to kawaii tori na no deshō.
何とかわいい鳥なのでしょう。

What cute birds!

nantō 南東 *the southeast* [→**tōnan** 東南]

nán-toka 何とか （〜**shite** 〜して） 《*managing*》*somehow* (*or other*)
¶Nan-to-ka Eigo de tegami o kakimashita.
何とか英語で手紙を書きました。
Somehow I wrote a letter in English.
¶Nan-to-ka ressha ni maniaimashita.
何とか列車に間に合った。
I somehow managed to be on time for the train.

nan-to-náku 何となく *for some reason, without really knowing why*
¶Nan-to-naku kono machi ga suki desu.
何となくこの町が好きです。
For some reason I like this town.

nan'yóbi 何曜日 *what day of the week*
¶Kyō wa nan'yōbi desu ka.
きょうは何曜日ですか。
What day of the week is it today?

náo 尚 ① *still,* 〈*not*〉 *yet* [→**mada** まだ①]
② *still more, even more* [→**issō** 一層]
¶Kinō mo atsukatta ga, kyō wa nao atsui.
きのうも暑かったが、きょうはなお暑い。
It was hot yesterday too, but today it's even hotter.

naóru 直る *to get repaired, to get mended, to get fixed*
¶Watashi no jitensha wa naorimashita ka.
私の自転車は直りましたか。
Is my bicycle fixed?

naóru 治る *to be cured, to heal, to get well, to recover*
¶Haha wa mō sukkari naorimashita.
母はもうすっかり治りました。
My mother has already completely recovered.

naósu 直す ① *to repair, to mend, to fix* [→**shūri suru** 修理する]
¶Chichi wa kowareta isu o naoshite kureta.
父は壊れたいすを直してくれた。

My father mended the broken chair for me.

② *to correct, to rectify* [→**teisei suru** 訂正する]

¶Kono bunshō no ayamari o naoshite kudasai.

この文章の誤りを直してください。

Please correct the errors in this passage.

③ *to translate* [→**hon'yaku suru** 翻訳する]

¶Kono bun o Nihongo ni naoshite kudasai.

この文を日本語に直してください。

Please translate this sentence into Japanese.

naósu 治す *to cure, to heal*

¶Hirata-sensei wa sono kanja o naoshite kureta.

平田先生はその患者を治してくれた。

Dr. Hirata cured that patient.

¶Haisha wa watashi no hidoi shitsū o naoshite kureta.

歯医者は私のひどい歯痛を治してくれた。

The dentist cured my terrible toothache.

nápukin ナプキン *napkin*

¶Napukin o hiza ni kakenasai.

ナプキンをひざにかけなさい。

Put the napkin on your lap.

nára なら ① *if it is, if it were* 《This word serves as the conditional (-**ba** form)of the copula **da** だ and follows a noun or a nominal adjective. The alternative form **naraba** ならば also occurs.》

¶Yasai nara daijōbu deshō.

野菜なら大丈夫でしょう。

Vegetables would probably be all right.

② *if (it is really the case that)* 《following a predicate》

¶"Shukudai wa mō owatta yo." "Owatta nara, misete chōdai."

「宿題はもう終わったよ」「終わったなら、見せてちょうだい」

"I already finished my homework."

"If you finished, show it to me."

naraberu 並べる ① *to put in a line, to arrange in a row*

② *to set out, to put out* 《a large number of items》

¶O-sara o tēburu ni narabete kudasai.

お皿をテーブルに並べてください。

Please set the dishes out on the table.

③ *to rank, to consider equally excellent*

narabu 並ぶ ① *to become arranged in a line, to form a row;* <*US*>*to line up,* <*UK*>*to queue up*

¶Shokken o kau tame ni narabimashita.

食券を買うために並びました。

I lined up to buy a meal ticket.

¶Yon-retsu ni narabinasai.

4列に並びなさい。

Line up in four lines.

• A to narande Aと並んで *side by side with A, beside A*

¶Akira-chan to narande aruita yo.

明ちゃんと並んで歩いたよ。

I walked side by side with Akira!

② *to rank, to be equal in excellence* [→**hitteki suru** 匹敵する]

naránai ならない *will not do* 《This word is the regular negative form of the verb **naru** 成る and has the predictable meanings as well. To have the meaning given here, it must occur in combination with a conditional clause of some kind. Translations into English ordinarily use *must not* or *may not* rather than *will not do if*, and *must* or *have to* rather than *will not do if not.*》

¶Sagyō o go-ji made ni oenakereba naranai.

作業を5時までに終えなければならない。

I have to finish this work by 5:00.

¶Chichi wa dekakenakereba narimasen deshita.

父は出かけなければなりませんでした。

My father had to go out.

¶Sonna koto o shite wa naranai.

そんな事をしてはならない。

You mustn't do such a thing.

narásu 鳴らす《The direct object is something that makes a sound.》 *to sound, to cause to make a sound; to ring* 《a bell》

¶Kanri-nin wa kasai-hōchi-ki o narashimashita.

管理人は火災報知器を鳴らしました。

The manager sounded the fire alarm.

¶Keiteki o narashimashita ne.

警笛を鳴らしましたね。

You sounded the horn, didn't you?

• yubi o narasu 指を鳴らす *to snap one's fingers*

narásu 慣らす，馴らす ① *to accustom*

¶Nihon-go ni mimi o narasu no wa jikan ga kakaru ne.

日本語に耳を慣らすのは時間がかかるね。

Accustoming one's ear to Japanese takes time, doesn't it.

② *to tame* 《*an animal*》

¶Yasei no dōbutsu o narasu no wa taihen desu.

野生の動物を慣らすのはたいへんです。

Taming wild animals is difficult.

naráu 習う *to study, to take lessons in* [→**osowaru** 教わる] [⇔**oshieru** 教える]

¶Ane wa ikebana o naratte imasu.

姉は生け花を習っています。

My older sister is studying flower arranging.

¶Ken-chan wa jūdō o naratte iru yo.

健ちゃんは柔道を習っているよ。

Ken is taking lessons in judo!

¶Narau yori narero.

習うより慣れろ。《*proverb*》

Practice makes perfect. 《*Literally: Rather than studying (something), get used to (it).*》

naréru 馴れる *to become tame*

¶Kono uma wa hito ni totemo narete iru.

この馬はとてもなれている。

This horse is very tame.

naréru 慣れる *to get accustomed, to get used* 〈*to*〉

¶Mō kono chihō no kikō ni naremashita.

もうこの地方の気候に慣れました。

I've already gotten used to the climate of this region.

¶Yumi-san wa wāpuro ni narete imasen.

由美さんはワープロに慣れていません。

Yumi is not used to word processing.

narḗtā ナレーター *narrator*

narikin 成金 *newly rich person, a nouveau riche* 《pejorative》

nariyuki 成り行き *course of events*

náru 生る *to grow, to be produced* 《The subject is a fruit, nut, etc., that appears on a tree or plant.》

¶Ano ki ni takusan no ringo ga narimasu.

あの木にたくさんのりんごがなります。

A lot of apples grow on that tree.

¶Kono mikan no ki wa yoku mi ga naru ne.

このみかんの木はよく実がなるね。

On this mandarin orange tree the fruit grows well.

naru 鳴る《The subject is something that makes a sound.》 *to sound, to make a sound; to ring* 《when the subject is a bell》

¶Shōgo no sairen ga natte imasu.

正午のサイレンが鳴っています。

The noon siren is sounding.

¶Denwa ga natte iru yo.

電話が鳴っているよ。

The telephone is ringing!

náru 成る ① *to become, to turn* 〈*into*〉

¶Hijō ni atsuku natta ne.

非常に暑くなったね。

It's become very hot, hasn't it.

¶Yamada-san no ojōsan wa gaka ni narimashita.

山田さんのお嬢さんは画家になりました。

Yamada's daughter became a painter.

¶Jirō wa zuibun se ga takaku natta ne.

次郎はずいぶん背が高くなったね。

Jiro has become very tall, hasn't he.

¶Raishu de jūgo-sai ni narimasu.

来週で15歳になります。

I will become fifteen years old next week.

¶Aki ni wa ko-no-ha ga aka ya kiiro ni narimasu.

秋には木の葉が赤や黄色になります。

In fall the tree leaves become red and yellow.

② *to be made up, to be composed,*

to consist
• A ga B kara naru AがBからなる *A is composed of B, A consists of B*
¶Shio wa natoryūmu to enso kara narimasu.
塩はナトリウムと塩素からなります。
Salt is composed of sodium and chlorine.
• A ga B kara natte iru AがBからなっている *A is composed of B, A consists of B*

narubeku なるべく *to the extent possible* [→**dekiru dake** できるだけ (s.v. **dekiru** 出来る)]
¶Narubeku isoide aruite kudasai.
なるべく急いで歩いてください。
Please walk as fast as possible.

naruhodo なるほど ① *Oh, I see* 《expressing a realization that something is so》
¶"Jōdan de itta n da yo." "Naruhodo."
「冗談で言ったんだよ」「なるほど」
"He said it as a joke!" "Oh, I see."
② *indeed, sure enough*
¶Naruhodo, jitsu ni utsukushii e desu ne.
なるほど、実に美しい絵ですね。
Indeed, it's a really beautiful picture, isn't it.

násake 情け *sympathy, compassion, pity*
• nasake-bukai 情け深い *compassionate, merciful*

nasakenái 情けない ① *miserable, pitiable, wretched*
¶Nasakenakute naki-takatta yo.
情けなくて泣きたかったよ。
I was so miserable I wanted to cry!
② *shameful, disgraceful*
¶Konna shiken ni ochiru no wa nasakenai yo.
こんな試験に落ちるのは情けないよ。
Failing this kind of test is embarrassing!

nasáru なさる 【HON. for **suru** する】

nashí 梨 *pear*

−**nashi** −無し ～**no** ～の *without, -less* 《Added to noun bases.》
¶Kuruma-nashi no seikatsu wa Amerika de wa konnan desu.
車なしの生活はアメリカでは困難です。

Life without a car is difficult in America.
• −nashi de／ni −なしで／に *without, in the absence of*
¶Kono hon wa jisho-nashi de yomemasu ka.
この本は辞書なしで読めますか。
Can you read this book without a dictionary?

nashitogeru 成し遂げる *to accomplish, to achieve, to carry through to completion*

násu 茄子 *eggplant*
• hama-nasu 浜茄子 *sweet brier*

natoryúmu ナトリウム 《Note the mismatch between the katakana spelling and the pronunciation.》 *sodium*
• enka-natoryūmu 塩化ナトリウム *sodium chloride*

natsú 夏 *summer* [⇔**fuyu** 冬]
¶Natsu ga ichiban suki desu.
夏がいちばん好きです。
I like summer best.
¶Natsu ni wa suiei o tanoshimimasu.
夏には水泳を楽しみます。
We enjoy swimming in summer.
• natsu-yasumi 夏休み <US>*summer vacation*, <UK>*the summer holidays*

natsukashíi 懐かしい *nostalgia-inducing, longed-for, dear old*
¶Ane wa tokidoki natsukashii gakusei-jidai o omoidasu.
姉は時々懐かしい学生時代を思い出す。
Whenever I look at my graduation photographs, I recall my dear old student days.

nattō 納豆 *fermented soybeans* 《a popular food in Japan》

nattoku 納得 *full understanding and assent*
• nattoku ga iku 納得がいく *one's assent is given upon full understanding*
• nattoku suru 納得する *to understand and give one's assent*

nawá 縄 *rope, cord* 《made of braided plant fibers》
¶Kono tsutsumi o nawa de shibatte

kudasai.

この包みを縄で縛ってください。

Please tie this package with rope.

¶Kono nawa o hodoite kureru?

この縄をほどいてくれる？

Will you untie these ropes for me?

nawatóbi 縄跳び *rope jumping*
• nawatobi o suru 縄跳びをする *to jump rope*

naya 納屋 *barn, shed*

nayamásu 悩ます *to afflict, to annoy, to bother*

¶Natsuo wa baka na shitsumon o shite sensei o nayamaseta.

夏生はばかな質問をして先生を悩ませた。

Natsuo often bothers the teacher with stupid questions.

• atama o nayamasu 頭を悩ます *to rack one's brains*

nayamí 悩み *anguish, distress, worry*

nayámu 悩む ① *to become worried, to become troubled*

• A ni／de nayande iru Aに／で悩んでいる *to be worried about A, to be troubled by A*

¶Yōko-san wa gakkō-seikatsu no koto de nayande iru.

洋子さんは学校生活のことで悩んでいる。

Yoko is worried about school life.

② *to become afflicted, to suffer* [→ **kurushimu** 苦しむ]

• A ni／de nayande iru Aに／で悩んでいる *to be afflicted by A, to be suffering from A*

¶Kokumin wa ue ni nayande imasu.

国民は飢えに悩んでいます。

The people are suffering from hunger.

náze なぜ *why*

¶Naze natsu ga suki na no?

なぜ夏が好きなの？

Why do you like summer?

¶Toshihiko ga naze konakatta ka shitte imasu ka.

俊彦がなぜ来なかったか知っていますか。

Do you know why Toshihiko didn't come?

• naze nara なぜなら *the reason is*

¶Ikanai hō ga ii to omoimasu. Naze nara abunai kara desu.

行かないほうがいいと思います。なぜなら危ないからです。

I think it would be better not to go. The reason is because it's dangerous.

nazo 謎 ① *riddle* «involving a play on words»

• nazo o kakeru なぞを掛ける *to ask a riddle, to pose a riddle*

• nazo o toku なぞを解く *to solve a riddle*

② *mystery, enigma*

¶Higaisha no shiin wa keisatsu ni totte nazo desu.

被害者の死因は警察にとってなぞです。

The reason for the victim's death is a mystery to the police.

nazukéru 名付ける *to name, to give a name*

• A ni／o B to nazukeru Aに／をBと名付ける *to name A B*

né 根 ① *root* «of a plant»

• ne o orosu 根を下ろす *to put down roots*

• ne ga tsuku 根が付く *roots form*

② *inborn characteristic, nature*

¶Egami-san wa ne wa ii hito desu.

江上さんは根はいい人です。

Mr. Egami is by nature a good person.

ne ね «This sentence-final particle is used to elicit agreement from the listener(s). With falling intonation, the speaker presumes agreement; with rising intonation, the speaker requests agreement.»

¶Kyō wa atsui desu ne. «falling intonation»

きょうは暑いですね。

It's hot today, isn't it.

¶Musuko-san wa dokusho ga o-suki desu ne. «rising intonation»

息子さんは読書がお好きですね。

Your son likes reading, isn't that right?

neagari 値上がり *price rise*

• neagari suru 値上がりする *to go up in price*

neage 値上げ *price raise* [⇔**nesage** 値下げ]

• neage suru 値上げする *to raise in price*
¶Basu-unchin ga sukoshi neage saremashita.

バス運賃が少し値上げされました。
The bus fare was raised a little.

nebáru 粘る ① *to be sticky; to be glutinous*

② *to persevere, to stick it out*
¶Saigo made nebaranakereba naranai yo.

最後まで粘らなければならないよ。
You have to stick it out to the end!

nebō 寝坊 ① *oversleeping, getting up late*

• nebō suru 寝坊する *to oversleep*
¶Nebō shite ressha ni noriokuremashita.

寝坊して列車に乗り遅れました。
I overslept and missed the train.

② *late riser*
¶Musuko wa aikawarazu nebō desu.

息子は相変わらず寝坊です。
My son, as ever, is a late riser.

nebokéru 寝ぼける *to become half-asleep, to become half-awake*
¶Ani wa nebokete okashii koto o iimashita.

兄は寝ぼけておかしいことを言いました。
My older brother was half-asleep and said something funny.

nebukuro 寝袋 *sleeping bag*

nebúsoku 寝不足 *lack of sleep, insufficient sleep*

nedan 値段 *price*
¶Kono tī-shatsu no nedan wa ikura desu ka.

このTシャツの値段はいくらですか。
How much is this T-shirt? 《*Literally: How much is the price of this T-shirt?*》
¶Kono rekōdo no nedan wa sanzen-en desu.

このレコードの値段は3000円です。
The price of this record is 3,000 yen.
¶Nedan mo tegoro desu.

値段も手ごろです。
The price is also reasonable.
¶Niku no nedan ga zuibun agarimashita ne.

肉の値段がずいぶん上がりましたね。

Meat prices have gone up a lot, haven't they.

nedáru 強請る *to press for, to importune for, to beg for*

• A ni B o nedaru AにBをねだる *to press A for B*
¶Musume wa haha-oya ni ningyō o nedarimashita.

娘は母親に人形をねだりました。
The girl pressed her mother for a doll.
¶Chichi ni motto kozukai ga hoshii to nedatta.

父にもっと小遣いが欲しいとねだった。
I begged Father for more pocket money.
《*Literally: I begged to Father that I want more pocket money.*》

nedoko 寝床 *bed*

néga ネガ (*photographic*)*negative*

negái 願い ① *wish, desire*
¶Watashi no negai ga kanatta yo.

私の願いがかなったよ。
My wish came true!

② *request, entreaty, favor* (*to ask*)
《*Typically occurs in the humble form; see* **o–negai** お願い.》

negáu 願う ① *to wish for, to desire*
¶O-shiawase o negatte imasu.

お幸せを願っています。
I am wishing for your happiness.
¶Watashi-tachi wa minna sekai-heiwa o negatte imasu.

私たちはみんな世界平和を願っています。
We're all wishing for world peace.

② *to ask for* [→**tanomu** 頼む]
《*Typically occurs in the humble form; see* **o–negai suru** お願いする(s.v. **o–negai** お願い).》

négi 葱 *green onion, scallion*

negoto 寝言 *talking in one's sleep*

• negoto o iu 寝言を言う *to talk in one's sleep*

neguríje ネグリジェ *negligee*

néji ねじ ① *screw* ((fastener))

• neji o shimeru 〔yurumeru〕ねじを締める〔緩める〕*to tighten* 〔*loosen*〕*a screw*

② *stem* 《of a clock or watch》

• neji o maku ねじを巻く *to wind the stem*

• neji-mawashi ねじ回し *screwdriver*

nejíru 捩じる {5} *to twist, to turn* 《*transitive*》

• totte o nejiru 取っ手をねじる *to turn a handle*

• neji o nejiru ねじをねじる *to screw a screw*

nekaseru 寝かせる ① *to put to bed; to put to sleep*
　② *to lay down, to lay horizontally*

nekasu 寝かす [☞**nekaseru** 寝かせる]

nekkachifu ネッカチーフ *neckerchief*

nékkuresu ネックレス *necklace* [→**kubi-kazari** 首飾り]

nekkyō 熱狂 *wild enthusiasm, excitement*

• nekkyō suru 熱狂する *to get wildly enthusiastic, to go wild with excitement*

¶Yakyū-bu no shōri ni minna nekkyō shite shimatta.
野球部の勝利にみんな熱狂してしまった。
Everyone got excited at the baseball team's victory.

• nekkyō-teki na 熱狂的な *enthusiastic, ardent*

¶Ozaki-san wa opera no nekkyō-teki na fan desu.
尾崎さんはオペラの熱狂的なファンです。
Mr. Ozaki is an ardent fan of the opera.

néko 猫 *cat*

¶Horikawa-san wa neko o ni-hiki katte imasu.
堀川さんは猫を2匹飼っています。
Ms. Horikawa keeps two cats.

¶Neko ga soto de nyānyā to naite imasu.
猫が外でニャーニャーと鳴いています。
A cat is meowing outside.

• ko-neko 子猫 *kitten*

nekojita 猫舌 *person whose tongue cannot stand hot food or drink*

nekoróbu 寝転ぶ *to lie down sprawlingly, to sprawl*

¶Takusan no hito ga suna-hama ni nekoronde imashita.
たくさんの人が砂浜に寝転んでいました。
A lot of people were sprawled on the sandy beach.

nékutai ネクタイ *necktie* 、

• nekutai-pin ネクタイピン *tiepin*

nemaki 寝巻 *kimono-like sleepwear*

nému ネーム *name* [→**namae** 名前]

• nému-purēto ネームプレート *nameplate*

nemui 眠い *sleepy, drowsy*

¶Nemukute hon ga yomenai desu.
眠くて本が読めないです。
I'm so sleepy I can't read the book.

nemuri 眠り *sleep*

¶Kodomo wa fukai nemuri ni ochimashita.
子供は深い眠りに落ちました。
The child fell into a deep sleep.

nemuru 眠る ① *to sleep*

¶Otōto wa itsu-mo ku-jikan nemurimasu.
弟はいつも9時間眠ります。
My younger brother always sleeps for nine hours.

¶Otōsan wa mada gussuri to nemutte iru yo.
お父さんはまだぐっすりと眠っているよ。
Dad is still sleeping soundly!

　② *to fall asleep* [⇔**mezameru** 目覚める]

¶Nan-ji ni nemurimashita ka.
何時に眠りましたか。
What time did you go to sleep?

nén 年 ① *year*

¶Nen ni yon-kai-gurai Fukuoka ni ikimasu.
年に4回ぐらい福岡に行きます。
I go to Fukuoka about four times a year.

• -nen −年《counter for year dates; see Appendix 2》

¶Taiheiyō-sensō wa sen-kyūhyaku-yon-jūgo-nen ni owarimashita.
太平洋戦争は1945年に終わりました。
The Pacific War ended in 1945.

¶Ikeda-san wa nan-nen ni umaremashita ka.
池田さんは何年に生まれましたか。
In what year was Mr. Ikeda born?

• -nen −年《counter for number of years; see Appendix 2》

¶Maiku-san wa Nihon ni kite chōdo ichi-nen da.

マイクさんは日本に来てちょうど１年だ。

It is exactly one year since Mike came to Japan.

¶Sono kōkai wa san-nen kakarimashita.

その航海は３年かかりました。

That voyage took three years.

② *year in school,* <US>*grade* [→**gakunen** 学年]

• nen-jū 年中 *all year round* [→**ichi-nen-jū** 一年中 (s.v. **ichinen** 一年)]

• nen-matsu 年末 *end of the year*

nén 念 ① *feeling, thought*

② [[→**chūi** 注意]] *attention, notice; care, caution*

• A ni nen o ireru Aに念を入れる *to pay careful attention to A; to exercise care in A*

• nen no tame 念のため *just in case*

nendai 年代 ① *age, period, era* [→**jidai** 時代]

• -nendai －年代 *the decade of* 《Added to number bases ending in zero.》

• sen-kyūhyaku-nanajū-nendai 1970年代 *the 1970's*

② *generation, age-group* [→**sedai** 世代]

• wakai nendai 若い年代 *the younger generation*

néndo 粘土 *clay*

• nendo o koneru 粘土をこねる *to knead clay*

nengájō 年賀状 *New Year's card*

nengáppi 年月日 *date* 《i.e., year, month, and day》

néngetsu 年月 *many years*

nengō 年号 *era name* 《In the case of Japan, this word refers to imperial era names.》

nenjūgyóji 年中行事 *annual event*

nenkan 年鑑 *year-in-review publication, yearbook*

nenkin 年金 *annuity, pension*

nenrei 年齢 *age* 《of a person or animal》 [→**toshi** 年②]

• nenrei-seigen 年齢制限 *age limit*

• heikin-nenrei 平均年齢 *average age*

• seishin-nenrei 精神年齢 *mental age*

nenryō 燃料 *fuel*

• nenryō-tanku 燃料タンク *fuel tank*

-nen-sei －年生 《counter for students in a given year of school; see Appendix 2》

• ichi-nen-sei １年生 *first-year student*

nenza 捻挫 *sprain*

• nenza suru ねんざする *to sprain*

¶Basuketto-senshu wa ashikubi o nenza shimashita.

バスケット選手は足首をねんざしました。

The basketball player sprained his ankle.

néon ネオン *neon*

• neon-sain ネオンサイン *neon sign*

nerau 狙う *to aim at, to aim for*

¶Shuryō-ka wa ōkami o jū de neraimashita.

狩猟家はおおかみを銃でねらいました。

The hunter aimed his gun at the wolf.

¶Kono chīmu wa yūshō o neratte imasu.

このチームは優勝をねらっています。

This team is aiming for the championship.

neru 寝る ① *to go to bed* [⇔**okiru** 起きる①]

¶Tokidoki yonaka no jūni-ji-sugi ni nemasu.

時々夜中の12時過ぎに寝ます。

I sometimes go to bed after 12:00 at night.

¶Mō neru jikan desu yo.

もう寝る時間ですよ。

It's already time for bed!

② *to sleep* [→**nemuru** 眠る①]

③ *to fall asleep* [→**nemuru** 眠る②]

néru 練る{5}① *to knead*

② *to train, to drill, to exercise* [→**kunren suru** 訓練する]

• waza o neru 技を練る *to exercise a skill*

③ *to think over and improve on*

• keikaku o neru 計画を練る *to think over and improve on a plan*

nesagari 値下がり *price decline*

• nesagari suru 値下がりする *to go down in price*

nesage 値下げ *lowering prices* [⇔**neage**

値上げ]
• nesage suru 値下げする *to lower the price of*
¶ Yunyū-hin ga nesage saremashita.
輸入品が値下げされました。
The price of imported goods has been lowered.

nḗsan 姉さん [☞**onḗsan** お姉さん]

nésshin 熱心 *enthusiasm, zeal*
• nesshin na 熱心な *enthusiastic, fervent, devoted, zealous, ardent*
¶ Akira-san wa nesshin na gakusei desu.
明さんは熱心な学生です。
Akira is an enthusiastic student.
¶ Hosokawa-sensei wa shokubutsu-gaku no kenkyū ni nesshin desu.
細川先生は植物学の研究に熱心です。
Dr. Hosokawa is devoted to botanical research.
¶ Megumi-san wa nesshin ni Eigo no renshū o shite iru.
恵子さんは熱心に英語の練習をしている。
Megumi is ardently practicing English.

nessuru 熱する{Irreg.} ① *to heat up* 《transitive or intransitive》
¶ Sono mizu o subayaku nesshite kudasai.
その水をすばやく熱してください。
Please heat up that water quickly.
② *to get excited* [→**kōfun suru** 興奮する]; *to get enthusiastic, to become zealous* [→**netchū suru** 熱中する]

netámu 妬む、嫉む *to become jealous of, to become envious of*
¶ Takuya wa Yumi no seikō o netande imasu.
拓也は由美の成功をねたんでいます。
Takuya is jealous of Yumi's success.

netchū 熱中 ～*no* ～の *enthusiastic, absorbed* [→**muchū no** 夢中の]
• netchū suru 熱中する *to get enthusiastic, to become absorbed*
¶ Chichi wa gorufu ni netchū shite imasu.
父はゴルフに熱中しています。
My father is enthusiastic about golf.
¶ Shujin wa shōsetsu o yomu koto ni netchū shite ita.

主人は小説を読むことに熱中していた。
My husband was absorbed in reading a novel.
¶ Kawamoto-sensei wa rekishi no kenkyū ni netchū shimashita.
川本先生は歴史の研究に熱中しました。
Dr. Kawamoto became absorbed in the study of history.

netsú 熱 ① *heat, thermal energy*
• netsu o kuwaeru 熱を加える *to add heat, to apply heat*
② *fever, (above-normal body) temperature*
¶ Kesa netsu o hakarimashita ka.
けさ熱を計りましたか。
Did you take your temperature this morning?
¶ Tomoko-san wa netsu ga takai yo.
友子さんは熱が高いよ。
Tomoko has a high temperature!

nettai 熱帯 *the tropics* [⇔**kantai** 寒帯]
• nettai-gyo 熱帯魚 *tropical fish*
• nettai-shokubutsu 熱帯植物 *tropical plant*
• nettai-ya 熱帯夜 *uncomfortably hot night*

nétto ネット *net* 《especially in tennis, volleyball, etc.》
• netto o haru ネットを張る *to put up a net*
• bakku-netto バックネット *backstop* 《on a baseball field》

nettō 熱湯 *boiling water*

nettowāku ネットワーク *network*
• terebi-nettowāku テレビネットワーク *television network*

neuchi 値打ち *worth, value* [→**kachi** 価値]

nezumi 鼠 *rat; mouse*
• nezumi-iro 鼠色 *gray* 《as a noun》
• nezumi-tori 鼠取り *rattrap; mousetrap*

nezuyói 根強い *deep-rooted, unchanging, firm*

ní 二 *two* 《see Appendix 2》
• Ni-gatsu 二月 *February*

ni に 《noun-following particle》 ① *at, on, in* 《a time》

¶Shichi-gatsu yokka no gozen chū ni shuppatsu shimashita.

7月4日の午前中に出発しました。

I started out on the morning of July 4th.

¶Itsu-mo jūichi-ji ni nemasu.

いつも11時に寝ます。

I always go to bed at 11:00.

¶Tahara-san wa Doyōbi ni takkyū o shimasu.

田原さんは土曜日に卓球をします。

Ms. Tahara plays table tennis on Saturdays.

¶Haha wa sen-kyūhyaku-yonjūhachi-nen ni umaremashita.

母は1948年に生まれました。

My mother was born in 1948.

② *at, on, in* «indicating a place where something is located»

¶Kyōko-san wa ima kōen ni imasu.

京子さんは今公園にいます。

Kyoko is at the park now.

¶Mekishiko wa Amerika-gasshūkoku no minami ni aru.

メキシコはアメリカ合衆国の南にある。

Mexico is south of the United States.

¶Nemuro wa Hokkaidō no tōbu ni arimasu.

根室は北海道の東部にあります。

Nemuro is in the eastern part of Hokkaido.

¶Ane wa Tōkyō ni sunde imasu.

姉は東京に住んでいます。

My older sister lives in Tokyo.

③ *to, for* [→**e** へ①]

¶Shōnen wa chichi-oya no tokoro ni hashitte ikimashita.

少年は父親の所に走っていきました。

The boy went running to his father.

④ *into, onto* [→**e** へ②]

¶Kutsu o geta-bako ni iremashita.

靴をげた箱に入れました。

I put the shoes into the shoe cupboard.

⑤ *by* «especially in combination with a passive verb»

¶Kono hon wa takusan no hito ni yomarete imasu.

この本はたくさんの人に読まれています。

This book is being read by a lot of people.

niáu 似合う *to become, to suit; to go well*

• A ni niau　Aに似合う *to become A, to suit A; to go well with A*

¶Kono akai sētā wa kare ni yoku niaimasu.

この赤いセーターは彼によく似合います。

This red sweater suits my boyfriend well.

¶Kono bōshi wa sono doresu ni niawanai yo.

この帽子はそのドレスに似合わないよ。

This hat doesn't match that dress!

nibúi 鈍い [[⇔**surudoi** 鋭い]]

① *dull, blunt, poor for cutting*

• nibui itami　鈍い痛み *dull pain*

② *insensitive, not keen* [→**donkan na** 鈍感な]

-**nichi** 一日 ① «counter for number of days; see Appendix 2»

¶Sono taikai wa jūni-nichi tsuzukimasu.

その大会は12日続きます。

That convention will last twelve days.

② «counter for days of the month; see Appendix 2»

¶Sugiyama-san wa Jū-gatsu jūgo-nichi ni kimasu.

杉山さんは10月15日に来ます。

Ms. Sugiyama will come on March 15th.

nichibotsu 日没 *sunset, nightfall*

ni chigai-nái に違いない *it is certain that, there is no doubt that, it must be the case that* «This expression generally follows an informal-style predicate, but the word preceding **ni chigai-nai** cannot be the copula form **da** だ. When **ni chigai-nai** is added to a clause that would end with **da**, the **da** does not appear.»

¶Hamada-san wa atama ga ii ni chigai-nai.

浜田さんは頭がいいに違いない。

There is no doubt that Ms. Hamada is smart.

¶Sumisu-san wa Igirisu-jin ni chigai nai yo.

スミスさんはイギリス人に違いないよ。

Mr. Smith must be an Englishman!

¶Ano hito wa jijitsu o shitte ita ni chigai nai.

あの人は事実を知っていたに違いない。

That person must have known the truth.

níchiji 日時 *the time and date*

¶Nichiji ga kimattara, shirasete kudasai.

日時が決まったら、知らせてください。

Please notify me as soon as the time and date are set.

nichijō 日常 〜no 〜の *everyday, daily*

• nichijō-kaiwa 日常会話 (*ordinary*) *everyday conversation*

• nichijō-seikatsu 日常生活 *everyday life*

¶Denwa wa nichijō-seikatsu no ichibu ni narimashita.

電話は日常生活の一部になりました。

The telephone has become a part of everyday life.

Nichiyō 日曜 [☞**Nichiyōbi** 日曜日]

• Nichiyō-gaka 日曜画家 *Sunday painter, week-end painter*

Nichiyōbi 日曜日 *Sunday*

¶Nichiyōbi wa taitei tenisu o shimasu.

日曜日はたいていテニスをします。

I usually play tennis on Sunday.

¶Tsugi no Nichiyōbi ni eiga ni ikō.

次の日曜日に映画に行こう。

Let's go to the movies next Sunday.

¶Chichi wa maishū Nichiyōbi ni kuruma o araimasu.

父は毎週日曜日に車を洗います。

My father washes the car every Sunday.

nichiyōhin 日用品 *daily necessities, things used every day*

nido-to 二度と *ever again* 《Always occurs in combination with a negative predicate.》

¶Nido-to soko ni wa ikitaku arimasen.

二度とそこには行きたくありません。

I don't want to go there ever again.

nieru 煮える *to be cooked by boiling*

¶Jagaimo ga yoku niemashita.

じゃがいもがよく煮えました。

The potatoes have been cooked well.

nífuda 荷札 *baggage tag*

nigái 苦い *bitter*

¶Kono kusuri wa nigai ne.

この薬は苦いね。

This medicine is bitter, isn't it.

¶Kinō nigai keiken o shimashita.

きのう苦い経験をしました。

I had a bitter experience yesterday.

• nigai kao 苦い顔 *sour face*

nigásu 逃がす ① *to set free, to let go* [→**hanasu** 放す②]

¶Nagata-san wa koi sū-hiki o nigashite yatta.

長田さんはこい数匹を逃がしてやった。

Mr. Nagata set several carp free.

② *to let escape, to fail to catch*

• chansu o nigasu チャンスを逃がす *to let an opportunity get away*

nigate 苦手 〜na 〜な ① *bad at, weak in* 《Used to describe both the people who are bad at something and the things they are bad at.》 [⇔**tokui no**／**na** 得意の／な]

¶Watashi wa ryōri ga nigate desu.

私は料理が苦手です。

I'm no good at cooking.

② 《Used to describe both the people who find someone or something hard to deal with and the people or things they find hard to deal with.》 *hard to deal with, hard to take; hard to beat* 《as an opponent》

¶Ōhara-san wa nigate desu.

大原さんは苦手です。

Ms. Ohara is hard for me to deal with.

nigéru 逃げる *to run away, to flee, to escape*

¶Dorobō wa kuruma de nigemashita.

泥棒は車で逃げました。

The thief fled in a car.

¶Kuma ga dōbutsu-en kara nigemashita.

熊が動物園から逃げました。

A bear escaped from the zoo.

nigiru 握る{5} ① *to grasp, to grip* 《with the hand》

¶Kodomo wa okāsan no te o nigirimashita.

子供はお母さんの手を握りました。

The child grasped his mother's hand.

¶Sono senshu wa batto o nigirimashita.
その選手はバットを握りました。
That player gripped the bat.

　② *to seize, to make one's own*
•kenryoku o nigiru 権力を握る *to take power*

nigiwáu 賑わう *to become lively, to become bustling* 《with people》
¶Hamabe wa wakamono de nigiwatte imashita.
浜辺は若者でにぎわっていました。
The beach was bustling with young people.

nigíyaka 賑やか 〜**na** 〜な *lively, bustling* 《with people》
¶Ano tōri wa nigiyaka desu.
あの通りはにぎやかです。
That street is bustling.
¶Kore wa nigiyaka na basho desu ne.
これはにぎやかな場所ですね。
This is a lively place, isn't it?

nigóru 濁る ① *to become muddy, to become turbid*
¶Kono kawa wa ō-ame no tame nigotte imasu.
この川は大雨のため濁っています。
This river is muddy because of heavy rain.

　② *to become spiritually impure, to become corrupt*

Nihón 日本 *Japan*
¶Ano hito wa Nihon de wa yūmei na kashu desu.
あの人は日本では有名な歌手です。
That person is a famous singer in Japan.
¶Sumisu-san wa Nihon bunka ni kyōmi ga arimasu.
スミスさんは日本文化に興味があります。
Mr. Smith is interested in Japanese culture.
•Nihon-go 日本語 *the Japanese language*
•Nihon-jin 日本人 *Japanese person*
•Nihon-kai 日本海 *the Japan Sea*
•Nihon-kairyū 日本海流 *the Japan Current*

•Nihon-koku-kenpō 日本国憲法 *the Constitution of Japan*
•Nihon-ma 日本間 *Japanese-style room*
•Nihon-rettō 日本列島 *the Japanese Islands, the Japanese Archipelago*
•Nihon-sankei 日本三景 *the three most famous scenic spots in Japan* 《**Matsushima** 松島, **Ama-no-hashidate** 天の橋立, **Itsukushima** 厳島》
•Nihon-sei no 日本製の *Japanese-made, made in Japan*
•Nihon-shu 日本酒 *(Japanese)sake* [→ **sake** 酒①]

niji 虹 *rainbow*
•niji ga kakaru にじがかかる *a rainbow appears*
¶Arashi no ato, sora ni niji ga kakarimashita.
あらしの後、空に虹がかかりました。
After the storm, a rainbow appeared in the sky.

nijímu にじむ *to blot, to run; to spread, to ooze*
¶Arau to, iro ga nijimimasu.
洗うと、色がにじみます。
When you wash it, the colors run.
¶Kono kami wa sugu ni inku ga nijimimasu.
この紙はすぐにインクがにじみます。
Ink blots easily on this paper.

nijū 二重 〜**no** 〜の *double, dual*
¶Kono heya ni wa nijū no mado ga tsuite imasu.
この部屋には二重の窓がついています。
This room has double windows.
•nijū-ago 二重顎 *double chin*
•nijū-shō 二重唱 *(vocal)duet*
•nijū-sō 二重奏 *(instrumental)duet*

ni kagítte に限って *out of all the possibilities, limited to this／that particular* 《following a noun》
¶Kyō ni kagitte dare mo kite imasen.
きょうに限ってだれも来ていません。
On this particular day nobody has come.

ni kakawárazu にかかわらず *regardless of, irrespective of* 《following a noun》

¶Kaigō wa tenkō ni kakawarazu hiraka-remasu.

会合は天候にかかわらず開かれます。

The meeting will be held regardless of the weather.

ni kákete にかけて [[→**made** まで①]]

until 《following a noun referring to a point in time》; *through* 《when a preceding noun refers to something longer than a point in time》

¶Shichi-gatsu kara Hachi-gatsu ni kakete Chūgoku o ryokō shimasu.

7月から8月にかけて中国を旅行します。

I am going to travel in China from July through August.

ni kánshite に関して *about, concerning* 《following a noun》 [→**ni tsuite** について]

ni kansúru に関する *about, concerning* 《following a noun and functioning as a noun modifier》

¶Dōbutsu ni kansuru hon wa arimasu ka.

動物に関する本はありますか。

Do you have any books about animals?

¶Ano hito wa toshi-mondai ni kansuru kōen o shita.

あの人は都市問題に関する講演をした。

That person gave a lecture about urban problems.

níkibi にきび *pimple*

¶Kao ni nikibi ga dekita yo.

顔ににきびができたよ。

A pimple appeared on my face!

nikka 日課 *daily task*

nikkan 日刊 〜**no** 〜の *(published) daily*

• nikkan-shi 日刊紙 *daily newspaper*

nikkeru ニッケル *nickel* ((metal))

nikki 日記 *diary*

• nikki o tsukeru 日記を付ける *to keep a diary*

¶Nishida-san wa go-nen-kan nikki o tsukete imasu.

西田さんは5年間日記をつけています。

Ms. Nishida has been keeping a diary for five years.

nikkō 日光 *sunlight, sunshine*

¶Kono taoru o nikkō de kawakashita yo.

このタオルを日光で乾かしたよ。

I dried this towel in the sunshine!

• nikkō o abiru 日光を浴びる *to sunbathe*

• nikkō-yoku 日光浴 *sunbathing*

• chokusha-nikkō 直射日光 *direct sunlight*

nikkóri にっこり（〜**to** 〜と）*with a big smile, beamingly*

¶Shōjo wa watashi ni nikkori to hohoe-mimashita.

少女は私ににっこりとほほえみました。

The little girl smiled beamingly at me.

nikkunému ニックネーム *nickname* [→**adana** あだ名; **aishō** 愛称]

nikochin ニコチン *nicotine*

níkoniko にこにこ（〜**to** 〜と）*smilingly, with a happy smile*

• nikoniko suru にこにこする *to smile happily*

nikú 肉 *meat*

• hiki-niku 挽き肉 *ground meat,* <*UK*>*minced meat*

nikúi 憎い *hateful, detestable*

¶Aitsu wa nikui yatsu da nā.

あいつは憎いやつだなあ。

Man, that guy's a hateful guy!

-nikui －にくい *hard to, difficult to* 《Added to verb bases.》 [⇔**-yasui** －やすい]

¶Kono pazuru wa toki-nikui desu.

このパズルは解きにくいです。

This puzzle is hard to solve.

nikúmu 憎む *to hate*

¶Raibaru o nikunde wa ikenai yo.

ライバルを憎んではいけないよ。

You must not hate your rivals!

nikurashíi 憎らしい *hateful, annoying, aggravating*

¶Sonna nikurashii koto o iwanai de.

そんな憎らしいことを言わないで。

Don't say such hateful things.

nikushimi 憎しみ *hatred, animosity, enmity*

nikushin 肉親 *blood relative*

nikutai 肉体 *the (living)body, the flesh*

《as opposed to the mind or spirit》[⇔**sei-shin** 精神]

• nikutai-bi 肉体美 *physical beauty*

• nikutai-rōdō 肉体労働 *physical labor*

ní mo kakawárazu にもかかわらず 【FORMAL】 *although* 《following a predicate》[→**noni** のに①]; *in spite of* 《following a noun》

¶Ame ni mo kakawarazu haha wa deka-kemashita.

雨にもかかわらず母は出かけました。

In spite of the rain my mother went out.

nímotsu 荷物 *baggage, luggage*

¶Kono nimotsu o hakonde kudasaimasen ka.

この荷物を運んでくださいませんか。

Won't you please carry this baggage for me?

ni mukatte に向かって 《following a noun》 ① *toward, for, in the direction of*

¶Herikoputā ga nishi ni mukatte tonde iru.

ヘリコプターが西に向かって飛んでいる。

A helicopter is flying west.

② *against, in opposition to*

¶Fune wa kaze ni mukatte susunde imasu.

船は風に向かって進んでいます。

The boat is moving forward against the wind.

-nin 一人 《counter for people; see Appendix 2》

nináu 担う *to carry on one's shoulder, to shoulder* [→**katsugu** 担ぐ①]

ningen 人間 *human being*

• ningen-kankei 人間関係 *human relationships*

• ningen-sei 人間性 *human nature*

níngyo 人魚 *mermaid, merman*

ningyō 人形 *doll*

• ningyō-geki 人形劇 *puppet show*

• ayatsuri-ningyō 操り人形 *puppet; marionette*

ninjin 人参 *carrot*

nínjō 人情 *human feelings, humanity*

¶Go-shujin wa totemo ninjō no aru hito desu.

ご主人はとても人情のある人です。

Your husband is a very warm-hearted person.

ninki 人気 *popularity*

• A ni ninki ga aru Aに人気がある *to be popular with A*

¶Yamada-sensei wa seito ni ninki ga arimasu.

山田先生は生徒に人気があります。

Mr. Yamada is popular with his students.

• ninki-kashu 人気歌手 *popular singer*

• ninki-mono 人気者 *a favorite, popular person*

• ninki-tōhyō 人気投票 *popularity vote*

-nin-mae 一人前 《counter for food portions; see Appendix 2》

ninmei 任命 *appointment* 《to a position》

• ninmei suru 任命する *to appoint*

ninshin 妊娠 *pregnancy*

• ninshin suru 妊娠する *to become pregnant*

¶Hayashi-san wa ninshin shite imasu.

林さんは妊娠しています。

Ms. Hayashi is pregnant.

níntai 忍耐 *patience, endurance, perseverance* [→**gaman** 我慢]

• nintai suru 忍耐する *to bear, to endure, to put up with*

• nintai-zuyoi 忍耐強い *very patient, persevering*

nínzu 人数 *the number* (*of people*)

¶Gakkō no seito no ninzu wa nan-nin desu ka.

学校の生徒の人数は何人ですか。

What is the number of school students?

• shō-ninzu 少人数 *a small number of people*

• ta-ninzu 多人数 *a large number of people*

nínzū 人数 [☞**ninzu** 人数]

niói 匂い, 臭い *odor, smell, scent*

¶Kono kōsui wa ii nioi ga shimasu.

この香水はいいにおいがします。

This perfume smells nice.

¶Kono heya wa gasu no nioi ga suru yo.

この部屋はガスのにおいがするよ。

This room smells of gas!

• nioi o kagu においをかぐ *to sniff an odor*

¶Sono gyūnyū no nioi o kaide mimashita.

その牛乳のにおいをかいでみました。

I tried smelling the milk.

ni ōjite に応じて *according to, in accordance with, in proportion to* 《following a noun》

¶Nōryoku ni ōjite sono shigoto o buntan shimashō.

能力に応じてその仕事を分担しましょう。

Let's divide up that work according to our abilities.

nióu 臭う *to give off a smell, to smell*

¶Kono sakana wa nioimasu.

この魚はにおいます。

This fish smells.

Nippón 日本 [☞**Nihon** 日本]

nirámu 睨む *to glare at, to look sharply at*

¶Sonna fū ni watashi o niramanai de.

そんなふうに私をにらまないで。

Don't glare at me in that way.

niru 似る *to become similar, to develop a resemblance*

• nite iru 似ている *to be similar, to bear a resemblance*

¶Akiko-san wa okāsan ni yoku nite imasu.

秋子さんはお母さんによく似ています。

Akiko closely resembles her mother.

niru 煮る *to cook by boiling*

¶Haha wa gyūniku to jagaimo o nite imasu.

母は牛肉とじゃがいもを煮ています。

My mother is boiling beef and potatoes.

nírui 二塁 *second base* [→**sekando** セカンド①]《in baseball》

• nirui-da 二塁打 *two-base hit, double*

• nirui-shu 二塁手 *second baseman* [→**sekando** セカンド②]

niryū 二流 ～**no** ～の *second-rate*

nīsan 兄さん [☞**onīsan** お兄さん]

nise 偽 ～**no** ～の *false, fake* [⇔**honmono no** 本物の]

• nise-mono 偽物 *an imitation, a fake* [⇔**honmono** 本物]

• nise-satsu 偽札 *counterfeit bill, counterfeit banknote*

nishi 西 *the west* [⇔**higashi** 東]

¶Taiyō wa nishi ni shizumimasu.

太陽は西に沈みます。

The sun sets in the west.

• nishi-bi 西日 *afternoon sunlight*

• Nishi-hankyū 西半球 *the Western Hemisphere*

• Nishi-Yōroppa 西ヨーロッパ *Western Europe* [→**Seiō** 西欧]

nishin 鰊 *herring*

ni shitagatte に従って ① *as, in accordance with, in proportion to* 《following a verb in the nonpast tense》 [→**ni tsurete** につれて]

¶Toshi o toru ni shitagatte, shiwa ga fuemasu.

年を取るにしたがって、しわがふえます。

As one grows older, one gets more wrinkles.

② *according to, in accordance with* 《following a noun》

¶Setsumei sho ni shitagatte denwa o setchi shimashita.

説明書にしたがって電話を設置しました。

I installed the telephone in accordance with the instructions.

ni shité wa にしては *for, with respect to being* 《following a noun》

¶Ogawa-san wa rokujūs-sai ni shite wa wakaku miemasu.

小川さんは60歳にしては若く見えます。

Mr. Ogawa looks young for sixty years old.

nisshabyō 日射病 *sunstroke*

nisshoku 日食 *solar eclipse*

• kaiki-nisshoku 皆既日食 *total solar eclipse*

ni sugínai に過ぎない [☞**sugiru** 過ぎる②]

ni táishite に対して《following a noun》 ① *toward, regarding*

¶Ano hito wa watshi-tachi ni taishite shinsetsu desu.

あの人は私たちに対して親切です。

He is kind toward us.

¶Go-shōtai ni taishite kokoro kara kansha shimasu.

ご招待に対して心から感謝します。

I thank you from my heart for your invitation. «Literally: Regarding your invitation, I give thanks from my heart.»

② *against, in opposition to*

¶Mura-bito wa sono keikaku ni taishite kōgi shimashita.

村人はその計画に対して抗議しました。

The villagers protested against that plan.

ni táisuru に対する《*following a noun and functioning as a noun modifier*》

① *toward, regarding*

¶Watashi ni taisuru taido wa totemo kōi-teki desu.

私に対する態度はとても好意的です。

Their attitude toward me is very friendly.

② *against, in opposition to*

nitchū 日中 *daytime, the daylight hours* [→**hiruma** 昼間]

¶Nitchū wa atataka desu ga, asa yū wa hiekomimasu.

日中は暖かですが、朝夕は冷え込みます。

It's warm in the daytime, but cool in the morning and evening.

ni tótte にとって *for, to, from the standpoint of*

¶Nihon-go o hanasu no wa watashi ni totte wa kantan desu.

日本語を話すのは私にとっては簡単です。

Speaking Japanese is very easy for me.

¶Sono tokei wa otōto ni totte taisetsu na mono desu.

その時計は弟にとって大切な物です。

That watch is important to my younger brother.

ni tsúite について *about, concerning* 《*following a noun*》

¶Sore ni tsuite sukoshi setsumei shite kudasai.

それについて少し説明してください。

Please explain a little about that.

¶Sensei wa Ōsutoraria ni tsuite hana-shita.

先生はオーストラリアについて話した。

The teacher talked about Australia.

¶Kōzan-shokubutsu ni tsuite no hon ga hitsuyō desu.

高山植物についての本が必要です。

I need a book about alpine plants.

ni tsurete につれて *as, in accordance with, in proportion to* 《*following a verb in the nonpast tense*》

¶Jikan ga tatsu ni tsurete, byōki wa yoku natta.

時がたつにつれて、病気はよくなった。

As time passed, the illness got better.

¶Yama o noboru ni tsurete, kūki ga usuku natta.

山を登るにつれて、空気が薄くなった。

As we climbed the mountain, the air became thinner and thinner.

nittei 日程 *schedule* 《*of what is to be done on what day*》

nítto ニット ～**no** ～の *knitted*

• nitto no sūtsu ニットのスーツ *knitted suit*

niwa 庭 *garden; yard*

• ura-niwa 裏庭 *back yard; back garden*

níwaka にわか ～**no** ～の *sudden* [→**totsuzen no** 突然の]

• niwaka-ame にわか雨 *sudden rainshower*

niwatori 鶏 *chicken*

• niwatori-goya 鶏小屋 *chicken coop*

ni yotte によって《*following a noun*》

① *by, by means of* [→**de** で②]

② *by* 《*in combination with a passive verb*》[→**ni** に⑤]

¶Shin-suisei ga aru kagaku-sha ni yotte hakken sareta.

新彗星がある科学者によって発見された。

A new comet has been discovered by a certain scientist.

③ *depending on*

¶Sore wa hito ni yotte chigaimasu.

それは人によって違います。

That differs depending on the person.

no の *of, having to do with* 《*noun-*

following particle》
• A no B AのB *B of A, B having to do with A, A's B*
¶Kore wa chichi no pen desu.
これは父のペンです。
This is my father's pen.
¶Kore wa kodomo-tachi no heya desu.
これは子供たちの部屋です。
This is the children's room.
¶Tokyō wa Nihon no shuto desu.
東京は日本の首都です。
Tokyo is the capital of Japan.
¶Kubo-sensei wa rika no sensei desu.
久保先生は理科の先生です。
Ms. Kubo is a science teacher.
¶Ashita Eigo no shiken ga arimasu.
あした英語の試験があります。
There will be an English examination tomorrow.
¶Rekishi no hon wa asoko ni arimasu.
歴史の本はあそこにあります。
The history books are over there.
¶Ane wa Hibiya no eiga-kan ni ikimashita.
姉は日比谷の映画館に行きました。
My older sister went to a movie theater in Hibiya.

no の ① *one, ones* 《as a pronoun》
¶Kuroi pen wa aru kedo, akai no wa nai ne.
黒いペンはあるけど、赤いのはないね。
There are black pens, but there are no red ones, are there.
¶Senjitsu katta no wa dame deshita.
先日買ったのはだめでした。
The one I bought the other day was no good.
② *-ing* 《Makes a preceding clause function as a noun.》
¶Hitori de iku no wa abunai desu yo.
独りで行くのは危ないですよ。
Going alone is dangerous!
¶Kono rajio o kumitateru no wa kantan desu.
このラジオを組み立てるのは簡単です。
Putting this radio together is simple.
nó 脳 *brain*

• nō-ha 脳波 *brain waves*
• nō-ikketsu 脳溢血 *cerebral hemorrhage, stroke*
• nō-miso 脳味噌 *brains, gray matter*
• nō-shi 脳死 *brain death*
nó 能 *noh* 《a kind of traditional Japanese drama》
nobásu 延ばす, 伸ばす ① *to postpone, to put off* [→**enki suru** 延期する]
¶Yakyū no shiai o is-shūkan nobashimashita.
野球の試合を1週間延ばしました。
We postponed the baseball game one week.
¶Ashita made henji o nobashimashita.
あしたまで返事を延ばしました。
I put off replying until tomorrow.
② *to prolong, to extend* 《in time》 [→**enchō suru** 延長する②]
¶Chichi wa Amerika-taizai o mō is-shūkan nobashita.
父はアメリカ滞在をもう1週間延ばした。
My father extended his stay in the United States by one week.
③ *to make longer, to extend* 《in space》 [→**enchō suru** 延長する①]
¶Sono tetsudō wa ato juk-kiro nobasu sō desu.
その鉄道はあと10キロ延ばすそうです。
I hear they're going to extend that railroad another ten kilometers.
④ *to reach out, to extend* 《transitive》
¶Imōto wa ningyō o torō to te o nobashimashita.
妹は人形を取ろうと手を伸ばしました。
My younger sister reached her hand out and tried to take the doll.
⑤ *to let grow* 《longer or taller》
¶Keiko-san wa kami-no-ke o nagaku nobashite imasu.
恵子さんは髪の毛を長く伸ばしています。
Keiko has let her hair grow long.
⑥ *to straighten; to smooth out* 《a wrinkle, etc.》
• sensuji o nobasu 背筋を伸ばす *to straighten one's back*
nobéru 述べる *to state, to tell*

¶ Tazawa-san mo keikaku ni tsuite iken o nobemasu.

田沢さんも計画について意見を述べます。

Ms. Tazawa will also state her opinion about the plan.

Nōberúshō ノーベル賞 *Nobel prize*

• Nōberushō-jushō-sha ノーベル賞受賞者 *Nobel prize winner*

nobí 延び, 伸び ① *growth* 《in length or height》

② *increase* [→**zōka** 増加]

③ *stretching* (*one's body*)

• nobi o suru 伸びをする *to stretch*

nobíru 延びる; 伸びる ① *to be postponed*

¶ Undō-kai wa raishū no Nichiyōbi made nobimashita.

運動会は来週の日曜日まで延びました。

The field day was postponed until next Sunday.

② *to be prolonged, to run overtime* [→**nagabiku** 長引く]

③ *to become longer, to extend, to stretch* 《in space》

④ *to grow* 《longer or taller》

• se ga nobiru 背が伸びる *one grows taller, one's height increases*

nobori 上り ① *going up, ascent* [⇔**kudari** 下り①]

② *going up* 《a river, etc.》 [⇔**kudari** 下り②]

③ *going to a capital from a provincial area* [⇔**kudari** 下り③]

• nobori-densha 上り電車 *inbound train*

• nobori-zaka 上り坂 *upward slope*

nobori 登り *climb; climbing*

• yama-nobori 山登り *mountain climbing*

nobori 昇り *rising* 《of the sun, moon, etc.》

noboru 上る ① *to rise, to amount, to add up* 《to a large total》

¶ Akaji wa hyakuman-en ni noborimashita.

赤字は100万円に上りました。

The deficit rose to one million yen.

¶ Gisei-sha wa gosen-nin ni noborimashita.

犠牲者は5000人に上りました。

The casualties amounted to 5,000 people.

② *to go up* 《a river, etc.》 [⇔**kudaru** 下る②]

¶ Bōto de kawa o nobotte ikimashita.

ボートで川を上っていきました。

We went up the river by boat.

③ *to go* 《to a capital from a provincial area》 [⇔**kudaru** 下る③]

¶ Musuko wa kyonen Tōkyō ni noborimashita.

息子は去年東京に上りました。

My son went to Tokyo last year.

noboru 登る *to climb up* [⇔**oriru** 下りる, 降りる①]

• A o noboru Aを登る *to climb up A*

• A ni noboru Aに登る *to climb up to the top* (*part*)*of A*

¶ Uchi no neko wa ki ni noboru no ga suki desu.

うちの猫は木に登るのが好きです。

Our cat likes to climb up trees.

noboru 昇る *to rise* 《when the subject is the sun, moon, etc.》

¶ Taiyō wa higashi kara noborimasu.

太陽は東から昇ります。

The sun rises from the east.

nochi 後 ① (〜**ni** 〜に) *later, afterwards*

¶ Hare, nochi kumori.

晴れ、後くもり。《a weather forecast》

Fair, later cloudy.

② *time after, time later* [→**ato** 後②]; *time in the future*

• nochi no 後の *later, subsequent; future* 《as a noun modifier》

• -nochi ni 一後に *later, from now* 《Added to number bases denoting periods of time.》

¶ Mikka-nochi ni mata Yumi-san ni aimasu.

3日後にまた由美さんに会います。

I will meet Yumi again in three days.

• nochi-hodo 後ほど *later, after a while*

¶ De-wa, nochi-hodo.

では、後ほど。

See you later. 《Literally: *Well then, later.*》

¶Nochi–hodo mata o–denwa itashimasu.
後ほどまたお電話いたします。
I'll telephone again later.

nóchi 農地 *farmland, agricultural land*

nóde ので *because, since* 《clause-conjoining particle》 [→**kara** から④]

¶Kibun ga warui node, kaisha o yasumimasu.
気分が悪いので、会社を休みます。
Since I don't feel well, I'll take time off work.

¶Totemo kōfun shite ita node, nemurenakatta.
とても興奮していたので、眠れなかった。
Since I was very excited, I couldn't sleep.

nódo 喉 *throat*

• nodo ga itai のどが痛い *one's throat hurts, one has a sore throat*

• nodo ga kawaku のどが渇く *to get thirsty*

• nodo–botoke 喉仏 *Adam's apple*

nódoka のどか ~**na** ~な *calm, peaceful* [→**odayaka na** 穏やかな]

nōen 農園 *farm* 《on which fruit, vegetables, etc., are raised》

nogaréru 逃れる *to evade, to elude*

nogásu 逃す [☞**nigasu** 逃がす]

nógyō 農業 *agriculture*

• nōgyō ni jūji suru 農業に従事する *to engage in agriculture*

• nōgyō–kōkō 農業高校 *agricultural high school*

• nōgyō–koku 農業国 *agricultural nation*

• nōgyō–kyōdō–kumiai 農業協同組合 *agricultural cooperative association*

nóhara 野原 *field, plain, prairie*

noiróze ノイローゼ *neurosis* [→**shinkei–shō** 神経症 (s.v. **shinkei** 神経)]

nōjó 農場 *farm*

nōka 農家 ① *farmhouse*
② *farmer; farm family*

noki 軒 *eaves*

nokkuáuto ノックアウト *knockout*

• nokkuauto suru ノックアウトする *to knock out*

nokogirí 鋸 *saw* ((tool))

¶Daiku–san wa ita o nokogiri de kitte

imasu.
大工さんは板をのこぎりで切っています。
The carpenter is cutting the board with a saw.

• A o nokogiri de hiku Aをのこぎりでひく *to saw A*

nōkómento ノーコメント ~**da** ~だ *to have no comment*

¶Sore ni tsuite wa nōkomento desu.
それについてはノーコメントです。
I have no comment about that.

nokorí 残り *the rest, remainder*

¶Miruku no nokori wa neko ni yarō.
ミルクの残りは猫にやろう。
I'll give the rest of the milk to the cat.

¶Inu wa ip–piki dake ga osu de, nokori wa mesu desu.
犬は1匹だけが雄で、残りは雌です。
Only one of the dogs is male, and the rest are female.

nokóru 残る ① *to stay, to remain*

¶Otōsan wa uchi ni nokotta yo.
お父さんはうちに残ったよ。
Dad stayed at home!

¶Senshu–tachi wa mada Ōsaka ni nokotte imasu.
選手たちはまだ大阪に残っています。
The players are still in Osaka.

② *to be left, to remain*

¶Shukudai ga takusan nokotte iru yo.
宿題がたくさん残っているよ。
I have a lot of homework left!

¶Satō wa dono kurai nokotte imasu ka.
砂糖はどのくらい残っていますか。
How much sugar is left?

nokósu 残す *to leave, to let remain, to have remain*

¶Sono neko wa esa o hanbun nokoshita yo.
その猫はえさを半分残したよ。
That cat left half its food!

¶Yamamoto–san wa kodomo–tachi ni zaisan o nokoshimashita.
山本さんは子供たちに財産を残しました。
Mr. Yamamoto left his fortune to his children.

¶Sensei wa Yōko–chan o hōkago

nokoshita yo.

先生は洋子ちゃんを放課後残したよ。

The teacher had Yoko remain after school!

nōkyō 農協 [☞**nōgyō-kyōdō-kumiai** 農業協同組合 (s.v. **nōgyō** 農業)]

nomí 蚤 *flea*

nómi 鑿 *chisel*

nómi のみ 【FORMAL】 *only, just* [→**dake** だけ①]

nomihṓdai 飲み放題 *as much as one wants to drink*

• nomihōdai no bā 飲み放題のバー *an all-you-can-drink bar*

nomikomu 飲み込む ① *to swallow* ② *to understand, to grasp* [→**rikai suru** 理解する]

nomímizu 飲み水 *water for drinking* [→**inryōsui** 飲料水]

nomímono 飲み物 *drink, beverage*

¶Nani-ka tsumetai nomimono o kudasai.

何か冷たい飲み物をください。

Please give me something cold to drink.

nōmin 農民 *farmer; peasant*

nóminarazu のみならず 【FORMAL】 *not only* [→**bakari de naku** ばかりでなく (s.v. **bakari** ばかり①)]

nominéto ノミネート ~**suru** ~する *to nominate*

nómu 飲む ① *to drink*

¶Akira-chan wa mai-asa gyūnyū o ip-pai nomu ne.

明ちゃんは毎朝牛乳を1杯飲むね。

Akira drinks a glass of milk every morning, doesn't he.

¶Kōhī o mō sukoshi nomimasen ka.

コーヒーをもう少し飲みませんか。

Won't you drink a little more coffee?

② *to take* 《medicine》

¶Kusuri o nomu no ga kirai desu.

薬を飲むのが嫌いです。

I dislike taking medicine.

nonbíri のんびり (~**to** ~と) *in a relaxed manner; free from worry*

• nonbiri suru のんびりする *to relax; to feel carefree*

¶Shiken ga owatte nonbiri shita kibun

desu.

試験が終わってのんびりした気分です。

I can relax now that the examination is all over. 《Literally: *The examination is over, and I feel carefree.*》

nonfíkushon ノンフィクション *nonfiction* [⇔**fikushon** フィクション]

nóni のに《clause-conjoining particle》 ① *although*

¶Kaze ga tsuyoi noni, tsuri ni ikimashita.

風が強いのに、釣りに行きました。

Although the wind was blowing hard, they went fishing.

② *in order to* [→**tame** 為①]

¶Nihon-go o oboeru noni, jikan ga kakarimasu.

日本語を覚えるのに、時間がかかります。

It takes time in order to learn Japanese.

nónki 呑気 ~**na** ~な *happy-go-lucky, easygoing, carefree*

¶Fukuda wa nonki na yatsu da nā.

福田はのんきなやつだなあ。

Boy, Fukuda's a happy-go-lucky guy.

nonpuro ノンプロ *a nonprofessional* [⇔**puro** プロ]

nóppo のっぽ 【COL.】 *tall and lanky person, beanpole* [⇔**chibi** ちび]

norainu 野良犬 *stray dog*

noraneko 野良猫 *stray cat*

noren 暖簾 *shop curtain* 《of the type that hangs down part way in the entry-way to a traditional Japanese store or restaurant》

norí 糊 ① *paste* ((adhesive))

• A ni B o nori de haru AをBにのりではる *to stick A on B with paste*

② *(laundry) starch*

norí 海苔 *laver* 《a kind of edible seaweed》

• nori-maki 海苔巻き *sushi rolled in laver*

• yaki-nori 焼き海苔 *baked laver*

norikae 乗り換え *change, transfer* 《from one vehicle to another》

¶Sonna ni tōku nai desu kedo, norikae wa ōi desu.

そんなに遠くないですけど、乗り換えは多

いです。

It isn't that far, but there are a lot of changes.

norikaéru 乗り換える *to change, to transfer* 《from one vehicle to another》

¶Ueno-eki de Aomori-yuki no tokkyū ni norikaeta.

上野駅で青森行きの特急に乗り換えた。

At Ueno Station I changed to the express for Aomori.

¶Nagoya de densha kara basu ni norikaemasu.

名古屋で電車からバスに乗り換えます。

We will change from a train to a bus at Nagoya.

noriki 乗り気 *enthusiasm, eagerness*

• A ni noriki ni naru Aに乗り気になる *to become enthusiastic about A*

norikósu 乗り越す *to ride past* 《one's stop or destination》

¶Shibuya made norikoshite shimatta yo.

渋谷まで乗り越してしまったよ。

I rode past as far as Shibuya!

norikumíin 乗組員 *crew member* 《on a ship or plane》

norimono 乗り物 *vehicle, vessel, conveyance*

Nōrinsuisánshō 農林水産省 *the Ministry of Agriculture, Forestry and Fisheries*

noriokuréru 乗り遅れる *to be too late for* 《getting in／on a vehicle》

• A ni noriokureru Aに乗り遅れる *to be too late for (and miss) A*

¶Saishū-ressha ni noriokuremashita.

最終列車に乗り遅れました。

I was too late for the last train.

nōritsu 能率 *efficiency*

• nōritsu-teki na 能率的な *efficient*

¶Eigo o shūtoku suru nōritsu-teki na hōhō wa nan desu ka.

英語を習得する能率的な方法は何ですか。

What is an efficient way to learn English?

norói 呪い *curse, malediction*

norói 鈍い *slow, sluggish*

nóronoro のろのろ （〜**to** 〜と）*slowly,*

sluggishly

noróu 呪う *to curse* 《transitive》

noru 乗る ① *to get* 《into／onto a means of transportation》 [⇔**oriru** 降りる②]

¶Koko kara wa Shibuya-yuki no basu ni norimasu.

ここからは渋谷行きのバスに乗ります。

From here I get on a bus for Shibuya.

¶Chichi no kuruma ni norimashita.

父の車に乗りました。

I got into my father's car.

• uma ni noru 馬に乗る *to get on a horse; to ride on a horse*

¶Keiko-san wa mai-asa shichi-ji go-fun no densha ni noru.

恵子さんは毎朝7時5分の電車に乗る。

Keiko takes the 7:05 train every morning.

¶Tarō-chan wa jitensha ni noreru yo.

太郎ちゃんは自転車に乗れるよ。

Taro can ride a bicycle!

② *to step up, to get up* 《onto something》

¶Kodomo ga chichi-oya no hiza ni norimashita.

子供が父親のひざに乗りました。

The child got up onto her father's lap.

③ *to take part, to get involved* 《in response to something》

• sōdan ni noru 相談に乗る *to give advice*

④ *to be deceived, to be taken in*

• keiryaku ni noru 計略に乗る *to be taken in by a scheme*

noru 載る ① *to be put, to be placed* 《on top of something》

¶Sono jisho wa tsukue ni notte imasu.

その辞書は机に載っています。

That dictionary is on top of the desk.

② *to be capable of being placed* 《on top of something》

¶Kono hako wa tana ni noru deshō.

この箱は棚に載るでしょう。

This box will probably go on the shelf.

③ *to be printed, to be published, to appear* 《in a newspaper, magazine, etc.》

• jisho ni noru 辞書に載る *to be listed in a dictionary*

nōryoku 能力 *ability, competence*

¶Neko ni wa kurayami no naka de mono o miru nōryoku ga aru.

猫には暗やみの中で物を見る能力がある。
A cat has the ability to see things in the dark.

nōsánbutsu 農産物 *agricultural product*

noseru 乗せる *to give a ride to; to put aboard, to take aboard*

¶Ani wa watashi-tachi o kuruma ni noseta yo.

兄は私たちを車に乗せたよ。
My older brother gave us a ride in the car!

noseru 載せる ① *to put, to place* 《on top of something》

¶Terebi no ue ni tokei o nosete wa ikemasen.

テレビの上に時計を載せてはいけません。
You mustn't put your watch on the TV.

② *to put, to print, to publish, to run* 《in a newspaper, magazine, etc.》

¶Kono kōkoku o ashita no shinbun ni nosemashō.

この広告をあしたの新聞に載せましょう。
Let's run this ad in tomorrow's newspaper.

nōson 農村 *farm village*

•nōson-chitai 農村地帯 *farm area*

nōto ノート ① *notebook*

② *note* 《i.e., a brief written record》

•nōto suru ノートする *to note down; to take notes on*

¶Terebi-kōen o nōto shimashita.

テレビ講演をノートしました。
I took notes on the TV lecture.

nottóru 乗っ取る *to seize, to take over; to hijack*

nozoku 除く [[⇔**fukumeru** 含める]]

① *to remove, to eliminate*

¶Sono hito no namae o meibo kara nozokimashō.

その人の名前を名簿から除きましょう。
Let's remove that person's name from the roster.

② *to omit, to leave out, to exclude* [→

habuku 省く①]

•A o nozoite Aを除いて *excluding A, except for A*

¶Onna-no-ko-tachi wa Keiko o nozoite minna kaetta.

女の子たちは恵子を除いてみんな帰った。
All the girls went home except for Keiko.

nozoku 覗く *to take a look at, to peek at, to peep at*

¶Shōnen wa hako no naka o nozokimashita.

少年は箱の中をのぞきました。
The boy peeped into the box. 《Literally: The boy peeped at the inside of the box.》

¶Imōto wa kāten no aida kara nozoite iru.

妹はカーテンの間からのぞいている。
My younger sister is peeking from between the curtains!

•kagami o nozoku 鏡をのぞく *to look into a mirror*

nozomi 望み [[→**kibō** 希望]] *wish, desire* [→**negai** 願い①]; *hope, expectation*

¶Yumi-san no nozomi wa ishi ni naru koto desu.

由美さんの望みは医師になることです。
Yumi's wish is to be a doctor.

¶Jōkyaku ga seizon shite iru nozomi wa arimasen.

乗客が生存している望みはありません。
There is no hope that the passengers survived.

nozomu 望む [[→**kibō suru** 希望する]] *to come to want, to come to desire; to hope for, to expect*

¶Haha wa boku ga kyōshi ni naru koto o nozonde imasu.

母は僕が教師になることを望んでいます。
My mother wants me to become a teacher.

¶Sekai-jū no hito-tachi ga heiwa o nozonde imasu.

世界中の人たちが平和を望んでいます。
People all over the world desire peace.

¶Musuko ga shiawase ni kurasu koto o nozonde imasu.

息子が幸せに暮らすことを望んでいます。
I am hoping for my son to lead a happy life.

nūdo ヌード ① (*portrait of*)*a nude*
② *the nude, nudity* [→**hadaka** 裸]

núgu 脱ぐ *to take off* «clothing» [⇔**kiru** 着る; **kaburu** 被る; **haku** 履く]
¶Dōzo kutsu o nuide kudasai.
どうぞ靴を脱いでください。
Take off your shoes, please.
¶Ken-chan wa fuku o nuide, pajama o kita.
健ちゃんは服を脱いで、パジャマを着た。
Ken took off his clothes and put on his pajamas.

nugúu 拭う *to wipe* [→**fuku** 拭く]

nuigurumi 縫いぐるみ *stuffed toy animal*
•kuma no nuigurumi くまの縫いぐるみ *teddy bear*

nuká 糠 *rice bran*
•nuka-miso 糠味噌 *salted rice-bran paste* «used in pickling»

nukarumi ぬかるみ *mire, muddy place*

nukasu 抜かす *to leave out, to fail to include, to skip over*
¶Go-pēji no renshū-mondai wa nukashi-mashō.
5ページの練習問題は抜かしましょう。
Let's leave out the exercises on page 5.

nukeme-nái 抜け目ない *shrewd, clever*

nukeru 抜ける ① *to come out, to fall out*
¶Kinō oku-ba ga nukemashita.
きのう奥歯が抜けました。
Yesterday a molar came out.
② *to come off, to fall off*
③ *to be omitted, to be left out, to be excluded*
¶Kono kyōkasho wa roku-pēji-bun ga nukete imasu.
この教科書は6ページ分が抜けています。
Six pages are missing from this textbook.
④ *to emerge on the other side of* «after passing through»
•tonneru o nukeru トンネルを抜ける *to*

emerge from a tunnel
•kiken o nukeru 危険を抜ける *to get out of danger*

nuku 抜く ① *to pull out, to draw out*
¶Kono toge o nuite kureru?
このとげを抜いてくれる？
Will you pull out this thorn for me?
¶Kono ha o nuita hō ga ii deshō.
この歯を抜いたほうがいいでしょう。
It would probably be better to pull out this tooth.
② *to remove, to take out, to eliminate* [→**nozoku** 除く①]
¶Dorai kurīningu de fuku no shimi o nuita.
ドライクリーニングで服のしみを抜いた。
The stains on the clothes were removed by dry cleaning.
③ *to omit, to leave out, to exclude* [→**habuku** 省く①]
④ *to pass, to overtake, to surpass* [→**oikosu** 追い越す]
¶Supōtsu-kā ga sukūru-basu o nuita.
スポーツカーがスクールバスを抜いた。
A sports car passed the school bus.

numá 沼 *swamp, marsh*
•numa-chi 沼地 *swampy place, marshy land*

nuno 布 *cloth, fabric*

nurasu 濡らす *to make wet, to wet, to moisten*
¶Zubon o nurasanai yō ni shinasai.
ズボンをぬらさないようにしなさい。
Make sure not to get your pants wet.

nureru 濡れる *to get wet*
¶Nureta taoru wa nikkō de kawakashi-mashō.
ぬれたタオルは日光で乾かしましょう。
Let's dry that wet towel in the sunshine.
•A ni／de nureru Aに／でぬれる *to get wet from A, to get wet with A*
¶Ame ni nuremashita.
雨にぬれました。
I got wet from the rain.
¶Kusa ga ame de nurete imasu.
草が雨でぬれています。
The grass is wet with rain.

nuru 塗る ① *to paint, to coat with paint*
¶Tonari no ojisan wa hei o chairo ni nutta ne.
隣のおじさんは塀を茶色に塗ったね。
The man next door painted the fence brown, didn't he.
　② *to apply, to spread* 《a liquid, paste, etc., onto a surface》
¶Kumi-san wa pan ni jamu o nurimashita.
久美さんはパンにジャムを塗りました。
Kumi spread jam on the bread.

nurúi 温い ① *insufficiently hot, lukewarm, tepid* 《describing a liquid that should be hot》
¶Furo ga nurui yo.
ふろがぬるい。
The bath is tepid!
¶Kono kōcha wa nurui desu ne.
この紅茶はぬるいですね。
This tea is lukewarm, isn't it.
　② *insufficiently cold, warm* 《describing a liquid that should be cold》
¶Bīru wa nuruku natte shimaimashita.
ビールはぬるくなってしまいました。
The beer has gotten warm.

nusúmu 盗む *to steal*
¶Dare-ka ga watashi no saifu o nusunda yo.
だれかが私の財布を盗んだよ。
Someone stole my wallet!

núu 縫う ① *to sew*
¶Haha wa mishin de sukāto o nutte imasu.
母はミシンでスカートを縫っています。
My mother is making a skirt on the sewing machine.
　② *to weave through, to pass through twisting and turning*

nyōbo 女房 [☞**nyōbō** 女房]
nyōbō 女房【COL. for **tsuma** 妻】 *wife* [⇔**teishu** 亭主]
nyúansu ニュアンス *nuance*
nyūgaku 入学 *matriculation, admission into a school*
• nyūgaku suru 入学する *to matriculate, to be admitted, to enter*

¶Imōto wa rainen chūgakkō ni nyūgaku shimasu.
妹は来年中学校に入学します。
My younger sister will enter junior high school next year.
• nyūgaku-gansho 入学願書 *application form for admission*
• nyūgaku-shiken 入学試験 *entrance examination* [→**nyūshi** 入試]
• nyūgaku-shiki 入学式 *matriculation ceremony*

nyūin 入院 *going into the hospital, hospitalization*
• nyūin suru 入院する *to go into the hospital, to be hospitalized*
¶Yōko-chan wa nyūin shite iru yo.
洋子ちゃんは入院しているよ。
Yoko is in the hospital!
• nyūin-kanja 入院患者 *inpatient*

nyūjō 入場 *entrance, admission* 《to a sporting event, concert, etc.》
• nyūjō suru 入場する *to enter*
¶Nyūjō o-kotowari
「入場お断り」《on a sign》
No Entrance
¶Nyūjō muryō
「入場無料」《on a sign》
Admission Free
• nyūjō-ken 入場券 *admission ticket; platform ticket* 《for seeing someone off at a train station》
• nyūjō-ryō 入場料 *admission fee*

nyūkai 入会 *admission, joining* 《a club, association, etc.》
• nyūkai suru 入会する *to join, to be admitted*
• nyūkai-kin 入会金 *admission fee, entrance fee*

nyūkoku 入国 *entry into a country* [⇔**shukkoku** 出国]
• nyūkoku suru 入国する *to make an entry (into a country)*

nyūryoku 入力 *input* [→**inputto** インプット] [⇔**shutsuryoku** 出力]

nyūsatsu 入札 <US>*bid*, <UK>*tender*
• nyūsatsu suru 入札する *to make a bid*

nyūshi 入試 (*school*)*entrance examination* [→**nyūgaku-shiken** 入学試験 (s.v. **nyūgaku** 入学)]

nyūsu ニュース *news*

¶Kore wa omoshiroi nyūsu desu.
これはおもしろいニュースです。
This is interesting news.

• nyūsu-bangumi ニュース番組 *news program*
• nyūsu-eiga ニュース映画 *newsreel*
• nyūsu-kaisetsu ニュース解説 *news commentary*
• nyūsu-kyasutā ニュースキャスター *newscaster*
• nyūsu-sokuhō ニュース速報 *news flash*
• kaigai-nyūsu 海外ニュース *foreign news*
• kokunai-nyūsu 国内ニュース *domestic news*
• supōtsu-nyūsu スポーツニュース *sports news*

O

o を ① 《noun-following particle marking the direct object of a clause》

¶Dare ga Nihon-go o benkyō shite imasu ka.
だれが日本語を勉強していますか。
Who is studying Japanese?

② 《noun-following particle marking the path of motion》

¶Kono basu wa tonneru o tōrimasu.
このバスはトンネルを通ります。
This bus passes through a tunnel.

ó 尾 *tail* [→**shippo** 尻尾]

¶Kono saru wa o ga nagai ne.
この猿は尾が長いね。
This monkey's tail is long, isn't it.

¶Inu wa o o furimashita.
犬は尾を振りました。
The dog wagged its tail.

ō 王 *king* [⇔**joō** 女王]

¶Ō ga sono kuni o osamete imasu.

王がその国を治めています。
A king is ruling that country.

• hyakujū no ō 百獣の王 *the king of beasts*
• ō-kan 王冠 *crown*
• ō-koku 王国 *kingdom*

o- 御 - 《This prefix is added to bases that are gramatically nouns, adjectival nouns, or adjectives. The prefix is typically honorific, but in some words it has lost its honorific force. It also appears in some humble forms.》

• o-kaki ni naru お書きになる 【HON. for **kaku** 書く】
• o-kane お金 *money*
• o-kotowari suru お断りする 【HUM. for **kotowaru** 断る】
• o-namae お名前 【HON. for **namae** 名前】 *name*

oáshisu オアシス *oasis*

ōbā オーバー [☞**ōbākōto** オーバーコート]

ōbā オーバー ① ～**suru** ～する *to exceed, to go over* 《a limit》

② ～**na** ～な *exaggerated, overstated* [→**ōgesa na** 大袈裟な]

oba 伯母 , 叔母 *aunt*

《Strictly speaking, this word should be written 伯母 if it refers to an aunt who is an older sister of a parent or the wife of an older brother of a parent, and should be written 叔母 if it refers to an aunt who is a younger sister of a parent or the wife of younger brother of a parent.》 [⇔**oji** 伯父, 叔父]

• oba-san 伯母さん, 叔母さん 【HON. for **oba** 伯母, 叔母】
• -oba-san - 伯母さん, - 叔母さん 《Added to a given name as a title.》

¶Hiroko-oba-san wa otōsan no onēsan.
広子伯母さんはお父さんのお姉さんです。
Aunt Hiroko is Father's older sister.

obáke お化け 【COL. for **yūrei** 幽霊】 *ghost*

• obake-yashiki お化け屋敷 *haunted house*

ōbākōto オーバーコート *overcoat*

obasan 小母さん *woman* 《This word typically refers to a middle-aged woman but a child may use it to refer to a young woman.》[⇔**ojisan** 小父さん]

obāsan おばあさん ① 【HON. for **sobo** 祖母】

   grandmother [⇔**ojīsan** おじいさん]

   ¶Obāsan wa ashi ga tassha desu ne.
   おばあさんは足が達者ですね。
   Your grandmother's legs are strong, aren't they.

   ② *old woman*

   ¶Obāsan ni seki o yuzurimashita.
   おばあさんに席を譲りました。
   I gave up my seat to an elderly woman.

   • hī-obāsan ひいおばあさん *great grand-mother*

Ōbei 欧米 *Europe and America*

   • Ōbei-jin 欧米人 *Europeans and Americans*

ōbí OB 《Generally not written out in katakana.》 *alumnus, old boy*

óbi 帯 *kimono sash, obi*

obieru 怯える *to become frightened*

   ¶Totsuzen no oto ni obiemashita.
   突然の音におびえました。
   I became frightened at the sudden noise.

ōbo 応募 *application* 《for a job, to a school, etc.》*;positive response to a solicitation for participation*

   • ōbo suru 応募する *to apply; to respond positively*

   ¶Ane wa sono shigoto ni ōbo shimasu.
   姉はその仕事に応募します。
   My older sister will apply for that job.

   • konkūru ni ōbo suru コンクールに応募する *to enter a contest*

   • ōbo-sha 応募者 *applicant*

oboé 覚え[[→**kioku** 記憶]] ① *memory, recollection*

   ¶Izen Ueda-san ni atta oboe ga arimasu.
   以前上田さんに会った覚えがあります。
   I have a recollection of having met Mr. Ueda before.

   ② *memory, ability to learn*

   ¶Kono ko wa oboe ga ii desu.
   この子は覚えがいいです。
   This child has a good memory.

oboéru 覚える ① *to commit to memory, to learn, to memorize* [→**kioku suru** 記憶する]

   ¶Mainichi tango o itsutsu-zutsu oboeru tsumori desu.
   毎日単語を五つずつ覚えるつもりです。
   I plan to learn five words every day.

   ¶Ashita made ni kono shi o oboenasai.
   あしたまでにこの詩を覚えなさい。
   Memorize this poem by tomorrow.

   • oboete iru 覚えている *to remember, to have a memory of*

   ¶Ano hito no namae o oboete imasu ka.
   あの人の名前を覚えていますか。
   Do you remember that person's name?

   ② *to feel, to experience*

   • itami o oboeru 痛みを覚える *to feel pain*

O–bón お盆 [☞**Bon** 盆]

oboreru 溺れる *to drown*

   ¶Futari no otoko no ko ga kawa de oboremashita.
   二人の男の子が川でおぼれました。
   Two little boys drowned in the river.

   ¶Oboreru mono wa wara o tsukamu.
   おぼれる者はわらをつかむ。《proverb》
   A drowning man will clutch at a straw.

obōsan お坊さん 【HON.】 *Buddhist priest, Buddhist monk*

ōbun オーブン *oven*

   • ōbun-tōsutā オーブントースター *toaster oven*

o–cha お茶 ① *tea* [→**cha** 茶]

   ¶O-cha o ip-pai ikaga desu ka.
   お茶を1杯いかがですか。
   How about a cup of tea?

   • usui〔koi〕o-cha 薄い〔濃い〕お茶 *weak〔strong〕tea*

   • o-cha o ireru お茶を入れる *to make tea*

   • o-cha ga hairu お茶が入る *tea becomes ready, tea is made*

   ② *green tea* [⇔**kōcha** 紅茶]

   ③ *the tea ceremony* [→**sadō** 茶道]

   • o-cha-zuke お茶漬 *tea poured over rice* 《a popular Japanese dish》

óchiba 落ち葉 *fallen leaf*

   • ochiba o kakiatsumeru 落ち葉をかき集

める *to rake up fallen leaves*

ochiiru 陥る{5} *to fall, to lapse* 《*into a bad condition or situation*》

• kiken ni ochiiru 危険に陥る *to fall into danger*

ochíru 落ちる ① *to fall, to drop, to plunge*

¶Basu ga kawa ni ochimashita.

バスが川に落ちました。

The bus fell into the river.

¶Papa ga hashigo kara ochita yo.

パパがはしごから落ちたよ。

Daddy fell from the ladder!

¶Koppu ga te kara ochimashita.

コップが手から落ちました。

The glass dropped from my hand.

¶Gakkō no seiseki mo ochimashita.

学校の成績も落ちました。

My school grades went down too.

② *to fail* 《*on a test, etc.*》 [⇔**ukaru** 受かる]; *to lose* 《*in an election*》

¶Boku mo shiken ni ochita yo.

僕も試験に落ちたよ。

I also failed the examination!

¶Katō-shichō wa kyonen no senkyo de ochimashita.

加藤市長は去年の選挙で落ちました。

Mayor Kato lost in last year's election.

③ *to come out* 《*when the subject is a stain, etc.*》

¶Kono yogore wa ochiru deshō.

この汚れは落ちるでしょう。

This dirt will probably come out.

ochitsuki 落ち着き *calmness; composure*

• ochitsuki ga aru〔nai〕落ち着きがある〔ない〕*to be calm*〔*restless*〕

¶Ano ko wa jugyō-chū ochitsuki ga nai desu.

あの子は授業中落ち着きがないです

That child is restless during class.

• ochitsuki o ushinau 落ち着きを失う *to lose one's composure*

ochitsuku 落ち着く ① *to calm* (*oneself*) *down*

¶Mā, ochitsukinasai.

まあ、落ち着きなさい。

Goodness, calm down.

② *to become settled, to become stable*

¶Sono kazoku wa atarashii ie ni ochitsuk-imashita.

その家族は新しい家に落ち着きました。

That family became settled in their new house.

o-chūgen お中元 [☞**chūgen** 中元]

ōdan 横断 *crossing, going across*

¶Ōdan kinshi

「横断禁止」《*on a sign*》

No Crossing 《*Literally: Crossing Forbidden*》

• ōdan suru 横断する *to cross, to go across*

¶Koko de dōro o ōdan shite wa ikemasen.

ここで道路を横断してはいけません。

You mustn't cross the street here.

• ōdan-hodō 横断歩道 *pedestrian crosswalk*

odáyaka 穏やか 〜**na** 〜な *peaceful, quiet, calm, gentle*

¶Tomoko-san wa odayaka na umi o mite imasu.

友子さんは穏やかな海を見ています。

Tomoko is looking at the calm sea.

¶Ano sensei wa odayaka na hito desu.

あの先生は穏やかな人です。

That teacher is a gentle person.

¶Nihon no kikō wa odayaka desu.

日本の気候は穏やかです。

The climate of Japan is mild.

¶Takako-san wa odayaka na han-ashi-kata o shimasu.

孝子さんは穏やかな話し方をします。

Takako has a quiet way of speaking.

odéko おでこ 【COL. for **hitai** 額】*forehead*

ōdio オーディオ *audio*

ōdíshon オーディション *an audition*

• ōdishon o ukeru オーディションを受ける *to undergo an audition*

ōdóburu オードブル *hors d'oeuvre*

odokasu 脅かす *to threaten, to menace* [→**odosu** 脅す]

ōdóri 大通り *main street, major street*

odori 踊り *dance; dancing*
- **odori-ko** 踊り子 *dancing girl, female dancer*

odorokásu 驚かす *to surprise*
¶Sono kekka wa shachō o odorokasu deshō.
その結果は社長を驚かすでしょう。
Those results will probably surprise the company president.

odoróku 驚く *to become surprised* [→ **bikkuri suru** びっくりする]
¶Sono shirase o kiite odorokimashita.
その知らせを聞いて驚きました。
I was surprised to hear that news.
¶Kodomo wa odoroite otōsan o miagemashita.
子供は驚いてお父さんを見上げました。
The child looked up at his father in surprise.
¶Ano hito no tegiwa no yosa ni wa odorokimashita.
あの人の手際のよさには驚きました。
I was surprised at that person's skill.

odoru 踊る *to dance*
¶Haruo wa Chieko to tango o odotte imasu.
春男は智恵子とタンゴを踊っています。
Haruo is dancing the tango with Chieko.
- **ongaku ni awasete odoru** 音楽に合わせて踊る *to dance to the music*

odosu 脅す *to threaten, to menace* [→ **odokasu** 脅かす]
¶Sono otoko wa jū de ten'in o odoshimashita.
その男は銃で店員を脅しました。
That man threatened the store employees with a gun.

ōen 応援 ① *help, assistance* [→**enjo** 援助]
¶Sū-nin no seinen ga ōen ni kite kuremashita.
数人の青年が応援に来てくれました。
Several young men came to our assistance.
- **ōen suru** 応援する *to help, to assist*
② *cheering for, rooting for; (moral) support, backing*

- **ōen suru** 応援する *to cheer for, to root for; to support, to back*
¶Watashi-tachi mo chīmu o ōen shimashita.
私たちもチームを応援しました。
We also cheered for the team.
- **ōen-dan** 応援団 *rooter group, cheering section*
- **ōen-dan-chō** 応援団長 *head rooter, cheering section leader*
- **ōen-enzetsu** 応援演説 *campaign speech (for a candidate)*

oeru 終える *to finish* 《transitive》
¶Sono shigoto o oeta tokoro desu.
その仕事を終えたところです。
I have just finished that work.

ōeru OL 《Generally not written out in katakana.》 *woman office worker* 《office lady》

ófisu オフィス *office(s)* 《where business or government office work is done》 [→ **jimu-sho** 事務所]

ōfuku 往復 *round trip, going and returning* [⇔**katamichi** 片道]
- **ōfuku suru** 往復する *to make a round trip, to go and return*
¶Mizuumi made aruite ōfuku suru to, gojup-pun kakaru yo.
湖まで歩いて往復すると、50分かかるよ。
If you go to the lake and back on foot, it takes 50 minutes!
- **ōfuku-hagaki** 往復葉書 *return postcard, postcard with a return card attached*
- **ōfuku-kippu** 往復切符 *round-trip ticket*

o-fúro お風呂 [☞**furo** 風呂]

ogámu 拝む *to pray to* 《with head bowed and hands together》
¶Gantan ni wareware wa hi-no-de o ogamimasu.
元日にわれわれは日の出を拝みます。
On New Year's Day we pray to the sunrise.
¶Sono toshiyori wa te o awasete ogamimashita.
その年寄りは手を合わせて拝みました。

That elderly person put his hands together and prayed.

Ogasawara-shótō 小笠原諸島 *the Bonin Islands*

ōgata 大型 ～**no** ～の *extra-large, large-scale, oversized*

¶Sono ōgata no taifū wa Honshū ni jōriku suru darō.

その大型の台風は本州に上陸するだろう。

That large-scale typhoon may come ashore on Honshu.

• ōgata-basu 大型バス *large bus*

ogawa 小川 *stream, creek, brook*

ōgesa 大袈裟 *exaggeration* [→**kochō** 誇張]

• ōgesa na 大げさな *exaggerated*

• ōgesa ni iu 大げさに言う *to exaggerate (what one says)*

ogináu 補う ① *to make up for, to compensate for*

¶Hitode-busoku o oginau hitsuyō ga arimasu.

人手不足を補う必要があります。

It is necessary to make up for the shortage of help.

② *to supply, to supplement with*

¶Kūsho ni tekitō na tango o oginainasai.

空所に適当な単語を補いなさい。

Fill in the blanks with appropriate words.

ōgóe 大声 *loud voice*

¶Ani wa itsu-mo ōgoe de hanashimasu.

兄はいつも大声で話します。

My older brother always speaks in a loud voice.

ōgon 黄金 *gold* [→**kin** 金]

ogoru 奢る *to treat* 《a person to food and／or drink》[→**gochisō suru** ご馳走する(s.v. **gochisō** ご馳走)]

¶Kyō wa boku ga ogorimasu.

きょうは僕がおごります。

Today I'll treat.

• A ni B o ogoru AにBをおごる *to treat A to B*

o-gyógi お行儀 [☞**gyōgi** 行儀]

ohayō おはよう *Good morning!*

• ohayō gozaimasu おはようございます

【FORMAL for **ohayō** (above)】

óhi 王妃 *king's wife, queen*

ói おい *Hey!* 《an interjection used to get another person's attention》

oi 甥 *nephew* [⇔**mei** 姪]

• oi-go-san 甥御さん 【HON. for **oi** (above)】

ōi 覆い *cover, covering*

ōi 多い *numerous, large in number, large in quantity* [⇔**sukunai** 少ない]

¶Tarō wa tomodachi ga ōi desu.

太郎は友達が多いです。

Taro has many friends.

¶Kono kawa ni wa sakana ga ōi desu.

この川には魚が多いです。

There are many fish in this river.

¶Tōkyō wa jinkō ga ōi desu.

東京は人口が多いです。

Tokyo's population is large.

¶Kono ko wa gakkō o yasumu koto ga ōi desu.

この子は学校を休むことが多いです。

This child is often absent from school.

¶Kono kuni wa jishin ga ōi desu.

この国は地震が多いです。

This country has many earthquakes.

¶Kotoshi wa ame ga amari ōku furimasen deshita.

今年は雨があまり多く降りませんでした。

This year there wasn't much rain.

oidásu 追い出す *to drive out, to force to go outside*

¶Sachiko wa neko o oidashita yo.

幸子は猫を追い出したよ。

Sachiko drove the cat out!

oide おいで ～**ni naru** ～になる

① 【HON. for **iku** 行く】 *to go*

② 【HON. for **kuru** 来る①】 *to come*

oiharáu 追い払う *to drive away, to make go away, to get rid of* [→**ou** 追う②]

¶Akio-san wa hae o oiharaimashita.

明夫さんははえを追い払いました。

Akio drove the flies away.

oikakéru 追い掛ける *to pursue, to follow, to go after* [→**ou** 追う①]

¶Inu wa bōru o oikakete imasu.

犬はボールを追いかけています。
The dog is going after the ball.

oikósu 追い越す *to pass, to overtake*
¶Basu ga watashi-tachi no migi-gawa o oikoshita.
バスが私たちの右側を追い越した。
A bus passed us on the right.
¶Oikoshi kinshi
「追い越し禁止」《on a sign》
No Passing 《Literally: *Passing Forbidden*》

ói-ni 大いに *very, greatly* [→**hijō ni** 非常に]
¶Sore wa ōi-ni kekkō desu.
それはおおいに結構です。
That's very fine.

óiru オイル ① *oil* [→**abura** 油]
② *petroleum* [→**sekiyu** 石油]
•oiru-shokku オイルショック *oil crisis*

oishii 美味しい *good-tasting, delicious*
《Can be used to describe a restaurant, cafeteria, etc., as well as food itself.》[⇔**mazui** まずい①]
¶Koko no piza wa oishii desu ne.
ここのピザはおいしいですね。
The pizza here is delicious, isn't it.
¶Kono resutoran wa amari oishiku nai yo.
このレストランはあまりおいしくないよ。
This restaurant isn't very good!
•oishi-sō na 美味しそうな *delicious-looking*
¶Oishi-sō da nā.
おいしそうだなあ。
Boy, it looks delicious!

oitsúku 追いつく *to catch up*
¶Sugu tomodachi ni oitsukimasu.
すぐ友達に追いつきます。
I'll catch up my friend right away.

o-jama お邪魔 [☞**jama** 邪魔]

óji 王子 *prince*

oji 伯父, 叔父 *uncle* 《Strictly speaking, this word should be written 伯父 if it refers to an uncle who is an older brother of a parent or the husband of an older sister of a parent, and should be written 叔父 if it refers to an uncle who is a

younger brother of a parent or the husband of younger sister of a parent.》[⇔**oba** 伯母, 叔母]
¶Asatte, oji ni aimasu.
あさって、叔父に会います。
I will see my uncle the day after tomorrow.
•oji-san 伯父さん, 叔父さん 【HON. for **oji** 伯父, 叔父】
•-oji-san -伯父さん, -叔父さん
《Added to a given name as a title.》
¶Watashi wa Shinji-oji-san ga dai-suki desu.
私は信治叔父さんが大好きです。
I love Uncle Shinji.

ojigi お辞儀 *bow* 《i.e., bending forward at the waist to show respect》
•ojigi suru おじぎする *to bow*
¶Seito wa sensei ni ojigi shimashita.
生徒は先生におじぎをしました。
The pupil bowed to the teacher.

ōjiru 応じる ① *to respond, to reply* [→**kotaeru** 答える]
¶Kaisha wa watashi no shitsumon ni ōjite kuremashita.
会社は私の質問に応じてくれました。
The company responded to my question.
② *to consent, to accede, to comply*
¶Tanaka-san no yōkyū ni ōjiru tsumori wa nai.
田中さんの要求に応じるつもりはない。
I have no intention of complying with Mr. Tanaka's demands.
•shōtai ni ōjiru 招待に応じる *to accept an invitation*

ojisan 小父さん *man* 《This word typically refers to a middle-aged man but a child may use it to refer to a young man.》[⇔**obasan** 小母さん]
¶Ano ojisan wa dare desu ka.
あのおじさんはだれですか。
Who is that man?

ojisan おじいさん ① 【HON. for **sofu** 祖父】 *grandfather* [⇔**obāsan** おばあさん]
② *old man*
•hī-ojīsan ひいおじいさん *great*

grandfather

ōjite 応じて［☞**ni ōjite** に応じて］

ōjo 王女 *princess*

ojōsan お嬢さん 【HON. for **musume**
娘】 ① *daughter*
¶Ojōsan wa o-ikutsu desu ka.
お嬢さんはおいくつですか。
How old is your daughter?
　② *young lady*
¶Kono ojōsan wa michi o oshite kuremashita.
このお嬢さんは道を教えてくれました。
This young lady told me the way.

oka 丘 *hill*

okage お陰, お蔭 *helpful influence*
• A no okage de Aのおかげで *thanks to*
A
¶Buchō no enjo no okage de, watashi wa
seikō shita.
部長の援助のおかげで、私は成功した。
Thanks to the department head's help, I
succeeded.
¶Kimi no okage de basu ni noriokureta
yo.
君のおかげでバスに乗り遅れたよ。
Thanks to you, I missed the bus!
• A no okage da Aのおかげだ *to be*
thanks to A
¶Watashi ga oyogeru no wa ani no okage
desu.
私が泳げるのは兄のおかげです。
It's thanks to my older brother that I can
swim.
• okage-same de おかげさまで 【HON.】
thanks to you
¶Okage-sama de tasukarimashita.
おかげさまで助かりました。
Thank you for your help.

ōkami 狼 *wolf*

o-kane お金 *money*［→**kane** 金］
¶Musuko wa manga-bon ni o-kane o takusan tsukaimasu.
息子は漫画本にお金をたくさん使います。
My son spends a lot of money on comic
books.
¶Kawaguchi-san wa o-kane o mōkeru no
ga jōzu desu.

川口さんはお金をもうけるのが上手です。
Mr. Kawaguchi is good at making mon-
ey.
¶Sono ryokōyō ni sukoshi o-kane o tame-
mashita.
その旅行用に少しお金をためました。
I saved some money for that trip.
¶Sono o-kane wa ashita haraimasu.
そのお金はあした払います。
I will pay that money tomorrow.

okáruto オカルト *the occult*
• okaruto-eiga オカルト映画 *occult movie*

okásan お母さん 【HON. for **haha**
母】 *mother*［⇔**otōsan** お父さん］
¶Ano hito wa Yoshiko-san no okāsan
desu.
あの人は義子さんのお母さんです。
That person is Yoshiko's mother.
¶Okāsan wa doko ni iru no?
お母さんはどこにいるの？
Where is Mother?

okashíi おかしい ① *funny, comical*［→
kokkei na 滑稽な］
¶Nani ga okashii n desu ka.
何がおかしいんですか。
What's funny?
　② *strange, odd*［→**hen na** 変な］
¶Satō-san ga okureru no wa okashii
desu.
佐藤さんが遅れるのはおかしいです。
For Mr. Sato to be late is strange.
¶Kikai no chōshi ga okashii yo.
機械の調子がおかしいよ。
There's someting wrong with the ma-
chine! 《Literally: The machine's condition
is strange!》

okásu 犯す ① *to commit* 《a crime, sin, error, etc.》
¶Sono hito wa hanzai o okashimashita.
その人は犯罪を犯しました。
That person committed a crime.
　② *to violate, to break*
¶Hōritsu o okashite wa ikenai desu.
法律を犯してはいけないです。
One must not break the law.
　③ *to rape*

okásu 侵す *to invade, to encroach upon*

• hito no puraibashī o okasu 人のプライバシーを侵す *to invade a person's privacy*

okásu 冒す ① *to brave, to face*

¶ Nozaki wa seimei no kiken o okashite jikken o shita.

野崎は生命の危険を冒して実験をした。

Nozaki made the experiment braving the danger to her life.

② *to affect, to attack* 《when the subject is an illness》

¶ Gan ga i o okashite imasu.

がんが胃を冒しています。

Cancer has affected the stomach.

okáwari お代わり *another helping, second helping*

¶ Okawari wa ikaga desu ka.

お代わりはいかがですか

How about another helping?

• okawari suru お代わりする *to have a second helping*

o-káwari お変わり [☞**kawari** 変わり①]

o-kayu お粥 [☞**kayu** 粥]

okazu おかず *supplementary dish in a traditional Japanese meal* 《A Japanese meal is thought of as consisting of a staple food (i.e., rice)and a variety of supplementary dishes. The word **okazu** refers to the latter.》

¶ Yūshoku no okazu wa nani ga ii desu ka.

夕食のおかずは何がいいですか。

What would be good for okazu at dinner?

ōkē オーケー ① *an OK*

¶ Boku wa chichi kara ōkē o moratta yo.

僕は父からオーケーをもらったよ。

I got an OK from my father!

• ōkē suru オーケーする *to okay*

② *OK* 《an interjection expressing agreement》

¶ Ōkē, kawari ni itte ageru yo.

オーケー、代わりに行ってあげるよ。

OK, I'll go in your place.

óke 桶 *tub; pail* [→**baketsu** バケツ]

• furo-oke 風呂桶 *bathtub* [→**yokusō** 浴槽]

ōkésutora オーケストラ ① *orchestra* [→**kangengaku-dan** 管弦楽団 (s.v. **kangengaku** 管弦楽)]

• *orchestral music* [→**kangengaku** 管弦楽]

ōki 大き ~**na** ~な《Used only as a modifier, never as a predicate.》 [[→**ōkii** 大きい]] [[⇔**chīsa na** 小さな]] *big, large; loud* 《sound》

¶ Shushō no hatsugen wa ōki na eikyō-ryoku o motsu darō

首相の発言は大きな影響力を持つだろう。

The prime minister's declaration will probably have a great influence on us.

¶ Sonna ni ōki na koe de utawanai de kudasai.

そんなに大きな声で歌わないでください。

Please don't sing in such a loud voice.

• ōki na kao o suru 大きな顔をする *to act big, to be haughty*

oki 沖 *the offshore*

¶ Yotto wa oki e demashita.

ヨットは沖へ出ました。

The sailboat went out offshore.

-oki －置き ~**no** ~の *at intervals skipping* 《Added to number bases. When the base is three or lower, -**oki** denotes intervals skipping that number in between, but there is disagreement among speakers when the base is larger than three. Some speakers interpret -**oki** after such larger numbers as meaning *each, every*.》

¶ Ichi-nen-oki no matsuri desu.

１年おきの祭りです。

It's an every-other-year festival.

¶ Watashi-tachi wa is-shūkan-oki ni eiga ni ikimasu.

私たちは１週間おきに映画に行きます。

We go to the movies every other week.

okiagaru 起き上がる *to sit up* 《from a lying position》*;to stand up* 《from a lying position》

ōkíi 大きい [[⇔**chīsai** 小さい]] *big, large; loud* 《sound》

¶ Ane no ryokō-kaban wa ōkii desu.

姉の旅行かばんは大きいです。

My older sister's travel bag is big.

¶Amerika wa sekai de mottomo ōkii kuni no hitotsu da.
アメリカは世界で最も大きい国の1つだ。
The United States is one of the largest countries in the world.

¶Sono shōjo wa toshi no wari ni ōkii desu ne.
その少女は年の割に大きいですね。
That girl is big for her age, isn't she.

¶Taiiku no sensei wa koe ga ōkii desu.
体育の先生は声が大きいです。
The physical education teacher has a loud voice.

¶Ōkiku kaite kudasai.
大きく書いてください。
Please write large.

¶Kono shashin o ōkiku shite kudasai.
この写真を大きくしてください。
Please make this photograph bigger.

¶Ōkiku nattara, gekisakka ni naritai desu.
大きくなったら、劇作家になりたいです。
When I grow up, I want to be a playwriter.

¶Sono mondai wa ōkiku narimashita.
その問題は大きくなりました。
That problem got bigger.

¶Sutereo no oto o ōkiku suru na.
ステレオの音を大きくするな。
Don't turn up the volume on the stereo.

• kuchi o ōkiku akeru 口を大きく開ける *to open one's mouth wide*

o-ki-ni-iri お気に入り *a favorite*

¶Yōko-chan wa sensei no o-ki-ni-iri da ne.
洋子ちゃんは先生のお気に入りだね。
Yoko is the teacher's favorite, isn't she.

• o-ki-ni-iri no お気に入りの *favorite*

¶Kore wa watashi no o-ki-ni-iri no raketto desu.
これは私のお気に入りのラケットです。
This is my favorite racket.

okíru 起きる ① *to get up* (*out of bed*) [⇔**neru** 寝る①]

¶Kyō wa nan-ji ni okimashita ka.
きょうは何時に起きましたか。
What time did you get up today?

• okite iru 起きている *to be up*

② *to wake up* 《intransitive》 [→**me o samasu** 目を覚ます (s.v. **samasu** 覚ます)] [⇔**neru** 寝る②]

• okite iru 起きている *to be awake*

¶Chichi wa yūbe osoku made okite imashita.
父はゆうべ遅熊で起きていました。
My father was awake until late last night.

③ [[→**okoru** 起こる]] *to happen, to occur; to break out* 《when the subject is a fire, war, etc.》

ōkisa 大きさ *size*

¶Kono hako no ōkisa wa onaji desu.
この箱の大きさは同じです
The size of this box is the same.

¶Kono ko no kutsu wa dono kurai no ōkisa desu ka.
この子の靴はどのくらいの大きさですか。
About what size are this child's shoes?

okiwasuréru 置き忘れる *to forget* (*to take*), *to leave behind* [→**wasureru** 忘れる②]

¶Basu no naka ni kamera o okiwasuremashita.
バスの中にカメラを置き忘れました。
I left my camera behind in the bus.

¶Chichi wa yoku pen o okiwasuremasu.
父はよくペンを置き忘れます。
My father often forgets to take his pen.

okkanái おっかない 【COL. for **kowai** 怖い】

okonai 行い *action* [→**kōdō** 行動]*;behavior, conduct* [→**furumai** 振る舞い]

¶Higoro no okonai ni ki o tsukete kudasai.
日ごろの行いに気をつけてください。
Be careful about your everyday behavior.

okonau 行う [[→**suru** する①]] *to do, to carry out; to hold* 《a meeting, ceremony, etc.》

¶Raishū Eigo no shiken o okonaimasu.
来週英語の試験を行います。
I will give an English test next week.

¶Kaigo wa ichi-ji kara kaigi-shitsu de okonaimasu.

会合は1時から会議室で行います。
The meeting will be held in the conference room from 1:00.

okóru 怒る *to get angry*

¶Suzuki-san wa kachō no kotoba ni okotte imasu.

鈴木さんは課長の言葉に怒っています。

Mr. Suzuki is angry at what the section chief said.

okóru 起こる [[→**okiru** 起きる③]] *to happen, to occur; to break out* «when the subject is a fire, war, etc.»

¶Nani-mo okoranai deshō.

何も起らないでしょう。

Nothing will probably happen.

¶Jishin ga okotte ōku no shisha ga deta.

地震が起こって多くの死者が出た。

There was an earthquake and there were many fatalities.

¶Yūbe kaji ga ni-ken okorimashita.

ゆうべ火事が2件起こりました。

Last night two fires broke out.

okósu 起こす ① *to wake* «transitive»

¶Roku-ji ni Morita-san o okoshite kudasai.

6時に森田さんを起こしてください。

Please wake Mr. Morita at 6:00.

② *to set upright, to bring to an upright position*

¶Kangofu wa rōjin o okoshimashita.

看護婦は老人を起こしました。

The nurse helped the elderly person up.

¶Kodomo wa taoreta jitensha o okoshimashita.

子供は倒れた自転車を起こしました。

The child set the fallen bicycle upright.

③ *to cause* [→**hikiokosu** 引き起こす]

¶Fuchūi de unten-shu wa kōtsū-jiko o okoshita.

不注意で運転手は交通事故を起こした。

The driver caused a traffic accident through carelessness.

okotáru 怠る *to neglect (to do), to fail to attend to*

•gimu o okotaru 義務を怠る *to neglect one's duty*

óku 多く «This word is the adverbial form

of **ōi** 多い and has the predictable meanings as well.» ① *large amount, large quantity*

¶Kono jiken ni kanshite ōku o kataru hitsuyō wa nai.

この事件に関して多くを語る必要はない。

It isn't necessary to say very much about this incident.

•ōku no 多くの *many, much* «as a noun modifier»

¶Kono ronbun ni wa ōku no mondai-ten ga arimasu.

この論文には多くの問題点があります。

This thesis has many problems.

② *majority, greater part* [→**daibubun** 大部分②]

¶Kega-nin no ōku wa gakusei desu.

けが人の多くは学生です。

Most of the injured are students.

óku 奥 *inner part, recesses*

•oku no heya 奥の部屋 *inner room, back room*

•kokoro no oku 心の奥 *the bottom of one's heart*

•mori no oku 森の奥 *the depths of a forest*

•oku-ba 奥歯 *back tooth, molar*

-oku －億 *hundred million* «see Appendix 2»

•ichi-oku 1億 *100 million*

•jū-oku 10億 *one billion*

oku 置く ① *to put, to place, to set*

¶Kabin o tana no ue ni okinasai.

花瓶を棚の上に置きなさい。

Put the vase on the shelf.

¶Denki-sutando o tsukue no ue ni okimashita.

電気スタンドを机の上に置きました。

I set a lamp on the desk.

② *to leave, to let remain* [→**nokosu** 残す]

¶Yamamoto-san wa haha ni memo o oite ikimashita.

山本さんは母にメモを置いていきました。

Ms. Yamamoto left a note for my mother and went.

③ *to do for some future purpose* «following the gerund (–te form) of another verb》

¶Bīru o mō sukoshi katte oite kudasai.

ビールをもう少し買っておいてください。

Please buy a little more beer (for later).

④ *to keep, to leave* 《following the gerund (–te form) of another verb》

¶Heya no doa o akete oite kudasai.

部屋のドアを開けておいてください。

Please leave the door of the room open.

okubyó 臆病 〜**na** 〜な *timid, cowardly*

okúgai 屋外 *the outdoors, the open air* [⇔**okunai** 屋内]

¶Kai wa okugai de hirakimashō

会は屋外で開きましょう。

Let's hold the meeting outdoors.

• okugai-supōtsu 屋外スポーツ *outdoor sports*

okujō 屋上 *rooftop*

• okujō-teien 屋上庭園 *roof garden*

okúnai 屋内 *inside, interior* 《of a building》 [⇔**okugai** 屋外]

¶Tsuyu no aida wa okunai de shimasu.

梅雨の間は屋内でします。

We do it indoors during the rainy season.

• okunai-pūru 屋内プール *indoor pool*

Ōkuráshō 大蔵省 *the Ministry of Finance*

okureru 遅れる, 後れる ① *to be late, to arrive late*

¶Shichi-ji no densha ni okuremashita.

7 時の電車に遅れました。

I was late for the 7:00 train.

¶Hikōki wa sanjup-pun-hodo okureru deshō.

飛行機は30分ほど遅れるでしょう。

The airplane will probably be about 30 minutes late.

② *to lose time, to become slow* 《when the subject is a clock》 [⇔**susumu** 進む③]

¶Watashi no tokei wa is-shūkan ni ip-pun okuremasu.

私の時計は 1 週間に 1 分遅れます。

My watch loses one minute a week.

¶Uchi no tokei wa ni-fun okurete imasu.

うちの時計は 2 分遅れています。

Our clock is two minutes slow.

③ *to lag behind*

¶Watashi wa tomodachi yori Eigo ga okurete imasu.

私は友達より英語が遅れています。

I am behind my friends in English.

¶Uchi no chichi wa jidai ni okurete iru yo.

うちの父は時代に遅れているよ。

My father is behind the times!

okurimono 贈り物 *present, gift*

¶Sensei e no okurimono desu.

先生への贈り物です。

It's a present for the teacher.

• Kurisumasu no okurimono クリスマスの贈り物 *Christmas present*

okuru 送る ① *to send* 《a thing》

¶Sono shashin o imōto ni okutte kudasai.

その写真を妹に送ってください。

Please send that photo to my younger sister.

② *to take, to escort* 《a person to a destination》

¶Hideo-kun wa kuruma de uchi made okutte kureta yo.

英男君は車でうちまで送ってくれたよ。

Hideo took me home in his car!

③ *to see off* 《a departing person》 [→**miokuru** 見送る①]

④ *to spend* 《a period of time》, *to live* 《a life》 [→**sugosu** 過ごす]

¶Sofu wa kōfuku na jinsei o okurimashita.

祖父は幸福な人生を送りました。

My grandfather lived a happy life.

okuru 贈る *to award, to give* 《as a gift》

¶Maitoshi shinnyūsei ni jisho o okurimasu.

毎年新入生に辞書を贈ります。

We give dictionaries to the new students every year.

ókusan 奥さん 【HON. for **tsuma** 妻】 *wife*

ókushon オークション *auction*

o-kyō お経 (*Buddhist*)*sutra*

omae お前 【COL.】 *you* 《There are

several Japanese words for *you*, but in general, Japanese speakers prefer to use names or titles rather than words for *you*. The word **omae** is generally used only by male speakers to address intimate social equals or intimate social inferiors. Used in other circumstances, **omae** is very insulting. Other words for *you* include **anata** あなた, **kimi** 君, and **kisama** 貴様.》

omake お負け ① *free gift, giveaway, premium* 《accompanying something one buys》［→**keihin** 景品①］
¶Kono enpitsu wa omake ni moratta mono da yo.
この鉛筆はおまけにもらったものだよ。
I got this pencil as a free gift.
•omake suru おまけする *to give as a free gift*
② *discount*［→**waribiki** 割引］
¶Ano mise de wa hyaku-en omake shitekureta.
あの店では100円おまけしてくれた。
I got a 100-yen discount at that store.
•omake suru おまけする *to discount, to lower in price*

omake-ni お負けに *in addition; to make matters worse*
¶Omake-ni yuki mo furi-hajimemashita.
おまけに雪も降りはじめました。
To make matters worse, it began to snow too.

omamori お守り *good-luck charm, talisman* 《Ordinarily bought at a Shinto shrine or Buddhist temple.》
¶Jinja de kōtsū-anzen no omamori o moratta.
神社で交通安全のお守りをもらった。
I got a traffic safety good-luck charm at the shrine.

o-matsuri お祭り［☞**matsuri** 祭り］
omáwarisan お巡りさん【COL. for **keikan** 警官】*police officer*
ōme 大目 ～**ni miru** ～に見る *to overlook, to tolerate*
o-me お目 ～**ni kakaru** ～にかかる【HUM. for **au** 会う】
•o-me ni kakeru お目にかける【HUM.

for **miseru** 見せる】
omedetō おめでとう *Congratulations!*
¶Gōkaku omedetō!
合格おめでとう！
Congratulations on passing!
¶Tanjōbi omedetō!
誕生日おめでとう！
Happy birthday!
¶Kurisumasu omedetō!
クリスマスおめでとう！
Merry Christmas!
•omedetō gozaimasu おめでとうございます
【FORMAL for **omedetō** (above)】
¶Akemashite omedetō gozaimasu.
明けましておめでとうございます。
Happy New Year! 《Said only after the new year has arrived.》

o-miai お見合い［☞**miai** 見合い］
o-míkoshi お神輿［☞**mikoshi** 神輿］
Ōmísoka 大晦日 *New Year's Eve*
o-miyage お土産［☞**miyage** 土産］
ómo 主 ～**na** ～な *main, chief, principal, leading*
¶Kongetsu no omo na supōtsu-gyōji wa nan desu ka.
今月の主なスポーツ行事は何ですか。
What are this month's main sports events?
¶Tone-gawa wa Nihon no omo na kawa no hitotsu desu.
利根川は日本の主な川の１つです。
The Tone River is one of Japan's principal rivers.
¶Sono kuni no omo na seiji-ka-tachi ga atsumarimashita.
その国の主な政治家たちが集まりました。
That country's leading politicians gathered.
•omo ni 主に *mainly, chiefly, mostly*
¶Kankyaku wa omo ni wakai onna no ko desu.
観客は主に若い女の子です。
The spectators are mainly young girls.
¶Natsu-yasumi wa omo ni kaigan de sugoshimasu.
夏休みは主に海岸で過ごします。
I spend the summer vacation mostly at

the seashore.

omócha おもちゃ *toy*

¶Kodomo-tachi wa omocha de asobu no ga suki desu.

子供たちはおもちゃで遊ぶのが好きです。

The children like playing with toys.

• omocha-bako おもちゃ箱 *toy box*

• omocha-ya おもちゃ屋 *toy store; toy-store proprietor*

omoi 重い ① *heavy* [⇔**karui** 軽い]

¶Kono hako wa te de hakobu ni wa omoi desu.

この箱は手で運ぶには重いです。

This box is heavy to carry by hand.

• kibun ga omoi 気分が重い *to feel depressed*

② *severe, serious*

• omoi batsu 重い罰 *severe punishment*

• omoi byōki 重い病気 *serious illness*

omoidásu 思い出す *to recall, to recollect, to remember*

¶Ano hito no namae o omoidashimashita ka.

あの人の名前を思い出しましたか。

Did you recall that person's name?

¶Yuki ga furu to, Hokkaidō o omoidashimasu.

雪が降ると、北海道を思い出します。

When it snows, I remember Hokkaido.

omoide 思い出 *reminiscence, memory*

¶Haha wa yoku gakusei-jidai no omoide o hanashimasu.

母はよく学生時代の思い出を話します。

My mother often talks about memories of her school days.

• tanoshii [kanashii] omoide 楽しい [悲しい] 思い出 *happy [sad] memories*

omoigakénai 思いがけない *unexpected, surprising*

¶Omoigakenai o-kyaku-san ga miemashita.

思いがけないお客さんが見えました。

An unexpected visitor came.

¶Sore wa omoigakenai koto desu.

それは思いがけないことです。

That's a surprising thing.

omoikiri 思いきり ① *without holding*

back, to one's heart's content, vigorously, hard

¶Omoikiri bōru o ketta yo.

思いきりボールをけったよ。

I kicked the ball hard!

② *resignation (to fate); decision, resolution*

• omoikiri ga ii 思い切りがいい *willing to resign oneself to fate;decisive, resolute*

• omoikiri ga warui 思い切りがいい *indecisive, irresolute*

• omoikiri-yoku 思い切りよく *resignedly;decisively, resolutely*

omoikítta 思い切った *bold, daring, resolute*

¶Shachō wa tokidoki omoikitta koto o shimasu.

社長は時々思い切ったことをします。

The company president sometimes does daring things.

omóikitte 思い切って *boldly, daringly, resolutely*

¶Yumiko wa omoikitte Ken ni tegami o kaita.

由美子は思い切って健に手紙を書いた。

Yumiko boldly wrote a letter to Ken.

omoikómu 思い込む *to come to a mistaken conclusion*

¶Ani wa kore ga honmono da to omoikonde imasu.

兄はこれが本物だと思い込んでいます。

My older brother mistakenly believes that this is the real thing.

omoitsúku 思い付く ① *to think of, to come up with* «when the subject is a person»

¶Chiji wa keikaku no setsumei-hōhō o omoitsukimashita.

知事は計画の説明方法を思いつきました。

The governor thought of a way to explain the plan.

② *to occur to one* «when the subject is a thought» [→**ukabu** 浮かぶ②]

¶Ii an ga omoitsukimasen.

いい案が思いつきません。

A good idea doesn't occur to me.

omoiyari 思いやり *sympathy, considera-*

tion, thoughtfulness

¶Akemi-san wa tanin ni taishite omoiyari ga aru.

明美さんは他人に対して思いやりがある。

Akemi has consideration for others.

ōmoji 大文字 *capital letter* [⇔**komoji** 小文字]

omomuki 趣 ① *gist, purport* [→**shushi** 趣旨]

② *appearance, look, air* [→**yōsu** 様子]

omonjíru 重んじる *to value, to think highly of*

¶Watashi no sensei wa nani yori mo kisoku o omonjimasu.

私の先生は何よりも規則を重んじます。

My teacher values rules more than anything else.

omosa 重さ *weight*

¶Sono sūtsukēsu no omosa wa juk-kiro desu.

そのスーツケースの重さは10キロです。

The weight of that suitcase is ten kilograms.

omoshirói 面白い *interesting* [→**kyōmi-bukai** 興味深い (s.v. **kyōmi** 興味)]; *amusing, fun* [→**tanoshii** 楽しい]

¶Kono hon wa watashi ni wa totemo omoshiroi desu.

この本は私にはとてもおもしろいです。

This book is very interesting to me.

¶Hitori de asobu no wa omoshiroku nai yo.

一人で遊ぶのはおもしろくないよ。

It's not fun playing alone!

¶Ōmori-san wa omoshiroi hito desu ne.

大森さんはおもしろい人ですね。

Mr. Omori is an interesting person, isn't he.

¶Sukētobōdo wa totemo omoshiroi yo.

スケートボードはとてもおもしろいよ。

Skateboarding is really fun!

omoté 表 ① *front side, face, obverse* [⇔**ura** 裏①]

¶Fūtō no omote ni namae o kakimashita.

封筒の表に名前を書きました。

I wrote the name on the face of the envelope.

② *outdoors, outside* [→**kogai** 戸外]

¶Kodomo-tachi wa omote de asonde imasu.

子供たちは表で遊んでいます。

The children are playing outdoors.

③ *top* «of an inning in baseball» [⇔**ura** 裏③]

¶Kyū-kai no omote desu.

9回の表です。

It's the top of the ninth inning.

omóu 思う *to think, to have the idea* [→**kangaeru** 考える①]

¶Haha wa densha ni maniawanai to omoimasu.

母は電車に間に合わないと思います。

I think that my mother will not make the train.

¶Yamada-san wa kuru to omoimasu ka.

山田さんは来ると思いますか。

Do you think that Mr. Yamada will come?

¶Inu o kaitai to omoimashita.

犬を飼いたいと思いました。

I thought that I would like to have a dog.

¶Kon'ya wa eiga o mi ni ikō to omotte imasu.

今夜は映画を見に行こうと思っています。

I'm thinking that I'll go to see a movie tonight.

¶Omotta hodo muzukashiku nai desu.

思ったほど難しくないです。

It's not as difficult as I had thought.

• A o B (da) to omou AをB(だ)と思う *to consider A (to be) B, to think A B*

¶Sono hito o baka da to omoimasu.

その人をばかだと思います。

I think that person is an idiot.

¶Kono keikaku o dō omoimasu ka.

この計画をどう思いますか。

What do you think of this plan?

omówazu 思わず *unintentionally, involuntarily, in spite of oneself*

¶Watashi wa omowazu waratte shimaimashita.

私は思わず笑ってしまいました。

I laughed unintentionally.

ōmu 鸚鵡 *parrot*

omuretsu オムレツ *omelet*

ón 恩 *kindness, favor; obligation for a favor received, debt of gratitude*

¶Go-on wa kesshite wasuremasen.

ご恩は決して忘れません。

I'll never forget your kindness.

• on o ukeru 恩を受ける *to receive a favor, to become obligated*

¶Harada-san ni wa tokubetsu ni on o ukete imasu.

原田さんには特別に恩を受けています。

I'm especially obligated to Mr. Harada.

• on ni naru 恩になる *to become obligated*

• on-gaeshi 恩返し *repaying a kindness*

• on-gaeshi suru 恩返しする *to repay a kindness*

ónā オーナー *owner* «especially of a professional sports team» [→**mochinushi** 持ち主, **shoyū-sha** 所有者]

onaji 同じ *same* «This word modifies a following noun with no intervening particle, but when used as a predicate, it requires a form of **da** だ.»

¶Keiko to watashi wa onaji gakkō ni kayotte imasu.

恵子と私は同じ学校に通っています。

Keiko and I go to the same school.

¶Watashi wa Yamada-san to onaji shigoto o shite imasu.

私は山田さんと同じ仕事をしています。

I do the same work as Ms. Tanaka.

¶Hayashi-san to Hayashi-san no haha oya wa kangae-kata ga onaji da.

林さんと林さんの母親は考え方が同じだ。

Ms. Hayashi and her mother's way of thinking are the same.

onaka お腹 *stomach*

¶Ima wa onaka ga ippai desu.

今はおなかがいっぱいです。

My stomach is full now.

¶Chichi wa onaka ga dete imasu.

父はおなかが出ています。

My father's stomach sticks out.

• onaka ga suku おなかがすく *to get hungry*

• onaka ga itai おなかが痛い *one's stomach is aching*

• onaka o kowasu おなかを壊す *to get an upset stomach*

onara おなら *fart* «This Japanese word is not as crude-sounding as the English translation.»

• onara o suru おならをする *to fart*

ónbu おんぶ 【COL.】 *carrying a person on one's back*

• onbu suru おんぶする *to carry on one's back*

ónchi 音痴 *tone-deafness*

• onchi no 音痴の *tone-deaf*

• hōkō-onchi 方向音痴 *lack of a sense of direction*

ondan 温暖 ～**na** ～な *warm, temperate, mild*

¶Nihon wa kikō ga ondan desu.

日本は気候が温暖です。

Japan's climate is mild.

• ondan-zensen 温暖前線 *warm front*

óndo 温度 *temperature*

¶Ondo wa Sesshi nijū-do desu.

温度は摂氏20度です。

The temperature is 20 degrees centigrade.

• ondo ga agaru 〔sagaru〕 温度上がる 〔下がる〕 *a temperature rises 〔falls〕*

• takai 〔hikui〕 ondo 高い 〔低い〕温度 *high 〔low〕 temperature*

• ondo-kei 温度計 *thermometer*

o-negai お願い 【HUM. for **tanomi** 頼み①】 *request, favor (to ask)*

¶Chotto o-negai ga aru n desu ga.

ちょっとお願いがあるんですが。

I have a favor to ask you. «Literally: I have a little bit of a request, but . . .»

• o-negai suru お願いする 【HUM. for **tanomu** 頼む】 *to request, to ask for*

¶O-tetsudai o o-negai dekimasu ka.

お手伝いをお願いできますか。

Can I ask you for your help?

onésan お姉さん 【HON. for **ane** 姉】 *older sister*

óngaku 音楽 *music*

¶Kono ko wa ongaku no sainō ga arimasu.

この子は音楽の才能があります。

This child has musical talent.

• ongaku-gakkō 音楽学校 *music school*

• ongaku-ka 音楽家 *musician*

• ongaku-kai 音楽会 *concert*

oni 鬼 *demon, ogre* 《A familiar figure in Japanese fairy tales, an **oni** has a human-like body with two horns on its head and fangs. In the game of tag, the person who is "it" is called the **oni**.》

¶Shigeo-san wa benkyō no oni desu.

茂男さんは勉強の鬼です。

Shigeo is a demon for studying.

¶Oni wa soto, fuku wa uchi.

鬼は外、福は内。

Demons out! Good luck in! 《Said as part of the bean throwing ritual traditionally performed on **Setsubun** (February 3). The beans are thrown to drive demons out of houses.》

¶Oni no inu ma ni sentaku.

鬼のいぬ間に洗濯。《proverb》

When the cat is away, the mice will play. 《Literally: *While the demon is away, no worries.*》

• oni-gokko 鬼ごっこ *(the game of)tag*

onisan お兄さん 【HON. for **ani** 兄】 *older brother*

onkyō 音響 *sound, acoustic vibrations*

• onkyō-gaku 音響学 *(the study of)acoustics*

• onkyō-kōka 音響効果 *acoustics* 《of a room, etc.》

onná 女 *woman, (human)female* [→**josei** 女性] [⇔**otoko** 男]

• onna no hito 女の人 *woman*

• onna no akachan 女の赤ちゃん *baby girl*

• onna no ko 女の子 *girl*

• onna-mono 女物 *item intended for women*

• onna-ppoi 女っぽい *womanly, feminine; womanish, effeminate*

• onna-rashii 女らしい *womanly, feminine*

• onna-tomodachi 女友達 *female friend*

óno 斧 *ax; hatchet*

onpu 音符 *note* 《in a musical score》

• nibu-onpu 二分音符 *half note*

• shibu-onpu 四分音符 *quarter note*

onsen 温泉 *hot spring, spa*

onshitsu 温室 *greenhouse, hothouse*

• onshitsu-shokubutsu 温室植物 *hothouse plant*

on'yomi 音読み *Chinese reading* 《of a **kanji**》

ópera オペラ *opera*

operḗtā オペレーター *operator* 《of a machine》*;(telephone)operator* [→ **denwa-kōkan-shu** 電話交換手 (s.v. **denwa** 電話)]

ṓpun オープン ～**suru** ～する [[→**kaiten suru** 開店する]]

① *to open* 《said of a store, restaurant, etc., for the business day》《transitive or intransitive》

② *to open* 《said of a newly established store, restaurant, etc.》《transitive or intransitive》

¶Raigetsu eki-mae ni depāto ga ōpun shimasu.

来月駅前にデパートがオープンします。

Next month a department store will open in front of the station.

ṓpunsen オープン戦 *preseason professional baseball game*

ōrai 往来 [[→**tōri** 通り]] ① *coming and going, traffic back and forth, traffic in both directions*

¶Kono tōri wa ōrai ga hageshii desu.

この通りは往来が激しいです。

The traffic on this street is heavy.

¶Koko wa kuraku naru to, kuruma no ōrai ga sukunai.

ここは暗くなると、車の往来が少ない。

When it gets dark, there is little automobile traffic here.

• ōrai suru 往来する *to come and go, to go in both directions*

② *road, street* [→**dōro** 道路]

oran'ũtan オランウータン *orangutan*

ore 俺 【COL.】 *I, me* 《There are several Japanese words for *I／me*. The word

ore is ordinarily restricted to male speakers addressing intimate social equals and intimate social inferiors. Other words for *I*/*me* include **watashi** 私, **watakushi** 私, **atashi** あたし, and **boku** 僕.》

o-rei お礼 [☞**rei** 礼]

orénji オレンジ ① *an orange*
② (*the color*)*orange*
• orenji-jūsu オレンジジュース *orange juice*

ōrénzu [凹]レンズ *concave lens* [⇔**totsurenzu** 凸レンズ]

oréru 折れる ① *to break* 《intransitive》
《The subject must be long and slender.》
¶Kono enpitsu wa shin ga sugu oreru ne.
この鉛筆はしんがすぐ折れるね。
This pencil lead breaks easily, doesn't it.
② *to fold up* 《intransitive》
③ *to turn* 《intransitive》 [→**magaru** 曲がる]
¶Soko de migi ni oreru to, gekijō ga arimasu.
そこで右に折れると、劇場があります。
If you turn to the right there, there is a theater.

orí 檻 *cage*
¶Ori no naka ni raion ga imasu.
おりの中にライオンがいます。
There's a lion in the cage.

oríbu オリーブ *olive*
• orību-yu オリーブ油 *olive oil*

orientéshon オリエンテーション *orientation* 《for people in a new environment》
¶Shinnyūsei wa oorientēshon o uketa.
新入生はオリエンテーションを受けた。
The new students received orientation.

origami 折り紙 ① *origami, paper folding* 《the traditional Japanese craft》
② *folding paper* (*for doing origami*)
• origami-tsuki no 折り紙付きの *certified, guaranteed, acknowledged*

oríjinaru オリジナル *an original* 《as opposed to a reproduction, copy, translation, etc.》
• orijinaru na オリジナルな *original, creative, inventive* [→**dokusō-teki na** 独創的な (s.v. **dokusō** 独創)]

Orinpíkku オリンピック *the Olympics*
¶Rokujūyo-nen no Orinpikku wa Tōkyō de hirakareta.
64年のオリンピックは東京で開かれた。
The '64 Olympics were held in Tokyo.
• Orinpikku-kiroku オリンピック記録 *Olympic record*
• Orinpikku-senshu オリンピック選手 *Olympic athlete*
• kaki-Orinpikku 夏季オリンピック *the Summer Olympics*
• tōki-Orinpikku 冬季オリンピック *the Winter Olympics*

oriru 降りる、下りる ① *to come down, to go down, to descend*
• kaidan o oriru 階段を降りる *to come*/*go down the stairs*
¶Sore kara oka o orimashita.
それから丘を降りました。
After that we went down the hill.
¶Neko ga ki no ue kara orite kimashita.
猫が木の上から降りてきました。
The cat came down from the tree.
② *to get off, to get out of* 《a means of transportation》 [⇔**noru** 乗る①]
¶Jōkyaku wa densha o orimashita.
乗客は電車を降りました。
The passengers got off the train.
¶Fumiko-san wa mon no mae de takushī kara orita.
文子さんは門の前でタクシーから降りた。
Fumiko got out of the taxi in front of the gate.
③ *to quit, to give up in the middle, to drop out of*
¶Kega o shita senshu wa shiai o orimashita.
けがをした選手は試合を降りました。
The injured player dropped out of the game.

óroka 愚か 〜**na** 〜な *foolish* [→**baka na** 馬鹿な①]
• oroka-mono 愚か者 *fool*

ōrora オーロラ *aurora* (*Borealis or Australis*)

oroshí 卸 *wholesale*
• oroshi-uri 卸売り *selling wholesale* [⇔

kouri 小売り]
 • oroshi-uri suru 卸売りする *to sell whole-sale*

orósu 下ろす ① *to take down, to get down; to lower*
 ¶Tana kara hako o oroshimashita.
棚から箱を下ろしました。
I took the box down from the shelf.
 ¶Buraindo o oroshite kudasai.
ブラインドを下ろしてください。
Please lower the blinds.
 ② *to withdraw* 《money》[→**hikidasu**
引き出す②]

orósu 降ろす *to let off, to let out of* 《a vehicle》[⇔**noseru** 乗せる]
 ¶Tsugi no kado de oroshite kudasai.
次の角で降ろしてください。
Let me off at the next corner, please.

ōru オール *oar*

óru 折る ① *to break, to snap* 《transitive》《The direct object must be long and slender.》
 ¶Otōto wa ki kara ochite ashi o otta yo.
弟は木から落ちて足を折ったよ。
My younger brother fell from a tree and broke his leg!
 ② *to bend* 《transitive》[→**mageru**
曲げる]
 • yubi o otte kazoeru 指を折って数える *to count by bending one's fingers*
 ③ *to fold* 《transitive》[→**tatamu** 畳む]
 ¶Sono tegami o yottsu ni orimashita.
その手紙を四つに折りました。
I folded that letter into four.

óru 織る *to weave*
 ¶Kono mura no onna-tachi wa jūtan o orimasu.
この村の女達はじゅうたんを織ります。
The women of this village weave carpets.

óru おる 【HUM. for **iru** 居る】

orugan オルガン *organ* ((musical instrument))
 • orugan-sōsha オルガン奏者 *organist*

orugóru オルゴール *music box*
 ¶Orugōru ga natte imasu.
オルゴールが鳴っています。
The music box is playing.

ōrunáito オールナイト 〜**no** 〜の
all-night
 • ōrunaito-eigyō オールナイト営業 *open for business all night*
 ¶Ōrunaito-eigyō no kusuri-ya wa arimasu ka.
オールナイト営業の薬屋はありますか。
Is there an all-night pharmacy?

ōrusutā– オールスター– *all-star–*
《Added to noun bases.》
 • ōrusutā-chīmu オールスターチーム
all-star team
 • ōrusutā-sen オールスター戦 *all-star game*

osaéru 押さえる ① *to hold down, to hold steady, to hold tight, to keep from moving*
 ¶Nagata-san wa ashi de doa o osaemashita.
長田さんは足でドアを押さえました。
Mr. Nagata held the door closed with his foot.
 ② *to cover* 《a part of one's body, usually with one or both hands》
 ¶Machiko-san wa kuchi o te de osaemashita.
真知子さんは口を手で押さえました。
Machiko covered her mouth with her hand.

osaéru 抑える *to control, to restrain, to suppress*
 ¶Sofu wa ikari o osaeru koto ga dekimasen.
祖父は怒りを抑えることができません。
My grandfather cannot control his anger.

oságari お下がり 【COL.】 *hand-me-down clothes*

oságe お下げ (*hair in a*) *braid, pigtail*

o–saki お先 〜**ni** 〜に [☞**saki ni** 先に③]

osamáru 治まる *to subside, to abate, to calm down*
 ¶Kusuri o nondara, itami wa osamarimashita.
薬を飲んだら、痛みは治まりました。
When I took the medicine, the pain subsided.

¶Kaze wa yatto osamarimashita.
風はやっと治まりました。
The wind finally subsided.

osamáru 収まる, 納まる ① *to be settled, to be taken care of*

¶Sono jiken wa osamarimashita.
その事件は収まりました。
That matter was settled.

② *to go, to be put* 《within a limited space》

¶O-miyage wa zenbu sono hako ni osamarimashita.
お土産は全部その箱に収まりました。
The souvenirs all went into that box.

③ *to be paid* 《when the subject is money owed》; *to be delivered* 《when the subject is goods》

¶Chūmon shita buhin ga kijitsu dōri ni osamatta.
注文した部品が期日通りに納まった。
The ordered parts were delivered on time.

osaméru 治める ① *to rule, to govern*

¶Joō ga ano kuni o osamete imasu.
女王があの国を治めています。
A queen rules that country.

② *to quell, to subdue, to settle, to quiet*

• kenka o osameru けんかを治める *to settle a quarrel*

osaméru 収める, 納める ① *to pay* 《money owed》; *to deliver* 《goods》

¶Chichi wa zeikin o osamemashita.
父は税金を納めました。
My father paid the taxes.

② *to accept* 《something offered》

• okurimono o osameru 贈り物を納める *to accept a gift*

③ *to obtain, to secure*

• shōri o osameru 勝利を収める *to win a victory*

• rieki o osameru 利益を収める *to make a profit*

④ *to put away, to store*

¶Shachō wa shorui o kinko ni osamemashita.
社長は書類を金庫に収めました。
The company president put the docu-

ments away in the safe.

o-san お産 *childbirth, giving birth* [→ **shussan** 出産]

osanái 幼い ① *very young*

¶Haraguchi-san wa osanai toki kara Beikoku ni sunde iru.
原口さんは幼い時から米国に住んでいる。
Ms. Haraguchi has lived in America since she was very young.

② *childish* [→**kodomo-ppoi** 子供っぽい (s.v. **kodomo** 子供)]

¶Sore wa osanai kangae desu.
それは幼い考えです。
That's a childish idea.

osananájimi 幼馴染み *childhood friend*

o-seibo お歳暮 [☞**seibo** 歳暮]

o-seji お世辞 *insincere compliment, flattery*

¶O-seji ga o-jōzu desu ne.
お世辞がお上手ですね。
You're good at flattery, aren't you.

• o-seji o iu お世辞を言う *to give compliments, to make flattering remarks*

osékkai お節介 *meddling*

• osekkai na おせっかいな *meddlesome*

• A no osekkai o yaku Aのおせっかいを焼く *to meddle in A's affairs*

¶Mita-san wa shotchū Ono-san no osekkai o yaite imasu.
三田さんはしょっちゅう小野さんのおせっかいを焼いています。
Miss Mita is always meddling in Miss Ono's affairs.

osen 汚染 *pollution*

• kankyō-osen 環境汚染 *environmental pollution* [→**kōgai** 公害]

ōsetsuma 応接間 *room in a home where visitors are received*

osháberi お喋り ① *chatting, (idle)talking*

¶Jugyō-chū no oshaberi wa yamenasai.
授業中のおしゃべりはやめなさい。
Stop that chattering during class.

• oshaberi suru おしゃべりする *to chat*

¶O-cha o nomi-nagara oshaberi shimashita.
お茶を飲みながらおしゃべりしました。

We chatted while drinking tea.
② *talkative person*
• oshaberi na おしゃべりな *talkative, garrulous* [⇔**mukuchi na** 無口な]
¶Kimi wa oshaberi da ne.
君はおしゃべりだね。
You're talkative, aren't you.

osháre お洒落 *dressing up, dressing stylishly*
• oshare na おしゃれな *stylish; stylishly dressed*
¶Oshare na seifuku desu ne.
おしゃれな制服ですね。
It's a stylish uniform, isn't it.
¶Mariko-san wa itsu-mo oshare desu.
真理子さんはいつもおしゃれです。
Mariko is always stylishly dressed.
• oshare suru おしゃれする *to dress up, to dress stylishly*
¶Sonna ni oshare shite doko e iku no?
そんなにおしゃれしてどこへ行くの？
Where are you going to go so dressed up?

oshíbori お絞り *moist hot towel* 《for cleaning hands before a meal》

oshie 教え ① *teaching, instruction, lessons*
② *(religious) teachings*
oshieru 教える ① *to teach*
¶Yoshida-sensei wa ongaku o oshiete imasu.
吉田先生は音楽を教えています。
Ms. Yoshida teaches music.
¶Eibun no tegami no kaki-kata o oshiete kudasai.
英文の手紙の書き方を教えてください。
Please teach me how to write letters in English.
② *to tell, to inform of; to show* 《how to do something》
¶Eki e iku michi o oshiete kudasai.
駅へ行く道を教えてください。
Please tell me the way to the station.
¶Kono dōgu no tsukai-kata o oshiete kuremasen ka.
この道具の使い方を教えてくれませんか。
Will you show me how to use this tool?

oshíi 惜しい ① *unfortunate, regrettable* [→**zannen na** 残念な]
¶Hareta hi ni benkyō shite iru no wa oshii desu.
晴れた日に勉強しているのは惜しいです。
It's unfortunate to be studying on a sunny day.
② *precious, too good to lose or waste*
¶Dare demo inochi wa oshii desu.
だれでも命は惜しいです。
Life is precious to everyone.
¶Kore wa mada suteru ni wa oshii yo.
これはまだ捨てるには惜しいよ。
This is still too valuable to throw away!

oshiire 押し入れ *closet* 《of the type used for storing bedding in a traditional Japanese-style room》

oshíkko おしっこ 【COL. for **shōben** 小便】 *pee-pee*

oshikómu 押し込む *to cram, to stuff* 《into a container》

o-shimai お仕舞い *end* [→**owari** 終わり]

oshímu 惜しむ ① *to begrudge, to be stingy with*
¶Chichi wa doryoku o oshimimasen.
父は努力を惜しみません。
My father does not begrudge effort.
② *to regret, to lament, to deplore*

o-shiri お尻 [☞**shiri** 尻]

oshitsubúsu 押しつぶす *to crush, to squash*
¶Bōshi no ue ni koshi o oroshite oshitsubushite shimaimashita.
帽子の上に腰を下ろして押しつぶしてしまいました。
I sat on top of my hat and crushed it.

oshitsukéru 押し付ける ① *to push, to press* 《one thing against another》
• A ni B o oshitsukeru AにBを押しつける *to push A against B, to press A against B*
¶Takahashi-san wa tsukue o kabe ni oshitsukemashita.
高橋さんは机を壁に押しつけました。
Mr. Takahashi pushed the desk against the wall.

② *to force* 《something on a person》 [→ **kyōsei suru** 強制する]

¶Ani wa itsu-mo watashi ni sono shigoto o oshitsukeru yo.

兄はいつも私にその仕事を押しつけるよ。

My older brother always forces that work on me!

O-shōgatsu お正月 [☞**Shōgatsu** 正月]

ōsodókkusu オーソドックス 〜**na** 〜な *orthodox*

osoi 遅い ① *late* [⇔**hayai** 早い]

¶Mō osoi kara, kaerimasu.

もう遅いから、帰ります。

It's already late, so I'll go home.

¶Osoi chōshoku o torimashita.

遅い朝食をとりました。

I had a late breakfast.

¶Hikōki wa osoku shuppatsu shimashita.

飛行機は遅く出発しました。

The plane departed late.

• osoku made 遅くまで *until late*

¶Ane wa maiban osoku made okite imasu.

姉は毎晩遅くまで起きています。

My older sister is up until late every night.

• osoku-tomo 遅くとも *at the latest*

¶Miyamoto wa osoku-tomo roku-ji made ni wa kaeru darō.

宮本は遅くとも6時までには帰るだろう。

Miyamoto will probably return by 6:00 at the latest.

② *slow* [⇔**hayai** 速い]

¶Tsuda-san wa osoku arukimasu.

津田さんは遅く歩きます。

Mr. Tsuda walks slowly.

¶Densha no supīdo ga osoku narimashita.

電車のスピードが遅くなりました。

The train slowed down.

osóraku 恐らく [[→**tabun** 多分]] *perhaps; probably*

《This word often occurs in sentences ending with an expression of probability (such as **darō**). Since such a sentence has virtually the same meaning whether or not **osoraku** is present, **osoraku** is redundant in a sense, but it serves as a signal of how a sentence will end.》

¶Osoraku yaku ni tatsu deshō.

恐らく役に立つでしょう。

Perhaps it will help.

¶Osoraku sore wa hontō desu.

恐らくそれは本当です。

Perhaps that's true.

osoré 恐れ ① *fear, terror*

• osore o shiranai 恐れを知らない *to know no fear*

② *fear, danger* 《that something bad will happen》

¶Sono fune wa chinbotsu no osore ga arimasu.

その船は沈没の恐れがあります。

That ship is in danger of sinking.

¶Daitōryō wa mata shippai suru osore ga arimasu.

大統領はまた失敗する恐れがあります。

There is fear that the president will fail again.

osoréru 恐れる *to be afraid of, to fear*

¶Dōbutsu wa hi o osoremasu.

動物は火を恐れます。

Animals are afraid of fire.

¶Gaikoku-go o hanasu toki, machigai o osorete wa ikemasen.

外国語を話すとき、まちがいを恐れてはいけません。

When speaking a foreign language, one mustn't be afraid of mistakes.

osoroshii 恐ろしい *terrible, frightful, frightening* [→**kowai** 怖い①]

¶Osoroshii yume o mita yo.

恐ろしい夢を見たよ。

I had a terrible dream!

¶Watashi wa kurayami ga osoroshii yo.

私は暗やみが恐ろしいよ。

I'm frightened of the dark!

• osoroshii jiko 恐ろしい事故 *terrible accident*

osóu 襲う ① *to attack, to assault*

¶Kuma ga murabito o osoimashita.

くまが村人を襲いました。

A bear attacked a villager.

② *to strike, to hit* 《when the subject is

a natural disaster, an illness, etc.》

¶Taifū ga Kyūshū o osoimashita.

台風が九州を襲いました。

A typhoon struck Kyushu.

osowaru 教わる *to receive instruction, to be taught*

• A ni B o osowaru AにBを教わる *to be taught B by A, to learn B from A*

¶Watashi wa Amerika-jin no josei ni Eigo o osowatta.

私はアメリカ人の女性に英語を教わった。

I learned English from an American woman.

ossháru おっしゃる{Irreg.}【HON. for iu 言う】

osú 雄 *a male* (*animal*) [⇔**mesu** 雌]

¶Kono neko wa osu desu ka, mesu desu ka.

この猫は雄ですか、雌ですか。

Is this cat a male or a female?

osu 押す ① *to push* [⇔**hiku** 引く①]

¶Abe-san wa beru no oshi-botan o oshimashita.

安部さんはベルの押しボタンを押しました。

Ms. Abe pushed the doorbell button.

② *to press down to leave a stamped mark*

¶Kakari-in wa shorui ni in o oshimashita.

係員は書類に印を押しました。

The clerk-in-charge pressed the seal down on the document.

o-susowake お裾分け *sharing a gift with another person*

• o-susowake suru おすそ分けする *to share a gift*

o-tagai お互い [☞**tagai** 互い]

otamajákushi お玉杓子 *tadpole, pollywog*

óte 大手 *major corporation*

otenba おてんば【COL.】*tomboy*

¶Yōko-chan wa otenba da ne.

洋子ちゃんはおてんばだね。

Yoko is a tomboy, isn't she?

otó 音 *sound* 《i.e., something audible》

• ōkii〔chīsai〕oto 大きい〔小さい〕音 *loud*〔*soft*〕*sound*

¶Ōki na oto o tatenai de kudasai.

大きな音を立てないでください。

Please don't make a loud sound.

¶Terebi no oto o chīsaku shinasai.

テレビの音を小さくしなさい。

Turn the TV volume down.

• takai oto 高い音 *high-volume sound;high-pitched sound*

• hikui oto 低い音 *low-volume sound;low-pitched sound*

ótóbai オートバイ *motorcycle*

• ōtobai ni noru オートバイに乗る *to get on a motorcycle;to ride a motorcycle*

otogibánashi おとぎ話 *fairy tale* [→**dōwa** 童話]

¶Kodomo-tachi wa otogibanashi o kiite imashita.

子供たちはおとぎ話を聞いていました。

The children were listening to fairy tales.

otokó 男 *man*, (*human*)*male* [→**dansei** 男性][⇔**onna** 女]

¶Koko ni wa otoko no ten'in wa nan-nin imasu ka.

ここには男の店員は何人いますか。

How many male salesclerks are there here?

• otoko no hito 男の人 *man*

¶Ano otoko no hito wa dare desu ka.

あの男の人はだれですか。

Who is that man?

• otoko no ko 男の子 *boy*

• otoko no akachan 男の赤ちゃん *baby boy*

• otoko-mono 男物 *item intended for men*

¶Kyōko-san wa otoko-mono no sētā o kite imasu.

京子さんは男物のセーターを着ています。

Kyoko is wearing a man's sweater.

• otoko-ppoi 男っぽい *manly; mannish*

• otoko-rashii 男らしい *manly*

• otoko-tomodachi 男友達 *male friend*

ōtomachíkku オートマチック ① 〜**na** 〜な *automatic* [→**jidō no** 自動の]

② *an automatic* (*device*)

③ *automatic transmission*

• ōtomachikku-sha オートマチック車 *vehi-*

cle with automatic transmission

otóme 乙女 ① *girl* [→**shōjo** 少女]
② *virgin, maiden* [→**shōjo** 処女]

ōtoméshon オートメーション *automation*

otona 大人 *adult* [→**seijin** 成人]
• otona ni naru 大人になる *to become an adult, to grow up*
¶Musuko wa mō otona ni narimashita.
息子はもう大人になりました。
My son has already become an adult.

otonashíi おとなしい ① *calm and quiet* «describing personality or behavior»
¶Kodomo-tachi wa otonashiku hon o yonde imasu.
子供たちはおとなしく本を読んでいます。
The children are reading quietly.
② *well-mannered, well-behaved*
¶Jirō-chan wa otonashii ko desu.
次郎ちゃんはおとなしい子です。
Jiro is a well-mannered child.

otoroéru 衰える *to become weak, to decline, to lose vigor*
¶Sofu wa ashi ga otoroemashita.
祖父は足が衰えました。
My grandfather's legs have become weak.
¶Haha no kenkō wa otoroemashita.
母の健康は衰えました。
My mother's health has declined.

otóru 劣る *to be／become inferior* [⇔**masaru** 勝る]
¶Watashi wa Eigo de wa imōto ni ototte imasu.
私は英語では妹に劣っています。
I am inferior to my younger sister in English.
¶Kono kōcha wa mae no yori hinshitsu ga ototte imasu.
この紅茶は前のより品質が劣っています。
The quality of this tea is inferior to the previous one.

otósan お父さん 【HON. for **chichi** 父】
father [⇔**okāsan** お母さん]
¶Otōsan wa doko?
お父さんはどこ？
Where's Father?
¶Otōsan wa byōin de hataraite iru no

desu ka.
お父さんは病院で働いているのですか。
Does your father work at hospital?

otoshidama お年玉 *gift of money given to children at New Year's*
¶Hiroshi-oji-san wa otoshidama ni nisen-en kureta yo.
弘叔父さんはお年玉に2000円くれたよ。
Uncle Hiroshi gave me 2,000 yen as a New Year's gift!

otoshimono 落とし物 *thing inadvertently dropped and lost*
¶Ishii-san wa mada otoshimono o sagashite imasu.
石井さんはまだ落とし物を探しています。
Mr. Ishii is still looking for the thing he lost.
• otoshimono-toriatsukai-jo 落とし物取扱所 *lost and found office*

otósu 落とす ① *to drop, to let fall, to make fall*
¶Sakki tamago o yuka ni otoshimashita.
さっき卵を床に落としました。
A little while ago I dropped an egg on the floor.
• supīdo o otosu スピードを落とす *to reduce speed*
② *to inadvertently drop and lose; to lose*
¶Doko-ka ni bōshi o otoshite shimaimashita.
どこかに帽子を落としてしまいました。
I lost my hat somewhere.
• inochi o otosu 命を落とす *to lose one's life*
• ninki o otosu 人気を落とす *to lose one's popularity*
• ki o otosu 気を落とす *to lose heart*
③ *to fail* «a student, etc.»
④ *to remove* «a stain, etc.»

otōtó 弟 *younger brother* [⇔**ani** 兄; **imōto** 妹]
¶Ichiban shita no otōto wa nana-sai desu.
いちばん下の弟は7歳です。
My youngest brother is seven years old.
• otōto-san 弟さん 【HON. for **otōto**

(above)】

ototói 一昨日 *the day before yesterday*
¶Sakurai-san wa ototoi no asa ni tsuki-mashita.
桜井さんはおとといの朝に着きました。
Mr. Sakurai arrived on the morning of the day before yesterday.
• saki-ototoi 一昨昨日 *the day before the day before yesterday*

otótoshi 一昨年 *the year before last*

otozuréru 訪れる *to visit, to pay a call on* [→hōmon suru 訪問する]

o-tsúmami おつまみ *snacks* «eaten while drinking beer, etc.»

o-tsuri お釣り *change* «returned in a transaction»
¶O-tsuri wa totte oite kudasai.
お釣りは取っておいてください。
Please keep the change.
¶O-tsuri o gojū-en moraimashita.
お釣りを50円もらいました。
I got 50 yen change.

otto 夫 *husband* [⇔tsuma 妻]

ottósei おっとせい *fur seal*

ou 追う ① *to pursue, to follow, to go after* [→oikakeru 追い掛ける]
¶Michiko-san wa ryūkō o otte imasu.
美知子さんは流行を追っています。
Michiko follows popular trends.
② *to drive away, to make go away, to get rid of* [→oiharau 追い払う]

ou 負う ① *to take, to assume* «an obligation, responsibility, etc.»
¶Takano-san wa sono jiko no sekinin o oimashita.
高野さんはその事故の責任を負いました。
Mr. Takano took responsibility for that accident.
② *to be indebted; to be due, to be attributable*
¶Otto no seikō wa tsuma no kyōryoku ni ou tokoro ga ōi.
夫の成功は妻の協力に負うところが多い。
There are many ways in which a husband's success is due to his wife's cooperation.
③ *to sustain* «an injury»

¶Kenji-san wa jiko de jūshō o oimashita.
健次さんは事故で重傷を負いました。
Kenji sustained a serious injury in the accident.

ōu 覆う *to cover*
¶Terebi o kono nuno de ōtte kudasai.
テレビをこの布で覆ってください。
Please cover the TV with this cloth.

óushi 雄牛 *bull*

owareru 追われる *to become very busy* «with work» «This word is the passive form of **ou** 追う and has the predictable meanings as well.»
¶Watashi wa kaji ni owarete imasu.
私は家事に追われています。
I am very busy with housework.

owari 終わり *end, finish* [⇔hajime 初め]
¶Raigetsu no owari ni shuppatsu shimasu.
来月の終わりに出発します。
I will leave at the end of next month.
¶Natsu-yasumi mo owari ni chikazukimashita.
夏休みも終わりに近づきました。
The summer vacation also has neared its end.
¶Hajime kara owari made damatte imashita.
初めから終わりまで黙っていました。
I kept silent from beginning to end.
¶Sono hon o owari made yomimashita ka.
その本を終わりまで読みましたか。
Did you read that book to the end?

owaru 終わる *to end, to finish* «transitive or intransitive»
¶Shiai wa ku-ji ni owarimashita.
試合は9時に終わりました。
The game ended at 9:00.
¶Kono shigoto o owattara, kaerimashō.
この仕事を終わったら、帰りましょう。
When we finish this work, let's go home.
¶Gakkō wa san-ji ni owarimasu.
学校は3時に終わります。
School ends at 3:00.

oyá 親 *parent*

¶Kono oya ni shite kono ko ari.
この親にしてこの子あり。《proverb》
Like father, like son. 《Literally: *Given this parent there will be this child.*》

• oya-go-san 親御さん 【HON. for **oya** 親 (above)】

• oya-omoi 親思い *love for one's parents, filial affection*

oya おや *Oh!* 《an exclamatory interjection expressing surprise or joy》
¶Oya, Kobayashi-kun mo kita yo.
おや、小林君も来たよ。
Oh, Kobayashi came too!

óya 大家 *landlord*

óyabun 親分 *boss* 《of henchmen》 [⇔ **kobun** 子分]

ōyake 公 ～**no** ～の ① *public, open*
¶Sono shirase o ōyake ni shimashita.
その知らせを公にしました。
They made that news public.
② *public, official, governmental*

óyako 親子 *parent and child*

• oyako-donburi 親子丼 *bowl of rice topped with chicken and egg*

oyakókō 親孝行 *filial piety*

oyasumi nasai お休みなさい *Good night.*

• oyasumi お休み 《a very informal version of **oyasumi nasai**》

oyátsu おやつ 【COL.】 *mid-afternoon snack*
¶Haha wa san-ji ni oyatsu o dashite kureta yo.
母は3時におやつを出してくれたよ。
My mother served us a mid-afternoon snack at 3:00!

oyayubi 親指 ① *thumb*
② *big toe*

ōyō 応用 *application, putting to a particular use*

• ōyō suru 応用する *to apply, to put to use*
¶Teko no genri wa ōku no mono ni ōyō saremasu.
てこの原理は多くの物に応用されます。
The principle of the lever is applied to many things.

• ōyō-han'i 応用範囲 *range of application*

• ōyō-mondai 応用問題 *application problem, question posed as an exercise for learners* [→**renshū-mondai** 練習問題 (s.v. **renshū** 練習)]

oyobu 及ぶ ① *to extend, to spread, to amount*
¶Sono kaigō wa 3-jikan ni oyobimashita.
その会合は3時間に及びました。
That meeting extended to three hours.
• A ni oyobanai Aには及ばない *to be unnecessary to do A*
② *to match, to equal* [→**hitteki suru** 匹敵する]
¶Eigo de wa Koyama-san ni oyobu mono wa imasen.
英語では小山さんに及ぶ者はいません。
In English there's no one who can match Mr. Koyama.

oyogí 泳ぎ *swimming* [→**suiei** 水泳]
¶Ogawa-san wa oyogi ga jōzu desu.
小川さんは泳ぎが上手です。
Ms. Ogawa is good at swimming.

oyógu 泳ぐ *to swim*
¶Ani wa umi de oyogu no ga suki desu.
兄は海で泳ぐのが好きです。
My older brother likes to swim in the ocean.

oyoso およそ *about, approximately* [→**yaku** 約]
¶Watashi wa mainichi oyoso ni-jikan benkyō shimasu.
私は毎日およそ2時間勉強します。
I study about two hours every day.

ōzáppa 大ざっぱ ～**na** ～な *rough, sketchy, approximate*

ōzéi 大勢 *a large number* 《of people》
¶Ōzei no shōnen-shōjo ga utatte imasu.
大勢の少年少女が歌っています。
A large number of boys and girls are singing.

ozōni お雑煮 *rice cakes with vegetables boiled in soup* 《a traditional Japanese New Year's dish》

P

pái パイ *pie*
- appuru-pai アップルパイ *apple pie*

paináppuru パイナップル *pineapple*

paiónia パイオニア *pioneer* [→**kaitaku-sha** 開拓者 (s.v. **kaitaku** 開拓)]

paipu パイプ ① *(tobacco)pipe*
② *pipe, tube* [→**kuda** 管]
- paipu-orugan パイプオルガン *pipe organ*

pairótto パイロット *pilot*
- pairotto-ranpu パイロットランプ *pilot lamp*

pájama パジャマ *pajamas*

pákingu パーキング *parking* [→**chūshajō** 駐車場]
- pākingu-mētā パーキングメーター *parking meter*

pákkēji パッケージ ① *packing* 《i.e., readying for transport》
- pakkēji suru パッケージする *to pack*
② *packaging* 《i.e., the box, paper, etc., in which an item is packed》
③ *package, parcel*
- pakkēji-tsuā パッケージツアー *package tour*

páma パーマ *permanent* (*wave*)
- pāma o kakeru パーマをかける *to get a permanent*

pán パン *bread*
¶Watashi wa gohan yori pan no hō ga suki desu.
私はご飯よりパンのほうが好きです。
I like bread better than rice.
¶Watashi wa chōshoku ni batā o nutta pan o tabeta.
私は朝食にバターを塗ったパンを食べた。
I had bread and butter for breakfast.
¶Ane wa yoku ōbun de pan o yakimasu.
姉はよくオーブンでパンを焼きます。
My older sister often bakes bread in the oven.

- pan-ko パン粉 *bread crumbs* 《used in cooking》
- pan-ya パン屋 *bakery; baker*

pánchi パンチ *punch, blow with the fist*

pánchi パンチ (*hole*)*punch*
- panchi-kādo パンチカード *punch card*

pánchi パンチ *punch* 《(beverage)》

pánda パンダ *panda*

pánfuretto パンフレット *pamphlet*

pánikku パニック *panic*
- panikku-jōtai パニック状態 *a state of panic*

panku パンク (*tire*)*puncture, blowout*
- panku suru パンクする *to get a flat tire* 《when the subject is a vehicle》*; to be punctured, to go flat* 《when the subject is a tire》
¶Chichi wa panku o shūri shite moraimashita.
父はパンクを修理してもらいました。
My father had the puncture fixed.

panorama パノラマ *panorama*

pansuto パンスト [☞**pantī-sutokkingu** パンティーストッキング (s.v. **pantī** パンティー)]

pantagúrafu パンタグラフ *pantograph*

pántī パンティー *panties*
- ichimai no pantī 1枚のパンティー *one pair of panties*
- pantī-sutokkingu パンティーストッキング *panty hose*

pantomáimu パントマイム *pantomime*

pántsu パンツ ① *underpants*
② *exercise pants*

pápa パパ *daddy, dad*

párafin パラフィン *paraffin*
- parafin-shi パラフィン紙 *paraffin paper*

parashúto パラシュート *parachute*
- parashūto de oriru パラシュートで降りる *to descend by parachute*

párasoru パラソル *parasol* [→**hi-gasa** 日傘 (s.v. **hi** 日)]

parḗdo パレード *parade*
- parēdo suru パレードする *to parade*
¶Yūshō-chīmu ga tōri o parēdo shimashita.
優勝チームが通りをパレードしました。

The championship team paraded along the street.

parétto パレット (*painter's*)*palette*

párodī パロディー *parody*

párupu パルプ (*wood*)*pulp*

pāsentēji パーセンテージ *percentage*

pāsénto パーセント *percent, percentage* [→**pāsentēji** パーセンテージ]

• -pāsento -パーセント《counter for percent; see Appendix 2》

¶Gakusei no gojūsan-pāsento ga josei desu.

学生の53パーセントが女性です。

Fifty-three percent of students are women.

pasokon パソコン *personal computer*

pásu パス ① (*free*)*pass;* <*US*>*commuter pass,* <*UK*>*season ticket* [→**teiki-ken** 定期券 (s.v. **teiki** 定期)]

② *pass* 《in basketball, football, etc.》

• pasu suru パスする *to pass*

• bōru o pasu suru ボールをパスする *to pass the ball*

③ *pass* 《when it is one's turn in a card game, etc.》

• pasu suru パスする *to pass*

④ ~**suru** ~する *to pass* 《a test, etc.》

• shiken ni pasu suru 試験にパスする *to pass an examination*

pasupóto パスポート *passport*

pasuteru パステル *pastel* (*crayon*)

• pasuteru-ga パステル画 *pastel* (*picture*)

patán パターン [☞**patan** パタン]

patán パタン *pattern*

pātī パーティー *party* ((social gathering))

¶Ashita pātī o hirakimashō.

あしたパーティーを開きましょう。

Let's have a party tomorrow.

pāto パート [☞**pātotaimu** パートタイム]

patokā パトカー *patrol car, police car*

pātonā パートナー *partner*

patorōru パトロール *patrol, patrolling*

• patorōru suru パトロールする *to patrol*

• patorōru-chū no パトロール中の *on-patrol*

¶Patorōru-chū no keikan ga hannin o

taiho shita.

パトロール中の警官が犯人を逮捕した。

An on-patrol police officer arrested the criminal.

• patorōru-kā パトロールカー [☞**patokā** パトカー]

pātotáimu パートタイム (*working*)*part time, part-time work*

¶Hirano-san wa pātotaimu de hataraite imasu.

平野さんはパートタイムで働いています。

Ms. Hirano works part-time.

• pātotaimu no shigoto パートタイムの仕事 *part-time work*

páwā パワー *power*

páwafuru パワフル ~**na** ~な *powerful*

pázuru パズル *puzzle*

• kurosuwādo-pazuru クロスワードパズル *crossword puzzle*

• jigusō-pazuru ジグソーパズル *jigsaw puzzle*

péa ペア *pair*

• pea o kumu ペアを組む *to get together to form a pair*

pedaru ペダル *pedal*

pēji ページ *page* 《of a book, etc.》

• pēji o mekuru ページをめくる *to turn over a page*

• -pēji -ページ

《counter for page numbers or number of pages; see Appendix 2》

¶Sono shashin wa jūgo-pēji ni aru ne.

その写真は15ページにあるね。

That photograph is on page 15, isn't it.

¶Mō hyaku-pēji yonda yo.

もう100ページ読んだよ。

I've already read 100 pages!

pén ペン *pen*

¶Jūsho o koko ni pen de kaite kudasai.

住所をここにペンで書いてください。

Please write your address here with a pen.

¶Pen wa ken yori tsuyoi.

ペンは剣より強い。《proverb》

The pen is mightier than the sword.

• pen-furendo ペンフレンド [☞**pen-paru** ペンパル (below)]

- pen-nēmu ペンネーム *pen name*
- pen-paru ペンパル *pen pal*
- sain-pen サインペン *felt-tip pen; roller-ball pen*

pénchi ペンチ *pliers*
péndanto ペンダント *pendant*
pengin ペンギン *penguin*
penishirin ペニシリン *penicillin*
- penishirin no chūsha ペニシリンの注射 *penicillin injection*

penki ペンキ *paint* 《for covering surfaces to improve appearance or protect》
- A o penki de nuru Aをペンキで塗る *to paint A with paint*
¶Hei o shiroi penki de nurimashita.
塀を白いペンキで塗りました。
I painted the fence white.
- A ni penki o nuru Aにペンキを塗る *to apply paint to A*
¶Penki nuritate
「ペンキ塗り立て」《on a sign》
Wet Paint
- penki-ya ペンキ屋 *painter; paint store*

pénshon ペンション *small home-like hotel*
pēpātésuto ペーパーテスト *written test* [→**hikki-shiken** 筆記試験 (s.v. **hikki** 筆記)]

perapera ぺらぺら 【COL.】 *fluently* 《describing speaking, ordinarily in a foreign language》
- perapera no ぺらぺらの *fluent* [→**ryu-chō na** 流暢な]
¶Kohho-san wa Nihon-go ga perapera desu.
コッホさんは日本語がぺらぺらです。
Ms. Koch's Japanese is fluent.

pésuto ペスト *bubonic plague*
pétto ペット *pet*
- petto-fūdo ペットフード *pet food*
- petto-shoppu ペットショップ *pet shop*

pianísuto ピアニスト *pianist*
piano ピアノ *piano*
- piano o hiku ピアノを弾く *to play the piano*
- piano o narau ピアノを習う *to study the piano, to take piano lessons*

piāru ピーアール *P.R.*
- piāru suru ピーアールする *to publicize, to advertise*

píero ピエロ *clown*
pikapika ぴかぴか *shiningly, twinkle-twinkle*
¶Hoshi ga pikapika hikatte imasu.
星がぴかぴか光っています。
The stars are twinkling.
- pikapika no ぴかぴかの *shiny*
¶Akiyama-san wa pikapika no kutsu o haite imasu.
秋山さんはぴかぴかの靴をはいています。
Mr. Akiyama is wearing shiny shoes.

píku ピーク *peak, maximum*
píkunikku ピクニック *picnic*
pín ピン *pin* 《(fastener)》
¶Sono e o pin de kabe ni tomete kudasai.
その絵をピンで壁に留めてください。
Please pin that picture on the wall.
- nekutai-pin ネクタイピン *tiepin*

pínattsu ピーナッツ *peanut*
- pīnattsu-batā ピーナッツバター *peanut butter*

pinboke ピンぼけ ~**no** ~の *out-of-focus, blurred*
pínchi ピンチ *pinch, jam, fix*
- pinchi o kirinukeru ピンチを切り抜ける *to get out of a pinch*
- pinchi ni ochiiru ピンチに陥る *to get into a pinch*
- pinchi-hittā ピンチヒッター *pinch hitter* 《in baseball》

pínku ピンク *pink* 《as a noun》
pinsétto ピンセット *tweezers*
- ippon no pinsetto 1本のピンセット *one pair of tweezers*

pinto ピント *photographic focus, camera lens focal point*
- pinto ga atte iru ピントが合っている *to be in focus*
¶Kono shashin wa pinto ga atte imasu ka.
この写真はピントが合っていますか。
Is this picture in focus?
- pinto ga hazurete iru ピントが外れている *to be out of focus*

• pinto o awaseru ピントを合わせる *to set the focus correctly*

¶Kamera no pinto o awasete shashin o totta.

カメラのピントを合わせて写真を撮った。

I focused the camera and took a picture.

pinto ぴんと 〜**kuru** 〜来る *to come home to one, to ring a bell*

piramíddo ピラミッド *pyramid*

píriodo ピリオド *period, <UK>full stop* ((punctuation mark)) [→**shūshifu** 終止符]

píriodo ピリオド *period* «in sports»

písuton ピストン *piston*

pisutoru ピストル *pistol*

pítchā ピッチャー *(baseball)pitcher* [→**tōshu** 投手]

pítchi ピッチ *pace, rate*

• pitchi o ageru ピッチを上げる *to quicken the pace*

• kyū-pitchi 急ピッチ *rapid pace*

pītíē ピーティーエー *PTA*

pittári ぴったり（〜**to** 〜と）① *tightly, snugly; exactly, perfectly, precisely*

• pittari no ぴったりの *tight, snug; exact, perfect-fitting*

¶Kono sunīkā wa boku ni pittari da yo.

このスニーカーは僕にぴったりだよ。

These sneakers fit me perfectly!

píza ピザ *pizza*

pointo ポイント ① *point (scored)* [→**tokuten** 得点]

• pointo o kasegu ポイントを稼ぐ *to earn a point, to gain a point*

② *(main)point, gist* [→**yōten** 要点]

¶O-hanashi no pointo o tsukamimashita.

お話のポイントをつかみました。

I got the point of what you said.

pointo ポイント <US>*(railroad) switch*, <UK>*(railroad)point*

pojíshon ポジション *position, place, location* [→**ichi** 位置]

pokétto ポケット *pocket*

¶Poketto ni saifu o irenasai.

ポケットに財布を入れなさい。

Put your wallet in your pocket.

¶Haruo wa poketto ni ryōte o tsukkonde

ita.

春男はポケットに両手を突っ込んでいた。

Haruo is walked with both hands in his pockets.

• zubon no poketto ズボンのポケット *pants pocket*

pomádo ポマード *pomade*

póndo ポンド *pound* ((unit of weight))

• -pondo ーポンド《counter for pounds; see Appendix 2》

póndo ポンド *pound* ((monetary unit))

• -pondo ーポンド《counter for pounds; see Appendix 2》

pónpu ポンプ *pump* «for liquid»

• ponpu de kumidasu ポンプでくみ出す *to pump out*

¶Ponpu de ido kara mizu o kumidashi-nasai.

ポンプで井戸から水をくみ出しなさい。

Pump out some water from the well.

poppukón ポップコーン *popcorn*

pópura ポプラ *poplar*

pópyurā ポピュラー 〜**na** 〜な *popular, of wide appeal* [→**taishū-muki no** 大衆向きの (s.v. **taishū** 大衆)]

• popyurā-myūjikku ポピュラーミュージック *popular music*

poriechiren ポリエチレン *polyethylene*

poroshatsu ポロシャツ *polo shirt*

póruno ポルノ *pornography*

• poruno-eiga ポルノ映画 *pornographic movie*

pósutā ポスター *poster*

¶Kashu no posutā o kabe ni harimashita.

歌手のポスターを壁にはりました。

I put up a poster of a singer on the wall.

pósuto ポスト <US>*mailbox*, <UK>*postbox*

• posuto ni ireru ポストに入れる *to drop in a mailbox*, <US>*to mail*, <UK>*to post*

¶Tochū de kono tegami o posuto ni irete ne.

途中でこの手紙をポストに入れてね。

Mail this letter on your way, won't you.

pósuto ポスト *post, position, job*

póteto ポテト *potato* [→**jagaimo**

じゃがいも]

• poteto-chippusu ポテトチップス *potato chip*

pótto ポット ① *pot* 《for coffee, tea, etc.》 ② *thermos bottle* [→**mahō-bin** 魔法瓶 (s.v. **mahō** 魔法)]

pōzu ポーズ *pose*

• shashin no pōzu o toru 写真のポーズを取る *to pose for a photo*

purachina プラチナ *platinum*

púragu プラグ (*electrical*)*plug*

puráibashī プライバシー *privacy*

• puraibashī no shingai プライバシーの侵害 *invasion of privacy*

puraido プライド *pride* [→**jisonshin** 自尊心]

purakādo プラカード *placard*

puramóderu プラモデル *plastic model*

púramu プラム *plum*

púran プラン ① *plan* (*of action*) [→**keikaku** 計画] ② *plan, drawing, blueprint* [→**sekkei-zu** 設計図 (s.v. **sekkei** 設計)]

puranetaryūmu プラネタリウム《Note the mismatch between the katakana spelling and the pronunciation.》 *planetarium*

puránkuton プランクトン *plankton*

púrasu プラス [[⇔**mainasu** マイナス]] ① *plus* (*sign*)

¶San purasu ni wa go desu.

3プラス2は5です。

Three plus two is five.

② *plus, gain, benefit*

purasuchíkku プラスチック *plastic*

¶Purasuchikku no omocha ga ōku natta ne.

プラスチックのおもちゃが多くなったね。

Plastic toys have increased, haven't they.

• purasuchikku-sei no プラスチック製の *manufactured out of plastic*

purattohōmu プラットホーム [☞**hōmu** ホーム]

purē プレー ① *play, the action* 《in a game or sport》

• purē o saikai suru プレーを再開する *to resume play*

② *a play* 《in a game or sport》

• umai purē うまいプレー *a skillful play*

• fain-purē ファインプレー *a fine play*

purehabu プレハブ *prefabricated house*

• purehabu-jūtaku プレハブ住宅 [☞**purehābu** プレハブ (above)]

pureigáido プレイガイド *entertainment ticket agency*

purēófu プレーオフ *play-off*

purésshā プレッシャー *psychological pressure, emotional pressure*

• presshā ni kurushimu プレッシャーに苦しむ *to suffer under emotional pressure*

purēto プレート ① *metal plate* ② (*home*)*plate* ③ *pitching rubber*

puréyā プレーヤー ① *player, athlete* [→**senshu** 選手] ② *instrument player, musical performer* [→**ensō-sha** 演奏者 (s.v. **ensō** 演奏)] ③ [☞**rekōdo-purēyā** レコードプレーヤー (s.v. **rekōdo** レコード)]

purézento プレゼント *present, gift* [→**okurimono** 贈り物]

¶Akira-chan e no purezento desu.

明ちゃんへのプレゼントです。

It's a present for Akira.

¶Murai-sensei ni purezento o okurimashō.

村井先生にプレゼントを贈りましょう。

Let's give Ms. Murai a present.

• purezento suru プレゼントする *to give as a present*

¶Yamanaka-san ni pen o purezento shimasu.

山中さんにペンをプレゼントします。

I will give a pen to Mr. Yamanaka as a present.

púrin プリン *pudding*

purínsesu プリンセス *princess* [→**ōjo** 王女]

purínsu プリンス *prince* [→**ōji** 王子]

puríntā プリンター *printer* ((machine))

purinto プリント ① *print* 《from a photographic negative》 ② *printing* 《from a photographic negative》

• purinto suru プリントする *to print* [→
yaku 焼く④]

③ (*mechanically*)*printed item*

④ *printing* 《of books, newspapers, etc.》
[→**insatsu** 印刷]

• purinto suru プリントする *to print*

purītsu プリーツ *pleat*

• purītsu-sukāto プリーツスカート *pleated
skirt*

purízumu プリズム *prism*

púro プロ *a professional* [⇔**amachua**
アマチュア]

• puro no プロの *professional*

• puro-senshu プロ選手 *professional athlete*

• puro-yakyū プロ野球 *professional baseball*

púro プロ [☞**purodakushon** プロ
ダクション]

purodákushon プロダクション ① *production company* 《for movies, television programs, etc.》

② *talent agency*

purodyūsā プロデューサー *producer* 《in
movies, television, etc.》

purofésshonaru プロフェッショナル [☞
puro プロ]

purofīru プロフィール [[→**yokogao**
横顔]] ① *profile, side-view of a face*

② *profile, brief description*

purogúramu プログラム ① *program* 《list
of participants, what is to be presented,
etc.》

② (*computer*)*program*

puropangásu プロパンガス *propane*
(*gas*)

puropera プロペラ *propeller*

• puropera-ki プロペラ機 *propeller plane*

puropōzu プロポーズ *marriage proposal*

• puropōzu suru プロポーズする *to propose marriage*

purorógu プロローグ *prologue*

Purotésutanto プロテスタント *a Protestant*

púru プール (*swimming*)*pool*

¶Pūru de oyogimashō.
プールで泳ぎましょう。

Let's swim in the pool.

pusshúhon プッシュホン *touch-tone
telephone*

R

ráberu ラベル *label* [→**retteru** レッテル]

¶Sono hako ni akai raberu o harimashita.
その箱に赤いラベルをはりました。
I put a red label on the box.

raburétā ラブレター *love letter*

rágubī ラグビー *rugby*

ráibaru ライバル *a rival*

¶Kudō-kun to boku wa sukēto no ii
raibaru da.
工藤君と僕はスケートのいいライバルだ。
*Kudo and I are friendly rivals in skat-
ing.*

ráiburarī ライブラリー *library* [→
tosho-kan 図書館 (s.v. **tosho** 図書)]

raichō 雷鳥 *ptarmigan* ((bird))

ráifuru ライフル *rifle*

• raifuru-jū ライフル銃 [☞**raifuru**
ライフル (above)]

raifuwāku ライフワーク *one's lifework*

ráigetsu 来月 *next month*

¶Tomu-san wa raigetsu no muika ni
kaerimasu.
トムさんは来月の6日に帰ります。
*Tom will go home on the sixth of next
month.*

¶Raigetsu Kyōto ni ikimasu.
来月京都に行きます。
I'm going to Kyoto next month.

ráin ライン ① *line* 《mark on a surface》
[→**sen** 線①]

② (*transportation*)*line, route* [→**sen**
線②]

③ *row,* <*US*>*line,* <*UK*>*queue*
《i.e., entities arranged in a row or line》
[→**retsu** 列]

• sutāto-rain スタートライン *starting line*

ráinā ライナー *line drive, liner* 《in baseball》

¶Tanabe-senshu wa sādo e rainā o utta.
田辺選手はサードへライナーを打った。
Tanabe hit a liner to third.

rainen 来年 *next year*

¶Sono kashu wa rainen Nihon ni kimasu.
その歌手は来年日本に来ます。
That singer will come to Japan next year.

¶Chichi wa rainen no San-gatsu ni Chūgoku kara kikoku shimasu.
父は来年の3月に中国から帰国します。
My father will come home from China next March.

rainichi 来日 *coming to Japan (on a visit)*

• rainichi suru 来日する *to come to Japan*

raion ライオン *lion*

ráisensu ライセンス [[→**menkyo** 免許]]
① *licensing, official permission*
② *license, permit*

raishū 来週 *next week*

¶Raishū no Kin'yōbi ni Kōbe ni ikimasu.
来週の金曜日に神戸に行きます。
I'm going to Kobe on next Friday.

¶Ani wa raishū Rondon ni iru deshō.
兄は来週ロンドンにいるでしょう。
My older brother will probably be in London next week.

• raishū no kyō 来週のきょう *a week from today*

ráitā ライター *(cigarette)lighter*

¶Chichi wa raitā de tabako ni hi o tsukemashita.
父はライターでたばこに火をつけました。
My father lit the cigarette with a lighter.

ráitā ライター *(professional)writer* [→**sakka** 作家]

• shinario-raitā シナリオライター *scenarist*

ráito ライト *lights, lighting, illumination* [→**shōmei** 照明]

• raito o tsukeru [kesu] ライトをつける [消す] *to turn on [off] the lights*

ráito ライト ① *right field* [→**uyoku** 右翼②]

② *right fielder* [→**uyoku-shu** 右翼手 (s.v. **uyoku** 右翼)] 《in baseball》

raitoban ライトバン <US>*station wagon;* <UK>*estate car*

ráiu 雷雨 *thunderstorm*

¶Kinō wa raiu ga arimashita.
きのうは雷雨がありました。
Yesterday there was a thunderstorm.

rajiētā ラジエーター *radiator*

rájio ラジオ ① *radio (broadcasting)* 《providing programs to the general public》

② *radio (receiver)* 《for listening to programs broadcast to the general public》

¶Haha wa rajio o yoku kikimasu.
母はラジオをよく聴きます。
My mother often listens to the radio.

¶Ōhashi-san wa rajio de ongaku o kiite imasu.
大橋さんはラジオで音楽を聴いています。
Ms. Ohashi is listening to music on the radio.

¶Rajio no oto o chīsaku shite kudasai.
ラジオの音を小さくしてください。
Please turn down the sound on the radio.

• rajio-bangumi ラジオ番組 *radio program*

• rajio-hōsō ラジオ放送 *radio broadcasting, radio broadcast*

• rajio-taisō ラジオ体操 *radio calesthenics*

rajūmu ラジウム《Note the mismatch between the katakana spelling and the pronunciation.》 *radium*

rakétto ラケット *racket* 《for tennis, badminton, etc.》*; paddle* 《for pingpong》

rakkan 楽観 *optimism* [→**rakuten** 楽天] [⇔**hikan** 悲観]

• rakkan suru 楽観する *to be optimistic*
• rakkan-teki na 楽観的な *optimistic*

rákkī ラッキー 〜**na** 〜な *lucky* [→**kōun na** 幸運な]

• rakkī-sebun ラッキーセブン *the lucky seventh (inning)*

rakko ラッコ *sea otter*

rakú 楽 〜**na** 〜な ① *easy, simple* [→**yasashii** 易しい]

¶Sore wa raku na shigoto desu.
それは楽な仕事です。
That is easy work.

¶Kyō no shukudai wa raku ni dekita yo.
きょうの宿題は楽にできたよ。
I was able to do today's homework easily!

② *comfortable, easy, at ease* [→**an-raku na** 安楽な]

¶Dōzo o-raku ni nasatte kudasai.
どうぞお楽になさってください。
Please make yourself comfortable.

• ki o raku ni motsu 気を楽に持つ *to take it easy*

rakuda らくだ *camel*

rakudai 落第 ① *failure* 《on an test》

• rakudai suru 落第する *to fail*

¶Ishihara-kun wa sono shiken ni rakudai shita yo.
石原君はその試験に落第したよ。
Ishihara failed on that test!

② *being held back, failure to be promoted* 《to the next grade in school》

• rakudai suru 落第する *to be held back*
• rakudai-sei 落第生 *student who has been held back*
• rakudai-ten 落第点 *failing score, failing grade*

¶Ani wa ni-kamoku de rakudai-ten o totta yo.
兄は2科目で落第点を取ったよ。
My older brother got failing grades in two subjects!

rakuen 楽園 *paradise*

rakugaki 落書き *graffiti, prank scribbling*

• rakugaki suru 落書きする *to write graffiti, to do scribbling as a prank*

¶Kokuban ni rakugaki shinai de.
黒板に落書きしないで。
Don't scribble on the blackboard.

¶Rakugaki kinshi
「落書き禁止」《on a sign》
No Graffiti

rakugo 落語 *traditional Japanese comic storytelling*

• rakugo-ka 落語家 *comic storyteller*

rakuten 楽天 *optimism* [→**rakkan** 楽観] [⇔**hikan** 悲観]

• rakuten-ka 楽天家 *optimist*
• rakuten-teki na 楽天的な *optimistic*

rāmen ラーメン *Chinese noodles* 《ordinarily served in broth》

rán 欄 *column* 《in a newspaper, etc.》

• supōtsu-ran スポーツ欄 *sports column*

rán 蘭 *orchid*

ranbō 乱暴 *violence, roughness; unruliness; rudeness*

¶Ranbō wa yoshita ho ga ii yo.
乱暴はよしたほうがいいよ。
It's better to not to use violence!

• ranbō na 乱暴な *violent, rough; unruly; rude*

¶Ano hito wa rekōdo o ranbō ni atsukaimasu.
あの人はレコードを乱暴に扱います。
That person handles records roughly.

• ranbō suru 乱暴する *to use violence; to behave wildly; to behave rudely*

ránchi ランチ *lunch* [→**chūshoku** 昼食]

• ranchi-taimu ランチタイム *lunchtime*
• o-ko-sama-ranchi お子様ランチ *special restaurant lunch for children*

rándebū ランデブー ① *date* 《with a person》 [→**dēto** デート]

② (*spacecraft*)*rendezvous*

rándorī ランドリー *laundry, cleaner's* (*shop*) [→**kurīningu-ya** クリーニング屋 (s.v. **kurīningu** クリーニング)]

• koin-randorī コインランドリー *laundromat*

rándoseru ランドセル *knapsack* 《This word refers specifically to a sturdy leather knapsack used by Japanese elementary-school children to carry books and supplies to and from school.》

ránkingu ランキング *ranking, standing* 《usually in sports》

ránku ランク *rank* [→**jun'i** 順位]

• ranku suru ランクする *to rank*

¶Ano hito wa shinjin-kashu no naka de dai-ichi-i ni ranku sarete imasu.
あの人は新人歌手の中で第1位にランクされています。

That person is ranked first among the new singers.

ránnā ランナー *runner* [→**sōsha** 走者]
- chō-kyori-rannā 長距離ランナー *long-distance runner*
- tan-kyori-rannā 短距離ランナー *short-distance runner, sprinter*

ranningu ランニング *running* 《in competition or for exercise》
- ranningu suru ランニングする *to run*
- ranningu-hōmā ランニングホーマー *inside-the-park home run* 《in baseball》
- ranningu-shatsu ランニングシャツ *sleeveless T-shirt*

ránpu ランプ *lamp, lantern* 《usually of the type that uses oil or batteries》

ranshi 乱視 (*eye*)*astigmatism*

rappa らっぱ *bugle*

rashíi らしい 《This word follows a predicate and functions grammatically as an adjective. The word preceding **rashii** cannot be the copula form **da** だ. Where **da** would be the appropriate predicate, **rashii** follows a noun or adjectival noun directly.》 ① *it seems that, it appears as if* [→**yō na** ような①]
¶Kaneda-san wa benkyō ni akita rashii.
金田さんは勉強にあきたらしい。
It seems that Ms. Kaneda has gotten tired of studying.
¶Sakamoto-san wa dōmo byōki rashii.
坂本さんはどうも病気らしい。
It really appears that Ms. Sakamoto is ill.
② *I hear that, people say that* [→**sō da** そうだ]
¶Tarō-san wa Amerika e iku rashii yo.
太郎さんはアメリカへ行くらしいよ。
I hear Taro will go to the United States!

-rashii -らしい *appropriate for, typical of, in accord with the true character of* 《Added to noun bases.》
¶Kyō wa haru-rashii tenki desu ne.
きょうは春らしい天気ですね。
Today's weather is typical of spring, isn't it.
¶Uso o tsuku no wa kimi-rashiku nai yo.

うそをつくのは君らしくないよ。
Telling lies isn't like you!

rasshuáwā ラッシュアワー *rush hour*
¶Ani wa asa no rasshuawā o sakete, roku-ji-han ni uchi o demasu.
兄は朝のラッシュアワーを避けて、6時半にうちを出ます。
My older brother leaves home at 6:30 to avoid the morning rush hour.

rasutoshín ラストシーン *last scene*

rasutosupáto ラストスパート *last spurt*
¶Marason-senshu wa rasutosupāto o kaketa.
マラソン選手はラストスパートをかけた。
The marathon runner made her last spurt.

Raten- ラテン- *Latin-* 《Added to noun bases.》
- Raten-amerika ラテンアメリカ *Latin America*
- Raten-go ラテン語 *the Latin language*
- Raten-ongaku ラテン音楽 *Latin music*

ráundo ラウンド ① *round* 《in boxing》
- -raundo -ラウンド《counter for rounds; see Appendix 2》
② *round* 《of golf》

rébā レバー *lever* [→**teko** 挺子]

rébā レバー *liver* 《(food)》

réberu レベル *level, degree* [→**suijun** 水準]
¶Sono kuni no bunka no reberu wa takai rashii.
その国の文化のレベルは高いらしい。
The level of culture in that country seems to be high.

rédā レーダー *radar*

réferī レフェリー *referee*

réfuto レフト ① *left field* [→**sayoku** 左翼②] 《in baseball》
② *left fielder* [→**sayoku-shu** 左翼手 (s.v. **sayoku** 左翼)]

régyurā レギュラー ① *regular* (*player*) [⇔**hoketsu-senshu** 補欠選手 (s.v. **hoketsu** 補欠②)]
- *regular* 《on a radio or TV program》

réi 礼 ① *bow* (*of respect*) [→**ojigi** お辞儀]

¶Kiritsu! Rei!

起立！礼！

Stand up! Bow! 《Typically used as instructions to a group by a person in charge, especially at schools to a body of students.》

• rei o suru 礼をする *to bow*

② (*expression of*)*thanks; token of gratitude, reward*

¶O-rei no kotoba mo arimasen.

お礼の言葉もありません。

I don't know how to thank you. 《Literally: I don't have even words of thanks.》

¶O-rei ni wa oyobimasen.

お礼には及びません。

It's not necessary to thank me.

¶Tetsudatta o-rei ni nisen-en moratta yo.

手伝ったお礼に2000円もらったよ。

I got two 2,000 yen as a reward for having helped!

• rei-jō 礼状 *thank-you letter*

réi 例 ① *example, instance*

• rei o ageru 例をあげる *to give an example*

② *habit, custom, usual practice*

• rei no 例の *the usual, the customary; the much-talked-about*

¶Rei no resutoran de o-hiru o tabemashō.

例のレストランでお昼を食べましょう。

Let's eat lunch at the usual restaurant.

• rei ni yotte 例によって *as usual, as always*

¶Sakata-kun wa rei ni yotte chikoku shimashita.

坂田君は例によって遅刻しました。

Sakata was late as usual.

• rei-bun 例文 *example sentence*

réi 零 *zero* [→**zero** ゼロ]

¶Sono shiken de rei-ten datta yo.

その試験で0点だったよ。

I got zero on that exam! 《Literally: On that exam I was zero!》

¶Go tai rei de watashi-tachi no chīmu ga shiai ni katta.

5対0で私たちのチームが試合に勝った。

Our team won the game five to zero.

reiáuto レイアウト *layout* 《on a printed page, etc.》

• reiauto suru レイアウトする *to lay out*

reibō 冷房 *air conditioning* [⇔**danbō** 暖房]

¶Reibō-kanbi

「冷房完備」《on a sign》

Air-conditioned

• reibō-sha 冷房車 *air-conditioned* (*train*)*car*

• reibō-sōchi 冷房装置 *air conditioner* [→**eakon** エアコン]

reidai 例題 *example problem, exercise* [→**renshū-mondai** 練習問題 (s.v. **renshū** 練習)]

reigai 例外 *exception, unusual case*

¶Kono kisoku ni wa ikutsu-ka no reigai ga arimasu.

この規則にはいくつかの例外があります。

There are several exceptions to this rule.

reigí 礼儀 *etiquette, manners* [→**sahō** 作法]

¶Sō suru no ga reigi desu.

そうするのが礼儀です。

It is etiquette to do so.

¶Ano ko wa reigi o shiranai ne.

あの子は礼儀を知らないね。

That child doesn't know her manners, does she.

• reigi-tadashii 礼儀正しい *polite, well-mannered* [⇔**burei na** 無礼な]

¶Toda-san wa reigi-tadashii hito desu.

戸田さんは礼儀正しい人です。

Ms. Toda is a well-mannered woman.

reihai 礼拝 *worship* (*of a deity*)*; worship service*

¶Ashita no reihai ni demasu.

あしたの礼拝に出ます。

I will attend tomorrow's worship service.

¶Ezaki-san-tachi wa kyōkai e reihai ni ikimasu.

江崎さんたちは教会へ礼拝に行きます。

Mr. Ezaki and the others will go to church to worship.

• reihai suru 礼拝する *to worship*

• reihai-dō 礼拝堂 *chapel*

réika 零下 (*the temperature range*)*be-*

low zero [→**hyōten-ka** 氷点下 (s.v. **hyōten** 氷点)]

¶Kesa wa reika ni-do datta yo.

けさは零下2度だったよ。

It was two degrees below zero this morning!

• reika no kion 零下の気温 *sub-zero temperature*

reikin 礼金 *money given as an expression of gratitude*

reinkōto レインコート *raincoat*

reisei 冷静 ~**na** ~な *calm, cool, composed*

¶Kōfun shinai de, reisei ni kangaete kudasai.

興奮しないで、冷静に考えてください。

Don't get excited; think about it calmly.

reitán 冷淡 ~**na** ~な *cold (-hearted), unfriendly* [→**tsumetai** 冷たい②]

¶Nozaki-san wa watashi ni reitan desu.

野崎さんは私に冷淡です。

Mr. Nozaki is cold to me.

reitō 冷凍 ~**suru** ~する *to freeze (in order to preserve)*

¶Kono niku wa reitō shimashō.

この肉は冷凍しましょう。

Let's freeze this meat.

• reitō-ko 冷凍庫 *freezer*

• reitō-shokuhin 冷凍食品 *frozen food*

reizóko 冷蔵庫 *refrigerator*

réjā レジャー ① *leisure time* [→**yoka** 余暇]

② *leisure-time activity*

réji レジ ① *cash register*

② *checkout counter*

¶Reji de haratte kudasai.

レジで払ってください。

Please pay at the checkout counter.

③ [☞**reji-gakari** レジ係 (below)]

• reji-gakari レジ係 *(register)cashier*

rekishi 歴史 *history*

¶Watashi-tachi no gakkō wa yonjū-nen no rekishi ga arimasu.

私たちの学校は40年の歴史があります。

Our school has a history of forty years.

• Nihon no rekishi 日本の歴史 *the history of Japan*

• rekishi-ka 歴史家 *historian*

• rekishi-teki na 歴史的な *historic*

¶Kore wa rekishi-teki ni yūmei na tatemono desu.

これは歴史的に有名な建物です。

This is a historically famous building.

rekkásha レッカー車 *wrecker, tow truck*

rekódo レコード ① *(phonograph)record*

¶Sono rekōdo o kakete kudasai.

そのレコードをかけてください。

Please play that record.

② ⟨*world*⟩ *record* [→**kiroku** 記録②]

• rekōdo-puréyā レコードプレーヤー *record player*

• rekōdo-ten レコード店 *record shop*

• erupī-rekōdo LPレコード *an LP*

rekuriḗshon レクリエーション *recreation, recreational activity*

¶Rekuriēshon ni haikingu ni itta.

レクリエーションにハイキングに行った。

We went hiking for recreation.

rémon レモン *lemon*

• remon-sukasshu レモンスカッシュ *lemon squash* ≪*an iced drink consisting of lemon juice mixed with soda water*≫

• remon-tī レモンティー *tea with a slice of lemon*

ren'ai 恋愛 *love, romantic attachment, being in love* [→**ai** 愛, **koi** 恋]

¶Machiko to no ren'ai wa itsu made mo tsuzuki-sō da.

真知子との恋愛はいつまでも続きそうだ。

It looks as if his romance with Machiko will continue forever, doesn't it.

• ren'ai-kekkon 恋愛結婚 *love marriage* [⇔**miai-kekkon** 見合い結婚 (s.v. **miai** 見合い)]

• ren'ai-shōsetsu 恋愛小説 *love story*

renchū 連中 【CRUDE】 *group of people, bunch*

rénga 煉瓦 *brick*

• renga-zukuri no 煉瓦造りの *built of bricks*

rengō 連合 *alliance, coalition*

• rengō suru 連合する *to form an alliance*

• rengō-koku 連合国 *the Allied Powers*

rénji レンジ (*kitchen*)*range*
- denshi-renji 電子レンジ *microwave oven*
- gasu-renji ガスレンジ *gas range*

renkō 連行 〜**suru** 〜する *to transport under custody* 《The direct object is ordinarily a criminal, prisoner, etc.》

renkon 蓮根 *lotus root*

renkyū 連休 *two or more holidays in succession*

renmei 連盟 *league, union, federation*
- Nihon-gakusei-yakyū-renmei 日本学生野球連盟 *the Students' Baseball League of Japan*

renpō 連邦 *federation*
- renpō-seifu 連邦政府 *federal government*

renraku 連絡 ① *contact, communication, touch*
- renraku suru 連絡する *to communicate, to let know*
- A ni B o renraku suru AにBを連絡する *to communicate B to A, to let A know B*
¶Atarashii jūsho o denwa de renraku shite kudasai.
新しい住所を電話で連絡してください。
Please let me know your new address by telephone.
- A to renraku o toru Aと連絡を取る *to get in touch with A*
¶Yōko-san to renraku o torimashita ka.
洋子さんと連絡を取りましたか。
Did you get in touch with Yoko?
② (*transportation*)*connection* [→**setsuzoku** 接続②]
- renraku suru 連絡する *to connect*
¶Kono densha wa Sendai-eki de tokkyū to renraku shite iru.
この電車は仙台駅で特急と連絡している。
This train connects with the express at Sendai station.
③ *connection, affiliation* [→**kankei** 関係]
- renraku-sen 連絡船 *connecting ferry-boat*

rensahánnnō 連鎖反応 *chain reaction*

renshū 練習 *practice, training*

- renshū suru 練習する *to practice*
¶Imōto wa mainichi san-jikan piano o renshū shimasu.
妹は毎日3時間ピアノを練習します。
My younger sister practices the piano three hours every day.
- renshū-mondai 練習問題 *example problem, exercise* [→**reidai** 例題]
- renshū-jiai 練習試合 *practice game*

rensō 連想 *association* (*of ideas*)
- rensō suru 連想する *to think of by association, to be reminded of*
¶Sairen no oto o kiku to, kūshū o rensō shimasu.
サイレンの音を聞くと、空襲を連想します。
Whenever I hear the sound of a siren, I am reminded of air raids.

rentakā レンタカー *rent-a-car, rental car*
¶Yoshio wa rentakā de mizuumi made doraibu shita.
良男はレンタカーで湖までドライブした。
Yoshio drove to the lake in a rental car.

réntaru レンタル *renting* (*to others*)
- rentaru-skī レンタルスキー *rental skis*

rentogen レントゲン ① *x-ray* (*radiation*) [→**ekkususen** エックス線]
② [☞**rentogen-shashin** レントゲン写真 (*below*)]
- rentogen-shashin レントゲン写真 *x-ray* (*photograph*)
- rentogen-shashin o toru レントゲン写真を撮る *to take an x-ray*

renzoku 連続 *uninterrupted continuity; succession, series*
- renzoku suru 連続する *to continue uninterrupted; to happen in succession, to happen consecutively*
- rensoku shite 連続して *continuously; in succession, consecutively*
¶Jiko ga renzoku shite okorimashita.
事故が連続して起こりました。
The accidents occurred in succession.
- renzoku-terebi-bangumi 連続テレビ番組 *television series*

rénzu レンズ *lens*
- bōen-renzu 望遠レンズ *telephoto lens*

- hyōjun-renzu 標準レンズ *standard lens*
- kōkaku-renzu 広角レンズ *wide-angle lens*
- kontakuto-renzu コンタクトレンズ *contact lens*

repátorī レパートリー *repertory, repertoire*

¶Sono pianisuto no repātorī ga hiroi.
このピアニストはレパートリーが広い。
That pianist's repertory is wide.

repóto レポート ① (*written*)*report* [→**ripóto** リポート, **hōkoku-sho** 報告書 (s.v. **hōkoku** 報告)]

② (*school*)*report*, (*term*)*paper*

¶Repōto o teishutsu shimashita ka.
レポートを提出しましたか。
Did you hand in your paper?

rēru レール (*metal*)*rail*

- rēru o shiku レールを敷く *to lay rails*
- kāten-rēru カーテンレール *curtain rail*

rḗsā レーサー *racing driver*

reshībā レシーバー *receiver* «i.e., the part of a telephone or other device held to the ear to hear a transmission» [→**juwaki** 受話器]

reshībā レシーバー *person who receives serve* «in tennis, volleyball, etc.»

reshību レシーブ *receiving serve* «in tennis, volleyball, etc.»

- reshību suru レシーブする *to receive serve*

reshíto レシート (*written*)*receipt* [→**ryōshūsho** 領収書]

réssha 列車 (*railroad*)*train*

¶Harada-san wa ressha ni noriokuremashita.
原田さんは列車に乗り遅れました。
Mr. Harada missed the train.

¶Keiko-san wa ressha ni maniaimashita.
恵子さんは列車に間に合いました。
Keiko was in time for the train.

¶Gogo go-ji-han no ressha de ikimashō.
午後5時半の列車で行きましょう。
Let's go on the 5:30 p.m. train.

- ressha-jikoku-hyō 列車時刻表 *train timetable*
- futsū-ressha 普通列車 *local train*

- kyūkō-ressha 急行列車 *express train*
- tokkyū-ressha 特急列車 *limited express train*

réssun レッスン *lesson, instruction*

¶Keiko-san wa Eigo no ressun o ukete iru.
恵子さんは英語のレッスンを受けている。
Keiko is taking English lessons.

rḗsu レース *lace*

- rēsu no tebukuro レースの手袋 *lace gloves*
- rēsu-ami レース編み *lacework*

rḗsu レース *race*

¶Tarō wa sono rēsu ni katsu darō.
太郎はそのレースに勝つだろう。
Taro will probably win that race.

- yotto-rēsu ヨットレース *sailboat race*

resukyūtai レスキュー隊 *rescue party* [→**kyūjo-tai** 救助隊 (s.v. **kyūjo** 救助)]

résuringu レスリング *wrestling*

résutoran レストラン *restaurant*

¶Koko wa pasuta de yūmei na resutoran desu.
ここはパスタで有名なレストランです。
This is a restaurant famous for pasta.

rétsu 列 *row*, <*US*>*line*, <*UK*>*queue* «i.e., entities arranged in a row or line»

¶Akemi-chan wa yon-ban-me no retsu ni imasu.
明美ちゃんは4番目の列にいます。
Akemi is in the fourth row.

- retsu ni warikomu 列に割り込む *to cut in line*
- retsu o tsukuru 列を作る *to form a line* [→**narabu** 並ぶ]

¶Kippu o kau tame ni retsu o tsukutte matte ita.
切符を買うために列を作って待っていた。
We formed and waited in a line in order to buy tickets.

retteru レッテル *label*

- retteru o haru レッテルをはる *to affix a label*

rettō 列島 *island chain, archipelago*

- Nihon-rettō 日本列島 *the Japanese*

Islands, the Japanese Archipelago

rettṓkan 劣等感 *inferiority complex* [⇔**yūetsukan** 優越感]

rḗzā レーザー *laser*
- rēzā–disuku レーザーディスク *laser disk*
- rēzā–kōsen レーザー光線 *laser beam*

ribáibaru リバイバル *revival* 《of an old movie, play, etc.》
- ribaibaru–eiga リバイバル映画 *revival film*

ribḗto リベート ① *rebate*
② *commission (payment); kickback*

ríbon リボン *ribbon*

rídā リーダー *leader* [→**shidō–sha** 指導者 (s.v. **shidō** 指導)]

rído リード ① *lead* 《in a competition》
- rīdo suru リードする *to take the lead*
¶Boku–tachi no chīmu wa ni–ten rīdo shite imasu.
僕たちのチームは 2 点リードしています。
Our team is leading by two points.
② *leading the way, guiding along*
¶Hayashi–san no rīdo de buji ni tsukimashita.
林さんのリードで無事に着きました。
With Mr. Hayashi leading the way, we arrived safely.
- rīdo suru リードする *to lead on the way, to guide along*

ríeki 利益 *profit, gain*

rífuto リフト *ski lift*

rígu リーグ *(sports)league*
- rīgu–sen リーグ戦 *league game, league match*
- Pashifikku–rīgu パシフィック・リーグ *the Pacific League* 《in Japanese professional baseball》
- Sentoraru–rīgu セントラル・リーグ *the Central League* 《in Japanese professional baseball》

rihabiri リハビリ [☞**rihabiritḗshon** リハビリテーション]

rihabiritḗshon リハビリテーション *rehabilitation*

rihā̆saru リハーサル *rehearsal*
¶Sono geki no rihāsaru wa ashita kara hajimaru.

その劇のリハーサルはあしたから始まる。
The rehearsals for that play will begin tomorrow.
- rihāsaru o suru リハーサルをする *to rehearse*

rihatsu 理髪 *haircutting, barbering*
- rihatsu–ten 理髪店 *barber shop* [→**tokoya** 床屋]

ríji 理事 *director, trustee*
- riji–kai 理事会 *board of directors, board of trustees*

ríka 理科 *(the study of)science*

ríkai 理解 *understanding, comprehension*
- A ni rikai ga aru Aに理解がある *to have an understanding of A; to have an appreciation of A; to be understanding toward A, to be sympathetic to A*
¶Chiji wa bunka–kōryū ni rikai ga aru jinbutsu desu.
知事は文化交流に理解がある人物です。
The governor is a figure who has an understanding of cultural exchange.
- rikai suru 理解する *to understand, to comprehend*
¶Kono bunshō o rikai shimashita ka.
この文章を理解しましたか。
Did you understand this text?.
¶Iin–chō no iu koto ga rikai dekimasu ka.
委員長の言う事が理解できますか。
Can you understand what the committee chairperson is saying?

rikkṓho 立候補 *candidacy*
- rikkōho suru 立候補する *to become a candidate, to run*
¶Uchi no Hiroshi wa seito–kai–chō ni rikkōho shimashita.
うちの宏は生徒会長に立候補しました。
Our Hiroshi ran for student council president.
- rikkōho–sha 立候補者 *candidate*

rikō 利口 ～**na** ～な *clever, bright, smart* [→**kashikoi** 賢い]
¶Oda–kun wa rikō na seinen desu ne.
小田君は利口な青年ですね。
Oda is a clever young man, isn't he.

¶Basu de iku no ga rikō da to omou yo.
バスで行くのが利口だと思うよ。
I think going by bus is smart!

rikon 離婚 *divorce*
• rikon suru 離婚する *to get divorced*

riku 陸 (*dry*)*land* [⇔**umi** 海]
¶Fune wa dandan riku ni chikazukimashita.
船はだんだん陸に近づきました。
The ship gradually approached the land.

rikuésuto リクエスト *request* [→**yōkyū** 要求]
• rikuesuto suru リクエストする *to request*
¶Efu emu kyoku ni daisuki na kyoku o rikuesuto shita.
FM 局に大好きな曲をリクエストした。
I requested on FM station to play my favorite song.
• rikuesuto-bangumi リクエスト番組 *request program*
• rikuesuto-kyoku リクエスト曲 *requested song, request*
¶Kashu wa watashi no rikuesuto-kyoku o utai mashita.
歌手は私のリクエスト曲を歌いました。
The singer sang my requests.

rikúgun 陸軍 *army*

rikujōkyōgi 陸上競技 *track and field events*

rikutsu 理屈 *logic, reasoning* [→**dōri** 道理]
• A ni rikutsu o iu A に理屈を言う *to reason with A*
• rikutsu ni au 理屈に合う *to be reasonable, to make sense*
¶Tsutsumi-san ga iu koto wa rikutsu ni atte imasu.
堤さんが言うことは理屈に合っています。
What Mr. Tsutsumi says is reasonable.

rimokon リモコン *remote control*

rimōtokontorōru リモートコントロール [☞**rimokon** リモコン]

-rin ー輪《counter for flowers; see Appendix 2》

ringo りんご *apple*
¶Kono ringo wa suppakute taberarenai yo.

このりんごは酸っぱくて食べられないよ。
This apple is so sour I can't eat it!
• ringo-jamu 林檎ジャム *apple jam*

ríngu リング ① (*finger*)*ring* [→**yubiwa** 指輪]
② *ring*《for boxing, wrestling, etc.》
¶Chanpion ga ringu ni agarimashita.
チャンピオンがリングに上がりました。
The champion entered the ring.
• engēji-ringu エンゲージリング *engagement ring*

ringyō 林業 *forestry*

rinji 臨時 ~**no** ~の *special, added out of unanticipated necessity*
• rinji-Kokkai 臨時国会 *special session of the Diet*
• rinji-nyūsu 臨時ニュース *special newscast*
• rinji-ressha 臨時列車 *special train*

rinkaigákkō 臨海学校 *seaside summer-school*

rinkaku 輪郭 *outline*

rinkangákkō 林間学校 *open-air summer-school*

rinpasen リンパ腺 *lymph gland*

rínri 倫理 *ethics*

ripóto リポート (*written*)*report* [→**repōto** レポート①, **hōkoku-sho** 報告書 (s.v. **hōkoku** 報告)]

rippa 立派 ~**na** ~な *fine, excellent, praiseworthy*
¶Uchida-san wa rippa na ie ni sunde imasu.
内田さんは立派な家に住んでいます。
Ms. Uchida lives in a fine house.
¶Onīsan wa rippa na isha ni narimashita.
お兄さんは立派な医者になりました。
Her older brother became a fine doctor.
¶Akira wa sūgaku de rippa na seiseki o osamemashita.
明は数学で立派な成績を収めました。
Akira got excellent grades in math.
¶Tazaki-san wa rippa ni shigoto o nashitogemashita.
田崎さんは立派に仕事を成し遂げました。
Mr. Tazaki accomplished the task very well.

rippō 立方 *cube* «of a number»
- rippō-kon 立方根 *cube root*
- rippō-mētoru 立方メートル *cubic meter*

rippōtai 立方体 *cube* ((geometrical figure))

rirákkusu リラックス ～**suru** ～する *to relax*
¶Ogata-san wa totemo rirakkusu shite iru yō ni miemashita.
尾形さんはとてもリラックスしているように見えました。
Ms. Ogata looked as if she were very relaxed.

rirē リレー *relay* (*race*)
- happyaku-mētoru-rirē 800メートルリレー *800-meter relay*
- medorē-rirē メドレーリレー *medley relay*

rirekisho 履歴書 *résumé, curriculum vitae*

rirífu リリーフ *relief* (*pitching*) «in baseball»
- ririfu suru リリーフする *to relieve*
¶Suzuki wa hachi-kai ni Tanaka o ririfu shimashita.
鈴木は8回に田中をリリーフしました。
Suzuki relieved Tanaka in the eighth inning.

ririku 離陸 *take-off* «of an airplane, etc.» [⇔**chakuriku** 着陸]
- ririku suru 離陸する *to take off*
¶Chichi no notta hikōki wa jū-ji ni ririku shita.
父の乗った飛行機は10時に離陸した。
The plane my father was on took off at 10:00.

ríron 理論 *theory*
- riron to jissen 理論と実践 *theory and practice*
- riron-ka 理論家 *theorist, theoretician*
- riron-teki na 理論的な *theoretical*

risáitaru リサイタル (*musical*)*recital*
¶Ane wa sengetsu, hajimete no risaitaru o hiraita.
姉は先月、初めてのリサイタルを開いた。
My older sister gave her first recital last month.

risei 理性 *reasoning ability, rationality*

- risei-teki na 理性的な *rational*

ríshi 利子 *interest* «paid on borrowed money»
¶Kono yokin wa go-pāsento no rishi ga tsuku.
この預金は5パーセントの利子がつく。
This deposit gets 5% interest.

risō 理想 *an ideal*
¶Yōko-san wa risō o jitsugen shimashita.
洋子さんは理想を実現しました。
Yoko realized her ideal.
- risō-shugi 理想主義 *idealism*
- risō-shugi-sha 理想主義者 *idealist*
- risō-teki na 理想的な *ideal*
¶Ezaki-sensei wa risō-teki na sensei desu.
江崎先生は理想的な先生です。
Ms. Ezaki is an ideal teacher.
¶Koko wa kyanpu ni wa risō-teki na basho desu.
ここはキャンプには理想的な場所です。
This is an ideal place for camping.

rísu りす *squirrel*

rísuto リスト *list* [→**ichiranhyō** 一覧表]
¶Kono na wa risuto ni notte imasu ka.
この名はリストに載っていますか。
Is this name on the list?

ritomasushikénshi リトマス試験紙 *litmus paper*

ritorurígu リトルリーグ *Little League*

rítsu 率 *rate, proportion, percentage*
¶Shiken ni gōkaku suru ritsu wa itsu-mo nana-wari-gurai da.
試験に合格する率はいつも7割ぐらいだ。
The passing rate of the examination is always about 70%. «Literally: *The rate of passing on the examination is always about 70%.*»
- da-ritsu 打率 *batting average*
- hanzai-ritsu 犯罪率 *crime rate*
- tōhyō-ritsu 投票率 *voting rate*
- waribiki-ritsu 割引率 *discount rate*

rittai 立体 (*geometrical*)*solid, three-dimensional figure*
- rittai-kōsa 立体交差 *two-level road intersection*

rittoru リットル *liter*
- -rittoru ーリットル «counter for liters; see

Appendix 2》

riyō 利用 *use, utilization*
- riyō suru 利用する *to use, to make use of*
¶Kongo wa taiyō-netsu o ōi ni riyō shimasu.
今後は太陽熱を大いに利用します。
From now on we will make use of solar heat a great deal.
- riyō-sha 利用者 *user*

riyū 理由 *reason, grounds*
¶Shippai no riyū wa wakarimasen.
失敗の理由はわかりません。
I don't understand the reason for the failure.
¶Byōki ga riyū de Yamazaki-san wa kesseki shimashita.
病気が理由で山崎さんは欠席しました。
Illness was the reason why Mr. Yamazaki was absent.

rizōto リゾート (*vacation*)*resort*

rízumu リズム *rhythm* [→**hyōshi** 拍子①]
¶Watashi-tachi wa taiko no rizumu ni awasete odotta.
私たちは太鼓のリズムに合わせて踊った。
We danced to the rhythm of the drums.

rō 蝋 *wax*
- rō-ningyō 蝋人形 *wax doll*
- rō-zaiku 蝋細工 *waxwork, wax craft*

róba 驢馬 *donkey*

róbī ロビー *lobby* 《of a building》

róbotto ロボット *robot*
- sangyō-yō-robotto 産業用ロボット *industrial robot*

rōdō 労働 *labor, work*
- rōdō suru 労働する *to labor, to work*
- rōdō-jikan 労働時間 *working hours*
- rōdō-kumiai 労働組合 <*US*>*labor union,* <*UK*>*trade union*
- rōdō-sha 労働者 *worker, laborer*
- Rōdō-shō 労働省 *the Ministry of Labor*
- jū-rōdō 重労働 *heavy labor*

rōdoku 朗読 *reading aloud*
- rōdoku suru 朗読する *to read aloud*

rōdoshō ロードショー (*a movie's*) *first run in selected theaters*

rōgan 老眼 *presbyopia*

rōhi 浪費 *waste, wasteful use*
¶Sore wa jikan no rōhi desu.
それは時間の浪費です。
That's a waste of time.
- rōhi suru 浪費する *to waste*
¶Sonna mono ni o-kane o rōhi shinai de.
そんな物にお金を浪費しないで。
Don't waste your money on such a thing.
- rōhi-ka 浪費家 *wasteful person*

roiyarubókkusu ロイヤルボックス *royal box*

rōjin 老人 *old person*
- rōjin-hōmu 老人ホーム *old people's home*
- rōjin-kurabu 老人クラブ *old people's club*

rójji ロッジ *mountain lodge*

rōka 廊下 *hallway, corridor*

rōkaru ローカル ~**na**~な *local; provincial* [→**chihō no** 地方の]
- rōkaru-nyūsu ローカルニュース *local news*
- rōkaru-sen ローカル線 *local* (*transportation*)*line*

rokéshon ロケーション (*filming*)*location*

rokétto ロケット *rocket*
¶Sengetsu roketto o uchiagemashita.
先月ロケットを打ち上げました。
They launched a rocket last month.
- tsuki-roketto 月ロケット *moon rocket*

rókkā ロッカー *locker*
- rokkā-rūmu ロッカールーム *locker room*
- koin-rokkā コインロッカー *coin-operated locker*

rókku ロック *rock* (*music*)

rokkunróru ロックンロール *rock'n'roll* (*music*)

rokú 六 *six* 《see Appendix 2》
- Roku-gatsu 六月 *June*

rokuga 録画 *video recording*
- rokuga suru 録画する *to videotape, to record*
¶Yakyū no shiai o rokuga shimashō.
野球の試合を録画しましょう。
Let's videotape the baseball game.

rokumakúen 肋膜炎 *pleurisy*

rokuon 録音 *audio recording*
- rokuon suru 録音する *to record, to tape*
¶Sono rajio-bangumi o rokuon shima-shita.
そのラジオ番組を録音しました。
I taped that radio program.
- rokuon-shitsu 録音室 *recording room, studio*
- rokuon-tēpu 録音テープ *magnetic tape, recording tape*

rōmáji ローマ字 *Roman letters, romanization*

romanchíkku ロマンチック 〜**na** 〜な *romantic*

rómansu ロマンス *romance, love affair*

rón ローン (*monetary*)*loan*
- ginkō-rōn 銀行ローン *bank loan*
- jūtaku-rōn 住宅ローン *home loan*

ronbun 論文 (*scholarly*)*paper, essay, article; thesis, dissertation*

róngi 論議 [[→**giron** 議論]] *argument, debate; discussion*
- rongi suru 論議する *to have an argument, to have a debate; to have a discussion*

rōnin 浪人 ① *masterless samurai*
② *person who has failed college entrance examinations and is studying to try again the following year*
- rōnin suru 浪人する *to study for the following year's college entrance examinations after having failed*

ronjiru 論じる *to discuss; to debate*
¶Watashi-tachi wa sono mondai o ronji-mashita.
私たちはその問題を論じました。
We discussed that problem.

rónri 論理 *logic*
- ronri-gaku 論理学 (*the study of*)*logic*
- ronri-teki na 論理的な *logical*
¶Sensei wa ronri-teki na setsumei o shi-mashita.
先生は論理的な説明をしました。
The teacher gave a logical explanation.

ronsō 論争 *verbal dispute, argument*
- ronsō suru 論争する *to dispute, to argue*

¶Shachō wa chingin ni tsuite kumiai-kanbu to ronsō shita.
社長は賃金について組合幹部と論争した。
The company president argued with the union leader about wages.

rópu ロープ *rope, cable* [→**tsuna** 綱, **nawa** 縄]

rōpuuē ロープウェー *ropeway, aerial cableway*

rōrāsukḗto ローラースケート ① *roller skating*
- rōrāsukēto o suru ローラースケートをする *to roller-skate*
② *roller skate*
- rōrāsukēto-jō ローラースケート場 *roller skating rink*

rōrupan ロールパン (*bread*)*roll*

rōryoku 労力 *hard work, effort, pains* [→**hone-ori** 骨折り(s.v. **hone** 骨)]
¶Ano daiku-san wa rōryoku o oshimanai ne.
あの大工さんは労力を惜しまないね。
That carpenter doesn't spare any effort, does he.

rosen 路線 ① *route* 《of a bus, train, etc.》
② *course* (*of action*) [→**hōshin** 方針]

rōsóku 蝋燭 *candle*
- rōsoku no akari ろうそくの明かり *candle-light*
- rōsoku o tsukeru ろうそくをつける *to light a candle*
- rōsoku o fukikesu ろうそくを吹き消す *to blow out a candle*
- rōsoku-tate 蝋燭立て *candlestick, candle holder*

rósu ロース *sirloin; pork loin*

rósu ロス *loss, disadvantageous outcome* [→**sonshitsu** 損失]
¶Pitchā no kega wa chīmu ni totte taihen na rosu desu.
ピッチャーのけがはチームにとってたいへんなロスです。
The pitcher's injury is a terrible loss to the team.
- rosu suru ロスする *to suffer the loss of*

rōtarī ロータリー *traffic circle,*

<*UK*>*roundabout*

rōtḗshon ローテーション *rotation, regularly recurring succession*
- rōtḗshon de ローテーションで *in rotation*

rúbi ルビ ① *small kana printed alongside or above a Chinese character to show its pronunciation* [→**furigana** 振り仮名]
② *the small-size type used to print such small kana*

rúbī ルビー *ruby*

rúi 塁 *base* 《*in baseball*》
- hon-rui 本塁 *home* (*base*)
- ichi-rui 一塁 *first base*
- ni-rui 二塁 *second base*
- san-rui 三塁 *third base*

rúi 類 *kind, sort, class* [→**shurui** 種類]
¶Rui wa tomo o yobu.
類は友を呼ぶ。《*proverb*》
Birds of a feather flock together. 《*Literally: A class invites its friends.*》

ruiji 類似 *resemblance*
- ruiji suru 類似する *to become similar* [→**niru** 似る]
¶Amerikan-futtobōru wa ragubī ni ruiji shite imasu.
アメリカンフットボールはラグビーに類似しています。
American football is similar to rugby.
- ruiji-hin 類似品 *an imitation; similar item*
- ruiji-ten 類似点 *point of similarity*

rúkī ルーキー *rookie*

rúmu ルーム *a room* [→**heya** 部屋]
- rūmu-kūrā ルームクーラー *room air conditioner*
- rūmu-sābisu ルームサービス *room service*

rúpo ルポ [☞**ruporutāju** ルポルタージュ]
- rupo-raitā ルポライター *on-the-scene reporter*

ruporutāju ルポルタージュ *on-the-scene reporting; on-the scene report*

rūru ルール *rule, regulation* [→**kisoku** 規則]
¶Rūru o mamoranakereba narimasen.
ルールを守らなければなりません。

One must obey the rules.

rúsu 留守 *being out, being away* 《*i.e., not at home or not at one's workplace*》
¶Ane wa ima rusu desu.
姉は今留守です。
My older sister is out now.
- uchi o rusu ni suru うちを留守にする *to go away from home*
- A no rusu ni kuru Aの留守に来る *to come while A is out*
¶Takano-san wa kachō no rusu ni kimashita.
高野さんは課長の留守に来ました。
Mr. Takano came while the section chief was out.

rusuban 留守番 ① *taking care of a house* (*while others are away*)
- rusuban o suru 留守番をする *to take care of a house*
② *person taking care of a house* (*while others are away*)
- rusuban-denwa 留守番電話 *telephone with an answering machine*

rūto ルート *route; channel*
¶Boku-tachi wa betsu no rūto de sanchō ni tasshimashita.
僕たちは別のルートで山頂に達しました。
We reached the summit by another route.
¶Shachō wa Ajia de no hanbai rūto o kaitaku shita.
社長はアジアでの販売ルートを開拓した。
The company president developed a sales route in Asia.

rūto ルート (*mathematical*)*root* 《*Ordinarily understood to mean square root unless otherwise specified.*》
¶Rūto kyū wa san desu.
ルート9は3です。
The square root of nine is three.
《*Although odd grammatically, this kind of sentence is a typical way of stating a fact of arithmetic.*》

rūtsu ルーツ *ancestry, roots*

rūzu ルーズ ～**na** ～な *careless, inattentive, sloppy, lax* [→**darashinai**

だらしない〕

¶Haha wa jikan ni rūzu desu.

母は時間にルーズです。

My mother is lax about time.

¶Fukui-san wa o-kane ni rūzu desu.

福井さんはお金にルーズです。

Mr. Fukui is careless about money.

rūzurīfu ルーズリーフ *loose-leaf note-book*

ryáku 略 [[→**shōryaku** 省略]] ① *abbreviation; abridgement*

② *omission, leaving out*

ryakúsu 略す ① *to abbreviate; to abridge*

¶"Gorubachofu" o "Go" to ryakushimashita.

「ゴルバチョフ」を「ゴ」と略しました。

I abbreviated "Gorubachofu" to "Go."

② *to omit, to leave out*

¶Ato wa ryakushite kekkō desu.

後は略して結構です。

You may omit the rest.

ryṓ 猟 *hunting* [→**kari** 狩, **shuryō** 狩猟〕

• ryō-ken 猟犬 *hunting dog*

• ryō-shi 猟師 *hunter*

ryṓ 量 *quantity, amount* [⇔**shitsu** 質〕

¶Naga-ame de mizuumi no mizu no ryō ga daibu fuemashita.

長雨で湖の水の量がだいぶ増えました。

The quantity of water in the lake greatly increased from the long rain.

• ryō-teki na 量的な *quantitative*

ryṓ 寮 *dormitory*

• ryō-sei 寮生 *student living in a dormitory*

ryṓ 漁 *(large-scale) fishing*

• ryō o suru 漁をする *to fish*

• ryō-shi 漁師 *fisherman*

• tai-ryō 大漁 *a big catch*

ryódo 領土 *territory* 《under a country's jurisdiction》

ryōgae 両替 ① *changing* 《money from large denominations to small》

• ryōgae suru 両替する *to change* [→**ku-zusu** 崩す②〕

¶Sen-en-satsu o hyaku-en-dama ni ryōgae shite kuremasu ka.

千円札を百円玉に両替してくれますか。

Will you change a 1000-yen bill into 100-yen coins for me?

② *(foreign) exchange* [→**gaikoku-kawase** 外国為替 (s.v. **kawase** 為替)〕

• ryōgae suru 両替する *to change*

¶Amerika ni iku hito wa en o doru ni ryōgae suru.

アメリカに行く人は円をドルに両替する。

People going to the United States change yen into dollars.

ryōgawa 両側 *both sides* 《i.e., the area to the right and to the left》

¶Dōro no ryōgawa ni namiki ga arimasu.

道路の両側に並木があります。

There are rows of trees on both sides of the road.

ryōhṓ 両方 *both; neither*

《in combination with a negative predicate》

¶Chichi wa Eigo mo Furansu-go mo ryōhō-tomo hanaseru.

父は英語もフランス語も両方とも話せる。

My father can speak both English and French.

¶Watashi no haha wa piano mo gitā mo ryōhō hikenai.

私の母はピアノもギターも両方弾けない。

My mother can play neither the piano nor the guitar.

ryōjíkan 領事館 *consulate* [→**sōryō-ji-kan** 総領事館 (s.v. **sōryōji** 総領事)〕

ryōkai 了解 *(considered) consent* [→**shōdaku** 承諾〕

• ryōkai suru 了解する *to consent to*

¶Fujimoto-kun mo tsui-ni sono keikaku o ryokai shita.

藤本君もついにその計画を了解した。

Fujimoto also finally consented to that plan.

¶Ryōkai!

了解！

《typically part of a conversation by two-way radio, etc.》

OK!, Roger!

ryokan 旅館 *inn*

ryōkin 料金 *charge, fee, fare, toll*
¶Ani wa hoteru no ryōkin o shiharaimashita.
兄はホテルの料金を支払いました。
My older brother paid the hotel charges.
¶Ryōkin wa ichi-jikan ikura desu ka.
料金は1時間いくらですか。
What is the charge for one hour?
• ryōkin-hyō 料金表 *price list*
• ryōkin-jo 料金所 *tollgate*
• basu-ryōkin バス料金 *bus fare*
• chūsha-ryōkin 駐車料金 *parking fee*
• nyūjō-ryōkin 入場料金 *admission fee*

ryokō 旅行 *travel; trip, journey, tour*
¶Okinawa e no ryokō wa dō datta?
沖縄への旅行はどうだった？
How was your trip to Okinawa?
• ryokō suru 旅行する *to take a trip; to travel*
• ryokō ni iku 旅行に行く *to go on a trip*
• ryokō-annai 旅行案内 *travel information; guidebook*
• ryokō-gaisha 旅行会社 *travel agency*
• ryokō-sha 旅行者 *traveler*
• dantai-ryokō 団体旅行 *group tour*
• kaigai-ryokō 海外旅行 *traveling abroad*
• pakku-ryokō パック旅行 *package tour*
• sekai-isshū-ryokō 世界一周旅行 *around the world trip*
• shinkon-ryokō 新婚旅行 *honeymoon*
• shūgaku-ryokō 修学旅行 *school excursion*
• uchū-ryokō 宇宙旅行 *space travel*

ryōmen 両面 *both sides, front and back*
• ryōmen-kopī 両面コピー *two-sided copy*

ryōri 料理 ① *cooking, preparing food*
¶Ane wa ryōri ga suki desu.
姉は料理が好きです。
My older sister likes cooking.
¶Chichi wa ryōri ga heta desu.
父は料理が下手です。
My father is poor at cooking.
• ryōri suru 料理する *to cook*
② *cuisine, dish(es)*
¶Ichiban suki na ryōri wa nan desu ka.

いちばん好きな料理は何ですか
What is your favorite dish?
• oishii ryōri おいしい料理 *delicious dish, delicious cuisine*
• assari shita ryōri あっさりした料理 *simple cuisine*
• ryōri-bangumi 料理番組 *cooking program*
• Chūgoku-ryōri 中国料理 *Chinese cuisine, Chinese dishes*
• Furansu-ryōri フランス料理 *French cuisine, French dishes*

ryōritsu 両立 ~**suru** ~する *to be compatible; to be combined harmoniously*
¶Heiki-kōgyō to sekai-heiwa wa ryōritsu shimasen.
兵器産業と世界平和は両立しません。
The armaments industry and world peace are not compatible.
• ryōritsu saseru 両立させる *to combine harmoniously, to do both well*
¶Isamu wa benkyō to arubaito o ryōritsu sasete iru.
勇は勉強とアルバイトを両立させている。
Isamu is doing both his studies and a part-time job well.

ryōshin 両親 *(both)parents* [→**oya** 親]

ryōshin 良心 *conscience*
¶Ryōshin ni hajinai kōdō o suru koto ga taisetsu da.
良心に恥じない行動をすることが大切だ。
It's important to act according to one's conscience. 《Literally: Acting so not to be ashamed in one's conscience is important.》
• ryōshin ga togameru 良心がとがめる *one's conscience troubles one*
• ryōshin-teki na 良心的な *conscientious*

ryōshūsho 領収書 *(written)receipt*

ryū 竜 *dragon*

ryūchō 流暢 ~**na** ~な *fluent*
¶Erikku-san wa ryūchō ni Nihon-go o hanashimasu.
エリックさんは流暢に日本語を話します。
Eric speaks Japanese fluently.

ryūgaku 留学 *study abroad*
¶Boku-tachi no Eigo no sensei wa ryūgaku no keiken ga aru.

僕たちの英語の先生は留学の経験がある。
Our English teacher has overseas study experience.

• ryūgaku suru 留学する *to study abroad; to go abroad to study*

¶Kyonen, Chikako wa Igirisu ni ryūgaku shimashita.
去年、千香子はイギリスに留学しました。
Last year, Chikako went to England to study English.

• ryūgaku-sei 留学生 *student studying abroad; foreign student* (*in Japan*)

ryū́ha 流派 *school, body of followers* 《of a traditional art form》

ryukkusákku リュックサック *rucksack, knapsack*

ryūkō 流行 [[→**hayari** はやり]]
① *fashion, vogue, popular trend, popularity*

• ryūkō suru 流行する *to come into fashion, to become popular* [→**hayaru** はやる]

¶Sono heasutairu ga ima ryūkō shite imasu.
そのヘアスタイルが今流行しています。
That hairstyle is in fashion now.

¶Kono sutairu ga kotoshi ryūkō suru deshō.
このスタイルが今年は流行するでしょう。
This style will probably come into fashion this year.

② *going around, prevalance* 《of a disease》

• ryūkō suru 流行する *to go around, to become prevalent, to become widespread*

¶Ima infuruenza ga ryūkō shite imasu.
今インフルエンザが流行しています。
The flu is going around now.

• ryūkō-byō 流行病 *epidemic disease*
• ryūkō-ka 流行歌 *popular song*
• ryūkō-okure no 流行遅れの *out of fashion*
• dai-ryūkō 大流行 *great popularity*
• saishin-ryūkō 最新流行 *the latest fashion*

Ryūkyū-shótō 琉球諸島 *the Ryukyu Islands*

ryūmachi リューマチ *rheumatism*

ryūsei 流星 *shooting star* [→ **nagare-boshi** 流れ星 (s.v. **nagare** 流れ)]

ryūtsū 流通 *circulation, flow; distribution* 《of products》

• ryūtsū suru 流通する *to circulate, to flow; to be distributed*

ryū́zan 流産 *miscarriage*

• ryūzan suru 流産する *to have a miscarriage*

S

sa 差 *difference, disparity, gap* [→ **chigai** 違い]

¶Dai-ichi-i to dai-ni-i to no sa wa ōkii desu.
第1位と第2位との差は大きいです。
The difference between the first place and second place is great.

sá さあ ① *all right now, come on* 《an interjection expressing encouragment or urging》

¶Sā, dekakeyō.
さあ、出かけよう。
All right now, let's go out.

¶Sā, minna isoide. Kōtei ni shūgō shiyō.
さあ、みんな急いで。校庭に集合しよう。
Come on, hurry everybody. Assemble in the schoolyard!

② *well, gee* 《an interjection expressing uncertainty》

¶Sā, shirimasen.
さあ、知りません。
Gee, I don't know.

¶Sā, tabun sore wa Pikaso deshō.
さあ、たぶんそれはピカソでしょう。
Well, that's probably a Picasso.

saba 鯖 *mackerel*

sabaku 砂漠 *desert*

sábetsu 差別 *discrimination*

• sabetsu suru 差別する *to discriminate against*

• jinshu–sabetsu 人種差別 *racial discrimination*

sabí 錆 *rust*

sabíru 錆びる *to rust*
• sabita kugi 錆びた釘 *rusty nail*

sabishíi 寂しい *lonely, lonesome*
¶Tōkyō de no hitori–gurashi wa sabishii desu.
東京での独り暮らしは寂しいです。
Living alone in Tokyo is lonely.
• sabishii basho 寂しい場所 *lonely place*

sā́bisu サービス ① *service* (*to customers*)
¶Kono mise wa sābisu ga ii desu.
この店はサービスがいいです。
This store's service is good.
② *free gift, premium* 《accompanying something one buys》 [→**omake** お負け①]
• sābisu–ryō サービス料 *service charge*

sabóru サボる 【COL.】 ① *to cut* 《class》, *to skip* 《school》
② *to do slowly on purpose* 《when the direct object refers to one's work》

saboten サボテン *cactus*

sā́bu サーブ *serve* 《in tennis, volleyball, etc.》
• sābu suru サーブする *to serve*

sā́chiráito サーチライト *searchlight*

sā́do サード ① *third base* [→**sanrui** 三塁] 《in baseball》
② *third baseman* [→**sanrui–shu** 三塁手 (s.v. **sanrui** 三塁)] 《in baseball》

sádō 茶道 *the tea ceremony*

saé さえ《This word can be used as a noun-following particle or following a gerund (-te form).》
① *even* 《indicating that what precedes is extreme》 《Often followed by **mo** も with no difference in meaning.》
¶Kono ko wa namae sae kakemasen.
この子は名前さえ書けません。
This child cannot even write his name.
② ⟨if⟩ *just* 《in combination with a -ba -ば conditional》
¶Kore sae oboereba, daijōbu desu yo.

これさえ覚えれば、大丈夫ですよ。
If you memorize just this, you'll be fine!

saegíru 遮る{5} *to interrupt, to obstruct*
¶O–hanashi o saegitte sumimasen.
お話を遮ってすみません。
I'm sorry to interrupt what you're saying.
¶Kono kāten wa hikari o saegitte imasu.
このカーテンは光を遮っています。
These curtains are obstructing the light.

saéru 冴える ① *to be clear; to be bright*
• saeta atama さえた頭 *clear head*
• saeta iro さえた色 *bright color*
• kibun ga saenai 気分がさえない *to feel depressed*
② *to become honed, to become mature* 《when the subject is a skill》
¶Noriko–san no piano no ude wa saete kimashita.
典子さんのピアノの腕は冴えてきました。
Noriko's piano skills have matured.

sáfā サーファー *surfer*

safáia サファイア *a sapphire*

sáfari サファリ *safari*

sáfin サーフィン *surfing*
• sāfin o suru サーフィンをする *to surf*

sāfubṓdo サーフボード *surfboard*

sagáru 下がる ① *to hang down, to be suspended*
¶Tenjō kara ranpu ga takusan sagatte iru.
天井からランプがたくさん下がっている。
Many lamps are hanging from the ceiling.
② *to go down, to become lower* [⇔ **agaru** 上がる①]
¶Netsu ga nakanaka sagaranai ne.
熱がなかなか下がらないね。
The fever just won't go down, will it.
¶Eigo no seiseki ga sagatte shimaimashita.
英語の成績が下がってしまいました。
My English grades went down.
③ *to step back, to move backward* [→ **shirizoku** 退く①]
¶Seito–tachi wa issei ni ushiro e sagarima-

shita.
生徒たちは一斉に後ろへ下がりました。
The students all stepped back together.

sagasu 捜す, 探す *to look for, to search for*
¶Nani o sagashite iru n desu ka.
何をさがしているんですか。
What are you looking for?

sagéru 下げる ① *to lower, to bring down*
¶Rajio no onryō o sagete kudasai.
ラジオの音量を下げてください。
Please turn down the volume on the radio.
• A ni atama o sageru Aに頭を下げる *to bow to A*
② *to hang, to suspend* [→**tsurusu** 吊るす]
¶Tenjō kara fūrin o sagemashō.
天井から風鈴を下げましょう。
Let's hang a wind-chime from the ceiling.

sági 詐欺 *swindle, fraud*
• sagi ni kakaru 詐欺にかかる *to be swindled*
• sagi-shi 詐欺師 *swindler*

saguru 探る ① *to feel around in, to grope around in*
¶Poketto o sagutte, kagi o toridashita.
ポケットを探って、かぎを取り出した。
I felt around in my pocket and took out the key.
② *to spy on, to investigate secretly*
¶Heitai wa teki no yōsu o sagutte kimashita.
兵隊は敵の様子を探ってきました。
The soldier spied on the enemy's situation and came back.
③ *to try to find out, to try to discover*
• gen'in o saguru 原因を探る *to try to find out the cause*

ságyō 作業 *work, working* [→**shigoto** 仕事]
• sagyō suru 作業する *to work*
• sagyō-ba 作業場 *workshop*
• sagyō-chū no 作業中の *at-work, working*
• sagyō-fuku 作業服 *work clothes*

sáhō 作法 *manners, etiquette*

sái さい *rhinoceros*

-sái 一歳《counter for years of age; see Appendix 2》
¶San-sai no onna no ko mo imashita.
３歳の女の子もいました。
There was also a three-year-old girl.
¶Nan-sai desu ka.
何歳ですか。
How old are you?
¶Otōto wa imōto yori ni-sai toshi shita desu.
弟は妹より２歳年下です。
My younger brother is two years younger than my younger sister.

saiaku 最悪 ~**no** ～の *worst, worst possible* [⇔**saijō no** 最上の①]
¶Saiaku no jitai ga shōjimashita.
最悪の事態が生じました。
The worst possible situation arose.
¶Saiaku no baai ni wa, ryokō wa chūshi ni narimasu.
最悪の場合には、旅行は中止になります。
In the worst possible case, the trip will be called off.

saibai 栽培 *growing, cultivation*
• saibai suru 栽培する *to grow, to cultivate*

sáiban 裁判 *(legal)trial*
• saiban ni naru 裁判になる *to come to trial, to go to court*
• saiban o ukeru 裁判を受ける *to stand trial*
• saiban-kan 裁判官 *judge, magistrate* [→**hanji** 判事]
• saiban-sho 裁判所 *court; courthouse*
• chihō-saiban-sho 地方裁判所 *district court*
• kan'i-saiban-sho 簡易裁判所 *summary court*
• katei-saiban-sho 家庭裁判所 *family court*
• kōtō-saiban-sho 高等裁判所 *high court*
• Saikō-saiban-sho 最高裁判所 *the Supreme Court*

saibō 細胞 *(organism)cell*

- saibō–bunretsu 細胞分裂 *cell division*

sáichū 最中 *midst, middle* 《of doing something》

¶Akiko-san wa ima benkyō no saichū desu.

明子さんは今勉強の最中です。

Akiko is in the middle of studying now.

¶Yumi wa eiga o mite iru saichū ni naki-dashita.

由美は映画を見ている最中に泣き出した。

Yumi began to cry in the middle of watching the movie.

sáidā サイダー *clear soda pop*

saidai 最大 ～no ～の *largest, maximum* [⇔**saishō no** 最小の]

- saidai-gen 最大限 *a maximum*
- Nihon-saidai no 日本最大の *largest in Japan*
- sekai-saidai no 世界最大の *largest in the world*

¶Biwa-ko wa Nihon-saidai no mizuumi desu.

琵琶湖は日本最大の湖です。

Lake Biwa is the largest lake in Japan.

sáido サイド ① [[→**yoko** 横①]] *side* (*part*); *the area beside*

② *side, standpoint*

- saido-bōdo サイドボード *sideboard*
- saido-kā サイドカー *sidecar*
- saido-surō サイドスロー *sidearm throw*
- shōhi-sha-saido 消費者サイド *the consumer side*

sáiensu サイエンス *science* [→**kagaku** 科学]

saifu 財布 *wallet*

saigai 災害 *disaster, calamity*

sáigo 最後 *the end, the last* [⇔**saisho** 最初]

¶Kono monogatari no saigo wa dō narimasu ka.

この物語の最後はどうなりますか。

How does the end of this story turn out?

- saigo no 最後の *final, last*

¶Kyō wa ichi-nen no saigo no hi desu.

きょうは1年の最後の日です。

Today is the last day of the year.

- saigo ni 最後に *at the end, ultimately; last*

¶Nan-kai mo yatte mite, saigo ni seikō shimashita.

何回もやってみて、最後に成功しました。

I tried doing it again and again, and ultimately succeeded.

saihō 裁縫 *sewing, needlework*

- saihō suru 裁縫する *to sew, to do needlework*
- saihō–dōgu 裁縫道具 *sewing implements*

saijitsu 祭日 ① *national holiday* [→**shukujitsu** 祝日]

② *festival day*

saijō 最上 ～no ～の ① *best, finest, supreme* [⇔**saiaku no** 最悪の]

- saijō no shinamono 最上の品物 *the finest goods*
- saijō no kōfuku 最上の幸福 *supreme happiness*

② *top, uppermost*

- saijō-kai 最上階 *top floor*

saikai 再開 *resumption, beginning again*

- saikai suru 再開する *to resume, to begin again* 《transitive or intransitive》

saiken 債券 *bond, debenture*

saikin 細菌 *bacteria, microbe*

saikin 最近 *recently, lately* [→**konogoro** このごろ]

¶Saikin go-nen-kan ni konna infure wa nakatta.

最近5年間にこんなインフレはなかった。

There hasn't been this kind of inflation in the last five years.

¶Saikin Yamanaka-san ni aimashita ka.

最近山中さんに会いましたか。

Have you seen Ms. Yamanaka lately?

¶Chichi wa saikin made Ōsaka ni imashita.

父は最近まで大阪にいました。

My father was in Osaka until recently.

- saikin no 最近の *the latest, recent*

¶Saikin no nyūsu o kikimashita ka.

最近のニュースを聞きましたか。

Have you heard the latest news?

¶Saikin no wakamono wa reigi-tadashiku

nai desu.

最近の若者は礼儀正しくないです。

Young people these days are not polite.

《*Literally: Recent young people are not polite*》

saikō 最高 [[⇔**saitei** 最低]] ① *maximum, highest point*

• saikō no 最高の *highest, maximum*

• saikō ni tassuru 最高に達する *to reach the maximum*

② 〜**no** 〜の *best* [→**saijō no** 最上の①] [⇔**saiaku no** 最悪の]

¶Kore wa ima made ni mita saikō no eiga desu.

これは今までに見た最高の映画です。

This is the best film I've seen up to now.

• saikō-kion 最高気温 *highest temperature*

• saikō-kiroku 最高記録 *best record*

• Saikō-saiban-sho 最高裁判所 *the Supreme Court*

• saikō-ten 最高点 *highest mark, highest score*

saikóro 骰子 *dice*

saikú 細工 ① *craftsmanship, handicrafting*

② *handcrafted item*

sáikuringu サイクリング *cycling, bicycle ride*

¶Ashita saikuringu ni ikō yo.

あしたサイクリングに行こうよ。

Let's go cycling tomorrow!

sáikuru サイクル *number of cycles per second*

¶Tōkyō to Ōsaka wa denki no saikuru ga chigaimasu.

東京と大阪は電気のサイクルが違います。

The number of cycles per second of electricity differs in Tokyo and Osaka.

• -saikuru −サイクル《*counter for cycles per second; see Appendix 2*》

sáimu 債務 *debt, liability, repayment obligation*

sáin サイン ① *signature* [→**shomei** 署名]; *autograph*

• sain suru サインする *to sign*

¶Koko ni namae o sain shite kudasai.

ここに名前をサインしてください。

Please sign your name here.

¶Sain shite itadakemasen ka.

サインしていただけませんか。

May I have you sign?

② *sign, signal* [→**aizu** 合図]

¶Hoshu wa tōshu ni sain o okurimashita.

捕手は投手にサインを送りました。

The catcher gave a sign to the pitcher.

• sain-chō サイン帳 *autograph album*

• sain-pen サインペン *felt-tip pen; roller-ball pen*

sainán 災難 *misfortune; calamity, disaster* [→**saigai** 災害]

sainō 才能 *talent, ability*

¶Musuko-san ni wa ongaku no sainō ga arimasu.

息子さんには音楽の才能があります。

Your son has musical talent.

• kakureta sainō 隠れた才能 *hidden talent*

• sainō no aru hito 才能のある人 *talented person*

sáiren サイレン *siren*

sairentoéiga サイレント映画 *silent movie*

sáiro サイロ *silo*

saisei 再生 ① *resuscitation; rebirth, reincarnation*

• saisei suru 再生する [[→**ikikaeru** 生き返る]] *to be resuscitated; to be reborn*

② *regeneration* 《*of a part of an organism*》

• saisei suru 再生する *to regenerate* 《*intransitive*》

¶Kono tokage no shippo wa saisei shimashita.

このとかげのしっぽは再生しました。

This lizard's tail regenerated.

③ *reclamation, recycling*

• saisei suru 再生する *to reclaim, to recycle*

④ *playback* 《*of a recording*》

• saisei suru 再生する *to play back*

saishin 最新 〜**no** 〜の *latest, newest, up-to-date*

• saishin no nyūsu 最新のニュース *the la-*

test news
• saishin-ryūkō 最新流行 *the latest fashion*

saisho 最初 *beginning* [⇔**saigo** 最後]
¶Eiga wa saisho kara saigo made omoshirokatta.
映画は最初から最後までおもしろかった。
The movie was interesting from beginning to end.
• saisho no 最初の *first, initial*
¶Washinton wa Amerika no saisho no daitōryō da.
ワシントンはアメリカの最初の大統領だ。
Washington was the first President of the United States.
• saisho ni 最初に *at the beginning; first*
¶Amunzen wa saisho ni Nankyokuten ni tōtatsu shita hito deshita.
アムンゼンは、最初に南極点に到達した人でした。
Amundsen was the person who reached the South Pole first.
¶Saisho ni hikōki de Okinawa ni iki-masu.
最初に飛行機で沖縄に行きます。
First I will go to Okinawa by plane.
• saisho wa 最初は *at first, initially*
¶Saisho wa boku-tachi no chīmu ga rīdo shite ita.
最初は僕たちのチームがリードしていた。
At first our team was leading.

saishō 最小 ～**no** ～の *smallest, minimum* [⇔**saidai no** 最大の]
• saishō-gen 最小限 *a minimum*
• saishō-ryō 最小量 *mimimum quantity*

saishū 採集 *collecting, gathering*
• saishū suru 採集する *to collect, to gather*

saishū 最終 ～**no** ～の *last, final* [→**saigo no** 最後の]
• saishū-densha 最終電車 *last train*
• saishū-kai 最終回 *last inning; last round*
• saishū-kettei 最終決定 *final decision*

sáisoku 催促 *pressing, demand*
• saisoku suru 催促する *to press for, to demand*

¶Tomodachi wa boku ni henji o saisoku shimashita.
友達は僕に返事を催促しました。
My friend pressed me for an answer.

saitei 最低 [⇔**saikō** 最高] ① *minimum, lowest point*
¶Kyūryō wa saitei de gojūman-en desu.
給料は最低で50万円です。
The salary is 500,000 yen at minimum.
• saitei no 最低の *lowest, minimum*
¶Kurasu de saitei no ten o totte shimatta.
クラスで最低の点を取ってしまった。
I got the lowest mark in the class.
② ～**no** ～の *worst* [→**saiaku no** 最悪の]
¶Watashi no shiru kagiri, kore wa saitei no shōsetsu desu.
私の知る限り、これは最低の小説です。
As for as I know, this is the worst novel.
• saitei-kion 最低気温 *lowest temperature*

saiten 採点 *marking, grading, scoring*
• saiten suru 採点する *to mark, to grade, to score*
¶Sensei wa mada tōan o saiten shite imasu.
先生はまだ答案を採点しています。
The teacher is still grading the examination papers.

saiwai 幸い ① [[→**shiawase** 幸せ]] *happiness; good fortune*
• saiwai na 幸いな *happy; fortunate*
¶O-yaku ni tateba saiwai desu.
お役に立てば幸いです。
I hope I can be of some help. 《*Literally: If I can be of help to you, I will be happy.*》
② （～**ni** ～に） *fortunately*
¶Saiwai shiken ni gōkaku shimashita.
幸い試験に合格しました。
Fortunately, I passed the examination.

saiyō 採用 ① *adoption, acceptance for use*
• saiyō suru 採用する *to adopt, to accept for use*
¶Rainen kara atarashii kyōkasho o saiyō suru yotei da.
来年から新しい教科書を採用する予定だ。

From next year they're planning to adopt new textbooks.

¶Kono teian ga saiyō saremashita.

この提案が採用されました。

This proposal was adopted.

② *hiring, employment*

• saiyō suru 採用する *to hire, to employ*

¶Sono kaisha wa kotoshi hitori dake saiyō shimashita.

その会社は今年1人だけ採用しました。

That company hired only one person this year.

• saiyō-shiken 採用試験 *employment examination*

saizen 最善 ① 〜no 〜の *best, most beneficial*

• saizen no hōhō 最善の方法 *the best method*

② *one's best, one's utmost*

• saizen o tsukusu 最善を尽くす *to do one's best*

sáizu サイズ (*clothing*)*size*

¶Kutsu no saizu wa ikutsu desu ka.

靴のサイズはいくつですか。

What is your shoe size?

¶Kore wa watashi no saizu ni aimasen.

これは私のサイズに合いません。

This isn't my size. 《*Literally: This doesn't match my size.*》

sají 匙 [→**supūn** スプーン]

• ko-saji 小匙 *teaspoon*

• ō-saji 大匙 *tablespoon*

saká 坂 *slope, sloping path*

¶Yōko-san no ie wa kono saka no ue ni aru ne.

洋子さんの家はこの坂の上にあるね。

Yōko's house is at the top of this slope, isn't it.

• kyū [yuruyaka] na saka 急〔緩やか〕な坂 *steep* [*gentle*] *slope*

• saka o noboru [kudaru] 坂を上る〔下る〕 *to go up* [*down*] *a slope*

• kudari-zaka 下り坂 *downward slope, descent*

• nobori-zaka 上り坂 *upward slope, ascent*

sakadachi 逆立ち *handstand; head-stand*

• sakadachi suru 逆立ちする *to do a handstand; to do a headstand*

sakaéru 栄える *to prosper, to flourish, to thrive* [→**han'ei suru** 繁栄する]

sakái 境 *border, boundary*

¶Kono kōen wa Tōkyō to Saitama no sakai ni arimasu.

この公園は東京と埼玉の境にあります。

This park is on the boundary between Tokyo and Saitama.

sakan 盛ん 〜na〜な *vigorous, energetic; thriving; popular*

¶Kono machi de wa shōgyō ga sakan desu.

この町では商業が盛んです。

Business is thriving in this town.

¶Kyūba de wa yakyū ga sakan desu ne.

キューバでは野球が盛んですね。

In Cuba baseball is popular, isn't it.

• sakan na hakushu 盛んな拍手 *thunderous applause*

• sakan ni moeru 盛んに燃える *to burn furiously*

sakana 魚 *fish*

¶Kono mizuumi ni wa sakana ga takusan iru yo.

この湖には魚がたくさんいるよ。

There are a lot of fish in this lake!

¶Watashi wa niku yori sakana no hō ga suki desu.

私は肉より魚のほうが好きです。

I like fish better than meat.

• sakana o tsuru 魚を釣る *to catch a fish* 《*with hook and line*》

• sakana-tsuri 魚釣り *fishing* 《*with hook and line*》

• sakana-ya 魚屋 *fish shop; fish dealer*

sakanobóru 遡る ① *to go upstream*

• kawa o sakanoboru 川をさかのぼる *to go up a river*

② *to go back, to date back* 《*to a time in the past*》; *to think back* 《*to a time in the past*》

¶Sono shūkan wa jūnana-seiki ni sakanoborimasu.

その習慣は17世紀にさかのぼります。

That custom dates back to the 17th century.

sakaráu 逆らう ① *to act against, to disobey*

• oya ni sakarau 親に逆らう *to disobey one's parents*

② *to move against* 《a flow or current of some kind》

¶Tama wa kaze ni sakaratte seki ni tobi-komimashita.

球は風に逆らって席に飛び込みました。

The ball moved against the wind and flew into the seats.

sakasama 逆様 ~**no** ~の ① *upside down, inverted*

¶Chizu o sakasama ni mite iru yo.

地図をさかさまに見ているよ。

You're looking at the map upside down!

② *backwards, reversed*

• junjo o sakasama ni suru 順序を逆様にする *to reverse the order*

sākasu サーカス *circus*

sáke 鮭 *salmon*

sake 酒 ① *sake, Japanese rice wine* [→**Nihon–shu** 日本酒 (s.v. **Nihon** 日本)]

② *alcoholic beverages, liquor*

• sake o nomu 酒を飲む *to drink alcohol*

sakébu 叫ぶ *to shout, to yell* [⇔**sasa-yaku** 囁く]

¶Sōnan-sha wa "Tasukete!" to sakebima-shita.

遭難者は「助けて！」と叫びました。

The accident victim shouted, "Help!"

sakéru 裂ける 《intransitive》 *to tear, to rip; to split, to crack*

¶Kono kāten wa sugu sakeru ne.

このカーテンはすぐ裂けるね。

This curtain tears easily, doesn't it.

sakéru 避ける *to avoid, to keep away from*

¶Matsumura-san wa watashi ni au no o sakete iru yo.

松村さんは私に会うのを避けているよ。

Mr. Matsumura is avoiding me!

• kiken o sakeru 危険は避ける *to avoid danger*

saki 先 ① *end, point, tip*

¶Pitchā wa hitosashi-yubi no saki o kega shita.

ピッチャーは人さし指の先をけがした。

The pitcher injured the tip of his forefinger.

• himo no saki ひもの先 *the end of a rope*

• enpitsu no saki 鉛筆の先 *the point of a pencil*

② *the future, later in time* [→**shōrai** 将来]

¶Saki no koto wa shinpai shinai de.

先の事は心配しないで。

Don't worry about the future. 《Literally: Don't worry about future things.》

• -saki －先 *from now* 《Added to bases denoting time periods.》

¶Kono gakkō mo go-nen-saki ni sō naru deshō.

この学校も５年先にそうなるでしょう。

This school will probably become like that too five years from now.

③ *the area ahead; the area beyond*

¶Yūbin-kyoku wa sūpā no saki ni ari-masu.

郵便局はスーパーの先にあります。

The post office is beyond the supermarket.

• saki ni tatsu 先に立つ *to take the lead*

• -saki －先 *ahead* 《Added to bases denoting distances.》

¶Shōgakkō wa gojū-mētoru-saki desu.

小学校は50メートル先です。

The elementary school is 50 meters ahead.

④ ~**ni** ~に *beforehand, first; ahead, earlier*

¶Dōzo o-saki ni.

どうぞお先に。

Please go ahead of me. 《Literally: Please, ahead》

¶O-saki ni shitsurei shimasu.

お先に失礼します。

Excuse me for leaving ahead of you. 《Literally: I will be rude earlier.》

¶Saki ni shukudai o yaranakereba nara-nai yo.

先に宿題をやらなければならないよ。
First I have to do my homework!
- saki-hodo 先程 【FORMAL for **sakki** さっき】 *a short while ago*

sakisófon サキソフォン *saxophone*

sákitto サーキット ① (*electrical*)*circuit* [→**kairo** 回路]
　② *auto racing track*

sakka 作家 *writer, novelist* [→**shōsetsu-ka** 小説家 (s.v. **shōsetsu** 小説)]

sákkā サッカー <*US*>*soccer,* <*UK*>*football*

sakkaku 錯覚 *illusion; hallucination*

sákki さっき *a little while ago*
　¶Sakki Jirō kara denwa ga atta yo.
さっき次郎から電話があったよ。
There was a phone call from Jiro a little while ago!

sakkyoku 作曲 *composing music* [⇔**sakushi** 作詞]
- sakkyoku suru 作曲する *to compose music, to write music*
- sakkyoku-ka 作曲家 *composer*

sakú 柵 *fence*

saku 咲く *to bloom, to blossom*
　¶Haru ni wa hana ga takusan sakimasu.
春には花がたくさん咲きます。
In the spring many flowers bloom.
　¶Ringo no ki ni mō sugu hana ga saku deshō.
りんごの木にもうすぐ花が咲くでしょう。
The blossoms will probably also bloom on the apple trees soon.
　¶Sakura ga mankai ni saite iru yo.
桜が満開に咲いているよ。
The cherry blossoms are in full bloom!

sáku 裂く《*transitive*》 *to tear, to rip; to split*
　¶Moderu wa sono shashin o zutazuta ni saita yo.
モデルはその写真をずたずたに裂いたよ。
The model tore that photograph to pieces!

sáku 割く *to spare, to share*
- jikan o saku 時間を割く *to spare some time*

sakúban 昨晩 *last night* [→**sakuya** 昨夜]

sakubun 作文 ① (*school*)*composition,* (*school*)*essay*
　¶Kazoku ni tsuite sakubun o kakimasu.
家族について作文を書きます。
I will write a composition about my family.
　② *writing compositions*
- Ei-sakubun 英作文 *English composition*

sakuhin 作品 *a work, opus*
- bungaku-sakuhin 文学作品 *a literary work*

sakuin 索引 *index* 《*of a book, etc.*》
- sakuin-kādo 索引カード *index card*

sakújitsu 昨日 *yesterday* [→**kinō** 昨日]

sakúmotsu 作物 *crops*
- sakumotsu o sodateru 作物を育てる *to raise crops*

sakunen 昨年 *last year* [→**kyonen** 去年]

sakura 桜 ① *cherry blossom*
　¶Sakura wa ima mankai desu.
桜は今満開です。
The cherry blossoms are now in full bloom.
　② *cherry tree*
- sakura-nbo さくらんぼう *cherry* ((*fruit*))

sákuru サークル ① *circle, ring* [→**wa** 輪]
　② *circle, club, group with a common interest*

sákusha 作者 *author, writer* [→**chosha** 著者]

sakushi 作詞 *writing the words to a song, writing lyrics* [⇔**sakkyoku** 作曲]
　¶Dare ga kono uta no sakushi o shimashita ka.
だれがこの歌の作詞をしましたか。
Who wrote the words to this song?
- sakushi suru 作詞する *to write the words to a song*
- sakushi-ka 作詞家 *lyricist*

sakúya 昨夜 *last night*
　¶Chichi wa sakuya jū-ji ni kaette kimashita.

父は昨夜10時に帰って来ました。
My father came home at 10:00 last night.

-samá －様 【HON. for **-san** －さん】 《Roughly equivalent to *Mr./Ms.* and neutral with respect to sex and marital status, this suffix can be added to a surname alone, to a given name alone, to a full name, and to many occupational titles.》

samásu 冷ます *to cool, to lower in temperature*
¶Sūpu o chotto samashimashō.
スープをちょっと冷ましましょう。
Let's cool the soup a bit.

samásu 覚ます **me o～** 目を～ *to wake up* 《intransitive》
¶Rajio no oto de me o samashimashita.
ラジオの音で目を覚ましました。
I woke up because of the sound of the radio.

samatage 妨げ *obstruction, hindrance, obstacle* [→**jama** 邪魔]
¶Ihō-chūsha ga kōtsū no samatage ni natte imasu.
違法駐車が交通の妨げになっています。
Illegal parking is an obstruction to traffic.

samatagéru 妨げる *to disturb, to obstruct, to hinder*
¶Oji no ibiki ga minna no suimin o samatageta.
叔父のいびきがみんなの睡眠を妨げた。
Uncle's snoring disturbed everyone's sleep.

samayóu 彷徨う *to wander, to roam*

samázama 様々 **～na** ～な *various* [→**iroiro na** 色々な]
¶Kono mondai ni tsuite samazama na iken ga aru.
この問題についてさまざまな意見がある。
There are various opinions about this problem.

same 鮫 *shark*

saméru 冷める *to get cool, to get cold*
¶Miso-shiru ga samete shimatta yo.
みそ汁が冷めてしまったよ。
The miso soup has gotten cold!

¶Musume no ongaku ni taisuru netsu wa sameta rashii desu.
娘の音楽に対する熱は冷めたらしいです。
It seems that my daughter's passion for music has cooled.

saméru 覚める **me ga～** 目が～ *to wake up* 《intransitive》
¶Kesa no jishin de me ga samemashita.
けさの地震で目が覚めました。
I woke up because of this morning's earthquake.

sámitto サミット *summit conference* [→**shunō-kaidan** 首脳会談 (s.v. **kaidan** 会談)]

sámo-nai to さもないと *otherwise, or else*
¶Isoginasai. Samo-nai-to densha ni okureru yo.
急ぎなさい。さもないと電車に遅れるよ。
Hurry up. Otherwise you'll be late for the train!

samúi 寒い *cold* 《describing a low air temperature or how a person feels when the air temperature is low》 [⇔**atsui** 暑い]
¶Kyō wa totemo samui ne.
きょうはとても寒いね。
It's very cold today, isn't it.
¶Sētā o kinai to samuku naru yo.
セーターを着ないと寒くなるよ。
Unless you wear a sweater, you'll get cold!

samuké 寒け *chill, sensation of cold*
• samuke ga suru 寒けがする *to feel a chill*

samurai 侍 *samurai* [→**bushi** 武士]

sámusa 寒さ *cold, coldness* 《i.e., low air temperature》
¶Samusa de te ga kajikande iru yo.
寒さで手がかじかんでいるよ。
My hands are numb from the cold!

san 三 *three* 《see Appendix 2》
• San-gatsu 三月 *March*
• san-kan-ō 三冠王 *triple crown winner*

-san －さん《Roughly equivalent to *Mr./Ms.* and neutral with respect to sex and marital status, this suffix can be added to a surname alone, to a given name alone, to a full name, and to many occupational titles.》

sán 酸 *acid* [⇔**arukari** アルカリ]
• san-sei 酸性 *acidity*

sanagi 蛹 *chrysalis, pupa*

sánba 産婆 *midwife*

sanbika 賛美歌 *hymn*

sanbutsu 産物 *product; result*
• doryoku no sanbutsu 努力の産物 *the result of one's efforts*
• fuku-sanbutsu 副産物 *by-product*
• kai-sanbutsu 海産物 *marine product*
• nō-sanbutsu 農産物 *agricultural product*
• toku-sanbutsu 特産物 *special product*

sánchi 産地 *producing area*
¶Yamanashi-ken wa budō no sanchi to shite yūmei desu.
山梨県はぶどうの産地として有名です。
Yamanashi-ken is famous as a grape producing area.

sanchō 山頂 *mountaintop, mountain summit*

sandántobi 三段跳び *triple jump* ((athletic event))

sandaru サンダル *sandal*

sandoítchi サンドイッチ *sandwich*

Sangíin 参議院 *the House of Councilors* 《the upper house in the Japanese Diet》[⇔**Shūgiin** 衆議院]
• Sangiin-giin 参議院議員 *member of the House of Councilors*

sángo 珊瑚 *coral*
• sango-shō 珊瑚礁 *coral reef*

sangúrasu サングラス *sunglasses*

sangyō 産業 *industry*
• Sangyō-kakumei 産業革命 *the Industrial Revolution*

San'in-chíhō 山陰地方 *The San'in region of Japan* 《Tottori, Shimane, and northern Yamaguchi Prefectures》

sanka 参加 *participation, taking part*
• sanka suru 参加する *to participate, to take part*
¶Takusan no kuni ga Orinpikku ni sanka suru.

たくさんの国がオリンピックに参加する。
Many countries take part in the Olympics.
• sanka-sha 参加者 *participant*

sánkaku 三角 *triangle*
• sankaku-jōgi 三角定規 *drafting triangle*
• sankaku-kei 三角形 *triangle, triangular figure*
• sankaku-su 三角洲 *river delta*

sankan 参観 *observation visit*
• sankan suru 参観する *to visit and observe*
¶Fubo wa kinō jugyō o sankan shimashita.
父母はきのう授業を参観しました。
Parents observed yesterday's classes!
• sankan-bi 参観日 *visiting day*

sankō 参考 *reference, source of information*
¶Sankō no tame ni sono shinbun o okutte kudasai.
参考のためにその新聞を送ってください。
Please send me that newspaper for reference.
• sankō ni suru 参考にする *to refer to, to consult*
• sankō ni naru 参考になる *to be instructive, to be helpful*
¶Ani no iken wa itsu-mo sankō ni naru yo.
兄の意見はいつも参考になるよ。
My older brother's opinions are always helpful!
• sankō-sho 参考書 *reference book*

sankyaku 三脚 *tripod*

sanma 秋刀魚 *mackerel pike*

sanmyaku 山脈 *mountain range*
• Himaraya-sanmyaku ヒマラヤ山脈 *the Himalayas*

sanpo 散歩 *walk, stroll*
• sanpo suru 散歩する *to take a walk, to stroll*
¶Watashi-tachi wa chōshoku o tabete, kaigan o sanpo shita.
私たちは朝食を食べて、海岸を散歩した。
We ate breakfast and strolled along the

beach.

• sanpo ni iku 散歩に行く *to go for a walk*

• inu o sanpo saseru 犬を散歩させる *to walk a dog*

sánpuru サンプル *sample* [→**mihon** 見本]

sanrínsha 三輪車 *tricycle*

sánrui 三塁 *third base* [→**sādo** サード①] 《in baseball》

• sanrui-da 三塁打 *three-base hit, triple*

• sanrui-shu 三塁手 *third baseman* [→**sādo** サード②]

sansei 賛成 *agreement, approval* [⇔**hantai** 反対]

¶Watashi mo sono keikaku ni sansei desu.
私もその計画に賛成です。
I am also in favor of that plan.

• sansei suru 賛成する *to agree, to be in favor*

¶Sakai-sensei ni wa sansei dekimasen.
酒井先生には賛成できません。
I cannot agree with Dr. Sakai.

sanshin 三振 *strikeout* 《in baseball》

• sanshin suru 三振する *to strike out* 《intransitive》

• karaburi-sanshin 空振り三振 *swinging strikeout*

• minogashi-sanshin 見逃し三振 *looking strikeout*

sanshō 参照 *reference, comparison*

• sanshō suru 参照する *to refer to, to compare*

¶Kono hon o sanshō shite kudasai.
この本を参照してください。
Please refer to this book.

sanshóuo 山椒魚 *salamander*

sanshutsu 産出 *production, output*

• sanshutsu suru 産出する *to produce, to yield*

¶Ano kōzan wa takusan no sekitan o sanshutsu shimasu.
あの鉱山はたくさんの石炭を産出します。
That mine produces a lot of coal.

sánso 酸素 *oxygen*

sansū́ 算数 *arithmetic*

Santakurósu サンタクロース *Santa Claus*

San'yō–chíhō 山陽地方 *the San'yō region of Japan* 《Okayama, Hiroshima, and southern Yamaguchi Prefectures》

saó 竿 *pole, rod*

• tsuri-zao 釣り竿 *fishing pole, fishing rod*

sapótā サポーター *athletic supporter*

sappári さっぱり ① ~**suru** ~する *to become refreshed; to become relieved*

¶Shawā o abite, sappari shimashita.
シャワーを浴びて、さっぱりしました。
I took a shower and felt refreshed.

② ~**shita** ~した *frank, open-hearted*

¶Ani wa sappari shita seikaku desu.
兄はさっぱりした性格です。
My older brother has a frank personality.

③ ~**shita** ~した *plain-tasting*

¶Sappari shita tabemono no hō ga ii desu.
さっぱりした食べ物のほうがいいです。
Plain food would be better.

④ ~**shita** ~した *neat, tidy*

¶Masako-san wa sappari shita fukusō o shite iru.
正子さんはさっぱりした服装をしている。
Masako is neatly dressed.

⑤ 〈*not*〉 *at all* 《in combination with a negative verb》

¶Sono setsumei wa sappari wakaranai yo.
その説明はさっぱりわからないよ。
I don't understand that explanation at all!

sara 皿 *dish; plate*

¶Kyōko wa tēburu ni o-sara o narabeta.
京子はテーブルにお皿を並べた。
Kyoko set the plates on the table.

• -sara 皿《counter for helpings, courses; see Appendix 2》

• sara-arai 皿洗い *dishwashing*

saraburéddo サラブレッド *a thoroughbred*

sárada サラダ *salad*

• sarada-yu サラダ油 *salad oil*

• yasai-sarada 野菜サラダ *vegetable salad*

sára-ni さらに *additionally, still more, further*

¶Watashi-tachi wa sanchō made sara-ni ichi-jikan aruita.

私たちは山頂までさらに1時間歩いた。

We walked a further hour to the summit.

¶Sono mondai o sara-ni rongi shimashō.

その問題をさらに論議しましょう。

Let's discuss that problem further.

sararīman サラリーマン *white-collar worker, salaried worker*

sáron サロン ① *salon, drawing room* ② *art exhibit room*

sáru 猿 *monkey; ape*

¶Saru mo ki kara ochiru.

猿も木から落ちる。《*proverb*》

Everybody makes mistakes. 《*Literally: Even monkeys fall from trees.*》

sáru 去る ① *to leave, to go away from*

¶Kaneko-san wa Ōsaka o saru koto ni kimeta.

金子さんは大阪を去ることに決めた。

Ms. Kaneko decided to leave Osaka.

¶Saru mono wa hibi ni utoshi.

去る者は日々に疎し。《*proverb*》

Out of sight, out of mind. 《*Literally: A person who leaves is more unfamiliar day by day.*》

② *to pass, to disappear*

• arashi ga saru あらしが去る *a storm passes*

• itami ga saru 痛みが去る *pain disappears*

③ *to elapse, to go by*

• tsukihi ga saru 月日が去る *the days and months go by*

sasa 笹 *bamboo grass*

sasaeru 支える *to support*

¶Komatta toki ni kibō ga sasaete kuremashita.

困ったときに希望が支えてくれました。

Hope supported me when I was in trouble.

• tsue de karada o sasaeru つえで体を支える *to support oneself with a cane*

sasageru 捧げる *to offer up, to devote, to dedicate*

¶Kyurī-fujin wa kagaku ni isshō o sasageta.

キュリー夫人は科学に一生をささげた。

Madame Curie devoted her life to science.

• inori o sasageru 祈りをささげる *to offer a prayer*

sásai ささい 〜**na** 〜な *trivial, petty*

sasayáku 囁く *to whisper* [⇔**sakebu** 叫ぶ]

• A no mimi-moto de sasayaku Aの耳もとでささやく *to whisper in A's ear*

saseru させる《This word is simply the causative form of **suru** する.》 *to make do, to have do; to let do*

¶Azuma-sensei wa ichi-nen-sei ni taiiku-kan no sōji o saseta.

東先生は1年生に体育館の掃除をさせた。

Mr. Azuma had the first-year students clean the gymnasium.

sasetsu 左折 *left turn* [⇔**usetsu** 右折]

• sasetsu suru 左折する *to turn left*

sashiageru 差し上げる 【HUM. for **ageru** 上げる】 *to give*

sashidashinin 差し出し人 *sender* 《of a letter, etc.》

sashidasu 差し出す ① *to hold out, to present*

¶Akira-san wa watashi ni te o sashidashimashita.

明さんは私に手を差し出しました。

Akira held out his hand to me.

② *to hand in, to submit* [→**teishutsu suru** 提出する]

• gansho o sashidasu 願書を差し出す *to submit an application*

sashie 挿絵 *illustration* 《in a book, newspaper, etc.》

sashikomu 差し込む ① *to thrust into, to insert*

¶Sono kagi o jō ni sashikonde kudasai.

そのかぎを錠に差し込んでください。

Please insert that key into the lock.

② *to shine into* 《intransitive》

¶Yūhi ga daidokoro ni sashikomimasu.

夕日が台所に差し込みます。

The evening sun shines into the kitchen.

sashimí 刺身 *sashimi, sliced raw fish*

sáshizu 指図 (*verbal*)*instructions,* (*verbal*)*directions;* (*verbal*)*orders* [→**meirei** 命令]

¶Minna ga shushō no sashizu ni shitagaimashita.

みんなが主将の指図に従いました。

Everyone followed the captain's instructions.

¶Aitsu no sashizu wa ukenai yo.

あいつの指図は受けないよ。

I won't take that guy's orders!

• sashizu suru 指図する *to direct; to give orders to*

sasori 蠍 *scorpion*

sasou 誘う ① *to invite*

¶Yōko-san ga konsāto ni sasotte kureta.

洋子さんがコンサートに誘ってくれた。

Yoko invited me to a concert.

② *to induce, to provoke* 《*a person's response*》

• namida o sasou 涙を誘う *to provoke tears*

• dōjō o sasou 同情を誘う *to induce sympathy*

sássa-to さっさと *quickly, promptly*

¶Oka-san wa sassa-to arukimasu ne.

岡さんはさっさと歩きますね。

Ms. Oka walks quickly, doesn't she.

¶Ame ga yanda kara, sassa-to kaerinasai.

雨がやんだから、さっさと帰りなさい。

It's stopped raining, so hurry home.

sásshi サッシ (*window*)*sash*

sassoku 早速 *at once, right away*

¶Sassoku Etsuko-san ni ai ni ikō.

早速悦子さんに会いに行こう。

Let's go to see Etsuko at once.

• sassoku no 早速の *prompt, immediate*

sásu 刺す ① *to prick, to stick, to stab*

¶Haha wa hari de yubi o sashimashita.

母は針で指を刺しました。

My mother pricked her finger with a needle.

② *to bite, to sting* 《*when the subject is an insect, etc.*》《*Ordinarily used in the passive.*》

¶Watashi-tachi wa hidoku ka ni sasareta yo.

私たちはひどく蚊に刺されたよ。

We were badly bitten by mosquitoes!

sásu 指す ① *to point at, to point to*

¶Gaido-san wa oka no ue no o-shiro o sashimashita.

ガイドさんは丘の上のお城を指しました。

The guide pointed to a castle on the hill.

② *to designate, to call on*

¶Tajima-sensei wa yoku Imai-kun o sasu ne.

田島先生はよく今井君を指すね。

Ms. Tajima often calls on Imai, doesn't she.

• A no na o sasu Aの名を指す *to call A's name*

sásu 差す ① *to pour, to let drip, to apply*

• megusuri o sasu 目薬を差す *to apply eye drops*

• kikai ni abura o sasu 機械に油を差す *to oil a machine*

② 《*intransitive*》 *to shine into; to shine on*

¶Kyōshitsu ni hi ga sashite imasu.

教室に日が差しています。

The sun is shining into the classroom.

③ **kasa o~** 傘を~ *to put an umbrella over one's head*

sasuga さすが ① (**~ni** ~に) *just as one would expect, exactly as one has heard, indeed* [→**yahari** やはり]

¶Sasuga Takahashi-san wa jōzu desu.

さすが高橋さんは上手です。

Just as one would expect, Ms. Takahashi is skillful.

② **~no** ~の *highly-reputed* 《Used only in the following pattern.》

• sasuga no A mo さすがのAも *even (the highly-reputed)A*

¶Sasuga no eiyū mo yaburemashita.

さすがの英雄も敗れました。

Even the hero was defeated.

sásupensu サスペンス *suspense*

satchūzai 殺虫剤 *insecticide*

sáte さて *now, well* 《an interjection indicating a shift in what is being talked about》

¶Sate, dō shimashō.

さて、どうしましょう。

Now, what shall we do?

¶Sate, mō kaeru jikan ni narimashita.

さて、もう帰る時間になりました。

Well, it's already time to leave.

satō 砂糖 *sugar*

¶Kōcha ni wa satō o nan-bai iremashō ka.

紅茶には砂糖を何杯入れましょうか。

How many spoonfuls of sugar shall I put in your tea?

• kaku-zatō 角砂糖 *sugar cube*

• kōri-zatō 氷砂糖 *sugar candy, rock candy*

sato 里 ① *village, hamlet* [→**mura** 村]

② *birthplace, hometown* [→**kokyō** 故郷]

③ *original family home* 《*of a wife, adopted child, etc.*》

satoimo 里芋 *taro*

satsu 札 <US> <dollar> *bill,* <UK>*bank note, note*

• satsu-ire 札入れ *wallet, billfold*

• satsu-taba 札束 *roll of bills*

• sen-en-satsu 千円札 *thousand-yenbill*

-**satsu** 一冊 《*counter for books, magazines, etc.; see Appendix 2*》

¶Sono hon ga ni-satsu hitsuyō desu.

その本が2冊必要です。

I need two copies of that book.

¶Ani wa hon o sanbyaku-satsu-gurai motte iru yo.

兄は本を300冊ぐらい持っているよ。

My older brother has about 300 books!

satsuei 撮影 *photographing, picture-taking; filming, shooting*

• satsuei suru 撮影する *to take a picture of, to photograph; to film, to shoot*

¶Kono eiga wa Pari de satsuei shimashō.

この映画はパリで撮影しましょう。

Let's shoot this movie in Paris.

¶Satsuei kinshi

「撮影禁止」《*on a sign*》

No Photographs

• satsuei-jo 撮影所 *movie studio*

satsujin 殺人 *murder*

• satsujin-jiken 殺人事件 *a murder*

satsumaimo 薩摩芋 *sweet potato*

sattō 殺到 ～**suru** ～する *to rush, to stampede, to throng, to flood*

¶Sono atarashii jisho ni chūmon ga sattō shite imasu.

その新しい辞書に注文が殺到しています。

Orders for that new dictionary are pouring in.

¶Kodomo-tachi wa mise ni sattō shimashita.

子供たちは店に殺到しました。

The children rushed into the store.

sausúpō サウスポー *a southpaw*

sawá 沢 ① *marsh*

② *stream in mountain ravine*

sawagashíi 騒がしい *noisy, boisterous*

¶Kōen wa sawagashii kodomo-tachi de ippai desu.

公園は騒がしい子供たちでいっぱいです。

The park is full of noisy children!

sáwagi 騒ぎ ① *din, racket, noise*

② *clamor, uproar, commotion*

• sawagi o okosu 騒ぎを起こす *to raise a clamor, to cause a commotion*

• ō-sawagi 大騒ぎ *great racket; great uproar*

sawágu 騒ぐ ① *to make noise, to make a racket*

¶Tosho-kan no naka de sonna ni sawaide wa ikenai.

図書館の中でそんなに騒いではいけない。

You mustn't make so much noise in the library.

② *to make a fuss, to make a clamor*

sawaru 触る ① *to put one's hand, to place one's hand in contact*

¶Keiko-chan wa watashi no ude ni sawatta.

恵子ちゃんは私の腕に触った。

Keiko put her hand on my arm.

② *to touch with one's hand, to feel*

¶Akachan wa okāsan no hana o sawatte imasu.

赤ちゃんはお母さんの鼻を触っています。

The baby is touching her mother's nose.
   ③ *to touch, to come into contact*
 《*when the subject is inanimate*》
 ¶Senaka ni nani-ka ga sawatta yo.
背中に何かが触ったよ。
Something touched my back!

sawáyaka 爽やか ～**na** ～な *fresh, refreshing*
 ¶Asa no kūki wa sawayaka desu ne.
朝の空気はさわやかですね。
The morning air is refreshing, isn't it.
 ¶Oyoidara kibun ga sawayaka ni narimashita.
泳いだら気分がさわやかになりました。
I felt refreshed after swimming.

sáyō 作用 *action, effect*
 • sayō suru 作用する *to produce an effect*
 • fuku-sayō 副作用 *side effect*
 • han-sayō 反作用 *reaction*

sáyoku 左翼 [[⇔**uyoku** 右翼]]
   ① (*political*)*left wing*
   ② *left field* 《*in baseball*》 [→**refuto**
レフト①]
 • sayoku-shu 左翼手 *left fielder* [→
refuto レフト②]

sayōnára さようなら [☞**sayonara**
さよなら]

sayonára さよなら *good-by*
 • sayonara o iu さよならを言う *to say
good-by*
 ¶Ano hito wa sayonara mo iwanakatta.
あの人はさよならも言わなかった。
*That person didn't even saying
good-by.*

sáyū 左右 *the right and the left*
 ¶Sayū o yoku mite kara dōro o
watarinasai.
左右をよく見てから道路を渡りなさい。
*After looking carefully left and right,
cross the street.*

sázae 栄螺 *turbo* ((*shellfish*))
sazanami さざ波 *ripple, small wave*
sazánka 山茶花 *sasanqua* ((*flower*))
sé 背 ① *back* 《*of the body*》 [→**senaka**
背中]
 ¶Keiko-san wa ano hito ni se o mukemashita.

恵子さんはあの人に背を向けました。
Keiko turned her back on that person.
 • isu no se いすの背 *chair back*
 • yama no se 山の背 *mountain ridge*
   ② *height, stature* [→**shinchō** 身長]
 ¶Se wa dono kurai desu ka.
背はどのくらいですか。
About how tall are you? 《*Literally:
About what is your height?*》
 ¶Imōto wa zuibun se ga nobimashita yo.
妹はずいぶん背が伸びましたよ。
My younger sister has grown quite tall!
 • se ga takai 〔hikui〕背が高い〔低い〕
to be tall 〔*short*〕
 • se-bangō 背番号 *number on the back
of a player's shirt*

sebiro 背広 (*business*)*suit*
sebone 背骨 *backbone*
sédai 世代 *a generation*
 • sedai no danzetsu 世代の断絶 *generation gap*
 • wakai sedai 若い世代 *the younger generation*

séfu セーフ ～**no** ～の *safe* 《*in baseball*》
[⇔**auto no** アウトの]
 ¶Rannā wa sanrui de sēfu ni natta.
ランナーは三塁でセーフになった。
The runner was safe at third.

séi 姓 *surname* [→**myōji** 名字]
séi 性 ① *sexuality*
   ② *sex* 《*i.e, male or female*》 [→**seibetsu**
性別]
 • sei-teki na 性的な *sexual*
 • sei-kyōiku 性教育 *sex education*

séi 背 *height, stature* [→**se** 背②]
séi 所為 *fault, cause for blame*
 ¶Sore wa watashi no sei ja nai yo.
それは私のせいじゃないよ。
That's not my fault!
 • A o B no sei ni suru AをBのせいにす
る *to blame B for A*
 ¶Otōto wa jibun no ayamari o watashi
no sei ni shimashita.
弟は自分の誤りを私のせいにしました。
*My younger brother blamed me for his
own mistake.*
 • A no sei de Aのせいで *because of A*

《when A is blamed》

¶Yuki no sei de ressha no daiya ga midaremashita.

雪のせいで列車のダイヤが乱れました。

Because of the snow, the train schedule became disrupted.

-sei －製 ① *made in* 《Added to noun bases denoting places.》

¶Doitsu-sei no kuruma wa ninki ga arimasu.

ドイツ製の車は人気があります。

German cars are popular.

¶Kono kamera wa Nihon-sei desu.

このカメラは日本製です。

This camera is Japanese-made.

② *made of* 《Added to noun bases denoting materials.》

• kōtetsu-sei no 鋼鉄製の *made of steel*

-sei －生 *student, pupil* 《Added to noun bases.》

¶Watashi wa kōritsu-chūgaku no ni-nen-sei desu.

私は公立中学の2年生です。

I am a second-year student at a public junior high school.

• daigaku-sei 大学生 *college student*

• daigaku-in-sei 大学院生 *graduate student*

• ichi-nen-sei 1年生 *first-year student*

• kōkō-sei 高校生 *high-school student*

seibetsu 性別 *sex* 《i.e, male or female》

séibi 整備 *repair, maintenance*

¶Ani no baiku wa seibi ga yuki-todoite imasu.

兄のバイクは整備が行き届いています。

My older brother's motorcycle is in good repair.

• seibi suru 整備する *to repair, to put in good condition*

¶Chichi wa kuruma o seibi shite moraimashita.

父は車を整備してもらいました。

My father had his car repaired.

• seibi-shi 整備士 *repairman; mechanic*

seibō 制帽 *regulation cap; school cap*

seibo 歳暮 ① *end of the year* [→ **nen-matsu** 年末 (s.v. **nen** 年)]

② *year-end gift*

séibu 西部 *the western part* [⇔**tōbu** 東部]

• Seibu-geki 西部劇 a *Western* (*drama*)

séibutsu 生物 *living thing*

¶Tsuki ni wa seibutsu ga imasu ka.

月には生物がいますか。

Are there living things on the moon?

• seibutsu-gaku 生物学 (*the study of*) *biology*

• seibutsu-gaku-sha 生物学者 *biologist*

seibyō 性病 *venereal disease*

seichō 生長 *growth* 《especially of plants》

¶Zassō wa seichō ga hayai desu ne.

雑草は生長が早いですね。

Weeds grow quickly, don't they. 《Literally: *As for weeds, growth is fast, isn't it.*》

• seichō suru 生長する *to grow*

seichō 成長 *growth* 《especially of animals》

• seichō suru 成長する *to grow*

¶Kuriyama-san wa chiteki na josei ni seichō shimashita.

栗山さんは知的な女性に成長しました。

Ms. Kuriyama has grown into an intellectual woman.

• keizai-seichō 経済成長 *economic growth*

seidai 盛大 ～**na** ～な *grand, splendid*

¶Seidai na kangei-kai o hirakimashita.

盛大な歓迎会を開きました。

We held a grand welcome party.

seidénki 静電気 *static electricity*

séido 制度 *system*

¶Kono gakkō ni wa shōgaku-kin no seido ga arimasu.

この学校には奨学金の制度があります。

At this school there is a scholarship system.

• shakai-seido 社会制度 *social system*

seidō 青銅 *bronze*

• Seidōki-jidai 青銅器時代 *the Bronze Age*

seien 声援 *cheering, shout of encouragement*

• seien suru 声援する *to cheer on, to shout encouragement to*

¶Jimoto no yakyū-chīmu o seien shi-masu.

地元の野球チームを声援します。

We cheer on the local baseball team.

séifu 政府 *the government*

• Nihon-seifu 日本政府 *the Japanese Government*

seifuku 制服 *a uniform* 《This word is typically used for school or company uniforms, but not for athletic uniforms.》

¶Yūbin-shūhai-nin wa nōkon no seifuku o kite imasu.

郵便集配人は濃紺の制服を着ています。

Mail carriers wear dark blue uniforms.

¶Ano seifuku o kita keikan ni tazune-mashō.

あの制服を着た警官に尋ねましょう。

Let's ask that uniformed police officer.

¶Kono gakkō no seifuku wa kakkō ga warui ne.

この学校の制服は格好が悪いね。

This school uniform is ugly, isn't it.

seifuku 征服 *conquest*

• seifuku suru 征服する *to conquer*

• seifuku-sha 征服者 *conqueror*

seigén 制限 *limit, restriction*

• seigen suru 制限する *to limit, to restrict*

¶Kotae wa hyaku-go ni seigen sarete imasu.

答えは100語に制限されています。

The answer is restricted to 100 words.

• seigen-jikan 制限時間 *restricted hours; time limit*

• seigen-sokudo 制限速度 *speed limit*

• jūryō-seigen 重量制限 *weight limit*

• nenrei-seigen 年齢制限 *age limit*

séigi 正義 *justice, righteousness*

¶Ano undō-ka wa seigi no tame ni tata-katte imasu.

あの運動家は正義のために戦っています。

That activist is fighting for justice.

• seigi-kan 正義感 *sense of justice*

seihántai 正反対 *the exact opposite*

seihin 製品 (*manufactured*)*product*

¶Kono kaisha no seihin wa hyōban ga ii desu.

この会社の製品は評判がいいです。

This company's products have a good reputation.

• gaikoku-seihin 外国製品 *foreign products*

• kōgyō-seihin 工業製品 *industrial products*

• shin-seihin 新製品 *new product*

seihókei 正方形 *a square* ((geometrical shape))

¶Kore wa ip-pen ga go-senchi no seihō-kei desu.

これは1辺が5センチの正方形です。

This is a square with sides of 5 centimeters.

seihoku 西北 *the northwest* [→**hokusei** 北西]

séii 誠意 *sincerity*

¶Daitōryō no seii o shinjimasu.

大統領の誠意を信じます。

I believe in the president's sincerity.

• seii no aru hito 誠意のある人 *sincere person*

• seii o motte 誠意をもって *sincerely, with sincerity*

¶Isha wa seii o motte kanja ni hanashima-shita.

医者は誠意をもって患者に話しました。

The doctor spoke sincerely to the patient.

seiíppai 精一杯 *as hard as one can, as best one can*

¶Seiippai benkyō shimasu.

精いっぱい勉強します。

I study as hard as I can.

¶Seiippai yarinasai.

精いっぱいやりなさい。

Do it as best you can.

seiji 政治 *politics, government*

¶Oji wa seiji ni kyōmi ga arimasu.

伯父は政治に興味があります。

My uncle is interested in politics.

• seiji-gaku 政治学 *political science*

• seiji-ka 政治家 *statesman, politician*

• minshu-seiji 民主政治 *democratic government*

seijin 成人 *adult* (*person*) [→**otona** 大人]

• seijin suru 成人する *to grow up, to*

reach adulthood

¶Uehara-san wa seijin shita musume-san mo imasu.

上原さんは成人した娘さんもいます。

Mr. Uehara also has a grown-up daughter.

• Seijin no hi 成人の日 *Coming-of-Age Day* 《a Japanese national holiday on January 15》

• seijin-muki no 成人向きの *intended for adults*

• seijin-shiki 成人式 *coming-of-age ceremony* 《Held on January 15th for people who have turned 20 during the preceding year.》

séijin 聖人 *saint*

seijitsu 誠実 〜**na** 〜な *sincere, faithful, honest*

¶Kyōko-san wa seijitsu na hito desu.

京子さんは誠実な人です。

Kyoko is a sincere person.

seijō 正常 〜**na** 〜な *normal* [⇔**ijō na** 異常な]

¶Musuko no taion wa yatto seijō ni modorimashita.

息子の体温はやっと正常に戻りました。

My son's temperature finally returned to normal.

Seijōki 星条旗 *the Stars and Stripes, the American flag*

seikai 正解 *correct answer*

¶Tsukamoto-san no kotae ga seikai desu yo.

塚本さんの答えが正解ですよ。

Mr. Tsukamoto's reply is the correct answer!

seikai 政界 *the political world, political circles*

seikaku 正確 〜**na** 〜な *correct, exact, accurate*

¶Seikaku na jikan o oshiete kuremasen ka.

正確な時間を教えてくれませんか。

Will you tell me the correct time?

¶Kono hōkokusho wa seikaku desu.

この報告書は正確です。

This report is accurate.

seikaku 性格 *character, personality, disposition*

¶Sono kyōdai wa seikaku ga zenzen chigau ne.

その兄弟は性格が全然違うね。

The personalities of those brothers are entirely different, aren't they.

¶Ani wa akarui seikaku desu.

兄は明るい性格です。

My older brother has a cheerful disposition.

seikatsu 生活 *life, living, livelihood*

¶Ano ryūgaku-sei wa shisso na seikatsu o okutte imasu.

あの留学生は質素な生活を送っています。

That foreign student is leading a simple life.

• seikatsu suru 生活する *to live, to lead a life, to make a living* [→**kurasu** 暮らす]

¶Oba wa Eigo o oshiete seikatsu shite imasu.

叔母は英語を教えて生活しています。

My aunt makes her living by teaching English.

• seikatsu-hi 生活費 *cost of living, living expenses*

• seikatsu-suijun 生活水準 *standard of living*

• gakkō-seikatsu 学校生活 *school life*

• katei-seikatsu 家庭生活 *home life*

• nichijō-seikatsu 日常生活 *everyday life, daily life*

• tokai-seikatsu 都会生活 *city life*

seikeigéka 整形外科 *plastic surgery*

seiketsu 清潔 〜**na** 〜な *clean, pure* [⇔**fuketsu na** 不潔な]

¶Seiketsu na taoru o tsukatte kudasai.

清潔なタオルを使ってください。

Please use a clean towel.

¶Te o seiketsu ni shite okanakereba ikemasen.

手を清潔にしておかなければいけません。

You must keep your hands clean.

séiki 世紀 *century*

• -seiki 一世紀《counter for centuries; see Appendix 2》

¶Nijūis-seiki wa nan-nen kara

hajimarimasu ka.

21世紀は何年から始まりますか。

From what year does the twenty-first century begin?

seikō 成功 *success* [⇔**shippai** 失敗]

¶Go-seikō o o-inori shimasu.

ご成功をお祈りします。

I wish you success.

¶Shippai wa seikō no moto.

失敗は成功のもと。《proverb》

Failure is but a stepping stone to success.《*Literally: Failure is the basis of success.*》

• seikō suru 成功する *to succeed*

¶Ani wa tsui ni shigoto o mitsukeru no ni seikō shita.

兄はついに仕事を見つけるのに成功した。

At last my older brother has succeeded in finding a job.

• dai-seikō 大成功 *great success*

¶Sono konsāto wa dai-seikō datta yo.

そのコンサートは大成功だったよ。

That concert was a great success!

seikyū 請求 *request; demand*

• seikyū suru 請求する *to ask for, to request; to demand*

¶Tēpu no daikin to shite sen-en o seikyū shimasu.

テープの代金として1000円を請求します。

We request 1,000 yen as the tape fee.

• seikyū-sho 請求書 *bill (to pay)*

séimei 生命 *life, animate existence* [→**inochi** 命]

¶Chichi oya wa seimei no kiken o okashite musume o sukutta.

父親は生命の危険を冒して娘を救った。

The father braved the danger to his life and saved his daughter.

¶Kanja no seimei wa kiken na jōtai ni arimasu.

患者の生命は危険な状態にあります。

The patient's life is in a critical condition.

• seimei-hoken 生命保険 *life insurance*

seimei 声明 *public statement*

• seimei o dasu 声明を出す *to make a public statement*

• kyōdō-seimei 共同声明 *joint statement*

séimei 姓名 *full name* [→**namae** 名前]

seimitsu 精密 ~**na** ~な *precise, detailed, minute*

¶Unten-shu wa seimitsu na chizu o hitsuyō to shite imasu.

運転手は精密な地図を必要としています。

The driver needs a detailed map.

• seimitsu-kensa 精密検査 *close medical examination*

• seimitsu-kikai 精密機械 *precision machine*

seinan 西南 *the southwest* [→**nansei** 南西]

seinen 青年 *young adult, a youth*《Typically used to refer to a young man.》

¶Akira-san wa zento-yūbō na seinen desu.

明さんは前途有望な青年です。

Akira is a promising young man.

• seinen-jidai 青年時代 *one's youth, one's young days*

¶Sono gaka wa seinen-jidai o Pari de sugoshita.

その画家は青年時代をパリで過ごした。

That painter spent his youth in Paris.

seinengáppi 生年月日 *date of birth*

seinō 性能 *capacity, ability*

• seinō no ii kikai 性能のいい機械 *efficient machine*

Seiō 西欧 *Western Europe* [⇔**Tōō** 東欧]

Seireki 西暦 *the Western calendar*《Typically used to mark years as A. D. by the Gregorian calendar.》[→**kigen** 紀元]

¶Kono shiro wa Seireki happyaku-gojū-nen ni tateraremashita.

この城は西暦850年に建てられました。

This castle was built in 850 A.D.

seiretsu 整列 ~**suru** ~する *to line up in orderly fashion, to form an orderly line*

¶Watashi-tachi wa yon-retsu ni seiretsu shimashita.

私たちは4列に整列しました。

We lined up in four lines.

séiri 整理 *putting in order, arranging;*

adjustment

• seiri suru 整理する *to put in order, to arrange; to rearrange, to adjust*

¶Tana no ue no hon o seiri shimashō.

棚の上の本を整理しましょう。

Let's rearrange the books that are on the shelf.

¶Mi-no-mawari no mono o seiri shite kudasai.

身の回りの物を整理してください。

Please put your belongings in order.

• seiri-bangō 整理番号 *reference number*

• seiri-ken 整理券 *numbered ticket*

• kōtsū-seiri 交通整理 *traffic control*

séiri 生理 ① *physiology* «*of an organism*»

② *mensuration* [→**gekkei** 月経, **mensu** メンス]

• seiri-gaku 生理学 (*the study of*)*physiology*

seiritsu 成立 *coming into existence, formation, completion*

• seiritsu suru 成立する *to come into existence, to be formed, to be completed*

seiryōínryō 清涼飲料 *soft drink*

séiryoku 勢力 *power, influence*

¶Taifū no seiryoku wa myōchō sukoshi yowamaru deshō.

台風の勢力は明朝少し弱まるでしょう。

The power of the typhoon will probably weaken a little tomorrow morning.

• seiryoku no aru hito 勢力のある人 *influential person*

• seiryoku-arasoi 勢力争い *power struggle*

séiryoku 精力 *energy, vigor, vitality*

¶Kōho-sha wa senkyo ni seiryoku o katamukemashita.

候補者は選挙に精力を傾けました。

The candidate applied his energy to the election.

• seiryoku-teki na 精力的な *energetic, vigorous*

seisaku 政策 (*government*)*policy*

seisaku 制作 (*artistic*)*production*

• seisaku suru 制作する *to make, to produce*

¶Ōku no terebi-dorama o seisaku shite imasu yo.

多くのテレビドラマを制作していますよ。

We produce many TV dramas!

• seisaku-sha 制作者 〈*movie*〉 *producer* [→**purodyūsā** プロデューサー]

seisaku 製作 *manufacturing, production* [→**seizō** 製造]

• seisaku suru 製作する *to make, to manufacture*

¶Kono kikai wa Amerika de seisaku saremashita.

この機械はアメリカで製作されました。

This machine was manufactured in America.

• seisaku-sha 製作者 *manufacturer* [→**mēkā** メーカー]; 〈*movie*〉 *producer* [→**purodyūsā** プロデューサー]

• seisaku-jo 製作所 *factory, manufacturing plant*

seisan 生産 *production, producing* [⇔**shōhi** 消費]

¶Kamera no seisan wa nobite imasu.

カメラの生産は伸びています。

The production of cameras is increasing.

• seisan suru 生産する *to make, to produce*

¶Kono kōjō wa nani o seisan shite iru no desu ka.

この工場は何を生産しているのですか。

What does this factory produce?

• seisan-butsu 生産物 *product*

• seisan-daka 生産高 *output*

• seisan-sha 生産者 *producer*

• kokumin-sō-seisan 国民総生産 *gross national product*

• tairyō-seisan 大量生産 *mass production*

seiseidōdō 正々堂々 (～**to** ～と) *fairly, in aboveboard fashion*

¶Seiseidōdō to shōbu shimashō.

正々堂々と勝負しましょう。

Let's compete fairly.

seiseki 成績 (*achieved*) *result, showing, performance*; (*school*)*mark*, <*US*>(*school*)*grade*

¶Kongetsu no eigyō no seiseki wa yoku

arimasen.

今月の営業の成績はよくありません。

This month's sales figures are not good.

¶Nagata-kun wa Eigo de ii seiseki o totta yo.

長田君は英語でいい成績をとったよ。

Nagata got a good grade in English!

¶Tomoko-chan no ongaku no seiseki wa go da yo.

友子ちゃんの音楽の成績は5だよ。

Tomoko's grade in music is an A!

《Many Japanese schools use a 1-5 grading scale with 5 being the highest.》

• seiseki-hyō 成績表 *report card*

seishiki 正式 ～**na**／**no** ～な／の *formal, official*

¶Yumi ni seishiki ni kekkon o mōshikonda yo.

由美に正式に結婚を申し込んだよ。

I formally proposed marriage to Yumi.

séishin 精神 [[⇔**nikutai** 肉体]] *spirit, soul; mind*

¶Fukumoto-san wa kagaku-teki na seishin no mochinushi desu.

福本さんは科学的な精神の持ち主です。

Ms. Fukumoto has a scientific mind.

¶Seishin ittō nanigoto-ka narazaran.

精神一到何事か成らざらん。《proverb》

Where there is a will, there is a way.

《Literally: With the spirit concentrated, something is bound to come of it.》

• seishin-byō 精神病 *mental illness*

• seishin-nenrei 精神年齢 *mental age*

• seishin-ryoku 精神力 *mental power*

• seishin-teki na 精神的な *spiritual* [⇔**busshitsu-teki na** 物質的な]*; mental*

seishitsu 性質 *nature, character, quality, property*

¶Gomu no motsu seishitsu no hitotsu wa dansei desu.

ゴムのもつ性質のひとつは弾性です。

One of the properties of rubber is elasticity.

• seishitsu no yoi hito 性質のよい人 *good-natured person*

Seisho 聖書 *the Bible*

• Kyūyaku-seisho 旧約聖書 *the Old Testament*

• Shin'yaku-seisho 新約聖書 *the New Testament*

seishun 青春 *youth, adolescence*

¶Seishun wa ni-do to konai yo.

青春は二度と来ないよ。

Youth will never come again!

• seishun-jidai 青春時代 *one's youth*

¶Chichi wa seishun-jidai o Kyōto de sugoshimashita.

父は青春時代を京都で過ごしました。

My father spent his youth in Kyoto.

seitai 声帯 *vocal cords*

seiteki 静的 ～**na** ～な *static, stationary* [⇔**dōteki na** 動的な]

seiten 晴天 *fair weather*

¶Honjitsu wa seiten nari.

本日は晴天なり。

Today is fair weather. 《This archaic sentence is used to test whether a microphone is turned on.》

séito 生徒 *student, pupil* [⇔**sensei** 先生]

¶Sono kurasu ni wa nan-nin no seito ga imasu ka.

そのクラスには何人の生徒がいますか。

How many students are there in that class?

• seito-kai 生徒会 *student council, students' association*

• seito-taikai 生徒大会 *students' meeting*

seitō 正当 ～**na** ～な *just, right, fair*

• seitō-bōei 正当防衛 *self-defense*

• seitō-ka 正当化 *justification*

• seitō-ka suru 正当化する *to justify*

seitō 政党 *political party*

¶Beikoku ni wa ōki na seitō ga futatsu arimasu.

米国には大きな政党が二つあります。

In the United States there are two major political parties.

• seitō-naikaku 政党内閣 *party cabinet*

• seitō-seiji 政党政治 *party government*

• hoshu-seitō 保守政党 *a conservative party*

• kakushin-seitō 革新政党 *a progressive party*

seiton 整頓 *putting in order* [→**seiri** 整理]

- seiton suru 整とんする *to put in order*

¶Heya o seiton shite okinasai.

部屋を整とんしておきなさい。

Keep your room in order.

Séiyō 西洋 *the West* [⇔**Tōyō** 東洋];

Europe [→**Yōroppa** ヨーロッパ]

- Seiyō-bunmei 西洋文明 *Western civilization; European civilization*
- Seiyō-jin 西洋人 *a Westerner; a European*

seiyō 静養 *rest; recuperation*

- seiyō suru 静養する *to rest quietly; to recuperate*

¶Isha wa kanja ni is-shūkan seiyō suru yō susumeta.

医者は患者に1週間静養するよう勧めた。

The doctor advised the patient to rest quietly for a week.

seiza 星座 *constellation*

seiza 正座 *to sit ceremonially on one's knees* 《This way of sitting, with the buttocks resting on the heels, is the formal posture for sitting on the floor in Japan.》

- seiza suru 正座する *to sit ceremonially*

séizei 精々 ① *at most, at best* [→**takadaka** 高々]

② *as hard as one can, as best one can* [→**seiippai** 精一杯]

seizō 製造 *manufacturing, production* [→**seisaku** 製作]

- seizō suru 製造する *to manufacture, to make*

seizon 生存 *being alive, existence*

¶Mizu wa seizon no tame ni hitsuyō desu.

水は生存のために必要です。

Water is necessary for existence.

- seizon suru 生存する *to exist, to live; to survive* [→**ikinokoru** 生き残る]
- seizon-kyōsō 生存競争 *the struggle for existence*
- seizon-sha 生存者 *survivor*

seizu 製図 *drafting, mechanical drawing*

sékai 世界 *world*

¶Pari wa sekai de mottomo utsukushii toshi no hitotsu desu.

パリは世界で最も美しい都市の一つです。

Paris is one of the world's most beautiful cities.

¶Yuasa-san wa sugureta pianisuto to shite sekai ni shirarete imasu.

湯浅さんはすぐれたピアニストとして世界に知られています。

Ms. Yuasa is known to the world as a great pianist.

- kodomo no sekai 子供の世界 *the world of children*
- yume no sekai 夢の世界 *the world of dreams*
- Sekai-ginkō 世界銀行 *The World Bank*
- sekai-heiwa 世界平和 *world peace*
- sekai-ichi no 世界一の *the best in the world*
- sekai-isshū-ryokō 世界一周旅行 *round-the-world trip*
- sekai-kiroku 世界記録 *world record*
- sekai-senshu-ken-taikai 世界選手権大会 *world championship* (*althletic event*)
- sekai-shi 世界史 *world history*
- sekai-taisen 世界大戦 *world war*

sekando セカンド ① *second base* [→**nirui** 二塁]

② *second baseman* [→**nirui-shu** 二塁手 (s.v. **nirui** 二塁)] 《*in baseball*》

séken 世間 *the world, the way the world is, society, people*

¶Imōto wa seken o amari shirimasen.

妹は世間をあまり知りません。

My younger sister doesn't know much about the world.

¶Ano seinen wa seken ni tsūjite imasu.

あの青年は世間に通じています。

That young man knows a lot about the world.

¶Tarō wa seken ga nani o itte mo ki ni shinai.

太郎は世間が何を言っても気にしない。

Taro isn't bothered by anything people say.

- seken-banashi 世間話 *gossip; small talk*

• seken-shirazu 世間知らず *knowing little of the ways of the world; person who knows little of the the ways of the world*

• seken-tei 世間体 *appearances, one's public reputation*

sekí 咳 *cough*

¶Sensei no seki ga hidoi desu ne.
先生のせきがひどいですね。
The teacher's cough is terrible, isn't it.

• seki o suru せきをする *to cough*

• seki-barai 咳払い *clearing one's throat*

• seki-barai o suru せきばらいをする *to clear one's throat*

• seki-dome 咳止め *cough suppresant*

séki 席 *seat, place to sit*

¶Kono seki ni suwatte mo yoroshii desu ka.
この席に座ってもよろしいですか。
May I sit in this seat?

¶Seki wa zenbu fusagatte imasu.
席は全部ふさがっています。
The seats are all occupied.

¶O-toshiyori ni seki o yuzuru yō ni shinasai.
お年寄りに席を譲るようにしなさい。
Make sure to give your seat to elderly people.

¶Yamamoto-san wa seki o machigaeta yō desu.
山本さんは席をまちがえたようです。
It appears that Mr. Yamamoto took the wrong seat.

• seki ni tsuku 席に着く *to take one's seat*

• seki o tatsu 席を立つ *to leave one's seat*

• shitei-seki 指定席 *reserved seat*

sekidō 赤道 *the equator*

sekigaisen 赤外線 *infrared rays*

sekihan 赤飯 *rice with red beans* 《Traditionally made to celebrate a happy occasion.》

Sekijūji 赤十字 *the Red Cross*

• Sekijūji-byōin 赤十字病院 *Red Cross hospital*

sekinin 責任 *responsibility*

¶Shachō ga sono shippai no sekinin o torimashita.
社長がその失敗の責任を取りました。
The company president took responsibility for that failure.

• sekinin no aru chii 責任のある地位 *a position with responsibility*

• sekinin-kan 責任感 *sense of responsibility*

¶Shimazaki-san wa sekinin-kan ga tsuyoi desu.
島崎さんは責任感が強いです。
Ms. Shimazaki's sense of responsibility is strong.

• sekinin-sha 責任者 *person in charge*

sekitán 石炭 *coal*

¶Koko de wa sekitan o taite heya o atatamemasu.
ここでは石炭をたいて部屋を暖めます。
Here they burn coal and warm the rooms.

sekiyu 石油 *petroleum, oil; kerosene* [→**tōyu** 灯油]

• sekiyu-gaisha 石油会社 *oil company*

• sekiyu-sutōbu 石油ストーブ *kerosene heater*

sékai 石灰 *lime* ((substance))

sekkaku 折角 *fruitlessly taking special trouble*

¶Haha ga sekkaku tsukutta ryōri mo muda ni natta.
母がせっかく作った料理も無駄になった。
The food that mother prepared was in vain.

• sekkaku no せっかくの *precious but not taken advantage of*

¶Sekkaku no o-maneki desu ga, konkai wa o-uke dekimasen.
せっかくのお招きですが、今回はお受けできません。
It's a kind invitation, but I can't accept this time.

sekkei 設計 *plan, design*

• sekkei suru 設計する *to plan, to design*

¶Yūmei na kenchiku-ka ga kono kōsha o sekkei shimashita.
有名な建築家がこの校舎を設計しました。
A famous architect designed this school building.

¶Kono hoteru wa umaku sekkei sarete imasu.

このホテルはうまく設計されています。

This hotel is well designed.

- sekkei-sha 設計者 *designer*
- sekkei-zu 設計図 *plan, blueprint*

sekken 石鹸 *soap*

¶Sekken de te o arainasai.

石けんで手を洗いなさい。

Wash your hands with soap.

- sekken-bako 石鹸箱 *soapbox*
- sekken-mizu 石鹸水 *soapy water*
- sengan-sekken 洗顔石鹸 *facial soap*
- sentaku-sekken 洗濯石鹸 *laundry soap*
- yokuyō-sekken 浴用石鹸 *bath soap*

sekkin 接近 *approach, nearing*

- sekkin suru 接近する *to approach, to get near*

¶Kono ōgata-taifū wa Kyūshū ni sekkin shite imasu.

この大型台風は九州に接近しています。

This large-scale typhoon is approaching Kyushu.

sékkusu セックス *sex, sexual intercourse*

- sekkusu suru セックスする *to have sex*

sekkyṓ 説教 ① *sermon, preaching*

- sekkyō suru 説教する *to preach, to give a sermon*

② *admonition, scolding* [→**kogoto** 小言]

- sekkyō suru 説教する *to admonish, to scold, to lecture*

¶Osoku kaette haha ni sekkyō saremashita.

遅く帰って母に説教されました。

I came home late and was scolded by my mother.

sekkyokuteki 積極的 〜**na** 〜な *positive, active, actively involved* [⇔**shōkyokuteki na** 消極的な]

¶Ani wa nani-goto ni mo sekkyokuteki desu.

兄は何事にも積極的です。

My older brother is actively involved in everything.

¶Sensei wa sekkyokuteki ni enjo shite

kudasaimashita.

先生は積極的に援助してくださいました。

The teacher helped us actively.

sekondo セコンド *a second* 《in boxing》

semái 狭い [[⇔**hiroi** 広い]]

① *narrow*

¶Ōgata-basu mo kono semai dōro o hashirimasu.

大型バスもこの狭い道路を走ります。

Big buses also run along this narrow road.

② *small (in area), cramped*

¶Kono heya wa semai desu ne.

この部屋は狭いですね。

This room is small, isn't it.

semáru 迫る ① *to approach, to draw near, to close in* [→**chikazuku** 近づく]

¶Shuppatsu no jikoku ga sematte imasu.

出発の時刻が迫っています。

The departure time is approaching.

② *to press for, to urge to give*

¶Kisha wa supōkusuman ni kaitō o sematta.

記者はスポークスマンに回答を迫った。

The reporter pressed the spokesperson for an answer.

semento セメント *cement*

¶Chichi wa semento de ishi no burokku o setsugō shita.

父はセメントで石のブロックを接合した。

Father joined the stone blocks with cement.

- semento-kōjō セメント工場 *cement factory*

seméru 攻める *to attack* [⇔**mamoru** 守る②]

¶Rikugun wa teki o sememashita.

陸軍は敵を攻めました。

The army attacked the enemy.

seméru 責める *to reproach, to censure; to say in reproach*

¶Jōkyaku wa jiko ga unten-shu no sei da to semeta.

乗客は事故が運転手のせいだと責めた。

The passengers said in reproach that the accident was the driver's fault.

sémete せめて *at least* [→**sukunaku-**

tomo 少なくとも]
¶Semete kutsu o migaita hō ga ii desu.
せめて靴を磨いたほうがいいです。
You should at least shine your shoes.

semi 蝉 *cicada*
¶Semi ga naki-hajimemashita.
せみが鳴き始めました。
The cicadas have begun to sing.

séminā セミナー *seminar* [→**zemi** ゼミ]

sén 千 *thousand* 《see Appendix 2》
• sen-en-satsu 千円札 *thousand-yen bill*

sén 栓 *stopper, plug, (wine)cork, (bottle)cap*
¶Wain no sen o nuite kuremashita ka.
ワインの栓を抜いてくれましたか。
Did you pull out the wine cork for me?
• sen-nuki 栓抜き *bottle opener; corkscrew*

sén 線 ① *line* 《mark on a surface》
• hosoi〔futoi〕sen 細い〔太い〕線 *fine〔bold〕line*
• sen o hiku 線を引 *to draw a line*
② *(transportation)line, route*
③ *(electrical)line, wire*
• denwa-sen 電話線 *telephone wire*
• heikō-sen 平行線 *parallel lines*
• kokusai-sen 国際線 *international route*
• kyoku-sen 曲線 *curved line*
• ten-sen 点線 *dotted line*

senaka 背中 *back (of the body)* [→**se** 背①]
¶Senaka ga mada itai yo.
背中がまだ痛いよ。
My back still hurts!
¶Boku wa tokidoki o-furo de otōto no senaka o nagashimasu.
僕は時々おふろで弟の背中を流します。
I sometimes wash my younger brother's back in the bath.
• senaka-awase ni 背中合わせに *back to back*

senbatsu 選抜 *selection, picking out* 《from a large pool of candidates》
• senbatsu suru 選抜する *to select, to pick out*
• senbatsu ni moreru 選抜に漏れる *to be left out of those selected*

• senbatsu-chīmu 選抜チーム *all-star team*

sénbei 煎餅 *Japanese rice cracker*

senchi センチ *centimeter*
• -senchi ーセンチ 《counter for centimeters; see Appendix 2》

senchiméntaru センチメンタル 〜**na** 〜な *sentimental* [→**kanshōteki na** 感傷的な]

senchimētoru センチメートル [☞**senchi** センチ]

sénchō 船長 *ship captain*

senden 宣伝 ① *advertising, publicity*
• senden suru 宣伝する *to advertise, to publicize*
¶Kono kusuri wa terebi de senden sarete imasu.
この薬はテレビで宣伝されています。
This medicine is being advertised on TV.
② *propaganda*
• senden suru 宣伝する *to propagandize*
• senden-bira 宣伝ビラ *advertising leaflet; propaganda leaflet*
• senden-posutā 宣伝ポスター *advertising poster*

sengén 宣言 *declaration, proclamation*
• sengen suru 宣言する *to declare, to proclaim*
¶Amerika wa nan-nen ni dokuritsu o sengen shimashita ka.
アメリカは何年に独立を宣言しましたか。
In what year did the United States declare independence?

séngetsu 先月 *last month*
¶Sengetsu wa ame ga ōkatta desu.
先月は雨が多かったです。
Last month there was a lot of rain.

sengo 戦後 *postwar period* [⇔**senzen** 戦前]

sén'i 繊維 *fiber*
¶Kore-ra wa yōmō no sen'i desu.
これらは羊毛の繊維です。
These are wool fibers.
• sen'i-kōgyō 繊維工業 *textile industry*
• sen'i-seihin 繊維製品 *textile goods*
• gōsei-sen'i 合成繊維 *synthetic fiber*
• kagaku-sen'i 化学繊維 *chemical fiber*

- tennen-sen'i 天然繊維 *natural fiber*

senjitsu 先日 *the other day*

¶Senjitsu Tsujimura-san no o-taku o tazunemashita.

先日辻村さんのお宅を訪ねました。

I visited Ms. Tsujimura's house the other day.

senjō 戦場 *battlefield*

senjutsu 戦術 *tactics*

- senjutsu-ka 戦術家 *tactician*

senkō 専攻 *major (field of study at a college)*

- senkō suru 専攻する *to major in*

sénkō 線香 *incense stick*

sénkyo 選挙 *election*

¶Rainen wa senkyo ga okonawaremasu.

来年は選挙が行われます。

The election will be held next year.

¶Tajima-kun ga senkyo de seito-kai no kaichō ni erabareta.

田島君が選挙で生徒会の会長に選ばれた。

Tajima was elected president of the student council in the election.

- senkyo suru 選挙する *to elect*
- senkyo-enzetsu 選挙演説 *campaign speech*
- senkyo-ken 選挙権 *the right to vote*
- senkyo-undō 選挙運動 *election campaign*
- sō-senkyo 総選挙 *general election*

senkyōshi 宣教師 *missionary*

senmen 洗面 ~**suru** ~する *wash one's face*

- senmen-dai 洗面台 *sink*
- senmen-dōgu 洗面道具 *toilet articles*
- senmen-jo 洗面所 *place for washing-up; bathroom* [→**toire** トイレ]
- senmen-ki 洗面器 *washbowl, portable washbasin*

senmon 専門 *specialty, area of expertise, field of specialization*

¶Tonari no mise wa kōhī ga senmon desu.

隣の店はコーヒーが専門です。

At the shop next-door coffee is the specialty.

¶Go-senmon wa nan desu ka.

ご専門は何ですか。

What is your field of specialization?

¶Sono mondai wa Kiyohara-sensei no senmon desu.

その問題は清原先生の専門です。

That problem is in Dr. Kiyohara's area of expertise.

- A o senmon ni suru Aを専門にする *to specialize in A; to major in A*
- senmon-gai no 専門外の *outside one's field of specialization*
- senmon-gakkō 専門学校 *vocational school*
- senmon-ka 専門家 *specialist, expert*

sennen 専念 ~**suru** ~する *to devote oneself*

¶Nashida-sensei wa shokubutsu no kenkyū ni sennen shite imasu.

梨田先生は植物の研究に専念しています。

Dr. Nashida is devoting himself to the study of botany.

sénobi 背伸び ~**suru** ~する *to stand on tiptoe*

senpai 先輩 *one's senior* «i.e., a person who entered the same organization earlier» [⇔**kōhai** 後輩]

¶Nakai-san wa bijutsu-bu no senpai desu.

中井さんは美術部の先輩です。

Mr. Nakai is my senior in the art club.

senpúki 扇風機 *(electric)fan*

- senpūki o kakeru [tomeru] 扇風機をかける [止める] *to turn on [off] a fan*

senrei 洗礼 *baptism*

- senrei o ukeru 洗礼を受ける *to receive baptism, to be baptized*

sénro 線路 *(railroad)track*

¶Senro ni hairanai de kudasai.

線路に入らないでください。

Please do not go on the tracks.

- senro-zutai ni 線路伝いに *along the tracks*

senryaku 戦略 *strategy*

- senryaku-ka 戦略家 *strategist*

senryō 占領 *(military)occupation*

- senryō suru 占領する *to occupy*

¶Kono toshi wa Doitsu-gun ni senryō

saremashita.
この都市はドイツ軍に占領されました。
This city was occupied by the German army.

sénryū 川柳 *satirical poem about people and daily life* 《with the same 5-7-5 format as a **haiku**》

sensā センサー *sensor*

senséi 先生 ① *teacher* [⇔**seito** 生徒; **gakusei** 学生]
¶Ryōshin wa futari-tomo kōkō no sensei desu.
両親は二人とも高校の先生です。
My parents are both high school teachers.
¶Ano kata wa Nihon-go no sensei desu.
あの方は日本語の先生です。
That person is a teacher of Japanese.
• -sensei －先生《Added to the surname of a teacher instead of **-san** －さん as a title of respect roughly equivalent to *Mr.*, *Ms.*, or *Dr.*》
¶Hayashi-sensei wa ongaku o oshiete irasshaimasu.
林先生は音楽を教えていらっしゃいます。
Ms. Hayashi teaches music.
② *Sir, Ma'am; the respected person*
《Used to address or refer to a person who is not a teacher but is accorded a similar kind of special respect, typically a doctor, lawyer, or elected official.》
• -sensei －先生《Added to the surname of such a person instead of **-san** －さん as a title of respect.》

sensei 宣誓 *oath*
• sensei suru 宣誓する *to take an oath, to swear*

sensei 専制 *despotism, autocracy*

senséshon センセーション *sensation, uproar*
¶Kono shōsetsu wa sekai-jū ni senséshon o makiokoshimashita.
この小説は世界中にセンセーションを巻き起こしました。
This novel created a sensation all over the world.

sénsha 戦車 *tank* ((vehicle))

senshi 戦死 *death in battle*
• senshi suru 戦死する *to die in battle*
¶Sofu wa Dai-niji-sekai-taisen de senshi shimashita.
祖父は第二次世界大戦で戦死しました。
My grandfather died in World War II.
• senshi-sha 戦死者 *person killed in battle*

senshínkoku 先進国 *advanced country* [⇔**hatten-tojō-koku** 発展途上国 (s.v. **hatten** 発展)]

senshitsu 船室 *ship cabin*

sénshu 選手 *player, athlete*
• yakyū no senshu 野球の選手 *baseball player*
• -senshu －選手《Added to an athlete's surname as an alternative to **-san** －さん; roughly equivalent to *Mr.* / *Ms.*》
• senshu-ken 選手権 *championship, title*
¶Morikawa-senshu wa sukī no senshu-ken o torimashita.
森川選手はスキーの選手権を取りました。
Ms. Morikawa took the skiing championship.
• senshu-ken-taikai 選手権大会 *championship competition*
• daihyō-senshu 代表選手 *representative player*
• sai-yūshū-senshu 最優秀選手 *most valuable player*

senshū 先週 *last week*
¶Senshū yuki ga sukoshi furimashita.
先週雪が少し降りました。
It snowed a little last week.
¶Senshū no Mokuyōbi ni tosho-kan ni ikimashita.
先週の木曜日に図書館に行きました。
I went to the library last Thursday.
• sen-senshū 先々週 *the week before last*

sensō 戦争 *war* [⇔**heiwa** 平和]
¶Sensō wa san-shūkan de owarimashita.
戦争は3週間で終わりました。
The war ended in three weeks.
¶Chichi wa sensō de fushō shimashita.
父は戦争で負傷しました。
My father was wounded in the war.
¶Sono sensō wa sen-kyūhyaku-sanju-

kyū-nen ni hajimarimashita.
その戦争は1939年に始まりました。
That war began in 1939.

¶Watashi-tachi wa sensō ni hantai desu.
私たちは戦争に反対です。
We are against war.

• sensō ni katsu 〔makeru〕 戦争に勝つ
〔負ける〕 *to win* 〔*lose*〕 *a war*

• sensō-eiga 戦争映画 *war movie*

• kaku-sensō 核戦争 *nuclear war*

sénsu センス *sense, sensitivity, judgment* 〔→**kankaku** 感覚②〕

¶Kishi-san ni wa iro no sensu ga arimasu.
岸さんには色のセンスがあります。
Ms. Kishi has a sense of color.

¶Oba wa fukusō no sensu ga ii yo.
伯母は服装のセンスがいいよ。
My aunt's judgment in clothing is good!

sensu 扇子 *folding fan*

sensui 潜水 〜**suru** 〜する *to dive, to become submerged* 《*from a starting point in the water*》 〔→**moguru** 潜る①〕

• sensui-fu 潜水夫 *diver, frogman*

• sensui-fuku 潜水服 *diving suit*

• sensui-kan 潜水艦 *a submarine*

séntā センター *center* 《(*institution*)》

• kenkyū-sentā 研究センター *research center*

• ryokō-sentā 旅行センター *tourist center*

séntā センター ① *center field* 《*in baseball*》
② *center fielder* 《*in baseball*》

• sentā-furai センターフライ *fly ball to center*

sentaku 洗濯 *washing clothes, doing laundry*

• sentaku suru 洗濯する *to wash clothes, to do the laundry; to launder, to wash*

¶Yogoreta tī-shatsu o sentaku shimashita.
汚れたTシャツを洗濯しました。
I washed the dirty T-shirts.

¶Watashi mo Nichiyōbi ni sentaku shimasu.
私も日曜日に洗濯します。
I also do the laundry on Sundays.

¶Kono doresu wa sentaku dekimasu ka.
このドレスは洗濯できますか。
Can this dress be laundered?

• sentaku-basami 洗濯鋏み *clothespin,* <*UK*>*clothes peg*

• sentaku-ki 洗濯機 *washing machine*

• sentaku-mono 洗濯物 *clothes to wash, laundry*

sentaku 選択 *choice, selection*

¶Mō sentaku no yochi wa nai to omoimasu.
もう選択の余地はないと思います。
I think that there is no longer any room for choice.

• sentaku suru 選択する *to choose* 〔→**erabu** 選ぶ〕

• sentaku-kamoku 選択科目 *elective subject*

sentō 先頭 *the head, the lead*

¶Morokko no senshu ga rēsu no sentō o kitta.
モロッコの選手がレースの先頭を切った。
The Moroccan athlete took the lead in the race.

• sentō ni tatsu 先頭に立つ *to lead, to go first*

¶Shushō wa senshu-tachi no sentō ni tatte kōshin shita.
主将が選手たちの先頭に立って行進した。
The captain is marching at the head of the players.

¶Chiagāru ga parēdo no sentō ni tachimasu.
チアガールがパレードの先頭に立ちます。
Cheerleaders will lead the parade.

• sentō-dasha 先頭打者 *lead-off hitter*

sénto セント *cent*

• -sento -セント《*counter for cents; see Appendix 2*》

séntō 銭湯 *public bathhouse* 〔→**furo-ya** 風呂屋 (s.v. **furo** 風呂)〕

sentoraruhítingu セントラルヒーティング *central heating*

sen'yō 専用 〜**suru** 〜する *to use exclusively*

• -sen'yō no -専用の *for the exclusivive use of* 《*Added to noun bases.*》

¶Koko wa jūgyōin-sen'yō no shokudō desu.

ここは従業員専用の食堂です。

This is a cafeteria for the exclusive use of employees.

¶Kono heya wa josei-sen'yō desu.

この部屋は女性専用です。

This room is for women only.

• sen'yō-sha 専用車 *car for personal use*

senzai 洗剤 *detergent, cleanser*

• gōsei-senzai 合成洗剤 *synthetic detergent*

sénzo 先祖 *ancestor* [→**sosen** 祖先] [⇔**shison** 子孫]

• senzo-denrai no 先祖伝来の *ancestral, handed down from one's ancestors*

seóu 背負う *to carry on one's back*

¶Seinen wa bakkupakku o seotte imashita.

青年はバックパックを背負っていました。

The young man was carrying a backpack on his back.

seóyogi 背泳ぎ *the backstroke* [→**haiei** 背泳]

separētsu セパレーツ *separates* ((women's clothing))

sépia セピア *sepia* 《as a noun》

seppuku 切腹 *harakiri*

• seppuku suru 切腹する *to commit harakiri*

sērāfuku セーラー服 *sailor suit* 《Typically worn as a uniform by girls in Japanese secondary schools.》

serenāde セレナーデ *serenade*

serifu 台詞 (*actor's*)*lines*

¶Joyū wa serifu o wasuremashita.

女優はせりふを忘れました。

The actress forgot her lines.

séron 世論 *public opinion* [→**yoron** 世論]

¶Seron wa sono keikaku ni hantai desu.

世論はその計画に反対です。

Public opinion is against that plan.

• seron-chōsa 世論調査 *public opinion poll*

serotēpu セロテープ *cellophane tape*

sēru セール (*bargain*)*sale* [→**yasuuri** 安売り]

• bāgen-sēru バーゲンセール *bargain sale*

serufusābisu セルフサービス *self-service*

¶Kono mise wa serufusābisu desu.

この店はセルフサービスです。

This store is self-service.

seruróido セルロイド *celluloid*

sērusúman セールスマン (*traveling*) *salesperson*

sērusupóinto セールスポイント *selling point*

¶Kono shōhin no sērusupointo wa nan desu ka.

この商品のセールスポイントは何ですか。

What is the selling point of this article?

Séshi セ氏 [☞**Sesshi** 摂氏]

sessen 接戦 *close game, close race*

¶Sessen no sue chanpion ga kachimashita.

接戦の末チャンピオンが勝ちました。

At the end of a close game the champion won.

sésse to せっせと *hard, diligently* [→**isshōkenmei** 一生懸命]

Sésshi 摂氏 *centigrade, Celsius* [⇔**Kashi** カ氏]

¶Saikō-kion wa Sesshi sanjū-do deshita.

最高気温は摂氏30度でした。

The high temperature was 30 degrees Celsius.

sesshoku 接触 ① (*physical*)*contact*

• sesshoku suru 接触する *to come into contact* [→**sessuru** 接する①]

¶Hazureta densen ga yane ni sesshoku shimashita.

外れた電線が屋根に接触しました。

The loose electric wire came into contact with the roof.

② (*social*)*contact, touch*

• sesshoku suru 接触する *to come into contact, to get in touch*

• sesshoku o tamotsu 接触を保つ *to keep in touch*

sessuru 接する{Irreg.} ① *to come into* (*physical*)*contact*

② *to border, to be adjacent, to touch*

¶Chokusen wa koko de en ni sessuru

deshō?

直線はここで円に接するでしょう？

The straight line touches the circle here, right?

③ *to come into (social)contact, to meet* [→**au** 会う]

¶Gaikoku-jin ni sessuru kikai ga arimasen deshita.

外国人と接する機会がありませんでした。

I had no chance to come into contact with foreigners.

sḗtā セーター *sweater*

setchakúzai 接着剤 *bonding agent, glue, adhesive*

¶Kono buhin o setchakuzai de tsukemashita.

この部品を接着剤でつけました。

I attached this part with glue.

• shunkan-setchakuzai 瞬間接着剤 *quick drying glue*

setomono 瀬戸物 *china, earthenware, pottery* [→**tōki** 陶器, **yakimono** 焼き物]

Setonáikai 瀬戸内海 *the Seto Inland Sea* 《surrounded by Honshu, Shikoku, and Kyushu》

sḗtsu 説 ① *theory; doctrine*

¶Gakusha wa atarashii setsu o tatemashita.

学者は新しい説を立てました。

The scholar advanced a new theory.

② *opinion, view* [→**iken** 意見]

¶Sore ni tsuite wa samazama na setsu ga arimasu.

それについてはさまざまな説があります。

There are various opinions about that.

sḗtsubi 設備 *equipment; facilities*

¶Ano hoteru wa setsubi ga hijō ni ii desu.

あのホテルは設備が非常にいいです。

That hotel's facilities are extremely good.

¶Kono gakkō wa danbō no setsubi ga arimasu.

この学校は暖房の設備があります。

This school has heating facilities.

• setsubi suru 設備する *to install, to provide*

setsubigo 接尾語 *suffix* [⇔**settōgo**

接頭語]

Setsubun 節分 《This name refers to the last day of winter according to the old lunar calendar. It now refers to February 3, the day on which the bean throwing ritual is performed. The beans are thrown to drive demons out of houses.》

setsumei 説明 *explanation*

¶Kono mondai wa setsumei no hitsuyō ga arimasen.

この問題は説明が必要ありません。

This problem needs no explanation.

• setsumei suru 説明する *to explain*

¶Watashi wa chikoku shita riyū o setsumei shimashita.

私は遅刻した理由を説明しました。

I explained the reason I was late.

¶Tosho-kan no riyō-hōhō o setsumei shite kudasai.

図書館の利用方法を説明してください。

Please the method of using the library.

• setsumei-sho 説明書 *(written)instructions*

setsunái 切ない *trying, distressing* [→**tsurai** 辛い]

setsuritsu 設立 *establishing, founding, setting up*

• setsuritsu suru 設立する *to establish, to found, to set up*

¶Kono gakkō wa gojū-nen-mae ni setsuritsu saremashita.

この学校は50年前に設立されました。

This school was founded fifty years ago.

• setsuritsu-sha 設立者 *founder*

setsuyaku 節約 *economy, saving, conservation*

• setsuyaku suru 節約する *to save, to economize on, to conserve*

¶O-kane o setsuyaku suru no wa muzukashii desu.

お金を節約するのは難しいです。

Saving money is difficult.

• setsuyaku-ka 節約家 *frugal person*

setsuzoku 接続 ① *connection, joining*

• setsuzoku suru 接続する *to connect, to join, to link*

② *(transportation)connection* [→**ren-**

raku 連絡②〕

• setsuzoku suru 接続する *to connect*
¶Kono densha wa Kyōto de shinkansen ni setsuzoku shimasu.
この電車は京都で新幹線に接続します。
This train connects with the Shinkansen at Kyoto.

• setsuzoku-shi 接続詞 *conjunction* ((part of speech))

settei 設定 *establishing, setting up, instituting*

• settei suru 設定する *to establish, to set up, to institute*

sétto セット ① *set* (*of things that go together*)

• kōhī-setto コーヒーセット *coffee set* 《i.e., coffee and accompanying extras treated as a single menu item》

② (*movie*)*set*

③ *set* 《in sports such as tennis》

• -setto ーセット《*counter for sets; see Appendix 2*》
¶Yūshō wa go-setto no shiai de kimarimashita.
優勝は5セットの試合で決まりました。
The championship was decided in a five-set match.

sétto セット ～**suru** ～する ① *to set* 《hair》
¶Kami o setto shite moraimashita.
髪をセットしてもらいました。
I had my hair set.

② *to set* 《a device》

settōgo 接頭語 *prefix* 〔⇔**setsubigo** 接尾語〕

settoku 説得 ～**suru** ～する *to persuade*
¶Chichi o settoku shite jitensha o katte moratta yo.
父を説得して自転車を買ってもらったよ。
I persuaded my father to buy me a bicycle!

• settoku-ryoku 説得力 *persuasiveness*

sewá 世話 ① *taking care, looking after*

• A no sewa o suru Aの世話をする *to take care of A, to look after A*
¶Chichi wa niwa no ueki no sewa o shite

imasu.
父は庭の植木の世話をしています。
My father is taking care of the garden shrubs.

¶Imōto wa kodomo-tachi no sewa o suru no ga suki desu.
妹は子供たちの世話をするのが好きです。
My younger sister likes to look after children.

② *help, aid, assistance*

• sewa ni naru 世話になる *to become obliged for having received help*
¶O-sewa ni narimashita.
お世話になりました。
I am much obliged to you.

• sewa-nin 世話人 *caretaker; sponsor*

shabéru 喋る{5} *to talk, to chat* 〔→**hanasu** 話す〕
¶Kyōko-san wa yoku shaberu ne.
京子さんはよくしゃべるね。
Kyoko talks a lot, doesn't she.
¶Gakusei-tachi wa o-cha o nomi-nagara shabetta.
学生たちはお茶を飲みながらしゃべった。
The students chatted while drinking tea.

shábeberu シャベル *shovel*

shābetto シャーベット *sherbet*

shabondama シャボン玉 *soap bubble*

shaburu しゃぶる *to suck on*

shachō 社長 *company president*

• fuku-shachō 副社長 *vice-president*

shagamu しゃがむ *to crouch, to squat*

shageki 射撃 *shooting, firing a gun*

• shageki o hajimeru 〔yameru〕 射撃を始める 〔やめる〕 *to open* 〔*cease*〕 *fire*

• shageki suru 射撃する *to shoot, to fire a gun*

sháin 社員 *company staff member, company employee*

shákai 社会 *society, the world*
¶Musuko wa rainen shakai ni demasu.
息子は来年社会に出ます。
My son will go out into the world next year.
¶Shakai no tame ni hataraki-tai desu.
社会のために働きたいです。
I want to work for the good of society.

- shakai-hōshi 社会奉仕 *social service*
- shakai-jin 社会人 *full-fledged member of society*
- shakai-kagaku 社会科学 *social science*
- shakai-mondai 社会問題 *social problem, social issue*
- shakai-shugi 社会主義 *socialism*
- shakai-seikatsu 社会生活 *social life*
- Shakai-tō 社会党 *the Socialist Party*

sháke 鮭 〔☞**sake** 鮭〕

shakkín 借金 *debt, borrowed money*
¶Gosen-en no shakkin o kaeshimashita.
5000円の借金を返しました。
I paid back a debt of 5,000 yen.
¶Tarō wa Jun ni jūman-en no shakkin ga aru yo.
太郎は淳に10万円の借金があるよ。
Taro has a debt of 100,000 yen to Jun!
- shakkin suru 借金する *to borrow money, to get a loan*

shákkuri しゃっくり *hiccup, the hiccups*
¶Shakkuri ga tomarimasen.
しゃっくりが止まりません。
My hiccups won't stop.
- shakkuri ga deru しゃっくりが出る *a hiccup comes out*

sháko 車庫 *garage; carport*

shakō 社交 *social interaction, socializing*
- shakō-dansu 社交ダンス *social dancing*
- shakō-sei 社交性 *sociability*
- shakō-teki na 社交的な *sociable*

shaku 癪 〜**ni sawaru** 〜にさわる *to be provoking, to be offensive, to get on one's nerves*
¶Komatsu-san wa shaku ni sawaru hito desu ne.
小松さんはしゃくにさわる人ですね。
Mr. Komatsu is a person who gets on one's nerves, isn't he.

shakuhachi 尺八 *shakuhachi* «a kind of bamboo flute»

shákushi 杓子 ① *ladle*
② *rice paddle*

shámen 斜面 *slope, hillside; sloping surface*
¶Kore kara wa kyū na shamen o

noborimasu.
これからは急な斜面を登ります。
From here on we're going to climb a steep slope.

shamisen 三味線 *shamisen* «a three-stringed, banjo-like musical instrument»

shámoji しゃもじ *rice paddle*

shandéria シャンデリア *chandelier*

shanpán シャンパン 〔☞**shanpen** シャンペン〕

shanpén シャンペン *champagne*

shánpū シャンプー *shampoo*
- shanpū suru シャンプーする *to shampoo*
¶Yūbe kami o shanpū shimashita.
ゆうべ髪をシャンプーしました。
I shampooed my hair last night.

shansón シャンソン *chanson, French-style popular song*

shápu シャープ *(musical)sharp* 〔⇔**furatto** フラット〕

share 洒落 *pun, play on words*
- share o iu しゃれを言う *to pun, to make a play on words*

shareru 洒落る *to get dressed up, to dress stylishly*
- shareta しゃれた *fashionable, stylish* «This word is the past-tense form of **shareru** and has the predictable range of meanings as well.» 〔→**oshare na** お洒落な〕

sharin 車輪 *vehicle wheel*

shasei 写生 ① *drawing/painting without embellishment, drawing/painting from life*
- shasei suru 写生する *to draw/paint without embellishment, to draw/paint from life*
¶Kōsha o ni- san-mai shasei shimashita.
校舎を2、3枚写生しました。
I drew two or three pictures of the school building.
② *sketching*
- shasei suru 写生する *to sketch, to make a sketch of*
- shasei-ga 写生画 *a drawing/painting from life; sketch*

shasen 車線 *lane* «marked on a road»

shasetsu 社説 (*newspaper*)*editorial*

shashin 写真 *photograph*

¶Shashin wa pinboke deshita.

写真はピンぼけでした。

The photograph was out of focus.

¶Shashin o genzō shite, yaite moraimashita.

写真を現像して、焼いてもらいました。

I had my photographs developed and printed.

¶Kono shashin o hikinobashite kudasai.

この写真を引き伸ばしてください。

Please enlarge this photograph.

• shashin o toru 写真を撮る *to take a photograph*

¶Tomodachi no shashin o torimashita.

友達の写真を撮りました。

I took a photograph of my friend.

• shashin ga toreru 写真が撮れる *a photograph is taken*

¶Kono shashin wa yoku torete imasu ne.

この写真はよく撮れていますね。

This is a good photograph, isn't it. 《Literally: This photograph is well taken, isn't it.》

• shashin o yakimasu 写真を焼き増す *to make a reprint of a photograph*

• shashin-ka 写真家 *photographer*

• shashin-ki 写真機 *camera* [→**kamera** カメラ]

• shashin-utsuri 写真うつり *the way one looks in photographs*

¶Imōto-san wa shashin-utsuri ga ii desu.

妹さんは写真うつりがいいです。

Your younger sister looks good in photographs.

• shashin-ya 写真屋 *camera store, photography shop*

• karā-shashin カラー写真 *color photograph*

• kinen-shashin 記念写真 *souvenir photo*

• shirokuro-shashin 白黒写真 *black-and-white photograph*

• supīdo-shashin スピード写真 *fast photo*

shashō 車掌 *conductor* 《on a train or bus》

shataku 社宅 *company housing*

shátsu シャツ *shirt*

• hansode-shatsu 半袖シャツ *short-sleeved shirt*

• ranningu-shatsu ランニングシャツ *sleeveless T-shirt*

• tī-shatsu ティーシャツ, Tシャツ *T-shirt*

sháttā シャッター ① (*camera*)*shutter*

¶Sumimasen ga, shattā o oshite kudasaimasen ka.

すみませんが、シャッターを押してくださいませんか。

Excuse me, won't you please press the shutter for us?

② *roll-up metal shutter* 《Used to secure an entryway or window.》

shattóáuto シャットアウト ① ~**suru** ~する *to shut out, to exclude*

② *shutout* 《in baseball》 [→**kanpū** 完封]

sháwā シャワー *shower* (*bath*)

• shawā o abiru シャワーを浴びる *to take a shower*

shepádo シェパード *German shepherd*

shérutā シェルター *a shelter*

shí 四 *four* 《see Appendix 2》 [→**yon** 四]

• Shi-gatsu 四月 *April*

• Shi-gatsu-baka 四月馬鹿 *an April fool*

shí 市 *city*

• shi-gikai 市議会 *city council*

• shi-ritsu no 市立の *administered by a city, municipal*

• shi-yakusho 市役所 *city hall*

• Kyōto-shi 京都市 *Kyoto City*

shí 死 *death*

• jiko-shi 事故死 *accidental death*

• kyū-shi 急死 *sudden death*

shi 詩 *poem; poetry*

• shi-jin 詩人 *poet*

• shi-shū 詩集 *collection of poems*

• shi-teki na 詩的な *poetic*

shi し *and, and besides that* 《sentence-conjoining particle》

¶Kono jisho wa yasui shi, totemo tsukai-yasui.

この辞書は安いし、とても使いやすい。

This dictionary is cheap, and really simple to use!

-shí -氏 【HON. for -**san** -さん】

《Roughly equivalent to *Mr./Ms.*; most commonly used for men.》

¶Nakamura-shi wa kaichō ni ninmei saremashita.

中村氏は会長に任命されました。

Mr. Nakamura was named chairperson.

shiagáru 仕上がる *to be completed* [→ **dekiagaru** 出来上がる]

¶Repōto ga yatto shiagarimashita.

レポートがやっと仕上がりました。

The report has finally been completed.

shiagéru 仕上げる *to finish, to complete*

¶Yūshoku-mae ni shukudai o shiagemashō.

夕食前に宿題を仕上げましょう。

Let's finish our homework before dinner!

shiai 試合 *competition, game, match, meet*

¶Ashita, Minami-kōkō to yakyū no shiai o shimasu.

明日、南高校と野球の試合をします。

Tomorrow we're going to play a baseball game with Minami High School.

shiawase 幸せ [[→**kōfuku** 幸福]] *happiness; good fortune*

• shiawase na 幸せな *happy; fortunate*

¶Akiyama-san wa kekkon shite, totemo shiawase da.

秋山さんは結婚して、とても幸せだ。

Mr. Akiyama got married and is very happy.

¶Mura no hito-tachi wa shiawase ni kurashimashita.

村の人たちは幸せに暮らしました。

The people of the village lived happily.

shibafu 芝生 *lawn, grass*

¶Otoko no ko ga shibafu ni nekoronde imasu.

男の子が芝生に寝転んでいます。

The boy is lying on the grass.

¶Shibafu ni hairanai de kudasai.

「芝生に入らないでください」《on a sign》

Keep off the grass. 《Literally: Please do not come on the grass.》

shibai 芝居 ① *play, drama, theatrical presentation*

• shibai o suru 芝居をする *to put on a play*

② *an act, faking*

• shibai o suru 芝居をする *to put on an act*

shibáraku 暫く ① *for a while*

¶Watashi-tachi wa shibaraku matte imashita.

私たちはしばらく待っていました。

We were waiting for a while.

② *for quite a while, for a long time*

¶Shibaraku desu ne.

しばらくですね。

It's been a long time (since I saw you last), hasn't it.

shibáru 縛る *to bind, to tie, to fasten*

¶Sono tsutsumi o himo de shibatte kudasai.

その包みをひもで縛ってください。

Please tie that package with string.

¶Shōjo wa kami o ribon de shibarimashita.

少女は髪をリボンで縛りました。

The girl tied her hair with a ribbon.

shíbashiba しばしば 【FORMAL for **tabitabi** 度々】 *often*

¶Shibashiba chichi to tsuri ni ikimasu.

しばしば父と釣りに行きます。

I often go fishing with my father.

shibiréru 痺れる *to become numb, to fall asleep*

¶Samusa de yubi ga shibirete shimatta.

寒さで指がしびれてしまった。

My fingers became numb with cold.

¶Ashi ga shibireta yo.

足がしびれたよ。

My legs have fallen asleep!

shibō 死亡 *death*

• shibō suru 死亡する *to die, to pass away* [→**shinu** 死ぬ]

• shibō-ritsu 死亡率 *death rate*

shibō 志望 *aspiration, desire, hope*

• shibō suru 志望する *to aspire to be*

¶Yōko-san wa kangofu o shibō shite imasu.

洋子さんは看護婦を志望しています。

Yoko is aspiring to be a nurse.

• shibō-gakkō 志望学校 *school one hopes*

to enter
- daiichi-shibō 第１志望 *one's first choice*

shibō 脂肪 *fat; grease*

¶Kono niku wa shibō ga ō-sugiru yo.

この肉は脂肪が多すぎるよ。

This meat has too much fat!

shibomu しぼむ ① *to wither, to wilt* 《when the subject is a plant》

¶Sono hana wa ichi-nichi dake de shibonde shimatta.

その花は１日だけでしぼんでしまった。

Those flowers wilted in just one day.

② *to become deflated*

¶Sono fūsen ga shibonda yo.

その風船がしぼんだよ。

That balloon deflated!

shibóru 絞る *to wring liquid out of, to squeeze liquid out of*

¶Sono nureta taoru o shibotte kudasai.

そのぬれたタオルを絞ってください。

Please wring out that wet towel.

¶Ane wa remon o shibotte jūsu ni shimashita.

姉はレモンを絞ってジュースにしました。

My older sister squeezed a lemon and made some lemon juice.

shibúi 渋い ① *astringent-tasting*

¶Kono kaki wa aji ga shibui desu.

この柿は味が渋いです。

This persimmon is astringent.

② *subdued, tasteful, refined*

¶Sensei wa shibui nekutai o shite imasu.

先生は渋いネクタイをしています。

The teacher is wearing a tasteful tie.

- shibui iro 渋い色 *subdued color*

shibukí 飛沫 *spray from splashing water*

shichí 七 *seven* 《see Appendix 2》 [→ nana 七]

- Shichi-gatsu 七月 *July*

Shichifukújin 七福神 *the Seven Gods of Good Fortune* 《These gods are traditionally said to sail into port on a ship filled with treasure on New Year's Eve. The seven are **Ebisu** 恵比寿 (god of fisherman and prosperous commerce), **Bishamon**

毘沙門 (god of war), **Daikoku** 大黒 (god of wealth), **Benten** 弁天 (goddess of eloquence and the arts), **Fukurokuju** 福禄寿 (god of wealth and longevity), **Jurōjin** 寿老人 (god of longevity), and **Hotei** 布袋 (god of happiness).》

Shichigosan 七五三 *the Seven-Five-Three Celebration* 《Boys aged three or five and girls aged three or seven put on their best clothes and visit a neighborhood Shinto shrine on November 15.》

shichimenchō 七面鳥 *turkey*

shichíya 質屋 *pawn shop*

shichō 市長 *(city)mayor*

¶Honma-san no otōsan wa shichō ni erabareta.

本間さんのお父さんは市長に選ばれた。

Mr. Honma's father was elected mayor.

- shichō-senkyo 市長選挙 *mayoral election*

shichóritsu 視聴率 *rating* 《of a TV program》

¶Kono terebi-bangumi no shichō-ritsu wa takai desu.

このテレビ番組の視聴率は高いです。

This TV program's rating is high.

shichū シチュー *stew*

shidai 次第 *circumstances* [→jijō 事情]

- shidai ni yotte 次第によって *depending on the circumstances*

-shidai 一次第 ① *as soon as* 《Added to verb bases.》

¶Tenki ni nari-shidai shuppatsu shimashō.

天気になり次第出発しましょう。

Let's start out as soon as it clears up.

② ~**da** ～だ *to depend on* 《Added to noun bases.》

¶Seikō wa doryoku-shidai desu.

成功は努力次第です。

Success depends on effort.

shidai-ni 次第に *gradually*

¶Tenkō ga shidai-ni kaifuku shite kimashita.

天候がしだいに回復してきました。

The weather has gradually improved.

shiden 市電 *streetcar*

shído シード *seed* 《in a tennis tournament, etc.》
- daiichi-shído 第1シード *the number one seed*

shidō 指導 *direction, guidance, leadership, instruction*
¶Sono kenkyū wa Ochiai-kyōju no shidō de susumerareta.
その研究は落合教授の指導で進められた。
That research progressed under Prof. Ochiai's leadership.
- shidō suru 指導する *to direct, to guide, to lead, to instruct*
¶Ueoka-san wa sakkā o shidō shite imasu.
上岡さんはサッカーを指導しています。
Mr. Ueoka is teaching soccer.
- shidō-in 指導員 *instructor*
- shidō-ryoku 指導力 *leadership ability*
- shidō-sha 指導者 *leader*

shiei 市営 ～**no** ～の *operated by a city, municipal*
- shiei-basu 市営バス *city bus*

shīemu CM 《Generally not written out in katakana.》 *commercial message* [→**komāsharu** コマーシャル]

shígai 市外 *area surrounding a town, outskirts, suburbs* [→**kōgai** 郊外]

shigaisen 紫外線 *ultraviolet rays*

shigamitsúku しがみつく *to clutch, to hold tightly*

shígan 志願 *aspiration; applying, requesting; volunteering*
- shigan suru 志願する *to apply for; to volunteer for*
¶Ani wa pairotto no shoku o shigan shimashita.
兄はパイロットの職を志願しました。
My older brother applied for a job as a pilot.
- shigan-sha 志願者 *applicant*

shigeki 刺激 *stimulus*
- shigeki suru 刺激する *to stimulate*
- shigeki-teki na 刺激的な *stimulating, exciting*
¶Kono hon wa kodomo ni wa

shigeki-teki-sugiru darō.
この本は子供には刺激的すぎるだろう。
This book may be too exciting for children.

shígen 資源 *resources*
¶Roshia wa shigen ga yutaka desu.
ロシアは資源が豊かです。
Russia's resources are abundant.
- chika-shigen 地下資源 *underground resources*
- tennen-shigen 天然資源 *natural resources*

shigéru 茂る{5} *to grow thick, to become luxuriant*
¶Niwa ni wa zassō ga shigette imasu.
庭には雑草がしげっています。
In the garden weeds are growing thick.

Shigósen 子午線 *the Prime Meridian*

shigoto 仕事 *work, task; job, employment, business*
¶Shinakereba naranai shigoto ga takusan aru.
しなければならない仕事がたくさんある。
There's a lot of work that I have to do.
¶Ane wa shigoto o sagashite imasu.
姉は仕事を捜しています。
My older sister is looking for a job.
¶Yasuda-san wa shigoto de Hiroshima ni imasu.
安田さんは仕事で広島にいます。
Ms. Yasuda is in Hiroshima on business.
¶Inu o sanpo ni tsurete iku no wa boku no shigoto desu.
犬を散歩に連れて行くのは僕の仕事です。
Taking the dog for a walk is my job.
¶Chichi wa asa hayaku shigoto ni dekakemasu.
父は朝早く仕事に出かけます。
My father goes to work early in the morning.
- shigoto o suru 仕事をする *to work* [→**hataraku** 働く]

shígunaru シグナル [[→**shingō** 信号]]
① *signal*
② *traffic signal* ((device))

shigure 時雨 *late autumn or early*

winter drizzle

shigyō 始業 [[⇔**shūgyō** 終業]]
① *the start of work or school each day*
② *the beginning of a new school term*
• shigyō-shiki 始業式 *start-of-the-term ceremony*

shíhai 支配 *rule, governing, control*
• shihai suru 支配する *to rule, to govern, to control*
¶ Sono kuni wa ō-sama ga shihai shite imasu.
その国は王様が支配しています。
A king rules over that country.
• shihai-nin 支配人 *manager*
• shihai-sha 支配者 *ruler*

shiharai 支払い *payment*
• shiharai-bi 支払い日 *date of payment*

shiharáu 支払う *to pay* 《The direct object is the money, charge, expense, etc.》 [→**harau** 払う①]

shiharáu 支払う *to pay* 《The direct object is the charge, expense, etc.》 [→**harau** 払う①]
• A ni B o shiharau AにBを支払う *to pay B to A*

shihatsu 始発 ① *the first train or bus departure of the day*
② *the first train or bus of the day*
¶ Kesawa Kyōto-yuki no shihatsu ni mani-aimashita.
けさは京都行きの始発に間に合いました。
This morning I was in time for the first Kyoto-bound train.
③ *starting point, origin* 《of a train or bus》
• shihatsu-eki 始発駅 *starting station*

shíhei 紙幣 *paper money,* <*US*>*bill,* <*UK*>*note*

shihó 四方 *every side, all sides; every direction, all directions*
¶ Mihari wa shihō o mimawashimashita.
見張りは四方を見回しました。
The guard looked around in every direction.
¶ Kodomo-tachi wa shihō ni nigemashita.
子供たちは四方に逃げました。
The children ran away in all directions.

shihon 資本 *capital, funds* [→**shikin** 資金]
• shihon-ka 資本家 *capitalist, financier*
• shihon-kin 資本金 *operating capital, capitalization*
¶ Sono dai-kigyō no shihon-kin wa nijū-oku-en desu.
その大企業の資本金は20億円です。
That big company's capitalization is two billion yen.
• shihon-shugi 資本主義 *capitalism*
• shihon-shugi-kokka 資本主義国家 *capitalist country*

shiin 子音 *a consonant* [⇔**boin** 母音]

shíji 支持 *support, backing*
• shiji suru 支持する *to support, to back*
¶ Dare-mo sono an o shiji shimasen deshita.
だれもその案を支持しませんでした。
No one supported that plan.
• shiji-sha 支持者 *supporter* ((person))

shiji 指示 ① *directions, instructions*
¶ Watashi-tachi wa shidō-sha no shiji ni shitagaimasu.
私たちは指導者の指示に従います。
We'll follow the leader's directions.
• shiji suru 指示する *to direct, to instruct*
② *indication, pointing to*
• shiji suru 指示する *to indicate, to point to*
¶ Kono ya-jirushi wa hōkō o shiji shite imasu.
この矢印は方向を指示しています。
This arrow indicates the direction.

shijin 詩人 *poet*

shijō 市場 *market*

shíjū 始終 *always* [→**tsune ni** 常に]; *often* [→**tabitabi** 度々]; *constantly, continually* [→**taezu** 絶えず]

shika 鹿 *deer*

shika しか *only, nothing but* 《Always occurs in combination with a negative predicate.》
¶ Ima jū-en shika nai desu.
今10円しかないです。
I only have ten yen now.
¶ Eigo wa sukoshi shika hanasemasen.

英語は少ししか話せません。
I can only speak a little English.
¶Watashi ni wa kore shika dekimasen.
私にはこれしかできません。
I̧ can only do this.

shikaeshi 仕返し *retaliation, getting back*
• shikaeshi suru 仕返しする *to retaliate, to get back*
¶Ano hito wa watashi ni shikaeshi suru deshō.
あの人は私に仕返しするでしょう。
That person will probably get back at me.

shikai 司会 *chairmanship, chairing; emceeing*
¶Iwasaki–san wa kaigi no shikai o shimasu.
岩崎さんは会議の司会をします。
Ms. Iwasaki will chair the meeting.
• shikai suru 司会する *to chair; to emcee*
• shikai-sha 司会者 *chairperson; master of ceremonies*

shikai 視界 *one's range of sight, one's view*
• shikai ni hairu 視界に入る *to come into view*
• shikai kara kieru 視界から消える *to disappear from view*

shikakú 四角 *a square* ((shape))

shikaku 資格 *qualifications, eligibility*
¶Ane wa chūgakkō no sensei no shikaku ga arimasu.
姉は中学校の先生の資格があります。
My older sister has the qualifications to be a junior–high–school teacher.

shikakúi 四角い *square* 《as an adjective》
¶Sono shikakui hako o tsukatte kudasai.
その四角い箱を使ってください。
Please use that square box.

shikámo しかも *besides, furthermore*
¶Kono kamera wa chīsaku te, shikamo, yasui.
このカメラは小さくて、しかも、安い。
This camera is small. Furthermore, it's inexpensive.

shikaru 叱る *to scold*
¶Sensei wa fuchūi na seito o shikarimashita.
先生は不注意な生徒をしかりました。
The teacher scolded the careless student.

shikáshi しかし *however, but*
¶Gorufu wa tanoshii. Shikashi, okane ga kakaru.
ゴルフは楽しい。しかし、お金がかかる。
Golf is fun. But, It's expensive.

shikata 仕方 *way of doing, how to do*
¶Kono ko wa mada ojigi no shikata wa shiranai.
この子はまだおじぎの仕方は知らない。
This child doesn't know how to bow yet.
¶Tadashii aisatsu no shikata o oshiete kudasai.
正しいあいさつの仕方を教えてください。
Please teach me the right way to greet people.
• shikata ga nai しかたがない *it can't be helped, there's nothing one can do*
¶Mō owatta kara, shikata ga nai ne.
もう終わったから、しかたがないね。
It's already ended, so there's nothing we can do, is there.
¶Kyō wa mushiatsukute shikata ga nai desu yo.
きょうは蒸し暑くてしかたがないですよ。
Today it's so hot and humid that I can't stand it! 《After a gerund (-te form), shikata ga nai often has an idiomatic meaning that might be translated a to such an extent that one can't stand it!》

shikéi 死刑 *death penalty*
¶Hannin wa shikei no senkoku o ukemashita.
犯人は死刑の宣告を受けました。
The criminal received the death sentence.

shikén 試験 [[→**tesuto** テスト]]
① *test, examination* 《to evaluate knowledge or ability》
¶Kyō wa Eigo no shiken ga arimasu.
きょうは英語の試験があります。
Today there is an English examination.
¶Yamada-sensei wa mainichi shiken o shimasu.

山田先生は毎日試験をします。
Ms. Yamada gives a test every day.
• maru-batsu-shiki no shiken ○×式の試験 *true-or-false test*

② *test, trial, experiment* 《to evaluate quality》
• shiken suru 試験する *to test, to experiment with*
• shiken-benkyō 試験勉強 *studying for a test*
• shiken-kan 試験管 *test tube*
• shiken-mondai 試験問題 *examination question*
• shiken-teki na 試験的な *experimental, trial*
• shiken-yōshi 試験用紙 *examination paper*
• chūkan-shiken 中間試験 *midterm examination*
• kimatsu-shiken 期末試験 *end-of-term examination, final examination*
• jitsuryoku-shiken 実力試験 *achievement test*

shikéru 湿気る{5} *to get soggy, to lose crispness* 《from absorbing moisture in the air》

shikí 式 ① *ceremony* [→**gishiki** 儀式]
• shiki-jō 式場 *place where a ceremony is held*
• heikai-shiki 閉会式 *closing ceremony*
• kaikai-shiki 開会式 *opening ceremony*
• sotsugyō-shiki 卒業式 *graduation ceremony*

② *expression, formula* 《in mathematics, chemistry, etc.》 [→**kōshiki** 公式]
• kagaku-shiki 化学式 *chemical formula*

-shiki 一式 *-type, -style* 《Added to noun bases.》
¶Amerika-shiki no seikatsu ni narete imasu.
アメリカ式の生活に慣れています。
I am used to an American-style way of life.

shikí 四季 *the four seasons*
¶Nihon no shizen wa shiki o tsūjite utsukushii desu.
日本の自然は四季を通じて美しいです。

Nature in Japan is beautiful throughout the four seasons.

shikí 指揮 *directing, leading, commanding; orders, instructions*
• shiki suru 指揮する *to direct, to conduct* 《an orchestra, etc.》, *to command* 《an army, etc.》
• shiki-kan 指揮官 *commander*
• shiki-sha 指揮者 *conductor, director, leader*

shikibúton 敷布団 *lower futon, mattress-type futon* 《The word **futon** 布団 refers to traditional Japanese bedding, which is folded up and put in closets during the day and laid out on the floor at night.》[⇔**kakebuton** 掛け布団]

shikíkin 敷金 *security deposit* 《paid to a landlord》

shikín 資金 *funds, capital* [→**shihon** 資本]

shikiri-ni 頻りに ① *frequently, repeatedly, often* [→**tabitabi** 度々]
¶Yūko wa shikiri-ni shi-yakusho ni denwa o kaketa.
夕子はしきりに市役所に電話をかけた。
Yuko phones the city hall very often.
② *hard, eagerly, keenly*
¶Ani ga shikiri-ni Aiko ni ai-ta-gatte iru.
兄がしきりに愛子に会いたがっている。
My older brother is eager to meet Aiko.

shikkaku 失格 *disqualification*
• shikkaku suru 失格する *to be disqualified*
¶Yazawa-senshu wa kesshō-sen de shikkaku ni narimashita.
矢沢選手は決勝戦で失格になりました。
Yazawa was disqualified from the finals.

shikkári しっかり （～ **to** ～と） *strongly, firmly, tightly, hard*
¶Shikkari benkyō shinasai.
しっかり勉強しなさい。
Study hard.
¶Seizon-sha wa shikkari tsuna ni tsukamarimashita.
生存者はしっかり綱に捕まりました。

The survivors held on to the rope tightly.

• shikkari suru しっかりする *to become strong, to become dependable*

¶ Tsuchida-san wa shikkari shite imasu ne.

土田さんはしっかりしていますね。

Ms. Tsuchida is dependable, isn't she.

shikke 湿気 *dampness; humidness*

• shikke ga ōi 湿気が多い *very damp; very humid*

shikki 湿気 [☞**shikke** 湿気]

shikō 思考 *thought, thinking*

• shikō-ryoku 思考力 *thinking power*

shikómu 仕込む ① *to give training in, to inculcate*

• A ni B o shikomu AにBを仕込む *to give training in B to A, to train A in B*

② *to stock, to lay in*

shikōsakugo 試行錯誤 *trial and error*

shiku 敷く *to spread out flat, to lay*

¶ Yuka ni midori no kāpetto o shikimashita.

床に緑のカーペットを敷きました。

I laid a green carpet on the floor.

¶ Sunahama ni goza o shiite, nikkō-yoku o shimasu.

砂浜にござを敷いて、日光浴をします。

We'll spread a mat on the beach and sunbathe.

¶ Watashi wa mainichi chichi no futon o shikimasu.

私は毎日父のふとんを敷きます。

I lay out my father's bedding every day.

• tetsudō o shiku 鉄道を敷く *to lay a railroad*

shikujíru しくじる {5} *to fail at, to fail to do*

shikumi 仕組み *structure, arrangement, set-up*

shikurámen シクラメン *cyclamen*

shikyū 至急（〜ni 〜に）*immediately, promptly, as soon as possible*

¶ Shikyū Tateishi-san ni renraku shite kudasai.

至急立石さんに連絡してください。

Please get in touch with Mr. Tateishi at once.

¶ Shikyū sore o shiagete kudasai.

至急それを仕上げてください。

Please finish that as soon as possible.

• shikyū no 至急の *urgent*

¶ Shikyū no yōji de dekakemashita.

至急の用事で出かけました。

I went out on urgent business.

shikyū 四球 *base on balls, walk 《in baseball》* [→**foabōru** フォアボール]

• shikyū de deru 四球で出る *to (reach base by a)walk*

shikyū 死球 *pitch that hits the batter* [→**deddobōru** デッドボール]

shikyū 子宮 *uterus*

shimá 縞 *stripe*

¶ Kono akai shima no sētā ga dai-suki desu.

この赤いしまのセーターが大好きです。

I love this sweater with the red stripes.

shimá 島 *island*

• shima-guni 島国 *island nation*

• hanare-jima 離れ島 *remote island*

shímai 姉妹 *sisters*

• shimai-kō 姉妹校 *sister school*

• shimai-toshi 姉妹都市 *sister city*

shimáru 閉まる *to close, to shut 《intransitive》* [⇔**aku** 開く]

¶ Doa wa jidō-teki ni shimarimasu.

ドアは自動的に閉まります。

The door closes automatically.

¶ Mado ga dōshite-mo shimaranai yo.

窓がどうしても閉まらないよ。

The window won't shut no matter what I do!

shimáru 締まる *to become tight; to become firm*

shímatsu 始末 ① *disposal, disposition, settling* [→**shobun** 処分①]

• shimatsu suru 始末する *to dispose of, to take care of, to settle*

② *circumstances, state of things*

shimau 仕舞う ① *to put away*

¶ Kono kēki o reizōko ni shimatte kudasai.

このケーキを冷蔵庫にしまってください。

Please put this cake away in the refrigerator.

• mise o shimau 店をしまう *to close a store; to go out of business*

② *to do ╱ happen to completion, to do ╱ happen beyond the point of no return* «following the gerund (-**te** form) of another verb»

¶Otōto wa kēki o zenbu tabete shimaimashita.

弟はケーキを全部食べてしまいました。

My younger brother ate up all the cake.

shimauma 縞馬 *zebra*

shímei 氏名 *full name, surname and given name*

shímei 使命 *mission, appointed task*

• shimei o hatasu 使命を果たす *to carry out one's mission*

shimei 指名 *nomination, naming, designation*

• shimei suru 指名する *to nominate, to name, to designate* «The direct object must be a person.»

¶Tanimoto-san wa gichō ni shimei saremashita.

谷本さんは議長に指名されました。

Ms. Tanimoto was nominated as chairperson.

• shimei-dasha 指名打者 *designated hitter* «in baseball»

shimekiri 締め切り *deadline*

¶Kyō ga mōshikomi no shimekiri desu.

きょうが申し込みの締め切りです。

Today is the deadline for applications.

¶Shimekiri wa gogo go-ji desu.

締め切りは午後5時です。

The deadline is 5:00 p.m.

shimekiru 閉め切る{5} ① *to close completely*

② *to keep closed*

¶Heya no to o shimekitte wa ikenai yo.

部屋の戸を閉め切ってはいけないよ。

You mustn't keep the door of the room closed!

shimekiru 締め切る{5} *to stop accepting* «something that must be submitted»

¶Nyūgaku-gansho no uketsuke o shimekirimasu.

入学願書の受け付けを締め切ります。

We will stop accepting applications for admission.

shimeru 湿る{5} *to get damp*

¶Ame de sentaku-mono ga shimette shimaimashita.

雨で洗濯物が湿ってしまいました。

The laundry got damp with rain.

shiméru 占める *to occupy, to get, to take* «a place, position, or proportion»

¶Suiden ga mura no hanbun o shimete imasu.

水田が村の半分を占めています。

Rice fields occupy half the village.

¶Nihon wa Orinpikku de dai-ichi-i o shimeta.

日本はオリンピックで第1位を占めた。

Japan took first place in the Olympics.

shiméru 閉める *to shut, to close* «transitive» [⇔**akeru** 開ける]

¶Mado o shimete kudasai.

窓を閉めてください。

Please close the window.

¶Mon wa roku-ji ni shimeru sō desu.

門は6時に閉めるそうです。

I hear they shut the gate at 6:00.

shiméru 締める ① *to fasten, to tie securely* «The direct object is often an article of clothing that is tied on. Like other verbs for putting on clothing, **shimeru** in the -**te iru** form can express the meaning *be wearing, have on.*»

¶Shīto-beruto o shimete kudasai.

シートベルトを締めてください。

Please fasten your seat belt.

¶Ani wa nekutai o shimete imasu.

兄はネクタイを締めています。

My older brother is wearing a tie.

② *to tighten* «transitive» [⇔**yurumeru** 緩める]

• neji o shimeru ねじを締める *to tighten a screw*

shimésu 示す *to show, to indicate, to point out*

¶Taira-san wa kono hon ni kyōmi o shimeshimashita.

平さんはこの本に興味を示しました。

Mr. Taira showed interest in this book.

¶Jitsurei o ikutsu-ka shimeshite kudasai.

実例をいくつか示してください。

Please show me a few actual examples.

¶Ya-jirushi ga chōjō e no michi o shime-shite imasu.

矢印が頂上への道を示しています。

The arrow indicates the way to the top.

¶Ondo-kei wa nijū-do o shimeshite imasu.

温度計は20度を示しています。

The thermometer is showing 20 degrees.

shimi 染み *stain, spot*

¶Kono shatsu ni shimi ga tsuite imasu.

このシャツに染みがついています。

There is a stain on this shirt.

• shimi-nuki 染み抜き *stain removal*

shímin 市民 *citizen*

• shimin-ken 市民権 *citizenship*

shimiru 染みる ① *to soak ⟨into⟩, to penetrate ⟨into⟩, to permeate ⟨into⟩*

¶Inku ga fuku ni shimimashita.

インクが服にしみました。

Ink soaked into the clothes.

¶Ame ga futte mo, sugu jimen ni shimiru darō.

雨が降っても、すぐ地面にしみるだろう。

Even if it rains, it will probably soak into the ground right away.

• mi ni shimiru 身にしみる *to touch one's heart; to feel piercing*

¶Sono shinsetsu ga mi ni shimimashita.

その親切が身にしみました。

That kindness touched my heart.

¶Samusa ga mi ni shimiru yo.

寒さが身にしみるよ。

The cold is piercing!

② *to come into contact with and cause to hurt*

¶Kemuri ga me ni shimimashita.

煙が目にしみました。

Smoke got in my eyes and made them hurt.

shimó 霜 *frost*

• shimo-bashira 霜柱 *frost needles on the ground*

• shimo-yake 霜焼け *frostbite*

• hatsu-shimo 初霜 *first frost of the year*

shimon 指紋 *fingerprint*

shimyurḗtā シミュレーター *simulator*

shín シーン *scene* ⟪in a movie, play, novel, etc.⟫

shín 芯 *core, pith, heart*

¶Kono ringo wa shin made kusatte iru yo.

このりんごはしんまで腐っているよ。

This apple is rotten to the core!

• rōsoku no shin ろうそくのしん *candle wick*

• enpitsu no shin 鉛筆のしん *pencil lead*

shin- 新 − *new* ⟪Added to noun bases.⟫ [⇔**kyū-** 旧−]

• shin-kiroku 新記録 *new record*

• shin-taisō 新体操 *rhythmic gymnastics*

shina 品 [[→**shinamono** 品物]] *useful article; item of merchandise*

¶Sono mise ni iroiro na shina ga arimasu.

その店にいろいろな品があります。

There is a variety of merchandise in that store.

• shina-gire no 品切れの *out-of-stock, sold-out*

shinamono 品物 [[→**shina** 品]] *useful article; item of merchandise*

shinario シナリオ *scenario, screenplay*

• shinario-raitā シナリオライター *scenario writer*

shínbaru シンバル *cymbals*

shínbō 辛抱 *patience, endurance* [→ **gaman** 我慢]

• shinbō suru 辛抱する *to put up with, to endure*

• shinbō-zuyoi 辛抱強い *patient*

¶Kodomo-tachi wa shinbō-zuyoku basu o machimashita.

子供たちは辛抱強くバスを待ちました。

The children waited patiently for the bus.

shínboru シンボル *symbol* [→**shōchō** 象徴]

• shinboru-māku シンボルマーク *symbol, logo*

shinbun 新聞 *newspaper*

¶Shinbun o mō yomimashita ka.

新聞をもう読みましたか。
Have you already read the newspaper?
¶Shinbun ni yoru to, tsuyu ga aketa sō desu.
新聞によると、梅雨が明けたそうです。
According to the newspaper, the rainy season has ended.
• shinbun-haitatsu 新聞配達 *newspaper delivery; person who delivers newspapers*
• shinbun-kiji 新聞記事 *newspaper article*
• shinbun-kisha 新聞記者 *newspaper reporter*
• shinbun-sha 新聞社 *newspaper company*

shinchō 身長 *stature, height*
¶Shinchō wa dono gurai desu ka.
身長はどのぐらいですか。
About how tall are you?

shinchō 慎重 *caution, prudence*
• shinchō na 慎重な *careful, cautious, prudent* [→**chūi-bukai** 注意深い (s.v. **chūi** 注意)]
¶Chichi wa totemo shinchō ni unten shimasu.
父はとても慎重に運転します。
My father drives very carefully.

shinchū 真鍮 *brass* ((metal))

shindai 寝台 *bed* [→**beddo** ベッド]; (*sleeping*)*berth*
• shindai-sha 寝台車 *sleeping car*

shindan 診断 ① *medical examination* [→**shinsatsu** 診察]
• shindan o ukeru 診断を受ける *to undergo a medical examination*
② *diagnosis*
• shindan suru 診断する *to diagnose*
• shindan-sho 診断書 *medical certificate*
• kenkō-shindan 健康診断 *medical check-up*

shindō 振動 *vibration; oscillation*
• shindō suru 振動する *to vibrate; to oscillate*

shíndo 震度 *seismic intensity* ((measured on the Japanese Metereological Agency 0–7 scale))

shínfonī シンフォニー *symphony* ((musi-cal piece)) [→**kōkyōkyoku** 交響曲]

shingā シンガー *singer*
• shingā-songuraitā シンガーソングライター *singer-songwriter*

shingaku 進学 *advancement, going on* ((to a higher-level school))
• shingaku suru 進学する *to advance, to go on*
¶Kōgyō-kōkō ni shingaku shi-tai desu.
工業高校に進学したいです。
I want to go on to a technical high school.

shingata 新型 *new model, new type*
¶Kore wa shingata no kuruma desu.
これは新型の車です。
This is a new-model car.

shíngetsu 新月 *new moon* [⇔**mangetsu** 満月]

shíngi 審議 *discussion, deliberation*
• shingi suru 審議する *to discuss, to deliberate on*
• shingi-kai 審議会 *deliberative council*

shingō 信号 ① *signal; signaling*
• shingō suru 信号する *to send a signal*
② *railroad signal; traffic light*
¶Shingō ga ao ni natte kara michi o watarimasu.
信号が青になってから道を渡ります。
We cross the street after the traffic light turns green.
• shingō o mamoru 〔mushi suru〕 信号を守る〔無視する〕 *to obey* 〔*disregard*〕 *a traffic light*
• shingō-ki 信号機 *signal* ((device))
• aka-shingō 赤信号 *red light*
• ao-shingō 青信号 *green light*

shíngu 寝具 *bedding* ((Refers to both beds and bedclothes.))

shíngurusu シングルス *singles* ((in sports)) [⇔**daburusu** ダブルス]

shínja 信者 *religious believer*

shinjin 新人 *newcomer* ((in a given field of endeavor)); *rookie*
• shinjin-kashu 新人歌手 *new singer*

shinjíru 信じる *to believe, to be sure of*
¶Hanaoka-san no iu koto o shinjimasu.
花岡さんの言う事を信じます。

I believe what Ms. Hanaoka says.
¶Chanpion no shōri o shinjite imasu.
チャンピオンの勝利を信じています。
I am sure of the champion's victory.

shínjitsu 真実 *truth*
¶Sensei ni shinjitsu o hanashimashita.
先生に真実を話しました。
We told the truth to the teacher.
• shinjitsu no 真実の *true, real* [→**hontō no** 本当の]

shinju 真珠 *pearl*
¶Ueno-san wa shinju no kubikazari o shite imasu.
上野さんは真珠の首飾りをしています。
Ms. Ueno is wearing a pearl necklace.

shinjū 心中 *two or more people committing suicide together*
• muri-shinjū 無理心中 *multiple suicide in which one person is unwilling*

shínka 進化 *evolution*
• shinka suru 進化する *to evolve*
• shinka-ron 進化論 *the theory of evolution*

Shinkánsen 新幹線 *the Shinkansen, the Bullet Train*
¶Shinkansen de Nagoya e ikimashita.
新幹線で名古屋へ行きました。
We went to Nagoya on the Shinkansen.
• Tōkaidō-shinkansen 東海道新幹線 *the Tokaido Shinkansen*

shínkei 神経 *a nerve*
• shinkei ga futoi 神経が太い *to have a lot of nerve, to be daring*
• shinkei ga surudoi 〔nibui〕 神経が鋭い 〔鈍い〕 *to be sensitive* 〔*insensitive*〕 《describing a person》
• shinkei-gaku 神経学 *neurology*
• shinkei-shitsu na 神経質な *nervous by temperament, high-strung*
• shinkei-shō 神経症 *neurosis* [→**noirōze** ノイローゼ]
• shinkei-tsū 神経痛 *neuralgia*

shinken 真剣 **na** ～な *serious, earnest* [→**honki no** 本気の]
¶Keikan wa shinken na kao o shite imasu.
警官は真剣な顔をしています。

The police officer has a serious look on his face.
¶Shinken ni sō iimashita yo.
真剣にそう言いましたよ。
I said so seriously!

shinkō 信仰 *religious faith, religious belief*
• shinkō suru 信仰する *to come to believe in, to come to have faith in*
¶Obāsan wa Bukkyo o shinkō shite imasu.
おばあさんは仏教を信仰しています。
Grandmother believes in Buddhism.

shinkō 進行 *progress, advance, forward movement*
• shinkō suru 進行する *to make progress, to proceed, to move forward*
¶Keikaku wa junchō ni shinkō shite imasu.
計画は順調に進行しています。
The plan is proceeding smoothly.

shinkoku 深刻 **na** ～な *serious, grave, severe*
¶Sore wa shinkoku na mondai desu ne.
それは深刻な問題ですね。
That's a serious problem, isn't it.
¶Shushō wa sono jiken o shinkoku ni uketomete iru.
首相はその事件を深刻に受けとめている。
The prime minister faced the incident seriously.

shinkon 新婚 **no** ～の *newly-married*
• shinkon-fūfu 新婚夫婦 *newly-married couple*
• shinkon-ryokō 新婚旅行 *honeymoon*
¶Ano futari wa Hawai ni shinkon-ryokō ni ikimasu.
あの二人はハワイに新婚旅行に行きます。
Those two will go to Hawaii on their honeymoon.

shinkū 真空 *vacuum*
• shinkū-kan 真空管 *vacuum tube*

shinkuronaizudosuímingu シンクロナイズドスイミング *synchronized swimming*

shinkyū 進級 *promotion* 《*to a higher grade in school or to a higher rank*》
• shinkyū suru 進級する *to be promoted,*

to move up

shínnā シンナー *paint thinner*

shínnen 信念 *belief, faith, conviction*

shínnen 新年 *new year*

¶Shinnen omedetō!

新年おめでとう！

Happy New Year!

• shinnen-kai 新年会 *New Year's party* 《Held after the new year has begun.》

shinnyū 侵入 *invasion, intrusion, break-in*

• shinnyū suru 侵入する *to invade, to intrude, to break in*

¶Yūbe kaisha ni dorobō ga shinnyū shimashita.

ゆうべ会社に泥棒が侵入しました。

A thief broke into the company last night.

• shinnyū-sha 侵入者 *invader, intruder*

shinnyūsei 新入生 *new student, student in the lowest class*

shinóbu 忍ぶ ① *to bear, to endure, to stand* [→**nintai suru** 忍耐する]

② *to conceal oneself from*

• hito-me o shinobu 人目を忍ぶ *to avoid being seen*

shinógu 凌ぐ ① *to endure, to bear, to stand* [→**nintai suru** 忍耐する]

② *to exceed, to surpass, to outstrip*

③ *to avoid, to take shelter from*

shinpai 心配 *anxiety, worry, concern* [⇔**anshin** 安心]

¶Haha no byōki ga shinpai desu.

母の病気が心配です。

My mother's illness is a worry.

• shinpai suru 心配する *to become anxious about, to get worried about*

¶Yumi-san wa sore o shinpai shite ita yo.

由美さんはそれを心配していたよ。

Yumi was worried about that!

• shinpai no tane 心配の種 *source of worry, cause of anxiety*

• A ni shinpai o kakeru Aに心配をかける *to cause A anxiety*

shinpan 審判 ① *umpire* [→**anpaia** アンパイア]; *referee* [→**referī**

レフェリー]; *judge* 《for a competition》 [→**jajji** ジャッジ]

② *umpiring; refereeing; judging* 《for a competition》; *decision, judgment*

• shinpan suru 審判する *to umpire; to referee; to judge*

shínpi 神秘 *mystery, something unexplained*

• shinpi-teki na 神秘的な *mysterious*

shinpin 新品 *new item* 《as opposed to something used or secondhand》

shínpo 進歩 *progress, improvement*

• shinpo suru 進歩する *to make progress, to improve*

¶Sawada-san no Eigo ryoku wa zuibun shinpo shita ne.

沢田さんの英語力はずいぶん進歩したね。

Mr. Sawada's English has improved a lot, hasn't it.

¶Kagaku-gijutsu ga kyūsoku ni shinpo shimashita.

科学技術が急速に進歩しました。

Technology progressed rapidly.

• shinpo-teki na 進歩的な *progressive*

shinpojūmu シンポジウム 《Note the mismatch between the katakana spelling and the pronunciation.》 *symposium*

shínpu 神父 (*Catholic*)*priest*

• -shinpu －神父 *Father* 《Added to a priest's name as a title.》

¶Rasāru-shinpu wa raigetsu o-kaeri ni narimasu.

ラサール神父は来月お帰りになります。

Father La Salle will go home next month.

shínpu 新婦 *bride* 《at a wedding》 [⇔**shinrō** 新郎]

shínpuru シンプル **na** ～な *simple, not ornate*

shinrai 信頼 *trust, confidence, reliance*

• shinrai suru 信頼する *to put trust in, to rely on*

¶Minna ga kōchi o shinrai shite imasu.

みんながコーチを信頼しています。

Everyone has trust in the coach.

¶Sono hito wa shinrai dekiru tomodachi desu.

その人は信頼できる友達です。
That person is a friend I can rely on.

shinreki 新暦 *the new (solar) calendar*
[→**taiyō-reki** 太陽暦 (s.v. **taiyō** 太陽]

shínri 心理 *psychology, mentality*
• shinri-gaku 心理学 *(the study of) psychology*
• shinri-gaku-sha 心理学者 *psychologist*

shínri 真理 *a truth, indisputable fact*

shinrin 森林 *forest, woods* [→**mori** 森]

shínro 進路 *course, way, path*
¶Mada shōrai no shinro o kimete imasen.
まだ将来の進路を決めていません。
I haven't yet decided on my future course.

shinrō 新郎 *groom* 《at a wedding》 [⇔ **shinpu** 新婦]
• shinrō-shinpu 新郎新婦 *the bride and groom*

shinrui 親類 *a relative* [→**shinseki** 親戚]
¶Senshū Shikoku no shinrui o tazunemashita.
先週四国の親類を訪ねました。
I visited a Shikoku relative last week.
¶Ano hito wa chikai shinrui desu.
あの人は近い親類です。
That person is a close relative.

shinryaku 侵略 *invasion* 《of another country》
• shinryaku suru 侵略する *to invade*
• shinryaku-sha 侵略者 *invader*

shinryōjo 診療所 *clinic*

shinsatsu 診察 *medical examination*
• shinsatsu suru 診察する *to examine*
¶Tajima-sensei ni shinsatsu shite itadakimashita.
田島先生に診察していただきました。
I had Dr. Tajima examine me.

shinsei 申請 *application* 《to the authorities》
• shinsei suru 申請する *to apply for*

shinsei 神聖 *sacredness, holiness*
• shinsei na 神聖な *sacred, holy*

shinseki 親せき *a relative* [→**shinrui** 親類]
¶Daigaku-sōchō wa watashi no tōi shin-

seki ni atarimasu.
大学総長は私の遠い親せきに当たります。
The university president is my distant relative.

shinsen 新鮮 *na* ～な *fresh*
¶Shinsen na kūki o chotto irete kudasai.
新鮮な空気をちょっと入れてください。
Please let in a little fresh air.
¶Kono ichigo wa shinsen desu.
このいちごは新鮮です。
These strawberries are fresh.

shinsesáizā シンセサイザー *(musical) synthesizer*

shínsetsu 親切 *kindness*
• shinsetsu na 親切な *kind, nice* [⇔**fu-shinsetsu na** 不親切な]
¶Yōko-san wa dare ni demo shinsetsu desu.
洋子さんはだれにでも親切です。
Yoko is kind to everyone.
¶Masao-kun wa shinsetsu ni nōto o misete kureta.
正男君は親切にノートを見せてくれた。
Masao kindly showed me his notebook.

shínshi 紳士 *gentleman*
• shinshi-fuku 紳士服 *men's wear*

shinshitsu 寝室 *bedroom*

shinshutsu 進出 *advance, making inroads*
• shinshutsu suru 進出する *to advance, to make inroads*

shíntai 身体 *body* 《of a living creature》 [→**karada** 体]
• shintai-kensa 身体検査 *medical check-up, physical examination*
• shintai-shōgai-sha 身体障害者 *physically handicapped person*

Shintō 神道 *Shinto, Shintoism* 《the indigenous Japanese religion》

shinu 死ぬ *to die* 《The subject must be a person or animal.》 [⇔**umareru** 生まれる]
¶Sofu wa gojūsan-sai de shinimashita.
祖父は53歳で死にました。
My grandfather died at 53.
¶Shushō wa byōki de shinimashita.
首相は病気で死にました。
The prime minister died of an illness.

¶Jidōsha-jiko de shinu hito ga ōi desu.

自動車事故で死ぬ人が多いです。

There are many people who die in auto-mobile accidents.

¶Ane wa shinda sobo no koto o yoku oboete iru.

姉は死んだ祖母のことをよく覚えている。

My older sister remembers our dead grandmother very well.

• shinde iru 死んでいる *to be dead*

shinwa 神話 *myth*

• Girisha-shinwa ギリシャ神話 *Greek myth*

shín'ya 深夜 *the middle of the night, the late night* [→**mayonaka** 真夜中]

¶Hayashi-san wa mai-ban shin'ya made benkyō shimasu.

林さんは毎晩深夜まで勉強します。

Ms. Hayashi studies until the middle of the night every night.

• shin'ya-hōsō 深夜放送 *late-night broadcasting; late-night program*

shin'yō 信用 ① *trust, confidence* [→ **shinrai** 信頼]

• shin'yō suru 信用する *to put confidence in, to put trust in*

② *reputability*

¶Are wa shin'yō no aru mēkā desu.

あれは信用のあるメーカーです。

That's a reputable manufacturer.

shin'yū 親友 *close friend, good friend*

¶Natori-kun wa boku no shin'yū no hi-tori desu.

名取君は僕の親友の一人です。

Natori is one of my close friends.

shinzen 親善 *friendship, amity, goodwill*

• shinzen-jiai 親善試合 *goodwill game, goodwill match*

• shinzen-shisetsu 親善使節 *goodwill mission*

• kokusai-shinzen 国際親善 *international friendship*

shinzō 心臓 *heart* ((bodily organ))

¶Sono tegami o uketotta toki, shinzō ga dokidoki shimashita.

その手紙を受け取ったとき、心臓がどきどき

しました。

My heart beat fast when I received that letter.

• shinzō ga tsuyoi 心臓が強い *to have a strong heart; to be brazen*

• shinzō ga yowai 心臓が弱い *to have a weak heart; to be timid*

• shinzō-byō 心臓病 *heart disease*

• shinzō-ishoku 心臓移植 *heart transplant*

• shinzō-mahi 心臓麻痺 *heart failure, heart attack*

shió 塩 *salt*

¶Shio o totte kudasai.

塩を取ってください。

Please pass the salt.

¶Shio o hito-tsumami iremasu.

塩を一つまみ入れます。

I'll put in a pinch of salt.

¶Kono sūpu wa shio ga kiki-sugite imasu.

このスープは塩がききすぎています。

This soup is too salty.

• shio-karai 塩辛い *salty*

• shio-zuke no 塩漬けの *salted, pre-served with salt*

shió 潮 ① (ocean)*tide*

¶Shio no nagare ga hayai ne.

潮の流れが速いね。

The tide's flow is fast, isn't it.

• shio ga michiru [hiku] 潮が満ちる [引く] *the tide rises* [*ebbs*]

② ~o fuku ~を吹く *to spout* 《The subject is ordinarily a whale.》

¶Ano kujira wa ima shio o fuite imasu.

あの鯨は今潮を吹いています。

That whale is spouting now.

• shio-kaze 潮風 *sea breeze*

• hiki-shio 引き潮 *low tide*

• michi-shio 満ち潮 *high tide*

shiohígari 潮干狩り *gathering sea-shells, etc., when the tide is out*

¶Enoshima ni shiohigari ni ikimashō.

江の島に潮干狩りに行きましょう。

Let's go gathering sea shells at Eno-shima.

shiómizu 塩水 *saltwater, brine* [⇔

mamizu 真水]

shíon 子音 [☞**shiin** 子音]

shioreru しおれる ① *to wither, to wilt* 《when the subject is a plant》 ② *to become dejected, to become downhearted*

shiori 栞, 枝折り ① *bookmark* ② *guidebook, handbook* [→**annai-sho** 案内書 (s.v. **annai** 案内)]

shippai 失敗 *failure* [⇔**seikō** 成功] ¶Shippai wa seikō no haha. 失敗は成功の母。《proverb》 *Failure is but a stepping stone to success.* 《Literally: Failure is the mother of success.》 •shippai suru 失敗する *to fail* 《intransitive》 ¶Saisho no keikaku wa kekkyoku shippai shimashita. 最初の計画は結局失敗しました。 *The first plan eventually failed.*

shippó 尻尾 *tail* [→**o** 尾]

shirabéru 調べる ① *to examine, to investigate, to look into, to look up* ¶Rekishi-ka wa mukashi no kiroku o shirabemashita. 歴史家は昔の記録を調べました。 *The historian examined the old records.* ¶Sono basho o chizu de shirabenasai. その場所を地図で調べなさい。 *Look up the place on the map.* ② *to search, to consult* ¶Tosho-kan de hyakkajiten o shirabemashita. 図書館で百科事典を調べました。 *I consulted an encyclopedia in the library.*

shiragá 白髪 *gray hair; white hair* ¶Ano shiraga no dansei wa dare desu ka. あの白髪の男性はだれですか。 *Who is that gray-haired man?* •shiraga ni naru 白髪になる *to become gray-haired*

shirakaba 白樺 *white birch*

shirakéru 白ける *to become uninteresting, to lose it's pleasant atmosphere*

shirami 虱 *louse*

shiránkao 知らん顔 *acting as if one doesn't know, attitude of indifference* •shirankao o suru 知らん顔をする *to act as if one doesn't know, to show indifference*

shirase 知らせ *notification, news* ¶Sono shirase o kiite odorokimashita. その知らせを聞いて驚きました。 *I heard that news and was surprised.*

shiraseru 知らせる *to tell, to report, to let know* •A ni B o shiraseru AにBを知らせる *to tell A B, to report B to A, to let A know B* ¶Atarashii jūsho o shirasete kudasai. 新しい住所を知らせてください。 *Please let me know your new address.*

shirewatáru 知れ渡る *to become widely known*

shirí 尻 *buttocks, bottom* •shiri-tori 尻取り *word-chain game* 《A game in which each player must say a word beginning with the last **kana** letter in the previous player's word. For example, if one player says **sakana**(さかな), perhaps the next player might say **natsu-yasumi** (なつやすみ).》 •shiri-mochi 尻餅 *slipping and falling on one's bottom* •shiri-mochi o tsuku 尻餅をつく *to slip and fall on one's bottom*

shiriai 知り合い *an acquaintance* ¶Miyashita-san wa watashi no shiriai desu. 宮下さんは私の知り合いです。 *Ms. Miyashita is an acquaintance of mine.*

shíritsu 市立 *no*~の *municipal, administered by a city* •shiritsu-kōkō 市立高校 *municipal high school* •shiritsu-tosho-kan 市立図書館 *municipal library*

shíritsu 私立 *no* ~の *private, privately administered* [⇔**kōritsu no** 公立の] ¶Musume wa shiritsu no joshi-chūgakkō ni kayotte imasu.

娘は私立の女子中学校に通っています。
My daughter is going to a private junior high school for girls.

• shiritsu-kōkō 私立高校 *private high school*

• shiritsu-tantei 私立探偵 *private detective*

shirizokéru 退ける ① *to repulse, to turn away*

② *to keep away, to prevent from approaching* [→**tōzakeru** 遠ざける①]

③ *to refuse, to reject* [→**kotowaru** 断る①]

shirizóku 退く ① *to move back, to step back*

② *to retire from, to resign from*

shírīzu シリーズ ① *series* 《of games between the same opponents》

② *series* 《of books, movies, etc.》

• Nihon-shirīzu 日本シリーズ *the Japan Series* 《the championship series in Japanese professional baseball》

• Shārokku-Hōmuzu no shirīzu シャーロック・ホームズのシリーズ *the Sherlock Holmes series*

shíro 白 *white* 《as a noun》

• shiro-ji 白地 *white background*

shiro 城 *castle*

shirói 白い ① *white* 《as an adjective》

¶Kaichō wa shiroi fuku o kite imasu.
会長は白い服を着ています。
The chairperson is wearing white clothes.

② *fair, light* 《describing a person's skin》

¶Masako-san wa hada ga shiroi desu.
正子さんは肌が白いです。
Masako's skin is fair.

shírokuro 白黒 ① *black and white*

② *right and wrong*

• shirokuro-terebi 白黒テレビ *black-and-white television*

shirómi 白身 ① *white* 《of an egg》 [⇔**kimi** 黄身]

② *white meat* 《of a fish》

• shiromi no sakana 白身の魚 *fish with white meat*

shíroppu シロップ *syrup*

shírōto 素人 *an amateur, a non-expert* [⇔**kuróto** 玄人]

shíru シール *sticker*

shíru 汁 ① *juice; sap*

• remon no shiru レモンの汁 *lemon juice*

② *soup; broth*

• miso-shiru 味噌汁 *miso soup*

shiru 知る {5} *to come to know, to find out*

¶Terebi de sore o shirimashita.
テレビでそれを知りました。
I found that out from TV.

• shitte iru 知っている *to know, to know about* 《The corresponding negative, however, is **shiranai** 知らない; the expected form **shitte inai** is not used.》

¶Akiko-san wa uta o takusan shitte iru yo.
明子さんは歌をたくさん知っているよ。
Akiko knows a lot of songs!

¶Zutto mae kara Sakata-san o shitte imasu.
ずっと前から坂田さんを知っています。
I've known Ms. Sakata since long ago.

¶Nihon no koto wa amari yoku shirimasen.
日本のことはあまりよく知りません。
I don't know very much about Japan.

¶Jun ga doko ni sunde iru ka shitte imasu ka.
純がどこに住んでいるか知っていますか。
Do you know where Jun lives?

shirubāshito シルバーシート *"silver" seat, priority seat* 《Provided for elderly and handicapped passengers on public transportation in Japan.》

shíruetto シルエット *silhouette*

shirukuhátto シルクハット *silk hat, top hat*

shirushi 印 ① *identifying mark*

• shirushi o tsukeru 印をつける *to put a mark*

¶Atarashii tango ni aka-enpitsu de shirushi o tsukemashita.
新しい単語に赤鉛筆で印をつけました。
I put marks on the new words with a red pencil.

② *sign, symbol, token*

¶Kachō wa dōi no shirushi ni unazukimashita.

課長は同意の印にうなずきました。

The section chief nodded as a sign of agreement.

shíryō 資料 *materials, data*

• shiryō o atsumeru 資料を集める *to collect data*

shíryoku 視力 *eyesight, vision, ability to see*

¶Kurata-san wa kōtsū-jiko de shiryoku o ushinaimashita.

倉田さんは交通事故で視力を失いました。

Mr. Kurata lost his eyesight in a traffic accident.

• shiryoku ga ii〔warui〕 視力がいい〔悪い〕 *one's eyesight is good〔bad〕*

• shiryoku-kensa 視力検査 *eye test*

shisei 姿勢 ① *posture*

• shisei ga ii 姿勢がいい *one's posture is good*

• shisei o tadasu 姿勢を正す *to straighten up, to stand ⁄ sit straight*

② *attitude, stance*〔→**taido** 態度〕

shiseki 史跡 *historic spot*

shisen 視線 *one's gaze, one's eyes*

¶Watashi-tachi wa shisen ga aimashita.

私たちは視線が合いました。

Our eyes met.

• shisen o sosogu 視線を注ぐ *to fix one's gaze*

• shisen o mukeru 視線を向ける *to direct one's gaze, to turn one's eyes*

shísetsu 施設 *institution, facility, installation*

• kōkyō-shisetsu 公共施設 *public facility*

shísha 支社 *branch office*

shísha 死者 *dead person, a fatality*

¶Sono jiko de ōku no shisha ga demashita.

その事故で多くの死者が出ました。

Many fatalities occurred in that accident.

shísha 使者 *messenger, envoy*

shíshi 獅子 *lion*〔→**raion** ライオン〕

shishū 刺繍 *embroidery*

• shishū o suru ししゅうをする *to do embroidery*

broidery

• shishū-ito 刺繍糸 *embroidery thread*

shishúnki 思春期 *adolescence*

shishutsu 支出 *expenditure, disbursement, outgo*〔⇔**shūnyū** 収入〕

¶Kongetsu wa shishutsu ga ōkatta ne.

今月は支出が多かったね。

This month there were a lot of expenditures, weren't there.

shīsō シーソー *seesaw*

• shīsō-gēmu シーソーゲーム *seesaw game*

shisō 思想 *thought, ideas*

• shisō-ka 思想家 *thinker*

shiso しそ *beefsteak plant*

shíson 子孫 *descendant*〔⇔**senzo** 先祖〕

shisshin 失神 ～**suru** ～する *to faint*〔→**kizetsu suru** 気絶する〕

¶Tsūkō-nin wa sono jiko o mite shisshin shimashita.

通行人はその事故を見て失神しました。

A passer-by saw that accident and fainted.

shísso 質素 ～**na** ～な *simple, plain, unostentatious*

¶Matsushima-san wa shisso na kurashi o shite imasu.

松島さんは質素な暮らしをしています。

Mr. Matsushima is living a simple life.

¶Kaichō wa shisso na minari o shite imasu.

会長は質素な身なりをしています。

The chairperson is dressed plainly.

shisú 指数 ① *(numerical)index*
② *exponent*《in mathematics》

shísutemu システム *system*

shita 下〔〔⇔**ue** 上〕〕 ① *bottom; lower part*

¶Shita kara ni-gyō-me o yominasai.

下から2行目を読みなさい。

Read the second line from the bottom.

¶Sono hon wa hon-dana no ichiban shita no dan ni aru.

その本は本棚のいちばん下の段にある。

That book is on the bottom shelf of the bookshelf.

② *the area under, the area below*

¶Atsukatta kara, ki no shita ni suwarimashita.

暑かったから、木の下に座りました。

It was hot, so I sat under a tree.

¶Oka ni tatsu to aoi umi ga shita ni miemasu.

丘に立つと青い海が下に見えます。

Standing on the hill the blue sea is visible below.

③ *the portion of a scale or ranking below*

¶Musuko wa sono hito no shita de hataraite imasu.

息子はその人の下で働いています。

My son is working under that person.

④ ~**no** ~の *younger*

¶Watashi wa ani yori mittsu shita desu.

私は兄より三つ下です。

I am three years younger than my older brother.

shitá 舌 *tongue*

shitagatte 従って《This word is the gerund (-**te** form)of **shitagau** 従う and has the predictable meanings as well.》

① *therefore, consequently* [→**dakara** だから]

¶Tōkyō wa jinkō ga ōku, shitagatte bukka ga takai.

東京は人口が多く、従って物価が高い。

Tokyo has a large population and consequently, prices are high.

② [☞**ni shitagatte** に従って]

shitagau 従う *to comply, to go along, to abide, to conform*

¶Heitai wa shiki-kan no meirei ni shitagaimasu.

兵隊は指揮官の命令に従います。

A soldier complies with his commander's orders.

¶Watashi-tachi wa sensei no chūkoku ni shitagaimashita.

私たちは先生の忠告に従いました。

We followed our teacher's advice.

shitagi 下着 *underwear, undergarment*

shitagókoro 下心 *ulterior motive*

shitai 死体 *dead body, corpse, carcass*

shitajiki 下敷き *underlay* 《placed under the paper one is writing on》

shitaku 支度, 仕度 *preparations, arrangements* [→**junbi** 準備]

¶Haha wa ima chōshoku no shitaku o shite imasu.

母は今朝食の仕度をしています。

My mother is now making the preparations for breakfast.

¶Shūgakuryokō no shitaku o shinakute wa narimasen.

修学旅行の仕度をしなくてはなりません。

I must make preparations for the school excursion.

• shitaku ga dekiru 支度が出来る *readiness is achieved, preparations are made complete*

¶Yūshoku no shitaku ga dekimashita.

夕食の仕度ができました。

Dinner is ready.

¶Watashi-tachi wa dekakeru shitaku ga dekite imasen.

私たちは出かける仕度ができていません。

We aren't ready to go out.

• shitaku suru 仕度する *to prepare, to make ready*

shitamachi 下町 *traditional shopping and entertainment district of a city, downtown* 《Typically located in a low-lying area of a Japanese city.》[⇔**yama-note** 山の手]

shitashíi 親しい *friendly, intimate, close*

¶Musuko ni wa shitashii tomodachi wa hotondo imasen.

息子には親しい友達はほとんどいません。

My son has almost no close friends.

¶Keiko-chan to shitashiku natta yo.

恵子ちゃんと親しくなったよ。

I've become friendly with Keiko!

shitatáru 滴る *to drip* 《intransitive》

¶Ase ga sono sōsha no hitai kara shitatatte imasu.

汗がその走者の額から滴っています。

Sweat is dripping from that runner's forehead.

shitate 仕立て *tailoring, making* 《major articles of clothing》

• shitate-ya 仕立屋 *tailor shop, dressmaker's; tailor, dressmaker*

shitatéru 仕立てる *to tailor, to make* 《major articles of clothing》

shitáu 慕う ① *to come to yearn for, to come to long for*
¶Bōmei-sha ga kokyō o shitau no wa tō-zen desu.
亡命者が故郷を慕うのは当然です。
It is natural for a defector to long for home.
　② *to come to adore, to come to idolize*
¶Kodomo-tachi wa ano wakai sensei o shitatte imasu.
子供たちはあの若い先生を慕っています。
The children adore that young teacher.

shitauke 下請け ① *subcontract work, subcontracting*
• shitauke suru 下請けする *to do as sub-contracting*
　② [☞**shitauke-gyōsha** 下請け業者（below）]
• shitauke-gyōsha 下請け業者 *subcontractor*

shitei 指定 *specification, designation*
• shitei no 指定の *specified, designated, set*
¶Shitei no jikan ni okuremashita.
指定の時間に遅れました。
I was late for the set time.
• shitei suru 指定する *to specify, to designate, to set*
¶Buchō wa kaigi no basho o shitei shima-shita.
部長は会議の場所を指定しました。
The department head designated the place for the meeting.
• shitei-seki 指定席 *reserved seat* [⇔ **jiyū-seki** 自由席（s.v. **jiyū** 自由）]

shiteki 私的 ～**na** ～な *private, personal*

shiteki 指摘 ～**suru** ～する *to point out, to indicate*
¶Chichi wa sono ayamari o shiteki shite kureta.
父はその誤りを指摘してくれた。
My father pointed out that mistake for me.

shiten 支店 *branch store, branch office*

• shiten-chō 支店長 *branch manager*

shitetsu 私鉄 *private railroad, non-government railroad*

shīto シート *seat, place to sit* [→**seki** 席]

shīto シート *waterproof canvas covering*

shīto シート *sheet* 《of paper, etc.》
¶Sono hikidashi ni kitte no shīto ga arimasu.
その引き出しに切手のシートがあります。
There is a sheet of stamps in that draw-er.
• -shīto -シート《counter for sheets; see Appendix 2》

shītsu シーツ （*bed*）*sheet*

shitsu 質 *quality* 《i.e., degree of goodness or badness》
¶Ryō yori shitsu ga taisetsu desu.
量より質が大切です。
Quality is more important than quantity.
¶Kono niku wa shitsu ga warui desu.
この肉は質が悪いです。
The quality of this meat is bad.

shitsū 歯痛 *toothache*

shitsubō 失望 *disappointment, discouragement*
¶Maketa chīmu no shitsubō wa ōkikatta desu.
負けたチームの失望は大きかったです。
The defeated team was extremely disappointed.
• shitsubō suru 失望する *to become disappointed, to become discouraged* [→**gak-kari suru** がっかりする]
¶Watashi-tachi wa sono shirase o kiite shitsubō shita.
私たちはその知らせを聞いて失望した。
We heard that news and were disappointed.
¶Sono keikaku ni shitsubō shimashita.
その計画に失望しました。
I was disappointed at that plan.

shitsúdo 湿度 *humidity*
• shitsudo-kei 湿度計 *hygrometer*

shitsugyō 失業 *unemployment*
• shitsugyō suru 失業する *to lose one's job*

- shitsugyō-chū no 失業中の
out-of-work, unemployed
- shitsugyō-ritsu 失業率 *unemployment rate*
- shitsugyō-sha 失業者 *unemployed person*

shitsuke 躾 *training in polite behavior, discipline*
¶Ryōshin wa shitsuke ga kibishii desu.
両親はしつけが厳しいです。
My parents' discipline is strict.
- shitsuke ga ii 〔warui〕 しつけがいい
〔悪い〕 *well-* 〔*ill-*〕 *bred*

shitsukéru 躾ける *to train in polite behavior, to discipline*

shitsukói しつこい ① *annoyingly persistent*
¶Kaichō wa sono keikaku o shitsukoku shuchō shite iru.
会長はその計画をしつこく主張している。
The chairperson is persistently advocating that plan.
② *too strong, too heavy* 《when describing a flavor, odor, color, etc.》
¶Tai-ryōri wa watashi ni wa shitsukoi desu.
タイ料理は私にはしつこいです。
Thai cuisine is too strong for me.

shitsumon 質問 *question, inquiry*
¶Nani-ka shitsumon ga arimasu ka.
何か質問がありますか。
Are there any questions?
¶Hōdōkan wa sono shitsumon ni assari kotaemashita.
報道官はその質問にあっさり答えました。
The press officer easily answered that question.
- shitsumon suru 質問する *to ask a question*
¶Shitsumon shite mo yoroshii desu ka.
質問してもよろしいですか。
May I ask a question?

shitsúnai 室内 *interior of a room*
- shitsunai no 室内の *indoor*
- shitsunai-pūru 室内プール *indoor swimming pool*
- shitsunai-supōtsu 室内スポーツ *indoor sports*

shitsúrei 失礼 *rudeness, impoliteness*
- shitsurei na 失礼な *rude, impolite*
¶Hito o yubi-sasu no wa shitsurei desu.
人を指さすのは失礼です。
It is rude to point at people.
¶Shitsurei desu ga, dochira-sama deshō ka.
失礼ですが、どちら様でしょうか。
May I ask who you are? 《Literally: *This is rude, but who are you?*》
- shitsurei suru 失礼する *to behave rudely* 《This expression is most often used to express politeness by saying that one's own behavior is rude.》
¶Shitsurei shimasu.
失礼します。
Pardon me (for what I about to do).
《Literally: *I will behave rudely.*》
¶Shitsurei shimashita.
失礼しました。
Pardon me (for what I did). 《Literally: *I behaved rudely.*》
¶Sorosoro shitsurei shimasu.
そろそろ失礼します。
I must be going soon. 《Literally: *I will soon behave rudely.*》

shitsuren 失恋 *unrequited love*
- shitsuren suru 失恋する *to be disappointed in love*

shitto 嫉妬 *jealousy*
- shitto suru しっとする *to become jealous*
¶Boku wa ani ni shitto shite inai yo.
僕は兄にしっとしていないよ。
I am not jealous of my older brother!
- shitto-bukai 嫉妬深い *jealous*

shiwa 皺 *wrinkle*

shiwaza 仕業 *act, deed,* 〈*a person's*〉 *doing*
¶Kore wa otōto no shiwaza ni chigai-nai yo.
これは弟の仕業に違いないよ。
This must be my younger brother's doing!

shíya 視野 ① *one's range of sight, one's field of view* [→**shikai** 視界]
- shiya ni hairu 視野に入る *to come into*

view

② *view of things, vision, way of looking at things*

¶Katō-san wa shiya ga semai desu.

加藤さんは視野が狭いです。

Mr. Kato's view of things is narrow.

shiyákusho 市役所 *city hall, town hall*

shiyō 私用 ① *private use, personal use*

② *private business, personal business*

¶Chichi wa shiyō de Kyōto ni ikimasu.

父は私用で京都に行きます。

My father will go to Kyoto on personal business.

shiyō 使用 *use*

• shiyō suru 使用する *to use* [→**tsukau** 使う]

¶Kono keisan-ki o shiyō shite mo ii desu ka.

この計算機を使用してもいいですか。

May I use this calculator?

• shiyō-chū no 使用中の *in-use*

• shiyō-hō 使用法 *way of using*

• shiyō-sha 使用者 *user*

shizen 自然 *nature*

¶Nihon no shizen wa utsukushii desu.

日本の自然は美しいです。

Nature in Japan is beautiful.

• shizen no／na 自然の／な *natural* [⇔ **fushizen na** 不自然な]

¶Kobayashi-san no taido wa goku shizen desu.

小林さんの態度はごく自然です。

Ms. Kobayashi's manner is quite natural.

• shizen ni 自然に *naturally; by itself, without anyone causing it*

¶Doa ga shizen ni shimatta yo.

ドアが自然に閉まったよ。

The door closed by itself!

• shizen-kagaku 自然科学 *natural science*

• shizen-shokuhin 自然食品 *natural food*

shízuka 静か ～**na** ～な ① *quiet, silent* [⇔**urusai** 煩い①]

¶Otaku no Akira-kun wa shizuka na ko desu ne.

お宅の明君は静かな子ですね。

Your Akira is a quiet child, isn't he.

¶Kōchō-sensei wa shizuka na kuchō de hanashimasu.

校長先生は静かな口調で話します。

The principal talks in a quiet voice.

• shizuka ni suru 静かにする *to be quiet, to stop making noise*

② *calm, still* [→**odayaka na** 穏やかな]

¶Asa no mizuumi wa totemo shizuka desu.

朝の湖はとても静かです。

The lake is very calm in the morning.

③ *gentle, slow-moving*

• shizuka na nagare 静かな流れ *gentle current*

shizukésa 静けさ ① *quietness, stillness*

② *tranquility, serenity*

shizukú 滴 *drop* 《of liquid》

¶Kasa kara shizuku ga tarete imasu.

傘から滴が垂れています。

Drops of water are dripping from the umbrella.

• ame no shizuku 雨の滴 *raindrop*

shizumarikáeru 静まり返る{5} *to become completely silent, to become deathly still*

¶Tōri ga shizumarikaette imasu.

通りは静まり返っています。

The street has become completely silent.

shizumáru 静まる, 鎮まる *become quiet; to calm down*

¶Yatto arashi ga shizumarimashita.

やっとあらしが静まりました。

At last the storm calmed down.

shizumu 沈む ① *to sink, to go down*

¶Sono fune wa taifū de shizumimashita.

その船は台風で沈みました。

That ship sank because of a typhoon.

• taiyō ga shizumu 太陽が沈む *the sun sets*

② *to sink into low spirits, to become depressed*

¶kono-goro dōshite shizunde iru no desu ka.

このごろどうして沈んでいるのですか。

Why are you in low spirits lately?

shízun シーズン *season* 《for something》

¶Koko wa aki ga kankō no shīzun desu.

ここは秋が観光のシーズンです。

Here autumn is the tourist season.

shō 省 *(government)ministry; department* 《in the U.S. federal government》

shō 章 *chapter*

• -shō 一章《counter for chapters; see Appendix 2》

shō 賞 *prize, award*

¶Musume wa shodō-ten de shō o torimashita.

娘は書道展で賞を取りました。

My daughter won a prize in the calligraphy exhibition.

• Akademī-shō アカデミー賞 *Academy Award*

• it-tō-shō 1 等賞 *first prize*

• Nōberu-shō ノーベル賞 *Nobel Prize*

shō ショー *a show*

• shō-uindō ショーウインドー *display window*

shōbai 商売 ① *business, buying and selling*

¶Sofu wa jūgo-sai de shōbai o hajimemashita.

祖父は15歳で商売を始めました。

My grandfather started a business at the age of fifteen.

¶Uchi no shōbai wa yaoya desu.

うちの商売は八百屋です。

My family's business is a vegetable store.

② *occupation, profession, trade* [→shokugyō 職業]

• shōbai-dōgu 商売道具 *tools of one's trade*

shōben 小便 *urine*

• shōben o suru 小便をする *to urinate*

• ne-shōben 寝小便 *bed wetting*

shōbō 消防 *fire fighting*

• shōbō-jidōsha 消防自動車 *fire engine*

• shōbō-shi 消防士 *fireman, <US>firefighter*

• shōbō-sho 消防署 *fire station, firehouse*

shōbu 勝負 *game, match, contest* [→shiai 試合]

¶Tsui ni shōbu ni katta.

ついに勝負に勝った。

At last we won the game

• shōbu suru 勝負する *to play a game, to have a match, to compete*

• shōbu ni katsu〔makeru〕勝負に勝つ〔負ける〕*to win〔lose〕a game*

• ii shōbu いい勝負 *evenly-matched contest*

• shōbu-goto 勝負事 *gambling*

shōbu 菖蒲 *iris* ((flower))

shōbun 処分 ① *disposal, disposition, settling* [→**shimatsu** 始末①]

• shobun suru 処分する *to dispose of, to take care of, to settle*

¶Kono aki-bako o dō shobun shimashō ka.

この空き箱をどう処分しましょうか。

How shall we dispose of these empty boxes?

② *punishment* [→**batsu** 罰]

• shobun suru 処分する *to punish* [→**bassuru** 罰する]

shōchi 承知 ① *consent, assent* [→**shōdaku** 承諾]

• shōchi suru 承知する *to consent to*

¶Wakasugi-san wa tenkin suru koto o shōchi shimashita.

若杉さんは転勤することを承知しました。

Mr. Wakasugi consented to being transferred.

¶Shōchi shimashita.

承知しました。

All right. 《Literally: I have consented.》

② *knowing, being aware*

• shōchi no ue de 承知の上で *knowingly, intentionally*

• shōchi suru 承知する *to come to know, to become aware of*

• go-shōchi no yō ni ご承知のように 【HON.】 *as you know*

shōchi 処置 *measure, step, action*

• shochi suru 処置する *to deal with, to take care of*

shōchō 象徴 *symbol, emblem*

¶Hato wa heiwa no shōchō desu.

はとは平和の象徴です。

The dove is the symbol of peace.
• shōchō suru 象徴する *to symbolize*

shōchū 焼酎 *shochu, Japanese distilled liquor* 《made from rice or sweet potatoes》

shōdaku 承諾 *consent, assent* [→**shōchi** 承知①]
• shōdaku suru 承諾する *to consent to*

shōdoku 消毒 *disinfection, sterilization*
• shōdoku suru 消毒する *to disinfect, to sterilize*

shōene 省エネ [☞**shōenerugī** 省エネルギー]

shōenérugī 省エネルギー *energy conservation*

shōga 生姜 *ginger* ((spice))

shōgai 生涯 *one's lifetime, one's whole life* [→**isshō** 一生]

shōgai 障害 *obstacle, impediment*
• shōgai-butsu-kyōsō 障害物競走 *obstacle race*
• gengo-shōgai 言語障害 *speech impediment*

shōgákkō 小学校 <*US*>*elementary school,* <*UK*>*primary school*
¶Otōto ga shōgakkō ni nyūgaku shimashita.
弟が小学校に入学しました。
My younger brother entered elementary school.
¶Imōto wa shōgakkō no go-nen-sei desu.
妹は小学校の５年生です。
My younger sister is a fifth-year pupil in elementary school.

shōgakukin 奨学金 *a scholarship*

shōgákusei 小学生 <*US*>*elementary school pupil,* <*UK*>*primary school pupil*
¶Imōto wa mada shōgakusei desu.
妹はまだ小学生です。
My younger sister is still an elementary-school pupil.

shō–ga–nái しょうがない 【COL. for **shikata ga nai** 仕方がない (s.v. **shikata** 仕方)】 *it can't be helped, there's nothing one can do*

Shōgatsú 正月 ① *the New Year season*
《the first several days of the new year》
¶O-shōgatsu o tanoshimi ni shite imasu.
お正月を楽しみにしています。
I'm looking forward to the New Year season.
② *New Year's Day* [→**ganjitsu** 元日]
¶O-shōgatsu ni wa ozōni o tabemasu.
お正月にはお雑煮を食べます。
On New Year's Day we eat ozoni.

shōgeki 衝撃 ① *shock, impact*
• shōgeki o ukeru 衝撃を受ける *to receive a shock, to receive an impact*
• shōgeki o ataeru 衝撃を与える *to give a shock, to make an impact*
② (*emotional*)*shock, trauma* [→**shokku** ショック]

shōgen 証言 (*court*)*testimony*
• shōgen-sha 証言者 *trial witness*

shōgi 将棋 *shogi, Japanese chess*

shōgo 正午 *noon*
¶Shōgo no nyūsu wa hōsō saremasen deshita.
正午のニュースは放送されませんでした。
The noon news was not broadcast.

shōgyō 商業 *commerce, business*
• shōgyō-Eigo 商業英語 *business English*
• shōgyō-kōkō 商業高校 *commercial high school*

shōhi 消費 *consumption, expending* [⇔**seisan** 生産]
• shōhi suru 消費する *to consume, to use up*
¶Kono sutōbu wa sekiyu o tairyō ni shōhi shimasu.
このストーブは石油を大量に消費します。
This heater consumes a lot of oil.
• shōhi-sha 消費者 *consumer*
• shōhi-zei 消費税 *consumption tax, sales tax*

shōhin 商品 *item for sale, item of merchandise*
• shōhin-ken 商品券 *gift certificate*

shōhin 賞品 *prize item*
¶Undō-kai de shōhin o takusan moratta yo.
運動会で賞品をたくさんもらったよ。

I got a lot of prizes in the athletic meet!

shóho 初歩 *rudiments, basics*

¶Watashi wa Itaria-go no shoho o fukushū shite imasu.

私はイタリア語の初歩を復習しています。
I'm reviewing the rudiments of Italian.

¶Imōto wa shoho kara piano o naraimasu.

妹は初歩からピアノを習います。
My younger sister is going to study piano from the basics.

shohyō 書評 *book review*

shōji 障子 *shoji* 《a sliding door or sliding screen made of translucent paper glued to a wooden lattice》

shōjíki 正直 *honesty, truthfulness, frankness*

• shōjiki na 正直な *honest, frank*

¶Tarō-chan wa shōjiki na shōnen desu.

太郎ちゃんは正直な少年です。
Taro is an honest boy.

¶Shōjiki ni itte, Ueda-san wa kirai desu.

正直に言って、上田さんは嫌いです。
Frankly speaking, I dislike Mr. Ueda.

¶San-do-me no shōjiki.

三度目の正直。《proverb》
Third time lucky. 《Literally: *Honesty of the third time.*》

shōjiru 生じる ① *to give rise to, to bring about*

② *to arise, to come about, to occur*

shójo 少女 *girl* [⇔**shōnen** 少年]

• shōjo-zasshi 少女雑誌 *girls' magazine*

shōjō 賞状 *certificate of merit, certificate of commendation*

shójo 処女 *virgin, maiden*

• shojo-saku 処女作 *maiden work, first work*

shōjō 症状 *symptoms, condition* 《of illness》

shojun 初旬 *the first third of a month* [→**jōjun** 上旬]

shōka 消化 *digestion*

• shōka suru 消化する *to digest*

¶Nama-yasai wa shōka suru made ni jikan ga kakaru.

生野菜は消化するまでに時間がかかる。

Raw vegetables take time to digest.

• shōka-kikan 消化器官 *digestive organs*

• shōka-furyō 消化不良 *indigestion*

shōka 消火 *fire extinguishing*

• shōka suru 消火する *to put out* 《The direct object must be a dangerous fire.》

• shōka ni ataru 消火に当たる *to fight a fire*

• shōka-ki 消火器 *fire extinguisher*

• shōka-sen 消火栓 *fire hydrant*

shōkai 紹介 *introduction, presentation*

• shōkai suru 紹介する *to introduce, to present*

¶Yumi-chan o ryōshin ni shōkai shimashita.

由美ちゃんを両親に紹介しました。
I introduced Yumi to my parents.

¶Kono kiji wa kongetsu no shinkan o shōkai shite imasu.

この記事は今月の新刊を紹介しています。
This article introduces this month's new books.

• shōkai-jō 紹介状 *letter of introduction*

• jiko-shōkai 自己紹介 *introducing oneself*

shōken 証券 *securities, stocks and bonds*

• shōken-gaisha 証券会社 *securities company*

shóki 初期 *beginning period, early stage*

¶Kono sakuhin wa Edo no shoki no mono desu.

この作品は江戸の初期の物です。
This work is from the beginning of the Edo period.

shoki 書記 *secretary, clerk*

• shoki-chō 書記長 *chief secretary*

shōkin 賞金 *prize money; reward money*

• A ni shōkin o dasu Aに賞金を出す *to offer prize ∕ reward money for A*

¶Shinobu wa maigo ni natta inu ni shōkin o dashita.

忍は迷子になった犬に賞金を出した。
Shinobu offered reward money for her lost dog.

shokki 食器 *tableware, dish*
- shokki-dana 食器棚 *dish cupboard*

shókku ショック（*emotional*）*shock, trauma* [→**shōgeki** 衝撃②]
¶Kawaigatte ita neko ga shinde, Umeki-san wa shokku deshita.
かわいがっていた猫が死んで、梅木さんはショックでした。
The cat she loved died, and Ms. Umeki was shocked.
- shokku-shi ショック死 *death from shock*

shōko 証拠 *evidence, proof*
¶Kono hito ga hannin da to iu shōko ga aru no ka.
この人が犯人だという証拠があるのか。
Is there any evidence that this person is a criminal?
¶Sore wa dare demo dekiru to iu shōko desu.
それはだれでもできるという証拠です。
That's proof that anyone can do it.
- shōko o atsumeru 証拠を集める *to gather evidence*

shoku 職 *job, position, employment*
¶Ani wa kotoshi no Shi-gatsu ni kono shoku ni tsukimashita.
兄は今年の4月にこの職に就きました。
My older brother took this job in April of this year.

shokuba 職場 *workplace, place of work*

shokúbutsu 植物 *plant, vegetation*
¶Haha wa shitsunai de shokubutsu o takusan sodatete imasu.
母は室内で植物をたくさん育てています。
My mother grows a lot of plants indoors.
- yasei no shokubutsu 野生の植物 *wild plant*
- shokubutsu-en 植物園 *botanical garden*
- shokubutsu-gaku 植物学 *botany*
- shokubutsu-gaku-sha 植物学者 *botanist*
- shokubutsu-ningen 植物人間 *vegetable* ((person))
- kōzan-shokubutsu 高山植物 *alpine plant*
- nettai-shokubutsu 熱帯植物 *tropical plant*

shokuchúdoku 食中毒 *food poisoning*

shokudō 食堂 ① *dining room* ② *restaurant; cafeteria*
- shokudō-sha 食堂車 *dining car*

shokúen 食塩 *table salt*
- shokuen-sui 食塩水 *salt-water solution*

shokúgyō 職業 *occupation, profession, vocation*
¶Otōsan no shokugyō wa nan desu ka.
お父さんの職業は何ですか。
What is your father's occupation?
- shokugyō-antei-sho 職業安定所 *employment security office*
- shokugyō-gakkō 職業学校 *vocational school*
- shokugyō-kyōiku 職業教育 *vocational education; professional education*

shokuhin 食品 *food item, grocery item*
- insutanto-shokuhin インスタント食品 *instant food*
- kakō-shokuhin 加工食品 *processed food*
- kenkō-shokuhin 健康食品 *health food*
- reitō-shokuhin 冷凍食品 *frozen food*
- shizen-shokuhin 自然食品 *natural food*

shokúin 職員 *staff member*
¶Osamu-san no otōsan wa kono byōin no shokuin desu.
治さんのお父さんはこの病院の職員です。
Osamu's father is a staff member of this hospital.
- shokuin-kaigi 職員会議 *staff meeting*
- shokuin-shitsu 職員室 *staff room*

shokuji 食事 *meal, repast*
¶Kuru mae ni karuku shokuji o torimashita.
来る前に軽く食事をとりました。
I had a light meal before I came.
¶Konishi-san wa watashi-tachi o shokuji ni maneite kureta.
小西さんは私たちを食事に招いてくれた。
Ms. Konishi invited us over for a meal.
- shokuji o suru 食事をする *to have a meal, to eat*
¶Watashi-tachi wa ichi-nichi ni san-do shokuji o shimasu.
私たちは1日に3度食事をします。

We eat three times a day.

¶Konban wa soto de shokuji o shimasu.

今晩は外で食事をします。

I will eat out tonight.

• shokuji-chū no 食事中の *in the middle of having a meal*

shokumin 植民 ① *colonization*

• shokumin suru 植民する *to start a colony, to settle*

② *colonist, settler*

• shokumin-chi 植民地 *colony*

shokúmotsu 食物 *food* [→**tabemono** 食べ物]

shokunin 職人 *craftsman, artisan*

• shokunin-gei 職人芸 *craftsmanship, skillful work*

shokupan 食パン *plain bread* 《i.e., bread without filling, frosting, etc.》

shokúryō 食料 *food* [→**tabemono** 食べ物]

• shokuryō ni naru 食料になる *to be edible*

• shokuryō-hin 食料品 *food item, grocery item* [→**shokuhin** 食品]

• shokuryō-hin-ten 食料品店 *grocery store*

shokúryō 食糧 *food, foodstuff*

¶Kyanpu no aida no shokuryō wa jūbun arimasu.

キャンプの間の食糧は十分あります。

We have plenty of food for camping.

• shokuryō-kiki 食糧危機 *food crisis*

• shokuryō-mondai 食糧問題 *food problem*

shokutaku 食卓 *dining table*

¶Dōzo shokutaku ni tsuite kudasai.

どうぞ食卓に着いてください。

Please sit at the dining table.

• shokutaku o yōi suru 食卓を用意する *to set the table*

• shokutaku o katazukeru 食卓を片付ける *to clear the table*

shokuyō 食用 *use as food, using for food*

• shokuyō no 食用の *edible*

• shokuyō-abura 食用油 *cooking oil*

shokuyoku 食欲 *appetite*

¶Kyō wa shokuyoku ga amari nai desu.

きょうは食欲があまりないです。

I don't have much appetite today.

• ōsei na shokuyoku おう盛な食欲 *hearty appetite, good appetite*

shōkyokuteki 消極的 ~**na** ~な *passive, not actively involved, lacking an active interest* [⇔**sekkyokuteki na** 積極的な]

¶Murayama-san wa shōkyokutei na seikaku desu.

村山さんは消極的な性格です。

Mr. Murayama has a passive personality.

¶Sono sakka no jinsei-kan wa shōkyokuteki desu.

その作家の人生観は消極的です。

That writer's view of life lacks an active interest.

shōkyū 昇給 *salary increase*

• shōkyū suru 昇給する *to receive a salary increase*

shokyū 初級 *beginning rank, beginning class* [⇔**jōkyū** 上級]

shōmei 証明 *proof, verification*

• shōmei suru 証明する *to prove, to verify*

¶Bengo-shi wa watashi ga soko ni ita koto o shōmei shita.

弁護士は私がそこにいたことを証明した。

The lawyer proved that I was there.

• shōmei-sho 証明書 *certificate*

shōmei 照明 *(artificial)lighting, (artificial)illumination*

• butai-shōmei 舞台照明 *stage lighting*

shomei 署名 *signature*

• shomei suru 署名する *to sign one's name*

¶O-kyaku-san wa kogitte ni shomei shimashita.

お客さんは小切手に署名しました。

The customer signed his name on the check.

• shomei-undō 署名運動 *signature-collecting campaign*

shōmén 正面 ① *front side, front surface*

¶Sono biru no shōmen wa dairiseki de de-

kite imasu.
そのビルの正面は大理石でできています。
The front of that building is marble.

② *the area straight in front, the area facing*

¶Eki no shōmen ni hana-ya ga arimasu.
駅の正面に花屋があります。
There is a flower shop opposite the station.

• shōmen-genkan 正面玄関 *front vestibule*

• shōmen-shōtotsu 正面衝突 *head-on collision*

shómin 庶民 *ordinary people, the general public, the masses*

• shomin-teki na 庶民的な *popular among the masses*

shonbén しょんべん 【CRUDE for **shōben** 小便】 *piss*

shōnen 少年 *boy* [⇔**shōjo** 少女]

¶Ichirō-kun wa rikō na shōnen desu.
一郎君は利口な少年です。
Ichiro is a bright boy.

• shōnen-jidai 少年時代 *one's boyhood years*

• shōnen-zasshi 少年雑誌 *boys' magazine*

shōnika 小児科 *pediatrics*

shōnin 商人 *merchant;* <US>*storekeeper, shopkeeper*

shōnin 証人 *witness, person who gives testimony*

shóppingu ショッピング *shopping* [→**kaimono** 買い物]

¶Kesa Ginza e shoppingu ni ikimashita.
けさ銀座へショッピングに行きました。
This morning I went shopping in Ginza.

shórai 将来 ① *the future* [→**mirai** 未来]

¶Shōrai no yume wa nan desu ka.
将来の夢は何ですか。
What are your dreams for the future?

¶Chikai shōrai ni uchū-ryokō ga dekiru deshō.
近い将来に宇宙旅行ができるでしょう。
We will probably be able to travel into space in the near future.

② *in the future*

¶Shōrai dezainā ni nari-tai to omoimasu.
将来デザイナーになりたいと思います。
In the future I think I'd like to be a designer.

shōri 勝利 *victory* [→**kachi** 勝ち] [⇔**haiboku** 敗北]

• shōri o eru 勝利を得る *to win a victory*

• shōri-sha 勝利者 *victor, winner*

• shōri-tōshu 勝利投手 *winning pitcher*

shóri 処理 *management, treatment, disposal* [→**shobun** 処分①]

• shori suru 処理する *to manage, to treat, to deal with, to take care of*

¶Sono mondai wa shori dekimasen.
その問題は処理できません。
I cannot deal with that problem.

shóru ショール *shawl*

shorudābággu ショルダーバッグ *shoulder bag*

shorui 書類 *documents, papers*

• jūyō-shorui 重要書類 *important documents*

shōrūmu ショールーム *showroom*

shōryaku 省略 ① *omission, leaving out*

• shōryaku suru 省略する *to omit, to leave out*

¶Kono bun no "that" wa shōryaku shite mo ii desu.
この文の「that」は省略してもいいです。
You may omit "that" in this sentence.

② *abbreviation; abridgement*

• shōryaku suru 省略する *to abbreviate; to abridge*

¶Rosanzerusu o shōryaku shite Rosu to yobimasu.
ロサンゼルスを省略してロスと呼びます。
One abbreviates Los Angeles and calls it Los.

shóryō 少量 ～**no** ～の *a little, a small amount of* [⇔**taryō no** 多量の]

shosai 書斎 *study* ((room))

shōsetsu 小説 *novel, story, work of fiction*

¶Kono shōsetsu wa besuto-serā ni naru deshō.
この小説はベストセラーになるでしょう。

This novel will probably become a best seller.

• shōsetsu-ka 小説家 *novelist*
• rekishi-shōsetsu 歴史小説 *historical novel*
• suiri-shōsetsu 推理小説 *mystery novel, detective story*

shōshin 昇進 *promotion, rise in rank*
• shōshin suru 昇進する *to be promoted, to advance in rank*

shoshínsha 初心者 *beginner, novice*

shōsho 証書 *deed; bond; certificate*
• sotsugyō-shōsho 卒業証書 *diploma*

shóshō 少々 *a little, a bit, slightly* [→ **yaya** やや]

shōsoku 消息 *news, tidings, word*
¶Furukawa-san kara wa nani-mo shōsoku ga arimasen.
古川さんからは何も消息がありません。
There is no word from Ms. Furukawa.

shōsū 小数 *decimal fraction*
• shōsū-ten 小数点 *decimal point*

shōsū 少数 [[⇔**tasū** 多数]] ① ～**no** ～の *few, a small number of*
¶Goku shōsū no gakusei ga sono koto o shitte imasu.
ごく少数の学生がその事を知っています。
A very small number of students know that fact.

② *minority*
• shōsū-iken 少数意見 *minority opinion*

shōtai 招待 *invitation*
• shōtai suru 招待する *to invite* [→**maneku** 招く①]
¶Tanjōbi-kai ni Hanako-chan o shōtai shimasu.
誕生日会に花子ちゃんを招待します。
I'll invite Hanako to my birthday party.
• shōtai-jō 招待状 *invitation, letter of invitation*
• shōtai-ken 招待券 *invitation ticket*

shotái 所帯 (*independent*)*household*

shotáimen 初対面 *first meeting* «between people»
¶Ikeguchi-san to wa kyō ga shotaimen desu.
池口さんとはきょうが初対面です。

Today will be the first time for me to meet Mr. Ikeguchi.

shótchū しょっちゅう 【COL. for **shijū** 始終】 *always; often; constantly*

shōten 商店 <*US*>*store, shop* [→ **mise** 店]
• shōten-gai 商店街 *shop-lined street; shopping center*
• shōten-shu 商店主 *storekeeper*

shóten 焦点 *focus, focal point*
• A no shōten o awaseru Aの焦点を合わせる *to focus A*
¶Kamera no shōten o tori ni awasemashita.
カメラの焦点を鳥に合わせました。
I focused my camera on the bird.
• shōten ga atte iru 焦点が合っている *to be in focus*
• shōten ga hazurete iru 焦点が外れている *to be out of focus*

shoten 書店 <*US*>*bookstore,* <*UK*>*bookshop*

shōto ショート *shortstop* [→**yūgekishu** 遊撃手]

shōto ショート *short* (*circuit*)
• shōto suru ショートする *to short-circuit* «*intransitive*»

shotoku 所得 *income* [→**shūnyū** 収入]
• shotoku-zei 所得税 *income tax*

shōtotsu 衝突 ① *collision*
• shōtotsu suru 衝突する *to collide*
¶Kuruma ga ki ni shōtotsu shimashita.
車が木に衝突しました。
The car collided into a tree.
② *clash, conflict*
¶Ani wa haha to yoku iken ga shōtotsu shimasu.
兄は母とよく意見が衝突します。
My older brother's opinion often clashes with my mother's.
• shōtotsu-jiko 衝突事故 *collision accident*
• shōmen-shōtotsu 正面衝突 *head-on collision*

shou しょう 【COL. for **seou** 背負う】 *to carry on one's back*

Shōwa 昭和 «*Japanese imperial era name*

for the period 1926–1989》
- Shōwa-jidai 昭和時代 *the Shōwa Era*
- Shōwa-tennō 昭和天皇 *the Shōwa Emperor*

shōyu 醤油 *soy sauce*

shoyū 所有 *possession, ownership*
- shoyū suru 所有する *to come to possess , to come to own*
  ¶Ikeda-san ga kono tatemono o shoyū shite imasu.
  池田さんがこの建物を所有しています。
  Mr. ikeda owns this building.
- shoyū-butsu 所有物 *belongings, possessions*
- shoyū-sha 所有者 *owner*

shōzō 肖像 *portrait, likeness* 《of a person》

shozoku 所属 *affiliation, membership*
- shozoku suru 所属する *to become affiliated, to become a member*
  ¶Watashi wa bijutsu-bu ni shozoku shite imasu.
  私は美術部に所属しています。
  I belong to the art club.

shū 州 *state, province*
  ¶Ōsutoraria ni wa ikutsu no shū ga arimasu ka.
  オーストラリアにはいくつの州がありますか。
  How many states are there in Australia?
- shū-gikai 州議会 *state／provincial legislature*
- Nyūyōku-shū ニューヨーク州 *New York State*
- Ontario-shū オンタリオ州 *Ontario Province*

shū 週 *week*
  ¶Shū ni san-kai Eigo no jugyō ga arimasu.
  週に3回英語の授業があります。
  There are English classes three times a week.
- kon-shū 今週 *this week*
- mai-shū 毎週 *every week*
  ¶Maishū tesuto ga aru yo.
  毎週テストがあるよ。
  There's a test every week!
- rai-shū 来週 *next week*

- sa-rai-shū さ来週 *the week after next*
- sen-shū 先週 *last week*
- sen-sen-shū 先々週 *the week before last*

shūban 週番 ① *week-long duty*
  ② *person on duty for the week*
  ¶Watashi wa konshū no shūban desu.
  私は今週の週番です。
  I am the person on duty this week.

shúbi 守備 ① *defense against attack*
- shubi suru 守備する *to defend, to guard*
  ② *defense* 《in sports》, *fielding* 《in baseball》
- shubi ni tsuku 守備に就く *to go on defense, to take the field*

shūbun 秋分 *autumnal equinox* [⇔ **shunbun** 春分]
- Shūbun no hi 秋分の日 *Autumnal Equinox Day* 《a national holiday in Japan》

shuchō 主張 *assertion, insistence*
- shuchō suru 主張する *to insist on, to assert*
  ¶Hikoku wa jibun ga tadashii to shuchō shimashita.
  被告は自分が正しいと主張しました。
  The defendant insisted that he was right.
  ¶Shimin wa kenri o shuchō shimashita.
  市民は権利を主張しました。
  The citizens asserted their rights.

shūchū 集中 *concentration, convergence*
- shūchū suru 集中する *to concentrate, to focus* 《transitive or intransitive》
  ¶Jibun no shigoto ni shūchū shite kudasai.
  自分の仕事に集中してください。
  Please concentrate on your own work.
  ¶Senshu-tachi wa kyō no shiai ni chūi o shūchū shite imasu.
  選手たちはきょうの試合に注意を集中して
  います。
  The players are focusing their attention on today's game.
- shūchū-ryoku 集中力 *ability to concentrate*

shudai 主題 *main subject, theme*

- shudai-ka 主題歌 *theme song*

shūdan 集団 *group, mass*

¶Nihon-jin wa yoku shūdan de kōdo suru sō desu.

日本人はよく集団で行動するそうです。

They say that Japanese people often act in groups.

- shūdan-seikatsu 集団生活 *group living*
- shūdan-teki na 集団的な *collective, group-oriented*

shúdan 手段 *means, way* [→**hōhō** 方法]

¶Isha wa akachan o sukuu tame ni, arayuru shudan o tsukushimashita.

医者は赤ちゃんを救うために、あらゆる手段を尽くしました。

The doctor exhausted every means to save the baby.

¶Sono mondai o kaiketsu suru shudan wa nai desu.

その問題を解決する手段はないです。

There is no way to settle that problem.

- shudan o toru 手段を取る *to take measures*

shuei 守衛 *security guard for a building*

shuen 主演 *leading role, starring role*

- shuen suru 主演する *to play the leading role, to star*

¶Mifune Toshirō wa ano eiga de shuen shimashita.

三船敏郎はあの映画で主演しました。

Toshiro Mifune starred in that movie.

shúfu 主婦 *housewife, homemaker*

shūgakuryókō 修学旅行 *school excursion, educational trip* «with one's teacher and fellow students»

¶San-nen-sei wa shūgakuryokō de Tōkyō ni ikimasu.

３年生は修学旅行で東京に行きます。

The third-year students will go to Tokyo on a school excursion.

shúgei 手芸 *handicraft*

shúgi 主義 *principle, doctrine*

- shugi o mamoru 主義を守る *to stick to one's principles*
- -shugi －主義 *-ism* «Added to noun

bases.»

- shakai-shugi 社会主義 *socialism*
- shihon-shugi 資本主義 *capitalism*

Shūgíin 衆議院 *the House of Representatives* «the lower house in the Japanese Diet» [⇔**Sangiin** 参議院]

- Shūgiin-giin 衆議院議員 *member of the House of Representatives*

shūgō 集合 *gathering, meeting, assembling*

- shūgō suru 集合する *to gather, to meet* «intransitive» [→**atsumaru** 集まる①]

¶Seito wa undō-jō ni shūgō shimashita.

生徒は運動場に集合しました。

The students gathered on the playground.

- shūgō-basho 集合場所 *meeting place*
- shūgō-jikoku 集合時刻 *meeting time*

shúgo 主語 *subject* «of a sentence» [⇔**jutsugo** 述語]

shūgyō 終業 [[⇔**shigyō** 始業]] ① *the end of work or school each day* ② *the end of a school term*

- shūgyō-shiki 終業式 *end-of-the-term ceremony*

shúi 周囲 [[→**mawari** 周り]] ① *circumference, distance around*

¶Kono ike wa shūi ga ni-kiro arimasu.

この池は周囲が２キロあります。

This pond is two kilometers around.

② *surroundings, environment, area around*

¶Gādoman wa shūi o mimawashimashita.

ガードマンは周囲を見回しました。

The guard looked around at the surroundings.

¶Ie no shūi wa ki de kakomarete imasu.

家の周囲は木で囲まれています。

The area around the house is surrounded by trees.

shūji 習字 *learning calligraphy; learning penmanship*

shújin 主人 ① *husband* [→**otto** 夫] ② *master; employer* ③ *proprietor, shop owner; head of the household*

- shujin-kō 主人公 *hero, heroine, pro-*

tagonist 《of a story》
• go-shujin ご主人 【HON. for **shujin** (above)】

shújutsu 手術 *surgery, operation*
• shujutsu o ukeru 手術を受ける *to undergo an operation*

shūkai 集会 *meeting, gathering, assembly*
• shūkai no jiyū 集会の自由 *freedom of assembly*

shūkaku 収穫 *harvest, crop, yield*
¶ Kotoshi wa kome no shūkaku ga ōkatta desu.
今年は米の収穫が多かったです。
This year the rice crop was large.
• shūkaku suru 収穫する *to harvest, to gather in*

shūkan 習慣 *habit, custom*
• shūkan ga tsuku 習慣が付く *a habit forms*
¶ Tanjōbi ni sekihan o taku no wa Nihon no shūkan desu.
誕生日に赤飯を炊くのは日本の習慣です。
Cooking rice with red beans on birthdays is a Japanese custom.

shūkan 週刊 〜no〜の *published weekly*
• shūkan-shi 週刊誌 *weekly magazine*

-**shūkan** 一週間 ① *week* 《Added to bases denoting an activity or purpose.》
• Kōtsū-anzen-shūkan 交通安全週間 *Traffic Safety Week*
② 《counter for weeks; see Appendix 2》
¶ Tarō-chan wa ni-shūkan gakkō o yasunde imasu.
太郎ちゃんは2週間学校を休んでいます。
Taro has been absent from school for two weeks.

shukanteki 主観的 〜na〜な *subjective* [⇔**kyakkanteki na** 客観的な]
¶ Kore wa watashi no shukanteki na inshō ni sugimasen.
これは私の主観的な印象にすぎません。
This is nothing more than my subjective impression.

shuken 主権 *sovereignty*

shukketsu 出血 *bleeding, hemorrhage*

• shukketsu suru 出血する *to bleed, to hemorrhage*

shukkin 出勤 *going to work, presence at work*
• shukkin suru 出勤する *to go to work, to appear at work*
¶ Chichi wa Doyōbi mo shukkin shimasu.
父は土曜日も出勤します。
My father goes to work on Saturday too.

shukkoku 出国 *departure from a country* [⇔**nyūkoku** 入国]
• shukkoku suru 出国する *to depart* 《from a country》

shukudai 宿題 *homework*
¶ Natsu-yasumi ni mo shukudai ga arimasu ka.
夏休みにも宿題がありますか。
Is there homework for the summer vacation too?
¶ Imōto no shukudai o tetsudatte yatta.
妹の宿題を手伝ってやった。
I helped my younger sister with her homework.

shukufuku 祝福 *blessing*
• shukufuku suru 祝福する *to bless*
¶ Shinpu-san wa akachan o shukufuku shimashita.
神父さんは赤ちゃんを祝福しました。
The priest blessed the child.

shukuhaku 宿泊 *lodging, staying* 《in a hotel, etc.》
• shukuhaku suru 宿泊する *to lodge, to stay*
¶ Watashi-tachi wa maitoshi kono hoteru ni shukuhaku shimasu.
私たちは毎年このホテルに宿泊します。
We stay at this hotel every year.
• shukuhaku-ryō 宿泊料 *room charge*

shukujitsu 祝日 *national holiday*

shūkurīmu シュークリーム *cream puff*

shukushō 縮小 *reduction, cutback*
• shukushō suru 縮小する *to reduce, to cut back*

shūkyō 宗教 *religion*

shūmatsu 週末 *weekend*
¶ Shūmatsu ni Nagasaki e ryokō shimashita.

週末に長崎へ旅行しました。
We made a trip to Nagasaki on the weekend.

shúmi 趣味 ① *hobby, pastime*
¶Watashi no shumi wa kitte-shūshū desu.
私の趣味は切手収集です。
My hobby is stamp collecting.

② *taste, preference, liking* [→**konomi** 好み]
¶Matsunami-san wa fuku no shumi ga ii desu.
松波さんは服の趣味がいいです。
Ms. Matsunami's taste in clothes is good.

shumoku 種目 *item of a particular type; event* 《in a competition》
• fīrudo-shumoku フィールド種目 *field events*
• torakku-shumoku トラック種目 *track events*

shunbun 春分 *vernal equinox* [⇔ **shūbun** 秋分]
• Shunbun no hi 春分の日 *Vernal Equinox Day* 《a national holiday in Japan》

shuniku 朱肉 *vermillion inkpad* 《used to ink signature seals》

shunkan 瞬間 ① *moment, instant*
• shunkan ni 瞬間に *instantaneously, in an instant*

② (~**ni** ~に) *the moment, the instant* 《following a past-tense verb》
¶Hebi o mita shunkan, otōto wa naki-dashita yo.
蛇を見た瞬間、弟は泣き出したよ。
The moment he saw the snake, my younger brother started crying!

shunō 首脳 *head, leader*
• shunō-kaidan 首脳会談 *summit meeting*

shúntō 春闘 *spring labor offensive* 《when Japanese labor unions traditionally demand wage increases and threaten strikes》

shūnyū 収入 *income* [⇔**shishutsu** 支出]
¶Gakkō no sensei no shūnyū wa sukunai desu.

学校の先生の収入は少ないです。
A schoolteacher's income is small.

shuppan 出版 *publishing, publication*
• shuppan suru 出版する *to publish*
¶Kono ehon wa kyonen shuppan saremashita.
この絵本は去年出版されました。
This picture book was published last year.
• shuppan-butsu 出版物 *a publication*
• shuppan-sha 出版社 *publishing company*

shuppatsu 出発 *departure, starting out* [⇔**tōchaku** 到着]
¶Enjin-koshō no tame shuppatsu ga ichi-jikan nobita.
エンジン故障のため出発が1時間延びた。
Because of engine trouble, the departure was delayed for an hour.
• shuppatsu suru 出発する *to depart, to leave, to start out*
¶Watashi-tachi wa hi-no-de-mae ni shuppatsu shimashita.
私たちは日の出前に出発しました。
We started out before sunrise.
• shuppatsu-jikoku 出発時刻 *departure time*
• shuppatsu-ten 出発点 *starting point*

shuppi 出費 *expenditure, outlay, expense*
• shuppi o kiritsumeru 出費を切り詰める *to cut down on one's expenses*

shūri 修理 *repair, fixing*
¶Kono tokei wa shūri ga hitsuyō desu.
この時計は修理が必要です。
This watch needs repair.
• shūri suru 修理する *to repair, to fix*
¶Chichi wa kowareta doa o shūri shimashita.
父は壊れたドアを修理しました。
My father repaired the broken door.
¶Kono jitensha o shūri shite moraimashita.
この自転車を修理してもらいました。
I had this bicycle fixed.

shúrui 種類 *kind, sort, type*
¶Kono shurui no hon o kaimashita.

この種類の本を買いました。
I bought a book of this kind.

¶Kono futatsu wa shurui ga onaji desu.
この二つは種類が同じです。
These two are the same kind.

• arayuru shurui あらゆる種類 *all kinds*

-shurui 一種類《counter for kinds; see Appendix 2》

¶Nan-shurui no ringo ga arimasu ka.
何種類のりんごがありますか。
How many kinds of apples are there?

shūryō 終了 *end, conclusion* [→**owari** 終わり]

• shūryō suru 終了する *to end, to conclude* 《transitive or intransitve》 [→ **owaru** 終わる]

shuryō 狩猟 *hunting*

• shuryō ni iku 狩猟に行く *to go hunting*

• shuryō-ka 狩猟家 *hunter*

shūsai 秀才 *brilliant person; talented person*

shusai 主催 *sponsorship, auspices*

¶Hana no tenji-kai wa terebi-kyoku no shusai desu.
花の展示会はテレビ局の主催です。
The flower show is sponsored by a TV station.

• shusai suru 主催する *to sponsor*

• shusai-sha 主催者 *sponsor, promoter*

shūshi 趣旨, 主旨 ① *main idea, point, purport*

¶Sono seiji-ka no enzetsu no shushi ga wakarimasen.
その政治家の演説の趣旨がわかりません。
I don't understand the point of that politician's speech.

② *aim, objective, purpose* [→**muku-teki** 目的]

¶Giin wa hōan no shushi o setsumei shimashita.
議員は法案の趣旨を説明しました。
The Diet member explained the aim of the bill.

shūshi 修士 *master's degree holder*

• shūshi-gō 修士号 *master's degree*

• shūshi-ronbun 修士論文 *master's thesis*

shūshífu 終止符 *period* 《(punctuation mark)》

• shūshifu o utsu 終止符を打つ *to put a period; to put an end*

shūshínkei 終身刑 *life sentence*

shushō 主将 *(team)captain*

¶Hayami-kun wa yakyū-bu no shushō desu.
早見君は野球部の主将です。
Hayami is captain of the baseball team.

shushō 首相 *prime minister*

• Shushō-kantei 首相官邸 *the Official Residence of the Prime Minister (of Japan)*

shūshoku 就職 *getting a job, being hired*

• shūshoku suru 就職する *to get a job, to find a job*

¶Ane wa ginkō ni shūshoku shimashita.
姉は銀行に就職しました。
My older sister got a job at a bank.

• shūshoku o mōshikomu 就職を申し込む *to apply for a job*

• shūshoku-guchi 就職口 *job, job opening*

• shūshoku-shiken 就職試験 *employment examination*

shushoku 主食 *principal food, staple food*

¶Nihon de wa kome ga shushoku desu.
日本では米が主食です。
In Japan rice is the staple food.

shussan 出産 *giving birth*

• shussan suru 出産する *to give birth to* [→**umu** 産む]

shusse 出世 *rising in the world, advancement in life*

• shusse suru 出世する *to rise in the world, to advance in life*

shusseki 出席 *presence, attendance* [⇔**kesseki** 欠席]

• shusseki suru 出席する *to be present, to attend*

¶Zen'in ga shusseki shite imasu.
全員が出席しています。
All the members are present.

¶Sono pātī ni shusseki suru tsumori

desu.

そのパーティーに出席するつもりです。

I plan to attend that party.

• shusseki o toru 出席を取る *to call the roll, to take attendance*

• shusseki-bo 出席簿 *roll, attendance book*

• shusseki-sha 出席者 *person who is present*

shusshin 出身 ① *origin, being born*

¶Go-shusshin wa dochira desu ka.

ご出身はどちらですか。

Where are you from?

　② *being a graduate*

¶Chichi wa Kyōto-daigaku no shusshin desu.

父は京都大学の出身です。

My father is a graduate of Kyoto University.

• shusshin-chi 出身地 *home town, birthplace*

• shusshin-kō 出身校 *alma mater*

shutchō 出張 *business trip*

• shutchō suru 出張する *to make a business trip*

¶Chichi wa ashita Fukuoka e shutchō shimasu.

父はあした福岡へ出張します。

My father is going to make a business trip to Fukuoka tomorrow.

shūten 終点 *last stop, terminal, <UK>terminus*

¶Watashi-tachi wa shūten de basu o orimashita.

私たちは終点でバスを降りました。

We got off the bus at the last stop.

shúto シュート *shot «in soccer, basketball, etc.»*

• shúto suru シュートする *to shoot*

shūto シュート *screwball (pitch) «in baseball»*

• shūto o nageru シュートを投げる *to throw a screwball*

shúto 首都 *capital*

¶Nihon no shuto wa Tōkyō desu.

日本の首都は東京です。

The capital of Japan is Tokyo.

• Shuto-ken 首都圏 *the Tokyo metropolitan area*

• Shuto-kōsoku-dōro 首都高速道路 *the (Tokyo)Metropolitan Expressway*

shūto 舅 *father-in-law* [→gifu 義父] [⇔shūtome 姑]

shūtoku 習得, 修得 *mastery, thorough learning*

• shūtoku suru 習得する *to master*

¶Ano tensai wa has-sai de daisū o shūtoku shimashita.

あの天才は8歳で代数を習得しました。

That genius mastered algebra at the age of eight.

shutoku 取得 *acquisition*

• shutoku suru 取得する *to acquire, to obtain*

shūtome 姑 *mother-in-law* [→gibo 義母] [⇔shūto 舅]

shutsuen 出演 *appearance as a performer*

• shutsuen suru 出演する *to appear as a performer, to perform*

¶Ano kashu wa ashita terebi ni shutsuen shimasu.

あの歌手はあしたテレビに出演します。

That singer will appear on TV tomorrow.

¶Musume wa gakkō no geki ni shutsuen shimasu.

娘は学校の劇に出演します。

My daughter will perform in a school play.

• shutsuen-ryō 出演料 *performance fee, appearance fee*

• shutsuen-sha 出演者 *performer, player*

shutsujō 出場 *taking part, participation «in a performance or contest»*

• shutsujō suru 出場する *to take part, to participate*

¶Marason ni shutsujō shiyo yo.

マラソンに出場しようよ。

Let's participate in the marathon!

shutsúryoku 出力 *output* [→autoputto アウトプット] [⇔nyūryoku 入力]

shuyaku 主役 *leading part, starring role*

¶Keiko-san wa geki de shuyaku o

enjimasu.
恵子さんは劇で主役を演じます。
Keiko will play the leading part in the play.

shūyō 収容 *accommodating, admitting, taking in*
• shūyō suru 収容する *to accomodate, to admit, to take in*
¶Kono kaikan wa sen-nin shūyō dekimasu.
この会館は1000人収容できます。
This public hall can accommodate 1,000 people.
• shūyō-jo 収容所 *asylum; internment camp, concentration camp*

shuyō 主要 〜**na** 〜な *main, chief, principal, major* [→**omo na** 主な]
• shuyō-sangyō 主要産業 *principal industries*
• shuyō-toshi 主要都市 *major cities*

shuzai 取材 *gathering information* 《for a book, news report, etc.》
• shuzai suru 取材する *to gather information for*
• A ni B o shuzai suru AにBを取材する *to gather information from A for B*

shūzen 修繕 *repair, fixing* [→**shūri** 修理]
• shūzen suru 修繕する *to repair, to fix*

sō そう *like that, in that way, so* 《Like other Japanese demonstratives beginning with so-, sō has two uses. One is to refer to something which is in sight and is relatively far from the speaker but relatively close to the listener(s). The other is to refer to something not in sight which is familiar only to the speaker or only to the listener(s).》 [⇔**kō** こう; **ā** ああ]
¶Sensei ni sō iimashō.
先生にそう言いましょう。
Let's say so to the teacher.
¶Watashi mo sō omoimasu.
私もそう思います。
I think so too.
¶Isshōkenmei benkyō shinasai. Sō sureba shiken ni ukaru deshō.
一生懸命勉強しなさい。そうすれば試験に

受かるでしょう。
Study hard. If you do so, you'll probably pass the examination.
• sō iu そういう *such, that kind of* [→**sonna** そんな]

sō そう 〜**da** 〜だ ① *to be that way; that's right, that's so* 《as an affirmative response to a question》
¶"Kon'ya yuki ni naru deshō ka" "Sō ka mo shiremasen."
「今夜雪になるでしょうか」「そうかもしれません」
"I wonder if it's going to snow tonight." "Maybe so."
¶"Keiko-san wa totemo shinsetsu desu ne." "Sō desu ne."
「恵子さんはとても親切ですね」「そうですね」
"Keiko is very kind, isn't she." "Yes, she is, isn't she."
¶"Tarō wa akarui ne." "Jirō mo sō da yo."
「太郎は明るいね」「次郎もそうだよ」
"Taro is cheerful, isn't he." "So is Jiro!"
¶"Kore wa kimi no bōshi desu ka." "Sō desu."
「これは君の帽子ですか」「そうです」
"Is this your hat?" "Yes, it is."
② *I hear that, they say that* 《following a clause》
¶Yokoyama-san wa Furansu-go ga hanaseru sō desu.
横山さんはフランス語が話せるそうです。
I hear that Ms. Yokoyama can speak French.
¶Yōko no otōsan wa pairotto da sō da yo.
洋子のお父さんはパイロットだそうだよ。
I hear that Yoko's father is a pilot!
¶Yūbe Ōsaka de dai-kaji ga atta sō desu.
ゆうべ大阪で大火事があったそうです。
They say that there was a big fire in Osaka last night.

-sō -そう 〜**na** 〜な *seeming to be, looking, appearing likely to* 《Added to verb, adjective, and adjectival noun bases.》

¶Ane wa totemo shiawase-sō desu.

姉はとても幸せそうです。

My older sister looks very happy.

¶Kono shitusmon wa muzukashi-sō desu ne.

この質問は難しそうですね。

This question seems difficult, doesn't it.

¶Yuki ga furi-sō da yo.

雪が降りそうだよ。

It looks like it's going to snow!

sóba 傍, 側 *the area nearby, the area beside*

¶Tosho-kan no soba ni kōen ga arimasu.

図書館のそばに公園があります。

There is a park by the library.

¶Neko wa watashi no soba ni suwarimashita.

猫は私のそばに座りました。

The cat sat beside me.

¶Tatematsu-san wa uchi no soba ni sunde imasu.

立松さんはうちのそばに住んでいます。

Mr. Tatematsu lives near my house.

¶Motto soba ni kinasai.

もっとそばに来なさい。

Come closer beside me.

¶Ano otoko no ko wa itsu-mo haha-oya no soba ni imasu.

あの男の子はいつも母親のそばにいます。

That boy is always near his mother.

sóba 蕎麦 ① *buckwheat*
　② *soba, buckwheat noodles*
- soba-ya 蕎麦屋 *soba shop; soba shop proprietor*

sōba 相場 ① *market price, quotation*
　② *market speculation, playing the market*

sobakásu そばかす *freckle*

sōbetsu 送別 *farewell, send-off*
- sōbetsu-kai 送別会 *farewell party*

sōbi 装備 ① *(installed)equipment*
　② *equipment installation*
- sōbi suru 装備する *to install as equipment*

¶Sono fune wa kaku-heiki o sōbi shite inai.

その船は核兵器を装備していない。

That ship has not been equipped with nuclear weapons.

sobiéru 聳える *to rise, to tower*

¶O-tera no tō ga takaku sobiete imasu.

お寺の塔が高くそびえています。

The temple tower rises high.

sóbo 祖母 *grandmother* [⇔**sofu** 祖父; **obāsan** おばあさん①]

soboku 素朴 ～**na** ～な *simple, unpretentious, artless*

¶Hanamura-san no soboku na hanashi-kata ga suki desu.

花村さんの素朴な話し方が好きです。

I like Mr. Hanamura's simple way of talking.

sóchi 装置 *device, apparatus, equipment*
- anzen-sōchi 安全装置 *safety device*
- butai-sōchi 舞台装置 *stage setting*
- danbō-sōchi 暖房装置 *heating apparatus*

sóchi 措置 *step, measure, action* [→ **shochi** 処置]
- sochi o toru 措置をとる *to take measures, to take action*

sochira そちら 【FORMAL】 《Like other Japanese demonstratives beginning with **so**-, sochira has two uses. One is to refer to something which is in sight and is relatively far from the speaker but relatively close to the listener(s). The other is to refer to something not in sight which is familiar only to the speaker or only to the listener(s).》 ① [[⇔**kochira** こちら①; **achira** あちら①]] *that way; there*

¶Mori-sensei wa sochira ni irasshaimasu ka.

森先生はそちらにいらっしゃいますか。

Is Ms. Mori there?

② [[⇔**kochira** こちら③]] *you; your family*

¶Sochira no go-iken wa ikaga deshō ka.

そちらのご意見はいかがでしょうか。

What is your opinion?

sóda ソーダ ① *soda, sodium carbonate*
　② *soda (pop)*

• sōda-sui ソーダ水 [☞**sōda** ソーダ②
(above)]

sōdan 相談 *consultation, talking over*
• sōdan suru 相談する *to consult, to talk
over, to have a talk*
¶Shōrai no shinro ni tsuite ryōshin to
sōdan shimashita.
将来の進路について両親と相談しました。
*I had a talk with my parents about my
future course.*
¶Noguchi-san wa sono mondai de
bengo-shi ni sōdan shita.
野口さんはその問題で弁護士に相談した。
*Mr. Noguchi consulted with a lawyer
about that matter.*
• sōdan ni noru 相談に乗る *to give advice*
• sōdan-aite 相談相手 *person to consult
with*

sodatéru 育てる ① *to grow* «transitive»
¶Haha no shumi wa bara o sodateru
koto desu.
母の趣味はばらを育てることです。
My mother's hobby is growing roses.
② *to bring up, to raise*
¶Ikemori-san wa san-nin no kodomo o
sodatemashita.
池森さんは3人の子供を育てました。
Ms. Ikemori raised three children.

sodátsu 育つ ① *to grow* «intransitive»
¶Mikan wa ondan na chihō ni sodachi-
masu.
みかんは温暖な地方に育ちます。
Mandarin oranges grow in warm regions.
② *to grow up, to reach maturity, to be
brought up*
¶Itoko wa Kyōto de umare, Kyōto de
sodachimashita.
いとこは京都で生まれ、京都で育ちました。
*My cousin was born and brought up in
Kyōto.*

sode 袖 *sleeve*
• sode o makuru そでをまくる *to roll up
one's sleeves*

sódō 騒動 *commotion, trouble, confusion; riot* [→**bōdō** 暴動]
• sōdō o okosu 騒動を起こす *to cause a*

commotion; to start a riot
• gakuen-sōdō 学園騒動 *campus riot*

soeru 添える *to attach, to add*
¶Sono okurimono ni tegami o soemasu
ka.
その贈り物に手紙を添えますか。
*Are you going to enclose a letter with
that present?*
¶Shashin o soete gansho o teishutsu
shimasu.
写真を添えて願書を提出します。
*I will attach a phonotograph and turn in
my application.*

sófā ソファー *sofa*
¶O-kyaku-san wa sofā ni suwatte imasu.
お客さんはソファーに座っています。
The guest is sitting on the sofa.

sófu 祖父 *grandfather* [⇔**sobo** 祖母;
ojisan おじいさん①]

sofutobōru ソフトボール ① (*the game
of*)*softball*
② *a softball*

sofutokurímu ソフトクリーム *soft ice
cream*

sofutouéa ソフトウエア *software* [⇔
hādouea ハードウエア]

sōgaku 総額 *total amount of money,
sum*
¶Hiyō no sōgaku wa sanman-en ni narimashita.
費用の総額は3万円になりました。
*The total expenditure came to 30,000
yen.*

sōgankyō 双眼鏡 *binoculars*

sōgo 相互 ～**no** ～の *mutual, reciprocal* [→**tagai no** 互いの]
• sōgo-rikai 相互理解 *mutual understanding*

sōgō 総合 ～**suru** ～する *to consolidate,
to synthesize*
¶Sā, minna no kangae o sōgō shite miyō.
さあ、みんなの考えを総合してみよう。
*Now, let's try consolidating everyone's
ideas.*
• sōgō-byōin 総合病院 *general hospital*
• sōgō-keikaku 総合計画 *overall plan*
• sōgō-ten 総合点 *total points*

sōi 相違 *difference* [→**chigai** 違い]

¶Haha to watashi no aida de wa iken no sōi ga arimasu.

母と私の間では意見の相違があります。

There is a difference of opinion between my mother and me.

soitsu そいつ 【CRUDE】 *that person* «Like other Japanese demonstratives beginning with **so-**, **soitsu** has two uses. One is to refer to a person who is in sight and is relatively far from the speaker but relatively close to the listener(s). The other is to refer to a person not in sight who is familiar only to the speaker or only to the listener(s).» [⇔**koitsu** こいつ; **aitsu** あいつ]

sōji 掃除 *cleaning* «by sweeping, wiping, etc.»

• sōji suru 掃除する *to clean*

¶Watashi wa mainichi heya o sōji shimasu.

私は毎日部屋を掃除します。

I clean my room every day.

• sōji-ki 掃除機 *vacuum cleaner*

sōjū 操縦 *operation, flying* 〈a plane〉, *driving* 〈a vehicle〉

• sōjū suru 操縦する *to operate, to fly, to drive*

• sōjū-seki 操縦席 *pilot seat, cockpit*

• sōjū-shi 操縦士 *pilot*

• sōjū-sōchi 操縦装置 *controls*

sōjuku 早熟 ~**na** ～な *precocious, early-maturing*

sōkai 総会 *general meeting*

• seito-sōkai 生徒総会 *general meeting of the students' association*

sokétto ソケット *electrical socket*

sōkin 送金 *remittance; sending money*

• sōkin suru 送金する *to remit*

sokki 速記 *shorthand, stenography*

¶Ane wa sokki o naratte imasu.

姉は速記を習っています。

My older sister is learning shorthand.

sokkúri そっくり ① ~**no** ～の *just like*

¶Musuko-san wa otōsan ni sokkuri desu.

息子さんはお父さんにそっくりです。

The son looks just like his father.

② *all, entirely*

¶Hōseki o akisu ni sokkuri nusumaremashita.

宝石を空き巣にそっくり盗まれました。

The jewels were all stolen by a sneak thief.

sókkusu ソックス *sock*

sōko 倉庫 *warehouse, storehouse*

soko 底 *bottom, lowermost part*

¶Kago no soko ga nukete shimaimashita

かごの底がぬけてしまいました。

The bottom of this basket has fallen out.

• kutsu no soko 靴の底 *sole of a shoe*

soko そこ *that place, there* «Like other Japanese demonstratives beginning with **so-**, **sono** has two uses. One is to refer to a place which is in sight and is relatively far from the speaker but relatively close to the listener(s). The other is to refer to a place not in sight which is familiar only to the speaker or only to the listener(s).» [⇔**koko** ここ; **asoko** あそこ]

¶Soko de nani o shite iru no?

そこで何をしているの？

What are you doing there?

¶Soko no seito ni kikinasai.

そこの生徒に聞きなさい。

Ask the student there.

¶Soko ni yūbin-posuto ga aru deshō?

そこに郵便ポストがあるでしょう？

There's a mailbox there, right?

¶Soko kara basu-tei made nan-pun-gurai desu ka.

そこからバス停まで何分ぐらいですか。

About how many minutes is it from there to the bus stop?

¶Haha wa soko made wa shitte imasu.

母はそこまでは知っています。

My mother knows that much. «Literally: *My mother knows up to there.*»

• soko de そこで *thus, thereupon, accordingly* «The literal meaning *at that place* is also possible.»

¶Tanaka-san wa kaisha o yamemashita. Soko de o-kane ni komatte imasu.

田中さんは会社を辞めました。そこでお金に困っています。

*Mr. Tanaka quit his company. So, he's
having money problems.*

sokonáu 損なう *to harm, to damage*

• A no kanjō o sokonau Aの感情を損な
う *to hurt A's feelings*

-sokonau －損なう *to miss doing, to
fail to do* 《Added to verb bases.》

¶Kesa chichi wa itsu-mo noru densha ni
nori-sokonatta.

けさ父はいつも乗る電車に乗り損なった。

*This morning my father missed the train
he usually takes.*

¶Dai-suki na terebi-bangumi o mi-sokon-
atta yo.

大好きなテレビ番組を見損なったよ。

I missed my favorite TV program!

-soku －足《counter for pairs of footwear; see Appendix 2》

sokubaku 束縛 *restriction, constraint*

• sokubaku suru 束縛する *to restrict, to
constrain*

sókudo 速度 *speed, velocity*

¶Kono ressha no sokudo wa jisoku yaku
nihyak-kiro desu.

この列車の速度は時速約200キロです。

*The speed of this train is approximately
200 kilometers an hour.*

• sokudo o ageru 速度を上げる *to speed
up*

• sokudo o otosu 速度を落とす *to slow
down*

• sokudo-kei 速度計 *speedometer*

• saikō-sokudo 最高速度 *maximum
speed, speed limit*

sokuryō 測量 *(land)survey, surveying*

• sokuryō suru 測量する *to survey*

• sokuryō-gishi 測量技師 *surveyor*

sokúryoku 速力 *speed* [→**sokudo** 速度]

sokuseki 即席 ～**no** ～の *impromptu;
instant* [→**insutanto-** インスタントー]

sokushi 即死 *instant death, death on
the spot*

• sokushi suru 即死する *to die instantly,
to be killed on the spot*

sokushin 促進 *promotion, encouragement*

• sokushin suru 促進する *to promote, to*

encourage

sokutatsu 速達 ＜*US*＞*special delivery*,
＜*UK*＞*express delivery*

¶Kono tegami o sokutatsu de okutte kudasai.

この手紙を速達で送ってください。

*Please send this letter by special de-
livery.*

• sokutatsu-ryōkin 速達料金 *special delivery charge*

sómatsu 粗末 ① ～**na** ～な *low-quality,
crude*

¶Kono mise de wa somatsu na mono o
urimasu.

この店では粗末な物を売ります。

They sell low-quality things in this store.

② ～**ni suru** ～にする *to treat carelessly, to use carelessly*

¶O-kane o somatsu ni shite wa ikenai yo.

お金を粗末にしてはいけないよ。

You mustn't use your money carelessly!

sómen そうめん *very thin wheat noodles, Japanese vermicelli*

someru 染める *to dye*

¶Haha wa kami-no-ke o kuroku somema-
shita.

母は髪の毛を黒く染めました。

My mother dyed her hair black.

sómosomo そもそも *in the first place, to
begin with*

• somosomo no そもそもの *original, initial*

somúku 背く *to act contrary, to disobey*

¶Ano futari wa kōsoku ni somuite
tabako o sutta.

あの二人は校則に背いてたばこを吸った。

*Those two disobey school regulations
and smoke cigarettes.*

• dentō ni somuku 伝統に背く *to act contrary to tradition*

són 損 *loss, disadvantageous outcome*
[⇔**toku** 得]

¶Sore o kau no wa son desu.

それを買うのは損です。

Buying that would be disadvantageous.

• son o suru 損をする *to incur a loss, to
suffer a loss*

¶Kekkyoku gosen-en no son o shita yo.

結局5000円の損をしたよ。
In the end I suffered 5,000 yen loss!
¶Sono kaisha wa hidoku son o shima-shita.
その会社はひどく損をしました。
The company incurred terrible losses.

• son o shite uru 損をして売る *to sell at a loss*

• son suru 損する [☞**son o suru** 損をする(above)]

sonaéru 備える ① *to provide, to furnish, to install*

¶Jimu-sho ni konpyūtā o sonaemashita.
事務所にコンピューターを備えました。
We installed a computer in the office.

② *to prepare oneself, to make provisions* [→**junbi suru** 準備する]

¶Yoshino-san wa shōrai ni sonaete cho-kin site imasu.
吉野さんは将来に備えて貯金しています。
Ms. Yoshino is saving to make provisions for the future.

¶Seito wa minna nyūshi ni sonaete ben-kyō shite iru.
生徒はみんな入試に備えて勉強している。
The students are all studying in preparation for the entrance examination.

sōnan 遭難 *life-threatening accident*

• sōnan suru 遭難する *to meet with an accident; to be wrecked* 《when the subject is a ship》

¶Nihon no tozan-tai ga Eberesuto-san de sōnan shita.
日本の登山隊がエベレスト山で遭難した。
A Japanese mountain-climbing team met with an accident on Mt. Everest.

¶Sono fune wa taihū de sōnan shima-shita.
その船は台風で遭難しました。
That ship was wrecked in a typhoon.

• sōnan-sha 遭難者 *accident victim*

• sōnan-shingō 遭難信号 *distress signal*

sónata ソナタ *sonata*

sónchō 村長 *village head*

sonchō 尊重 *respect, esteem* 《for a thing》

• sonchō suru 尊重する *to respect, to*
have a high regard for

¶Shikashi, saiban-kan no iken o sonchō shimasu.
しかし、裁判官の意見を尊重します。
However, I respect the judge's opinion.

songai 損害 *damage, harm, loss*

¶Sono songai wa gohyakuman-en ni noborimashita.
その損害は500万円に上りました。
That loss amounted to 5 million yen.

• songai o ukeru 損害を受ける *to be damaged, to suffer a loss*

• songai o ataeru 損害を与える *to cause damage, to cause a loss*

sonkei 尊敬 *respect, esteem* 《for a person》 [⇔**keibetsu** 軽蔑]

• sonkei suru 尊敬する *to come to respect, to come to revere*

¶Watashi wa chichi o sonkei shite iru yo.
私は父を尊敬しているよ。
I respect my father!

¶Senshu-tachi wa Hiroshi o kantoku to shite sonkei shite iru.
選手たちは浩を監督として尊敬している。
The players respect Hiroshi as their coach.

• sonkei-go 尊敬語 *honorific word* 《one type of respectful vocabulary in Japanese》 [⇔**kenjō-go** 謙譲語]

sonna そんな *that kind of* 《Like other Japanese demonstratives beginning with so-, **sonna** has two uses. One is to refer to something which is in sight and is relatively far from the speaker but relatively close to the listener(s). The other is to refer to something not in sight which is familiar only to the speaker or only to the listener(s).》 [⇔**konna** こんな; **anna** あんな]

¶Sonna koto wa iwanakatta yo.
そんなことは言わなかったよ。
I didn't say such a thing!

¶Sonna dōbutsu wa imasu ka.
そんな動物はいますか。
Is there such an animal?

• sonna ni そんなに *to that extent, that much*

¶Sonna ni hayaku hashiranai de.
そんなに速く走らないで。
Don't run so fast.

sono その *that* 《as a noun modifier》
《Like other Japanese demonstratives beginning with so-, **sono** has two uses. One is to refer to something which is in sight and is relatively far from the speaker but relatively close to the listener(s). The other is to refer to something not in sight which is familiar only to the speaker or only to the listener(s).》 [⇔**kono** この; **ano** あの]

¶Sono mado o akete kudasai.
その窓を開けてください。
Please open that window.

¶Sono hi wa totemo kaze ga tsuyokatta yo.
その日はとても風が強かったよ。
That day the wind was very strong!

¶Sono toori desu.
そのとおりです。
That's right. 《Literally: *It is that way.*》

• sono ue その上 *besides that, moreover*
¶Yumi wa totemo yasashiku, sono ue rikō da.
由美はとてもやさしく、そのうえ利口だ。
Yumi is very kind. Besides that, she is bright.

• sono uchi そのうち *sometime soon, before long, by and by*
¶Sono uchi Hawai ni ikō to omotte imasu.
そのうちハワイに行こうと思っています。
I'm thinking of going to Hawaii sometime soon.

• sono go その後 *after that, since then*
¶Sono go Matsukawa-san kara wa tayori ga arimasen.
その後松川さんからは便りがありません。
Since then there haven't been any letters from Ms. Matsukawa.

¶Sono go mata jiko o okoshite shimaimashita.
その後また事故を起こしてしまいました。
After that I caused another accident again.

• sono koro そのころ *in those days, at that time*
¶Sono koro Seki-san wa Kyōto ni sunde imashita.
そのころ関さんは京都に住んでいました。
In those days Ms. Seki was living in Kyoto.

• sono toki その時 *then, at that time*
¶Sono toki o-furo ni haitte imashita.
その時おふろに入っていました。
I was in the bath at that time.

• sono ba de その場で *on the spot*
¶Suri wa sono ba de tsukamatta yo.
すりはその場で捕まったよ。
The pickpocket was caught on the spot!

• sono mama そのまま *as is, as things are*
¶Subete sono mama ni shite okinasai.
すべてそのままにしておきなさい。
Leave everything as it is.

¶Sono mama o-machi kudasai.
そのままお待ちください。《on the telephone》
Hold the line, please. 《Literally: *Please wait as is.*》

sonshitsu 損失 *loss, detrimental occurrence*
¶Shachō no kyūshi wa kaisha ni totte ōki na sonshitsu da.
社長の急死は会社にとって大きな損失だ。
The president's sudden death was a great loss to the company.

sōnyū 挿入 *insertion*
• sōnyū suru 挿入する *to insert*

sonzai 存在 *existence, being*
¶Maeyama-san wa kami no sonzai o shinjite imasu.
前山さんは神の存在を信じています。
Mr. Maeyama believes in the existence of God.

• sonzai suru 存在する *to exist*
¶Sono shōjo wa yūrei ga sonzai suru to shinjite iru.
その少女は幽霊が存在すると信じている。
That girl believes that ghosts exist.

¶Sono yō na mono wa kono yo ni sonzai shinai yo.
そのような物はこの世に存在しないよ。

That kind of thing does not exist in this world!

sōon 騒音 *noise, annoying sound*
- sōon-kōgai 騒音公害 *noise pollution*

sopurano ソプラノ ① *soprano* (*voice*)
② *soprano* (*singer*)
③ *soprano* (*part*)

sóra 空 *sky*
¶Sora wa sugu ni hareru deshō.
空はすぐに晴れるでしょう。
The sky will probably clear up soon.
¶Sora ni wa kumo ga hitotsu mo nai ne.
空には雲が一つもないね。
There's not a cloud in the sky, is there.
¶Sora no tabi wa yahari mada kōka desu ne.
空の旅はやはりまだ高価ですね。
As you'd expect, air travel is still expensive, isn't it.
- sora-iro 空色 *sky blue* «as a noun»
- sora-moyō 空模様 *the look of the sky, the weather*
- sora-takaku 空高く *high up in the sky; high into the sky*
¶Jetto-ki ga sora-takaku tonde imasu.
ジェット機が空高く飛んでいます。
A jet is flying high up in the sky.

sorámame 空豆 *broad bean*

sore それ *that* (*one*) «Like other Japanese demonstratives beginning with so–, **sore** has two uses. One is to refer to something which is in sight and relatively far from the speaker but relatively close to the listener(s). The other is to refer to something not in sight which is familiar only to the speaker or only to the listener(s).» [⇔**kore** これ; **are** あれ]
¶Oji ga sore o kureta yo.
叔父がそれをくれたよ。
My uncle gave that to me!
¶Itsu sore o sutemashita ka.
いつそれを捨ててましたか。
When did you throw that away?
¶Sore wa dare no kutsu desu ka.
それはだれの靴ですか。
Whose shoes are those?
- sore kara それから«The literal meaning

from that is also possible.» [[→**soshite** そして]] *after that, since then; and, and also*
¶Chichi wa Ōsaka ni iki, sore kara Fukuoka e mukau tsumori desu.
父は大阪に行き、それから福岡へ向うつもりです。
Father will go to in Osaka, and after that he will head for Fukuoka.
¶Watashi-tachi wa sore kara hanashiatte imasen.
私たちはそれから話し合っていません。
We haven't talked to each other since then.
- sore de それで«The literal meaning *by that, using that* is also possible.» *for that reason, so; and then, and so* «Used in questions.»
¶Netsu ga arimashita. Sore de kesseki shita n desu.
熱がありました。それで欠席したんです。
I had a fever. For that reason, I was absent
¶"Yūbe eiga o mi ni ikimashita yo."
"Sore de nan-ji ni owarimashita ka."
「ゆうべ映画を見に行きましたよ」「それで何時に終わりましたか」
"I went to see a movie last night!" "And so what time did it end?"
- sore ni それに *besides that, moreover* «The literal meanings *to that, on that*, etc., are also possible.»
¶Atsui desu ne. Sore ni kaze mo nai desu ne.
暑いですね。それに風もないですね。
It's hot, isn't it. Besides that, there's no wind, is there.
- sore dokoro-ka それどころか *on the contrary, quite the opposite of that*
¶"Tanimori-san wa sore o kiite kanashimimashita ka." "Sore dokoro-ka yorokobimashita yo."
「谷森さんはそれを聞いて悲しみましたか」「それどころか喜びましたよ」
"Was Ms. Tanimori sad to hear that?" "On the contrary, she was glad!"
- sore hodo それほど *that much, to that*

extent, so

¶Mondai wa sore hodo muzukashiku nai desu.

問題はそれほど難しくないです。

The problem is not so difficult.

• sore made それまで *until then*

¶Sore made matanakereba narimasen yo.

それまで待たなければなりませんよ。

You'll have to wait until then!

• sore made ni それまでに *by then*

¶Sore made ni shukudai o shiagemasu.

それまでに宿題を仕上げます。

I will finish my homework by then.

sore-dé-wa それでは *well then, in that case*

¶Sore-de-wa, oyasumi nasai.

それでは、お休みなさい。

Well then, good night.

¶Sore-de-wa, Ono-san ni au hitsuyō wa nai.

それでは、小野さんに会う必要はない。

In that case, there's no need to see Mr. Ono.

sore-tómo それとも *or* 《connecting alternative questions》

¶Kono pen wa sensei no desu ka, sore-tomo Ogura-san no desu ka.

このペンは先生のですか、それとも小倉さんのですか。

Is this pen yours, or is it Mr. Ogura's?

sorézore それぞれ *each, each respectively*

¶Sanka-sha wa sorezore jibun no iken ga arimasu.

参加者はそれぞれ自分の意見があります。

The participants each have their own opinion.

¶Sensei wa seito-tachi ni sorezore nōto o is-satsu-zutsu agemashita.

先生は生徒たちにそれぞれノートを1冊ずつあげました。

The teacher gave the students one notebook each.

• sorezore no それぞれの *each, each respective*

¶Sorezore no kuni ni wa dokutoku no shūkan ga arimasu.

それぞれの国には独特の習慣があります。

Each country has its own unique customs.

Sóri 総理 [☞**Sōridaijin** 総理大臣]

• Sōri-fu 総理府 *the Prime Minister's Office*

sóri そり *sled; sleigh*

Sōridáijin 総理大臣 *the Prime Minister (of Japan)*

sóritsu 創立 *founding, establishment* [→**setsuritsu** 設立]

• sōritsu suru 創立する *to found, to establish*

¶Kono gakkō wa sen-kyu-hyaku-gojū-nen ni sōritsu saremashita.

この学校は1950年に創立されました。

This school was founded in 1950.

• sōritsu-kinen-bi 創立記念日 *anniversary of the founding*

• sōritsu-sha 創立者 *founder*

sóro ソロ *a solo* [→**dokushō** 独唱; **dokusō** 独奏]

• piano-soro ピアノソロ *piano solo*

soroban 算盤 *abacus*

soroéru 揃える ① *to arrange, to place in orderly fashion*

¶Tēburu no ue no shinbun o soroete kudasai.

テーブルの上の新聞をそろえてください。

Please arrange the newspapers on the table.

¶Tsukue o kichin-to soroemashita.

机をきちんとそろえました。

We arranged the desks neatly.

② *to make the same, to make uniform*

• ashinami o soroeru 足並みをそろえる *to get in step*

③ *to get a complete set of, to get a wide assortment of*

• zairyō o soroeru 材料をそろえる *to get all the ingredients*

sórosoro そろそろ （〜to 〜と） ① *soon* [→**ma-mo-naku** 間も無く]

¶Sorosoro gādoman ga arawareru deshō.

そろそろガードマンが現れるでしょう。

The guard will probably appear soon.

¶Sorosoro shichi-ji ni narimasu.

そろそろ 7 時になります。
It will soon be 7:00.

② *slowly, little by little*

¶Tozan-tai wa sorosoro chōten ni noborimashita.

登山隊はそろそろ頂点に登りました。
The mountain-climbing party climbed slowly to the summit.

soróu 揃う ① *to gather, to come to the same place* [→**atsumaru** 集まる]

¶Minna soroimashita ka.

みんなそろいましたか。
Is everybody here? 《*Literally: Has everybody gathered?*》

② *to become the same, to become uniform*

¶Kono kurasu no seito wa Eigo no chikara ga hotonodo sorotte imasu.

このクラスの生徒は英語の力がほとんどそろっています。
The English ability of the students in this class is almost uniform.

③ *to be gathered into a complete set, to be gathered into a wide assortment*

¶Toshokan ni wa gengo-gaku no hon ga sorotte imasu.

図書館には言語学の本がそろっています。
There is a wide selection of linguistics books in the library.

sóru 反る *to warp, to bend* 《intransitive》

¶Sono ita wa netsu de sotte shimaimashita.

その板は熱で反ってしまいました。
That board warped in the heat.

sóru 剃る *to shave* 《The direct object can be a part of the body or a kind of hair.》

¶Ano hito wa ichi-nichi ni ni-kai hige o sorimasu.

あの人は 1 日に 2 回ひげをそります。
That person shaves twice a day.

• kao o soru 顔をそる *to shave one's face*
• atama o soru 頭をそる *to shave one's head*

sóryō 送料 *freight charge; postage*

¶Kono kozutsumi no sōryō wa ikura desu ka.

この小包の送料はいくらですか。
How much is the postage for this package?

¶Kono nimotsu no sōryō wa uketori-nin ga shiharau.

この荷物の送料は受け取り人が支払う。
The freight charge for baggage will be paid by the receiver.

sōryōji 総領事 *consul general*

• sōryōji-kan 総領事館 *consulate general* [→**ryōjikan** 領事館]

sōsa 捜査 *criminal investigation*

• sōsa suru 捜査する *to investigate*
• sōsa-honbu 捜査本部 *investigation headquarters*

sōsa 操作 *operation, manipulation, running*

• sōsa suru 操作する *to operate, to manipulate, to run*

¶Kono kikai o sōsa suru no wa muzukashii.

この機械を操作するのは難しい。
Operating this machine is difficult.

sōsaku 創作 ① *creation, origination*

• sōsaku suru 創作する *to create, to originate*

② *creative writing, original writing*

• sōsaku suru 創作する *to write (as an original work)*

③ *an original written work, a work of creative writing*

• sōsaku-katsudō 創作活動 *creative activity*

sōsaku 捜索 *search, searching*

• sōsaku suru 捜索する *to search* 《a place》

¶Sū-nin no keikan ga sono ie o sōsaku shimashita.

数人の警官がその家を捜索しました。
Several police officers searched that house.

• sōsaku-tai 捜索隊 *search party*

sōséiji 双生児 *twins* [→**futago** 双子]

• ichiransei-sōseiji 一卵性双生児 *identical twins*
• Shamu-sōseiji シャム双生児 *Siamese twins*

sōsēji ソーセージ *sausage*

sósen 祖先 *ancestor* [→**senzo** 先祖] [⇔ **shison** 子孫]

sōsénkyo 総選挙 *general election*

sósha 走者 *runner*
- saishū-sōsha 最終走者 *anchor runner*

sōshiki 葬式 *funeral*
- sōshiki ni sanretsu suru 葬式に参列する *to attend a funeral*
- sōshiki o itonamu 葬式を営む *to hold a funeral*

sóshiki 組織 *organization*
- soshiki suru 組織する *to organize*
¶Menbā wa iin-kai o soshiki shimashita.
メンバーは委員会を組織しました。
The members organized a committee.

sōshite そうして [☞**soshite** そして]

soshite そして ① *and then, after that*
¶Ani wa Kyōto, Ōsaka, soshite Kōbe ni shutchō shita.
兄は京都、大阪、そして神戸に出張した。
My older brother went on business to Kyoto, Osaka, and then Kobe.
② *and, and also*
¶Bankoku wa atsuku, soshite shitsudo mo takai.
バンコクは暑く、そして湿度も高い。
Bangkok is hot and also humid.

soshitsu 素質 *the makings, aptitude*
¶Ojōsan wa dai-kashu ni naru soshitsu ga arimasu.
お嬢さんは大歌手になる素質があります。
Your daughter has the makings of a great singer.

sōsho 草書 *grass style* 《of Japanese calligraphy》 [⇔**gyōsho** 行書; **kaisho** 楷書]

soshō 訴訟 *lawsuit*
- soshō o okosu 訴訟を起こす *to file suit*

sōshoku 装飾 *decoration, adornment*
- sōshoku suru 装飾する *to decorate, to adorn* [→**kazaru** 飾る①]
¶Kono e wa watashi no heya no ii sōshoku ni narimasu.
この絵は私の部屋のいい装飾になります。
This picture will be a nice decoration for my room.
- sōshoku-hin 装飾品 *decoration, ornament*
- shitsunai-sōshoku 室内装飾 *interior decoration*

sosogu 注ぐ ① *to pour* 《transitive》《The direct object must be a liquid.》
¶Ane wa koppu ni kōra o sosoide kureta.
姉はコップにコーラを注いでくれた。
My older sister poured some cola into a glass for me.
② *to flow, to empty* 《into a lake》
¶Tone-gawa wa Taiheiyō ni sosogimasu.
利根川は太平洋に注ぎます。
The Tone River flows into the Pacific Ocean.
③ *to concentrate, to focus, to devote*
- chūi o sosogu 注意を注ぐ *to focus one's attention*
- zenryoku o sosogu 全力を注ぐ *to devote all one's energy*

sosokkashíi そそっかしい *careless*

sosonokásu 唆す *to tempt, to entice*
¶Yakuza ga shōnen o sosonokashite, suri o saseta.
やくざは少年を唆して、すりをさせた。
The gangster enticed the boy and made him pick pockets.

sósu ソース *sauce*
¶Sutēki ni sōsu o kakemasu ka.
ステーキにソースをかけますか。
Shall I put sauce on your steak?
- howaito-sōsu ホワイトソース *white sauce*
- usutā-sōsu ウスターソース *Worcestershire sauce*

sōtaiteki 相対的 〜**na** 〜な *relative, comparative*

sotchí そっち 【COL.for **sochira** そちら】

sotchoku 率直 〜**na** 〜な *frank, candid, outspoken*
¶Shushō wa sotchoku na iken o nobemashita.
首相は率直な意見を述べました。
The prime minister stated his candid opinion.

sōtō 相当 ① (〜**ni** 〜に) *considerably, fairly, quite* [→**kanari** かなり]
¶Ani wa gitā ga sōtō umai desu.

兄はギターが相当うまいです。
My older brother is quite good at the guitar.

¶Kesa wa sōtō samui ne.
けさは相当寒いね。
It's quite cold this morning, isn't it.

• sōtō na／no 相当な／の *considerable, fair*

¶Tsuki ni ichiman-en wa sōtō na o-kozukai da yo.
月に1万円は相当なお小遣いだよ。
10,000 yen a month is considerable pocket money!

② ～**suru** ～する *to be equivalent, to correspond* [→**ataru** 当たる⑥]

¶Ichi-doru wa Nihon-en de ikura ni sōtō shimasu ka.
1ドルは日本円でいくらに相当しますか。
How many Japanese yen are there to the dollar?

¶"Hana" ni sōtō suru Eigo wa nan desu ka.How many Japanese en equal dollar?
「花」に相当する英語は何ですか。
What is the English that corresponds to "hana"?

• -sōtō no ―相当の *worth* 《Added to bases denoting amounts of money.》

¶Kore wa jūman-en-sōtō no kabin desu.
これは10万円相当の花瓶です。
This is a vase worth 100,000 yen.

③ ～**na**／**no** ～な／の *appropriate, suitable, befitting* [→**tekitō na** 適当な]

• sōtō suru 相当する *to be appropriate, to suit, to befit*

¶Sore wa gakusei ni sōtō na shigoto desu.
それは学生に相当な仕事です。
That's work appropriate for a student.

sóto 外 ① *the outside* [⇔**uchi** 内①]

¶Dare-ka ga soto kara doa o akemashita.
だれかが外からドアを開けました。
Somebody opened the door from the outside.

② *outside, outdoors*

¶Yōko-chan wa soto ni iru yo.
洋子ちゃんは外にいるよ。
Yoko's outside!

¶Shōjo wa mado kara soto o nagamete imasu.
少女は窓から外を眺めています。
The girl is looking out of the window.

¶Soto e asobi ni ikō.
外へ遊びに行こう。
Let's go outside to play.

sotogawa 外側 *the outside, the outer side* [⇔**uchigawa** 内側]

¶Hako no sotogawa o shiroku nuru tsumori desu.
箱の外側を白く塗るつもりです。
I intend to paint the outside of the box white.

sotsugyō 卒業 *graduation* 《i.e., successful completion of a course of study》

• sotsugyō suru 卒業する *to graduate from*

¶Michiko no ani wa rainen daigaku o sotsugyō suru.
美知子の兄は来年大学を卒業する。
Michiko's older brother will graduate from college next year.

• sotsugyō-shiki 卒業式 *graduation ceremony*

• sotsugyō-shōsho 卒業証書 *diploma*

• sotsugyō-sei 卒業生 *graduate*

sotto そっと ① *quietly, softly, gently, lightly*

• sotto suru そっとする *to leave undisturbed, to leave alone*

¶Naoko-chan o sotto shite okimashō.
直子ちゃんをそっとしておきましょう。
Let's leave Naoko alone.

② *secretly, stealthily* [→**kossori** こっそり]

¶Oka-san wa sotto Tarō ni mekubase shimashita.
岡さんはそっと太郎に目くばせしました。
Mr. Oka secretly signaled Taro with his eyes.

sou 沿う《used in connection with roads, rivers, etc.》 *to be alongside; to follow*

¶Watashi-tachi wa kawa ni sotte hashitte imashita.
私たちは川に沿って走っていました。
We were running along the river.

sówasowa そわそわ ～**suru** ～する *to*

become restless; to become nervous
¶Musuko wa sowasowa shita kodomo desu.
息子はそわそわした子供です。
My son is a restless child.
¶Kyōko-san wa sowasowa shita yōsu deshita ne.
京子さんはそわそわした様子でしたね。
Kyoko looked nervous, didn't she.

sōzō 創造 *creation*
• sōzō suru 創造する *to create*
• Sōzō-sha 創造者 *the Creator*
• sōzō-teki na 創造的な *creative*
• Tenchi-sōzō 天地創造 *the Creation*

sōzō 想像 *imagination, imagining; surmise, guess* [→**suisoku** 推測]
¶Sore wa dokusha no sōzō ni makasemasu.
それは読者の想像に任せます。
I will leave that to the reader's imagination.
• sōzō suru 想像する *to imagine; to surmise*
¶Mukashi no hitobito no seikatsu o sōzō shite mimashō.
昔の人々の生活を想像してみましょう。
Let's try imagining the life of people long ago.
• sōzō ga tsuku 想像がつく *one can imagine*
• sōzō-ryoku 想像力 *imagination, imaginativeness*
¶Yōko-chan wa sōzō-ryoku ga yutaka desu.
洋子ちゃんは想像力が豊かです。
Yoko's imagination is rich.
• sōzō-ryoku o hatarakaseru 想像力を働かせる *to use one's imagination*
• sōzō-jō no 想像上の *imaginary*

sōzoku 相続 *inheritance, succession*
• sōzoku suru 相続する *to inherit, to succeed to*
¶Chichi wa sofu kara sono zaisan o sōzoku shimashita.
父は祖父からその財産を相続しました。
My father inherited that fortune from my grandfather.

• sōzoku-nin 相続人 *heir*
• sōzoku-zaisan 相続財産 *inherited fortune*

sōzōshíi 騒々しい *noisy, boisterous* [→ **sawagashii** 騒がしい]
¶Ano otoko-no-ko-tachi wa itsu-mo sōzōshii yo.
あの男の子たちはいつも騒々しいよ。
Those boys are always noisy!

su 巣 *nest; web; hive*
• su-bako 巣箱 *birdhouse*

sú 酢 *vinegar*
• su-no-mono 酢の物 *side dish with vinegar as the seasoning*

sū 数 *number* [→**kazu** 数]
• gū-sū 偶数 *even number*
• ki-sū 奇数 *odd number*

sū 数－ *several* 《Generally added to a counter; see Appendix 2.》
• sū-jitsu 数日 *several days* 《This word is exceptional because –**jitsu** is not the counter for days.》
• sū-nen 数年 *several years*
• sū-nin 数人 *several* 《when counting people》

-sū －数 *number, quantity* 《Added to the counter appropriate for what is being counted; see Appendix 2.》
¶Enpitsu no hon-sū o tashikamete kudasai.
鉛筆の本数を確かめてください。
Please check the number of pencils.
¶Kuruma no dai-sū wa koko ni kaite arimasu.
車の台数はここに書いてあります。
The number of cars is written here.

subarashíi 素晴らしい *wonderful, splendid, magnificent*
¶Yūbe wa subarashiku tanoshikatta yo.
ゆうべはすばらしく楽しかったよ。
Last night was wonderfully enjoyable!
¶Subarashii eiga deshita ne.
すばらしい映画でしたね。
It was a wonderful movie, wasn't it.

subayái 素早い *quick-moving, quick-acting, agile, nimble*

suberídai 滑り台 *(playground)slide*

suberikómu 滑り込む *to slide into*

¶Rannā wa nirui ni suberikomimashita.

ランナーは二塁に滑り込みました。

The runner slid into second base.

subéru 滑る{5} ① *to slide* «*intransitive*»; *to skate, to ski*

¶Hanako to sukī-jō ni itte, ichi-nichi-jū subetta.

花子とスキー場に行って、一日中滑った。

I went to a ski resort with Hanako and skied all day long.

② *to slip* «*intransitive*»

¶Kōtta michi de suberanai yō ni ki o tsukete ne.

凍った道で滑らないように気をつけてね。

Take care not to slip on the frozen road.

• kuchi ga suberu 口が滑る *the tongue slips, something unintended is said*

③ *to be slippery* «*when the subject is a surface*»

¶Yuki ga futte, michi ga suberu yo.

雪が降って、道が滑るよ。

It snowed and the road is slippery!

• suberi-yasui 滑りやすい *slippery, easy to slip on*

¶Kono yuka wa suberi-yasui yo.

この床は滑りやすいよ。

This floor is slippery!

súbete すべて *all, everything* [→**zenbu** 全部]

¶Kore ga nyūshu dekita jōhō no subete desu.

これが入手できた情報のすべてです。

This is all of the information that I could get hold of.

¶Amerika-jin ga subete Eigo o hanasu to iu wake de wa nai.

アメリカ人がすべて英語を話すというわけではない。

It is not the case that Americans all speak English.

• subete no すべての *all, every*

¶Subete no seito ga taiiku-kan ni shūgō shimashita.

すべての生徒が体育館に集合しました。

All the students gathered in the gym.

suchímu スチーム ① *steam* [→**jōki** 蒸気]

② *steam heat; steam heating*

¶Sono heya wa suchīmu ga tōtte imasu.

その部屋はスチームが通っています。

That room is steam-heated. «*Literally: As for that room, steam heat passes through.*»

suchuwádesu スチュワーデス *stewardess*

súde-ni 既に ① *already* [→**mō** もう①]

¶Ken ni denwa shita toki ni wa, sude-ni dete ita.

健に電話したときには、すでに出ていた。

When I telephoned Ken, he had already left.

② ⟨*no*⟩ *longer,* ⟨*not*⟩ *any more* «*in combination with a negative predicate*» [→**mō** もう②]

¶Megumi wa sude-ni sono apāto ni sunde inai.

恵はすでにそのアパートに住んでいない。

Megumi was no longer living in that apartment.

sue 末 ① *end, close* [→**owari** 終わり]

¶Sobo wa sengetsu no sue ni taiin shimashita.

祖母は先月の末に退院しました。

My grandmother was discharged from the hospital at the end of last month.

② *after, as a result*

¶Sū-nen no doryoku no sue, kin-medaru o kakutoku shimashita.

数年の努力の末、金メダルを獲得しました。

As a result of many years of effort, she won the gold medal.

¶Yoku kangaeta sue, iku koto ni shimashita.

よく考えた末、行くことにしました。

After thinking about it a lot, I decided to go.

③ *the future*

• A no iku sue Aの行く末 *A's future, how A's future will go*

• sue-kko 末っ子 *the youngest child in a family*

¶Boku wa yo-nin-kyōdai no suekko desu.

僕は4人兄弟の末っ子です。

I'm the youngest of four children.

sueru 据える ① *to place, to set, to lay*
[→**oku** 置く①]

② *to appoint, to place* 《a person in a job or position》

sufínkusu スフィンクス *sphinx*

sūgaku 数学 *mathematics*

¶Kyō wa sūgaku no jugyō ga aru yo.

きょうは数学の授業があるよ。

We have math class today!

• sūgaku-sha 数学者 *mathematician*

súgao 素顔 *face without make-up, true face*

sugasugashíi 清々しい *refreshing, fresh*
[→**sawayaka na** 爽やかな]

¶Yūdachi no ato wa kūki ga sugasugashii desu.

夕立の後は空気がすがすがしいです。

The air is refreshing after a late afternoon rainshower.

súgata 姿 *form, appearance, figure*

¶Sono uma wa hontō ni utsukushii sugata o shite iru.

その馬はほんとうに美しい姿をしている。

That horse really has a fine figure.

¶Haiyū wa kagami ni jibun no sugata o utsushimashita.

俳優は鏡に自分の姿を映しました。

The actor looked at his appearance in the mirror.

• sugata o arawasu 姿を現わす *to appear, to come in sight*

• sugata o kesu 姿を消す *to disappear*

sugi 杉 *Japanese cedar*

-sugi －過ぎ ① *past, after* 《Added to bases denoting times or ages.》

¶Jū-ji jūgo-fun-sugi desu.

10時15分過ぎです。

It's 10:15.

¶Mayonaka-sugi made okite imashita.

真夜中過ぎまで起きていました。

I was up until after midnight.

¶Ojīsan wa nanajū-sugi da yo.

おじいさんは70過ぎだよ。

Grandfather is past 70!

② *excess, too much* 《Added to verb bases.》

• nomi-sugi 飲みすぎ *excessive drinking*

sugíru 過ぎる ① *to pass by, to pass through* [→**tsūka suru** 通過する]

¶Hikōki ga zujō o sugite ikimashita.

飛行機が頭上を過ぎていきました。

A plane passed overhead.

② *to exceed, to pass* 《a time or age》

¶Mō o-hiru o sugita yo.

もうお昼を過ぎたよ。

It's already past noon!

• ni suginai に過ぎない *to be nothing more than, to be merely* 《following a noun or a clause》

¶Sore wa chosha no iken ni suginai desu.

それは著者の意見に過ぎないです。

That's nothing more than the author's opinion.

¶Shachō wa han o oshita ni sugimasen.

社長は判を押したに過ぎません。

The company president did nothing more than stamp it with his seal.

③ *to elapse, to pass* [→**tatsu** 経つ]

¶Kono gakkō ni nyūgaku shite kara ni-nen ga sugita.

この学校に入学してから2年が過ぎた。

Two years have passed since we entered this school.

¶Fuyu ga sugite, haru ni narimashita.

冬が過ぎて、春になりました。

Winter passed, and it became spring.

-sugiru －過ぎる *to excess, over-*
《Added to verb, adjective, and adjectival noun bases.》

¶Hataraki-sugiru no wa kenkō ni warui desu.

働きすぎるのは健康に悪いです。

Overworking is bad for one's health.

¶Kono shiken wa kantan-sugiru deshō.

この試験は簡単すぎるでしょう。

This examination is probably too simple.

¶Sono pasokon wa taka-sugite, totemo kaenai.

そのパソコンは高すぎて、とても買えない。

That personal computer is too expensive and I can't possibly buy it.

sugói 凄い *amazing, tremendous, astounding, startling*

¶Sugoi!

すごい！

Wow!

¶Supōtsu-kā ga sugoi sokudo de hashitte iru.

スポーツカーがすごい速度で走っている。

The sports car is moving at a tremendous speed.

sugósu 過ごす *to spend, to pass* 《a period of time》

¶Kotoshi wa fuyu-yasumi o Kyōto de sugoshimasu.

今年は冬休みを京都で過ごします。

This year I will spend the winter vacation in Kyoto.

¶Pātī de tanoshiku sugoshimashita ka.

パーティーで楽しく過ごしましたか。

Did you have a good time at the party?

súgu すぐ ① 《～ni ～に》 *at once, <US>right away, <UK>straight away*

¶Sugu shuppatsu shimashō.

すぐ出発しましょう。

Let's start out at once.

•mō sugu (ni) もうすぐ（に）*soon, any time now*

•to sugu (ni) とすぐ（に）*as soon as* 《following a nonpast-tense verb》

¶Otōto wa kaette kuru to sugu ni terebi o tsukemashita.

弟は帰って来るとすぐにテレビをつけました。

As soon as my younger brother came home, he switched on the TV.

② *right, directly*

¶Sugu mae no hito ni kikimashita.

すぐ前の人に聞きました。

I asked the person right in front of me.

•sugu no すぐの *nearby, close*

¶Sono kōjō wa minato kara sugu desu.

その工場は港からすぐです。

That factory is close to the port.

③ 《～ni ～に》 *easily, readily*

¶Kono ko wa sugu naku yo.

この子はすぐ泣くよ。

This child cries easily!

suguréru 優れる *to become superior*

¶Kono sakuhin wa mae no yori sugurete imasu.

この作品は前のより優れています。

This work is superior to the previous one.

•sugureta すぐれた *excellent, superior* 《when modifying a following noun》

¶Wakamatsu-san wa sugureta sakkyoku-ka desu.

若松さんは優れた作曲家です。

Ms. Wakamatsu is an excellent composer.

súibun 水分 *water content, moisture content*

•suibun no ōi kudamono 水分の多い果物 *very juicy fruit*

suichoku 垂直 ～na/no ～な/の ① *perpendicular*

② *vertical*

•suichoku-sen 垂直線 *vertical line; perpendicular line*

suidō 水道 *water service, public water-supply facilities*

•suidō no mizu 水道の水 *tap water, city water*

•suidō o hiku 水道を引く *to connect the water service*

•suidō-kan 水道管 *water pipe*

•suidō-ryōkin 水道料金 *water charges*

suiei 水泳 *swimming*

¶Yumiko-san wa suiei ga jōzu desu.

由美子さんは水泳が上手です。

Yumiko is good at swimming.

•suiei o suru 水泳をする *to swim*

•suiei-kyōshitsu 水泳教室 *swimming class*

•suiei-pantsu 水泳パンツ *swimming trunks*

•suiei-taikai 水泳大会 *swimming meet*

suigai 水害 *flood damage, flooding*

¶Kono machi wa kyonen suigai o ukemashita.

この町は去年水害を受けました。

This town suffered flood damage last year.

suigara 吸殻 *cigarette butt*

suigin 水銀 *mercury, quicksilver*

suigyū 水牛 *water buffalo*

suihei 水平 ～**na**／**no** ～な／の *level, horizontal*

• suihei-sen 水平線 *the horizon* (*between sky and sea*) [⇔**chiheisen** 地平線]; *horizontal line*

• suihei-sen-jō ni 水平線上に *above the horizon*

súihei 水兵 (*navy*)*sailor*

suiji 炊事 *cooking, kitchen work* [→ **ryōri** 料理①]

• suiji suru 炊事する *to cook, to do the cooking*

suijōki 水蒸気 *steam; water vapor*

suijun 水準 *level, position on a scale*

• bunka-suijun 文化水準 *cultural level*

suika 西瓜 *watermelon*

suikómu 吸い込む *to suck in; to inhale, to breathe in* 《transitive》

¶Shinsen na kūki o mune-ippai suikonda.

新鮮な空気を胸いっぱい吸い込んだ。

I took a deep breath of fresh air. 《Literally: I breathed in a chestful of fresh air.》

suikyū 水球 *water polo*

suimin 睡眠 *sleep, slumber*

¶Yūbe wa jūbun ni suimin o torimashita.

ゆうべは十分に睡眠をとりました。

I got plenty of sleep last night.

• suimin-busoku 睡眠不足 *lack of sleep, insufficient sleep*

suimono 吸い物 *clear soup* 《This is one kind of soup commonly served with traditional Japanese meals, and it typically consists of vegetables with fish or chicken in a fish broth flavored with salt and a small amount of soy sauce.》

suíngu スイング ① *swing* 《of an athlete》

¶Sono battā no suingu wa subarashii ne.

そのバッターのスイングはすばらしいね。

That batter's swing is wonderful, isn't it.

② *swing* (*music*)

suiren 水蓮 *water lily*

súiri 推理 *reasoning, inference*

¶Sono suiri wa machigatte imasu.

その推理はまちがっています。

That reasoning is mistaken.

• suiri suru 推理する *to infer*

• suiri-shōsetsu 推理小説 *mystery novel, detective story*

súiryoku 水力 *waterpower*

• suiryoku-hatsuden 水力発電 *hydroelectricity generation*

• suiryoku-hatsuden-sho 水力発電所 *hydroelectric power plant*

suisaiga 水彩画 *watercolor painting*

Suisei 水星 (*the planet*)*Mercury*

suisei 彗星 *comet*

• suisei no o 〔kaku〕 彗星の尾〔核〕 *the tail* 〔*nucleus*〕 *of a comet*

• Harē-suisei ハレー彗星 *Halley's comet*

suisen 水仙 *narcissus*

• rappa-suisen らっぱ水仙 *daffodil*

suisen 推薦 *recommendation*

• suisen suru 推薦する *to recommend*

¶Sensei ga kono hon o suisen shite kudasaimashita.

先生がこの本を推薦してくださいました。

The teacher recommended this book to us.

• suisen-jō 推薦状 *letter of recommendation*

súisha 水車 *waterwheel*

• suisha-goya 水車小屋 *waterwheel-powered mill*

suishin 推進 ① *propulsion*

• suishin suru 推進する *to propel*

② *promotion, furthering*

• suishin suru 推進する *to promote, to further*

súishō 水晶 *quartz crystal*

súiso 水素 *hydrogen*

• suiso-bakudan 水素爆弾 *hydrogen bomb*

suisō 水槽 *water tank, cistern*

suisoku 推測 *guess, conjecture*

¶Kore wa suisoku ni suginai yo.

これは推測にすぎないよ。

This is no more than conjecture!

• suisoku ga ataru 〔hazureru〕 推測が当たる〔外れる〕 *a guess proves right* 〔*wrong*〕

• suisoku suru 推測する *to guess, to conjecture*

súitchi スイッチ (*electrical*)*switch*

• denki no suitchi o ireru 〔kiru〕 電気の
スイッチを入れる〔切る〕*to switch
on* 〔*off*〕 *the lights*

suitō 水筒　*canteen, flask*

suītópī スイートピー　*sweet pea*

Suiyō 水曜〔☞**Suiyōbi** 水曜日〕

Suiyōbi 水曜日　*Wednesday*

suizókukan 水族館　*aquarium* ((institution))

sūji 数字　*numeral, figure*

• Rōma-sūji ローマ数字　*Roman numerals*

súji 筋　① *muscle* [→**kinniku** 筋肉]*;
tendon, sinew*

• suji o chigaeru 筋を違える *to pull a
muscle, to strain a muscle*

② *line* 《mark on a surface》 [→**sen**
線①]*; stripe* [→**shima** 縞]

③ *plot* 《of a story》

¶Kono shōsetsu no suji wa tanjun-sugimasu.
この小説の筋は単純すぎます。
The plot of this novel is too simple.

④ 〜**ga tōtte iru** 〜が通っている *to
make sense, to be coherent*

¶Kono setsumei wa suji ga tōtte iru to
omoimasu.
この説明は筋が通っていると思います。
*I think that this explanation makes
sense.*

sukáfu スカーフ　*scarf*

sukánku スカンク　*skunk*

sukáto スカート　*skirt*

sukáuto スカウト　①（*personnel*）*scout*

② *scouting for personnel*

• sukauto suru スカウトする *to scout for
personnel*

sukéjūru スケジュール　*schedule*

¶Ashita wa sukejūru ga tsumatte imasu.
あしたはスケジュールが詰まっています。
Tomorrow my schedule is crowded.

sukéru スケール　*scale, extent, proportionate size* [→**kibo** 規模]

sukétchi スケッチ　① *sketching*

• suketchi suru スケッチする *to sketch, to
make a sketch of*

¶Watashi wa panda o suketchi shimashita.

私はパンダをスケッチしました。
I sketched the panda.

② *sketch, rough drawing*

• suketchi-bukku スケッチブック *sketchbook*

sukḗto スケート　① *skating*

• sukēto o suru スケートをする *to skate*

② *skate*

• sukēto-jō スケート場 *skating rink*

sukí 好き　〜**na** 〜な 《This adjectival
noun is used to describe both the people
who like and the people or things that are
liked.》　*liked; fond* [⇔**kirai na** 嫌い
な]

¶Niku wa amari suki ja nai desu.
肉はあまり好きじゃないです。
I don't like meat very much.

¶Yagi-san wa fuyu yori natsu no hō ga
suki desu.
八木さんは冬より夏のほうが好きです。
Mr. Yagi likes summer better than winter.

¶Ichiban suki na kudamono wa banana
da yo.
いちばん好きな果物はバナナだよ。
The fruit I like best is the banana!

¶Suki na dake tabete kudasai.
好きなだけ食べてください。
Please eat as much as you like.

¶Suki na yō ni shinasai.
好きなようにしなさい。
Do as you like.

¶Nattō ga suki na hito wa imasu ka.
納豆が好きな人はいますか。
Is there anyone who like natto?

¶Otōto wa terebi o miru no ga suki desu.
弟はテレビを見るのが好きです。
My younger brother likes watching TV.

suki 隙　① *opening, gap* [→**sukima**
透き間]

② *chance, opportunity* [→**kikai** 機会]

¶Nigeru suki ga nakatta yo.
逃げるすきがなかったよ。
I had no chance to escape!

③ *unguarded point, weak point; unguarded moment*

¶Jūdō no senshu wa aite no suki o nera-

imasu.

柔道の選手は相手のすきをねらいます。

Judo contestants aim for their opponent's unguarded point.

sukí スキー ① *skiing*

¶Boku wa tomodachi to Zaō ni sukī ni ikimashita.

僕は友達と蔵王にスキーに行きました。

I went skiing at Zao with my friend.

• sukī o suru スキーをする *to ski*

② *ski*

• sukī-gutsu スキー靴 *ski boot*

• sukī-jō スキー場 *ski resort*

sukíkirai 好き嫌い *likes and dislikes*

¶Kono ko wa sukikirai ga hageshii desu.

この子は好き嫌いがはげしいです。

This child's likes and dislikes are intense.

sukima 透き間 *opening, gap, crack*

¶Hei no sukima kara neko ga haitte kimashita.

塀の透き間から猫が入ってきました。

A cat came in through an opening in the fence.

• sukima-kaze 透き間風 *draft, wind coming in through a crack*

sukinshíppu スキンシップ *close physical contact and the resulting emotional bond* 《typically between parent and child》

sukíppu スキップ *skipping* (*gait*)

• sukippu suru スキップする *to skip*

sukitóru 透き通る *to be transparent*

sukíyā スキーヤー *skier*

sukiyaki すき焼き *sukiyaki* 《This popular Japanese dish consists of thinly sliced beef and various other ingredients cooked in broth in a shallow pan. The pan is usually set on a burner in the center of the table.》

sukkári すっかり *completely, entirely, utterly*

¶Chichi wa mō sukkari genki ni narimashita.

父はもうすっかり元気になりました。

My father has already gotten completely better.

¶Kono kutsu wa sukkari nurete shimaimashita.

この靴はすっかりぬれてしまいました。

These shoes got completely wet.

• sukkari wasureru すっかり忘れる *to forget completely*

sukóa スコア *score* 《of a contest》

¶Boku no chīmu wa go-tai-ichi no sukoa de katta yo.

僕のチームは5対1のスコアで勝ったよ。

Our team won by a score of 5 to 1!

• sukoa-bōdo スコアボード *scoreboard*

sukóppu スコップ *shovel* [→**shaberu** シャベル]

sukŏru スコール *squall*

sukóshi 少し *a few, a little, a small amount* [⇔**takusan** たくさん]

¶Ringo mo sukoshi katte kudasai.

りんごも少し買ってください。

Please buy a few apples too.

¶Taiiku-kan ni wa seito ga sukoshi shika imasen.

体育館には生徒が少ししかいません。

In the gym there are only a few students.

¶Kono sūpu ni shio o sukoshi irete kudasai.

このスープに塩を少し入れてください。

Please put a little salt in this soup.

¶Eigo ga sukoshi hanasemasu.

英語が少し話せます。

I can speak a little English.

• sukoshi-zutsu 少しずつ *little by little*

¶Kanja wa sukoshi-zutsu naotte kimashita.

患者は少しずつ治ってきました。

The patient got better little by little.

• sukoshi-mo 少しも 〈*not*〉 *at all*, 〈*not*〉 *even a little*, 〈*not*〉 *even a few* 《Always occurs in combination with a negative predicate.》

¶Sukoshi-mo tsukarete inai yo.

少しも疲れていないよ。

I am not tired at all!

suku 空く *to become empty; to become uncrowded* [⇔**komu** 込む]

¶Kono basu wa suite imasu.

このバスはすいています。

This bus is uncrowded.

• onaka ga suku おなかがすく *to get hungry* 《Literally: *one's stomach becomes empty*》

sukui 救い *help, rescue*
¶Bōya wa sukui o motomete sakebimashita.
坊やは救いを求めて叫びました。
The little boy yelled for help.

sukúizu スクイズ *squeeze* (*play*) 《in baseball》

sukunái 少ない *small in number, small in quantity* [⇔**ōi** 多い]
¶Kono machi ni wa ki ga totemo sukunai desu.
この町には木がとても少ないです。
There are very few trees in this town.
¶Kyonen wa yuki ga sukunakatta desu.
去年は雪が少なかったです。
There was little snow last year.
¶Seikō suru nozomi wa sukunai desu.
成功する望みは少ないです。
There is little hope of succeeding.
¶Chichi ga Nichiyōbi ni uchi ni iru koto wa sukunai.
父が日曜日にうちにいることは少ない。
There are few times when my father is at home on Sunday.

sukúnaku-tomo 少なくとも *at least* [→**semete** せめて]
¶Sukunaku-tomo ichi-nen ni ik-kai wa ryokō shimasu.
少なくとも1年に1回は旅行します。
I take a trip at least once a year.

sukūpu スクープ (*news*)*scoop* [→**tokudane** 特種]
• sukūpu suru スクープする *to get a scoop about*

sukúramu スクラム *scrum*
• sukuramu o kumu スクラムを組む *to form a scrum*

sukuráppu スクラップ ① *scrap* (*metal*) ② <*US*> 〈*newspaper*〉 *clipping*, <*UK*> 〈*newspaper*〉 *cutting* [→**kirinuki** 切り抜き]
• sukurappu-bukku スクラップブック *scrapbook*

sukurín スクリーン (*movie*)*screen*

sukūrubásu スクールバス *school bus*

sukúryū スクリュー *screw, propeller* 《of a ship》

sukūtā スクーター *motor scooter*

sukuu 救う *to help, to rescue, to save*
¶Komatte ita ga, tomodachi ga sukutte kureta.
困っていたが、友達が救ってくれた。
I was having trouble, but my friend helped me.
¶Sensei wa oborete iru kodomo o sukuimashita.
先生はおぼれている子供を救いました。
The teacher saved the drowning child.

sukuu 掬う *to scoop up*
¶Kodomo-tachi wa ami de kingyo o sukuimashita.
子供たちは網で金魚をすくいました。
The children scooped up goldfish with nets.
• A no ashi o sukuu Aの足をすくう *to trip A up*

sukyándaru スキャンダル *scandal*

súmai 住まい *residence, dwelling*

sumásshu スマッシュ *smash* 《in tennis, etc.》
• sumasshu suru スマッシュする *to hit a smash*

sumásu 済ます ① *to finish, to complete* [→**oeru** 終える]
¶Watashi-tachi wa mō chūshoku o sumasemashita.
私たちはもう昼食を済ませました。
We have already finished our lunch.
② *to make do, to get by* [→**sumu** 済む②]
¶Yūshoku wa rāmen de sumashemashō.
夕食はラーメンで済ませましょう。
Let's make do with noodles for dinner.

sumáto スマート 〜**na** 〜な ① *slim, slender*
¶Eiko-san wa totemo sumāto ni narimashita.
英子さんはとてもスマートになりました。
Eiko has gotten very slim.
② *smart, stylish*

sumí 炭 *charcoal*
- sumi-bi 炭火 *charcoal fire*

súmi 隅 *corner* «within an enclosed or delimited area», *nook*
¶Heya no sumi ni isu ga arimasu.
部屋の隅にいすがあります。
There is a chair in the corner of the room.
- sumi ni tatsu 隅に立つ *to stand in the corner*

sumí 墨 <*US*>*India ink*, <*UK*>*Indian ink, Chinese ink; ink stick*
¶Sobo wa sumi de tegami o kaite imasu.
祖母は墨で手紙を書いています。
My grandmother is writing a letter in India ink.
- sumi-e 墨絵 *traditional India-ink painting*

sumimasen すみません ① *I'm sorry; Excuse me* [→**gomen nasai** ご免なさい]
¶"Hontō ni sumimasen." "Dō itashimashite."
「ほんとうにすみません」「どういたしまして」
"I'm very sorry." "Not at all."
¶Chikoku shite sumimasen.
遅刻してすみません。
I'm sorry I'm late.
¶Sumimasen ga, ryōgae o o-negai dekimasu ka.
すみませんが、両替をお願いできますか。
Excuse me, but can you exchange some money?
  ② *Thank you* «In this use, the speaker expresses thanks by apologizing for putting the listener to trouble.»
¶"Dōzo go-enryo-naku meshiagatte kudasai." "Sumimasen."
「どうぞ遠慮なく召し上がってください」「すみません」
"Help yourself, please." "Thank you."

sumire 菫 *violet* ((flower))
- sanshoku-sumire 三色菫 *pansy*

sumō 相撲 *sumo* (*wrestling*)
- sumō o toru 相撲を取る *to do sumo*
- sumō-tori 相撲取り *sumo wrestler*

sumóggu スモッグ *smog*

- kō-kagaku-sumoggu 光化学スモッグ *photochemical smog*

súmu 住む *to reside, to live*
¶Doko ni sunde imasu ka.
どこに住んでいますか。
Where are you living?
¶Imōto wa ima oba to issho ni sunde imasu.
妹は今伯母といっしょに住んでいます。
My younger sister is now living with my aunt.
¶Hokkaidō ni sunde mi-tai desu.
北海道に住んでみたいです。
I want to try living in Hokkaido.

súmu 済む ① *to become finished, to become over*
¶Heya no sōji wa shichi-ji made ni wa sumu deshō.
部屋の掃除は7時までには済むでしょう。
Room cleaning will probably be finished by 7:00.
¶Eigo no shiken wa sumimashita.
英語の試験は済みました。
The English examination is over.
  ② *to make do, to get by* [→**sumasu** 済ます②]
¶Nani-mo kawanai de sumimashita.
何も買わないで済みました。
I got by without buying anything.

súmu 澄む *to become clear, to become transparent*
¶Yama no sunda kūki wa kimochi ga ii desu.
山の澄んだ空気は気持ちがいいです。
The fresh mountain air feels good.

sumúzu スムーズ 〜na 〜な *smooth, free from difficulty* [→**nameraka na** 滑らかな②]
¶Banji ga sumūzu ni hakobimashita.
万事がスムーズに運びました。
Everything progressed smoothly.

suna 砂 *sand*
¶Kutsu ni suna ga haitta yo.
靴に砂が入ったよ。
Sand got in my shoes!
- suna-ba 砂場 *sandbox*, <*UK*>*sandpit*
- suna-hama 砂浜 *sandy beach*

sunákku スナック ① *snack food*
② 《A kind of bar where the bill includes a nominal table charge for a small appetizer which is automatically served to all customers.》

súnao 素直 〜**na** 〜な *gentle, meek; obedient, unresisting*
¶Akira-chan wa sunao na shōnen desu.
明ちゃんは素直な少年です。
Akira is an obedient boy.
¶Sofu no iu koto o sunao ni kikimashita.
祖父の言うことを素直に聞きました。
I listened meekly to what my grandfather said.
¶Otōto wa sunao na seikaku desu.
弟は素直な性格です。
My younger brother has a gentle nature.

sunáppu スナップ ① *snap (fastener)*
② *snap of the wrist* 《in throwing or hitting a ball》
③ *snapshot*

sunáwachi 即ち *that is (to say)*
¶Yamamoto-hakase wa senshū no Kin'yōbi, sunawachi Jūni-gatsu tōka ni shuppatsu shimashita.
山本博士は先週の金曜日、すなわち12月10日に出発しました。
Dr. Yamamoto started out last Friday, that is, on December 10.

suné 脛 *lower leg* 《below the knee and above the ankle》
¶Imōto wa watashi no sune o ketta yo.
妹は私のすねをけったよ。
My younger sister kicked my lower leg!

sunīkā スニーカー *sneakers*

sunpō 寸法 *measurements (for clothing)*
¶Yōfuku-ya-san wa uwagi no sunpō o torimashita.
洋服屋さんは上着の寸法を取りました。
The tailor took the measurements for a jacket.

sūpā スーパー [☞**sūpāmāketto** スーパーマーケット]

supagétti スパゲッティ *spaghetti*

supái スパイ *spy*

supáiku スパイク ① *(athletic-shoe) spike*

• supaiku suru スパイクする *to spike* 《a player》
② *spiked shoe*

supáiku スパイク *spike, spiking* 《in volleyball》
• supaiku suru スパイクする *to spike*

sūpāmāketto スーパーマーケット *supermarket*

sūpāman スーパーマン *superman*

supána スパナ <*US*> *wrench,* <*UK*> *spanner*

supāto スパート *spurt* 《in a race》
• supāto suru スパートする *to spurt*
• supāto o kakeru スパートをかける *to put on a spurt*

supéa スペア *a spare (item)*
• supea-kī スペアキー *spare key*
• supea-taiya スペアタイヤ *spare tire*

supēdo スペード *spades* ((playing-card suit))

supékutakuru スペクタクル *spectacle, spectacular show*
• supekutakuru-eiga スペクタクル映画 *movie spectacular*

supēsu スペース *space, room*

supēsushátoru スペースシャトル *space shuttle*

supīdo スピード *(rate of) speed* [→**sokudo** 速度]
¶Sono kuruma wa supīdo ga demasen.
その車はスピードが出ません。
That car cannot produce speed.
• supīdo o dasu スピードを出す *to increase speed, to speed up*
• supīdo o otosu スピードを落とす *to reduce speed, to slow down*
• supīdo-ihan スピード違反 *speeding violation*

supīkā スピーカー *speaker, loudspeaker*

supoito スポイト *(medicine) dropper*

supókusuman スポークスマン *spokesperson*

suponji スポンジ *sponge*
• suponji-kēki スポンジケーキ *sponge cake*

supónsā スポンサー *sponsor*

supótsu スポーツ *sport, sports*
¶Tarō-kun wa donna supōtsu ga suki

desu ka.
太郎君はどんなスポーツが好きですか。
What kind of sports does Taro like?
¶Junko-san wa supōtsu ga tokui desu.
順子さんはスポーツが得意です。
Junko is good at sports.
• supōtsu-bangumi スポーツ番組 *sports program*
• supōtsu-jaketto スポーツジャケット *sport jacket*
• supōtsu-kā スポーツカー *sports car*
• supōtsu-nyūsu スポーツニュース *sports news*
• supōtsu-shatsu スポーツシャツ *sport shirt*
• supōtsu-uea スポーツウエア *sportswear*
• supōtsu-yōhin スポーツ用品 *sporting goods*

supōtsúman スポーツマン *person who participates in sports, athlete*

supōtsumanshíppu スポーツマンシップ *sportsmanship*

supottoráito スポットライト *spotlight*

suppái 酸っぱい *sour*
¶Kono aoi ringo wa suppai yo.
この青いりんごは酸っぱいよ。
This green apple is sour!

sūpu スープ *soup*
• sūpu o nomu スープを飲む *to eat soup* 《Literally: *to drink soup*》
• yasai-sūpu 野菜スープ *vegetable soup*

supún スプーン *spoon*
¶Karēraisu wa supūn de tabemasu.
カレーライスはスプーンで食べます。
One eats curry and rice with a spoon.
¶Kōcha ni supūn ip-pai no satō o iremashita.
紅茶にスプーン1杯の砂糖を入れました。
I put a spoonful of sugar in my tea.

supurḗ スプレー ① *spray, atomized liquid* [→**kiri** 霧②]; *spraying*
• supurē suru スプレーする *to spray* 《transitive》
② *sprayer, atomizer*

supuringu スプリング（*metal*)*spring* [→**bane** ばね]

supurínkurā スプリンクラー *sprinkler*

suraidingu スライディング *sliding* 《in baseball》

suraido スライド（*photographic*)*slide*
¶Rondon no suraido o misete kudasai.
ロンドンのスライドを見せてください。
Please show us the slides of London.
• suraido-eisha-ki スライド映写機 *slide projector*

suráisu スライス ① *slicing, cutting in slices*
• suraisu suru スライスする *to slice*
② *slice*
• suraisu-chīzu スライスチーズ *sliced cheese*

suráisu スライス《in tennis, golf, etc.》 *hitting a slice; slice*
• suraisu suru スライスする *to hit a slice*

surákkusu スラックス *slacks*

suránpu スランプ ① （*emotional*)*slump*
¶Murakami tōshu wa suranpu de nayande iru sō da.
村上投手はスランプで悩んでいるそうだ。
Murakami, the pitcher seems to be worried about his slump.
• suranpu ni ochiiru スランプに陥る *to fall into a slump*
② （*economic*)*slump* [→**fukeiki** 不景気]

súrasura すらすら（〜**to** 〜と）*smoothly, easily, fluently*
¶Haruo wa sono muzukashii shitsumon ni surasura kotaeta.
春男はその難しい質問にすらすら答えた。
Haruo answered that difficult question easily.

surechigau 擦れ違う *to pass by each other going in opposite directions*
¶Tōri de Sugiyama-san to surechigatta deshō.
通りで杉山さんとすれ違ったでしょう。
I probably passed by Mr. Sugiyama on the street.
¶Kono semai dōro de kuruma ga surechigau no wa konnan da.
この狭い道路で車がすれ違うのは困難だ。
It's dangerous for cars to pass each other on this narrow road.

súri スリ ① *pickpocketing*
② *pickpocket*
¶Suri ni go-yōjin
「スリにご用心」《on a sign》
Beware of Pickpockets

suríbachi すりばち *earthenware mortar*
[⇔**surikogi** すりこぎ]

surikireru 擦り切れる *to become worn out*（*from abrasion*）
¶Kono kiji wa sugu ni surikiremasu.
この生地はすぐに擦り切れます。
This cloth wears out easily.
¶Sono hito wa surikireta kōto o kite ita.
その人は擦り切れたコートを着ていた。
That person was wearing a worn-out coat.

suríkizu 擦り傷 *scratch, abrasion*（（injury））

surikógi すりこぎ *wooden pestle* [⇔**suribachi** すりばち]

súrippa スリッパ（*house*）*slippers*《backless slippers worn in rooms without **tatami**（floor mats）》

suríppu スリップ *slip*（（underwear））

suríppu スリップ *slip, skid*
• surippu suru スリップする *to slip, to skid* [→**suberu** 滑る②]

súrirā スリラー *thriller*

súriru スリル *thrill*
¶Kinō suriru ni michita eiga o mimashita.
きのうスリルに満ちた映画を見ました。
Yesterday I saw a movie full of thrills.
• suriru ga aru スリルがある *to be thrilling*

surógan スローガン *slogan*

surōmóshon スローモーション *slow motion*

surópu スロープ *slope, hillside* [→**shamen** 斜面]

súru 擦る *to rub, to chafe, to abrade*
《transitive》
• matchi o suru マッチをする *to strike a match*

suru する{Irreg.} ① *to do, to engage in* [→**okonau** 行う]
¶Nani o shite iru n desu ka.
何をしているんですか。

What are you doing?
¶Kyō wa suru koto ga takusan arimasu.
きょうはする事がたくさんあります。
I have a lot of things to do today.
¶Kaisha no tame nara, nan demo shimasu.
会社のためなら、何でもします。
I'll do anything if it's for the company.
¶Seiji-ka wa enzetsu o shimashita.
政治家は演説をしました。
The politician made a speech.
¶Chichi wa sanpo o shite imasu.
父は散歩をしています。
My father is taking a walk.
¶Sā, toranpu o shimashō.
さあ、トランプをしましょう。
Well, let's play cards.

② **A o B ni**~ AをBに~ *to make A into B*
¶Iin-tachi wa Nakayama-san o iin-chō ni shimashita.
委員たちは中山さんを委員長にしました。
The committee members made Mr. Nakayama the chairperson.

③ *to come to have*《when the direct object is a feature》
¶Ano ko wa kawaii kao o shite imasu.
あの子はかわいい顔をしています。
That child has a cute face.
¶Kono ie wa piramiddo no katachi o shite imasu.
この家はピラミッドの形をしています。
This house has a pyramid shape.

④ *to be noticeable, to be felt*
¶Hidoi zutsū ga shimasu.
ひどい頭痛がします。
I have a bad headache.
¶Hen na oto ga shimashita.
変な音がしました。
There was a strange sound.

⑤ *to cost*
¶Kono tokei wa hassen-en shimashita.
この時計は8000円しました。
This watch cost 8,000 yen.

⑥ *time passes*
¶Ato jup-pun shitara daijōbu da yo.
あと10分したら大丈夫だよ。

After another ten minutes, it'll be fine!

surudói 鋭い [[⇔**nibui** 鈍い]]

① *sharp, good for cutting*

¶Motto surudoi naifu o tsukainasai.

もっと鋭いナイフを使いなさい。

Use a sharper knife.

• surudoi kotoba 鋭い言葉 *sharp words, scathing words*

• surudoi hihyō 鋭い批評 *sharp criticism*

• surudoi itami 鋭い痛み *sharp pain*

• surudoi me 鋭い目 *piercing look*

② *keen, acute, sensitive*

¶Inu wa hana ga surudoi desu.

犬は鼻が鋭いです。

Dogs' noses are keen.

sushí 寿司, 鮨 *sushi*

• sushi-ya 寿司屋 *sushi shop; sushi restaurant*

suso 裾 *portion at the lower hem* «of a kimono, skirt, pants leg, etc.»

• yama no suso 山のすそ *the foot of a mountain*

• suso-wake 裾分け [☞**o-susowake** お裾分け]

súsu 煤 *soot*

¶Shōbō-shi no kao wa susu de makkuro desu.

消防士の顔はすすで真っ黒です。

The firefighter's face is completely black with soot.

susugu 濯ぐ *to rinse*

¶Shanpū no ato wa yoku kami o susuginasai.

シャンプーの後はよく髪をすすぎなさい。

Rinse your hair well after the shampoo.

• kuchi o susugu 口をすすぐ *to rinse out one's mouth*

susukéru 煤ける *to become sooty*

susumeru 進める ① *to make go forward, to send forward*

• gun o susumeru 軍を進める *to send troops forward*

② *to go ahead with, to cause to progress*

¶Watashi-tachi wa samazama na konnan o norikoete, sono keikaku o susumemashita.

私たちはさまざまな困難を乗り越えて、その計画を進めました。

We overcame various difficulties and went ahead with that plan.

③ *to set forward* «a clock»

¶Tokei o go-fun susumemashita.

時計を5分進めました。

I set the clock forward five minutes.

susumeru 勧める ① *to advise, to encourage, to suggest*

¶Kyōju wa gakusei-tachi ni kono hon o yomu yō susumemashita.

教授は学生たちにこの本を読むよう勧めました。

The professor advised the students to read this book.

② *to offer*

¶Tomodachi no okāsan ga kōcha o susumete kuremashita.

友達のお母さんが紅茶を勧めてくれました。

My friend's mother offered me some tea.

susumeru 薦める *to recommend* [→**suisen suru** 推薦する]

susumu 進む ① *to go forward, to move ahead* [→**zenshin suru** 前進する]

¶Tomaranai de, susunde kudasai.

止まらないで、進んでください。

Don't stop, please move ahead.

¶Watashi-tachi wa yukkuri susumimashita.

私たちはゆっくり進みました。

We went forward slowly.

¶Mō sukoshi mae e susunde kudasai.

もう少し前へ進んでください。

Please move forward a little more.

② *to progress, to advance* [→**shinpo suru** 進歩する]

¶Kensetsu-sagyō wa junchō ni susunde imasu.

建設作業は順調に進んでいます。

Construction is making smooth progress.

¶Sore wa susunda kangae desu.

それは進んだ考えです。

That's an advanced idea.

③ *to gain, to become fast* «when the subject is a clock» [⇔**okureru** 遅れる②]

¶Kono tokei wa ichi-nichi ni ichi-byō

susumu sō desu.

この時計は 1 日に 1 秒進むそうです。

I hear that this clock gains one second a day.

sutā スター *star* (*performer*)
- eiga-sutā 映画スター *movie star*
- dai-sutā 大スター *big star*

sutáffu スタッフ *staff; staff member*

sutairísuto スタイリスト ① *hair stylist; wardrobe stylist*

② *person who dresses stylishly*

sutáiru スタイル ① *style, fashion*

¶Mizusawa-san wa itsu-mo saishin no sutairu no fuku o kite imasu.

水沢さんはいつも最新のスタイルの服を着ています。

Mr. Mizusawa always wears the latest style of clothes.

② *personal appearance*

¶Tomoko-san wa sutairu ga ii desu ne.

友子さんはスタイルがいいですね。

Tomoko's appearance is nice, isn't it.

sutájiamu スタジアム *stadium*

sutajio スタジオ 〈*movie*〉 *studio*

sutamina スタミナ *stamina*

¶Ano pitchā wa sutamina ga nai yo.

あのピッチャーはスタミナがないよ。

That pitcher has no stamina!

sutandádo スタンダード ～na～な *standard, typical*

sutando スタンド *stands* 《in a stadium, etc.》

sutando スタンド *electric lamp* [→ **denki-sutando** 電気スタンド (s.v. **denki** 電気)]

sutánpu スタンプ ① *stamp* 《for making an ink impression》
- sutanpu o osu スタンプを押す *to apply a stamp*

② *stamp* 《i.e., an ink impression》

sutareru 廃れる *to go out of use; to go out of fashion*

sutáto スタート *start, start-off*
- sutāto suru スタートする *to start, to make a start*
- sutāto no aizu スタートの合図 *start signal*

- sutāto o kiru スタートを切る *to make a start*

¶Sono rannā wa ii sutāto o kirimashita.

そのランナーはいいスタートを切りました。

That runner made a good start.

- sutāto-gakari スタート係 *starter* ((person))
- sutāto-rain スタートライン *starting line*

sutéji ステージ (*theater*)*stage* [→**butai** 舞台]

sutéki ステーキ *steak*
- bīfu-sutēki ビーフステーキ *beefsteak*
- sāroin-sutēki サーロインステーキ *sirloin steak*

suteki 素敵 ～**na** ～な *splendid, wonderful, nice*

¶Sensei wa suteki na sētā o kite imasu ne.

先生はすてきなセーターを着ていますね。

The teacher is wearing a nice sweater, isn't she.

sutékkā ステッカー *sticker, adhesive label*

sutékki ステッキ *walking stick, cane* [→ **tsue** 杖]

sutendogúrasu ステンドグラス *stained glass*

suténresu ステンレス *stainless steel*

sutéppu ステップ ① (*dance*)*step*

② *step* 《in a process》

③ *steps* 《on a bus, train, etc.》

sutereo ステレオ ① *a stereo*

¶Sutereo de kono rekōdo o kakete kure.

ステレオでこのレコードをかけてくれ。

Play this record on the stereo.

② *stereo, stereophonic sound reproduction*

- sutereo-hōsō ステレオ放送 *stereo broadcasting*

suteru 捨てる ① *to throw away, to discard*

¶Kono furu-zasshi o sutemashō.

この古雑誌を捨てましょう。

Let's throw away these old magazines.

¶Sore o kuzu-ire ni sutenai de kudasai.

それをくず入れに捨てないでください。

Don't throw that away in the wastebasket.

② *to abandon, to desert, to give up on*
• kazoku o suteru 家族を捨てる *to abandon one's family*

súto スト 【COL. for **sutoraiki** ストライキ】

sutōbu ストーブ *room heater*
• denki-sutōbu 電気ストーブ *electric heater*
• gasu-sutōbu ガスストーブ *gas heater*
• sekiyu-sutōbu 石油ストーブ *oil heater*

sutókkingu ストッキング *stocking*

sutókku ストック *stock (of unsold goods)* [→**zaiko** 在庫]

sutókku ストック *ski pole*

sutoppuuótchi ストップウォッチ *stopwatch*

sutoráiki ストライキ *(labor)strike*
• sutoraiki o suru ストライキをする *to go on strike*
• chin'age-sutoraiki 賃上げストライキ *strike for higher wages*

sutoráiku ストライク *strike 《in baseball》*

sutoráipu ストライプ *stripe* [→**shima** 縞]
• sutoraipu no nekutai ストライプのネクタイ *striped necktie*

sutóresu ストレス *stress, strain*

sutoréto ストレート ① *fastball 《in baseball》*
② ～**na** ～な *straight, consecutive, uninterrupted*
• sutoreto de katsu ストレートで勝つ *to win in straight games, sets, etc.*

sutórō ストロー *(drinking)straw*
¶Kodomo wa sutorō de miruku o nomimashita.
子供はストローでミルクを飲みました。
The child drank milk through a straw.

sutorobo ストロボ ① *strobe light*
② *electric flash 《(camera attachment)》*

sutoróku ストローク *stroke 《in sports》*

sútsu スーツ *suit 《(clothing)》*
¶Mori-san wa kyō atarashii sūtsu o kite iru.
森さんはきょう新しいスーツを着ている。
Ms. Mori is wearing a new suit today.

sūtsukésu スーツケース *suitcase*

sutsūru スツール *stool 《(seat)》*

suu 吸う ① *to suck in; to inhale*
¶Shinsen na kūki o fukaku suimashita.
新鮮な空気を深く吸いました。
I deeply inhaled the fresh air.
• iki o suu 息を吸う *to take in a breath*
② *to suck on 《in order to draw out a liquid or gas》*
¶Akachan ga okāsan no chichi o sutte imasu.
赤ちゃんがお母さんの乳を吸っています。
The baby is sucking on her mother's breast.
• tabako o suu たばこを吸う *to smoke (cigarettes)*
③ *to absorb* [→**kyūshū suru** 吸収する]
¶Kono suponji wa amari mizu o suimasen.
このスポンジはあまり水を吸いません。
This sponge doesn't absorb very much water.

súwan スワン *swan* [→**hakuchō** 白鳥]

suwaru 座る ① *to sit, to take a seat* [→**koshikakeru** 腰掛ける]
¶Mikami-san wa benchi ni suwatte imasu.
三上さんはベンチに座っています。
Ms. Mikami is sitting on a bench.
¶Gaido wa ichiban mae no seki ni suwatta.
ガイドはいちばん前の席に座った。
The guide sat in the frontmost seat.
② *to sit on one's knees 《This way of sitting, with the buttocks resting on the heels, is the formal posture for sitting on the floor in Japan.》*
¶Tatami ni kichin-to suwatte kudasai.
畳にきちんと座ってください。
Please sit straight on the tatami.

suzu 鈴 *bell 《usually the type consisting of a small bead inside a metal shell》*

súzu 錫 *tin 《(metal)》*

suzume 雀 *sparrow*

suzúran 鈴蘭 *lily of the valley*

suzurí 硯 *inkstone 《used in Japanese caligraphy》*

suzushíi 涼しい *cool* [⇔**atatakai**

暖かい, 温かい]

¶Oka no ue ni wa suzushii kaze ga fuite imasu.

丘の上には涼しい風が吹いています。

A cool wind is blowing on top of the hill.

¶Firumu wa suzushii basho ni hokan shinasai.

フィルムは涼しい場所に保管しなさい。

Keep the film in a cool place.

T

tá 田 *rice field, rice paddy*
• ta-ue 田植え *rice planting*

tá 他 ～**no** ～の *other, another* [→**hoka no** 外の, 他の]

tába 束 *bundle; bunch*
• -taba － 束《*counter for bundles, bunches; see Appendix 2*》

¶Obāchan wa hito-taba no furui tegami o yaita.

おばあちゃんは1束の古い手紙を焼いた。

Grandma burned a bundle of old letters.

• taba-neru 束ねる *to bundle together*

¶Furu-zasshi o tabanete kuremasen ka.

古雑誌を束ねてくれませんか。

Won't you bundle together the old magazines for me?

tabako たばこ *cigarette; cigar; tobacco*

¶Chichi wa tabako o yamemashita.

父はたばこをやめました。

My father gave up smoking.

• tabako o suu たばこを吸う *to smoke* (*cigarettes*)

¶Ōtaki-kyōju wa tabako o sui-sugimasu ne.

大滝教授はたばこを吸いすぎますね。

Professor Otaki smokes too much, doesn't she.

• tabako-ya たばこ屋 *tobacconist's; tobacconist*

tabehódai 食べ放題 *as much as one wants to eat*

• tabehōdai no baikingu 食べ放題のバイキング *all-you-can-eat smorgasbord*

tabemóno 食べ物 *food*

¶Donna tabemono ga ichiban suki desu ka.

どんな食べ物がいちばん好きですか。

What kind of food do you like best?

¶Sashimi wa watashi no suki na tabemono no hitotsu desu.

刺身は私の好きな食べ物の一つです。

Sashimi is one of my favorite foods.

¶Nani-ka tabemono o motte kimashita ka.

何か食べ物を持ってきましたか。

Did you bring some food?

tabéru 食べる *to eat*

¶O-hiru ni wa nani o tabemashita ka.

お昼には何を食べましたか。

What did you eat for lunch?

¶Kēki o tabemasen ka.

ケーキを食べませんか。

Won't you have some cake?

tabesugi 食べ過ぎ *eating too much*

tabí 旅 *trip, journey, travel* [→**ryokō** 旅行]

tábi 足袋 *tabi, Japanese split-toed sock*

• jika-tabi 地下足袋 *worker's tabi* 《long **tabi** with rubber soles typically worn by construction workers and other laborers》

tabí-ni 度に *every time* 《Always follows a verb in the nonpast tense.》

¶Ane wa kikyō suru tabi-ni sono oka ni noborimasu.

姉は帰郷するたびにその丘に登ります。

My elder sister climbs that hill every time she goes back home.

tabitabi 度々 *often*

¶Hideo wa tabitabi gakkō ni okureru yo.

英雄はたびたび学校に遅れるよ。

Hideo is often late for school!

¶Ani wa tabitabi tosho-kan ni ikimasu.

兄はたびたび図書館に行きます。

My older brother often goes to the library.

tabū タブー *a taboo*

tábun 多分《This word typically occurs in

sentences ending with an expression of possibility (such as **to omou** と思う) or probability (such as **darō** だろう). Since such a sentence has virtually the same meaning whether or not **tabun** is present, **tabun** is redundant in a sense, but it serves as a signal of how a sentence will end.》 *perhaps; probably*

¶Tabun ashita wa hareru deshō.

たぶんあしたは晴れるでしょう。

It will probably clear up tomorrow.

¶Kitagawa-san wa tabun kuru to omoimasu.

北川さんはたぶん来ると思います。

I think perhaps Ms. Kitagawa will come.

-tachi 一達《This suffix indicates the plural and is added to noun bases referring to people or to personified animals. When the base refers to a specific individual, the combination with **-tachi** that individual and those associated with that individual.》

• watashi-tachi 私たち *we, us*

tachiagaru 立ち上がる *to stand up, to rise to one's feet*

¶Minna sugu ni tachiagarimashita.

みんなすぐに立ち上がりました。

They all stood up immediately.

tachibá 立場 *standpoint, place, position*

• A no tachiba ni naru Aの立場になる *to put oneself in A's position*

¶Kōchō-sensei no tachiba ni natte kangaete kudasai.

校長先生の立場になって考えてください。

Please put yourself in the principal's place and think about it.

tachidomaru 立ち止まる *to stop walking*

¶Otōsan wa tachidomatte, chizu o mimashita.

お父さんは立ち止まって、地図を見ました。

Dad stopped walking and looked at the map.

tachigiki 立ち聞き *eavesdropping*

• tachigiki suru 立ち聞きする *to eavesdrop on*

¶Tanin no hanashi o tachigiki shite wa ikenai yo.

他人の話を立ち聞きしてはいけないよ。

You mustn't eavesdrop on other people's conversations!

tachigui 立ち食い 【COL.】 *eating while standing up*

• tachigui suru 立ち食いする *to eat standing up*

tachiiri 立ち入り *entering, setting foot in*

¶Tachiiri kinshi

「立入禁止」《on a sign》

Keep Out 《Literally: *Entering prohibited*》

tachisaru 立ち去る *to leave, to go away from*

¶Hōdō-jin wa ku-ji-goro ni genba o tachisatta.

報道陣は9時ごろに現場を立ち去った。

The press left the scene at about 9:00.

tachiyomi 立ち読み *reading while standing up* 《This word typically refers to reading at a bookstore without buying anything.》

• tachiyomi suru 立ち読みする *to read standing up*

tachiyoru 立ち寄る *to drop in, to stop by*

¶Tokidoki gakkō no kaeri ni hon-ya ni tachiyorimasu.

時々学校の帰りに本屋に立ち寄ります。

I sometimes drop in at a bookstore on my way home from school.

táda 唯、只 ① *only, just, merely* [→**tan ni** 単に]

¶Ani wa tada koibito ni au tame ni yatte kita.

兄はただ恋人に会うためにやってきた。

My older brother only came to see his girlfriend.

• tada no ただの *mere; ordinary, run-of-the-mill* [→**futsū no** 普通の]

② *however* [→**shikashi** しかし]

③ ~**no** ~の *free (of charge)* [→**muryō no** 無料の]

• tada de ただで *for free, without charge*

¶Kono nōto o tada de moratta yo.

このノートをただでもらったよ。

I got this notebook for free!

tadáima 只今 [[→**ima** 今]] *now; just now* «in combination with a past-tense verb»

¶Chichi wa tadaima nyūyoku-chū desu.

父はただいま入浴中です。

My father is taking a bath right now.

¶Haha wa tadaima modotta tokoro desu.

母はただいま戻ったところです。

My mother has just now returned.

tadaima ただいま *I'm home, I'm back* «Japanese etiquette requires this announcement upon one's return.»

¶Okāsan, tadaima.

お母さん、ただいま。

Mom, I'm home.

tádashi 但し *however* [→**shikashi** しかし]

tadashíi 正しい *right, correct*

¶Oda-san no iu koto wa itsumo tadashii.

小田さんの言うことはいつも正しい。

What Ms. Oda says is always right.

¶Tadashii jikan o oshiete kudasai.

正しい時間を教えてください。

Please tell me the correct time.

¶Jirō wa watashi no kotoba o tadashiku rikai shite kureta.

次郎は私の言葉を正しく理解してくれた。

Jiro understood my words correctly.

¶Sono tango o tadashiku hatsuon shinasai.

その単語を正しく発音しなさい。

Pronounce that word correctly.

tadásu 正す *to correct, to rectify*

¶Ayamari ga areba, tadashite kudasai.

誤りがあれば、正してください。

If there are errors, please correct them.

tadayóu 漂う *to drift*

¶Bōto ga kaijō ni tadayotte imasu.

ボートが海上に漂っています。

A rowboat is drifting on the sea.

tadōshi 他動詞 *transitive verb* [⇔ **jidōshi** 自動詞]

taéru 耐える、堪える ① *to stand, to endure, to bear, to put up*

• A ni taeru Aに耐える *to stand A, to endure A, to bear A, to put up with A*

¶Watashi wa hito-ban-jū ha no itami ni taemashita.

私は一晩中歯の痛みに耐えました。

I put up with a toothache all night long.

¶Kono atsusa ni wa taerarenai yo.

この暑さには耐えられないよ。

I can't stand this heat!

② *to withstand*

• A ni taeru Aに耐える *to withstand A*

¶Kono ie wa ōki na jishin ni mo taemasu.

この家は大きな地震にも耐えます。

This house will withstand even a big earthquake.

taéru 絶える ① *to come to an end, to end*

¶Haha-oya no shinpai-goto wa taemasen.

母親の心配事は絶えません。

A mother's worries never end.

② *to die out* [→**zetsumetsu suru** 絶滅する]

táezu 絶えず *continually, incessantly*

táfu タフ ～**na** ～な *tough, hardy*

¶Masao wa tafu na yatsu da.

正男はタフなやつだ。

Masao is a tough guy.

tagai 互い ～**no** ～の *mutual*

• tagai ni 互いに *each other, mutually*

¶Kyōdai wa tagai ni tasuke-awanakereba naranai.

兄弟は互いに助け合わなければならない。

Brothers and sisters must help each other.

¶Ano futari wa tagai ni okurimono o kōkan shimashita.

あの二人は互いに贈り物を交換しました。

Those two exchanged gifts.

-ta-garu －たがる [☞**-garu** －がる]

tagayásu 耕す *to plow, to till*

• hatake o tagayasu 畑を耕す *to plow a field*

tágui 類い *sort, type, kind* [→**shurui** 種類]

tái 鯛 *sea bream*

tái 対 ① *versus*

¶Nihon tai Chūgoku no shiai wa ashita desu.

日本対中国の試合はあしたです。
The Japan vs. China game is tomorrow.

② *to* 《Typically used in giving scores.》
¶Watashi-tachi no chīmu wa san tai ichi de katta yo.
私たちのチームは 3 対 1 で勝ったよ。
Our team won by 3-to-1!

¶Sono shiai wa san tai san no dōten de owarimashita.
その試合は 3 対 3 の同点で終わりました。
The game ended in a 3-to-3 tie.

-tai ーたい *to want to* 《Added to verb bases to form words that are grammatically adjectives. To express the desire of a third person, **-garu** ーがる is added to the base of an adjective formed with **-tai**. When **-tai** is added to a verb with a direct object, the object can be marked either with **o** を or with **ga** が。》
¶Ashita mo tenisu o shi-tai.
あしたもテニスをしたい。
I want to play tennis tomorrow too.

¶Nani-mo nomi-taku nai.
何も飲みたくない。
I don't want to drink anything.

¶Yōroppa ni iki-tai nā.
ヨーロッパに行きたいなあ。
Boy, I want to go to Europe.

¶Ani ni tetsudatte morai-tai no desu.
兄に手伝ってもらいたいのです。
I want my older brother to help me.

¶Shachō to hanashi-tai to omoimasu.
社長と話したいと思います。
I'd like to talk with the company president. 《Adding to **omou** after **-tai** softens the assertion of desire, but the literal translation *I think I want to* usually sounds rather unnatural. In most cases, the less literal *I'd like to* is preferable.》
¶Otōto wa kono kēki o tabe-ta-garu deshō.
弟はこのケーキを食べたがるでしょう。
My younger brother will probably want to eat this cake.

taiátari 体当たり ① *throwing oneself* 《against something》
• taiatari suru 体当たりする *to throw one-self*

¶Otoko no hito wa doa ni taiatari shima-shita.
男の人はドアに体当たりしました。
The man threw himself against the door.

② *devoting all one's energy, throwing oneself* 《into something》
• taiatari de yaru 体当たりでやる *to do with all one's energy*

taibatsu 体罰 *corporal punishment*

táido 態度 *attitude, manner, bearing, deportment*
¶Watashi-tachi ni taisuru taido wa kōi-teki desu.
私たちに対する態度は好意的です。
Their attitude toward us is friendly.

¶Hiromi-chan wa jugyō-chū no taido ga hijō ni yoi.
弘美ちゃんは授業中の態度が非常によい。
Hiromi's class manner is very good.

taifú 台風 *typhoon*
¶Kyūshū wa yoku taifū ni osowaremasu.
九州はよく台風に襲われます。
Kyushu is often hit by typhoons.

• taifū no me 台風の目 *eye of a typhoon*
• Taifū-go-gō 台風 5 号 *Typhoon No. 5*
《Typhoons are given numbers rather than names in Japan.》

taigai 大概 ① *generally, usually* [→ **futsū** 普通①]
• taigai no 大概の *general, usual*
② *for the most part, almost completely* [→**hotondo** 殆ど①]
• taigai no 大概の *most, almost all*
③ [[→**tabun** 多分]] *perhaps; probably*
④ ～**no** ～の *moderate, reasonable*

Taihéiyō 太平洋 *the Pacific Ocean* [⇔ **Taiseiyō** 大西洋]
• Taiheiyō-sensō 太平洋戦争 *the Pacific War* 《Refers to the part of World War II between Japan and the Allies in 1941–45.》
• Minami-Taiheiyō 南太平洋 *the South Pacific*

taihen 大変 ① *very, extremely* [→**hijō ni** 非常に]
¶Sono shirase ni taihen odorokimashita.

その知らせにたいへん驚きました。
I was very surprised at that news.

② 〜**na** 〜な *terrible; terribly difficult*
¶Sore wa taihen na mondai desu ne.
それはたいへんな問題ですね。
That's a terribly difficult problem, isn't it.
¶Shido-sha wa taihen na ayamari o shimashita.
指導者はたいへんな誤りをしました。
The leader made a terrible mistake.
¶Taihen da!
たいへんだ！
Good Heavens! 《Literally: It's terrible!》

táiho 逮捕 *arrest*
• taiho suru 逮捕する *to arrest*
• taiho-jō 逮捕状 *arrest warrant*

taihō 大砲 *artillery gun, cannon*

táii 大意 *gist, general idea*

táiiku 体育 *physical training; physical education*
• Taiiku no hi 体育の日 *Health-Sports Day 《a Japanese national holiday on October 10》*
• taiiku-kan 体育館 *gymnasium*

taiin 退院 *leaving the hospital, being discharged from the hospital* [⇔**nyūin** 入院]
• taiin suru 退院する *to leave the hospital, to be discharged from the hospital*
¶Kono kanja wa ashita taiin dekiru deshō.
この患者はあした退院できるでしょう。
This patient will probably be able to leave the hospital tomorrow.

taiji 退治 *extermination 《of a pest》*
• taiji suru 退治する *to exterminate, to get rid of*
¶Mazu nezumi o taiji shimashō.
まずねずみを退治しましょう。
First let's get rid of the rats.

taijō 退場 *leaving 《a sporting event, concert, etc.》* [⇔**nyūjō** 入場]
• taijō suru 退場する *to leave*

taijū 体重 *(body)weight*
¶Taijū wa dono gurai arimasu ka.
体重はどのぐらいありますか。

About how much do you weigh?
¶Taijū ga ni-kiro fuemashita.
体重が２キロ増えました。
I've gained two kilograms.
• taijū-kei 体重計 *(body-weight)scale*

taikai 大会 ① *mass meeting; general meeting* [→**sōkai** 総会]; *convention*
② *tournament, meet, competition*
• benron-taikai 弁論大会 *speech contest*
• rikujō-taikai 陸上大会 *track meet*
• marason-taikai マラソン大会 *large marathon race*
• seito-taikai 生徒大会 *students' meeting*
• suiei-taikai 水泳大会 *swim meet*

taikaku 体格 *build, physique*
¶Tasaka-sensei wa gasshiri shita taikaku no hito desu.
田坂先生はがっしりした体格の人です。
Mr. Tasaka is a person of strong build.
• taikaku ga ii 体格がいい *one's build is good*

taiken 体験 *an experience*
¶Tomodachi wa Rōma de no taiken o hanashite kureta.
友達はローマでの体験を話してくれた。
My friend told me about her experiences in Rome.
• taiken suru 体験する *to experience*

táiki 大気 *atmosphere, the air*
• taiki-ken 大気圏 *atmosphere, atmospheric zone*
• taiki-osen 大気汚染 *air pollution*

taikin 大金 *large amount of money*

taiko 太鼓 *drum ((musical instrument))*
• ko-daiko 小太鼓 *snare drum*
• ō-daiko 大太鼓 *bass drum*

taikō 対抗 *opposition; rivalry*
• taikō suru 対抗する *to match, to rival* [→**hitteki suru** 匹敵する]; *to oppose* [→**hantai suru** 反対する]
¶Karate de wa Saitō-kun ni dare-mo taikō dekinai yo.
空手では斉藤君にだれも対抗できないよ。
Nobody can match Saito in karate!

taikoku 大国 *great country, powerful country*

taikutsu 退屈 ～**na** ～な *boring, dull*
¶Kore wa taikutsu na terebi-bangumi desu.
これは退屈なテレビ番組です。
This is a boring TV program.
• taikutsu suru 退屈する *to get bored*
¶Kaichō no nagai supīchi ni taikutsu shimashita.
会長の長いスピーチに退屈しました。
We got bored with the chairperson's long speech.

taimingu タイミング *timing* 《with which something is done》
¶Jitsu ni ii taimingu de Sekiguchi-san ga heya ni haitte kita.
実にいいタイミングで関口さんが部屋に入ってきた。
Mr. Sekiguchi came into the room with truly good timing.

táimurī タイムリー ～**na** ～な *timely, well-timed*
• taimurī-hitto タイムリーヒット *timely hit* 《in baseball》

táion 体温 *(body)temperature*
• taion o hakaru 体温を計る *to take a temperature*
• taion-kei 体温計 *(clinical) thermometer*

taipísuto タイピスト *typist*

táipu タイプ ① *type, style, model* [→ **kata** 型①]
¶Musuko wa kono taipu no jitensha ga suki desu.
息子はこのタイプの自転車が好きです。
My son likes this type of bicycle.
② *type* 《of person》
¶Uemura-san wa boku no suki na taipu desu.
上村さんは僕の好きなタイプです。
Ms. Uemura is the type I like.

táipu タイプ [☞**taipuraitā** タイプライター]

taipuráitā タイプライター *typewriter*
• taipuraitā o utsu タイプライターを打つ *to do typing, to type*

taira 平ら ～**na** ～な *flat, level* [→**hira-tai** 平たい]
¶Rōdō-sha wa undō-jō o taira ni shima-shita.
労働者は運動場を平らにしました。
The workers made the playground level.
• taira na tochi 平らな土地 *flat land*

tairagéru 平らげる ① *to put down, to suppress; to subjugate*
② 【COL.】 *to eat up completely*

tairiku 大陸 *continent*
• Ajia-tairiku アジア大陸 *the Asian Continent*

tairitsu 対立 *mutual opposition, mutual antagonism* [⇔**itchi** 一致]
• tairitsu suru 対立する *to be opposed (to each other)*
¶Futari no iken wa tairitsu shite imasu.
二人の意見は対立しています。
The opinions of the two are opposed.

táiru タイル *tile* 《of the type used on floors and walls》
• tairu o haru タイルを張る *to lay tiles*
• tairu no yokushitsu タイルの浴室 *tiled bathroom*

tairyō 大量 *large quantity*
¶Nihon wa tairyō no sekiyu o yunyū shite imasu.
日本は大量の石油を輸入しています。
Japan imports large quantities of oil.
• tairyō ni 大量に *in large quantities*
• tairyō-seisan 大量生産 *mass production*

táiryoku 体力 *physical strength, stamina*
¶Obāsan no tairyoku wa otoroeta ne.
おばあさんの体力は衰えたね。
Grandmother's stamina has weakened, hasn't it.
• tairyoku-tesuto 体力テスト *physical strength test*

taisaku 対策 *countermeasure*

taisei 体制 *organization, system, structure* 《ordinarily of a society or country》
• keizai-taisei 経済体制 *economic structure*
• seiji-taisei 政治体制 *political system*

Taiséiyō 大西洋 *the Atlantic Ocean* [⇔ **Taiheiyō** 太平洋]

táiseki 体積 *(cubic)volume*

taisetsu 大切 〜**na** 〜な [[→**daiji na** 大事な]] *important* [→**jūyō na** 重要な]; *precious* [→**kichō na** 貴重な]

¶Dokusho o suru koto wa taisetsu desu.
読書をすることは大切です。
Reading books is important.

¶Kore wa taisetsu na gakkō-gyōji desu.
これは大切な学校行事です。
This is an important school event.

¶Kenkō wa totemo taisetsu desu.
健康はとても大切です。
Good health is precious.

• taisetsu ni 大切に *carefully, with care*
¶Taisetsu ni atsukatte kudasai.
大切に扱ってください。
Handle with care.

• taisetsu ni suru 大切にする *to value; to take good care of*

táishi 大使 *ambassador*
• taishi-kan 大使館 *embassy*
• chūBei-Nihon-taishi 駐米日本大使 *Japanese ambassador to the United States*
• chūNichi-Amerika-taishi 駐日アメリカ大使 *American ambassador to Japan*

táishita 大した *great, outstanding; serious, important*
¶Ano kata wa taishita geijutsu-ka desu.
あの方は大した芸術家です。
That person is a great artist.

¶Taishita kega de wa nai desu.
大したけがではないです。
It's not a serious injury.

táishite 大して 〈*not*〉 *very,* 〈*not*〉 *especially* 《Always occurs in combination with a negative predicate.》
¶Kyō wa taishite atsuku nai.
きょうは大して暑くない。
It is not especially hot today.

táishite 対して [☞**ni taishite** に対して]

taishō 対象 *object, target*
¶Murai-sensei no kenkyū no taishō wa konchū desu.
村井先生の研究の対象は昆虫です。
The object of Dr. Murai's research is insects.

taishō 対照 *contrast*
• taishō suru 対照する *to contrast* 《transitive》
• A o B to taishō suru AをBと対照する *to contrast A with B*

táishō 大将 (*army*)*general; admiral*

Taishō 大正《Japanese imperial era name for the period 1912–1926》
• Taishō-jidai 大正時代 *the Taishō Era*
• Taishō-tennō 大正天皇 *the Taishō Emperor*

taishoku 退職 *leaving one's job*
• taishoku suru 退職する *to retire; to resign*
¶Oji wa rokujūgo-sai de taishoku shimasu.
叔父は65歳で退職します。
My uncle will retire at sixty-five.

• taishoku-kin 退職金 *retirement allowance*

taishū 大衆 *the general public, the masses*
• taishū-muki no 大衆向きの *popular, of wide appeal*
• taishū-sakka 大衆作家 *popular writer*
• taishū-shōsetsu 大衆小説 *popular novel*

taisō 体操 ① *gymnastics* ② *calesthenics*
• taisō-bu 体操部 *gymnastics club; gymnastics team*
• biyō-taisō 美容体操 *shape-up calesthenics*
• kikai-taisō 機械体操 *apparatus gymnastics*

taisúru 対する [☞**ni taisuru** に対する]

taitei 大抵 ① *usually, generally* [→**futsū** 普通]
¶Watashi wa taitei roku-ji ni okimasu.
私はたいてい6時に起きます。
I usually get up at 6:00.

¶Haha wa gozen-chū wa taitei uchi ni imasu.
母は午前中はたいていうちにいます。
My mother is usually at home in the morning.

② *for the most part, almost complete-*

ly [→**hotondo** 殆ど①]

• taitei no 大抵の *most, almost all*

③ [[→**tabun** 多分]] *probably; perhaps*

④ ～no ～の 〈*no*〉 *ordinary* 《in combination with a negative predicate》

¶Sore wa taitei no nōryoku de wa arimasen.

それはたいていの能力ではありません。

That's no ordinary ability.

táitoru タイトル ① *title* 《of a book, etc.》 [→**dai** 題]

② (*championship*)*title* [→**senshu-ken** 選手権 (s.v. **senshu** 選手)]

• taitoru-matchi タイトルマッチ *title match*

táitsu タイツ *tights*

taiwa 対話 *conversation* [→**kaiwa** 会話]; *dialog*

¶Kono kyōju wa gakusei to no taiwa ga suki da.

この教授は学生との対話が好きだ。

This professor likes to have conversations with his students.

• taiwa suru 対話する *to have a conversation; to have a dialog*

taiya タイヤ *tire*

¶Kono taiya ga panku shita yo.

このタイヤがパンクしたよ。

This tire went flat!

• sunō-taiya スノータイヤ *snow tire*

• supea-taiya スペアタイヤ *spare tire*

táiyō 太陽 *sun*

¶Taiyō wa nishi ni shizumu deshō?

太陽は西に沈むでしょう？

The sun sets in the west, right?

• taiyō-denchi 太陽電池 *solar battery*

• taiyō-enerugī 太陽エネルギー *solar energy*

• taiyō-kei 太陽系 *solar system*

• taiyō-reki 太陽暦 *solar calendar*

taizai 滞在 *stay* (*away from home*), *sojourn*

• taizai suru 滞在する *to stay*

¶Pari ni wa itsu made taizai suru tsumori desu ka.

パリにはいつまで滞在するつもりですか。

Until when are you planning to stay in Paris?

taka たか *hawk*

takadaka 高々 *at most, at best* [→**seizei** 精々①]

takái 高い ① [[⇔**hikui** 低い①]] *high; tall*

¶Kētsū wa sekai de ni-ban-me ni takai yama desu.

K２は世界で２番目に高い山です。

K2 is the second highest mountain in the world.

¶Ani wa chichi yori san-senchi se ga takai desu.

兄は父より３センチ背が高いです。

My older brother is three centimeters taller than my father.

¶Jetto-ki ga takaku tonde iru yo.

ジェット機が高く飛んでいるよ。

A jet is flying high!

¶Chiagāru wa totemo takaku janpu shita.

チアガールはとても高くジャンプした。

The cheerleader jumped very high.

• takai hana 高い鼻 *prominent nose*

② *loud* [⇔**hikui** 低い②]

③ *expensive* [⇔**yasui** 安い]

¶Kono hon wa takai desu ne.

この本は高いですね。

This book is expensive, isn't it.

¶Sono jitensha wa takakute kaenai yo.

その自転車は高くて買えないよ。

That bicycle is expensive, so I can't buy it!

¶Kono yō na furui kitte wa takaku uremasu.

このような古い切手は高く売れます。

This kind of old stamp sells at a high price.

takamáru 高まる *to rise, to increase*

takaméru 高める *to raise, to increase*

takará 宝 *treasure, precious thing*

• takara-kuji 宝くじ *public lottery; lottery ticket*

• takara-mono 宝物 *precious thing*

• takara-sagashi 宝捜し *treasure hunt*

tákasa 高さ ① *height*

¶Kono biru no takasa wa yaku gojū-mētoru desu.

このビルの高さは約50メートルです。
The height of this building is approximately 50 meters.
　② *loudness*
　③ *expensiveness*

take 竹 *bamboo*
- take-no-ko 竹の子 *bamboo shoot*
- take-yabu 竹薮 *bamboo grove*
- take-zao 竹竿 *bamboo pole*

takeuma 竹馬 *bamboo stilts* 《on which a person walks》
¶Jirō wa takeuma ni noru no ga umai yo.
次郎は竹馬に乗るのがうまいよ。
Jiro is good at walking on stilts!

taki 滝 *waterfall*
¶Sono taki wa takasa ga san-jū-mētoru arimasu.
その滝は高さが30メートルあります。
The height of that waterfall is 30 meters.
- Naiagara no taki ナイアガラの滝 *Niagara Falls*

takibi 焚き火 *fire (built on the ground); bonfire*
¶Nohara de takibi o shimashita.
野原でたき火をしました。
We built a fire in the field.

takigi 薪 *firewood* [→**maki** 薪]

tákkuru タックル *tackle, tackling*
- takkuru suru タックルする *to tackle*

takkyū 卓球 *table tennis, pingpong*
- takkyū o suru 卓球をする *to play table tennis*
- takkyū-dai 卓球台 *ping-pong table*

táko 凧 *kite* ((toy))
- tako-age 凧揚げ *kite flying*

táko 蛸 *octopus*

táko たこ *callus*

taku 焚く ① *to make, to build* 《The direct object is a fire.》
- hi o taku 火をたく *to make a fire*
　② *to burn (as fuel)*
¶Kono fune wa sekitan o taite hashirimasu.
この船は石炭をたいて走ります。
This ship runs by burning coal.
　③ *to heat* 《a bath to the appropriate

temperature》[→**wakasu** 沸かす②]
- furo o taku ふろをたく *to heat a bath*

taku 炊く *to cook* 《by boiling until the liquid is absorbed》
¶Imōto ga gohan o takimashita.
妹がご飯をたきました。
My younger sister cooked rice.

takumashíi 逞しい ① *robust, sturdy, powerfully built*
　② *strong-minded, resolute*

takumi 巧み ～**na** ～な *skillful, clever, ingenious*

takusán たくさん *many, much, a lot* [⇔ **sukoshi** 少し]
¶Takusan no gakusei ga tenisu-bu ni hairimasu.
たくさんの学生がテニス部に入ります。
Many students join the tennis club.
¶Hako no naka ni orenji ga takusan arimasu.
箱の中にオレンジがたくさんあります。
There are a lot of oranges in the box.
¶Kyō wa shukudai ga takusan arimasu.
きょうは宿題がたくさんあります。
Today I have a lot of homework.
¶Roku-gatsu ni wa ame ga takusan furimasu.
6月には雨がたくさん降ります。
In June it rains a lot.

tákushī タクシー *taxi*
¶Takushī ni norimashō.
タクシーに乗りましょう。
Let's take a taxi.
¶Eki made takushī de ikimashita.
駅までタクシーで行きました。
I went to the station by taxi.
¶Takushī o yonde kudasai.
タクシーを呼んでください。
Please call a taxi.
- takushī-dai タクシー代 *taxi fare*
- takushī-noriba タクシー乗り場 *taxi stand* <*UK*>*taxi rank*
- takushī-unten-shu タクシー運転手 *taxi driver*

takuwae 蓄え ① *savings, money put away* [→**chokin** 貯金②]
　② *store, stock, supply*

takuwaéru 蓄える *to store, to save* [→ **tameru** 貯める]

tamá 玉 ① *spherical object, ball (-shaped object); bead*
- keito no tama 毛糸の玉 *ball of yarn*

② *lens* [→**renzu** レンズ]
- megane no tama 眼鏡の玉 *glasses lens*

tamá 球 ① *ball* 《*used in a game*》
- tama o nageru 球を投げる *to throw a ball*

② *light bulb* [→**denkyū** 電球]

tamá 弾 *bullet; cannonball*

tama たま ～**no** ～の *occasional, infrequent*
- tama ni たまに *occasionally, infrequently*

¶Takegawa-san wa tama ni baiorin o hikimasu.

竹川さんはたまにバイオリンを弾きます。

Ms. Takekawa occasionally plays the violin.

tamágo 卵 *egg*
- tamago no shiromi 〔kimi〕卵の白身 〔黄身〕*egg white* 〔*yolk*〕
- nama-tamago 生卵 *raw egg*

tamamushi 玉虫 *jewel beetle*

tamanégi 玉葱 *onion*

tamaranai 堪らない *to be unable to stand, to be unable to bear* 《This word is grammatically a negative verb form and it ordinarily follows a clause ending in a gerund (-**te** form) of an adjective.》

¶Horibe-kun wa sono bokushingu no shiai o mitakute tamaranai.

堀部君はそのボクシングの試合を見たくてたまらない。

Horibe wants to see that boxing match so much he can't stand it.

¶Samukute tamarimasen.

寒くてたまりません。

I'm so cold I can't stand it.

tamaru 溜まる , 貯まる *to collect, to accumulate* 《intransitive》

¶Tēburu no ue ni hokori ga tamatte imasu.

テーブルの上にほこりがたまっています。

Dust has settled on the table.

¶Chokin ga nihyakuman-en tamatta yo.

貯金が200万円たまったよ。

I've saved up 2,000,000 yen! 《Literally: *Savings of 2,000,000 yen have accumulated!*》

támashī 魂 *soul*

tamatama たまたま ① *by chance, unexpectedly, coincidentally* [→**gūzen** 偶然②]

② *occasionally, infrequently* [→**tama ni** たまに]

tamé 為 ① (～**ni** ～に) *in order to* 《following a verb in the nonpast tense》 [→**noni** のに②]

¶Shashin o toru tame ni kōen ni ikimasu.

写真を撮るために公園に行きます。

I'm going to go to the park to take pictures.

② (～**ni** ～に) *because, since* 《following a clause》 [→**node** ので]

¶Ame ga futta tame ni suzushiku narimashita.

雨が降ったために涼しくなりました。

Because it rained, it got cool.

③ **no**～(**ni**) の～ (に) *because of, due to* 《following a noun》

¶Ame no tame ni yakyū no shiai wa chūshi ni natta.

雨のために野球の試合は中止になった。

The baseball game was called off due to the rain.

④ *benefit, sake*

¶Akira wa watashi no tame ni piano o hiite kureta.

明は私のためにピアノを弾いてくれた。

Akira played the piano for me.

- tame ni naru ためになる *to be beneficial*

taméiki 溜息 *sigh*
- tameiki o tsuku ため息をつく *to sigh, to heave a sigh*

tamerai ためらい *hesitation, wavering*
- tamerai mo naku ためらいもなく *without hesitation*

tameráu ためらう *to hesitate about, to waver about*

¶Shitsumon o suru no o tameratte imashita.

質問をするのをためらっていました。
I hesitated to ask a question.

tameru 貯める *to save, to store* [→**ta-kuwaeru** 蓄える]

¶Wāpuro o kau tame ni o-kane o tame-masu.

ワープロを買うためにお金をためます。
I am saving up to buy a word processor.

tamésu 試す *to try out, to sample, to test*

¶Kono atarashii reitō-shokuhin o tame-shite mimashō.

この新しい冷凍食品を試してみましょう。
Let's try this new frozen food.

táminaru ターミナル (*transportation*)*terminal*

tamótsu 保つ *to keep, to maintain, to preserve*

¶Kenkō o tamotsu tame ni nani o shite imasu ka.

健康を保つために何をしていますか。
What are you doing to maintain your health?

¶Densha wa zutto onaji supīdo o tamotte iru.

電車はずっと同じスピードを保っている。
The train is maintaining a constant speed.

tan 痰 *phlegm*

tana 棚 *shelf*

• hon-dana 本棚 *bookshelf*

Tanabata 七夕 *Tanabata Festival, the Star Festival* 《July 7》

tánbarin タンバリン *tambourine*

tanbo 田んぼ *rice field, rice paddy* [→**ta** 田]

tanchō 単調 〜**na** 〜な *monotonous, dull*

táne 種 ① *seed; stone* 《of a cherry, etc.》; *pit* 《of a peach, etc.》

¶Tane kara me ga dete kimashita.

種から芽が出てきました。
The seeds have started sprouting.

• tane o maku 種をまく *to sow seeds, to plant seeds*

¶Haha wa niwa ni asagao no tane o ma-kimashita.

母は庭に朝顔の種をまきました。
My mother planted morning-glory seeds in the garden.

② *cause, source* [→**gen'in** 原因]

• shinpai no tane 心配の種 *source of anxiety*

③ *material* 《to talk or write about》

• hanashi no tane 話の種 *topic of conversation*

④ *the secret* 《of a magic trick, etc.》

tango 単語 *word, vocabulary item*

• tango-hyō 単語表 *vocabulary list*

• Ei-tango 英単語 *English word*

• kihon-tango 基本単語 *basic word*

taní 谷 *valley*

• tani-gawa 谷川 *mountain stream*

tán'i 単位 ① *unit* 《of calculation》

② *unit,* <*US*>*credit* 《of academic work》

• -tan'i －単位《counter for units of academic work; see Appendix 2》

tánin 他人 ① *other person*

¶Tanin ni tayoru no wa yoku nai yo.

他人に頼るのはよくないよ。
It's not good to depend on others!

② *unrelated person, non-relative*

③ *outsider, third party, person not involved*

④ *stranger, person one does not know*

• tanin-atsukai 他人扱い *treating as a stranger*

• tanin-atsukai suru 他人扱いする *to treat as a stranger*

tanjō 誕生 *birth*

• tanjō suru 誕生する *to be born* [→**umareru** 生まれる]

• tanjō-pātī 誕生パーティー *birthday party*

• tanjō-seki 誕生石 *birthstone*

tanjōbi 誕生日 *birthday*

¶Tanjōbi wa itsu?

誕生日はいつ？
When's your birthday?

¶Kyō wa watashi no jūyon-sai no tanjōbi desu.

きょうは私の14歳の誕生日です。
Today is my fourteenth birthday.

¶O-tanjōbi omedetō.

お誕生日おめでとう。

Happy birthday.

¶Chichi wa tanjōbi no purezento ni tokei o kureta.

父は誕生日のプレゼントに時計をくれた。

My father gave me a watch as a birthday present.

tanjun 単純 〜**na** 〜な ① *simple, uncomplicated* [⇔**fukuzatsu na** 複雑な]

¶Sore wa goku tanjun na koto desu.

それはごく単純な事です。

That's a very simple matter.

② *simple-minded, simple-hearted*

¶Ueda-san wa kodomo no yō ni tanjun desu.

上田さんは子供のように単純です。

Mr. Ueda is simple-minded like a child.

tánka 担架 *stretcher*

tánkā タンカー *tanker*

tanken 探検 *exploration, expedition*

• tanken suru 探検する *to explore*

• tanken-ka 探検家 *explorer*

• tanken-tai 探検隊 *expedition team*

tánki 短気 *short temper*

• tanki na 短気な *short-tempered*

• tanki o okosu 短気を起こす *to lose one's temper*

tánki 短期 *short period of time* [⇔ **chōki** 長期]

tankō 炭鉱 *coal mine*

tánku タンク *tank* ((container))

• tank-rōrī タンクローリー <*US*>*tank truck*

tankyóri 短距離 *short distance* [⇔**chū-kyori** 中距離; **chōkyori** 長距離]

• tankyori-kyōsō 短距離競走 *short-distance race, sprint*

tanmatsu 端末 (*computer*)*terminal*

• tanmatsu-sōchi 端末装置 [☞**tanmatsu** 端末 (above)]

tán-ni 単に *only, merely* [→**tada** 唯, 只①]

tánnin 担任 ① *charge, responsibility*

② *teacher in charge, homeroom teacher*

¶Watashi-tachi no tannin wa Katō-sensei desu.

私たちの担任は加藤先生です。

Our homeroom teacher is Mr. Kato.

tánomi 頼み ① *request, favor* (*to ask*) [→**irai** 依頼]

¶Sugimoto-san no tanomi de koko e kimashita.

杉本さんの頼みでここへ来ました。

I came here at Ms. Sugimoto's request.

¶Kimi ni tanomi ga aru yo.

君に頼みがあるよ。

I have a favor to ask you!

② *reliance, trust* [→**shinrai** 信頼]

• tanomi ni naru 頼みになる *to be reliable*

• tanomi ni suru 頼みにする *to rely on, to put one's trust in*

• tanomi no tsuna 頼みの綱 *one's only hope*

tanomoshíi 頼もしい ① *reliable, dependable, trustworthy*

¶Ken-san wa tanomoshii hito desu.

健さんは頼もしい人です。

Ken is a reliable person.

② *promising* 《*describing a person*》

tanomu 頼む [[→**irai suru** 依頼する]] ① *to request, to ask for*

¶Boku wa ane ni kēki no okawari o tanonda yo.

僕は姉にケーキのお代わりを頼んだよ。

I asked my older sister for another piece of cake!

¶Keikan wa higai-sha ni tēpu o kiku yō tanonda.

警官は被害者にテープを聴くよう頼んだ。

The police officer asked the victim to listen to a tape.

¶Sonna ni hayaku hashiranai de to tomodachi ni tanonda.

そんなに速く走らないでと友達に頼んだ。

I asked my friend not to run so fast.

② *to importune to handle, to ask to take care of*

¶Kachō wa Katō-san ni sono shigoto o tanomimashita.

課長は加藤さんにその仕事を頼みました。

The section chief asked Ms. Kato to

handle that job.

tanoshíi 楽しい *pleasant, fun, delightful*

¶Minna tanoshii toki o sugoshimashita.
みんな楽しい時を過ごしました。
Everyone had a pleasant time.

¶Ensoku wa tanoshikatta desu ka.
遠足は楽しかったですか。
Was the excursion fun?

tanoshími 楽しみ *pleasure, enjoyment*

¶Suiei wa sofu no tanoshimi no hitotsu desu.
水泳は祖父の楽しみの一つです。
Swimming is one of my grandfather's pleasures.

• tanoshimi ni suru 楽しみにする *to look forward to*

¶Boku-tachi wa natsu-yasumi o tanoshimi ni shite imasu.
僕たちは夏休みを楽しみにしています。
We are looking forward to the summer vacation.

tanoshímu 楽しむ *to enjoy, to take pleasure in*

¶Musume-san wa ryokō o tanoshinda sō desu ne.
娘さんは旅行を楽しんだそうですね。
I hear your daughter enjoyed her trip.

¶Kodomo-tachi wa yakyū no shiai o mite tanoshinda.
子供たちは野球の試合を見て楽しんだ。
The children enjoyed watching the baseball game.

tánpa 短波 *a shortwave*

• tanpa-hōsō 短波放送 *shortwave broadcasting*

tanpakúshitsu 蛋白質 *protein*

tanpen 短編 *a short work* 《story or movie》

• tanpen-eiga 短編映画 *short film*

• tanpen-shōsetsu 短編小説 *short story*

tánpo 担保 *collateral, security* 《for a loan》

tánpopo たんぽぽ *dandelion*

tansan 炭酸 *carbonic acid*

• tansan-gasu 炭酸ガス *carbon dioxide (gas)*

• tansan-sui 炭酸水 *soda water*

tánsho 短所 *fault, weak point* [⇔ **chōsho** 長所]

¶Takagi-san ni wa tansho ga arimasen.
高木さんには短所がありません。
Ms. Takagi has no faults.

tanshuku 短縮 *shortening, reduction*

• tanshuku suru 短縮する *to shorten, to reduce*

¶Jugyō ga jup-pun-zutsu tanshuku saremashita.
授業が10分ずつ短縮されました。
Each class was reduced by ten minutes.

tánso 炭素 *carbon*

tansu 箪笥 *chest of drawers; wardrobe; cupboard*

• cha-dansu 茶箪笥 *cupboard, sideboard*

• yōfuku-dansu 洋服箪笥 *dresser*

tansū 単数 *the singular* [⇔**fukusū** 複数]

tansui 淡水 *fresh water* [→**mamizu** 真水] [⇔**shio-mizu** 塩水 (s.v. **shio** 塩)]

tansuikábutsu 炭水化物 *carbohydrate*

tantei 探偵 (*private*)*detective*

• tantei-shōsetsu 探偵小説 *detective story*

tantō 担当 *charge, being in charge*

• tantō suru 担当する *to take charge of* [→**ukemotsu** 受け持つ]

• tantō-sha 担当者 *person in charge*

tánuki 狸 *raccoon dog*

taoréru 倒れる ① *to fall over, to topple over*

¶Sono shōnen wa aomuke ni jimen ni taoremashita.
その少年はあおむけに地面に倒れました。
That boy fell over on the ground backwards.

② *to fall ill, to collapse*

táoru タオル *towel*

• basu-taoru バスタオル *bath towel*

taósu 倒す ① *to make fall over*

¶Kodomo ga kabin o taoshimashita.
子供が花瓶を倒しました。
The child knocked over a vase.

② *to defeat* [→**makasu** 負かす]

tappúri たっぷり ① (～**to** ～と) *plenti-*

fully, plenty

¶Tappuri jikan ga aru yo.

たっぷり時間があるよ。

There's plenty of time!

¶Penki o tappuri nutte kudasai.

ペンキをたっぷり塗ってください。

Please apply plenty of paint.

②*fully, a full*

¶Kaigan e iku no ni tappuri san-jikan wa kakaru.

海岸へ行くのにたっぷり3時間はかかる。

It takes a full three hours to go to the beach.

•jishin-tappuri no 自信たっぷりの *self-assured, very confident*

tára 鱈 *cod*

tarai たらい *washtub*

taráppu タラップ *gangway*

-tarazu －足らず *less than* 《Added to bases denoting specific quantities.》

¶Jup-pun-tarazu de basu-tei ni tsuki-masu.

10分足らずでバス停に着きます。

You will arrive at the bus stop in less than ten minutes.

tarento タレント ① *talent* [→**sainō** 才能]
②*star, show-business personality* 《who appears on television or radio》

•terebi-tarento テレビタレント *TV star*

taréru 垂れる ① *to hang down, to droop, to dangle*

¶Shōjo no kami wa senaka ni tarete ima-shita.

少女の髪は背中に垂れていました。

The girl's hair was hanging down her back.

②*to drip* [→**shitataru** 滴る]

¶Tenjō kara mizu ga tarete imasu.

天井から水が垂れています。

Water is dripping from the ceiling.

tariru 足りる *to be enough, to suffice*

¶Seito ga go-nin ireba, tarimasu.

生徒が5人いれば、足ります。

If there are five students, that's enough.

¶Sen-en de tariru deshō.

1000円で足りるでしょう。

1,000 yen will probably be enough.

¶Sono kuni wa shokuryō ga tarinai sō desu.

その国は食糧が足りないそうです。

I hear there is not enough food in that country.

taru 樽 *barrel, cask, keg*

tarumu 弛む ① *to become loose, to slacken*

¶Rōpu ga sukoshi tarunde imasu.

ロープが少したるんでいます。

The rope is a little slack.

② *to become indolent*

¶Musuko wa konogoro tarunde imasu.

息子はこのごろたるんでいます。

My son is indolent recently.

taryō 多量 ～*no* ～の *much, large quantity of* [⇔**shōryō no** 少量の]

•taryō ni 多量に *in great quantity*

táshika 確か *if I remember correctly*

¶Kekkon-shiki wa tashika raishū no Doyōbi desu.

結婚式は確か来週の土曜日です。

The wedding is definitely next Saturday.

•tashika na 確かな *sure, certain, beyond doubt*

¶Miyagi-san no seikō wa tashika da to omoimasu.

宮城さんの成功は確かだと思います。

I think Ms. Miyagi's success is beyond doubt.

•tashika ni 確かに *surely, certainly, definitely*

¶Tashika ni Tomomi-chan ni kagi o wa-tashita yo.

確かに友美ちゃんにかぎを渡したよ。

I definitely handed the key to Tomomi!

tashikaméru 確かめる *to make sure of, to confirm, to verify*

¶Kaigō no nichiji o tashikamete kudasai.

会合の日時を確かめてください。

Please verify the date of the meeting.

¶Tojimari o tashikamemashita ka.

戸締まりを確かめましたか。

Did you make sure the doors were locked? 《Literally: *Did you make sure of the door locking?*》

tashízan 足し算 *addition* 《in arithmetic》

[⇔**hikizan** 引き算]

• tashizan suru 足し算する *to add* [→ **tasu** 足す②]

¶Kono hyō no sūji o tashizan shinasai.

この表の数字を足し算しなさい。

Add up the figures on this chart.

tashō 多少 *to some extent, somewhat*

¶Kubota-kun no tōan ni wa tashō ayamari ga arimasu.

久保田君の答案には多少誤りがあります。

There are some mistakes on Kubota's examination paper.

¶Kore kara wa tashō raku ni narimasu.

これからは多少楽になります。

It will get somewhat easier from now on.

tasogare 黄昏 *dusk, twilight*

tassuru 達する{Irreg.} ① *to reach, to arrive*

¶Ashita no asa sanchō ni tassuru deshō.

あしたの朝山頂に達するでしょう。

They will probably reach the summit tomorrow morning.

¶Tanken-ka wa ik-kagetsu de Nankyoku-ten ni tasshimashita.

探検家は1か月で南極点に達しました。

The explorer reached the South Pole in one month.

② *to attain, to accomplish, to achieve*

¶Shushō wa tsui-ni mokuteki o tasshimashita.

首相はついに目的を達しました。

The prime minister finally achieved his aim.

tasu 足す ① *to add; to supply, to supplement with* [→**oginau** 補う②]

② *to add* «in arithmetic» [⇔**hiku** 引く④]

¶Ni tasu san wa go.

2足す3は5。

Two plus three is five. «Although odd grammatically, this kind of sentence is a typical way of stating a fact of arithmetic.»

tasū 多数 [[⇔**shōsū** 小数]] ① ～**no** ～ の *many, a large number of*

② *majority*

• tasū-ketsu 多数決 *decision by majority*

tasukáru 助かる ① *to be rescued, to be saved*

¶Kanja wa shujutsu o ukete tasukarimashita.

患者は手術を受けて助かりました。

The patient had an operation and was saved.

② *to be helped*

¶Sore de kakei ga ōi ni tasukatta yo.

それで家計が大いに助かったよ。

The family budget was greatly helped by that!

¶Okage-sama de tasukarimashita.

おかげ様で助かりました。

Thank you for your help.

tasuké 助け *help, assistance*

¶Higai-sha wa tasuke o motomemashita ga, dare-mo ōjimasen deshita.

被害者は助けを求めましたが、だれも応じませんでした。

The victim asked for help, but no one responded.

¶Sensei no chūkoku wa ōki na tasuke ni naru deshō.

先生の忠告は大きな助けになるでしょう。

The teacher's advice will probably be a big help.

tasukéru 助ける ① *to help, to lend a helping hand to*

¶Nakano-san wa itsu-mo komatta hito o tasukemasu.

中野さんはいつも困った人を助けます。

Mr. Nakano always helps people in trouble.

② *to help with*

¶Shukudai o tasukete kureru?

宿題を助けてくれる？

Will you help me with my homework?

③ *to rescue, to save*

¶Shōbō-shi wa akachan o hi no naka kara tasuketa.

消防士は赤ちゃんを火の中から助けた。

The firefighter rescued the baby from the fire.

tatakai 戦い *fight, battle*

• tatakai ni katsu〔makeru〕戦いに〔勝つ〕負ける *to win〔lose〕a battle*

tatakau 戦う *to fight, to battle, to struggle*

¶Tsūkō-nin wa gōtō to yūkan ni tatakaimashita.

通行人は強盗と勇敢に戦いました。

A passer-by fought bravely with the robber.

¶Sanka-sha wa heiwa no tame ni tatakatte imasu.

参加者は平和のために戦っています。

The participants are fighting for peace.

tataku 叩く *to strike, to hit* [→**utsu** 打つ]*; to pat; to knock on*

¶Tomodachi wa watashi no atama o tataita yo.

友達は私の頭をたたいたよ。

My friend hit me on the head!

¶Fan wa senshu no senaka o tatakimashita.

ファンは選手の背中をたたきました。

The fan patted the player on the back.

¶Dare-ka ga doa o tataite imasu.

だれかがドアをたたいています。

Someone is knocking on the door.

tatami 畳 *tatami, straw floor mat*

tatamu 畳む *to fold* (*over onto itself*), *to fold up* «transitive»

¶Meido wa tēburu-kurosu o tatamimashita.

メイドはテーブルクロスを畳みました。

The maid folded up the tablecloth.

¶Hankachi o yottsu ni tatande kudasai.

ハンカチを四つに畳んでください。

Please fold the handkerchief in four.

• kasa o tatamu 傘を畳む *to close an umbrella*

tátchi タッチ ① *tag* «in baseball»

• tatchi suru タッチする *to make the tag*

¶Nirui-shu wa rannā ni tatchi dekinakatta.

二塁手はランナーにタッチできなかった。

The second baseman couldn't make the tag on the runner.

② (*artistic*) *touch, manner of execution*

③ ～**suru** ～する *to touch upon, to have to do with*

táte 縦 ① [[⇔**yoko** 横②]] *length* «as opposed to width»; *height* «as opposed to width»

¶Kono tēburu wa tate ga san-mētoru de, yoko ga ichi-mētoru desu.

このテーブルは縦が3メートルで、横が1メートルです。

This table is three meters long and one meter wide.

② ～**no** ～の [[⇔**yoko no** 横の③]] *vertical; end-to-end*

• tate no sen 縦の線 *vertical line*

táte 盾 (*hand-held*) *shield*

tatéfuda 立て札 (*freestanding*) *signboard*

¶Kanri-nin wa "Kinen" no tatefuda o tatemashita.

管理人は「禁煙」の立て札を立てました。

The manager set up a "No smoking" signboard.

tatémae 建て前, 立て前 *outwardly expressed feelings, stated motivation* [⇔**honne** 本音]

tatémono 建物 *a building*

tatéru 立てる *to stand, to set up*

¶Sono hon o hondana ni tatenasai.

その本を本棚に立てなさい。

Stand those books on the bookshelf.

¶Kōchi wa takai sao o jimen ni tatemashita.

コーチは高いさおを地面に立てました。

The coach stood a tall pole in the ground.

tatéru 建てる *to build, to erect*

¶Ani wa ōki na ie o tatemashita.

兄は大きな家を建てました。

My older brother built a large house.

¶Mochinushi wa garēji o tatemashita.

持ち主はガレージを建てました。

The owner built a garage.

tatoé たとえ *even if* «This word introduces a clause ending in a gerund (-**te** form) plus **mo**. Since the clause has the same meaning whether or not **tatoe** is present, **tatoe** is redundant in a sense, but it serves as a signal that the clause will end this way.»

¶Tatoe ashita ame ga futte mo shuppatsu shimasu.

たとえあした雨が降っても出発します。

Even if it rains tomorrow, I will start out.

¶Tatoe ano hito ga nani o itte mo shinjinai yo.

たとえあの人が何を言っても信じないよ。

I wouldn't believe anything that person says!

tatóeba 例えば *for example, for instance*

tatoéru 例える *to liken, to compare*

¶Kono sakka wa yoku jinsei o kōkai ni tatoemasu.

この作家はよく人生を航海に例えます。

This writer often compares life to a voyage.

tátorunékku タートルネック *turtleneck* (*sweater*)

tátsu 立つ ① *to stand; to stand up, to rise to one's feet* [→**tachiagaru** 立ち上がる]

¶Okusan wa mon no tokoro ni tatte imasu.

奥さんは門の所に立っています。

A lady is standing at the gate.

¶Mado no soba ni tatte iru josei ga Nakao-san da.

窓のそばに立っている女性が中尾さんだ。

The woman standing by the window is Ms. Nakao.

¶Oka no ue ni chīsa na ie ga tatte imasu.

丘の上に小さな家が立っています。

A little house stands on the hill.

② *to leave, to depart from* [⇔**tsuku** 着く①]

¶Sono densha wa hachi-ji ni Tōkyō o tachimasu.

その電車は8時に東京を立ちます。

That train leaves Tokyo at 8:00.

tátsu 建つ *to be built, to be erected*

¶Takai biru ga eki-mae ni tatsu sō desu.

高いビルが駅前に建つそうです。

I hear that a tall building is going to be built in front of the station.

tátsu 経つ *to elapse, to pass*

¶Watashi ga Tōkyō ni kite kara go-nen ga tachimashita.

私が東京に来てから5年がたちました。

Five years have passed since I came to Tokyo.

tatsumaki 竜巻 *whirlwind, tornado*

tatsu-no-otoshígo 竜の落とし子 *seahorse*

tatta たった 【COL. for **tada** 唯, 只①】 *only, just, merely*

¶Watashi wa tatta nihyaku-en shika motte inai yo.

私はたった200円しか持っていないよ。

I only have 200 yen!

¶Shokuin-shitsu ni wa sensei ga tatta futari shika inai.

職員室には先生がたった二人しかいない。

There were only two teachers in the staff room.

• tatta hitori de たった一人で *all by oneself, all alone*

• tatta no たったの *mere; ordinary, run-of-the-mill*

tattaíma たった今 【COL.】 *just now* 《always in combination with a past-tense verb》

¶Ichikawa-kun wa tattaima dekaketa yo.

市川君はたった今出かけたよ。

Ichikawa just went out!

táwā タワー *tower*

• Tōkyō-tawā 東京タワー *Tokyo Tower*

táyori 便り *news, word, tidings, correspondence*

¶Nagai aida Sachiko-san kara tayori ga arimasen.

長い間幸子さんから便りがありません。

There hasn't been any word from Sachiko for a long time.

táyori 頼り *thing/person to rely on*

• tayori ni naru 頼りになる *to be reliable*

¶Sono isha wa tayori ni narimasu.

その医者は頼りになります。

That doctor is reliable.

• tayori ni suru 頼りにする *to rely on, to depend on*

¶Tanin no tasuke o tayori ni shinai de.

他人の助けを頼りにしないで。

Don't rely on the help of others.

• A o tayori ni　A を頼りに *with the help of A, relying on A*

¶Chizu o tayori ni sono byōin o saga-shimashita.

地図を頼りにその病院を探しました。

With the aid of a map, I looked for that hospital.

tayóru 頼る *to rely, to depend*

¶Mizutani-san wa onīsan ni tayotte imasu.

水谷さんはお兄さんに頼っています。

Mr. Mizutani is depending on his older brother.

tazuna 手綱 *reins*

tazunéru 訪ねる *to visit, to call on*

¶Senshū oji o tazunemashita.

先週伯父を訪ねました。

I visited my uncle last week.

¶Ashita Fukuchi-san no tokoro o tazuneru tsumori desu.

あした福地さんの所を訪ねるつもりです。

I intend to visit Mr. Fukuchi's place tomorrow.

tazunéru 尋ねる *to ask, to inquire* [→kiku 聞く③]

• A ni B o tazuneru　A に B を尋ねる *to ask A about B*

¶Eki e iku michi o keikan ni tazunemashita.

駅へ行く道を警官に尋ねました。

I asked a police officer the way to the station.

té 手 ① *hand*

¶Akira-san ni mo te o futta yo.

明さんにも手を振ったよ。

I waved my hand to Akira too!

¶Kodomo-tachi wa te o tsunaide aru-kimashita.

子供たちは手をつないで歩きました。

The children walked hand in hand.

• te o ageru 手を上げる *to raise one's hand*

• te o kasu 手を貸す *to lend a hand*

• te ni hairu 手に入る *to come into one's possession*

• te ga kakaru 手が掛かる *to require a lot*

of work, to be laborious

② *arm «including the hand»*

③ *means, method* [→shudan 手段]

¶Hoka no te o tsukatte mimashō.

ほかの手を使ってみましょう。

Let's try using another method.

④ *kind, sort* [→shurui 種類]

¶Sono te no mono wa yushutsu dekinai deshō.

その手の物は輸出できないでしょう。

One probably cannot export that kind of thing.

• te-kubi 手首 *wrist*

• te-no-hira 手の平 *palm of the hand*

• te-no-kō 手の甲 *back of the hand*

teárai 手洗い *washroom, bathroom, restroom* «Toilets and bathtubs are traditionally in separate rooms in Japan. This word refers to a room containing a toilet.» [→toire トイレ]

téashi 手足 ① *arms and legs*

② *hands and feet*

teatarishídai 手当たり次第（〜ni 〜に）*at random*

¶Natsu-yasumi no aida wa teatarishidai ni hon o yonda.

夏休みの間は手当たり次第に本を読んだ。

During the summer vacation I read books at random.

teáte 手当 ① *medical treatment* [→chiryō 治療]

¶Shōjo wa byōin de teate o ukemashita.

少女は病院で手当を受けました。

The girl was treated at the hospital.

• teate suru 手当する *to treat*

② *salary supplement, allowance*

• kazoku-teate 家族手当 *family allowance*

• ōkyū-teate 応急手当 *first-aid*

teatsui 手厚い *warm, solicitous*

tebanásu 手放す *to part with, to let someone else have*

¶Kono rekōdo wa zettai ni tebanasansai yo.

このレコードは絶対に手放さないよ。

I absolutely will not part with this record!

tébiki 手引き ① *guidance, guiding*
② *guide* ((person))
③ *primer, manual, guide*

tebúkuro 手袋 *gloves; mittens*
¶Migi no tebukuro o nakushite shimaimashita.
右の手袋を無くしてしまいました。
I lost my right glove.

tēburu テーブル *table*
¶Tēburu no ue o katazukete kudasai.
テーブルの上を片づけてください。
Please clear the table. 《*Literally: Please tidy the top of the table.*》
• tēburu ni tsuku テーブルに着く *to take a seat at a table*
• tēburu-chāji テーブルチャージ *cover charge*
• tēburu-kurosu テーブルクロス *table-cloth*
• tēburu-manā テーブルマナー *table manners*
• tēburu-supīchi テーブルスピーチ *after-dinner speech*

techō 手帳 *small notebook for reminders,* <UK>*pocketbook*

tegákari 手掛かり *clue, trace*

tegami 手紙 *letter* ((message))
¶Yōko-chan kara tegami o moratta yo.
洋子ちゃんから手紙をもらったよ。
I got a letter from Yoko!
¶O-tegami o dōmo arigatō gozaimashita.
お手紙をどうもありがとうございました。
Thank you very much for your letter.

tegará 手柄 *feat, meritorious deed, exploit*
• tegara o tateru 手柄を立てる *to distinguish oneself, to do a meritorious deed*

tegaru 手軽 〜**na** 〜な [[→**kantan na** 簡単な]] *simple; easy*
¶Kesa wa tegaru na chōshoku o tabemashita.
けさは手軽な朝食を食べました。
I ate a simple breakfast this morning.
¶Sore wa tegaru na shigoto desu.
それは手軽な仕事です。
That's an easy task.

tegiwá 手際 〜**ga ii** 〜がいい *to be skillful*
• tegiwa ga warui 手際が悪い *to be unskillful*
• tegiwa-yoku 手際よく *skillfully*

tegoro 手頃 〜**na** 〜な ① *handy, easy to handle*
¶Kono jisho wa tegoro na ōkisa desu.
この辞書は手ごろな大きさです。
This dictionary is a handy size.
② *reasonable, inexpensive*
¶Kono gurōbu wa tegoro na nedan desu.
このグローブは手ごろな値段です。
This glove is reasonably price. 《*Literally: As for this glove, it's a reasonable price.*》

tehón 手本 ① *example, model*
¶Ano hito o tehon ni shimashō.
あの人を手本にしましょう。
Let's make that person our example.
② *copybook, book of model characters* 《*for Japanese calligraphy*》
¶Tehon o minagara kono ji o kakimashita.
手本を見ながらこの字を書きました。
I wrote this character while looking at the copybook.

teian 提案 *proposal, suggestion*
¶Riji-kai wa watashi no teian ni sansei shimashita.
理事会は私の提案に賛成しました。
The board of directors agreed to my proposal.
• teian suru 提案する *to propose, to suggest*
¶Ichikawa-san wa ii keikaku o teian shimashita.
市川さんはいい計画を提案しました。
Ms. Ichikawa proposed a good plan.

teibō 堤防 *embankment, dike, levee* [→**tsutsumi** 堤]

teiden 停電 *electrical outage, power failure*
¶Yūbe nijup-pun-kan no teiden ga arimashita.
ゆうべ20分間の停電がありました。
There was a twenty-minute power failure last night.

téido 程度 *degree, extent; level* [→**sui-**

jun 水準]

¶Kaichō no iu koto wa aru teido made wakarimasu.

会長の言う事はある程度までわかります。

I understand what the chairperson says to some extent.

¶Kono renshū-mondai wa watashi ni wa teido ga taka-sugiru yo.

この練習問題は私には程度が高すぎるよ。

The level of this exercise is too high for me!

teien 庭園 *(spacious and decorative) garden*

téigi 定義 *a definition*

• teigi suru 定義する *to define*

teiin 定員 *number of persons set by rule; maximum number of persons allowed, capacity*

¶Kono basu no teiin wa rokujū-mei desu.

このバスの定員は60名です。

The capacity of this bus is 60 people.

téiji 定時 *fixed time, set time*

¶Gakkō wa teiji ni hajimarimasu.

学校は定時に始まります。

School starts at a set time.

• teiji-sei-kōkō 定時制高校 *part-time high school 《Japanese schools of this type are ordinarily in session from 6:00 to 10:00 p.m.》*

teika 定価 *list price, regular price*

¶Kono tokei no teika wa gosen-en desu ga, tokubai de kaimashita.

この時計の定価は5000円ですが、特売で買いました。

The list price of this watch is 5,000 yen, but I bought it on sale.

¶Kono jitensha o teika de kaimashita ka.

この自転車を定価で買いましたか。

Did you buy this bicycle at list price?

téiki 定期 ① *fixed time period*

• teiki no 定期の *regular, regularly scheduled*

¶Kumiai-in wa teiki no kaigō o hirakimasu.

組合員は定期の会合を開きます。

The union members will hold their regular meeting.

② [☞**teiki-ken** 定期券 (below)]

• teiki-ire 定期入れ *commuter-pass holder*

• teiki-ken 定期券 <*US*>*commuter pass,* <*UK*>*season ticket*

• teiki-shiken 定期試験 *regular examination*

• teiki-teki na 定期的な *regular, occurring at regular intervals*

¶Yutaka wa tsuki ni ni-kai teiki-teki ni oya ni tegami o kaku.

豊は月に2回定期的に親に手紙を書く。

Yutaka writes a letter to his parents regularly twice a month.

• teiki-yokin 定期預金 *time deposit*

• fu-teiki no 不定期の *irregular, not regularly scheduled*

teikíatsu 低気圧 [[⇔**kōkiatsu** 高気圧]] ① *low atmospheric pressure* ② *low pressure (weather) system*

teikō 抵抗 *resistance, opposition*

¶Teki-gun wa nan no teikō mo shimasen deshita.

敵軍は何の抵抗もしませんでした。

The enemy forces put up no resistance.

• teikō suru 抵抗する *to resist, to oppose*

¶Gakusei-tachi wa keikan-tai ni teikō shimashita.

学生たちは警官隊に抵抗しました。

The students resisted the police force.

téikoku 帝国 *empire*

teikyō 提供 *providing, furnishing; offer*

• teikyō suru 提供する *to provide, to furnish; to offer*

¶Okumura-san mo shiryō o teikyō shite kuremashita.

奥村さんも資料を提供してくれました。

Mr. Okumura also provided data for me.

teikyúbi 定休日 *regular day to be closed for business*

téinei 丁寧 ～**na** ～な ① *polite* [→ **reigi-tadashii** 礼儀正しい (s.v. **reigi** 礼儀)]

¶Nagao-san wa dare ni taishite mo teinei

desu.

長尾さんはだれに対してもていねいです。
Mr. Nagao is polite to everybody.

¶Teinei na henji o uketorimashita.

ていねいな返事を受け取りました。
I received a polite reply.

¶Supōkusuman wa teinei ni kotaemashita.

スポークスマンはていねいに答えました。
The spokesperson answered politely.

　② *careful, attentive to details*

¶Motto teinei ni kakinasai.

もっとていねいに書きなさい。
Write more carefully.

• teinei-go 丁寧語 *polite word* 《one type of respectful vocabulary in Japanese》

teinen 定年 *mandatory retirement age*

teiré 手入れ ① *taking care, maintenance*

• teire ga yukitodoku 手入れが行き届く *maintenance is scrupulous*

• teire suru 手入れする *to take care of, to maintain*

¶Undō-jō wa yoku teire shite arimasu.

運動場はよく手入れしてあります。
The playground has been well taken care of.

　② *police raid*

¶Yūbe sono bā ni teire ga arimashita.

ゆうべそのバーに手入れがありました。
There was a police raid on that bar last night.

teiryūjo 停留所 *stop* 《where a bus or streetcar stops》

• basu no teiryūjo バスの停留所 *bus stop*

teisei 訂正 *correction, rectification*

• teisei suru 訂正する *to correct, to rectify*

¶Shiryō no ayamari o teisei shimasu.

資料の誤りを訂正します。
I will correct the mistakes in the data.

teisetsu 定説 *generally accepted theory*

teisha 停車 *stop, stopping* 《by a train, bus, car, etc.》

• teisha suru 停車する *to come to a stop, to make a stop*

¶Kono densha wa kaku-eki ni teisha shimasu.

この電車は各駅に停車します。
This train stops at every station.

• kyū-teisha 急停車 *sudden stop*

teishi 停止 ① *stopping, cessation of movement*

• teishi suru 停止する *to come to a stop*

¶Basu wa teishi shimashita.

バスは停止しました。
The bus came to a stop.

　② *suspension, interruption*

• teishi suru 停止する *to suspend, to interrupt*

¶Kono kaisha wa kinō eigyō o teishi shimashita.

この会社はきのう営業を停止しました。
This company suspended operations yesterday.

teishoku 定食 *set restaurant meal*

téishu 亭主 【COL. for **otto** 夫】 *husband* [⇔**nyōbō** 女房]

teishutsu 提出 *handing in, turning in* 《of documents, etc.》

• teishutsu suru 提出する *to hand in, to turn in*

¶Dewa, tōan o teishutsu shinasai.

では、答案を提出しなさい。
All right, hand in your examination papers.

téjina 手品 *magic trick*

¶Mori-sensei wa toranpu no tejina ga jōzu desu.

森先生はトランプの手品が上手です。
Mr. Mori is good at card tricks.

• tejina-shi 手品師 *magician*

teki 敵 *enemy* [⇔**mikata** 味方]; *adversary, opponent*

• teki-gun 敵軍 *enemy military force, enemy troops*

• teki-mikata 敵味方 *friends and enemies*

• teki-nashi no 敵無しの *unrivaled*

-teki －的 *-like, -ish, -ic, -al* 《Added to noun bases to form adjectival nouns.》

• kagaku-teki na 科学的な *scientific*

• ongaku-teki na 音楽的な *musical*

• tensai-teki na 天才的な *genius-like*

tékido 適度 ～**no** ～の *moderate*

tékii 敵意 *hostility*

tekiō 適応 ① *adaptation*
- tekiō suru 適応する *to adapt oneself*
¶Sono ryūgaku-sei wa Nihon no sei-katsu-yōshiki ni sugu tekiō shimashita.
その留学生は日本の生活様式にすぐ適応しました。
That foreign student soon adapted herself to the Japanese lifestyle.
② *suitability*
- tekiō suru 適応する *to become suitable, to become suited*

tékipaki てきぱき（〜to 〜と）*quickly, promptly, with dispatch*

tekisetsu 適切 〜na 〜な *appropriate, proper, apt* [→**fusawashii** 相応しい]
¶Tekisetsu na shochi o totte kudasai.
適切な処置を取ってください。
Please take appropriate measures.

tekisúru 適する{Irreg.} *to be fit, to be appropriate*
¶Kono mizu wa nomu noni tekisuru sō desu.
この水は飲むのに適するそうです。
They say this water is fit to drink.
¶Tsukamoto-san wa sono shigoto ni teki-shite imasu.
塚本さんはその仕事に適しています。
Ms. Tsukamoto is right for that job.
¶Kono basho wa tsuri ni tekishite iru to omoimasu.
この場所は釣りに適していると思います。
I think this place is suitable for fishing.

tékisuto テキスト *textbook* [→**kyōkasho** 教科書]
¶Kore wa Eigo no tekisuto desu.
これは英語のテキストです。
This is an English textbook.

tekitō 適当 〜na〜な *appropriate, suitable* [→**fusawashii** 相応しい]
¶Kore wa chūgaku-sei ni tekitō na hon desu.
これは中学生に適当な本です。
This is an appropriate book for junior high school students.
¶Sono fuku wa undō suru noni tekitō ja nai yo.

その服は運動するのに適当じゃないよ。
Those clothes aren't appropriate for doing exercise!

tekkō 鉄鋼 *steel* [→**kōtetsu** 鋼鉄]

tekkyō 鉄橋 *iron bridge, <US>railroad bridge, <UK>railway bridge*

teko てこ *lever*

tékubi 手首 *wrist*

tékunikku テクニック *technique*
¶Sono rēsā wa sugureta unten no teku-nikku o motte imasu.
そのレーサーはすぐれた運転のテクニックを持っています。
The racer has excellent driving technique.

tēma テーマ *theme, subject matter* [→**shudai** 主題]
- tēma-songu テーマソング *theme song*

temá 手間 *time and effort, trouble, labor* [→**tesū** 手数]
¶Kono shigoto wa tema ga kakaru ne.
この仕事は手間がかかるね。
This work takes time and effort, doesn't it.

temae 手前 ① *the area on this side, the area nearer*
¶Kōen no temae ni chūsha-jō ga ari-masu.
公園の手前に駐車場があります。
There is a parking lot on this side of the park.
¶Hayashi-san wa Nagoya no hitotsu temae no eki de orita.
林さんは名古屋の一つ手前の駅で降りた。
Mr. Hayashi got off one station this side of Nagoya.
② *consideration of decorum* «in front of other people»; *out of consideration for decorum* «in front of other people»
¶O-kyaku-san no temae okoru wake ni wa ikimasen.
お客さんの手前怒るわけには行きません。
Out of consideration for decorum in front of guests, I can't very well get angry.

témane 手真似 *hand gesture*
¶Kachō wa temane de watashi o yobima-shita.

課長は手まねで私を呼びました。
The section chief beckoned me with a gesture.

• temane de hanasu 手まねで話す *to talk by gestures*

temotó 手元 *the area near at hand, the area within reach*

• temoto ni 手もとに *at hand, within reach*

¶Itsu-mo nōto o temoto ni oite imasu.
いつもノートを手もとに置いています。
I always keep a notebook at hand.

tén 天 ① *the sky, the heavens* [→**sora** 空]

¶Maketa senshu wa ten o aogi, tameiki o tsuita.
負けた選手は天を仰ぎ、ため息をついた。
The defeated athlete looked up at the sky and sighed.

② *heaven, God, the gods; fate, destiny*

• ten to chi 天と地 *heaven and earth*

• ten ni makaseru 天に任せる *to leave up to God; to leave up to fate*

ten 点 ① *point, dot*

• ten o utsu 点を打つ *to make a dot, to write a point*

¶Sensei wa chizu ni ten o uchimashita.
先生は地図に点を打ちました。
The teacher made a dot on the map.

② *spot, speck, blot*

¶Uchi no neko no Tama ni wa shiro-ji ni kuroi ten ga madara ni tsuite imasu.
うちの猫のタマには白地に黒い点がまだらについています。
Our cat, Tama, is white with black spots.

③ *(scored)point; mark, <US>grade* «expressed as a number»

¶Hosokawa-kun wa Eigo de ii ten o totta yo.
細川君は英語でいい点を取ったよ。
Hosokawa got a good grade in English!

• -ten 一点《counter for points; see Appendix 2》

¶Kono kurasu no heikin wa hachijut-ten desu.
このクラスの平均は80点です。

This class's average is 80 points.

④ *point, respect; viewpoint*

¶Sono ten de wa shachō mo onaji iken desu.
その点では社長も同じ意見です。
On that point the company president also has the same opinion.

• man-ten 満点 *perfect score,* <UK>*full marks*

• shōsū-ten 小数点 *decimal point*

-ten 一点《counter for items; see Appendix 2》

ténā テナー [☞**tenōru** テノール]

• tenā-sakkusu テナーサックス *tenor saxophone*

tenbō 展望 *sweeping view, vista* [→**nagame** 眺め]

• tenbō suru 展望する *to get a sweeping view of*

• tenbō-dai 展望台 *observation platform, observation deck*

téngoku 天国 *heaven, paradise* [⇔**jigoku** 地獄]

tengu 天狗 *long-nosed goblin* 《A familiar character in folk tales, a **tengu** is human in form with a red face and wings and is said to live deep in mountains.》

tenímotsu 手荷物 *hand-baggage, luggage*

¶Mazu tenimotsu o azuketai no desu.
まず手荷物を預けたいのです。
First I want to check my luggage.

• tenimotsu-ichiji-azukari-sho 手荷物一時預かり所 *baggage room,* <US>*checkroom,* <UK>*cloakroom*

ten'in 店員 <US>*salesclerk,* <UK>*shop assistant*

¶Ane wa depāto no ten'in o shite imasu.
姉はデパートの店員をしています。
My older sister is working as a salesclerk in a department store.

ténisu テニス *tennis*

• tenisu o suru テニスをする *to play tennis*

¶Nichiyōbi wa tomodachi to tenisu o shimasu.
日曜日は友達とテニスをします。

On Sundays I play tennis with a friend.
- tenisu-bōru テニスボール *tennis ball*
- tenisu-kōto テニスコート *tennis court*
- tenisu-raketto テニスラケット *tennis racket*
- tenisu-shūzu テニスシューズ *tennis shoes*
- nanshiki-tenisu 軟式テニス *rubber-ball tennis*

tenji 点字 *braille*

tenji 展示 *exhibiting, display* [→**chinretsu** 陳列]
- tenji suru 展示する *to put on display, to exhibit*
¶Atarashii kuruma ga takusan tenji sarete iru yo.
新しい車がたくさん展示されているよ。
A lot of new cars are being exhibited!
- tenji-kai 展示会 *show, exhibition* [→**tenrankai** 展覧会]

tenjō 天井 *ceiling*
¶Tenjō ni utsukushī shanderia ga tsuite imasu.
天井に美しいシャンデリアがついています。
A beautiful chandelier is attached to the ceiling.
¶Kono heya wa tenjō ga hikui desu ne.
この部屋は天井が低いですね。
This room's ceiling is low, isn't it.

tenka 点火 *ignition, lighting*
- tenka suru 点火する *to provide ignition, to set fire*
- A ni tenka suru Aに点火する *to ignite A, to light A*

ténka 天下 ① *the whole world, everything under heaven*
② *the whole country, the realm*
- tenka o toru 天下を取る *to take power, to bring the whole country under one's rule*
③ *having one's own way, being in one's element*

tenkai 展開 *development; expansion, spread*
- tenkai suru 展開する《transitive or intransitive》*to develop; to expand, to spread*

tenkei 典型 *typical example, perfect example*
- tenkei-teki na 典型的な *typical*
¶Kore wa tenkei-teki na Nihon-ryōri desu.
これは典型的な日本料理です。
This is typical Japanese cuisine.

tenken 点検 *inspection, examination, check*
- tenken suru 点検する *to inspect, to examine, to check*
¶Uchi o deru mae ni kaimono no risuto o tenken shita.
うちを出る前に買物のリストを点検した。
I checked my shopping list before leaving home.

ténki 天気 ① *the weather*
¶Kyō no tenki wa dō desu ka.
きょうの天気はどうですか。
How is today's weather?
¶Tenki wa yoku nari-sō desu.
天気はよくなりそうです。
It looks as if the weather will improve.
¶Yama no tenki wa kawari-yasui desu.
山の天気は変わりやすいです。
Mountain weather is easily changeable.
② *fair weather*
- tenki ni naru 天気になる *to become fair, to clear up*
- tenki-yohō 天気予報 *weather forecast*
¶Tenki-yohō de wa ashita wa yuki da sō desu.
天気予報ではあしたは雪だそうです。
According to the weather forecast, it will snow tomorrow.
¶Tenki-yohō ga atarimashita.
天気予報が当たりました。
The weather forecast proved correct.
- tenki-zu 天気図 *weather map, weather chart*

tenkin 転勤 *changing jobs, taking a different job*
- tenkin suru 転勤する *to change jobs, to be transferred* (*to a different job*)
¶Chichi wa Takasaki-shiten ni tenkin shimashita.
父は高崎支店に転勤しました。

My father was transferred to the Takasaki branch.

tenkō 天候 (*short-term*)*weather pattern*

tenkō 転校 *changing schools, moving to a different school*
- tenkō suru 転校する *to change schools, to transfer* (*to a different school*)
¶Kyonen kono gakkō ni tenkō shimashita.
去年この学校に転校しました。
I transferred to this school last year.
- tenkō-sei 転校生 *transfer student*

tenmetsu 点滅《*involving a light*》 *going on and off, flashing; turning on and off*
- tenmetsu suru 点滅する *to go on and off; to turn on and off*

tenmon 天文 *astronomical phenomena*
- tenmon-dai 天文台 *astronomical observatory*
- tenmon-gaku 天文学 *astronomy*
- tenmon-gaku-sha 天文学者 *astronomer*

tennen 天然 〜**no** 〜の *natural*
- tennen-gasu 天然ガス *natural gas*
- tennen-kinen-butsu 天然記念物 *natural monument*
- tennen-shigen 天然資源 *natural resources*

Tennó 天皇 *the Emperor* (*of Japan*)
- Tennō-hai 天皇杯 *the Emperor's Trophy*《Presented to the winner of each Grand Sumo tournament.》
- Tennō-heika 天皇陛下 *His Majesty the Emperor*
- Tennō-tanjō-bi 天皇誕生日 *the Emperor's Birthday*《a Japanese national holiday (on December 23 in the Heisei Era)》
- Shōwa-tennō 昭和天皇 *the Showa Emperor*

Tennōsei 天王星 (*the planet*)*Uranus*
te-no-hira 手のひら *palm of the hand*
te-no-kō 手の甲 *back of the hand*
tenóru テノール ① *tenor* (*voice*)
② *tenor* (*singer*)
③ *tenor* (*part*)
- tenōru-kashu テノール歌手 [☞**tenōru**

テノール② (*above*)]
ténpi 天火 *oven* [→**ōbun** オーブン]
ténpo テンポ *tempo*
tenpuku 転覆 *overturning, capsizing*
- tenpuku suru 転覆する *to overturn, to capsize*《intransitive》
¶Kaze de yotto ga tenpuku shimashita.
風でヨットが転覆しました。
The sailboat capsized in the wind.

tenpura てんぷら *tempura*《a dish consisting of relatively small pieces of food (typically seafood and vegetables)dipped in a flour–and–egg batter and deep fried in vegetable oil》

tenránkai 展覧会 *exhibition, show*
¶Kyō Mone no e no tenrankai o mi ni ikimasu.
きょうモネの絵の展覧会を見に行きます。
Today I'm going to go to see an exhibition of Monet's pictures.

tensai 天才 ① *genius, great talent* ((attribute))
② *genius* ((person))
¶Mōtsaruto wa ongaku no tensai deshita.
モーツァルトは音楽の天才でした。
Mozart was a musical genius.
- tensai-teki na 天才的な *highly gifted*
¶Okada-san wa tensai-teki na pianisuto desu.
岡田さんは天才的なピアニストです。
Ms. Okada is a highly gifted pianist.

tensai 天災 *natural calamity, natural disaster*

tensaku 添削 *correction*《of a text》
- tensaku suru 添削する *to correct*
tensen 点線 *dotted line*
ténshi 天使 *angel* [⇔**akuma** 悪魔]
tentai 天体 *heavenly body*
- tentai-bōenkyō 天体望遠鏡 *astronomical telescope*
- tentai-kansoku 天体観測 *astronomical observation*

tenteki 点滴 *intravenous drip injection*
ténto テント *tent*
- tento o haru テントを張る *to put up a tent, to pitch a tent*
- tento o tatamu テントを畳む *to fold up*

a tent, to strike a tent

tentōmushi てんとう虫 <US>*ladybug*,
<UK>*ladybird*

tenugui 手拭い *hand towel*
- tenugui-kake 手拭い掛け *hand-towel hanger*

teókure 手遅れ 〜**no** 〜の *too late (to do any good)*
¶Ima kara hajimete mo teokure da yo.
今から始めても手遅れだよ。
Even if you start now it's too late!

teppan 鉄板 *iron sheet*
- teppan-yaki 鉄板焼き *cooking on an iron-sheet grill*

teppén 天辺 *top, highest point*

teppō 鉄砲 *gun*

tēpu テープ ① *magnetic tape, recording tape*
¶Kashu wa sono uta o tēpu ni rokuon shimashita.
歌手はその歌をテープに録音しました。
The singer recorded that song on tape.
- tēpu ni toru テープにとる *to get on tape*
② *finish-line tape*
- tēpu o kiru テープを切る *to break the tape*
③ *adhesive tape*
④ *paper streamer*
- tēpu-rekōdā テープレコーダー *tape recorder*

terá 寺 *(Buddhist)temple*

terásu 照らす *to illuminate, to shine on*
¶Shanderia ga hōru o terashite imasu.
シャンデリアがホールを照らしています。
Chandeliers are illuminating the hall.
¶Tsuki ga nohara o terashite imasu.
月が野原を照らしています。
The moon is shining on the field.

térasu テラス *terrace* 《adjoining a building》

térebi テレビ ① *television (broadcasting)*
¶Gakusei-tachi wa itsu-mo yūshoku-go ni terebi o miru.
学生たちはいつも夕食後にテレビを見る。
The students always watch television after supper.

② *television (set)*
¶Chichi wa terebi de yakyū o mite imasu.
父はテレビで野球を見ています。
My father is watching baseball on television.
¶Tarō-chan, terebi no oto o chīsaku shite ne.
太郎ちゃん、テレビの音を小さくしてね。
Taro, turn down the volume on the TV.
- terebi o tsukeru 〔kesu〕 テレビをつける 〔消す〕 *to turn on* 〔*off*〕 *the television*
- terebi-bangumi テレビ番組 *television program*
- terebi-denwa テレビ電話 *videophone*
- terebi-gēmu テレビゲーム *video game*
- terebi-kyoku テレビ局 *television station*
- terebi-kamera テレビカメラ *television camera*
- karā-terebi カラーテレビ *color TV*

terehonkádo テレホンカード *telephone card* 《a debit card for use in public telephones in Japan》

terekkusu テレックス *telex*
¶Ani wa jimu-sho ni hōkoku o terekkusu de okutta.
兄は事務所に報告をテレックスで送った。
My older brother sent his report to the office by telex.

terépashī テレパシー *telepathy*

teréru 照れる *to come to feel shy, to get embarrassed*
¶Sensei no mae de piano o hiite, teremashita.
先生の前でピアノを弾いて、照れました。
I played the piano in front of the teacher and got embarrassed.

teréya 照れ屋 *shy person*

téro テロ *terrorism*

terorísuto テロリスト *terrorist*

téru 照る{5} *to shine* 《The subject must be the sun or the moon.》
¶Kon'ya wa mangetsu ga akaruku tette imasu.
今夜は満月が明るく照っています。
The full moon is shining brightly tonight.

teságuri 手探り *groping*
- tesaguri de susumu 手探りで進む *to go*

forward gropingly, to feel one's way along

teshitá 手下 *follower, underling, subordinate*

tesó 手相 *the pattern of lines on the palm of the hand*
- tesó o miru 手相を見る *to read a person's palm*

tesū 手数 *time and effort, trouble, bother* [→**tema** 手間]
¶O-tesū desu ga, kono tegami o soku-tatsu de dashite kudasaimasen ka.
お手数ですが、この手紙を速達で出してくださいませんか。
I'm sorry to trouble you, but will you mail this letter by special delivery for me? 《Literally: *It's a bother, but will you mail this letter by special delivery for me?*》
- A ni tesū o kakeru Aに手数をかける *to trouble A, to impose on A*
- tesū ga kakaru 手数がかかる *to be a lot of trouble*
- tesū-ryō 手数料 *handling charge, commission fee*

tesurí 手すり *handrail*

tésuto テスト [[→**shiken** 試験]] ① *test* 《to evaluate knowledge or ability》
¶Kinō Eigo no tesuto ga atta yo.
きのう英語のテストがあったよ。
There was an English test yesterday!
② *test, trial* 《to evaluate quality》
¶Atarashii hikōki no tesuto wa ik-kagetsu tsuzukimasu.
新しい飛行機のテストは1か月続きます。
The tests of the new plane will continue for a month.
- tesuto suru テストする *to test*
- gakuryoku-tesuto 学力テスト *scholastic achievement test*

tetsu 鉄 *iron* 《(metal)》
¶Tetsu wa atsui uchi ni ute.
鉄は熱いうちに打て。《proverb》
Strike while the iron is hot.
- tetsu-kuzu 鉄屑 *scrap iron*

tetsubō 鉄棒 ① *iron bar*
② *horizontal bar* 《in gymnastics》

tetsudái 手伝い ① *help, assistance*

《with a task》
② *helper, assistant*

tetsudáu 手伝う ① *to help, to assist*
¶Kyō wa uchi de haha o tetsudaimasu.
きょうはうちで母を手伝います。
I'll help my mother at home today.
② *to help with, to assist with*
¶Ani wa shukudai o tetsudatte kurema-shita.
兄は宿題を手伝ってくれました。
My older brother helped me with my homework.

tetsudō 鉄道 *railroad, railway*
- tetsudō-jiko 鉄道事故 *railroad accident*

tetsúgaku 哲学 *(the study of)philosophy*
- tetsugaku-sha 哲学者 *philosopher*

tetsuya 徹夜 *staying up all night*
- tetsuya suru 徹夜する *to stay up all night*
¶Ashita ga shimekiri dakara konban wa tetsuya shimasu.
あしたが締め切りだから今晩は徹夜します。
Tomorrow is the deadline, so I'll stay up all night tonight.
- tetsuya no 徹夜の *all-night*
- tetsuya de 徹夜で *all night long*
¶Yūbe wa tetsuya de benkyō shimashita.
ゆうべは徹夜で勉強しました。
Last night I studied all night long.

tetsúzuki 手続き *procedure, course of action*

tettei 徹底 ～**suru** ～する *to be thorough, to be exhaustive*
- tettei-teki na 徹底的な *thorough, exhaustive*

tettoribayái 手っ取り早い *quick and not involving much exertion*

tewatásu 手渡す *to hand, to pass* [→**watasu** 渡す①]

tezáwari 手触り *feel, perception triggered by touching*
¶Kore wa kegawa no yō na tezawari desu.
これは毛皮のような手触りです。
This feels like fur. 《Literally: *As for this, it's a feel like fur*》

tezúkuri 手作り 〜**no** 〜の *handmade; homemade*

¶Kono tezukuri no ningyō wa Nanbei de kaimashita.

この手作りの人形は南米で買いました。

I bought this handmade doll in South America.

¶Tezukuri no aisukurīmu wa oishii ne.

手作りのアイスクリームはおいしいね。

Homemade ice cream is delicious, isn't it.

tīn'éjā ティーンエージャー *teenager*

tīshatsu ティーシャツ、Tシャツ *T-shirt*

tísshu ティッシュ [☞**tisshupēpā** ティッシュペーパー]

tisshupēpā ティッシュペーパー *tissue, kleenex*

to 戸 *door*

¶Dare-ka ga to o tataite iru yo.

だれかが戸をたたいているよ。

Someone is knocking on the door!

• to o akeru [shimeru] 戸を開け [閉める] *to open [close] a door*

• to-guchi 戸口 *doorway*

Tó 都 [☞**Tōkyō-to** 東京都 (below)]

• To-chiji 都知事 *Governor of Tokyo*

• To-min 都民 *citizen of Tokyo*

• Tōkyō-to 東京都 *Tokyo (Metropolitan)Prefecture*

to と 《noun-following particle》① *and* 《Connects nouns but not clauses; optional after the last item mentioned.》

¶Watashi wa Eigo to rekishi to ongaku ga suki desu.

私は英語と歴史と音楽が好きです。

I like English and history and music.

¶Miki-chan to Yūko-chan wa naka-yoshi desu.

美紀ちゃんと祐子ちゃんは仲よしです。

Miki and Yuko are good friends.

② 《indicating a partner, opponent, etc.》 *with; against*

¶Toshiko-san wa sensei to tenisu o shite imasu.

敏子さんは先生とテニスをしています。

Toshiko is playing tennis with the teacher.

¶Itsu-mo otōto to kenka shimasu.

いつも弟とけんかします。

I always quarrel with my younger brother.

③ *with* 《when a comparison is involved》; *from* 《when a difference is involved》

¶Kotoshi no akaji o kyonen no to kurabemashō.

今年の赤字を去年のと比べましょう。

Let's compare this year's deficit with last year's.

¶Kore wa furui no to chigaimasu.

これは古いのと違います。

This differs from the old one.

to と《This clause-conjoining particle always follows a predicate in the nonpast tense.》 *when, whenever; if*

¶Ame ga furu to, uchi no neko wa soto ni demasen.

雨が降ると、うちの猫は外に出ません。

My cat doesn't go outside, when it rains.

¶Isoganai to, ressha ni maniawanai yo.

急がないと、列車に間に合わないよ。

If you don't hurry, you'll miss the train!

to と *that* 《This quotative particle follows what is said or thought and precedes a verb of saying or thinking.》

¶Nishiyama-san wa kuru to iimashita.

西山さんは来ると言いました。

Ms. Nishiyama said that she would come.

¶Jaiantsu wa maketa to omoimasu.

ジャイアンツは負けたと思います。

I think that the Giants lost.

tō 党 *(political)party* [→**seitō** 政党]; *clique*

• tō-in 党員 *party member*

• ya-tō 野党 *opposition party*

• yo-tō 与党 *government party, party in power*

tō 塔 *tower; pagoda* 《at a Buddhist temple》

• gojū no tō 五重の塔 *five-storied pagoda*

• kansei-tō 管制塔 *control tower*

• Rondon-tō ロンドン塔 *The Tower of*

London

• terebi-tō テレビ塔 *television tower*

-tō 一等《counter for classes, rankings, etc.; see Appendix 2》

¶Tsuchida-san wa kyōsō de it-tō ni narimashita.

土田君は競走で 1 等になりました。

Tsuchida was first in the race.

• it-tō-shō 1 等賞 *first prize*

tō 等 *and so on, etcetera* 《noun-following particle》 [→**nado** など①]

-tō 一頭《counter for large animals; see Appendix 2》

tō 十 *ten* 《See Appendix 2.》

tōan 答案 *examination paper*

tōban 当番 ① *one's turn on duty*
② *person whose turn on duty it is*

¶Kyō wa dare ga tōban desu ka.

きょうはだれが当番ですか。

Who is on duty today?

• sōji-tōban 掃除当番 *cleaning duty*

tobasu 飛ばす ① *to let fly, to make fly, to fly; to throw* [→**nageru** 投げる]; *to send flying*

¶Kodomo-tachi ga kami-hikōki o tobashite imasu.

子供たちが紙飛行機を飛ばしています。

Children are flying paper planes.

¶Tsuyoi kaze ga kanban o tobashimashita.

強い風が看板を飛ばしました。

The strong wind sent the signboard flying.

② *to make go very fast*

• kuruma o tobasu 車を飛ばす *to drive a car very fast*

③ *to skip, to pass over*

¶Dekinai mondai o tobasu koto ni shimashita.

できない問題を飛ばすことにしました。

I decided to skip the problems I couldn't do.

tóbi 鳶 *kite* ((bird))

tobiagáru 跳び上がる *to jump up*

¶Akira wa tobiagatte, bōru o ukemashita.

晃は跳び上がって、ボールを受けました。

Akira jumped up and caught the ball.

tobibako 跳び箱 *vaulting horse*

• tobibako o tobu とび箱を跳ぶ *to vault over a vaulting horse*

tobidásu 飛び出す *to rush out, to run out, to jump out*

¶Beru ga naru to, watashi wa kyōshitsu kara tobidashita.

ベルが鳴ると、私は教室から飛び出した。

When the bell rang, I ran out of the classroom.

tobikómu 飛び込む *to jump 〈into〉, to dive 〈into〉*

¶Koizumi-san wa pūru ni tobikomimashita.

小泉さんはプールに飛び込みました。

Ms. Koizumi dived into the pool.

¶Hannin wa hashi kara kawa ni tobikomimashita.

犯人は橋から川に飛び込みました。

The criminal jumped from the bridge into the river.

tobinóru 飛び乗る *to jump, to jump* 《into／onto a vehicle》

¶Hirokawa-kun wa jitensha ni tobinotte nigeta yo.

広川君は自転車に飛び乗って逃げたよ。

Hirokawa jumped on his bicycle and escaped!

tobiokíru 飛び起きる *to jump out of bed*

tobioríru 飛び降りる *to jump down*

¶Dorobō wa mado kara tobiorimashita.

泥棒は窓から飛び降りました。

The burglar jumped down from the window.

tobira 扉 *door* [→**to** 戸]

tobitsúku 飛び付く *to jump 〈at／on〉* 《in an attempt to catch》

¶Neko wa suzume ni tobitsukimashita.

猫はすずめに飛びつきました。

The cat jumped on the sparrow.

tobiuo 飛び魚 *flying fish*

tobokéru とぼける 【COL.】 *to pretend ignorance*

toboshíi 乏しい *scanty, meager, scarce* [⇔**yutaka na** 豊かな①]

¶Kono kuni wa tennen-shigen ga toboshii.

この国は天然資源が乏しい。

This country's natural resources are meager.

• A ga B ni toboshii AがBに乏しい *A is lacking in B, A has meager B*

¶Taguchi-san wa isha to shite no keiken ni toboshii.

田口さんは医者としての経験に乏しい。

Mr. Taguchi is lacking in experience as a doctor.

tōbu 東部 *eastern part* [⇔**seibu** 西部]

tobu 飛ぶ *to fly* «intransitive»

¶Suenaga-san wa ashita Hawai ni tobi masu.

末永さんはあしたハワイに飛びます。

Mr. Suenaga will fly to Hawaii tomorrow.

¶Kono tori wa Shiberia kara tonde kimashita.

この鳥はシベリアから飛んできました。

This bird flew from Siberia.

tobu 跳ぶ *to jump, to leap*

¶Hiroshi wa hashirihabatobi de rokumētoru-ijō tonda.

浩は走り幅跳びで6メートル以上跳んだ。

Hiroshi jumped over six meters in the long jump.

tōbun 当分 *for a while; for the present, for the time being*

tōbun 糖分 *sugar content*

tōchaku 到着 *arrival* [⇔**shuppatsu** 出発]

• tōchaku suru 到着する *to arrive*

¶Densha wa jikan-dōri ni Hakata-eki ni tōchaku shita.

電車は時間どおりに博多駅に到着した。

The train arrived at Hakata Station on time.

¶Ichi-jikan de Kōbe ni tōchaku shimashita.

1時間で神戸に到着しました。

We arrived in Kobe in an hour.

• tōchaku-hōmu 到着ホーム *arrival platform*

• tōchaku-jikoku 到着時刻 *arrival time*

tochi 土地 ① *land, ground, lot; soil* [→ **tsuchi** 土]

¶Oji wa Kōbe ni tochi o kau tsumori desu.

伯父は神戸に土地を買うつもりです。

My uncle intends to buy land in Kobe.

② *region, locality* [→**chihō** 地方①]

• tochi-tsuki no 土地付きの *including land, with a lot*

tochū 途中 *the way between departure point and destination; the time between start and finish*

¶Uchi e kaeru tochū desu.

うちへ帰る途中です。

I'm on my way home.

• tochū de 途中で *on the way; in the middle*

¶Gakkō e iku tochū de tomodachi ni deaimashita.

学校へ行く途中で友達に出会いました。

On the way to school, I ran into a friend.

¶Benkyō o tochū de yamete wa ikenai yo.

勉強を途中でやめてはいけないよ。

You mustn't give up studying in the middle!

tōdai 灯台 *lighthouse*

todana 戸棚 *cupboard*

todoké 届け *notification, notice, report*

• kesseki-todoke 欠席届け *notification of absence*

todokéru 届ける ① *to send, to have delivered* [→**okuru** 送る①]

¶Kono shima ni wa shokuryō o fune de todokemasu.

この島には食料を船で届けます。

They send food to this island by boat.

② *to deliver, to take*

¶Tarō-chan wa sono saifu o kōban ni todoketa yo.

太郎ちゃんはその財布を交番に届けたよ。

Taro took that wallet to the police box!

③ *to report, to give notice of*

¶Mō yūbin kyoku ni jūsho no henkō o todokemashita ka.

もう郵便局に住所の変更を届けましたか。

Have you already notified the post office of your change of address?

todóku 届く ① *to be delivered, to arrive*
¶Watashi no tegami wa todokimashita ka.
私の手紙は届きましたか。
Did my letter arrive?
　② *to reach, to extend*
• te ga todoku 手が届く *one's hand reaches, one is able to reach*
¶Kodomo wa kono beru ni te ga todokanai deshō.
子供はこのベルに手が届かないでしょう。
A child probably cannot reach this bell.

tōfú 豆腐 *tofu, bean curd*
¶Tōfu o it-chō katte kimashita.
豆腐を1丁買ってきました。
I went and bought one block of tofu.

tōgárashi 唐辛 *red pepper, cayenne pepper*

togátta 尖った *pointed, sharp*

tōgé 峠 *mountain pass*

togé 棘 *thorn; splinter*
• A ni toge ga sasaru Aにとげが刺さる *a thorn / splinter gets stuck in A*
¶Yubi ni toge ga sasatta yo.
指にとげが刺さったよ。
I got a splinter in my finger! 《*Literally: A splinter got stuck in my finger.*》
• toge o nuku とげを抜く *to remove a thorn / splinter*

togéru 遂げる *to achieve, to attain, to accomplish*
• nozomi o togeru 望みを遂げる *to attain one's desire*

tōgi 討議 *discussion*
• tōgi suru 討議する *to discuss; to have a discussion*
¶Sensei-gata wa kōsoku ni tsuite nagai aida tōgi shita.
先生方は校則について長い間討議した。
The teachers discussed the school rules for a long time.
¶Kono mondai o kōchō-sensei to tōgi shimashita.
この問題を校長先生と討議しました。
We discussed this problem with the principal.

tōgō 統合 *synthesis, unification, unity*

[→**tōitsu** 統一]
• tōgō suru 統合する *to synthesize, to unify, to combine*

tógu 研ぐ *to whet, to hone, to sharpen by grinding*

tōgyū 闘牛 *bullfight; bullfighting*
• tōgyū-shi 闘牛士 *bullfighter*

tóho 徒歩 ～**de** ～で *on foot* [→**aruite** 歩いて (s.v. **aruku** 歩く)]
¶Soko made toho de jūgo-fun kakarimasu.
そこまで徒歩で15分かかります。
It takes fifteen minutes to there on foot.
• toho-ryokō 徒歩旅行 *walking tour, hike*

tohō 途方 ① ～**ni kureru** ～に暮れる *to be left at a loss, to become perplexed*
¶Morinaga-san wa shitsugyō shite tohō ni kurete imasu.
森永さんは失業して途方に暮れています。
Mr. Morinaga became unemployed and is at a loss.
　② ～**mo nai** ～もない *absurd, ludicrous, outrageous* [→**tonde-mo-nai** とんでもない]
¶Yoneda-san wa tohō mo nai nedan de ie o katta.
米田さんは途方もない値段で家を買った。
Mr. Yoneda bought a house at an outrageous price.

tōhoku 東北 *the northeast* [→**hokutō** 北東]
• Tōhoku-chihō 東北地方 *the Tohoku region* (*of Japan*) 《Aomori, Akita, Iwate, Yamagata, Miyagi, and Fukushima Prefectures》

tōhyō 投票 *voting, casting a vote*
¶Tōhyō de iin-chō o erabimashō.
投票で委員長を選びましょう。
Let's choose the committee chairperson by voting.
¶Sono keikaku ni sansei no tōhyō o shimasu.
その計画に賛成の投票をします。
I'm going to vote for that plan. 《*Literally: I will cast a vote of agreement for that plan.*》

• tōhyō suru 投票する *to vote*
¶Watashi mo Itō-san ni tōhyō shima-shita.
私も伊藤さんに投票しました。
I also voted for Mr. Ito.
• tōhyō-bi 投票日 *election day*
• tōhyō-jo 投票所 *polling place*
• tōhyō-yōshi 投票用紙 *ballot*

toi 問い *question, inquiry* [→**shitsumon** 質問]

tōi 遠い *far, distant* [⇔**chikai** 近い]
¶Shōgakkō wa koko kara tōi desu ka.
小学校はここから遠いですか。
Is the elementary school far from here?
¶Yōko-chan wa watashi no tōi shinseki desu.
洋子ちゃんは私の遠い親せきです。
Yoko is my distant relative.
• mimi ga tōi 耳が遠い *to be hard of hearing*
• tōi mukashi 遠い昔 *the distant past*

toiawaséru 問い合わせる *to inquire about, to ask about*
• A ni B o toiawaseru AにBを問い合わせる *to ask A about B*
¶Shuppatsu-jikoku o Nozaki-san ni toiawaseyō.
出発時刻を野崎さんに問い合わせよう。
Let's ask Ms. Nozaki about the departure time.

tóire トイレ *bathroom, restroom, lavatory* 《Toilets and bathtubs are traditionally in separate rooms in Japan. This word refers to a room containing a toilet.》 [→ **tearai** 手洗い]
¶Toire o karite ii desu ka.
トイレを借りていいですか。
May I use your bathroom?

tóiretto トイレット [☞**toire** トイレ]
• toiretto-pēpā トイレットペーパー *toilet paper*

tōitsu 統一 *unity; uniformity; unification*
¶Kono chīmu wa tōitsu o kaite imasu.
このチームは統一を欠いています。
This team lacks unity.
• tōitsu suru 統一する *to unify*

to iu という [☞**iu** 言う]

tōji 冬至 *winter solstice* [⇔**geshi** 夏至]

tōji 当時 *the time in question, that time, then, those days*
¶Tōji no Sōridaijin wa Fukuda-san de-shita.
当時の総理大臣は福田さんでした。
The Prime Minister at that time was Mr. Fukuda.

tojikoméru 閉じ込める *to shut up, to confine* 《The direct object must be a person or animal.》
¶Terorisuto wa hitojichi o koya ni tojiko-meta.
テロリストは人質を小屋に閉じ込めた。
The terrorist shut the hostage up in a hut.

tojikomóru 閉じ籠る *to shut oneself up, to confine oneself*
¶Musuko wa heya ni tojikomorimashita.
息子は部屋に閉じこもりました。
My son shut himself up in his room.
¶Kaze de mikka-kan ie ni tojikomotte imashita.
かぜで3日間家に閉じこもっていました。
I stayed in the house for three days because of a cold.

tojímari 戸締まり *closing and locking the doors*
• tojimari suru 戸締まりする *to close and lock the doors, to lock up*
¶Dekakeru mae ni tojimari shinasai.
出かける前に戸締まりしなさい。
Lock up before you go out.

tojíru 閉じる *to close, to shut* 《transitive or intransitive》 [⇔**hiraku** 開く①]
¶Sā, hon o tojimashō.
さあ、本を閉じましょう。
All right, let's close our books.
• me o tojiru 目を閉じる *to close one's eyes*
• mon ga tojiru 門が閉じる *a gate closes*

tojíru 綴じる *to bind together* 《The direct object must be sheets of paper, etc., or something containing such sheets.》
¶Sono shinbun o tojite oite kudasai.
その新聞をとじておいてください。

Please bind those newspapers together.

• hon o tojiru 本をとじる *to bind a book*

tōjitsu 当日 *the day in question, that day*

¶Tōjitsu wa subarashii tenki deshita.

当日はすばらしい天気でした。

It was wonderful weather that day.

tōjō 搭乗 *boarding, getting on／in* 《a vehicle, especially an airplane》

• tōjō suru 搭乗する *to get* 《on／in a vehicle》

• tōjō-ken 搭乗券 *boarding pass*

tōjō 登場 ① *appearance* 《as a character in a play, novel, etc.》

• tōjō suru 登場する *to appear, to make one's appearance*

¶Ano haiyū wa yoku terebi ni tōjō shimasu.

あの俳優はよくテレビに登場します。

That actor often appears on TV.

② *appearance* 《of a new public figure or product》

• tōjō suru 登場する *to appear*

• tōjō-jinbutsu 登場人物 *character*

tōka 十日 《see Appendix 2》 ① *ten days* ② *the tenth* 《day of a month》

tokage とかげ *lizard*

tokai 都会 *city* [→**toshi** 都市]

¶Musume wa tokai ni sunde imasu.

娘は都会に住んでいます。

My daughter lives in a city.

• tokai-ka 都会化 *urbanization*

• tokai-seikatsu 都会生活 *city life*

tokásu 溶かす ① *to melt* 《transitive》

¶Kōnetsu wa tetsu o tokashimasu.

高熱は鉄を溶かします。

High heat melts iron.

② *to dissolve* 《transitive》

¶Kusuri o mizu ni tokashite nomimashita.

薬を水に溶かして飲みました。

I dissolved the medicine in water and drank it.

tōkei 統計 *statistics*

• tōkei ni yoru to 統計によると *according to statistics*

tokei 時計 *clock; watch*

¶Tokei ga san-ji o uchimashita.

時計が３時を打ちました。

The clock struck three.

¶Sono tokei de wa ima nan-ji desu ka.

その時計では今何時ですか。

What time is it now by that clock?

¶Kono tokei wa atte imasu ka.

この時計は合っていますか。

Is this clock correct?

• tokei ga susumu 時計が進む *a clock／watch becomes fast, a watch／clock gains time*

¶Watashi no tokei wa ni-fun susunde imasu.

私の時計は２分進んでいます。

My watch is two minutes fast.

• tokei ga okureru 時計が遅れる *a clock／watch becomes slow, a watch／clock loses time*

¶Kono tokei wa ichi-nichi ni san-byō okuremasu.

この時計は１日に３秒遅れます。

This clock loses three seconds a day.

• tokei no chōshin〔tanshin〕 時計の長針〔短針〕 *minute hand*〔*hour hand*〕*of a clock*

• tokei-dai 時計台 *clock tower*

• tokei-ten 時計店 *watch store, clock store*

• dejitaru-dokei デジタル時計 *digital watch, digital clock*

• hato-dokei 鳩時計 *cuckoo clock*

• mezamashi-dokei 目覚まし時計 *alarm clock*

tokekomu 溶け込む *to blend* 〈into〉*, to mix* 〈with〉 《intransitive》

tokéru 溶ける ① *to melt* 《intransitive》

¶Yuki-daruma wa sukoshi-zutsu tokete imasu.

雪だるまは少しずつ溶けています。

The snowman is melting little by little.

② *to dissolve* 《intransitive》

¶Sono kusuri wa mizu ni tokeru deshō?

その薬は水に溶けるでしょう？

That medicine dissolves in water, right?

tōki 陶器 *china, earthenware, pottery* [→**setomono** 瀬戸物, **yakimono** 焼き物]

tokí 時 ① (amount of)time, time span
[→**jikan** 時間②]

¶Toki ga tatsu ni tsurete, sono kioku mo usureta.

時がたつにつれて、その記憶も薄れた。

As time passes, that memory also faded.

¶Yūbe wa tanoshii toki o sugoshima-shita.

ゆうべは楽しい時を過ごしました。

I had a pleasant time last night.

¶Toki wa kane nari.

時は金なり。《proverb》

Time is money.

② time, occasion; (time)when

¶Sono toki watashi wa benkyō-chū de-shita.

そのとき私は勉強中でした。

At that time I was studying.

¶Ken-san wa go-sai no toki ni Kōbe ni kimashita.

健さんは5歳のときに神戸に来ました。

Ken came to Kobe when he was five years old.

¶Kibun ga warui toki wa, byōin ni iki-nasai.

気分が悪いときは、病院に行きなさい。

When you feel sick, go to the hospital.

¶Ashita dekakeru toki ni denwa shite kudasai.

あした出かけるときに電話してください。

Please telephone me when you go out to-morrow.

•toki ni wa 時には *sometimes, occasion-ally* [→**tokidoki** 時々]

tóki 鴇 *Japanese crested ibis*

tóki 冬季 *wintertime, the winter season*
[⇔**kaki** 夏季]

•tōki-Orinpikku 冬季オリンピック *the Winter Olympics*

tokidoki 時々 *sometimes, now and then*

¶Tokidoki Kurosaki-san ni denwa shi-masu.

時々黒崎さんに電話します。

I sometimes telephone Ms. Kurosaki.

¶Umi wa tokidoki aremasu.

海は時々荒れます。

The sea sometimes gets rough.

¶Tokidoki sono hito ni aimasu.

時々その人に会います。

I sometimes see that person.

tokka 特価 *special price*

•tokka-hin 特価品 *bargain item*

tokkú-ni とっくに 【COL.】 *long ago, long since*

tokkuri 徳利 *ceramic bottle for heating and pouring sake*

tókkyo 特許 *patent*

tokkyū 特急 *a limited express, a spe-cial express*

tōkō 登校 *going to school, attending school*

•tōkō suru 登校する *to go to school, to attend school*

¶Mainichi jitensha de tōkō shimasu.

毎日自転車で登校します。

I go to school by bicycle every day.

•tōkō-kyohi 登校拒否 *refusal to attend school*

toko 床 *bed*

•toko ni tsuku 床につく *to go to bed; to become confined to bed*

¶Chichi wa byōki de is-shūkan toko ni tsuite imasu.

父は病気で1週間床についています。

My father has been confined to bed for a week because of illness.

tokonoma 床の間 *alcove* 《in a tradition-al Japanese-style room》

tokoro 所 ① *place, location* [→**basho** 場所]

¶Koko wa Sōseki ga umareta tokoro desu.

ここは漱石が生まれた所です。

This is the place where Soseki was born.

¶Andō-san no sunde iru tokoro ga wa-karimasu ka.

安藤さんの住んでいる所がわかりますか。

Do you know where Mr. Ando lives?

¶Yōko-san wa doa no tokoro ni imasu.

洋子さんはドアの所にいます。

Yoko is by the door. 《Literally: *Yoko is at the place of the door.*》

② point in time 《In this meaning **tokoro** follows a verb. When the action is referred to by verb is already completed, **tokoro** is typically translated as *having just*. When the action has not yet begun, **tokoro** is typically translated as *being about to*. When the action is in progress, **tokoro** is typically translated as *being in the middle of*.»

¶Megumi ni tegami o kakō to shite iru tokoro desu.

恵に手紙を書こうとしているところです。

I'm about to write a letter to Megumi.

¶Chichi wa sono shigoto o chōdo oeta tokoro da.

父はその仕事をちょうど終えたところだ。

My father has just finished that job.

¶Kyō no fukushū o shite iru tokoro desu.

きょうの復習をしているところです。

I'm in the middle of reviewing today's lesson.

tokoró-de ところで ① *well, now* «indicating a shift in what is being talked about» [→**sate** さて]

¶Tokoro-de, sorosoro dekakemashō ka.

ところで、そろそろ出かけましょうか。

Well, shall we start out soon?

② *by the way*

¶Tokoro-de, ashita no gogo wa isogashii desu ka.

ところで、あしたの午後は忙しいですか。

By the way, are you busy tomorrow afternoon?

tokorodókoro 所々 *here and there, various places* [→**achikochi** あちこち]

tokoya 床屋 ① *barber*
② *barbershop*

tōkú 遠く *an area far away, the distance* «The adverbial form of **tōi** 遠い differs in being unaccented.»

¶Fuji-san ga tōku ni miemasu.

富士山が遠くに見えます。

Mt. Fuji is visible in the distance.

toku 得 *profit, gain, benefit* [⇔**son** 損]

¶Kore o benkyō shite mo toku ni narimasen.

これを勉強しても得になりません。

Even if you study this, it won't be any

benefit.

• toku o suru 得をする *to profit, to benefit*

• toku-suru 得する [☞**toku o suru** 得をする (above)]

tóku 解く ① *to solve, to resolve, to clear up* [→**kaiketsu suru** 解決する]

• gokai o toku 誤解を解く *to clear up a misunderstanding*

② *to solve* «a puzzle, arithmetic problem, etc.»

¶Atsuko-chan wa kokuban no mondai o zenbu toita yo.

淳子ちゃんは黒板の問題を全部解いたよ。

Atsuko solved all the problems on the blackboard!

③ *to untie, to unfasten, to undo* [→**hodoku** 解く]

④ *to cancel, to remove*

• keikoku o toku 警告を解く *to cancel a warning*

• kinshi o toku 禁止を解く *to remove a prohibition*

tokubai 特売 *selling at a bargain; bargain sale*

• tokubai de kau 特売で買う *to buy on sale*

• tokubai-hin 特売品 *bargain, item on sale*

tokubetsu 特別 ～**no**／**na**～の／な *special, particular*

¶Tokubetsu no riyū wa arimasen deshita.

特別の理由はありませんでした。

There was no special reason.

• tokubetsu ni 特別に *especially, particularly*

¶Kyō wa tokubetsu ni atsuraeta fuku o kimasu.

今日は特別にあつらえた服を着ます。

Today I will wear specially-ordered clothes.

• tokubetsu-bangumi 特別番組 *special program*

• tokubetsu-gō 特別号 *special issue*

• tokubetsu-kyūkō 特別急行 *a special express*

• tokubetsu-seki 特別席 *special seat*

tokuchō 特長 *strong point, merit* [→ **chōsho** 長所]

tokuchō 特徴 *distinctive characteristic, special feature* [→**tokushoku** 特色]

¶Nibui dōsa wa panda no tokuchō no hitotsu desu.

鈍い動作はパンダの特徴の一つです。

Clumsy movement is one of the panda's distinctive characteristics.

tokudane 特種 *exclusive news story, scoop*

tókugi 特技 *one's special ability*

tokuháin 特派員 *correspondent «for a newspaper, etc.»*

tokúi 得意 ① ～**no**／**na** ～の／な *good at* «This noun modifier is used to describe both the people who are skillful and the things they are skillful at.» [→ **jōzu na** 上手な]

¶Ōishi-san wa Eigo ga tokui desu.

大石さんは英語が得意です。

Ms. Oishi is good at English.

② ～**no** ～の *proud, triumphant, elated*

¶Ano hito o homeru to, tokui ni naru yo.

あの人を褒めると、得意になるよ。

When you praise that person, she becomes elated!

③ *customer who buys regularly*

tokumei 匿名 ～**no** ～の *anonymous*

• tokumei no tegami 匿名の手紙 *anonymous letter*

tóku-ni 特に *especially, particularly*

¶Kyō wa toku ni atsui ne.

きょうは特に暑いね。

It's especially hot today, isn't it?

¶Ani wa ongaku, toku ni jazu ga dai-suki desu.

兄は音楽、特にジャズが大好きです。

My older brother loves music, particularly jazz.

tokushoku 特色 *distinctive characteristic, special feature* [→**tokuchō** 特徴]

tokushu 特殊 ～**na** ～な *special, particular* [→**tokubetsu no** 特別の]

tokushū 特集 ① *special edition focusing on a particular topic*

¶Hachi-gatsu-gō wa Orinpikku no tokushū desu.

8月号はオリンピックの特集です。

The August issue is a special edition on the Olympics.

② *compiling a special edition focusing on a particular topic*

• tokushū suru 特集する *to compile a special edition*

• tokushū-gō 特集号 *special issue*

• tokushū-kiji 特集記事 *feature article*

tokuten 得点 *scored point; score*

• tokuten suru 得点する *to score, to score a point*

• tokuten-keiji-ban 得点掲示板 *scoreboard*

tokuyū 特有 ～**no** ～の *unique, special* [→**dokutoku no** 独特の]

• -tokuyū no －特有の *unique to, peculiar to* «Added to noun bases.»

• Nihon-tokuyū no 日本特有の *unique to Japan*

tókyoku 当局 *the authorities*

tomaru 止る ① *to stop (moving), to halt* «intransitive»

¶Sono patokā wa ginkō no mae de kyū ni tomatta.

そのパトカーは銀行の前で急に止まった。

That patrol car stopped suddenly in front of the bank.

¶Kono tokei wa tomatte imasu ne.

この時計は止まっていますね。

This watch has stopped, hasn't it?

② *to stop, to cease* «intransitive»

¶Kanja no myaku ga tomarimashita.

患者の脈が止りました。

The patient's pulse stopped.

③ *to alight, to perch*

¶Densen ni tori ga tomatte imasu.

電線に鳥が止っています。

A bird is perched on the power line.

tomaru 泊まる *to lodge, to stay (over)*

¶Ikkō wa Pari no hoteru ni tomatte imasu.

一行はパリのホテルに泊まっています。

The party is staying at a hotel in Paris.

¶Ashita wa shinseki no ie ni tomarimasu.
あしたは親せきの家に泊まります。
Tomorrow I'm going to stay at a relative's house.

tómato トマト *tomato*

tōmáwari 遠回り *making a detour, taking the long way*

• tōmawari suru 遠回りする *to make a detour, to take the long way*

¶Sono michi wa tsūkō-dome datta node, tōmawari shinakereba narimasen deshita.
その道は通行止めだったので、遠回りしなければなりませんでした。
The road was blocked, so we had to make a detour.

tōmáwashi 遠回し ～**na**／**no** ～な／の *indirect, roundabout*

• tōmawashi ni iu 遠回しに言う *to say in a roundabout way*

tōmei 透明 ～**na** ～な *transparent, clear*

tomeru 止める ① *to stop (the motion of), to halt* 《transitive》*; to stop the flow of, to turn off*

¶Chichi wa gakkō no mae ni kuruma o tomemashita.
父は学校の前に車を止めました。
My father stopped the car in front of the school.

¶Gasu o tomeru no o wasurenai de kudasai.
ガスを止めるのを忘れないでください。
Please don't forget to turn off the gas.

② *to stop, to bring to an end* 《intransitive》

• kenka o tomeru けんかを止める *to break up a fight*

tomeru 泊める *to provide lodging for, to let stay over, to put up*

¶Kon'ya dake tomete kudasai ne.
今夜だけ泊めてくださいね。
Please let me stay over just tonight, OK?

tomeru 留める *to affix, to fasten; to fasten together; to fix in place*

¶Musuko wa kashu no shashin o kabe ni tomemashita.
息子は歌手の写真を壁に留めました。

My son stuck a singer's photo to the wall.

tómi 富 *riches*

tōmin 冬眠 *hibernation*

• tōmin ni hairu 冬眠に入る *to go into hibernation*

• tōmin kara sameru 冬眠から覚める *to come out of hibernation*

tómo 友 *friend* [→**tomodachi** 友達]

-tomo ―とも *both, all* 《Added to bases denoting more than one entity.》

¶Watashi-tachi wa futari-tomo Eigo ga hanasemasu.
私たちは二人とも英語が話せます。
Both of us can speak English.

¶Otōto wa dōnatsu o goko-tomo tabeta yo.
弟はドーナツを5個とも食べたよ。
My younger brother ate all five doughnuts!

tomodachi 友達 *friend* 《Unless otherwise specified, this word is ordinarily understood to mean the speaker's friend, i.e., my friend.》

¶Kochira wa tomodachi no Yōko-san desu.
こちらは友達の洋子さんです。
This is my friend Yoko.

¶Oka-san wa haha no mukashi kara no tomodachi desu.
岡さんは母の昔からの友達です。
Ms. Oka is a friend of my mother's from long ago.

¶Watashi-tachi wa Pōru-san to tomodachi ni narimashita.
私たちはポールさんと友達になりました。
We became friends with Paul.

• shitashii tomodachi 親しい友達 *close friend*

tómokaku ともかく *anyway, anyhow, in any case* [→**tonikaku** とにかく]

tomonáu 伴う ① *to involve, to have as a concomitant*

¶Sono jikken wa kiken o tomonaimasu.
その実験は危険を伴います。
That experiment involves danger.

② *to travel with as one's companion*

《Ordinarily occurs as a gerund (-te form) followed by a verb of motion.》[→ **tsureru** 連れる]

¶Tomodachi o tomonatte Kyūshū ni ikimashita.

友達を伴って九州に行きました。

I went to Kyushu with a friend.

③ *to go along, to be concomitant, to accompany*

¶Taifū ni wa ō-ame ga tomonaimasu.

台風には大雨が伴います。

Heavy rain accompanies a typhooon.

tomo-ni 共に *together, collectively* [→ **issho ni** 一緒に]

tōmórokoshi とうもろこし *<US>corn, <UK>maize*

¶Tōmorokoshi o san-bon tabemashita.

とうもろこしを3本食べました。

I ate three ears of corn.

tómu 富む *to become rich, to come to abound*

¶Sono kuni wa tennen-shigen ni tonde imasu.

その国は天然資源に富んでいます。

That country is rich in natural resources.

tón トン *(metric)ton*《＝1,000 kilograms》

• -ton －トン《counter for (metric)tons; see Appendix 2》

tonaéru 唱える ① *to advocate; to advance, to voice*

② *to recite, to chant*

tónamento トーナメント *tournament*

tōnan 東南 *the southeast* [→**nantō** 南東]

• Tōnan-Ajia 東南アジア *Southeast Asia*

tōnan 盗難 *robbery*

• tōnan-hin 盗難品 *stolen item*

tonari 隣 *the area directly beside; the area next door*

¶Tonari no ie wa totemo furui desu.

隣の家はとても古いです。

The house next door is very old.

¶Sūtsukēsu wa tonari no heya ni aru yo.

スーツケースは隣の部屋にあるよ。

The suitcase is in the next room!

¶Hon-ya wa hana-ya no tonari ni arimasu.

本屋は花屋の隣にあります。

The bookstore is next to the flower shop.

¶Tonari ni suwatte ii desu ka.

隣に座っていいですか。

May I sit next to you?

¶Koike-san wa Kishi-san no tonari ni sunde imasu.

小池さんは岸さんの隣に住んでいます。

Mr. Koike lives next door to Mr. Kishi.

• tonari-kinjo 隣近所 *the neighborhood; the neighbors*

tonbo とんぼ *dragonfly*

tonchínkan 頓珍漢 【COL.】 ～**na** ～ な *incoherent, illogical; irrelevant*

tonde-mo-nái とんでもない *absurd, preposterous, outrageous*

¶Tonde-mo-nai koto ga atta yo.

とんでもないことがあったよ。

A preposterous thing happened!

¶"Shinji to kekkon suru no?"

"Tonde-mo-nai!"

「真二と結婚するの？」「とんでもない！」

"Are you going to marry Shinji?" "Of course not."《In this use, labeling a suggestion preposterous serves as an emphatic denial.》

¶"Dōmo arigatō gozaimashita."

"Tonde-mo-arimasen."

「どうもありがとうございました」「とんでもありません」

"Thank you very much for your kindness." "Not at all."《In this use, labeling a thank-you preposterous serves as a polite denial that one deserves any thanks. English *Don't be silly* has a similar use but is not as polite.》

tónikaku とにかく *anyway, anyhow, in any case*

¶Tonikaku mō ichi-do yatte mimashō.

とにかくもう一度やってみましょう。

Anyway, let's try doing it one more time.

tonkatsu とんかつ *pork cutlet*

tonneru トンネル *tunnel*

tonosama 殿様 ① *Japanese feudal lord*

② *liege lord; nobleman*

③ *generous and unworldly person of leisure*

tónton とんとん (〜**to** 〜と) *with a tap–tap, tappingly*
¶Dare-ka ga to o tonton to tatakimashita.
だれかが戸をとんとんとたたきました。
Someone tapped on the door.

ton'ya 問屋 ① *wholesale store*
② *wholesaler*

tōnyōbyō 糖尿病 *diabetes*

Tōō 東欧 *Eastern Europe* [⇔**Seiō** 西欧]

tópikku トピック *topic, subject* [→**wadai** 話題]

toppa 突破 〜**suru** 〜する ① *to break through; to surmount, to overcome*
• nankan o toppa suru 難関を突破する *to overcome a difficulty*
② *to exceed, to go over* [→**uwamawaru** 上回る]
¶Kono kuni no jinkō wa ichi oku-nin o toppa shimashita.
この国の人口は１億人を突破しました。
The population of this country exceeded one hundred million.

tóppu トップ *top, head, lead*
¶Chiemi-chan wa itsu-mo kurasu no toppu da.
知恵美ちゃんはいつもクラスのトップだ。
Chiemi is always top of the class.

tora 虎 *tiger*

toraberāzuchékku トラベラーズチェック *traveler's check* [→**ryokō–kogitte** 旅行小切手 (s.v. **kogitte** 小切手)]

toráburu トラブル *trouble, discord*
• toraburu o okosu トラブルを起こす *to cause trouble*

torái トライ *try* 《in rugby》
• torai suru トライする *to score a try*

toraiánguru トライアングル *triangle* ((musical instrument))

torákku トラック *truck*
¶Watashi no ani wa torakku no untenshu desu.
私の兄はトラックの運転手です。
My older brother is a truck driver.

torákku トラック (*running*)*track*
• torakku-kyōgi トラック競技 *track events*

torákutā トラクター *tractor*

toranjísutā トランジスター *transistor*

toránku トランク *trunk, suitcase*

tora–no–maki 虎の巻 【COL.】 *book explaining the content of a textbook in simplified terms*

toranpétto トランペット *trumpet*

toránporin トランポリン *trampoline*

toránpu トランプ *playing card*
• toranpu o suru トランプをする *to play cards*

toranshíbā トランシーバー *transceiver*

torénā トレーナー ① *sweat shirt*
② *trainer* 《in sports》

toréningu トレーニング *training* 《in sports》
¶Shiai ni sonaete torēningu ni hagende iru.
試合に備えてトレーニングに励んでいる。
We are training hard in preparation for the match.
• torēningu suru トレーニングする *to train*
• torēningu-kyanpu トレーニングキャンプ *training camp*
• torēningu-pantsu トレーニングパンツ *sweat pants*
• torēningu-shatsu トレーニングシャツ *sweat shirt* [→**torénā** トレーナー①]

torérā トレーラー *trailer* ((vehicle))

toréru 取れる ① *to come off, to come loose*
¶Kōto no botan ga hitotsu toreta yo.
コートのボタンが一つ取れたよ。
One of my coat buttons came off!
② *to be produced, to be obtained*
¶Kono chihō de wa ringo ga takusan toremasu.
この地方ではりんごがたくさん取れます。
Many apples are produced in this area.
③ *to disappear, to go away*
¶Kata no itami wa toremashita ka.
肩の痛みは取れましたか。
Has the pain in your shoulder gone away?

toréru 撮れる *to be taken, to be captured on film*
¶Kono shashin wa yoku torete imasu ne.

この写真はよく撮れていますね。
This is a good photograph, isn't it. ⟪Literally: This photograph is well taken, isn't it.⟫

tōrí 通り〔〔→**ōrai** 往来〕〕 ① *street, road* 〔→**dōro** 道路〕

¶Tōri de yūjin ni aimashita.
通りで友人に会いました。
I met a friend on the street.

¶Kono kyōshitsu wa tōri ni menshite imasu.
この教室は通りに面しています。
This classroom faces the street.

• tōri o yokogiru 通りを横切る *to cross the street*

② *coming and going, traffic in both directions*

¶Kono kōsa-ten wa kuruma no tōri ga ōi desu.
この交差点は車の通りが多いです。
This intersection has a lot of automobile traffic.

tóri 通り（〜**ni** 〜に）*as, like, in accordance* ⟪modifiying a predicate⟫

¶Otōto wa itsu-mo no tōri jū-ji ni nemashita.
弟はいつものとおり10時に寝ました。
My younger brother went to bed at 10:00 as usual.

¶Isha no iu tōri ni shinasai.
医者の言うとおりにしなさい。
Do as the doctor says.

¶Sono tōri desu.
そのとおりです。
It's as you say.

• tōri no とおりの *as, like* ⟪modifiying a noun⟫

tori 鳥 *bird*

¶Tori ga eda ni tomarimashita.
鳥が枝に止まりました。
A bird alighted on a branch.

• tori-kago 鳥籠 *bird cage*
• tori-niku 鳥肉 *chicken (meat)*

toriáezu とりあえず ① *for the time being, for the present* 〔→**tōbun** 当分〕
② *immediately, at once* 〔→**sassoku** 早速〕

toriageru 取り上げる ① *to pick up with one's hand*

¶Haha ga juwaki o toriagete, watashite kureta.
母が受話器を取り上げて、渡してくれた。
Mother picked up the receiver and handed it to me.

② *to take away, to confiscate*

¶Sensei wa boku ga yonde ita hon o toriageta.
先生はぼくが読んでいた本を取り上げた。
The teacher took away the book I was reading.

③ *to take up, to consider*

• mondai o toriageru 問題を取り上げる *to take up a problem*

toriatsukai 取り扱い *handling, treatment* 〔→**atsukai** 扱い〕

¶Toriatsukai chūi
「取扱注意」⟪on a label⟫
Handle With Care

toríbun 取り分 *share, portion* ⟪that one is entitled to take⟫

toridasu 取り出す *to take out with one's hand*

¶Gakusei wa poketto kara tango-chō o toridashita.
学生はポケットから単語帳を取り出した。
The student took a vocabulary notebook out of his pocket.

torié 取り柄 *merit, good point* 〔→**chōsho** 長所〕

torihada 鳥肌 *goose-flesh*

• torihada ga tatsu 鳥肌が立つ *one gets goose-flesh*

toríhiki 取り引き *transaction, buying and selling, business*

• torihiki suru 取り引きする *to transact business, to do business*

torii 鳥居 *(Shinto shrine)gateway*

toriire 取り入れ *harvesting, harvest*

toriireru 取り入れる ① *to harvest, to gather in*

¶Hachi-gatsu wa tōmorokoshi o toriiremasu.
8月にはとうもろこしを取り入れます。
In August we harvest the corn.

② *to gather and take inside*

¶Ame ga futte kita node sentaku-mono o toriireta.

雨が降ってきたので洗濯物を取り入れた。
Since it started raining, I took the laundry inside.

③ *to adopt, to accept*

¶Kono teian o toriiremashō ka.

この提案を取り入れましょうか。
Shall we adopt this proposal?

torikaeru 取り替える *to exchange, to trade* [→**kōkan suru** 交換する]

• A o B to torikaeru A を B と取り替える *to exchange A for B, to trade A for B*

¶Kōichi wa jitensha o atarashii tokei to torikaeta.

光一は自転車を新しい時計と取り替えた。
Koichi exchanged the bike for a new watch.

torikaesu 取り返す *to get back, to take back, to regain* [→**torimodosu** 取り戻す]

¶Tomodachi ni kashita o-kane o torikaeshite kudasai.

友達に貸したお金を取り返してください。
Get back the money you lent to your friend.

torikakaru 取り掛かる *to start in, to set about*

¶Chichi wa sugu ni shigoto ni torikakatta.

父はすぐに仕事に取りかかった。
My father started in on the work right away.

¶Yūshoku o tabete kara shukudai ni torikakatta.

夕食を食べてから宿題に取りかかった。
After eating dinner I started in on my homework.

torikakomu 取り囲む *to surround, to gather around*

¶Fan ga kashu no kuruma o torikakomimashita.

ファンが歌手の車を取り囲みました。
The fans surrounded the singer's car.

torikesu 取り消す *to cancel, to call off, to revoke*

¶Denwa de yakusoku o torikeshimashita.

電話で約束を取り消しました。

I canceled the appointment by telephone.

toríkku トリック *trick, deception*

• torikku-satsuei トリック撮影 *trick photography*

torikumu 取り組む *to grapple, to wrestle*

torimodosu 取り戻す *to get back, to take back, to regain* [→**torikaesu** 取り返す]

¶Yatto sono o-kane o torimodoshimashita.

やっとそのお金を取り戻しました。
I finally got that money back.

torinozoku 取り除く *to remove, to take away*

¶Seito-tachi wa guraundo no ishi o torinozoita.

生徒たちはグラウンドの石を取り除いた。
The students removed the playground stones.

tōrinukéru 通り抜ける *to pass through and emerge from*

¶Sōnan-sha wa mori o tōrinukemashita.

遭難者は森を通り抜けました。
The accident victims passed through the woods.

tório トリオ *trio*

torishirabe 取り調べ *examination, investigation, inquiry*

torishiraberu 取り調べる *to examine, to investigate, to inquire into*

tōrisugíru 通り過ぎる *to go past, to pass beyond*

¶Ukkari shite Kanda-eki o tōrisugimashita.

うっかりして神田駅を通り過ぎました。
I carelessly went past Kanda Station.

Tóritsu 都立 ～**no** ～の *administered by Tokyo Prefecture, Tokyo metropolitan*

• Toritsu-kōkō 都立高校 *a Tokyo metropolitan high school*

toriyoseru 取り寄せる *to have sent, to have brought*

¶Chichi wa kono zasshi o Amerika kara toriyoseta.

父はこの雑誌をアメリカから取り寄せた。

My father had this magazine sent from the United States.

tōrō 灯籠 *Japanese garden lantern*

tōroku 登録 *registration*

- tōroku suru 登録する *register* 《transitive》
- tōroku-shōhyō 登録商標 *registered trademark*

tóron 討論 *discussion, debate*

- tōron suru 討論する *to discuss, to debate about*
- tōron-kai 討論会 *debate contest*

torónbōn トロンボーン *trombone*

tororībásu トロリーバス *trolleybus*

tóru 通る ① *to pass by, to pass through*

¶Kinō kono mise no mae o tōrimashita.

きのうこの店の前を通りました。

I passed by this store yesterday.

- hōan ga tōru 法案が通る *a bill passes*
- koe ga tōru 声が通る *a voice carries*

② *to pass* 《on a test, etc.》 [→**gōkaku suru** 合格する]

- A ni tōru Aに通る *to pass A*

¶Nyūgaku-shiken ni tōrimashita ka.

入学試験に通りましたか。

Did you pass the entrance examination?

③ *to pass, to be accepted* (*as adequate*)

¶Sonna iiwake wa tōranai deshō.

そんな言い訳は通らないでしょう。

That kind of excuse will probably not be accepted.

④ *to be known* 〈*as*〉; *to go* 《by a name》

- A de tōru Aで通る *to be known as A; to go by A*

¶Hannin wa Jimī to iu namae de tōtte itta.

犯人はジミーという名前で通っていた。

The criminal went by the name of Jimmy.

tóru 取る ① *to take hold of; to pick up*

¶Otōto no te o totte, michi o watarimashita.

弟の手を取って、道を渡りました。

I took my younger brother's hand and crossed the street.

- juwaki o toru 受話器を取る *to pick up the receiver*

② *to obtain, to get*

¶Haha wa asa hayaku narande, ii seki o torimashita.

母は朝早く並んで、いい席を取りました。

My mother lined up early in the morning and got a good seat.

- totte kuru 取って来る *to go and get*

¶Jisho o totte kite mo ii desu ka.

辞書を取ってきてもいいですか。

May I go and get my dictionary?

- gakui o toru 学位を取る *to get an academic degree*
- totte oku 取っておく *to keep, to set aside*

③ *to steal, to take away*

¶Hannin wa saifu o totte nigemashita.

犯人は財布を取って逃げました。

The culprit stole the wallet and ran away.

④ *to take, to choose, to pick*

¶Zenbu suki deshita ga, chīsai no o totta.

全部好きでしたが、小さいのを取った。

I liked them all, but I took the small one.

⑤ *to pass, to hand* [→**tewatasu** 手渡す]

¶Koshō o totte kudasai.

こしょうを取ってください。

Please pass the pepper.

¶Sono kanazuchi o totte kureru?

その金づちを取ってくれる？

Will you hand me that hammer?

⑥ *to take down, to write down*

¶Sono setsumei no memo o torimashita ka.

その説明のメモを取りましたか。

Did you take notes on that explanation?

⑦ *to eat, to have* 《a meal》

¶Kyō wa ni-ji-sugi ni chūshoku o torimashita.

きょうは２時過ぎに昼食をとりました。

Today I had lunch after 2:00.

⑧ *to take off, to remove; to take out, to delete*

¶Heya no naka de wa bōshi o torinasai.

部屋の中では帽子を取りなさい。
Take off your hat inside the room.

⑨ *to take, to subscribe to*

¶Dono shinbun o totte imasu ka.
どの新聞を取っていますか。
Which newspaper do you take?

tóru 捕る *to catch, to capture*

¶Uchi no neko wa nezumi o torimasen.
うちの猫はねずみを捕りません。
Our cat does not catch mice.

tóru 採る ① *to gather, to search for and collect*

• hana o toru 花を採る *to gather flowers*

② *to employ, to hire* [→**yatou** 雇う]

¶Ano kaisha wa dai-sotsu shika torimasen.
あの会社は大卒しか採りません。
That company only hires college graduates.

tōrui 盗塁 *stealing a base* 《in baseball》

• tōrui suru 盗塁する *to advance by stealing a base*

¶Rannā wa ni-rui ni tōrui shimashita.
ランナーは二塁に盗塁しました。
The runner advanced to second base by stealing.

• tōrui-ō 盗塁王 *base-stealing champion*

tōsen 当選 ① *being elected*

• tōsen suru 当選する *to be elected*

¶Yamada-san ga seito-kaichō ni tōsen shimashita.
山田さんが生徒会長に当選しました。
Ms. Yamada was elected student council president.

② *winning a prize*

• tōsen suru 当選する *to win a prize*

• tōsen-bangō 当選番号 *winning number*

• tōsen-sha 当選者 *winning candidate; prize winner*

tōshi 凍死 *death from freezing*

• tōshi suru 凍死する *to freeze to death*

tōshi 闘志 *fight, fighting spirit*

¶Ano sumō-tori wa tōshi o ushinatta yō desu.
あの相撲取りは闘志を失ったようです。
It seems as if that sumo wrestler has lost his fighting spirit.

• tōshi-manman no 闘志満々の *full of fighting spirit*

toshí 年 ① *year*

¶Yoi o-toshi o o-mukae kudasai.
よいお年をお迎えください。
Have a happy New Year! 《Literally: Please greet a good year.》

• toshi no hajime [kure] 年の始め[暮れ] *beginning [end] of the year*

② *age* 《of a person or animal》 [→**nen-rei** 年齢]

¶O-toshi wa ikutsu desu ka.
お年はいくつですか。
How old are you?

¶Okāsan wa toshi no wari ni wakaku miemasu ne.
お母さんは年の割に若く見えますね。
Your mother looks young for her age, doesn't she.

¶Haruko-san to Kyōko-san no toshi wa onaji nijūgo-sai desu.
春子さんと京子さんの年は同じ25歳です。
Haruko and Kyoko are the same age of 25 years.

• toshi o toru 年を取る *to get older*

• toshi-totta 年取った *old, elderly* [⇔**wakai** 若い]

tóshi 都市 *city* [→**tokai** 都会]

¶Pari wa Furansu de ichiban ōki na toshi da.
パリはフランスでいちばん大きな都市だ。
Paris is the largest city in France.

• toshi-gasu 都市ガス *city gas*

• toshi-keikaku 都市計画 *city planning*

• kōgyō-toshi 工業都市 *industrial city*

tōshi 投資 *investment*

• tōshi suru 投資する *to invest*

toshigoro 年ごろ ① *(approximate) age* 《of a person or animal》

¶Sono futari no shōjo wa hobo onaji toshigoro desu.
その二人の少女はほぼ同じ年ごろです。
Those two girls are about the same age.

② *marriageable age* 《of a woman》

¶Tanaka-san ni wa toshigoro no musume-san ga imasu.
田中さんには年ごろの娘さんがいます。

Mr. Tanaka has a daughter of marriageable age.

toshishita 年下 ～**no** ～の *younger* [⇔ **toshiue no** 年上の]

¶Hiroko-san wa Keiko-san yori san-sai toshishita desu.

弘子さんは桂子さんより3歳年下です。

Hiroko is three years younger than Keiko.

to shite として *as, in the capacity of; for, with respect to being*

¶Runowāru wa gaka to shite yūmei desu.

ルノワールは画家として有名です。

Renoir is famous as a painter.

¶Kazama-san wa gaido to shite dōkō shimashita.

風間さんはガイドとして同行しました。

Ms. Kazama went along as a guide.

¶Watashi to shite wa nani-mo iu koto wa arimasen.

私としては何も言うことはありません。

As for me, I have nothing to say.

toshiue 年上 ～**no** ～の *older* 《when describing a person or animal》 [⇔**toshishita no** 年下の]

¶Ane wa ani yori go-sai toshiue desu.

姉は兄より5歳年上です。

My older sister is five years older than my older brother.

¶Hideko to Sachiko to dochira ga toshiue desu ka.

秀子と幸子とどちらが年上ですか。

Who is older, Hideko or Sachiko?

¶San-nin no uchi de Hiroshi ga ichiban toshiue desu.

3人のうちで弘がいちばん年上です。

Hiroshi is the oldest of the three.

toshiyori 年寄り *elderly person*

¶Toshiyori ni shinsetsu ni shinasai.

年寄りに親切にしなさい。

Be kind to elderly people.

tōsho 投書 *letter to the editor; written suggestion to an institution*

•tōsho suru 投書する *to send a letter to the editor; to send in a suggestion*

¶Chichi wa yoku shinbun ni tōsho shimasu.

父はよく新聞に投書します。

My father often sends letters to the newspaper editor.

•tōsho-bako 投書箱 *suggestion box*

•tōsho-ran 投書欄 *readers' column, letters-to-the-editor column*

tósho 図書 *books*

•toshō-kan 図書館 *library* ((building))

•tosho-kan-in 図書館員 *librarian*

•tosho-mokuroku 図書目録 *catalog of books*

•tosho-shitsu 図書室 *reading room, library* ((room))

tóshu 投手 (baseball)*pitcher* [→**pitchā** ピッチャー]

tōsō 闘争 *struggle, conflict*

•tōsō suru 闘争する *to struggle, to fight* [→**tatakau** 戦う]

tosō 塗装 *coating with paint*

•tosō suru 塗装する *to paint, to coat with paint*

tosshin 突進 *rush, dash, charge*

•tosshin suru 突進する *to rush, to dash, to charge*

¶Senshu-tachi wa gōru ni mukatte tosshin shita.

選手たちはゴールに向かって突進した。

The players charged toward the goal.

tósu 通す ① *to make pass by, to make pass through; to let pass by, to let pass through*

¶Chotto tōshite kudasai.

ちょっと通してください。

Please let me pass.

•hari ni ito o tōsu 針に糸を通す *to thread a needle*

•hōan o tōsu 法案を通す *to pass a bill* ② *to show in, to usher in*

¶O-kyaku-san o heya ni tōshimashita.

お客さんを部屋に通しました。

I showed the guest into the room.

tósu トス ① *toss, light throw*

•tosu suru トスする *to toss* ② *coin toss, coin flip*

tósutā トースター *toaster*

tósuto トースト *toast*

totan トタン *galvanized sheet iron*

• totan-yane トタン屋根 *tin roof*

totan 途端 ～**ni** ～に *just as, as soon as* «following a past-tense verb»

¶Erebētā ni notta totan ni teiden shita.
エレベーターに乗ったとたんに停電した。
Just as I got on the elevator, there was a power failure.

tōtei 到底 〈*not*〉 *possibly, absolutely* «Always occurs in combination with a negative predicate or a predicate with a negative meaning.»

¶Yamane-san ni wa tōtei sonna koto wa dekinai.
山根さんには到底そんなことはできない。
Mr. Yamane cannot possibly do such a thing.

¶Sore wa tōtei muri da to omoimasu.
それは到底無理だと思います。
I think that's absolutely impossible.

totemo とても ① *very* [→**hijō ni** 非常に]
② 〈*not*〉 *possibly* «in combination with a negative predicate»

¶Sonna koto wa totemo dekinai yo.
そんなことはとてもできないよ。
I can't possibly do such a thing!

tōtō 到頭 [[→**tsui-ni** 遂に]] ① *at last, finally*
② *in the end , after all*

totonoéru 整える、調える ① *to prepare, to ready* [→**yōi suru** 用意する]*; to supply oneself with, to provide oneself with*

¶Yūshoku o totonoeru no wa jikan ga kakarimasu.
夕食を整えるのは時間がかかります。
Preparing supper takes time.

② *to put in order, to adjust*
• A no chōshi o totonoeru Ａの調子を整える *to tune A*
• taichō o totonoeru 体調を整える *to get oneself in good physical condition*

totsurénzu 凸レンズ *convex lens* [⇔**ō-renzu** 凹レンズ]

totsuzen 突然 *suddenly*

¶Basu wa totsuzen tomarimashita.
バスは突然止まりました。
The bus stopped suddenly.

¶Totsuzen tenki ga kawatta yo.
突然天気が変わったよ。
Suddenly the weather changed!

• totsuzen no 突然の *sudden*

totté 取っ手 *handle, knob*

tótte とって [☞**ni totte** にとって]

tottemo とっても 【COL. for **totemo** とても】

tótte oku 取っておく [☞**toru** 取る②]

Tōyō 東洋 *the East, the Orient* [⇔**Seiyō** 西洋]

• Tōyō-bijutsu 東洋美術 *Oriental art*
• Tōyō-bunmei 東洋文明 *Oriental civilization*
• Tōyō-jin 東洋人 *an Oriental*

tōyu 灯油 *kersosene; lamp oil*

tōzai 東西 *east and west* [⇔**nanboku** 南北]

• kokon-tōzai 古今東西 *all times and places*

tōzakáru 遠ざかる ① *to move away, to recede into the distance*

¶Hikōki wa dandan tōzakatte ikimashita.
飛行機はだんだん遠ざかって行きました。
The airplane gradually receded into the distance.

② *to stay away, to distance oneself*

¶Sore igo Koizumi-san kara tōzakatte imasu.
それ以後小泉さんから遠ざかっています。
Since then I've been staying away from Mr. Koizumi.

tōzakéru 遠ざける [[⇔**chikazukeru** 近付ける]] ① *to keep away, to prevent from approaching*

② *to keep at arm's length, to refrain from associating with*

¶Imagawa-san wa Sugie-san o tōzakete imasu.
今川さんは杉江さんを遠ざけています。
Ms. Imagawa is keeping Mr. Sugie at arm's length.

tózan 登山 *mountain climbing*

¶Chichi wa tozan ga suki desu.
父は登山が好きです。
My father likes mountain climbing.

• tozan suru 登山する *to climb a*

mountain
- tozan-ka 登山家 *mountaineer, alpinist*

tōzen 当然 *as a matter of course, naturally, not surprisingly*
- tōzen no 当然の *natural, obvious, unsurprising* [→**atarimae no** 当たり前の]

¶Kachō wa keisan-misu o mitsuke, tōzen okotta.

課長は計算ミスを見つけ、当然怒った。

The section chief found a miscalculation, and naturally he got angry.

¶Kokumin ga sō kangaeru no wa tōzen desu.

国民がそう考えるのは当然です。

It's natural for the people to think so.

-tsū 一通《counter for letters, documents; see Appendix 2》

tsúā ツアー *group tour*

¶Ani wa ni-shūkan no tsuā ni ikimasu.

兄は2週間のツアーに行きます。

My older brother will go on a two-week group tour.

tsúba 唾 *spittle, saliva*
- tsuba o haku つばを吐く *to spit*

tsúbaki 椿 *camellia* ((flower))

tsubakí 唾 [☞**tsuba** 唾]

tsubame 燕 *swallow* ((bird))

tsubasa 翼 *wing* [→**hane** 羽②]

tsuberukurinkénsa ツベルクリン検査 *tuberculin test*

tsubo 壺 *pot; jar*

tsubo 坪《a unit of area (=approx. 3.3 m²)》
- -tsubo 一坪《counter for **tsubo**; see Appendix 2》

tsubomí 蕾 *(flower)bud*

¶Momo no tsubomi ga fukurande iru yo.

桃のつぼみが膨らんでいるよ。

The peach blossom buds are swelling!

tsúbu 粒 *grain*《of rice, etc.》; *drop* 《of liquid》 [→**shizuku** 滴]
- -tsubu 一粒《counter for grains, drops; see Appendix 2》

¶Kono kusuri o asa yū futa-tsubu zutsu nonde kudasai.

この薬を朝夕2粒ずつ飲んでください。

Take two drops of this medicine morning

and evening.
- ō-tsubu 大粒 *large drops*

tsubureru 潰れる ① *to get crushed, to get smashed, to get squashed*

¶Danbōru-bako ga tsuburemashita.

段ボール箱がつぶれました。

The cardboard box got crushed.

¶Tamago ga zenbu tsubureta yo!

卵が全部つぶれたよ。

All the eggs got smashed!

② *to go bankrupt, to go out of business* [→**hasan suru** 破産する]

¶Eki-mae no pan-ya ga tsubureta sō desu.

駅前のパン屋がつぶれたそうです。

They say the bakery in front of the station went out of business.

tsubusu 潰す *to crush, to smash, to squash*

¶Wain o tsukuru tame ni budō o tsubushimasu.

ワインを作るためにぶどうをつぶします。

To make wine you crush grapes.
- tamago o tsubusu 卵をつぶす *to smash an egg*
- jikan o tsubusu 時間をつぶす *to kill time*

tsubuyáku 呟く *to mutter, to murmur*

¶Haha wa "Tsukareta wa"to tsubuyakimashita.

母は「つかれたわ」とつぶやきました。

My mother muttered, "I'm tired!"

tsūchi 通知 *notification, report*
- tsūchi suru 通知する *to notify of, to report*
- tsūchi-hyō 通知表 *report card* [→**tsūshin-bo** 通信簿 (s.v. **tsūshin** 通信)]

tsuchí 土 *earth, soil; the ground*

¶Tsuchi de sono ana o umenasai.

土でその穴を埋めなさい。

Fill that hole with earth.

¶Kaizoku wa sono takara-mono o tsuchi no naka ni umemashita.

海賊はその宝物を土の中に埋めました。

The pirates buried that treasure in the ground.
- tsuchi ga koete 〔yasete〕 iru 土が肥えて

〔やせて〕いる the soil is rich 〔poor〕

tsuchikáu 培う to cultivate, to foster

tsūchō 通帳 passbook

tsúe 杖 walking stick, cane

tsūgaku 通学 commuting (back and forth)to school, attending school
- tsūgaku suru 通学する to go to school, to commute to school

¶Musume wa basu de tsūgaku shite imasu.

娘はバスで通学しています。

My daughter commutes to school by bus.

¶Watashi wa kyonen kara aruite tsūgaku shite imasu.

私は去年から歩いて通学しています。

Since last year I've been going to school on foot.

tsugeguchi 告げ口 tattling
- tsugeguchi suru 告げ口する to tattle about

¶Mari wa watashi-tachi no koto o sensei ni tsugeguchi shita.

真里は私たちのことを先生に告げ口した。

Mari tattled about us to the teacher.

tsugeru 告げる to tell, to announce

¶Sono himitsu wa dare ni mo tsugenai de ne.

その秘密はだれにも告げないでね。

Don't tell anybody that secret, OK?

tsugí 次 the next one

¶Tsugi wa dare desu ka.

次はだれですか。

Who's next?

- tsugi no 次の next (in order), following

¶Tsugi no densha ni norimashō.

次の電車に乗りましょう。

Let's take the next train.

¶Tsugi no pēji o minasai.

次のページを見なさい。

Look at the next page.

- tsugi ni 次に next «as an adverb»

¶Ichiban hayai iki-kata wa chikatetsu de, tsugi ni hayai no wa basu desu.

いちばん早い行き方は地下鉄で、次に早いのはバスです。

The fastest way of going is the subway, and the next fastest is the bus.

¶Tsugi ni nani o shimashō ka.

次に何をしましょうか。

What shall we do next?

tsugi 継ぎ patch (for repairing clothes)

¶Haha wa zubon ni tsugi o atete kuremashita.

母はズボンに継ぎを当ててくれました。

My mother put a patch on my pants.

tsugime 継ぎ目 joint, juncture, seam

tsugítsugi 次々 ~ni／to ～に／と one after another, in close succession

¶Watashi-tachi wa tsugitsugi ni sensei to akushu shimashita.

私たちは次々に先生と握手しました。

We shook hands with the teacher one after another.

tsugō 都合 ① circumstances, conditions 〔→**jijō** 事情〕

¶Shigoto no tsugō de shusseki dekimasen deshita.

仕事の都合で出席できませんでした。

Because of circumstances at work, I was unable to attend.

- tsugō ga ii 〔warui〕 都合がいい〔悪い〕 circumstances are favorable 〔unfavorable〕
  ② (one's)convenience
- tsugō ga ii 〔warui〕 都合がいい〔悪い〕 to be convenient 〔inconvenient〕 for one

¶Tsugō no ii toki ni denwa shite kudasai.

都合のいいときに電話してください。

Please phone at your convenience.

¶Watashi-tachi wa ashita ga tsugō ga ii desu.

私たちはあしたが都合がいいです。

Tomorrow is convenient for us.

tsugu 注ぐ to pour «into a container» «transitive»

¶Mō ippai kōhī o tsuide kudasai.

もう１杯コーヒーをついでください。

Please pour me another cup of coffee.

tsugu 継ぐ to succeed to, to inherit

¶Chōnan ga otōsan no shigoto o tsugu deshō.

長男がお父さんの仕事を継ぐでしょう。

The oldest son will probably inherit his father's business.

• A no ato o tsugu Aの後を継ぐ *to succeed A*

¶Tarō ga chichi oya no ato o tsuide shachō ni natta.

太郎が父親の後を継いで社長になった。

Taro succeeded his father and became the company president.

tsugunáu 償う *to make up for, to make amends for*

¶Kimi wa mō sono shippai o tsugunatta yo.

君はもうその失敗を償ったよ。

You already made up for that mistake!

tsui 対 *pair*

¶Kore-ra no pendanto wa tsui ni natte imasu.

これらのペンダントは対になっています。

These pendants make a pair.

• -tsui 一対《counter for pairs; see Appendix 2》

¶Haha wa it-tsui no kokeshi-ningyō o kaimashita.

母は1対のこけし人形を買いました。

My mother bought a pair of kokeshi dolls.

tsúi つい ① *just, only* 《modifying a time or distance》

¶Tsui kinō Nagata-san ni aimashita.

ついきのう長田さんに会いました。

I saw Mr. Nagata just yesterday.

② *carelessly* [→**ukkari shite** うっかりして]; *unintentionally, inadvertently* [→**omowazu** 思わず]

tsuide 序で 〜**ni** 〜に *while one is at it;* (*since it's convenient*)*in addition to* 《following a clause》

¶Tsuide ni oiru mo chekku shite kudasai.

ついでにオイルもチェックしてください。

While at it, please have them check the oil too.

¶Eki e iku tsuide ni kono tegami o dasu yo.

駅へ行くついでにこの手紙を出すよ。

I'll mail this letter on my way to the station!

tsuihō 追放 *expulsion, banishment, exile, deportation*

• tsuihō suru 追放する *to expel, to banish, to exile, to deport*

tsuika 追加 *addition, supplement, addendum*

• tsuika no 追加の *additional, supplementary*

• tsuika suru 追加する *to add, to append*

• tsuika-ryōkin 追加料金 *additional charge*

tsuikyū 追及 *pursuit, search*

• tsuikyū suru 追及する *to pursue, to seek after*

tsúi-ni 遂に ① *at last, finally* [→**yatto** やっと①]

¶Tsui-ni sono yume wa jitsugen shimashita.

ついにその夢は実現しました。

At last that dream became true.

② *after all, in the end* [→**kekkyoku** 結局]

¶Tsui-ni mae no sōsha ni wa oitsukenakatta.

ついに前の走者には追いつけなかった。

In the end I wasn't able to catch up with the runner ahead.

tsuiraku 墜落 *fall, drop* 《from a high place》; *crash* 《of an airplane, etc.》

• tsuiraku suru 墜落する *to fall, to drop; to crash*

tsuiseki 追跡 *chase, pursuit*

• tsuiseki suru 追跡する *to chase, to pursue*

¶Sū-dai no patokā ga akai kuruma o tsuiseki shite iru.

数台のパトカーが赤い車を追跡している。

Several patrol cars are chasing a red car.

tsuitachí 一日 *the first* 《day of a month》《see Appendix 2》

¶Tsuda-san wa Go-gatsu tsuitachi ni Kyōto e ikimasu.

津田さんは5月1日に京都へ行きます。

Mr. Tsuda will go to Kyoto on the first of May.

tsúite ついて [☞**ni tsuite** について]

tsúite iku 付いて行く [☞**tsuku** 付く]

tsúite kuru 付いて来る［☞**tsuku** 付く］

tsuitotsu 追突 *rear-end collision*
• tsuitotsu suru 追突する *to collide from behind*
¶Ōtobai ga kuruma ni tsuitotsu shimashita.
オートバイが車に追突しました。
A motorcycle crashed into the back of a car.

tsuiyásu 費やす *to spend, to expend*
［→**tsukau** 使う②］
¶Mainichi shukudai ni ni-jikan o tsuiyashimasu.
毎日宿題に２時間を費やします。
I spend two hours every day on homework.

tsūjiru 通じる ① *to lead* «when the subject is a path, etc.»
¶Kono michi wa kōen ni tsūjite imasu.
この道は公園に通じています。
This road leads to the park.
② *to run, to provide transportation* «when the subject is a vehicle»
¶Basu wa koko kara Tōkyō-eki ni tsūjite imasu.
バスはここから東京駅に通じています。
The buses run from here to Tokyo Station.
③ **denwa ga~** 電話が~ *a telephone call goes through*
④ *to be understood, to be intelligible*
¶Sono kuni de Eigo wa tsūjimasu ka.
その国で英語は通じますか。
Is English understood in that country?

tsūjō 通常 *usually, ordinarily, generally*［→**futsū** 普通］
• tsūjō no 通常の *usual, ordinary, regular*

tsūka 通過 *passing by; passing through*
• tsūka suru 通過する *to pass by; to pass through*
¶Mō Kyōto o tsūka shimashita ka.
もう京都を通過しましたか。
Have we already passed through Kyoto?
¶Sono hōan wa Kokkai o tsūka suru deshō.
その法案は国会を通過するでしょう。
That bill will probably pass the Diet.

tsúka 通貨 *currency, money in circulation*

tsuká 塚 *mound*

tsukai 使い ① *errand for another person*
¶Tsukai ni itte kureru?
使いに行ってくれる？
Will you go on an errand for me?
② *person who does an errand for another person*

tsukamaeru 捕まえる ① *to take hold of, to grab onto with one's hand*
¶Otōto no te o tsukamaete, dōro o watarimashita.
弟の手を捕まえて、道路を渡りました。
I took hold of my younger brother's hand and crossed the road.
② *to capture, to catch; to arrest*［→**taiho suru** 逮捕する］
¶Neko ga nezumi o tsukamaeta yo.
猫がねずみを捕まえたよ。
The cat caught a mouse!
¶Keikan ga suri o tsukamaemashita.
警官がすりを捕まえました。
The police officer arrested a pickpocket.

tsukamaru 捕まる ① *to be captured, to be caught; to be arrested*
¶Morimoto-san wa supīdo-ihan de tsukamatta yo.
森本さんはスピード違反で捕まったよ。
Mr. Morimoto was caught for a speeding violation!
② *to take hold, to grab*
• A ni tsukamaru Aに捕まる *to take hold of A, to grab onto A*
¶Sono rōpu ni tsukamarinasai.
そのロープに捕まりなさい。
Take hold of that rope.

tsukámu つかむ ① *to grasp, to grip with one's hand*
¶Matsuno-san wa totsuzen watashi no te o tsukamimashita.
松野さんは突然私の手をつかみました。
Mr. Matsuno suddenly grasped my hand.

② *to grasp, to understand*

tsukaré 疲れ *fatigue, weariness*

tsukaréru 疲れる *to get tired, to get fatigued*

¶Aruite totemo tsukareta yo.
歩いてとても疲れたよ。
I got tired from walking!

¶Tsukarete ugokenai yo.
疲れて動けないよ。
I'm so tired I can't move!

tsukau 使う *to use*

¶Kono kasa o tsukatte mo ii desu ka.
この傘を使ってもいいですか。
May I use this umbrella?

¶Kono hako wa nan ni tsukau no desu ka.
この箱は何に使うのですか。
What are you going to use this box for?

¶Wāpuro o tsukau no wa muzukashii desu ka.
ワープロを使うのは難しいですか。
Is it difficult to use a word processor?

tsukau 遣う *to spend* [→**tsuiyasu** 費やす]

¶Tomodachi wa o-kozukai zenbu o hon ni tsukatte shimau.
友達はお小遣い全部を本に遣ってしまう。
My friend will spend all of her allowance on books.

tsukemono 漬け物 *pickle*

tsukéru 付ける ① *to attach, to affix; to make part of, to add*

¶Jitensha ni jō o tsukete kudasai.
自転車に錠を付けてください。
Please attach a lock to the bicycle.

• namae o tsukeru 名前を付ける *to give a name*

• aji o tsukeru 味を付ける *to add flavoring*

• hito no ato o tsukeru 人の後を付ける *to follow a person, to tail a person*

② *to write, to enter*

• gōkei o tsukeru 合計を付ける *to enter the total*

③ *to make regular entries in, to keep*

• nikki o tsukeru 日記を付ける *to keep a diary*

tsukéru 点ける ① *to light* «a fire» [⇔ **kesu** 消す①]

• tabako ni hi o tsukeru たばこに火をつける *to light a cigarette*

② *to turn on* «a device» [⇔**kesu** 消す②]

• rajio o tsukeru ラジオをつける *to turn on the radio*

tsukéru 着ける *to put on* «The direct object is ordinarily an incidental item or accessory that a person wears. Like other verbs for putting on clothing, **tsukeru** in the -te iru form can express the meaning *be wearing, have on*.»

¶Joyū wa nekkuresu o tsukemashita.
女優はネックレスを着けました。
The actress put on a necklace.

tsukí 月 ① *the moon*

¶Hikō-shi-tachi wa tsuki ni chakuriku shimashita.
飛行士たちは月に着陸しました。
The astronauts landed on the moon.

¶Akarui tsuki ga demashita.
明るい月が出ました。
A bright moon came out.

② *month*

¶Tsuki ni ichi-do haha ni tegami o dashimasu.
月に1度母に手紙を出します。
I send a letter to my mother once a month.

• tsuki no hajime [nakaba, owari] 月の初め〔半ば、終わり〕 *the beginning [middle, end] of the month*

• tsuki-akari 月明かり *moonlight*

• tsuki-yo 月夜 *moonlit night*

• mai-tsuki 毎月 *every month*

tsukiai 付き合い *personal association, social contact*

• tsukiai ga ii 付き合いがいい *sociable*

• tsukiai ga hiroi 付き合いが広い *circle of friends is wide*

tsukiatari 突き当たり *end* «of a path, etc., so that one cannot continue going straight ahead»

¶Tōri no tsukiatari ni kyōkai ga arimasu.
通りの突き当たりに教会があります。

There is a church at the end of the street.

tsukiatáru 突き当たる ① *to run into, to bump into* [→**butsukaru** ぶつかる]

¶Omocha no jidōsha wa kabe ni tsukiatatta.

おもちゃの自動車は壁に突き当たった。

The toy car ran into the wall.

② *to come to an end* 《when the subject is a path, etc.》

¶Kono michi wa chūsha-jō ni tsukiatarimasu.

この道は駐車場に突き当たります。

This street ends at a parking lot.

③ *to go along to the end* 《of a path》

¶Kono rōka o tsukiatatte, hidari e magaru to kōchō-shitsu ga arimasu.

この廊下を突き当たって、左へ曲がると校長室があります。

If you go to the end of this hall and turn left, there is the principal's office.

tsukiáu 付き合う ① *to associate, to carry on social contact, to keep company*

¶Kachō wa Amano-san to tsukiatte iru yo.

課長は天野さんと付き合っているよ。

The section chief is going out with Ms. Amano!

② *to go along, to do together* 《to keep a person company》

¶Kaimono ni tsukiatte kureru?

買い物に付き合ってくれる？

Will you come shopping with me?

¶Shokuji o tsukiatte kudasai.

食事を付き合ってください。

Please dine with me.

tsukidásu 突き出す ① *to thrust out*

② *to turn over* 《a person to the police》

tsukidéru 突き出る *to protrude, to stick out*

tsukíhi 月日 *time, the days and months*

• tsukihi ga tatsu 月日がたつ *time passes*

tsūkin 通勤 *commuting (back and forth)to work*

• tsūkin suru 通勤する *to commute to work*

¶Chichi wa chikatetsu de tsūkin shite imasu.

父は地下鉄で通勤しています。

My father commutes to work by subway.

tsukíru 尽きる *to run out, to be used up, to be exhausted* [→**nakunaru** 無くなる②]

tsukisásu 突き刺す ① *to stick, to stab, to poke* 《one thing into another》

¶Ani wa niku ni naifu o tsukisashimashita.

兄は肉にナイフを突き刺しました。

My older brother stabbed a knife into the meat.

② *to stab, to pierce* 《one thing with another》

¶Paburofu-san wa fōku de jagaimo o tsukisashite tabemashita.

パブロフさんはフォークでじゃがいもを突き刺して食べました。

Mr. Pavlov stabbed a potato with his fork and ate it.

tsukisoi 付き添い ① *attending (to be of service), accompanying (to be of service); escorting*

¶Tsukisoi no kangofu-san mo imashita.

付き添いの看護婦さんもいました。

There was also an attending nurse.

② *attendant; escort*

tsukisóu 付き添う *to attend (to take care of); to escort*

¶Ane wa byōki no kodomo ni tsukisotte imasu.

姉は病気の子供に付き添っています。

My older sister is attending a sick child.

tsukkómu 突っ込む ① *to thrust into, to stuff into*

¶Kensa-kan wa kaban no naka ni te o tsukkonda.

検査官はかばんの中に手を突っ込んだ。

The inspector thrust her hand into the bag.

② *to plunge into* 《intransitive》

¶Sono kuruma wa ike ni tsukkomimashita.

その車は池に突っ込みました。

That car plunged into the pond.

tsūkō 通行 *passing along, going along;*

traffic

• tsūkō suru 通行する *to pass along, to go along*

• tsūkō o samatageru 通行を妨げる *to obstruct traffic*

¶Tsūkō kinshi
「通行禁止」《on a sign》
No Passage 《Literally: Passing along prohibited》

• tsūkō-dome no 通行止めの *closed-to-traffic*

• tsūkō-ken 通行権 *right of way*

• tsūkō-nin 通行人 *passer-by*

• tsūkō-ryōkin 通行料金 *road toll*

• hidari-gawa-tsūkō 左側通行 *left-side traffic* 《Typically used on signs to mean Keep left.》

• ippō-tsūkō 一方通行 *one-way traffic*

tsúku 付く *to become attached, to become affixed; to become part of, to be added*

¶Kono shatsu ni shimi ga tsukimashita.
このシャツに染みが付きました。
This shirt got stained. 《Literally: A stain attached itself to this shirt》

¶Sono tsukue ni wa hikidashi ga itsutsu tsuite imasu.
その机には引き出しが5つ付いています。
That desk has five drawers.

• tsuite iku 付いて行く *to go along, to follow, to accompany*

¶Saki ni itte kudasai. Watashi wa ato kara tsuite ikimasu.
先に行ってください。私は後から付いていきます。
Please go ahead. I'll follow after you.

• tsuite kuru 付いて来る *to come along, to follow, to accompany*

¶Watashi ni tsuite kite kudasai.
私に付いてきてください。
Please follow me.

tsúku 点く [[⇔**kieru** 消える①]] *to start burning* 《when the subject is a fire》; *to catch on fire, to light; to go on* 《when the subject is an electric light, appliance, etc.》

¶Tonari no ie ni hi ga tsukimashita.
隣の家に火がつきました。
The house next-door caught on fire.

¶Terebi wa mada tsuite iru yo.
テレビはまだついているよ。
The television is still turned on!

• denki ga tsuku 電気がつく *lights go on*

• matchi ga tsuku マッチがつく *a match lights*

tsúku 着く ① *to arrive* [→**tōchaku suru** 到着する] [⇔**tatsu** 立つ②]

¶Ōshima-san wa kinō Hakata ni tsukimashita.
大島さんはきのう博多に着きました。
Mr. Oshima arrived in Hakata yesterday.

¶Sā, tsuita yo.
さあ、着いたよ。
Well, we've arrived!

② *to sit down, to take one's place*

¶Dōzo seki ni tsuite kudasai.
どうぞ席に着いてください。
Please take a seat.

• shokutaku ni tsuku 食卓に着く *to sit down at the dining table*

tsúku 就く *to take up, to go into* 《The direct object is a job.》

• shokugyō ni tsuku 職業に就く *to take up an occupation*

tsuku 突く ① *to prick, to stab* 《one thing with another》 [→**tsukisasu** 突き刺す②]

¶Pin de yubi o tsukimashita.
ピンで指を突きました。
I pricked my finger with a pin.

② *to poke, to jab, to prod*

¶Itō-san wa yubi de sono hito no mune o tsukimashita.
伊藤さんは指でその人の胸を突きました。
Mr. Ito poked that person in the chest with his finger.

③ *to use as a support*

• tsue o tsuku つえを突く *to use a cane*

• hiji o tsuku ひじを突く *to prop one's elbows*

tsukue 机 *desk*

¶Shioda-san wa tsukue ni mukatte benkyō shite imasu.
塩田さんは机に向かって勉強しています。

Ms. Shioda is studying at her desk.

tsukuribánashi 作り話 *made-up story*

tsukuróu 繕う *to mend, to fix*

tsukúru 作る ① *to make, to create*

¶Emi-chan wa kinō yūshoku o tsukutta yo.

恵美ちゃんはきのう夕食を作ったよ。

Emi made dinner yesterday!

¶Haha wa kono doresu o tsukutte kuremashita.

母はこのドレスを作ってくれました。

My mother made me this dress.

¶Wain wa budō kara tsukurimasu.

ワインはぶどうから作ります。

They make wine from grapes.

• ongaku o tsukuru 音楽を作る *to write music*

② *to form, to organize*

¶San-nen-sei wa dokusho-kurabu o tsukuru sō desu.

3年生は読書クラブを作るそうです。

I hear the third-year students are going to form a reading club.

③ *to grow, to raise* [→**saibai suru** 栽培する]

¶Haha wa yasai o tsukuru no ga shumi desu.

母は野菜を作るのが趣味です。

My mother's hobby is growing vegetables.

tsukúru 造る ① *to manufacture, to produce* [→**seizō suru** 製造する]

¶Kono kōjō de wain o tsukurimasu.

この工場でワインを造ります。

They produce wine at this factory.

② *to build, to construct*

¶Kono shitauke-gyōsha wa hashi o tsukutte imasu.

この下請け業者は橋を造っています。

This subcontractor is building a bridge.

tsukúsu 尽くす ① *to use up, to exhaust*

• besuto o tsukusu ベストを尽くす *to do one's best*

• zenryoku o tsukusu 全力を尽くす *to do everything in one's power*

② *to make great efforts, to persevere tirelessly*

¶Oda-sensei wa kagaku no tame ni tsukushimashita.

小田先生は科学のために尽くしました。

Dr. Oda perservered for the sake of science.

tsúma 妻 *wife* [⇔**otto** 夫; **okusan** 奥さん]

tsumamu 摘む *to take hold of with the fingertips*

¶Poteto-chippusu o tsumande tabemashita.

ポテトチップスをつまんで食べました。

I ate potato chips with my fingers.

¶Hidoi nioi ni hana o tsumamimashita.

ひどいにおいに鼻をつまみました。

I held my nose at the terrible smell.

tsumaránai つまらない ① *dull, boring* [→**taikutsu na** 退屈な]

¶Kono pātī wa tsumaranai nā.

このパーティーはつまらないなあ。

Boy, this party is dull.

¶Mattaku tsumaranai eiga datta yo.

まったくつまらない映画だったよ。

It was a really boring movie!

② *trifling, trivial* [→**sasai na** 些細な]

¶Imōto-tachi wa tsumaranai koto de kenka suru.

妹たちはつまらない事でけんかする。

My younger sisters quarrel about trivial things.

③ *worthless, good-for-nothing*

¶Tsumaranai mono ni o-kane o tsukawanai de.

つまらない物にお金を遣わないで。

Don't spend money on worthless things.

¶Tsumaranai mono desu ga, dōzo.

つまらない物ですが、どうぞ。

This is for you; I hope you like it. ≪Literally: It's a worthless thing, but please.≫

≪Japanese etiquette calls for denigrating a gift one gives as a way of showing respect for the recipient. The implication is that the recipient deserves better.≫

tsúmari つまり ① *in other words, that is (to say)* [→**sunawachi** 即ち]

¶Gantan, tsumari Ichigatsu tsuitachi wa watashi no tanjōbi desu.

元旦、つまり1月1日は私の誕生日です。
New Year's Day, that is, January 1st, is my birthday.

② *in short, to sum up* [→**yōsuru-ni** 要するに]

¶Tsumari, sono otoko ni damasareta wake desu.
つまり、その男にだまされたわけです。
In short, the fact is that we were deceived by that man.

tsumáru 詰まる ① *to become stopped up, to become clogged, to become blocked* [→**fusagaru** 塞がる①]

¶Mata gesui ga tsumatte iru yo.
また下水が詰まっているよ。
The drain is blocked up again.

② *to be packed, to be crammed* 《into a container》

¶Sono kaban ni wa o-miyage ga ippai tsumatte iru.
その鞄にはお土産がいっぱい詰まっている。
That bag is packed full of souvenirs.

③ *to become full, to become jam-packed*

¶Kono honbako wa manga-bon de tsumatte imasu.
この本箱は漫画本で詰まっています。
This bookcase is full of comic books.

④ *to become shorter, to shrink* [→**chijimaru** 縮まる]

• hi ga tsumaru 日が詰まる *the days become shorter*

tsumasaki 爪先 *toe tip*

• tsumasaki de aruku つま先で歩く *to walk on tiptoe*

tsumayōji 爪楊枝 *toothpick* [→**yōji** 楊枝]

tsumazuku つまずく *to stumble*

¶Shōjo wa ishi ni tsumazuite korobimashita.
少女は石につまずいて転びました。
The girl stumbled on a stone and fell down.

tsume 爪 〈finger-〉 *nail; claw*

• tsume o kiru つめを切る *to cut nails*

• tsume-kiri 爪切り *nail clipper*

tsumekomu 詰め込む *to cram, to pack* 《into a container》

¶Kono kuruma ni ushi jut-tō o tsume-komu no wa muri da.
この車に牛10頭を詰め込むのは無理だ。
It's impossible to cram ten cows into this truck.

tsuméru 詰める ① *to pack, to put* 《into a container》

¶Kono hako ni orenji o tsumemashita.
この箱にオレンジを詰めました。
They packed oranges in this box.

② *to move closer, to move closer together* 《transitive》

¶Seki o chotto tsumete kudasai.
席をちょっと詰めてください。
Please move your seats a little closer together.

③ *to make shorter, to shrink* [→**tanshuku suru** 短縮する]

• yōfuku o tsumeru 洋服を詰める *to shorten clothes*

tsumetai 冷たい ① *cold* 《describing an object or tangible substance at a low temperature》 [⇔**atsui** 熱い]

¶Soto wa tsumetai kaze ga fuite iru yo.
外は冷たい風が吹いているよ。
A cold wind is blowing outside!

¶Nani-ka tsumetai nomimono o kudasai.
何か冷たい飲み物をください。
Please give me something cold to drink.

② *cold (-hearted), unfriendly* [→**reitan na** 冷淡な] [⇔**atatakai** 温かい③]

¶Yuzawa wa sono tegami ni tsumetai henji o dashita.
湯沢はその手紙に冷たい返事を出した。
Yuzawa sent a cold answer to that letter.

¶Miyuki-san wa boku ni wa tsumetai yo.
美幸さんは僕には冷たいよ。
Miyuki is cold to me!

tsúmi 罪 *crime, offense; sin*

¶Hito o damasu no wa tsumi desu.
人をだますのは罪です。
To deceive people is a sin.

• tsumi na 罪な *cruel, heartless*

• tsumi no aru [nai] hito 罪のある［ない］人 *guilty [innocent] person*

• tsumi o okasu 罪を犯す *to commit a*

crime

tsumiki 積み木 *(toy)building block*

tsumori つもり ① *intention*

• tsumori da つもりだ *to intend to, to be planning to* 《following a clause ending in a nonpast-tense verb》

¶Ashita wa tenisu o suru tsumori desu.

あしたはテニスをするつもりです。

Tomorrow I intend to play tennis.

¶Shōrai nan ni naru tsumori desu ka.

将来何になるつもりですか。

What do you plan to become in the future?

• tsumori ga nai つもりがない *to have no intention of, not to be planning to* 《following a clause ending in a nonpast-tense verb》

¶Sono hoken ni kanyū suru tsumori wa arimasen.

その保険に加入するつもりはありません。

I have no intention of subscribing to that insurance policy.

② *(possibly mistaken)belief*

• tsumori da つもりだ *to think (perhaps mistakenly)* 《following a clause ending in a past-tense verb》

¶Denki o keshita tsumori desu ga, tashikamemasu.

電気を消したつもりですが、確かめます。

I think I turned out the lights, but I'll make sure.

tsumoru 積もる *to accumulate, to pile up* 《intransitive》

¶Kono yuki wa amari tsumoranai deshō.

この雪はあまり積もらないでしょう。

This snow will probably not accumulate very much.

tsumu 摘む *to pick, to pluck*

¶Kazoku de hatake de ichigo o tsumimashita.

家族で畑でいちごを摘みました。

They picked strawberries in the field as a family.

tsumu 積む ① *to load* 《as freight》

¶Kono torakku ni kome o tsumimashō.

このトラックに米を積みましょう。

Let's load the rice onto this truck.

② *to pile up, to stack; to amass, to accumulate*

¶Sensei wa tsukue no ue ni hon o tsumimashita.

先生は机の上に本を積みました。

The teacher piled up books on her desk.

• okane o tsumu お金を積む *to accumulate money*

tsuná 綱 *rope, cord; cable*

¶Akira-san wa ni-hon no ki no aida ni tsuna o harimashita.

明さんは2本の木の間に綱を張りました。

Akira stretched a rope between the two trees.

• tsuna-hiki 綱引き *tug of war*

• tsuna-watari 綱渡り *tightrope walking; tightrope walker*

tsunagu 繋ぐ ① *to tie, to fasten, to tether*

¶Kaubōi wa uma o ki ni tsunagimashita.

カウボーイは馬を木につなぎました。

The cowboy tied his horse to a tree.

② *to tie together, to connect, to join*

• te o tsunagu 手をつなぐ *to join hands*

③ *to connect* 《a phone call》

¶Suzuki-sensei ni tsunaide kudasai.

鈴木先生につないでください。

Please connect me with Dr. Suzuki.

tsunami 津波 *tsunami, tidal wave*

tsundora ツンドラ *tundra*

tsúne 常 *the usual, the ordinary course of things*

• yo no tsune 世の常 *the way of the world*

• tsune no 常の *usual, ordinary, common*

• tsune ni 常に [[→**itsu-mo** いつも (s.v. **itsu** いつ)]] *always; usually*

tsunó 角 *horn, antler*

• tsuno-bue 角笛 *horn* 《i.e., an animal's horn made into a musical instrument》

tsūpīsu ツーピース *woman's suit consisting of a jacket and skirt*

tsurai 辛い *hard, trying, bitter*

¶Maiasa go-ji ni okiru no wa tsurai yo.

毎朝5時に起きるのはつらいよ。

It is hard to get up at 5:00 every morning!

• tsurai me ni au つらい目にあう *to have a trying experience*

tsuranúku 貫く ① *to pierce through, to penetrate through; to pass through*

¶Kono ya wa mato o tsuranukimashita.

この矢は的を貫きました。

This arrow penetrated the target.

¶Kawa wa machi o tsuranuite nagarete imasu.

川は町を貫いて流れています。

The river flows through the city.

② *to carry through, to accomplish* [→ **yaritogeru** やり遂げる]

• mokuteki o tsuranuku 目的を貫く *to accomplish an objective*

tsurara つらら *icicle*

tsureru 連れる *to travel with as one's companion* 《Ordinarily occurs as a gerund (-**te** form) followed by a verb of motion.》

• tsurete iku 連れて行く *to take* 《an animate being along》

¶Itoko wa watashi o kōen ni tsurete itte kureta.

いとこは私を公園に連れていってくれた。

My cousin took me to the park.

¶Itoko wa Kyōto no iroiro na tokoro e tsurete itte kuremashita.

いとこは京都のいろいろな所へ連れていってくれました。

My cousin took me to a lot of places in Kyoto.

• tsurete kuru 連れて来る *to bring* 《an animate being along》

¶Imōto-san o tsurete kite kudasai.

妹さんを連れてきてください。

Please bring your younger sister with you.

tsurete つれて [☞**ni tsurete** につれて]

tsurete iku 連れて行く [☞**tsureru** 連れる]

tsurete kuru 連れて来る [☞**tsureru** 連れる]

tsuri 釣り *fishing* (*with hook and line*), *angling*

• tsuri o suru 釣りをする *to fish*

¶Ani wa tsuri ga dai-suki desu.

兄は釣りが大好きです。

My older brother loves fishing.

¶Ashita wa kawa e tsuri ni iku tsumori desu.

あしたは川へ釣りに行くつもりです。

Tomorrow I'm planning to go to the river for fishing.

• tsuri–bari 釣り針 *fish hook*

• tsuri–bori 釣り堀 *fishing pond*

• tsuri–ito 釣り糸 *fishing line*

• tsuri–zao 釣り竿 *fishing rod, fishing pole*

tsuri 釣り [☞**o-tsuri** お釣り]

tsuriai 釣り合い *balance, equilibrium*

• tsuriai o toru 釣り合いを取る *to attain balance*

¶Heikindai no ue de tsuriai o totte aruita.

平均台の上で釣り合いを取って歩いた。

I attained balance and walked along the beam.

• tsuriai o tamotsu 釣り合いを保つ *to maintain balance*

tsuriáu 釣り合う *to balance, to become in balance*

tsurikawa 吊り革 *hanging strap* 《for standing passengers on a bus or train》

¶Densha ni nottara, tsurikawa ni tsukamatte ne.

電車に乗ったら、つり革につかまってね。

When you get on the train, hold on to a hanging strap, OK?

tsúro 通路 *passageway; aisle*

¶Kono nimotsu ga tsūro o fusaide imasu.

この荷物が通路をふさいでいます。

This luggage is blocking the aisle.

• tsūro–gawa 通路側 *side by the aisle*

• tsūro–gawa no seki 通路側の席 *aisle seat*

tsurú 蔓 *vine*

tsúru 鶴 *crane* ((bird))

tsuru 釣る *to catch* (*with a hook and line*)

¶Kono kawa de sakana o tsurimasu.

この川で魚を釣ります。

I catch fish in this river.

¶Kinō masu o go-hiki tsutta yo.

きのうますを 5 匹釣ったよ。
I caught five trout yesterday!

tsuru 吊る [☞**tsurusu** 吊るす]

tsurúhashi つるはし *pick, pickaxe*

tsurusu 吊るす *to hang, to suspend*
¶Noki-shita ni fūrin o tsurushimashita.
軒下に風鈴をつるしました。
I hung a wind chime under the eave.

tsúrutsuru つるつる ① ~**no** ~の *smooth* (*-surfaced*) [→**nameraka na** 滑らかな①]
• tsurutsuru suru つるつるする *to become smooth*
• tsurutsuru ni hagete iru つるつるにはげている *to be completely bald*
 ② *slippingly, slidingly*
• tsurutsuru no つるつるの *slippery*
• tsurutsuru suru つるつるする *to become slippery*
• tsurutsuru suberu つるつる滑る *to slide slippingly*

Tsūsánshō 通産省 [☞**Tsūshōsangyōshō** 通商産業省]

tsūshin 通信 (*long-distance*)*communication, correspondence*
• tsūshin suru 通信する *to communicate*
• tsūshin-bo 通信簿 *report card* [→**tsūchi–hyō** 通知表 (s.v. **tsūchi** 通知)]
• tsūshin-eisei 通信衛星 *communications satellite*
• tsūshin-hanbai 通信販売 *mail-order selling*
• tsūshin-kyōiku 通信教育 *correspondence course*
• tsūshin-sha 通信社 *news agency*

Tsūshōsangyóshō 通商産業省 *the Ministry of International Trade and Industry* (*MITI*)

tsutá 蔦 *ivy*

tsutaeru 伝える ① *to tell, to report, to communicate* [→**shiraseru** 知らせる]
¶Sono shirase o minna ni tsutaemashō.
その知らせをみんなに伝えましょう。
Let's tell that news to everybody.
¶Watashi ni denwa suru yō ni Koike-san ni tsutaete itadakemasu ka.
私に電話するように小池さんに伝えていた

だけますか。
Will you tell Mr. Koike to phone me?
 ② *to transmit, to hand down, to impart, to teach; to introduce* «*from abroad*»
• densetsu o tsutaeru 伝説を伝える *to hand down a legend*
• chishiki o tsutaeru 知識を伝える *to impart knowledge*
 ③ *to transmit* «*vibrations*», *to conduct* «*electricity*»
¶Kūki wa onpa o tsutaemasu.
空気は音波を伝えます。
Air transmits sound waves.

tsutawaru 伝わる ① *to be widely communicated, to spread*
¶Sono uwasa wa gakkō-jū ni tsutawarimashita.
そのうわさは学校中に伝わりました。
That rumor has spread all over the school.
 ② *to be transmitted, to be handed down, to be imparted; to be introduced* «*from abroad*»
¶Zen wa jūni-seiki ni Chūgoku kara Nihon ni tsutawatta.
禅は12世紀に中国から日本に伝わった。
In the 12th century Zen was introduced into Japan from China.
 ③ *to be transmitted, to be conveyed, to travel* «*when the subject is sound, electricity, etc.*»
¶Denki wa kono sen o tsutawarimasu.
電気はこの線を伝わります。
The electricity is transmitted through this line.

tsutomé 勤め (*white-collar*)*job*
¶Ani wa sono kaisha ni tsutome ga mitsukarimashita.
兄はその会社に勤めが見つかりました。
My older brother found a job at that company.
• tsutome-nin 勤め人 *salaried worker, white-collar worker*
• tsutome-saki 勤め先 *one's workplace*

tsutomé 務め *duty* (*to be performed*)
• tsutome o hatasu 務めを果たす *to ful-*

fill one's duties

tsutoméru 勤める *to work* (*in a white-collar job*)

¶Ishikawa-san wa ginkō ni tsutomete imasu.

石川さんは銀行に勤めています。

Ms. Ishikawa works at a bank.

tsutoméru 務める *to serve in the role of, to serve in the post of*

¶Inoue-san wa ima kaichō o tsutomete imasu.

井上さんは今会長を務めています。

Ms. Inoue is now serving as chairperson.

tsutoméru 努める *to exert oneself, to make efforts, to work hard* [→**doryoku suru** 努力する]

¶Mainichi undō suru yō ni tsutomete imasu.

毎日運動するように努めています。

I am making efforts to do exercise every day.

tsutsu 筒 *tube, empty cylinder*

tsutsúji ツツジ *azalea* ((flower))

tsutsúku 突く ① *to poke* 《one thing with another》

② *to peck*

tsutsumí 包み <US>*package*, <UK>*parcel, bundle*

¶Hon no tsutsumi o uketorimashita.

本の包みを受け取りました。

I received a package of books.

•tsutsumi-gami 包み紙 *wrapping paper*

tsutsumí 堤 *dike, embankment, levee* [→**teibō** 堤防]

tsutsúmu 包む *to wrap* 《in a covering》

¶Kore o kirei na kami ni tsutsunde kudasai.

これをきれいな紙に包んでください。

Please wrap this in pretty paper.

tsutsushímu 慎む ① *to be careful about, to be prudent about*

•kotoba o tsutsushimu 言葉を慎む *to be careful about one's words*

② *to refrain from, to abstain from*

•tabako o tsutsushimu たばこを慎む *to refrain from smoking*

tsuya 艶 *gloss, shine, luster*

tsūyaku 通訳 ① (*language-to-language*)*interpretation*

•tsūyaku suru 通訳する *to interpret*

¶Toda-san ga tsūyaku shite kureru deshō.

戸田さんが通訳してくれるでしょう。

Ms. Toda will probably interpret for us.

② *interpreter*

•dōji-tsūyaku 同時通訳 *simultaneous interpretation; simultaneous interpreter*

tsūyō 通用 *current use; current usability*

•tsūyō suru 通用する *to be in current use; to be usable at present*

¶Ōsutoraria de wa Eigo ga tsūyō shimasu.

オーストラリアでは英語が通用します。

English is used in Australia.

¶Kono kōka wa mō tsūyō shinai yo.

この硬貨はもう通用しないよ。

This coin is no longer in use!

tsuyói 強い *strong* [⇔**yowai** 弱い]

¶Tsuyoi kaze ga fuite iru yo.

強い風が吹いているよ。

A strong wind is blowing!

¶Doa o tsuyoku oshite akete kudasai.

ドアを強く押して開けてください。

Please push the door strongly and open it.

¶Ame ga tsuyoku futte imasu.

雨が強く降っています。

It's raining hard.

•A ni tsuyoi Aに強い *strong in A, good at A; not easily affected adversely by A*

¶Yamane-san wa kagaku ni tsuyoi ne.

山根さんは科学に強いね。

Ms. Yamane is good at science, isn't she.

tsuyomáru 強まる *to become stronger* [⇔**yowamaru** 弱まる]

tsuyoméru 強める *to make stronger* [⇔**yowameru** 弱める]

tsúyosa 強さ *strength*

tsúyu 露 *dew*

•tsuyu ga oriru 露が降りる *dew settles, dew forms*

tsuyu 梅雨 *the Japanese rainy season* 《typically mid-June through mid-July》

• tsuyu ni hairu 梅雨に入る *to enter the rainy season*

• tsuyu ga akeru 梅雨が明ける *the rainy season ends*

tsuzukeru 続ける *to continue, to keep doing*

¶Sono shigoto o tsuzukete kudasai.
その仕事を続けてください。
Please continue that work.

-tsuzukeru −続ける *to continue to*
《Added to both transitive and intransitive verb bases.》

¶Musuko wa nan-jikan mo benkyō shi-tsuzukemashita.
息子は何時間も勉強し続けました。
My son continued studying for many hours.

¶Ato sanjup-pun-gurai aruki-tsuzukete kudasai.
あと30分ぐらい歩き続けてください。
Please continue walking for about 30 minutes.

tsuzuku 続く *to continue, to last, to go on*

¶Arashi wa ichi-nichi-jū tsuzukimashita.
あらしは1日中続きました。
The storm continued all day.

tsuzuri 綴り ① *spelling* 《in an alphabet》
② *binding together* 《typically said of papers》
③ *bound pad, bound of sheaf* 《typically said of papers》

tsuzuru 綴る ① *to spell* 《in an alphabet》

¶Sono tango wa dō tsuzurimasu ka.
その単語はどうつづりますか。
How do you spell that word?

② *to write, to compose* 《a text》

• sakubun o tsuzuru 作文をつづる *to write a composition*

③ *to bind together* 《The direct object is typically papers.》

¶Sono shorui wa tsuzutte teishutsu shite kudasai.
その書類はつづって提出してください。
Bind and submit those documents please.

U

ú 鵜 *cormorant*

• u-nomi 鵜呑み *gulping down; gullibly accepting as true*

• u-nomi ni suru 鵜呑みにする *to gulp down; to gullibly accept as true*

ubáu 奪う ① *to take forcibly*

¶Gōtō wa rōjin kara o-kane o ubaimashita.
強盗は老人からお金を奪いました。
The robber took money from an elderly person.

② *to engross, to captivate* 《a person's mind, attention, etc.》

¶Sono geki ni kokoro o ubawaremashita.
その劇に心を奪われました。
I was engrossed in that play.

uchi 内 ① *the inside* [→**naibu** 内部] [⇔ **soto** 外]

② *time during, time while, time within* [→**aida** 間①]

¶Fuyu no uchi wa zutto koko ni imasu.
冬のうちはずっとここにいます。
We will stay here all winter.

¶Kuraku naranai uchi ni kaerimasu.
暗くならないうちに帰ります。
I'm going to go home before it gets dark.
《Literally: I'm going to go home while it has not gotten dark.》

¶Ane wa ni-, san-nichi no uchi ni genki ni naru darō.
姉は2、3日のうちに元気になるだろう。
My older sister will probably get well within two or three days.

¶Sūjitsu no uchi ni kaette kimasu.
数日のうちに帰ってきます。
I'll come back within a few days.

¶Tetsu wa atsui uchi ni ute.
鉄は熱いうちに打て。《proverb》
Strike while the iron is hot.

③ *included membership, included*

range [→**naka** 中②]

• A no uchi de Aのうちで *among A, of A* 《in combination with a superlative》

¶Taro wa go-nin no uchi de ichiban se ga takai.

太郎は5人のうちでいちばん背が高い。

Taro is the tallest among the five.

uchi 家 ① *house* [→**ie** 家①]

¶Yamamoto-san-tachi wa ōki na uchi ni sunde iru.

山本さんたちは大きなうちに住んでいる。

The Yamamotos live in a big house.

¶Uchi no naka de asobanai de.

うちの中で遊ばないで。

Don't play inside the house.

② *my home; my family*

¶Tokidoki sono kodomo-tachi o uchi ni manekimasu.

時々その子供たちをうちに招きます。

I sometimes invite those children to my home.

¶Mō uchi ni kaerō yo.

もううちに帰ろうよ。

Let's go home now!

¶Uchi wa minna hayaoki desu.

うちはみんな早起きです。

My family are all early risers.

uchiageru 打ち上げる ① *to launch, to shoot up*

¶Natsu ni wa kaigan de hanabi o uchiage-masu.

夏には海岸で花火を打ち上げます。

We shoot up fireworks at the seashore in the summer.

¶Raigetsu, roketto ga uchiageraremasu.

来月、ロケットが打ち上げられます。

A rocket will be launched next month.

② *to pop up* 《in baseball》

¶Sentā ni furai o uchiageta.

センターにフライを打ち上げた。

I popped up to center field.

uchiakeru 打ち明ける *to tell, to bring into the open, to reveal*

¶Kanojo wa sono himitsu o boku ni uchiaketa.

彼女はその秘密を僕に打ち明けた。

My girlfriend told me that secret.

uchigawa 内側 *the inside, the inner side* [⇔**sotogawa** 外側]

¶Uchigawa wa midori-iro desu.

内側は緑色です。

The inside is green.

¶Dare-ka ga mon no uchigawa ni tatte imasu.

だれかが門の内側に立っています。

Somebody is standing inside the gate.

uchiki 内気 ～**na** ～な *shy, timid*

¶Sono shōnen wa uchiki desu.

その少年は内気です。

That boy is shy.

uchiwa うちわ *fan* 《a round, non-folding fan made of paper on a bamboo frame》

• uchiwa de aogu うちわであおぐ *to fan with a fan*

uchiwa 内輪 ～**no** ～の *private, internal*

úchū 宇宙 *the universe; (outer)space*

¶Taiyō ya hoshi wa uchū no ichibu desu.

太陽や星は宇宙の一部です。

The sun and stars are part of the universe.

• uchū-fuku 宇宙服 *spacesuit*

• uchū-hikō-shi 宇宙飛行士 *astronaut, cosmonaut*

• uchū-jidai 宇宙時代 *the Space Age*

• uchū-jin 宇宙人 *(space)alien*

• uchū-ryokō 宇宙旅行 *space travel*

• uchū-sen 宇宙船 *spaceship, spacecraft*

• uchū-shoku 宇宙食 *space food*

• uchū-sutēshon 宇宙ステーション *space station*

udé 腕 ① *arm* 《from shoulder to wrist》

¶Ano futari wa ude o kunde aruite imasu.

あの二人は腕を組んで歩いています。

Those two are walking arm in arm.

② *skill, ability* [→**nōryoku** 能力]

¶Mitsuko-san no skī no ude wa taishita mono desu.

光子さんのスキーの腕は大したものです。

Mitsuko's skiing ability is really something.

• ude-dokei 腕時計 *wristwatch*

• ude-tate-fuse 腕立て伏せ *pushup*

• ude-zumō 腕相撲 *arm wrestling*

udon うどん *udon* «a kind of wheat noodles popular in Japan»

• udon-ya うどん屋 *udon shop, udon restaurant*

ue 上 [[⇔**shita** 下]] ① *top; upper part*
¶Oka no ue made noborimashita.
丘の上まで登りました。
I climbed to the top of the hill.
¶Ue no kai ni oji ga sunde imasu.
上の階に伯父が住んでいます。
My uncle lives on the upper floor.
¶Piano no ue ni ningyō ga arimasu.
ピアノの上に人形があります。
There is a doll on top of the piano.
¶Tēburu no ue ni shiroi kabā o kakenasai.
テーブルの上に白いカバーをかけなさい。
Spread a white cover on top of the table.

• ue no gakunen 上の学年 *the upper grades* (*in school*)
② *the area above*
¶Tako ga ki no ue ni agatte imasu.
たこが木の上に上がっています。
A kite is flying above the tree.
¶Tanabe-san wa odoroite tobiagarimashita.
田辺さんは驚いて跳び上がりました。
Mr. Tanabe jumped up in surprise.
¶Ue ni ikinasai.
上に行きなさい。
Go upstairs.
③ *the part of a scale or ranking above*
¶Tenisu no ude wa otōto no hō ga ue desu.
テニスの腕は弟のほうが上です。
As for skill at tennis, my younger brother is better.
④ ~**no** ~の *older*
¶Ichiban ue no musuko wa jūgo-sai desu.
いちばん上の息子は15歳です。
My oldest son is 15.
¶Jirō-san wa Yumiko-san yori futatsu ue desu.
次郎さんは由美子さんより二つ上です。
Jiro is two years older than Yumiko.

ué 飢え *hunger*

¶Takusan no dōbutsu ga ue de shinimashita.
たくさんの動物が飢えで死にました。
Many animals died of hunger.

ueki 植木 *garden tree, garden plant; potted plant*
• ueki-bachi 植木鉢 *flowerpot*
• ueki-ya 植木屋 *gardener*

ueru 植える *to plant*
¶Chichi wa niwa ni bara o uemashita.
父は庭にばらを植えました。
My father planted roses in the garden.

uéru 飢える *to get very hungry; to starve*

uésuto ウエスト *waist*
¶Musume wa uesuto ga hosoi desu.
娘はウエストが細いです。
My daughter's waist is slender.

uétā ウエーター *waiter*

ueto ウエート *weight* ((athletic equipment))
• uēto-rifutingu ウエートリフティング *weight lifting* [→**jūryō-age** 重量挙げ(s.v. **jūryō** 重量)]
• uēto-torēningu ウエートトレーニング *weight training*

uétoresu ウエートレス *waitress*

uétto ウエット ~**na** ~な *sentimental, tender-hearted* [⇔**dorai na** ドライな]

ugai うがい *gargling*
• ugai suru うがいする *to gargle*
• ugai-gusuri うがい薬 *mouthwash, gargle*

ugokásu 動かす ① *to move* «transitive»
¶Tsukue o ugokashinasai.
机を動かしなさい。
Move your desk.
• kokoro o ugokasu 心を動かす *to move one's heart, to move one*
¶Haha no kotoba wa watashi no kokoro o ugokashimashita.
母の言葉は私の心を動かしました。
My mother's words moved me.
• te o ugokasu 手を動かす *to move one's hands*
② *to operate, to run* «transitive» [→**sōsa suru** 操作する]

¶Kono kikai o ugokasu koto ga dekimasu ka.

この機械を動かすことができますか。

Can you operate this machine?

ugokí 動き *movement; action* [→**kōdō** 行動]

• me no ugoki 目の動き *eye movement*

• ugoki ga torenai 動きが取れない *to be unable to move, to be stuck*

ugóku 動く ① *to move* 《intransitive》

¶Mō chotto hidari ni ugoite kudasai.

もうちょっと左に動いてください。

Please move a little more to the left.

② *to work, to run, to function*

¶Erebētā wa ugoite imasen.

エレベーターは動いていません。

The elevator is not working.

¶Kono kikai wa gasorin de ugokimasu.

この機械はガソリンで動きます。

This machine runs on gasoline.

¶Kono tokei wa ugoite imasu ka.

この時計は動いていますか。

Is this clock running?

ugúisu 鶯 *Japanese nightingale*

uīku ウイーク *week* [→**shū** 週]

• uīku-dē ウイークデー *weekday* [→**heijitsu** 平日]

• uīku-endo ウイークエンド *weekend* [→**shūmatsu** 週末]

• Gōruden-uīku ゴールデンウイーク *Golden Week* 《the period of April 29 through May 5 when three Japanese national holidays fall in close succession: **Midori no hi** みどりの日(April 29), **Kenpō-kinen-bi** 憲法記念日(May 3), and **Kodomo no hi** こどもの日(May 5)》

uīkupóinto ウイークポイント *weak point* [→**jakuten** 弱点]

uíndō ウインドー *window* [→**mado** 窓]

• uindō-shoppingu ウインドーショッピング *window shopping*

¶Yoku Keiko to Shibuya ni uindō-shoppingu ni ikimasu.

よく恵子と渋谷にウインドーショッピングに行きます。

I often go to Shibuya with Keiko for window-shopping.

uindosáfin ウインドサーフィン *windsurfing*

• uindosāfin o suru ウインドサーフィンをする *to windsurf*

uínku ウインク *wink*

• uinku suru ウインクする *to wink*

¶Okada-kun ga kirei na onna no ko ni uinku shita.

岡田君がきれいな女の子にウインクした。

Okada winked at that pretty girl.

uírusu ウイルス *virus*

uisúkī ウイスキー *whiskey*

ukaberu 浮かべる ① *to float, to sail* 《transitive》

¶Watashi-tachi wa mizuumi ni yotto o ukabemashita.

私たちは湖にヨットを浮かべました。

We sailed a sailboat on the lake.

② *to show outwardly* 《on one's face》 《transitive》

• me ni namida o ukaberu 目に涙を浮かべる *to show tears in one's eyes*

¶Shōjo wa me ni namida o ukabete iru yo.

少女は目に涙を浮かべているよ。

The girl has tears in her eyes!

③ *to call, to recall* 《to mind》

• atama ni ukaberu 頭に浮かべる *to call to mind, to recall*

• kokoro ni ukaberu 心に浮かべる *to call to mind, to recall*

ukabu 浮かぶ ① *to float* 《intransitive》 [→**uku** 浮く]

¶Shiroi kumo ga ao-zora ni ukande iru.

白い雲が青空に浮かんでいる。

White clouds are floating in the blue sky.

② *to occur to one*

¶Ii kangae ga ukabimashita.

いい考えが浮かびました。

A good idea occurred to me.

ukagau 伺う ① 【HUM. for **tazuneru** 訪ねる】 *to visit, to pay a call*

¶Ashita ukagaimasu.

あした伺います。

I'll visit you tomorrow.

② 【HUM. for **tazuneru** 尋ねる, **kiku**

聞く③】 *to ask, to inquire*

¶Ukagaitai koto ga arimasu.

伺いたい事があります。

There is something I want to ask you.

¶Chotto ukagaimasu ga, ginkō wa doko desuka.

ちょっと伺いますが、銀行はどこですか。

Pardon me, but where is the bank?

《*Literally: I am going to ask you, but where is the bank?*》

③ 【HUM. for **kiku** 聞く①】 *to hear, to be told*

ukai 迂回 *detour; making a detour* [→**tōmawari** 遠回り]

• ukai suru 迂回する *to make a detour*

ukáru 受かる *to pass, to succeed* 《*on a test*》[→**gōkaku suru** 合格する] [⇔ **ochiru** 落ちる②]

¶Imōto wa shiken ni ukatta yo.

妹は試験に受かったよ。

My younger sister passed the examination!

ukeireru 受け入れる *to accept*

¶Sono enjo no mōshide o ukeiremasu.

その援助の申し出を受け入れます。

I will accept that offer of help.

ukemí 受け身 ① *the defensive*

② *the passive* 《*in grammar*》

ukemotsu 受け持つ *to take charge of, to accept charge of*

¶Katō-sensei ga watashi-tachi no kurasu o ukemotsu yo.

加藤先生が私たちのクラスを受け持つよ。

Mr. Kato is in charge of our class!

¶Tanaka-sensei wa san-nensei no sūgaku o ukemotta.

田中先生は3年生の数学を受け持った。

Ms. Tanaka took charge of third-year math.

ukéru 受ける ① *to receive*

¶Watashi-tachi wa dai-kangei o ukemashita.

私たちは大歓迎を受けました。

We received a big welcome.

② *to accept* [→**ukeireru** 受け入れる]

¶Sono shōtai o yorokonde ukemasu.

その招待を喜んで受けます。

I'll gladly accept that invitation.

③ *to take* 《*lessons*》

¶Shū san-jikan Eigo no jugyō o ukete iru yo.

週3時間英語の授業を受けているよ。

I'm taking three hours of English classes a week.

④ *to undergo, to experience*

¶Kono kanja wa kesa shujutsu o ukemashita.

この患者はけさ手術を受けました。

This patient underwent surgery this morning.

• shiken o ukeru 試験を受ける *to take an examination*

¶Ashita sono shiken o ukemasu.

あしたその試験を受けます。

I will take that examination tomorrow.

• songai o ukeru 損害を受ける *to suffer damage*

¶Sono mura wa taifū de dai-songai o ukemashita.

その村は台風で大損害を受けました。

That village suffered great damage in the typhoon.

⑤ *to catch* 《*a ball, etc.*》

¶Refuto wa bōru o ryōte de ukemashita.

レフトはボールを両手で受けました。

The left fielder caught the ball with both hands.

⑥ *to become popular*

¶Kono uta ga wakai hito ni ukete imasu.

この歌が若い人に受けています。

This song is popular with young people.

uketoru 受け取る *to receive, to get, to accept*

¶Suzuki-san wa ojīsan kara maishū tegami o uketorimasu.

鈴木さんはおじいさんから毎週手紙を受け取ります。

Mr. Suzuki receives a letter from his grandfather every week.

¶Sensei wa seito-tachi kara okurimono o uketotta.

先生は生徒たちから贈り物を受け取った。

The teacher accepted a present from the students.

uketsugu 受け継ぐ *to inherit, to succeed to* [→**tsugu** 継ぐ]

uketsuke 受付 ① *acceptance, receiving,
reception*
　② *information desk, reception desk*
　③ *receptionist*

uketsukeru 受け付ける *to accept, to receive*
　¶Mōshikomi wa ashita kara uketsuke-
masu.
申し込みはあしたから受け付けます。
*They will accept applications starting to-
morrow.*

ukibúkuro 浮き袋 *life preserver* [→
kyūmei-gu 救命具 (s.v. **kyūmei** 救命)];
life buoy

ukiyóe 浮世絵 *ukiyoe* 《i.e., a traditional
Japanese woodblock print》

ukkári うっかり（〜**shite** 〜して）*carelessly, absent-mindedly*
　¶Ukkari shite kyōkasho o motte konakatta.
うっかりして教科書を持ってこなかった。
I carelessly didn't bring my textbook.

uku 浮く *to float* 《intransitive》 [→**ukabu**
浮かぶ①]

umá 馬 *horse; pony*
　• uma ni noru 馬に乗る *to mount a
horse; to ride a horse*
　• uma kara oriru 馬から降りる *to dis-
mount from a horse*
　• uma kara ochiru 馬から落ちる *to fall
from a horse*

umái うまい ① *skillful, good* (*at*) 《This
adjective is used to describe both people
who are skillful and the things they are
skillful at.》 [→**jōzu na** 上手な]
　¶Hiromi-san wa tenisu ga umai desu.
弘美さんはテニスがうまいです。
Hiromi is good at tennis.
　¶Arai-san wa Eigo o hanasu no ga totemo umai.
荒井さんは英語を話すのがとてもうまい。
*Mr. Arai is very good at speaking Eng-
lish.*
　• umaku iku うまく行く *to go well*
　¶Subete umaku ikimashita.

すべてうまく行きました。
Everything went well.
　② *good-tasting, delicious* [→**oishii**
美味しい]

umare 生まれ *birth*
　¶Umare wa doko desu ka.
生まれはどこですか。
Where were you born?
　• -umare no −生まれの *born in／at／on*
《Added to bases denoting a place or
date.》
　¶Jon-san wa Beikoku-umare no hito
desu.
ジョンさんは米国生まれの人です。
*John is a person born in the United
States.*
　¶Kono ko wa Ichi-gatsu-tsuitachi-umare
desu.
この子は1月1日生まれです。
This child was born on January 1st.

umarekawáru 生まれ変わる *to be
reincarnated*

umareru 生まれる *to be born* [⇔**shinu**
死ぬ]
　¶Kawada-san wa Kyōto de umaremashita.
川田さんは京都で生まれました。
Ms. Kawada was born in Kyoto.
　¶Doko de umareta n desu ka.
どこで生まれたんですか。
Where were you born?
　¶Umarete kara zutto koko ni sunde
imasu.
生まれてからずっとここに住んでいます。
*I have been living here ever since I was
born.*
　¶Koko ga watashi no umareta machi
desu.
ここが私の生まれた町です。
This is the town where I was born.
　• umarete hajimete 生まれて初めて *for the
first time in one's life*
　¶Umarete hajimete hikōki ni norimashita.
生まれて初めて飛行機に乗りました。
*I rode on an airplane for the first time in
my life.*

umaretsuki 生まれつき *by nature, as an inborn characteristic*

¶Maeda-san wa umaretsuki kinben desu.

前田さんは生まれつき勤勉です。

Mr. Maeda is diligent by nature.

• umaretsuki no 生まれつきの *born, natural*

¶Hiroshi-san wa umaretsuki no shijin desu.

弘さんは生まれつきの詩人です。

Hiroshi is a born poet.

ume 梅 ① *ume, Japanese apricot, plum* 《The translation *plum* is traditional, although misleading.》

② *ume tree*

③ *ume blossoms*

• ume-boshi 梅干し *pickled ume*

umeru 埋める ① *to bury*

¶Chichi wa sono tsubo o umemashita.

父はそのつぼを埋めました。

My father buried that pot in the ground.

② *to fill in* 《transitive》

• ike o umeru 池を埋める *to fill in a pond*

• kūran o umeru 空欄を埋める *to fill in a blank*

úmi 海 ① *sea, ocean*

¶Umi ga arete imasu.

海が荒れています。

The ocean is rough.

¶Sono umi o fune de watarimashita.

その海を船で渡りました。

We crossed that sea by boat.

② *seaside, beach*

¶Natsu wa umi e ikimasu.

夏は海へ行きます。

In summer we go to the beach.

umí 膿 *pus*

umu 産む, 生む ① *to give birth to*

¶Naomi-san wa onna no ko o umimashita.

直美さんは女の子を産みました。

Naomi gave birth to a girl.

¶Nezumi wa dondon ko o umu dōbutsu desu.

ねずみはどんどん子を産む動物です。

Rats are animals that give birth to young

in great numbers.

② *to lay* 《an egg》

¶Kono niwatori wa tamago o umanai yo.

この鶏は卵を産まないよ。

This chicken doesn't lay eggs!

③ *to produce, to give rise to* [→ **shōjiru** 生じる①]

¶Natsume Sōseki wa Nihon no unda idai na sakka desu.

夏目漱石は日本の生んだ偉大な作家です。

Soseki Natsume is a great writer that Japan produced.

ún 運 *fortune, luck*

• un ga ii 〔warui〕 運がいい〔悪い〕 *to have good 〔bad〕 luck*

• un-yoku 運よく *luckily*

¶Un-yoku sensei ni aemashita.

運よく先生に会えました。

Luckily I was able to meet the teacher.

unagi 鰻 *eel*

• unagi no kabayaki うなぎのかば焼き *broiled eel*

• unagi-nobori 鰻登り *steady increase, rapid increase*

unáru 唸る ① *to groan, to moan*

② *to growl; to howl*

¶Inu ga watashi o mite unatta yo.

犬が私を見てうなったよ。

A dog looked at me and growled!

unazuku 頷く *to nod (in affirmation)*

¶Tomoko-chan wa damatte, tada unazukimashita.

友子ちゃんはだまって、ただうなずきました。

Tomoko, just nodded without speaking.

únchin 運賃 *fare*

¶Basu no unchin ga raigetsu neage ni naru deshō.

バスの運賃が来月値上げになるでしょう。

The bus fares will probably be raised next month.

• katamichi-unchin 片道運賃 *one-way fare*

• ōfuku-unchin 往復運賃 *round-trip fare*

undō 運動 ① *(physical)exercise*

¶Suiei wa ii undō desu.

水泳はいい運動です。

Swimming is good exercise.
¶Motto undō o shita hō ga ii desu.
もっと運動をしたほうがいいです。
It would be better to do more exercise.
• undō suru 運動する *to exercise, to get exercise*
② *campaign, movement* 《for a political or social cause》
• undō suru 運動する *to campaign*
③ *movement, motion* 《in physics》
• undō no hōsoku 運動の法則 *the laws of motion*
• undō suru 運動する *to move, to go into motion*
• undō-busoku 運動不足 *insufficient exercise, lack of exercise*
• undō-gu 運動具 *sporting goods*
• undō-gutsu 運動靴 *sneakers, athletic shoes*
• undō-jō 運動場 *playground*
• undō-kai 運動会 *athletic meet; field day, sports day* 《at a school》
• kōtsū-anzen-undō 交通安全運動 *traffic safety campaign*
• rōdō-undō 労働運動 *labor movement*
únga 運河 *canal*
• Suezu-unga スエズ運河 *the Suez Canal*
• Panama-unga パナマ運河 *the Panama Canal*
úni うに ① *sea urchin*
② *seasoned sea urchin eggs*
únmei 運命 *destiny, fate*
¶Fushigi na unmei deshita.
不思議な運命でした。
It was a strange fate.
unten 運転 *driving* 《a vehicle》; *operating* 《a machine》
¶Kuruma no unten ga dekimasu ka.
車の運転ができますか。
Can you drive a car?
¶Kono kikai no unten no shikata ga wakarimasen.
この機械の運転の仕方がわかりません。
I don't know how to operate this machine.
• unten suru 運転する *to drive; to operate*

• unten-menkyo-shō 運転免許証 *driver's license*
• unten-sha 運転者 *driver* 《of a car, etc.》
• unten-shu 運転手 *driver* 《of a vehicle as an occupation》
unubore 自惚れ *overconfidence, conceit*
• unubore no tsuyoi hito うぬぼれの強い人 *very conceited person*
unuboreru 自惚れる *to become conceited*
• unuboreta hito うぬぼれた人 *conceited person*
ún'yu 運輸 *transportation*
• Un'yu-shō 運輸省 *the Ministry of Transport*
unzári うんざり ～**suru** ～する *to get fed up, to get sick and tired*
¶Taro wa shigoto ni unzari shite imasu.
太郎は仕事にうんざりしています。
Taro is fed up with his job.
• unzari da うんざりだ *to be fed up, to be sick and tired*
¶Sonna jiman-banashi ni wa mō unzari desu.
そんな自慢話にはもううんざりです。
I'm already sick and tired of that kind of boasting.
uo 魚 *fish* [→**sakana** 魚]
• tobi-uo 飛び魚 *flying fish*
uókka ウォッカ *vodka*
uōminguáppu ウォーミングアップ *warming-up* (*exercises*)
• uōminguappu suru ウォーミングアップする *to warm up*
urá 裏 ① *back, other side, opposite side* [⇔**omote** 表①]
¶Kono meishi no ura ni nani-ka ga kaite arimasu.
この名刺の裏に何かが書いてあります。
Something is written on the back of this business card.
¶Ura mo mite kudasai.
裏も見てください。
Please look at the other side, too.
② *the area behind* [→**ushiro** 後ろ①]
¶Uchi no ura ni kōen ga arimasu.
うちの裏に公園があります。

There is a park behind my house.

③ *bottom «of an inning»* [⇔**omote** 表③]

¶Nana-kai no ura desu.

7回の裏です。

It's the bottom of the 7th inning.

• ura-bangumi 裏番組 *program on a different channel*

• ura-dōri 裏通り *back street, alley*

• ura-guchi 裏口 *back door*

• ura-guchi-nyūgaku 裏口入学 *gaining admission to a school dishonestly*

• ura-ji 裏地 *lining «of a coat, etc.»*

• ura-mon 裏門 *back gate*

uragáeshi 裏返し 〜**no** 〜の *inside-out; opposite-face-down*

¶Ken-chan wa kutsushita o uragaeshi ni haite ita yo.

健ちゃんは靴下を裏返しにはいていたよ。

Ken was wearing his socks inside out!

uragáesu 裏返す ① *to turn over, to turn opposite face down «transitive»* [→ **hikkurikaesu** ひっくり返す①]

¶Sono ni-mai no toranpu o uragaeshite kudasai.

その2枚のトランプを裏返してください。

Please turn those two cards over.

② *to turn inside out «transitive»*

uragirí 裏切り *betrayal, treachery*

• uragiri-mono 裏切り者 *betrayer, traitor*

uragíru 裏切る{5} *to betray*

¶Ano hito wa tomodachi o uragiru ka mo shiremasen.

あの人は友達を裏切るかもしれません。

That person might betray his friends.

¶Kekka wa wareware no kitai o uragirimashita.

結果はわれわれの期待を裏切りました。

The results betrayed our hopes.

uramí 恨み *grudge*

¶Ano hito ni nan no urami mo nai yo.

あの人に何の恨みもないよ。

I don't have any kind of grudge against that person!

urámu 恨む *to have a grudge against*

úran ウラン *uranium*

uranái 占い *fortunetelling*

¶Okusan wa toranpu de uranai o shimasu.

奥さんはトランプで占いをします。

The wife does fortunetelling with cards.

• uranai-shi 占い師 *fortune-teller*

uranáu 占う *to foretell, to divine by fortunetelling*

urayamashíi 羨ましい *envious «This adjective is used to describe both people who are envious and the things they are envious of.»*

¶Ano hito no seikō ga urayamashii desu.

あの人の成功がうらやましいです。

I am envious of that person's success.

¶Otōto mo urayamashii yō desu.

弟もうらやましいようです。

My younger brother also seems to be envious.

urayámu 羨む *to envy*

urazukéru 裏付ける *to provide support for, to back up*

ureru 売れる ① *to sell «intransitive»*

¶Kono hon wa yoku uremasu.

この本はよく売れます。

This book sells well.

¶Sono e wa gojū-man-en de uremashita.

その絵は50万円で売れました。

That picture sold for 500,000 yen.

② *to become popular, to become well known*

¶Āchā wa yoku urete iru sakka desu.

アーチャーはよく売れている作家です。

Archer is a very popular writer.

ureshíi 嬉しい *glad, happy «This adjective is ordinarily restricted to describing the speaker's happiness. To describe another person's (apparent) happiness requires a form such as **ureshi-sō** (below).»* [⇔ **kanashii** 悲しい]

¶Gōkaku shite taihen ureshii desu.

合格してたいへんうれしいです。

I am very glad that I passed.

• ureshi-sō na 嬉しそうな *happy-looking, happy-seeming «This adjective is ordinarily used to describe another person's (apparent) happiness.»*

úri 瓜 *melon*

uriba 売り場 *sales counter; department* 《of a large store》
- bunbōgu-uriba 文房具売り場 *stationery counter*
- kippu–uriba 切符売り場 *ticket office; ticket counter*
- omocha-uriba おもちゃ売り場 *toy department*

uridashi 売り出し ① *putting on sale, putting on the market*
② (*bargain*)*sale* [→**tokubai** 特売]
- ō–uridashi 大売り出 *big sale*
¶Honjitsu ō–uridashi
「本日大売り出し」《on a sign》
Big Sale Today
- nenmatsu-dai–uridashi 年末大売り出し
big year–end sale

uridásu 売り出す *to put on sale, to put on the market*
¶Sono shingata-kamera wa raishū uridashimasu.
その新型カメラは来週売り出します。
They will put that new-model of camera on sale next week.

urikire 売り切れ *being sold out*
¶Kippu wa urikire desu.
切符は売り切れです。
The tickets are sold out.

urikiréru 売り切れる *to become sold out*

uroko うろこ *scale* 《on the skin of a fish, reptile, etc.》

urotsuku うろつく *to loiter, to hang around*

ū̃ru ウール *wool* (*cloth*) [→**keito** 毛糸]
¶Kono kutsushita wa ūru desu.
この靴下はウールです。
These socks are wool.
¶Noguchi-san wa ūru no sētā o kite iru.
野口さんはウールのセーターを着ている。
Ms. Noguchi is wearing a woolen sweater.

uru 売る *to sell* 《transitive》 [⇔**kau** 買う]
¶Ano mise de wa hana o utte imasu.
あの店では花を売っています。
They're selling flowers at that store.

¶Oba wa Tanaka-san ni kuruma o yonjū-man-en de utta.
叔母は田中さんに車を40万円で売った。
My aunt sold a car to Ms. Tanaka for 400,000 yen.

urū̃doshi 閏年 *leap year*

urusái 煩い ① *noisy* [→**sawagashii** 騒がしい] [⇔**shizuka na** 静かな①]
¶Rajio ga urusai ne.
ラジオがうるさいね。
The radio is noisy, isn't it.
¶Urusai!
うるさい！
Be quiet! 《Literally: You're noisy!》
② *given to nagging, given to complaining*
¶Haha wa itsu-mo urusai desu.
母はいつもうるさいです。
My mother is always given to nagging.
③ *particular, fussy*
¶Chichi wa tabemono ni urusai desu.
父は食べ物にうるさいです。
My father is particular about food.
④ *annoying, bothersome*
¶Hae wa urusai ne.
はえはうるさいね。
The flies are annoying, aren't they.

usagi 兎 *rabbit; hare*

usetsu 右折 *right turn* [⇔**sasetsu** 左折]
- usetsu suru 右折する *to turn right*

ushi 牛 *cow; ox; bull*
¶Ojīsan wa ushi no chichi o shibotte iru.
おじいさんは牛の乳を搾っている。
Grandfather is milking the cows.
- ko–ushi 子牛 *calf*

ushinau 失う *to lose, to be deprived of* [→**nakusu** 無くす]
¶Mattaku nozomi o ushinaimashita.
まったく望みを失いました。
I completely lost hope.
- chansu o ushinau チャンスを失う *to lose a chance*

ushiro 後ろ *the area behind* [⇔**mae** 前②]
¶Sono ie no ushiro ni taiboku ga aru.
その家の後ろに大木がある。
There is a big tree behind that house.

¶Inu wa shujin no ushiro o tsuite ikima-shita.

犬は主人の後ろをついていきました。

The dog followed behind its master.

¶Kono kuruma no ushiro no seki wa semai desu.

この車の後ろの席は狭いです。

The back seat of this car is cramped.

• ushiro o furikaeru 後ろを振り返る *to look back, to look behind one*

• ushiro-ashi 後ろ足 *hind leg*

• ushiro-sugata 後ろ姿 *appearance from behind*

úso 嘘 *lie, falsehood* 《Japanese **uso** is not as insulting as English *lie*.》

¶Uso!

うそ！

You're kidding! 《Literally: *A lie!*》

• uso o tsuku うそをつく *to tell a lie, to stretch the truth*

¶Seiji-ka wa yoku uso o tsukimasu.

政治家はよくうそをつきます。

Politicians often tell lies.

• uso-tsuki 嘘つき *liar* 《Japanese **uso-tsuki** is not as insulting as English *liar*.》

úsu 臼 *mortar* 《used with a pestle》

usugurai 薄暗い *dim, slightly dark*

¶Usuguraku natte kimashita.

薄暗くなってきました。

It has gotten a little dark.

• usugurai hikari 薄暗い光 *dim light*

usui 薄い ① *thin, small from front to back* [⇔**atsui** 厚い①]

¶Sono pan o usuku kitte kudasai.

そのパンを薄く切ってください。

Please slice that bread thin.

② [[⇔**koi** 濃い]] *light, pale* 《describing a color》; *thin, sparse* 《describing liquid, hair, etc.》; *weak* 《describing coffee, tea, etc.》

¶Iro wa usui ao desu.

色は薄い青です。

The color is a light blue.

¶Koko no sūpu wa usukute mazui desu yo.

ここのスープは薄くてまずいですよ。

The soup here is thin and bad tasting!

utá 歌 *song*

¶Nihon no uta o utaimashō.

日本の歌を歌いましょう。

Let's sing a Japanese song.

• uta-goe 歌声 *singing voice*

utagai 疑い ① *doubt*

¶Ano gakusei no seikō wa utagai ga nai desu.

あの学生の成功は疑いがないです。

There is no doubt about that student's success.

② *suspicion; mistrust*

¶Minna ga watashi o utagai no me de mite iru yo.

みんなが私を疑いの目で見ているよ。

Everybody is looking at me suspiciously! 《Literally: *Everybody is looking at me with eyes of suspicion.*》

• utagai-naku 疑いなく *undoubtedly*

utagau 疑う ① *to doubt*

¶Jibun no me o utagatta yo.

自分の目を疑ったよ。

I doubted my own eyes!

② *to suspect; to mistrust*

¶Yoshida ga yatta no de wa nai ka to uta-gaimashita.

吉田がやったのではないかと疑いました。

We suspected that Yoshida had done it.

utagawashii 疑わしい ① *doubtful, questionable* [→**ayashii** 怪しい②]

¶Kachō ga hontō ni shutchō ni itta ka dō ka utagawashii desu.

課長がほんとうに出張に行ったかどうか疑わしいです。

It is doubtful whether the section chief really went on the business trip or not.

② *suspicious, suspicion-arousing, suspicious-looking* [→**ayashii** 怪しい①]

¶Unten-shu wa utagawashii hito desu.

運転手は疑わしい人です。

The driver is a suspicious-looking person.

utau 歌う *to sing*

¶Keiko-chan wa uta o utau koto ga suki desu.

恵子ちゃんは歌を歌うことが好きです。

Keiko likes to sing songs.

¶Watashi-tachi wa orugan ni awasete uta-imasu.

私たちはオルガンに合わせて歌います。

We sing along with the organ.

• hana-uta o utau 鼻歌を歌う *to hum*

útsu 打つ *to strike, to hit, to beat, to knock* [→**tataku** 叩く]

¶Ani wa boku no atama o utta yo.

兄は僕の頭を打ったよ。

My older brother hit me on the head!

¶Senshu wa batto de bōru o uchimashita.

選手はバットでボールを打ちました。

The player hit the ball with the bat.

¶Otoko no ko wa taiko o utte imasu.

男の子は太鼓を打っています。

The boy is beating a drum.

¶Tokei ga san-ji o uchimashita.

時計が3時を打ちました。

The clock struck three.

• hito no kokoro o utsu 人の心を打つ *to move a person, to impress a person*

¶Sono hanashi wa ōi ni kokoro o uchima-shita.

その話は大いに心を打ちました。

That story moved me greatly.

útsu 撃つ ① *to shoot* 《a person, animal, etc.》

¶Hannin wa keikan o kenjū de uchima-shita.

犯人は警官をけん銃で撃ちました。

The criminal shot the police officer with a pistol.

　② *to fire, to shoot* 《a gun》 [→**hassha suru** 発射する]

¶Mainichi shōgo ni taihō o uchimasu.

毎日正午に大砲を撃ちます。

They fire a cannon every day at noon.

¶Ute!

撃て！

Fire!

utsubuse うつぶせ 〜**ni** 〜に *on one's face, on one's stomach, prone* [⇔ **aomuke ni** 仰向けに]

¶Jirō-chan wa utsubuse ni taoreta yo.

次郎ちゃんはうつぶせに倒れたよ。

Jiro fell on his face.

• utsubuse ni naru うつぶせになる *to lie on one's stomach*

utsukushíi 美しい *beautiful, lovely*

¶Kono hana wa totemo utsukushii ne.

この花はとても美しいね。

This flower is very beautiful, isn't it.

¶Nan-to utsukushii keshiki deshō.

何と美しい景色でしょう。

What a lovely view!

¶Onēsan wa utsukushii koe o shite imasu ne.

お姉さんは美しい声をしていますね。

Your older sister has a beautiful voice, doesn't she.

utsumúku うつむく *to look down; to hang one's head*

¶Sono ko wa hazukashi-sō ni utsumuk-imashita.

その子は恥ずかしそうにうつむきました。

That child looked down shyly.

utsúru 写る *to be taken, to come out* 《The subject is a photograph or something photographed.》

¶Hamano-san no shashin wa itsu-mo yoku utsurimasu.

浜野さんの写真はいつもよく写ります。

Ms. Hamano's photographs always come out well.

¶Fuji-san wa kono shashin ni kirei ni ut-sutte iru.

富士山はこの写真にきれいに写っている。

Mt. Fuji looks beautiful in this picture.

utsúru 映る ① *to be reflected*

¶Shiroi kumo ga mizuumi ni utsutte ima-shita.

白い雲が湖に映っていました。

White clouds were reflected on the lake.

　② *to be shown, to be projected* 《on a screen》; *to come in* 《on a television, etc.》

¶Kono terebi wa yoku utsuranai ne.

このテレビはよく映らないね。

(The picture on)this television doesn't come in well, does it.

utsúru 移る ① *to move* 《from one place to another》 《intransitive》 [→**idō suru** 移動する]

¶Watanabe-san wa atarashii ie ni

utsurimashita.

渡辺さんは新しい家に移りました。

Mr. Watanabe moved to a new house.

② *to change, to turn, to shift* 《from one thing to another》 《intransitive》

¶Kisetsu wa natsu kara aki ni utsurimashita.

季節は夏から秋に移りました。

The season changed from summer to fall.

¶Wadai wa tenisu ni utsurimashita.

話題はテニスに移りました。

The topic shifted to tennis.

③ *to be transmitted* 《when the subject is an illness》

¶Otōto no kaze ga haha ni utsurimashita.

弟のかぜが母にうつりました。

My younger brother's cold was transmitted to my mother.

utsúsu 写す ① *to copy; to trace*

¶Sono shi o nōto ni utsushimasu.

その詩をノートに写します。

I'll copy that poem in my notebook.

② *to take* 《a photograph》 [→**toru** 撮る]

¶Kamera-man wa yama no shashin o utsushimashita.

カメラマンは山の写真を写しました。

The photographer took a picture of the mountains.

utsúsu 映す ① *to reflect* 《transitive》

¶Suimen ga tsuki o utsushite imasu.

水面が月を映しています。

The water is reflecting the moon.

② *to project, to show* 《on a screen》

¶Sensei wa suraido o utsushite imasu.

先生はスライドを映しています。

The teacher is showing slides.

utsúsu 移す ① *to move* 《from one place to another》 《transitive》

¶Kore-ra no tsukue o tonari no kyōshitsu ni utsushinasai.

これらの机を隣の教室に移しなさい。

Move these desks to the next classroom.

② *to give, to transmit* 《an illness》

¶Tomodachi ni kaze o utsushite

shimatta.

友達にかぜをうつしてしまった。

I gave my friend my cold.

utsuwa 器 *container, vessel, receptacle*

uttaéru 訴える ① *to appeal for* [→**yobikakeru** 呼び掛ける②]

¶Watashi-tachi wa sekai ni heiwa o uttaete imasu.

私たちは世界に平和を訴えています。

We are appealing to the world for peace.

② *to complain of*

¶Musume wa yoku zutsū o uttaemasu.

娘はよく頭痛を訴えます。

My daughter often complains of headaches.

③ *to make an accusation*

¶Kimura wa kono otoko ga hōseki o nusunda to uttaeta.

木村はこの男が宝石を盗んだと訴えた。

Ms. Kimura made the accusation that this man stole the jewels.

④ *to sue*

¶Higai-sha wa shachō o uttaemashita.

被害者は社長を訴えました。

The vicitim sued the company president.

uttóri うっとり 〜**to** 〜と *absorbedly, with rapture, enchantedly*

¶Imōto wa opera o uttori to kiite iru yo.

妹はオペラをうっとりと聴いているよ。

My younger sister is listening enchantedly to opera!

• uttori suru うっとりする *to be captivated*

uwagi 上着 (*suit*)*coat*, (*sport*)*jacket*

uwamawaru 上回る *to exceed* [→**koeru** 越える②, **kosu** 越す②]

uwasa 噂 *rumor; gossip, idle talk*

• uwasa ni mimi o kasu うわさに耳を貸す *to listen to rumors*

• uwasa o tateru うわさを立てる *to start a rumor*

• uwasa o hiromeru うわさを広める *to spread a rumor*

• hito no uwasa o suru 人のうわさをする *to gossip about a person, to talk about a person*

¶Uwasa o sureba kage.

うわさをすれば影。《proverb》

Speak of the devil and he will appear.
《Literally: *If one talks (about a person),
(that person's)shadow (looms).*》

• uwasa-banashi 噂話 *gossip*

uyamáu 敬う ① *to respect, to esteem* 《a
person》[→**sonkei suru** 尊敬する]
② *to worship* 《a deity》[→**ogamu**
拝む]

úyoku 右翼 [[⇔**sayoku** 左翼]]
① (*political*)*right wing*
② *right field* 《in baseball》[→**raito**
ライト①]
• uyoku-dantai 右翼団体 *right-wing
group*
• uyoku-shu 右翼手 *right fielder* [→
raito ライト②]

uzúmaki 渦巻き *whirlpool, eddy*

uzura 鶉 *quail*

W

wa は《This particle marks the preceding
phrase as the topic of a sentence or as con-
trasting with something else. Although
the phrase preceding **wa** frequently ends
in a noun, there are other possibilities as
well.》
¶Mizuno-san wa san-nen-sei desu.
水野さんは3年生です。
Ms. Mizuno is a third-year student.
¶Amai mono wa tabemasen.
甘い物は食べません。
I don't eat sweet things.
¶Koko ni wa dare-mo imasen.
ここにはだれもいません。
There's no one here.
¶Shumi to shite wa gorufu no hō ga suki
desu.
趣味としてはゴルフのほうが好きです。
As a hobby, I like golf better.
¶Ano eiga o mitai to wa omoimasen.
あの映画を見たいとは思いません。
I don't think I want to see that movie.

¶Yasuku wa nai kedo, kaimashō.
安くはないけど、買いましょう。
It's not cheap, but let's buy it.
¶Osoku nete wa ikemasen.
遅く寝てはいけません。
You mustn't go to bed late.

wá 輪 *circle, ring*
¶Kodomo-tachi wa te o tsunaide wa ni
narimashita.
子供たちは手をつないで輪になりました。
*The children joined hands and formed a
circle.*

wa わ《This sentence-final particle is spoken with rising intonation and expresses
mild exclamation. It is generally used only
by female speakers, and it often occurs in
combination with a following **yo** よ or **ne**
ね.》
¶Kore wa dekinai wa.
これはできないわ。
I can't do this!

wá 和 *peace, harmony* 《between people》

-wa 一羽《counter for birds; see Appendix
2》

wǎ わっ [☞**wā** わあ]

wā わあ《an interjection expressing sur-
prise, hearty approval, or dismay》 *Oh!,
Gee!, Heavens!, Gosh!; Yay!, Hurray!*
¶Wā, kusai!
わあ、臭い！
Gosh, it's smelly!
¶Wā, ureshii!
わあ、うれしい！
Oh, I'm happy!

wabí 詫び *apology*

wabíru 詫びる *to apologize for* [→
ayamaru 謝る]

wabishíi 佗びしい ① *lonely, lonesome*
[→**sabishii** 寂しい]
② *wretched-looking* [→**misuborashii**
みすぼらしい]

wadai 話題 *topic, subject*
¶Wadai o kaemashō.
話題を変えましょう。
Let's change the subject.

wādopuroséssā ワードプロセッサー *word
processor*

Waeijíten 和英辞典 *Japanese-English dictionary*

wafū 和風 *Japanese style, Japanese type*
- wafū no ie 和風の家 *Japanese-style house*

wafuku 和服 *traditional Japanese clothes* [⇔**yōfuku** 洋服②]

wagamáma わがまま *selfishness*
- wagamama na わがままな *selfish*
- ¶Yamakawa-kun wa jitsu ni wagamama da yo.
  山川君は実にわがままだよ。
  Yamakawa is really selfish!

wágo 和語 *native Japanese word* [⇔**gairaigo** 外来語; **kango** 漢語]

wagomu 輪ゴム *rubber band*

waidosukurín ワイドスクリーン *wide (movie)screen*

wáin ワイン *wine* [→**budō-shu** 葡萄酒 (s.v. **budō** 葡萄)]
- wain-gurasu ワイングラス *wineglass*
- aka-wain 赤ワイン *red wine*
- roze-wain ロゼワイン *rosé wine*
- shiro-wain 白ワイン *white wine*

wáipā ワイパー *windshield wiper*

wáiro 賄賂 *bribe*
- wairo o okuru わいろを贈る *to give a bribe*
- wairo o toru わいろを受け取る *to take a bribe*

waishatsu ワイシャツ *dress shirt* «the type typically worn with a suit»

wákaba 若葉 *young leaves, new leaves*

wakái 若い *young* [⇔**toshi-totta** 年取った (s.v. **toshi** 年)]
- ¶Ano kashu wa wakai hito-tachi no aida ni ninki ga aru.
  あの歌手は若い人たちの間に人気がある。
  That singer is popular among young people.
- ¶Abe-san wa toshi no wari ni wa waka-ku miemasu.
  安部さんは年の割には若く見えます。
  Mr. Abe looks young for his age.
- ¶Sofu wa wakai koro jazu ga suki de-shita.
  祖父は若いころジャズが好きでした。
  My grandfather liked jazz when he was young.

wakáme 若布 *wakame* «a kind of edible seaweed»

wakamono 若者 *young person*

wakaré 別れ *parting, farewell, good-by*
- ¶Eiko-san wa tomodachi ni wakare o tsugemashita.
  英子さんは友達に別れを告げました。
  Eiko said good-by to her friends.
- o-wakare-pātī お別れパーティー *farewell party*

wakareme 分かれ目 *turning point*
- ¶Sore ga daitōryō no jinsei no wakareme deshita.
  それが大統領の人生の分かれ目でした。
  That was the turning point in the president's life.

wakaréru 分かれる *to become divided; to branch*
- ¶Sono hon wa san-bu ni wakarete imasu.
  その本は3部に分かれています。
  That book is divided into three parts.
- ¶Kurasu no iken wa kono ten de wakare-te imasu.
  クラスの意見はこの点で分かれています。
  Class opinion is divided on this point.

wakaréru 別れる ① *to part, to say good-by*
- ¶Eki de Kyōko-san to wakaremashita.
  駅で京子さんと別れました。
  I parted from Kyoko at the station.
- ¶Koko de wakaremashō.
  ここで別れましょう。
  Let's say good-by here.
  ② *to get divorced* [→**rikon suru** 離婚する]

wakáru 分かる ① *to understand* «What is understood is treated as a grammatical subject and marked with **ga** が rather than with **o** を.»
- ¶Nihon-go ga wakarimasu ka.
  日本語がわかりますか。
  Do you understand Japanese?
- ¶Hamada-san wa kono bun no imi ga wa-karu darō.

浜田さんはこの文の意味がわかるだろう。
Ms. Hamada probably understands the meaning of this sentence.

¶Ano hito no itte iru koto ga wakarimasu ka.
あの人の言ってることがわかりますか。
Do you understand what that person is saying?

② *to come to know, to find out; to realize, to know* «What is known or realized is treated as a grammatical subject and marked with **ga** が rather than with **o** を.»

¶Yamada-san ga yameta riyū ga wakarimashita.
山田さんが辞めた理由がわかりました。
I found out the reason why Mr. Yamada resigned.

¶Dō sureba ii ka wakarimasen.
どうすればいいかわかりません。
I don't know what I should do.

• wakari-nikui 分かりにくい *hard to understand*

¶Kono hon wa wakari-nikui yo.
この本はわかりにくいよ。
This book is hard to understand!

• wakari-yasui 分かり易い *easy to understand*

¶Kono setsumei wa wakari-yasui.
この説明はわかりやすい。
This explanation is easy to understand.

wákasa 若さ *youth, youthfulness*

¶Kono yo no naka de wakasa ni masaru mono wa arimasen.
この世の中で若さに勝る物はありません。
In this world there is nothing better than youth.

wakasu 沸かす ① *to bring to a boil, to heat until boiling* «The direct object must be a liquid.»

¶O-yu o wakashite kudasai.
お湯を沸かしてください。
Please boil some water.

② *to heat* «a bath to the appropriate temperature»

¶O-furo o wakasu no o wasurenai de.
おふろを沸かすのを忘れないで。

Don't forget to heat the bath.

wake 訳 ① *reason* [→**riyū** 理由]; *cause* [→**gen'in** 原因]

¶Yasunda wake o iinasai.
休んだ訳を言いなさい。
Tell me the reason you stayed home.

¶Dō iū wake de soko e itta no desu ka.
どういう訳でそこへ行ったのですか。
Why did you go there? «Literally: *For what reason did you go there?*»

② *meaning, sense* [→**imi** 意味]

¶Kono Eibun wa wake ga wakarimasen.
この英文は訳がわかりません。
I don't understand the meaning of this English sentence.

③ *the case* «that something is true»

¶Wasureta wake ja nai yo.
忘れた訳じゃないよ。
It's not (the case)that I forgot!

④ ~**ni wa ikanai** ～にはいかない *cannot very well* «following a verb in the nonpast tense»

¶Tochū de akirameru wake ni wa ikanai darō?
途中であきらめる訳にはいかないだろう？
I can't very well give up in the middle, right?

wakéru 分ける *to divide* «something into parts» [→**bunkatsu suru** 分割する]; *to share*

¶Haha wa sono kēki o yattsu ni wakemashita.
母はそのケーキを8つに分けました。
My mother divided the cake into eight pieces.

¶Misako wa chokorēto o Junko to waketa.
美佐子はチョコレートを順子と分けた。
Misako shared the chocolate with Junko.

wakí 脇 ① *the area beside* [→**yoko** 横①]

¶Aite wa boku no waki ni tatte imashita.
相手は僕のわきに立っていました。
My opponent was standing beside me.

¶Jirō wa Tarō no waki ni suwarimashita.
次郎は太郎のわきに座りました。
Jiro sat down beside Taro.

② *armpit, underarm* [→**waki-no-shita**
脇の下]

¶Midori-san wa raketto o waki ni kakaete imasu.

緑さんはラケットをわきに抱えています。
*Midori is holding a racket under her
arm.*

wakidéru 湧き出る *to gush out, to
spurt out, to flow out*

¶Koko ni onsen ga wakidete imasu.

ここに温泉がわき出ています。
A hot spring flows out here.

wakimí 脇見 *looking aside*

• wakimi suru わき見をする *to look aside*

waki-nó-shita 脇の下 *armpit, underarm* [→**waki** 脇②]

wákkusu ワックス *wax* 《used to make a
surface shiny and smooth》

wakú 枠 *frame, enclosing edge*

• waku-gumi 枠組み *framework*

• mado-waku 窓枠 *window frame*

waku 沸く ① *to come to a boil* 《The subject must be a liquid.》

¶O-yu ga waite imasu.

お湯が沸いています。
The water is boiling.

② *to become heated* 《to the appropriate
temperature when the subject is a bath》

¶O-furo ga waite imasu yo.

おふろが沸いていますよ。
The bath is heated!

wákuchin ワクチン *vaccine*

• infuruenza no wakuchin インフルエンザ
のワクチン *influenza vaccine*

wakusei 惑星 *planet*

waméku 喚く *to yell, to scream* [→**sakebu** 叫ぶ]

wán 湾 *bay; gulf*

• Tōkyō-wan 東京湾 *Tokyo Bay*

• Mekishiko-wan メキシコ湾 *the Gulf of
Mexico*

wána 罠 *trap, snare*

• wana ni kakaru わなにかかる *to become
caught in a trap*

• wana o shikakeru わなを仕掛ける *to set
a trap*

¶Suzume o toru tame ni wana o shika-

keyō.

すずめを捕るためにわなをしかけよう。
Let's set a trap to catch sparrows.

wáni わに *crocodile; alligator*

wanmanshő ワンマンショー *one-man
show, solo performance*

wanpaku 腕白 【COL.】 *naughtiness,
brattiness, unruliness* 《of a child》

• wanpaku na わんぱくな *naughty, bratty,
mischievous, unruly*

• wanpaku-bōzu 腕白坊主 *naughty boy*

wanpísu ワンピース *one-piece dress*

wánryoku 腕力 ① *arm strength*

• wanryoku no tsuyoi hito 腕力の強い人
person with strong arms

② *force, violence* [→**bōryoku** 暴力]

¶Gōtō wa wanryoku de Ken kara kaban
o ubaitotta.

強盗は腕力で健からかばんを奪いとった。
*The thief took the bag away from Ken
by force!*

wanshō 腕章 *arm-band*

wánwan わんわん ① *bow-wow,
woof-woof*

¶Sono inu wa watashi ni mukatte wanwan to hoeta.

その犬は私に向かってわんわんとほえた。
That dog barked at me.

② *doggie*

wāpuro ワープロ [☞**wādopurosessā**
ワードプロセッサー]

wára 藁 *straw* 《plant stem》

• wara-buki 藁葺き *straw thatching*

wárabi 蕨 *bracken*

warai 笑い ① *laugh, laughter*

¶Okashikute warai ga tomarimasen.

おかしくて笑いが止りません。
It's so funny I can't stop laughing.

《Literally: *It's funny, and my laughter
won't stop.*》

② *smile* [→**hohoemi** 微笑み]

• warai o ukaberu 笑いを浮かべる *to
wear a smile*

• warai-banashi 笑い話 *joke, funny story*
[→**jōdan** 冗談]

• warai-goe 笑い声 *laughing voice*

• ō-warai 大笑い *big laugh, good laugh*

- ō-warai suru 大笑いする *to have a good laugh*

warau 笑う ① *to laugh*

¶Iin wa minna ōgoe de waraimashita.

委員はみんな大声で笑いました。

The committee members all laughed loudly.

- kusukusu warau くすくす笑う *to chuckle*
- kerakera warau けらけら笑う *to chortle*
- geragera warau げらげら笑う *to guffaw*

② *to smile* [→**hohoemu** 微笑む]

- nikoniko warau にこにこ笑う *to smile beamingly, to beam*

¶Akachan wa watashi o mite nikoniko waratte ita.

赤ちゃんは私を見てにこにこ笑っていた。

The baby was looking at me and beaming.

- nikkori warau にっこり笑う *to smile broadly*
- nitanita warau にたにた笑う *to grin*

wáre 我 *oneself*

- ware ni kaeru 我に返る *to come to, to regain consciousness*

¶Ware ni kaeru to watashi wa byōshitsu no beddo ni nete ita.

我に返ると私は病室のベッドに寝ていた。

When I came to, I was lying in a hospital bed.

- ware o wasureru 我を忘れる *to forget oneself*

¶Ware o wasurete dokusho ni fukette imashita.

我を忘れて読書にふけっていました。

I was so absorbed in reading that I forgot myself.

waremono 割れ物 *fragile item*

wareru 割れる ① *to break into pieces* 《intransitive》; *to crack open* 《intransitive》; *to split* 《intransitive》

¶Sono furui chawan ga waremashita.

その古い茶わんが割れました。

That old teacup broke.

② *to become divided*

wareware 我々 *we, us* [→**watashi**-**tachi** 私たち (s.v. **watashi** 私)]

wari 割 *rate; proportion, ratio* [→**hiri-**

tsu 比率]

¶Ichi-jikan gohyaku-en no wari de haraimashō.

1時間500円の割で払いましょう。

I'll pay at the rate of 500 yen an hour.

- A no wari ni Aの割に *in proportion to A, for A*

¶Chichi wa toshi no wari ni wa wakaku miemasu.

父は年の割には若く見えます。

My father looks young for his age.

- wari ni 割に *relatively, rather* [→**hikaku-teki** (**ni**) 比較的 (に) (s.v. **hikaku**)]

-**wari** 一割 《counter for tenths; see Appendix 2》

¶Seito no ni-wari ga infuruenza ni katta.

生徒の2割がインフルエンザにかかった。

Two tenths of the students have influenza.

wariai 割合 ① [[→**wari** 割]] *rate; proportion, ratio* [→**hiritsu** 比率]

¶Is-shūkan ni ni-satsu no wariai de hon o yonde imasu.

1週間に2冊の割合で本を読んでいます。

I'm reading at the rate of two books a week.

¶Go-tai-san no wariai de su to satō o mazenasai.

5対3の割合で酢と砂糖を混ぜなさい。

Please mix vinegar and sugar in a proportion of 5 to 3.

② (~**ni** ~に) *relatively, rather* [→ **wari ni** 割に]

wariate 割り当て *allotment, quota*

wariatéru 割り当てる *to assign, to allot, to apportion*

¶Haha wa watashi ni o-sara o arau yaku o wariatemashita.

母は私にお皿を洗う役を割り当てました。

My mother assigned the role of washing the dishes to me.

waribashi 割り箸 *disposable wooden chopsticks* 《Provided for customers in most restaurants and for guests at a home meal, these chopsticks are wrapped in paper and must be split apart for use.》

waribiki 割引 *discount*
- waribiki suru 割引する *to discount, to give a discount on*
  - -waribiki −割引《*counter for discounts in steps of 10%; see Appendix 2*》
  ¶Kono tokei o ichi-waribiki de kaimashita.
  この時計を 1 割引で買いました。
  I bought this watch at a 10 percent discount.
  ¶Kono shina wa ni-waribiki desu.
  この品は 2 割引です。
  There is a 20 percent discount on this item. 《*Literally: This item is a 20 percent discount.*》
- waribiki-ken 割引券 *discount ticket*

warikan 割り勘 【COL.】 *splitting the cost*
- warikan ni suru 割り勘にする *to split the cost of*
  ¶Pikunikku no hiyō o warikan ni shimashō.
  ピクニックの費用を割り勘にしましょう。
  Let's split the picnic expenses.

warikómu 割り込む *to cut* 《*in line*》; *to break* 《*into a conversation*》
  ¶Retsu ni warikomanai de kudasai.
  列に割り込まないでください。
  Please don't cut in line.

warízan 割り算 *division* 《*in arithmetic*》 [⇔**kakezan** 掛け算]
- warizan o suru 割り算をする *to divide* [→**waru** 割る③]; *to do division*

waru 割る ① *to break into pieces* 《*transitive*》; *to crack open* 《*transitive*》; *to chop, to split*
  ¶Dare ga kono koppu o watta no desu ka.
  だれがこのコップを割ったのですか。
  Who broke this glass?
- tamago o waru 卵を割る *to crack open an egg*
  ② *to divide* 《*something into parts*》 [→**wakeru** 分ける]; *to apportion* [→**wariateru** 割り当てる]
  ③ *to divide* 《*in arithmetic*》

¶Kyū waru san wa san.
9 割る 3 は 3 。
Nine divided by three is three. 《*Although odd grammatically, this kind of sentence is a typical way of stating a fact of arithmetic.*》

warugí 悪気 *malice, ill will*
- warugi ga atte 悪気があって *out of malice, with ill will*
  ¶Warugi ga atte shita wake ja nai yo.
  悪気があってしたわけじゃないよ。
  It's not that I did it out of malice.

warúguchi 悪口 [☞**warukuchi** 悪口]

warúi 悪い ① *bad* [⇔**ii** いい①]
  ¶Kyō wa tenki ga warui desu ne.
  きょうは天気が悪いですね。
  Today the weather is bad, isn't it.
  ¶Tabako wa kenkō ni warui desu yo.
  たばこは健康に悪いですよ。
  Tobacco is bad for your health!
  ¶Uso o tsuku no wa warui koto da.
  うそをつくのは悪いことだ。
  Telling lies is a bad thing.
  ② *at fault, to blame*
  ¶Sono toki wa boku ga warukatta no desu.
  そのときは僕が悪かったのです。
  That time I was to blame.

warúkuchi 悪口 *bad-mouthing, speaking ill*
- A no warukuchi o iu Aの悪口を言う *to speak ill of A, to bad-mouth A*
  ¶Tanin no warukuchi o itte wa ikenai yo.
  他人の悪口を言ってはいけない。
  You mustn't speak ill of others.

warumono 悪者 *villain, rascal*

wárutsu ワルツ *waltz*
- warutsu o odoru ワルツを踊る *to dance a waltz*

wásabi わさび *Japanese horseradish, wasabi*

washi 鷲 *eagle*

washitsu 和室 *Japanese-style room* [⇔**yōshitsu** 洋室]

washoku 和食 *Japanese cuisine* [⇔**yōshoku** 洋食]

wasuremono 忘れ物 *thing forgotten*

and left behind
- wasuremono o suru 忘れ物をする *to forget something and leave it behind*

wasureppói 忘れっぽい *forgetful*

¶Sofu wa toshi o totte wasureppoku natta.

祖父は年を取って忘れっぽくなった。

My grandfather has grown old and become very forgetful.

wasureru 忘れる ① *to forget, to cease to remember*

¶Hashimoto-san no denwa-bangō o wasurete shimatta.

橋本さんの電話番号を忘れてしまった。

I forgot Mr. Hashimoto's telephone number.

¶Ashita memo-chō o wasurenai de kudasai.

あしたメモ帳を忘れないでください。

Please don't forget your notebooks tomorrow.

② *to leave behind, to forget* (*to take*) [→**okiwasureru** 置き忘れる]

¶Basu no naka ni kamera o wasuremashita.

バスの中にカメラを忘れました。

I forgot my camera in the bus.

¶Dare-ka ga kasa o wasurete ikimashita.

だれかが傘を忘れていきました。

Somebody left an umbrella behind.

watá 綿 ① *cotton* (*plant*), *raw cotton*
② *cotton wadding*
- wata-gashi 綿菓子 *cotton candy*

watakushi 私 【FORMAL for **watashi** 私】

watarídori 渡り鳥 *migratory bird*

wataru 渡る *to cross, to go over, to go across*

¶Nakanishi-san wa Taiheiyō o yotto de watarimashita.

中西さんは太平洋をヨットで渡りました。

Ms. Nakanishi crossed the Pacific in a sailboat.

¶Koko de dōro o watarimashō.

ここで道路を渡りましょう。

Let's cross the road here.

- A no te ni wataru Aの手に渡る *to pass*

into A's possession

wataru 亘る *to extend, to range, to spread* [→**oyobu** 及ぶ]

¶Sono kenkyū wa sanjū-nen ni watarimashita.

その研究は30年にわたりました。

That research extended over 30 years.

watashi 私, *I, me* 《There are several Japanese words for *I*／*me*, and **watashi** is the most commonly used in translation from English. Particularly for male speakers, **watashi** is rather formal. Other words for *I*／*me* include **watakushi** 私, **atashi** あたし, **boku** 僕, and **ore** 俺.》

¶Watashi wa chūgaku-sei desu.

私は中学生です。

I am a junior-high-school student.

¶Kore wa watashi no pen ja nai wa.

これは私のペンじゃないわ。

This isn't my pen!

¶Chichi wa watashi o shikatta yo.

父は私をしかったよ。

My father scolded me!

¶Yumiko-san no tokei wa watashi no yori ii ne.

由美子さんの時計は私のよりいいね。

Yumiko's watch is better than mine, isn't it.

- watashi-tachi 私たち *we, us*

¶Kojima-sensei wa watashi-tachi no Eigo no sensei desu.

小島先生は私たちの英語の先生です。

Ms. Kojima is our English teacher.

watasu 渡す ① *to hand, to pass* [→**tewatasu** 手渡す]

¶Kyōko-san wa sensei ni tegami o watashimashita.

京子さんは先生に手紙を渡しました。

Kyoko handed the teacher a letter.

② *to ferry across*

③ *to place across, to position so as to span*

¶Ano ojisan ga mizo ni ita o watashite kureta.

あのおじさんが溝に板を渡してくれた。

That man put a board across the ditch for us.

wátto わっと ① *with a sudden burst of noise*

¶Katta hito wa watto naki-dashimashita.
勝った人はわっと泣き出しました。
The person who won burst out crying.

② *as a throng, in a crowd*

¶Tokubai ga hajimaru to, kyaku ga watto atsumatta.
特売が始まると、客がわっと集まった。
When the sale starts, the customers will gather in a crowd.

wátto ワット *watt*

• -watto －ワット《counter for watts; see Appendix 2》

¶Hyaku-watto no denkyū mo arimasu ka.
100ワットの電球もありますか。
Do you also have a 100-watt light bulb?

wayaku 和訳 *translation into Japanese*

• wayaku suru 和訳する *to translate into Japanese*

¶Kono Eibun o wayaku shite kudasai.
この英文を和訳してください。
Please translate these English sentences into Japanese.

• Eibun-wayaku 英文和訳 *translation from English into Japanese*

wazá 技 *skill, art, technique* [→**gijutsu** 技術]

¶Ōuchi-san wa jūdō de subarashii waza o miseta.
大内さんは柔道ですばらしい技を見せた。
Mr. Ouchi showed us wonderful judo techniques.

wazá 業 ① *deed, act* [→**kōi** 行為]
② *task* [→**shigoto** 仕事]

wáza-to わざと *on purpose*

¶Waza-to sō itta no desu ka.
わざとそう言ったのですか。
Did you say so on purpose?

• waza-to-rashii わざとらしい *forced, unnatural*

¶Haiyū no warai wa waza-to-rashikatta desu ne.
俳優の笑いはわざとらしかったですね。
The actor's smile was unnatural, wasn't it.

wázawaza わざわざ *to go to all the trouble of* 《in combination with a verb》

¶Oji wa Kōbe kara wazawaza chichi ni ai ni kita.
伯父は神戸からわざわざ父に会いに来た。
My uncle went to all the trouble of coming from Kobe to see my father.

wázuka 僅か ① *a few, a little* [→**sukoshi** 少し]

¶O-kane wa wazuka shika motte imasen.
お金はわずかしか持っていません。
I have only a little money.

② *merely, only*

¶Eki kara aruite wazuka go-fun desu.
駅から歩いてわずか5分です。
It's only five minutes on foot from the station.

• wazuka na わずかな *paltry, scanty, meager, slight*

¶Wazuka ni oboete imasu.
わずかに覚えています。
I remember slightly.

• wazuka na kyūryō わずかな給料 *meager salary*

• wazuka na chigai わずかな違い *slight difference*

Y

yá 矢 *arrow* 《used with a bow》

¶Kōin, ya no gotoshi.
光陰矢のごとし。《proverb》
Time flies. 《Literally: *Time is like an arrow.*》

• ya o hanatsu 矢を放つ *to shoot an arrow*

¶Ryōshi wa sono shika o neratte, ya o hanatta yo.
猟師はその鹿をねらって、矢を放ったよ。
The hunter took aim at that deer and fired an arrow!

• ya-jirushi 矢印 *arrow (-shaped indicator)*

ya や *and* 《Unlike **to** と, the noun-conjoining particle **ya** implies that there are items in addition to those actually mentioned.》

¶Boku wa supagetti ya piza ga suki desu.
僕はスパゲッティやピザが好きです。
I like (things such as) spaghetti and pizza.

yā やあ 【COL.】 *Hi!* 《This greeting is ordinarily restricted to male speakers and is not appropriate for addressing a social superior.》

¶Yā, genki?
やあ、元気？
Hi! How are you?

yaban 野蛮 ～**na** ～な *savage, barbarous*
• yaban-jin 野蛮人 *a savage, a barbarian*

yabu 薮 *thicket*

yabukéru 破ける *to tear* 《intransitive》 [→**yabureru** 破れる①]

yabúku 破く *to tear* [→**yaburu** 破る①] 《transitive》

yaburéru 敗れる *to be defeated, to lose* [→**makeru** 負ける①]

¶Boku-tachi no chīmu wa kesshō de yaburemashita.
僕たちのチームは決勝で敗れました。
Our team was defeated in the final.

yaburéru 破れる ① *to tear* 《intransitive》 [→**sakeru** 裂ける]

¶Kaganda toki ni zubon ga yaburemashita.
かがんだときにズボンが破れました。
When I bent down my pants tore.

¶Sono kāten wa yaburete iru yo.
そのカーテンは破れているよ。
That curtain is torn!

② *to break, to get damaged* [→**kowareru** 壊れる]

yabúru 破る ① *to tear* 《transitive》 [→**saku** 裂く]

¶Jirō wa ano tegami o yabutta yo.
次郎はあの手紙を破ったよ。
Jiro tore that letter!

② *to break, to damage* [→**kowasu** 壊す①]

¶Inu ga kakine o yabutte haitta yo.
犬が垣根を破って入ったよ。
A dog broke the fence and went in!

③ *to break* 《a previous record》

¶Sekiguchi-senshu wa marason de sekai-kiroku o yabutta.
関口選手はマラソンで世界記録を破った。
Sekiguchi broke the world record in the marathon.

④ *to break, to violate*
• yakusoku o yaburu 約束を破る *to break a promise*

⑤ *to defeat, to beat* [→**makasu** 負かす]

¶Seibu wa san tai ichi de Kintetsu o yaburimashita.
西武は3対1で近鉄を破りました。
Seibu beat Kintetsu 3 to 1.

yáchin 家賃 *rent (payment)*

¶Tōkyō no oji wa takai yachin o haratte imasu.
東京の叔父は高い家賃を払っています。
My uncle in in Tokyo is paying high rent.

yachō 野鳥 *wild bird*

yādo ヤード *yard* ((unit of measure))
• -yādo ーヤード 《counter for yards; see Appendix 2》

yagate やがて *soon, before long, by and by* [→**sono uchi** そのうち]

¶Chichi mo yagate wakatte kureru deshō.
父もやがてわかってくれるでしょう。
My father will probably understand me soon.

¶Yagate hi ga kuremashita.
やがて日が暮れました。
Before long it got dark.

¶Yagate haru ga yatte kuru ne.
やがて春がやってくるね。
Spring will come before long, won't it.

¶Ano hito ga koko ni kite yagate ichi-nen ni naru.
あの人がここに来てやがて1年になる。
It'll soon be a year since that person came here.

yági 山羊 *goat*

yahári やはり *as one might expect; just*

as I thought, sure enough

¶Watashi mo yahari kurashikku ga suki desu.

私もやはりクラシックが好きです。

As you might expect, I also like classical music.

¶Kondō-san wa ima mo yahari Kōfu ni sunde iru.

近藤さんは今もやはり甲府に住んでいる。

Just as I thought, Mr. Kondo is still living in Kofu.

¶Isshōkenmei renshū shita ga, yahari dame datta.

一生懸命練習したが、やはりだめだった。

I practiced as hard as I could, but sure enough it was no good.

yáji 野次 *jeering, heckling*
- yaji-uma 野次馬 *curiousity seeker* «*who rushes to see fires, accidents, etc.*»

yajíru 野次る{5} *to jeer, to heckle*

yakamashíi やかましい ① *noisy* [→**urusai** 煩い①]
　② *given to nagging, given to complaining* [→**urusai** 煩い②]
　③ *particular, fussy* [→**urusai** 煩い③]

yakan 夜間 *nighttime, the night hours* [⇔**hiruma** 昼間]
- yakan-hikō 夜間飛行 *night (plane)flight*

yakan やかん *tea kettle*

yáke やけ *desperation, despair*
- yake ni naru やけになる *to despair, to fall into despair*

¶Hiroshi wa yake ni natte, hon o yuka ni tataki-tsuketa.

浩はやけになって本を床にたたきつけた。

Hiroshi fell into despair and threw the book on the floor.

yakedo 火傷 *burn; scald*
- yakedo suru やけどする *to get burned／scalded; to burn／scald* «*The direct object is part of the subject's body.*»

¶Sutōbu ni chikazuki-sugiru to, yakedo suru yo.

ストーブに近づきすぎるとやけどするよ。

If you go too near the heater, you'll get burned.

¶O-yu de te o yakedo shimashita.

お湯で手をやけどしました。

I scalded my hand with hot water.

- yakedo o suru やけどをする *to get a burn／scald*

¶Mata yubi ni yakedo o shita yo.

また指にやけどをしたよ。

I burned my finger again!

yakeru 焼ける ① *to burn* «*intransitive*» [→**moeru** 燃える]

¶Tonari no ie wa yūbe kaji de yakemashita.

隣の家はゆうべ火事で焼けました。

The house next door burned down last night.

　② *to roast, to broil* «*intransitive*»; *to bake* «*intransitive*»

¶Sono sakana ga yakeru made matte kudasai.

その魚が焼けるまで待ってください。

Please wait until that fish is broiled.

　③ *to become suntanned; to become sunburned*

¶Sukī de sonna ni yaketa no?

スキーでそんなに焼けたの？

Did you get so suntanned from skiing?

- hi ni yakeru 日に焼ける *to get tanned in the sun; to get burned in the sun*

yakimono 焼き物 *pottery, ceramic ware*

yakitori 焼き鳥 *small pieces of chicken grilled on bamboo skewers*

yákkai 厄介 *trouble, annoyance* [→**mendō** 面倒]
- A no yakkai ni naru Aのやっかいになる *to become reliant on A* «*for care, support, etc.*»
- yakkai na やっかいな *troublesome, bothersome*

yakkyoku 薬局 *pharmacy*, <*US*>*drugstore*, <*UK*>*chemist's*

yakō 夜行 *overnight train*

¶Boku wa jū-ji-hatsu, Kumamoto-yuki no yakō ni notta.

僕は10時発、熊本行きの夜行に乗った。

I took the 10:00 night train for Kumamoto.

yakú 役 ① *post, office, position, job*

• yaku ni tsuku 役に就く *to take up a post, to assume a position*
¶Ishii-san wa shihai-nin no yaku ni tsukimashita.
石井さんは支配人の役に就きました。
Mr. Ishii took up the post of manager.
② *role, function* [→**yakuwari** 役割]
• yaku o tsutomeru 役を勤める *to play a role, to serve a function*
• yaku ni tatsu 役に立つ *to be useful, to be helpful, to serve a purpose*
¶Kono hon wa yaku ni tatsu shi, omoshiroi yo.
この本は役に立つし、おもしろいよ。
This book is useful and also interesting!
¶Kono hako wa yaku ni tatanai ne.
この箱は役に立たないね。
This box is no use, is it.
③ *part, role* «in a play, etc.»
¶Ane wa Jurietto no yaku o enjimashita.
姉はジュリエットの役を演じました。
My older sister played the part of Juliet.
• yaku-datsu 役立つ [☞**yaku ni tatsu** 役に立つ (above)]

yáku 約 *approximately, about* [→**oyoso** およそ]
¶Koko kara eki made yaku ichi-kiro arimasu.
ここから駅まで約１キロあります。
It's approximately one kilometer from here to the station.

yáku 訳 *translation* [→**hon'yaku** 翻訳]

yaku 焼く ① *to burn* «transitive» [→**moyasu** 燃やす]
¶Otōsan wa ochiba o yaita yo.
お父さんは落ち葉を焼いたよ。
Dad burned the fallen leaves!
② *to roast, to broil* «transitive»; *to bake* «transitive»
¶Haha wa gyūniku o yaite imasu.
母は牛肉を焼いています。
My mother is roasting beef.
¶Keiko-san wa appurupai o yakimashita.
恵子さんはアップルパイを焼きました。
Keiko baked an apple pie.
¶Yūshoku ni sakana o yakimashō.
夕食に魚を焼きましょう。

Let's broil some fish for supper.
③ *to tan* «one's skin»
• hada o yaku 肌を焼く *to tan one's skin*
④ *to print* «from a photographic negative»

yakubá 役場 *public office* (*building*) «in a small town or village»
• machi-yakubi 町役場 *town office*
• mura-yakuba 村役場 *village office*

yakuhin 薬品 ① *medicine, drug* [→**kusuri** 薬]
¶Kono jikken ni wa go-shurui no yakuhin o tsukaimasu.
この実験には５種類の薬品を使います。
We will use five kinds of drugs in this experiment.
② *chemical* (*agent*)

yakúin 役員 *officer, director, executive*

yakumé 役目 *job, role, function* [→**yakuwari** 役割]
¶Sara-arai wa kimi no yakume da yo.
皿洗いは君の役目だよ。
Washing the dishes is your job!
• yakume o hatasu 役目を果たす *to carry out a job, to play a role, to serve a function*
¶Susumu wa gakkō no daihyō to shite no yakume o hatashita.
進は学校の代表としての役目を果たした。
Susumu fulfilled his duties as a school representative.

yakunin 役人 (*government*)*official*

yakusha 役者 *actor, actress* [→**haiyū** 俳優]
• ninki-yakusha 人気役者 *popular actor*

yakushó 役所 *public office* (*building*), *government office* (*building*)
• ku-yakusho 区役所 *ward office*
• shi-yakusho 市役所 *city office*

yakusoku 約束 ① *promise*
¶Kitano-san wa itsu-mo yakusoku o mamorimasu.
北野さんはいつも約束を守ります。
Mr. Kitano always keeps his promises.
¶Maeda-san wa yakusoku o yaburu koto wa arimasen.
前田さんは約束を破ることはありません。

Ms. Maeda never breaks a promise.

• yakusoku suru 約束する *to promise, to give one's word*

¶Noboru-chan wa hayaku okiru to yakusoku shita ne.

登ちゃんは早く起きると約束したね。

Noboru promised that he would get up early, didn't he.

② *appointment, engagement, promise to meet*

¶Sumimasen ga, hoka ni yakusoku ga arimasu.

すみませんが、ほかに約束があります。

I'm sorry, but I have another engagement.

¶San-ji no yakusoku datta ga, Yumi wa konakatta.

3時の約束だったが、由美は来なかった。

It was a 3:00 date, but Yumi didn't come.

• yakusoku suru 約束する *to make an appointment*

yakúsu 訳す *to translate* [→**hon'yaku suru** 翻訳する]

¶Sore o Nihon-go ni yakushite kudasai.

それを日本語に訳してください。

Please translate that into Japanese.

yakuwari 役割 *role, part, function* [→ **yakume** 役目]

• yakuwari o hatasu 役割を果たす *to play a role, to play a part, to serve a function*

¶Akimoto-kun wa seito-kai de jūyō na yakuwari o hatashita.

秋元君は生徒会で重要な役割を果たした。

Akimoto played an important role in the student council.

yákuza やくざ *(Japanese)gangster, yakuza*

yakuzáishi 薬剤師 *pharmacist*

yakyū 野球 *(the game of)baseball*

¶Boku wa yakyū no chīmu ni haitte iru yo.

僕は野球のチームに入っているよ。

I'm on the baseball team!

• yakyū o suru 野球をする *to play baseball*

• yakyū-bu 野球部 *baseball club, baseball team*

• yakyū-fan 野球ファン *baseball fan*

• yakyū-jō 野球場 *baseball stadium, ball park*

• yakyū-senshu 野球選手 *baseball player*

yamá 山 ① *mountain*

¶Kotoshi no natsu wa yama e ikimashō.

今年の夏は山へ行きましょう。

This summer let's go to the mountains.

¶Watashi-tachi wa takai yama ni noborimashita.

私たちは高い山に登りました。

We climbed a high mountain.

② *speculation, venture*

• yama o kakeru 山をかける *to take a calculated risk*

• yama-goya 山小屋 *mountain hut*

• yama-hodo 山ほど *as much as a mountain, amounting to a great deal*

¶Suru koto ga yama-hodo aru n desu.

する事が山ほどあるんです。

I have a mountain of things to do.

• yama-kaji 山火事 *mountain forest fire*

• yama-kuzure 山崩れ *mountain landslide*

• yama-michi 山道 *mountain path*

• yama-mori 山盛り *large serving*

• yama-nobori 山登り *mountain climbing*

yamábiko やまびこ *echo* [→**kodama** こだま]

yama-no-te 山の手 *hillier residential sections of a city, uptown* 《The desirable residential neighborhoods of a Japanese city are typically in hilly areas away from a low-lying downtown area.》 [⇔ **shitamachi** 下町]

yameru 止める ① *to stop (doing)*

¶Kenka o yamete kudasai.

けんかをやめてください。

Please stop quarreling.

¶Yoru osoku neru no o yamenasai.

夜遅く寝るのをやめなさい。

Stop going to bed late at night.

② *to give up, to stop indulging in*

¶Chichi wa tabako o yamemashita.

父はたばこをやめました。

My father gave up smoking.

③ *to give up on, to abandon* «a planned activity»

¶ Totsuzen samuku natta kara, ensoku o yamemashita.

突然寒くなったから、遠足をやめました。

It suddenly got cold, so we gave up the excursion.

yameru 辞める *to resign from, to quit*

¶ Raigetsu tenisu-bu o yameru tsumori desu.

来月テニス部を辞めるつもりです。

I'm planning to quit the tennis club next month.

¶ Uehara-san wa mō sugu gichō o yamemasu.

上原さんはもうすぐ議長を辞めます。

Mr. Uehara will resign from the chair soon.

yamí 闇 *darkness, the dark* [→**kurayami** 暗闇]

¶ Yami no naka o tesaguri de susumimashita.

やみの中を手探りで進みました。

I went forward through the dark by groping.

• yami-yo 闇夜 *dark night*

yámori やもり *gecko*

yamu 止む *to stop, to cease, to end, to die down*

¶ Yuki ga yamimashita.

雪がやみました。

The snow stopped.

¶ Hageshii ame desu ga, ma-mo-naku yamu deshō.

激しい雨ですが、まもなくやむでしょう。

It is violent rain, but it will probably die down soon.

¶ Ame ga futtari yandari shite imasu.

雨が降ったりやんだりしています。

It's raining on and off. 《Literally: Rain is alternately falling and stopping.》

yamu-o-énai やむを得ない *cannot be helped, to be unavoidable*

¶ Tashō no konran wa yamu-o-enai darō.

多少の混乱はやむをえないだろう。

A certain amount of confusion can't be avoided.

¶ Yamu-o-enai jijō de Kōji wa kaisha o yasunda.

やむをえない事情で浩二は会社を休んだ。

Koji was absent from work due to unavoidable circumstances.

yanagi 柳 *willow*

yáne 屋根 *roof*

¶ Yane ni agatte wa ikenai yo.

屋根に上がってはいけないよ。

You mustn't go up on the roof!

• yane-ura-beya 屋根裏部屋 *attic, loft*

yángu ヤング *young person* [→**wakamono** 若者]

yaní 脂 ① *resin* «from a tree»
② *tar* «from burned tobacco»

yaochō 八百長 【COL.】 *fixed game, fixed contest*

¶ Ano shiai wa yaochō datta yo.

あの試合は八百長だったよ。

That game was fixed!

yaoya 八百屋 ① <US>*vegetable store,* <UK>*greengrocer's*
② <US>*vegetable store proprietor,* <UK>*greengrocer*

yappári やっぱり 【COL. for **yahari** やはり】

yáreyare やれやれ *whew* «an interjection expressing relief, fatigue, or disappointment»

yari 槍 *spear; javelin*

• yari-nage 槍投げ *the javelin throw*

yarikata やり方 *way of doing* [→**shikata** 仕方]

¶ Shōgi no yarikata o oshiete kudasai.

将棋のやり方を教えてください。

Please teach me how to play shogi.

¶ Shimada-san wa nan demo jibun no yarikata de yaru.

島田さんは何でも自分のやり方でやる。

Mr. Shimada does everything in his own way.

yarinaósu やり直す *to do over, to redo*

¶ Shachō wa mō ichi-do yarinoasu yō ni itta.

社長はもう一度やり直すように言った。

The company president said to do it over again.

yaritogéru やり遂げる *to accomplish, to complete, to carry through*

¶Kaichō wa sono keikaku o hitori de yaritogemashita.

会長はその計画を一人でやり遂げました。

The chairperson carried through that plan by himself.

yarítori やり取り *giving and taking, reciprocal exchange*

yaru 遣る《In either use of this word the recipient must not be the speaker, the speaker's group, or a person or group with whom the speaker is identifying. In contrast to **ageru** 上げる, the use of **yaru** implies that the recipient is inferior in status to or on very intimate terms with the giver.》 ① *to give* 《to a recipient》

¶Inu ni mizu o yaru no o wasurenai de ne.

犬に水をやるのを忘れないでね。

Don't forget to give water to the dog, OK?

② *to do the favor of* 《following the gerund (-te form) of another verb》

¶Musuko ni kuruma o katte yarimashita.

息子に車を買ってやりました。

I bought a car for my son.

yaru 遣る 【COL. for **suru** する①】 *to do, to engage in*

¶Ima shukudai o yatte iru tokoro da yo.

今宿題をやっているところだよ。

I'm in the middle of doing my homework now!

¶Yūgata made ni kore o yatte shimaimashō.

夕方までにこれをやってしまいましょう。

Let's finish this by late afternoon.

• yatte iku やって行く *to get along, to live*

¶Ōtani-san nara buchō to umaku yatte ikeru.

大谷さんなら部長とうまくやっていける。

If it's Mr. Otani, he can get along well with the department head.

yasai 野菜 *vegetable*

¶Chichi wa niwa de yasai o tsukutte imasu.

父は庭で野菜を作っています。

My father grows vegetables in the garden.

• yasai-sarada 野菜サラダ *vegetable salad*

• yasai-sūpu 野菜スープ *vegetable soup*

yasashii 優しい *kind, nice* [→**shinsetsu na** 親切な]; *gentle, mild*

¶Kono inu wa totemo yasashii me o shite imasu.

この犬はとても優しい目をしています。

This dog has very gentle eyes.

¶Sono obāsan wa shōjo ni totemo yasashiku hanashita.

おばあさんは少女にとても優しく話した。

That old woman spoke to the little girl very kindly.

yasashii 易しい *easy, simple* [→**kantan na** 簡単な①] [⇔**muzukashii** 難しい]

¶Tekisuto wa yasashii Eigo de kaite arimasu.

テキストは易しい英語で書いてあります。

The textbook is written in simple English.

¶Sono shukudai wa omotta yori yasashikatta yo.

その宿題は思ったより易しかったよ。

The homework was easier than I thought!

yasei 野生 〜**no** 〜の *wild, untamed* 《describing an animal》; *wild, uncultivated* 《describing a plant》

¶Yama-michi de yasei no saru o mimashita.

山道で野生の猿を見ました。

I saw a wild monkey on the mountain path.

yaseru 痩せる *to lose weight, to become thinner* [⇔**futoru** 太る]

¶Haha wa ni-kagetsu de go-kiro yasemashita.

母は2か月で5キロやせました。

My mother lost five kilograms in two months.

• yasete iru やせている *to be slender, to be thin*

¶Kyōko-san wa yasete iru ne.

京子さんはやせているね。

Kyoko is slim, isn't she.

- yaseta hito やせた人 *slender person, thin person*

yáshi やし *palm ((tree))*
- yashi no ki やしの木 *palm tree*
- yashi no mi やしの実 *coconut*

yáshin 野心 *ambition, aspiration*
¶Ano wakamono wa yashin ni moete imasu.
あの若者は野心に燃えています。
That young person is burning with ambition.
- yashin-saku 野心作 *an ambitious work*

yashinau 養う ① *to support, to provide a living for* «a family, etc.»
¶Mori-san wa sukunai shūnyū de kazoku o yashinatte iru.
森さんは少ない収入で家族を養っている。
Mr. Mori supports his family on a small income.
② *to bring up, to rear, to raise* [→sodateru 育てる②]
¶Takeda-san wa san-nin no koji o yashinaimashita.
武田さんは3人の孤児を養いました。
Ms. Takeda brought up three orphans.
③ *to train, to cultivate* «an ability, capacity, etc.»
- shūkan o yashinau 習慣を養う *to cultivate a habit*

yasúi 安い *inexpensive, cheap* [⇔takai 高い③]
¶Kono tokei wa yasui desu ne.
この時計は安いですね。
This watch is cheap, isn't it.
¶Motto yasui no o misete kudasai.
もっと安いのを見せてください。
Please show me a cheaper one.
¶Ano mise de wa kamera ga yasuku kaeru yo.
あの店ではカメラが安く買えるよ。
You can buy cameras cheap at that store!

-yasui −やすい *easy to* «Added to verb bases.» [⇔-nikui −にくい]
¶Kono hon wa yomi-yasui yo.
この本は読みやすいよ。
This book is easy to read!

¶Otōto wa kaze o hiki-yasui taishitsu desu.
弟はかぜをひきやすい体質です。
My younger brother easily catches cold.

yasumí 休み ① *rest, break, recess* [→kyūkei 休憩]
¶Jugyō to jugyō no aida ni jup-pun-kan no yasumi ga aru.
授業と授業の間に10分間の休みがある。
There is a ten-minute break between classes.
② *holiday, day off* [→kyūjitsu 休日]; *vacation* [→kyūka 休暇]
¶Kyō wa gakkō wa yasumi desu.
きょうは学校は休みです。
There's no school today. «Literally: Today, as for school, it's a day off.»
③ *absence* «from school, work, etc.» [→kesseki 欠席]
¶Yōko-san wa kyō wa yasumi desu.
洋子さんはきょうは休みです。
Yoko is absent today.

yasúmu 休む ① *to rest, to take a break* [→kyūkei suru 休息する]; *to take a break from*
¶Sukoshi no aida yasumimashō.
少しの間休みましょう。
Let's rest for a while.
¶Sukoshi benkyō o yasumō yo.
少し勉強を休もうよ。
Let's take a break from studying for a little while!
② *to be absent from, to stay home from* [→kesseki suru 欠席する]
¶Kinō wa gakkō o yasunda yo.
きのうは学校を休んだよ。
Yesterday I was absent from school!
③ *to go to bed* [→neru 寝る①]; *to sleep* [→neru 寝る②]
¶Kyō wa hayaku yasumimashō.
きょうは早く休みましょう。
Let's go to bed early tonight.
¶Hayashi-san wa mada yasunde imasu.
林さんはまだ休んでいます。
Mr. Hayashi is still sleeping.

yasúraka 安らか 〜**na** 〜な *peaceful, tranquil*

yasuri 鑢 *file* ((tool))
- A ni yasuri o kakeru Aにやすりをかける *to use a file on A*
- kami-yasuri 紙やすり *sandpaper*

yasuuri 安売り *(bargain)sale* [→**bāgen** バーゲン]
- yasuuri o suru 安売りをする *to have a sale*

¶Ano mise de wa kagu no yasuuri ga arimasu.
あの店では家具の安売りがあります。
At that store they're having a furniture sale.

¶Maishū Doyōbi ni yasuuri ga arimasu.
毎週土曜日に安売りがあります。
They have a sale every Saturday.
- yasuuri suru 安売りする *to sell at a reduced price*

yátai 屋台 ① *roofed street stall* 《Food vendors perpare and serve simple dishes in these stalls, usually on roadsides. The stalls are often on wheels for easy transport.》
② *outdoor dance platform* 《sometimes on a parade float》
- yatai-mise 屋台店 [☞**yatai** 屋台① (above)]

yatō 野党 *opposition party, party out of power* [⇔**yotō** 与党]

yatóu 雇う *to hire, to employ*
¶Sono kaisha de wa keibiin o hachi-nin yatotte imasu.
その会社では警備員を8人雇っています。
At that company they employ eight security guards.

yátsu 奴 【CRUDE for **hito** 人】 *guy, gal*
¶Akira wa ii yatsu da yo.
明はいいやつだよ。
Akira's a nice guy!

yatte kúru やってくる *to come, to come along, to turn up*
¶Hageshii arashi ga yatte kita yo.
激しいあらしがやってきたよ。
A violent storm came along!

¶Mata tsuyu ga yatte kita ne.
また梅雨がやってきたね。
The rainy season has come again, hasn't it.

yatto やっと ① *at last, finally* [→**tsui-ni** 遂に①]
¶Yatto yama-goya ni tōchaku shimashita.
やっと山小屋に到着しました。
At last we arrived at the mountain hut.
② *just barely* [→**karōjite** 辛うじて]
¶Yatto jugyō ni maniaimashita.
やっと授業に間に合いました。
I was just barely in time for class.

yattoko やっとこ *pincers, pliers*

yattsú 八つ *eight* 《see Appendix 2》

yattsukéru やっつける 【COL.】 *to successfully attack, to get; to finish off, to take care of*

yawaragéru 和らげる *to soften, to moderate, to ease*
¶Kono kusuri wa itami o yawaragemasu.
この薬は痛みを和らげます。
This medicine will ease the pain.
- koe o yawarageru 声を和らげる *to soften one's voice*

yawarakái 柔らかい, 軟らかい ① [[⇔**katai** 堅い, 固い, 硬い①]] *soft; flexible, pliant; tender* 《describing meat, etc.》
¶Kono kusshon wa totemo yawarakai yo.
このクッションはとてもやわらかいよ。
This cushion is very soft!

¶Aki no yawarakai hizashi ga dai-suki desu.
秋のやわらかい日ざしが大好きです。
I love the soft sunshine of autumn.

¶Kono sutēki wa yawarakai desu ne.
このステーキはやわらかいですね。
This steak is tender, isn't it.
② *gentle, mild*
- yawarakai koe やわらかい声 *gentle voice*

yáya やや *a little, somewhat, slightly*
¶Aite wa yaya tsukareta yō desu.
相手はやや疲れたようです。
My opponent seems to have gotten somewhat tired.

¶Sore wa yaya ringo ni nite imasu.

それはややりんごに似ています。
That looks a little like an apple.

yayakoshíi ややこしい *complicated* [→ **fukuzatsu na** 複雑な]; *troublesome* [→ **mendō na** 面倒な]

¶Kore wa taihen yayakoshii mondai desu.
これはたいへんややこしい問題です。
This is a very complicated problem.

yó 世 ① *the world, the way the world is, society* [→**seken** 世間]

• kono yo この世 *this world, this life*

• ano yo あの世 *the next world, life after death*

¶Boku wa ano yo o shinjinai yo.
僕はあの世を信じないよ。
I don't believe in the next world!

• yo o saru 世を去る *to leave this world, to die*

¶Sono shijin wa wakai toki ni yo o sarimashita.
その詩人は若いときに世を去りました。
That poet died when he was young.

② [[→**jidai** 時代]] *era; the times*

yó 夜 *night* [→**yoru** 夜]

• yo ga akeru 夜が明ける *day breaks* 《*Literally: Night brightens.*》

¶Mō sugu yo ga akeru deshō.
もうすぐ夜が明けるでしょう。
It will be probably be daybreak soon.

• yo-dōshi 夜通し *all night long*

¶Tanaka-san wa yo-dōshi okite imashita.
田中さんは夜通し起きていました。
Ms. Tanaka was up all night long.

yó 用 *matter to attend to, business, errand* [→**yōji** 用事]

¶Konban wa yō ga arimasu.
今晩は用があります。
I have a matter to attend to this evening.

¶Chichi wa kaisha no yō de Ōsaka e ikimasu.
父は会社の用で大阪へ行きます。
My father is going to go to Osaka on company business.

yó 様 ① ～**na** ～な《The word yō follows a predicate and functions grammatically as an adjectival noun. The word preceding yō cannot be the copula form da だ.

Where da would be the appropriate predicate, **no** の (following a noun) or **na** な (following an adjectival noun) appears instead. It is also possible to use the demonstratives **kono** この, **sono** その, **ano** あの, and **dono** どのbefore yō.》 *like, seeming, apparent, as if* [→**rashii** らしい①]

• A no yō na B AのようなB *a B like A*

¶Tori no yō ni sora o tobu no wa tanoshii deshō.
鳥のように空を飛ぶのは楽しいでしょう。
Flying through the sky like a bird is probably fun.

¶Kono yō na kami ga origami ni wa saiteki desu.
このような紙が折り紙には最適です。
Paper like this is the most suitable for origami.

¶Chichi wa itsu-mo no yō ni shichi-ji ni kitaku shita.
父はいつものように7時に帰宅した。
My father returned home at 7:00 as usual.

¶Jirō wa onīsan no yō ni isshōkenmei benkyō shita.
次郎は兄さんのように一生懸命勉強した。
Jiro studied hard like his older brother.

¶Ishikawa-san wa nani-mo dekinai yō na hito desu ne.
石川さんは何もできないような人ですね。
Mr. Ishikawa is a person who appears unable to do anything.

¶Erebētā ga kowarete iru yō desu.
エレベーターが壊れているようです。
It seems that the elevator is broken.

¶Ame ga furu yō da ne.
雨が降るようだね。
It looks as if it's going to rain, doesn't it.

② ～**ni** ～に *so that, in order to* 《following a verb in the nonpast tense》 [→**tame** 為①]

¶Kyūkō ni maniau yō ni hayaku uchi o deta.
急行に間に合うように早くうちを出た。
I left home early so that I would be in time for the express.

• yō ni suru ようにする *to make sure that,*

to bring it about that «following a verb in the nonpast tense»

¶Zenbu tsukau yō ni shimashō.

全部使うようにしましょう。

Let's make sure that we use it all.

• yō ni naru ようになる *to come about that, to get to the point that* «following a verb in the nonpast tense»

¶Midori wa yatto jitensha ni noreru yō ni natta.

緑はやっと自転車に乗れるようになった。

Midori was finally able to ride a bicycle.

③（〜**ni** 〜に）《Following a verb in the nonpast tense and preceding a verb of requesting, **yō** is used to report a request.》

¶Chichi wa otōto ni ki o tsukeru yō ni chūi shimashita.

父は弟に気をつけるように注意しました。

My father warned my younger brother to be careful.

- **yō** －様 *way of doing, way to do* 《Added to verb bases.》[→**kata** －方]

¶Furui jitensha wa mō naoshi-yō ga arimasen.

古い自転車はもう直しようがありません。

There is no longer any way to fix the old bicycle.

- **yō** －用 〜**no** 〜の *for use in; for use by* 《Added to noun bases.》

¶Ie no mae ni kōji-yō no torakku ga tomatte ita.

家の前に工事用のトラックが止まっていた。

A truck for construction-use was parked in front of the house.

¶Dansei-yō no keshō-hin mo arimasu.

男性用の化粧品もあります。

There are also cosmetics for men.

yo よ《sentence-final particle indicating exclamation》

¶Hitori de ikimashita yo.

一人で行きましたよ。

I went alone!

yoaké 夜明け *dawn, daybreak*

¶Watashi-tachi wa yoake ni shuppatsu shimashita.

私たちは夜明けに出発しました。

We started out at dawn.

yóbi 予備 *reserve, extra supply*

• yobi no 予備の *spare, extra*

¶Yobi no taiya wa nai yo.

予備のタイヤはないよ。

There's no spare tire!

• yobi-chishiki 予備知識 *background knowledge, peliminary knowledge*

• yobi-kō 予備校 *cram school* 《to prepare students for college entrance examinations》

• yobi-senkyo 予備選挙 *primary election*

yobidásu 呼び出す *to call over, to summon over; to page*

¶Hoshino-san o denwa-guchi ni yobidashite kudasai.

星野さんを電話口に呼び出してください。

Please call Ms. Hoshino over to the phone.

¶O-yobidashi itashimasu. Suzuki-sama.

お呼び出しいたします。鈴木様。《public address announcement》

Paging Mr. Suzuki. 《Literally: *I summon. Mr. Suzuki.*》

yobikakéru 呼び掛ける ① *to call out* 《to a person》

¶Kōchō-sensei ga ni-kai kara watashi ni yobikakemashita.

校長先生が２階から私に呼びかけました。

The headmaster called out to me from the second floor.

② *to appeal for* [→**uttaeru** 訴える①]

¶Daitōryō wa kokumin ni shiji o yobikakemashita.

大統領は国民に支持を呼びかけました。

The president appealed to the people for support.

yobō 予防 *prevention*

¶Kaze no yobō ni bitamin-shī o torinasai.

かぜの予防にビタミンＣをとりなさい。

Take vitamin C for prevention of colds.

• yobō suru 予防する *to prevent*

• yobō-chūsha 予防注射 *preventive injection, inoculation*

• Kasai-yobō-shūkan 火災予防週間 *Fire Prevention Week*

yobu 呼ぶ ① *to call, to hail*
¶Takushī o yonda ga tomaranakatta.
タクシーを呼んだが止まらなかった。
I hailed the taxi but it didn't stop.
　② *to call for, to summon, to send for*
¶Sugu o-isha-san o yonde kudasai.
すぐお医者さんを呼んでください。
Please send for the doctor at once!
¶Denwa de takushī o yonde kudasai.
電話でタクシーを呼んでください。
Please telephone for a taxi.
¶Yanagisawa-kun, Katō-sensei ga yonde
iru yo.
柳沢君、加藤先生が呼んでいるよ。
*Yanagisawa, Ms. Kato is calling for
you!*
　③ *to invite* [→**shōtai suru** 招待する]
¶Uno-san o shokuji ni yobimashita.
宇野さんを食事に呼びました。
I invited Ms. Uno to dinner.
　④ *to call out, to say out loud*
¶Sensei wa seito no namae o yobimashita.
先生は生徒の名前を呼びました。
*The teacher called out the student's
name.*
　⑤ *to call, to name*
¶Masa to yonde kudasai.
マサと呼んでください。
Please call me Masa.

yobun 余分 *an excess, a surplus*
• yobun no 余分の *extra, spare, surplus*
[→**yokei na** 余計な②]
¶Ikura-ka yobun no o-kane o motte
imasu ka?
いくらか余分のお金を持っていますか？
Do you have any extra money?

yōchi 幼稚 ～**na** ～な *childish, infantile*
¶Sore wa yōchi na iken desu ne.
それは幼稚な意見ですね。
That is a childish opinion, isn't it.

yóchi 余地 (*available*)*room, margin,
leeway* [→**yoyū** 余裕]
¶Soko ni mō ichi-dai no jitensha o oku
yochi ga aru.
そこにもう1台自転車を置く余地がある。
*There's room to put one more bicycle
there.*

yōchíen 幼稚園 *pre-school, kindergarten*

yōdái 容体, 容態 *condition* 《*of one who
is ill*》
¶Sofu no yōdai ga akka shimashita.
祖父の容体が悪化しました。
My grandfather's condition got worse.

yodare 涎 *drool*
• yodare ga deru よだれが出る *drool
comes out*

yōfuku 洋服 ① *clothes* [→**fuku** 服]
¶Kawada-san no yōfuku wa nurete
imasu.
川田さんの洋服はぬれています。
Mr. Kawada's clothes are wet.
　② *Western-style clothes* [⇔**wafuku**
和服]
• yōfuku-dansu 洋服だんす (*clothes-stor-
age*)*wardrobe*
• yōfuku-ya 洋服屋 *tailor; tailor shop*

yógan 溶岩 *lava*

yogen 予言 *prophecy, prediction*
¶Keizai-gaku-sha no yogen ga atarimashita.
経済学者の予言が当たりました。
The economist's prediction proved true.
• yogen suru 予言する *to foretell, to pre-
dict*
¶Senkyo no kekka wa dare mo yogen dekimasen.
選挙の結果はだれも予言できません。
*No one can foretell the results of the elec-
tion.*
• yogen-sha 予言者 *prophet*

yōgi 容疑 *suspicion of having commit-
ed a crime*
¶Ano hito wa satsujin no yōgi de taiho
saremashita.
あの人は殺人の容疑で逮捕されました。
*That person was arrested on suspicion of
murder.*
• yōgi-sha 容疑者 (*crime*)*suspect*

yogi-nái 余儀ない *unavoidable*

yōgo 用語 *term, terminology*
• senmon-yōgo 専門用語 *technical term,
technical terminology*

yogore 汚れ *dirt, grime; stain* [→**shimi**

染み〕

•yogore o otosu 汚れを落とす *to wash off dirt; to get out a stain*

¶Ani wa jitensha no yogore o otoshimashita.

兄は自転車の汚れを落としました。

My older brother washed the dirt off his bicycle.

•yogore-mono 汚れ物 *dirty things; dirty clothes*

yogoreru 汚れる *to become dirty, to become stained*

¶Sono hankachi wa yogorete imasu.

そのハンカチは汚れています。

That handkerchief is dirty.

¶Shiroi kuruma wa ame no hi ni wa sugu yogoremasu.

白い車は雨の日にはすぐ汚れます。

A white car soon gets dirty on a rainy day.

¶Yogoreta te de sawaranai de.

汚れた手で触らないで。

Don't touch it with dirty hands.

¶Kono atari no kūki wa yogorete iru ne.

この辺りの空気は汚れているね。

The air around here is dirty, isn't it.

yogosu 汚す *to make dirty, to stain*

¶Fuku o yogoshite wa dame yo.

服を汚してはだめよ。

You mustn't get your clothes dirty!

¶Junko-chan wa kono kami o inku de yogoshita yo.

順子ちゃんはこの紙をインクで汚したよ。

Junko stained this paper with ink!

yōgúruto ヨーグルト *yogurt*

yohō 予報 *forecast*

•tenki-yohō 天気予報 *weather forecast*

yohodo 余程 ① *very, extremely* [→**hijō ni** 非常に]

¶Ano kashu wa yohodo kanemochi ni chigai-nai.

あの歌手はよほど金持ちに違いない。

That singer must be very rich.

② *by far, much* [→**zutto** ずっと③]

¶Kono heya no hō ga yohodo suzushii desu ne.

この部屋のほうがよほど涼しいですね。

This room is much cooler, isn't it.

yói 良い [☞**ii** いい]

yói 用意 *preparation* [→**junbi** 準備]

•yōi o suru 用意をする *to make preparations, to get ready*

¶Haha wa yūshoku no yōi o shite imasu.

母は夕食の用意をしています。

My mother is making the preparations for supper.

•yōi ga dekiru 用意ができる *preparations become completed*

¶Chōshoku no yōi ga dekimashita.

朝食の用意ができました。

Breakfast is ready. 《Literally: *Breakfast preparations have been completed.*》

¶Shuppatsu no yōi wa dekimashita ka.

出発の用意はできましたか。

Are you ready to start out? 《Literally: *Have the preparations for starting out been completed?*》

¶Yōi, don.

用意、どん。

Ready, go! 《when starting a race》

•yōi suru 用意する *to prepare, to get ready* 《transitive or intransitive》

yōi 容易 ～**na** ～な *easy, not difficult* [→**yasashii** 易しい]

yōji 用事 *matter to attend to, business, errand* [→**yō** 用]

yōji 幼児 *young child, preschool child*

yōji 楊枝 *toothpick* [→**tsumayōji** 爪楊枝]

yōjin 用心 *heed, caution, prudence* [→**chūi** 注意②]

•yōjin suru 用心する *to take care, to be careful; to take care with, to be careful of*

¶Tabe-suginai yō ni yōjin shinasai.

食べすぎないように用心しなさい。

Be careful not to eat too much.

•yōjin-bukai 用心深い *very careful, very cautious*

¶Gādoman wa yōjin-bukaku atari o mimawashita.

ガードマンは用心深く辺りを見回した。

The guard looked around very carefully.

yóka 余暇 *leisure time, spare time* [→

hima 暇②〕

¶Chichi wa yoka ni e o kaku no ga shumi desu.

父は余暇に絵をかくのが趣味です。

My father's hobby is painting in his leisure time.

yōka 八日《see Appendix 2》 ① *eight days*

② *the eighth* 《day of a month》

yokei 余計 ① (〜**ni** 〜に) *more than ordinarily; even more* 〔→**issō** 一層〕

¶Kurai kara, yokei kowai n desu.

暗いから、よけい怖いんです。

Because it's dark, it's even more frightening.

② 〜**na** 〜な *excess, surplus, extra* 〔→**yobun no** 余分の〕

¶Yokei na o-kane wa zenzen nai yo.

よけいなお金は全然ないよ。

I don't have any extra money!

¶Denwa-dai o gojū-en yokei ni haratte shimatta.

電話代を50円よけいに払ってしまった。

I paid 50 yen too much for the telephone bill.

③ 〜**na** 〜な *unnecessary, uncalled-for*

¶Yokei na koto wa iwanai hō ga ii yo.

よけいな事は言わないほうがいいよ。

It's better not to say uncalled-for things!

yokéru 避ける *to avoid* 〔→**sakeru** 避ける〕; *to make way for*

¶Hodō ni tatte, kuruma o yokenasai.

歩道に立って、車をよけなさい。

Stand on the sidewalk and make way for the car.

yōki 陽気 ① 〜**na** 〜な *cheerful, merry* 〔⇔**inki na** 陰気な〕

¶Yōki na uta o utaō yo.

陽気な歌を歌おうよ。

Let's sing cheerful songs!

¶Keiko-chan wa totemo yōki na ko desu.

恵子ちゃんはとても陽気な子です。

Keiko is a very cheerful child.

¶Yōko-san wa yōki ni waratte imashita.

洋子さんは陽気に笑っていました。

Yoko was laughing merrily.

② *seasonal weather, (short-term) weather pattern* 〔→**tenkō** 天候〕

yokin 預金 ① *depositing money* 《in a bank, etc.》

• yokin suru 預金する *to deposit money; to deposit* 《money》

¶Haha wa ginkō ni goman-en yokin shimashita.

母は銀行に5万円預金しました。

My mother deposited 50,000 yen in the bank.

② *money on deposit*

¶Yūbin-kyoku ni yokin ga niman-en arimasu.

郵便局に預金が2万円あります。

I have 20,000 yen on deposit in the post office.

¶Ginkō kara yokin o ichiman-en hiki-dashimashita.

銀行から預金を1万円引き出しました。

I withdrew 10,000 yen from the bank.

• yokin-tsūchō 預金通帳 *bankbook, passbook*

• futsū-yokin 普通預金 *ordinary deposit*

• teiki-yokin 定期預金 *fixed-time deposit*

yokka 四日《see Appendix 2》 ① *four days*

② *the fourth* 《day of a month》

yoko 横 ① *side (part); the area beside*

¶Mama no yoko ni suwaritai yo.

ママの横に座りたいよ。

I want to sit beside Mama!

¶Yoko no iriguchi kara tatemono ni hairimashita.

横の入口から建物に入りました。

I entered the building from the side entrance.

• yoko o muku 横を向く *to turn one's face to the side*

② *width* 《as opposed to height or length》〔⇔**tate** 縦①〕

¶Kono hako wa yoko ga gojū-roku senchi arimasu.

この箱は横が56センチあります。

The width of this box is 56 centimeters.

③ 〜**no** 〜の [→**tate no** 縦の②] *hoŗizontal; side-by-side*
- yoko no sen 横の線 *horizontal line*
- yoko ni naru 横になる *to lie down* [→**yokotawaru** 横たわる]

yokogao 横顔 ① *profile, side-view of a face*
② *profile, brief description*

yokogíru 横切る{5} *to cross, to go across* 《the short way from one side to the other of something long and narrow》
¶Koko de dōro o yokogitte wa ikemasen.
ここで道路を横切ってはいけません。
You must not cross the street here.

yokoku 予告 *advance notice*
- yokoku suru 予告する *to give advance notice of, to announce in advance*
- yokoku-hen 予告編 *preview* 《of a movie, television program, etc.》

yōkoso ようこそ *welcome* 《as a greeting》
¶Yōkoso Nihon e.
ようこそ日本へ。
Welcome to Japan.
¶Yōkoso irasshaimashita.
ようこそいらっしゃいました。
I'm glad you came. 《Literally: Welcome you came.》

yokotaéru 横たえる *to lay down, to put down horizontally*
¶Byōnin wa beddo ni karada o yokotaemashita.
病人はベッドに体を横たえました。
The ill person laid himself on the bed.

yokotawáru 横たわる *to lie down*
¶Chichi wa sofā ni yokotawarimashita.
父はソファーに横たわりました。
My father lay down on the sofa.

yokú 欲 *desire, want*
¶Yumi-san wa yoku no nai hito desu.
由美さんは欲のない人です。
Yumi is a person of no wants.
- chishiki-yoku 知識欲 *desire for knowledge*
- shoku-yoku 食欲 *appetite*

yóku 良く ① *well* 《This word is the regular adverbial form of **yoi** 良い, but it is also used as the (irregular) adverbial

form of **ii** いい》
¶Yūbe wa yoku nemuremashita ka.
ゆうべはよく眠れましたか。
Were you able to sleep well last night?
¶Fujimori-san no koto wa yoku shitte imasu.
藤森さんのことはよく知っています。
I know Mr. Fujimori well.
¶Kono shashin o yoku mite kudasai.
この写真をよく見てください。
Please look at this picture carefully.
¶Yoku yatta yo.
よくやったよ。
Well done! 《Literally: You did it well!》
¶Yoku kimashita ne.
よく来ましたね。
How nice of you to come. 《Literally: You came well, didn't you.》
② *often* [→**tabitabi** 度々]
¶Hideko-chan wa yoku chikoku suru ne.
秀子ちゃんはよく遅刻するね。
Hideko is often late, isn't she.
¶Ani to yoku tsuri ni iku yo.
兄とよく釣りに行くよ。
I often go fishing with my older brother!

yoku− 翌− *the next, the following* 《Added to bases denoting regularly recurring time spans.》
- yoku-asa 翌朝 *the next morning, the following morning*
- yoku-jitsu 翌日 *the next day, the following day*
- yoku-nen 翌年 *the next year, the following year*

yokubarí 欲張り ① *greed*
- yokubari na 欲張りな *greedy*
② *greedy person*

yokubō 欲望 *desire, want* [→**yoku** 欲]

yokushitsu 浴室 *bathroom* 《Toilets and the bathtubs are traditionally in separate rooms in Japan. This word refers to a room for taking a bath.》 [→**furo−ba** 風呂場 (s.v. **furo** 風呂)]

yokusō 浴槽 *bathtub* [→**yubune** 湯船]

yōkyū 要求 [[→**seikyū** 請求]] *demand; request*
- yōkyū suru 要求する *to demand; to*

request

• A ni B o yōkyū suru AにBを要求する
*to demand B from／of A to request B
from／of A*

¶Higai-sha wa basu-gaisha ni o-kane o
yōkyū shimashita.

被害者はバス会社にお金を要求しました。
*The victim demanded money from the
bus company.*

¶Shichō ni yakusoku o mamoru yō yōkyū shimashita.

市長に約束を守るよう要求しました。
*We requested that the mayor keep his
promise.*

yome 嫁 ① *bride* [→**hanayome** 花嫁]；
wife [→**tsuma** 妻]

② *daughter-in-law* [⇔**muko** 婿]

• o-yome-san お嫁さん 【HON. for
yome (above)】

yomikatá 読み方 ① *way of reading*

② *reading, pronunciation* 《*of a Chinese
character*》

yōmō 羊毛 *wool*

• yōmō-seihin 羊毛製品 *woolen manufactured article*

yómu 読む *to read*

¶Tokidoki beddo de hon o yomimasu.

時々ベッドで本を読みます。
I sometimes read a book in bed.

¶Ani wa manga no hon o yonde imasu.

兄は漫画の本を読んでいます。
*My older brother is reading a comic
book.*

¶Koe o dashite yonde kudasai.

声を出して読んでください。
Please read aloud.

¶Imōto wa kodomo-tachi ni hon o yonde
imasu.

妹は子供たちに本を読んでいます。
*My younger sister is reading a book to
the children.*

¶Igirisu no shōsetsu o yonda koto ga
arimasu ka.

イギリスの小説を読んだことがありますか。
Have you ever read an English novel?

yón 四 *four* [→**shi** 四] 《see Appendix 2》

yonaká 夜中 *the late night hours*

yo-nó-naka 世の中 *the world, the way
the world is, society* [→**seken** 世間]

¶Yo-no-naka wa semai mono desu ne.

世の中は狭いものですね。
It's a small world, isn't it.

¶Yo-no-naka ga kawarimashita.

世の中が変わりました。
The world has changed.

yopparai 酔っぱらい 【COL.】 *drunk-
en person*

• yopparai-unten 酔っぱらい運転 *drunk-
en driving*

• yopparai-unten-sha 酔っぱらい運転者
drunken driver

yopparau 酔っ払う 【COL. for you
酔う①】 *to get drunk*

¶Hirokawa-san wa sono toki yopparatte
ita yo.

広川さんはそのとき酔っぱらっていたよ。
Ms. Hirokawa was drunk then!

yoppodo よっぽど 【COL. for **yohodo**
余程】

yōrei 用例 *usage example*

¶Sensei wa ikutsu-ka no yōrei o agete
setsumei shita.

先生はいくつかの用例をあげて説明した。
*The teacher explained it by giving several
usage examples.*

yóri より ① *than* 《This word is used in
comparisons and can follow either a noun
or a verb.》

¶Chichi wa haha yori toshishita desu.

父は母より年下です。
My father is younger than my mother.

¶Kono hon wa ano hon yori omoshiroi
yo.

この本はあの本よりおもしろいよ。
*This book is more interesting than that
one!*

¶Eigo yori sūgaku ga suki desu.

英語より数学が好きです。
I like mathematics better than English.

¶Shōsetsu wa yomu yori kaku hō ga tanoshii yo.

小説は読むより書くほうが楽しいよ。
*Writing novels is more fun than reading
them!* 《*Literally: As for novels, writing is*

more enjoyable than reading!»

② 【FORMAL for **kara** から①】
from, out of, off of «noun-following particle»

③ 【FORMAL for **kara** から②】
from, since, 〈*beginning*〉 *at,* 〈*beginning*〉 *on* «noun-following particle»

yoridori 選り取り *choosing and taking what one likes*
¶Yoridori sen-en
「選り取り1000円」《on a sign in a store》
Your choice, 1,000 yen

yorikakáru 寄り掛かる *to lean* (*for support*) «intransitive»
¶Tantei wa ki ni yorikakatte imashita.
探偵は木に寄りかかっていました。
The detective was leaning against the tree.
¶Tesuri ni yorikakaranai de kudasai.
手すりに寄りかからないでください。
Please don't lean on the handrail.

yorimichi 寄り道 *stopping off on the way*
•yorimichi suru 寄り道する *to stop off on the way*
¶Yorimichi shinai de massugu kaerinasai.
寄り道しないでまっすぐ帰りなさい。
Come straight home without stopping off on the way.

yoroi 鎧 *armor*

yorokobaséru 喜ばせる *to please, to make happy* «This word is the regular causative form of **yorokobu** 喜ぶ.»
¶Sono akachan o yorokobaseru no wa kantan desu.
その赤ちゃんを喜ばせるのは簡単です。
Pleasing that baby is easy.

yorokobi 喜び *joy, pleasure, delight*
¶Go-ryōshin wa yorokobi de ippai deshita.
ご両親は喜びでいっぱいでした。
The parents were filled with joy.
¶Ongaku o kiku koto ga ane no nani-yori no yorokobi desu.
音楽を聴くことが姉の何よりの喜びです。
Listening to music is my older sister's greatest pleasure.

yorokóbu 喜ぶ *to become glad, to become pleased; to become glad about, to become pleased at*
¶Keiko mo Yūji no seikō o totemo yorokonde imasu.
恵子も雄二の成功をとても喜んでいます。
Keiko is also very pleased with Yuji's success.
¶Kimi wa sono shirase o kiite yorokonda yo.
喜美はその知らせを聞いて喜んだよ。
Kimi heard that news and was glad!
•yorokonde 喜んで *with pleasure, gladly* «This form is the gerund (-**te** form) of **yorokobu**, and it has the predictable range of meanings as well.»
¶Yorokonde oshiete ageru yo.
喜んで教えてあげるよ。
I'll gladly teach you!

yóron 世論 *public opinion* [→**seron** 世論]
•yoron-chōsa 世論調査 *public opinion poll*

Yōróppa ヨーロッパ *Europe*
•Yōroppa-jin ヨーロッパ人 *a European*

yoroshii 宜しい 【FORMAL for **ii** いい②】 *all right, very well*
¶Yoroshii, mō ichi-do mimashō.
よろしい、もう一度見ましょう。
Very well, I will look one more time.
¶Kore de yoroshii desu ka.
これでよろしいですか。
Is this all right?

yoroshiku 宜しく《This word is the regular adverbial form of **yoroshii** 宜しいand has the predictable range of meanings as well.》 ① ～**onegai shimasu** ～お願いします *I humbly beg you, I ask you kindly* 《This statement is a polite way of asking for a favor when it is clear what that favor is. When addressed to a person one has just met, the favor is understood to be something like *treating me well in the future.* The statement is often preceded by **dōzo** どうぞ, and it is frequently abbreviated by omitting **onegai shimasu**.》
¶Hajimemashite. Suzuki desu. Dōzo yoro-

shiku.

始めまして。鈴木です。どうぞよろしく。

How do you do? I'm Suzuki. Glad to meet you.

② ～**tsutaete kudasai** ～伝えてください

Please say hello, Please give my best 《This request is frequently abbreviated by omitting **tsutaete kudasai.**》

¶Yōko-san ni yoroshiku tsutaete kudasai.

洋子さんによろしく伝えてください。

Please say hello to Yoko.

yóru 夜 *night, nighttime* [→**ban** 晩][⇔ **hiru** 昼②]

¶Yoru osoku made benkyō shite imashita.

夜遅くまで勉強していました。

I was studying until late at night.

¶Ani wa Kin'yō no yoru ni hikōki de Pari ni mukatta.

兄は金曜の夜に飛行機でパリに向かった。

My older brother will go to Paris by plane on Friday night.

¶Kinō no yoru wa jū-ji ni nemashita.

きのうの夜は10時に寝ました。

Last night I went to bed at 10:00.

¶Yoru hachi-ji made ni modorinasai.

夜8時までに戻りなさい。

Come back by 8:00 p.m.

• yoru-gohan 夜ご飯 *evening meal, dinner, supper* [→**yūshoku** 夕食]

yoru 因る, 拠る ① *to be due, to be caused*

¶Jiko wa unten-shu no fuchūi ni yoru mono deshita.

事故は運転手の不注意によるものでした。

The accident was due to the driver's carelessness.

② *to be based* [→**motozuku** 基づく]

¶Kono keikaku wa kachō no kangae ni yoru mono desu.

この計画は課長の考えによるものです。

This plan is based on the section chief's idea.

• A ni yoru to Aによると *according to A*

¶Kyō no shinbun ni yoru to, Nagoya de taika ga atta sō desu.

きょうの新聞によると、名古屋で大火があったそうです。

According to today's paper, there was a big fire in Nagoya.

• A ni yoreba Aによれば *according to A*

③ *to depend, to be contingent*

¶Shiai ga okonawareru ka dō ka wa tenkō ni yoru.

試合が行われるかどうかは天候による。

Whether the game will be played or not depends on the weather.

yoru 寄る ① *to get near, to approach close* [→**chikazuku** 近付く]

¶Motto hi ni yorinasai.

もっと火に寄りなさい。

Get nearer to the fire.

② *to drop in, to stop by* [→**tachiyoru** 立ち寄る]

¶Kyō kaeri ni ano mise e yoru yo.

きょう帰りにあの店へ寄るよ。

I'll stop by at that store today on my way home!

③ *to gather, to get together* 《intransitive》《The subject must be animate.》

yóryō 要領 ① *the point, the gist* [→ **yōten** 要点]

• yōryō o eru 要領を得る *to become to the point*

¶Ōkura-daijin no kotae wa yōryō o ete ita.

大蔵大臣の答えは要領を得ていた。

The Finance Minister's answers were to the point.

② *knack* [→**kotsu** こつ]

• yōryō ga ii 要領がいい *efficient* 《describing a person》; *shrewd*

yōsai 洋裁 *dressmaking, sewing Western-style clothes*

yosan 予算 *budget, estimate of expenditures*

• yosan o tateru 予算を立てる *to prepare a budget*

¶Haha wa ryokō no yosan o tatemashita.

母は旅行の予算を立てました。

My mother prepared a budget for the trip.

yōsan 養蚕 *sericulture*

yōsei 妖精 *fairy*

yōseki 容積 *capacity, volume* 《of a container》

yosen 予選 *preliminary (competition); primary (election)*
¶Fuji-senshu wa hyaku-mētoru no yosen o tsūka shita.
藤選手は100メートルの予選を通過した。
Sato got through the 100-meter preliminary.

yoseru 寄せる [[→**chikazukeru** 近付ける①]] *to bring near, to put close; to let come near, to let approach*
¶Seito-tachi wa tsukue o mado-giwa ni yosemashita.
生徒たちは机を窓ぎわに寄せました。
The students put their desks close to the windows.
• A ni kokoro o yoseru Aに心を寄せる *to feel for A; to take to A* 《A is ordinarily a person.》

yōshi 用紙 *paper* 《for a specific use》; *form* 《to fill in》
¶Kono yōshi ni kinyū shite kudasai.
この用紙に記入してください。
Please fill in this form.
• kaitō-yōshi 解答用紙 *answer sheet*
• shiken-yōshi 試験用紙 *examination paper*

yōshi 養子 *adopted child*

yōshi 陽子 *proton* [⇔**denshi** 電子; **chūsei-shi** 中性子 (s.v. **chūsei** 中性)]

yōshi よし *All right, OK* 《an interjection expressing resolve, agreement, or solace》

yōshiki 様式 *style, form, mode*
¶Kono jiin wa romanesuku yōshiki de taterareta.
この寺院はロマネスク様式で建てられた。
This temple has been built in Roman style.
• seikatsu-yōshiki 生活洋式 *lifestyle*

yōshitsu 洋室 *Western-style room* [⇔**washitsu** 和室]

yōshoku 養殖 *raising, culture, farming* 《in the sense of increasing the yield of a marine product by artificial means》
• yōshoku suru 養殖する *to raise, to cul-*

ture, to farm
• shinju no yōshoku 真珠の養殖 *pearl culture*
• yōshoku-jō 養殖場 〈*fish*〉 *farm,* 〈*oyster*〉 *bed*

yōshoku 洋食 *Western-style food* [⇔ **washoku** 和食]

yoshū 予習 *preparing what is to be learned, studying beforehand* [⇔**fukushū** 復習]
• yoshū suru 予習する *to prepare, to study beforehand*
¶Ashita no yoshū o shimashō.
あしたの予習をしましょう。
Let's prepare for tomorrow's lesson.
《Literally: Let's do tomorrow's preparation.》

yōso 要素 *element, factor*

yoso 余所 *another place, somewhere else*
¶Pen o doko-ka yoso ni wasureta ni chigai-nai.
ペンをどこかよそに忘れたに違いない。
I must have forgotten the pen somewhere else.
¶Tabako wa doko-ka yoso de sutte kudasai.
たばこはどこかよそで吸ってください。
Please smoke somewhere else.
• yoso no hito よその人 *stranger, outsider*

yosō 予想 *expectation, anticipation, supposition*
¶Watashi no yosō ni hanshite Yoshioka-kun wa shiken ni ochita.
私の予想に反して吉岡君は試験に落ちた。
Contrary to my expectations, Yoshioka failed on the examination.
• yosō suru 予想する *to expect, to anticipate*
• yosō-dōri 予想通り *as expected*

yosomi 余所見 *looking away*
• yosomi suru 余所見する *to look away*

yōsu 様子 ① *state of affairs, situation, condition* [→**jōtai** 状態]
¶Tokuhain ga sensō no yōsu o hōkoku shimashita.
特派員が戦争の様子を報告しました。

The correspondent reported the war situation.

② *appearance; air, manner; sign, indication*

¶Suchuwādesu wa hidoku tsukareta yōsu desu.

スチュワーデスはひどく疲れた様子です。

The stewardess appears to be terribly tired.

¶Ano hito no yōsu wa okashii ne.

あの人の様子はおかしいね。

That person's manner is strange, isn't it.

¶Kono sora no yōsu de wa, ashita wa ame deshō.

この空の様子では、あしたは雨でしょう。

By the appearance of this sky, tomorrow it will probably rain.

¶Yuki ga furi-sō na yōsu desu.

雪が降りそうな様子です。

It looks likes snow. 《*Literally: It's an appearance that it looks as if snow will fall.*》

yósu 止す [[→**yameru** 止める]] ① *to stop* (*doing*)

¶Sonna koto wa yoshinasai.

そんなことはよしなさい。

Stop doing that kind of thing.

② *to give up, to stop indulging in*

¶Chichi wa sake o yoshimashita.

父は酒をよしました。

My father gave up liquor.

③ *to give up on, to abandon* 《*a planned activity*》

¶Kyō no tozan wa yoshimasu.

きょうの登山はよします。

We will abandon today's mountain climb.

yōsúru-ni 要するに *in short, to sum up* [→**tsumari** 詰まり②]

¶Yōsuru-ni, sono kangae wa ayamari datta no da.

要するに、その考えは誤りだったのだ。

In short, that idea was mistaken.

yotei 予定 *plan*(*s*), *arrangement, schedule*

¶Kondo no Nichiyōbi wa nani-ka yotei ga arimasu ka.

今度の日曜日は何か予定がありますか。

Do you have any plans this coming Sunday?

¶Shachō wa yotei o henkō shimashita.

社長は予定を変更しました。

The company president changed his plans.

¶Hikōki wa yotei yori sanjup-pun okurete tsukimasu.

飛行機は予定より30分遅れて着きます。

The plane will arrive 30 minutes behind schedule.

• yotei o tateru 予定を立てる *to make plans, to make a schedule*

¶Natsu-yasumi no yotei wa mō tatemashita ka.

夏休みの予定はもう立てましたか。

Have you already made plans for the summer vacation?

¶Eki-mae ni atsumaru yotei desu.

駅前に集まる予定です。

The arrangement is to gather in front of the station.

• yotei suru 予定する *to arrange, to plan, to schedule*

¶Shiai wa Doyōbi no gogo ni yotei sarete imasu.

試合は土曜日の午後に予定されています。

The match is scheduled for Saturday afternoon.

• yotei-dōri 予定どおり *on schedule, as planned*

• yotei-hyō 予定表 (*written*)*schedule*

yōtén 要点 *the point, the gist*

¶O-hanashi no yōten ga wakarimasen.

お話の要点がわかりません。

I don't understand the point of what you are saying.

yotō 与党 *ruling party, party in power* [⇔**yatō** 野党]

yotsukado 四つ角 *intersection where two roads cross at right angles*

yotte よって [☞**ni yotte** によって]

yótto ヨット *sailboat, sailing yacht*

¶Oji wa Biwa-ko de yotto o hashirasemasu.

伯父は琵琶湖でヨットを走らせます。

My uncle sails his sailboat on Lake

Biwa.

¶Shinbun-kisha wa Taiheiyō o yotto de ōdan shita.

新聞記者は太平洋をヨットで横断した。

The newspaper reporter crossed the Pacific in a sailboat.

• yotto-hābā ヨットハーバー *yacht harbor*
• yotto-rēsu ヨットレース *(sailing)yacht race*

yottsú 四つ *four* 《see Appendix 2》

yóu 酔う ① *to get drunk*

¶Chichi wa you to, kuchi-kazu ga ōku narimasu.

父は酔うと、口数が多くなります。

When my father gets drunk, he becomes talkative.

② *to get motion sickness*

¶Boku wa hikōki de wa yoimasen yo.

僕は飛行機では酔いませんよ。

I don't get motion sickness on planes!

• fune ni you 船に酔う *to get seasick*
• kuruma ni you 車に酔う *to get carsick*

yowái 弱い *weak* [⇔**tsuyoi** 強い]

¶Kono ko wa umaretsuki karada ga yowai no desu.

この子は生まれつき体が弱いのです。

This child is weak by nature. 《Literally: As for this child, the body is weak by nature.》

• A ni yowai Aに弱い *weak in A, bad at A; easily affected adversely by A*

¶Boku wa sūgaku ni yowai.

僕は数学に弱い。

I'm weak in math.

¶Uchi no musume wa norimono ni yowai no ga nayami desu.

うちの娘は乗り物に弱いのが悩みです。

The fact our daughter gets motion sickness in vehicles is a worry. 《Literally: The fact that our daughter is easily affected adversely by vehicles is a worry.》

• ki ga yowai 気が弱い *to be timid*
• ishi ga yowai 意志が弱い *to be weak-willed*

yowamáru 弱まる *to become weaker* [⇔ **tsuyomaru** 強まる]

yowaméru 弱める *to make weaker* [⇔

tsuyomeru 強める]

yowamí 弱み *weakness, weak point*

¶Oyabun wa kesshite yowami o misenai yo.

親分は決して弱みを見せないよ。

The boss never shows his weaknesses!

yowámushi 弱虫 【COL.】 *coward*

yowáru 弱る ① *to lose vigor, to get weaker*

¶Jūbyō no chichi wa hi-mashi ni yowatte imasu.

重病の父は日増しに弱っています。

My critically-ill father is getting weaker day by day.

② *to get into difficulty, to get into a quandary, to become troubled* [→ **komaru** 困る]

yōyaku 漸く ① *at last, finally* [→**tsui-ni** 遂に]

② *just barely* [→**karōjite** 辛うじて]

③ *gradually* [→**shidai-ni** 次第に]

yoyaku 予約 ① *reservation* 《at a hotel, restaurant, etc.》

¶Kyōto no hoteru no yoyaku o shimashita ka.

京都のホテルの予約をしましたか。

Did you make reservations at the hotel in Kyoto?

• yoyaku o uketsukeru 予約を受け付ける *to take a reservation*
• yoyaku o torikesu 予約を取り消す *to cancel a reservation*
• yoyaku suru 予約する *to reserve*

¶Kaigi ni sono heya o yoyaku shimashita.

会議にその部屋を予約しました。

I reserved that room for the meeting.

② *subscription* 《to a magazine, newspaper, etc.》

• yoyaku suru 予約する *to subscribe to*

③ *appointment* 《with a doctor, dentist, etc.》

¶O-isha-san ni denwa shite, gogo yo-ji no yoyaku o torimashita.

お医者さんに電話して、午後4時の予約をとりました。

I phoned the doctor and got a 4:00 p.m.

appointment.

• yoyaku-seki 予約席 *reserved seat*

yoyū 余裕 *(available)*room, margin, leeway* [→**yochi** 余地]

¶Kuruma ni watashi ga noru yoyū ga arimasu ka.

車に私が乗る余裕がありますか。

Is there room for me in the car?

¶Jikan no yoyū ga arimasu ka.

時間の余裕がありますか。

Is there any leeway in the time?

• kau yoyū 買う余裕 *leeway to buy, ability to afford*

¶Shinsha o kau yoyū wa nai yo.

新車を買う余裕はないよ。

I can't afford to buy a new car!

yú 湯 *hot water, warm water* [⇔**mizu** 水②]

¶O-yu de te o arainasai.

お湯で手を洗いなさい。

Wash your hands with warm water.

¶Haha wa kōcha o ireru tame ni o-yu o wakashita.

母は紅茶を入れるためにお湯を沸かした。

My mother boiled water to make tea.

¶Furo ni yu o irete kuremasu ka?

ふろに湯を入れてくれますか？

Will you put hot water in the bath for me?

• yu-bune 湯船 *bathtub* [→**yokusō** 浴槽]

• yu-dōfu 湯豆腐 *tofu boiled in water*

• yu-nomi 湯飲み *teacup*

• yu-wakashi-ki 湯沸かし器 *water heater*

yū 言う [☞**iu** 言う] 《In spite of the hiragana spelling いう, this word is pronounced yū except in unnaturally precise speech.》

yūbé 夕べ *evening*

¶Boku-tachi wa ongaku no yūbe o moyōshimashita.

僕たちは音楽の夕べを催しました。

We held a musical evening.

¶Oji no uchi de tanoshii yūbe o sugoshimashita.

叔父のうちで楽しい夕べを過ごしました。

We spent a pleasant evening at my

uncle's home.

yūbe 昨夜 *last night, yesterday night* [→**sakuya** 昨夜]

¶Yūbe wa yoku nemuremashita ka.

ゆうべはよく眠れましたか。

Did you sleep well last night?

yubí 指 *finger; toe*

¶Ane wa hossori shita yubi o shite iru yo.

姉はほっそりした指をしているよ。

My older sister has slender fingers!

¶Kodomo wa ichi kara go made yubi de kazoemashita.

子供は1から5まで指で数えました。

The child counted from one to five on his fingers.

• yubi-ori no 指折の *leading, prominent*

• yubi-saki 指先 *fingertip; toe tip*

• hito-sashi-yubi 人差し指 *index finger*

• ko-yubi 小指 *little finger; little toe*

• kusuri-yubi 薬指 *ring finger*

• naka-yubi 中指 *middle finger*

• oya-yubi 親指 *thumb; big toe*

yūbin 郵便 ① <US>*mail (service),* *postal service*

¶Kesa no yūbin de kono tegami ga kimashita.

けさの郵便でこの手紙が来ました。

This letter came in the morning mail.

¶Kono nimotsu o yūbin de okutte kudasai.

この荷物を郵便で送ってください。

Please send this package by mail.

¶Rondon made yūbin wa nan-nichi kakarimasu ka.

ロンドンまで郵便は何日かかりますか。

How many days does mail take to London?

② <US>*(item sent in the)mail,* <UK>*(item sent in the)post*

¶Kyō wa yūbin ga takusan todoite imasu.

きょうは郵便がたくさん届いています。

A lot of mail has come today.

• yūbin-bangō 郵便番号 <US>*zip code,* <UK>*postcode*

• yūbin-butsu 郵便物 [☞**yūbin** 郵便② (above)]

- yūbin-hagaki 郵便葉書 *postcard*
- yūbin-haitatsu-nin 郵便配達人 *<US>mail carrier, postman*
- yūbin-kitte 郵便切手 *postage stamp* [→**kitte** 切手]
- yūbin-kyoku 郵便局 *post office*
- yūbin-kyoku-in 郵便局員 *post-office clerk*
- yūbin-ryōkin 郵便料金 *postage (charge)*
- yūbin-uke 郵便受け *<US>mailbox, <UK>letter box 《in which mail is received》*

yubiwa 指輪 *(finger)ring*

¶Akatsuka-san wa rubī no yubiwa o shite imasu.
赤塚さんはルビーの指輪をしています。
Ms. Akatsuka is wearing a ruby ring.

- kekkon-yubiwa 結婚指輪 *wedding ring*
- kon'yaku-yubiwa 婚約指輪 *engagement ring* [→**engējiringu** エンゲージリング]

yūbō 有望 ～**na** ～な *promising, likely to turn out well*

- yūbō na zento 有望な前途 *a promising future*

yūdachi 夕立 *sudden evening rainshower*

¶Kinō yūdachi ga furimashita.
きのう夕立が降りました。
There was a sudden evening rainshower yesterday.

- yūdachi ni au 夕立にあう *to get caught in a sudden evening rainshower*

yūdai 雄大 ～**na** ～な *grand, majestic, magnificent*

¶Chōjō kara no yūdai na nagame o tanoshimimashita.
頂上からの雄大な眺めを楽しみました。
We enjoyed the magnificent view from the summit.

yudan 油断 *carelessness, negligence*

- yudan suru 油断する *to be careless, to let one's guard down*

¶Yudan suru to, kega o suru yo.
油断すると、けがをするよ。
If you're careless, you'll get injured!

yuden 油田 *oil field*

yudéru ゆでる *to boil (in plain water)* 《transitive》

¶Haha wa tamago o kataku yudemashita.
母は卵を固くゆでました。
My mother boiled the eggs hard.

yūdoku 有毒 ～**na** ～な *poisonous*

- yūdoku-gasu 有毒ガス *poisonous gas*

yūeki 有益 ～**na** ～な *rewarding, instructive, useful*

yūénchi 遊園地 *amusement park*

yūetsúkan 優越感 *superiority complex* [⇔**rettōkan** 劣等感]

yūfō ユーフォー *UFO*

yūfuku 裕福 ～**na** ～な *rich, wealthy* [→**kanemochi no** 金持ちの]

¶Hagiwara-san wa yūfuku na ie ni umaremashita.
萩原さんは裕福な家に生まれました。
Mr. Hagiwara was born into a wealthy family.

yūga 優雅 ～**na** ～な *elegant, refined*

¶Sadō ya ikebana wa yūga na shumi desu ne.
茶道や生け花は優雅な趣味ですね。
The tea ceremony and flower arrangement are elegant pursuits, aren't they.

yūgai 有害 ～**no** ～の *harmful, injurious* [⇔**mugai no** 無害の]

¶Tabako wa kenkō ni yūgai desu.
たばこは健康に有害です。
Tobacco is harmful to one's health.

yugameru 歪める *to distort, to twist, to make crooked*

¶Tsūyaku wa daitōryō no kotoba o yugamemashita.
通訳は大統領の言葉をゆがめました。
The interpreter distorted the president's words.

yugamu 歪む *to become distorted, to become twisted, to become crooked*

¶Kyatchā no kao wa kutsū de yugande ita.
キャッチャーの顔は苦痛でゆがんでいた。
The catcher's face was twisted with pain.

¶Terebi no gamen ga yugande iru yo.
テレビの画面がゆがんでいるよ。
The (picture on the) TV screen is

distorted!

yūgata 夕方 *late afternoon, early evening* «Typically understood to mean the period from an hour or two before sunset until the end of twilight.»

¶Ane wa taitei yūgata ni wa kitaku shimasu.

姉はたいてい夕方には帰宅します。

My older sister usually comes home in the early evening.

¶Ani wa yūgata roku-ji-goro ni gaishutsu shimashita.

兄は夕方6時ごろに外出しました。

My older brother went out at about 6:00 in the evening.

¶Chichi wa kinō no yūgata ryokō ni dekakemashita.

父はきのうの夕方旅行に出かけました。

My father left on a trip late yesterday afternoon.

yúge 湯気 *(visible)steam, vapor*

yūgekíshu 遊撃手 *shortstop* [→**shōto** ショート] «in baseball»

yūgi 遊戯 ① *playing, game, recreation* [→**asobi** 遊び]

② *directed group play* «combining exercise and recreation for young children at a day-care center or school»

¶Yōchien no kodomo-tachi wa yūgi o shite imasu.

幼稚園の子供たちは遊戯をしています。

The children in the kindergarten are doing group play.

•yūgi-jō 遊戯場 *playground* [→**undō-jō** 運動場 (s.v. **undō** 運動)]*; recreation center*

yūgure 夕暮れ *the time of evening around sunset, dusk*

yūhan 夕飯 *evening meal* [→**yūshoku** 夕食]

yūhi 夕日 *evening sun, setting sun* [⇔**asahi** 朝日]

¶Yūhi ga sono heya ni sashikonde imasu.

夕日がその部屋に差し込んでいます。

The setting sun is shining into that room.

yūigi 有意義 ～**na** ～な *significant, worthwhile, valuable*

¶Kono shippai wa yūigi na keiken ni naru deshō.

この失敗は有意義な経験になるでしょう。

This failure will probably be a valuable experience.

yuigon 遺言 *last words, dying wishes, will*

•yuigon-jō 遺言状 *(written)will* [→**isho** 遺書]

yúiitsu 唯一 ～**no** ～の *the (one and)only*

¶Kore wa Hanshin ni totte yuiitsu no chansu desu.

これは阪神にとって唯一のチャンスです。

This is the only chance for Hanshin.

yūjin 友人 *friend* [→**tomodachi** 友達]

yūjō 友情 *friendship, fellowship*

¶Mina-san no atatakai yūjō o kesshite wasuremasen.

皆さんの温かい友情を決して忘れません。

I will never forget everyone's warm friendship.

•yūjō ni atsui 友情に厚い *friendly*

yuka 床 *floor* «i.e., bottom surface of a room»

•yuka-undō 床運動 *floor exercise* «in gymnastics»

yúkai 愉快 ～**na** ～な [[⇔**fuyukai na** 不愉快な]] ① *pleasant, delightful, merry*

¶Sensei to oshaberi suru no wa jitsu ni yukai desu.

先生とおしゃべりするのは実に愉快です。

Chatting with the teacher is really pleasant.

¶Kyō wa totemo yukai datta ne.

きょうはとても愉快だったね。

Today was really delightful, wasn't it.

② *cheerful, pleased*

yūkai 誘拐 *kidnapping, abduction*

•yūkai suru 誘拐する *to kidnap, to abduct*

yūkan 夕刊 *evening edition of a newspaper* [⇔**chōkan** 朝刊]

yūkan 勇敢 ～**na** ～な *brave* [→**isamashii** 勇ましい]

¶Ano tanken-ka wa yūkan na otoko da

ne.

あの探検家は勇敢な男だね。

That explorer is a brave man, isn't he.

¶Heitai wa kuni no tame ni yūkan ni tatakaimashita.

兵隊は国のために勇敢に戦いました。

The soldier fought bravely for his country.

yukata 浴衣 *informal cotton kimono* 《A **yukata** is usually worn in summer as a bathrobe and for sleeping. Hotels generally provide them for guests.》

yūkénsha 有権者 *person with the right to vote, voter*

yuketsu 輸血 *blood transfusion*

• yuketsu suru 輸血する *to give a blood transfusion*

¶Isha wa sono kanja ni yuketsu shimashita.

医者はその患者に輸血しました。

The doctor gave that patient a blood transfusion.

yūki 勇気 *courage*

¶Ishikawa-san wa yūki no aru hito desu ne.

石川さんは勇気のある人ですね。

Ms. Ishikawa is a courageous woman, isn't she.

¶Boku ni wa sore o suru yūki ga nai yo.

僕にはそれをする勇気がないよ。

I don't have the courage to do that!

• yūki o dasu 勇気を出す *to muster one's courage*

• yūki o ushinau 勇気を失う *to lose one's courage*

• yūki-zukeru 勇気づける *to encourage*

¶Tomodachi no kotoba ni yūki-zukeraremashita.

友達の言葉に勇気づけられました。

I was encouraged by my friend's words.

yuki 雪 *snow*

¶Ame ga yuki ni kawarimashita.

雨が雪に変わりました。

The rain has changed to snow.

¶Kotoshi wa yuki ga ōi.

今年は雪が多い。

There's a lot of snow this year.

¶Yama ni wa yuki ga jus-senchi tsumotte imasu.

山には雪が10センチ積もっています。

On the mountain ten centimeters of snow have accumulated.

• yuki ga furu 雪が降る *snow falls*

¶Yuki ga furi-sō desu ne.

雪が降りそうですね。

It looks as if it's going to snow, doesn't it.

¶Yuki ga hageshiku futte iru yo.

雪が激しく降っているよ。

It's snowing hard!

• yuki ga yamu 雪がやむ *snow stops falling*

• yuki-daruma 雪だるま *snowman*

• yuki-doke 雪解け *snow thaw*

• yuki-gassen 雪合戦 *snowball fight*

• yuki-guni 雪国 *snowy region*

• hatsu-yuki 初雪 *the first snow of the season*

• ō-yuki 大雪 *heavy snowfall*

¶Kinō ō-yuki ga furimashita yo.

きのう大雪が降りましたよ。

There was a heavy snowfall yesterday!

–yuki －行き 〜**no** 〜の *bound for, going to* 《Added to nouns denoting places.》

¶Matsumoto de Shinjuku-yuki no ressha ni norikaemashita.

松本で新宿行きの列車に乗り換えました。

In Matsumoto I transferred to a train bound for Shinjuku.

¶Kono basu wa Mishima-yuki desu.

このバスは三島行きです。

This bus is going to Mishima.

yukisaki 行き先 *destination*

yukkúri ゆっくり （〜**to** 〜と） *slowly, in a leisurely manner, without hurrying*

¶Mō sukoshi yukkuri hanashite itadakemasu ka.

もう少しゆっくり話していただけますか。

Could we have you speak a little more slowly?

¶Awatenai de, yukkuri yatte kudasai.

あわてないで、ゆっくりやってください。

Don't rush, please take your time doing it.

• yukkuri nemuru ゆっくり眠る *to sleep well*

• yukkuri maniau ゆっくり間に合う *to be in plenty of time*

• yukkuri suru ゆっくりする *to take one's time; to stay a long time*

¶ Dōzo go-yukkuri.
どうぞごゆっくり。
Please stay as long as you like.

yūkō 有効 〜**na** 〜な [[⇔**mukō** 無効]]
① *effective, fruitful*

¶ Kōzui o fusegu yūkō na shudan o oshiete kudasai.
洪水を防ぐ有効な手段を教えてください。
Teach us effective measures to prevent floods.

¶ Natsu-yasumi o yūkō ni tsukainasai.
夏休みを有効に使いなさい。
Use of your summer vacation fruitfully.
② *valid, in effect*

¶ Kono ōfuku-kippu wa muika-kan yūkō desu.
この往復切符は6日間有効です。
This round-trip ticket is valid for six days.

yūkō 友好 *friendship, amity*

• yūkō-teki na 友好的な *friendly, amicable*

¶ Ima no yūkō-teki na kankei o tsuzukeru koto ga jūyō da.
今の友好的な関係を続けることが重要だ。
It is important that we continue the present friendly relations.

yuku 行く {Irreg.} [☞**iku** 行く]

yukue 行方 *whereabouts, where one has gone*

¶ Taishi no yukue ga wakarimasen.
大使の行方がわかりません。
They don't know the ambassador's whereabouts.

¶ Yukue no wakaranakatta shōjo wa buji deshita.
行方のわからなかった少女は無事でした。
The girl who had been missing was safe.

• yukue-fumei no 行方不明の *whereabouts unknown, missing*

¶ Uchi no inu wa mada yukue-fumei

desu.
うちの犬はまだ行方不明です。
Our dog is still missing.

yumé 夢 *dream*

¶ Yakusha ni naru no ga watashi no yume desu.
役者になるのが私の夢です。
Becoming an actor is my dream.

¶ Yume ga genjitsu ni narimashita.
夢が現実になりました。
The dream became reality.

• yume o miru 夢を見る *to dream, to have a dream*

¶ Nakunatta haha no yume o mita yo.
亡くなった母の夢を見たよ。
I dreamed about my deceased mother!

• yume ni mo omowanai 夢にも思わない *to never dream*

¶ Katsu to wa yume ni mo omowanakatta yo.
勝つとは夢にも思わなかったよ。
I never dreamed that I would win!

yūmei 有名 〜**na** 〜な *famous, well-known*

¶ Hayata-san wa shōrai yūmei na sakka ni naru darō.
早田さんは将来有名な作家になるだろう。
Ms. Hayata will probably become a famous writer in the future.

¶ Arimori-san wa sekai-teki ni yūmei na kagakusha desu.
有森さんは世界的に有名な科学者です。
Mr. Arimori is a world-famous scientist.

¶ Kono tera wa teien de yūmei desu.
この寺は庭園で有名です。
This temple is famous for its garden.

• yūmei-jin 有名人 *famous person, celebrity*

• yūmei-kō 有名校 *big-name school*

yumí 弓 *bow* 《used to shoot arrows》

¶ Ācherī no senshu wa yumi ni ya o tsugaeta.
アーチェリーの選手は弓に矢をつがえた。
The archery competitor fitted an arrow to the bow.

¶ Ryōshi wa yumi o hiite ya o hanatta.
猟師は弓を引いて矢を放った。

The hunter drew the bow and shot the arrow.

yúmoa ユーモア *humor, wit*

¶Tanimura-san wa yūmoa ga wakaranai ne.

谷村さんはユーモアがわからないね。

Mr. Tanimura doesn't understand humor, does he.

yúmorasu ユーモラス 〜**na** 〜な *humorous*

¶Oda-san wa yūmorasu na hanashi o shite kureta.

小田さんはユーモラスな話をしてくれた。

Mr. Oda told us a humorous story.

yúnihōmu ユニホーム *a uniform*

¶Unten-shu wa yunihōmu o kite imashita.

運転手はユニホームを着ていました。

The chauffer was wearing his uniform.

yunīku ユニーク 〜**na** 〜な *unique; unusual*

¶Hashimoto-san no kangae-kata wa totemo yunīku desu.

橋本さんの考え方はとてもユニークです。

Ms. Hashimoto's way of thinking is very unusual.

yūnō 有能 〜**na** 〜な *able, capable, competent*

¶Morita-san wa yūnō na kisha desu.

森田さんは有能な記者です。

Ms. Morita is a capable reporter.

yunyū 輸入 *importation* [⇔**yushutsu** 輸出]

•yunyū suru 輸入する *to import*

¶Nihon wa Amerika kara komugi o yunyū shite imasu.

日本はアメリカから小麦を輸入しています。

Japan imports wheat from America.

•yunyū-hin 輸入品 *import, imported item*

yurai 由来 *origin, derivation, past history*

•yurai suru 由来する *to originate, to derive, to date back*

yūran 遊覧 *excursion, going around to see the sights*

•yūran suru 遊覧する *to go around and*

see the sights of, to make an excursion through*

•yūran-basu 遊覧バス *sightseeing bus*

•yūran-sen 遊覧船 *excursion ship, pleasure boat*

yūrei 幽霊 *dead person's spirit, ghost* [→**bōrei** 亡霊]

¶Yūrei nante shinjinai yo.

幽霊なんて信じないよ。

I don't believe in such things as ghosts!

yureru 揺れる *to shake* 《intransitive》; *to sway* 《intransitive》; *to rock* 《intransitive》

¶Jishin de ie ga yureru no o kanjimashita.

地震で家が揺れるのを感じました。

I felt the house sway in the earthquake.

¶Fune ga hageshiku yuremashita.

船が激しく揺れました。

The ship rocked terribly.

yúri 有利 〜**na** 〜な *advantageous, favorable, profitable* [⇔**furi na** 不利な]

¶Ima nara seimei hoken ni kanyū suru no ga yūri desu.

今なら生命保険に加入するのが有利です。

If it's now, taking out life insurance would be advantageous.

¶Sono kettei wa watashi-tachi ni yūri na mono deshita.

その決定は私たちに有利なものでした。

That decision was favorable to us.

yuri 百合 *lily*

yurikago 揺り籠 *cradle*

•yurikago kara hakaba made 揺りかごから墓場まで *from the cradle to the grave*

yurúi 緩い ① *loose, slack; loose-fitting* [⇔**kitsui** きつい①]

¶Kono zubon wa boku ni wa yurui yo.

このズボンは僕には緩いよ。

These pants are loose on me!

② *lax, lenient* 《describing a restriction, regulation, etc.》

¶Kono gakkō wa kōsoku ga yurui.

この学校は校則が緩い。

This school's rules are lax.

yuruméru 緩める *to loosen, to slacken* 《transitive》

¶Daiku wa mazu neji o yurumemashita.
大工はまずねじを緩めました。
The carpenter first loosened the screw.

• ki o yurumeru 気を緩める *to relax one's attention*

yurúmu 緩む ① *to become loose, to slacken*

¶Aruite iru uchi ni kutsu no himo ga yurumimashita.
歩いているうちに靴のひもが緩みました。
While I was walking my shoelaces became loose.

② *to abate*

¶Kizu no itami ga dandan yurumimashita.
傷の痛みがだんだん緩みました。
The pain of the wound gradually abated.

yurushí 許し ① *permission* [→**kyoka** 許可]

¶Ten'in wa yurushi o ezu ni gaishutsu shimashita.
店員は許しを得ずに外出しました。
The store clerk went out without getting permission.

② *forgiveness, pardon*

yurúsu 許す ① *to allow, to permit* [→**kyoka suru** 許可する]

¶Chichi wa tsuri ni iku no o yurushite kureta yo.
父は釣りに行くのを許してくれたよ。
My father let me go fishing!

② *to forgive, to pardon*

¶Ani wa watashi no machigai o yurushite kuremashita.
兄は私のまちがいを許してくれました。
My older brother forgave my mistake.

¶Watashi no fuchūi o yurushite kudasai.
私の不注意を許してください。
Please forgive my carelessness.

yurúyaka 緩やか ~**na** ~な ① [[⇔**kyū na** 急な③]] *gentle* «describing a slope»; *gentle* «describing a curve»

¶Koko kara wa yuruyaka na saka o noborimasu.
ここからは緩やかな坂を上ります。
From here we're going to go up a gentle slope.

② *slow, gentle* «describing a flow» [⇔**kyū na** 急な④]

¶Bōto wa yuruyaka na nagare o kudarimashita.
ボートは緩やかな流れを下りました。
The boat went down a slow stream.

yūryō 有料 ~**no** ~の *requiring payment, involving a fee, not free* [⇔**muryō no** 無料の]

¶Sono kyōgi-kai wa yūryō desu.
その競技会は有料です。
That athletic meet isn't free.

• yūryō-chūsha-jō 有料駐車場 *pay parking lot*

• yūryō-dōro 有料道路 *toll road*

• yūryō-toire 有料トイレ *pay toilet*

yūryoku 有力 ~**na** ~な ① *strong, powerful, influential*

¶Otōsan wa yūryoku na seiji-ka desu.
お父さんは有力な政治家です。
His father is an influential politician.

② *strong, convincing, compelling*

¶Yūryoku na shōko wa nani-mo arimasen.
有力な証拠は何もありません。
There is no strong evidence. «Literally: As for strong evidence, there is nothing.»

• yūryoku-sha 有力者 *influential person, powerful person*

Yūséishō 郵政省 *the Ministry of Postal Service and Telecommunications*

yūsen 優先 *priority, preference*

• yūsen suru 優先する *to have priority, to take precedence*

• yūsen-jun'i 優先順位 *order of priority*

yūshō 優勝 *winning the championship*

• yūshō suru 優勝する *to win the championship*

¶Watashi-tachi no kurasu wa takkyū no shiai de yūshō shita.
私たちのクラスは卓球の試合で優勝した。
Our class won the table tennis championship.

• yūshō-chīmu 優勝チーム *champion team*

• yūshō-kappu 優勝カップ *championship trophy, championship cup*

- yūshō-ki 優勝旗 *championship flag, championship pennant*
- yūshō-sha 優勝者 *champion*

yūshoku 夕食 *evening meal, supper, dinner* [→**yoru-gohan** 夜ご飯 (s.v. **yoru** 夜), **ban-gohan** 晩ご飯 (s.v. **ban** 晩)]
- Kinō watashi wa yūshoku o tsukurimashita.
きのう私は夕食を作りました。
Yesterday I made supper.
¶Yūshoku no mae ni ni-jikan benkyō shimasu.
夕食の前に2時間勉強します。
I study for two hours before supper.
¶Uchi de wa yūshoku wa shichi-ji desu.
うちでは夕食は7時です。
At our house dinner is at 7:00.

yūshū 優秀 ～**na** ～な *excellent, superior*
¶Kyōko-chan wa totemo yūshū na chūgakusei deshita.
京子ちゃんはとても優秀な中学生でした。
Kyoko was an excellent junior high school student.
¶Ani wa yūshū na seiseki de kōkō o sotsugyō shimashita.
兄は優秀な成績で高校を卒業しました。
My older brother graduated from high school with excellent grades.
- sai-yūshū-senshu 最優秀選手 *most valuable player*

yushutsu 輸出 *exportation* [⇔**yunyū** 輸入]
- yushutsu suru 輸出する *to export*
¶Amerika wa Nihon e komugi o yushutsu shite imasu.
アメリカは日本へ小麦を輸出しています。
The United States exports wheat to Japan.
- yushutsu-hin 輸出品 *export, exported item*

yūsō 郵送 <US>*mailing*, <UK>*posting*
- yūsō suru 郵送する *to send by mail, to mail*
¶Sono hon o ashita yūsō shimasu.
その本をあした郵送します。

I will mail that book tomorrow.
- yūsō-ryō 郵送料 *postage (charge)*

yusō 輸送 *transporting*
- yusō suru 輸送する *to transport*
¶Sono shima ni shū ni ichi-do shokuryō o fune de yusō shimasu.
その島に週に一度食糧を船で輸送します。
They transport food to that island by boat once a week.

yusugu 濯ぐ *to rinse* [→**susugu** 濯ぐ]
¶Shokugo wa kuchi o yoku yusuginasai.
食後は口をよくゆすぎなさい。
After meals rinse your mouth well.

yūsuhósuteru ユースホステル *youth hostel*

yusuru 揺する *to shake «transitive»; to rock «transitive»*
¶Ki o yusutte kuri no mi o otoshimashita.
木を揺すってくりの実を落としました。
We shook the tree and made the chestnuts fall.

yútaka 豊か ～**na** ～な [[⇔**mazushii** 貧しい]] ① *abundant, ample, rich* [→**hōfu na** 豊富な] [⇔**toboshii** 乏しい]
¶Sono kuni wa sekiyu ga yutaka desu.
その国は石油が豊かです。
In that country oil is abundant.
¶Kono ko wa sōzō-ryoku ga yutaka desu.
この子は想像力が豊かです。
This child has a rich imagination.
　② *rich, wealthy* [→**yūfuku na** 裕福な] [⇔**binbō na** 貧乏な]
¶Kanada wa yutaka na kuni desu.
カナダは豊かな国です。
Canada is a wealthy country.

yūtán ユーターン *U-turn*
yūtópia ユートピア *utopia*
yūtósei 優等生 *honor student*
yūutsu 憂鬱 ～**na** ～な *gloomy* [⇔**kaikatsu na** 快活な]
¶Raishū wa shiken na node, yūutsu desu.
来週は試験なので、憂うつです。
I'm depressed because we have exams next week.
¶Kono goro yūutusu na tenki ga tsuzuite

imasu.

このごろ憂うつな天気が続いています。

These days gloomy weather continues.

yūwaku 誘惑 *temptation, enticement; seduction*

- yūwaku ni katsu 誘惑に勝つ *to overcome a temptation*
- yūwaku ni makeru 誘惑に負ける *to give in to temptation*
- yūwaku to tatakau 誘惑と戦う *to fight temptation*
- yūwaku suru 誘惑する *to tempt, to entice; to seduce*

¶Yakuza wa o-kane de sono seinen o yūwaku shimashita.

やくざはお金でその青年を誘惑しました。

The gangster enticed that young man with money.

yūyake 夕焼け *sunset (colors)*

¶Boku to shinobu wa utsukushii yūyake o nagamete imashita.

僕と忍は美しい夕焼けを眺めていました。

Shinobu and I were looking at the beautiful sunset.

yūzai 有罪 *(criminal) guilt* [⇔**muzai** 無罪]

- yūzai no 有罪の *guilty*

yúzu 柚 *citron*

yuzuru 譲る *to yield, to let have*

- A ni B o yuzuru AにBを譲る *to yield B to A, to let A have B*

¶Densha de obāsan ni seki o yuzurimashita.

電車でおばあさんに席を譲りました。

I let an old woman have my seat on the train.

¶Chichi wa usetsu suru kuruma ni michi o yuzurimashita.

父は右折する車に道を譲りました。

My father yielded the roads to the car turning right.

¶Izawa-san wa musume-san ni zenzaisan o yuzurimashita.

井沢さんは娘さんに全財産を譲りました。

Mr. Izawa let his daughter have his whole fortune.

¶Tomodachi ni piano o rokuman-en de

yuzutta yo.

友達にピアノを6万円で譲ったよ。

I let my friend have the piano for 60,000 yen!

Z

zabúton 座布団 *floor cushion «for a person to sit on»*

zadánkai 座談会 *round-table discussion, symposium*

záiaku 罪悪 [[→**tsumi** 罪]] *sin; crime*

- zaiaku-kan 罪悪感 *sense of guilt*

zaigaku 在学 *being enrolled in school*

- zaigaku suru 在学する *to become enrolled in school*

¶Yokomizo-kun wa kotoshi wa zaigaku shite imasu.

横溝君は今年は在学しています。

Yokomizo is enrolled in school this year.

- zaigaku-chū no 在学中の *enrolled-in-school*
- zaigaku-shōmei-sho 在学証明書 *school enrollment certificate*

zaikai 財界 *the financial world, financial circles*

zaiko 在庫 *stock (of unsold goods)*

zaimoku 材木 *<US> lumber, <UK> timber* [→**mokuzai** 木材]

záiru ザイル *mountain-climbing rope*

zairyō 材料 *materials; ingredient*

¶Miso-shiru no zairyō wa arimasu ka.

みそ汁の材料はありますか。

Do you have the ingredients for miso soup?

- kenchiku-zairyō 建築材料 *building materials*

záisan 財産 *fortune, estate, accumulated wealth*

¶Sono kigyō-ka wa bakudai na zaisan o kizukimashita.

その企業家はばく大な財産を築きました。

That industrialist built up a large

fortune.

zaisei 財政 *government finances*

zakkubaran ざっくばらん 【COL.】
~**na** ~な *frank, open, candid*

zákuro ざくろ *pomegranate*

zandaka 残高 *balance, remaining money* [→**zankin** 残金]

zangyō 残業 *overtime work*
• zangyō suru 残業する *to work overtime*

zánkin 残金 *balance, remaining money* [→**zandaka** 残高]

zankoku 残酷 ~**na** ~な *cruel*

zannén 残念 ~**na** ~な *regrettable, unfortunate, too bad*
¶Satō-san ga kai ni sanka dekinai no wa zannen da.
佐藤さんが会に参加できないのは残念だ。
It's unfortunate that Ms. Sato can't attend the meeting.
• zannnen-nagara 残念ながら *unfortunately, regrettably*
• zannen-shō 残念賞 *consolation prize*

zánsho 残暑 *lingering summer heat, late summer heat*

zaseki 座席 *seat, place to sit* [→**seki** 席]
• zaseki-shitei-ken 座席指定券 *reserved-seat ticket*

zashikí 座敷 *room with a tatami (mat)floor*

zasshi 雑誌 *magazine, periodical*
¶Kono zasshi o totte imasu.
この雑誌を取っています。
I subscribe to this magazine.

zassō 雑草 *weed*
• zassō o toru 雑草を取る *to pull weeds*

zátsu 雑 ~**na** ~な *sloppily done*

zatsudan 雑談 *small talk, chat*
• zatsudan suru 雑談する *to chat*

zatsuon 雑音 *noise, static*

zatto ざっと ① *cursorily, briefly, roughly*
¶Kachō wa keikaku o zatto setsumei shimashita.
課長は計画をざっと説明しました。
The section chief roughly explained the plan.

¶Kenchiku-ka wa zatto ie no shasei o shimashita.
建築家はざっと家の写生をしました。
The architect roughly sketched the house.
② *approximately, about* [→**oyoso** およそ]
¶Kono daigaku ni wa zatto ni-man-nin no gakusei ga iru.
この大学にはざっと2万人の学生がいる。
This college has about 20,000 students.

zazen 座禅 *sitting in Zen meditation*
• zazen o kumu 座禅を組む *to sit in Zen meditation*

zéhi 是非 *by all means, at any cost, without fail*
¶Ashita no shiai ni wa zehi kachitai yo.
あしたの試合にはぜひ勝ちたいよ。
I want to win the tomorrow's game without fail!

zéi 税 *tax* [→**zeikin** 税金]
• chihō-zei 地方税 *local tax*
• shōhi-zei 消費税 *consumption tax, sales tax*
• shotoku-zei 所得税 *income tax*

zeikan 税関 *customs* 《where import duties are collected》
¶Ikkō wa Narita-kūkō de zeikan o tsūka shimashita.
一行は成田空港で税関を通過しました。
The party went through customs at Narita Airport.

zeikin 税金 *tax*
¶Chichi wa takusan no o-kane o zeikin ni haraimashita.
父はたくさんのお金を税金に払いました。
My father paid a lot of money in taxes.
¶Kono kamera wa zeikin ga kakarimasen.
このカメラは税金がかかりません。
Tax does not apply to this camera.

zéimu 税務 *taxation work, tax collection*
• zeimu-sho 税務署 *taxation office*

zeitakú 贅沢 *extravagance*
• zeitaku na ぜいたくな *extravagant*
¶Sono kanemochi wa zeitaku ni kurashite ita.

その金持ちはぜいたくに暮らしていた。
That rich person was living extravagantly.

zékken ゼッケン *racing number*
《attached to the front or back of an athlete's shirt》

zekkō 絶好 〜**no** 〜の *best, ideal, excellent*
¶Zekkō no chansu o nogashite shimaimashita.
絶好のチャンスを逃してしまいました。
I missed the best chance.
• zekkō-chō 絶好調 *best condition, top form*

zémi ゼミ *seminar*

zemináru ゼミナール [☞**zemi** ゼミ]

zén 善 *goodness* [⇔**aku** 悪]
¶Zen wa isoge.
善は急げ。《proverb》
Don't hesitate to do good. 《Literally: As for goodness, hurry.》
• zen-aku 善悪 *good and evil*

Zén 禅 *Zen* (*Buddhism*)
• Zen-shū 禅宗 *the Zen sect*

-zen 一膳 ①《counter for pairs of chopsticks; see Appendix 2》
②《counter for bowlfuls of rice; see Appendix 2》

zén'aku 善悪 *go and evil, right and wrong*

zénbu 全部 *all, the whole, the total* [→ **subete** 全て]
¶Koppu wa zenbu warete shimaimashita.
コップは全部割れてしまいました。
All the glasses broke.
¶Kono kitte wa zenbu watashi no desu.
この切手は全部私のです。
These stamps are all mine.
¶Chichi wa sono sakana o zenbu tabemashita.
父はその魚を全部食べました。
My father ate that whole fish.
¶Kono hon o zenbu yonda wake de wa arimasen.
この本を全部読んだわけではありません。
I haven't read all these books.
• zenbu de 全部で *in all, all together*

¶Zenbu de sanzen-en motte imasu.
全部で3000円持っています。
I have 3,000 yen in all.

zéngo 前後 ① *the time periods before and after*
¶Yūshoku no zengo ni Eigo o benkyō shimashita.
夕食の前後に英語を勉強しました。
I studied English before and after supper.
② *the areas in front and behind*
¶Ashi o zengo ni ugokashimashō.
足を前後に動かしましょう。
Let's move our legs back and forth.

-zengo 一前後 ① *about, approximately*
《Added to bases denoting points in time.》[→**-goro** 一ごろ]
¶Mensetsu wa jū-ji-zengo ni owaru deshō.
面接は10時前後に終わるでしょう。
The interview will probably end at about 10:00.
② *about, approximately* 《Added to bases denoting specific quantities.》[→ **-gurai** 一ぐらい]
¶Sono hito no taijū wa rokujuk-kiro-zengo desu.
その人の体重は60キロ前後です。
That person's weight is about 60 kilograms.

zenhan 前半 *the first half* [⇔**kōhan** 後半]
¶Shiai no zenhan ga miraremasen deshita.
試合の前半が見られませんでした。
I could not watch the first half of the game.

zén'i 善意 *good will, good intentions*
• zen'i de 善意で *out of good will, with good intentions*
¶Zen'i de ano hito ni tegami o kakimashita.
善意であの人に手紙を書きました。
I wrote a letter to that person out of good will.

zen'in 全員 *everyone involved, all*
¶Daihyō wa zen'in sono an ni sansei

shimashita.
代表は全員その案に賛成しました。
The representatives all agreed to the proposal.

zenjitsu 前日 *the preceding day*
¶Shiken no zenjitsu wa terebi o minakatta yo.
試験の前日はテレビを見なかったよ。
I didn't watch television the day before the examination!

zénkoku 全国 *the whole country*
¶Senshu-tachi wa zenkoku kara atsumarimashita.
選手たちは全国から集まりました。
The athletes gathered from all over the country.
• zenkoku-taikai 全国大会 *national convention; national meet*
• zenkoku-teki na 全国的な *nationwide*
¶Murakami wa sakka to shite zenkoku-teki ni shirarete iru.
村上は作家として全国的に知られている。
Murakami is known as a writer nationwide.

zenmai ぜんまい (*metal*)*spring* [→ **bane** ばね]
¶Orugōru no zenmai o maite kudasai.
オルゴールのぜんまいを巻いてください。
Please wind the spring of the music box.

zenmetsu 全滅 *complete destruction, annihilation*
• zenmetsu suru 全滅する *to be completely destroyed*
¶Sono mura wa yama-kuzure de zenmetsu shimashita.
その村は山崩れで全滅しました。
That village was completely destroyed by a landslide.

zennín 善人 *good person, virtuous person* [⇔**akunin** 悪人]

zenpō 前方 *the area ahead*
¶Zenpō ni shima ga miemasu.
前方に島が見えます。
We can see an island ahead.
¶Gojū-mētoru zenpō ni basu-tei ga arimasu.
50メートル前方にバス停があります。

There is a bus stop 50 meters ahead.

zenryoku 全力 *all one's strength, all one's might*
• zenryoku de 全力で *with all one's might*
• zenryoku o tsukusu 全力を尽くす *to do one's utmost*
¶Zenryoku o tsukushite shiken o oemashita.
全力を尽くして試験を終えました。
I did my utmost and finished the exam.

zensen 前線 ① (*weather*)*front*
② *front line* 《*in a battle*》

zenshin 全身 *whole body*
¶Makiko wa zenshin zubunure de furuete ita yo.
真紀子は全身ずぶぬれで震えていたよ。
Makiko got soaked, and her whole body was shivering!
• zenshin-zō 全身像 *full-length portrait*

zenshin 前進 *advance, going forward*
• zenshin suru 前進する *to advance, to go forward*

zenshū 全集 *the complete works*
• Shēkusupia-zenshū シェークスピア全集 *the complete works of Shakespeare*

zensoku 喘息 *asthma*

zentai 全体 *the whole, entire thing* [⇔ **bubun** 部分]
• zentai to shite 全体として *as a whole, on the whole*
¶Kono keikaku wa zentai to shite umaku itte imasu.
この計画は全体としてうまくいっています。
This plan is going well as a whole.
• -zentai −全体 *the whole* 《Added to noun bases.》
¶Machi-zentai ga odayaka desu.
町全体が穏やかです。
The whole town is quiet.
• zentai-teki na 全体的な *overall* 《as a noun modifier》
¶Kono sakubun wa zentai-teki ni jōzu ni kakete imasu.
この作文は全体的に上手に書けています。
This composition is well written overall.

zentei 前提 *premise*

zénto 前途 *one's future, one's*

prospects

• yūbo na zento 有望な前途 *a promising future*

• zento-yūbō na 前途有望な *promising*

¶O-jōsan wa zento-yūbō na pianisuto desu.

お嬢さんは前途有望なピアニストです。

Their daughter is a promising pianist.

zén'ya 前夜 *preceding night, eve*

¶Kimatsu-shiken no zen'ya ni kaze o hikimashita.

期末試験の前夜にかぜをひきました。

I caught a cold the night before the final examinations.

• Kurisumasu-zen'ya クリスマス前夜 *Christmas Eve*

zenzen 全然 ⟨*not*⟩ *at all, completely* [→**mattaku** 全く]

¶Kyō wa zenzen shigoto o suru ki ni narimasen.

きょうは全然仕事をする気になりません。

I don't feel like doing any work at all today.

¶Watashi wa sore ni tsuite zenzen shirimasen.

私はそれについて全然知りません。

I don't know anything at all about that.

¶Sore wa zenzen betsu no koto desu yo.

それは全然別の事ですよ。

That's a completely different matter!

zerachin ゼラチン *gelatin*

zérī ゼリー *jelly*

zéro ゼロ *zero* [→**rei** 零]

zésuchā ゼスチャー [☞**jesuchā** ジェスチャー]

zésuchua ゼスチュア [☞**jesuchā** ジェスチャー]

zetsubō 絶望 *despair, hopelessness*

• zetsubō suru 絶望する *to despair, to give up hope*

¶Otōto wa zetsubō shite kitaku shimashita.

弟は絶望して帰宅しました。

My younger brother came home in despair.

¶Kesshite zetsubō shite wa ikenai yo.

決して絶望してはいけないよ。

You must never give up hope!

• zetsubō-teki na 絶望的な *hopeless*

¶Kono shiai wa zetsubō-teki da to kanjimashita.

この試合は絶望的だと感じました。

I felt that this game was hopeless.

zetsuen 絶縁 ① *breaking the connection, disconnection*

• zetsuen suru 絶縁する *to break the connection*

② (*electrical*)*insulation*

• zetsuen suru 絶縁する *to insulate*

• zetsuen-tai 絶縁体 (*electrical*)*insulator*

zetsumetsu 絶滅 *extinction, dying out*

• zetsumetsu suru 絶滅する *to become extinct, to die out*

¶Nihon de wa kono tori wa zetsumetsu shimashita.

日本ではこの鳥は絶滅しました。

This bird died out in Japan.

zettai 絶対 (～**ni** ～に) *absolutely, unconditionally, positively*

¶Kono hakari-kata wa zettai ni machigatte iru yo.

この計り方は絶対にまちがっているよ。

This way of measuring is positively wrong!

¶Watashi-tachi wa sensō ni wa zettai hantai desu.

私たちは戦争には絶対反対です。

We are absolutely against war.

¶Sūjitsu wa zettai ni ansei ni shita hō ga ii desu.

数日は絶対に安静にしたほうがいいです。

You should get absolute rest for a few days.

• zettai no 絶対の *absolute, unconditional*

• zettai-tasū 絶対多数 *absolute majority*

zṓ 象 *elephant*

zṓ 像 *image; portrait; statue*

¶Chōkoku-ka wa ki de zō o hotte imashita.

彫刻家は木で像を彫っていました。

The sculptor was carving an image out of wood.

• dairiseki no zō 大理石の像 *marble*

statue

• Jiyū no megami-zō 自由の女神像 *the Statue of Liberty*

• seki-zō 石像 *stone image*

zo ぞ《This sentence-final particle expresses strong exclamation and is generally used only by male speakers.》

¶Dame da zo.

だめだぞ.

It's no good!

zōge 象牙 *ivory*

• zōge-zaiku 象牙細工 *ivory (craft)work*

-zoi －沿い ～**no** ～の *alongside, on*

《Added to noun bases denoting roads, rivers, etc.》

¶Kokudō-zoi no mise de shokuji shimashita.

国道沿いの店で食事しました.

They ate at a shop alongside the national highway.

¶Kawa-zoi ni arukimashō.

川沿いに歩きましょう.

Let's walk along the river.

zōka 増加 *increase* [⇔**genshō** 減少]

• zōka suru 増加する *to increase* 《intransitive》 [→**fueru** 増える]

¶Daigaku-sei no kazu ga zōka shite imasu.

大学生の数が増加しています.

The number of college students has increased.

zōki 雑木 *mixture of various kinds of trees*

• zōki-bayashi 雑木林 *thicket of various kinds of trees*

zōkin 雑巾 *dusting cloth; floor-wiping cloth*

• zōkin-gake 雑巾掛け *cleaning with a cloth*

• zōkin-gake suru 雑巾掛けする *to clean with a cloth*

zokugo 俗語 *slang*

zokusúru 属する{Irreg.} *to belong, to be affiliated; to be categorizable*

¶Uchi no Akira wa yakyū-bu ni zokushite imasu.

うちの明は野球部に属しています.

Our Akira belongs to the baseball club.

zókuzoku ぞくぞく ～**suru** ～する *to shiver*

¶Soto wa samukute zokuzoku shimashita.

外は寒くてぞくぞくしました.

I was shivering because it was cold outside.

zokuzoku 続々 （～**to** ～と) *one after another, in succession* [→**aitsuide** 相次いで]

zonjiageru 存じ上げる 【HUM. for **shiru** 知る when the direct object is a person】

zonjíru 存じる ① 【HUM. for **shiru** 知る when the direct object is not a person】

② 【HUM. for **omou** 思う】

zōri 草履 *Japanese sandals* 《with a flat sole and a thong fitting between the big toe and the second toe》

zōsen 造船 *shipbuilding*

• zōsen-jo 造船所 *shipbuilding yard*

zotto ぞっと ～**suru** ～する *to shudder* 《The subject is a person.》

¶Hebi o mite zotto shita yo.

蛇を見てぞっとしたよ.

I saw a snake and shuddered!

zu 図 *figure, diagram, illustration*

• dai-ichi-zu 第１図 *figure 1*

zubári ずばり （～**to** ～と) *frankly, unreservedly*

zubón ズボン *pants, trousers, slacks*

¶Zubon o ip-pon kaimashita.

ズボンを１本買いました.

I bought a pair of pants.

• zubon o haku 〔nugu〕 ズボンをはく 〔脱ぐ〕 *to put on* 〔*take off*〕 *one's pants*

• zubon-tsuri ズボン吊り ＜*US*＞*suspenders*, ＜*UK*＞*braces*

• han-zubon 半ズボン *short pants, shorts*

zubunure ずぶ濡れ ～**no** ～の *soaked-to-the-skin*

¶Yūdachi de zubunure ni natta yo.

夕立でずぶぬれになったよ.

I got soaked to the skin in the afternoon rainshower!

zúga 図画《This word is ordinarily used when the drawing or painting is done in school.》 ① *drawing* 〈*pictures*〉, *painting* 〈*pictures*〉

② *picture, drawing, painting*

zugáikotsu 頭蓋骨 *skull*

zuhyō 図表 *chart, graph*

zúi 髄 *marrow*

zúibun 随分 *very, a lot* [→**hijō ni** 非常に]

¶Kesa wa zuibun samukatta yo.
けさはずいぶん寒かったよ。
It was very cold this morning!

¶Sumō no koto o zuibun shitte iru ne.
相撲の事をずいぶん知っているね。
You know a lot about sumo, don't you.

zuihitsu 随筆 *essay* 〈*consisting of the writer's random thoughts*〉

• zuihitsu-ka 随筆家 *essayist*

zukai 図解 *explanation by diagram*

• zukai suru 図解する *to explain by a diagram*

zukan 図鑑 *illustrated book*

-zuke －付け *dated*《Added to bases denoting dates.》

¶Jūni-gatsu-nijūgo-nichi-zuke no tegami ga todokimashita.
12月25日付けの手紙が届きました。
A letter dated December 25 was delivered.

zukín 頭巾 *hood, cowl* 《(cloth head covering)》; *skullcap*

zúkku ズック *canvas* 《(cloth)》

zúnō 頭脳 *brains, thinking ability*

zurásu ずらす ① *to shift, to move slightly by sliding* 《transitive》

② *to shift out of overlap* 《in space or time》 《transitive》

zuréru ずれる ① *to shift out of overlap* 《in space or time》 《intransitive》

② *to shift out of proper position* 《in space or time》 《intransitive》

zurúi 狡い *sly, tricky; unfair*

• zurui koto o suru ずるい事をする *to do something unfair, to cheat*

-zútsu －ずつ *in amounts of*《Added to bases denoting quantities.》

¶Hitori-zutsu kyōshitsu ni hairinasai.
一人ずつ教室に入りなさい。
Enter the classroom one by one.

¶Enpitsu o ni-hon-zutsu totte kudasai.
鉛筆を2本ずつ取ってください。
Please take two pencils each.

¶Sukoshi-zutsu hakobimashō.
少しずつ運びましょう。
Let's carry it little by little.

zutsū 頭痛 *headache*

• zutsū ga suru 頭痛がする *to have a headache*

zutto ずっと ① *all along, all the way, the whole time*

¶Hito-ban-jū zutto yuki ga futte imashita.
一晩中ずっと雪が降っていました。
It was snowing all through the night.

¶Zutto Okazaki-san to issho deshita.
ずっと岡崎さんといっしょでした。
I was with Ms. Okazaki the whole time.

¶Ima made zutto doko ni ita no desu ka.
今までずっとどこにいたのですか。
Where were you all this time until now?

¶Taro wa kono mae no Kin'yōbi kara zutto yasumi da.
太郎はこの前の金曜日からずっと休みだ。
Taro has been off since last Friday.

② *far, extremely* 《preceding a word denoting a separation in space or time》

• zutto mae ni ずっと前に *a long time ago*

③ *by far, much*

¶Chūgoku wa Nihon yori zutto hiroi desu.
中国は日本よりずっと広いです。
China is much larger than Japan.

zūzūshii ずうずうしい *impudent, shameless, brazen*

APPENDIX 1: Conjugation

Japanese predicate words can be divided into three types: verb, adjective, and copula. There are, of course, many different verbs and many different adjectives, but there is only one copula. Each predicate word has a variety of different forms, and this set of forms is sometimes called a conjugation. This appendix provides a brief description of the conjugations of of each type of predicate word.

1. Regular Verbs

Most Japanese verbs have conjugations that can be classified as one of two traditionally recognized regular types.

a. **Ichidan** Verbs

A verb of the first regular type has an informal nonpast affirmative form (the form listed in dictionaries) that ends in the sequence –**iru** or –**eru**. The verbs **ochiru** 落ちる and **taberu** 食べる are typical examples, and several forms of each are listed below. Notice that the portions **ochi**– and **tabe**– are common to every form.

ochi–ru	informal nonpast affirmative
ochi–nai	informal nonpast negative
ochi–masu	semi-formal nonpast affirmative
ochi–tai	informal nonpast affirmative desiderative
ochi–ta	informal past affirmative
ochi–tara	–**tara** conditional
ochi–tari	alternative
ochi–te	gerund
ochi–reba	–**ba** conditional
ochi–ro	imperative
ochi–yō	informal volitional
tabe–ru	informal nonpast affirmative
tabe–nai	informal nonpast negative
tabe–masu	semi-formal nonpast affirmative

tabe–**tai**	informal nonpast affirmative desiderative
tabe–**ta**	informal past affirmative
tabe–**tara**	–**tara** conditional
tabe–**tari**	alternative
tabe–**te**	gerund
tabe–**reba**	–**ba** conditional
tabe–**ro**	imperative
tabe–**yō**	informal volitional

The traditional name **ichidan** 一段 means *one-row* and comes from the fact that in **kana** spelling, the same letter occurs before the ending in every form of a given verb (**chi** ち in the case of **ochiru** and **be** べ in the case of **taberu**). In the traditional 10–column 5–row arrangement of the **kana** syllabary, the letters for syllables containing the same vowel are in the same row, so the letter before the endings in the forms of an **ichidan** verb represents only one row of the syllabary.

As noted above, the form of an **ichidan** verb that is listed in a dictionary ends in –**iru** or –**eru**. Unless there is an explicit notation to the contrary, any verb listed in this dictionary with final –**iru** or –**eru** is **ichidan** and has a conjugation like **ochiru** and **taberu**.

b. **Godan** Verbs

A verb of the second regular type has an informal nonpast affirmative form (the form listed in dictionaries) that ends in one of the following syllables: –**u**, –**ku**, –**gu**, –**su**, –**tsu**, –**nu**, –**bu**, –**mu**, –**ru**. The traditional name **godan** 五段 means *five-row* and comes from the fact that the stem is followed by each of the five vowels in at least one form. Thus, in the **kana** spelling of the forms of a **godan** verb, at least five different letters occur to represent the final consonant of the stem (if any) and the initial vowel of an ending. In the traditional 10–column 5–row arrangement of the **kana** syllabary, the letters for syllables containing the same vowel are in the same row, so the relevant letters in the forms of a **godan** verb represent all five rows of the syllabary.

Although all **godan** verbs share certain obvious similarities in their conjugations, it is convenient to describe each of the nine subtypes separately.

i. Final –**u** Subtype

Any verb listed in this dictionary with final –**u** following a vowel has a conjugation like **arau** 洗う.

ara–**u**	informal nonpast affirmative
araw–**a**–**nai**	informal nonpast negative
ara–**i**–**masu**	semi-formal nonpast affirmative

ara–i–tai	informal nonpast affirmative desiderative
arat–ta	informal past affirmative
arat–tara	–**tara** conditional
arat–tari	alternative
arat–te	gerund
ara–eba	–**ba** conditional
ara–e	imperative
ara–ō	informal volitional

ii. Final –**ku** Subtype

Unless there is an explicit notation to the contrary, any verb listed in this dictionary with final –**ku** has a conjugation like **aruku** 歩く.

aruk–u	informal nonpast affirmative
aruk–a–nai	informal nonpast negative
aruk–i–masu	semi–formal nonpast affirmative
aruk–i–tai	informal nonpast affirmative desiderative
aru–i–ta	informal past affirmative
aru–i–tara	–**tara** conditional
aru–i–tari	alternative
aru–i–te	gerund
aruk–eba	–**ba** conditional
aruk–e	imperative
aruk–ō	informal volitional

iii. Final –**gu** Subtype

Any verb listed in this dictionary with final –**gu** has a conjugation like **isogu** 急ぐ.

isog–u	informal nonpast affirmative
isog–a–nai	informal nonpast negative
isog–i–masu	semi–formal nonpast affirmative
isog–i–tai	informal nonpast affirmative desiderative
iso–i–da	informal past affirmative
iso–i–dara	–**tara** conditional
iso–i–dari	alternative
iso–i–de	gerund
isog–eba	–**ba** conditional
isog–e	imperative
isog–ō	informal volitional

iv. Final –**su** Subtype

Any verb listed in this dictionary with final –**su** has a conjugation like **hanasu** 話す.

hanas–u	informal nonpast affirmative
hanas–a–nai	informal nonpast negative
hanash–i–masu	semi–formal nonpast affirmative
hanash–i–tai	informal nonpast affirmative desiderative
hanash–i–ta	informal past affirmative
hanash–i–tara	–**tara** conditional
hanash–i–tari	alternative
hanash–i–te	gerund
hanas–eba	–**ba** conditional
hanas–e	imperative
hanas–ō	informal volitional

v. Final –tsu Subtype

Any verb listed in this dictionary with final –**tsu** has a conjugation like **tamotsu** 保つ.

tamots–u	informal nonpast affirmative
tamot–a–nai	informal nonpast negative
tamoch–i–masu	semi–formal nonpast affirmative
tamoch–i–tai	informal nonpast affirmative desiderative
tamot–ta	informal past affirmative
tamot–tara	–**tara** conditional
tamot–tari	alternative
tamot–te	gerund
tamot–eba	–**ba** conditional
tamot–e	imperative
tamot–ō	informal volitional

vi. Final –nu Subtype

The only Japanese verb that ends with –**nu** is **shinu** 死ぬ.

shin–u	informal nonpast affirmative
shin–a–nai	informal nonpast negative
shin–i–masu	semi–formal nonpast affirmative
shin–i–tai	informal nonpast affirmative desiderative
shin–da	informal past affirmative
shin–dara	–**tara** conditional
shin–dari	alternative
shin–de	gerund
shin–eba	–**ba** conditional
shin–e	imperative
shin–ō	informal volitional

vii. Final –**bu** Subtype

Any verb listed in this dictionary with final –**bu** has a conjugation like **asobu** 遊ぶ.

asob–u	informal nonpast affirmative
asob–a–nai	informal nonpast negative
asob–i–masu	semi-formal nonpast affirmative
asob–i–tai	informal nonpast affirmative desiderative
ason–da	informal past affirmative
ason–dara	–**tara** conditional
ason–dari	alternative
ason–de	gerund
asob–eba	–**ba** conditional
asob–e	imperative
asob–ō	informal volitional

viii. Final –**mu** Subtype

Any verb listed in this dictionary with final –**mu** has a conjugation like **tanomu** 頼む.

tanom–u	informal nonpast affirmative
tanom–a–nai	informal nonpast negative
tanom–i–masu	semi-formal nonpast affirmative
tanom–i–tai	informal nonpast affirmative desiderative
tanon–da	informal past affirmative
tanon–dara	–**tara** conditional
tanon–dari	alternative
tanon–de	gerund
tanom–eba	–**ba** conditional
tanom–e	imperative
tanom–ō	informal volitional

ix. Final –**ru** Subtype

Any verb listed in this dictionary with final –**uru**, or –**oru** has a conjugation like **mamoru** 守る (see below).

Unless there is an explicit notation to the contrary, any verb listed in this dictionary with final –**aru** has a conjugation like **mamoru** 守る (see below).

As noted above in Section 1.a, unless there is an explicit notation to the contrary, any verb listed in this dictionary with final –**iru** or –**eru** is **ichidan** and has a conjugation like **ochiru** and **taberu**. If a verb ending in –**iru** or –**eru** is **godan** (and therefore has a conjugation like **mamoru** below), its entry in this dictionary contains the notation {5} immediately after the ordinary Japanese writing of the entry word. For example, the verb hashiru 走る is **godan**, and its entry in this dictionary begins: **hashīru** 走る {5}.

mamor–u	informal nonpast affirmative
mamor–a–nai	informal nonpast negative
mamor–i–masu	semi-formal nonpast affirmative
mamor–i–tai	informal nonpast affirmative desiderative
mamot–ta	informal past affirmative
mamot–tara	**–tara** conditional
mamot–tari	alternative
mamot–te	gerund
mamor–eba	**–ba** conditional
mamor–e	imperative
mamor–ō	informal volitional

2. Irregular Verbs

Any verb listed in this dictionary which is neither **ichidan** nor **godan** is marked with the notation {Irreg.} to indicate that it is irregular.

a. aru ある

The verb **aru** has a conjugation like that of a final –**ru** subtype **godan** verb (see Section 1.b.ix above) in most respects, but the informal negative forms lack the expected initial **ara–**. For example, the informal nonpast negative is **nai** (instead of the expected but nonexistent **ar–a–nai**), the informal past negative is **na–katta** (instead of the expected but nonexistent **ar–a–nakatta**), etc.

b. Irregular Verbs Ending in –aru

There are five verbs ending in –**aru** which have conjugations similar to those of final –**ru** subtype **godan** verbs (see Section 1.b.ix above). These five irregular verbs are all honorific or formal in terms of speech level, and each has some forms that deviate from the regular **godan** pattern.

i. kudasaru くださる, nasaru なさる, ossharu おっしゃる

These three verbs are all honorific and share the same conjugation pattern. The forms of **kudasaru** are given below as illustrations.

kudasar–u	informal nonpast affirmative
kudasar–a–nai	informal nonpast negative
kudasa–i–masu	semi-formal nonpast affirmative
kudasar–i–tai	informal nonpast affirmative desiderative
kudasat–ta	informal past affirmative
kudasat–tara	**–tara** conditional
kudasat–tari	alternative
kudasat–te	gerund
kudasar–eba	**–ba** conditional
kudasa–i	imperative

ii. **irassharu** いらっしゃる

This honorific verb has forms parallel to those of the three verbs just above in Section 1.b.i, but it also has additional alternative forms for the informal past affirmative and for the forms that are historically related to the informal past affirmative (i.e., the **-tara** conditional, the alternative, and the gerund).

irasshar–u	informal nonpast affirmative
irasshar–a–nai	informal nonpast negative
irassha–i–masu	semi–formal nonpast affirmative
irasshar–i–tai	informal nonpast affirmative desiderative
irasshat–ta ∼ **irash–i–ta**	informal past affirmative
irasshat–tara ∼ **irash–i–tara**	**-tara** conditional
irasshat–tari ∼ **irash–i–tari**	alternative
irasshat–te ∼ **irash–i–te**	gerund
irasshar–eba	**-ba** conditional
irassha–i	imperative

iii. **gozaru** ござる

The formal verb **gozaru** has a conjugation pattern parallel to that of the three verbs above in Section 1.b.i, but **gozaru** is now archaic except in forms with semi–formal endings (i.e., **-masu**, **-mashita**, **-masen**, **-mashō**, etc.). The semi–formal nonpast affirmative, for example, is **goza–i–masu**.

c. **iku** 行く and **yuku** 行く

The verb **iku** and its somewhat archaic equivalent **yuku** have a conjugation pattern like that of final **-ku** subtype **godan** verbs (see Section 1.b.ii above) except for the informal past affirmative and the forms that are historically related to the informal past affirmative (i.e., the **-tara** conditional, the alternative, and the gerund). Illustrative forms of **iku** are given below.

ik–u	informal nonpast affirmative
ik–a–nai	informal nonpast negative
ik–i–masu	semi–formal nonpast affirmative
ik–i–tai	informal nonpast affirmative desiderative
it–ta	informal past affirmative
it–tara	**-tara** conditional
it–tari	alternative
it–te	gerund
ik–eba	**-ba** conditional
ik–e	**imperative**
ik–ō	informal volitional

d. kureru くれる

The verb **kureru** has a conjugation pattern like that of an **ichidan** verb (see Section 1.a above) except for the imperative form, which is **kure** (instead of the expected but nonexistent **kure-ro**).

e. kuru 来る and suru する

These two verbs are, for practical purposes, completely irregular. Each has a unique conjugation pattern.

ku-ru	informal nonpast affirmative
ko-nai	informal nonpast negative
ki-masu	semi-formal nonpast affirmative
ki-tai	informal nonpast affirmative desiderative
ki-ta	informal past affirmative
ki-tara	-**tara** conditional
ki-tari	alternative
ki-te	gerund
ku-reba	-**ba** conditional
ko-i	imperative
ko-yō	informal volitional

su-ru	informal nonpast affirmative
shi-nai	informal nonpast negative
shi-masu	semi-formal nonpast affirmative
shi-tai	informal nonpast affirmative desiderative
shi-ta	informal past affirmative
shi-tara	-**tara** conditional
shi-tari	alternative
shi-te	gerund
su-reba	-**ba** conditional
shi-ro	imperative
shi-yō	informal volitional

f. Verbs Ending in -**suru**

A number of Japanese verbs can be analyzed as a single element of Chinese origin (written with a single Chinese character) combined into a compound with **suru**. However, there are differences of opinion among native speakers of Japanese about the conjugations of these verbs, and an individual speaker's opinion will not be consistent from verb to verb. The verb **bassu-ru** 罰する is a typical example, and several forms are listed below. The differences of opinion involve the alternative forms for the informal nonpast affirmative and the informal nonpast negative (and other forms based on it). For the informal nonpast affirmative, a speaker may or may not accept the shorter alternative (**bassu** for this verb). For the informal nonpast negative, a speaker may accept one or both of the two alternative forms (**basshinai** and **bassanai** for this verb).

bassu–ru ~ bass–u	informal nonpast affirmative
basshi–nai ~ bass–a–nai	informal nonpast negative
basshi–masu	semi–formal nonpast affirmative
basshi–tai	informal nonpast affirmative desiderative
basshi–ta	informal past affirmative
basshi–tara	**–tara** conditional
basshi–tari	alternative
basshi–te	gerund
bassu–reba	**–ba** conditional
basshi–ro	imperative
basshi–yō	informal volitional

3. Verb Bases

In this dictionary, the term *verb base* refers to what precedes the informal nonpast affirmative desiderative ending **–tai**. For example, the base of **taberu** (see Section A.1.a above) is **tabe**, and the base of **hanasu** (see Section A.1.b.iv above) is **hanashi**.

4. Adjectives

Every Japanese adjective has an informal nonpast affirmative form (the form listed in dictionaries) that ends in **–i**.

a. Regular Adjectives

All Japanese adjectives except **ii** (see Section B.2 below) have the same conjugation pattern. The adjective **takai** 高い is a typical example, and several forms are listed below.

taka–i	informal nonpast affirmative
taka–ku	adverbial
taka–kute	gerund
taka–kereba	**–ba** conditional
taka–katta	informal past affirmative
taka–kattara	**–tara** conditional
taka–kattari	alternative

b. ii いい

The adjective **ii** is derived historically from **yoi**, which is still used as a somewhat more formal alternative. The conjugations of the two words differ only in the informal nonpast affirmative form. For all other forms, the regular forms of **yoi** are used. Several form of **ii** are listed below to illustrate.

i–i	informal nonpast affirmative
yo-ku	adverbial
yo-kute	gerund
yo-kereba	–**ba** conditional
yo-katta	informal past affirmative
yo-kattara	–**tara** conditional
yo-kattari	alternative

c. Negative Forms

The negative forms of an adjective are made by combining the adverbial form with forms of the separate word **nai**, and **nai** itself has the conjugation of an adjective. For example the informal nonpast negative of **takai** is **takaku na-i**, the informal past negative is **takaku na-katta**, etc.

d. Adjective Bases

In this dictionary, the term *adjective base* refers to what precedes the endings other than the informal nonpast affirmative ending –**i**. For example, the base of **takai** (see Section B.1. above) is **taka**, and the base of **ii** (see Section B.2 above) is **yo**.

5. The Copula

a. Affirmative Forms

When a noun or adjectival noun is used as a predicate, it is followed by a form of the copula. The Japanese copula thus has a function analogous to some uses of the English verb *to be*. Several forms of the copula are listed below.

da	informal nonpast affirmative
desu	semi–formal nonpast affirmative
datta	informal past affirmative
deshita	semi–formal past affirmative
dat-tara	–**tara** conditional
dattari	alternative
de	gerund
nara(–**ba**)	–**ba** conditional

darō	informal tentative
deshō	semi-formal tentative

b. Negative Forms

The negative forms of the copula are made by combining the gerund with forms of the separate word **nai**, usually with the particle **wa** は in between. The word **nai** itself has the conjugation of an adjective. For example the informal nonpast negative of the copula is **de(wa)na-i**, the informal past negative is **de(wa)na-katta**, etc. In conversation, **de wa** typically contracts to **ja** じゃ.

APPENDIX 2: Numerals, Counters, and Numbers

1. Numerals

A number in Japanese ordinarily consists of a numeral followed by a counter. Two sets of numerals are in use, one native and one borrowed from Chinese. The only native numerals still used in modern Japanese are those denoting 1–10, and with the exception of **nana**(7) and the variant forms **yon**(4) and **tō** (10), they do not occur as independent words. Still other variant forms appear in certain numeral + counter combinations, but the basic native numerals are:

hito	一	*one*
futa	二	*two*
mi	三	*three*
yo	四	*four*
itsu	五	*five*
mu	六	*six*
nana	七	*seven*
ya	八	*eight*
kokono	九	*nine*
to	十	*ten*

The borrowed numerals can generally occur as independent words. (Those denoting very large quantities— **man, oku, chō** —occur only in combinations with another numeral preceding, but these combinations can function as independent words; see below.) They are used independently in activities such as counting to ten or doing arithmetic. A number of variant forms appear in certain numeral + counter combinations, but the basic borrowed numerals are:

ichi	一	*one*
ni	二	*two*
san	三	*three*
shi	四	*four*
go	五	*five*

roku	六	*six*
shichi	七	*seven*
hachi	八	*eight*
ku / kyū	九	*nine*
jū	十	*ten*
hyaku	百	*hundred*
man	万	*ten thousand*
oku	億	*hundred million*
chō	兆	*trillion*

Large numerals are made by combining these elements. (Users unfamiliar with the principles for forming such combinations should consult a textbook.) Many combinations involving large numerals show variations in a form like those found in numeral + counter combinations. These combinations are listed below. (Note that some of these combinations contain native numerals as their first elements.)

hyaku	百	*one hundred*
ni–hyaku	二百	*two hundred*
san–byaku	三百	*three hundred*
yon–hyaku	四百	*four hundred*
go–hyaku	五百	*five hundred*
rop–pyaku	六百	*six hundred*
nana–hyaku	七百	*seven hundred*
hap–pyaku	八百	*eight hundred*
kyū–hyaku	九百	*nine hundred*
sen / is–sen	千／一千	*one thousand*
ni–sen	二千	*two thousand*
san–zen	三千	*three thousand*
yon–sen	四千	*four thousand*
go–sen	五千	*five thousand*
roku–sen	六千	*six thousand*
nana–sen	七千	*seven thousand*
has–sen	八千	*eight thousand*
kyū–sen	九千	*nine thousand*
ichi–man	一万	*ten thousand*
ni–man	二万	*twenty thousand*
san–man	三万	*thirty thousand*
yon–man	四万	*forty thousand*
go–man	五万	*fifty thousand*

roku–man	六万	*sixty thousand*
nana–man	七万	*seventy thousand*
hachi–man	八万	*eighty thousand*
kyū–man	九万	*ninety thousand*
jū–man	十万	*one hundred thousand*
hyaku–man	百万	*one million*
sen–man / is–sen–man	千万／一千万	*ten million*
ichi–oku	一億	*one hundred million*
ni–oku	二億	*two hundred million*
san–oku	三億	*three hundred million*
yon–oku	四億	*four hundred million*
go–oku	五億	*five hundred million*
roku–oku	六億	*six hundred million*
nana–oku	七億	*seven hundred million*
hachi–oku	八億	*eight hundred million*
kyū–oku	九億	*nine hundred million*
jū–oku	十億	*one billion*
hyaku–oku	百億	*ten billion*
sen–oku / is–sen–oku	千億／一千億	*one hundred billion*
it–chō	一兆	*one trillion*
ni–chō	二兆	*two trillion*
san–chō	三兆	*three trillion*
yon–chō	四兆	*four trillion*
go–chō	五兆	*five trillion*
roku–chō	六兆	*six trillion*
nana–chō	七兆	*seven trillion*
hat–chō	八兆	*eight trillion*
kyū–chō	九兆	*nine trillion*
jut–chō / jit–chō	十兆	*ten trillion*
hyaku–chō	百兆	*one hundred trillion*
sen–chō / is–sen–chō	千兆／一千兆	*one quadrillion*

2. Counters

When actually counting something rather than using numbers as abstract quantities, numbers consisting of numeral + counter are generally required. Choosing the appropriate counters for different situations is not a simple matter in Japanese. There is a degree of arbitrariness in the conventions for counting certain things with certain counters, and in many cases there is more than one acceptable choice of counter. Users who are unfamiliar with the counter system should consult a textbook for a more detailed explanation.

When no specific counter is available (or when a specific counter is possible but not chosen), the counter –**tsu** is used. This counter combines with native numerals, but if the number is greater than 9, –**tsu** does not appear. The variant native form **tō** is used for 10, and the numerals borrowed from Chinese, with no counter attached, are pressed into service for numbers greater than 10. (Users who are unfamiliar with this complication in the counter system should consult a textbook for further explanation.) The numbers in this series are listed below.

hito–tsu	一つ	*one*
futa–tsu	二つ	*two*
mit–tsu	三つ	*thrre*
yot–tsu	四つ	*four*
itsu–tsu	五つ	*five*
mut–tsu	六つ	*six*
nana–tsu	七つ	*seven*
yat–tsu	八つ	*eight*
kokono–tsu	九つ	*nine*
tō	十	*ten*
jū–ichi	十一	*eleven*
jū–ni	十二	*twelve*
iku–tsu	いくつ	*how many*

Years of age can also be counted with this series of numbers, but the special irregular form **hatachi** is used for twenty years old, whereas the regular form **ni–jū** is used for twenty of anything else counted with this series.

In addition to the problem of choosing appropriate counters, numeral + counter combinations exhibit a bewildering variety in their forms. The catalog below contains an entry for each counter listed in the body of this dictionary, and each catalog entry lists the important numeral + counter combinations (from which the forms of other combinations can be inferred).

Each catalog entry begins with a counter in its basic form (the form in which it is listed in the body of this dictionary) and a brief indication of the kinds of things it is typically used to count. When a single counter has two clearly distinct uses, each use is numbered.

Each use is marked as cardinal(C), ordinal(O), or both(C/O). A cardinal counter forms cardinal numbers, that is, numbers specifying quantities. For example, the counter –**mētoru** is cardinal, so the combination **ichi–mētoru** 一メートル means *one meter* (not *meter one*). An ordinal counter forms ordinal numbers, that is, numbers naming something at a given position in a series. For example, the counter **-ban-sen** is ordinal, so the combination **ichi-ban-sen** 一番線 means *track one* (not *one track*). An example of a counter that can be either cardinal or ordinal is **-pēji**. The combination **ichi-pēji** 一ページ can mean either *one page* or *page one*. More general ordinal numbers can be formed by adding the suffix **-me** to cardinal numbers. For example, **ichi-pēji-me** 一ページ目 means *first page* (which may or may not be *page one*). The prefix **dai-** 第一 can also combine with many cardinal numbers to form ordinals. For example, **dai-ip-po** 第一歩 means *first step*.

In most catalog entries, the combinations for 1–10, 100, and 1,000 are given. In addition, each entry provides the word for *how many* using the counter in question (marked with the notation[?]). Certain counters are seldom or never used with certain numerals, and such combinations are omitted. In a few cases, combinations other than those for 1–10, 100, and 1,000 are provided.

For counters introduced in Jorden & Noda, the numeral + counter combinations listed in the catalog generally follow the forms given there (Eleanor Harz Jorden & Mari Noda, *Japanese: The Spoken Language*, 3 vols. Yale University Press, 1987–1990.). Otherwise, the combinations generally follow the commentary by Sakurai & Akinaga in the NHK accent and pronunciation dictionary （桜井茂治，秋永一枝「数詞・助数詞の発音とアクセント」『日本語発音アクセント辞典』日本放送出版協会）. In all cases, however, native speakers have been consulted for judgments, and these judgments have served as the final authority. Alternative forms are listed for many combinations, and in real-life situations, forms that do not appear below often occur.

3. Catalog of Counters and Numeral + Counter Combinations

-anpea 一アンペア *amperes*(C)
[1] ichi-anpea [2] ni-anpea [3] san-anpea [4] yon-anpea [5] go-anpea [6] roku-anpea [7] nana-anpea/shichi-anpea [8] hachi-anpea [9] kyū-anpea [10] jū-anpea [100] hyaku-anpea [1,000] sen-anpea [?] nan-anpea

-aru 一アール *ares*(C)
[1] ichi-āru [2] ni-āru [3] san-āru [4] yon-āru [5] go-āru [6] roku-āru [7] nana-āru/ shichi-āru [8] hachi-āru [9] kyū-āru [10] jū-āru [100] hyaku-āru [1,000] sen-āru [?] nan-āru

-bai 一倍 *multiples* (i.e., *n times as much/many*) (C)
[2] ni-bai [3] san-bai [4] yon-bai [5] go-bai [6] roku-bai [7] nana-bai/shichi-bai [8] hachi-bai [9] kyū-bai [10] jū-bai [100] hyaku-bai [1,000] sen-bai [?] nan-bai

-ban —番 *numbers in a series*(O)
[1] ichi-ban [2] ni-ban [3] san-ban [4] yon-ban/yo-ban [5] go-ban
[6] roku-ban [7] nana-ban/shichi-ban [8] hachi-ban [9] kyū-ban/ku-ban
[10] jū-ban [100] hyaku-ban [1,000] sen-ban [?] nan-ban

-ban —晩 *nights*(C)
[1] hito-ban [2] futa-ban [3] mi-ban [4] yo-ban [?] iku-ban

-banchi —番地 *lot numbers* (*used in addresses*)(O)
[1] ichi-banchi [2] ni-banchi [3] san-banchi [4] yon-banchi [5] go-banchi
[6] roku-banchi [7] nana-banchi/shichi-banchi [8] hachi-banchi [9] kyū-
banchi/ku-banchi [10] jū-banchi [?] nan-banchi

-ban-sen —番線 *railroad station track numbers*(O)
[1] ichi-ban-sen [2] ni-ban-sen [3] san-ban-sen [4] yon-ban-sen [5] go-
ban-sen [6] roku-ban-sen [7] nana-ban-sen/shichi-ban-sen [8] hachi-ban-
sen [9] kyū-ban-sen [10] jū-ban-sen [?] nan-ban-sen

-bariki —馬力 *horsepower*(C)
[1] ichi-bariki [2] ni-bariki [3] san-bariki [4] yon-bariki [5] go-bariki
[6] roku-bariki [7] nana-bariki/shichi-bariki [8] hachi-bariki [9] kyū-
bariki [10] jū-bariki [100] hyaku-bariki [1,000] sen-bariki [?] nan-bariki

-bin —便 *airline flights*(C/O)
[1] ichi-bin [2] ni-bin [3] san-bin [4] yon-bin/yo-bin [5] go-bin [6] roku-
bin [7] nana-bin/shichi-bin [8] hachi-bin [9] kyū-bin [10] jū-bin
[100] hyaku-bin [1,000] sen-bin [?] nan-bin

-boruto —ボルト *volts*(C)
[1] ichi-boruto [2] ni-boruto [3] san-boruto [4] yon-boruto [5] go-boruto
[6] roku-boruto [7] nana-boruto/shichi-boruto [8] hachi-boruto [9] kyū-
boruto [10] jū-boruto [100] hyaku-boruto [1,000] sen-boruto [?] nan-
boruto

-bu —部 *parts*(C)
[1] ichi-bu [2] ni-bu [3] san-bu [4] yon-bu [5] go-bu [6] roku-bu
[7] nana-bu/shichi-bu [8] hachi-bu [9] kyū-bu [10] jū-bu [100] hyaku-bu
[1,000] sen-bu [?] nan-bu

-bu —部 *copies* (*of documents, books, etc.*)(C)
See -**bu** above.

-bun —分 *parts, portions*(C)
[1] ichi-bun [2] ni-bun [3] san-bun [4] yon-bun [5] go-bun [6] roku-bun
[7] nana-bun/shichi-bun [8] hachi-bun [9] kyū-bun/ku-bun [10] jū-bun
[100] hyaku-bun [1,000] sen-bun [?] nan-bun

-byo —秒 *seconds*(C)
[1] ichi-byō [2] ni-byō [3] san-byō [4] yon-byō [5] go-byō [6] roku-byō
[7] nana-byo/shichi-byo [8] hachi-byō [9] kyū-byō [10] jū-byō
[100] hyaku-byō [1,000] sen-byō [?] nan-byō

-channeru —チャンネル *broadcast channels*(C/O)
[1] it-channeru [2] ni-channeru [3] san-channeru [4] yon-channeru
[5] go-channeru [6] roku-channeru [7] nana-channeru/shichi-channeru
[8] hat-channeru/hachi-channeru [9] kyū-channeru [10] jut-channeru
[100] hyaku-channeru [?] nan-channeru

-dai —台 *vehicles, machines*(C)
[1] ichi-dai [2] ni-dai [3] san-dai [4] yon-dai [5] go-dai [6] roku-dai
[7] nana-dai/shichi-dai [8] hachi-dai [9] kyū-dai [10] jū-dai [100] hyaku-
dai [1,000] sen-dai [?] nan-dai

-dai —代 *people in succession to a headship*(C)
[1] ichi-dai [2] ni-dai [3] san-dai [4] yon-dai [5] go-dai [6] roku-dai
[7] nana-dai/shichi-dai [8] hachi-dai [9] kyū-dai [10] jū-dai [100] hyaku-
dai [1,000] sen-dai [?] nan-dai

-dāsu —ダース *dozens*(C)
[1] ichi-dāsu [2] ni-dāsu [3] san-dāsu [4] yon-dāsu [5] go-dāsu [6] roku-
dāsu [7] nana-dāsu/shichi-dāsu [8] hachi-dāsu [9] kyū-dāsu/ku-dāsu
[10] jū-dāsu [100] hyaku-dāsu [1,000] sen-dāsu [?] nan-dāsu

-do —度　① *times, occurrences*(C)　② *degrees (of temperature or arc)*(C)
[1] ichi-do [2] ni-do [3] san-do [4] yon-do [5] go-do [6] roku-do
[7] nana-do/shichi-do [8] hachi-do [9] kyū-do/ku-do [10] jū-do
[100] hyaku-do [1,000] sen-do [?] nan-do

-doru —ドル *dollars*(C)
[1] ichi-doru [2] ni-doru [3] san-doru [4] yon-doru [5] go-doru [6] roku-
doru [7] nana-doru/shichi-doru [8] hachi-doru [9] kyū-doru [10] jū-doru
[100] hyaku-doru [1,000] sen-doru [?] nan-doru

-en —円 *yen*(C)
[1] ichi-en [2] ni-en [3] san-en [4] yon-en/yo-en [5] go-en [6] roku-en
[7] nana-en [8] hachi-en [9] kyū-en [10] jū-en [100] hyaku-en [1,000] sen-
en [?] nan-en

-fīto —フィート *feet (i.e., units of linear measure)*(C)
[1] ichi-fīto [2] ni-fīto [3] san-fīto [4] yon-fīto [5] go-fīto [6] roku-fīto
[7] nana-fīto [8] hachi-fīto [9] kyū-fīto [10] jū-fīto/juf-fīto/jif-fīto
[100] hyaku-fīto [1,000] sen-fīto [?] nan-fīto

-fun 一分　① *minutes*(C)　② *minutes past the hour* (*when telling time*)(O)
[1] ip-pun [2] ni-fun [3] san-pun [4] yon-pun [5] go-fun [6] rop-pun
[7] nana-fun/shichi-fun [8] hap-pun/hachi-fun [9] kyū-fun [10] jup-pun/jip-pun [100] hyap-pun [?] nan-pun

-garon 一ガロン *gallons*(C)
[1] ichi-garon [2] ni-garon [3] san-garon [4] yon-garon [5] go-garon
[6] roku-garon [7] nana-garon/shichi-garon [8] hachi-garon [9] kyū-garon
[10] jū-garon [100] hyaku-garon [1,000] sen-garon [?] nan-garon

-gatsu 一月 *months of the calendar*(O)
[1(January)] Ichi-gatsu [2(February)] Ni-gatsu [3(March)] San-gatsu
[4(April)] Shi-gatsu [5(May)] Go-gatsu [6(June)] Roku-gatsu [7(July)]
Shichi-gatsu [8(August)] Hachi-gatsu [9(September)] Ku-gatsu [10(October)] Jū-gatsu [11(Novermber)] Jūichi-gatsu [12(December)] Jūni-gatsu
[?] nan-gatsu

-go 一語 *words*(C)
[1] ichi-go [2] ni-go [3] san-go [4] yon-go [5] go-go [6] roku-go
[7] nana-go/shichi-go [8] hachi-go [9] kyū-go [10] jū-go [100] hyaku-go [1,000] sen-go [?] nan-go

-gō 一号 *train numbers, magazine issues*(O)
[1] ichi-gō [2] ni-gō [3] san-gō [4] yon-gō [5] go-gō [6] roku-gō
[7] nana-gō/shichi-gō [8] hachi-gō [9] kyū-gō [10] jū-gō [100] hyaku-gō [1,000] sen-gō [?] nan-gō

-guramu 一グラム *grams*(C)
[1] ichi-guramu [2] ni-guramu [3] san-guramu [4] yon-guramu
[5] go-guramu [6] roku-guramu [7] nana-guramu/shichi-guramu
[8] hachi-guramu [9] kyū-guramu [10] jū-guramu [100] hyaku-guramu
[1,000] sen-guramu [?] nan-guramu

-gyō 一行 *lines of text*(C)
[1] ichi-gyō [2] ni-gyō [3] san-gyō [4] yon-gyō [5] go-gyō [6] roku-gyō
[7] nana-gyō/shichi-gyō [8] hachi-gyō [9] kyū-gyō [10] jū-gyō
[100] hyaku-gyō [1,000] sen-gyō [?] nan-gyō

-hai 一杯 *cupfuls, glassfuls, bowlfuls, spoonfuls*(C)
[1] ip-pai [2] ni-hai [3] san-bai [4] yon-hai [5] go-hai [6] rop-pai
[7] nana-hai/shichi-hai [8] hap-pai/hachi-hai [9] kyū-hai [10] jup-pai/jip-pai [100] hyap-pai [1,000] sen-bai [?] nan-bai

-hako 一箱 *boxes, boxfuls*(C)
[1] hito-hako [2] futa-hako [3] mi-hako/san-pako [4] yon-hako [5] go-hako [6] rop-pako [7] nana-hako/shichi-hako [8] hachi-hako/hap-pako

[9] kyū-hako [10] jup-pako/jip-pako [100] hyap-pako [1,000] sen-pako
[?] nan-pako

-haku 一泊 *nights of a stayover*(C)
[1] ip-paku [2] ni-haku [3] san-paku [4] yon-paku [5] go-haku
[6] rop-paku [7] nana-haku/shichi-haku [8] hap-paku/hachi-haku
[9] kyū-haku [10] jup-paku/jip-paku [?] nan-paku

-heihō-mētoru 一平方メートル *square meters*(C)
[1] ichi-heihō-mētoru [2] ni-heihō-mētoru [3] san-heihō-mētoru
[4] yon-heihō-mētoru [5] go-heihō-mētoru [6] roku-heihō-mētoru
[7] nana-heihō-mētoru/shichi-heihō-mētoru [8] hachi-heihō-mētoru
[9] kyū-heihō-mētoru [10] jū-heihō-mētoru [100] hyaku-heihō-mētoru
[1,000] sen-heihō-mētoru [?] nan-heihō-mētoru

-hekutāru 一ヘクタール *hectares*(C)
[1] ichi-hekutāru [2] ni-hekutāru [3] san-hekutāru [4] yon-hekutāru
[5] go-hekutāru [6] roku-hekutāru [7] nana-hekutāru/shichi-hekutāru
[8] hachi-hekutāru [9] kyū-hekutāru [10] jū-hekutāru [100] hyaku-
hekutāru [1,000] sen-hekutāru [?] nan-hekutāru

-hen 一辺 *polygon sides*(C)
[1] ip-pen [2] ni-hen [3] san-ben/san-hen [4] yon-hen [5] go-hen
[6] rop-pen/roku-hen [7] nana-hen/shichi-hen [8] hap-pen/hachi-hen
[9] kyū-hen [10] jup-pen/jip-pen [100] hyap-pen [?] nan-ben

-hen 一遍 *times, occurrences*(C)
[1] ip-pen [2] ni-hen [3] san-ben [4] yon-hen [5] go-hen [6] rop-pen/
roku-hen [7] nana-hen/shichi-hen [8] hap-pen/hachi-hen [9] kyū-hen
[10] jup-pen/jip-pen [100] hyap-pen [?] nan-ben

-hiki 一匹 *animals*(C)
[1] ip-piki [2] ni-hiki [3] san-biki [4] yon-hiki/shi-hiki [5] go-hiki
[6] rop-piki/roku-hiki [7] nana-hiki/shichi-hiki [8] hap-piki/hachi-hiki
[9] kyū-hiki [10] jup-piki/jip-piki [100] hyap-piki [1,000] sen-biki
[?] nan-biki

-ho 一歩 *steps, paces*(C)
[1] ip-po [2] ni-ho [3] san-po/san-bo [4] yon-po [5] go-ho [6] rop-po
[7] nana-ho/shichi-ho [8] hap-po/hachi-ho [9] kyū-ho [10] jup-po/jip-
po [100] hyap-po [1,000] sen-po [?] nan-po

-hon 一本 *long objects*(C)
[1] ip-pon [2] ni-hon [3] san-bon [4] yon-hon [5] go-hon [6] rop-pon
[7] nana-hon/shichi-hon [8] hap-pon/hachi-hon [9] kyū-hon [10] jup-
pon/jip-pon [100] hyap-pon [1,000] sen-bon [?] nan-bon

-hyō 一票 *votes*(C)
[1] ip-pyō [2] ni-hyō [3] san-byō [4] yon-hyō [5] go-hyō
[6] rop-pyō/roku-hyō [7] nana-hyō/shichi-hyō [8] hap-pyō/hachi-
hyō [9] kyū-hyō [10] jup-pyō/jip-pyō [100] hyap-pyō [1,000] sen-byō
[?] nan-byō

-inchi 一インチ *inches*(C)
[1] ichi-inchi [2] ni-inchi [3] san-inchi [4] yon-inchi [5] go-inchi
[6] roku-inchi [7] nana-inchi/shichi-inchi [8] hachi-inchi [9] kyū-inchi
[10] jū-inchi [100] hyaku-inchi [1,000] sen-inchi [?] nan-inchi

-ji 一時 *hours on the clock, o'clock*(O)
[1] ichi-ji [2] ni-ji [3] san-ji [4] yo-ji [5] go-ji [6] roku-ji [7] shichi-
ji/nana-ji [8] hachi-ji [9] ku-ji [10] jū-ji [11] juichi-ji [12] juni- ji
[?] nan-ji

-ji 一字 *letters, characters*(C)
[1] ichi-ji [2] ni-ji [3] san-ji [4] yo-ji/yon-ji [5] go-ji [6] roku-ji
[7] nana-ji/shichi-ji [8] hachi-ji [9] kyū-ji [10] jū-ji [100] hyaku-ji
[1,000] sen-ji [?] nan-ji

-jikan 一時間 *hours*(C)
[1] ichi-jikan [2] ni-jikan [3] san-jikan [4] yo-jikan [5] go-jikan
[6] roku-jikan [7] nana-jikan/shichi-jikan [8] hachi-jikan [9] ku-jikan
[10] jū-jikan [100] hyaku-jikan [1,000] sen-jikan [?] nan-jikan

-jō 一畳 *tatami mats* (*traditional unit of measure for room size*)(C)
[1] ichi-jō [2] ni-jō [3] san-jō [4] yo-jō/yon-jō [5] go-jō [6] roku-jō
[7] nana-jō/shichi-jō [8] hachi-jō [9] kyū-jō/ku-jō [10] jū-jō [100] hyaku-
jō [?] nan-jō

-kabu 一株 *shares of stock*(C)
[1] hito-kabu [2] futa-kabu [3] mi-kabu/san-kabu
[4] yo-kabu/yon-kabu [5] go-kabu [6] rok-kabu
[7] nana-kabu/shichi-kabu [8] hachi-kabu/hak-kabu
[9] kyū-kabu [10] juk-kabu/jik-kabu [100] hyak-kabu
[1,000] sen-kabu [?] nan-kabu

-kagetsu 一か月 *months*(C)
[1] ik-kagetsu [2] ni-kagetsu [3] san-kagetsu [4] yon-kagetsu
[5] go-kagetsu [6] rok-kagetsu [7] nana-kagetsu/shichi-kagetsu
[8] hak-kagetsu/hachi-kagetsu [9] kyū-kagetsu [10] juk-kagetsu/jik-
kagetsu [100] hyak-kagetsu [?] nan-kagetsu

-kai 一回 ① *times, occurences*(C) ② *innings*(C/O)
[1] ik-kai [2] ni-kai [3] san-kai [4] yon-kai [5] go-kai [6] rok-kai
[7] nana-kai/shichi-kai [8] hak-kai/hachi-kai [9] kyū-kai

652

[10] juk-kai/jik-kai [100] hyak-kai [1,000] sen-kai [?] nan-kai

-kai —階 *building stories*(C/O)
[1] ik-kai [2] ni-kai [3] san-gai [4] yon-kai [5] go-kai [6] rok-kai
[7] nana-kai/shichi-kai [8] hak-kai/hachi-kai [9] kyū-kai
[10] juk-kai/jik-kai [100] hyak-kai [?] nan-gai

-kairi —海里 n*autical miles*(C)
[1] ichi-kairi [2] ni-kairi [3] san-kairi [4] yon-kairi [5] go-kairi
[6] rok-kairi [7] nana-kairi/shichi-kairi [8] hachi-kairi/hak-kairi
[9] kyū-kairi [10] juk-kairi/jik-kairi [100] hyak-kairi [1,000] sen-kairi
[?] nan-kairi

-kakoku —ヵ国 *countries*(C)
[1] ik-kakoku [2] ni-kakoku [3] san-kakoku [4] yon-kakoku
[5] go-kakoku [6] rok-kakoku [7] nana-kakoku/shichi-kakoku
[8] hachi-kakoku/hak-kakoku [9] kyū-kakoku [10] juk-kakoku/jik-
kakoku [100] hyak-kakoku [?] nan-kakoku

-kakoku-go —ヵ国語 *languages*(C)
[1] ik-kakoku-go [2] ni-kakoku-go [3] san-kakoku-go
[4] yon-kakoku-go [5] go-kakoku-go [6] rok-kakoku-go
[7] nana-kakoku-go/shichi-kakoku-go [8] hachi-kakoku-
go/hak-kakoku-go [9] kyū-kakoku-go [10] juk-kakoku-
go/jik-kakoku-go [100] hyak-kakoku-go [1,000] sen-kakoku-
go [?] nan-kakoku-go

-kan —巻 *volumes* (*in a set of books*)(C)
[1] ik-kan [2] ni-kan [3] san-kan [4] yon-kan [5] go-kan [6] rok-kan
[7] nana-kan [8] hachi-kan [9] kyū-kan[10] juk-kan/jik-kan
[100] hyak-kan [1,000] sen-kan [?] nan-kan

-karatto —カラット *carats*(C)
[1] ichi-karatto [2] ni-karatto [3] san-karatto [4] yon-karatto
[5] go-karatto [6] roku-karatto [7] nana-karatto/shichi-karatto
[8] hachi-karatto [9] kyū-karatto [10] juk-karatto/jik-karatto
[100] hyaku-karatto/hyak-karatto [1,000] sen-karatto [?] nan-karatto

-karorī —カロリー *calories*(C)
[1] ichi-karorī [2] ni-karorī [3] san-karorī [4] yon-karorī [5] go-karorī
[6] rok-karorī/roku-karorī [7] nana-karorī/shichi-karorī [8] hachi-karorī
[9] kyū-karorī [10] juk-karorī/jik-karorī [100] hyaku-karorī/hyak-karorī
[1,000] sen-karorī [?] nan-karorī

-kasho —箇所 *places*(C)
[1] ik-kasho [2] ni-kakoku [3] san-kasho [4] yon-kasho [5] go-kasho

[6] rok-kasho [7] nana-kasho/shichi-kasho [8] hachi-kasho/hak-kasho
[9] kyū-kasho [10] juk-kasho/jik-kasho [100] hyak-kasho [1,000] sen-kasho
[?] nan-kasho

-ken —件 *incidents*(C)
[1] ik-ken [2] ni-ken [3] san-ken/san-gen [4] yon-ken [5] go-ken [6] rok-
ken [7] nana-ken/shichi ken [8] hachi-ken/hak-ken [9] kyū-ken
[10] juk-ken/jik-ken [100] hyak-ken [1,000] sen-ken [?] nan-ken

-ken —軒 *houses, small buildings*(C)
[1] ik-ken [2] ni-ken [3] san-gen/san-ken [4] yon-ken [5] go-ken [6] rok-
ken [7] nana-ken/shichi-ken [8] hak-ken/hachi-ken [9] kyū-ken
[10] juk-ken/jik-ken [100] hyak-ken [1,000] sen-gen [?] nan-gen

-keta —桁 *digit, figure* (*in an Arabic numeral*)(C)
[1] hito-keta [2] ni-keta/futa-keta [3] san-keta/mi-keta [4] yon-keta/yo-
keta [5] go-keta [6] rok-keta [7] nana-keta/shichi-keta [8] hachi-keta/hak-
keta [9] kyū-keta [10] juk-keta/jik-keta [100] hyak-keta/hyaku-keta
[1,000] sen-keta [?] nan-keta

-kire —切れ *slices, cut pieces*(C)
[1] hito-kire [2] futa-kire [3] mi-kire/san-kire [4] yo-kire/yon-kire
[5] go-kire [6] rok-kire/roku-kire [7] nana-kire/shichi-kire
[8] hachi-kire/hak-kire [9] kyū-kire [10] juk-kire/jik-kire
[100] hyak-kire/hyaku-kire [1,000] sen-kire [?] nan-kire

-kiro —キロ ① *kilograms*(C) ② *kilometers*(C)
[1] ichi-kiro [2] ni-kiro [3] san-kiro [4] yon-kiro [5] go-kiro
[6] rok-kiro [7] nana-kiro/shichi-kiro [8] hachi-kiro/hak-kiro
[9] kyū-kiro [10] juk-kiro/ji-kiro [100] hyak-kiro [1,000] sen-kiro
[?] nan-kiro

-kiroguramu —キログラム *kilograms*(C)
  See **-kiro** above.

-kirometoru —キロメートル *kilometers*(C)
  See **-kiro** above.

-kirowatto —キロワット *kilowatts*(C)
[1] ichi-kirowatto [2] ni-kirowatto [3] san-kirowatto
[4] yon-kirowatto [5] go-kirowatto [6] rok-kirowatto
[7] nana-kirowatto/shichi-kirowatto [8] hachi-kirowatto [9] kyū-kirowatto
[10] juk-kirowatto/ji-kirowatto [100] hyak-kirowatto [1,000] sen-kirowatto
[?] nan-kirowatto

-ko 一個 *objects (especially spherical or cube-shaped)*(C)
[1] ik-ko [2] ni-ko [3] san-ko [4] yon-ko [5] go-ko [6] rok-ko
[7] nana-ko/shichi-ko [8] hak-ko [9] kyū-ko [10] juk-ko/jik-ko
[100] hyak-ko [1,000] sen-ko [?] nan-ko

-kōnen 一光年 *light years*(C)
[1] ichi-kōnen [2] ni-kōnen [3] san-kōnen [4] yon-kōnen
[5] go-kōnen [6] rok-kōnen/roku-kōnen [7] nana-kōnen
[8] hachi-kōnen [9] kyū-kōnen [10] juk-kōnen/jik-kōnen
[100] hyak-kōnen [1,000] sen-kōnen [?] nan-kōnen

-kumi 一組 *sets, pairs*(C)
[1] hito-kumi [2] futa-kumi [3] mi-kumi/san-kumi [4] yon-kumi
[5] go-kumi [6] rok-kumi [7] nana-kumi/shichi-kumi [8] hachi-
kumi/hak-kumi [9] kyū-kumi [10] juk-kumi/jik-kumi [100] hyak-
kumi [1,000] sen-kumi [?] nan-kumi

-kyoku 一曲 *musical pieces*(C)
[1] ik-kyoku [2] ni-kyoku [3] san-kyoku [4] yon-kyoku
[5] go-kyoku [6] rok-kyoku [7] nana-kyoku [8] hachi-kyoku/hak-
kyoku [9] kyū-kyoku [10] juk-kyoku/jik-kyoku [100] hyak-kyoku
[1,000] sen-kyoku [?] nan-kyoku

-kyū 一級 *classes, grades, ranks*(C/O)
[1] ik-kyū [2] ni-kyū [3] san-kyu [4] yon-kyū [5] go-kyū
[6] rok-kyū [7] nana-kyū/shichi-kyū [8] hachi-kyū/hak-kyū
[9] kyū-kyū [10] juk-kyū/jik-kyū [100] hyak-kyū
[1,000] sen-kyū [?] nan-kyū

-ma 一間 *rooms*(C)
[1] hito-ma [2] futa-ma [3] mi-ma [4] yon-ma/yo-ma [5] go-ma
[6] roku-ma [7] nana-ma/shichi-ma [8] hachi-ma [9] kyū-ma
[10] jū-ma [100] hyaku-ma [1,000] sen-ma [?] nan-ma

-mai 一枚 *flat objects*(C)
[1] ichi-mai [2] ni-mai [3] san-mai [4] yon-mai [5] go-mai
[6] roku-mai [7] nana-mai/shichi-mai [8] hachi-mai [9] kyū-mai
[10] jū-mai [100] hyaku-mai [1,000] sen-mai [?] nan-mai

-mairu 一マイル *miles*(C)
[1] ichi-mairu [2] ni-mairu [3] san-mairu [4] yon-mairu
[5] go-mairu [6] roku-mairu [7] nana-mairu/shichi-mairu
[8] hachi-mairu [9] kyū-mairu [10] jū-mairu [100] hyaku-mairu
[1,000] sen-mairu [?] nan-mairu

-maku ―幕 *acts of a play*(C)
[1] hito-maku [2] futa-maku [3] san-maku/mi-maku [4] yon-maku
[5] go-maku [6] roku-maku [7] nana-maku/shichi-maku
[8] hachi-maku [9] kyū-maku [10] jū-maku [?] nan-maku

-mei ―名 *people*(C)
[1] ichi-mei [2] ni-mei [3] san-mei [4] yon-mei [5] go-mei
[6] roku-mei [7] nana-mei/shichi-mei [8] hachi-mei [9] kyū-mei
[10] jū-mei [100] hyaku-mei [1,000] sen-mei [?] nan-mei

-men ―面 *polyhedron facets*(C)
[1] ichi-men [2] ni-men [3] san-men [4] yon-men/shi-men
[5] go-men [6] roku-men [7] nana-men/shichi-men [8] hachi-men
[9] kyū-men/ku-men [10] jū-men [100] hyaku-men [1,000] sen-men
[?] nan-men

-mētā ―メーター *meters* (*i.e., units of linear measure*)(C)
See **-mētoru** below.

-mētoru ―メートル *meters* (*i.e., units of linear measure*)(C)
[1] ichi-mētoru [2] ni-mētoru [3] san-mētoru [4] yon-mētoru
[5] go-mētoru [6] roku-mētoru [7] nana-mētoru/shichi-mētoru
[8] hachi-mētoru [9] kyū-mētoru [10] jū-mētoru [100] hyaku-mētoru
[1,000] sen-mētoru [?] nan-mētoru

-miri ―ミリ ① *millimeters*(C) ② *milliliters*(C)
[1] ichi-miri [2] ni-miri [3] san-miri [4] yon-miri [5] go-miri
[6] roku-miri [7] nana-miri/shichi-miri [8] hachi-miri [9] kyū-miri
[10] jū-miri [100] hyaku-miri [1,000] sen-miri [?] nan-miri

-mirimetoru ―ミリメートル *millimeters*(C)
See **-miri** above.

-miririttoru ―ミリリットル *milliliters*(C)
See **-miri** above.

-nen ―年 ① *years*(C) ② *years of an era* (*A.D. unless otherwise specified*)
(O)
[1] ichi-nen [2] ni-nen [3] san-nen [4] yo-nen [5] go-nen
[6] roku-nen [7] nana-nen/shichi-nen [8] hachi-nen
[9] kyū-nen/ku-nen [10] jū-nen [100] hyaku-nen [1,000] sen-nen [?] nan-
nen

-nichi ―日 ① *days*(C) ② *days of a month*(O)
[1(cardinal)] tsuitachi [1(ordinal)] ichi-nichi [2] futsu-ka
[3] mik-ka [4] yok-ka [5] itsu-ka [6] mui-ka [7] nano-ka [8] yō-ka
[9] kokono-ka [10] tō-ka [11] jūichi-nichi [12] jūni-nichi

[13] jūsan-nichi [14] jūyok-ka [15] jūgo-nichi [16] jūroku-nichi
[17] jūshichi-nichi [18] jūhachi-nichi [19] jūku-nichi [20] hatsu-ka
[21] nijūichi-nichi [22] nijūni-nichi [23] nijūsan-nichi
[24] nijūyok-ka [25] nijūgo-nichi [26] nijūroku-nichi
[27] nijūshichi-nichi [28] nijūhachi-nichi [29] nijūku-nichi
[30] sanjū-nichi [31] sanjūichi-nichi [100] hyaku-nichi
[1,000] sen-nichi [?] nan-nichi

-nin 一人 *people*(C)
[1] hito-ri [2] futa-ri [3] san-nin [4] yo-nin [5] go-nin
[6] roku-nin [7] nana-nin/shichi-nin [8] hachi-nin [9] ku-nin/kyū-nin [10]
jū-nin [100] hyaku-nin [1,000] sen-nin [?] nan-nin

-nin-mae 一人前 *portions of food for people*(C)
[1] ichi-nin-mae [2] ni-nin-mae [3] san-nin-mae [4] yo-nin-mae
[5] go-nin-mae [6] roku-nin-mae [7] nana-nin-mae/shichi-nin-mae
[8] hachi-nin-mae [9] ku-nin-mae/kyū-nin-mae [10] jū-nin-mae
[100] hyaku-nin-mae [1,000] sen-nin-mae [?] nan-nin-mae

-pāsento 一パーセント *prcent*(C)
[1] ichi-pāsento/ip-pāsento [2] ni-pāsento [3] san-pāsento
[4] yon-pāsento [5] go-pāsento [6] roku-pāsento/rop-pāsento
[7] nana-pāsento/shichi-pāsento [8] hachi-pāsento/hap-pāsento
[9] kyū-pāsento [10] jup-pāsento/jip-pāsento
[100] hyaku-pāsento [?] nan-pāsento

-pēji 一ページ *pages*(C/O)
[1] ichi-pēji/ip-pēji [2] ni-pēji [3] san-pēji [4] yon-pēji [5] go-pēji
[6] roku-pēji [7] nana-pēji/shichi-pēji [8] hachi-pēji [9] kyū-pēji
[10] jup-pēji/jip-pēji [100] hyaku-pēji [1,000] sen-pēji [?] nan-pēji

-pondo 一ポンド *pounds* (*i.e.*, *units of weight*)(C)
[1] ichi-pondo/ip-pondo [2] ni-pondo [3] san-pondo [4] yon-pondo
[5] go-pondo [6] roku-pondo [7] nana-pondo/shichi-pondo
[8] hachi-pondo [9] kyū-pondo [10] jup-pondo/jip-pondo
[100] hyaku-pondo [1,000] sen-pondo [?] nan-pondo

-pondo 一ポンド *pounds* (*i.e.*, *monetary units*)(C)
See **-pondo** above.

-raundo 一ラウンド *boxing rounds*(C)
[1] ichi-raundo [2] ni-raundo [3] san-raundo [4] yon-raundo
[5] go-raundo [6] roku-raundo [7] nana-raundo/shichi-raundo
[8] hachi-raundo [9] kyū-raundo [10] jū-raundo
[100] hyaku-raundo [1,000] sen-raundo [?] nan-raundo

-rippō-mētoru 一立方メートル *cubic meters*(C)
[1] ichi-rippō-mētoru [2] ni-rippō-mētoru [3] san-rippō-mētoru
[4] yon-rippō-mētoru [5] go-rippō-mētoru [6] roku-rippō-mētoru
[7] nana-rippō-mētoru/shichi-rippō-mētoru [8] hachi-rippō-mētoru
[9] kyū-rippō-mētoru [10] jū-rippō-mētoru [100] hyaku-rippō-mētoru
[1,000] sen-rippō-mētoru [?] nan-rippō-mētoru

-rittoru 一リットル *liters*(C)
[1] ichi-rittoru [2] ni-rittoru [3] san-rittoru [4] yon-rittoru
[5] go-rittoru [6] roku-rittoru [7] nana-rittoru/shichi-rittoru
[8] hachi-rittoru [9] kyū-rittoru [10] jū-rittoru [100] hyaku-rittoru
[1,000] sen-rittoru [?] nan-rittoru

-sai 一歳 *years of age*(C)
[1] is-sai [2] ni-sai [3] san-sai [4] yon-sai [5] go-sai [6] roku-sai
[7] nana-sai/shichi-sai [8] has-sai [9] kyū-sai [10] jus-sai/jis-sai
[100] hyaku-sai [?] nan-sai

-saikuru 一サイクル *cycles per second*(C)
[1] ichi-saikuru [2] ni-saikuru [3] san-saikuru [4] yon-saikuru
[5] go-saikuru [6] roku-saikuru [7] nana-saikuru/shichi-saikuru
[8] hachi-saikuru/has-saikuru [9] kyū-saikuru
[10] jus-saikuru/jis-saikuru [100] hyaku-saikuru
[1,000] sen-saikuru [?] nan-saikuru

-sara 一皿 *helpings, courses* (*of food*)(C)
[1] hito-sara [2] futa-sara [3] mi-sara [4] yon-sara/yo-sara
[5] go-sara [6] roku-sara [7] nana-sara [8] hachi-sara/has-sara
[9] kyū-sara [10] jus-sara/jis-sara [100] hyaku-sara [1,000] sen-sara
[?] nan-sara

-satsu 一冊 *books, magazines*(C)
[1] is-satsu [2] ni-satsu [3] san-satsu [4] yon-satsu [5] go-satsu
[6] roku-satsu [7] nana-satsu/shichi-satsu [8] has-satsu [9] kyū-satsu
[10] jus-satsu/jis-satsu [100] hyaku-satsu [1,000] sen-satsu
[?] nan-satsu

-seiki 一世紀 ① *centuries*(C) ② *centuries of an era* (*A.D. unless otherwise specified*)(O)
[1] is-seiki [2] ni-seiki [3] san-seiki [4] yon-seiki [5] go-seiki
[6] roku-seiki [7] nana-seiki/shichi-seiki [8] has-seiki/hachi-seiki
[9] kyū-seiki [10] jus-seiki/jis-seiki [100] hyaku-seiki
[1,000] sen-seiki [?] nan-seiki

-senchi ―センチ *centimeters*(C)
[1] is-senchi [2] ni-senchi [3] san-senchi [4] yon-senchi
[5] go-senchi [6] roku-senchi [7] nana-senchi/shichi-senchi
[8] has-senchi/hachi-senchi [9] kyū-senchi [10] jus-senchi/jis-senchi
[100] hyaku-senchi [1,000] sen-senchi [?] nan-senchi

-senchimētoru ―センチメートル *centimeters*(C)
See **-senchi** above.

-sento ―セント *cents*(C)
[1] is-sento [2] ni-sento [3] san-sento [4] yon-sento [5] go-sento
[6] roku-sento [7] nana-sento/shichi-sento [8] has-sento [9] kyū-sento
[10] jus-sento/jis-sento [100] hyaku-sento [?] nan-sento

-setto ―セット *sets (in sports)*(C)
[1] ichi-setto/is-setto [2] ni-setto [3] san-setto [4] yon-setto
[5] go-setto [6] roku-setto [7] nana-setto/shichi-setto
[8] has-setto/hachi-setto [9] kyū-setto [10] jus-setto/jis-setto
[100] hyaku-setto [1,000] sen-setto [?] nan-setto

-shīto ―シート *sheets (of stamps, etc.)*(C)
[1] ichi-shīto [2] ni-shīto [3] san-shīto [4] yon-shīto [5] go-shīto
[6] roku-shīto [7] nana-shīto/shichi-shīto [8] hachi-shīto
[9] kyū-shīto [10] jus-shīto/jis-shīto
[100] hyaku-shīto [1,000] sen-shīto [?] nan-shīto

-shō ―章 *book chapters*(C)
[1] is-shō [2] ni-shō [3] san-shō [4] yon-shō [5] go-shō [6] roku-shō
[7] nana-shō [8] has-shō [9] kyū-shō [10] jus-shō/jis-shō
[100] hyaku-shō [1,000] sen-shō [?] nan-shō

-shūkan ―週間 *weeks*(C)
[1] is-shūkan [2] ni-shūkan [3] san-shūkan [4] yon-shūkan
[5] go-shūkan [6] roku-shūkan [7] nana-shūkan [8] has-shūkan
[9] kyū-shūkan [10] jus-shūkan/jis-shūkan [100] hyaku-shūkan
[?] nan-shūkan

-shurui ―種類 *kinds, sorts, types*(C)
[1] is-shurui/hito-shurui [2] ni-shurui/futa-shurui [3] san-shurui
[4] yon-shurui [5] go-shurui [6] roku-shurui [7] nana-shurui/shichi-shurui
[8] has-shurui/hachi-shurui [9] kyū-shurui [10] jus-shurui/jis-shurui
[100] hyaku-shurui [1,000] sen-shurui [?] nan-shurui

-soku ―足 *pairs of footwear*(C)
[1] is-soku [2] ni-soku [3] san-zoku [4] yon-soku [5] go-soku
[6] roku-soku [7] nana-soku/shichi-soku [8] has-soku

[9] kyū–soku [10] jus–soku/jis–soku [100] hyaku–soku
[1,000] sen–zoku [?] nan–zoku

-taba 一束 *bundles, bunches*(C)
[1] hito–taba [2] futa–taba [3] mi–taba/san–taba [4] yon–taba
[5] go–taba [6] roku–taba [7] nana–taba/shichi–taba
[8] hachi–taba/hat–taba [9] kyū–taba [10] jut–taba/jit–taba
[100] hyaku–taba [1,000] sen–taba [?] nan–taba

-tan'i 一単位 *units of academic work*(C)
[1] ichi–tan'i/it–tan'i [2] ni–tan'i [3] san–tan'i [4] yon–tan'i
[5] go–tan'i [6] roku–tan'i [7] nana–tan'i/shichi–tan'i
[8] hachi–tan'i/hat–tan'i [9] kyū–tan'i [10] jut–tan'i/jit–tan'i
[100] hyaku–tan'i [1,000] sen–tan'i [?] nan–tan'i

-ten 一点 ① *scored points*(C) ② *items*(C)
[1] it–ten [2] ni–ten [3] san–ten [4] yon–ten [5] go–ten [6] roku–ten
[7] nana–ten/shichi–ten [8] hat–ten/hachi–ten [9] kyū–ten
[10] jut–ten/jit–ten [100] hyaku–ten [1,000] sen–ten [?] nan–ten

-ton 一トン *(metric) tons*(C)
[1] it–ton [2] ni–ton [3] san–ton [4] yon–ton [5] go–ton
[6] roku–ton [7] nana–ton/shichi–ton [8] hachi–ton/hat–ton [9] kyū–ton
[10] jut–ton/jit–ton [100] hyaku–ton [1,000] sen–ton [?] nan–ton

-tsū 一通 *letters (of correspondence)*(C)
[1] it–tsū [2] ni–tsū [3] san–tsū [4] yon–tsū [5] go–tsū [6] roku–tsū
[7] nana–tsū/shichi–tsū [8] hat–tsū [9] kyū–tsū [10] jut–tsū/jit–tsū
[100] hyaku–tsū [1,000] sen–tsū [?] nan–tsū

-tsubo 一坪 *tsubo (units of area of approximately* 3.3 m²) (C)
[1] hito–tsubo [2] futa–tsubo [3] mi–tsubo/san–tsubo
[4] yo–tsubo/yon–tsubo [5] itsu–tsubo/go–tsubo [6] roku–tsubo
[7] nana–tsubo [8] hat–tsubo [9] kyū–tsubo [10] to–tsubo
[100] hyaku–tsubo [1,000] sen–tsubo [?] nan–tsubo

-tsubu 一粒 *grains, drops*(C)
[1] hito–tsubu [2] futa–tsubu [3] mi–tsubu/san–tsubu
[4] yo–tsubu/yon–tsubu [5] itsu–tsubu/go–tsubu [6] roku–tsubu
[7] nana–tsubu/shichi–tsubu [8] hachi–tsubu/hat–tsubu [9] kyū–tsubu
[10] jut–tsubu/jit–tsubu [100] hyaku–tsubu [1,000] sen–tsubu
[?] nan–tsubu

-tsui 一対 *pairs*(C)
[1] it–tsui [2] ni–tsui [3] san–tsui [4] yon–tsui [5] go–tsui
[6] roku–tsui [7] nana–tsui [8] hat–tsui [9] kyū–tsui

[10] jut-tsui/jit-tsui [100] hyaku-tsui [1,000] sen-tsui [?] nan-tsui

-tō —頭 *large animals*(C)
[1] it-tō [2] ni-tō [3] san-tō [4] yon-tō [5] go-tō [6] roku-tō
[7] nana-tō/shichi-tō [8] hat-tō/hachi-tō [9] kyū-tō [10] jut-tō/jit-tō
[100] hyaku-tō [1,000] sen-tō [?] nan-tō

-tō —等 *classes, rankings*(O)
[1] it-tō [2] ni-tō [3] san-tō [4] yon-tō [5] go-tō [6] roku-tō
[7] nana-tō/shichi-tō [8] hat-to/hachi-tō [9] kyū-tō [10] jut-tō/jit-tō
[100] hyaku-tō [1,000] sen-tō [?] nan-tō

-wa —羽 *birds, rabbits*(C)
[1] ichi-wa [2] ni-wa [3] san-ba/san-wa [4] yon-wa/yon-ba/shi-wa
[5] go-wa [6] rop-pa/roku-wa [7] nana-wa/shichi-wa [8] hachi-wa
[9] kyū-wa [10] jup-pa/jip-pa [100] hyap-pa [1,000] sen-ba [?] nan-ba

-wari —割 *tenths*(C)
[1] ichi-wari [2] ni-wari [3] san-wari [4] yon-wari [5] go-wari
[6] roku-wari [7] nana-wari/shichi-wari [8] hachi-wari
[9] kyū-wari/ku-wari [10] jū-wari [?] nan-wari

-waribiki —割引 *discounts in steps of 10%*(C)
[1] ichi-waribiki [2] ni-waribiki [3] san-waribiki [4] yon-waribiki
[5] go-waribiki [6] roku-waribiki [7] nana-waribiki/shichi-waribiki
[8] hachi-waribiki [9] kyū-waribiki [10] jū-waribiki
[?] nan-waribiki

-watto —ワット *watts*(C)
[1] ichi-watto [2] ni-watto [3] san-watto [4] yon-watto [5] go-watto
[6] roku-watto [7] nana-watto/shichi-watto [8] hachi-watto
[9] kyū-watto [10] jū-watto [100] hyaku-watto [1,000] sen-watto
[?] nan-watto

-yādo —ヤード *yards* (*i.e., units of linear measure*)(C)
[1] ichi-yādo [2] ni-yādo [3] san-yādo [4] yon-yādo [5] go-yādo
[6] roku-yādo [7] nana-yādo/shichi-yādo [8] hachi-yādo [9] kyū-yādo
[10] jū-yādo [100] hyaku-yādo [1,000] sen-yādo [?] nan-yādo

-zen —膳 ① *pairs of chopsticks*(C) ② *bowls of rice*(C)
[1] ichi-zen [2] ni-zen [3] san-zen [4] yon-zen [5] go-zen
[6] roku-zen [7] nana-zen [8] hachi-zen [9] kyū-zen [10] jū-zen
[100] hyaku-zen [1,000] sen-zen [?] nan-zen

APPENDIX 3: Place Names

1. JAPANESE PREFECTURES

Aichi(-ken) 愛知（県）
Akita(-ken) 秋田（県）
Aomori(-ken) 青森（県）
Chiba(-ken) 千葉（県）
Ehime(-ken) 愛媛（県）
Fukui(-ken) 福井（県）
Fukuoka(-ken) 福岡（県）
Fukushima(-ken) 福島（県）
Gifu(-ken) 岐阜（県）
Gunma(-ken) 群馬（県）
Hiroshima(-ken) 広島（県）
Hokkaidō 北海道
Hyōgo(-ken) 兵庫（県）
Ibaragi(-ken) 茨城（県）
Ishikawa(-ken) 石川（県）
Iwate(-ken) 岩手（県）
Kagawa(-ken) 香川（県）
Kagoshima(-ken) 鹿児島（県）
Kanagawa(-ken) 神奈川（県）
Kōchi(-ken) 高知（県）
Kumamoto(-ken) 熊本（県）
Kyōto(-fu) 京都（府）
Mie(-ken) 三重（県）
Miyagi(-ken) 宮城（県）

Miyazaki(-ken) 宮崎（県）
Nagano(-ken) 長野（県）
Nagasaki(-ken) 長崎（県）
Nara(-ken) 奈良（県）
Niigata(-ken) 新潟（県）
Ōita(-ken) 大分（県）
Okayama(-ken) 岡山（県）
Okinawa(-ken) 沖縄（県）
Ōsaka(-fu) 大阪（府）
Saga(-ken) 佐賀（県）
Saitama(-ken) 埼玉（県）
Shiga(-ken) 滋賀（県）
Shimane(-ken) 島根（県）
Shizuoka(-ken) 静岡（県）
Tochigi(-ken) 栃木（県）
Tokushima(-ken) 徳島（県）
Tōkyō(-to) 東京（都）
Tottori(-ken) 鳥取（県）
Toyama(-ken) 富山（県）
Wakayama(-ken) 和歌山（県）
Yamagata(-ken) 山形（県）
Yamaguchi(-ken) 山口（県）
Yamanashi(-ken) 山梨（県）

2. Selected Japanese Cities

Akita(-shi) 秋田（市）
Aomori(-shi) 青森（市）
Chiba(-shi) 千葉（市）
Fukui(-shi) 福井（市）
Fukuoka(-shi) 福岡（市）
Fukushima(-shi) 福島（市）
Gifu(-shi) 岐阜（市）
Hakodate(-shi) 函館（市）
Hiroshima(-shi) 広島（市）
Kagoshima(-shi) 鹿児島（市）
Kanazawa(-shi) 金沢（市）
Kita-Kyūshū(-shi) 北九州（市）
Kōbe(-shi) 神戸（市）
Kōchi(-shi) 高知（市）
Kofu(-shi) 甲府（市）
Kumamoto(-shi) 熊本（市）
Kyōto(-shi) 京都（市）
Maebashi(-shi) 前橋（市）
Matsue(-shi) 松江（市）
Matsuyama(-shi) 松山（市）
Mito(-shi) 水戸（市）
Miyazaki(-shi) 宮崎（市）
Morioka(-shi) 盛岡（市）
Nagano(-shi) 長野（市）
Nagasaki(-shi) 長崎（市）

Nagoya(-shi) 名古屋（市）
Naha(-shi) 那覇（市）
Nara(-shi) 奈良（市）
Niigata(-shi) 新潟（市）
Ōita(-shi) 大分（市）
Okayama(-shi) 岡山（市）
Ōsaka(-shi) 大阪（市）
Saga(-shi) 佐賀（市）
Sapporo(-shi) 札幌（市）
Sendai(-shi) 仙台（市）
Shimonoseki(-shi) 下関（市）
Shizuoka(-shi) 静岡（市）
Takamatsu(-shi) 高松（市）
Tokushima(-shi) 徳島（市）
Tōkyō(-to) 東京（都）
Tottori(-shi) 鳥取（市）
Toyama(-shi) 富山（市）
Tsu(-shi) 津（市）
Urawa(-shi) 浦和（市）
Utsunomiya(-shi) 宇都宮（市）
Wakayama(-shi) 和歌山（市）
Yamagata(-shi) 山形（市）
Yamaguchi(-shi) 山口（市）
Yokohama(-shi) 横浜（市）

3. Selected Foreign Countries and Cities

Afuganisutan アフガニスタン
  Afghanistan
Airurando アイルランド *Ireland*
Aisurando アイスランド *Iceland*
Ajisuabeba アジスアベバ
  Addis-Ababa
Akura アクラ *A*ccra
Amerika アメリカ *America*
Amusuterudamu アムステルダム
  Amsterdam
Angora アンゴラ *Angola*
Ankara アンカラ *Ankara*
Antowāpu アントワープ *Antwerp*
Arubania アルバニア *Albania*
Aruje アルジェ *Algiers*
Arujeria アルジェリア *Algeria*
Aruzenchin アルゼンチン *Argentina*
Asunshion アスンシオン *Asuncion*
Atene アテネ *Athens*

Bachikan バチカン *the Vatican*
Bagudaddo バグダッド *Baghdad*
Bahama バハマ *the B*ahamas
Bāmingamu バーミンガム
  Birmingham
Banguradeshu バングラデシュ
  Bangladesh
Bankoku バンコク *Bangkok*
Bankūbā バンクーバー *Vancouver*
Banuatsu バヌアツ *Vanuatu*
Bārēn バーレーン *Bahrain*
Barubadosu バルバドス *Barbados*
Baruserona バルセロナ *Barcelona*
Beirūto ベイルート *Beirut*
Benin ベニン *Benin*
Benechia ベネチア *Venice*
Benezuera ベネズエラ *Venezuela*
Beogurādo ベオグラード *Belgrade*
Berīzu ベリーズ *Belize*
Berufasuto ベルファスト *Belfast*
Berugī ベルギー *Belgium*
Berurin ベルリン *Berlin*
Betonamu ベトナム *Vietnam*
Bogota ボゴタ *Bogota*
Bon ボン *Bonn*
Bonbei ボンベイ *Bombay*
Boribia ボリビア *Bolivia*
Boruchimoa ボルチモア *Baltimore*

Bosuton ボストン *Boston*
Botsuwana ボツワナ *Botswana*
Budapesuto ブダペスト *Budapest*
Buenosuairesu ブエノスアイレス
  Buenos Aires
Bukaresuto ブカレスト *Bucharest*
Burajiru ブラジル *Brazil*
Burugaria ブルガリア *Bulgaria*
Burunei ブルネイ *Brunei*
Burunji ブルンジ *Burundi*
Buryusseru ブリュッセル *Brussels*
Būtan ブータン *Bhutan*

Chado チャド *Chad*
Chibetto チベット *Tibet*
Chiri チリ *Chile*
Chōsen-Minshushugi-Jinmin-
  Kyōwakoku 朝鮮民主主義人民共和国
  People's Republic of Korea
Chūgoku 中国 *China*
Chunijia チュニジア *Tunisia*
Chunisu チュニス *Tunis*
Chūrihhi チューリッヒ *Zurich*

Daburin ダブリン *Dublin*
Daikan-Minkoku 大韓民国
  Republic of Korea
Darasu ダラス *Dallas*
Denbā デンバー *Denver*
Denmakū デンマーク *Denmark*
Detoroito デトロイト *Detroit*
Doitsu ドイツ *Germany*
Dominika ドミニカ *Dominica*
Dyusserudorufu デュッセルドルフ
  Dusseldorf

Echiopia エチオピア *Ethiopia*
Edinbara エディンバラ *Edinburgh*
Eikoku 英国 *Great Britain*
Ejiputo エジプト *Egypt*
Ekuadoru エクアドル *Ecuador*
Erusarubadoru エルサルバドル
  El Salvador
Erusaremu エルサレム *Jerusalem*

Fijī フィジー *Fiji*
Finrando フィンランド *Finland*
Firaderufia フィラデルフィア
  Philadelphia

Firentse フィレンツェ Florence
Firipin フィリピン the Philippines
Furankufuruto フランクフルト Frankfurt
Furansu フランス France

Gabon ガボン Gabon
Gaiana ガイアナ Guyana
Gāna ガーナ Ghana
Ganbia ガンビア Gambia
Ginia ギニア Guinea
Girisha ギリシャ Greece
Guatemara グアテマラ Guatemala
Gurasugō グラスゴー Glasgow
Gurenada グレナダ Grenada
Gurīnrando グリーンランド Greenland

Habana ハバナ Havana
Hāgu ハーグ the Hague
Haichi ハイチ Haiti
Hanburugu ハンブルグ Hamburg
Hangarī ハンガリー Hungary
Hanoi ハノイ Hanoi
Herushinki ヘルシンキ Helsinki
Honjurasu ホンジュラス Honduras
Honkon 香港 Hong Kong
Honoruru ホノルル Honolulu
Hyūsuton ヒューストン Houston

Iemen イエメン Yemen
Igirisu イギリス Great Britain
Indo インド India
Indoneshia インドネシア Indonesia
Iraku イラク Iraq
Iran イラン Iran
Isuraeru イスラエル Israel

Isutanbūru イスタンブール Istanbul
Itaria イタリア Italy

Jakaruta ジャカルタ Jakarta
Jamaika ジャマイカ Jamaica
Jibuchi ジブチ Djibouti
Jinbabue ジンバブエ Zimbabwe
Junēbu ジュネーブ Geneva

Kabūru カブール Kabul
Kairo カイロ Cairo
Kamerūn カメルーン Cameroon

Kanada カナダ Canada
Kanbojia カンボジア Cambodia
Kanton 広東 Canton
Karachi カラチ Karachi
Karakasu カラカス Caracas
Karukatta カルカッタ Calcutta
Katāru カタール Qatar
Katomanzu カトマンズ Kathmandu
Kebekku ケベック Quebec
Kenia ケニア Kenya
Kēputaun ケープタウン Cape Town
Kiefu キエフ Kiev
Kipurosu キプロス Cyprus
Kiribasu キリバス Kiribati
Kongo コンゴ Congo
Kopenhāgen コペンハーゲン Copenhagen
Koronbia コロンビア Colombia
Koronbo コロンボ Colombo
Kosutarika コスタリカ Costa Rica
Kuararunpūru クアラルンプール Kuala Lumpur
Kuwēto クウェート Kuwait
Kyanbera キャンベラ Canberra
Kyūba キューバ Cuba

Madagasukaru マダガスカル Madagascar
Madorasu マドラス Madras
Madorīdo マドリード Madrid
Maiami マイアミ Miami
Makao マカオ Macao
Managua マナグア Managua
Manira マニラ Manila
Maraui マラウィ Malawi
Marēshia マレーシア Malaysia
Mari マリ Mali
Maruseiyu マルセイユ Marseilles
Maruta マルタ Malta
Māsharu-shotō マーシャル諸島 Marshall Islands
Mekishiko メキシコ Mexico
Mekka メッカ Mecca
Meruborun メルボルン Melbourne
Mikuroneshia ミクロネシア Micronesia
Minami-Afurika 南アフリカ South Africa
Mirano ミラノ Milan

Moko 蒙古 *Mongolia*
Monako モナコ *Monaco*
Mongoru モンゴル *Mongolia*
Montekaruro モンテカルロ
Monte Carlo
Montoriōru モントリオール
Montreal
Mōrishasu モーリシャス *Mauritius*
Mōritania モーリタニア *Mauritania*
Morokko モロッコ *Morocco*
Morujibu モルジブ *Maldives*
Mosukuwa モスクワ *Moscow*
Mozanbīku モザンビーク
Mozambique
Myanmā ミャンマー *Myanmar*
Myunhen ミュンヘン *Munich*

Naijeria ナイジェリア *Nigeria*
Nairobi ナイロビ *Nairobi*
Nankin 南京 *Nanjing*
Napori ナポリ *Naples*
Nauru ナウル *Nauru*
Nepāru ネパール *Nepal*
Nijēru ニジェール *Niger*
Nikaragua ニカラグア *Nicaragua*
Nishi–Samoa 西サモア
Western Samoa
Noruwē ノルウェー *Norway*
Nyūderī ニューデリー *New Delhi*
Nyūginia ニューギニア *New Guinea*
Nyūjīrando ニュージーランド
New Zealand
Nyūorinzu ニューオリンズ
New Orleans
Nyūyōku ニューヨーク *New York*

Omān オマーン *Oman*
Oranda オランダ *Holland*
Osuro オスロ *Oslo*
Ōsutoraria オーストラリア
Australia
Ōsutoria オーストリア *Austria*
Otawa オタワ *Ottawa*

Pakisutan パキスタン *Pakistan*
Panama パナマ *Panama*
Paraguai パラグアイ *Paraguay*
Pari パリ *Paris*
Paresuchina パレスチナ *Palestine*
Pekin 北京 *Beijing*

Perū ペルー *Peru*
Pittsubāgu ピッツバーグ *Pittsburgh*
Pōrando ポーランド *Poland*
Porutogaru ポルトガル *Portugal*
Pōtorando ポートランド *Portland*
Puraha プラハ *Prague*
Pyonyan 平壌 *Pyongyang*

Rangūn ラングーン *Rangoon*
Raosu ラオス *Laos*
Rapasu ラパス *La Paz*
Rasubegasu ラスベガス *Las Vegas*
Ratobia ラトビア *Latvia*
Rebanon レバノン *Lebanon*
Reikyabiku レイキャビク *Reykjavik*
Ribapūru リバプール *Liverpool*
Riberia リベリア *Liberia*
Ribia リビア *Libya*
Rihitenshutain リヒテンシュタイン
Liechtenstein
Rima リマ *Lima*
Risubon リスボン *Lisbon*
Ritoania リトアニア *Lithuania*
Riyon リヨン *Lyon*
Rōma ローマ *Rome*
Rondon ロンドン *London*
Rosanzerusu ロサンゼルス
Los Angeles
Rosshia ロシア *Russia*
Rotterudamu ロッテルダム
Rotterdam
Rukusenburuku ルクセンブルク
Luxembourg
Rūmania ルーマニア *Rumania*
Ruwanda ルワンダ *Rwanda*

Sanchiago サンチアゴ *Santiago*
Sanfuranshisuko サンフランシスコ
San Francisco
Sanpauro サンパウロ *Sao Paulo*
Sansarubadoru サンサルバドル
San Salvador
Santodomingo サントドミンゴ
Santo Domingo
Saujiarabia サウジアラビア
Saudi Arabia
Seisheru セイシェル *Seychelles*
Senegaru セネガル *Senegal*
Sentoruisu セントルイス *St. Louis*

Shanhai 上海 *Shanghai*
Shiatoru シアトル *Seattle*
Shidonī シドニー *Sydney*
Shierareone シエラレオネ
　Sierra Leone
Shikago シカゴ *Chicago*
Shingapōru シンガポール
　Singapore
Shiria シリア *Syria*
Somaria ソマリア *Somalia*
Soromon-shotō ソロモン諸島
　Solomon Islands
Sorutorēkushiti ソルトレークシティ
　Salt Lake City
Souru ソウル *Seoul*
Sūdan スーダン *Sudan*
Suisu スイス *Switzerland*
Sukottorando スコットランド
　Scotland
Supein スペイン *Spain*
Surinamu スリナム *Surinam*
Suriranka スリランカ *Sri Lanka*
Sutokkuhorumu ストックホルム
　Stockholm
Suwēden スウェーデン *Sweden*

Tahichi タヒチ *Tahiti*
Tai タイ *Thailand*
Taihoku 台北 *Taipei*

Taiwan タイワン *Taiwan*
Tanjīru タンジール *Tangier*
Tanzania タンザニア *Tanzania*
Teheran テヘラン *Teheran*
Teruabibu テルアビブ *Tel Aviv*
Tōgo トーゴ *Togo*
Tonga トンガ *Tonga*
Torinidādo-Tobago トリニダード・
　トバゴ *Trinidad and Tobago*
Torino トリノ *Turin*
Toripori トリポリ *Tripoli*
Toronto トロント *Toronto*
Toruko トルコ *Turkey*

Uēruzu ウェールズ *Wales*
Uīn ウィーン *Vienna*
Uganda ウガンダ *Uganda*
Ukuraina ウクライナ *Ukraine*
Uruguai ウルグアイ *Uruguay*

Warushawa ワルシャワ *Warsaw*
Washinton ワシントン *Washington*

Yohanesuburuku ヨハネスブルク
　Johannesburg
Yorudan ヨルダン *Jordan*

Zaīru ザイール *Zaire*
Zanbia ザンビア *Zambia*